Real Options and Investment under Uncertainty

Real Options and Investment under Uncertainty
Classical Readings and Recent Contributions

Edited by Eduardo S. Schwartz and Lenos Trigeorgis

The MIT Press
Cambridge, Massachusetts
London, England

This book was set in Times New Roman on '3B2' by Asco Typesetters, Hong Kong.
Printed and bound in the United States of America.

Library of Congress Cataloging-in-Publication Data

Real options and investment under uncertainty : classical readings and recent contributions / edited by Eduardo S. Schwarz and Lenos Trigeorgis.
    p.   cm.
  Includes bibliographical references and index.
  ISBN 0-262-19446-5 (alk. paper)
  1. Options (Finance) 2. Capital investments. 3. Uncertainty. I. Schwarz, Eduardo S. II. Trigeorgis, Lenos.
HG6024 .R427 2001
332.64′5—dc21   2001037064

Contents

Contents

Preface

This edited book provides a neatly bound collection and integration of all the classical papers and important recent contributions to the literature on real options and capital investment under uncertainty that has been revolutionizing modern investment decision making. All the important thought leaders in finance and economics that made substantial contributions to the development of real options theory and practice are represented here.

Corporate resource allocation, capital budgeting or investment under uncertainty has been a stagnant field for several decades, until the recent developments in real options have provided the tools and unlocked the possibilities to revolutionize the field. The insights and techniques derived from option pricing are capable of quantifying the elusive elements of managerial operating flexibility and strategic interactions thus far ignored or underestimated by conventional Net Present Value (NPV) and other quantitative approaches.

The book includes sections on identifying reasons for the underinvestment problem and general/conceptual frameworks for viewing productive investment opportunities as real options; useful building blocks; quantifying various types of real options separately and in combination; competitive and strategic aspects of investment under uncertainty; various useful numerical analysis techniques; a variety of applications, including valuing natural resources (mines, oil properties, etc.), R&D and pioneer ventures, land development, strategic acquisitions, power plants, flexible manufacturing and multinational operations; and empirical evidence from oil leases, land prices, and discontinued operations.

Both academic and practitioner interest in these developments is unusually high. The book can serve as reference/supplementary material for researchers and students (e.g., in advanced/elective finance courses in option pricing, capital budgeting or corporate finance, doctoral seminars, and as a library resource). It should also be of significant interest and value to the newcomer as well as the seasoned professional (e.g., to corporate planners and finance executives).

It is our hope that a synthesized collection of these classical pieces and recent developments may help spark further interest and subsequent developments and applications in this important and rapidly growing field that is expected to become the dominant valuation paradigm as we enter the uncertainties and challenges of the twenty-first century.

1 Real Options and Investment under Uncertainty: An Overview

Eduardo S. Schwartz and Lenos Trigeorgis

1 Real Options: Main Ideas

The application of option concepts to value real assets has been an important and exciting growth area in the theory and practice of finance. It has revolutionized the way academics and practitioners think about investment projects by explicitly incorporating management flexibility into the analysis. This flexibility can represent a substantial part of the value of many projects. Neglecting it can grossly undervalue these investments and induce a miss-allocation of resources in the economy.[1]

The traditional approach to valuing investment projects, based on net present value (NPV), essentially involves discounting the expected net cash flows from a project at a discount rate that reflects the risk of those cash flows (the "risk-adjusted" discount rate). In this approach the adjustment for risk is made to the discount rate. An alternative approach is to make the adjustment for risk to the cash flows and to discount the resulting certainty-equivalent cash flows, instead of the expected cash flows, at the risk-free rate of interest.[2] The net-present-value approach is usually used in practice because it is thought normally to be easier to estimate the risk-adjusted discount rate than the certainty-equivalent cash flows.[3] However, in certain cases, such as in the case of commodities for which futures contracts exist, the certainty-equivalent cash flows are clearly easier to calculate since they can be obtained from future (or forward) prices.[4] So, when valuing projects in which the main uncertainty is the commodity price and future prices for the commodity exist, it is much easier to use the certainty-equivalent approach. Instead of having to obtain subjective forecasts of future spot prices of the commodity, which are highly volatile, market-traded future prices can be used. This approach bypasses the need to compute a risk-adjusted discount rate. Once the adjustment for risk has been appropriately made to the cash flows, the relevant discount rate is the risk-free rate of interest.

These results are more general than the above example might seem to indicate. Harrison and Kreps (1979), Harrison and Pliska (1981), and others have shown that, in perfect markets, the absence of arbitrage implies the existence of a probability distribution such that securities are priced based on their discounted (at the risk free rate) expected cash flows, where expectation is determined under this risk-neutral or risk-adjusted probability measure (also called the "equivalent martingale measure"). If markets are complete and all risks can be hedged, these probabilities are unique. Such would be the case, for example, when we are pricing a call option on a stock by forming a portfolio between the underlying stock and a riskless bond which dynamically replicates the payoff of the call option. If markets are not complete these risk-neutral probabilities are not necessarily unique, but any one of the (possibly infinite number of) probability distributions would determine the same market value of the security. Such would be the case, for example, when we are pricing a corporate bond subject to default risk when default can occur suddenly (with a certain probability per unit of time). When future contracts exist, futures prices are the expected spot prices at the maturity of the futures contract under this risk-neutral probability distribution. In the above discussion we have implicitly assumed that interest rates are constant, but these results also apply when interest rates are stochastic.

The critical advantage of working in this risk-neutral environment in which the relevant discount rate is the risk-free rate of interest is that it is an appropriate and convenient environment for option pricing. This allows the multiple operating options available in a typical investment project to be naturally incorporated in the analysis. These options include the optimal time to invest in a project, options to stop and restart production in response to price changes, the option to abandon the project if prices are too low to justify maintaining ongoing operations, the option to expand production, corporate growth options etc.

Option pricing theory, developed by Black and Scholes (1973), Merton (1973) and Cox and Ross (1976), introduced the concept of pricing securities by arbitrage methods. Since the option is valued *relative* to the underlying asset (and can in principle be replicated synthetically), it has the same value in the actual world as in a risk-neutral environment. For the purpose of valuing an option, *it can be assumed* that the expected rate of return on the underlying asset (as well as the option) is the risk-free rate of interest in such a risk-neutral environment. The expected value of the option at maturity, under the risk-neutral probability distribution, can then be discounted at the risk-free rate to obtain the current value of the option. If the market is complete the risk-neutral distribution is unique and can be obtained simply by replacing the actual (true) expected rate of return on the underlying asset by the risk-free rate of return.

Using this risk-neutral framework to value investment projects has three major advantages. First, it allows properly taking into account all the flexibilities (options) that the project might have. Second, it uses all the information contained in market prices (e.g., futures prices) when such prices exist. Third, it allows using the powerful analytical tools developed in contingent claims analysis to determine both the value of the investment project as well as its optimal operating policy (i.e., optimal exercise of the many real options the project might have).

These methods have been first successfully applied in the valuation of natural resource investments, such as gold and copper mines and oil deposits. A main reason for this is the existence of well-developed futures markets for these commodities from which essential market information can be extracted that makes use of the certainty-equivalent and risk-neutral approaches quite convenient.

In the first attempts to value investment projects in natural resources using this new approach (e.g., see Brennan and Schwartz 1985), the spot price of the commodity was assumed to follow geometric Brownian motion similar to the process assumed for stock prices in the option pricing literature. This allowed for straightforward extension of the option pricing framework to value real assets. Futures prices were used to determine the average convenience yield, which plays a similar role in the commodity spot price process as the dividend yield does in the stock price process.[5]

The stochastic process initially assumed for the spot commodity price, however, had some drawbacks. First, if the convenience yield is assumed constant, the model is unable to capture changes in the term structure of futures prices (for example, from backwardation to contango or vice-versa). In reality, the convenience yield experiences significant changes through time. Second, the model implies that the volatility of all futures returns is equal to the volatility of spot returns. The data shows, however, that the volatility of futures returns decreases with the time to maturity of the futures contract. Third, geometric Brownian motion implies that the variance of the distribution of spot prices grows linearly with time, whereas supply and demand adjustments to changing prices would suggest some type of mean reversion in spot commodity prices. In the last few years there have been several attempts to address the drawbacks of the basic natural-resource valuation model discussed above.[6,7]

In most capital investment situations, however, the sources of uncertainty in a project do not have futures prices from which to easily obtain the risk-adjusted process needed for valuation. In many cases the sources of uncertainty in the project are state variables that are not traded assets. Examples of this are product demand uncertainty, geological uncertainty, technological uncertainty, and cost uncertainty.

If a claim is contingent on the value of one or more state variables that are not traded assets, an equilibrium model of asset prices can be used to value the contingent claim. Generalizing Merton's (1973b) intertemporal capital asset pricing model, Cox, Ingersoll, and Ross (1985) derive a fundamental partial differential equation that must be satisfied by the value of all such general claims. This analysis implies that, for the purposes of pricing the contingent claim, a "risk-adjusted drift" for the stochastic process of the state variables can again be used such that the expected option payoff at maturity can be discounted at the riskless interest rate. In this case, the risk-adjusted drift is equal to the original drift minus an adjustment for risk (risk premium) that comes from the equilibrium model. The drift of the process and the risk adjustment from the equilibrium model now enter into the valuation model. In order to implement this approach it is necessary to know the correlation between changes in the state variables and aggregate wealth (the "beta").[8]

These general ideas can be applied to investment project valuation. For assets which do not have traded futures contracts or for other state variables that may affect output, such as uncertainty shocks on demand or costs, one must adjust the drift of the corresponding stochastic process using an equilibrium model to enable risk-free discounting. If a time series of the state variable is available to estimate the parameters of its stochastic process, it can be used to compute the correlation of changes in this state variable with the market portfolio. This correlation can then be used in an equilibrium model for determining the appropriate risk adjustment.

In practice, most real option problems must be solved using numerical methods. In many cases they can be modeled using partial differential equations (PDE's) and boundary conditions which the value of the project must satisfy. Their numerical solution gives not only the value of the project, but also the optimal strategy for exercising the options embedded in the analysis. The simplest real option problems involving one or two state variables can also be more conveniently solved using binomial or trinomial trees in one or two dimensions. But if the problems involve more state variables and/or are path-dependent, the more practical solution is to use Monte Carlo simulation methods. Until very recently simulation methods were not available for solving American-type options, which are the type typically encountered in real option problems. But in the last few years, methods have been developed which allow using simulation for solving American-style options.[9] For example, Longstaff and Schwartz (1998) developed a least-squares Monte Carlo approach to value American-type options by simulation. At every point in time the problem is to compare the value of immediate exercise with the conditional expected value (under the risk neutral measure) from continuation. The conditional expected value of continuation, for each path at each point in time, can be obtained from the fitted value of the linear regression of the discounted value (at the risk free rate) of the cash flows obtained from the simulation following the optimal policy in the future, on a set of basis functions of the state variables. Since this is a recursive procedure starting from the maturity of the option, the outcome is the optimal stopping time for each path in the simulation. Knowing the optimal stopping time for each path, the American option can then be easily valued. Chapter 27 by Cortazar reviews these developments and the use of numerical methods in general.

We pointed out a number of major advantages that real options valuation has over the traditional net present value approach. It explicitly allows for managerial flexibility in the form of options in the valuation procedure. It does not require the estimation of a risk-adjusted discount rate and uses the risk-free rate of interest as the discount rate. When market (e.g., future) prices exist, it avoids the need to make assumptions about the trajectory of spot prices in the future since it uses the information contained in futures prices.

Academic articles dealing with the application of option pricing theory to valuing real assets have appeared in the finance literature for more than fifteen years. The practical application of these ideas has mainly been taking place in the last several years. Although the methodology was first applied to natural resource investments, more recently we started seeing applications in a range of other areas, including research and development, development of new technologies, company valuation and M&As, intellectual property rights/intangible assets, etc. We predict that the real options approach to valuation will have a significant impact in the practice of finance and strategy over the next 5–10 years.

2   Real Options: Literature in Perspective

The sections that follow describe various stages in the development and evolution of the real options literature, organized around several broad themes. This classification should provide the reader with both a historical and a contextual perspective for the development of the ideas, problems, and techniques in real options analysis. The role and position in the literature of the selected readings in this book (with relevant chapter in parenthesis) is indicated when appropriate.

2.1   Underinvestment and Conceptual Options Approaches

The real options revolution arose in part as a response to the dissatisfaction of corporate practitioners, strategists, and some academics with traditional capital budgeting techniques. Well before the development of real options, corporate managers and strategists were grappling intuitively with the elusive elements of managerial operating flexibility and strategic interactions. Early critics (e.g., Dean [1951], Hayes and Abernathy [1980], Hayes and Garvin [1982]) recognized that standard discounted cash flow (DCF) criteria often undervalued investment opportunities, leading to myopic decisions, underinvestment and eventual loss of competitive position, because they either ignored or did not properly value important strategic considerations. Decision scientists further maintained that the problem lied in the application of the wrong valuation techniques altogether, proposing instead the use of simulation and decision tree analysis (see Hertz [1964], Magee [1964]) to capture the value of future operating flexibility associated with many projects. Proponents (e.g., Hodder and

Riggs [1985], Hodder [1986]) have argued that the problem rather arises from misuse of DCF techniques as commonly applied in practice. Myers (chapter 2), while confirming that part of the problem results from various misapplications of the underlying theory, acknowledges that traditional DCF methods have inherent limitations when it comes to valuing investments with significant operating or strategic options (e.g., in capturing the sequential interdependence among investments over time), suggesting that option pricing holds the best promise of valuing such investments. Trigeorgis and Mason (chapter 4) clarify that option valuation can be seen operationally as a special, economically-corrected version of decision tree analysis that is better suited in valuing a variety of corporate operating and strategic options. Baldwin and Clark (1992) discuss the importance of organizational capabilities in strategic capital investment, while Baldwin and Trigeorgis (1993) propose remedying the underinvestment problem and restoring competitiveness by developing specific adaptive capabilities viewed as an infrastructure for acquiring and managing real options.

Building on Myers's (1977) initial idea of thinking of discretionary investment opportunities as "growth options," Kester (chapter 3) conceptually discusses strategic and competitive aspects of growth opportunities. Dixit and Pindyck (chapter 5) and Trigeorgis (chapter 6) provide alternative conceptual real options frameworks for capital budgeting decisions. Other general conceptual frameworks are presented in Mason and Merton (1985), Trigeorgis and Mason (chapter 4), Brealey and Myers (2000), and Kulatilaka and Marcus (1988, 1992). Mason and Merton (1985), for example, provide a good discussion of many operating as well as financing options, and integrate them in a project financing for a hypothetical, large-scale energy project.

2.2 Review of Some Basic Models

The quantitative origins of real options derive from the seminal work of Black and Scholes (1973) and Merton (1973) in pricing financial options. Cox, Ross, and Rubinstein's (1979) binomial approach enabled a more simplified valuation of options in discrete-time. Margrabe (1978) values an option to exchange one risky asset for another, while Stulz (1982) analyzes options on the maximum (or minimum) of two risky assets and Johnson (1987) extends it to several risky assets. These papers opened up the potential to help analyze the generic option to switch among alternative uses and related options (e.g., abandon for salvage value or switch among alternative inputs or outputs). Geske (1979) values a compound option (i.e., an option to acquire another option), which in principle may be applied in valuing growth opportunities which become available only if earlier investments are undertaken. Carr (1988) combines the above two building blocks to value sequential (compound) exchange options, involving an option to acquire a subsequent option to exchange the underlying asset for another risky alternative. The above line of work opened up the potential, in principle, to value investments with a series of investment outlays that can be switched to alternative states of operation, and particularly to eventually help value strategic inter-project dependencies.

The book includes a number of papers as a review of some basic models more directly relevant to the valuation of capital investment opportunities or real options. Trigeorgis (chapter 7) reviews the basic principles of valuing various real options (e.g., to defer, expand, abandon) via simple binomial trees. Brennan and Schwartz (chapter 8) provide a clear exposition of natural resource valuation based on the certainty-equivalent approach using futures contracts. Dixit (chapter 9) uses real options theory to explain why firms often do not invest until price rises substantially above long-run average cost and do not exit a business for lengthy periods, sustaining operating losses, even after price falls substantially below this cost (hysteresis). Kulatilaka and Trigeorgis (chapter 10) present a simple, discrete-time model of the generic flexibility to switch between alternative technologies or operating project "modes", also illustrating a hysteresis effect where, even though immediate switching may seem attractive, it may be long-term optimal to wait. Pindyck (chapter 11) shows how to value in continuous time the option value of waiting under investment irreversibility and uncertainty, modeled using option pricing or dynamic programming.

2.3   Valuing Various Real Options

A number of seminal papers gave a boost to the real options literature by focusing on valuing quantitatively—in many cases deriving analytic, closed-form solutions—one type after another of a variety of real options, although each option was typically analyzed in isolation. The option to defer or initiate investment has been examined by McDonald and Siegel (chapter 12), by Paddock, Siegel, and Smith (chapter 37) in valuing offshore petroleum leases, and by Tourinho (1979) in valuing reserves of natural resources. Ingersoll and Ross (1992) reconsider the decision to wait in light of the beneficial impact of a potential future interest rate decline on project value. Majd and Pindyck (chapter 13) value the option to delay sequential construction for projects that take time to build, or there is a maximum rate at which investment can proceed. Carr (1988) and Trigeorgis (1993a) also deal with valuing sequential or staged (compound) investments. Trigeorgis and Mason (chapter 4), and Pindyck (chapter 15) examine options to alter (e.g., expand or contract) operating scale or capacity choice. The option to temporarily shut down and restart operations was analyzed by McDonald and Siegel (1985), and by Brennan and Schwartz (chapter 8).

Myers and Majd (chapter 14) analyze the option to permanently abandon a project for its salvage value seen as an American put option. Options to switch use (e.g., outputs or inputs) have been examined, among others, by Margrabe (1978), Kensinger (1987), Kulatilaka (1988), and Kulatilaka and Trigeorgis (chapter 10). Baldwin and Ruback (1986) show that future price uncertainty creates a valuable switching option that benefits short-lived projects. Future investment opportunities seen as corporate growth options are discussed in Myers (1977), Brealey and Myers (2000), Kester (chapter 3), Trigeorgis and Mason (chapter 4), Trigeorgis (chapter 6), Pindyck (chapter 15), and Chung and Charoenwong (1991).

Despite its enormous theoretical contribution, the focus of the earlier literature on valuing individual real options (i.e., one type of option at a time) has nevertheless limited its practical value. Real-life projects are often more complex in that they involve a collection of multiple real options, whose values may interact. An early exception is Brennan and Schwartz (chapter 8), who determine the combined value of the options to shut down (and restart) a mine, and to abandon it for salvage. They recognize that partial irreversibility resulting from costs of switching the mine's operating state may create a hysteresis or inertia effect making it long-term optimal to remain in the same operating state even if short-term cash flow considerations seem to favor early switching. Although hysteresis is a form of interaction between early and later decisions, however, Brennan and Schwartz do not explicitly address the interactions among individual option values. Trigeorgis (chapter 17) focuses explicitly on the nature of real option interactions pointing out, for example, that the presence of subsequent options can increase the value of the effective underlying asset for earlier options, while exercise of prior real options may alter (e.g., expand or contract) the underlying asset itself, and hence the value of subsequent options on it. Thus, the combined value of a collection of real options may differ from the sum of separate option values. Trigeorgis identifies conditions for when option interactions are small or large, negative or positive. Kulatilaka (1994) subsequently examines the impact of interactions among such options on their optimal exercise schedules. The recent recognition of real option interdependencies should enable a smoother transition from a theoretical stage to an application phase.

2.4 Strategy and Competition

An area of immense importance is that of competition and strategy. Sustainable competitive advantages resulting from patents, proprietary technologies, ownership of valuable natural resources, managerial capital, reputation or brand name, scale and market power, empower companies with valuable options to grow through future profitable investments and to more effectively respond to unexpected adversity or opportunities in a changing technological, competitive, or general business environment. A number of economists have addressed several competitive and strategic aspects of capital investment early on. For example, Roberts and Weitzman (1981) find that in sequential decision making, it may be worthwhile to undertake investments with negative NPV when early investment can provide information about future project benefits, especially when their uncertainty is greater. Baldwin (1982) finds that optimal sequential investment for firms with market power facing irreversible decisions may require a positive premium over NPV to compensate for the loss in value of future opportunities that results from undertaking an investment. Pindyck (chapter 15) analyzes options to choose capacity under product price uncertainty when investment is, again, irreversible. Dixit (1989) considers firm entry and exit decisions under uncertainty, showing that in the presence of sunk or costly switching costs it may not be long-term optimal to reverse a decision even when prices appear attractive in the short term. Kogut and Kulatilaka (chapter 36) analyze the international plant location option in the presence of mean-reverting exchange rate volatility.

From a more explicit real options perspective, a number of authors (e.g., Myers [1987], Kester [1984, 1993], Trigeorgis and Mason [1987], Trigeorgis [1988], Brealey and Myers [2000], and Trigeorgis and Kasanen [1991]) have initially dealt with competitive and strategic options rather conceptually. For example, Kester (chapter 3) develops qualitatively various competitive and strategic aspects of inter-project growth options, while Kester (1993) proposes a planned sequential, rather than parallel, implementation of a collection of interrelated consumer products when learning results from early product introductions (e.g., about available shelf space needed for similar subsequent products) and when competitive advantage is eroding. Trigeorgis and Kasanen (1991) also examine sequential project interdependencies and synergies as part of an ongoing strategic planning and control process. Kasanen (1993) also deals with the strategic problem of the interaction between current investments and future opportunities, using a spawning matrix structure to determine the optimal mix of strategic and operating projects.

In section IV of the book, Luehrman (chapter 18) discusses a conceptual framework for viewing strategy as managing a portfolio of real options. Strategic acquisitions of other companies also often involve a number of growth, divestiture, and other flexibility options, as discussed in Smith and Triantis (chapter 19). Childs, Ott, and Triantis (chapter 20) provide an intuitive and interesting discussion for managing portfolios of interrelated (e.g., R&D) projects.

More quantitatively, Trigeorgis (1991a) uses option pricing techniques to examine early investment that may preempt anticipated competitive entry, and to value the option to defer investment when impacted by random competitive entry (Trigeorgis, 1990b). Further departing from the common assumption of perfect competition, Smit and Trigeorgis (chapter 21) and Kulatilaka and Perotti (chapter 22) examine how the investment decisions of a firm will influence competitive reactions and the equilibrium market price or quantity when early investment generates a strategic (e.g., cost) advantage. Grenadier and Weiss (chapter 23) use option pricing to value investment in technological innovations. A simpler game-theoretic treatment of competitive reactions under different market structures in a real options framework is also given in Smit and Ankum (1993). Supplementing options analysis with game theoretic tools capable of incorporating strategic competitive counteractions promises to be an important and challenging direction for future research.

2.5 Numerical Techniques

In the more complex real-life option situations, such as those involving multiple interacting real options, analytic solutions may not exist and one may not even be always able to write down the set of partial differential equations describing the underlying stochastic processes. The ability to value such complex option situations has been enhanced, however, with various numerical analysis techniques, many of which take advantage of risk neutral valuation. Generally, there are two types of numerical techniques for option valuation: (1) those that approximate the underlying stochastic processes directly, and are generally more intuitive; and (2) those approximating the resulting partial differential equations. The first category includes various lattice approaches such as Cox, Ross and Rubinstein's (1979) standard binomial lattice and Trigeorgis's (chapter 24) log-transformed binomial method, which are particularly well suited to valuing complex projects with multiple embedded real options, a series of investment outlays, dividend-like effects, as well as option interactions; it also includes Monte Carlo simulation, initially used by Boyle (1977). Cortazar (chapter 27) reviews simulation techniques in the context of real options problems and applications in the context of broader numerical methods. Boyle (1988) shows how lattice frameworks can be extended to handle two state variables, while Hull and White (1988) suggest a control variate technique to improve computational efficiency when a similar derivative asset with an analytic solution is available. Examples of the second category include numerical integration, and implicit or explicit finite difference schemes used by Brennan (1979), Brennan and Schwartz (chapter 25), and Majd and Pindyck (1987). Finally, a number of analytic approximations are also available. A comprehensive review of such numerical techniques is given in the articles by Geske and Shastri (chapter 26), Trigeorgis (chapter 24), and Cortazar (chapter 27).

2.6 Applications

A variety of real options applications is provided in section VI, starting with Merton's (chapter 28) overview of options applications (part of his Nobel prize address). Nichols's (chapter 29) celebrated interview about real options applications at Merck is another natural apetizer. Kemna (chapter 30) describes actual cases involving the timing of developing an offshore oil field, valuing a growth option in a manufacturing venture, and the abandonment decision of a refining production unit.

In the area of *flexible manufacturing*, the flexibility provided by flexible manufacturing systems, flexible production technology or other machinery having multiple uses has been analyzed from an options perspective by Kulatilaka (1988, 1993), Triantis and Hodder (1990), Aggarwal (1991), and Kulatilaka and Trigeorgis (chapter 10), among others. Kulatilaka (chapter 31) values the flexibility of an actual dual-fuel industrial steam boiler over a rigid alternative. Baldwin and Clark (1993) studied the flexibility created by modularity in design that connects components of a larger system through standard interfaces.

Of course, early applications arose in the area of *natural resource investments* due to the availability of traded resource or commodity prices, high volatilities and long durations, resulting in higher and better option value estimates. Brennan and Schwartz (chapters 8 and 16) first utilized the convenience yield derived from futures and spot prices of a commodity to value the options to shut down or abandon a mine. Paddock, Siegel, and Smith (chapter 37) valued options embedded in undeveloped oil reserves and provided the first empirical evidence that option values are better than actual DCF-based bids in valuing offshore oil leases. Trigeorgis (chapter 32) values an actual minerals project considered by a major multinational company involving several options. Bjerksund and Ekern (chapter 33) value a Norwegian oil field with options to defer and abandon. Morck, Schwartz and Stangeland (1989) valued forestry resources under stochastic inventories and prices. Laughton and Jacoby (1993) studied biases in the valuation of certain commodity projects of different duration characterized by a mean-reverting price process rather than the standard random walk assumption.

In the area of *land development*, Titman (chapter 34), Quigg (chapter 38), and other authors have shown that the value of vacant urban land should reflect not only its value based on its best immediate use, but also its option value if development is delayed and the land is converted into its best alternative use in the future. In a different context, McLaughlin and Taggart (1992) view the opportunity cost of using excess capacity as the change in the value of the firm's options caused by diverting capacity to an alternative use. In *leasing*, a number of authors valued various operating options embedded in leasing contracts.

In the area of *large-scale energy projects and regulation*, Mason and Baldwin (1988) valued government subsidies to large-scale energy projects as put options, while Teisberg (1994) provides an option valuation analysis of investment choices by a regulated firm. In *research and development*, Kolbe, Morris, and Teisberg (1991) discuss option elements embedded in R&D projects. Option elements involved in the staging of *start-up ventures* are discussed in Sahlman (1998) and Trigeorgis (1993). Pindyck (chapter 35) discusses capital investments when the cost is uncertain in the context of a power plant application.

In *foreign investment*, Baldwin (1977) discusses various location, timing and staging options present when firms scan the global marketplace. Bell (1995) and Kogut and Kulatilaka (chapter 36), among others, examine entry, capacity, and switching options for firms with multinational operations under exchange rate volatility. Various other option applications are found in areas ranging from valuing mean-reverting cash flows in *shipping*, studied by Bjerksund and Ekern (1995), to *global warming* (e.g., Hendricks [1991]) and *environmental pollution compliance* options, analyzed by Edleson and Reinhardt (1995). The potential for future applications is clearly a growth option itself.

2.7 Empirical Evidence

Empirical evidence on the explanatory power of real options started to emerge only quite recently. Kester (chapter 3) estimates that the value of a firm's growth options is more than half the market value of equity for many firms, even 70–80% for more volatile industries. Similarly, Pindyck (chapter 15) also suggests that growth options represent more than half of firm value if demand volatility exceeds 0.2. An early application in valuing offshore petroleum leases and explaining market bids has been provided by Paddock, Siegel, and Smith (chapter 37). Quick (chapter 38) reports empirical results indicating that option-based land valuations are better approximations of market prices. Berger, Ofek, and Swary (chapter 39) provide evidence of market valuation of the abandonment option in plant closing decisions. Moel and Tufano (1999) provide evidence that mine operating decisions are consistent with real option theory. More evidence is clearly forthcoming. We hope that this work will help stimulate further applications and more evidence in the years ahead.

Notes

1. Calculating the values of multiple options embedded in investment projects separately and adding the results may lead to substantial overvaluation of project value, however.

2. The certainty-equivalent cash flows are the certain amounts which would have the same value as the uncertain cash flows.

3. Fama and French (1997) have recently emphasized the difficulties of accurately estimating risk-adjusted discount rates.

4. Here, we do not distinguish between forward and future prices, i.e., we assume that the interest rate is deterministic or that commodity prices are uncorrelated with interest rates.

5. The convenience yield is the flow of services that accrue to the holder of the spot commodity but not to the holder of a futures contract. In practice, the convenience yield is the adjustment needed in the drift rate of the spot price process to properly price existing futures contracts.

6. See for example Brennan (1991), Gibson and Schwartz (1990 and 1991), Ross (1997), Cortazar and Schwartz (1994), and Bessembinder, Coughenour, Seguin, and Smoller (1995).

7. Schwartz (1997) compares three models of the stochastic behavior of commodity prices in terms of their ability to price the term structure of futures prices and the term structure of futures return volatility. The first model is a one-factor model in which the log of the spot price of the commodity is assumed to follow a mean-reverting process. The second model assumes that the convenience yield is also stochastic and follows a mean-reverting process. In this model the convenience yield plays the role of a stochastic dividend in the spot price process. The third model extends the second by assuming also stochastic interest rates. For the two commercial commodities considered, copper and oil, the one-factor model does a poor job in explaining the characteristics of the data. The other two models, however, are able to capture many of the characteristics of the term structure of futures prices and volatilities. This type of approach is now being used to model the behavior of commodity prices.

8. For example, Brennan and Schwartz (1982) apply this framework to the valuation of a regulated firm in which the underlying state variable is the rate of return on the rate base.

9. See Longstaff and Schwartz (1988).

References

Baldwin, C. 1987. "Competing for Capital in a Global Environment." *Midland Corporate Finance Journal* 5, no. 1: 43–64.

Baldwin, C., and K. Clark. 1993. "Modularity and Real Options." Working paper, Harvard Business School.

Baldwin, C., and L. Trigeorgis. 1993. Real Options, Capabilities, TQM, and Competitiveness. Working paper 93-025, Harvard Business School.

Bell, G. 1995. "Volatile Exchange Rates and the Multinational Firm: Entry, Exit, and Capacity Options." In *Real Options in Capital Investment: Models, Strategies, and Applications*, ed. L. Trigeorgis. Praeger.

Bjerksund, P., and S. Ekern. 1990. "Managing Investment Opportunities Under Price Uncertainty: From 'Last Chance' to 'Wait and See' Strategies." *Financial Management* 19, no. 3: 65–83.

Bjerksund, P., and S. Ekern. 1995. "Contingent Claims Evaluation of Mean-Reverting Cash Flows in Shipping." In *Real Options in Capital Investment: Models, Strategies, and Applications*, ed. L. Trigeorgis. Praeger.

Black, F., and M. Scholes. 1973. "The Pricing of Options and Corporate Liabilities," *Journal of Political Economy* 81 (May–June): 637–659.

Brealey, R., and S. C. Myers. 2000. Principles of Corporate Finance. McGraw-Hill.

Brennan, M., and E. Schwartz. 1985. "Evaluating Natural Resource Investments." *Journal of Business* 58, no. 2: 135–157.

Brennan, M., and L. Trigeorgis. 1999. *Project Flexibility, Agency, and Product Market Competition*. Oxford University Press.

Capozza, D., and G. Sick. 1994. "The Risk Structure of Land Markets." *Journal of Urban Economics* 35: 297–319.

Carr, P. 1988. "The Valuation of Sequential Exchange Opportunities." *Journal of Finance* 43, no. 5: 1235–1256.

Childs, P., S. Ott and A. Triantis. 1998. "Capital Budgeting for Interrelated Projects: A Real Options Approach." *Journal of Financial and Quantitative Analysis* 33, no. 3: 305–334.

Copeland T., and J. F. Weston. 1982. "A Note on the Evaluation of Cancellable Operating Leases." *Financial Management* 11, no. 2: 60–67.

Dixit, A. 1980. "The Role of Investment in Entry Deterrence." *Economic Journal* 90 (March): 95–106.

Dixit, A. 1992. "Investment and Hysteresis." *Journal of Economic Perspectives* 6 (Winter): 107–132.

Dixit, A., and R. S. Pindyck. 1994. *Investment Under Uncertainty*. Princeton University Press.

Geske, R. 1979. "The Valuation of Compound Options." *Journal of Financial Economics* 7, no. 1: 63–81.

Grenadier, S., and A. M. Weiss. 1997. "Investment in Technological Innovations: An Option Pricing Approach." *Journal of Financial Economics* 44: 397–416.

Hendricks, D. 1991. Optimal Policy Responses to an Uncertain Threat: The Case of Global Warming. Working paper, Kennedy School of Government, Harvard University.

Hiraki, T. 1995. "Corporate Governance, Long-term Investment Orientation, and Real Options in Japan." In *Real Options in Capital Investment: Models, Strategies, and Applications*, ed. L. Trigeorgis. Praeger.

Ingersoll, J., and S. Ross. 1992. "Waiting to Invest: Investment and Uncertainty." *Journal of Business* 65, no. 1: 1–29.

Kemna, A. 1993. "Case Studies on Real Options." *Financial Management* 22, no. 3: 259–270.

Kester, W. C. 1984. "Today's Options for Tomorrow's Growth." *Harvard Business Review* 62, no. 2: 153–160.

Kogut, B., and N. Kulatilaka. 1994. "Operating Flexibility, Global Manufacturing, and the Option Value of a Multinational Network." *Management Science* 40, no. 1: 123–139.

Kolbe, A. L., P. A. Morris, and E. O. Teisberg. 1991. "When Choosing R&D Projects, Go with Long Shots." *Research-Technology Management* (January–February).

Kulatilaka, N. 1993. "The Value of Flexibility: The Case of a Dual-Fuel Industrial Steam Boiler." *Financial Management* 22, no. 3: 271–279.

Kulatilaka, N. 1995. "The Value of Flexibility: A General Model of Real Options." In *Real Options in Capital Investment: Models, Strategies, and Applications*, ed. L. Trigeorgis. Praeger.

Kulatilaka, N., and L. Trigeorgis. 1994. "The General Flexibility to Switch: Real Options Revisited." *International Journal of Finance* 6, no. 2: 778–798.

Laughton, D. G., and H. D. Jacoby. 1993. "Reversion, Timing Options, and Long-term Decision-Making." *Financial Management* 22, no. 3: 225–240.

Luehrman, T. 1998. "Strategy as a Portfolio of Real Options." *Harvard Business Review* (September–October): 89–99.

Martzoukos, S., and L. Trigeorgis. 1998. General Multi-stage Capital Investment Problems with Multiple Uncertainties. Working paper, University of Chicago.

Mason, S. P., and C. Baldwin. 1988. "Evaluation of Government Subsidies to Large-scale Energy Projects: A Contingent Claims Approach." *Advances in Futures and Options Research* 3: 169–181.

Mason, S. P., and R. C. Merton. 1985. "The Role of Contingent Claims Analysis in Corporate Finance." In *Recent Advances in Corporate Finance*, ed. E. Altman and M. Subrahmanyam. Irwin.

McConnel, J., and J. Schallheim. 1983. "Valuation of Asset Leasing Contracts." *Journal of Financial Economics* 12, no. 2: 237–261.

McDonald, R., and D. Siegel. 1985. "Investment and the Valuation of Firms When There is an Option to Shut Down." *International Economic Review* 26, no. 2: 331–349.

McDonald, R., and D. Siegel. 1986. "The Value of Waiting to Invest." *Quarterly Journal of Economics* 101, no. 4: 707–727.

McLaughlin, R., and R. Taggart. 1992. "The Opportunity Cost of Using Excess Capacity." *Financial Management* 21, no. 2: 12–23.

Merton, R. C. 1973. "Theory of Rational Option Pricing." *Bell Journal of Economics and Management Science* 4, no. 1: 141–183.

Merton, R. C. 1998. "Applications of Option-Pricing Theory: Twenty-Five Years Later." *American Economic Review* 88, no. 3: 336–340.

Morck, R., E. Schwartz, and D. Stangeland. 1989. "The Valuation of Forestry Resources under Stochastic Prices and Inventories." *Journal of Financial and Quantitative Analysis* 24, no. 4: 473–487.

Myers, S. C. 1987. "Finance Theory and Financial Strategy." *Midland Corporate Finance Journal* 5, no. 1: 6–13.

Myers, S. C., and S. Majd. 1990. "Abandonment Value and Project Life." *Advances in Futures and Options Research* 4: 1–21.

Paddock, J., D. Siegel, and J. Smith. 1988. "Option Valuation of Claims on Physical Assets: The Case of Offshore Petroleum Leases." *Quarterly Journal of Economics* 103, no. 3: 479–508.

Panayi, S., and L. Trigeorgis. 1998. "Multi-stage Real Options: The Cases of Information Technology Infrastructure and International Bank Expansion." *Quarterly Review of Economics and Finance* 38: 675–692.

Pindyck, R. 1988. "Irreversible Investment, Capacity Choice, and the Value of the Firm." *American Economic Review* 78, no. 5: 969–985.

Pindyck, R. 1991. "Irreversibility, Uncertainty, and Investment." *Journal of Economic Literature* 29, no. 3: pp. 1110–1148.

Quigg, L. 1993. "Empirical Testing of Real Option-Pricing Models." *Journal of Finance* 48, no. 2: 621–640.

Quigg, L. 1995. "Optimal Land Development." In *Real Options in Capital Investment: Models, Strategies, and Applications*, ed. L. Trigeorgis. Praeger.

Sahlman, W. 1988. "Aspects of Financial Contracting in Venture Capital." *Journal of Applied Corporate Finance* 1: 23–36.

Schwartz, E., and L. Trigeorgis. 2000. *Real Options and Investment under Uncertainty: Classical Readings and Recent Contributions.* MIT Press.

Sick, G. 1989. *Capital Budgeting With Real Options.* Monograph, Salomon Brothers Center, New York University.

Smit, H. T. J., and L. A. Ankum. 1993. "A Real Options and Game-Theoretic Approach to Corporate Investment Strategy under Competition." *Financial Management* 22, no. 3: 241–250.

Smit, H. T. J., and L. Trigeorgis. 1993. Flexibility and Commitment in Strategic Investment. Working paper, Tinbergen Institute, Erasmus University, Rotterdam.

Smit, H. T. J., and L. Trigeorgis. 1997. R&D Option Strategies. Working paper, University of Chicago.

Smit, H. T. J., and L. Trigeorgis. 1999. Flexibility, Strategic Options and Dynamic Competition in Technology Investments. In Real Options Applications, ed. A. Micalizzi and L. Trigeorgis. Egea.

Smith, K. W., and A. Triantis. 1995. "The Value of Options in Strategic Acquisitions." In *Real Options in Capital Investment: Models, Strategies, and Applications*, ed. L. Trigeorgis. Praeger.

Spence, M. 1979. "Investment Strategy and Growth in a New Market." *Bell Journal of Economics* 10 (spring): 1–19.

Teisberg, E. 1994. "An Option Valuation Analysis of Investment Choices by a Regulated Firm." *Management Science* 40, no. 4: 535–548.

Titman, S. 1985. "Urban Land Prices Under Uncertainty." *American Economic Review* 75, no. 3: 505–514.

Triantis A., and J. Hodder. 1990. "Valuing Flexibility as a Complex Option." *Journal of Finance* 45, no. 2: 549–565.

Trigeorgis, L. 1988. "A Conceptual Options Framework for Capital Budgeting." *Advances in Futures and Options Research* 3: 145–167.

Trigeorgis. L. 1990. "A Real Options Application in Natural Resource Investments." *Advances in Futures and Options Research* 4: 153–164.

Trigeorgis, L. 1991a. "Anticipated Competitive Entry and Early Preemptive Investment in Deferrable Projects." *Journal of Economics and Business* 43, no. 2: 143–156.

Trigeorgis, L. 1991b. "A Log-Transformed Binomial Numerical Analysis Method for Valuing Complex Multi-Option Investments." *Journal of Financial and Quantitative Analysis* 26, no. 3: 309–326.

Trigeorgis, L. 1993a. "The Nature of Option Interactions and the Valuation of Investments with Multiple Real Options." *Journal of Financial and Quantitative Analysis* 28, no. 1: 1–20.

Trigeorgis, L. 1993b. "Real Options and Interactions with Financial Flexibility." *Financial Management* 22, no. 3: 202–224.

Trigeorgis, L., ed. 1995a. *Real Options in Capital Investment: Models, Strategies, and Applications.* Praeger.

Trigeorgis, L. 1995b. "Evaluating Leases with Complex Operating Options." *European Journal of Operational Research* (Special Issue on Financial Modelling) 75.

Trigeorgis, L. 1996. *Real Options: Managerial Flexibility and Strategy in Resource Allocation.* MIT Press.

Trigeorgis, L. Forthcoming. *Innovation and Strategy, Flexibility, Natural Resources and Foreign Investment: New Developments and Applications in Real Options.* Oxford University Press.

Trigeorgis, L., and S. P. Mason. 1987. "Valuing Managerial Flexibility." *Midland Corporate Finance Journal* 5, no. 1: 14–21.

I UNDERINVESTMENT AND CONCEPTUAL OPTIONS APPROACHES

2 Finance Theory and Financial Strategy

Stewart C. Myers

Strategic planning is many things, but it surely includes the process of deciding how to commit the firm's resources across lines of business. The financial side of strategic planning allocates a particular resource, capital.

Finance theory has made major advances in understanding how capital markets work and how risky real and financial assets are valued. Tools derived from finance theory, particularly discounted cash-flow analysis, are widely used. Yet finance theory has had scant impact on strategic planning.

I attempt here to explain the gap between finance theory and strategic planning. Three explanations are offered:

1. Finance theory and traditional approaches to strategic planning may be kept apart by differences in language and "culture."

2. Discounted cash flow analysis may have been misused, and consequently not accepted, in strategic applications.

3. Discounted cash flow analysis may fail in strategic applications even if it is properly applied.

Each of these explanations is partly true. I do not claim that the three, taken together, add up to the whole truth. Nevertheless, I will describe both the problems encountered in applying finance theory to strategic planning, and the potential payoffs if the theory can be extended and properly applied.

The first task is to explain what is meant by "finance theory" and the gap between it and strategic planning.

The Relevant Theory

The financial concepts most relevant to strategic planning are those dealing with firms' capital investment decisions, and they are sketched here at the minimum level of detail necessary to define "finance theory."

Think of each investment project as a "mini-firm," all-equity financed. Suppose its stock could be actively traded. If we know what the mini-firm's stock would sell for, we know its present value. We calculate net present value (NPV) by subtracting the required investment.

In other words, we calculate each project's present value to investors who have free access to capital markets. We should therefore use the valuation model which best explains the prices of similar securities. However, the theory is usually boiled down to a single model, discounted cash flow (DCF):

$$\mathrm{PV} = \sum_{t=1}^{T} \frac{C_t}{(1+r)^t},$$

where

PV = present (market) value;

C_t = forecasted incremental cash flow after corporate taxes—strictly speaking the mean of the distribution of possible $\tilde{C}_t$'s;

T = project life (C_T includes any salvage value);

r = the opportunity cost of capital, defined as the equilibrium expected rate of return on securities equivalent in risk to the project being valued.

NPV equals PV less the cash outlay required at $t = 0$.

Since present values add, the value of the firm should equal the sum of the values of all its mini-firms. If the DCF formula works for each project separately, it should work for any collection of projects, a line of business, or the firm as a whole. A firm or line of business consists of intangible as well as tangible assets, and growth opportunities as well as assets-in-place. Intangible assets and growth opportunities are clearly reflected in stock prices, and in principle can also be valued in capital budgeting. Projects bringing intangible assets or growth opportunities to the firm have correspondingly higher NPVs. I will discuss whether DCF formulas can capture this extra value later.

The opportunity cost of capital varies from project to project, depending on risk. In principle, each project has its own cost of capital. In practice, firms simplify by grouping similar projects in risk classes, and use the same cost of capital for all projects in a class.

The opportunity cost of capital for a line of business, or for the firm, is a value-weighted average of the opportunity costs of capital for the projects it comprises.

The opportunity cost of capital depends on the use of funds, not on the source. In most cases, financing has a second-order impact on value: you can make much more money through smart investment decisions than smart financing decisions. The advantage, if any, of departing from all-equity financing is typically adjusted for through a somewhat lowered discount rate.

Finance theory stresses cash flow and the expected return on competing assets. The firm's investment opportunities compete with securities stockholders can buy.

Investors willingly invest or reinvest cash in the firm only if it can do better, risk considered, than the investors can do on their own.

Finance theory thus stresses fundamentals. It should not be deflected by accounting allocations, except as they affect cash taxes. For example, suppose a positive-NPV project sharply reduces book earnings in its early stages. Finance theory would recommend forging ahead, trusting investors to see through the accounting bias to the project's true value. Empirical evidence indicates that investors do see through accounting biases; they do not just look naively at last quarter's or last year's EPS. (If they did, all stocks would sell at the same price-earnings ratio.)

All these concepts are generally accepted by financial economists. The concepts are broadly consistent with an up-to-date understanding of how capital markets work. Moreover, they seem to be accepted by firms, at least in part: any time a firm sets a hurdle rate based on capital market evidence and uses a DCF formula, it must implicitly rely on the logic I have sketched. So the issue here is not whether managers accept finance theory for capital budgeting (and for other financial purposes). It is why they do not use the theory in strategic planning.

The Gap Between Finance Theory and Strategic Planning

I have resisted referring to strategic planning as "capital budgeting on a grand scale" because capital budgeting in practice is a bottom-up process. The aim is to find and undertake specific assets or projects that are worth more than they cost.

Picking valuable pieces does not ensure maximum value for the whole. Piecemeal, bottom-up capital budgeting is not strategic planning.

Capital budgeting techniques, however, ought to work for the whole as well as the parts. A strategic commitment of capital to a line of business is an investment project. If management does invest, they must believe the value of the firm increases by more than the amount of capital committed—otherwise they are throwing money away. In other words, there is an implicit estimate of net present value.

This would seem to invite application of finance theory, which explains how real and financial assets are valued. The theory should have direct application not only to capital budgeting, but also to the financial side of strategic planning.

Of course it has been applied to some extent. Moreover, strategic planning seems to be becoming more financially sophisticated. Financial concepts are stressed in several recent books on corporate strategy.[1] Consulting firms have developed the concepts' strategic implications.[2]

Nevertheless, I believe it is fair to say that most strategic planners are not guided by the tools of modern finance. Strategic and financial analyses are not reconciled, even when the analyses are of the same major project. When low net present value projects are nurtured "for strategic reasons," the strategic analysis overrides measures of financial value. Conversely, projects with apparently high net present values are passed by if they don't fit in with the firm's strategic objectives. When financial and strategic analyses give conflicting answers, the conflict is treated as a fact of life, not as an anomaly demanding reconciliation.

In many firms, strategic analysis is partly or largely directed to variables finance theory says are irrelevant. This is another symptom of the gap, for example:

· Many managers worry about a strategic decision's impact on book rate of return or earnings per share. If they are convinced the plan adds to the firm's value, its impact on accounting figures should be irrelevant.

· Some managers pursue diversification to reduce risk—risk as they see it. Investors see a firm's risk differently. In capital markets, diversification is cheap and easy. Investors who want to diversify do so on their own. Corporate diversification is redundant; the market will not pay extra for it.

If the market were willing to pay extra for diversification, closed-end funds would sell at premiums over net asset value, and conglomerate firms would be worth more to investors than their components separately traded. Closed-end funds actually sell at discounts, not premiums. Conglomerates appear to sell at discounts, too, although it is hard to prove it since the firm's components are not traded separately.

Much of the literature of strategic planning seems extremely naive from a financial point of view. Sometimes capital markets are ignored. Sometimes firms are essentially viewed as having a stock of capital, so that "cash cows" are needed to finance investment in rapidly growing lines of business. (The firms that pioneered in strategic planning actually had easy access to capital markets, as do almost all public companies.) Firms may not like the price they pay for capital, but that price is the opportunity cost of capital, the proper standard for new investment by the firm.

The practical conflicts between finance and strategy are part of what lies behind the recent criticism of U.S. firms for allegedly concentrating on quick payoffs at the expense of value. U.S. executives, especially MBAs, are said to rely too much on purely financial analysis, and too little on building technology, products, markets, and production efficiency. The financial world is not the real world, the argument goes; managers succumb to the glamour of high finance. They give time and talent to mergers, spinoffs, unusual securities, and complex financing packages when they should be out on the factory floor. They pump up current earnings per share at the expense of long-run values.

Much of this criticism is not directed against finance theory, but at habits of financial analysis that financial economists are attempting to reform. Finance theory of course concentrates on the financial world—that is, capital markets. However, it fundamentally disagrees with the implicit assumption of the critics who say that the financial world is not the real world and that financial analysis diverts attention from, and sometimes actively undermines, real long-run values. The professors and textbooks actually say that financial values rest on real values and that most value is created on the left-hand side of the balance sheet, not on the right.

Finance theory, however, is under attack, too. Some feel that any quantitative approach is inevitably short-sighted. Hayes and Garvin, for example, have blamed discounted cash flow for a significant part of this country's industrial difficulties. Much of their criticism seems directed to misapplications of discounted cash flow, some of which I discuss later. But they also believe the underlying theory is wanting; they say that "beyond all else, capital investment represents an act of faith."[3] This statement offends most card-carrying financial economists.

I do not know whether "gap" fully describes all of the problems noted, or hinted at, in the discussion so far. In some quarters, finance theory is effectively ignored in strategic planning. In others, it is seen as being in conflict, or working at cross-purposes, with other forms of strategic analysis. The problem is to explain why.

Two Cultures and One Problem

Finance theory and strategic planning could be viewed as two cultures looking at the same problem. Perhaps only differences in language and approach make the two appear incompatible. If so, the gap between them might be bridged by better communication and a determined effort to reconcile them.

Think of what can go wrong with standard discounted cash flow analyses of a series of major projects:

• Even careful analyses are subject to random error. There is a 50 percent probability of a positive NPV for a truly border line project. Firms have to guard against these errors dominating project choice.

• Smart managers apply the following check. They know that all projects have zero NPV in long-run competitive equilibrium. Therefore, a positive NPV must be explained by a short-run deviation from equilibrium or by some permanent competitive advantage. If neither explanation applies, the positive NPV is suspect. Conversely, a negative NPV is suspect if a competitive advantage or short-run deviation from equilibrium favors the project.

In other words, smart managers do not accept positive (or negative) NPVs unless they can explain them.

Strategic planning may serve to implement this check. Strategic analyses look for market opportunities—that is, deviations from equilibrium—and try to identify the firm's competitive advantages.

Turn the logic of the example around. We can regard strategic analysis which does not explicitly compute NPVs as showing absolute faith in Adam Smith's invisible hand. If a firm, looking at a line of business, finds a favorable deviation from long-run equilibrium, or if it identifies a competitive advantage, then (efficient) investment in that line must offer profits exceeding the opportunity cost of capital. No need to calculate the investment's NPV: the manager knows in advance that NPV is positive.

The trouble is that strategic analyses are also subject to random error. Mistakes are also made in identifying areas of competitive advantage or out-of-equilibrium markets. We would expect strategic analysts to calculate NPVs explicitly, at least as a check; strategic analysis and financial analysis ought to be explicitly reconciled. Few firms attempt this. This suggests the gap between strategic planning and finance theory is more than just "two cultures and one problem."

The next step is to ask why reconciliation is so difficult.

Misuse of Finance Theory

The gap between strategic and financial analysis may reflect misapplication of finance theory. Some firms do not try to use theory to analyze strategic investments. Some firms try but make mistakes.

I have already noted that in many firms capital investment analysis is partly or largely directed to variables finance theory says are irrelevant. Managers worry about projects' book rates of return or impacts on book earnings per share. They worry about payback, even for projects that clearly have positive NPVs. They try to reduce risk through diversification.

Departing from theoretically correct valuation procedures often sacrifices the long-run health of the firm for the short, and makes capital investment choices arbitrary or unpredictable. Over time, these sacrifices appear as disappointing growth, eroding market share, loss of technological leadership, and so forth.

The non-financial approach taken in many strategic analyses may be an attempt to overcome the short horizons and arbitrariness of financial analysis as it is often misapplied. It may be an attempt to get back to fundamentals. Remember, however: finance theory never left the fundamentals. Discounted cash flow should not in principle bias the firm against long-lived projects, or be swayed by arbitrary allocations.

However, the typical mistakes made in applying DCF do create a bias against long-lived projects. I will note a few common mistakes.

Ranking on Internal Rate of Return

Competing projects are often ranked on internal rate of return rather than NPV. It is easier to earn a high rate of return if project life is short and investment is small. Long-lived, capital-intensive projects tend to be put down the list even if their net present value is substantial.

The internal rate of return does measure bang per buck on a DCF basis. Firms may favor it because they think they have only a limited number of bucks. However, most firms big enough to do formal strategic planning have free access to capital markets. They may not like the price, but they can get the money. The limits on capital expenditures are more often set inside the firm, in order to control an organization too eager to spend money. Even when a firm does have a strictly limited pool of capital, it should not use the internal rate of return to rank projects. It should use NPV per dollar invested, or linear programming techniques when capital is rationed in more than one period.[4]

Inconsistent Treatment of Inflation

A surprising number of firms treat inflation inconsistently in DCF calculations. High nominal discount rates are used but cash flows are not fully adjusted for future inflation. Thus accelerating inflation makes projects—especially long-lived ones—look less attractive even if their real value is unaffected.

Unrealistically High Rates

Some firms use unrealistically high discount rates, even after proper adjustment for inflation. This may reflect ignorance of what normal returns in capital markets really are. In addition:

· Premiums are tacked on for risks that can easily be diversified away in stockholders' portfolios.

· Rates are raised to offset the optimistic biases of managers sponsoring projects. This adjustment works only if the bias increases geometrically with the forecast period. If it does not, long-lived projects are penalized.

· Some projects are unusually risky at inception, but only of normal risk once the start-up is successfully passed. It is easy to classify this type of project as "high-risk," and to add a start-up risk premium to the discount rate for all future cash flows. The risk premium should be applied to the start-up period only. If it is applied after the start-up period, safe, short-lived projects are artificially favored.

Discounted cash flow analysis is also subject to a difficult organizational problem. Capital budgeting is usually a bottom-up process. Proposals originate in the organization's midriff, and have to survive the trip to the top, getting approval at every stage. In the process political alliances form, and cash flow forecasts are bent to meet known standards. Answers—not necessarily the right ones—are worked out for anticipated challenges. Most projects that get to the top seem to meet profitability standards set by management.

According to Brealey and Myers's Second Law, "The proportion of proposed projects having positive NPV is independent of top management's estimate of the opportunity cost of capital."[5]

Suppose the errors and biases of the capital budgeting process make it extremely difficult for top management to verify the true cash flows, risks, and present value of capital investment proposals. That would explain why firms do not try to reconcile the results of capital budgeting and strategic analyses. However, it does not explain why strategic planners do not calculate their own NPVs.

We must ask whether those in top management—the managers who make strategic decisions—understand finance theory well enough to use DCF analysis effectively. Although they certainly understand the arithmetic of the calculation, they may not understand the logic of the method deeply enough to trust it or to use it without mistakes.

They may also not be familiar enough with how capital markets work to use capital market data effectively. The widespread use of unrealistically high discount rates is probably a symptom of this.

Finally, many managers distrust the stock market. Its volatility makes them nervous, despite the fact that the volatility is the natural result of a rational market. It may be easier to underestimate the sophistication of the stock market than to accept its verdict on how well the firm is doing.

Finance Theory May Have Missed the Boat

Now consider the firm that understands finance theory, applies DCF analysis correctly, and has overcome the human and organizational problems that bias cash

flows and discount rates. Carefully estimated net present values for strategic investments should help significantly. However, would they fully grasp and describe the
firm's strategic choices? Perhaps not.

There are gaps in finance theory as it is usually applied. These gaps are not necessarily intrinsic to finance theory generally. They may be filled by new approaches to
valuation. However, if they are the firm will have to use something more than a
straightforward discounted cash flow method.

An intelligent application of discounted cash flow will encounter four chief
problems:

· Estimating the discount rate,

· Estimating the project's future cash flows,

· Estimating the project's impact on the firm's other assets' cash flows—that is,
through the cross-sectional links between projects, and

· Estimating the project's impact on the firm's future investment opportunities. These
are the time-series links between projects.

The first three problems, difficult as they are, are not as serious for financial
strategy as the fourth. However, I will review all four.

Estimating the Opportunity Cost of Capital

The opportunity cost of capital will always be difficult to measure, since it is an
expected rate of return. We cannot commission the Gallup Poll to extract probability
distributions from the minds of investors. However, we have extensive evidence on
past average rates of return in capital markets and the corporate sector.[6] No long-run
trends in "normal" rates of return are evident. Reasonable, ballpark cost of capital
estimates can be obtained if obvious traps (for example, improper adjustments for
risk or inflation) are avoided. In my opinion, estimating cash flows properly is more
important than fine-tuning the discount rate.

Forecasting Cash Flow

It's impossible to forecast most projects' actual cash flows accurately. DCF calculations do not call for accurate forecasts, however, but for accurate assessments of the
mean of possible outcomes.

Operating managers can often make reasonable subjective forecasts of the operating variables they are responsible for—operating costs, market growth, market share,
and so forth—at least for the future that they are actually worrying about. It is difficult for them to translate this knowledge into a cash flow forecast for, say, year

seven. There are several reasons for this difficulty. First, the operating manager is asked to look into a far future he is not used to thinking about. Second, he is asked to express his forecast in accounting rather than operating variables. Third, incorporating forecasts of macroeconomic variables is difficult. As a result, long-run forecasts often end up as mechanical extrapolations of short-run trends. It is easy to overlook the long-run pressures of competition, inflation, and technical change.

It should be possible to provide a better framework for forecasting operating variables and translating them into cash flows and present value—a framework that makes it easier for the operating manager to apply his practical knowledge and that explicitly incorporates information about macroeconomic trends. There is, however, no way around it: forecasting is intrinsically difficult, especially when your boss is watching you do it.

Estimating Cross-Sectional Relationships Between Cash Flows

Tracing "cross-sectional" relationships between project cash flows is also intrinsically difficult. The problem may be made more difficult by inappropriate project definitions or boundaries for lines of businesses. Defining business units properly is one of the tricks of successful strategic planning.

However, these inescapable problems in estimating profitability standards, future cash returns, and cross-sectional interactions are faced by strategic planners even if they use no financial theory. They do not reveal a flaw in existing theory. Any theory or approach encounters them. Therefore, they do not explain the gap between finance theory and strategic planning.

The Links Between Today's Investments and Tomorrow's Opportunities

The fourth problem—the link between today's investments and tomorrow's opportunities—is much more difficult.

Suppose a firm invests in a negative-NPV project in order to establish a foothold in an attractive market. Thus a valuable second-stage investment is used to justify the immediate project. The second stage must depend on the first: if the firm could take the second project without having taken the first, then the future opportunity should have no impact on the immediate decision. However, if tomorrow's opportunities depend on today's decisions, there is a time-series link between projects.

At first glance, this may appear to be just another forecasting problem. Why not estimate cash flows for both stages, and use discounted cash flow to calculate the NPV for the two stages taken together?

You would not get the right answer. The second stage is an option, and conventional discounted cash flow does not value options properly. The second stage is an option because the firm is not committed to undertake it. It will go ahead if the first stage works and the market is still attractive. If the first stage fails, or if the market sours, the firm can stop after Stage 1 and cut its losses. Investing in Stage 1 purchases an intangible asset: a call option on Stage 2. If the option's present value offsets the first stage's negative NPV, the first stage is justified.

The Limits of Discounted Cash Flow

The limits of DCF need further explanation. Think first of its application to four types of securities:

1. DCF is standard for valuing bonds, preferred stocks and other fixed-income securities.

2. DCF is sensible, and widely used, for valuing relatively safe stocks paying regular dividends.

3. DCF is not as helpful in valuing companies with significant growth opportunities. The DCF model can be stretched to say that Apple Computer's stock price equals the present value of the dividends the firm may eventually pay. It is more helpful to think of Apple's price, P_0, as:

$$P_0 = \frac{\text{EPS}}{r} + \text{PVGO}, \quad \text{where}$$

EPS   = normalized current earnings

r = the opportunity cost of capital

PVGO = the net present value of future growth opportunities.

Note that PVGO is the present value of a portfolio of options—the firm's options to invest in second-stage, third-stage, or even later projects.

4. DCF is never used for traded calls or puts. Finance theory supplies option valuation formulas that work, but the option formulas look nothing like DCF.

Think of the corporate analogues to these securities:

· There are few problems in using DCF to value safe flows, for example, flows from financial leases.

· DCF is readily applied to "cash cows"—relatively safe businesses held for the cash they generate rather than for strategic value. It also works for "engineering investments," such as machine replacements, where the main benefit is reduced cost in a clearly-defined activity.

• DCF is less helpful in valuing businesses with substantial growth opportunities or intangible assets. In other words, it is not the whole answer when options account for a large fraction of a business's value.

• DCF is no help at all for pure research and development. The value of R&D is almost all option value. Intangible assets' value is usually option value.

The theory of option valuation has been worked out in detail for securities—not only puts and calls, but warrants, convertibles, bond call options, and so forth. The solution techniques should be applicable to the real options held by firms. Several preliminary applications have already been worked out, for example:

• Calculations of the value of a Federal lease for offshore exploration for oil or gas. Here the option value comes from the lessee's right to delay the decisions to drill and develop, and to make these decisions after observing the extent of reserves and the future level of oil prices. [7]

• Calculating an asset's abandonment or salvage value: an active second-hand market increases an asset's value, other things equal. The second-hand market gives the asset owner a put option which increases the value of the option to bail out of a poorly performing project. [8]

The option "contract" in each of these cases is fairly clear: a series of calls in the first case and a put in the second. However, these real options last longer and are more complex than traded calls and puts. The terms of real options have to be extracted from the economics of the problem at hand. Realistic descriptions usually lead to a complex implied "contract," requiring numerical methods of valuation.

Nevertheless, option pricing methods hold great promise for strategic analysis. The time-series links between projects are the most important part of financial strategy. A mixture of DCF and option valuation models can, in principle, describe these links and give a better understanding of how they work. It may also be possible to estimate the value of particular strategic options, thus eliminating one reason for the gap between finance theory and strategic planning.

Lessons for Corporate Strategy

The task of strategic analysis is more than laying out a plan or plans. When time-series links between projects are important, it's better to think of strategy as managing the firm's portfolio of real options.[9] The process of financial planning may be thought of as:

• Acquiring options, either by investing directly in R&D, product design, cost or quality improvements, and so forth, or as a by-product of direct capital investment (for example, investing in a Stage 1 project with negative NPV in order to open the door for stage 2).

• Abandoning options that are too far "out of the money" to pay to keep.

• Exercising valuable options at the right time—that is, buying the cash-producing assets that ultimately produce positive net present value.

There is also a lesson for current applications of finance theory to strategic issues. Several new approaches to financial strategy use a simple, traditional DCF model of the firm.[10] These approaches are likely to be more useful for cash cows than for growth businesses with substantial risk and intangible assets.

The option value of growth and intangibles is not ignored by good managers even when conventional financial techniques miss them. These values may be brought in as "strategic factors," dressed in non-financial clothes. Dealing with the time-series links between capital investments, and with the option value these links create, is often left to strategic planners. But new developments in finance theory promise to help.

Bridging the Gap

We can summarize by asking how the present gap between finance theory and strategic planning might be bridged.

Strategic planning needs finance. Present value calculations are needed as a check on strategic analysis and vice versa. However, the standard discounted cash flow techniques will tend to understate the option value attached to growing, profitable lines of business. Corporate finance theory requires extension to deal with real options. Therefore, to bridge the gap we on the financial side need to:

• Apply existing finance theory correctly.

• Extend the theory. I believe the most promising line of research is to try to use option pricing theory to model the time-series interactions between investments.

Both sides could make a conscious effort to reconcile financial and strategic analysis. Although complete reconciliation will rarely be possible, the attempt should uncover hidden assumptions and bring a generally deeper understanding of strategic choices. The gap may remain, but with better analysis on either side of it.

Notes

1. See, for example, W. E. Fruhan, Jr., *Financial Strategy: Studies in the Creation, Transfer and Destruction of Shareholder Value* (Homewood, Illinois: Richard D. Irwin, Inc., 1979); M. S. Salter and W. A. Weinhold, *Diversification Through Acquisition* (New York: The Free Press, 1979); and H. Bierman, *Strategic Financial Planning* (New York: The Free Press, 1980).

2. See Alberts, W. A. and McTaggart, James M. 1984, "Value-based Strategic Investment Planning," *Interfaces*, Vol. 14, No. 1 (January–February), pp. 138–151.

3. R. H. Hayes and D. A. Garvin, "Managing as If Tomorrow Mattered," *Harvard Business Review*, Vol. 60, No. 3 (May–June), 1982, pp. 70–79.

4. See R. A. Brealey and S. C. Myers, *Principles of Corporate Finance* (New York: McGraw-Hill Book Company, 1981), pp. 101–107.

5. Brealey and Myers, *Principles of Corporate Finance*, cited in note 4, p. 238.

6. For estimates of capital market returns over the period 1926 to the present, see R. G. Ibbotson and R. A. Sinquefield, *Stocks, Bonds, Bills and Inflation: The Past and the Future*, Financial Analysts Research Foundation, Charlottesville, Virginia, 1982. For estimates of historical returns on capital from a corporate perspective, see D. M. Holland and S. C. Myers, "Trends in Corporate Profitability and Capital Costs," in R. Lindsay, ed., *The Nation's Capital Needs: Three Studies*, Committee on Economic Development, Washington, DC, 1979.

7. See the article in this issue by James Paddock, Daniel Siegel, and James Smith, which deals with the use of option pricing models in valuing offshore petroleum leases.

8. See S. C. Myers and S. Majd, "Applying Option Pricing Theory to the Abandonment Value Problem," Sloan School of Management, MIT, Working Paper, 1983.

9. See W. C. Kester, "Today's Options for Tomorrow's Growth," *Harvard Business Review* (March–April 1984).

10. See, for example, Chapter 2 of W. E. Fruhan, Jr., *Financial Strategy: Studies in the Creation, Transfer and Destruction of Shareholder Value* (Homewood, Illinois: Richard D. Irwin, Inc., 1979).

3 Today's Options for Tomorrow's Growth

W. Carl Kester

Since the rise in the use of discounted cash flow techniques, most managers face an increasingly difficult choice in evaluating complex investment decisions. Should they pursue risky projects that offer a below-target rate of return but could create valuable strategic opportunities later? Or should they stick with a less risky and more immediately profitable bet?

Whether it's a diversified company trying to keep pace in a fast-growing market or a smokestack company struggling to regain its competitive edge, the choice must be made. Take the case of a large, technology-based company. Despite a cut in spending plans to avoid outside financing, the capital appropriations committee decided to consider a special project that would require a plant for the large-scale manufacture of a new, proprietary material that had been successfully produced in a pilot plant.

On an ordinary net present value basis, high construction costs, low projected cash flows, and a high sensitivity to cyclical fluctuation combined to make the project unattractive. Opponents argued it would hurt reported earnings, diminish near-term cash flows, and depress an already low stock price.

Proponents pointed out the project's long-term strategic benefits. Wide acceptance of the material would produce a virtual cascade of new commercial development and capacity expansion projects. The project's value came not so much from cash flows directly attributable to the new plant as from opportunities for growth. In the end, the proponents prevailed by falling back on the corporate culture. They recalled a similar project the company had pursued just before World War II—one on which much of its postwar success was built.

The committee finally approved the project but, because of uncertainty and the lack of stronger analytic support, it deferred final appropriation for one year. Ultimately, the new material succeeded. Production efficiencies were achieved, user acceptance developed, and new applications proliferated. But the initial delay proved costly. A competitor's substitute product gained an early foothold in the new material's primary market, forcing the first company to spend more money than originally planned.

How could the project's proponents have made their argument more convincing so that funds would have been committed at once? More to the point, what if a manager doesn't have history to back up his argument? What analytic framework can be used to give a hard edge to the "soft" strategic side of the investment argument?

Based on my research into the investment and capital budgeting decisions of companies, I've concluded that one answer is to think of future investment opportunities as analogous to ordinary call options on securities.[1] Most managers are familiar with call options since they trade actively on public exchanges and such options are often an important part of a compensation package.

Securities options give the owner the *right* (as distinct from an obligation) to buy a security at a fixed, predetermined price (called the exercise price) on or before some fixed date (the maturity date). By way of analogy, a discretionary opportunity to invest capital in productive assets like plant, equipment, and brand names at some future point in time is like a call option on real assets, or a "growth option." The cost of the investment represents the option's exercise price. The value of the option (its underlying "security") is the present value of expected cash flows plus the value of any new growth opportunities expected through ownership and employment of the assets. The time to maturity is the amount of time available before the opportunity disappears.

Like call options on securities, growth options represent real value to those companies fortunate enough to possess them. Any investment project whose implementation can be deferred, that can be modified by the company, or that creates new investment opportunities can be analyzed using this framework. This would include opportunities to:

• Expand capacity, make new product introductions, or acquire other companies.

• Increase budgets for advertising, basic research, and commercial development programs (insofar as these budgets represent investment in assets like brand names or technical expertise).

• Make outlays for maintenance and replacement projects (since these too are discretionary projects that can be forgone if management decides to shrink or leave a business).

Just as securities traders would price a bond-warrant unit to reflect both of its sources of value—that is, the cash from the bond and the option value from the attached warrant—so too should a company analyze an investment in such a way as to delineate all its sources of value.

The importance of growth options can be recognized by looking at the difference between the total market value of a company's equity and the capitalized value of its current earnings stream (see table 3.1). The difference is an estimate of the value of its growth options. As the last column indicates, valuable growth options constitute well over half the market value of many companies' equity.

While only large, publicly traded companies are represented in this exhibit, small, privately held organizations share similar characteristics. In fact, growth options

Table 3.1
Growth option value as a component of selected companies' total equity value

	Market value of equity* ($ millions)	Anticipated earnings* ($ millions)	Capitalized value of earnings using various discount rates** ($ millions)			Estimated value of growth options† ($ millions)	Percent of market value represented by growth options
			15%	20%	25%		
Electronics							
Motorola	5,250	210	1,400	1,050	840	3,850–4,410	73–84
Genrad	550	17	113	85	68	437–482	79–88
RCA	2,200	240	1,600	1,200	960	600–1,240	27–56
Computers and peripheral							
Apple Computer	2,000	99	660	495	396	1,340–1,604	67–80
Digital Equipment	5,690	285	1,900	1,425	1,140	3,790–4,550	67–80
IBM	72,890	5,465	36,433	27,325	21,860	36,457–51,030	50–70
Chemicals							
Celanese	1,010	78	520	390	312	490–698	49–69
Monsanto	4,260	410	2,733	2,050	1,640	1,527–2,620	36–62
Union Carbide	4,350	280	1,867	1,400	1,120	2,483–3,230	57–74
Tires and rubber							
Firestone	1,090	88	587	440	352	503–738	46–68
Goodyear	2,520	300	2,000	1,500	1,200	520–1,320	21–52
Uniroyal	400	47	313	235	188	87–212	22–53
Food processing							
Carnation	1,790	205	1,367	1,025	820	423–970	24–54
Consolidated Foods	1,190	171	1,140	855	684	50–506	4–43
General Foods	2,280	317	2,113	1,585	1,268	167–1,012	7–44

* Source: *Value Line Investment Survey*, August 12, 1983.
** Anticipated earnings are treated as a perpetuity.
† Ranges of growth option value are determined by subtracting the high and low values of capitalized earnings from the market value of the equity.

probably dominate the equity value of small, high-growth companies marketing innovative products. The plethora of companies making initial public offerings at high price-earnings multiples attests to this fact. Genentech went public with annual revenues of $9 million and an operating cash flow of only 6¢ per share. At the initial public offering of $35 (a level quickly surpassed in the immediate aftermarket), the market value of its equity was $262 million—almost entirely based on options for future growth, not on the attractions of its current cash flow.

Strategic Capital Budgeting

While some strategically important investments allow for straightforward evaluation using ordinary discounted cash flow (DCF) techniques (for example, a cost-reduction project for a company whose competitive advantage rests exclusively on being the low-cost producer), others seem to defy such analysis. This is true because they are but the first link in a long chain of subsequent investment decisions. Future events often make it desirable to modify an initial project by expanding it or introducing a new production technology at some later date. Other spin-off opportunities such as the conversion of by-products to usable goods or the development of complementary products to fill out a line may also arise.

Precisely how and when subsequent investment decisions will be made depend on future events. But the array—and attractiveness—of future investment opportunities at the company's disposal depends critically on the assets put in place in the present.

Realizing the importance of strategic investments and the difficulty of using quantitative techniques to analyze them, companies have developed a number of other methods of evaluation. Unfortunately, none has proved totally successful in practice.

In fact, existing cures for quantitative shortcomings may be worse than the disease. What is needed in their place is an approach that overcomes both the restrictiveness of ordinary net present value (NPV) analysis and the lack of analytic discipline that characterizes qualitative evaluation.

Take the opening case example. Proponents of production of the new material understood the value of the opportunity but could not convince skeptics without recalling a precedent. Lacking that precedent, their unstructured application of intuition and judgment would not have overcome formal, quantitative arguments.

The proponents should have organized their arguments around the concept of growth options. They could have argued more effectively that:

Discounted cash flow analysis understates the value of the project.

The risk associated with the project was one of the best reasons to preserve, not reject, it.

In an environment of high and rising interest rates, the capital budget should have been weighted in favor of such projects.

The options approach might have spared the company its subsequent mistake in delaying the capital commitment. In particular, it would have enabled the committee to recognize those conditions under which it should implement the project quickly and those under which it would be safe to defer.

How Valuable Are Growth Options?

The value of a call option on an asset depends on the value of the asset itself and the cost of exercising the option. If, for example, IBM's stock traded at $120, a call option, giving its owner the right to purchase a share of IBM at $100, would be worth at least $20 and probably more.

The same logic applies to growth options. The opportunity to undertake a project is worth at least the present value of the project's cash inflow less the present value of its outflow. But the *opportunity* to invest can be worth even more than the project's NPV. How much more depends on:

The Length of Time the Project Can Be Deferred   Time is valuable when deciding whether to exercise an option. The ability to defer the decision gives the decision maker time to examine the course of future events and the chance to avoid costly errors if unfavorable developments occur. It also provides an interval during which a positive turn of events can make a project dramatically more profitable. The longer the interval, the more likely it is that this will happen; hence, the longer a project can be deferred the more valuable a growth option will be.

Even a project with a negative NPV can be a valuable "out-of-the-money" growth option if the company can put off the investment decision for a while. A company might maintain such out-of-the-money options even if they require ongoing spending for engineering, product development, market research, and so on, provided there is a realistic chance that future events will make the project more valuable.

Project Risk   Paradoxically, risk is a *positive* factor in the determination of a growth option's worth. If two investment opportunities have identical NPVs and can be deferred for the same amount of time, the riskier of the two projects will be a more valuable growth option. This is because of an asymmetry between potential upside

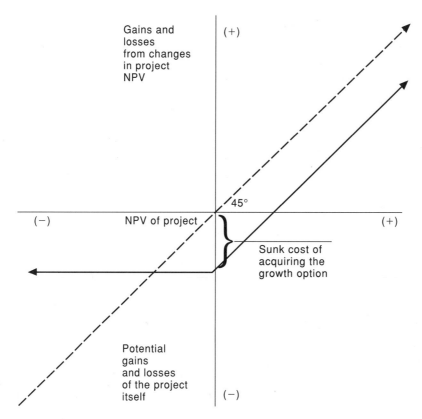

Figure 3.1
The asymmetry between upside gains and downside losses in option ownership

gains and downside losses when an option matures. As figure 3.1 illustrates, large gains are possible if a project's NPV increases. However, losses can be cut by simply choosing not to exercise the option whenever the project's NPV is negative. This ability means that high risk increases the chance of eventually realizing a large gain without equally increasing the chance of incurring a large loss.

The Level of Interest Rates   High interest rates generally translate into higher discount rates and lower present values of future cash flows for any given project. Clearly, that should depress the value of an option to undertake a project.

But higher discount rates also imply a lower present value of the future capital necessary to exercise an option. Such a countervailing effect helps to buoy the option's value as interest rates rise. This can give certain kinds of projects—specifically, those that create new growth options—a crucial comparative advantage in the capital budgeting process.

How Exclusive the Owner's Right is to Exercise the Option   Unlike call options on securities, there are two types of growth options: *proprietary* and *shared*. Proprietary options provide highly valuable, exclusive rights of exercise. These result from patents or the company's unique knowledge of a market or a technology that competitors cannot duplicate.

Shared growth options are less valuable "collective" opportunities of the industry, like the chance to enter a market unprotected by high barriers or to build a new plant to service a particular geographic market. Projects to cut costs are also shared options since competitors usually can and will respond with cost reductions of their own, thus minimizing the benefits to any one company.

Shared growth options are less attractive than proprietary ones because counter investments by the competition can erode or even preempt profits. Only if a company is in a sufficiently strong competitive position to ward off assaults and grab the lion's share of a project's value can a shared growth option be valuable.

Implications for Capital Budgeting

Thinking of investments as growth options challenges conventional wisdom about capital budgeting. For example, a company may be justified in accepting projects with a negative NPV. Some projects, such as the one in the opening example, may initially drain cash flows. But they may also create options for future growth. If the growth option's value more than offsets that lost from the project's cash flows, then it is worthwhile.

Suppose a company found the present value of construction and future operating costs for a genetic engineering lab to total $5 million. As a basic research lab, it would not, of course, generate positive cash flows, only opportunities for future commercial development of new discoveries. Still, the project would be justifiable if, in management's judgment, these growth options were worth $5 million or more.

If new growth options are involved, high-risk projects might be preferable to low-risk ones. In light of the beneficial impact of risk on growth option value, companies should hold options on projects whose value swings widely rather than only slightly over time. Projects that create new growth options in risky environments should have an advantage in the capital budgeting process. As an executive of a major consumer products company noted:

"If you know everything there is to know about a [new] product, it's not going to be a good business. *There have to be some major uncertainties to be resolved.* This is the only way to get a product with a major profit opportunity." [Emphasis added.]

When capital is scarce and interest rates rise, projects that create new growth options may be less adversely affected than those that generate only cash. This makes them relatively more attractive in the capital budgeting process. Normally, companies tilt their preferences toward projects that generate cash when capital is tight. But one large technology-based company discovered a different kind of comparative advantage during a capital squeeze in the late 1970s. A member of the capital appropriation committee described the problem:

"Allocating capital would be easy if you could do it just 'by the numbers,' but you must consider 'directional' factors as well. The idea of a hurdle-rate [to evaluate projects] becomes even less important in periods of tight capital because directional factors take precedence. When capital is tight, we take a longer-haul view and pick up the savings and cost-reduction projects later."

These "directional" factors are valuable growth options that the company looks for in new or growing markets.

Deciding when to exercise a growth option depends on a comparative analysis of the advantages and disadvantages of going ahead with a project as soon as possible. Because this *option* to invest is worth more than the NPV of the underlying project, a company should wait until the last possible moment before committing funds. That preserves the option's premium while protecting the company from costly and avoidable mistakes. A decision to commit funds to a project any earlier than necessary sacrifices this value.

When to Invest Early

Experience shows that companies often commit investment funds at a very early date despite their ability to defer a final decision. Companies that do so must believe that the cost of deferring the decision exceeds the value sacrificed from early exercise. For instance, a competitor may preempt the move or take action that raises the cost of the project, as happened to the company in the opening example. In general, a company will find it pays to exercise its growth options earlier than necessary when: competitors have access to the same option; the project's net present value is high; the level of risk and interest rates are low; and industry rivalry is intense.

Figure 3.2 shows how a company should time the exercise of its growth options based on the extent of industry rivalry and on the exclusiveness of a company's right to exercise the options. The upper right and lower left quadrants offer straight-

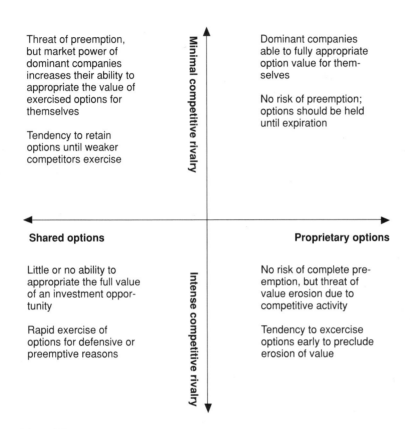

Figure 3.2
Timing the commitment of capital

forward directions for companies. The other two present intermediate cases with less obvious results. A company may wish to exercise even proprietary growth options early, for example, if the industry is intensely competitive and a timely commitment is likely to discourage attack.

A company generally tries to obtain a dominant competitive position in order to achieve and protect high returns on investment. But by giving a company the right to *time* the investment more selectively, the growth option provides an important, though often overlooked, motive for dominating the market. One executive stated:

What you're really trying to do with capital is create a strong competitive position.... We say [to our division managers] 'Do what you have to do to retain a leadership position in the short run.' Of course, over the long run, you can stay a leader only if you have the best cost position, so we must pay attention to that. But get the strongest leadership position, and *that* is what is going to pay off.

The advantage of being number one in an industry is the opportunity to initiate changes in technology and pricing. If one initiates change, one is in a much better position to take advantage of it because one can, in effect, control the timing and anticipate the outcome.

Using the Framework

Given the determinants of a growth option's value and the many different characteristics it can display, no single formula can embody its value reliably. Consequently, the first assessment of a project expected to generate new growth options might best be qualitative, although rooted in established principles of option valuation.

As a first step, the company should classify projects more accurately according to their growth option characteristics. Classification along traditional functional lines such as replacement, cost reduction, capacity expansion, and new product introduction provides little guidance. A more appropriate classification begins by distinguishing between projects whose future benefits are realized primarily through cash flows (simple options) and those whose future benefits include opportunities for further discretionary investment (compound options). Simple growth options—like routine cost reduction and maintenance and replacement projects—create value only through the cash flows stemming from the underlying assets.

Compound growth options—like research and development projects, a major expansion in an existing market, entry into a new market, and acquisitions—lead to new investment opportunities and affect the value of existing growth options.

A simple growth option requires only that the company evaluate cash flows according to net present value or rate of return methods. The complexity of compound options, their role in shaping a company's strategy, and even their impact on the survival of the organization all demand a broader analysis. A company must consider these projects as part of a larger cluster of projects or as a stream of investment decisions that extends over time. Given the company's strategy, executives should question whether a particular option will bring the right investment opportunities in the right markets—within a time frame suitable to their company's needs.

The company must separate projects that require an immediate decision from those on which it can defer final action. For growth options with a shorter time frame, executives need to focus only on the value gained or lost from acceptance. However, deferrable projects should be analyzed according to the relative costs and benefits of deferral.

Finally, the company must ask whether it can capture the option's benefits for itself or whether they will be available to other competitors as well.

Disciplining Project Evaluations

To illustrate, let's look at a generic chemical investment and alter it to fit different circumstances. A chemical company wants to build a facility for producing a toxic chemical next to a user's plant. The chemical is a commodity, the facility is to be owned and operated by the company, and the user is scheduled to purchase a fixed percentage of the plant's capacity output under a take-or-pay contract. If the company doesn't construct the facility immediately, however, the offer expires and the user will build and manage a plant on its own.

The chemical company's opportunity is a *simple, expiring, proprietary* growth option. The company should evaluate it by calculating the net present value of cash flows. The project's stand-alone cash value in the present is the only measure of the project's worth needed, since that is the value to be gained or lost.

Suppose this offer does not expire within a year and the potential exists for a relaxation of regulations controlling production of the toxic chemical. Under these circumstances, the company now realizes the new facility can be built at a much lower cost in the future. At the same time, the company discovers that the user has approached other chemical companies with the same offer. The company classifies the project as a *simple, deferrable, shared* growth option. Again, the company needs to evaluate only cash flows but must study the impact of deferral on cash since it shares the option with competitors. The company should channel project evaluation into a comparison of potential costs and benefits from either immediate exercise or deferral.

Finally, suppose that the toxic chemical is actually a new compound developed by the company. As a substitute for existing chemicals, it offers users significant cost savings. If the facility can produce the new compound in volume and the company can prove the cost savings, it can expect demand to grow rapidly, and realize new opportunities to build additional production facilities. On the negative side, the compound is difficult to produce, and government regulations could change radically. Moreover, the user continues to consider proposals from producers of a conventionally used chemical.

This last growth option is *shared, compound*, and *deferrable*. Even if cash flow analysis indicates that the company should reject or defer the project, top management may accept it immediately if preemption by competitors could seriously erode the worth of future growth options.

A New Perspective

The key advantage of the growth-option perspective is that it integrates capital budgeting with long-range planning. Within the framework, capital budgeting is simply the execution of a company's long-range plan.

Because investment decisions today can create the basis for investment decisions tomorrow, capital allocations made in any year are vital steps in the ultimate achievement of strategic objectives. By the same token, a long-range plan necessarily implies the cultivation of particular investment opportunities and can have a direct, dollars-and-cents impact on a company's stock price in the near term as well. The two activities are different but related means to the same end: maximizing the value of the company's equity.

To explicitly link capital budgeting and long-range planning, a company should place them both under the supervision of a single executive or an executive committee. Top management will impose a strategic perspective on what might otherwise be an uncoordinated aggregation of isolated capital expenditures.

Operating with a growth option perspective allows responsible executives to focus on the single, overriding objective of enhancing the value of the company's equity. The capital budgeting process will not be confused by linking the seemingly divergent and mutually exclusive aims of investing for future growth and maintaining a high stock price in the present. Once headquarters understands that some of the strategic benefits of investments are valuable options on future growth, it becomes clear that such investments add to the value of the company's equity, just as do projects that yield immediate cash flow. The only difference: value comes initially in the form of growth options rather than cash flows.

Such recognition will mark a critical shift in executive attention. A company should not spend time and effort trading off growth with ROI or market share with profitability. Rather, the company's focus should be on the kind of value the investment will create, its durability, and the auxiliary decisions required to protect or enhance it over time.

An executive of a *Fortune* "500" company once claimed that, "You simply can't put a dollar sign on a technological future that may have a tremendous payoff." The executive may be right. But that does not mean future investment opportunities have no value for the company's shareholders. Moreover, it certainly does not mean a company should abandon or distort the one approach available to put a dollar sign on the future—the discounting of expected cash flows using appropriate discount rates.

To be consistent with the objective of maximizing equity value, executives must broaden their perspective on the process of resource allocation so that they can integrate "strategic" factors logically and systematically into the capital budgeting process.

By thinking of discretionary investment opportunities as options on real assets, executives will address other relevant questions that have received little attention so far. How, for example, are growth options created, and which will be most valuable? How permanent and how liquid are growth options as components of company value? Does it matter whether a company owns a growth option exclusively or as a collective option of the industry? What influence do industry structure and competitive interaction have on growth option value? What auxiliary financial decisions are required to permit the future conversion of growth options to real assets?

The answers to questions such as these will vary from one situation to another. Thus, the growth-option framework reaffirms the potentially valuable role that executive judgment and experience can play in the resource allocation process. But regardless of the specific situation, the growth option framework establishes a common basis for the analysis needed to answer fundamental questions and provides a coherent structure for organizing the application of executive judgment.

Research Methodology

Clinical data and impetus for this article came from my involvement in field research on financial goals and resource allocation conducted in 1979–80 by Professors Gordon Donaldson and Jay Lorsch at the Harvard Graduate School of Business Administration. Twelve *Fortune* "500"-size companies with varying degrees of product market diversity and ownership concentration were studied. I interviewed managers at each company ranging from financial analyst to chairman of the board, including the chief executive officer, the chief financial officer, and the director of planning (or an officer with more or less equivalent responsibilities). I also reviewed documents such as capital budgeting manuals, annual plans throughout the 1970s, and internal records of capital expenditure and performance by line of business. The result of this field research was an extensive clinical data base of corporate documents and interview transcripts, rich in practical perspectives on corporate planning and resource allocation processes.

Notes

1. This analogy was first drawn by Stewart Myers in "Determinants of Corporate Borrowing," *Journal of Financial Economics*, no. 5 (Rochester, NY: University of Rochester, 1977), p. 147.

4 Valuing Managerial Flexibility

Lenos Trigeorgis and Scott P. Mason

Many are dissatisfied with the current practice of capital budgeting. Oftentimes corporate managers are willing to overrule conventional net present value (NPV) analysis or other discounted cash flow (DCF) techniques in order to accommodate major strategic considerations. In the early 1980s, academic critics of DCF such as Robert Hayes, William Abernathy, and David Garvin argued that such techniques systematically undervalue projects by ignoring strategic concerns.[1] For this reason, they proposed that important investment decisions be made on the basis of executive judgement so as to avoid the "distortions" of quantitative techniques. More recently, James Hodder and Henry Riggs have argued that the dissatisfaction with NPV is due rather to the misinterpretation and misuse of DCF techniques as commonly applied in practice—for example, through improper treatment of inflation effects or excessive risk adjustments.[2] Decision scientists, on the other hand, see the problem as lying not in the misuse of NPV, but rather in the application of the wrong valuation techniques altogether. They argue that DCF does not recognize the value of the flexibility management has in operating productive assets. In place of DCF they propose the use of techniques such as Monte Carlo simulation[3] and decision tree analysis[4] which recognize the possibility of different operating decisions given future events and thus capture the value of future flexibility.

One need not embrace the position of any of the above critics to accept as a valid concern that current capital budgeting practices are unable to capture all sources of value associated with a given project. Specifically, there are two aspects of extra value or economic desirability that are inadequately captured by a standard NPV analysis: first, the "operating flexibility" available within a single project which enables management to make or revise decisions at a future time (such as, for example, options to defer, expand, or abandon the project); and second, the "strategic" option value of a project resulting from its interdependence with future and follow-up investments.

(Chapter 2 in this volume) Stewart Myers points to the inability to capture the sequential interdependence between investments as the most serious shortcoming of traditional DCF approaches. Carl Kester, building on Myers' idea of thinking of discretionary investment opportunities as "growth options," more fully develops the interactive strategic and competitive aspects of inter-project options.[5] Both Myers and Kester suggest that the practice of capital budgeting should be extended by the use of option valuation techniques to deal with real investment opportunities and so help bridge the gap between financial theory and strategic planning.

There have been at least two negative reactions to the proposals of Myers and Kester. The first concerns the issue of practicability. The reaction of a number of professional managers has been that while the analogy relating managerial flexibility to options has intuitive appeal, the actual application of option-based techniques to capital budgeting must be too complex (or certainly more complex than DCF) for practical application. The second negative reaction has come from decision scientists who argue that all that is needed to capture the value of managerial flexibility is the use of traditional decision tree analysis (DTA), a technique which has existed for over 20 years. It is among the goals of this paper to address both of these concerns by showing that options techniques (1) can be practically used to quantify the value of the flexibility implicit in a variety of projects and (2) can be seen operationally as a special, though economically-corrected, version of DTA that recognizes market opportunities to trade and borrow.

Managerial Flexibility and Asymmetry

The basic inadequacy of the NPV or DCF approaches to capital budgeting is that they ignore, or cannot properly capture, management's ability to revise its original operating strategy if and when, as uncertainty is resolved, future events turn out differently from what management expected at the outset. Unlike other approaches, the options-based technique of contingent claims analysis (CCA) explicitly recognizes that management's flexibility to adapt its future actions, contingent on future events, introduces an "asymmetry" or "skewedness" in the distribution of the value of the project. This asymmetry results in an expansion of the investment opportunity's value vis-a-vis standard NPV analysis because future management decisions can improve upside potential while at the same time limiting downside losses. This asymmetry introduced by managerial flexibility calls for an expanded NPV criterion that reflects both sources of a project's value, the traditional "static" NPV of directly measurable cash flows and a premium for the flexibility embedded in its operating options.[6] That is,

Expanded NPV = Static NPV + Option Premium.

Notice that the use of "expanded" NPV or CCA analysis does not result in the scrapping of static NPV or DCF techniques. Rather static NPV analysis is a crucial and necessary input to an expanded NPV approach to capital budgeting.

A Generic Example

Consider an opportunity to invest $104 (all equity) to build a plant that a year later will have a realizable value of either $180 or $60 with equal probability. For sim-

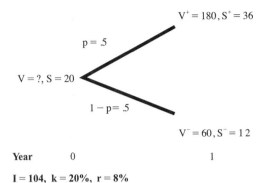

$V^+ = 180, S^+ = 36$

$p = .5$

$V = ?, S = 20$

$1 - p = .5$

$V^- = 60, S^- = 12$

Year   0   1

I = 104, k = 20%, r = 8%

V: present Value of subsequent expected cash flows from project
S: 'twin Security' price
I: required Investment outlay
E: value of investment opportunity to firm's Equityholders
k: discount rate (expected rate of return)
r: Risk-free interest rate

Figure 4.1
Decision tree for the generic plant and its "twin security"

plicity, assume that, once constructed, the plant will operate indefinitely, and continuously, at a constant output rate and require no future follow-on investment. Following traditional practice, let *S* be the listed stock price of an *identical* plant. Recall that the existence of such a "twin security" is implicitly assumed in traditional NPV analysis for purposes of estimating the required rate of return on a project. The twin security is assumed to have a value of $36 if the realized value of the project is $180 and a value of $12 if the realized value of the project turns out to be $60. Finally, assume both the plant and its "twin security" have an expected rate of return (or discount rate) of 20 percent, while the risk-free interest rate is assumed to be 8 percent. The above conditions are summarized in figure 4.1.

Traditional Approaches

Traditional DCF techniques, including net present value (NPV) analysis, would discount the plant's expected cash flows using the expected rate of return of the plant's twin security as the appropriate discount rate. The discount rate would be estimated by determining the project's beta coefficient from the prices of its "twin security" and applying the Capital Asset Pricing Model (CAPM).[7] The *gross* value of the project, *V*, would then be given by the expression:

$$V = E(V_1)/(1 + k) = [pV^+ + (1 - p)V^-]/(1 + k)$$
$$= [.5 \times 180 + .5 \times 60]/(1 + .20)$$
$$= 100^8$$

Subtracting the present value of investment costs gives the project's NPV:

$$NPV = V - I = 100 - 104 = -4.$$

Thus the value of this investment opportunity is a *negative* $4. In the absence of managerial flexibility, traditional DCF would correctly reject this project. As we will see shortly, however, if managerial flexibility or various kinds of operating options are present, investment in the plant may actually become economically desirable despite its negative static NPV.

Traditional DCF is unable properly to capture the value of operating options because of their dependence on future events that are uncertain at the time of the initial decision. Decision scientists attempt to overcome the shortcomings of conventional DCF analysis by taking into account the possibility of later actions that could be taken by the firm's management as future uncertainty resolves itself. Simulation techniques of the Monte Carlo type, for example, can allow explicit recognition of uncertainty by using repeated random sampling from the probability distributions for the various cash flow components of a project to generate output probability distributions of NPV (or IRR) for a given management strategy. The profile of resulting outcomes, however, is difficult to translate into clear-cut decisions for action. Decision tree analysis (DTA) helps management structure the decision problem by mapping out all feasible alternative actions contingent on the possible states of nature (chance events) in a hierarchical, or "tree-like," manner. DTA can actually be seen as an advanced version of DCF or NPV—one that correctly computes unconditional expected cash flows by properly taking account of their conditional probabilities given each state of nature. As such, DTA is correct in principle and particularly useful for analyzing complex sequential investment decisions. Its main shortcoming, however, is the problem of determining the appropriate discount rate to be used in working back through the decision tree.

As will be shown, the problem with traditional approaches to capital budgeting lies in the valuation of investment opportunities whose claims are not symmetric. The asymmetry resulting from operating flexibility options and other strategic aspects of various projects can nevertheless be properly analyzed by thinking of discretionary investment opportunities as collections of options on real assets (or as "real options") through the technique of Contingent Claims Analysis.

Contingent Claims Analysis

Contingent Claims Analysis (CCA) enables management to quantify properly the additional value of a project's operating flexibility. In the absence of such flexibility CCA gives results identical to those of traditional DCF. As we shall see next, the economic foundation of CCA rests with the explicit recognition of market opportunities to trade and create desired payoff patterns through securities transactions.

To see what insights CCA can provide, suppose that the gross value of the plant, fully constructed, V, and the price of the plant's "twin security," S, move over the next year as follows:

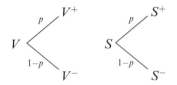

The gross value of the completed plant should not be confused with the value of the (possibly complex) opportunity to initiate construction of a new plant. The value of the opportunity to start construction on a new plant, E, will then move in a manner that is perfectly correlated with the movements in V or S:

Now consider some of the open market transactions that would be possible. Specifically, following a standard option pricing hedging strategy, management could construct a portfolio consisting of n shares of the "twin security" S partly financed by borrowings of amount B at the rate r. This portfolio can be chosen such that it will exactly replicate the opportunity to build a new plant, independently of whether the project does well (S^+) or poorly (S^-):

$$E = nS - B \underset{1-p}{\overset{p}{<}} \begin{matrix} E^+ = nS^+ - (1+r)B \\ \\ E^- = nS^- - (1+r)B \end{matrix}$$

Thus, if this portfolio can be specified precisely (that is, how many shares (n) financed by how much borrowing (B)), then the investment opportunity, E, must have the same value as the equivalent portfolio or profitable arbitrage opportunities will exist. Treating the conditions of equal payoffs as two equations, the two unknowns n and B can be solved for as follows:

$$n = (E^+ - E^-)/(S^+ - S^-); \quad \text{and}$$

$$B = [E^+ S^- - E^- S^+]/(S^+ - S^-)(1 + r)$$

In other words, management can replicate the payoff to the new investment opportunity by (a) purchasing n shares of the "twin security" and (b) financing this purchase in part by borrowing an amount B at the risk-free rate r.

The current (beginning of the period) value of the opportunity (obtained by simply substituting for n and B in the equation $E = nS - B$ and then rearranging terms) is given as follows:

$$E = [p'E^+ + (1 - p')E^-]/(1 + r), \quad \text{with}$$

$$p' = [(1 + r)S - S^-]/(S^+ - S^-).$$

Note that the value of the opportunity does not explicitly involve the actual probabilities (p)s. Instead, it is expressed in terms of "risk-neutral" probabilities (p')s—that is, adjusted probabilities that allow expected values to be discounted at the risk-free rate. Essentially, then, instead of discounting expected future values using the actual probabilities of .5 at the expected risk-adjusted rate of return (in this case, 20 percent), CCA equivalently discounts expected future values using the risk-neutral probability of .4 at the riskless rate (here, 8 percent). To demonstrate, by substituting into the expression for the risk-neutral probability,

$$p' = [(1 + r)S - S^-]/(S^+ - S^-)$$

$$= [(1.08 \times 20) - 12]/(36 - 12)$$

$$= 0.4 \text{ (as distinct from } p = 0.5)$$

and applying this probability and the risk-free rate we obtain

$$V = [p'V^+ + (1 - p')V^-]/(1 + r)$$

$$= [.4 \times 180 + .6 \times 60]/1.08 = 100$$

This is identical with the (gross) project value obtained using traditional DCF with the actual probability p and the discount rate k,

$$V = [pV^+ + (1 - p)V^-]/(1 + k)$$

$$= [.5 \times 180 + .5 \times 60]/1.20 = 100$$

As this example illustrates, in the absence of operating flexibility or asymmetry, CCA gives the same results as traditional DCF. When operating flexibility is present, however, such as in those cases when management has the option to defer, abandon, expand, or contract a project, traditional DCF is unable to handle the resulting asymmetries and may result in significantly misleading prescriptions for capital budgeting.

Simple Examples of Managerial Flexibility (Operating Options)

Continuing with our basic example, we will assume throughout that the value of the plant, V, and its twin security, S, move through time as follows:

$$V = 100, \quad S = 20 \quad \overbrace{}^{p} \quad V^+ = 180, \quad S^+ = 36$$
$$\underbrace{}_{1-p} \quad V^- = 60, \quad S^- = 12$$

Year   0   1

In the examples that follow, we also assume that if any part of the required investment outlay (having present value of $104) is to be spent in the future, an allowance for it is made by placing that amount in an escrow account earning the riskless interest rate. We will now illustrate how various kinds of operating options can enhance the value (i.e., the NPV) of the opportunity to invest in the above project.

The Option to Defer the Investment

Suppose the firm has a one-year license granting it the exclusive right to construct a new plant of the same kind being considered. What is the value of the investment *opportunity* provided by the license, given that undertaking the project *immediately* was shown to have a negative NPV? With the flexibility to defer undertaking the project provided by the exclusive license, management maintains the right to benefit from favorable random movements in project value; at the same time they cannot be hurt by unfavorable market circumstances because they have no symmetric obligation to invest. To determine the exact positive amount of the option to defer provided by the license, we simply substitute the appropriate values for the payoffs to the investment opportunity, E^+ and E^-, in the risk-neutral relationship above.

Because the option to defer the project for a year gives management the right, but not the obligation, to make the investment by next year, they will wait and make the investment if the project value next year turns out to exceed the necessary investment at that time. In other words, the option to wait can be seen as a call option on the project V with an exercise price equal to the required outlay next year (I_1). This translates into the right to choose the maximum of the project value minus the required investment or zero, since management would simply allow the license or option to expire if project value turns out not to cover the necessary costs. That is,

$$E^+ = \max(V^+ - I_1, 0) = \max(180 - 112.32, 0) = 67.68,$$

$$E^- = \max(V^- - I_1, 0) = \max(60 - 112.32, 0) = 0$$

(with $I_0 = 104$ growing in one year at 8% to $I_1 = 112.32$).

Thus, with the option to defer the investment, the payoff structure would be as follows:

$$V = 100, \quad E = ? \quad \overset{p}{\underset{1-p}{\diagdown}} \quad \begin{matrix} V^+ = 180, \quad E^+ = 67.68 \\ \\ V^- = 60, \quad E^- = 0 \end{matrix}$$

Year   0   1

Again, with $p' = [(1+r)S - S^-]/(S^+ - S^-) = 0.4$, the total value of the investment opportunity (the expanded NPV that incorporates the value of the option to defer) can be expressed as follows:

$$E = [p'E^+ + (1 - p')E^-]/(1 + r)$$

$$= [.4 \times 67.68 + .6 \times 0]/1.08 = 25.07$$

It is worth emphasizing once more that although the project per se has a negative (static) NPV of $4 if taken immediately, the investment proposal should not be rejected because the *opportunity* to invest in the project within a year (that is, when the value of the license is taken into consideration) is worth a positive $25.07. The value of the option to defer provided by the license itself is thus the following:

Option Premium = Expanded NPV – Static NPV = 25.07 – (−4) = 29.07, which, incidentally, is equal to almost one third of the project's gross value.

It should be clear from the above example that CCA is operationally identical to decision tree analysis, but with the key difference that the probabilities are transformed so as to allow the use of a risk-free discount rate. Therefore, CCA visits no new implementation problems on DTA.

Of course, one may claim that this value of waiting can be captured equally well by traditional DCF or DTA approaches. Simply recognize that you can wait for a year and then take the project only if its value next year exceeds the necessary investment (so that again $E^+ = 67.68$, $E^- = 0$); then determine its expected value using the actual probabilities and discount back at the expected rate of return ($k = 20\%$) to determine the current value of the investment opportunity (including the value of the option to wait) as follows:

$$E = [pE^+ + (1 - p)E^-]/(1 + k)$$

$$= [.5 \times 67.68 + .5 \times 0]/1.20 = 28.20$$

Notice that the DCF/DTA value of waiting is different than that given by contingent claims analysis. (Discounting backward at the lower risk-free rate of 8 percent while using the actual probabilities also produces an answer, $E = 31.33$, that is different from CCA's.)

To show that $28.20 given by the traditional approach is not the correct value for this investment opportunity, simply refer back to the arbitrage argument. Would anyone be willing to pay $28.20 for the license? The answer is "no" because any prospective buyer could instead purchase 2.82 $[(67.68 - 0)/(36 - 12)]$ shares of the "twin security" at its current price of $20 per share for a total cost of $56.40, while financing the remaining part of that purchase by borrowing $B = \$31.33$ at the riskless rate; and next year his investment will be worth $67.68 or 0:

$$E^+ = nS^+ - (1 + r)B = 2.82 \times 36 - 1.08 \times 31.33 = 67.68$$

$$E^- = nS^- - (1 + r)B = 2.82 \times 12 - 1.08 \times 31.33 = 0$$

Thus, he would have been able to exactly replicate the payoff of the investment in any state of the world for an out-of-pocket expense of $25.07. Clearly he would not pay $28.20 for an opportunity that can be replicated for $25.07. Therefore, to eliminate the possibility of arbitrage opportunities, the value of this investment opportunity must be $25.07 as given by the CCA approach.

The error in the traditional DTA approach arises from use of a single (or constant) risk-adjusted discount rate. Asymmetric claims on an asset do not have the same expected rate of return as the underlying asset itself. CCA corrects for this error by transforming the probabilities. With the above demonstration CCA can therefore be seen as operationally equivalent to decision tree analysis. Following the insights of option pricing theory, however, it takes account of open market opportunities to buy or sell and borrow or lend. In so doing, it provides an economically corrected version of the conventional DTA.

The Option to Expand

Once a project is undertaken, management may have the flexibility to alter it in various ways at different times during its life. The option to expand is an excellent example of the strategic dimension of a project. Management may find it desirable, for example, to make additional follow-on investment if it turns out that its product is more enthusiastically received in the market than originally expected. In this sense the original investment opportunity can be thought of as the initial scale project plus a call option on a future opportunity.[9]

Suppose that in our example management has the option to invest an additional $80 one year after the initial investment (that is, $I_1' = \$80$) which would double the scale and value of the plant. Then in year 1 management has the option either to maintain the same scale of operation or double the scale and receive twice the project value by paying the additional cost. In this case,

$$E = \max(V, 2V - I_1') = V + \max(V - I_1', 0), \text{ so that:}$$

$$E^+ = \max(V^+, 2V^+ - I_1') = \max(180, 360 - 80) = 280$$

$$E^- = \max(V^-, 2V^- - I_1') = \max(60, 120 - 80) = 60$$

Thus, management will exercise its option to expand if market conditions turn out favorably, but will otherwise let it expire unexercised. The value of the investment opportunity (including the value of the option to expand if market conditions turn better than expected) is then given as follows:

$$E = [p'E^+ + (1 - p')E^-]/(1 + r) - I$$

$$= [.4 \times 280 + .6 \times 60]/1.08 - 104 = 33.04,$$

and thus the value of the option to expand $= 33.04 - (-4) = 37.04$, or 37 percent of the gross project value.

The Option to Contract

Analogous to the option to expand a project is the option to contract the scale of a project's operation by forgoing planned future expenditures if the product is not as well received in the market as initially expected. The option to contract can thus be seen as a put option on part of the project with an exercise price equal to the value of the planned expenditures that can be cancelled.

Suppose that in our example part of the investment cost having a $104 present value necessary to initiate and maintain the given scale of the plant's operation is to be spent next year. Specifically, $50 will have to be paid immediately and an investment of $58.32 (the future value of $54) is planned in one year. Suppose also that in one year, as an alternative to making the full $58.32 investment necessary to maintain the current scale of operations, management has the option to halve the scale and value of the project by not making the $58.32 outlay. Clearly, if market conditions next year turn out unfavorably, management may find it valuable to exercise its option to contract the scale of the project's operation. In this case,

$$E^+ = \max(V^+ - I_1, .5V^+) = \max(180 - 58.32, 90) = 121.68,$$

$$E^- = \max(V^- - I_1, .5V^-) = \max(60 - 58.32, 30) = 30$$

The investment opportunity, incorporating the option to contract, is then worth:

$E = [.4 \times 121.68 + .6 \times 30]/1.08 - 50 = 11.73$, so that the value of the option to contract $= 11.73 - (-4) = 15.73$ or about 16% of project value.

Other Types of Operating Options

Contingent claims analysis can similarly handle many other types of operating flexibility problems. Examples of such options are the option to shut down operations temporarily, to switch use, or to abandon a project early when future market conditions turn out worse than originally expected.

The flexibility to shut down production temporarily, or not to operate at all, in any given year of the project's life becomes valuable if cash revenues are not adequate to cover the variable cost of operating in that year. Thus, in a given year, management could either operate and obtain the difference between cash revenues and total costs of operating or shut down and pay the fixed costs associated with the project for that year. One may thus look at the flexibility to operate (or not) in any year as an option to acquire that year's cash revenue by paying the variable costs as the exercise price.

In addition to the option not to operate in a given year, management may also have the flexibility to terminate or redeploy a project. For example, consider a chemical plant or oil refinery that can use a number of different inputs to produce a variety of different outputs.[10] As market conditions change and the relative prices of inputs, outputs, or the plant resale value (in a "secondhand" market) fluctuate, management may find it valuable to abandon the current project's use by switching to a cheaper input, a more profitable output, or simply to sell the plant's assets in the secondhand market. This flexibility to switch use or abandon a project early in exchange for its "salvage value" enables management to select the maximum of the project's value in its present use or in its best alternative use. Thus, an investment opportunity with the flexibility to switch use can be seen as the sum of the project in its current use plus a put option on it with an exercise price equal to the value of its best alternative use.

Management may also find it justifiable to abandon a project during construction to save any subsequent investment cost. This will happen when the current required investment exceeds the value of continuing the project. Thus, when the necessary investment outlay is not simply a single expenditure at the outset, but rather a sequence of investment "installments" extending throughout the project's life, the investment opportunity can actually be seen as a compound option in which each investment "installment" represents the exercise price that must be paid in order to acquire a subsequent option to continue operating the project for the next stage until the next installment comes due, and so on.[11]

Project Interdependence

Many projects are not independent, as assumed by traditional DCF procedures, but should rather be seen as necessary links in a chain of interrelated projects. Making an investment outlay to acquire the first project in such a sequence of contingent investments is a prerequisite for opening up the opportunity to acquire the benefits of the next investment in line by paying its own "exercise price" or cost installment. In essence such investment opportunities are options on options (that is, options whose payoff are other options) or "compound" options. This notion of project interdependence is remarkably similar in structure when looking at a sequence of projects to the intra-project relationships present in the options to expand or abandon; and thus it would be analyzed in essentially the same manner. The principal difference is that each investment cost "installment" now provides the opportunity to begin a new project rather than continue with a new stage of the same project.

Project interdependence may have considerable strategic import since it may justify acceptance of projects with a negative static NPV on the basis of their potential to open up subsequent new investment opportunities in the future. A research and development project, a lease for an undeveloped tract with potential oil reserves, or an acquisition of an unrelated company are only a few examples of such real compound options that may be undertaken not so much for their directly measurable cash flows (there may be none, as in the case of some speculative research projects), but rather for the new opportunities they may open up (a new technological break-through, large oil reserves, or access to a new market). In general, such inter-project options are associated with investments intended to place the firm on a growth path or to improve its strategic position in the industry by, say, entering a new geographic market or employing a new technology.

Implications for Capital Budgeting

This paper has addressed the proposal that capital budgeting procedures be extended to recognize the options present in real projects. We have demonstrated that the options-based technique of contingent claims analysis can actually be seen as a special, economically-adjusted version of DTA that recognizes market opportunities to trade and borrow (and is therefore no more difficult to use than DTA).

Looking at opportunities to invest as collections of options on real assets offers new insight into resource allocation decision-making that in some respects challenges conventional thinking. It broadens management's horizon by moving toward an "expanded NPV" analysis whereby the total value of an investment opportunity is explicitly quantified as the sum of the "static" NPV of direct expected cash flows and an option premium reflecting the value of managerial flexibility.

By viewing investment opportunities from the perspective of options valuation, management is in a better position to recognize that

• conventional, static NPV may indeed undervalue projects by suppressing the "option premium" component;

• it may be correct to accept projects with negative NPVs if the option premium associated with the value of managerial flexibility exceeds the negative NPV of the project's measurable expected cash flows;

• the magnitude of undervaluation, and the extent to which managers should justifiably invest more than that dictated by conventional DCF standards, can be quantified using CCA (unlike other suggestions by critics).

The options framework indicates that the value of managerial flexibility is greater in more uncertain environments—again, a direct result of the asymmetry it introduces. It may also be greater, all else equal, during periods of higher interest rates and in the case of investment opportunities of longer duration. Thus, contrary to popular belief, higher uncertainty, higher interest rates, and longer investment horizons (when part of the actual investment can be deferred) are not necessarily damaging to the value of an investment opportunity. While these effects do reduce a project's static NPV component, they may also lead to an increase in the value of a project's option premium (or managerial flexibility) which may outweigh the negative effect.

Notes

1. R. Hayes and W. Abernathy, "Managing Our Way to Economic Decline," *Harvard Business Review* (July–August 1980); and R. Hayes and D. Garvin, "Managing As If Tomorrow Mattered," *Harvard Business Review* (May–June 1982).

2. J. Hodder and H. Riggs, "Pitfalls in Evaluating Risky Projects," *Harvard Business Review* (January–February 1985), pp. 128–135.

3. For applications of Monte Carlo simulation to capital budgeting, see D. Hertz, "Risk Analysis in Capital Investment," *Harvard Business Review* 42 (January–February 1964), pp. 95–106.

4. See J. Magee, "How to Use Decision Trees in Capital Investment," *Harvard Business Review* (September–October 1964).

5. W. C. Kester, "Today's Options for Tomorrow's Growth," *Harvard Business Review* (March–April 1984).

6. See L. Trigeorgis, "Valuing Real Investment Opportunities: An Options Approach to Strategic Capital Budgeting," Unpublished doctoral dissertation, Harvard University (1986).

7. See David Mullins, "Does the Capital Asset Pricing Model Work?," *Harvard Business Review* (January–February 1982), pp. 105–114.

8. Valuing the plant at 100 also follows from the fact that the scale of the publicly traded ($20) plant is one fifth that of the proposed plant (i.e., $5 \times 20 = 100$).

9. This is Stewart Myers's concept of corporate "growth options," as first presented in his article, "The Determinants of Corporate Borrowing," *Journal of Financial Economics* 5 (November 1977).

10. This type of flexibility is discussed in Scott Mason and Robert C. Merton, "The Role of Contingent Claims Analysis in Corporate Finance," in E. Altman and M. Subrahmanyam (eds.), *Recent Advances in Corporate Finance*, Irwin, (1985).

11. This is the idea of compoundness within the same project—an intra-project interaction.

5 The Options Approach to Capital Investment

Avinash K. Dixit and Robert S. Pindyck

Companies make capital investments in order to create and exploit profit opportunities. Investments in research and development, for example, can lead to patents and new technologies that open up those opportunities. The commercialization of patents and technologies through construction of new plants and expenditures for marketing can allow companies to take advantage of profit opportunities. Somewhat less obviously, companies that shut down money-losing operations are also investing: The payments they make to extract themselves from contractual agreements, such as severance pay for employees, are the initial expenditure. The payoff is the reduction of future losses.

Opportunities are *options*—rights but not obligations to take some action in the future. Capital investments, then, are essentially about options. Over the past several years, economists including ourselves have explored that basic insight and found that thinking of investments as options substantially changes the theory and practice of decision making about capital investment. Traditionally, business schools have taught managers to operate on the premise that investment decisions can be reversed if conditions change or, if they cannot be reversed, that they are now-or-never propositions. But as soon as you begin thinking of investment opportunities as options, the premise changes. Irreversibility, uncertainty, and the choice of timing alter the investment decision in critical ways.

The purpose of this chapter is to examine the shortcomings of the conventional approaches to decision making about investment and to present a better framework for thinking about capital investment decisions. Any theory of investment needs to address the following question: How should a corporate manager facing uncertainty over future market conditions decide whether to invest in a new project? Most business schools teach future managers a simple rule to apply to such problems. First, calculate the present value of the expected stream of cash that the investment will generate. Then, calculate the present value of the stream of expenditures required to undertake the project. And, finally, determine the difference between the two—the net present value (NPV) of the investment. If it's greater than zero, the rule tells the manager to go ahead and invest.

Of course, putting NPV into practice requires managers to resolve some key issues early on. How should you estimate the expected stream of operating profits from the investment? How do you factor in taxes and inflation? And, perhaps most critical, what discount rate or rates should you use? In working out those issues, managers sometimes run into complications. But the basic approach is fairly straightforward:

calculating the net present value of an investment project and determining whether it is positive or negative.

Unfortunately, this basic principle is often wrong. Although the NPV rule is relatively easy to apply, it is built on faulty assumptions. It assumes one of two things: either that the investment is reversible (in other words, that it can somehow be undone and the expenditures recovered should market conditions turn out to be worse than anticipated); or that, if the investment is *ir*reversible, it is a now-or-never proposition (if the company does not make the investment now, it will lose the opportunity forever).

Although it is true that some investment decisions fall into those categories, most don't. In most cases, investments are irreversible and, in reality, capable of being delayed. A growing body of research shows that the ability to delay an irreversible investment expenditure can profoundly affect the decision to invest. Ability to delay also undermines the validity of the net present value rule. Thus, for analyzing investment decisions, we need to establish a richer framework, one that enables managers to address the issues of irreversibility, uncertainty, and timing more directly.

Instead of assuming that investments are either reversible or that they cannot be delayed, the recent research on investment stresses the fact that companies have *opportunities* to invest and that they must decide how to exploit those opportunities most effectively. The research is based on an important analogy with financial options. A company with an opportunity to invest is holding something much like a financial call option: It has the right but not the obligation to buy an asset (namely, the entitlement to the stream of profits from the project) at a future time of its choosing. When a company makes an irreversible investment expenditure, it "exercises," in effect, its call option. So the problem of how to exploit an investment opportunity boils down to this: How does the company exercise that option optimally? Academics and financial professionals have been studying the valuation and optimal exercising of financial options for the past two decades.[1] Thus we can draw from a large body of knowledge about financial options.

The recent research on investment offers a number of valuable insights into how managers can evaluate opportunities, and it highlights a basic weakness of the NPV rule. When a company exercises its option by making an irreversible investment, it effectively "kills" the option. In other words, by deciding to go ahead with an expenditure, the company gives up the possibility of waiting for new information that might affect the desirability or timing of the investment; it cannot disinvest should market conditions change adversely. The lost option value is an opportunity cost that must be included as part of the cost of the investment. Thus the simple NPV rule needs to be modified: Instead of just being positive, the present value of the expected stream of cash from a project must exceed the cost of the project by an amount equal to the value of keeping the investment option alive.[2]

Numerous studies have shown that the cost of investing in an opportunity can be large and that investment rules that ignore the expense can lead the investor astray. The opportunity cost is highly sensitive to uncertainty over the future value of the project; as a result, new economic conditions that may affect the perceived riskiness of future cash flows can have a large impact on investment spending—much larger than, say, a change in interest rates. Viewing investment as an option puts greater emphasis on the role of risk and less emphasis on interest rates and other financial variables.

Another problem with the conventional NPV rule is that it ignores the value of creating options. Sometimes an investment that appears uneconomical when viewed in isolation may, in fact, create options that enable the company to undertake other investments in the future should market conditions turn favorable. An example is research and development. By not accounting properly for the options that R&D investments may yield, naïve NPV analyses lead companies to invest too little.

Option value has important implications for managers as they think about their investment decisions. For example, it is often highly desirable to delay an investment decision and wait for more information about market conditions, even though a standard analysis indicates that the investment is economical right now. On the other hand, there may be situations in which uncertainty over future market conditions should prompt a company to speed up certain investments. Such is the case when the investments create additional options that give a company the ability (although not the obligation) to do additional future investing. R&D could lead to patents, for example; land purchases could lead to development of mineral reserves. A company might also choose to speed up investments that would yield information and thereby reduce uncertainty.

As a practical matter, many managers seem to understand already that there is something wrong with the simple NPV rule as it is taught—that there is a value to waiting for more information and that this value is not reflected in the standard calculation. In fact, managers often require that an NPV be more than merely positive. In many cases, they insist that it be positive even when it is calculated using a discount rate that is much higher than their company's cost of capital. Some people have argued that when managers insist on extremely high rates of return they are being myopic. But we think there is another explanation. It may be that managers understand a company's options are valuable and that it is often desirable to keep those options open.

In order to understand the thought processes such managers may be using, it is useful to step back and examine the NPV rule and how it is used. For anyone analyzing an investment decision using NPV, two basic issues need to be addressed: first, how to determine the expected stream of profits that the proposed project will generate and the expected stream of costs required to implement the project; and, second, how to choose the discount rate for the purpose of calculating net present value. Textbooks don't have a lot to say about the best way to calculate the profit and cost streams. In practice, managers often seek a *consensus* projection or use an average of high, medium, and low estimates. But however they determine the expected streams of profits and costs, managers are often unaware of making an implicit faulty assumption. The assumption is that the construction or development will begin at a fixed point in time, usually the present. In effect, the NPV rule assumes a fixed scenario in which a company starts and completes a project, which then generates a cash flow during some expected lifetime—without *any* contingencies. Most important, the rule anticipates no contingency for delaying the project or abandoning it if market conditions turn sour. Instead, the NPV rule compares investing today with *never* investing. A more useful comparison, however, would examine a range of possibilities: investing today, or waiting and perhaps investing next year, or waiting longer and perhaps investing in two years, and so on.

As for selecting the discount rate, a low discount rate gives more weight to cash flows that a project is expected to earn in the distant future. On the other hand, a high discount rate gives distant cash flows much less weight and hence makes the company appear more myopic in its evaluation of potential investment projects.

Introductory corporate-finance courses give the subject of selecting discount rates considerable attention. Students are generally taught that the correct discount rate is simply the opportunity cost of capital for the particular project—that is, the expected rate of return that could be earned from an investment of similar risk. In principle, the opportunity cost would reflect the nondiversifiable, or *systematic*, risk that is associated with the particular project. That risk might have characteristics that differ from those of the company's other individual projects or from its average investment activity. In practice, however, the opportunity cost of a specific project may be hard to measure. As a result, students learn that a company's weighted average cost of capital (WACC) is a reasonable substitute. The WACC offers a good approximation as long as the company's projects do not differ greatly from one another in their nondiversifiable risk.[3]

Most students leave business school with what appears to be a simple and powerful tool for making investment decisions: Estimate the expected cash flows for a project; use the company's weighted average cost of capital (perhaps adjusted up or down to reflect the risk characteristics of the particular project) to calculate the project's NPV; and then, if the result is positive, proceed with the investment.

But both academic research and anecdotal evidence bear out time and again the hesitancy of managers to apply NPV in the manner they have been taught. For example, in a 1987 study, Harvard economist Lawrence Summers found that companies were using hurdle rates ranging from 8% to 30%, with a median of 15% and a mean of 17%. Allowing for the deductibility of interest expenses, the nominal interest rate during the period in question was only 4%, and the real rate was close to zero. Although the hurdle rate appropriate for investment with a nondiversifiable risk usually exceeds the riskless rate, it is not enough to justify the large discrepancies found. More recent studies have confirmed that managers regularly and consciously set hurdle rates that are often three or four times their weighted average cost of capital.[4]

Evidence from corporate *dis*investment decisions is also consistent with that analysis. In many industries, companies stay in business and absorb large operating losses for long periods, even though a conventional NPV analysis would indicate that it makes sense to close down a factory or go out of business. Prices can fall far below average variable cost without inducing significant disinvestment or exit from the business. In the mid-1980s, for example, many U.S. farmers saw prices drop drastically, as did producers of copper, aluminum, and other metals. Most did not disinvest, and their behavior can be explained easily once irreversibility and option value are taken into account. Closing a plant or going out of business would have meant an irreversible loss of tangible and intangible capital: The specialized skills that workers had developed would have disappeared as they dispersed to different industries and localities, brand name recognition would have faded, and so on. If market conditions had improved soon after and operations could have resumed profitably, the cost of reassembling the capital would have been high. Continuing to operate keeps the capital intact and preserves the option to resume profitable production later. The option is valuable, and, therefore, companies may quite rationally choose to retain it, even at the cost of losing money in the meantime.

The slow response of U.S. imports to changes in the exchange rate during the early 1980s is another example of how managers deviate from the NPV rule. From mid-1980 to the end of 1984, the real value of the U.S. dollar increased by about 50%. As a result, the ability of foreign companies to compete in the U.S. market soared. But the volume of imports did not begin to rise substantially until the beginning of 1983, when the stronger dollar was already well established. In the first quarter of 1985, the dollar began to weaken; by the end of 1987, it had almost declined to its 1978 level. However, import volume did not decline for another two years; in fact, it rose a little.

Once established in the U.S. market, foreign companies were slow to scale back or close their export operations when the exchange rate moved unfavorably. That behavior might seem inconsistent with traditional investment theory, but it is easy to understand in the light of irreversibility and option value: The companies were willing to suffer temporary losses to retain their foothold in the U.S. market and keep alive their option to operate profitably in the future if the value of the dollar rose.

So far, we have focused on managers who seem shortsighted when they make investment decisions, and we have offered an explanation based on the value of the option for waiting and investing later. But some managers appear to override the NPV rule in the opposite direction. For example, entrepreneurs sometimes invest in seemingly risky projects that would be difficult to justify by a conventional NPV calculation using an appropriately risk-adjusted cost of capital. Such projects generally involve R&D or some other type of exploratory investment. Again, we suggest that option theory provides a helpful explanation because the goal of the investments is to reveal information about technological possibilities, production costs, or market potential. Armed with this new information, entrepreneurs can decide whether to proceed with production. In other words, the exploratory investment creates a valuable option. Once the value of the option is reflected in the returns from the initial investment, it may turn out to have been justified, even though a conventional NPV calculation would not have found it attractive.

Before proceeding, we should elaborate on what we mean by the notions of irreversibility, ability to delay an investment, and option to invest. What makes an investment expenditure irreversible? And how do companies obtain their options to invest?

Investment expenditures are irreversible when they are specific to a company or to an industry. For example, most investments in marketing and advertising are company specific and cannot be recovered. They are sunk costs. A steel plant, on the other hand, is industry specific in that it cannot be used to produce anything but steel. One might think that, because in principle the plant could be sold to another steel producer, investment in a plant is recoverable and is not a sunk cost. But that is not necessarily true. If the industry is reasonably competitive, then the value of the plant will be approximately the same for all steel companies, so there is little to be gained from selling it. The potential purchaser of the steel plant will realize that the seller has been unable to make money at current prices and considers the plant a bad investment. If the potential buyer agrees that it's bad investment, the owner's ability to sell the plant will not be worth much. Therefore, an investment in a steel plant (or any other industry-specific capital project) should be viewed largely as a sunk cost: that is, irreversible.

Even investments that are not company or industry specific are often partly irreversible because buyers of used equipment, unable to evaluate the quality of an item, will generally offer to pay a price that corresponds to the average quality in the market. Sellers who know the quality of the item they are selling will resist unloading above-average merchandise at a reduced price. The average quality of used equipment available in the market will go down and, therefore, so will the market price. Thus cars, trucks, office equipment, and computers (items that are not industry specific and can be sold to buyers in other industries) are apt to have resale values that are well below their original purchase costs, even if they are almost new.

Irreversibility can also arise because of government regulations, institutional arrangements, or differences in corporate culture. For example, capital controls may make it impossible for foreign (or domestic) investors to sell their assets and reallocate their funds. By the same token, investments in new workers may be partly irreversible because of the high costs of hiring, training, and firing. Hence most major investments are to a large extent irreversible.

The recognition that capital investment decisions can be irreversible gives the ability to delay investments added significance. In reality, companies do not always have the opportunity to delay their investments. For example, strategic considerations can make it imperative for a business to invest quickly in order to preempt investment by existing or potential competitors. In most cases, though, it is at least feasible to delay. There may be a cost—the risk of entry by other companies or the loss of cash flows—but the cost can be weighted against the benefits of waiting for new information. And those benefits are often substantial.

We have argued that an irreversible investment opportunity is like a financial call option. The holder of the call option has the right, for a specified period, to pay an exercise price and to receive in return an asset—for example, a share of stock—that has some value. Exercising the option is irreversible; although the asset can be sold to another investor, one cannot retrieve the option or the money that was paid to exercise it. Similarly, a company with an investment opportunity has the option to spend money now or in the future (the exercise price) in return for an asset of some value (the project). Again, the asset can be sold to another company, but the investment itself is irreversible. As with the financial call option, the option to make a capital investment is valuable in part because it is impossible to know the future value of the asset obtained by investing. If the asset rises in value, the net payoff from investing increases. If the value declines, the company can decide not to invest and will lose only what it has spent to obtain the investment opportunity. As long as there are *some* contingencies under which the company would prefer not to invest, that is, when there is some probability that the investment would result in a loss, the opportunity to delay the decision—and thus to keep the option alive—has value. The question, then, is when to exercise the option. The choice of the most appropriate time is the essence of the optimal investment decision.

Recognizing that an investment opportunity is like a financial call option can help managers understand the crucial role uncertainty plays in the timing of capital investment decisions. With a financial call option, the more volatile the price of the stock on which the option is written, the more valuable the option and the greater the incentive to wait and keep the option alive rather than exercise it. This is true because of the asymmetry in the option's net payoffs: The higher the stock price rises the greater the net payoff from exercising the option; however, if the stock price falls, one can lose only what one paid for the option.

The same goes for capital investment opportunities. The greater the uncertainty over the potential profitability of the investment, the greater the value of the opportunity and the greater the incentive to wait and to keep the opportunity alive rather than exercise it by investing at once. Of course, uncertainty also plays a role in the conventional NPV rule—the fact that a risk is nondiversifiable creates an uncertainty that is added on to the discount rate used to compute present values. But in the option view of investment, uncertainty is far more important and fundamental. A small increase in uncertainty (nondiversifiable or otherwise) can lead managers to delay some investments (those that involve the exercising of options, such as the construction of a factory). At the same time, uncertainty can prompt managers to accelerate other investments (those that generate options or reveal information, such as R&D programs).

In addition to understanding the role of irreversibility and uncertainty, it is also important to understand how companies obtain their investment opportunities (their options to invest) in the first place. Sometimes investment opportunities result from patents or from ownership of land or natural resources. In such cases, the opportunities are probably the result of earlier investments. Generally, however, investment opportunities flow from a company's managerial resources, technological knowledge, reputation, market position, and possible scale, each of which may have been built up gradually. Such resources enable the company to undertake in a productive way investments that individuals or other companies cannot undertake.

Regardless of where a company gets its options to invest, the options are valuable. Indeed, a substantial part of the market value of most companies can be attributed to their options to invest and grow in the future, as opposed to the capital they already have in place. That is particularly true for companies in very volatile and unpredictable industries, such as electronics, telecommunications, and biotechnology. Most of the economic and financial theory of investment has focused on how companies should (and do) exercise their options to invest. But managers also need to understand how their companies can obtain investment opportunities in the first place. The knowledge will help them devise better long-term competitive strategies to determine how to focus and direct their R&D, how much to bid for mineral rights, how early to stake out competitive positions, and so on.

To illustrate the implications of the option theory of investment and the problems inherent in the traditional net present value rule, let us work through the process of making a capital investment decision at a hypothetical pharmaceutical company.

Suppose that you are the CEO of a company considering the development and production of a new drug. Both the costs and the revenues from the venture are highly uncertain. The costs will depend on, among other things, the purity of the output of the chemical process and the compound's overall effectiveness. The revenues will depend on the company's ability to find a principal market for the compound (and for whatever secondary uses might be discovered) and the time frame within which rival companies are able to introduce similar products.

Suppose that you must decide whether to make an initial investment of $15 million in R&D. You realize that later, if you decide to continue the project, additional money will have to be invested in a production facility. There are three possible scenarios for the cost of production: low ($40 million), middle ($80 million), and high ($120 million). To keep matters simple, we will assume that each of the scenarios is equally likely (in other words, that each has a $\frac{1}{3}$ probability of occurring). Let us also assume that there are two equally likely cases for the revenue (probability $\frac{1}{2}$ each): low ($50 million) and high ($130 million). To focus on the question of how uncertainty and option values modify the usual NPV analysis and to keep the example simple, we will also assume that the time frame is short enough that the usual discounting to reflect the time value of money can be ignored.

Should you make the $15 million investment in R&D? First, let us analyze the problem by using a simple NPV approach. The expected value (i.e., the probability-weighted average) of the cost of the production facility is ($\frac{1}{3} \times$ $40 million) + ($\frac{1}{3} \times$ $80 million) + ($\frac{1}{3} \times$ $120 million) = $80 million. Likewise, the expected value of the revenue is ($\frac{1}{2} \times$ $50 million) + ($\frac{1}{2} \times$ $130 million) = $90 million. Therefore, the expected value of the operating profit is $10 million, which does not justify the expenditure of $15 million on R&D. So the conventional thinking would kill the project at the outset.

However, suppose that by doing the R&D, you are able to narrow the uncertainty by finding out which of the three possibilities for the cost of the production facility is closest to reality. After learning about the cost, you would be able to make a decision to go ahead and continue the project or to drop it. Thus the $15 million you invest in R&D creates an option—a right with no obligation to proceed with the actual production and marketing.

For a moment, we will put aside the market uncertainty and suppose that the revenue will always be $90 million. If the high-cost ($120 million) scenario is the one that materializes, you will decide not to proceed with the production and your operating profit will be zero. In the other two cases, however, you will proceed. The operating profit is $90 million − $80 million = $10 million in the middle-cost case and $90 million − $40 million = $50 million in the low-cost case. The probability-weighted average of your operating profit across all three possible outcomes is $(\frac{1}{3} \times 0) + (\frac{1}{3} \times \$10 \text{ million}) + (\frac{1}{3} \times \$50 \text{ million}) = \$20$ million. That exceeds your research and development cost of $15 million, and, therefore, the investment in R&D would be justified.

The logic shows that an action to *create* an option should be valued more highly than a naïve NPV approach would suggest. The gap between the naïve calculation and the correct one arises because the option itself is valuable. You can exercise it selectively when doing so is to your advantage, and you can let it lapse when exercising it would be unprofitable. The amount that an option should be valued over and above the $10 million expected profit (calculated on the assumption of immediate go-ahead) depends on the sizes and the probabilities of the losses that you are able to avoid.

Now let us reintroduce the notion of uncertainty with regard to the expected revenue. Suppose that you have found out that the middle-cost scenario ($80 million) is the reality. If you need to make a go-or-no-go decision about production at this point, you will choose to proceed because the expected revenue of $(\frac{1}{2} \times \$130 \text{ million}) + (\frac{1}{2} \times \$50 \text{ million}) = \$90$ million exceeds the production cost of $80 million, resulting in an operating profit of $10 million. But suppose you can postpone the production decision until you have found out the true market potential. By waiting, you can choose to go ahead only if the revenue is high, and you can avoid the loss-making case where the revenue turns out to be low. If revenue is high (which occurs with probability $\frac{1}{2}$), you will earn an operating profit of $130 million − $80 million = $50 million, and if revenue is low (also probability $\frac{1}{2}$), you will earn zero, for an average or expected value of $25 million, which is more than the $10 million you would get if you went ahead at once.

Here the opportunity to proceed with production is like a call option. Making a go-or-no-go decision amounts to exercising that option. If you can identify some eventualities that would cause you to rethink a go-ahead decision (such as a drop in market demand for your product), then the ability to wait and avoid those eventualities is valuable: The option has a time value or a holding premium. The fact that the option is "in the money" (going ahead would yield a positive NPV) does not necessarily mean that you should exercise the option (in this case, proceeding with production). Instead, you should wait until the option is deeper in the money—that is, until the net present value of going ahead is large enough to offset the loss of the value of the option.

In this example, we have intentionally left out any explicit cost of waiting. But you can easily include potential waiting costs in the calculation. Suppose that while you wait to gauge the market potential, a rival will grab $20 million worth of your anticipated revenues. The revenues under your most favorable scenario will be only $110 million and under the unfavorable one only $30 million. Now, if you wait, you can expect an outcome of $110 million − $80 million = $30 million with probability $\frac{1}{2}$ and an outcome of zero with probability $\frac{1}{2}$, for an expected value of $15 million. That is still better than the $10 million you get if you go ahead at once.

There's an important lesson here: Just as an action that creates an option needs to be valued more than the NPV analysis would indicate, an action that *exercises* or *uses up* an option should be valued *less* than a simple NPV approach would suggest. The reason is that the option itself is valuable. You can exercise an option selectively when the action is to your advantage, or you can let it lapse when such a course would be unprofitable. Again, the extra value gain depends on the sizes and the probabilities of the losses you are able to avoid.

It is even possible to put the revenue uncertainty and the cost uncertainty together. Thus if the R&D investment reveals that costs will be at the high end, you should again wait for the resolution of the revenue uncertainty before you proceed, earning $\frac{1}{2} \times$ ($130 million − $120 million) = $5 million. If the costs fall in the middle, it is best to wait, as we saw above; the expected operating profit will be $25 million. If the cost is at the low end ($40 million), however, the operating profit is positive at both revenue levels. In that case, it is best to proceed with production at once because the expected profit is $(\frac{1}{2} \times \$130$ million$) + (\frac{1}{2} \times \$50$ million$) - \$40$ million $= \$50$ million. The proper calculation for NPV that results from the $15 million R&D investment is $(\frac{1}{3} \times \$5$ million$) + (\frac{1}{3} \times \$25$ million$) + (\frac{1}{3} \times \$50$ million$) = \$26.7$ million, which is even bigger than the $20 million we calculated when we left out the revenue uncertainty. We are now valuing the production options correctly, whereas earlier we assumed, in effect, that those options would be exercised immediately; in the high-cost and middle-cost scenarios, exercising the options wouldn't have been optimal.

All of the numbers in this pharmaceutical example were chosen to facilitate simple calculations. But the basic ideas represented in the case can be applied in a variety of real-life situations. As long as there are contingencies under which the company would not wish to proceed to production, the R&D that conveys information about which contingency will materialize creates an option. And insofar as there is a positive probability that production would be unprofitable, building the plant (rather than waiting) exercises an option.

The option theory of investing also has clear implications for companies attempting to raise capital. If financial market participants understand the nature of the options correctly, they will place greater value on the investments that *create* options, and they will be more hesitant to finance those that *exercise* options. Therefore, as the pharmaceutical company proceeds from exploratory R&D (which creates options) to production and marketing (which exercises them), it will find the hurdle rate rising and sources of eager venture capital drying up. It is interesting to note that this is exactly what has been going on recently in the biotechnology industry as it has progressed from searching for several new products to trying to exploit the few it has found.[5] The increased difficulty of finding venture capital for biotechnology can be explained in other ways—disappointments over earlier biotechnology products, problems securing and enforcing patents, the risk of a health care cost crunch, to name a few. But we believe that, to a large extent, the market is making an astute differentiation between the creation of options and the exercising of options.

As companies in a broad range of industries are learning, opportunities to apply option theory to investments are numerous. Below are a few examples to illustrate the kinds of insight that the options theory of investment can provide.

Investments in Oil Reserves

Nowhere is the idea of investments as options better illustrated than in the context of decisions to acquire and exploit deposits of natural resources. A company that buys deposits is buying an asset that it can develop immediately or later, depending on market conditions. The asset, then, is an option—an opportunity to choose the future development timetable of the deposit. A company can speed up production when the price is high, and it can slow it down or suspend it altogether when the price is low. Ignoring the option and valuing the entire reserve at today's price (or at future prices following a preset rate of output) can lead to a significant underestimation of the value of the asset.

The U.S. government regularly auctions off leases for offshore tracts of land, and oil companies perform valuations as part of their bidding process. The sums involved are huge—an individual oil company can easily bid hundreds of millions of dollars.

It should not be surprising, then, that unless a company understands how to value an undeveloped oil reserve as an option, it may overpay, or it may lose some very valuable tracts to rival bidders.[6]

Consider what would happen if an oil company manager tried to value an undeveloped oil reserve using the standard NPV approach. Depending on the current price of oil, the expected rate of change of the price, and the cost of developing the reserve, he might construct a scenario for the timing of development and hence the timing (and size) of the future cash flows from production. He would then value the reserve by discounting these numbers and adding them together. Because oil price uncertainty is not completely diversifiable, the greater the perceived volatility of oil prices, the higher the discount rate that he would use; the higher the discount rate, the lower the estimated value of the undeveloped reserve.

But that would grossly underestimate the value of the reserve. It completely ignores the flexibility that the company has regarding when to develop the reserve—that is, when to exercise the reserve's option value. And note that, just as options are more valuable when there is more uncertainty about future contingencies, the oil reserve is more valuable when the price of oil is more volatile. The result would be just the opposite of what a standard NPV calculation would tell us: In contrast to the standard calculation, which says that greater uncertainty over oil prices should lead to *less* investment in undeveloped oil reserves, option theory tells us it should lead to *more*.

By treating an undeveloped oil reserve as an option, we can value it correctly, and we can also determine when is the best time to invest in the development of the reserve. Developing the reserve is like exercising a call option, and the exercise price is the cost of development. The greater the uncertainty over oil prices, the longer an oil company should hold undeveloped reserves and keep alive its option to develop them.

Scale Versus Flexibility in Utility Planning

The option view of investment can also help companies value flexibility in their capacity expansion plans. Should a company commit itself to a large amount of production capacity, or should it retain flexibility by investing slowly and keeping its options for growth open? Although many businesses confront the problem, it is particularly important for electric utilities, whose expansion plans must balance the advantages of building large-scale plants with the advantages of investing slowly and maintaining flexibility.

Economies of scale can be an important source of cost savings for companies. By building one large plant instead of two or three smaller ones, companies might be able to reduce their average unit cost while increasing profitability. Perhaps companies should respond to growth opportunities by bunching their investments—that is, investing in new capacity only infrequently but adding large and efficient plants each time. But what should managers do when demand growth is uncertain, as it often is? If the company makes an irreversible investment in a large addition to capacity and then demand grows slowly or even shrinks, it will find itself burdened with capital it doesn't need. When the growth of demand is uncertain, there is a trade-off between scale economies and the flexibility that is gained by investing more frequently in small additions to capacity as they are needed.

Electric utilities typically find that it is much cheaper per unit of capacity to build large coal-fired power plants than it is to add capacity in small amounts. But at the same time, utilities face considerable uncertainty about how fast demand will grow and what the fuel to generate the electricity will cost. Adding capacity in small amounts gives the utility flexibility, but it is also more costly. As a result, knowing how to value the flexibility becomes very important. The options approach is well suited to the purpose.

For example, suppose a utility is choosing between a large coal-fired plant that will provide enough capacity for demand growth over the next 10 to 15 years or adding small oil-fired generators, each of which will provide for about a year's worth of demand growth as needed. The utility faces uncertainty over demand growth and over the relative prices of coal and oil in the future. Even if a straightforward NPV calculation favors the large coal-fired plant, that does not mean that it is the more economical alternative. The reason is that if it were to invest in the coal-fired plant, the utility would commit itself to a large amount of capacity and to a particular fuel. In so doing, it would give up its options to grow more slowly (should demand grow more slowly than expected) or to grow with at least some of the added capacity fueled by oil (should oil prices, at some future date, fall relative to coal prices). By valuing the options using option-pricing techniques, the utility can assess the importance of the flexibility that small oil-fired generators would provide.

Utilities are finding that the value of flexibility can be large and that standard NPV methods that ignore flexibility can be extremely misleading. A number of utilities have begun to use option-pricing techniques for long-term capacity planning. The New England Electric System (NEES), for example, has been especially innovative in applying the approach to investment planning. Among other things, the company has used option-pricing techniques to show that an investment in the repowering of a hydroelectric plant should be delayed, even though the conventional NPV calculation for the project is positive. It has also used the approach to value contract provisions for the purchase of electric capacity and to determine when to retire a generating unit.[7]

Price Volatility in Commodities

Commodity prices are notorious for their volatility. Copper prices, for example, have been known to double or drop by half in the space of several months. Why are copper prices so volatile, and how should producers decide whether to open new mines and refineries or to close old ones in response to price changes? The options approach to investment helps provide answers to such questions.

Investment and disinvestment in the copper industry involve large sunk costs. Building a new copper mine, smelter, or refinery involves a large-scale commitment of financial resources. Given the volatility of copper prices, managers understand that there is value to waiting for more information before committing resources, even if the current price of copper is relatively high. As we showed in the earlier pharmaceutical example, a positive NPV is not sufficient to justify investment. The price of copper and, correspondingly, the NPV of a new copper mine must be high enough to cover the opportunity cost of giving up the option to wait. The same is true with disinvestment. Once a mine, smelter, or refinery is closed, it cannot be reopened easily. As a result, managers will keep these facilities open even if they are losing money at current prices. They recognize that by closing a facility, they incur an opportunity cost of giving up the option to wait for higher future prices. Thus many copper mines built during the 1970s, when copper prices were high, were kept open during the mid-1980s, when copper prices fell to their lowest levels in real terms since the Great Depression.

Given the large sunk costs involved in building or closing copper-producing facilities and given the volatility of copper prices, it is essential to account for option value when making investment decisions. In reality, copper prices must rise far above the point of positive NPV to justify building new facilities and fall far below average variable cost to justify closing down existing facilities. Outside observers might see that approach as a form of myopia. We believe, however, that it reflects a rational response to option value.

Understanding option value and its implications for irreversible investment in the copper industry can also help us understand why copper prices are so volatile in the first place. Corporate inertia in building and closing down facilities feeds back into prices. Suppose that the demand for copper rises in response to higher-than-average

GNP growth, causing the price of copper to rise. Knowing that the price might fall later, producers typically wait rather than respond immediately with new additions to capacity. Since greater supply is not readily forthcoming, the pressure of demand translates into rapid increases in price. Similarly, during downturns in demand, as mines remain open to preserve their options, the price collapses. Recent history has illustrated this phenomenon: The reluctance of producers to close mines during the mid-1980s, when demand was weak, allowed the price to fall even more than it would have otherwise. Thus the reaction of producers to price volatility in turn sustains the magnitude of price volatility, and any underlying fluctuations of demand or costs will appear in an exaggerated way as price fluctuations.

The economic environment in which most companies must now operate is far more volatile and unpredictable than it was 20 years ago—in part because of growing globalization of markets coupled with increases in exchange-rate fluctuations, in part because of more rapid technology-induced changes in the marketplace. Whatever its cause, however, uncertainty requires that managers become much more sophisticated in the ways they assess and account for risk. It's important for managers to get a better understanding of the options that their companies have or that they are able to create. Ultimately, options create flexibility, and, in an uncertain world, the ability to value and use flexibility is critical.

Decisions that enhance a company's flexibility by creating and preserving options (decisions, for example, about R&D and test marketing) have value that transcends a naïve calculation of NPV. More readily than conventional calculations suggest, managers should make decisions that increase flexibility. Choices that reduce flexibility by exercising options and committing resources to irreversible uses (construction of specific plants and equipment, advertising of particular products) will be valued less than their conventional NPV. Such choices should be made more hesitantly— and subjected to stiffer hurdle rates than the cost of capital—or delayed until circumstances are exceptionally favorable.

The bottom line for managers is that learning how to apply the net present value rule is not sufficient. To make intelligent investment choices, managers need to consider the value of keeping their options open. In this case, we don't think there is any option.

Notes

1. For an overview of financial options and their valuation see John C. Cox and Mark Rubinstein, *Options Markets* (Englewood Cliffs, N.J.: Prentice-Hall, 1985); John C. Hull, *Options, Futures, and Other Deriva-*

tive Securities (Englewood, Cliffs, N.J.: Prentice-Hall, 1989); or Hans R. Stoll and Robert E. Whaley, *Futures and Options: Theory and Applications* (Cincinnati, Ohio: South-Western Publishing Co., 1993).

2. Of course, one can always redefine NPV by subtracting from the conventional calculation the opportunity cost of exercising the option to invest and then saying that the rule "invest if NPV is positive" holds. But to do so is to accept our criticism. To highlight the importance of valuing the option, we prefer to keep it separate from the conventional NPV. But if others prefer to continue to use positive NPV terminology, they should be careful to include all relevant option values in their definition of NPV.

3. For a more comprehensive discussion of the standard techniques of capital budgeting, see a corporate finance textbook such as Richard A. Brealey and Stewart C. Myers, *Principles of Corporate Finance*, 6th ed. (New York: McGraw-Hill, 2000).

4. See Lawrence H. Summers, "Investment Incentives and the Discounting of Depreciation Allowances," in *The Effects of Taxation on Capital Accumulation.* ed. Martin Feldstein (University of Chicago Press, 1987) p. 300; James M. Poterba and Lawrence H. Summers, "Time Horizons of American Firms: New Evidence from a Survey of CEOs" (MIT Working Paper, October 1991); Michael L. Dertouzos, Richard K. Lester, Robert M. Solow, and the MIT Commission on Industrial Productivity, *Made in America* (Harper Paperback, 1990) p. 61; and Robert H. Hayes and David A. Garvin, "Managing As If Tomorrow Mattered," HBR May–June 1982, pp. 70–9.

5. See "Panic in the petri dish," *The Economist*, July 23, 1994, pp. 61–2.

6. The application of option theory to offshore petroleum reserves was pioneered by James L. Paddock, Daniel R. Siegel, and James L. Smith, "Option Valuation of Claims on Real Assets: The Case of Offshore Petroleum Leases," *Quarterly Journal of Economics* 103, August 1988, pp. 479–508.

7. For a more detailed discussion of utility industry applications and NEES's experience in this area, see Thomas Kaslow and Robert S. Pindyck, "Valuing Flexibility in Utility Planning." *The Electricity Journal* 7, March 1994, pp. 60–5.

6 A Conceptual Options Framework for Capital Budgeting

Lenos Trigeorgis

I   Introduction

Recent studies of the practice of corporate management verify that there continues to be a discrepancy between traditional finance theory and corporate practice. Many managers, dissatisfied with the current state of capital budgeting, are often willing to overrule conventional net present value (NPV) analysis or other discounted cash flow (DCF) techniques because they see additional value in projects beyond that resulting from directly measurable cash flows.

Specifically, many practitioners recognize two aspects of extra value that are not adequately addressed in a conventional NPV analysis: (1) the "operating flexibility" of a project that is simply a collection of options enabling management to make or revise decisions at some future time (e.g., to defer, expand, or abandon a project early), and (2) the "strategic value" of a project resulting from its interdependencies with future, follow-up investments and from competitive interaction.

Several academics have also recognized that traditional capital budgeting techniques may often misvalue projects due to the presence of such strategic interactions and managerial operating options. For example, Myers [20] notes the inability of conventional DCF techniques to capture the time-series interactions among contingent investments. Kester [12] uses Myers' initial concept of looking at growth investment opportunities as options on real assets to explore qualitatively the "strategic" and competitive interaction aspects of real projects. Trigeorgis and Mason [33] use options-based contingent claims analysis to practically quantify the value of managerial operating flexibility embedded in a variety of operating options. All agree that corporate finance theory needs to be extended by using option valuation techniques to deal with real investment opportunities and bridge the existing gap between traditional financial theory and strategic planning.

Other approaches that have been proposed to overcome the shortcomings of static NPV analysis such as simulation (Hertz [8]) and decision tree analysis (DTA), as applied to capital budgeting by Magee [13], basically stumble on the problem of determining the appropriate discount rate.[1] The fundamental problem, as we will see next, lies in the valuation of investment opportunities whose claims are not symmetric. In general, asymmetric claims on the value of a project do not have the same discount rate as the project value itself. More specifically, using a constant risk-adjusted discount rate is incorrect if uncertainty is not resolved continuously at a constant rate over time as is the case with growth or compound investment opportunities where early stages of a project are contingent (or can be seen as options) on follow-up stages. It is time to recognize that managerial flexibility creates several interacting real options in most investment projects that may add value due to their inherent asymmetry.[2]

II NPV and Managerial Flexibility/Asymmetry

The basic inadequacy of the NPV or other DCF approaches to capital budgeting is that they ignore, or cannot properly capture, management's flexibility to adapt and revise later decisions. Traditional NPV in particular makes implicit assumptions concerning an "expected scenario" of cash flows and presumes management's commitment to a certain "operating strategy." Typically, an *expected* pattern of cash flows over a *prespecified* life is discounted at a risk-adjusted rate to arrive at the project's NPV. Treating projects as *independent* investment opportunities, an *immediate* accept or reject decision is then made by accepting all projects for which NPV is positive. In effect, it is as if management makes at the outset an irrevocable commitment to an "operating strategy"—e.g., to take the project immediately and operate it continuously until the end of its prespecified expected useful life—from which it cannot depart regardless of whether nature remains faithful to or deviates from its expected scenario of cash flows.

In the real world of uncertainty and competitive interactions, however, the realization of cash flows will probably differ from what management originally expected. As new information arrives and uncertainty about future cash flows is gradually resolved, management may find that various projects allow it varying degrees of flexibility to depart from and revise the operating strategy it originally anticipated to follow. For example, management may be able to defer, expand, abandon, or in various other ways alter a project at different stages during its useful life.

Management's flexibility to adapt its future actions depending on the future environment introduces an asymmetry or skewness in the probability distribution of NPV that expands the investment opportunity's true value by improving its upside potential while limiting downside losses relative to management's initial expectations (see figure 6.1).[3] This asymmetry necessitates using an expanded NPV rule reflecting both components of an opportunity's value, the traditional (static or passive) NPV of direct cash flows and a premium for the flexibility inherent in its operating options, i.e.,

Expanded NPV = Static (Passive) NPV + Option Premium.

Note that such an "expanded NPV" framework does not seek to do away with traditional (static) NPV but rather uses it as a necessary (although not necessarily the only) value component.

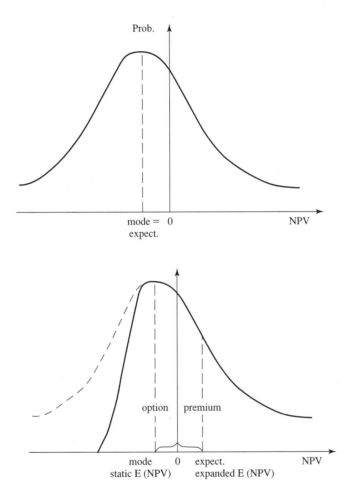

Figure 6.1
Managerial flexibility/options introduce asymmetry in the probability distribution of NPV

III Toward a Conceptual Real Options Framework

As we just pointed out, the operating flexibility and strategic value aspects of various projects cannot be properly captured by traditional DCF techniques due to their discretionary asymmetric nature and dependence on future events that are uncertain at the time of the initial decision. These important aspects can, nevertheless, be properly analyzed by thinking of investment opportunities as being bundles of options on real assets (or "real options") through the options-based technique of contingent claims analysis (CCA) (see, for instance, Trigeorgis and Mason [33]). Just as the owner of an American call option on a financial asset has the right—but not the obligation—to acquire the asset by paying a prespecified price (the "exercise price") on or before a predetermined date (the "exercise or maturity date"), and he will exercise the option if and when it is to his best interest to do so, so will the holder of options on real assets. The owner of a discretionary investment opportunity has the right—but not the obligation—to acquire the (gross) present value of expected cash flows by making an investment outlay on or before the anticipated date when the investment opportunity will cease to exist.[4] Thus, there exists a close analogy between such real investment opportunities (or real options) and call options on stocks (as shown in figure 6.2).[5,6]

Even if no other associated real options exist, the *flexibility to defer* or decide when to initiate the project, as may be provided by a lease to drill for oil, the property rights to extract mineral reserves, or a patent to develop a new product, has a positive value even if immediate undertaking of the project has a negative (static) NPV of cash flows. Such flexibility gives management the right to wait and make the investment (i.e., exercise the option) only if (for instance, the price of the oil or the mineral rises, or the demand for the new product develops enough so that) project value turns out to exceed the necessary outlay, without imposing any symmetric obligation to invest and lose if the opposite scenario occurs.[7]

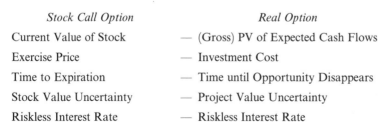

Stock Call Option	Real Option
Current Value of Stock	— (Gross) PV of Expected Cash Flows
Exercise Price	— Investment Cost
Time to Expiration	— Time until Opportunity Disappears
Stock Value Uncertainty	— Project Value Uncertainty
Riskless Interest Rate	— Riskless Interest Rate

Figure 6.2
Comparison between call options on stocks and real options

More generally, when other real options in addition to the option to defer the investment are present, a discretionary investment opportunity can be seen as a call option on a collection or portfolio consisting of the project value, V, and other real call or put options. For example, the *option to expand* the scale of a project by $e\%$ by making an additional investment I' can be formally seen as analogous to a call option to acquire $e\%$ of the (gross) project value (the underlying "asset") with exercise price of I'. If market conditions are uncertain, management may, for example, find it preferable to build excess production capacity enabling it to produce at a faster rate, on a larger scale, or for a longer period if, as uncertainty resolves itself, it turns out that its product is more enthusiastically received in the market than originally anticipated.

Similarly, the *option to contract* the scale of a project's operation by $c\%$ to save on certain preplanned advertising or maintenance expenditures of magnitude I'' can be seen as a put option on $c\%$ of the project value with exercise price I''. For instance, management may find it justifiable to build a plant with lower initial construction costs and higher maintenance expenditures in order to acquire the flexibility to contract operations by cutting down on maintenance costs if the product turns out to do worse than initially expected. Management may also have the *flexibility to temporarily shut down* production (or not to operate) in any given year if cash revenues are not adequate to cover the variable costs of operating in that year; one may thus look at operation in each year as a call option on that year's cash revenue with exercise price the variable cost of operating.[8]

Management may also have the flexibility to terminate a project in its current use earlier than initially expected by switching to its future best alternative use (switching between alternative inputs/outputs) or selling its assets in a second-hand market for their "salvage value." Consider, for example, the decision to build a chemical plant involving the choice between a plant with lower initial construction costs that can use only a single input (e.g., electricity) to produce a single output (e.g., vitamins), and an otherwise identical plant with somewhat higher costs (and higher resale value) but allowing the flexibility to receive diverse inputs (either electricity or coal) to produce a variety of outputs (say vitamins or aspirins). Even though the first plant may have a higher (static) NPV, management may find the second plant more desirable as market conditions change and the relative prices of inputs, outputs, or the plant resale value fluctuate as it may switch to a cheaper input, a more profitable output, or sell the plant's assets in a second-hand market. This *option to switch use* can be seen as a put option on the opportunity's value (in its current use) with exercise price its value in the best alternative use. Furthermore, management may also have the *option to abandon* a project during construction by "defaulting" on subsequent preplanned investment cost "installments" if a coming "installment" exceeds the value from continuing the project. This option to abandon can be looked at either as a compound call option on the opportunity with exercise prices the set of individual investment "installments" or alternatively as a put option on the opportunity with exercise price the cumulative value of subsequent cost savings.[9]

Most of the important payoffs of managerial flexibility can be captured by combining these simple options as building blocks. If many such real options are present simultaneously then the total investment opportunity can be seen as a collection of such real call and put options and can be, in most cases, analyzed numerically via a more involved contingent claims analysis.[10] But even in complex cases when numerical routines are not available, an options-based conceptual framework can offer significant payoffs to qualitative understanding.

IV   Developing a New Project Classification

In practice, firms often classify projects according to risk or functional characteristics (e.g., replacement or new product introduction) to simplify the capital budgeting process. These schemes are incomplete, however, in that they overlook the option aspects of projects described earlier. To motivate a new options-based classification and be better able to appreciate the various elements that it encompasses, let us first start from simple NPV and gradually build up the framework highlighting one aspect at a time. After introducing the flexibility to defer or abandon a project, we will then focus on the concept of compoundness first within and later among projects, and finally highlight interactions introduced by competition.

To see things in a broader perspective, let us first distinguish between two basic types of decision problems that a manager may face: (1) "games against nature," in which the manager's problem is to optimize in the face of random fluctuations in the (gross) value of cash flows from the investment, V (mostly applicable to fully competitive markets), and (2) "strategic games against competition," in which the manager's investment decisions are made with the explicit recognition that they would invite competitive reaction that would in turn impact the value of the investment opportunity (generally found in oligopolistic markets).

A   Static (Passive) NPV

Traditional NPV addresses decision problems of the first type since it typically ignores strategic competitive interactions. But even in dealing with "games against nature" passive NPV is limited in that it implicitly presumes that all decisions are unequivocally taken up front as if management did not have the flexibility to review its original plans in response to nature's deviation from its expected scenario of cash flows. As explained earlier, in the absence of such managerial flexibility or real options, static NPV would be correct: management would make an *immediate* investment outlay, I (considering for now the simplest case of a *single* one-time expenditure), only in return for a higher present value of expected cash inflows, V. The difference, i.e., NPV $(= V - I)$ is of course the current value of the *investment*, provided the manager had no other choice but to "take it (immediately) or leave it."

B Opportunity to Defer

What should really be of interest, however, is not the value of immediate investment per se, but rather the value of the investment *opportunity*. As explained earlier, in a world of uncertainty where nature can play games (V may fluctuate randomly) the opportunity to invest can be more valuable than immediate investment since it allows management the flexibility to defer undertaking the investment until circumstances turn most favorable or back out altogether if they turn unsatisfactory. The investment *opportunity* is thus formally *equivalent* to a call *option* on V with exercise price the one-time investment outlay I. The value of this opportunity to invest therefore exceeds the NPV of cash flows from immediate investment by the value of the flexibility to defer the investment. Such an investment opportunity may thus be economically desirable even if the investment itself may have a negative NPV (i.e., $V < I$). It would therefore be very useful to distinguish between opportunities that allow management the flexibility to defer their undertaking (such as projects with patents or leases) and projects that do not (such as an expiring offer to immediately expand capacity to meet extra demand by an impatient client).

Even if management lacks the flexibility to defer the undertaking of a project when faced with an immediate accept/reject decision, it may still have the flexibility to abandon a once undertaken project for its "salvage value" before the end of its expected life if it turns out to perform worse than expected.[11] The flexibility to abandon a project early should therefore be explicitly accounted for in the investment decision whenever appropriate.

C Intraproject Compoundness

Let us, for the moment, suppress the flexibility to defer undertaking the project or abandon it for its salvage value. Consider, however, the investment outlay, I, no longer as a single one-time expenditure at the outset but rather as a sequence of investment "installments" starting immediately and extending throughout (much of) the life of the investment (e.g., annual maintenance expenditures during the life of a machine or plant). In such a case the investment is actually a compound option where an earlier investment cost installment represents the exercise price required to acquire a subsequent option to continue operating the project until the next installment comes due, and so on. This is the idea of compoundness within the same project —an intraproject interaction. If managerial flexibility is reintroduced, then intraproject compoundness highlights a series of distinct points in time—just before a subsequent investment installment comes due—when the project might be better discontinued if it turns out not to perform satisfactorily. DCF techniques and particularly NPV that deal with the sequence of investment installments simply by subtracting their present value from that of the expected cash inflows or even by including all but the first investment installment costs in the so called "net cash flows" clearly undervalue such compound investments.

D Interproject Compoundness

Let us now return to the simple case of a single one-time investment outlay at the start of each project. Consider, however, the case of contingent projects where undertaking the first is a prerequisite for the next or provides the opportunity to acquire at maturity the benefits of the new investment by making a new outlay (e.g., a research project provides at completion the opportunity to acquire the revenues of the developed product upon incurring a production outlay). This idea of interproject compoundness is remarkably similar in structure when looking at a sequence of projects to the intraproject compoundness described above (see figure 6.3), with the difference that each "investment installment" now provides the opportunity to begin a new project rather than continue the same one. Compoundness between projects is an interaction of strategic importance since it may justify the undertaking of projects with negative NPV of direct cash flows on the basis of opening up subsequent future investment opportunities.

E Competitive Interaction

Another dimension to the valuation of investment opportunities is introduced by competitive interaction. Here we may distinguish between two forms of analysis depending on the type of interaction between competitors. If the impact of competitive entry can be considered exogenous and pertains basically to the threat of capturing part of the value of the investment away from the incumbent firm, then its management still faces an "optimization problem"—although a more complex one—in that it has to incorporate the impact of competition in its own investment decision but can ignore any reciprocal effects of that decision on competitors' actions.

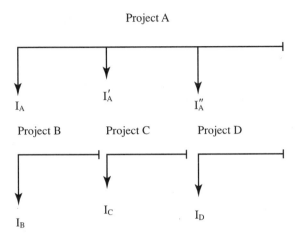

Figure 6.3
Intraproject compoundness

If, however, each competitor's investment decisions are contingent upon and sensitive to the other's moves then a more complex "game-theoretic" treatment becomes necessary. Investing earlier than one otherwise would to preempt competitive entry is a simple case of such "strategic games against competition". The absence or presence (and type) of competitive interaction can therefore serve as another "cut" for classifying and valuing real investment opportunities. We are thus led to propose the set of "strategic questions" for corporate management presented in figure 6.4.

V "Strategic Questions" for Capital Budgeting Analysis

The first question that management must address in the evaluation process refers to the *exclusiveness of option ownership* and the *effect of competition* on the firm's ability to fully appropriate for itself the option value. If the firm retains an exclusive right as to whether and when to invest, unaffected by competitive initiatives, then its investment opportunity is classified as a *proprietary option*. Investment opportunities with high barriers of entry for competitors such as a patent for developing a product having no close substitutes, or a unique knowhow of a technological process, or market conditions that competitors are unable to duplicate for at least some time, are just a few examples of such real proprietary options. In such cases, management may have the flexibility to abandon a project early (i.e., the project has additional "abandonment value"), or even temporarily interrupt the project's operation in certain

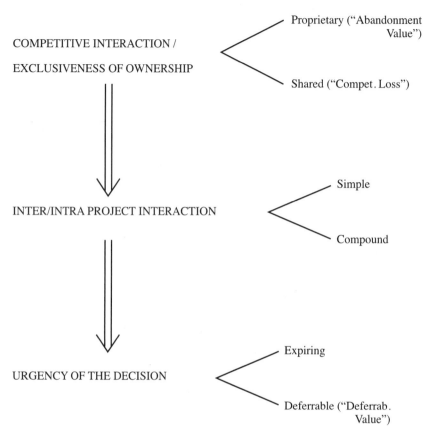

Figure 6.4
Set of strategic questions

"unprofitable" periods.[12] If, however, competitors share the right to exercise and may be able to take part (or all) of the project's value away from the firm, then the option is *shared*.[13] Shared real options can be seen as jointly held opportunities of a number of competing firms or of a whole industry, and can be exercised by any one of their collective owners. Such shared real options are, for example, the opportunity to introduce a new product unprotected by possible introduction of close substitutes, or to penetrate a new geographic market without barriers to competitive entry. The loss in value suffered by an incumbent firm as a result of competitive interaction when a competitive firm exercises its shared rights will be subsequently called "competitive loss."

The second question concerns *inter- (or intra-) project interactions*, specifically compoundness.[14] Is an investment opportunity valuable in and of itself or is it a prerequisite for subsequent investment opportunities? If the opportunity is a real option leading upon exercise to further discretionary investment opportunities or an option whose payout is another option then it is classified as *compound*. Such real options on options may have a more "strategic" impact on a firm and are more complicated to analyze; they can no longer be looked at as independent investments, but rather as links in a chain of interrelated projects the earlier of which are prerequisites for the ones to follow. A research and development (R&D) investment, a lease for an undeveloped tract with potential oil reserves, and an acquisition of an unrelated company are just a few examples of such compound options that may be undertaken not just for their direct cash flows but also (or perhaps primarily) for the new opportunities that they may open up (a new technological breakthrough, large reserves of oil, or access to a new market). On the other hand, if the project can be evaluated as a stand-alone investment opportunity, it is called a *simple option*. Such independent opportunities whose value upon exercise is limited only to the underlying project in and of itself are, for instance, standard replacement or maintenance projects.

The last "strategic question" refers to the *urgency of the decision*. Management must distinguish between those projects that need an immediate accept/reject decision, i.e., *expiring* investment opportunities, and those that management can defer for future action, i.e., *deferrable* options. We will subsequently refer to the value of the flexibility to defer undertaking a project as the "deferrability value" of the project. Deferrable projects require a more extensive analysis of the optimal timing of investment since management must compare the net value of taking the project today with the net value of taking it at all possible future years. Thus, management must analyze the relative benefits and costs of waiting in association with other strategic considerations (e.g., the threat of competitive entry in a shared-deferrable option may justify early capital commitment for preemptive purposes). This mode of analysis leads us to the real options classification scheme shown in figure 6.5.[15]

This eight-fork classification scheme is intended to focus management's attention on the important characteristics of investment opportunities as options on real assets as described above. And although the distinctions between the various categories may at times be more relative rather than absolute, most real investment opportunities including strategic can find a place in one of the eight branches of the options-based classification tree. For example, routine maintenance could be classified and analyzed as a proprietary–simple–expiring (P–S–E) option, plant modernization as proprietary–simple–deferrable, bidding for purchase of assets as shared–simple–

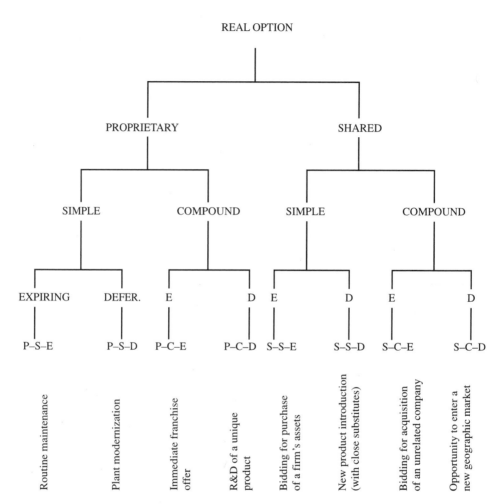

Figure 6.5
Proposed real options classification

expiring, a new product introduction with close substitutes as shared–simple–deferrable, an immediate franchise offer as proprietary–compound–expiring, research and development of a unique product as proprietary–compound–deferrable, bidding for the acquistion of an unrelated company as shared–compound–expiring, and the opportunity to enter a new geographic market as shared–compound–deferrable.

It is worth noting that under this real options classification scheme conventional (static) NPV investments are properly seen as a special case under the leftmost branch of proprietary–simple–expiring options since such investments are typically evaluated as if they were exclusively owned (hence "proprietary"), independent (hence "simple"), and immediate (hence "expiring") opportunities.

VI Options Classification, Operating Strategy, and Value Components

The options-based classification scheme also helps uncover management's implicit "operating strategy" as well as the different value components comprising the "option premium" part of an investment opportunity's "expanded NPV." Figure 6.6 shows different "operating strategies" and the corresponding real option value ("expanded NPV") for various simple investment categories under the options classification scheme. Again, the proposed framework should be seen as a practical aid in recognizing and understanding some frequently recurring options combinations.

In figure 6.6, Part A shows the basic operating strategy assumed (appropriately so in the absence of managerial flexibility) by conventional (static) DCF techniques: management starts the project (indicated by "↓") at time 0 and operates it continuously (indicated by a solid line "—") until the end (indicated by "↑") of its pre-estimated expected useful life (T). The value of the real opportunity in this case is adequately captured by the static NPV component (since there is no "option premium" in the absence of real options).

In Part B different operating strategies may be found preferable when circumstances turn out differently from what was originally expected. In a proprietary–simple–expiring opportunity the possibility of abandonment at an earlier time ($T' < T$) may become valuable. The value of the real opportunity would then be its value if no departure from the expected scenario and operating strategy were to occur (i.e., the static NPV) plus the value of abandonment. In a shared–simple–expiring real option, the project is again taken immediately but competitive entry (denoted by "⇂") may cause erosion in project value, so the option premium may actually have negative value (competitive loss). In a proprietary–simple–deferrable opportunity the option premium results from management's flexibility to defer the project (until T_1)

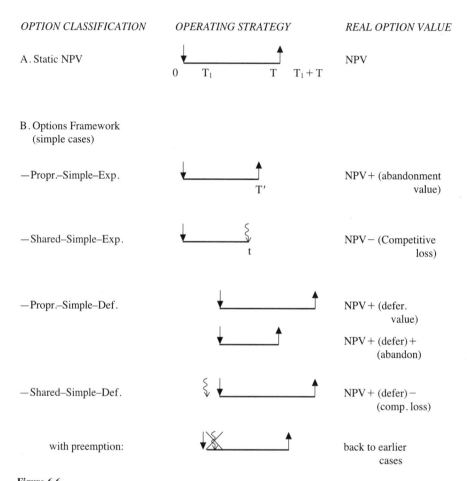

Figure 6.6
Option classification, "operating strategies," and components of real option value. T, expected project life; T_1, period to defer (e.g., duration of patent or lease); ↓, management's decision to start the project; ↑, management's decision to end the project; ⌇, competitive entry (out of management's control).

and possibly from its additional incremental ability to abandon it early, i.e., "option premium" = "deferrability value" + "abandonment value."

Finally, in a shared–simple–deferrable investment opportunity the value of the real option ("expanded NPV") is

static NPV + ("deferrability value" − "competitive loss").

If this "expanded NPV" turns positive before the investment opportunity expires, the project should be undertaken. Exactly when, however, would depend on the trade-off between "deferrability value" and "competitive loss": the longer management defers the investment, the higher its deferrability value, but also the greater the risk of competitive loss.

Figure 6.7, based on an analogy with call options, is intended to give a simplified visual impression of the various components of value for the last case of the shared–simple–deferrable option. It shows total real option value (expanded NPV), R, as a function of (gross) project value, V, and is based on the assumption that a competitor's entry causes a drop in project value from V to V', with the exact magnitude of the drop (which may, for instance, be due to loss of market share to the competitor) depending on market structure characteristics. This project value drop translates into a smaller damage in real option value attributed to competition from $R(V)$ to $R(V')$ (the "competitive loss").

Notice that the real option value exceeds the static NPV component of project value (given by the vertical distance to the 45 degree line which equals $V − I$), and is nonnegative even if the project's NPV is negative. The "deferrability value" component of the option premium is here represented by the vertical distance equivalent to $R(V) − \text{NPV}$. Observe that either the "deferrability value" or the "competitive loss" parts of the option premium may dominate, depending on the severity of the impact of competitive entry on (gross) project value.

VII Implications for Capital Budgeting

Viewing opportunities to invest as collections of options on real assets provides new insight into investment decision making and enables managers to draw several important implications for capital budgeting, some of which may provide direct challenge to established popular beliefs.

1. An "expanded NPV" analysis. Management should broaden its valuation horizon by moving toward an "expanded NPV" criterion in order to capture the flexibility of operating strategies it may implement as well as other strategic interactions. Under

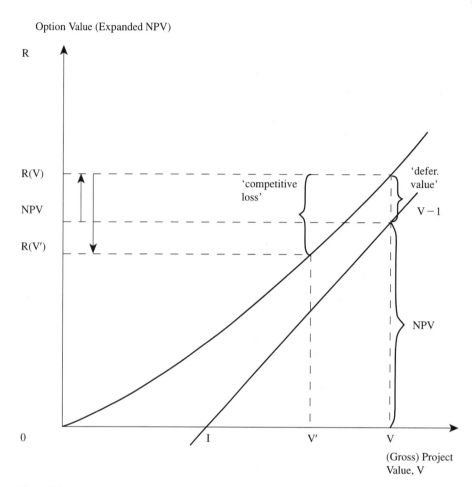

Figure 6.7
Value components for a shared-simple-deferrable investment opportunity

the expanded framework, the total economic desirability of an investment opportunity is explicitly seen as the sum of its static NPV of directly measurable expected cash flows and of the option premium reflecting the value of managerial operating flexibility and strategic interactions. The incremental contribution of (and any interactions among) these additional sources of value (e.g., "deferrability value," "abandonment value," "competitive loss") comprising the "option premium" should be added to the static NPV, so that an investment opportunity is now desirable if

expanded NPV = static NPV + option premium > 0.

By looking at real investment opportunities through this expanded conceptual options valuation lens managers can now better appreciate that:

(a) traditional (static) NPV may indeed undervalue projects (by suppressing the "option premium" or flexibility component of total value), as previously suggested by Kester [12] and other critics, mainly from corporate strategy;

(b) it may be justified to accept projects with negative (static) NPV if the value of managerial flexibility (i.e., the option premium) exceeds the negative NPV of the project's direct expected cash flows;[16]

(c) the value of managerial flexibility—and the extent to which managers should make investment outlays in excess of what is dictated by traditional standards—can now be quantified through options pricing, unlike other suggestions by previous critics.

2. The options framework also indicates that, other things remaining the same, the value of managerial flexibility ("option premium"):

(a) is higher in more uncertain environments, again a direct consequence of the asymmetry it introduces. (This beneficial impact of risk on real option value implies that in more uncertain environments real compound options, having a higher option premium component, are relatively more valuable than, say, simple deferrable investment opportunities, which in turn are more valuable than simple expiring projects);

(b) may be higher during periods of high real interest rates;

(c) may be higher for investment opportunities of longer duration. (This implies that in the special case of a proprietary real option without any form of "dividends"—such as competitive arrivals or intermediate cash flows—management may find it optimal to wait until close to maturity before deciding whether to exercise its real option or not.[17] The value implicit in having control over the timing of exercising such a proprietary real option may help explain the striving by many firms to achieve a dominant competitive position in their industry.)

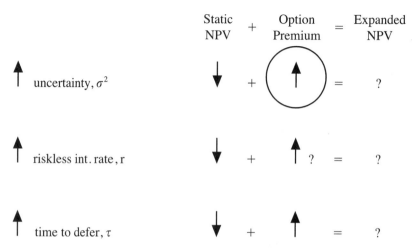

Figure 6.8
Impact of various factors on investment opportunity value components

Note that, contrary to conventional popular belief, higher uncertainty, greater interest rates, or more time before undertaking a project (though implying more distant cash flows) are not necessarily hurting the value of an investment opportunity. Although all these factors do certainly damage its (static) NPV component as traditionally recognized—their negative impact shown by down-pointing arrows in figure 6.8—they may nevertheless substantially enhance managerial flexibility and bear the opposite effect on the "option premium" component of value—the possibility of a positive impact indicated by upward-pointing arrows. Thus, the overall impact of these factors is not clear-cut a priori, although it *may* prove beneficial for the total value of an investment opportunity or "expanded NPV" (if it increases the "option premium" more than it reduces the "static NPV" component of value).

3. The presence of competitive interactions in shared options may justify earlier exercise.[18]

As Kester [10] first recognized, competitive actions may cause erosion in a real option's value that may not be avoidable simply by selling the option to others (as most real options may not be tradeable) so that an early preemptive investment may at times be the only available response to prevent such undesirable competitive value losses. The effect of such competitive erosions in real option value in a preemptive equilibrium setting may be thought of as analogous to the effect of dividends on the value of a call option in justifying early exercise.[19]

In general, management may find it justifiable to exercise relatively early (a) when its real option is shared with competitors and the anticipated loss in project value due to competitive entry is large and can be preempted, (b) when competitive pressure is intense, (c) when project uncertainty and, generally, interest rates are low, and (d) when the "competitive loss" preempted exceeds the "deferrability value" sacrificed by early exercise, or more generally when the value of managerial flexibility (or option premium) is low relative to the (static) NPV of the project.

VIII Conclusion

This chapter sought to describe a general conceptual framework for analyzing investment opportunities seen as collections of options on real assets, with special emphasis on the operating flexibility and strategic/competitive dimensions that are left out of conventional discounted cash flow analyses. A new project classification scheme and strategic questions for capital budgeting analysis have been proposed, and their use in helping uncover management's implicit operating strategy and the various option value components has been described. Our framework is intended as a practical aid in recognizing and understanding the frequently encountered combinations of real options.

The options-based framework presented here promises to offer an expanded and unifying evaluation approach for all real investment decisions by integrating capital budgeting and strategic planning under the single roof of value maximization. Moreover, since the options methodology has been used already in the valuation of most financial securities, options-based analysis has the potential not only to integrate all real investment decisions ("strategic" with "normal"), but also to marry the real with the financing decisions of the firm under a common paradigm.

Notes

I am grateful to W. Carl Kester, Scott P. Mason, and Stewart C. Myers who, through their writings and discussions, left their marks on the following pages. Any errors are my own.

1. In decision analysis the tree is built forward using the actual probabilities and expected rate of return; thus, when moving backward to calculate project value, it is inconsistent to discount at the riskless rate of return and the appropriate discount rate remains indeterminable.

In option pricing, however, the no-arbitrage hedge attainable under continuous trading allows a solution that is independent of risk attitudes and that therefore may be conveniently obtained in a world of risk neutrality. In essence, we may obtain the solution by building forward an equivalent tree using "risk-neutral" probabilities so that when moving backward we may consistently discount the expected terminal cash flows at the risk-free rate. Thus, in its discrete form options pricing can be seen as a special though economically corrected version of DTA that recognizes open market opportunities to trade and borrow (see Trigeorgis and Mason [33]).

2. Option pricing techniques can simultaneously compute the correct discount rate and determine the optimal exercise of operating options inherent in a project.

3. In the absence of such managerial flexibility, the probability distribution of NPV would be reasonably symmetric, in which case the (static) expected NPV (or mean of the symmetric distribution) would coincide with its mode or most likely estimate (see top part of figure 6.1). When managerial flexibility (such as the options to defer or abandon a project early) is significant, however, by basically providing a protection against (or adaptation to) future events turning out differently from what management expected at the outset, it introduces a truncation (typically at or below the mode) so that the resulting actual distribution is skewed to the right (bottom part of figure 6.1). The true expected value of such an asymmetric distribution—which we will refer to as the "expanded" expected NPV, "expanded" in that it incorporates managerial flexibility—exceeds its mode—which is the same as the mode of the corresponding symmetric distribution and hence the static expected NPV—by an "option premium" reflecting the value of managerial flexibility.

4. The "investment outlay" does not necessarily have to be a single one-time investment, but may actually be a series of investment "installments."

5. The value of a call option on a stock is of course higher, other things constant, the greater the stock price and the lower the required exercise price, the greater the volatility of stock returns (since it increases the upside profit potential while the downside risk is limited due to the option asymmetry), the higher the risk-free interest rate (since it lowers the present value of the future exercise cost), and the longer the time to maturity (both through a higher total uncertainty of stock returns and a lower present value of the exercise cost). For a more detailed exposition of option pricing see Cox and Rubinstein [4] or Brealey and Myers [2, chapter 20].

6. Although the analogy between stock call options and real options is a close one, it is not exact. Some of the main differences that we incorporate in our framework later are (1) stock call options are proprietary (exclusively owned) while real options may often be shared with competitors; (2) unlike stock call options, real options are generally not tradeable (which may motivate early exercise to preempt competitors); (3) real options may often be interdependent (compound options).

7. The option to initiate has been examined by Tourinho [30] in valuing reserves of natural resources, by McDonald and Siegel [19], and by Siegel, Smith, and Paddock [27] in valuing offshore petroleum leases. The latter found, for example, that longer leases allowing more flexibility as to when, if at all, to develop the petroleum tracts are more valuable, especially when oil prices are highly uncertain. Majd and Pindyck [14] recently value the option to delay sequential construction (or time to build).

8. The option to shut down has been analyzed by McDonald and Siegel [18] using quantitative option pricing techniques.

9. The option to abandon has first been treated by Robichek and Van Horn [25] using simulation techniques. Recently Myers and Majd [21] employ quantitative option pricing methodology to analyze the same option seen as formally equivalent to an American put on a dividend-paying stock.

The problem of switching between inputs or outputs has not yet been solved explicitly, although some related work has appeared in the literature. Margrabe [15], for example, values an option to exchange one asset for another, while Stultz [29] analyzes options on the maximum (or minimum) of two risky assets, which incidentally provides an approach for valuing opportunities allowing the flexibility to choose upon exercise among two mutually exclusive uses (or related risky streams of cash flows). A good example would be the opportunity to buy a piece of land that can be used either for a house or office space. Recently, Kensinger [9] examines the option to exchange [convert] one set of commodities for [into] another.

10. The simultaneous presence of several such real options may give rise to (typically negative) interaction effects (such as between the options to expand and abandon), necessitating the use of options-based numerical analysis techniques for solving the more complex problems. See Trigeorgis [32] for a numerical analysis of projects with multiple interacting real options.

11. "Salvage value" or value in the best alternative use may come from the value of expected cash flows from switching use (or inputs/outputs), a market price for which the project may sell in a second-hand market or, in situations where subsequent expenditures are due, the value of subsequent cost savings from discontinuing the project.

12. To simplify exposition we will ignore for the rest of the paper the option (not) to operate, as well as the options to expand/contract the scale of operations.

13. As pointed out earlier, shared options can be differentiated further depending on whether the impact of competition is taken as exogenous or causes endogenous strategic counteractions.

14. There are, of course, other forms of interproject dependence such as "mutually exclusive" projects where undertaking of one project precludes undertaking the other, or "synergistic" projects that enhance each other's cash flows when taken together; we will choose to ignore these interactions in this paper and concentrate instead on compoundness.

15. The basic form of this classification is similar to that first proposed by Kester [12].

16. It may also be justified to defer projects with positive NPV if the benefits of deferral would exceed associated costs (as can be more clearly seen in the shared–simple–deferrable situation described earlier).

17. This, of course, holds under the assumed Weiner diffusion dynamics for an asset earning an equilibrium expected rate of return. Other authors using different dynamic structures have similarly found, for example, that a monopolist firm would delay exercising its option to innovate or explore relative to a competitive situation (see, for example, Dasgupta and Stiglitz [5] and Pindyck [22]). If competition is present or if the project earns an expected return below the market equilibrium, then the "dividend effect" may turn premature exercise into an optimal action.

18. The idea that competition will induce premature exercise is also supported in the economic literature. For example, Dasgupta and Stiglitz [5] show that competitive threat may induce a firm to innovate earlier, and Reinganum [24] finds that competitors may stimulate innovation through their provocation of incumbent firms.

19. See Trigeorgis [31] for a quantitative treatment of the impact of competitive entry seen as analogous to dividends.

References

1. Black, F., and M. Scholes, "The Pricing of Options and Corporate Liabilities." *Journal of Political Economy* 3 (1973), 637–659.

2. Brealey, R., and S. Myers, *Principles of Corporate Finance*, 6th ed. New York: McGraw-Hill, 2000.

3. Brennan, M., and E. Schwartz, "A New Approach to Evaluating Natural Resource Investments," *Midland Corporate Finance Journal* (Spring 1985).

4. Cox, J., and M. Rubinstein, *Options Markets*. Englewood Cliffs, N.J.: Prentice-Hall, 1985.

5. Dasgupta, P., and J. Stiglitz, "Uncertainty, Industrial Structure and the Speed of R/D," *Bell Journal of Economics* 11 (Autumn 1980), 1–28.

6. Gehr, A., Jr, "Risk Adjusted Capital Budgeting Using Arbitrage," *Financial Management* (Winter 1981), 14–19.

7. Geske, R., "The Valuation of Compound Options," *Journal of Financial Economics* 7 (1979), 63–82.

8. Hertz, D., "Risk Analysis in Capital Investment," *Harvard Business Review* 42 (January–February 1964), 95–106.

9. Kensinger, J. W., "Adding the Value of Active Management into the Capital Budgeting Equation," *Midland Corporate Finance Journal* (Spring 1987), 31–42.

10. Kester, W. C., "Evaluating Growth Options: A New Approach to Strategic Capital Budgeting," Working Paper 83-38, Harvard Business School (November 1982).

11. Kester, W. C., "Turning Growth Options into Real Assets," Harvard Business School (January 1984).

12. Kester, W. C., "Today's Options for Tomorrow's Growth," *Harvard Business Review* (March/April 1986).

13. Magee, J., "How to Use Decision Trees in Capital Investment," *Harvard Business Review* (September–October 1964).

14. Majd, S., and R. Pindyck, "Time to Build, Option Value, and Investment Decisions," *Journal of Financial Economics* (March 1987), 7–27.

15. Margrabe, W., "The Value of an Option to Exchange One Asset for Another," *Journal of Finance* 33, 1 (March 1978), 177–186.

16. Mason, S. P., and C. Y. Baldwin, "Evaluation of Government Subsidies to Large-Scale Energy Projects: A Contingent Claims Approach," *Advances in Futures and Options Research*, 3: 169–181.

17. Mason, S. P., and R. C. Merton, "The Role of Contingent Claims Analysis in Corporate Finance," in *Recent Advances in Corporate Finance* (E. Altman and M. Subrahmanyam, eds.). Irwin, 1985.

18. McDonald, R., and D. Siegel, "Investment and the Valuation of Firms When There Is an Option to Shut Down," *International Economic Review* (1985).

19. McDonald, R., and D. Siegel, "The Value of Waiting to Invest," *Quarterly Journal of Economics* (November 1986), 707–727.

20. Myers, S., "Finance Theory and Financial Strategy," *Interfaces* 14, 1 (January–February 1984), 126–137; reprinted in *Midland Corporate Finance Journal* (Spring 1987), 6–13.

21. Myers, S., and S. Majd, "Calculating Abandonment Value Using Option Pricing Theory," Working Paper No. 1462-83, Sloan School of Management, MIT, Cambridge, MA (revised January 1984).

22. Pindyck, R., "Uncertainty and Exhaustible Resource Markets," *Journal of Political Economy* 86 (December 1980), 1203–1225.

23. Rao, R., and J. Martin, "Another Look at the Use of Option Pricing Theory to Evaluate Real Asset Investment Opportunities," *Journal of Business Finance and Accounting* 8, 3 (Autumn 1981), 421–430.

24. Reinganum, J., "Uncertain Innovation and the Persistence of Monopoly," *American Economic Review* 73, 4 (September 1983), 741–748.

25. Robichek, A., and J. Van Horn, "Abandonment Value and Capital Budgeting," *Journal of Finance* (December 1967), 577–590.

26. Schwab, B., and P. Lusztig, "A Note on Investment Evaluations in Light of Uncertain Future Opportunities," *Journal of Finance* 27, 5 (December 1972), 1093–1100.

27. Siegel, D., J. Smith, and J. Paddock, "Valuing Offshore Oil Properties with Option Pricing Models," *Midland Corporate Finance Journal* (Spring 1987), 22–30.

28. Smith, C., "Option Pricing: A Review," *Journal of Financial Economics* 3 (January/March 1976), 3–51.

29. Stultz, R., "Options on the Minimum or Maximum of Two Risky Assets: Analysis and Applications," *Journal of Financial Economics* 10, 2 (January 1982), 161–185.

30. Tourinho, O., "The Option Value of Reserves of Natural Resources," Working Paper, University of California, Berkeley (1979).

31. Trigeorgis, L., "The Impact of Competitive Interaction on the Value of Real Investment Opportunities," Harvard Business School (December 1984).

32. Trigeorgis, L., "Projects with Multiple Real Options: A Numerical Investigation," Harvard Business School (December 1985).

33. Trigeorgis, L., and S. P. Mason, "Valuing Managerial Flexibility," *Midland Corporate Finance Journal* (Spring 1987), 14–21.

II REVIEW OF SOME BASIC MODELS

7 Real Options: An Overview

Lenos Trigeorgis

Many academics and practicing managers now recognize that the net present value (NPV) rule and other discounted cash flow (DCF) approaches to capital budgeting are inadequate in that they cannot properly capture management's flexibility to adapt and revise later decisions in response to unexpected market developments. Traditional NPV makes implicit assumptions concerning an "expected scenario" of cash flows and presumes management's passive commitment to a certain "operating strategy" (e.g., to initiate the project immediately, and operate it continuously at base scale until the end of its prespecified expected useful life).

In the actual marketplace, characterized by change, uncertainty and competitive interactions, however, the realization of cash flows will probably differ from what management expected initially. As new information arrives and uncertainty about market conditions and future cash flows is gradually resolved, management may have valuable flexibility to alter its operating strategy in order to capitalize on favorable future opportunities or mitigate losses. For example, management may be able to defer, expand, contract, abandon, or otherwise alter a project at different stages during its useful operating life.

Management's flexibility to adapt its future actions in response to altered future market conditions expands an investment opportunity's value by improving its upside potential while limiting downside losses relative to management's initial expectations under passive management. The resulting asymmetry caused by managerial adaptability calls for an "expanded NPV" rule reflecting both value components: the traditional (static or passive) NPV of direct cash flows, and the option value of operating and strategic adaptability. This does not mean that traditional NPV should be scrapped, but rather should be seen as a crucial and necessary input to an options-based, expanded NPV analysis, i.e.,

Expanded (strategic) NPV = static (passive) NPV of expected cash flows

$$+ \text{ value of options from active management.} \qquad (1)$$

An options approach to capital budgeting has the potential to conceptualize and even quantify the value of options from active management. This value is manifest as a collection of real (call or put) options embedded in capital investment opportunities, having as an underlying asset the gross project value of expected operating cash flows. Many of these real options occur naturally (e.g., to defer, contract, shut down or abandon), while others may be planned and built-in at some extra cost (e.g., to expand capacity or build growth options, to default when investment is staged

Table 7.1
Common Real Options

Category	Description	Important In	Analyzed By
Option to defer	Management holds a lease on (or an option to buy) valuable land or resources. It can wait (x years) to see if output prices justify constructing a building or plant, or developing a field.	All natural resource extraction industries; real estate development; farming; paper products.	Tourinho [98]; Titman [97]; McDonald & Siegel [76]; Paddock, Siegel & Smith [83]; Ingersoll & Ross [44].
Time to build option (staged investment)	Staging investment as a series of outlays creates the option to abandon the enterprise in midstream if new information is unfavorable. Each stage can be viewed as an option on the value of subsequent stages, and valued as a compound option.	All R&D intensive industries, especially pharmaceuticals; long-development capital-intensive projects, e.g., large-scale construction or energy-generating plants; start-up ventures.	Majd & Pindyck [68]; Carr [22]; Trigeorgis [106].
Option to alter operating scale (e.g., to expand; to contract; to shut down and restart)	If market conditions are more favorable than expected, the firm can expand the scale of production or accelerate resource utilization. Conversely, if conditions are less favorable than expected, it can reduce the scale of operations. In extreme cases, production may temporarily halt and start up again.	Natural resource industries such as mine operations; facilities planning and construction in cyclical industries; fashion apparel; consumer goods; commercial real estate.	Brennan & Schwartz [19]; McDonald & Siegel [75]; Trigeorgis & Mason [110]; Pindyck [84].
Option to abandon	If market conditions decline severely, management can abandon current operations permanently and realize the resale value of capital equipment and other assets in secondhand markets.	Capital intensive industries, such as airlines and railroads; financial services; new product introductions in uncertain markets.	Myers & Majd [82].

Option to switch (e.g., outputs or inputs)	If prices or demand change, management can change the output mix of the facility ("product" flexibility). Alternatively, the same outputs can be produced using different types of inputs ("process" flexibility).	*Output shifts:* any good sought in small batches or subject to volatile demand, e.g., consumer electronics; toys; specialty paper; machine parts; autos. *Input shifts:* all feedstock-dependent facilities, e.g., oil; electric power; chemicals; crop switching; sourcing.	Margrabe [69]; Kensinger [50]; Kulatilaka [55]; Kulatilaka & Trigeorgis [63].
Growth options	An early investment (e.g., R&D, lease on undeveloped land or oil reserves, strategic acquisition, information network/infrastructure) is a prerequisite or link in a chain of interrelated projects, opening up future growth opportunities (e.g., new generation product or process, oil reserves, access to new market, strengthening of core capabilities). Like interproject compound options.	All infrastructure-based or strategic industries, especially high-tech, R&D, or industries with multiple product generations or applications (e.g., computers, pharmaceuticals); multi-national operations; strategic acquisitions.	Myers [80]; Brealey & Myers [16]; Kester [51], [52]; Trigeorgis [100]; Pindyck [84]; Chung & Charoenwong [23].
Multiple interacting options	Real-life projects often involve a "collection" of various options, both upward-potential enhancing calls and downward-protection put options present in combination. Their combined option value may differ from the sum of separate option values, i.e., they interact. They may also interact with financial flexibility options.	Real-life projects in most industries discussed above.	Brennan & Schwartz [19]; Trigeorgis [106]; Kulatilaka [58].

sequentially, or to switch between alternative inputs or outputs). Table 7.1 describes briefly the most common categories of encountered real options, the types of industries they are important in, and lists representative authors that have analyzed them.[1] A more comprehensive review of the real options literature is given in the first section.

This chapter provides a comprehensive overview of the existing real options literature and applications, and presents practical principles for quantifying the value of various real options. The comprehensive literature review traces the evolution of the real options revolution, organized around thematic developments covering the early criticisms, conceptual approaches, foundations and building blocks, risk-neutral valuation and risk adjustment, analytic contributions in valuing different options separately, option interactions, numerical techniques, competition and strategic options, various applications, and future research directions. An example is then used to conceptually discuss the basic nature of the various real options that may be embedded in capital investments. Initially assuming all-equity financing, the paper presents principles useful for valuing both upside-potential operating options, such as to defer an investment or expand production, as well as various downside-protection options, such as to abandon for salvage value or switch use (inputs/outputs), and abandon project construction by defaulting on planned, staged future outlays.

The [original] paper extends the analysis in the presence of financial leverage within a venture capital context and examines the improvement in equityholders' value as a result of additional financial flexibility, noting potential interactions with operating flexibility. The beneficial impact of staging venture capital financing in installments (thereby creating an option to abandon by the lender, as well as an option to revalue later at potentially better terms by each party), and other issues related to the mix of debt and equity venture capital financing are also explored.

The chapter is organized as follows. Following the comprehensive literature review in Section I, Section II uses an example to motivate discussion of various real options and presents practical principles for valuing several such options. The last section concludes and discusses some extensions.

I   A Review of the Real Options Literature

Corporate value creation and competitive position in different markets are critically determined by corporate resource allocation and the evaluation of investment opportunities. The field of capital budgeting remained stagnant for several decades, until recent developments in real options provided the tools and unlocked the possibilities to revolutionize the field. In what follows, I will attempt to describe briefly some stages in the development and evolution of the real options literature, while organizing the presentation around several broad themes. This is not an easy task, and I apologize to those authors and readers who may find my treatment here rather subjective and non-exhaustive.

A Symptoms, Diagnosis, and Traditional Medicine: Early Critics, the Underinvestment Problem, and Alternative Valuation Paradigms

The real options revolution arose in part as a response to the dissatisfaction of corporate practitioners, strategists, and some academics with traditional capital budgeting techniques. Well before the development of real options, corporate managers and strategists were grappling intuitively with the elusive elements of managerial operating flexibility and strategic interactions. Early critics (e.g., Dean [28], Hayes and Abernathy [34], and Hayes and Garvin [35]) recognized that standard discounted cash flow (DCF) criteria often undervalued investment opportunities, leading to myopic decisions, underinvestment and eventual loss of competitive position, because they either ignored or did not properly value important strategic considerations. Decision scientists further maintained that the problem lay in the application of the wrong valuation techniques altogether, proposing instead the use of simulation and decision tree analysis (see Hertz [37] and Magee [65]) to capture the value of future operating flexibility associated with many projects. Proponents (e.g., Hodder and Riggs [40] and Hodder [39]) have argued that the problem arises from misuse of DCF techniques as commonly applied in practice. Myers [78], while confirming that part of the problem results from various misapplications of the underlying theory, acknowledges that traditional DCF methods have inherent limitations when it comes to valuing investments with significant operating or strategic options (e.g., in capturing the sequential interdependence among investments over time), suggesting that option pricing holds the best promise of valuing such investments. Later, Trigeorgis and Mason [108] explain that option valuation can be seen operationally as a special, economically corrected version of decision tree analysis that is better suited in valuing a variety of corporate operating and strategic options, while Teisberg [93] provides a practical comparative discussion of the DCF, decision analysis, and real option valuation paradigms. Baldwin and Clark [5] discuss the importance of organizational capabilities in strategic capital investment, while Baldwin and Trigeorgis [8] propose remedying the underinvestment problem and restoring competitiveness by developing specific adaptive capabilities viewed as an infrastructure for acquiring and managing real options.

B A New Direction: Conceptual Real Options Approaches

Building on Myers' [77] initial idea of thinking of discretionary investment opportunities as "growth options," Kester [50] conceptually discusses strategic and competitive aspects of growth opportunities. Other general, conceptual real options
frameworks are presented in Mason and Merton [69], Trigeorgis and Mason [108],
Trigeorgis [98], Brealey and Myers [16], and Kulatilaka and Marcus [58], [59].
Mason and Merton [69], for example, provide a good discussion of many operating
as well as financing options, and integrate them in a project financing for a hypothetical, large-scale energy project.

C Generic Medicine: Foundations and Building Blocks

The quantitative origins of real options, of course, derive from the seminal work of
Black and Scholes [13] and Merton [75] in pricing financial options. Cox, Ross, and
Rubinstein's [26] binomial approach enabled a more simplified valuation of options
in discrete time. Margrabe [67] values an option to exchange one risky asset for
another, while Stulz [92] analyzes options on the maximum (or minimum) of two
risky assets and Johnson [44] extends it to several risky assets. These papers have the
potential to help analyze the generic option to switch among alternative uses and
related options (e.g., abandon for salvage value or switch among alternative inputs or
outputs). Geske [30] values a compound option (i.e., an option to acquire another
option), which, in principle, may be applied in valuing growth opportunities which
become available only if earlier investments are undertaken. Carr [21] combines the
above two building blocks to value sequential (compound) exchange options, involving an option to acquire a subsequent option to exchange the underlying asset for
another risky alternative. Kulatilaka [54] and [56] describes an equivalent dynamic
programming formulation for the option to switch among operating modes. The
above line of work has the potential, in principle, to value investments with a series of
investment outlays that can be switched to alternative states of operation, and particularly to eventually help value strategic interproject dependencies.

D Slightly Different Medicine: Risk-Neutral Valuation and Risk Adjustment

The actual valuation of options in practice has been greatly facilitated by Cox
and Ross's [25] recognition that an option can be replicated (or a "synthetic option"
created) from an equivalent portfolio of traded securities. Being independent of risk
attitudes or capital market equilibrium considerations, such risk-neutral valuation
enables present-value discounting, at the risk-free interest rate, of expected future
payoffs (with actual probabilities replaced with risk-neutral ones), a fundamental

characteristic of "arbitrage-free" price systems involving traded securities. Rubinstein [86] further showed that standard option pricing formulas can be alternatively derived under risk aversion, and that the existence of continuous trading opportunities enabling a riskless hedge or risk neutrality are not really necessary. Mason and Merton [69] and Kasanen and Trigeorgis [47] maintain that real options may, in principle, be valued similar to financial options, even though they may not be traded, since in capital budgeting we are interested in determining what the project cash flows would be worth if they were traded in the market, i.e., their contribution to the *market* value of a publicly traded firm. The existence of a traded "twin security" (or dynamic portfolio) that has the same risk characteristics (i.e., is closely correlated) with the nontraded real asset in complete markets is sufficient for real option valuation. More generally, Constantinides [23], Cox, Ingersoll, and Ross [27, lemma 4], and Harrison and Kreps [33], among others, have suggested that any contingent claim on an asset, traded or not, can be priced in a world with systematic risk by replacing its actual growth rate with a certainty-equivalent rate (by subtracting a risk premium that would be appropriate in market equilibrium), and then behaving as if the world were risk-neutral. This is analogous to discounting certainty-equivalent cash flows at the risk-free rate, rather than actual expected cash flows at a risk-adjusted rate. For traded assets in equilibrium or for those real assets with no systematic risk (e.g., R&D, exploration or drilling for certain precious metals or natural resources), the certainty-equivalent or risk-neutral rate just equals the risk-free interest rate (minus any dividends). However, if the underlying asset is not traded, as may often be the case in capital budgeting associated options, its growth rate may actually fall below the equilibrium total expected return required of an equivalent-risk traded financial security, with the difference or "rate of return short-fall" necessitating a dividend-like adjustment in option valuation (e.g., see McDonald and Siegel [71] and [72]). If the underlying asset is traded in futures markets, though, this dividend- (or convenience-yield-) like return shortfall or rate of foregone earnings can be easily derived from the futures prices of contracts with different maturities (see Brennan and Schwartz [19]). In other cases, however, estimating this return shortfall may require use of a market equilibrium model (e.g., see McDonald and Siegel [72]).

E   A Tablet for Each Case: Valuing Each Different Real Option Separately

There came a series of papers which gave a boost to the real options literature by focusing on valuing quantitatively—in many cases, deriving analytic, closed-form solutions—one type after another of a variety of real options, although each option was typically analyzed in isolation. As summarized in table 7.1, the option to defer or initiate investment has been examined by McDonald and Siegel [73], by Paddock,

Siegel, and Smith [80] in valuing offshore petroleum leases, and by Tourinho [96] in valuing reserves of natural resources. Ingersoll and Ross [43] reconsider the decision to wait in light of the beneficial impact of a potential future interest rate decline on project value. Majd and Pindyck [66] value the option to delay sequential construction for projects that take time to build, or there is a maximum rate at which investment can proceed. Carr [21] and Trigeorgis [104] also deal with valuing sequential or staged (compound) investments. Trigeorgis and Mason [108] and Pindyck [81] examine options to alter (i.e., expand or contract) operating scale or capacity choice. The option to temporarily shut down and restart operations was analyzed by McDonald and Siegel [72] and by Brennan and Schwartz [19]. Myers and Majd [79] analyze the option to permanently abandon a project for its salvage value seen as an American put option. Options to switch use (i.e., outputs or inputs) have been examined, among others, by Margrabe [67], Kensinger [49], Kulatilaka [54], and Kulatilaka and Trigeorgis [62]. Baldwin and Ruback [7] show that future price uncertainty creates a valuable switching option that benefits short-lived projects. Future investment opportunities that are seen as corporate growth options are discussed in Myers [77], Brealey and Myers [16], Kester [50] and [51]. Trigeorgis and Mason [108], Trigeorgis [98], Pindyck [81], and Chung and Charoenwong [22].

F   The Tablets Interact: Multiple Options and Interdependencies

Despite its enormous theoretical contribution, the focus of the earlier literature on valuing individual real options (i.e., one type of option at a time) has nevertheless limited its practical value. Real-life projects are often more complex in that they involve a collection of multiple real options whose values may interact. An early exception is Brennan and Schwartz [19], who determine the combined value of the options to shut down (and restart) a mine, and to abandon it for salvage. They recognize that partial irreversibility resulting from the costs of switching the mine's operating state may create a persistence, inertia or *hysteresis* effect, making it long-term optimal to remain in the same operating state even though short-term considerations (i.e., current cash flows) may seem to favor immediate switching. Although hysteresis can be seen as a form of interaction between early and later decisions, Brennan and Schwartz do not explicitly address the interactions among individual option values. Trigeorgis [104] focuses on the nature of real option interactions, pointing out, for example, that the presence of subsequent options can increase the value of the effective underlying asset for earlier options, while exercise of prior real options may alter (e.g., expand or contract) the underlying asset itself, and hence the value of subsequent options on it. Thus, the combined value of a collection of real options may differ from the sum of separate option values. Using a numerical analysis method suitable for valuing complex multi-option investments (Trigeorgis [102]), he presents the valuation of options to defer, abandon, contract or expand investment, and switch use in the context of a generic investment, first with each option in isolation and later in combination. He shows, for example, that the incremental value of an additional option, in the presence of other options, is generally less than its value in isolation and declines as more options are present. More generally, he identifies situations where option interactions can be small or large and negative as well as positive. Kulatilaka [57] subsequently examines the impact of interactions among three such options on their optimal exercise schedules. The recent recognition of real option interdependencies should subsequently enable a smoother transition from a theoretical stage to an application phase.

G   The Bitter Pill: Numerical Techniques

In the more complex real-life option situations, such as those involving multiple interacting real options, analytic solutions may not exist and one may not even be always able to write down the set of partial differential equations describing the underlying stochastic processes. The ability to value such complex option situations has been enhanced, however, with various numerical analysis techniques, many of which take advantage of risk-neutral valuation. Generally, there are two types of numerical techniques for option valuation: (i) those that approximate the underlying stochastic processes directly and are generally more intuitive; and (ii) those approximating the resulting partial differential equations. The first category includes Monte Carlo simulation used by Boyle [14], and various lattice approaches such as Cox, Ross, and Rubinstein's [26] standard binomial lattice method, and Trigeorgis' [102] log-transformed binomial method; the latter are particularly well-suited to valuing complex projects with multiple embedded real options, a series of investment outlays, dividend-like effects, as well as option interactions. Boyle [15] shows how lattice frameworks can be extended to handle two state variables, while Hull and White [42] suggest a control variate technique to improve computational efficiency when a similar derivative asset with an analytic solution is available. Examples of the second category include numerical integration, and implicit or explicit finite difference schemes used by Brennan [17], Brennan and Schwartz [18], and Majd and Pindyck [66]. Finally, a number of analytic approximations are also available: Geske and Johnson [31] have proposed a compound-option analytic polynomial approximation approach; Barone-Adesi and Whaley [9] have suggested a quadratic approximation, while others have used various problem-specific heuristic approximations. A comprehensive review of such numerical techniques is given in the articles by Geske and Shastri [32] and Trigeorgis [102], as well as in a book by Hull [41].

H   The General Environment: Competition and Strategic Options

An important area that deserves more attention, and where real options have the potential to make a significant difference, is that of competition and strategy. Sustainable competitive advantages resulting from patents, proprietary technologies, ownership of valuable natural resources, managerial capital, reputation or brand name, scale, and market power, empower companies with valuable options to grow through future profitable investments and to more effectively respond to unexpected adversity or opportunities in a changing technological, competitive, or general business environment. A number of economists have addressed several competitive and strategic aspects of capital investment early on. For example, Roberts and Weitzman [85] find that in sequential decision-making, it may be worthwhile to undertake investments with negative NPV when early investment can provide information about future project benefits, especially when their uncertainty is greater. Baldwin [3] finds that optimal sequential investment for firms with market power facing irreversible decisions may require a positive premium over NPV to compensate for the loss in value of future opportunities that results from undertaking an investment. Pindyck [81] analyzes options to choose capacity under product price uncertainty when investment is, again, irreversible. Dixit [29] considers firm entry and exit decisions under uncertainty, showing that in the presence of sunk or switching costs it may not be long-term optimal to reverse a decision even when prices appear attractive in the short-term. Bell [10] combines Dixit's entry and exit decisions with Pindyck's capacity options for the multinational firm under volatile exchange rates. Kogut and Kulatilaka [52] analyze the international plant location option in the presence of mean-reverting exchange rate volatility, while Kulatilaka and Marks [60] examine the strategic bargaining value of flexibility in the firm's negotiations with input suppliers.

From a more explicit real options perspective, a number of authors (e.g., Myers [78], Kester [50] and [51], Trigeorgis and Mason [108], Trigeorgis [98], Brealey and Myers [16], and Trigeorgis and Kasanen [107]) have initially dealt with competitive and strategic options rather conceptually. For example, Kester [50] develops qualitatively various competitive and strategic aspects of interproject growth options, while Kester [51] proposes a planned sequential, rather than parallel, implementation of a collection of interrelated consumer products when learning results from early product introductions (e.g., about available shelf space needed for similar subsequent products) and when competitive advantage is eroding. Trigeorgis and Kasanen [107] also examine sequential project interdependencies and synergies as part of an ongoing strategic planning and control process. In this issue of *Financial Management*, Kasanen [46] also deals with the strategic problem of the interaction between current investments and future opportunities, using the rather novel concept of a spawning matrix structure (capturing the firm's ability to generate investment opportunities *across* projects through feedback effects) to determine an optimal mix of strategic and operating projects.

Trigeorgis [101] uses quantitative option pricing techniques to examine early investment that may preempt anticipated competitive entry, and to value the option to defer investment when impacted by random competitive entry (Trigeorgis [100]). Ang and Dukas [2] incorporate both competitive and asymmetric information, arguing that the time pattern of discounted cash flows also matters due to the possibility of premature project termination as a result of random competitive entry. Further departing from the common assumption of perfect competition, Kulatilaka and Perotti [61] examine how the investment decisions of a firm will influence the production decisions of competitors and the market price when early investment generates a cost advantage. In this issue, Smit and Ankum [89] combine the real options approach to investment timing with basic principles from game theory and industrial organization to explore various investment timing strategies in follow-up projects based on the reaction of competitors under different market structures. Supplementing options analysis with game theoretic tools capable of incorporating strategic competitive counteractions promises to be an important and challenging direction for future research.

I   Cure for All Kinds of Cases: A Variety of Applications

Besides theoretical developments, real option applications are currently also receiving increased attention. Real options valuation has been applied in a variety of contexts, such as in natural resource investments, land development, leasing, flexible manufacturing, government subsidies and regulation, R&D, new ventures and acquisitions, foreign investment and strategy, and elsewhere.

Early applications naturally arose in the area of *natural resource investments* due to the availability of traded resource or commodity prices, high volatilities and long durations, resulting in higher and better option value estimates. Brennan and Schwartz [19] first utilize the convenience yield derived from futures and spot prices of a commodity to value the options to shut down or abandon a mine. Paddock, Siegel, and Smith [80] value options embedded in undeveloped oil reserves and provide the first empirical evidence that option values are better than actual DCF-based bids in valuing offshore oil leases. Trigeorgis [99] values an actual minerals project considered by a major multinational company involving options to cancel during construction, expand production, and abandon for salvage. Bjerksund and Ekern [11] value a Norwegian oil field with options to defer and abandon. Mørck, Schwartz, and Stangeland [76] value forestry resources under stochastic inventories and prices. Stensland and Tjostheim [91] also discuss some applications of dynamic programming to natural resource exploration. In this volume, Laughton and Jacoby [63] examine biases in the valuation of real options and long-term decision-making when a mean-reversion price process is more appropriate, as may be the case in certain commodity projects, than the traditional Brownian motion or random walk assumption. They find that ignoring reversion would overestimate long-term uncertainty, but may over- or undervalue associated timing options. On the more applied side, Kemna [48] shares her experiences with Shell in analyzing actual cases involving the timing of developing an offshore oil field, valuing a growth option in a manufacturing venture, and the abandonment decision of a refining production unit, and discusses problem formulation and implementation issues in the process of adapting option theory in practice.

In the area of *land development*, Titman [95], Williams [109], Capozza and Sick [20], and Quigg [84] show that the value of vacant land should reflect not only its value based on its best immediate use (e.g., from constructing a building now), but also its option value if development is delayed and the land is converted into its best alternative use in the future. It may thus pay to hold land vacant for its option value even in the presence of currently thriving real estate markets. Quigg [83] reports empirical results indicating that option-based land valuation that incorporates the option to wait to develop land provides better approximations of actual market prices. In a different context, McLaughlin and Taggart [74] view the opportunity cost of using excess capacity as the change in the value of the firm's options caused by diverting capacity to an alternative use. In *leasing*, Copeland and Weston [24], Lee, Martin, and Senchack [64], McConnell and Schallheim [70], and Trigeorgis [103] value various operating options embedded in leasing contracts.

In the area of *flexible manufacturing*, the flexibility provided by flexible manufacturing systems, flexible production technology or other machinery having multiple uses has been analyzed from an options perspective by Kulatilaka [54], Triantis and Hodder [97], Aggarwal [1], Kulatilaka and Trigeorgis [62], and Kamrad and Ernst [45], among others. In this issue, Kulatilaka [55] values the flexibility provided by an actual dual-fuel industrial steam boiler that can switch between alternative energy inputs (natural gas and oil) as their relative prices fluctuate, and finds that the value of this flexibility far exceeds the incremental cost over a rigid, single-fuel alternative. Baldwin and Clark [6] study the flexibility created by modularity in design that connects components of a larger system through standard interfaces.

In the area of *government subsidies and regulation*, Mason and Baldwin [68] value government subsidies to large-scale energy projects as put options, while Teisberg

[94] provides an option valuation analysis of investment choices by a regulated firm. In *research and development*, Kolbe, Morris, and Teisberg [53] discuss option elements embedded in R&D projects. Option elements involved in the staging of *start-up ventures* are discussed in Sahlman [87], Willner [110], and this article. Strategic *acquisitions* of other companies also often involve a number of growth, divestiture, and other flexibility options, as discussed by Smith and Triantis [100]. Other applications of options in the strategy area were discussed in Section I.H. earlier. On the empirical side, Kester [50] estimates that the value of a firm's growth options is more than half the market value of equity for many firms, even 70–80% for more volatile industries. Similarly, Pindyck [81] also suggests that growth options represent more than half of firm value if demand volatility exceeds 20%. In *foreign investment*, Baldwin [4] discusses various location, timing and staging options present when firms scan the global marketplace. Bell [10] and Kogut and Kulatilaka [52], among others, examine entry, capacity, and switching options for firms with multinational operations under exchange rate volatility. Hiraki [38] suggests that the Japanese bank-oriented corporate governance system serves as the basic infrastructure that enables companies to jointly develop corporate real options.

Various other option applications can be found in areas ranging from *shipping* (Bjerksund and Ekern [12]) to *environmental pollution and global warming* (e.g., Hendricks [36]). The potential for future applications itself seems like a growth option.

J Other Sources and Future Research Directions

Other comprehensive treatments of real options can be found in the articles by Mason and Merton [69] and Trigeorgis and Mason [108], a monograph by Sick [88], an economics review article by Pindyck [82], as well as in a volume edited by Trigeorgis [105] and a book by MIT Press [Trigeorgis [106]). The Spring 1987 Issue of the *Midland Corporate Finance Journal* and a 1991 Special Issue of *Managerial Finance* (Vol. 17, No. 2/3) have also been devoted to real options and capital budgeting. In the present issue of *Financial Management* (Autumn 1993), the articles by Laughton and Jacoby [63], Smit and Ankum [89], and Kasanen [46] are indicative of an active literature that is evolving in several new directions in modelling, competition and strategy, while the articles by Kemna [48] and Kulatilaka [55] represent recent attempts to implement real options valuation in actual case applications. Clearly, an increased attention to application and implementation issues is the next stage in the evolution of real options.

In addition to more actual case applications and tackling real-life implementation issues and problems, fruitful directions for future research, in both theory and practice, include:

(i) Focusing more on investments (such as in R&D, pilot or market tests, or excavations) that can "generate" information and learning (e.g., about the project's prospects) by extending/adjusting option pricing and risk-neutral valuation with Bayesian analysis or alternative (e.g., jump) processes.

(ii) Exploring in more depth endogenous competitive counteractions and a variety of competitive/market structure and strategic issues using a combination of game-theoretic industrial organization with option valuation tools.

(iii) Modelling better the various strategic and growth options.

(iv) Extending real options in an agency context recognizing that the potential (theoretical) value of real options may not be realized in practice if managers, in pursuing their own agenda (e.g., expansion or growth, rather than firm value maximization), misuse their discretion and do not follow the optimal exercise policies implicit in option valuation. This raises the need to design proper corrective incentive contracts by the firm (taking also into account asymmetric information).

(v) Recognizing better that real options may interact not only among themselves but with financial flexibility options as well, and understanding the resulting implications for the combined, interdependent corporate investment and financing decisions. [In Section III of the original article, we take a first step toward recognizing such interactions among real and financial flexibility options.]

(vi) On the practical side, applying real options to the valuation of flexibility in related areas, such as in competitive bidding, information technology or other platform investments, energy and R&D problems, international finance options, and so on.

(vii) Using real options to explain empirical phenomena that are amenable to observation or statistical testing, such as examining empirically whether managements of firms that are targets for acquisition may sometimes turn down tender offers in part due to the option to wait in anticipation of receiving better future offers.

(viii) Conducting more field, survey, or empirical studies to test the conformity of theoretical real option valuation and its implications with management's intuition and experience, as well as with actual price data when available.

II Real Options: An Example and Valuation Principles

This section discusses conceptually the basic nature of different real options through a comprehensive example, and then illustrates some practical principles for valuing such options. To facilitate our discussion of the various real options that may be embedded in capital investments, consider first the following example.

A   Example: An Oil Extraction and Refinery Project

A large oil company has a one-year lease to start drilling on undeveloped land with potential oil reserves. Initiating the project may require certain exploration costs, to be followed by construction of roads and other infrastructure outlays, I_1. This would be followed by outlays for the construction of a new processing facility, I_2. Extraction can begin only after construction is completed, i.e., cash flows are generated only during the "operating stage" that follows the last outlay. During construction, if market conditions deteriorate, management can choose to forego any future planned outlays. Management may also choose to reduce the scale of operation by $c\%$, saving a portion of the last outlay, I_C, if the market is weak. The processing plant can be designed upfront such that, if oil prices turn out higher than expected, the rate of production can be enhanced by $x\%$ with a follow-up outlay of I_E. At any time, management may salvage a portion of its investment by selling the plant and equipment for their salvage value or switch them to an alternative use value, A. An associated refinery plant—which may be designed to operate with alternative sources of energy inputs—can convert crude oil into a variety of refined products. This type of project presents the following collection of real options:

(i) *The option to defer investment.*   The lease enables management to defer investment for up to one year and benefit from the resolution of uncertainty about oil prices during this period. Management would invest I_1 (i.e., exercise its option to extract oil) *only if* oil prices increase sufficiently, but would not commit to the project, saving the planned outlays, if prices decline. Just before expiration of the lease, the value creation will be $\max(V - I_1, 0)$. The option to defer is thus analogous to an American call option on the gross present value of the completed project's expected operating cash flows, V, with the exercise price being equal to the required outlay, I_1. Since early investment implies sacrificing the option to wait, this option value loss is like an additional investment opportunity cost, justifying investment only if the value of cash benefits, V, actually exceeds the initial outlay by a substantial premium. As noted in Exhibit 1, the option to wait is particularly valuable in resource extraction industries, farming, paper products, and real estate development due to high uncertainties and long investment horizons.

(ii) *The option to default during construction (or the time-to-build option).*   In most real-life projects, the required investment is not incurred as a single upfront outlay. The actual staging of capital investment as a series of outlays over time creates valuable options to "default" at any given stage (e.g., after exploration if the reserves or oil prices turn out very low). Thus, each stage (e.g., building necessary infrastructure) can be viewed as an option on the value of subsequent stages by incurring the installment cost outlay (e.g., I_1) required to proceed to the next stage, and can therefore be valued similar to compound options. This option is valuable in all R&D intensive industries, especially pharmaceuticals, in highly uncertain, long-development capital intensive industries, such as energy-generating plants or large-scale construction, and in venture capital.

(iii) *The option to expand.*   If oil prices or other market conditions turn out more favorable than expected, management can actually accelerate the rate or expand the scale of production (by $x\%$) by incurring a follow-up cost outlay (I_E). This is similar to a call option to acquire an additional part ($x\%$) of the base-scale project, paying I_E as exercise price. The investment opportunity with the option to expand can be viewed as the base-scale project plus a call option on future investment, i.e., $V + \max(xV - I_E, 0)$. Given an initial design choice, management may deliberately favor a more expensive technology for the built-in flexibility to expand production if and when it becomes desirable. As discussed further below, the option to expand may also be of strategic importance, especially if it enables the firm to capitalize on future growth opportunities. As noted, when the firm buys vacant undeveloped land, or when it builds a small plant in a new geographic location (domestic or overseas) to position itself to take advantage of a developing large market, it essentially installs an expansion/growth option. This option, which will be exercised only if future market developments turn out favorable, can make a seemingly unprofitable (based on static NPV) base-case investment worth undertaking.

(iv) *The option to contract.*   If market conditions are weaker than originally expected, management can operate below capacity or even reduce the scale of operations (by $c\%$), thereby saving part of the planned investment outlays (I_C). This flexibility to mitigate loss is analogous to a put option on part ($c\%$) of the base-scale project, with exercise price equal to the potential cost savings (I_C), giving $\max(I_C - cV, 0)$. The option to contract, just as the option to expand, may be particularly valuable in the case of new product introductions in uncertain markets. The option to contract may also be important, for example, in choosing among technologies or plants with a different construction to maintenance cost mix, where it may be preferable to build a plant with lower initial construction costs and higher maintenance expenditures in order to acquire the flexibility to contract operations by cutting down on maintenance if market conditions turn out unfavorable.

(v) *The option to shut down (and restart) operations.*   In real life, the plant does not have to operate (i.e., extract oil) in each and every period automatically. In fact, if oil prices are such that cash revenues are not sufficient to cover variable operating (e.g., maintenance) costs, it might be better not to operate temporarily, especially if the costs of switching between the operating and idle modes are relatively small. If prices rise sufficiently, operations can start again. Thus, operation in each year can be seen as a call option to acquire that year's cash revenues (C) by paying the variable costs of operating (I_V) as exercise price, i.e., $\max(C - I_V, 0)$.[2] Options to alter the operating scale (i.e., expand, contract, or shut down) are typically found in natural resource industries, such as mine operations, facilities planning and construction in cyclical industries, fashion apparel, consumer goods, and commercial real estate.

(vi) *The option to abandon for salvage value.*   If oil prices suffer a sustainable decline or the operation does poorly for some other reason, management does not have to continue incurring the fixed costs. Instead, management may have a valuable option to abandon the project permanently in exchange for its salvage value (i.e., the resale value of its capital equipment and other assets in secondhand markets). As noted, this option can be valued as an American put option on current project value (V) with exercise price the salvage or best alternative use value (A), entitling management to receive $V + \max(A - V, 0)$ or $\max(V, A)$. Naturally, more general-purpose capital assets would have a higher salvage and option abandonment value than special-purpose assets. Valuable abandonment options are generally found in capital intensive industries, such as in airlines and railroads, in financial services, as well as in new product introductions in uncertain markets.

(vii) *The option to switch use (i.e., inputs or outputs).*   Suppose the associated oil refinery operation can be designed to use alternative forms of energy inputs (e.g., fuel oil, gas, or electricity) to convert crude oil into a variety of output products (e.g., gasoline, lubricants, or polyester). This would provide valuable built-in flexibility to switch from the current input to the cheapest future input, or from the current output to the most profitable future product mix, as the relative prices of the inputs or outputs fluctuate over time. In fact, the firm should be willing to pay a certain positive premium for such a flexible technology over a rigid alternative that confers no choice or less choice. Indeed, if the firm can in this way develop extra uses for its assets over its competitors, it may be at a significant advantage. Generally, "process" flexibility can be achieved not only via technology (e.g., by building a flexible facility that can switch among alternative energy "inputs"), but also by maintaining relationships with a variety of suppliers, changing the mix as their relative prices change. Subcontracting policies may allow further flexibility to contract the scale of future operations at a low cost in case of unfavorable market developments. As noted, a multinational oil company may similarly locate production facilities in various countries in order to acquire the flexibility to shift production to the lowest-cost producing facilities, as the relative costs, other local market conditions, or exchange rates change over time.

Process flexibility is valuable in feedstock-dependent facilities, such as oil, electric power, chemicals, and crop switching. "Product" flexibility, enabling the firm to switch among alternative "outputs," is more valuable in industries such as automobiles, consumer electronics, toys or pharmaceuticals, where product differentiation and diversity are important and/or product demand is volatile. In such cases, it may be worthwhile to install a more costly flexible capacity to acquire the ability to alter product mix or production scale in response to changing market demands.

(viii) *Corporate growth options.* As noted, another version of the earlier option to expand of considerable strategic importance are corporate growth options that set the path of future opportunities. Suppose, in the above example, that the proposed refinery facility is based on a new, technologically superior "process" for oil refinement developed and tested internally on a pilot plant basis. Although the proposed facility in isolation may appear unattractive, it could be only the first in a series of similar facilities if the process is successfully developed and commercialized, and may even lead to entirely new oil by-products. More generally, many early investments (e.g., R&D, a lease on undeveloped land or a tract with potential oil reserves, a strategic acquisition, or an information technology network) can be seen as prerequisites or links in a chain of interrelated projects. The value of these projects may derive not so much from their expected directly measurable cash flows, but rather from unlocking future growth opportunities (e.g., a new-generation product or process, oil reserves, access to a new or expanding market, strengthening of the firm's core capabilities or strategic positioning). An opportunity to invest in a first-generation high-tech product, for example, is analogous to an option on options (an interproject compound option). Despite a seemingly negative NPV, the infrastructure, experience, and potential by-products generated during the development of the first-generation product may serve as springboards for developing lower-cost or improved-quality future generations of that product, or even for generating new applications into other areas. But unless the firm makes that initial investment, subsequent generations or other applications would not even be feasible. The infrastructure and experience gained can be proprietary and can place the firm at a competitive advantage, which may even reinforce itself if learning cost curve effects are present. Growth options are found in all infrastructure-based or strategic industries, especially in high-tech, R&D, or industries with multiple product generations or applications (e.g., semiconductors, computers, pharmaceuticals), in multinational operations, and in strategic acquisitions.

In a more general context, such operating and strategic adaptability represented by corporate real options can be achieved at various stages during the value chain, from switching the factor input mix among various suppliers and subcontracting practices, to rapid product design (e.g., computer-aided design) and modularity in design, to shifting production among various products rapidly and cost-efficiently in a flexible manufacturing system. The next section illustrates, through simple numerical examples, basic practical principles for valuing several of the above real options. For expositional simplicity, we will subsequently ignore any return shortfall or other dividend-like effects (see Section I.D. above for appropriate adjustments).

B   Principles of Valuing Various Real Options

Consider, as in Trigeorgis and Mason [108],[3] valuing a generic investment opportunity (e.g., similar to the above oil extraction project). Specifically, suppose we are faced with an opportunity to invest $I_0 = \$104$ (in millions) in an oil project whose (gross) value in each period will either move up by 80% or down by 40%, depending on oil price fluctuations: a year later, the project will have an expected value (from subsequent cash flows) of $180 (million) if the oil price moves up ($C^+ = 180$) or $60 if it moves down ($C^- = 60$).[4] There is an equal probability ($q = 0.5$) that the price of oil will move up or down in any year. Let S be the price of oil, or generally of a "twin security" that is traded in the financial markets and has the same risk characteristics (i.e., is perfectly correlated) with the real project under consideration (such as the stock price of a similar operating unlevered oil company). Both the project and its twin security (or oil prices) have an expected rate of return (or discount rate) of $k = 20\%$, while the risk-free interest rate is $r = 8\%$.

In what follows, we assume throughout that the value of the project (i.e., the value, in millions of dollars, in each year, t, of its subsequent expected cash flows appropriately discounted back to that year), V_t, and its twin security price (e.g., a twin oil stock price in $ per share, or simply the price of oil in $ per barrel), S_t, move through time as follows:

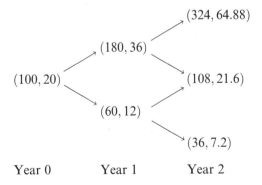

Year 0   Year 1   Year 2

For example, the pair (V_0, S_0) above represents a current gross project value of $100 million, and a spot oil price of $20 a barrel (or a $20 per share twin oil stock price). Under traditional (passive) NPV analysis, the current gross project value would be obtained first by discounting the project's end-of-period values (derived from subsequent cash flows), using the expected rate of return of the project's twin security (or, here, of oil prices) as the appropriate discount rate, i.e., $V_0 = (0.5 \times 180 + 0.5 \times 60)/1.20 = 100$. Note that this gross project value is, in this case, exactly proportional to the twin security price (or the spot oil price). After subtracting the current investment costs, $I_0 = 104$, the project's NPV is finally given by:

$$\text{NPV} = V_0 - I_0 = 100 - 104 = -4 \ (<0). \tag{2}$$

In the absence of managerial flexibility or real options, traditional DCF analysis would have rejected this project based on its negative NPV. However, passive DCF is unable to properly capture the value of embedded options because of their discretionary asymmetric nature and dependence on future events that are uncertain at the time of the initial decision. The fundamental problem, of course, lies in the valuation of investment opportunities whose claims are not symmetric or proportional and whose discount rates vary in a complex way over time.

Nevertheless, such real options can be properly valued using contingent claims analysis (CCA) within a backward risk-neutral valuation process.[5] Essentially, the same solution can be obtained in our actual risk-averse world as in a "risk-neutral" world in which the current value of any contingent claim could be obtained from its expected future values—with expectations taken over the risk-neutral probabilities, p, imputed from the twin security's (or oil) prices—discounted at the riskless rate, r. In such a risk-neutral world, the current (beginning of the period) value of the project (or of equityholders' claim), E, is given by:

$$E = \frac{pE^+ + (1 - p)E^-}{(1 + r)},$$

where

$$p = \frac{(1 + r)S - S^-}{(S^+ - S^-)}. \tag{3}$$

The probability, p, can be estimated from the price dynamics of the twin security (or of oil prices):

$$p = \frac{(1.08 \times 20) - 12}{36 - 12} = 0.4.$$

Note that the value for $p = 0.4$ is distinct from the actual probability, $q = 0.5$, and can be used to determine "certainty-equivalent" values (or expected cash flows) which can be properly discounted at the risk-free rate. For example,

$$V_0 = \frac{pC^+ + (1-p)C^-}{(1+r)} = \frac{0.4 \times 180 + 0.6 \times 60}{1.08} = 100. \qquad (4)^6$$

In what follows, we assume that if any part of the required investment outlay (having present value of $104 million) is not going to be spent immediately but in future installments, that amount is placed in an escrow account earning the riskless interest rate.[7] We next illustrate how various kinds of both upside-potential options, such as to defer or expand, and downside-protection options, such as to abandon for salvage or default during construction, can enhance the value of the opportunity to invest (i.e., the value of equity or NPV) in the above generic project, under the standard assumption of all-equity financing. Our focus here is on basic practical principles for valuing one kind of operating option at a time.

1 The Option to Defer Investment The company has a one-year lease providing it a proprietary right to defer undertaking the project (i.e., extracting the oil) for a year, thus benefiting from the resolution of uncertainty about oil prices over this period. Although undertaking the project immediately has a negative NPV (of -4), the opportunity to invest afforded by the lease has a positive worth since management would invest *only* if oil prices and project value rise sufficiently, while it has no obligation to invest under unfavorable developments. Since the option to wait is analogous to a call option on project value, V, with an exercise price equal to the required outlay next year, $I_1 = 112.32 \, (= 1.04 \times 1.08)$:

$$E^+ = \max(V^+ - I_1, 0) = \max(180 - 112.32, 0) = 67.68,$$
$$E^- = \max(V^- - I_1, 0) = \max(60 - 112.32, 0) = 0. \qquad (5)$$

The project's total value (i.e., the expanded NPV that includes the value of the option to defer) from Equation (3) is:

$$E_0 = \frac{pE^+ + (1-p)E^-}{(1+r)} = \frac{0.4 \times 67.68 + 0.6 \times 0}{1.08} = 25.07. \qquad (6)$$

From Equation (1), the value of the option to defer provided by the lease itself is thus given by:

Option to defer = expanded NPV − passive NPV = 25.07 − (−4) = 29.07 $\qquad$ (7)

which, incidentally, is equal to almost one-third of the project's gross value.[8]

2 The Option to Expand (Growth Option)   Once the project is undertaken, any necessary infrastructure is completed and the plant is operating, management may have the option to accelerate the rate or expand the scale of production by, say, 50% ($x = 0.50$) by incurring a follow-up investment outlay of $I_E = 40$, provided oil prices and general market conditions turn out better than originally expected. Thus, in year 1 management can choose either to maintain the base scale operation (i.e., receive project value, V, at no extra cost) or expand by 50% the scale and project value by incurring the extra outlay. That is, the original investment opportunity is seen as the initial-scale project plus a call option on a future opportunity, or $E = V + \max(xV - I_E, 0) = \max(V, (1 + x)V - I_E)$:

$$E^+ = \max(V^+, 1.5V^+ - I_E) = \max(180, 270 - 40) = 230$$

i.e., expand;

$$E^- = \max(V^-, 1.5V^- - I_E) = \max(60, 90 - 40) = 60 \tag{8}$$

i.e., maintain base scale. The value of the investment opportunity (including the value of the option to expand if market conditions turn out better than expected) then becomes:

$$E_0 = \frac{pE^+ + (1 - p)E^-}{(1 + r)} - I_0 = \frac{0.4 \times 230 + 0.6 \times 60}{1.08} - 104 = 14.5, \tag{9}$$

and thus the value of the option to expand is:

Option to expand = $14.5 - (-4) = 18.5,$ \tag{10}

or 18.5% of the gross project value.

3 Options to Abandon for Salvage Value or Switch Use   In terms of downside protection, management has the option to abandon the oil extraction project at any time in exchange for its salvage value or value in its best alternative use, if oil prices suffer a sustainable decline. The associated oil refinery plant also can use alternative energy inputs and has the flexibility to convert crude oil into a variety of products. As market conditions change and the relative prices of inputs, outputs or the plant resale value in a secondhand market fluctuate, equityholders may find it preferable to abandon the current project's use by switching to a cheaper input, a more profitable output, or simply sell the plant's assets to the secondhand market. Let the project's value in its best alternative use, A, (or the salvage value for which it can be exchanged) fluctuate over time as:

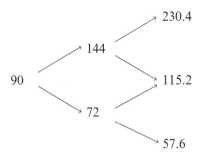

Year 0   Year 1   Year 2

Note that the project's current salvage or alternative use value ($A_0 = 90$) is below the project's value in its present use ($V_0 = 100$)—otherwise management would have switched use immediately—and has the same expected rate of return (20%); it nevertheless has a smaller variance so that if the market keeps moving up it would not be optimal to abandon the project early for its salvage value, but if it moves down management may find it desirable to switch use (e.g., in year 1 exchange the present use value of $V_1 = 60$ for a higher alternative use value of $A_1 = 72$).[9] Thus, equityholders can choose the maximum of the project's value in its present use, V, or its value in the best alternative use, A, i.e., $E = \max(V, A)$:

$$E^+ = \max(V^+, A^+) = \max(180, 144) = 180 = V^+,$$

i.e., continue;

$$E^- = \max(V^-, A^-) = \max(60, 72) = 72 = A^-, \tag{11}$$

i.e., switch use. The value of the investment (including the option to abandon early or switch use) is then:

$$E_0 = \frac{pE^+ + (1-p)E^-}{(1+r)} - I_0$$

$$= \frac{0.4 \times 180 + 0.6 \times 72}{1.08} - 104 = +2.67 \tag{12}$$

so that the project with the option to switch use is now desirable. The value of the option itself is:

$$\text{Option to switch use} = 2.67 - (-4) = 6.67, \tag{13}$$

or almost seven percent of the project's gross value. This value is clearly dependent on the schedule of salvage or alternative use values.

4 The Option to Default (on Planned Staged Cost Installments) During Construction

Even during the construction phase, management may abandon a project to save any subsequent investment outlays, if the coming required investment exceeds the value from continuing the project (including any future options). Suppose that the investment (of \$104 present value) necessary to implement the oil extraction project can be staged as a series of "installments": $I_0 = \$44$ out of the \$104 allocated amount will need to be paid out immediately (in year 0) as a start-up cost for infrastructure, with the \$60 balance placed in an escrow account (earning the risk-free rate) planned to be paid as a $I_1 = \$64.8$ follow-up outlay for constructing the processing plant in year 1. Next year management will then pay the investment cost "installment" as planned only in return for a higher project value from continuing, else it will forego the investment and receive nothing. Thus, the option to default when investment is staged sequentially during construction translates into $E = \max(V - I_1, 0)$:

$$E^+ = \max(V^+ - I_1, 0) = \max(180 - 64.8, 0) = 115.2,$$

i.e., continue;

$$E^- = \max(V^- - I_1, 0) = \max(60 - 64.8, 0) = 0, \tag{14}$$

i.e., default. The value of the investment opportunity (with the option to default on future outlays) is given by:

$$E_0 = \frac{pE^+ + (1-p)E^-}{(1+r)} - I_0$$

$$= \frac{0.4 \times 115.2 + 0.6 \times 0}{1.08} - 44 = -1.33 \tag{15}$$

and the option to abandon by defaulting during construction is:

$$\text{Option to abandon by defaulting} = -1.33 - (-4) = 2.67, \tag{16}$$

or about three percent of project value. This value is of course dependent on the staged cost schedule.

For simplicity, the above examples were based on a one-period risk-neutral backward valuation procedure. This procedure can be easily extended to a discrete multi-period setting with any number of stages. Starting from the terminal values, the process would move backwards calculating option values one step earlier (using the up and down values obtained in the preceding step), and so on. A two-period extension is illustrated in the next section. As the number of steps increases, the discrete-time solution naturally approaches its continuous Black-Scholes-type equivalent (with appropriate adjustments), when it exists.

III   Summary, Conclusions and Extensions

Following a comprehensive thematic overview of the evolution of real options, this paper has illustrated, through simple examples, how to quantify in principle the value of various types of operating options embedded in capital investments, both for enhancing upside potential (e.g., through options to defer or expand), as well as for reducing downside risk (e.g., via options to abandon for salvage value or switch use, and to default on staged planned outlays). We have also noted a number of fruitful future research directions, including more applications and implementation problems, empirical and field studies, theoretical extensions combining options theory with Bayesian analysis to model learning, with game theory to model competitive and strategic interactions, with agency theory/asymmetric information to model/ correct misuse of managerial discretion, as well as interactions between operating and financial flexibility.

Taking a first step in the latter direction, [in the original article] we extended the analysis in the presence of leverage within a venture capital context and examined the potential improvement in equityholders' value as a result of additional financial flexibility, starting from the equityholders' option to default on debt payments deriving from limited liability. The beneficial impact of staging venture capital financing in installments, thereby creating an option to abandon by the lender, and when using a mix of debt and equity venture capital was also examined. Staging capital financing may be beneficial not only to venture capitalists (by preserving an option to abandon), but also to entrepreneurs as well, since it allows potentially better financing terms in later stages. In later-stage debt financing, for example, better terms may be achieved in the form of lower interest costs. If later-stage financing is to be provided in the form of an equity ownership share based on the project's market value as would be revealed at an interim stage, entrepreneurs could gain by suffering less equity dilution when a higher project value is assessed in reallocating the claims in the good interim state. Even in a bad interim state, entrepreneurs might still gain if they can prevent imminent abandonment of the venture (assuming they still believe it is worthwhile to pursue) by the venture capitalists by renegotiating more appropriate terms given the higher risks (either offering a greater equity share or a higher interest rate). The option to actively revalue the terms of a financing deal as operating project uncertainties get resolved over successive stages is clearly valuable, compared to a passive alternative where the financing terms are irrevocably committed to from the very beginning under less complete information. Building-in flexibility in a financing deal may determine whether the venture will continue and eventually succeed or fail when interim performance does not meet initial expectations.

Thus, contrary to what is often popularly assumed, the value of an investment deal may not depend solely on the amount, timing, and operating risk of its measurable cash flows. The future operating outcomes of a project can actually be impacted by future decisions (by either equityholders or lenders) depending on the inherent or built-in operating and financial options and the way the deal is financed (e.g., the staging of financing or the allocation of cash flows among debt and equity claimants). In such cases, interactions between a firm's operating and financial decisions can be quite significant, as exemplified by the typical venture capital case. These interactions are likely to be more pronounced for large, uncertain, long-development and multi-staged investments or growth opportunities, especially when substantial external (particularly debt) multistaged financing is involved. Understanding these inter-actions and designing a proper financing deal that recognizes their true value, while being flexible enough to better reflect the evolution of a project's operating risks as it moves through different stages, can mean the difference between success or failure. Options-based valuation can thus be a particularly useful tool to corporate managers and strategists by providing a consistent and unified approach toward incorporating the value of both the real and financial options associated with the combined invest-ment and financial decision of the firm.

Notes

I would like to thank George M. Constantinides, Nalin Kulatilaka, Scott P. Mason, Stewart C. Myers, Martha A. Schary, Han Smit, two anonymous reviewers, and the editor, James S. Ang, for useful com-ments on earlier versions of parts of this work. The usual disclaimer applies.

1. Parts of table 7.1 are adapted from Baldwin and Trigeorgis [8].

2. Alternatively, management has an option to obtain project value V (net of fixed costs, I_F) minus vari-able costs (I_V), or shut down and receive project value minus that year's foregone cash revenue (C), i.e., $\max(V - I_V, V - C) - I_F = (V - I_F) - \min(I_V, C)$. The latter expression implies that the option not to operate enables management to acquire project value (net of fixed costs) by paying the minimum of vari-able costs (if the project does well and management decides to operate) or the cash revenues (that would be sacrificed if the project does poorly and it chooses not to operate).

3. Trigeorgis and Mason [108] use a similar example to show how options-based valuation can be seen operationally as a special, though economically corrected, version of decision tree analysis (DTA) that recognizes open-market opportunities to trade and borrow.

4. All project values are hereafter assumed to be in millions of dollars (with "millions" subsequently dropped).

5. As noted, the basic idea is that management can replicate the payoff to equity by purchasing a specified number of shares of the "twin security" and financing the purchase in part by borrowing a specific amount at the riskless interest rate, r. This ability to construct a "synthetic" claim or an equivalent/replicating portfolio (from the "twin security" and riskless bonds) based on no-arbitrage equilibrium principles enables the solution for the current value of the equity claim to be independent of the actual probabilities (in this case, 0.5) or investors' risk attitudes (the twin security's expected rate of return or discount rate, $k = 0.20$).

6. This confirms the gross project value, $V_0 = 100$, obtained earlier using traditional DCF with the actual probability ($q = 0.5$) and the risk-adjusted discount rate ($k = 0.20$).

7. This assumption is intended to make the analysis somewhat more realistic and invariant to the cost structure make-up, and is not at all crucial to the analysis.

8. The above example confirms that CCA is operationally identical to decision tree analysis (DTA), with the key difference that the probabilities are transformed so as to allow the use of a risk-free discount rate. Note, however, that the DCF/DTA value of waiting may differ from that given by CCA. The DCF/DTA approach in this case will overestimate the value of the option if it discounts at the constant 20% rate required of securities comparable in risk to the "naked" (passive) project:

$$E_0 = \frac{qE^+ + (1-q)E^-}{(1+k)} = \frac{0.5 \times 67.68 + 0.5 \times 0}{1.20} = 28.20.$$

Again, the error in the traditional DTA approach arises from the use of a single (or constant) risk-adjusted discount rate. Asymmetric claims on an asset do not have the same riskiness (and hence expected rate of return) as the underlying asset itself. CCA corrects for this error by transforming the probabilities.

9. We assume here for simplicity that the project's value in its current use and in its best alternative use (or salvage value) are perfectly positively correlated. Of course, the option to switch use would be even more valuable the lower the correlation between V and A.

References

1. R. Aggarwal, "Justifying Investments in Flexible Manufacturing Technology," *Managerial Finance* (May 1991), pp. 77–88.

2. J. S. Ang and S. Dukas, "Capital Budgeting in a Competitive Environment," *Managerial Finance* (May 1991), pp. 6–15.

3. C. Baldwin, "Optimal Sequential Investment When Capital is Not Readily Reversible," *Journal of Finance* (June 1982), pp. 763–782.

4. C. Baldwin, "Competing for Capital in a Global Environment," *Midland Corporate Finance Journal* (Spring 1987), pp. 43–64.

5. C. Baldwin and K. Clark, "Capabilities and Capital Investment: New Perspectives on Capital Budgeting," *Journal of Applied Corporate Finance* (Summer 1992), pp. 67–87.

6. C. Baldwin and K. Clark, "Modularity and Real Options," Working Paper, Harvard Business School, 1993.

7. C. Baldwin and R. Ruback, "Inflation, Uncertainty, and Investment," *Journal of Finance* (July 1986), pp. 657–669.

8. C. Baldwin and L. Trigeorgis, "Toward Remedying the Underinvestment Problem: Competitiveness, Real Options, Capabilities, and TQM," Working Paper #93-025, Harvard Business School, 1993.

9. G. Barone-Adesi and R. Whaley, "Efficient Analytic Approximation of American Option Values," *Journal of Finance* (June 1987), pp. 301–320.

10. G. Bell, "Volatile Exchange Rates and the Multinational Firm: Entry, Exit, and Capacity Options," in *Real Options in Capital Investment: New Contributions*, L. Trigeorgis (ed.), New York, NY, Praeger, 1995.

11. P. Bjerksund and S. Ekern, "Managing Investment Opportunities Under Price Uncertainty: from 'Last Chance' to 'Wait and See' Strategies," *Financial Management* (Autumn 1990), pp. 65–83.

12. P. Bjerksund and S. Ekern, "Contingent Claims Evaluation of Mean-Reverting Cash Flows in Shipping," in *Real Options in Capital Investment: New Contributions*, L. Trigeorgis (ed.), New York, NY, Praeger, 1995.

13. F. Black and M. Scholes, "The Pricing of Options and Corporate Liabilities," *Journal of Political Economy* (May/June 1973), pp. 637–659.

14. P. Boyle, "Options: A Monte Carlo Approach," *Journal of Financial Economics* (May 1977), pp. 323–338.

15. P. Boyle, "A Lattice Framework for Option Pricing with Two State Variables," *Journal of Financial and Quantitative Analysis* (March 1988), pp. 1–12.

16. R. Brealey and S. C. Myers, *Principles of Corporate Finance*, New York, NY, McGraw-Hill, 6th edition, 2000, Ch. 21.

17. M. Brennan, "The Pricing of Contingent Claims in Discrete Time Models," *Journal of Finance* (March 1979), pp. 53–68.

18. M. Brennan and E. Schwartz, "Finite Difference Methods and Jump Processes Arising in the Pricing of Contingent Claims: A Synthesis," *Journal of Financial and Quantitative Analysis* (September 1978), pp. 461–474.

19. M. Brennan and E. Schwartz, "Evaluating Natural Resource Investments," *Journal of Business* (April 1985), pp. 135–157.

20. D. Capozza and G. Sick, "Risk and Return in Land Markets," Working Paper, University of British Columbia, 1992.

21. P. Carr, "The Valuation of Sequential Exchange Opportunities," *Journal of Finance* (December 1988), pp. 1235–1256.

22. K. Chung and C. Charoenwong, "Investment Options, Assets in Place, and the Risk of Stocks," *Financial Management* (Autumn 1991), pp. 21–33.

23. G. Constantinides, "Market Risk Adjustment in Project Valuation," *Journal of Finance* (May 1978), pp. 603–616.

24. T. Copeland and J. F. Weston, "A Note on the Evaluation of Cancellable Operating Leases," *Financial Management* (Summer 1982), pp. 60–67.

25. J. Cox and S. Ross, "The Valuation of Options for Alternative Stochastic Processes," *Journal of Financial Economics* (January 1976), pp. 145–166.

26. J. Cox, S. Ross, and M. Rubinstein, "Option Pricing: A Simplified Approach," *Journal of Financial Economics* (September 1979), pp. 229–263.

27. J. Cox, J. Ingersoll, and S. Ross, "An Intertemporal General Equilibrium Model of Asset Prices," *Econometrica* (March 1985), pp. 363–384.

28. J. Dean, *Capital Budgeting*, New York, NY, Columbia University Press, 1951.

29. A. Dixit, "Entry and Exit Decisions Under Uncertainty," *Journal of Political Economy* (June 1989), pp. 620–638.

30. R. Geske, "The Valuation of Compound Options," *Journal of Financial Economics* (March 1979), pp. 63–81.

31. R. Geske and H. Johnson, "The American Put Option Valued Analytically," *Journal of Finance* (December 1984), pp. 1511–1524.

32. R. Geske and K. Shastri, "Valuation by Approximation: A Comparison of Alternative Option Valuation Techniques," *Journal of Financial and Quantitative Analysis* (March 1985), pp. 45–71.

33. J. M. Harrison and D. M. Kreps, "Martingales and Arbitrage in Multiperiod Securities Markets," *Journal of Economic Theory* (June 1979), pp. 381–408.

34. R. Hayes and W. Abernathy, "Managing Our Way to Economic Decline," *Harvard Business Review* (July–August 1980), pp. 66–77.

35. R. Hayes and D. Garvin, "Managing as if Tomorrow Mattered," *Harvard Business Review* (May–June 1982), pp. 71–79.

36. D. Hendricks, "Optimal Policy Responses to an Uncertain Threat: The Case of Global Warming," Working Paper, Harvard University Kennedy School of Government, 1991.

37. D. Hertz, "Risk Analysis in Capital Investment," *Harvard Business Review* (January–February 1964), pp. 95–106.

38. T. Hiraki, "Corporate Governance, Long-term Investment Orientation, and Real Options in Japan," in *Real Options in Capital Investment: New Contributions*, L. Trigeorgis (ed.), New York, NY, Praeger, 1995.

39. J. Hodder, "Evaluation of Manufacturing Investments: A Comparison of U.S. and Japanese Practices," *Financial Management* (Spring 1986), pp. 17–24.

40. J. Hodder and H. Riggs, "Pitfalls in Evaluating Risky Projects," *Harvard Business Review* (January–February 1985), pp. 128–135.

41. J. Hull, *Options, Futures, and Other Derivative Securities*, Englewood Cliffs, NJ, Prentice-Hall, 1989, Ch. 9.

42. J. Hull and A. White, "The Use of the Control Variate Technique in Option Pricing," *Journal of Financial and Quantitative Analysis* (September 1988), pp. 697–705.

43. J. Ingersoll and S. Ross, "Waiting to Invest: Investment and Uncertainty," *Journal of Business* (January 1992), pp. 1–29.

44. H. Johnson, "Options on the Maximum or the Minimum of Several Assets," *Journal of Financial and Quantitative Analysis* (September 1987), pp. 277–284.

45. B. Kamrad and R. Ernst, "Multiproduct Manufacturing with Stochastic Input Prices and Output Yield Uncertainty," in *Real Options in Capital Investment: New Contributions*, L. Trigeorgis (ed.), New York, NY, Praeger, 1995.

46. E. Kasanen, "Creating Value by Spawning Investment Opportunities," *Financial Management* (Autumn 1993), pp. 251–258.

47. E. Kasanen and L. Trigeorgis, "A Market Utility Approach to Investment Valuation," *European Journal of Operational Research* (Special Issue on Financial Modelling), pp. 294–309.

48. A. Kemna, "Case Studies on Real Options," *Financial Management* (Autumn 1993), pp. 259–270.

49. J. Kensinger, "Adding the Value of Active Management into the Capital Budgeting Equation," *Midland Corporate Finance Journal* (Spring 1987), pp. 31–42.

50. W. C. Kester, "Today's Options for Tomorrow's Growth," *Harvard Business Review* (March–April 1984), pp. 153–160.

51. W. C. Kester, "Turning Growth Options Into Real Assets," in *Capital Budgeting Under Uncertainty*, R. Aggarwal (ed.), Englewood Cliffs, NJ, Prentice-Hall, 1993, pp. 187–207.

52. B. Kogut and N. Kulatilaka, "Operating Flexibility, Global Manufacturing, and the Option Value of a Multinational Network," *Management Science*, 1994, pp. 123–139.

53. A. L. Kolbe, P. A. Morris, and E. O. Teisberg, "When Choosing R&D Projects, Go with Long Shots," *Research-Technology Management* (January–February 1991).

54. N. Kulatilaka, "Valuing the Flexibility of Flexible Manufacturing Systems," *IEEE Transactions in Engineering Management* (1988), pp. 250–257.

55. N. Kulatilaka, "The Value of Flexibility: The Case of a Dual-Fuel Industrial Steam Boiler," *Financial Management* (Autumn 1993), pp. 271–280.

56. N. Kulatilaka, "The Value of Flexibility: A General Model of Real Options," in *Real Options in Capital Investment: New Contributions*, L. Trigeorgis (ed.), New York, NY, Praeger, 1995.

57. N. Kulatilaka, "Operating Flexibilities in Capital Budgeting: Substitutability and Complementarity in Real Options," in *Real Options in Capital Investment: New Contributions*, L. Trigeorgis (ed.), New York, NY, Praeger, 1995.

58. N. Kulatilaka and A. Marcus, "A General Formulation of Corporate Operating Options," *Research in Finance*, JAI Press, 1988, pp. 183–200.

59. N. Kulatilaka and A. Marcus, "Project Valuation Under Uncertainty: When Does DCF Fail?," *Journal of Applied Corporate Finance* (Fall 1992), pp. 92–100.

60. N. Kulatilaka and S. Marks, "The Strategic Value of Flexibility: Reducing the Ability to Compromise," *American Economic Review* (June 1988), pp. 574–580.

61. N. Kulatilakà and E. Perotti, "Strategic Investment Timing Under Uncertainty," Working Paper, Boston University, 1992.

62. N. Kulatilaka and L. Trigeorgis, "The General Flexibility to Switch: Real Options Revisited," *International Journal of Finance*, pp. 776–798.

63. D. G. Laughton and H. D. Jacoby, "Reversion, Timing Options, and Long-Term Decision-Making," *Financial Management* (Autumn 1993), pp. 225–240.

64. W. Lee, J. Martin, and A. Senchack, "The Case for Using Options to Evaluate Salvage Values in Financial Leases," *Financial Management* (Autumn 1982), pp. 33–41.

65. J. Magee, "How to Use Decision Trees in Capital Investment," *Harvard Business Review* (September–October 1964).

66. S. Majd and R. Pindyck, "Time to Build, Option Value, and Investment Decisions," *Journal of Financial Economics* (March 1987), pp. 7–27.

67. W. Margrabe, "The Value of an Option to Exchange One Asset for Another," *Journal of Finance* (March 1978), pp. 177–186.

68. S. P. Mason and C. Baldwin, "Evaluation of Government Subsidies to Large-scale Energy Projects: A Contingent Claims Approach," *Advances in Futures and Options Research*, 1988, pp. 169–181.

69. S. P. Mason and R. C. Merton, "The Role of Contingent Claims Analysis in Corporate Finance," in *Recent Advances in Corporate Finance*, E. Altman and M. Subrahmanyam (eds.), Homewood, IL, Richard D. Irwin, 1985, pp. 7–54.

70. J. McConnell and J. Schallheim, "Valuation of Asset Leasing Contracts," *Journal of Financial Economics* (August 1983), pp. 237–261.

71. R. McDonald and D. Siegel, "Option Pricing When the Underlying Asset Earns a Below-Equilibrium Rate of Return: A Note," *Journal of Finance* (March 1984), pp. 261–265.

72. R. McDonald and D. Siegel, "Investment and the Valuation of Firms When There is an Option to Shut Down," *International Economic Review* (June 1985), pp. 331–349.

73. R. McDonald and D. Siegel, "The Value of Waiting to Invest," *Quarterly Journal of Economics* (November 1986), pp. 707–727.

74. R. McLaughlin and R. Taggart, "The Opportunity Cost of Using Excess Capacity," *Financial Management* (Summer 1992), pp. 12–23.

75. R. C. Merton, "Theory of Rational Option Pricing," *Bell Journal of Economics and Management Science* (Spring 1973), pp. 141–183.

76. R. Mørck, E. Schwartz, and D. Stangeland, "The Valuation of Forestry Resources under Stochastic Prices and Inventories," *Journal of Financial and Quantitative Analysis* (December 1989), pp. 473–487.

77. S. C. Myers, "Determinants of Corporate Borrowing," *Journal of Financial Economics* (November 1977), pp. 147–176.

78. S. C. Myers, "Finance Theory and Financial Strategy," *Midland Corporate Finance Journal* (Spring 1987), pp. 6–13.

79. S. C. Myers and S. Majd, "Abandonment Value and Project Life," *Advances in Futures and Options Research*, 1990, pp. 1–21.

80. J. Paddock, D. Siegel, and J. Smith, "Option Valuation of Claims on Physical Assets: The Case of Offshore Petroleum Leases," *Quarterly Journal of Economics* (August 1988), pp. 479–508.

81. R. Pindyck, "Irreversible Investment, Capacity Choice, and the Value of the Firm," *American Economic Review* (December 1988), pp. 969–985.

82. R. Pindyck, "Irreversibility, Uncertainty, and Investment," *Journal of Economic Literature* (September 1991), pp. 1110–1148.

83. L. Quigg, "Empirical Testing of Real Option-Pricing Models," *Journal of Finance* (June 1993), pp. 621–640.

84. L. Quigg, "Optimal Land Development," in *Real Options in Capital Investment: New Contributions*, L. Trigeorgis (ed.), New York, NY, Praeger, 1995.

85. K. Roberts and M. Weitzman, "Funding Criteria for Research, Development, and Exploration Projects," *Econometrica* (September 1981), pp. 1261–1288.

86. M. Rubinstein, "The Valuation of Uncertain Income Streams and the Pricing of Options," *Bell Journal of Economics* (Autumn 1976), pp. 407–425.

87. W. Sahlman, "Aspects of Financial Contracting in Venture Capital," *Journal of Applied Corporate Finance* (1988), pp. 23–36.

88. G. Sick, *Capital Budgeting With Real Options*, Monograph, New York University, Salomon Brothers Center, 1989.

89. H. T. J. Smit and L. A. Ankum, "A Real Options and Game-Theoretic Approach to Corporate Investment Strategy Under Competition, *Financial Management* (Autumn 1993), pp. 241–250.

90. K. W. Smith and A. Triantis, "The Value of Options in Strategic Acquisitions," in *Real Options in Capital Investment: New Contributions*, L. Trigeorgis (ed.), New York, NY, Praeger, 1995.

91. G. Stensland and D. Tjostheim, "Some Applications of Dynamic Programming to Natural Resource Exploration," *Stochastic Models and Option Values*, in D. Lund and B. Oksendal (eds.), Amsterdam, North-Holland, 1990.

92. R. Stulz, "Options on the Minimum or the Maximum of Two Risky Assets: Analysis and Applications," *Journal of Financial Economics* (July 1982), pp. 161–185.

93. E. Teisberg, "Methods for Evaluating Capital Investment Decisions Under Uncertainty," in *Real Options in Capital Investment: New Contributions*, L. Trigeorgis (ed.), New York, NY, Praeger, 1995.

94. E. Teisberg, "An Option Valuation Analysis of Investment Choices by a Regulated Firm," *Management Science*, (1994), pp. 535–548.

95. S. Titman, "Urban Land Prices Under Uncertainty," *American Economic Review* (June 1985), pp. 505–514.

96. O. Tourinho, "The Option Value of Reserves of Natural Resources," Working Paper No. 94, University of California at Berkeley, 1979.

97. A. Triantis and J. Hodder, "Valuing Flexibility as a Complex Option," *Journal of Finance* (June 1990), pp. 549–565.

98. L. Trigeorgis, "A Conceptual Options Framework for Capital Budgeting," *Advances in Futures and Options Research*, 1988, pp. 145–167.

99. L. Trigeorgis, "A Real Options Application in Natural Resource Investments," *Advances in Futures and Options Research*, 1990, pp. 153–164.

100. L. Trigeorgis, "Valuing the Impact of Uncertain Competitive Arrivals on Deferrable Real Investment Opportunities," Working Paper, Boston University, 1990.

101. L. Trigeorgis, "Anticipated Competitive Entry and Early Preemptive Investment in Deferrable Projects," *Journal of Economics and Business* (May 1991), pp. 143–156.

102. L. Trigeorgis, "A Log-Transformed Binomial Numerical Analysis Method for Valuing Complex Multi-Option Investments," *Journal of Financial and Quantitative Analysis* (September 1991), pp. 309–326.

103. L. Trigeorgis, "Evaluating Leases with a Variety of Operating Options," Working Paper, Boston University, 1992.

104. L. Trigeorgis, "The Nature of Option Interactions and the Valuation of Investments with Multiple Real Options," *Journal of Financial and Quantitative Analysis* (March 1993), pp. 1–20.

105. L. Trigeorgis (ed.), *Real Options in Capital Investment: New Contributions*, New York, NY, Praeger, 1995.

106. L. Trigeorgis, *Options in Capital Budgeting: Managerial Flexibility and Strategy in Resource Allocation*, Cambridge, MA, The MIT Press, 1996.

107. L. Trigeorgis and E. Kasanen, "An Integrated Options-Based Strategic Planning and Control Model," *Managerial Finance* (May 1991), pp. 16–28.

108. L. Trigeorgis and S. P. Mason, "Valuing Managerial Flexibility," *Midland Corporate Finance Journal* (Spring 1987), pp. 14–21.

109. J. Williams, "Real Estate Development as an Option," *Journal of Real Estate Finance and Economics* (June 1991), pp. 191–208.

110. R. Willner, "Valuing Start-Up Venture Growth Options," in *Real Options in Capital Investment: New Contributions*, L. Trigeorgis (ed.), New York, NY, Praeger, 1995.

8 A New Approach to Evaluating Natural Resource Investments

Michael J. Brennan and Eduardo S. Schwartz

The plight of the contemporary capital budgeting analyst may be compared to that of the 19th-century physician. Long on learning, he is short on technique, and such technique as he does possess can be acquired in a matter of weeks by the intelligent layman. For, while understanding of the operation of capital markets has progressed rapidly during the past two decades, significant innovations in corporate capital budgeting techniques have been markedly absent. Such innovations as have been proposed—linear programming, simulation and decision-tree analysis—have failed to win widespread acceptance; and the implementation of corporate capital budgeting rules remains largely a matter of reaching for the discount tables or the pocket calculator.

The object of capital budgeting is to find investment projects whose value exceeds their cost. Setting aside difficulties associated with determination of the cost of projects,[1] the essential problem is that of appraising or valuing the asset which will be created by an investment, be it an oil refinery, a ship or a computer assembly plant. In this sense the task of the financial analyst is not unlike that of the appraiser or realtor who ventures opinions on the value of real properties. It is instructive to note that real estate appraisals typically start from the known prices at which similar properties have changed hands in the recent past and then make marginal adjustments to reflect differences in location, size and so on.

At first blush this approach bears no relation to the procedures followed by financial analysts in appraising investment projects. As is often the case, however, first impressions are misleading. In fact the financial analyst also proceeds by adjustment from the known values of some assets to an estimate of the value of the hypothetical asset—that is, the outcome of the investment project under consideration. The difference is simply that while the realtor makes modest interpolations from the prices of neighbouring properties, the financial analyst typically makes enormous extrapolations from the known values of completely unrelated assets: in fact, from the value of a portfolio of riskless bonds whose time pattern of cash flows corresponds to that of the investment project.

We shall argue that the whole apparatus of the classical discounted cash flow approach to capital budgeting is predicated upon an analogy between a real investment project and a portfolio of riskless bonds. Such an analogy may be appropriate in some contexts—one thinks naturally of public utilities—but it is obviously inappropriate in many other cases (and nowhere perhaps more so than in the realm of natural resource investments, our primary concern in this paper). The challenge to the financial analyst is to choose an asset of known value which is closest in characteristics to the asset whose value is to be determined. Since this choice must contain an element of judgment, capital budgeting is as much a matter of art as of technique. Unfortunately, many text books leave the mistaken impression that capital budgeting is simply a question of mechanical application of the rules of discounting.

In the case of natural resource investments, the relevant asset whose value is known will often be a portfolio consisting of riskless bonds and either the commodity which is to be produced by the investment project—be it gold, oil or lead—or a futures contract on that commodity. This is most easily seen in the case of a gold mine which will produce a known output at a known cost. If the costs are known, they can be discounted, like the payments on a Treasury bond, at the riskless interest rate, leaving only the problem of valuing the output. This latter task is simple if there exists a market for forward delivery, or a futures market for the commodity. The present value of an ounce of future production is equal simply to the appropriate current futures price discounted at the riskless interest rate (to reflect the fact that payment is deferred). Indeed it turns out that this discounted futures price for gold is almost exactly equal to the current spot price because of arbitrage considerations which we shall elucidate below. This means that for any commodity which, like gold, is held for investment or speculative purposes, future output can be evaluated at the current spot price without any discounting.

For commodities which are held in inventory for commercial rather than investment purposes, the situation is somewhat more complex, since it is necessary to take account of the net benefits yielded by an inventory of the commodity. The principal benefits of the inventory are, first, production cost savings made possible by avoidance of the interruptions in production which would be inevitable in the absence of an inventory and, second, the ability to take advantage of unforeseen local increases in the demand for the commodity. Collectively these benefits, net of the costs of storage of the inventory, are known as the "convenience yield" of an inventory of the commodity. It is the *marginal* convenience yield, then, or the extra services yielded by an additional unit of inventory, which must be taken into account in valuing future units of production.

It turns out that the present value of a unit of future production of the commodity is equal to the current spot price discounted by the marginal convenience yield. Moreover this marginal convenience yield may be inferred from the relation between the spot and futures prices of the commodity.

Note that this convenience yield approach avoids simultaneously the twin problems of assessing the expected future spot price at which the commodity will be sold, and of assigning a discount rate appropriate to the risk of these revenues. On the other hand it is necessary to estimate the convenience yield, which may itself be a function of the spot price of the commodity. The scope for error in estimating the convenience yield, however, is much less than in estimating future spot prices and discount rates.

Thus far we have assumed that the future output of the project is known; however, this assumption is unlikely to be the case in most situations. Future output will depend upon a number of factors which are unknown at the time the project is evaluated: most notably, on geological features which will be revealed only as production takes place, and on future market conditions. Depending on actual future prices, production may be changed, or a project shut down or even abandoned with resulting costs of closure, redundancy and so on.

These operating options are extremely difficult to evaluate under the classical present value approach. They may be valued in a quite straightforward manner, however, and the optimal operating policies determined, by treating the project as an *option* on the commodity, and adapting the option pricing paradigm originally developed by Fischer Black and Myron Scholes (1973) and elaborated by Robert Merton (1973). Indeed so flexible is this approach that it is possible to value individual components of the cash flows from a project—for example, to calculate the present value of a royalty, an income tax or redundancy payments—and, even more important, to determine the effect of alternative fiscal arrangements on the optimal operating policies of the projects. However, before we present this new approach to capital budgeting for natural resource investments, it will prove useful to consider in more detail the limitations of the classical discounted cash flow model.

The Classical Discounted Cash Flow Model

The classical Discounted Cash Flow or Present Value procedure for capital budgeting has now almost everywhere replaced cruder payback or accounting rate of return methods. It involves a comparison between the cost of an investment project and the present value of the cash flows the project will generate, which is calculated according to the well-known formula:

$$\text{PV} = \frac{C_1}{1+k} + \frac{C_2}{(1+k)^2} + \cdots \frac{C_n}{(1+k)^n} \tag{1}$$

where C_t is the cash flow expected in period t and k is the appropriate discount rate. Formula (1) is also the one used to arrive at the value of a bond, where C_t is the coupon payment, C_n is the final repayment of principal and k is the interest rate. This is not fortuitous, since the origin of the formula and its only rigorous justification is precisely in its application to bonds or known cash flows.

The application of the formula to the valuation of real risky assets is made possible by two more or less tacit assumptions or conventions. The first is that uncertain future cash flows can be replaced by their expected values and that these expected cash flows can be treated as given at the outset. The second is that the discount rate is known and constant, and that it depends solely upon the risk of the project. Let us consider the limitations of an approach based on these assumptions and see why the underlying bond analogy may be a poor one for some investment projects, especially in the field of natural resources.

First, the classical approach, by assuming that the cash flows to be discounted are given at the outset, presupposes a static approach to investment decision-making—one which ignores the possibility of future management decisions that will be made in response to the market conditions encountered. Over the life of a project, decisions can be made to change the output rate, to expand or close the facility, or even to abandon it. The flexibility afforded by these decision possibilities may contribute significantly to the value of the project.

To introduce an analogy which we shall develop further below, the classical approach may be likened to valuing a stock option contract while ignoring the right of the holder not to exercise when it is unprofitable. To some extent this drawback of the classical approach may be overcome by employing a scenario or simulation approach in which alternative scenarios—involving for example different price outcomes and management responses—are generated and the resulting cash flows estimated. These cash flows are then averaged across scenarios and discounted to arrive at the present value.

Unfortunately this scenario or simulation approach gives rise to two further problems. First, it requires that the appropriate policy for each scenario be determined in advance. Sometimes this will be possible. For example, if the output rate can be adjusted costlessly, the simple rule of setting marginal cost equal to price may sometimes be optimal.[2] But more generally this will not be possible. If it is costly to close or abandon a project, then the decision to close is itself an investment decision with uncertain future cash flows depending on commodity prices. The optimal closure policy must therefore be determined simultaneously with the original capital budgeting decision.

Even more fundamentally, the degree of managerial discretion in making future operating decisions will tend to affect the risk of the project under consideration. A project which can be abandoned under adverse circumstances will be less risky than one that cannot; it will be even less risky if part of the initial capital investment can be recovered in the event of abandonment. The classical approach offers no way of allowing for this risk effect except through some *ad hoc* adjustment of the discount rate.

In fact the tacit assumption concerning the discount rate is the second Achilles' heel of the classical approach. Given any set of expected cash flows, there almost always exists some discount rate which will yield the correct present value. But the determination of this discount rate presents an almost insurmountable task, and current procedures cannot be regarded as any more than highly imperfect rules of thumb. Thus these procedures all assume that the discount rate is constant, which is tantamount to assuming that the risk of the project is constant over its life. And this is, of course, highly unlikely. Not only will the risk depend in general upon the remaining life of the project, it will almost certainly depend upon the current profitability of the project through an operating leverage effect. Hence, not only will the discount rate vary with time, it will also be uncertain.

Even if the appropriate discount rate were deterministic and constant, the problems of estimation would still be formidable. In principle the discount rate should depend upon the risk of the project, but how is this risk to be assessed? The generally approved procedure is to use the Capital Asset Pricing Model and to base the discount rate on the beta of the project as estimated from other firms with similar projects. In practice these other firms consist in effect of portfolios of projects, sometimes in unrelated industries, and this makes the assignment of betas to individual projects a hazardous undertaking.[3] Transferring these betas to the project under consideration creates further problems, for a new project is likely to have a cost structure which differs in a systematic fashion from existing, mature projects. The problem is compounded by the consideration, mentioned above, that the latitude of future operating decisions inherent in a project will affect its risk, and is unlikely to be duplicated in existing projects.

Of course these problems are often ignored in practice and a single corporate discount rate based on the weighted average cost of capital is employed for all projects, regardless of risk. As is well known, however, the price of this simplification is a capital budgeting decision system which contains systematic biases as between projects with different risks and different lives. And, as we have argued, such a decision system will lead to the systematic undervaluation of projects with significant operating options.

A final practical difficulty with the classical approach is the necessity to forecast expected output prices for many years into the future. This problem is particularly acute for natural resource industries, where annual price fluctuations of 25 to 50 percent are not uncommon. Under these conditions a wide range of possibilities for the path of expected future spot prices will appear plausible, and the calculated present value of the project will depend upon some arbitrary selection among them.

The foregoing appears to constitute a fairly strong indictment of the classical discounted cash flow approach to capital budgeting. It would be premature, however, to conclude that the approach is without merit, or that it should be discarded in favour of some even worse approach, such as the old payback rule. The limitations of the classical approach arise because it is based fundamentally on an analogy between a portfolio of riskless bonds and a real investment project. In many cases this analogy may be useful; for example, in situations in which the scope for future managerial discretion is limited, and the fiction of other similar risk projects can be maintained. Moreover, even if these conditions are not satisfied, the bond analogy underlying the classical approach may still be the best method available.

In general the appropriate analogy will depend upon the type of project under consideration. For natural resource projects, as we shall show, a better analogy than the classical model is provided by the option pricing or contingent claims paradigm. This approach treats a natural resource extraction project or mine as an option on the underlying commodity. It will prove helpful first, however, to consider the principles involved in valuing a simple gold mine assuming no scope for future managerial discretion.

A Simple Gold Mine

Consider a gold mine which will produce a known output of 1000 ounces at a cost of $200,000 over each of the next two years. The present value of the mine is simply the difference between the present value of the reserves, which will depend upon the future spot price of gold, and the present value of the costs. Since the costs are certain, the bond analogy applies precisely to them, and they may be discounted at the current bond rate, R, say 10 percent, to yield as follows:

$$\text{PV (Costs)} = \frac{200,000}{1.1} + \frac{200,000}{1.1^2} = \$347,107. \tag{2}$$

To value the output or revenues of the mine, let us suppose initially there exist futures markets for gold deliverable in one and two years, and that the current futures prices are F_1 and F_2. Now an individual who goes long in a one-year futures contract agrees to take delivery of one ounce of gold in one year in return for a payment of F_1, which will also take place in one year.[4] He is effectively buying gold for future delivery at a *current*, or present value, price of $F_1/(1 + R)$, where the discounting reflects the fact that payment is deferred for one year. Similarly, an individual who goes short in a futures contract agrees to make delivery of the gold in one year in return for receiving F_1 at that time. He is effectively selling gold for future delivery at a current or present value price of $F_1/(1+R)$. Thus the futures market reveals to us directly the present value of an ounce of gold deliverable in t years as $F_t/(1+R)^t$.

Now the owner of the gold mine owns nothing but the right to deliver 1000 ounces of gold in one and two years after incurring the necessary extraction costs dealt with above. It follows that the present value of this gold for future delivery is given by the equation:

$$\text{PV (Revenues)} = \frac{1000\, F_1}{1.1} + \frac{1000\, F_2}{1.1^2} \tag{3}$$

where the interest rate, R, is 10 percent. It follows that the present value of the mine is simply the difference between expressions (3) and (2), and the gold mine is equivalent to a portfolio consisting of gold futures and riskless bonds.

Note that this approach obviates any need either to forecast the future spot price of gold, an exceedingly difficult task, or to determine an appropriate discount rate for revenues from sales of gold, which is also a difficult task. Instead, the present value of the mine is expressed solely in terms of observables, the futures prices and the interest rate.

It may be objected that the value of the mine yielded by this approach does not correspond to that obtained by an analyst using his own forecasts of future gold prices. This is quite possible. The value does correspond, however, to the price at which the gold mine could be sold today—a price which depends solely on current market expectations about future gold prices, which in turn are reflected in futures prices. Thus it is important to distinguish between the current market value of the mine, which is what the present value analysis is intended to yield, and deviations between the market's and the analyst's expectations about the future spot price of gold. If the analyst believes that gold is undervalued by the market, then it is quite possible for him to speculate on his hunches in the futures market; but he should not confuse his hunches with his estimate of the current market value of the mine.

A second objection that may be made to the foregoing analysis is that there do not exist futures markets for delivery beyond a couple of years, and yet the mine may have a production life of many more years. As we shall see, however, the existence of a futures market is not critical to our analysis. For a commodity which is held for investment purposes, such as gold, the futures price is always equal to the current spot price compounded forward at the interest rate. Thus the futures price for delivery in t years, F_t, may be written as

$$F_t = S_0(1 + R)^t \tag{4}$$

where S_0 is the current spot price of gold. Relation (4) permits us to infer what the futures would be, from the current spot price and the interest rate, even if no futures contract of the relevant maturity is actually traded.

To see why relation (4) must hold, consider an individual who is holding gold for investment purposes as part of his portfolio. If the futures price is less than the value given by expression (4), it will pay him to sell his gold at the current spot price, S_0, and enter into a future's contract to repurchase the gold in t years at F_t. The proceeds of the gold sale invested in bonds will yield $S_0(1 + R)^t$ at a time t and he will require only F_t to make good on the futures contract, leaving him with a certain profit $S_0(1 + R)^t - F_t$. So long as F_t is below the value implied by (4), it will pay all holders of gold to sell spot and repurchase in the futures market. But since the world stocks of gold must be held by someone, it cannot be profitable for them all to sell gold and repurchase it via a futures market transaction. Thus the futures price cannot be less than the value given by expression (4). Moreover, the futures price cannot exceed this value either, for then unlimited riskless profits would follow from a strategy of purchasing gold to hold in inventory and simultaneously selling futures contracts.

Therefore, the only equilibrium price for gold for future delivery is the compounded value of the current spot price as given by (4). Substituting this value for the futures price in expression (3) for the present value of the mine revenues, we find

$$
\begin{aligned}
\text{PV (Revenues)} &= \frac{1000 \times S_0(1.1)}{1.1} + \frac{1000 \times S_0(1.1)^2}{1.1^2} \\
&= 1000 \times S_0 + 1000 \times S_0 \\
&= 2000 \times S_0.
\end{aligned}
\tag{5}
$$

To express this in words, the present value of the mine revenues is obtained by valuing the future output at the *current spot price* of gold without discounting. Thus, careful reasoning reveals that it is possible to value a gold mine without making any of the hazardous assumptions about future prices of gold which would be required under the classical present value approach. Instead of treating the gold mine as analogous to a portfolio of bonds, as the classical approach does, we recognize that it is more akin to a portfolio of gold and of bonds sold short—with the latter corresponding to the production costs.

Now gold is something of a special case since its high value and imperishability make the costs of storing it in inventory negligible, and since individuals do in fact store it in safety deposit boxes for investment purposes. The situation is somewhat different for most other metals. No one, as far as we know, holds ingots of lead, zinc or aluminum in their safety deposit boxes. Instead these metals are held in commercial inventories by refiners and fabricators who use the metals in their production processes. We consider next how the foregoing analysis must be modified to account for the holding of commercial inventories.

A Simple Copper Mine

Let us consider next the example of copper held in inventory not by individual investors, but by manufacturers of copper wire and piping and others who have a commercial interest in the metal. These inventories are held, like inventories of any raw material, because they permit production to proceed smoothly without interruptions caused by shortages of raw materials. Some inventories will continue to be held even if the spot price is expected to decline; the decline in the value of the inventory is offset by the convenience of having the inventory on hand. This benefit of having an inventory on hand is referred to as the *convenience yield* of the inventory. The marginal convenience yield is the benefit yielded by the marginal unit of inventory net of any costs of physical storage, deterioration, etc.

Commercial holders will add to their inventories until the marginal convenience yield, C, is equal to the financial costs of carrying inventory. These costs consist of the interest on the funds tied up in inventory, $S_0 \times R$, less the capital gain, $(F_1 - S_0)$, which is realized if a futures contract is entered into to eliminate the inventory price risk:

$$C = S_0 \times R + (S_0 - F_1) \tag{6}$$

Solving for the one period futures price,

$$F_1 = S_0(1 + R) - C. \tag{7}$$

Comparing expression (7) with the corresponding expression (4) for gold futures, we see that the only difference lies in the convenience yield, C, which tends to reduce the futures relative to the spot price.

The *marginal* convenience yield will depend on the size of the total inventories in the economy. When commercial inventories are large, the benefit of an additional unit of inventory will be correspondingly small. At the same time spot prices will also be low because of the excess supply of the commodity. Therefore it is reasonable to take the convenience yield as proportional to the current spot price, $C = cS_0$.[5] Substituting into (7) we find that the futures price for delivery in t periods is

$$F_t = S_0(1 + R - c)^t. \tag{8}$$

We are able to use expression (8) to evaluate the revenues from a copper mine in just the same way we could evaluate the revenues from the gold mine. The only difference is that we must value the future output at the current spot price discounted at the convenience yield.[6] For example, if our copper mine will produce 100 pounds of copper in each of the following two years and the convenience yield is 2 percent we find that

$$\text{PV (Reserves)} = \frac{100 \times S_0}{1.02} + \frac{100 \times S_0}{1.02^2} = 194 \times S_0.$$

There is only one remaining problem, and that is the appropriate convenience yield. Fortunately this can be computed from the current spot and futures prices and the interest rate using expression (8).

The Mine as an Option

To this point we have seen how to value a mine whose output rate is predetermined, regardless of the price at which the output can be sold. In practice the owner of a mine generally has the right to choose the optimal output rate, to close the mine, to re-open it, or even to abandon it as circumstances dictate. Because of these decision possibilities, a mine is most appropriately regarded as a complex option on the resources contained in the mine. Just as a stock option gives the holder the right to acquire shares at a fixed exercise price, ownership of a mine confers the right to acquire the output of the mine at a fixed exercise price equal to the variable cost of production. Consequently, a mine may be valued by combining the valuation principles already presented with the option pricing approach pioneered by Black-Scholes (1973) and Merton (1973). The option pricing approach implies that the value of the mine satisfies a certain differential equation subject to a set of boundary conditions which we shall now consider.

The value of the mine will depend upon whether it is currently open and producing or closed and incurring maintenance costs. It will also depend upon the unexploited inventory remaining in the mine. And just as in the case of the fixed output mines already discussed, it will depend upon the current spot price of the commodity. Finally, the mine value will also depend upon an index of operating costs.

To be more specific, we will begin by defining the following symbols:

Q	the remaining mine inventory
S	the current spot price of the commodity
OC	an index of mine operating costs
$V(Q, S, OC)$	the current value of an operating mine
$N(Q, S, OC)$	the current value of a non-operating mine.

Then we have the following boundary conditions:

Mine Exhaustion: When the inventory in the mine is exhausted, the mine can no longer operate. In this case its value depends solely on the salvage value, which may be negative.

$N(Q, S, OC) = $ Salvage Value

Premature Abandonment: If output prices are sufficiently low, and the cost of maintaining a non-operating mine are sufficiently high, it may pay to abandon a mine even though there is a positive remaining inventory. The abandonment possibility places a floor under the value of the mine so that

$N(Q, S, OC) \geq $ Salvage Value

Operating Decisions: If the variable costs of operation are constant, and the mine has no influence on the price at which output can be sold, it will always be optimal either to operate the mine at its full capacity rate, q, or to shut it down temporarily. There will generally be costs involved with shutting the mine—redundancy payments and so on. However, the ability to shut down means that the value of an operating mine can never be less than the value of the mine shut less the costs of shutting:

$O(Q, S, OC) \geq N(Q, S, OC) - $ Shutting Costs.

Similarly, since a shut mine can always be re-opened at a cost, the value of a non-operating mine cannot be less than the value of an operating mine minus the costs of re-opening, so that

$N(Q, S, OC) \geq O(Q, S, OC) - $ Re-opening Costs.

Cash Flows: When the mine is operating it generates a cash flow which is given by

$$q(S(1 - r) - A(OC))(1 - t_c) - t_r O$$

where q is the capacity output rate, r is a royalty rate which is charged on the value of output, $A(OC)$ is the average cash cost of production at the capacity output, t_c is the corporate tax rate, and t_r is the real estate tax rate, which is assumed to be charged on the value of the mine, O. When the mine is shut the cash flow is given by the negative of the maintenance costs and real estate taxes.

Given these conditions the equation for the mine value may be solved simply on a personal computer. The nature of the solution is illustrated in figure 8.1, which plots the mine value as a function of the spot price for a given level of mine inventory, Q, and level of operating costs, OC. To understand this figure suppose that the mine is initially shut and that the spot price is between S_1 and S_2. As the spot price rises, the value of the operating mine begins to exceed the value of the mine shut, but may not be enough to justify incurring the costs of opening the mine. It is not optimal to open the mine until the spot price reaches S_2, at which point the value of the mine in operation exceeds its value shut by just the amount of the opening costs. Once opened, the mine will remain in operation even if the spot price drops. It will not be optimal to shut the mine unless the price drops to S_1, at which point the value of the shut mine exceeds the value of the operating mine by the amount of the shutting costs. If the salvage value of the mine is zero, it will not be optimal to actually cease maintenance and abandon the mine until the spot price falls to S_0.

Valuing a Gold Mine

To gain some further insight into our valuation procedure and the data inputs required to implement it, we shall consider a specific numerical example. The data for our hypothetical gold mine are presented in table 8.1. It is instructive to compare the data required here with those required for a classical discounting analysis. First, we do not require any projections for the price of gold or specification of a "cost of capital" for the mine. We require instead that the convenience yield of gold be specified.[7] Additional data required by this approach, but not by the classical discounting approach, are the standard deviation or risk of the gold price per unit time,[8] the maintenance costs for a shut mine, the costs of opening and shutting the mine and the salvage value. The reason these data are not required for a classical discounting is that the options of shutdown or abandonment are never explicitly included in this type of analysis.

Table 8.2 shows the value of the mine when it has a 20-year inventory of production for different gold prices.[9] Note that the value of the mine depends upon whether it is currently open and operating or shut-down. If the mine is currently operating it is

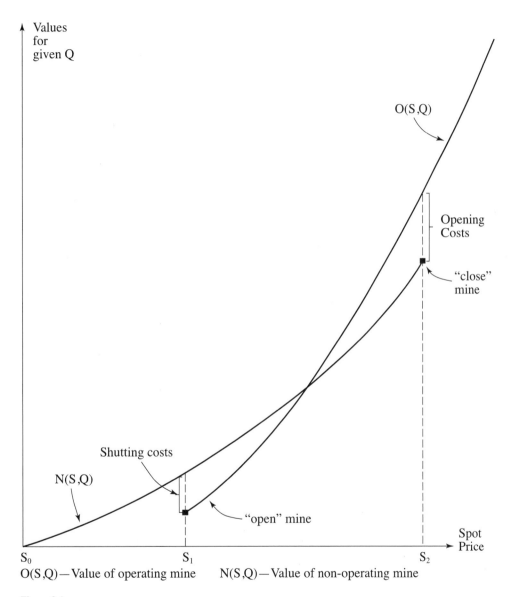

Figure 8.1
The value of a mine in terms of the current spot price of the commodity

Table 8.1
Data for a hypothetical gold mine

Mine	Gold
Capacity output rate: 50 thousand ounces per year	Convenience yield: 0% per year
Current mine inventory: 1 million ounces	Price risk: 20% per year
Average production costs (current prices): $250 per ounce	**Taxes**
Opening cost (current prices): $1 m	Real estate: 2% per year
Shutting cost (current prices): $1 m	Income: 48%
Annual maintenance cost (current prices): $1 m per year	Royalty: 2%
Salvage value: —0—	**Interest rate:** 9% per year
Cost inflation rate: 9% per year	

Table 8.2
Value of gold mine for different gold prices

Gold price $/ounce	Mine value ($m)			Value of[1] options ($m)	Risk[2] % per year
	Open		Shut		
100	—0—		—0—	—	—
150	1.08	—	2.08	—	154
200	8.65	—	9.65	—	82
250	20.02		20.85	24.36	68
300	34.86		34.78	17.22	57
350	51.82		50.96	9.75	49
400	70.04		69.04	9.29	43
450	89.05	—	88.05	7.73	40
500	108.58	—	107.58	6.51	37
550	128.47	—	127.47	5.57	35
600	148.60	—	147.60	4.81	33

— Indicates it is optimal to open mine if currently shut.
— Indicates it is optimal to shut mine if currently open.
1. Options to open/shut and to abandon.
2. Standard deviation of rate of return.

optimal to shut it down if the gold price falls below $230. Since the variable cost of production is $250, this implies that it is optimal to maintain production even when the mine is operating at a loss in order to avoid the costs of shutdown and possible subsequent reopening. On the other hand, if the mine is currently closed, it is not optimal to open it until the gold price has risen to $380, which is substantially above the variable costs of production.

The column "Value of options" represents the difference between the value of our hypothetical mine when it is open and in production, and the value of an otherwise identical mine which must be operated at full capacity until it is exhausted in 20

Table 8.3
Valuing the components of mine revenue

Gross revenue	$m. 322.5
Royalty	6.5
Net revenue	316.0
Operating cost	159.0
Taxable income	157.0
Corporate tax	75.4
After tax cash flow	81.6
Opening costs	.3
Shutdown costs	.7
Maintenance costs	6.9
Salvage value	—
Real estate tax	21.9
Net cash flow	51.8
Current gold price: $350 per ounce	

years. This comparison is of interest because the assumption of continuous production is implicit in the classical discounting approach. It is clear that the value of the options to shut the mine and subsequently re-open it, or even to abandon it, is a very substantial fraction of the total value of the mine, particularly when the gold price is in the neighborhood of the variable cost of production. Valuation approaches which ignore these operating options are likely to under-estimate substantially the value of the mine.

The final column of the table shows how the risk of the mine varies with the price of gold: when the price is low, the operating leverage is high. As the price rises the operating leverage declines and the risk of the mine falls until for very high gold prices it approaches the price risk of gold itself, 20 percent.

While table 8.2 shows the value of the complete mine for a range of gold prices, table 8.3 shows how, given a particular current gold price of $350, the present values of the different elements of the cash flow combine to yield the value of the mine. This type of analysis is likely to be particularly useful in evaluating cost-saving investments for a given mine. We can see immediately, for example, that a 10 percent saving in operating cost will have a pre-tax present value of $15.9 m and an after-tax present value of $15.9 m $\times$ (1 − .48) = $8.27 m.

The model also makes possible an analysis of the effects of alternative tax and royalty arrangements, taking into account the fact that these not only affect the shares of risk borne by the government and the owner of the mine, but also change the mine owner's optimal policy for operating the mine.

Conclusion

We have argued in this paper that traditional approaches to capital budgeting suffer from some severe limitations. These are particularly acute in the natural resource sector, where output prices are especially volatile. The problems include the forecasting of future output prices, the determination of an appropriate discount rate, and the inability to allow for management flexibility in future operating decisions. The alternative approach we have described largely overcomes these problems by using the hitherto neglected information contained in futures prices—the convenience yield—and by recognizing that a mine can be treated as a type of option on the underlying commodity.[10] The approach has already been applied with some success to the analysis of a large resource project in Canada.

While our focus here has been on natural resource projects where futures markets for the underlying commodity exist, the basic principles underlying the analysis lend themselves with appropriate modification to applications in other contexts in which the role of management in influencing future operations and cash flows is significant. This is the typical case, we believe, and while the traditional analysis views capital investments, like children, as hostages to fortune, our approach recognizes that, like children also, they are often amenable to their progenitors' guidance.

Notes

1. These may be far from trivial as recent experience with nuclear power plants reveal.

2. For an extractive industry even this may not be the case, for it may be better to leave the resource in the ground in the expectation of more favourable prices in the future.

3. Fuller and Kerr (1981) describe well the difficulties of arriving at a beta estimate even for a division of a corporation.

4. We are ignoring the technical distinctions between futures markets and forward markets.

5. More complex relations between the convenience yield and the spot price can also be taken into account.

6. A technical note: this approach is exact only for continuous compounding. In practice discrete compounding makes a negligible difference.

7. The futures/spot price relation for gold reveals a zero convenience yield.

8. In general the standard deviation of the rate of return on the commodity can be obtained from an historical time series of commodity prices. For those commodities, like gold, on which traded options exist, an implied standard deviation can also be obtained using an appropriate option pricing model [Black and Scholes (1973)].

9. Note that we have neglected the effects of depreciation allowances associated with the investment in the mine. The present value of tax savings due to these allowances should be added to the figures in the table.

10. For a more detailed description of this approach see Brennan and Schwartz (1985).

References

Black, F. and M. Scholes, "The Pricing of Options and Corporate Liabilities," *Journal of Political Economy* 81, 637–657, (1973).

Brennan, M. and E. Schwartz, "Evaluating Natural Resource Investments," *The Journal of Business*, 58, 2, 135–157 (1985).

Fuller, R. and H. Kerr, "Estimating the Divisional Cost of Capital: An Analysis of the Pure-Play Technique," *The Journal of Finance*, 36, 5 (December), 997–1009, (1981).

Merton, R., "Theory of Rational Option Pricing," *Bell Journal of Economics And Management Science* 4, 141–183, (1973).

9 Investment and Hysteresis

Avinash Dixit

The economic theory of investment under competitive conditions rests on the foundations of Marshall's analysis of long and short run equilibria. If price exceeds long run average cost, this induces existing firms to expand, and new ones to enter. If price falls below average variable cost, then firms suspend operations or even exit from the market.

Reality is very different. Firms invest in projects that they expect to yield a return in excess of a required or "hurdle" rate. Observers of business practice find that such hurdle rates are three or four times the cost of capital.[1] In other words, firms do not invest until price rises substantially above long run average cost. The hurdle rate appropriate for investment with systematic risk will exceed the riskless rate, but it seems hard to justify the large discrepancies observed. On the downside, firms stay in business for lengthy periods while absorbing operating losses, and price can fall substantially below average variable cost without inducing disinvestment or exit. Many U.S. farmers in the mid-1980s were in this situation.[2]

An example that combines upside and downside aspects is the very slow response of U.S. imports to the exchange rate. From 1980 to the end of 1984, the real value of the U.S. dollar increased by about 50 percent. The competitive advantage of foreign firms in the U.S. market rose dramatically. But import volume began its persistent rise only at the start of 1983: a lag far longer than the year or 18 months previously believed to be typical. In the first quarter of 1985 the dollar started to fall, and by the end of 1987 was almost back to its 1978 level. But import volume did not decrease for another two years; if anything it rose a little (Krugman and Baldwin, 1987, figures 1 and 2). Once established in the U.S. market, foreign firms were very slow to scale down or shut down their export operations when the exchange rate moved unfavorably.

Some recent developments in the theory of investment under uncertainty have offered an interesting new explanation of these phenomena. This new approach suggests that textbook pictures of the dynamics of a competitive industry need substantial redrawing. More generally, it says that a great deal of inertia is optimal when dynamic decisions are being made in an uncertain environment. It builds on an interesting analogy between real investments and options in financial markets. The main merit of this approach is that it brings many disparate phenomena into a common framework. Most intriguingly, it even sheds new light on some non-economic matters. In this article I shall give a brief outline of the new view, and discuss several of its applications.

Timing of Investment and the Value of Waiting

Three features are common to most investment decisions, and they combine to yield effects like those in the examples above. First, almost as a matter of definition, an investment entails some sunk cost, an expenditure that cannot be recouped if the action is reversed at a later date. Second, the economic environment has ongoing uncertainty, and information arrives gradually. Finally, an investment opportunity does not generally disappear if not taken immediately; the decision is not only whether to invest, but also when to invest. The qualitative implication is easily stated. When these three conditions are present, waiting has positive value. In the evolving environment, time brings more information about the future prospects of the project. As long as the opportunity to invest remains available, a later decision can be a better one. And because there are sunk costs, it does not always pay to take a less perfect action now and change it later.

Of course, the value of waiting must be set against the sacrifice of current profit. If current conditions become sufficiently favorable, one should eventually take the action that is optimal according to the current calculation, and not wait any longer. But the "trigger" level of currently expected profit that makes it optimal to proceed exceeds the Marshallian normal return. Similarly, waiting has value when contemplating disinvestment. The Marshallian criterion of failing to cover variable cost should not trigger abandonment; the correct point is a critical negative level of operating profit.

This view of investment under uncertainty can be summarized as "a theory of optimal inertia," or "a benevolent tyranny of the status quo." It says that firms that refuse to invest even when the currently available rates of return are far in excess of the cost of capital may be optimally waiting to be surer that this state of affairs is not transitory. Likewise, farmers who carry large losses may be rationally keeping their operation alive on the chance that the future may be brighter.

The verbal argument above is purely qualitative; it says that waiting has a positive value, but not whether this value is typically large enough to have a significant impact on investment and disinvestment decisions. In the subsequent sections I shall show in some illustrative calculations that the effect can be very large indeed, and therefore merits serious attention.

The Example of a Discrete Investment Project

My first illustrative example is the simplest, namely a single discrete investment project. Suppose the project can be launched by incurring a sunk cost K, and once launched, lasts forever. Let R denote its flow of net operating revenues per unit time.

This is where the uncertainty comes in. Future revenues are only imperfectly predictable from the current observation. The probability distribution of future net revenues is determined by the present, but the actual path remains uncertain. This probabilistic law of evolution of R can take many forms, but a particularly simple specification proves insightful as well as realistic for many applications. We suppose that each period, R can either increase or decrease by a fixed percentage. The probabilities of increase and decrease need not be equal, so there can be a positive or a negative trend to R. In other words, R follows a random walk, whose steps are of equal proportions, that is, they form a geometric series. If the time period for each step of R is very short, then the distribution of the logarithm of R_t at a future time t, given the initial R_0 at time 0, is approximately normal. Then, R is said to follow a proportional or geometric Brownian motion.

Many economic time-series—exchange rates, prices of natural resources, prices of common stocks, and others—can to a reasonable first approximation be described as geometric random walks or Brownian motions. That makes the assumption particularly natural for this illustrative example.[3] Thus, the discrete project might be an oil well, whose future revenues are random as the price of oil fluctuates. Or it may be a manufacturing plant whose output is exported, so the future revenues fluctuate with the exchange rate. Purely for expository simplicity, I shall suppose that the trend rate of growth of R is zero. This does not affect the qualitative results, and I shall mention how a non-zero trend affects the quantitative ones.[4]

The Effect of Waiting

Suppose the aim is to maximize the expected (in the statistical sense of the mean or probability-weighted average) present value of profits. Let future revenues be discounted at a positive rate $\rho > 0$, the opportunity cost of riskless capital specified exogenously. Then, given a current level R of revenues, the expected present value of the discounted future stream of perpetual revenues is R/ρ. Observe that by focusing on the expected value of profits, I am making an implicit assumption that the investor is risk-neutral. The purpose of this assumption is to show that the value of waiting has nothing to do with risk-aversion. It is rather an intertemporal trade-off of present risk vs. future risk.[5]

The textbook or Marshallian criterion would be to invest when the project has positive expected net worth (present value net of the sunk cost K), that is, when $R/\rho > K$. The borderline level M of the current revenue flow that would make one indifferent between investing and not investing is given by

$$M = \rho K. \tag{1}$$

The textbook recommends investment when the current revenue flow exceeds M; I shall call M the "Marshallian investment trigger."

But this criterion comes from thinking that the choice is between acting right now to get $R/\rho - K$, and not investing at all, which gets 0. What happens if the true menu of choices is wider, and waiting for a while and then reassessing the decision is also possible? Now at the Marshallian trigger, waiting is better than either investing right away or not investing at all. To see this, consider a particular alternative strategy: Wait for a fixed interval of time, and observe the value of R, say R_1, at its end. If $R_1 > M$ invest at once, otherwise never invest. (Of course, the alternative strategy is not itself optimal, but by showing it does better, we prove that the Marshallian criterion is not optimal when waiting is possible.) If the return at the end of the fixed waiting time exceeds the Marshallian trigger ($R_1 > M$), then the net worth of the investment must be positive at that time, and remains positive when discounted back to the starting time. If the expected return is less than the Marshallian trigger ($R_1 < M$), the net worth is zero because we do not invest. The probability-weighted average of a positive number and zero is of course positive. Therefore the proposed alternative strategy does better than either investing right away or not investing at all, each of which yields zero when the current revenue is exactly at the Marshallian trigger. By continuity, waiting remains better than investing for initial values of R slightly in excess of M.

The point is that waiting for a certain amount of time enables an investor to avoid the downside risk in revenues over that interval, while realizing the upside potential. This selective reduction in risk over time generates a positive value of waiting. On the other side, the cost of waiting is the sacrifice of the profit flow over the period of waiting. Therefore, if the current net revenue flow reaches a sufficiently high level, it won't pay to wait any longer. There is still a critical or trigger level, say H, such that investment is optimal when the current revenue exceeds it. But this H is larger than the Marshallian level M.

We can make the argument more precise, and explore what parameters determine the size of the difference between the optimal decision to wait and the Marshallian criterion for investment. As a first step, we see how the net worth of a project might be changed by a strategy of waiting until the expected revenue exceeds an exogenously given investment trigger H. This will furnish the tools for explaining how the investment trigger H itself should be optimally chosen.[6] Figure 9.1 illustrates the calculation.

The upward-sloping straight line labelled $i_1 i_2$ in figure 9.1 represents the value to be received from investing immediately; that is, $R/\rho - K$. If the return R is zero, then the project would lose K. Otherwise, the value of this function increases with slope $1/\rho$ as the return R increases.

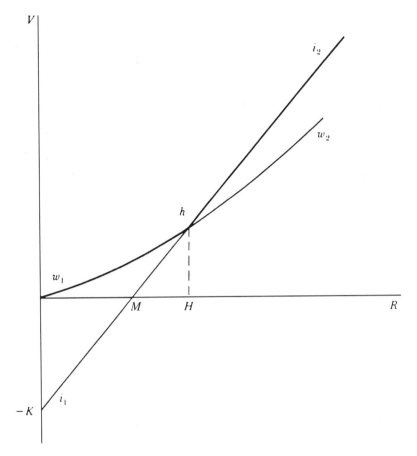

Figure 9.1
Values of waiting and investing

Now consider how the expected return from this project changes if the rule is applied that investment will occur only if the expected return R exceeds a trigger H. If the trigger is surpassed, then the investment project takes place, and the return is given by the thickly drawn portion of the line $i_1 i_2$ above the point h, where $R = H$. If the expected return is equal to the trigger, then the firm will be indifferent between waiting and investing immediately. If the expected return is less than the trigger, $R < H$, the rule tells us to wait. But there is a positive probability that at some future time R will climb above H and generate a positive net worth. Of course we rationally anticipate this possibility, so the net worth is positive even now. The value is merely the value of waiting, or that of the opportunity or "option" to invest at some future time.[7]

Calculation of this option value needs some mathematical reasoning, which I relegate to the Appendix. Here is some intuition for its general form. The option value should approach zero if the current R is very low, because then the event of R climbing to H is unlikely except in the far future, and the discounted present value of that is quite small. Successively higher current values of R should raise the value of waiting increasingly rapidly. For R close to H but just below it, the probability of reaching H in the very near future approaches one, and the option value approaches the net worth of a live project at H. The result is shown as the convex curve labelled w_1w_2 in figure 9.1, starting at the origin and meeting the straight line i_1i_2 at the point h. Only the thickly drawn portion w_1h to the left of H gives the value of waiting; beyond h investment takes place and the value of waiting is irrelevant.

The overall value of the opportunity to invest is then given by the thick curve w_1h and the thick line hi_2 taken together. The algebra of the Appendix gives the functional forms of these curves as

$$V(R) = \begin{cases} BR^\beta & \text{if } R \leq H \\ R/\rho - K & \text{if } R \geq H. \end{cases} \tag{2}$$

The upper formula is the value of waiting (the convex curve w_1w_2 of figure 9.1). The expression involves two constants, B and β, whose meaning will be explained soon. For now, just note that B is positive and β exceeds unity. The lower expression is the value of investing (the straight line i_1i_2 of figure 9.1). The thickly drawn portions correspond to the value of waiting or investing in its range of validity, and the light portions show the continuation of the separate parts into the irrelevant regions. At H there is indifference, so the two expressions are equal.

There are two new terms in the first expression, showing the value of waiting, that require explanation. The power β depends on the discount rate ρ, and on the volatility of the revenue, which is measured by the variance σ^2 of the logarithm of R per unit time. The Appendix shows that

$$\beta = \frac{1}{2}\left[1 + \sqrt{1 + \frac{8\rho}{\sigma^2}}\right] > 1. \tag{3}$$

B is a multiplicative constant. It is determined by the condition that the two expressions for net worth $V(R)$ must be equal when R equals H. Therefore $BH^\beta = H/\rho - K$. Or to rephrase in a formulation which will be useful presently,

$$H/\rho = K + BH^{\beta}. \tag{4}$$

The intuitive meaning of B will be explored more in the next section.

The Optimal Policy

In the previous example, the investment trigger H was exogenously given. Now consider how the trigger should optimally be chosen. If the trigger value H is increased slightly above its value in figure 9.1, that shifts the junction point h between the thickly drawn curve and line to the right. This can only be accomplished by raising the whole curve w_1w_2 representing the value of waiting. In equation (2), this corresponds to raising B in the upper formula.

To maximize value, such increase should be pushed as far as possible, that is, until the graph of the value of waiting—the curved line given by BR^{β}—becomes tangential to that of the straight-line return of investing immediately: $R/\rho - K$. Thus, the choice of an optimal trigger H is defined by the requirement that the graphs of the two formulas of the expression (2) should meet tangentially at H. This is called the "smooth pasting" condition.

Figure 9.2 shows the optimum H. The corresponding $V(R)$ function is drawn thicker, with the convex curve w_1h of the value of waiting to the left of H, and the straight line hi_2 of the net worth of the project to the right of that point. The Marshallian trigger M is where the value of investing just becomes positive, that is, where the straight line i_1i_2 crosses the horizontal axis. The optimum trigger H is obviously to the right of this.

The observant reader will have noted that the curve BR^{β} lies above the line $R/\rho - K$ to the right of H, and wondered if this means that investment is optimal only at the point H, and waiting again the preferred policy for higher values of R. The answer is no. The point is that the expression BR^{β} ceases to have a valid interpretation as the value of waiting when $R > H$. Otherwise it would create a pure speculative bubble; the value of waiting would be high because the prospect of reaching an even higher R would offer an even higher value of waiting, with no actual investment ever in sight. In the same way, increasing B even farther to lift the curve BR^{β} clean above the line $R/\rho - K$ is not a meaningful policy.

A sharper intuition into the relationship between the Marshallian and the optimal triggers for investment can be gleaned with some algebra. The smooth pasting condition equates the slopes of the value of waiting and the value of investing at the optimal trigger H. Therefore we differentiate each formula in (2) with respect to R, evaluate the derivatives at H, and equate the two expressions. This gives

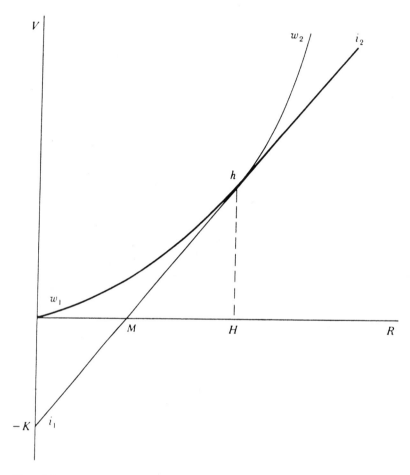

Figure 9.2
Optimal investment policy

$$\beta BH^{\beta-1} = 1/\rho. \tag{5}$$

Then use equations (4) and (5) to solve for H and eliminate B. We find that the optimal H is given by

$$H = \frac{\beta}{\beta - 1}\rho K. \tag{6}$$

Remember the Marshallian investment trigger M was to invest when $M = \rho K$. Therefore we have a very simple relation between the Marshallian and the optimal triggers: the latter is $\beta/(\beta - 1)$ times the former.

We can express the optimal trigger in a way that parallels the Marshallian formula even more closely. Define a new discount or hurdle rate ρ' that incorporates a correction for the value of waiting. Once this correction has been made, one can proceed in the Marshallian way; the project is worth undertaking when its net worth calculated using the corrected discount rate becomes positive. For this, we need $H = \rho' K$, or

$$\rho' = \frac{\beta}{\beta - 1}\rho. \tag{7}$$

This formulation will be applied in the next section to develop some estimates of the potential difference between the optimal and Marshallian triggers.

The reader should also be able to make greater intuitive sense of equation (4) at this point. Instead of correcting the discount rate for the value of waiting, we could correct the cost of investment. Immediate action has an opportunity cost, namely loss of the option to wait. This is valued at BR^β, and we must add it to the actual cost of investment K to get the full cost of immediate action. Then such action is justified when the benefit R/ρ exceeds this full cost. As (4) shows, this happens when the current revenue R reaches the trigger H.

Readers who happen to be familiar with elementary concepts of financial options—from theoretical study or their own practical investment experience—can sharpen their intuition by exploiting an analogy with financial options.[8] The opportunity to make a real investment is akin to an American call option—a right but not an obligation to buy a stock at a preset price called the strike price or exercise price. For the real investment project I am considering, the exercise price is the sunk cost K of the project. If the option is exercised, the firm acquires ownership of a stock that pays a dividend stream of expected present value R/ρ. The net worth, $R/\rho - K$, is called the "intrinsic value" of the option. But exercising the option at the instant its intrinsic value becomes positive is not optimal, because the option also has a value of waiting, called the "holding premium" or "time value." One should wait until the holding premium falls to zero. The "smooth pasting" condition that helps determine the optimal point of exercise has long been known in the theory of financial options. In fact, option pricing theory can claim credit for developing this condition that is now standard in the general theory of control of Brownian motion (Merton, 1973, fn. 60).[9]

The Importance of Option Values

Is the difference between the Marshallian trigger M and the optimal trigger H, or equivalently, the difference between the conventional discount rate ρ and the modified discount rate ρ', quantitatively so large that economists should alter our orthodox views on investment and rewrite our textbooks? Of course, the answer depends on the parameters. If the uncertainty is low, there can be only little value in waiting. If the uncertainty is high, on the other hand, setting a high trigger before taking action may avoid some very bad outcomes. If the discount rate is low, the future is valued relatively more and options that help avoid bad future outcomes become more valuable. Here are some sample calculations to show that for plausible parameter values the effect can be very large indeed.

For export projects whose revenues fluctuate with exchange rates, a coefficient of variation of 10 percent over one year fits the recent experience of exchange rate volatility (Frankel and Meese, 1987). If the project is an oil well or a copper mine, a much higher figure of 25 to 40 percent per year is closer to the experience of fluctuations in the prices of these resources (Brennan and Schwartz, 1985). Therefore, let us use a value in this range, say $\sigma = 0.2$, as a base case. Suppose the discount rate is 5 percent per year. Then we find $\beta = 2.15$, and the multiple $\beta/(\beta - 1)$ equals 1.86. Thus current revenues have to rise to nearly double the level that ensures a positive net worth before waiting ceases to be optimal. Using the alternative method of adjusting the discount rate, we find $\rho' = 9.3$ percent, which is quite a big correction to $\rho = 5$ percent.

For a more general sense of how the underlying parameters affect β and ρ', note from the definition of β given earlier in equation (3) that a lower discount rate ρ or a higher standard deviation σ of the revenues yield a lower β. In turn, a smaller β means a larger factor $\beta/(\beta - 1)$, and therefore the longer it is optimal to wait.

It is intuitively evident that when the future is less heavily discounted, the value of waiting for more information goes up. As an example, if in the above calculation we reduce ρ to 2 percent, which is closer to historic riskless real rates of interest, then β drops to 1.62, and the multiple $\beta/(\beta - 1)$ rises to 2.61. It is equally intuitive that greater uncertainty means a higher value of waiting. If in the numerical example we raise σ to 0.4 (while keeping ρ at 5 percent), then $\beta = 1.43$, $\rho' = 16.6$ percent and H is 3.32 times M.

Two limiting cases are worth mention. If the future is very heavily discounted (ρ large) or very certain (σ small), then β goes to infinity and $\beta/(\beta - 1)$ goes to 1. Option values becomes unimportant in this limit and the Marshallian criterion applies. In the opposite extreme, as ρ goes to 0 or σ goes to infinity, β goes to 1 and $\beta/(\beta - 1)$ goes to infinity; Marshallian analysis becomes totally misleading.[10]

To sum up, even when the cost of capital is as low as 5 percent per year, the value of waiting can quite easily lead to adjusted hurdle rates of 10 to 15 percent. Summers' (1987) finding of median hurdle rates of 15 percent is no longer a puzzle.

Extensions and Qualifications

The above example of a discrete investment project was deliberately oversimplified to highlight the value of waiting. In practical applications, of course, various complications and countervailing considerations must be recognized. Here I shall briefly outline some important matters of this kind.

The example can readily be generalized in many respects, and the essential lesson of the importance of the value of waiting survives unscathed. We can allow the scale of the initial investment to be a matter of choice, introduce some cost to varying this scale, and also allow a choice of the level of operation at each instant by varying labor or other inputs. If the net revenues can sometimes become negative, we can allow temporary suspension or abandonment. This last extension raises some interesting new issues, and is considered in the next section.

The assumption that net revenues follow a Brownian motion embodies a restriction: uncertainty is roughly symmetric around the trend. In practice, distributions of future outcomes are sometimes quite lopsided. Therefore, we should know what they do to investment decisions.

Bernanke (1983) found the answer and called it the *bad news principle*: "of possible future outcomes, only the unfavorable ones have a bearing on the current propensity to undertake a given project." In other words, the downside risk is the primary force governing optimal investment decisions when waiting is possible. To be more precise, the total upside probability matters, but not the shape of the distribution of revenues to the right of the optimal trigger. The technical proof of this is in an additional Appendix available from the author. But the intuition is not difficult. Remember that when we decide whether to proceed or to wait a little more, what is at stake is not the uncertainty per se, but how it will resolve in the next small amount of time; that is, the tradeoff between current and future risks. Most of the upside potential remains whether action occurs right away, or after a small delay. The possibility of a downturn, and the ability to avoid an action that could thereby prove to be a mistake, is what makes waiting valuable. That is why the downside risk matters most when deciding whether to wait.

Let us turn to some other issues that were left out of the model. In the simple example, waiting had a positive value because it allowed further observations of the revenue fluctuations. More generally, the point is that the passage of time reveals more information. In reality there are other forces that also bear on the issue of whether to wait.

First, there may be a race to seize a scarce opportunity. In the simple example, the opportunity to invest was assigned to just one firm. But if it is available to any of several firms, then waiting is no longer feasible. The option to wait will expire because some competitor will seize the opportunity. Then some firm will invest as soon as the expected present value crosses zero, and the Marshallian trigger will be valid.

But when there are several firms, a more interesting scenario is that more than one firm can invest. When they do so, industry supply increases and price falls along the demand curve. This, or the expectation of such price fall, places a limit on the equilibrium investment. In other words, we have a competitive industry in a dynamic environment. This is the natural setting in which to explore the validity of the Marshallian story of entry at long run average cost and exit at short run variable cost. I consider this in the later section titled "Competitive Industry Dynamics." The outcome of the correct melding of each firm's choice of waiting or investing into a dynamic equilibrium process turns out to be quite far from the Marshallian picture.

Second, there are strategic situations where making the first move has a commitment value. The role of investment in altering the outcome of a Cournot oligopoly is well known; see Dixit (1980), and a richer dynamic version in Fudenberg and Tirole (1983). In practice, strategic considerations may call for early investment at the same time that information aspects suggest waiting; the optimal choice then has to balance the two.

Finally, when there are several firms, their information may differ. Then each firm has to consider how it can infer other firms' information from their actions, and in turn how its information may leak to others through its actions. For example, suppose each firm independently evaluates the prospects of a project, and the evaluation is subject to error. If one firm observes that no other firm has invested, it infers that their evaluations were insufficiently favorable, and adjusts its own evaluation downward. When all firms do this, they may all decide to wait. Conversely, once one firm invests, others conclude that its evaluation must have been very strongly favorable, and adjust their own judgments upward. Therefore the first firm may quickly be followed by others, resulting in a bunching of investment. For discussions of such matters, see Stiglitz (1989) and Leahy (1990, Chapter 3).

Abandonment and Hysteresis

In the simple example of the previous section, the net revenue flow from the project was always positive; therefore, there was no reason to suspend or abandon a project once it was launched. In reality, we see firms suffering operating losses. To capture this, let R now be *gross* revenue, and introduce a flow cost C of operation. Let R follow a geometric Brownian motion. For simplicity of exposition, suppose R has zero trend, and that C is constant. This does not alter the qualitative results; the former assumption is relaxed in the Appendix.

If temporary suspension of operation is possible, this will be done whenever R falls below C. This looks like the textbook Marshallian theory: disinvestment should take place when operating losses are being made. But suspension is not disinvestment. Most typically, if a firm ceases operation, it cannot restart at will without incurring some further cost. It is as if the machinery rusts when unused. To highlight this feature, I shall suppose that rusting is total and immediate. Then, suspension is the same as outright abandonment. If one ever wants to restart in the future, the whole sunk cost K must be incurred over again.[11]

The possibility of waiting now influences the decision to abandon, just as it affected the decision to invest. The gross revenue R has to fall some way below the operating cost C before abandonment becomes optimal. The intuition is similar to that for investment. The investor is willing to tolerate some operating loss to keep alive the option of future profitable operation should R turn upward. Only when the current loss exceeds the value of the option does it pay to abandon. Let L be the critical low value of revenue that just triggers abandonment when option value is taken into account properly. Then our intuitive reasoning says that L must be less than C.

The expected present value of operating profits when the current revenue flow is R equals $(R - C)/\rho$. The Marshallian investment criterion would tell the firm to go ahead when this exceeds K, that is, when current revenue exceeds the trigger level $M = C + \rho K$. The right-hand side is just Marshall's long run cost, being the sum of the variable cost and the interest on the sunk cost. When the option value of waiting to invest is recognized, the trigger H is higher. Thus we have the chain of inequalities

$$L < C < C + \rho K < H. \tag{8}$$

In the earlier simple example, we could explicitly show the solution for the investment trigger H. But here, L and H are determined by a more complicated system of nonlinear equations that does not permit a closed-form solution. The derivation of this system is sketched in the Appendix; more details are in Dixit (1989b). Here I shall merely mention some numerical results.

First, let us estimate the quantitative significance of the option values. Let $\rho = 0.05$ and $\sigma = 0.2$ as in the base case of the previous section. Choose units of account so that $C = 1$, and suppose that $K = 2$. Then the normal return to capital or the interest on sunk costs is $\rho K = 0.1$. The long run average cost, or the Marshallian investment trigger, is $M = 1.1$. With these values we find $L = 0.72$ and $H = 1.62$. At the truly optimal entry trigger H, the operating profit is 0.62, which is more than six times the normal return to capital. At the exit trigger L, losses equal to nearly a third of variable costs are being sustained. Once again the departure from Marshallian theory is very dramatic for quite plausible values of the parameters. Dixit (1989b) considers a wide range of parameter values and finds similar results.

It is important to recognize that the triggers L and H are jointly determined by all the parameters of the problem. An increase in the sunk cost K will obviously raise the investment trigger H. But it will also lower the abandonment trigger L; the project will be continued through periods of greater losses for the option of keeping alive the larger sunk stake. Conversely, if abandonment is costly—for example, severance payments to workers or the cost of restoring the site of a mine—then the entry trigger is higher; firms are more cautious in undertaking a venture they may have to abandon later at a cost.

Optimal Inertia

Sunk costs alone will produce a zone of inaction between the two Marshallian triggers of the variable cost C and the total cost $M = C + \rho K$. If the current revenue flow is between these levels, then the optimal policy is to maintain the status quo. The project is not launched, but if already active, is not canceled.

But with uncertainty, the zone of inaction that takes option values into account is wider, expanding to between the triggers L and H. The numerical calculations show how big the gap can be. In the example just above, the Marshallian range of inertia extends from 1 to 1.1, while the optimal range goes from 0.72 to 1.62, which is quite a dramatic difference. Other plausible values of the parameters ρ, σ and so on have equally substantial effects. Dynamic economic choices should exhibit much greater inertia when there is uncertainty.

This has potentially important implications for macroeconomics. Small nominal or real frictions can produce even larger rigidities than those suggested by models that ignore evolving information, for example the "menu cost" models of Mankiw (1985) and Akerlof and Yellen (1985) or the "portfolio" model of Greenwald and Stiglitz (1989).

The implications for labor markets are also potentially dramatic. Tangible costs of hiring and firing workers are significant in almost all occupations, and quite large in some countries. If wages are sticky, then the response of employment to output demand fluctuations will be slower when employers, recognizing the option value of the status quo, hoard labor in downturns, and are slow to hire in upturns. Alternatively, very large wage fluctuations will be needed to maintain classical full employment.

If wages are sticky and employment responds slowly, the marginal product of labor may go quite some way above the wage without any hiring taking place, and below it without any firing (Bentolila and Bertola, 1990). Contrary to conventional theory, the wage in any occupation is not constantly equated to opportunity cost of labor. Economists usually dismiss the popular concern about a "loss of jobs" by invoking just such an equation: the person out of a job only ceases to earn in this occupation just about what he or she could have earned elsewhere. The view presented here suggests that the popular concern may have more justification.

Hysteresis

Picture a particular path of the stochastic evolution of net revenues through time. Let the numerical values be as above. Suppose the initial R equals 1, and it starts to rise. It crosses the Marshallian trigger of 1.1, but no investment takes place. Finally it rises above 1.62, and the project is launched. Then the revenue starts to fall, and comes back all the way down to 1. But this does not justify abandonment. The driving force behind the investment decision, namely the currently observed revenue, has been restored to its initial level. But its meandering along the way has left its mark, namely an active project where there was none before.

Similar effects have long been known in physics and other sciences. The closest for our purpose comes from electromagnetism. Take an iron bar and loop an insulated wire around it. Pass an electric current through the wire; the iron will become magnetized. Now switch the current off. The magnetism is not completely lost; some residual effect remains. The cause (the current) was temporary, but left some lasting effect (the magnetized bar). This phenomenon is called hysteresis, and by analogy the failure of investment decisions to reverse themselves when the underlying causes are fully reversed can be called economic hysteresis.

If some electric current is passed through the wire in the opposite direction, the residual magnetism will be lost. With a strong enough opposing current, magnetism will be induced in the reverse direction. Similarly, if our project's current revenue falls even more, it will eventually be abandoned. Then a subsequent rise back to 1 in revenues will not restore the project; there is hysteresis in the reverse direction, too.

Sunk costs alone can cause hysteresis in textbook Marshallian analysis, as R moves in and out of the Marshallian zone of inaction between variable and total costs. But if such fluctuations are occurring, it behooves us to let the firm have rational expectations about its stochastic environment. When that is done, the uncertainty magnifies the effect quite dramatically; very large changes in R in the opposite direction are needed to reverse the effects of a temporary move in either direction.

In this light, the slowness of the U.S. imports to respond to the dollar appreciation of the early 1980s, and the even greater slowness to improve despite the subsequent fall back to the 1980 level, become quite understandable and even intuitive. Krugman (1989, Chapter 2) and Dixit (1989a) discuss this case in greater detail.

U.S. vs. Japan

Observers of America's relative decline in manufacturing—for example, Dertouzos et al. (1990, pp. 61–65)—attribute part of the problem to the dominance of short-term thinking among U.S. managers, which causes them to apply high "hurdle" rates when considering investment decisions. The explanations given for this short-term emphasis include fear of hostile takeovers, high mobility of managers, and various kinds of uncertainty including that in the government's taxation, regulation, and trade policies. Our analysis of the effect of option values on investment suggests that uncertainty is even more important than previously realized. It can explain much or even all of the gap between typical hurdle rates and the cost of capital. The high rates might actually be optimal responses to uncertainty.

But the explanation is inadequate as it stands. The option value effect raises the optimal entry point, but by the same token it lowers the optimal exit point. If American firms are more hesitant to invest or enter new ventures because of uncertainty, they should be more ready to ride out bad periods. But the same observers find exactly the opposite tendency. In many sectors including color TVs, VCRs, and semiconductors, American firms have abandoned the field after short periods of losses, while Japanese firms hang in there (Dertouzos et al., 1990, especially Industry Studies C and F).

A common explanation of Japanese firms' willingness to absorb losses is the life-time employment system. This makes labor a quasi-fixed factor, and reduces the variable component of cost. Conventional theory points out that lower variable costs mean that revenues must fall farther to cause abandonment. But by the same token, these larger sunk costs of Japanese firms should make them more reluctant investors! Reality is the opposite; they are particularly aggressive investors.

A better explanation may be found in Bernanke's bad news principle. Suppose the uncertainty facing Japanese firms is more lopsided; they are protected from the downside risk because the government supports them in various ways, including cartelization to avoid destructive competition in recessions. Then the value of waiting to invest, which is governed mainly by the downside risk, is quite small, and they invest more aggressively. For disinvestment, of course, the argument turns around and becomes the good news principle. The option value of keeping the operation alive is governed primarily by the upside potential, which is relatively more important for Japanese firms, and induces them to ride out bad periods that would drive American firms into dissolution.

This analysis is not intended to be comprehensive, but it does allow some conditional statements on policy. If the aim is to induce quicker new investment or entry of firms, it is especially important to reduce the downside risk. If the aim is to prevent disinvestment or exit, it is especially important to improve the upside potential.

Competitive Industry Dynamics

The analysis so far has dealt with a single project or a single firm, taking its revenues as exogenously determined. Now consider what happens to an industry populated by many active price-taking firms, and identical potential entrants. Each takes the price as evolving exogenously over time, albeit with some uncertainty. But the actions of all of them in turn determine the price path. What will be the overall equilibrium of this process?

Consider a simple structure that serves to bring out the essential points. The source of the uncertainty must now be something exogenous to all the firms; I shall suppose this to be a demand shock. Specifically, suppose an inverse demand curve for the industry, expressing price P as a function of quantity Q and the shock to demand X; assume this takes the algebraic form $P = XD(Q)$. Each firm has a very Marshallian technology. It becomes active by making an initial sunk investment of K. While active, it has a standard rising short run marginal cost curve that becomes its supply curve. Temporary suspension of operations is again assumed away. The industry supply curve at an instant is found by the usual horizontal summation of the supply curves of all active firms. Write C for the minimum short run average variable cost and M for the minimum long run average cost.

Figure 9.3 enables us to trace out the dynamics of the industry. Suppose the firms that are originally active generate the industry supply curve S_1. Fluctuations in the demand shock variable X will induce movements along S_1, leading to fluctuations in

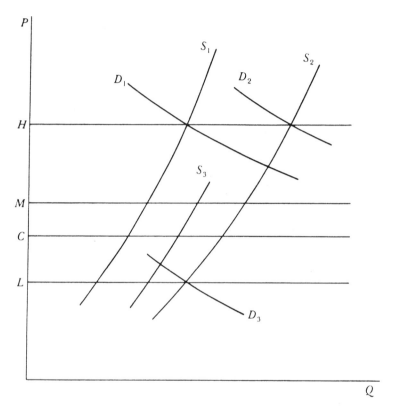

Figure 9.3
Competitive industry dynamics

the price P. Suppose new entry is triggered when the price rises to the critical level H.
Along S_1, this happens when demand rises to the position D_1. When some new firms
enter, the supply curve shifts to the right; let S_2 be its new position. The price falls
along the demand curve D_1. Thereafter, new demand shocks will cause movements
along S_2, until either the critical high price H is reached again, triggering more entry,
or a critical low price L is reached, triggering some exit. In the figure, the former
occurs if the demand curve rises to the position D_2, and the latter if the demand curve
falls to the position D_3. For the whole range of demand curves between these
extremes, the number of firms stays unchanged and the price and quantity fluctuate
with the shocks to demand. If demand hits the upper limit, further entry shifts the
supply curve to the right of S_2; if it hits the lower limit, the supply curve shifts to the
left to a position like S_3. The process then goes on.[12]

Consider the picture from the perspective of a potential firm. It knows that new entry will prevent the price from ever rising above H, exit will stop it from falling below L, and within this range the price will fluctuate as demand shocks evolve. Given this price process, it must choose its own entry and exit strategies, which will consist of an entry trigger H' and an exit trigger L'. For the industry's equilibrium with rational expectations and identical firms, the entry and exit triggers chosen by each firm should be the same as the ceiling and floor on the price process that each assumes in arriving at its optimal decision. That is, $H' = H$ and $L' = L$.

Determining such an equilibrium requires some mathematics (Lippman and Rumelt, 1985; Edleson and Osband, 1989; Leahy, 1990; Dixit, 1991b). But one important general property is easy to see: the entry trigger will allow supernormal profit, and the exit trigger will allow some operating losses. The reason is evident when we consider the net worth of a firm contemplating entry or exit. Suppose, contrary to the above assertion, that the equilibrium ceiling price coincides with the Marshallian long run average cost M. Now, each firm knows that new entry will prevent the price from ever rising above this level, but adverse demand shocks can drive the price below M from time to time. Then each firm expects that the operating profit will never be more than normal, but can be less at times. Therefore the expected average return to capital must be below normal, and net worth must be negative. Firms will not enter under such circumstances. The investment trigger H must exceed the long run average cost, to give firms the prospect of periods of supernormal returns mixed with periods of subnormal ones. The equilibrium level of H must be such as to ensure exactly normal average return, or zero net worth, for a potential investor.

Similarly, if the equilibrium floor price were the Marshallian average variable cost C, then firms at this point would see non-negative operating profit at all future dates, and positive at some dates. This does not call for exit. The equilibrium trigger for exit L must be sufficiently below C to make the consequences of staying in, namely operating losses for some periods and profits for other periods, average out to exactly zero net worth, and make each firm indifferent between staying and leaving.

The ranking of L, C, M and H in the industry's equilibrium is the same as the earlier ranking (8) when there was just one monopoly firm. Therefore we should explore the connection between the above reasoning based on zero net worth, and the earlier analysis based on the value of waiting. When the entry of new firms places a ceiling at H on the price, this cuts off each firm's upside profit potential. That reduces the value of investing and waiting alike. In equilibrium, the reductions are such that the pure waiting value for each firm is zero, as it should be when there is a potential infinity of identical entrants and no firm has any scarce privilege. Likewise, the floor

L cuts off the downside risk, and raises the value of exiting and staying alike. In fact, when the demand shock follows a geometric Brownian motion, the changes in the values of investing and waiting are equal, and each firm's entry and exit triggers L and H are exactly the same as they would have been if it were the only firm in the market, and therefore not subject to the ceilings and floors that result from other firms' entry and exit (Leahy, 1991).

Therefore we can take the previous numerical calculations for individual firms and apply them to the industry equilibrium. We see that the no-entry-no-exit range of prices in a competitive industry is likely to be quite wide. Remember that in our base case, the Marshallian range of inaction extended from 1 to 1.1, and the one that accounts for option values went from 0.72 to 1.62. Therefore we are likely to see significant periods of supernormal profits with no new entry, and of operating losses without exit, in the course of a competitive industry's equilibrium evolution.

This picture calls for a very fundamental rethinking, particularly in the matter of regulation and other industry policies. It is most important to regard the equilibrium of an industry as an organic process over time. Drawing inferences from snapshots at particular instants can be seriously misleading.

Suppose we observe such an industry at an instant when the price is between the Marshallian long run average cost M and the entry trigger H. We see established firms making supernormal profits, but no new entry taking place. Given our training in conventional microeconomics or industrial organization theory, we suspect the presence of monopoly power or entry barriers. We might be inclined to suggest anti-trust action. But we would be wrong; the process viewed as a whole is fully competitive, and long run expected returns are normal.

Likewise, if the price is below the minimum average variable cost, that need not signal predatory dumping by the firms that are making the losses. They may merely and rationally be riding out the bad period to keep their sunk capital alive.

Only be observing the evolution of the industry for a long time can we spot genuine departures from the competitive norm. Basing policies on snapshots can result in harm despite the policy-maker's best intentions. In the picture above, temporary large profits are merely due to the swings of demand in a competitive industry that permits only normal profit as a long run average. If the government tries to reduce these supernormal returns using antitrust action or price-ceilings, this merely depresses new entry to suboptimal levels. The resultant reduction of supply can actually raise the long run average price; see Dixit (1991c). Similarly, if the government pursues policies to support firms in bad periods, firms will anticipate this, leading to additional entry, which will aggravate the losses when bad times arrive.

Non-Economic Applications

Many personal, social, and political decisions that are not narrowly economic share the features of investment: they are costly to reverse, they must be made in an uncertain environment, and their timing is a matter of choice. Therefore option values and optimal inertia are significant for them, too. Quantification is a lot harder, but useful qualitative lessons can be drawn. I share the economist's usual temptation to indulge in amateur sociology, and will offer two quick examples.

The first is a dramatic example of the value of waiting. Hamermesh and Soss (1974) offer a Beckerian model of suicide. This involves comparing the expected utility of the rest of one's life and a suitable standard of zero. Far from being an excessively rational model, this is not rational enough, because it leaves out the option value of staying alive. We have seen that exit decisions are governed by Bernanke's good news principle: the prospect of an upturn is the primary determinant of the option value. As Micawber said in *David Copperfield*, "something will be turning up."

The second example shows how other considerations may offset the value of waiting. Once upon a time in New York City, there lived an Assistant Professor of Finance. He and his "spouse-equivalent" had separate rent-controlled apartments. Their relationship progressed to a point when the woman suggested that they should keep one of the apartments and give up the other. He explained to her the importance of keeping options alive: it was unlikely that they would split up, but given a positive probability, and so on. She took this very badly and ended the relationship.

Financial economists who hear this story say that it just proves how right the man was about option values. But the economics of information offers a more convincing explanation. The man misunderstood the situation. This was not a decision problem under uncertainty, but a signalling game. The woman was unsure how highly he valued her, and it was precisely his willingness to undertake the costly irreversible action of giving up the apartment that had value as a signal.[13] The man overlooked this, tried to sit on the fence, and fell flat on his face.

Further Reading

For readers whose appetite is whetted by this sampling of new ideas on investment under uncertainty and their applications, the next stop should be Pindyck (1991). He gives a full survey of the literature, to which readers can then turn for even more details. Pindyck also develops the analogy with financial options particularly thoroughly.

Readers sufficiently intrigued to attempt their own research in this area must make a little investment in techniques. I hope they have learned the basic lesson of the story, and will be duly cautious in making this decision. For those who decide to go ahead, Dixit (1991a) provides a relatively gentle introduction aimed at economists, and gives references to rigorous but harder mathematical treatises.

Acknowledgment

I am very grateful to the editors—Carl Shapiro, Joseph Stiglitz, and Timothy Taylor —for their excellent suggestions to improve the exposition. I also thank Ben Bernanke, Alan Blinder, Gene Grossman, James Hines, Eric Rasmusen, Lars Svensson, Timothy Taylor, and Christopher Williams for comments on earlier drafts, and the National Science Foundation for financial support under Grant No. SES-8803300.

Appendix: Value of Waiting

Here I derive the expression for the value of waiting. I shall allow the net revenue R to have a non-zero trend growth rate μ. The proportional variance per unit time is σ^2. Consider the opportunity to invest as an asset that is held for a small interval of time dt while R stays below H. It pays no dividend, but its value $V(R)$ changes with R, so it may make a capital gain or loss. The change dR in R over this interval is random, with mean and variance

$$\mathrm{E}[dR] = \mu R\, dt, \quad \mathrm{Var}[dR] = \sigma^2 R^2\, dt.$$

Then

$$\mathrm{E}[dR^2] = (E[dR])^2 + \mathrm{Var}[dR] = \mu^2 R^2\, dt^2 + \sigma^2 R^2\, dt.$$

Therefore the expected capital gain is

$$\mathrm{E}[dV] = V'(R)\mathrm{E}[dR] + \tfrac{1}{2}V''(R)\mathrm{E}[dR^2]$$

$$= V'(R)\mu R\, dt + \tfrac{1}{2}V''(R)[\mu^2 R^2\, dt^2 + \sigma^2 R^2\, dt].$$

In equilibrium, this should equal the normal return $\rho V\, dt$. Writing this equation, dividing by dt, and letting dt go to zero, we get the differential equation

$$\tfrac{1}{2}\sigma^2 R^2 V''(R) + \mu R V'(R) - \rho V(R) = 0. \tag{A.1}$$

This is a simple equation of the Cauchy–Euler type. Try a solution of the form $V(R) = R^x$. By substituting in (A.1), x must satisfy the associated quadratic equation

$$\tfrac{1}{2}\sigma^2 x(x-1) + \mu x - \rho = 0. \tag{A.2}$$

The left-hand side of (A.2) is negative at $x = 0$ when $\rho > 0$. It is also negative when $x = 1$ provided $\rho > \mu$, which we assume to ensure convergence of the expected discounted present value of the revenues. Then one root of (A.2) is negative, and the other exceeds 1. Call them α and β respectively. Then the general solution of (A.1) is

$$V(R) = AR^\alpha + BR^\beta, \tag{A.3}$$

where A and B are constants to be determined.

The value of waiting should go to zero as R goes to zero. Since α is negative, we see from (A.3) that we must have $A = 0$. That leaves $V(R) = BR^\beta$, which is just the expression in equation (2) of the text.

In the text I assumed $\mu = 0$. Then (A.2) becomes

$$x(x-1) = 2\rho/\sigma^2, \quad \text{or} \quad (x - \tfrac{1}{2})^2 = [1 + 8\rho/\sigma^2]/4.$$

This immediately gives equation (4) of the text for β.

Adjusted Discount Rates

When $\mu \neq 0$, the future revenue stream is expected to grow at rate μ and is discounted back at rate ρ, so its expected present value is $R/(\rho - \mu)$. The net worth of investing is $R/(\rho - \mu) - K$. The Marshallian trigger is $M = (\rho - \mu)K$. Otherwise the calculation proceeds as in the text, and the optimal trigger H is still $\beta/(\beta - 1)$ times M. Therefore the adjusted discount rate ρ' is defined by

$$\rho' - \mu = \frac{\beta}{\beta - 1}(\rho - \mu).$$

Investment and Abandonment

Here it proves convenient to label the value of waiting and the value of a live project separately as functions of R; call them $V_0(R)$ and $V_1(R)$ separately.

The value of waiting still satisfies the same equality of capital gain and normal return, leading to

$$V_0(R) = B_0 R^\beta, \tag{A.4}$$

where the constant B_0 is to be determined. The value of an active project now includes the value of the option to abandon. To find it, follow the same steps as above, but note that the asset now pays a dividend, namely the revenue flow R. The normal return $\rho V_1(R)\,dt$ should now equal the sum of the dividend $R\,dt$ and the expected capital gain $E[dV_1]$. This leads to the differential equation

$$\tfrac{1}{2}\sigma^2 R^2 V_1''(R) + \mu R V_1'(R) - \rho V_1(R) + R = 0. \tag{A.5}$$

The general solution now includes a term corresponding to a particular solution of the non-homogeneous equation. Trying a linear form kR, we find that k must equal $1/(\rho - \mu)$. Therefore

$$V_1(R) = R/(\rho - \mu) + A_1 R^\alpha + B_1 R^\beta.$$

The first term is just the expected present value of revenues; the rest is the value of the option to abandon. This option is very far from being exercised if R goes to infinity, so the option value should go to zero there. For that we need $B_1 = 0$, leaving us with

$$V_1(R) = R/(\rho - \mu) + A_1 R^\alpha. \tag{A.6}$$

At the investment trigger H the increase in value upon investing should equal the cost of investing:

$$V_1(H) - V_0(H) = K, \tag{A.7}$$

and the two value functions should meet tangentially, leading to the "smooth pasting condition"

$$V_1'(H) - V_0'(H) = 0. \tag{A.8}$$

Similarly, at the abandonment trigger L, we have

$$V_1(L) - V_0(L) = 0; \tag{A.9}$$

if there is a direct cost of abandonment such as severance payment, then minus that will appear on the right-hand side. There is also the smooth pasting condition

$$V_1'(L) - V_0'(L) = 0. \tag{A.10}$$

Substituting the functional forms (A.4) and (A.6) into equations (A.7)–(A.10), we get four equations that must be solved simultaneously for the two constants A, B and the two triggers H, L. An explicit analytical solution is not possible, but some properties of the solution can be obtained by analytical methods, see Dixit (1989b). Numerical solution is quite easy using simultaneous nonlinear equation solving routines such as the one available in GAUSS.

Notes

1. Summers (1987, p. 300) found hurdle rates ranging from 8 to 30 percent, with a median of 15 and a mean of 17 percent. The cost of riskless capital was much lower; allowing for the deductibility of interest expenses, the nominal interest rate was 4 percent, and the real rate was close to zero. Summers' concern was the discount rate applied to depreciation allowances. But he found that almost all firms used the same rate to discount all components of cash flow. See also Dertouzos et al. (1990, p. 61).

2. In 1983, average net income per farm operator was $6,000. Even if rent and mortgage payments on land are excluded from costs on the theory that the land had no alternative use, the figure rises to only $13,500 (figures from the *Statistical Abstract of the United States*, 1990). These being national averages, there must have been many farming families who were earning much less than the opportunity cost of their own labor.

3. The qualitative results are valid much more generally. What we need is "positive persistence" in R: a higher value today should shift the distribution of future values to the right. An additional Appendix, available by writing to the author, explains this point. Most investment problems will have this feature. It might fail when uncertainty is due to shocks to intertemporal preferences: a higher demand today then signals lower demand in the future.

4. The appendixes develop the analysis with a general trend μ. See also McDonald and Siegel (1986), and Pindyck (1988).

5. In fact, the case of a risk-averse investor can be treated using similar techniques and yields similar results. We need only modify ρ to take into account the project's systematic risk (beta); see Pindyck (1991).

6. This whole procedure is very rough and heuristic, and is adopted for ease of exposition. Readers who wish to see more rigorous arguments that the optimal policy takes this "trigger level" form, and fuller explanations of the subsequent mathematics, should read the additional Appendix, available by writing to the author, and the references cited there.

7. I have assumed without stating so explicitly that the opportunity to invest is owned by a single firm or individual. If it is freely available to any of the usual infinity of potential entrants waiting in the wings, it cannot have a positive value. See the sections "Extensions and Qualifications" and "Competitive Industry Dynamics" later in this article.

8. Other interested readers can find the basic concepts explained in the Symposium on Arbitrage in the Fall 1987 issue of the *Journal of Economic Perspectives*.

9. For experts in financial economics, I should clarify that the project of my example is an option with an infinite expiry date; the finite-horizon case is treated by McDonald and Siegel (1986). Also, the stock (project) pays dividend (revenue flow); that is why exercise before the expiry date can be optimal.

10. I have set the trend growth rate of revenues at zero in the above analysis, but this is a good place to mention its twofold effect. On the one hand, a faster expected rate of future revenue growth makes investment more attractive. If the trend rate of growth is μ, then the discounted present value of future revenues starting at R is $R/(\rho - \mu)$, so the Marshallian trigger is $M = (\rho - \mu)K$. On the other, the consequences of a given difference in the current revenue level become magnified as time goes on. Therefore the value of avoiding a given amount of downside risk increases, and with it the value of waiting. The adjusted dis-

count rate ρ' is explicitly derived in the Appendix. The adjusted discount rate is given by $\rho' - \mu = [\beta/(\beta - 1)](\rho - \mu)$, and the optimal trigger is $H = (\rho' - \mu)K$. Now μ also affects β, and an increase in μ lowers β; this is the waiting effect. Numerical calculations show that the waiting effect generally wins. For example, if we keep the basic values $\rho = 5$ percent and $\sigma = 0.2$, but raise the trend growth rate from zero to 2 percent per year, then β falls from 2.15 to 1.58, and ρ' rises from 9.3 to 13.6 percent per year, and H is 3.9 times M.

11. For an analysis of the case where temporary suspension is possible, see McDonald and Siegel (1985).

12. Actually there is a further subtlety when the demand shocks follow Brownian motion. Time being continuously variable for this process, a little entry quickly drops the price slightly below H. From there, the probability of demand rising to take the price to H again in a short interval is quite high. That induces some further entry, and so on. In other words, once the price hits the entry trigger, it is quite likely to keep on bouncing close to this level for a while, with gradual entry and increase in quantity.

13. Barry Nalebuff suggested a more fully game-theoretic resolution: the man knew what game was being played, and *meant* to send the signal that the woman correctly interpreted. But in my judgment, if he had wanted to convey such a signal, he could have done so in many other and more unambiguous ways.

References

Akerlof, George, and Janet Yellen, "A Near-Rational Model of the Business Cycle with Wage and Price Inertia," *Quarterly Journal of Economics*, Supplement, 1985, *100*, 823–838.

Bentolila, Samuel, and Giuseppe Bertola, "Firing Costs and Labor Demand: How Bad Is Eurosclerosis?," *Review of Economic Studies*, July 1990, *57*, 381–402.

Bernanke, Ben S., "Irreversibility, Uncertainty, and Cyclical Investment," *Quarterly Journal of Economics*, February 1983, *98*, 85–106.

Brennan, Michael J., and Eduardo S. Schwartz, "Evaluating Natural Resource Investments," *Journal of Business*, April 1985, *58*, 135–157.

Dertouzos, Michael, Richard K. Lester, and Robert M. Solow, *Made in America*, New York: Harper Paperback Edition, 1990.

Dixit, Avinash, "The Role of Investment in Entry Deterrence," *Economic Journal*, March 1980, *90*, 95–106.

Dixit, Avinash, "Hysteresis, Import Penetration, and Exchange Rate Passthrough," *Quarterly Journal of Economics*, May 1989 (a), *104*, 205–228.

Dixit, Avinash, "Entry and Exit Decisions Under Uncertainty," *Journal of Political Economy*, June 1989 (b), *97*, 620–638.

Dixit, Avinash, "The Art of Smooth Pasting," working paper, Princeton University, 1991 (a).

Dixit, Avinash, "Irreversible Investment and Competition Under Uncertainty," working paper, Princeton University, 1991 (b).

Dixit, Avinash, "Irreversible Investment with Price Ceilings," *Journal of Political Economy*, June 1991 (c), *99*, 541–557.

Edleson, Michael, and Kent Osband, "Competitive Markets with Irreversible Investment," working paper, Rand Corporation, 1989.

Frankel, Jeffrey, and Kenneth Meese, "Are Exchange Rates Too Variable?" In Fischer, Stanley, ed., *NBER Macroeconomics Annual*, Volume II. Cambridge: MIT Press, 1987, 117–153.

Fudenberg, Drew, and Jean Tirole, "Capital as Commitment: Strategic Investment to Deter Mobility," *Journal of Economic Theory*, December 1983, *31*, 227–250.

Greenwald, Bruce, and Joseph E. Stiglitz, "Toward a Theory of Rigidities," *American Economic Review*, Papers and Proceedings, 1989, *79*, 364–369.

Hamermesh, Daniel S., and Neal M. Soss, "An Economic Theory of Suicide," *Journal of Political Economy*, January–February 1974, *82*, 83–90.

Krugman, Paul, *Exchange Rate Instability*, Cambridge: MIT Press, 1989.

Krugman, Paul, and Richard Baldwin, "The Persistence of the U.S. Trade Deficit," *Brookings Papers on Economic Activity*, 1987, No. 1, 1–44.

Leahy, John, *Aggregation and Adjustment Costs*, Doctoral Dissertation, Princeton University, 1990.

Leahy, John, "The Optimality of Myopic Behavior in a Competitive Model of Entry and Exit," working paper, Harvard University, 1991.

Lippman, Stephen A., and R. P. Rumelt, "Demand Uncertainty and Investment In Industry-Specific Capital," working paper, UCLA Graduate School of Management, 1985.

Mankiw, N. Gregory, "Small Menu Costs and Large Business Cycles: A Macroeconomic Model," *Quarterly Journal of Economics*, May 1985, *100*, 529–539.

McDonald, Robert, and Daniel Siegel, "Investment and the Valuation of Firms when There Is an Option to Shut Down," *International Economic Review*, June 1985, *26*, 331–349.

McDonald, Robert, and Daniel Siegel, "The Value of Waiting to Invest," *Quarterly Journal of Economics*, November 1986, *101*, 707–727.

Merton, Robert C., "The Theory of Rational Option Pricing," *Bell Journal of Economics and Management Science*, Spring 1973, *4*, 141–183.

Pindyck, Robert S., "Irreversible Investment, Capacity Choice, and the Value of the Firm," *American Economic Review*, December 1988, *78*, 969–985.

Pindyck, Robert S., "Irreversibility, Uncertainty, and Investment," *Journal of Economic Literature*, September 1991, *26*:3, 1110–1148.

Stiglitz, Joseph E., "Incentives, Information and Organizational Design," *Empirica—Austrian Economic Papers*, 1989, *16*:1, 3–29.

Summers, Lawrence H., "Investment Incentives and the Discounting of Depreciation Allowances," in *The Effects of Taxation on Capital Accumulation*, Martin Feldstein, ed., Chicago: University of Chicago Press, 1987.

10 The General Flexibility to Switch: Real Options Revisited

Nalin Kulatilaka and Lenos Trigeorgis

I Introduction

Consider a firm that produces multiple output products with uncertain demand. The firm faces an explicit or implicit choice between producing each product utilizing specialized, cost efficient but rigid capital, versus a more flexible (though more costly) alternative with a built-in option to switch the operating mode among the various products in response to changing market conditions. Another firm may consider building a new power plant. Should the plant be built to operate only on oil? How about on natural gas instead? Or should the plant be designed up front with the flexibility to use either input? Clearly, an investment with more potential choices would be more valuable than one that restricts choices. Is the resulting value of flexibility worth the extra cost?

Complex analyses of this type of problems have appeared earlier in the literature (e.g., see Kulatilaka (1986, 1988), Triantis and Hodder (1990), Fine and Freund (1990), and He and Pindyck (1992)). In this paper we present a rather simple analysis of generic options which enable management to switch, possibly at specified switching costs, between alternative "modes" of operation. We show that, without switching costs, the value of a flexible project can be seen as the value of a rigid project, plus the sum of the values of the options to switch in future periods, i.e., option value additivity holds. The presence of asymmetric switching costs, however, may create compound interactions that can cause such option value additivity to break down. We note that the valuation of the flexible project must be determined simultaneously with the optimal operating (switching) policy. Our simple analysis also captures the *hysteresis* effect which states that, even though immediate switching may seem attractive based on short-term considerations (i.e., current cash flows), it may in fact be long-term optimal to wait.

This general framework has natural applications in flexible manufacturing systems and, with appropriate interpretation of the operating "modes" and switching costs, it can subsume as special cases most other known real options. We take the opportunity to revisit, as special case of our framework, the real options to defer investment, expand or contract production, temporarily shut down and restart operations, abandon for salvage, and default during construction.

The rest of the paper is organized as follows. Section II presents a generic flexibility example and determines the value of inflexible technology projects as a benchmark. Section III then determines the value of the flexibility to switch operating modes, first when there are no switching costs and option value additivity holds, and later when there are asymmetric switching costs with compound interactions. Section IV presents a generalized model, and revisits known real options as special cases. The last section discusses other applications and concludes.

II   A Generic Flexibility Example

In order to clarify the main ideas, we will first present a simple illustrative example. Consider two alternative (mutually exclusive) projects, A and B, whose net cash flows depend on a single exogenous state variable, such as oil price. For example, one may think of an auto manufacturer using alternative *rigid* technologies to produce a small car. The decision horizon is divided into two time periods spanned by three decision times ($t = 0, 1$ and 2). We assume a binomial evolution of oil prices, i.e., in each period the oil price can take one of two possible values conditional on each previous value. Let P_t^s be the price of oil at time t and state s (where $s = +$ or $-$ at the end of period 1, or $++, +-, --$ at the end of period 2). The binomial "tree" of oil prices is given below:

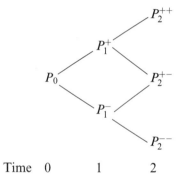

Time   0   1   2

The net cash flows of the projects are contingent on the oil price realization and the operating mode employed. Let $c_t^s(m)$ be the net cash flow generated at time t if state s is realized when operating in mode m ($m = A, B$), i.e.,

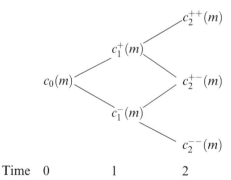

Time   0   1   2

Suppose, for example, that project *A* utilizes a more energy efficient technology that uses less oil, but has higher fixed costs. During periods of high oil prices the increased demand for small cars would generate higher net cash flows. In our notation, the project using *rigid* technology *A* will generate the following cash flows, $c_t^s(A)$, in *each* period:

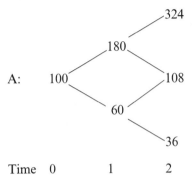

A:
```
                    324
              180
        100         108
              60
                    36
```

Time   0   1   2

Project *B*, by contrast, employs a less energy efficient technology that uses more oil, but would require lower fixed costs. Hence, in low oil price states, project *B* would generate higher cash flows and dominate project *A*, while the opposite occurs for high oil price states. Suppose the net cash flows from the project using rigid technology *B*, $c_t^s(B)$, are:

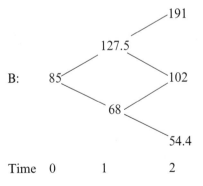

B:
```
                    191
            127.5
       85           102
             68
                    54.4
```

Time   0   1   2

Note that in the above example the cash flows under projects *A* and *B* are positively (although not perfectly) correlated, since they involve alternative technologies to produce *small* cars that would both benefit, although in somewhat different ways, from higher oil prices. One can think of other situations where the cash flows under the two alternative projects may be negatively correlated. For example, project *A* may still represent an energy efficient technology to build *small* cars, but project *B* may involve an energy efficient technology to build *large* cars. In this case, the demand and cash flows for A would be high when oil prices are high, while the demand and cash flows for B would be high when oil prices are low. When the correlation between the cash flows is negative, the value of the flexibility to switch between technologies A and B would be even higher. Before considering the value of the flexibility to switch among alternative technologies or operating "modes", however, it is useful to first establish as a benchmark the value of each rigid technology.

The Value of Rigid Technology Projects

Under traditional discounted cash flow (DCF) techniques, the present value of cash flows from each project can generally be obtained from discounting expected future cash flows at the risk-adjusted rate of return. Alternatively, and more appropriately in the presence of managerial flexibility, a risk-neutral valuation approach can be used in which present values can be obtained from expected future values using risk-neutral probabilities to compute expectations, discounted at the risk-free rate. In our example, suppose the *actual* probability of an oil price increase is .5 and the risk-adjusted discount rate is 20%. The corresponding risk-neutral probabilities when the risk-free rate is 8% are $p = 0.4$ in the "up" state and $1 - p = 0.6$ in the "down" state.[1]

The present value of net cash flows from the project using rigid technology A can thus be obtained as follows:

$$PV(A) = 100 + [.5 \times 180 + .5 \times 60]/1.20 + 144/1.20^2 \quad \text{(using actual rates)}$$

$$= 100 + [.4 \times 180 + .6 \times 60]/1.08 \quad \text{(using risk-neutral rates)}$$

$$+ [.4^2 \times 324 + 2(.4)(.6)108 + .6^2 \times 36]/1.08^2$$

$$= 100 + 100 + 100 = 300 \tag{1}$$

Similarly, for the project using rigid technology B:

$$PV(B) = 85 + 85 + 85 = 255. \tag{2}$$

III   The Value of the Flexibility to Switch Technologies

We now turn to the valuation of a flexible project, F, that allows management to choose between technologies A and B. When oil prices are high, technology A dominates, but when oil prices are low B is the dominant technology. In our preliminary analysis we consider the simpler case where switching can be done costlessly. In this case, the combined flexibility to switch can simply be determined as the sum of the options to switch at various times. We later introduce asymmetric costs of switching and show that compound interaction effects cause this option value additivity to break down.

A. No Switching Costs: Option Additivity

Consider first the case where switching between technologies A and B involves no costs. Obviously, the right (with no obligation) to switch between the two technologies makes the value of the flexible project, $V(F)$, greater than the value of either of the rigid projects whose operation is restricted to a single technology. That is, $V(F) \geq \max(\text{PV}(A), \text{PV}(B))$.

Actually, the value of the flexible project exceeds that of rigid project A (which is committed to using only technology A) by the value of the flexibility to switch operation from A to B, denoted by $F(A \rightarrow B)$, whenever the value of cash flows from operating technology B turns out to be higher, i.e., $V(F) = \text{PV}(A) + F(A \rightarrow B)$. In the case with no switching costs, this combined flexibility value is the sum of the three (European) options to switch from A to B, denoted by $S_t(A \rightarrow B)$, at times 0, 1, and 2, respectively. That is, $F(A \rightarrow B) = S_0(A \rightarrow B) + S_1(A \rightarrow B) + S_2(A \rightarrow B)$.

To confirm this, let $c_t^s(A \rightarrow B)$ be the *incremental* or additional cash payoff from voluntarily switching from technology A to B at time t and state s, if it is beneficial to do so. That is, $c_t^s(A \rightarrow B) \equiv \max(c_t^s(B) - c_t^s(A), 0)$. In the above example, $S_0(A \rightarrow B) = \max(85 - 100, 0) = 0$, i.e., the option to switch from A to B immediately is worthless. Switching from A to B in year 1, however, results in the following incremental cash flow pattern in each state:

$$
\begin{array}{lll}
 & \nearrow & c_1^+(A \rightarrow B) = \max(127.5 - 180, 0) = 0 \\
S_1(A \rightarrow B) & & \\
[4.4] & & \\
 & \searrow & c_1^-(A \rightarrow B) = \max(68 - 60, 0) = 8 \\
\end{array}
$$

$t = 0 \qquad\qquad 1$

Thus, the value today of the option to switch from A to B in year 1 is given by:

$$S_1(A \rightarrow B) = [pc_1^+(A \rightarrow B) + (1-p)c_1^-(A \rightarrow B)]/(1+r)$$

$$= [.4 \times 0 + .6 \times 8]/1.08 = 4.4$$

Similarly, for year 2 switching:

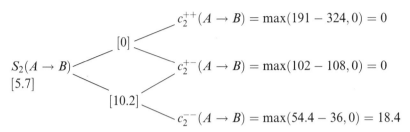

$$c_2^{++}(A \to B) = \max(191 - 324, 0) = 0$$

$$c_2^{+-}(A \to B) = \max(102 - 108, 0) = 0$$

$$c_2^{--}(A \to B) = \max(54.4 - 36, 0) = 18.4$$

The discounted values of the terminal ($t = 2$) cash flows one period earlier (at $t = 1$) are given in brackets, as 0 and 10.2, respectively. (For example, for the down state ($-$) in year 1: $[.4 \times 0 + .6 \times 18.4]/1.08 = 10.2$.) Discounting one more time to the beginning,

$$S_2(A \to B) = [.4 \times 0 + .6 \times 10.2]/1.08 = 5.7$$

The combined value of the flexibility to switch operation from technology A to B at any of the three decision times is given by:

$$F(A \to B) = S_0(A \to B) + S_1(A \to B) + S_2(A \to B)$$

$$= 0 + 4.4 + 5.7 = 10.1. \tag{3}$$

Thus, one should prefer the flexible project F over the rigid project A as long as the incremental cost of acquiring F ($I(F)$) over A ($I(A)$) is less than the value of flexibility, i.e.,

$$I(F) - I(A) < F(A \to B) \ (= V(F) - \mathrm{PV}(A) = 10.1), \text{ or}$$

$$V(F) - I(F) > \mathrm{PV}(A) - I(A) \equiv \mathrm{NPV}(A) \tag{4}$$

(i.e., as long as the flexible project, F, has a greater "expanded NPV" than the rigid one).

The total value of the flexible project (using either technology A or B) is therefore given, from (1) and (3), by:

$$V(F) = \mathrm{PV}(A) + F(A \to B) = 300 + 10.1 = 310.1. \tag{5}$$

The flexible project can also be thought of as equivalent (in the absence of switching costs) to using technology B, with the flexibility to switch from technology B to A when profitable (under high oil price states), i.e., $V(F) = \mathrm{PV}(B) + F(B \to A)$. The combined value of the flexibility to switch operation from B to A is similarly given by:

$$F(B \to A) = S_0(B \to A) + S_1(B \to A) + S_2(B \to A)$$

$$= 15 + 19.4 + 20.7 = 55.1. \tag{6}$$

Therefore, $V(F) = PV(B) + F(B \to A) = 255 + 55.1 = 310.1$, confirming that, in the absence of switching costs, $PV(A) + F(A \to B) = V(F) = PV(B) + F(B \to A)$. The breakdown of value into various components (and their additivity) is summarized below for each rigid technology separately, as well as for the flexible project:

Time	Rigid Technology A	Option $A \to B$	Rigid Technology B	Option $B \to A$	Flexible Project A/B
0	100	0	85	15	100
1	100	4.4	85	19.4	104.4
2	100	5.7	85	20.7	105.7
Total	300	10.1	255	55.1	310.1

Alternatively, the flexible project can be valued directly as a package by noting that its cash flows in each period will be the highest of those from the two technologies, e.g., $c_2^s(F) = \max(c_2^s(A), c_2^s(B))$. In this case, this would result in the following "decision tree" (with the brackets in the top lines, added next to the *best* (max) current cash flow, capturing the value as of that time of subsequent cash flows given optimal future operation):

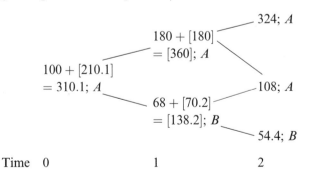

The optimal technology to use (A or B) at each decision node is noted (after the semicolon) along with the optimal total value (which is confirmed to be 310.1 at $t = 0$). Basically, without switching costs the general dynamic problem is equivalent to a series of simpler myopic problems, with the combined package value being equal to the sum of the separate component values. This equivalence may no longer hold in the presence of asymmetric switching costs.

B.   With Switching Costs: Compound Interactions

In the earlier case with no switching costs the exercise of a switching option affects only the current payoff but has no effect on subsequent decisions, hence option value additivity holds. When there are costs associated with switching from one operating mode to another, the switching options are no longer independent, and their values no longer add up to the combined flexibility value (i.e., option value additivity breaks down). Switching costs not only affect the current cash payoff and optimal operating decision, but also alter the exercise costs and, hence, the switching decisions in future periods. Basically, exercise of a prior option (i.e., switching operating modes in an earlier period) creates a series of nested new options (to switch in the future), analogous to a *compound option*. This invalidates option value additivity.

Let $I(A \rightarrow B)$ be the cost of switching from technology A to B. In the presence of such switching costs, the incremental cash flow of switching from A to B then becomes $c_t^s(A \rightarrow B) \equiv \max(c_t^s(B) - c_t^s(A) - I(A \rightarrow B), 0)$. For example, suppose $I(A \rightarrow B) = 8$, and $I(B \rightarrow A) = 2$. Revisiting our example above with such asymmetric switching costs, each separate switching option is now valued as follows:

$$S_0(A \rightarrow B) = \max(85 - 100 - 8, 0) = 0$$

$$c_1^+(A \rightarrow B) = \max(127.5 - 180 - 8, 0) = 0$$

$S_1(A \rightarrow B)$
$[0]$

$$c_1^-(A \rightarrow B) = \max(68 - 60 - 8, 0) = 0$$

$t = 0$ 1

so the option to switch from A to B at time 1 by paying an \$8 switching cost also becomes worthless ($S_1(A \rightarrow B) = 0$). Similarly, we value the time-2 option to switch from A to B:

$$c_2^{++}(A \rightarrow B) = 0$$

$[0]$

$S_2(A \rightarrow B)$
$[3.2]$

$$c_2^{+-}(A \rightarrow B) = 0$$

$[5.78]$

$$c_2^{--}(A \rightarrow B) = \max(54.4 - 36 - 8, 0) = 10.4$$

Thus, the sum of the three options to switch from A to B is:

$$S_0(A \rightarrow B) + S_1(A \rightarrow B) + S_2(A \rightarrow B) = 0 + 0 + 3.2 = 3.2. \tag{7}$$

Similarly, the sum of the option values for switching from B to A is as follows:

$$S_0(B \rightarrow A) + S_1(B \rightarrow A) + S_2(B \rightarrow A) = 13 + 18.7 + 19.6 = 51.3. \tag{8}$$

It therefore can be seen that $\text{PV}(A) + \sum S_t(A \rightarrow B) = 300 + 3.2 = 303.2$, which is no longer equivalent to $\text{PV}(B) + \sum S_t(B \rightarrow A) = 255 + 51.3 = 306.3$. That is, in the presence of switching costs, the flexible project can no longer be viewed as being equivalent to one of the rigid technologies plus the set (or sum) of simple (European) options to switch to the other technology.

In fact, the value of the flexible project, $V(F)$, differs from either of the above values. Since a current decision to switch or not would affect the technology under which the firm would operate as it enters future periods, it would impact on the future switching costs (i.e., the exercise price of future options) and the set of future switching decisions, necessitating the use of *dynamic programming*. Future choices will be path (history) dependent. In such cases, the flexible project *value*, V, must be determined *simultaneously* with the schedule of *optimal operating modes, m*.

Specifically, the management of the flexible project has two basic choices: continue operating in the current mode (e.g., technology A) for one more period—and receive the current cash payoff, $c_t^s(A)$, plus any expected future benefits assuming optimal future operation—, or switch immediately (to B) by paying the specified switching cost in exchange for receiving B's current cash flow and its expected future benefits. A mode switch would be optimal only if the value from switching exceeds the value from delaying potential switching. That is,

$$V_t^s(A) = \max(c_t^s(A) + \hat{E}[V_{t+1}^s(A)]/(1+r), c_t^s(B)$$
$$+ \hat{E}[V_{t+1}^s(B)]/(1+r) - I(A \rightarrow B)) \tag{9}$$

where $\hat{E}[V_{t+1}^s(i)] \equiv pV_{t+1}^+(i) + (1-p)V_{t+1}^-(i)$, $i = A$ or B;

$c_t^s(m)$: cash flow at time t and state s when operating in technology or "mode" m;

$V_t^s(m)$: flexible project value as of time t given that state s is entered while operating in technology m, assuming optimal future switching decisions;

$m_t^s(i)$: optimal operating technology or "mode" at time t given that state s is entered while operating in mode i (here, $i = A$ or B);

$\hat{E}[.]$: risk-neutral expectations operator (using the risk-neutral probability, p).

The backward iterative process begins from the terminal time, T (here $T = 2$), where the above expression is simplified to:

$$V_T^s(A) = \max(c_T^s(A), c_T^s(B) - I(A \to B))$$
$$= c_T^s(A) + \max([c_T^s(B) - c_T^s(A)] - I(A \to B), 0), \qquad (10)$$

where the latter expression resembles a call option to pay the switching costs as exercise price in order to acquire the incremental cash flows of B over A.

Applying this to our earlier example, we obtain the following terminal values for each state s, $V_2^s(A)$, assuming operation is entered using technology A:

$V_2^{++}(A) = \max(324, 191 - 8) = 324;\quad m_2^{++}(A) = A$ (i.e., stay in A)

$V_2^{+-}(A) = \max(108, 102 - 8) = 108;\quad m_2^{+-}(A) = A$ (stay in A)

$V_2^{--}(A) = \max(36, 54.4 - 8) = 46.4;\quad m_2^{--}(A) = B$ (*switch* to B)

Similarly, if operation is entered using technology B:

$V_2^{++}(B) = \max(191, 324 - 2) = 322;\quad m_2^{++}(B) = A$ (*switch* to A)

$V_2^{+-}(B) = \max(102, 108 - 2) = 106;\quad m_2^{+-}(B) = A$ (*switch* to A)

$V_2^{--}(B) = \max(54.4, 36 - 2) = 54.4;\quad m_2^{--}(B) = B$ (stay in B)

The above backward process would then result in the following two "decision trees," each with a set of project values, $V_t^s(i)$, and optimal operating technology or modes, $m_t^s(i)$, depending on whether time-0 operation is entered using technology A or B ($i = A, B$):

if operation is entered using technology A,

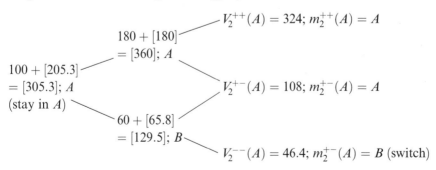

while if operation is entered using technology B,

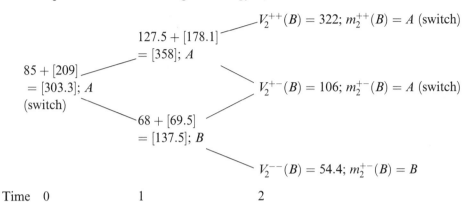

$$V_2^{++}(B) = 322; \ m_2^{++}(B) = A \ (\text{switch})$$

$$127.5 + [178.1]$$
$$= [358]; \ A$$

$$85 + [209]$$
$$= [303.3]; \ A$$
$$(\text{switch})$$

$$V_2^{+-}(B) = 106; \ m_2^{+-}(B) = A \ (\text{switch})$$

$$68 + [69.5]$$
$$= [137.5]; \ B$$

$$V_2^{--}(B) = 54.4; \ m_2^{+-}(B) = B$$

Time   0   1   2

The discounted risk-neutral expected value of future payoffs one period earlier is shown in the top line brackets at that time. For each operating mode or technology, we would then add to the current cash flow the discounted risk-neutral expectation of the future benefits from operating in that mode (net of any switching costs), and select the technology resulting in the higher project value. That is,

$$c_1^+(B) + [\{pV_2^{++}(B) + (1-p)V_2^{+-}(B)\}/(1+r)] - I(A \rightarrow B))$$

$$= \max(180 + [\{.4 \times 324 + .6 \times 108\}/1.08],$$

$$127.5 + [\{.4 \times 322 + .6 \times 106\}/1.08] - 8)$$

$$= \max(180 + [180], 127.5 + [178.1] - 8) = \max(360, 297.6)$$

$$= 360; \ m_1^+(A) = A(\text{stay in } A)$$

Similarly,

$$V_1^-(A) = \max(60 + [65.8], 68 + [69.5] - 8) = \max(125.8, 129.5)$$

$$= 129.5; m_1^-(A) = B \ (\textit{switch to } B)$$

If operation is entered using technology B,

$$V_1^+(B) = 358; \quad m_1^+(B) = A \ (\textit{switch to } A); \text{ and}$$

$$V_1^-(B) = 137.5; \quad m_1^-(B) = B \ (\text{stay in } B)$$

Finally, moving similarly one step earlier to the beginning:

$$V_0(A) = \max(100 + [205.3], 85 + [209] - 8)$$

$$= 305.3; \quad m_0(A) = A \tag{11}$$

(i.e., if enter using technology A, stay in A)

$$V_0(B) = \max(85 + [209], 100 + [205.3] - 2)$$

$$= 303.3; \quad m_0(B) = A \tag{12}$$

(i.e., if enter using B, switch immediately to A).

(If immediate switching is not possible, then $V_0(B) = 294$.)

The current value of the flexible project is, of course, the most beneficial of the above initial operating choices, i.e.,

$$V(F) = \max(V_0(A), V_0(B)) = \max(305.3, 303.3) = 305.3, \tag{13}$$

and the optimal initial technology is A. The optimal operating schedule (or time sequence of optimal $m_i^s(i)$, $i = A$ or B) is as follows:

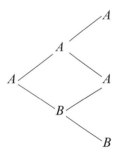

That is, start operating using technology A; in case of an up state, stay in A; else (if down state), switch to B; if another down state occurs stay in B, else (if up) switch back to A.

We can now confirm that the compoundness effect introduced by switching costs causes the separate switching options to interact, violating their value additivity. For example, the combined switching flexibility afforded by the flexible project beyond rigid project A (or B) is given by:

$$F(A \rightarrow B) = V(F) - \mathrm{PV}(A) = 305.3 - 300 = 5.3$$

$$F(B \rightarrow A) = V(F) - \mathrm{PV}(B) = 305.3 - 255 = 50.3$$

$$(= 294 - 255 = 39, \tag{14}$$

excluding immediate switching)—that is, to acquire the flexible project with the given switching costs one should be willing to pay \$5.3 beyond the cost of rigid project A, \$50.3 (or \$39) more than the cost of project B, and \$4.8 ($= 310.1 - 305.3$) *less* than the cost of a comparable flexible project with costless switching. The combined flexibility value clearly differs from the sum of separate values determined above:

$S_0(A \to B) + S_1(A \to B) + S_2(A \to B) = 0 + 0 + 3.2 = 3.2$
(vs. a combined value of 5.3)

$S_0(B \to A) + S_1(B \to A) + S_2(B \to A) = 13 + 18.7 + 19.6 = 51.3$ (vs. 50.3)

(or, $S_1(B \to A) + S_2(B \to A) = 18.7 + 19.6 = 38.3$, vs. 39 if immediate switching is excluded).

When compound options are involved, as was the case above, often positive interactions or complementarities result that make the value of the whole greater than the sum of the parts.

IV   A Generalization with Known Real Options as Special Cases

The above approach can be generalized for more than three periods ($t = 0, 1, 2, \ldots, T$) to cover any number of states ($s = 0, 1, 2, \ldots, n$), and for more than just two technologies or operating "modes" ($i = 0, 1, 2, \ldots, M$, rather than just A or B) within a backward iterative process seen as a discrete, economically-adjusted version of the known Bellman equation of dynamic programming. Starting from the end and moving backwards, the value of a flexible project in state s at any time, $t - 1$, would be obtained from the expected future values in the up ($s + 1$) and down ($s - 1$) states calculated one step earlier (at time t) as follows:

$$V_{t-1}^s(m) = \max_i \{c_{t-1}^s(i) + [pV_t^{s+1}(i) + (1 - p)V_t^{s-1}(i)]/(1 + r) - I(m \to i)\} \qquad (15)$$

with $I(m \to i) = 0$ for $i = m$ (i.e., there are no costs when staying in the same mode). At the terminal period ($t = T$) when the process starts, the expression becomes

$$V_T^s(m) = \max_i \{c_T^s(i) - I(m \to i)\} \qquad (16)$$

with $c_T^s(i)$ being the terminal cash flow (or salvage value) when entering state s while operating in mode i. The process can be applied iteratively, moving backwards step by step until the beginning ($t = 0$) project value is obtained, along with the optimal operating schedule. Kulatilaka (1986, 1988) provides a numerical analysis of this general problem based on a set of simultaneous stochastic dynamic programs.

As we noted, in the absence of switching costs, the solution to the general dynamic problem would be equivalent to a series of simple myopic solutions: in each period, simply choose the operating mode (i) with the highest current cash flow benefit, $c_t^s(i)$; in this case, the value of flexibility *can* be determined independently of the operating schedule. The presence of asymmetric switching costs, however, may create a compoundness effect that requires a more complex, *forward-looking* dynamic analysis, where the value of flexibility must be determined *simultaneously* with the optimal operating schedule or switching "exercise" policy.

One consequence of the interdependence between current and future decisions in the presence of switching costs is that a *range of inaction* known as a *hysteresis* band may arise whereby, even though immediate switching may appear attractive based on static analysis (i.e., current cash flows), it may in fact be long-term optimal to wait due to dynamic considerations (e.g., a high cost of immediate switching, or a high probability and cost of re-switching back in later stages).[2] By waiting, the firm maintains its option to switch later, if it becomes sufficiently attractive, instead of being "absorbed" into a mode out of which later re-switching, no-matter how desirable, would be excessively costly. For example, in the case of irreversible projects, McDonald and Siegel (1986) have shown that it may be optimal to defer investment (i.e., wait to invest) even though immediate undertaking of the project may result in a positive NPV, or it may be optimal to continue operating (i.e., wait to abandon) a currently unprofitable project. Shutting down and re-opening operations, or switching among alternative inputs or outputs of a production process may be subject to similar "inertia" effects.

As Kulatilaka (1986) points out, with appropriate interpretation of the operating "modes" and switching costs (and other parameters, such as cash flows), most of the known real options can be valued as special cases of the above generic switching flexibility—being, in essence, a complex compound exchange option. The operating "modes" are now defined more broadly as various decision alternatives, rather than just technologies. For example, one may think of operating a project in the following "modes":

i operating *"mode" (decision alternative)*

0 do not operate (e.g., *defer* investment or temporarily *shut down*)

1 operate base-scale project (*invest* or *produce*)

2 *expand* the scale of production

3 *contract* operations

4 *abandon* for salvage value or *default* during construction

5 *switch* (e.g., outputs or inputs)

Given the above definition of operating "modes," let us revisit some of the known real options with appropriate interpretation of switching costs and other parameters.

A. Option to Defer Investment

The firm considers the optimal timing to invest, i.e., when to make the initial investment outlay, I_0. The current operating mode is 0 (i.e., "do not operate" or "wait") and the alternative mode to switch to is 1 ("operate", "invest" or "produce"). The switching cost involved is the initial investment outlay, so $I(0 \rightarrow 1) = I_0$. No re-switching is possible (i.e., investment is irreversible), so $I(1 \rightarrow 0) = \infty$. No cash flows can be generated while in the current waiting mode (0), i.e., $c_t(0) = 0$; after converting to the production mode (1), a stream of positive cash flows will be generated, $c_t(1) \geq 0$, with a present value $PV_0(1)$. In the absence of switching costs, immediate investment would be optimal if $PV_0(1) > I_0$ or $NPV \equiv PV_0(1) - I_0 > 0$. However, the presence of insurmountable re-switching costs ($I(1 \rightarrow 0) = \infty$) may make it long-term optimal for the firm to wait to invest (i.e., remain in an "out-of-the-money" mode) even if immediate investing would generate attractive current benefits in the form of a positive current net present value (i.e., even if $NPV > 0$).

B. Option to Expand

The firm has already made the initial investment enabling it to produce, i.e., operate the base-scale project. Given that it is found in the "up" states (e.g., facing a better than expected demand for its product in the market), the firm considers whether to make an additional outlay, I_E, enabling to expand the production scale (e.g., through adding plant capacity) by $e\%$. That is, the firm is currently in mode 1 and considers switching to 2. The switching cost is the cost of expanding, i.e., $I(1 \rightarrow 2) = I_E$. Again, switching is irreversible, so $I(2 \rightarrow 1) = \infty$. The cash flows (and project value) in the expanded "mode" would be $e\%$ higher than in the base-scale mode, so $c_t(2) = (1 + e)c_t(1)$.

C. Option to Contract

The firm considers contracting operations by $c\%$ from the current base-scale production, in order to save on certain variable operating costs (I_C). The switching cost is the operating cost saving, i.e., $I(1 \rightarrow 3) = -I_C$. The cash flows (and value) in the contracted mode (3) are by $c\%$ lower relative to those in the base-scale mode, i.e., $c_t(3) = (1 - c)c_t(1)$.

D. Option to Temporarily Shut Down and Restart Operations

The firm considers switching back and forth between "operating" (mode 1) and "not operating" (mode 0), as in the case of shutting down and re-opening a mine. There are no cash flows generated in the "shut down" mode, so $c_t(0) = 0$. Switching to the "production" mode involves variable operating costs, $I(0 \rightarrow 1) = I_V$, in exchange for positive cash revenues (R), i.e., $c_t(1) = R_t - I_V > 0$. Switching to the "idle" mode may involve specific shut down costs (I_S), so $I(1 \rightarrow 0) = I_S$. If no switching costs are involved whatsoever (i.e., if $I(0 \rightarrow 1) = I(1 \rightarrow 0) = 0$) then the firm would operate whenever profits are positive, and its value would be the sum of simple call options to pay the variable costs and acquire the cash revenues in each year, as in McDonald and Siegel (1985). However, the presence of non-zero switching costs would violate this additivity due to the compoundness effect we discussed earlier.

E.   Option to Abandon for Salvage Value

The firm, currently in the production mode (1) but facing bad prospects, considers abandoning in exchange for a specified salvage value, S (i.e., switching to mode 4). Although the firm currently generates positive cash flows $(c_t(1) > 0)$ and would produce no cash flows in case of abandonment (i.e., $c_t(4) = 0$), it is nevertheless facing negative switching "costs" in the amount of the salvage value, (i.e., $I(1 \rightarrow 4) = -S$). If abandonment is irreversible, $I(4 \rightarrow 1) = \infty$. This switching cost asymmetry may induce firms to continue operating currently unprofitable projects.

F.   Option to Default During Construction (or the Time-to-Build Option)

Once it decides to initiate investment (mode 1), the firm needs to make a series of investment outlays in stages, say I_0 at $t = 0$ and I_1 at $t = 1$, before completing construction at time T (here, $T = 1$). Positive cash revenues will be generated only after project completion (i.e., for $t \geq T + 1$). That is, $c_t(1) = -I_t$ for $t \leq T$ (i.e., $t = 0, 1$); and $c_t(1) \geq 0$ thereafter. However, the firm may choose to abandon the project during construction by defaulting on a coming investment outlay, thereby switching to mode 4; in this mode, no cash flows would be produced, i.e., $c_t(4) = 0$ for all t.

Of course, real-life projects may allow switching between more than just two operating modes during their lifetime. For example, the opportunity to invest in a mine may collectively involve the following operating modes: wait to invest (mode 0), expand (mode 2) or contract production (mode 3), shut down (mode 0) and re-open (mode 1), or even completely abandon the mine (mode 4). Brennan and Schwartz (1985) consider the operation of such a mine with the options to open, shut down, and abandon. As noted, the presence of asymmetric switching costs and interactions among various such real options would make their values non-additive, and would render project valuation and optimal operating policy non-trivial.

V   Conclusions

We have presented a rather simple analysis of generic options that enable management to switch between alternative technologies or "modes" of operation. We have shown that, without switching costs, the value of a flexible project can be seen as the value of a rigid project plus the sum of the values of the options to switch in future periods. The presence of asymmetric switching costs, however, may create compound interactions that can violate such option value additivity. We also noted that valuation of the flexible project must be determined simultaneously with the optimal operating policy.

The general framework presented here has wide applicability. In the earlier section, we have seen how, with appropriate interpretation of the operating "modes" and switching costs, it can subsume as special cases most other known real options. The early part of this paper has focused on an example of *product flexibility*, enabling a firm to switch among alternative technologies for producing various *outputs*. Additional examples would include chemical plants or oil refineries that can easily vary their output mix (e.g., a refinery may convert crude oil into gasoline, fuel oil or lubricants), or even switching agricultural crop depending on relative prices. A natural application of product flexibility is in flexible manufacturing systems (FMS). The trade-off here lies in selecting between a more expensive but flexible manufacturing system that allows changing operating modes rapidly at very low switching costs in response to uncertain market developments, versus a high-volume, specialized and inflexible alternative. In a low-uncertainty environment, the specialized alternative may be more cost-effective, but the value of flexibility may justify the additional cost of the flexible system under higher uncertainty.

The above framework finds applications in a variety of other situations as well. A noted application is the *process flexibility* of switching among alternative *inputs*. Of course, the flexibility to select the cheapest alternative would be acquired or built-in at some extra cost. Such is the case of the power plant that can operate with alternative forms of energy, shifting among oil, natural gas, coal, or electricity as their relative prices fluctuate. Similarly, a multi-national corporation can position plants globally in various countries so that it can switch production to the lowest-cost producing plant as the relative exchange rates or other factors change over time.

Real-life valuation, of course, can be rather complex. As noted, compoundness effects related to asymmetric switching costs and other interactions among various such real options would make their values non-additive, and would render project valuation and optimal operating policy non-trivial. As noted earlier, in the absence of switching costs, exercising a switching option affects only the current payoff but not any subsequent decisions, so that option value additivity is preserved. In the presence of switching costs, however, the switching options are no longer independent and their values no longer add up to the combined flexibility value. Switching costs not only affect the current cash payoff and decision, but also alter the exercise costs and, hence, the future switching decisions. In principle, exercise of a prior option (i.e., switching operating modes in an earlier period) creates a series of nested new options to switch in future periods which, like *compound options*, cause option value additivity to break down.[3]

Another noted consequence of this type of interdependence between current and future decisions in the presence of switching costs is that a *hysteresis range* may arise whereby it may be long-term optimal to wait, maintaining the option to switch later if it becomes sufficiently attractive. Noted examples include waiting to invest even though immediate investment may have a positive NPV, or delaying abandonment of a currently unprofitable project. Shutting down and re-opening operations, or switching among alternative inputs or outputs of a production process may be subject to similar inertia or hysteresis effects. All these elements, however, can be captured in principle within a generalized model of flexibility, as described in this paper.

Notes

1. The risk-neutral probability can be obtained from market information, namely the prices of the underlying asset, P, in the up $(+)$ and down $(-)$ states and the interest rate, r, as follows: $P = [(1 + r)P - P^-]/(P^+ - P^-)$. See Trigeorgis and Mason (1987) for a simple exposition. In the case of commodity prices (such as for oil), the risk-neutral adjustment may require accounting for a net convenience yield than can be inferred from futures market information. See Brennam and Schwartz (1985).

2. See Baldwin and Krugman (1989), Kogut and Kulatilaka (1993), and Bell (1993) for a detailed discussion on hysteresis effects in international trade.

3. For other kinds of interaction among multiple real options, see also Trigeorgis (1992).

References

1. Aggarwal, R., "Justifying Investments in Flexible Manufacturing Technology: Adding Strategic Analysis to Capital Budgeting Under Uncertainty," *Managerial Finance*, 17 (1991), 77–88.

2. Baldwin, R. and P. Krugman, "Persistent Trade Effects of Large Exchange Rate Shocks," *Quarterly Journal of Economics*, 104 (1989), 636–654.

3. Bell, G., "Volatile Exchange Rates and the Multinational Firm: Entry, Exit, and Capacity Options," in L. Trigeorgis (ed.), *Real Options in Capital Investment: New Contributions*, New York, NY: Praeger, forthcoming 1993.

4. Brennan, M. and E. Schwartz, "Evaluating Natural Resource Investments," *Journal of Business*, 58 (1985), 135–157.

5. Fine, C. and R. Freund, "Optimal Investment in Product-flexible Manufacturing Capacity," *Management Science*, 36 (1990), 449–466.

6. He, H. and R. Pindyck, "Investments in Flexible Production Capacity," *Journal of Economic Dynamics and Control*, 16 (1992), 575–599.

7. Kensinger, J., "Adding the Value of Active Management into the Capital Budgeting Equation," *Midland Corporate Finance Journal*, 5 (Spring 1987), 31–42.

8. Kogut, B. and N. Kulatilaka, "Operating Flexibility, Global Manufacturing, and the Option Value of a Multinational Network," *Management Science*, 40, 1 (1994), 123–139.

9. Kulatilaka, N., "The Value of Flexibility," MIT-EL working paper 86-014 (1986).

10. Kulatilaka, N., "Valuing the Flexibility of Flexible Manufacturing Systems," *IEEE Transactions in Engineering Management*, 35 (1988), 250–257.

11. McDonald, R. and D. Siegel, "The Value of Waiting to Invest," *Quarterly Journal of Economics*, 101 (1986), 707–727.

12. Ritchken, P. and G. Rabinowitz, "Capital Budgeting Using Contingent Claims Analysis," *Advances in Futures and Options Research*, 3 (1988), 119–143.

13. Triantis, A. and J. Hodder, "Valuing Flexibility as a Complex Option," *Journal of Finance*, 45 (1990), 549–565.

14. Trigeorgis, L., "Option Interactions and the Valuation of Investments with Multiple Real Options," *Journal of Financial and Quantitative Analysis*, 28, 1 (March 1993), 1–20.

15. Trigeorgis, L. and S. P. Mason, "Valuing Managerial Flexibility," *Midland Corporate Finance Journal*, 5 (Spring 1987), 14–21.

11 Irreversibility, Uncertainty, and Investment

Robert S. Pindyck

I Introduction

Despite its importance to economic growth and market structure, the investment behavior of firms, industries, and countries remains poorly understood. Econometric models have had limited success in explaining and predicting changes in investment spending, and we lack a clear explanation of why some countries or industries invest more than others.

One problem with existing models is that they ignore two important characteristics of most investment expenditures. First, the expenditures are largely irreversible; that is, they are mostly sunk costs that cannot be recovered. Second, the investments can be delayed, giving the firm an opportunity to wait for new information to arrive about prices, costs, and other market conditions before it commits resources.

As an emerging literature has shown, the ability to delay an irreversible investment expenditure can profoundly affect the decision to invest. It also undermines the theoretical foundation of standard neoclassical investment models, and invalidates the net present value rule as it is usually taught to students in business school: "Invest in a project when the present value of its expected cash flows is at least as large as its cost." This rule—and models based on it—are incorrect when investments are irreversible and decisions to invest can be postponed.

Irreversibility may have important implications for our understanding of aggregate investment behavior. It makes investment especially sensitive to various forms of risk, such as uncertainty over the future product prices and operating costs that determine cash flows, uncertainty over future interest rates, and uncertainty over the cost and timing of the investment itself. Irreversibility may therefore have implications for macroeconomic policy; if a goal is to stimulate investment, stability and credibility could be much more important than tax incentives or interest rates.

What makes an investment expenditure a sunk cost and thus irreversible? Usually it is the fact that the capital is firm or industry specific, that is, it cannot be used productively by a different firm or in a different industry. For example, most investments in marketing and advertising are firm specific, and hence are clearly sunk costs. A steel plant is industry specific—it can only be used to produce steel. Although in principle the plant could be sold to another steel company, its cost should be viewed as mostly sunk, particularly if the industry is competitive. The reason is that the value of the plant will be about the same for all firms in the industry, so there is likely to be little gained from selling it. (If the price of steel falls so that a plant turns out, ex post, to have been a "bad" investment, it will also be viewed as a bad investment by other steel companies, so that the ability to sell the plant will not be worth much.)

Even investments that are not firm or industry specific are often partly irreversible because of the "lemons" problem. For example, office equipment, cars, trucks, and computers are not industry specific, but have resale value well below their purchase cost, even if new. Irreversibility can also arise because of government regulations or institutional arrangements. For example, capital controls may make it impossible for foreign (or domestic) investors to sell assets and reallocate their funds. And investments in new workers may be partly irreversible because of high costs of hiring, training, and firing.

Firms do not always have an opportunity to delay investments. For example, there can be occasions in which strategic considerations make it imperative for a firm to invest quickly and thereby preempt investment by existing or potential competitors. (Richard Gilbert 1989 surveys the literature on strategic aspects of investment.) But in most cases, delay is at least feasible. There may be a cost to delay—the risk of entry by other firms, or simply foregone cash flows—but this cost must be weighed against the benefits of waiting for new information.

An irreversible investment opportunity is much like a financial call option. A call option gives the holder the right, for some specified amount of time, to pay an exercise price and in return receive an asset (e.g., a share of stock) that has some value. Exercising the option is irreversible; although the asset can be sold to another investor, one cannot retrieve the option or the money that was paid to exercise it. A firm with an investment opportunity likewise has the option to spend money (the "exercise price") now or in the future, in return for an asset (e.g., a project) of some value. Again, the asset can be sold to another firm, but the investment is irreversible. As with the financial call option, this option to invest is valuable in part because the future value of the asset obtained by investing is uncertain. If the asset rises in value, the net payoff from investing rises. If it falls in value, the firm need not invest, and will only lose what it spent to obtain the investment opportunity.

How do firms obtain investment opportunities? Sometimes they result from patents, or ownership of land or natural resources. More generally, they arise from a firm's managerial resources, technological knowledge, reputation, market position, and possible scale, all of which may have been built up over time, and which enable the firm to productively undertake investments that individuals or other firms cannot undertake. Most important, these options to invest are valuable. Indeed, for most firms, a substantial part of their market value is attributable to their options to invest and grow in the future, as opposed to the capital they already have in place. (For discussions of growth options as sources of firm value, see Stewart Myers 1977; W. Carl Kester 1984; and my 1988 article.)

When a firm makes an irreversible investment expenditure, it exercises, or "kills," its option to invest. It gives up the possibility of waiting for new information to arrive that might affect the desirability or timing of the expenditure; it cannot disinvest should market conditions change adversely. This lost option value is an opportunity cost that must be included as part of the cost of the investment. As a result, the NPV rule "Invest when the value of a unit of capital is at least as large as its purchase and installation cost" must be modified. The value of the unit must *exceed* the purchase and installation cost, by an amount equal to the value of keeping the investment option alive.

Recent studies have shown that this opportunity cost of investing can be large, and investment rules that ignore it can be grossly in error.[1] Also, this opportunity cost is highly sensitive to uncertainty over the future value of the project, so that changing economic conditions that affect the perceived riskiness of future cash flows can have a large impact on investment spending, larger than, say, a change in interest rates. This may help to explain why neoclassical investment theory has failed to provide good empirical models of investment behavior.

This chapter has several objectives. First, I will review some basic models of irreversible investment to illustrate the option-like characteristics of investment opportunities, and to show how optimal investment rules can be obtained from methods of option pricing, or alternatively from dynamic programming. Besides demonstrating a methodology that can be used to solve a class of investment problems, this will show how the resulting investment rules depend on various parameters that come from the market environment.

A second objective is to survey briefly some recent applications of this methodology to a variety of investment problems, and to the analysis of firm and industry behavior. Examples will include the effects of sunk costs of entry, exit, and temporary shutdowns and restartups on investment and output decisions, the implications of construction time (and the option to abandon construction) for the value of a project, and the determinants of a firm's choice of capacity. I will also show how models of irreversible investment have helped to explain the prevalence of "hysteresis," that is, the tendency for an effect (such as foreign sales in the U.S.) to persist well after the cause that brought it about (an appreciation of the dollar) has disappeared.

Finally, I will briefly discuss some of the implications that the irreversibility of investment may have for policy. For example, given the importance of risk, policies that stabilize prices or exchange rates may be particulary effective ways of stimulating investment. Similarly, a major cost of political and economic instability may be its depressing effect on investment.

Section II uses a simple two-period example to illustrate how irreversibility can affect an investment decision, and how option pricing methods can be used to value a firm's investment opportunity, and determine whether or not the firm should invest. Section III then works through a basic continuous-time model of irreversible investment that was first examined by McDonald and Siegel (1986). Here a firm must decide when to invest in a project whose value follows a random walk. I first solve this problem using option pricing methods and then by dynamic programming, and show how the two approaches are related. Section IV extends this model so that the price of the firm's output follows a random walk, and the firm can (temporarily) stop producing if price falls below variable cost. I show how both the value of the project and the value of the firm's option to invest in the project can be determined, and derive the optimal investment rule and examine its properties.

Sections III and IV require the use of stochastic calculus, but I explain the basic techniques and their application in the Appendix. However, readers who are less technically inclined can skip directly to Section V. That section surveys a number of extensions that have appeared in the literature, as well as other applications of the methodology, including the analysis of hysteresis. Section VI discusses policy implications and suggests future research, and Section VII concludes.

II   A Simple Two-Period Example

The implications of irreversibility and the option-like nature of an investment opportunity can be demonstrated most easily with a simple two-period example. Consider a firm's decision to invest irreversibly in a widget factory. The factory can be built instantly, at a cost I, and will produce one widget per year forever, with zero operating cost. Currently the price of widgets is $100, but next year the price will change. With probability q, it will rise to $150, and with probability $(1 - q)$ it will fall to $50. The price will then remain at this new level forever. (See figure 11.1.) We will assume that this risk is fully diversifiable, so that the firm can discount future cash flows using the risk-free rate, which we will take to be 10 percent.

For the time being we will set $I = \$800$ and $q = .5$. (Later we will see how the investment decision depends on I and q.) Given these values for I and q, is this a good investment? Should we invest now, or wait a year and see whether the price goes up or down? Suppose we invest now. Calculating the net present value of this investment in the standard way, we get

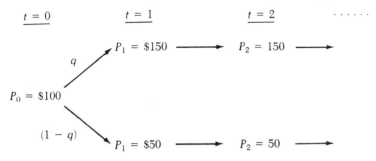

Figure 11.1
Price of widgets

$$\text{NPV} = -800 + \sum_{t=0}^{\infty} 100/(1.1)^t$$

$$= -800 + 1,100 = \$300.$$

The NPV is positive; the current value of a widget factory is $V_0 = 1,100 > 800$. Hence it would seem that we should go ahead with the investment.

This conclusion is incorrect, however, because the calculations above ignore a cost—the opportunity cost of investing now, rather than waiting and keeping open the possibility of not investing should the price fall. To see this, calculate the NPV of this investment opportunity, assuming instead that we wait one year and then invest only if the price goes up:

$$\text{NPV} = (.5)\left[-800/1.1 + \sum_{t=1}^{\infty} 150/(1.1)^t\right]$$

$$= 425/1.1 = \$386.$$

(Note that in year 0, there is no expenditure and no revenue. In year 1, the $800 is spent only if the price rises to $150, which will happen with probability .5.) The NPV today is higher if we plan to wait a year, so clearly waiting is better than investing now.

Note that if our only choices were to invest today or never invest, we would invest today. In that case there is no option to wait a year, and hence no opportunity cost to killing such an option, so the standard NPV rule would apply. We would likewise invest today if next year we could disinvest and recover the $800 should the price fall. Two things are needed to introduce an opportunity cost into the NPV calculation—

irreversibility, and the ability to invest in the future as an alternative to investing today. There are, of course, situations in which a firm cannot wait, or cannot wait very long, to invest. (One example is the anticipated entry of a competitor into a market that is only large enough for one firm. Another example is a patent or mineral resource lease that is about to expire.) The less time there is to delay, and the greater the cost of delaying, the less will irreversibility affect the investment decision. We will explore this point again in Section III in the context of a more general model.

How much is it worth to have the flexibility to make the investment decision next year, rather than having to invest either now or never? (We know that having this flexibility is of some value, because we would prefer to wait rather than invest now.) The value of this "flexibility option" is easy to calculate; it is just the difference between the two NPVs, that is, $386 − $300 = $86.

Finally, suppose there exists a futures market for widgets, with the futures price for delivery one year from now equal to the expected future spot price, $100.[2] Would the ability to hedge on the futures market change our investment decision? Specifically, would it lead us to invest now, rather than waiting a year? The answer is no. To see this, note that if we were to invest now, we would hedge by selling short futures for five widgets; this would exactly offset any fluctuations in the NPV of our project next year. But this would also mean that the NPV of our project today is $300, exactly what it is without hedging. Hence there is no gain from hedging, and we are still better off waiting until next year to make our investment decision.

A Analogy to Financial Options

Our investment opportunity is analogous to a call option on a common stock. It gives us the right (which we need not exercise) to make an investment expenditure (the exercise price of the option) and receive a project (a share of stock) the value of which fluctuates stochastically. In the case of our simple example, next year if the price rises to $150, we exercise our option by paying $800 and receive an asset that will be worth $V_1 = \$1,650 \ (= \sum_0^\infty 150/1.1^t)$. If the price falls to $50, this asset will be worth only $550, so we will not exercise the option. We found that the value of our investment opportunity (assuming that the actual decision to invest can indeed be made next year) is $386. It will be helpful to recalculate this value using standard option pricing methods, because later we will use such methods to analyze other investment problems.

To do this, let F_0 denote the value today of the investment opportunity, that is, what we should be willing to pay today to have the option to invest in the widget factory, and let F_1 denote its value next year. Note that F_1 is a random variable; it depends on what happens to the price of widgets. If the price rises to $150, then F_1

will equal $\sum_0^\infty 150/(1.1)^t - \$800 = \$850$. If the price falls to \$50, the option to invest will go unexercised, so that F_1 will equal 0. Thus we know all possible values for F_1. The problem is to find F_0, the value of the option today.

To solve this problem, we will create a portfolio that has two components: the investment opportunity itself, and a certain number of widgets. We will pick this number of widgets so that the portfolio is risk-free, that is, so that its value next year is independent of whether the price of widgets goes up or down. Because the portfolio will be risk-free, we know that the rate of return one can earn from holding it must be the risk-free rate. By setting the portfolio's return equal to that rate, we will be able to calculate the current value of the investment opportunity.

Specifically, consider a portfolio in which one holds the investment opportunity, and sells short n widgets. (If widgets were a traded commodity, such as oil, one could obtain a short position by borrowing from another producer, or by going short in the futures market. For the moment, however, we need not be concerned with the actual implementation of this portfolio.) The value of this portfolio today is $\Phi_0 = F_0 - nP_0 = F_0 - 100n$. The value next year, $\Phi_1 = F_1 - nP_1$, depends on P_1. If $P_1 = 150$ so that $F_1 = 850$, $\Phi_1 = 850 - 150n$. If $P_1 = 50$ so that $F_1 = 0$, $\Phi_1 = -50n$. Now, let us choose n so that the portfolio is risk-free, that is, so that Φ_1 is independent of what happens to price. To do this, just set

$$850 - 150n = -50n,$$

or, $n = 8.5$. With n chosen this way, $\Phi_1 = -425$, whether the price goes up or down.

We now calculate the return from holding this portfolio. That return is the capital gain, $\Phi_1 - \Phi_0$, minus any payments that must be made to hold the short position. Because the expected rate of capital gain on a widget is zero (the expected price next year is \$100, the same as this year's price), no rational investor would hold a long position unless he or she could expect to earn at least 10 percent. Hence selling widgets short will require a payment of $.1P_0 = \$10$ per widget per year.[3] Our portfolio has a short position of 8.5 widgets, so it will have to pay out a total of \$85. The return from holding this portfolio over the year is thus $\Phi_1 - \Phi_0 - 85 = \Phi_1 - (F_0 - nP_0) - 85 = -425 - F_0 + 850 - 85 = 340 - F_0$.

Because this return is risk-free, we know that it must equal the risk-free rate, which we have assumed is 10 percent, times the initial value of the portfolio, $\Phi_0 = F_0 - nP_0$:

$$340 - F_0 = .1(F_0 - 850).$$

We can thus determine that $F_0 = \$386$. Note that this is the same value that we obtained before by calculating the NPV of the investment opportunity under the assumption that we follow the optimal strategy of waiting a year before deciding whether to invest.

We have found that the value of our investment opportunity, that is, the value of the option to invest in this project, is \$386. The payoff from investing (exercising the option) today is \$1,100 − \$800 = \$300. But once we invest, our option is gone, so the \$386 is an opportunity cost of investing. Hence the *full cost* of the investment is \$800 + \$386 = \$1,186 > \$1,100. As a result, we should wait and keep our option alive, rather than invest today. We have thus come to the same conclusion as we did by comparing NPVs. This time, however, we calculated the value of the option to invest, and explicitly took it into account as one of the costs of investing.

Our calculation of the value of the option to invest was based on the construction of a risk-free portfolio, which requires that one can trade (hold a long or short position in) widgets. Of course, we could just as well have constructed our portfolio using some other asset, or combination of assets, the price of which is perfectly correlated with the price of widgets. But what if one cannot trade widgets, and there are no other assets that "span" the risk in a widget's price? In this case one could still calculate the value of the option to invest the way we did at the outset—by computing the NPV for each investment strategy (invest today versus wait a year and invest if the price goes up), and picking the strategy that yields the highest NPV. That is essentially the dynamic programming approach. In this case it gives exactly the same answer, because all price risk is diversifiable. In Section III we will explore this connection between option pricing and dynamic programming in more detail.

B   Changing the Parameters

So far we have fixed the direct cost of the investment, I, at \$800. We can obtain further insight by changing this number, as well as other parameters, and calculating the effects on the value of the investment opportunity and on the investment decision. For example, by going through the same steps as above, it is easy to see that the short position needed to obtain a risk-free portfolio depends on I as follows:

$$n = 16.5 - .01I.$$

The current value of the option to invest is then given by

$$F_0 = 750 - .455I.$$

The reader can check that as long as $I > \$642$, F_0 exceeds the net benefit from investing today (rather than waiting), which is $V_0 - I = \$1,100 - I$. Hence if $I > \$642$, one should wait rather than invest today. However, if $I = \$642$, $F_0 = \$458 =$

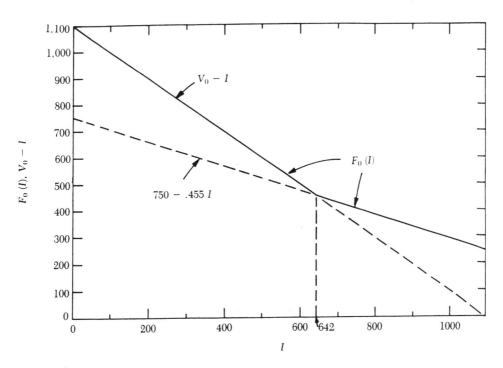

Figure 11.2
Option to invest in widget factory

$V_0 - I$, so that one would be indifferent between investing today and waiting until next year. (This can also be seen by comparing the NPV of investing today with the NPV of waiting until next year.) And if $I <$ \$642, one should invest today rather than wait. The reason is that in this case the lost revenue from waiting exceeds the opportunity cost of closing off the option of waiting and not investing should the price fall. This is illustrated in figure 11.2, which shows the value of the option, F_0, and the net payoff, $V_0 - I$, both as functions of I. For $I >$ \$642, $F_0 = 750 - .455I >$ $V_0 - I$, so the option should be kept alive. However, if $I <$ \$642, $750 - .455I <$ $V_0 - I$, so the option should be exercised, and hence its value is just the net payoff, $V_0 - I$.

We can also determine how the value of the investment option depends on q, the probability that the price of widgets will rise next year. To do this, let us once again set $I =$ \$800. The reader can verify that the short position needed to obtain a risk-free portfolio is independent of q, that is, $n = 8.5$. The payment required for the short position, however, does depend on q, because the expected capital gain on a widget depends on q. The expected rate of capital gain is $[E(P_1) - P_0]/P_0 = q - .5$, so the required payment per widget in the short position is $.1 - (q - .5) = .6 - q$. By following the same steps as above, it is easy to see that the value today of the option to invest is $F_0 = 773q$. This can also be written as a function of the current value of the project, V_0. We have $V_0 = 100 + \sum_1^\infty (100q + 50)/(1.1)^t = 600 + 1000q$, so $F_0 = .773V_0 - 464$. Finally, note that it is better to wait rather than invest today as long as $F_0 > V_0 - I$, or $q < .88$.

There is nothing special about the particular source of uncertainty that we introduced in this problem. There will be a value to waiting (i.e., an opportunity cost to investing today rather than waiting for information to arrive) whenever the investment is irreversible and the net payoff from the investment evolves stochastically over time. Thus we could have constructed our example so that the uncertainty arises over future exchange rates, factor input costs, or government policy. For example, the payoff from investing, V, might rise or fall in the future depending on (unpredictable) changes in policy. Alternatively, the cost of the investment, I, might rise or fall, in response to changes in materials costs, or to a policy change, such as the granting or taking away of an investment subsidy or tax benefit.

In our example, we made the unrealistic assumption that there is no longer any uncertainty after the second period. Instead, we could have allowed the price to change unpredictably *each period*. For example, we could posit that at $t = 2$, if the price is \$150, it could increase to \$225 with probability q or fall to \$75 with probability $(1 - q)$, and if it is \$50 it could rise to \$75 or fall to \$25. Price could rise or fall in a similar way at $t = 3, 4$, and so on. One could then work out the value of the option to invest, and the optimal rule for exercising that option. Although the algebra is messier, the method is essentially the same as for the simple two-period exercise we carried out above. (This is the basis for the binomial option pricing model. See John Cox, Stephen Ross, and Mark Rubinstein 1979 and Cox and Rubinstein 1985 for detailed discussions.) Rather than take this approach, in the next section we extend our example by allowing the payoff from the investment to fluctuate *continuously* over time.

The next two sections make use of continuous-time stochastic processes, as well as Ito's Lemma (which is essentially a rule for differentiating and integrating functions of such processes). These tools, which are becoming more and more widely used in economics and finance, provide a convenient way of analyzing investment timing and option valuation problems. I provide an introduction to the use of these tools in the Appendix for readers who are unfamiliar with them. Those readers might want to review the Appendix before proceeding. (Introductory treatments can also be found in Robert Merton 1971; Gregory Chow 1979; John Hull 1989; and A. G. Malliaris and William Brock 1982.) Readers who would prefer to avoid this technical material altogether can skip directly to Section V, although they will miss some insights by doing so.

III   A More General Problem of Investment Timing

One of the more basic models of irreversible investment is that of McDonald and Siegel (1986). They considered the following problem: At what point is it optimal to pay a sunk cost I in return for a project whose value is V, given that V evolves according to a geometric Brownian motion:

$$dV = \alpha V\,dt + \sigma V\,dz \tag{1}$$

where dz is the increment of a Wiener process, that is, $dz = \varepsilon(t)(dt)^{1/2}$, with $\varepsilon(t)$ a serially uncorrelated and normally distributed random variable. Equation (1) implies that the current value of the project is known, but future values are log-normally distributed with a variance that grows linearly with the time horizon. (See the Appendix for an explanation of the Wiener process.) Thus although information arrives over time (the firm observes V changing), the future value of the project is always uncertain.

McDonald and Siegel pointed out that the investment opportunity is equivalent to a perpetual call option, and deciding when to invest is equivalent to deciding when to exercise such an option. Thus, the investment decision can be viewed as a problem of option valuation (as we saw in the simple example presented in the previous section). I will rederive the solution to their problem in two ways, first using option pricing (contingent claims) methods, and then via dynamic programming. This will allow us to compare these two approaches and the assumptions that each requires. We will then examine the characteristics of the solution.

A   The Use of Option Pricing

As we have seen, the firm's option to invest, that is, to pay a sunk cost I and receive a project worth V, is analogous to a call option on a stock. Unlike most financial call options, it is *perpetual*—it has no expiration date. We can value this option and determine the optimal exercise (investment) rule using the same methods used to value financial options. (For an overview of option pricing methods and their application, see Cox and Rubinstein 1985; Hull 1989; and Mason and Merton 1985.)

This approach requires one important assumption, namely that stochastic changes in V are spanned by existing assets. Specifically, it must be possible to find an asset or construct a dynamic portfolio of assets (i.e., a portfolio whose holdings are adjusted continuously as asset prices change), the price of which is perfectly correlated with V. This is equivalent to saying that markets are sufficiently complete that the firm's decisions do not affect the opportunity set available to investors. The assumption of spanning should hold for most commodities, which are typically traded on both spot and futures markets, and for manufactured goods to the extent that prices are correlated with the values of shares or portfolios. However, there may be cases in which this assumption will not hold; an example might be a new product unrelated to any existing ones.

With the spanning assumption, we can determine the investment rule that maximizes the firm's market value without making any assumptions about risk preferences or discount rates, and the investment problem reduces to one of contingent claim valuation. (We will see shortly that if spanning does not hold, dynamic programming can still be used to maximize the present value of the firm's expected flow of profits, subject to an arbitrary discount rate.)

Let x be the price of an asset or dynamic portfolio of assets perfectly correlated with V, and denote by ρ_{Vm} the correlation of V with the market portfolio. Then x evolves according to

$$dx = \mu x\, dt + \sigma x\, dz,$$

and by the capital asset pricing model (CAPM), its expected return is $\mu = r + \phi\rho_{Vm}\sigma$, where r is the risk-free rate and ϕ is the market price of risk. We will assume that α, the expected percentage rate of change of V, is *less* than its risk-adjusted return μ. (As will become clear, the firm would never invest if this were not the case. No matter what the current level of V, the firm would always be better off waiting and simply holding on to the option to invest.) We denote by δ the difference between μ and α, that is, $\delta = \mu - \alpha$.

A few words about the meaning of δ are in order, given the important role it plays in this model. The analogy with a financial call option is helpful here. If V were the price of a share of common stock, δ would be the dividend rate on the stock. The total expected return on the stock would be $\mu = \delta + \alpha$, that is, the dividend rate plus the expected rate of capital gain.

If the dividend rate δ were zero, a call option on the stock would always be held to maturity, and never exercised prematurely. The reason is that the entire return on the stock is captured in its price movements, and hence by the call option, so there is no cost to keeping the option alive. But if the dividend rate is positive, there is an opportunity cost to keeping the option alive rather than exercising it. That opportunity cost is the dividend stream that one forgoes by holding the option rather than the stock. Because δ is a proportional dividend rate, the higher the price of the stock, the greater the flow of dividends. At some high enough price, the opportunity cost of forgone dividends becomes high enough to make it worthwhile to exercise the option.

For our investment problem, μ is the expected rate of return from owning the completed project. It is the equilibrium rate established by the capital market, and includes an appropriate risk premium. If $\delta > 0$, the expected rate of capital gain on the project is less than μ. Hence δ is an opportunity cost of delaying construction of the project, and instead keeping the option to invest alive. If δ were zero, there would be no opportunity cost to keeping the option alive, and one would never invest, no matter how high the NPV of the project. That is why we assume $\delta > 0$. On the other hand, if δ is very large, the value of the option will be very small, because the opportunity cost of waiting is large. As $\delta \to \infty$, the value of the option goes to zero; in effect, the only choices are to invest now or never, and the standard NPV rule will again apply.

The parameter δ can be interpreted in different ways. For example, it could reflect the process of entry and capacity expansion by competitors. Or it can simply reflect the cash flows from the project. If the project is infinitely lived, then equation (1) can represent the evolution of V during the operation of the project, and δV is the rate of cash flow that the project yields. Because we assume δ is constant, this is consistent with future cash flows being a constant proportion of the project's market value.[4]

Equation (1) is, of course, an abstraction from most real projects. For example, if variable cost is positive and the project can be shut down temporarily when price falls below variable cost, V will not follow a log-normal process, even if the output price does. Nonetheless, equation (1) is a useful simplification that will help to clarify the main effects of irreversibility and uncertainty. We will discuss more complicated (and hopefully more realistic) models later.

B Solving the Investment Problem

Let us now turn to the valuation of our investment opportunity, and the optimal investment rule. Let $F = F(V)$ be the value of the firm's option to invest. To find $F(V)$ and the optimal investment rule, consider the return on the following portfolio: Hold the option, which is worth $F(V)$, and go short dF/dV units of the project (or equivalently, of the asset or portfolio x). Using subscripts to denote derivatives, the value of this portfolio is $P = F - F_V V$. Note that this portfolio is dynamic; as V changes, F_V may change, in which case the composition of the portfolio will be changed.

The short position in this portfolio will require a payment of $\delta V F_V$ dollars per time period; otherwise no rational investor will enter into the long side of the transaction. (To see this, note that an investor holding a long position in the project will demand the risk-adjusted return μV, which includes the capital gain *plus* the dividend stream δV. Because the short position includes F_V units of the project, it will require paying out $\delta V F_V$.) Taking this into account, the total return from holding the portfolio over a short time interval dt is

$$dF - F_V \, dV - \delta V F_V \, dt.$$

We will see shortly that this return is risk-free. Hence to avoid arbitrage possibilities it must equal $r(F - F_V V) \, dt$:

$$dF - F_V \, dV - \delta V F_V \, dt = r(F - F_V V) \, dt. \tag{2}$$

To obtain an expression for dF, use Ito's Lemma:

$$dF = F_V \, dV + (1/2)F_{VV}(dV)^2. \tag{3}$$

(Ito's Lemma is explained in the Appendix. Note that higher-order terms vanish.) Now substitute (1) for dV, with α replaced by $\mu - \delta$, and $(dV)^2 = \sigma^2 V^2 \, dt$ into equation (3):

$$dF = (\mu - \delta)V F_V \, dt + \sigma V F_V \, dz + (1/2)\sigma^2 V^2 F_{VV} \, dt. \tag{4}$$

Finally, substitute (4) into (2), rearrange terms, and note that all terms in dz cancel out, so the portfolio is indeed risk-free:

$$(1/2)\sigma^2 V^2 F_{VV} + (r - \delta)V F_V - rF = 0. \tag{5}$$

Equation (5) is a differential equation that $F(V)$ must satisfy. In addition, $F(V)$ must satisfy the following boundary conditions:

$$F(0) = 0. \tag{6a}$$

$$F(V^*) = V^* - I. \tag{6b}$$

$$F_V(V^*) = 1. \tag{6c}$$

Condition (6a) says that if V goes to zero, it will stay at zero—an implication of the process (1)—so the option to invest will be of no value. V^* is the price at which it is optimal to invest, and (6b) just says that upon investing, the firm receives a net payoff $V^* - I$. Condition (6c) is called the "smooth pasting" condition. If $F(V)$ were not continuous and smooth at the critical exercise point V^*, one could do better by exercising at a different point.[5]

To find $F(V)$, we must solve equation (5) subject to the boundary conditions (6a–6c). In this case we can guess a functional form, and determine by substitution if it works. It is easy to see the solution to equation (5) that also satisfies condition (6a) is

$$F(V) = aV^\beta \tag{7}$$

where a is a constant, and β is given by[6]

$$\beta = 1/2 - (r - \delta)/\sigma^2 + \{[(r - \delta)/\sigma^2 - 1/2]^2 + 2r/\sigma^2\}^{1/2}. \tag{8}$$

The remaining boundary conditions, (6b) and (6c), can be used to solve for the two remaining unknowns: the constant a, and the critical value V^* at which it is optimal to invest. By substituting (7) into (6b) and (6c), it is easy to see that

$$V^* = \beta I/(\beta - 1) \tag{9}$$

and

$$a = (V^* - I)/(V^*)^\beta. \tag{10}$$

Equations (7–10) give the value of the investment opportunity, and the optimal investment rule, that is, the critical value V^* at which it is optimal (in the sense of maximizing the firm's market value) to invest. We will examine the characteristic of this solution below. Here we simply point out that we obtained this solution by showing that a hedged (risk-free) portfolio could be constructed consisting of the option to invest and a short position in the project. However, $F(V)$ must be the solution to equation (5) even if the option to invest (or the project) does not exist and could not be included in the hedge portfolio. All that is required is spanning, that is, that one could find or construct an asset or dynamic portfolio of assets (x) that replicates the stochastic dynamics of V. As Merton (1977) has shown, one can replicate the value function with a portfolio consisting only of the asset x and risk-free bonds, and because the value of this portfolio will have the same dynamics as $F(V)$, the solution to (5), $F(V)$ must be the value function to avoid dominance.

As discussed earlier, spanning will not always hold. If that is the case, one can still solve the investment problem using dynamic programming. This is shown below.

C Dynamic Programming

To solve the problem by dynamic programming, note that we want a rule that maximizes the value of our investment opportunity, $F(V)$:

$$F(V) = \max E_t[(V_T - I)e^{-\mu T}] \tag{11}$$

where E_t denotes the expectation at time t, T is the (unknown) future time that the investment is made, μ is the discount rate, and the maximization is subject to equation (1) for V. We will assume that $\mu > \alpha$, and as before denote $\delta = \mu - \alpha$.

Because the investment opportunity, $F(V)$, yields no cash flows up to the time T that the investment is undertaken, the only return from holding it is its capital appreciation. As shown in the Appendix, the Bellman equation for this problem is therefore

$$\mu F = (1/dt)E_t \, dF. \tag{12}$$

Equation (12) just says that the total instantaneous return on the investment opportunity, μF, is equal to its expected rate of capital appreciation.

We used Ito's Lemma to obtain equation (3) for dF. Now substitute (1) for dV and $(dV)^2$ into equation (3) to obtain the following expression for dF:

$$dF = \alpha V F_V \, dt + \sigma V F_V \, dz + (1/2)\sigma^2 V^2 F_{VV} \, dt.$$

Because $E_t(dz) = 0$, $(1/dt)E_t \, dF = \alpha V F_V + (1/2)\sigma^2 V^2 F_{VV}$, and equation (12) can be rewritten as:

$$(1/2)\sigma^2 V^2 F_{VV} + \alpha V F_V - \mu F = 0$$

or, substituting $\alpha = \mu - \delta$,

$$(1/2)\sigma^2 V^2 F_{VV} + (\mu - \delta) V F_V - \mu F = 0. \tag{13}$$

Observe that this equation is almost identical to equation (5); the only difference is that the discount rate μ replaces the risk-free rate r. The boundary conditions (6a–6c) also apply here, and for the same reasons as before. (Note that (6c) follows from the fact that V^* is chosen to maximize the net payoff $V^* - I$.) Hence the contingent claims solution to our investment problem is equivalent to a dynamic programming solution, under the assumption of risk neutrality.[7]

Thus if spanning does not hold, we can still obtain a solution to the investment problem, subject to some discount rate. The solution will clearly be of the same form, and the effects of changes in σ or δ will likewise be the same. One point is worth noting, however. Without spanning, there is no theory for determining the "correct" value for the discount rate μ (unless we make restrictive assumptions about investors' or managers' utility functions). The CAPM, for example, would not hold, so it could not be used to calculate a risk-adjusted discount rate.

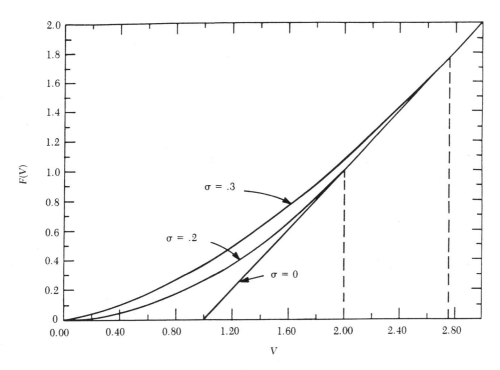

Figure 11.3
$F(V)$ for $\sigma = 0.2, 0.3$

D Characteristics of the Solution

Assuming that spanning holds, let us examine the optimal investment rule given by equations (7–10). A few numerical solutions will help to illustrate the results and show how they depend on the values of the various parameters. As we will see, these results are qualitatively the same as those that come out of standard option pricing models. Unless otherwise noted, in what follows we set $r = .04$, $\delta = .04$, and the cost of the investment, I, equal to 1.

Figure 11.3 shows the value of the investment opportunity, $F(V)$, for $\sigma = .2$ and .3. (These values are conservative for many projects; in volatile markets, the standard deviation of annual changes in a project's value can easily exceed 20 or 30 percent.) The tangency point of $F(V)$ with the line $V - I$ gives the critical value of V, V^*; the firm should invest only if $V \geq V^*$. For any positive σ, $V^* > I$. Thus the standard NPV rule, "Invest when the value of a project is at least as great as its cost," must be modified to include the opportunity cost of investing now rather than waiting. That opportunity cost is exactly $F(V)$. When $V < V^*$, $V < I + F(V)$, that is, the value of the project is less than its *full* cost, the direct cost I plus the opportunity cost of "killing" the investment option.

Note that $F(V)$ increases when σ increases, and so too does the critical value V^*. Thus uncertainty increases the value of a firm's investment opportunities, but decreases the amount of actual investing that the firm will do. As a result, when a firm's market or economic environment becomes more uncertain, the stock market value of the firm can go up, even though the firm does less investing and perhaps produces less! This should make it easier to understand the behavior of oil companies during the mid-1980s. During this period oil prices fell, but the perceived uncertainty over future oil prices rose. In response, oil companies paid more than ever for off-shore leases and other oil-bearing lands, even though their development expenditures fell and they produced less.

Finally, note that our results regarding the effects of uncertainty involve no assumptions about risk preferences, or about the extent to which the riskiness of V is correlated with the market. Firms can be risk-neutral, and stochastic changes in V can be completely diversifiable; an increase in σ will still increase V^* and hence tend to depress investment.

Figures 11.4 and 11.5 show how $F(V)$ and V^* depend on δ. Observe that an increase in δ from .04 to .08 results in a *decrease* in $F(V)$, and hence a decrease in the critical value V^*. (In the limit as $\delta \to \infty$, $F(V) \to 0$ for $V < I$, and $V^* \to I$, as Figure 5 shows.) The reason is that as δ becomes larger, the expected rate of growth of V falls, and hence the expected appreciation in the value of the option to invest and acquire V falls. In effect, it becomes costlier to wait rather than invest now. To see this, consider an investment in an apartment building, where δV is the net flow of rental income. The total return on the building, which must equal the risk-adjusted market rate, has two components—this income flow plus the expected rate of capital gain. Hence the greater the income flow relative to the total return on the building, the more one forgoes by holding an option to invest in the building, rather than owning the building itself.

If the risk-free rate, r, is increased, $F(V)$ increases, and so does V^*. The reason is that the present value of an investment expenditure I made at a future time T is Ie^{-rT}, but the present value of the project that one receives in return for that expenditure is $Ve^{-\delta T}$. Hence with δ fixed, an increase in r reduces the present value of the cost of the investment but does not reduce its payoff. But note that while an increase in r raises the value of a firm's investment options, it also results in fewer of those options being exercised. Hence higher (real) interest rates reduce investment, but for a different reason than in the standard model.

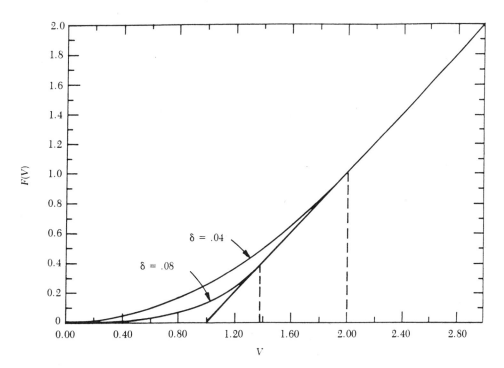

Figure 11.4
$F(V)$ for $\delta = 0.04, 0.08$

IV   The Value of a Project and the Decision to Invest

As mentioned earlier, equation (1) abstracts from most real projects. A more realistic model would treat the price of the project's output as a geometric random walk (and possibly one or more factor input costs as well), rather than making the value of the project a random walk. It would also allow for the project to be shut down (permanently or temporarily) if price falls below variable cost. The model developed in the previous section can easily be extended in this way. In so doing, we will see that option pricing methods can be used to find the value of the project, as well as the optimal investment rule.

Suppose the output price, P, follows the stochastic process:

$$dP = \alpha P \, dt + \sigma P \, dz. \tag{14}$$

We will assume that $\alpha < \mu$, where μ is the market risk-adjusted expected rate of return on P or an asset perfectly correlated with P, and let $\delta = \mu - \alpha$ as before. If the

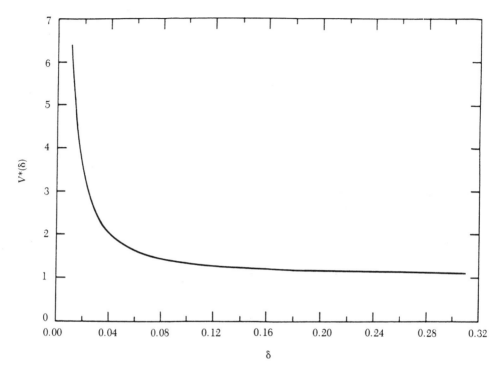

Figure 11.5
V^* as a function of δ

output is a storable commodity (e.g., oil or copper), δ will represent the *net marginal convenience yield* from storage, that is, the flow of benefits (less storage costs) that the marginal stored unit provides. We assume for simplicity that δ is constant. (For most commodities, marginal convenience yield in fact fluctuates as the total amount of storage fluctuates.)

We will also assume the following: (i) Marginal and average production cost is equal to a constant, c. (ii) The project can be costlessly shut down if P falls below c, and later restarted if P rises above c. (iii) The project produces one unit of output per period, is infinitely lived, and the (sunk) cost of investing in the project is I.

We now have two problems to solve. First, we must find the value of this project, $V(P)$. To do this, we can make use of the fact that the project itself is a set of options.[8] Specifically, once the project has been built, the firm has, for each future time t, an option to produce a unit of output, that is an option to pay c and receive P. Hence the project is equivalent to a large number (in this case, infinite, because the project is assumed to last indefinitely) of *operating* options, and can be valued accordingly.

Second, given the value of the project, we must value the firm's option to invest in it, and determine the optimal exercise (investment) rule. This will boil down to finding a critical P^*, where the firm invests only if $P \geq P^*$. As shown below, the two steps to this problem can be solved sequentially by the same methods used in the previous section.[9]

A Valuing the Project

If we assume that uncertainty over P is spanned by existing assets, we can value the project (as well as the option to invest) using contingent claim methods. Otherwise, we can specify a discount rate and use dynamic programming. We will assume spanning and use the first approach.

As before, we construct a risk-free portfolio: long the project and short V_P units of the output. This portfolio has value $V(P) - V_P P$, and yields the instantaneous cash flow $j(P - c)\,dt - \delta V_P P\,dt$, where $j = 1$ if $P \geq c$ so that the firm is producing, and $j = 0$ otherwise. (Recall that $\delta V_P P\,dt$ is the payment that must be made to maintain the short position.) The total return on the portfolio is thus $dV - V_P\,dP + j(P - c)\,dt - \delta V_P P\,dt$. Because this return is risk-free, set it equal to $r(V - V_P P)\,dt$. Expanding dV using Ito's Lemma, substituting (14) for dP, and rearranging yields the following differential equation for V:

$$(1/2)\sigma^2 P^2 V_{PP} + (r - \delta)P V_P - rV + j(P - c) = 0. \tag{15}$$

This equation must be solved subject to the following boundary conditions:

$$V(0) = 0. \tag{16a}$$

$$V(c^-) = V(c^+). \tag{16b}$$

$$V_P(c^-) = V_P(c^+). \tag{16c}$$

$$\lim_{P \to \infty} V = P/\delta - c/r. \tag{16d}$$

Condition (16a) is an implication of equation (14); that is, if P is ever zero it will remain zero, so the project then has no value. Condition (16d) says that as P becomes very large, the probability that over any finite time period it will fall below cost and production will cease becomes very small. Hence the value of the project approaches the difference between two perpetuities: a flow of revenue (P) that is discounted at the risk-adjusted rate μ but is expected to grow at rate α, and a flow of cost (c), which is constant and hence is discounted at the risk-free rate r. Finally, conditions (16b) and (16c) say that the project's value is a continuous and smooth function of P.

The solution to equation (15) will have two parts, one for $P < c$, and one for $P \geq c$. The reader can check by substitution that the following satisfies (15) as well as boundary conditions (16a) and (16d):

$$V(P) = \begin{cases} A_1 P^{\beta_1}; & P < c \\ A_2 P^{\beta_2} + P/\delta - c/r; & P \geq c \end{cases} \qquad (17)$$

where:[10]

$$\beta_1 = 1/2 - (r - \delta)/\sigma^2 + \{[(r - \delta)/\sigma^2 - 1/2]^2 + 2r/\sigma^2\}^{1/2}$$

and

$$\beta_2 = 1/2 - (r - \delta)/\sigma^2 - \{[(r - \delta)/\sigma^2 - 1/2]^2 + 2r/\sigma^2\}^{1/2}.$$

The constants A_1 and A_2 can be found by applying boundary conditions (16b) and (16c):

$$A_1 = \frac{r - \beta_2(r - \delta)}{r\delta(\beta_1 - \beta_2)} c^{(1-\beta_1)}.$$

$$A_2 = \frac{r - \beta_1(r - \delta)}{r\delta(\beta_1 - \beta_2)} c^{(1-\beta_2)}.$$

The solution (17) for $V(P)$ can be interpreted as follows: When $P < c$, the project is not producing. Then, $A_1 P^{\beta_1}$ is the value of the firm's options to produce in the future, if and when P increases. When $P \geq c$, the project is producing. If, irrespective of changes in P, the firm had no choice but to continue producing throughout the future, the present value of the future flow of profits would be given by $P/\delta - c/r$. However, should P fall, the firm can stop producing and avoid losses. The value of its options to stop producing is $A_2 P^{\beta_2}$.

A numerical example will help to illustrate this solution. Unless otherwise noted, we set $r = .04$, $\delta = .04$, and $c = 10$. Figure 11.6 shows $V(P)$ for $\sigma = 0$, .2, and .4. When $\sigma = 0$, there is no possibility that P will rise in the future, so in this case the firm will never produce (and has no value) unless $P > 0$. If $P > 10$, $V(P) = (P - 10)/.04 = 25P = 250$. However, if $\sigma > 0$, the firm always has some value as long as $P > 0$; although the firm may not be producing today, it is likely to produce at some point in the future. Also, because the upside potential for future profit is unlimited while the downside is limited to zero, the greater is σ, the greater is the expected future flow of profit, and the higher is V.

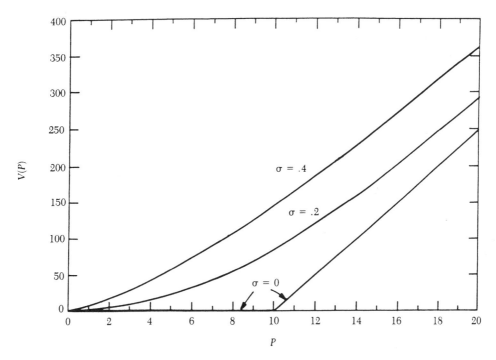

Figure 11.6
$F(P)$ for $\sigma = 0, 0.2, 0.4$

Figure 11.7 shows $V(P)$ for $\sigma = .2$ and $\delta = .02$, $.04$, and $.08$. For any fixed risk-adjusted discount rate, a higher value of δ means a lower expected rate of price appreciation, and hence a lower value for the firm.

B   The Investment Decision

Now that we know the value of this project, we must find the optimal investment rule. Specifically, what is the value of the firm's option to invest as a function of the price P, and at what critical price P^* should the firm exercise that option by spending an amount I to purchase the project?

By going through the same steps as above, the reader can check that the value of the firm's option to invest, $F(P)$, must satisfy the following differential equation:

$$(1/2)\sigma^2 P^2 F_{PP} + (r - \delta)PF_P - rF = 0. \tag{18}$$

$F(P)$ must also satisfy the following boundary conditions:

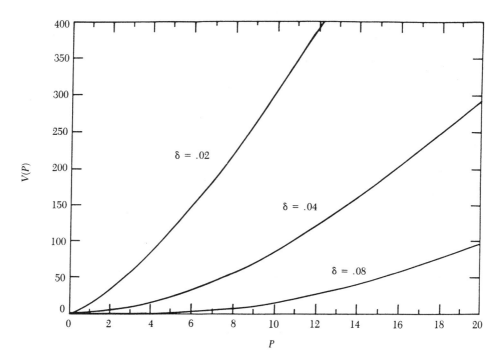

Figure 11.7
$F(P)$ for $\delta = 0.02, 0.04, 0.08$

$$F(0) = 0. \tag{19a}$$

$$F(P^*) = V(P^*) - I. \tag{19b}$$

$$F_P(P^*) = V_P(P^*). \tag{19c}$$

These conditions can be interpreted in the same way as conditions (6a–6c) for the model presented in Section III. The difference is that the payoff from the investment, V, is now a function of the price P.

The solution to equation (18) and boundary condition (19a) is

$$F(P) = \begin{cases} aP^{\beta_1}, & P \le P^* \\ V(P) - I, & P > P^* \end{cases} \tag{20}$$

where β_1 is given above under equation (17). To find the constant a and the critical price P^*, we use boundary conditions (19b) and (19c). By substituting equation (20) for $F(P)$ and equation (17) for $V(P)$ (for $P \geq c$) into (19b) and (19c), the reader can check that the constant a is given by

$$a = \frac{\beta_2 A_2}{\beta_1}(P^*)^{(\beta_2 - \beta_1)} + \frac{1}{\delta \beta_1}(P^*)^{(1-\beta_1)} \tag{21}$$

and the critical price P^* is the solution to

$$\frac{A_2(\beta_1 - \beta_2)}{\beta_1}(P^*)^{\beta_2} + \frac{(\beta_1 - 1)}{\delta \beta_1}P^* - \frac{c}{r} - I = 0. \tag{22}$$

Equation (22), which is easily solved numerically, gives the optimal investment rule. (The reader can check first, that (22) has a unique positive solution for P^* that is larger than c, and second, that $V(P^*) > I$, so that the project must have an NPV that exceeds zero before it is optimal to invest.)

This solution is shown graphically in figure 11.8, for $\sigma = .2$, $\delta = .04$, and $I = 100$. The figure plots $F(P)$ and $V(P) - I$. Note from boundary condition (19b) that P^* satisfies $F(P^*) = V(P^*) - I$, and note from boundary condition (19c) that P^* is at a point of tangency of the two curves.

The comparative statics for changes in σ or δ are of interest. As we saw before, an increase in σ results in an increase in $V(P)$ for any P. (The project is a set of call options on future production, and the greater the volatility of price, the greater the value of these options.) But although an increase in σ raises the value of the project, it also increases the critical price at which it is optimal to invest, that is, $\partial P^* / \partial \sigma > 0$. The reason is that for any P, the opportunity cost of investing, $F(P)$, increases even more than $V(P)$. Hence as with the simpler model presented in the previous section, increased uncertainty reduces investment. This is illustrated in figure 11.9, which shows $F(P)$ and $V(P) - I$ for $\sigma = 0$, .2, and .4. When $\sigma = 0$, the critical price is 14, which just makes the value of the project equal to its cost of 100. As σ is increased, both $V(P)$ and $F(P)$ increase; P^* is 23.8 for $\sigma = .2$ and 34.9 for $\sigma = .4$.

An increase in δ also increases the critical price P^* at which the firm should invest. There are two opposing effects. If δ is larger, so that the expected rate of increase of P is smaller, options on future production are worth less, so $V(P)$ is smaller. At the same time, the opportunity cost of waiting to invest rises—the expected rate of growth of $F(P)$ is smaller—so there is more incentive to exercise the investment option, rather than keep it alive. The first effect dominates, so that a higher δ results in a higher P^*. This is illustrated in figure 11.10, which shows $F(P)$ and $V(P) - I$ for $\delta = .04$ and .08. Note that when δ is increased, $V(P)$ and hence $F(P)$ fall sharply, and the tangency at P^* moves to the right.

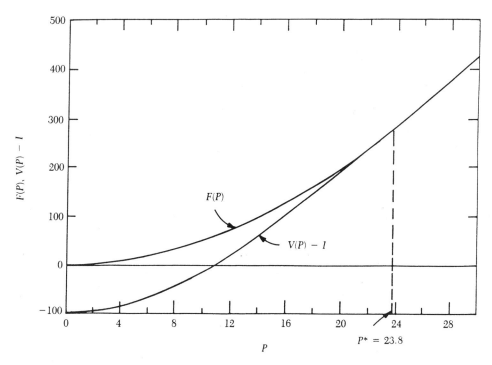

Figure 11.8
$V(P) - I$ and $F(P)$ for $\sigma = 0.2$, $\delta = 0.04$

This result might at first seem to contradict what the simpler model of Section III tells us. Recall that in that model, an increase in δ reduces the critical value of the *project*, V^*, at which the firm should invest. But while in this model P^* is higher when δ is larger, the corresponding value of the project, $V(P^*)$, is lower. This can be seen from figure 11.11, which shows P^* as a function of σ for $\delta = .04$ and .08, and figure 11.12, which shows $V(P^*)$. If, say, σ is .2 and δ is increased from 0.4 to .08, P^* will rise from 23.8 to 29.2, but even at the higher P^*, V is lower. Thus $V^* = V(P^*)$ is declining with δ, just as in the simpler model.

This model shows how uncertainty over future prices affects both the value of a project and the decision to invest. As discussed in the next section, the model can easily be expanded to allow for fixed costs of temporarily stopping and restarting production, if such costs are important. Expanded in this way, models like this can have practical application, especially if the project is one that produces a traded commodity, like copper or oil. In that case, σ and δ can be determined directly from futures and spot market data.

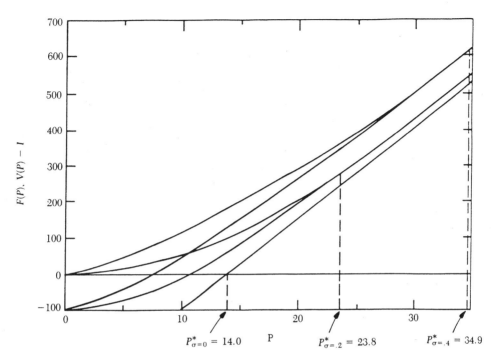

Figure 11.9
$V(P) - 1$ and $F(P)$ for $\sigma = 0, 0.2, 0.4$

C   Alternative Stochastic Processes

The geometric random walk of equation (14) is convenient in that it permits an analytical solution, but one might believe that the price, P, is better represented by a different stochastic process. For example, one could argue that over the long run, the price of a commodity will follow a mean-reverting process (for which the mean reflects long-run marginal cost, and might be time-varying). Our model can be adapted to allow for this or for alternative stochastic processes for P. However, in most cases numerical methods will then be necessary to obtain a solution.

As an example, suppose P follows the mean-reverting process:

$$dP/P = \lambda(\bar{P} - P)\, dt + \sigma\, dz. \tag{23}$$

Here, P tends to revert back to a "normal" level $\bar{P}$ (which might be long-run marginal cost in the case of a commodity like copper or coffee). By going through the same arguments as we did before, it is easy to show that $V(P)$ must then satisfy the

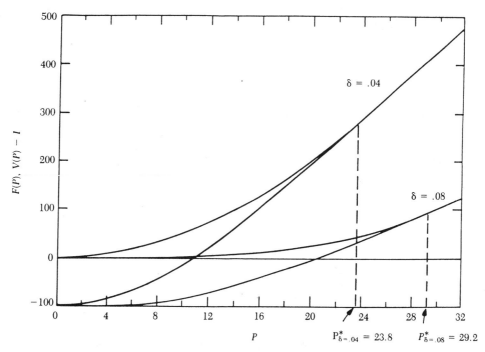

Figure 11.10
$V(P) - 1$ and $F(P)$ for δ

following differential equation:

$$(1/2)\sigma^2 P^2 V_{PP} + [(r - \mu - \lambda)P + \lambda\bar{P}]PV_P - rV + j(P - c) = 0 \qquad (24)$$

together with boundary conditions (16a–16c). The value of the investment option, $F(P)$, must satisfy

$$(1/2)\sigma^2 P^2 F_{PP} + [(r - \mu - \lambda)P + \lambda\bar{P}]PF_P - rF = 0 \qquad (25)$$

with boundary conditions (19a–19c). Equations (24) and (25) are ordinary differential equations, so solution by numerical methods is relatively straightforward.

V   Extensions

The models presented in the previous two sections are fairly simple, but illustrate how a project and an investment opportunity can be viewed as a set of options, and valued

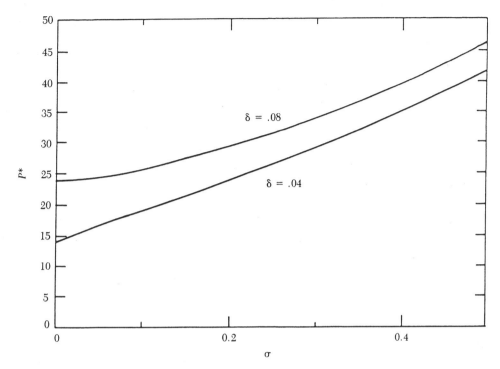

Figure 11.11
P^* vs. σ for $\delta = 0.04, 0.08$

accordingly. These insights have been extended to a variety of problems involving investment and production decisions under uncertainty. This section reviews some of them.

A   Sunk Costs and Hysteresis

In Sections III and IV, we examined models in which the investment expenditure is a sunk cost. Because the future value of the project is uncertain, this creates an opportunity cost to investing, which drives a wedge between the current value of the project and the direct cost of the investment.

In general, there may be a variety of sunk costs. For example, there may be a sunk cost of exiting an industry or abandoning a project. This could include severance pay for workers, land reclamation in the case of a mine, and so on.[11] This creates an opportunity cost of shutting down, because the value of the project might rise in the future. There may also be sunk costs associated with the operation of the project. In

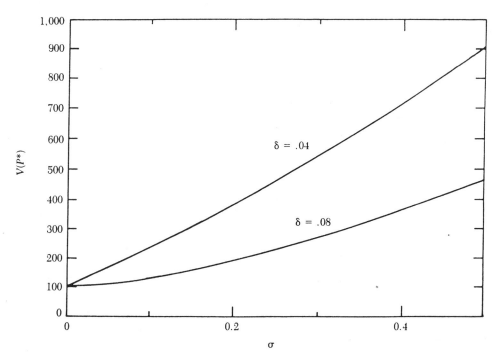

Figure 11.12
$V(P^*)$ vs. σ for $\delta = 0.04, 0.08$

Section IV, we assumed that the firm could stop and restart production costlessly. For most projects, however, there are likely to be substantial sunk costs involved in even temporarily shutting down and restarting.

The valuation of projects and the decision to invest when there are sunk costs of this sort have been studied by Brennan and Schwartz (1985) and Dixit (1989a). Brennan and Schwartz (1985) find the effects of sunk costs on the decision to open and close (temporarily or permanently) a mine, when the price of the resource follows equation (14). Their model accounts for the fact that a mine is subject to cave-ins and flooding when not in use, and a temporary shutdown requires expenditures to avoid these possibilities. Likewise, reopening a temporarily closed mine requires a substantial expenditure. Finally, a mine can be permanently closed. This will involve costs of land reclamation (but avoids the cost of a temporary shutdown).

Brennan and Schwartz obtained an analytical solution for the case of an infinite resource stock. (Solutions can also be obtained when the resource stock is finite, but then numerical methods are required.) Their solution gives the value of the mine as a function of the resource price and the curent state of the mine (i.e., open or closed). It also gives the decision rule for changing the state of the mine (i.e., opening a closed mine or temporarily or permanently closing an open mine). Finally, given the value of the mine, Brennan and Schwartz show how (in principle) an option to invest in the mine can be valued and the optimal investment rule determined, using a contingent claim approach like that of Section IV.[12]

By working through a realistic example of a copper mine, Brennan and Schwartz showed how the methods discussed in this paper can be applied in practice. But their work also shows how sunk costs of opening and closing a mine can explain the "hysteresis" often observed in extractive resource industries: During periods of low prices, managers often continue to operate unprofitable mines that had been opened when prices were high; at other times managers fail to reopen seemingly profitable ones that had been closed when prices were low. This insight is further developed in Dixit (1989a, 1991), and is discussed below.

Dixit (1989a) studies a model with sunk costs k and l, respectively, of entry and exit. The project produces one unit of output per period, with variable cost w. The output price, P, follows equation (14). If $\sigma = 0$, the standard result holds: Enter (i.e., spend k) if $P \geq w + \rho k$, and exit if $P \leq w - \rho l$, where ρ is the firm's discount rate.[13] However, if $\sigma > 0$, there are opportunity costs to entering or exiting. These opportunity costs raise the critical price above which it is optimal to enter, and lower the critical price below which it is optimal to exit. (Furthermore, numerical simulations show that σ need not be large to induce a significant effect.)

These models help to explain the prevalence of hysteresis—effects that persist after the causes that brought them about have disappeared. In Dixit's model, firms that entered an industry when price was high may remain there for an extended period of time even though price has fallen below variable cost, so they are losing money. (Price may rise in the future, and to exit and later reenter involves sunk costs.) And firms that leave an industry after a protracted period of low prices may hesitate to reenter, even after prices have risen enough to make entry seem profitable. Similarly, the Brennan and Schwartz model shows why many copper mines built during the 1970s when copper prices were high were kept open during the mid-1980s when copper prices had fallen to their lowest levels (in real terms) since the Great Depression.

The fact that exchange rate movements during the 1980s left the U.S. with a persistent trade deficit at the end of that decade can also be seen as a result of hysteresis. For example, Dixit (1989b) models entry by Japanese firms into the U.S. market when the exchange rate follows a geometric Brownian motion. Again, there are sunk costs of entry and exit. The Japanese firms are ordered according to their variable costs, and all firms are price takers. As with the models discussed above, the sunk costs combined with exchange rate uncertainty create opportunity costs of entering or exiting the U.S. market. As a result, there will be an exchange rate band within which Japanese firms neither enter nor exit, and the U.S. market price will not vary as long as exchange rate fluctuations are within this band. Richard Baldwin (1988) and Baldwin and Paul Krugman (1989) developed related models that yield similar results. These models help to explain the low rate of exchange rate passthrough observed during the 1980s, and the persistence of the U.S. trade deficit even after the dollar depreciated. (Baldwin 1988 also provides empirical evidence that the over-valuation of the dollar during the early 1980s was indeed a hysteresis-inducing shock.)

Sunk costs of entry and exit can also have hysteretic effects on the exchange rate itself, and on prices. Baldwin and Krugman (1989), for example, show how the entry and exit decisions described above feed back to the exchange rate. In their model, a policy change (e.g., a reduction in the money supply) that causes the currency to appreciate sharply can lead to entry by foreign firms, which in turn leads to an equilibrium exchange rate that is *below* the original one. (These ideas are also discussed in Krugman 1989.) Similar effects occur with prices. In the case of copper, the reluctance of firms to close down mines during the mid-1980s, when demand was weak, allowed the price to fall even more than it would have otherwise.

Finally, sunk costs may be important in explaining the dependence of consumer spending, particularly for durable goods, on income and wealth. Most purchases of consumer durables are at least partly irreversible. Poksang Lam (1989) developed a model that accounts for this, and shows how irreversibility results in a sluggish adjustment of the stock of durables to income changes. Sanford Grossman and Guy Laroque (1990) study consumption and portfolio choice when consumption services are generated by a durable good and a transaction cost must be paid when the good is sold. Unlike in standard models (e.g., Merton 1971), optimal consumption is not a smooth function of wealth; a large change in wealth must occur before a consumer changes his holdings of durables and hence his consumption. As a result, the consumption-based CAPM fails to hold (although the market portfolio-based CAPM does hold).

B   Sequential Investment

Many investments occur in stages that must be carried out in sequence, and sometimes the payoffs from or costs of completing each stage are uncertain. For example, investing in a new line of aircraft begins with engineering, and continues with prototype production, testing, and final tooling stages. And an investment in a new drug by a pharmaceutical company begins with research that (with some probability) leads to a new compound, continues with extensive testing until FDA approval is obtained, and concludes with the construction of a production facility and marketing of the product.

Sequential investment programs like these can take substantial time to complete—five to ten years for the two examples mentioned above. In addition, they can be temporarily or permanently abandoned midstream if the value of the end product falls, or the expected cost of completing the investment rises. Hence these investments can be viewed as compound options; each stage completed (or dollar invested) gives the firm an option to complete the next stage (or invest the next dollar). The problem is to find a contingent plan for making these sequential and irreversible expenditures.

Majd and Pindyck (1987) solve this problem for a model in which a firm invests continuously (each dollar spent buys an option to spend the next dollar) until the project is completed, investment can be stopped and later restarted costlessly, and there is a maximum rate at which outlays and construction can proceed (i.e., it takes "time to build"). The payoff to the firm upon completion is V, the value of the operating project, which follows the geometric Brownian motion of equation (1). Letting K be the total remaining expenditure required to complete the project, the optimal rule is to keep investing at the maximum rate as long as V exceeds a critical value $V^*(K)$, with $dV^*/dK < 0$. Using the methods of Sections III and IV, it is straightforward to derive a partial differential equation for $F(V, K)$, the value of the investment opportunity. Solutions to this equation and its associated boundry conditions, which are obtained by numerical methods, yield the optimal investment rule $V^*(K)$.[14]

These solutions show how time to build magnifies the effects of irreversibility and uncertainty. The lower the maximum rate of investment (i.e., the longer it takes to complete the project), the higher is the critical $V^*(K)$ required for construction to proceed. This is because the project's value upon completion is more uncertain, and the expected rate of growth of V over the construction period is less than μ, the risk-adjusted rate of return (δ is positive). Also, unlike the model of Section III where the critical value V^* declines monotonically with δ, with time to build, V^* will increase with δ when δ is large. The reason is that while a higher δ increases the opportunity cost of waiting to begin construction, it also reduces the expected rate of growth of V during the construction period, so that the (risk-adjusted) expected payoff from completing construction is reduced. Finally, by computing $F(V, K)$ for different maximum rates of investment, one can value construction time flexibility, that is, what one would pay to be able to build the project faster.[15]

In the Majd-Pindyck model, investment occurs as a continuous flow; that is, each dollar spent gives the firm an option to spend another dollar, up to the last dollar, which gives the firm a completed project. Often, however, sequential investments occur in discrete stages, as with the aircraft and pharmaceutical examples mentioned above. In these cases, the optimal investment rules can be found by working backward from the completed project, as we did with the model of Section IV.

To see how this can be done, consider a two-stage investment in new oil production capacity. First, reserves of oil must be obtained, through exploration or outright purchase, at a cost I_1. Second, development wells (and possibly pipelines) must be built, at a cost I_2. Let P be the price of oil and assume it follows the geometric Brownian motion of equation (14). The firm thus begins with an option, worth $F_1(P)$, to invest in reserves. Doing so buys an option, worth $F_2(P)$, to invest in development wells. Making this investment yields production capacity, worth $V(P)$.

Working backward to find the optimal investment rules, first note that as in the model of Section IV, $V(P)$ is the value of the firm's operating options, and can be calculated accordingly. Next, $F_2(P)$ can be found; it is easy to show that it must satisfy equation (18) and boundary conditions (19a–19c), with I_2 replacing I, and P^* becoming the critical price at which the firm should invest in development wells. Finally, $F_1(P)$ can be found. It also satisfies (18) and (19a–19c), but with $F_2(P)$ replacing $V(P)$ in (19b) and (19c), I_1 replacing I, and P^{**} replacing P^*. (P^{**} is the critical price of oil at which the firm should invest in reserves.) If marginal production cost is constant and there is no cost to stopping or restarting production, an analytical solution can be obtained.[16]

In this example there is no time to build; each stage (obtaining reserves, and building development wells) can be completed instantly. For many projects each stage of the investment takes time, and the firm can stop investing in the middle of a stage. Then the problem must be solved numerically, using a method like the one in Majd and Pindyck (1987).[17]

In all of the models discussed so far, no learning takes place, in the sense that future prices (or project values, V) are always uncertain, and the degree of uncertainty depends only on the time horizon. For some sequential investments, however, early stages provide information about costs or net payoffs in later stages. Synthetic fuels was a much debated example of this; oil companies argued that demonstration plants were needed (and deserved funding by the government) to determine production costs. The aircraft and pharmaceutical investments mentioned above also have these characteristics. The engineering, prototype production, and testing stages in the development of a new aircraft all provide information about the ultimate cost of production (as well as the aircraft's flight characteristics, which will help determine its market value). Likewise, the R&D and testing stages of the development of a new drug determine the efficacy and side effects of the drug, and hence its value.

Kevin Roberts and Martin Weitzman (1981) developed a model of sequential investment that stresses this role of information gathering. In their model, each stage of investment yields information that reduces the uncertainty over the value of the completed project. Because the project can be stopped in midstream, it may pay to go ahead with the early stages of the investment even though ex ante the net present value of the entire project is negative. Hence the use of a simple net present value rule can reject projects that should be undertaken. This is just the opposite of our earlier finding that a simple NPV rule can *accept* projects that should be rejected. The crucial assumption in the Roberts-Weitzman model is that prices and costs do not evolve stochastically. The value of the completed project may not be known (at least until the early stages are completed), but that value does not change over time, so there is no gain from waiting, and no opportunity cost to investing now. Instead, information gathering adds a shadow value to the early stages of the investment.[18]

This result applies whenever information gathering, rather than waiting, yields information. The basic principle is easily seen by modifying our simple two-period example from Section II. Suppose that the widget factory can only be built this year, and at a cost of $1,200. However, by first spending $50 to research the widget market, one could determine whether widget prices will rise or fall next year. Clearly one should spend this $50, even though the NPV of the entire project (the research plus the construction of the factory) is negative. One would then build the factory only if the research showed that widget prices will rise.

C   Incremental Investment and Capacity Choice

So far we have examined decisions to invest in single, discrete projects, for example, the decision to build a new factory or develop a new aircraft. Much of the economics literature on investment, however, focuses on *incremental* investment; firms invest to the point that the cost of the marginal unit of capital just equals the present value of the revenues it is expected to generate. The cost of the unit can include adjustment costs (reflecting the time and expense of installing and learning to use new capital) in addition to the purchase cost. In most models, adjustment costs are a convex function of the rate of investment, and are thus a crucial determinant of that rate. (For an overview, see Stephen Nickell 1978 or the more recent survey by Andrew Abel 1990.)

Except for work by Kenneth Arrow (1968) and Nickell (1974), which is in a deterministic context, this literature generally ignores the effects of irreversibility. As with discrete projects, irreversibility and the ability to delay investment decisions change the fundamental rule for investing. The firm must include as part of the total cost of an incremental unit of capital the opportunity cost of investing in that unit now rather than waiting.

Giuseppe Bertola (1989) and Pindyck (1988) developed models of incremental investment and capacity choice that account for irreversibility. In Pindyck's model, the firm faces a linear inverse demand function, $P = \theta(t) - \gamma Q$, where θ follows a geometric Brownian motion, and has a Leontief production technology. The firm can invest at any time at a cost k per unit of capital, and each unit of capital gives it the capacity to produce up to one unit of output per period. The investment problem is solved by first determining the value of an incremental unit of capital, given θ and an existing capital stock, K, and then finding the value of the option to invest in this unit and the optimal exercise rule. This rule is a function $K^*(\theta)$—invest whenever $K < K^*(\theta)$—which determines the firm's optimal capital stock. Pindyck shows that an increase in the variance of θ increases the value of an incremental unit of capital (that unit represents a set of call options on future production), but increases the value of the option to invest in the unit even more, so that investment requires a higher value of θ. Hence a more volatile demand implies that a firm should hold less capital, but have a higher market value.[19]

In Bertola's model, the firms' net revenue function is of the form $AK^{1-\beta}Z$, with $0 < \beta < 1$. (This would follow from a Cobb-Douglas production function and an isoelastic demand curve.) The demand-shift variable Z and the purchase price of capital follow correlated geometric Brownian motions. Bertola solves for the optimal investment rule, and shows that the marginal profitability of capital that triggers investment is higher than the user cost of capital as conventionally measured. The capital stock, K, is nonstationary, but Bertola finds the steady-state distribution for the ratio of the marginal profitability of capital to its price. Irreversibility and uncertainty reduce the mean of this ratio; that is, on average capital intensity is higher. Although the firm has a higher threshold for investment, this is outweighed on average by low outcomes for Z.

The finding that uncertainty over future demand can increase the value of a marginal unit of capital is not new. All that is required is that the marginal revenue product of capital be convex in price. This is the case when the unit of capital can go unutilized (so that it represents a set of operating options). But as Richard Hartman (1972) pointed out, it is also the case for a competitive firm that combines capital and labor with a linear homogeneous production function. Hartman shows that as a result, price uncertainty increases the firm's investment and capital stock.

Andrew Abel (1983) extends Hartman's result to a dynamic model in which price follows a geometric Brownian motion and there are convex costs of adjusting the capital stock, and again shows that uncertainty increases the firm's rate of investment. Finally, Ricardo Caballero (1991) introduces asymmetric costs of adjustment to allow for irreversibility (it can be costlier to reduce K than to increase it), and shows that again price uncertainty increases the rate of investment. However, the Abel and Caballero results hinge on the assumptions of constant returns and perfect competition, which make the marginal revenue product of capital independent of the capital stock. Then the firm can ignore its future capital stock (and hence irreversibility) when deciding how much to invest today. As Caballero shows, decreasing returns or imperfect competition will link the marginal revenue products of capital across time, so that the basic result in Pindyck (1988) and Bertola (1989) holds.[20]

The assumption that the firm can invest incrementally is extreme. In most industries, capacity additions are lumpy, and there are scale economies (a 400 room hotel usually costs less to build and operate than two 200 room hotels). Hence firms must decide when to add capacity, and how large an addition to make. This problem was first studied in a stochastic setting by Alan Manne (1961). He considered a firm that must always have enough capacity to satisfy demand, which grows according to a simple Brownian motion with drift. The cost of adding an amount of capacity x is kx^a, with $0 < a < 1$; the firm must choose x to minimize the present value of expected capital costs. Manne shows that with scale economies, uncertainty over demand growth leads the firm to add capacity in larger increments, and increases the present value of expected costs.

In Manne's model (which might apply to an electric utility that must always satisfy demand) the firm does not choose when to invest, only how much. Most firms must choose both. Pindyck (1988) determined the effects of uncertainty on these decisions when there are no scale economies in construction by extending his model to a firm that must decide when to build a single plant and how large it should be.[21] As with Manne's model, uncertainty increases the optimal plant size. However, it also raises the critical demand threshold at which the plant is built. Thus demand uncertainty should lead firms to delay capacity additions, but makes those additions larger when they occur.

Sometimes capacity choice is accompanied by a technology choice. Consider a firm that produces two products, A and B, with interdependent demands that vary stochastically. It can produce these products by (irreversibly) installing and utilizing product-specific capital, or by (irreversibly) installing a more costly flexible type of capital that can be used to produce either or both products. The problem is to decide which type and how much capital to install. Hua He and Pindyck (1989) solve this for a model with linear demands by first valuing incremental units of capital (output-specific and flexible), and then finding the optimal investment rule, and hence optimal amounts of capacity. By integrating the value of incremental units of specific and flexible capital, one can determine the preferred type of capital, as well as the value (if any) of flexibility.

In all of the studies cited so far, the stochastic state variable (the value of the project, the price of the firm's output, or a demand- or cost-shift variable) is specified exogenously. In a competitive equilibrium, firms' investment and output decisions are dependent on the price process, but also collectively generate that process. Hence we would like to know whether firms' decisions are consistent with the price processes we specify.

At least two studies have addressed this issue. Steven Lippman and Richard P. Rumelt (1985) model a competitive industry where firms face sunk costs of entry and exit, and the market demand curve fluctuates stochastically. They find an equilibrium consisting of optimal investment and production rules for firms (with uncertainty, they hold less capacity), and a corresponding process for market price. John Leahy (1989) extends Dixit's (1989a) model of entry and exit to an industry setting in which price is endogenous. He shows that price will be driven by demand shocks until an entry or exit barrier is reached, and then entry or exit prevent it from moving further. Hence price follows a regulated Brownian motion. Surprisingly, it makes no difference whether firms take entry and exit into account, or simply assume that price will follow a geometric Brownian motion; the same entry and exit barriers result. This suggests that models in which price is exogenous may provide a reasonable description of industry investment and capacity.

VI Investment Behavior and Economic Policy

Nondiversifiable risk plays a role in even the simplest models of investment, by affecting the cost of capital. But the findings summarized in this paper suggest that risk may be a more crucial determinant of investment. This is likely to have implications for the explanation and prediction of investment behavior at the industry- or economy-wide level, and for the design of policy.

The role of interest rates and interest rate stability in determining investment is a good example of this. Jonathan Ingersoll and Stephen Ross (1988) have examined irreversible investment decisions when the interest rate evolves stochastically, but future cash flows are known with certainty. As with uncertainty over future cash flows, this creates an opportunity cost of investing, so that the traditional NPV rule will accept too many projects. Instead, an investment should be made only when the interest rate is below a critical rate, r^*, which is *lower* than the internal rate of return, r^o, which makes the NPV zero. Furthermore, the difference between r^* and r^o grows as the volatility of interest rates grows.

Ingersoll and Ross also show that for long-lived projects, a decrease in expected interest rates for all future periods need not accelerate investment. The reason is that such a change also lowers the cost of waiting, and thus can have an ambiguous effect on investment. This suggests that the level of interest rates may be of only secondary importance as a determinant of aggregate investment spending; interest rate volatility may be more important.

In fact, investment spending on an aggregate level may be highly sensitive to risk in various forms: uncertainties over future product prices and input costs that directly determine cash flows, uncertainty over exchange rates, and uncertainty over future tax and regulatory policy. This means that if a goal of macroeconomic policy is to stimulate investment, stability and credibility may be more important than the particular levels of tax rates or interest rates. Put another way, if uncertainty over the economic environment is high, tax and related incentives may have to be very large to have any significant impact on investment.

Similarly, a major cost of political and economic instability may be its depressing effect on investment. This is likely to be particularly important for the developing economies. For many LDCs, investment as a fraction of GDP has fallen dramatically during the 1980s, despite moderate economic growth. Yet the success of macroeconomic policy in these countries requires increases in private investment. This has created a catch-22 that makes the social value of investment higher than its private value. The reason is that if firms do not have confidence that macro policies will succeed and growth trajectories will be maintained, they are afraid to invest, but if they do not invest, macro policies are indeed doomed to fail. It is therefore important to understand how investment might depend on risk factors that are at least partly under government control, for example, price, wage, and exchange rate stability, the threat of price controls or expropriation, and changes in trade regimes.[22]

The irreversibility of investment also helps to explain why trade reforms can turn out to be counterproductive, with a liberalization leading to a decrease in aggregate investment. As Rudiger Dornbusch (1987) and Sweder Van Wijnbergen (1985) have noted, uncertainty over future tariff structures, and hence over future factor returns, creates an opportunity cost to committing capital to new physical plants. Foreign exchange and liquid assets held abroad involve no such commitment, and so may be preferrable even though the expected rate of return is lower.[23] Likewise, it may be difficult to stem or reverse capital flight if there is a perception that it may become more difficult to take capital out of the country than to bring it in.

Irreversibility is also likely to have policy implications for specific industries. The energy industry is an example. There, the issue of stability and credibility arises with the possibility of price controls, "windfall" profit taxes, or related policies that might be imposed should prices rise substantially. Investment decisions must be made taking into account that price is evolving stochastically, but also the probability that price may be capped at some level, or otherwise regulated.

A more fundamental problem is the volatility of market prices themselves. For many raw commodities (oil is an example), price volatility rose substantially in the early 1970s, and has been high since. Other things equal, we would expect this to increase the value of land and other resources needed to produce the commodity, but have a depressing effect on construction expenditures and production capacity. Most studies of the gains from price stabilization focus on adjustment costs and the curvature of demand and (static) supply curves. (See David Newbery and Joseph Stiglitz 1981 for an overview.) The irreversibility of investment creates an additional gain which must be accounted for.

The existing literature on these effects of uncertainty and instability is a largely theoretical one. This may reflect the fact that models of irreversible investment under uncertainty are relatively complicated, and so are difficult to translate into well-specified empirical models. In any case, the gap here between theory and empiricism is disturbing. While it is clear from the theory that increases in the volatility of, say, interest rates or exchange rates should depress investment, it is not at all clear how large these effects should be. Nor is it clear how important these factors have been as explanators of investment across countries and over time. Most econometric models of aggregate economic activity ignore the role of risk, or deal with it only implicitly. A more explicit treatment of risk may help to better explain economic fluctuations, and especially investment spending.[24] But substantial empirical work is needed to determine whether the theoretical models discussed in this paper have predictive power.[25]

One step in this direction is the recent paper by Bertola and Caballero (1990). They solve the optimal irreversible capital accumulation problem for an individual firm with a Cobb-Douglas production function, and then characterize the behavior of *aggregate* investment when there are both firm-specific and aggregate sources of uncertainty. Their model does well in replicating the behavior of postwar U.S. investment.

Simulation models may provide another vehicle for testing the implications of irreversibility and uncertainty. The structure of such a model might be similar to the model presented in Section IV, and parameterized so that it "fits" a particular industry. One could then calculate predicted effects of observed changes in, say, price volatility, and compare them to the predicted effects of changes in interest rates or tax rates. Models of this sort could likewise be used to predict the effect of a perceived possible shift in the tax regime, the imposition of price controls, and so on. Such models may also be a good way to study uncertainty of the "peso problem" sort.

VII Conclusions

I have focused largely on investment in capital goods, but the principles illustrated here apply to a broad variety of problems involving irreversibility. For example, as Dornbusch (1987) points out, the same issues arise in labor markets, where firms face high (sunk) costs of hiring, training, and sometimes firing workers. (Samuel Bentolila and Giuseppe Bertola 1990 have recently developed a formal model that explains how hiring and firing costs affect employment decisions.)

Another important set of applications arises in the context of natural resources and the environment. If future values of wilderness areas and parking lots are uncertain, it may be better to wait before irreversibly paving over a wilderness area. Here, the option value of waiting creates an opportunity cost, and this must be added to the current direct cost of destroying the wilderness area when doing a cost-benefit analysis of the parking lot. This point was first made by Arrow and Anthony Fisher (1974) and Claude Henry (1974), and has since been elaborated upon in the environmental economics literature.[26] It has become especially germane in recent years because of concern over possible irreversible long-term environmental changes such as ozone depletion and global warming.

While this insight is important, actually measuring these opportunity costs can be difficult. In the case of a well-defined project (a widget factory), one can construct a model like the one in Section IV. But it is not always clear what the correct stochastic process is for, say, the output price. Even if one accepts equation (14), the opportunity cost of investing now (and the investment rule) will depend on parameters, such as α and σ, that may not be easy to measure. The problem is much greater when applying these methods to investment decisions involving resources and the environment. Then one must model, for example, the stochastic evolution of society's valuation of wilderness areas.

On the other hand, models like the ones discussed in this chapter can be solved (by numerical methods) with alternative stochastic processes for the relevant state variables, and it is easy to determine the sensitivity of the solution to parameter values, as we did in Sections III and IV. These models at least provide some insight into the importance of irreversibility, and the ranges of opportunity costs that might be implied. Obtaining such insight is clearly better than ignoring irreversibility.

Appendix

This appendix provides a brief introduction to the tools of stochastic calculus and dynamic programming that are used in Sections III and IV. For more detailed introductory discussions, see Stuart Dreyfus (1965),

Merton (1971), Chow (1979), Malliaris and Brock (1982), or Hull (1989). For more rigorous treatments, see Harold Kushner (1967) or Wendell Fleming and Raymond Rishel (1975). I first discuss the Wiener process, then Ito's Lemma, and finally stochastic dynamic programming.

Wiener Processes

A Wiener process (also called a Brownian motion) is a continuous-time Markov stochastic process whose increments are independent, no matter how small the time interval. Specifically, if $z(t)$ is a Wiener process, then any change in z, Δz, corresponding to a time interval Δt, satisfies the following conditions:

(i) The relationship between Δz and Δt is given by

$$\Delta z = \varepsilon_t \sqrt{\Delta t}$$

where ε_t is a normally distributed random variable with a mean of zero and a standard deviation of 1.

(ii) ε_t is serially uncorrelated, that is, $E(\varepsilon_t \varepsilon_s) = 0$ for $t \neq s$. Thus the values of Δz for any two different intervals of time are independent, so $z(t)$ follows a Markov process.

Let us examine what these two conditions imply for the change in z over some finite interval of time T. We can break this interval into n units of length Δt each, with $n = T/\Delta t$. Then the change in z over this interval is given by

$$z(s + T) - z(s) = \sum_{i=1}^{n} \varepsilon_i (\Delta t)^{1/2}.$$

Because the ε_i's are independent of each other, the change $z(s + T) - z(s)$ is normally distributed with mean 0, and variance $n\Delta t = T$. This last point, which follows from the fact that Δz depends on $\sqrt{\Delta t}$ and not on Δt, is particulary important; *the variance of the change in a Wiener process grows linearly with the time interval.*

Letting the Δt's become infinitesimally small, we write the increment of the Wiener process as $dz = \varepsilon(t)(dt)^{1/2}$. Because $\varepsilon(t)$ has zero mean and unit standard deviation, $E(dz) = 0$, and $E[(dz)^2] = dt$. Finally, consider two Wiener processes, $z_1(t)$ and $z_2(t)$. Then we can write $E(dz_1 dz_2) = \rho_{12} \, dt$, where ρ_{12} is the coefficient of correlation between the two processes.

We often work with the following generalization of the Wiener process:

$$dx = a(x, t) \, dt + b(x, t) \, dz. \tag{A.1}$$

The continuous-time stochastic process $x(t)$ represented by equation (A.1) is called an *Ito process*. Consider the mean and variance of the increments of this process. Because $E(dz) = 0$, $E(dx) = a(x, t) \, dt$. The variance of dx is equal to $E\{[dx - E(dx)]^2\} = b^2(x, t) \, dt$. Hence we refer to $a(x, t)$ as the expected drift rate of the Ito process, and we refer to $b^2(x, t)$ as the variance rate.

An important special case of (A.1) is the *geometric Brownian motion with drift*. Here $a(x, t) = \alpha x$, and $b(x, t) = \sigma x$, where α and σ are constants. In this case (A.1) becomes

$$dx = \alpha x \, dt + \sigma x \, dz. \tag{A.2}$$

(This is identical to equation (1) in Section III, but with V replaced by x.) From our discussion of the Wiener process, we know that over any finite interval of time, *percentage* changes in x, $\Delta x/x$, are normally distributed. Hence absolute changes in x, Δx, are *log-normally* distributed. We will derive the expected value of Δx shortly.

An important property of the Ito process (A.1) is that while it is continuous in time, it is not differentiable. To see this, note that dx/dt includes a term with $dz/dt = \varepsilon(t)(dt)^{-1/2}$, which becomes infinitely large as dt becomes infinitesimally small. However, we will often want to work with functions of x (or z), and we will need to find the differentials of such functions. To do this, we make use of Ito's Lemma.

Ito's Lemma

Ito's Lemma is mostly easily understood as a Taylor series expansion. Suppose x follows the Ito process (A.1), and consider a function $F(x, t)$ that is at least twice differentiable. We want to find the total differential of this function, dF. The usual rules of calculus define this differential in terms of first-order changes in x and t: $dF = F_x \, dx + F_t \, dt$, where subscripts denote partial derivatives, that is, $F_x = \partial F / \partial x$, and so on. But suppose that we also include higher-order terms for changes in x:

$$dF = F_x \, dx + F_t \, dt + (1/2)F_{xx}(dx)^2 + (1/6)F_{xxx}(dx)^3 + \cdots. \tag{A.3}$$

In ordinary calculus, these higher-order terms all vanish in the limit. To see whether that is the case here, expand the third and fourth terms on the right-hand side of (A.3). First, substitute (A.1) for dx to determine $(dx)^2$:

$$(dx)^2 = a^2(x, t)(dt)^2 + 2a(x, t)b(x, t)(dt)^{3/2} + b^2(x, t) \, dt.$$

Terms in $(dt)^{3/2}$ and $(dt)^2$ vanish as dt becomes infinitesimal, so we can ignore these terms and write $(dx)^2 = b^2(x, t) \, dt$. As for the fourth term on the right-hand side of (A.3), every term in the expansion of $(dx)^3$ will include dt raised to a power greater than 1, and so will vanish in the limit. This is likewise the case for any higher-order terms in (A.3). Hence Ito's Lemma gives the differential dF as

$$dF = F_x \, dx + F_t \, dt + (1/2)F_{xx}(dx)^2, \tag{A.4}$$

or, substituting from (A.1) for dx,

$$dF = [F_t + a(x, t)F_x + \tfrac{1}{2}b^2(x, t)F_{xx}] \, dt + b(x, t)F_x \, dz. \tag{A.5}$$

We can easily extend this to functions of several Ito processes. Suppose $F = F(x_1, \ldots, x_m, t)$ is a function of time and the m Ito processes, $x_1, \ldots, x_m$, where

$$dx_i = a_i(x_1, \ldots, x_m, t) \, dt + b_i(x_1, \ldots, x_{m,t}) \, dz_i, \quad i = 1, \ldots, m \tag{A.6}$$

and $E(dz_i dz_j) = \rho_{ij} \, dt$. Then, letting F_i denote $\partial F / \partial x_i$ and F_{ij} denote $\partial^2 F / \partial x_i \partial x_j$, Ito's Lemma gives the differential dF as

$$dF = F_t \, dt + \sum_i F_i \, dx_i + \frac{1}{2}\sum_i \sum_j F_{ij} \, dx_i \, dx_j \tag{A.7}$$

or, substituting for dx_i:

$$dF = \left[F_t + \sum_i a_i(x_1, \ldots, t)F_i + \frac{1}{2}\sum_i b_i^2(x_1, \ldots, t)F_{ii} + \sum_{i \neq j} \rho_{ij} b_i(x_1, \ldots, t) b_j(x_1, \ldots, t)F_{ij} \right] dt$$

$$+ \sum_i b_i(x_1, \ldots, t)F_i \, dz_i. \tag{A.8}$$

Example: Geometric Brownian Motion Let us return to the process given by equation (A.2). We will use Ito's Lemma to find the process followed by $F(x) = \log x$. Because $F_t = 0$, $F_x = 1/x$, and $F_{xx} = -1/x^2$, we have from (A.4):

$$dF = (1/x) \, dx - (1/2x^2)(dx)^2$$

$$= \alpha \, dt + \sigma \, dz - \tfrac{1}{2}\sigma^2 \, dt$$

$$= (\alpha - \tfrac{1}{2}\sigma^2) \, dt + \sigma \, dz. \tag{A.9}$$

Hence, over any finite time interval T, the change in $\log x$ is normally distributed with mean $(\alpha - \frac{1}{2}\sigma^2)T$ and variance $\sigma^2 T$.

The geometric Brownian motion is often used to model the prices of stocks and other assets. It says returns are normally distributed, with a standard deviation that grows with the square root of the holding period.

Example: Correlated Brownian Motions   As a second example of the use of Ito's Lemma, consider a function $F(x, y) = xy$, where x and y each follow geometric Brownian motions:

$$dx = \alpha_x x\, dt + \sigma_x x\, dz_x$$

$$dy = \alpha_y y\, dt + \sigma_y y\, dz_y$$

with $E(dz_x dz_y) = \rho$. We will find the process followed by $F(x, y)$, and the process followed by $G = \log F$. Because $F_{xx} = F_{yy} = 0$ and $F_{xy} = 1$, we have from (A.7):

$$dF = x\, dy + y\, dx + (dx)(dy). \tag{A.10}$$

Now substitute for dx and dy and rearrange:

$$dF = (\alpha_x + \alpha_y + \rho\sigma_x\sigma_y)F\, dt + (\sigma_x\, dz_x + \sigma_y\, dz_y)F. \tag{A.11}$$

Hence F also follows a geometric Brownian motion. What about $G = \log F$? Going through the same steps as in the previous example, we find that

$$dG = (\alpha_x + \alpha_y) - \tfrac{1}{2}\sigma_x^2 - \tfrac{1}{2}\sigma_y^2)\, dt + \sigma_x\, dz_x + \sigma_y\, dz_y. \tag{A.12}$$

From (A.12) we see that over any time interval T, the change in $\log F$ is normally distributed with mean $(\alpha_x + \alpha_y - \tfrac{1}{2}\sigma_x^2 - \tfrac{1}{2}\sigma_y^2)T$ and variance $(\sigma_x^2 + \sigma_y^2 + 2\rho\sigma_x\sigma_y)T$.

Stochastic Dynamic Programming

Ito's Lemma also allows us to apply dynamic programming to optimization problems in which one or more of the state variables follow Ito processes. Consider the following problem of choosing $u(t)$ over time to maximize the value of an asset that yields a flow of income $\Pi = \Pi[x(t), u(t)]$:

$$\max_u E_0 \int_0^\infty \Pi[x(t), u(t)]e^{-\mu t}\, dt, \tag{A.13}$$

where $x(t)$ follows the Ito process given by

$$dx = a(x, u)\, dt + b(x, u)\, dz. \tag{A.14}$$

Let J be the value of the asset assuming $u(t)$ is chosen optimally,

$$J(x) = \max_u E_t \int_t^\infty \Pi[x(\tau), u(\tau)]e^{-\mu\tau}\, d\tau. \tag{A.15}$$

Because time appears in the maximand only through the discount factor, the Bellman equation (the fundamental equation of optimality) for this problem can be written as

$$\mu J = \max_u [\Pi(x, u) + (1/dt)E_t\, dJ]. \tag{A.16}$$

Equation (A.16) says that the total return on this asset, μJ, has two components, the income flow $\Pi(x, u)$, and the expected rate of capital gain, $(1/dt)E_t\, dJ$. (Note that in writing the expected capital gain, we apply the expectation operator E_t, which eliminates terms in dz, *before* taking the time derivative.) The optimal $u(t)$ balances current income against expected capital gains to maximize the sum of the two components.

To solve this problem, we need to take the differential dJ. Because J is a function of the Ito process $x(t)$, we apply Ito's Lemma. Using equation (A.4),

$$dJ = J_x \, dx + \tfrac{1}{2} J_{xx} (dx)^2. \tag{A.17}$$

Now substitute (A.14) for dx into (A.17):

$$dJ = [a(x,u)J_x + \tfrac{1}{2} b^2(x,u)J_{xx}] \, dt + b(x,u)J_x \, dz. \tag{A.18}$$

Using this expression for dJ, and noting that $E(dz) = 0$, we can rewrite the Bellman equation (A.16) as

$$\mu J = \max_u \left[\Pi(x,u) + a(x,u)J_x + \frac{1}{2} b^2(x,u)J_{xx} \right]. \tag{A.19}$$

In principle, a solution can be obtained by going through the following steps. First, maximize the expression in curly brackets with respect to u to obtain an optimal $u^* = u^*(x, J_x, J_{xx})$. Second, substitute this u^* back into (A.19) to eliminate u. The resulting differential equation can then be solved for the value function $J(x)$, from which the optimal feedback rule $U^*(x)$ can be found.

Example: Bellman Equation for Investment Problem   In Section III we examined an investment timing problem in which a firm had to decide when it should pay a sunk cost I to receive a project worth V, given that V follows the geometric Brownian motion of equation (1). To apply dynamic programming, we wrote the maximization problem as equation (11), in which $F(V)$ is the value function, that is, the value of the investment opportunity, assuming it is optimally exercised.

It should now be clear why the Bellman equation for this problem is given by equation (12). Because the investment opportunity yields no cash flow, the only return from holding it is its expected capital appreciation, $(1/dt)E_t \, dF$, which must equal the total return μF, from which (12) follows. Expanding dF using Ito's Lemma results in equation (13), a differential equation for $F(V)$. This equation is quite general, and could apply to a variety of different problems. To get a solution $F(V)$ and investment rule V^* for our problem, we also apply the boundary conditions (6a–6c).

Example: Value of a Project   In Section IV we examined a model of investment in which we first had to value the project as a function of the output price P. We derived a differential equation (15) for $V(P)$ by treating the project as a contingent claim. Let us rederive this equation using dynamic programming.

The dynamic programming problem is to choose an operating policy ($j = 0$ or 1) to maximize the expected sum of discounted profits. If the firm is risk-neutral, the problem is

$$\max_{j=0,1} E_0 \int_0^\infty j[P(t) - c]e^{-rt} \, dt, \tag{A.20}$$

given that P follows the geometric Brownian motion of equation (14). The Bellman equation for the value function $V(P)$ is then

$$rV = \max_{j=0,1}[j(P - c) + (1/dt)E_t \, dV]. \tag{A.21}$$

By Ito's Lemma, $(1/dt)E_t \, dV = \tfrac{1}{2}\sigma^2 P^2 V_{PP} + \alpha P V_P$. Maximizing with respect to j gives the optimal operating policy, $j = 1$ (i.e., operate) if $P > c$, and $j = 0$ (i.e., do not operate) otherwise. Substituting $\alpha = r - \delta$ and rearranging gives equation (15).

Acknowledgment

My thanks to Prabhat Mehta for his research assistance, and to Ben Bernanke, Vittorio Corbo, Nalin Kulatilaka, Robert McDonald, Louis Serven, Andreas Solimano, and two anonymous referees for helpful comments and suggestions. Financial support was provided by MIT's Center for Energy Policy Research, by the World Bank, and by the National Science Foundation under Grant No. SES-8618502. Any errors are mine alone.

Notes

1. See, for example, Robert McDonald and Daniel Siegel (1986), Michael Brennan and Eduardo Schwartz (1985), Saman Majd and Pindyck (1987), and Pindyck (1988). Ben Bernanke (1983) and Alex Cukierman (1980) have developed related models in which firms have an incentive to postpone irreversible investments so that they can wait for new information to arrive. However, in their models, this information makes the future value of an investment less uncertain; we will focus on situations in which information arrives over time, but the future is always uncertain.

2. In this example, the futures price would equal the expected future price because we assumed that the risk is fully diversifiable. (If the price of widgets were positively correlated with the market portfolio, the futures price would be less than the expected future spot price.) Note that if widgets were storable and aggregate storage is positive, the marginal convenience yield from holding inventory would then be 10 percent. The reason is that because the futures price equals the current spot price, the net holding cost (the interest cost of 10 percent less the marginal convenience yield) must be zero.

3. This is analogous to selling short a dividend-paying stock. The short position requires payment of the dividend, because no rational investor will hold the offsetting long position without receiving that dividend.

4. A constant payout rate, δ, and required return, μ, imply an infinite project life. Letting CF denote the cash flow from the project,

$$V_0 = \int_0^T CF_t e^{-\mu t}\, dt = \int_0^T \delta V_0 e^{(\mu-\delta)t} e^{-\mu t}\, dt,$$

which implies $T = \infty$. If the project has a finite life, equation (1) cannot represent the evolution of V during the operating period. However, it can represent its evolution prior to construction of the project, which is all that matters for the investment decision. See Majd and Pindyck (1987, pp. 11–13), for a detailed discussion of this point.

5. Avinash Dixit (1988) provides a heuristic derivation of this condition.

6. The general solution to equation (5) is

$$F(V) = a_1 V^{\beta_1} + a_2 V^{\beta_2},$$

where

$$\beta_1 = 1/2 - (r-\delta)/\sigma^2 + \{[(r-\delta)/\sigma^2 - 1/2]^2 + 2r/\sigma^2\}^{1/2} > 1,$$

and

$$\beta_2 = 1/2 - (r-\delta)/\sigma^2 - \{[(r-\delta)/\sigma^2 - 1/2]^2 + 2r/\sigma^2\}^{1/2} < 0.$$

Boundary condition (6a) implies that $a_2 = 0$, so the solution can be written as in equation (7).

7. This result was first demonstrated by Cox and Ross (1976). Also, note that equation (5) is the Bellman equation for the maximization of the net payoff to the hedge portfolio that we constructed. Because the portfolio is risk-free, the Bellman equation for that problem is

$$rP = -\delta V F_V + (1/dt) E_t\, dP. \tag{i}$$

That is, the return on the portfolio, rP, equals the per period cash flow that it pays out (which is negative, because $\delta V F_V$ must be paid in to maintain the short position), plus the expected rate of capital gain. By substituting $P = F - F_V V$ and expanding dF as before, one can see that (5) follows from (i).

8. This point and its implications are discussed in detail in McDonald and Siegel (1985).

9. Note that the option to invest is an option to purchase a package of call options (because the project is just a set of options to pay c and receive P at each future time t). Hence we are valuing a compound option. For examples of the valuation of compound financial options, see Robert Geske (1979) and Peter Carr (1988). Our problem can be treated in a simpler manner.

10. By substituting (17) for $V(P)$ into (15), the reader can check that β_1 and β_2 are the solutions to the following quadratic equation:

$$(1/2)\sigma^2\beta_1(\beta_1 - 1) + (r - \delta)\beta_1 - r = 0.$$

Because $V(0) = 0$, the positive solution $(\beta_1 > 1)$ must apply when $P < c$, and the negative solution $(\beta_2 < 0)$ must apply when $P > c$. Note that β_1 is the same as β in equation (8).

11. Of course the scrap value of the project might exceed these costs. In this case, the owner of the project holds a *put option* (an option to "sell" the project for the net scrap value), and this raises the project's value. This has been analyzed by Myers and Majd (1985).

12. Jeffrey MacKie-Mason (1990) developed a related model of a mine that shows how nonlinear tax rules (such as a percentage depletion allowance) affect the value of the operating options as well as the investment decision.

13. As Dixit points out, one would find hysteresis if, for example, the price began at a level between w and $w + pk$, rose above $w + pk$ so that entry occurred, but then fell to its original level, which is too high to induce exit. However, the firm's price expectations would then be irrational (because the price is in fact varying stochastically).

14. Letting k be the maximum rate of investment, this equation is

$$\tfrac{1}{2}\sigma^2 V^2 F_{VV} + (r - \delta)VF_V - rF - x(kF_K + k) = 0$$

where $x = 1$ when the firm is investing and 0 otherwise. $F(V, K)$ must also satisfy the following boundary conditions:

$$F(V, 0) = V,$$

$$\lim_{V \to \infty} F_V(V, K) = e^{-\delta K/k},$$

$$F(0, K) = 0$$

and $F(V, K)$ and $F_V(V, K)$ continuous at the boundary $V^*(K)$. For an overview of numerical methods for solving partial differential equations of this kind, see Geske and Kuldeep Shastri (1985).

15. The production decisions of a firm facing a learning curve and stochastically shifting demand is another example of this kind of sequential investment. Here, part of the firm's cost of production is actually an (irreversible) investment, which yields a reduction in future costs. Because demand fluctuates, the future payoffs from this investment are uncertain. Majd and Pindyck (1989) introduce stochastic demand into a learning curve model, and derive the optimal production rule. They show how uncertainty over future demand reduces the shadow value of cumulative production generated by learning, and thus raises the critical price at which it is optimal for the firm to produce.

16. James Paddock, Daniel Siegel, and James Smith (1988) value oil reserves as options to produce oil, but ignore the development stage. Octavio Tourinho (1979) first suggested that natural resource reserves can be valued as options.

17. In a related paper, Carliss Baldwin (1982) analyzes sequential investment decisions when investment opportunities arrive randomly, and the firm has limited resources to invest. She values the sequence of opportunities, and shows that a simple NPV rule will lead to overinvestment.

18. Weitzman (1981) used this model to evaluate the case for building demonstration plants for synthetic fuel production, and found that learning about costs could justify these early investments. Much of the debate over synthetic fuels has had to do with the role of government, and in particular whether subsidies (for demonstration plants or for actual production) could be justified. These issues are discussed in Paul Joskow and Pindyck (1979) and Richard Schmalensee (1980).

19. This means that the ratio of a firm's market value to the value of its capital in place should always exceed one (because part of its market value is the value of its growth options), and this ratio should be higher for firms selling in more volatile markets. Kester's (1984) study suggests that this is indeed the case.

20. Even if firms are perfectly competitive and have constant returns, stochastic fluctuations in demand will depress irreversible investment if there can be entry by new firms in response to price increases. See Pindyck (1990b) for a discussion of this point. Also, Abel, Bertola, Caballero, and Pindyck examine the effects of increased demand or price uncertainty holding the discount rate fixed. As Roger Craine (1989) points out, an increase in demand uncertainty is likely to be accompanied by an increase in the systematic riskiness of the firm's capital, and hence an increase in its risk-adjusted discount rate.

21. The firm has an option, worth $G(K, \theta)$, to build a plant of arbitrary size K. Once built, the plant has a value $V(K, \theta)$ (the value of the firm's operating options), which can be found using the methods of Section IV. $G(K, \theta)$ will satisfy equation (18), but with boundary conditions $G(K^*, \theta^*) = V(K^*, \theta^*) - kK^*$ and $G_\theta(K^*, \theta^*) = V_\theta(K^*, \theta^*)$, where θ^* is the critical θ at which the plant should be built, and K^* is its optimal size. See the Appendix to Pindyck (1988).

22. Ricardo Caballero and Vittorio Corbo (1988), for example, have shown how uncertainty over future real exchange rates can depress exports.

23. But Van Wijnbergen is incorrect in claiming (1985, p. 369) that "there is only a gain to be obtained by deferring commitment if uncertainty decreases over time so that information can be acquired about future factor returns as time goes by." He bases his analysis on the models of Bernanke (1983) and Cukierman (1980), in which there is indeed a reduction in uncertainty over time. But as we have seen from the models in Sections III and IV of this paper, this is not necessary. In those models, the future value of the project or price of output is *always* uncertain, but there is nonetheless an opportunity cost to committing resources.

24. The sharp jumps in energy prices in 1974 and 1979–80 clearly contributed to the 1975 and 1980–82 recessions. They reduced the real incomes of oil-importing countries, and caused adjustment problems—inflation and further drops in income due to rigidities that prevented wages and nonenergy prices from quickly equilibrating. But energy shocks also raised uncertainty over future economic conditions; it was unclear whether energy prices would fall or keep rising, what impact higher energy prices would have on the marginal products of various types of capital, how long-lived the inflationary impact of the shocks would be, and so on. Much more volatile exchange rates and interest rates also made the economic environment more uncertain, especially in 1979–82. This may have contributed to the decline in investment spending that occurred, a point made by Bernanke (1983) with respect to changes in oil prices. Also, see Paul Evans (1984) and John Tatom (1984) for discussions of the effects of increased interest rate volatility.

25. See Pindyck (1990a) for a more detailed discussion of this issue.

26. Recent examples are Anthony Fisher and W. Michael Hanemann (1987) and Hanemann (1989). This concept of option value should be distinguished from that of Schmalensee (1972), which is more like a risk premium that is needed to compensate risk-averse consumers because of uncertainty over future valuations of an environmental amenity. For a recent discussion of this latter concept, see Mark Plummer and Hartman (1986).

References

Abel, Andrew B. "Optimal Investment Under Uncertainty," *Amer. Econ. Rev.*, Mar. 1983, *73*(1), pp. 228–33.

———. "Consumption and Investment," in *Handbook of monetary economics*. Eds.: Benjamin Friedman and Frank Hahn. NY: North-Holland, 1990, pp. 726–78.

Arrow, Kenneth J. "Optimal Capital Policy with Irreversible Investment," in *Value, capital and growth, papers in honour of Sir John Hicks*. Ed.: James N. Wolfe. Edinburgh: Edinburgh U. Press, 1968, pp. 1–19.

Arrow, Kenneth J. and Fisher, Anthony C. "Environmental Preservation, Uncertainty, and Irreversibility," *Quart. J. Econ.*, May 1974, *88*(2), pp. 312–19.

Baldwin, Carliss Y. "Optimal Sequential Investment When Capital Is Not Readily Reversible," *J. Finance*, June 1982, *37*(3), pp. 763–82.

Baldwin, Richard. "Hysteresis in Import Prices: The Beachhead Effect," *Amer. Econ. Rev.*, Sept. 1988, *78*(4), pp. 773–85.

Baldwin, Richard and Krugman, Paul. "Persistent Trade Effects of Large Exchange Rate Shocks," *Quart. J. Econ.*, Nov. 1989, *104*(4), pp. 635–54.

Bentolila, Samuel and Bertola, Giuseppe. "Firing Costs and Labor Demand: How Bad Is Eurosclerosis?" *Rev. Econ. Stud.*, July 1990, *57*(3), pp. 381–402.

Bernanke, Ben S. "Irreversibility, Uncertainty, and Cyclical Investment," *Quart. J. Econ.*, Feb. 1983, *98*(1), pp. 85–106.

Bertola, Giuseppe. "Irreversible Investment." unpublished working paper, Princeton U., 1989.

Bertola, Giuseppe and Caballero, Ricardo J. "Irreversibility and Aggregate Investment." unpublished, Princeton U., June 1990.

Brennan, Michael J. and Schwartz, Eduardo S. "Evaluating Natural Resource Investments," *J. Bus.*, Apr. 1985, *58*(2), pp. 135–57.

Caballero, Ricardo J. "Competition and the Non-Robustness of the Investment-Uncertainty Relationship," *Amer. Econ. Rev.*, Mar. 1991, *81*(1), pp. 279–88.

Caballero, Ricardo and Corbo, Vittorio. "Real Exchange Rate Uncertainty and Exports: Multi-Country Empirical Evidence." Columbia U. Dept. of Economics Discussion Paper No. 414, Dec. 1988.

Carr, Peter. "The Valuation of Sequential Exchange Opportunities," *J. Finance*, Dec. 1988, *43*(5), pp. 1235–56.

Chow, Gregory C. "Optimal Control of Stochastic Differential Equation Systems," *J. Econ. Dynam. Control*, May 1979, *1*, pp. 143–75.

Cox, John C. and Ross, Stephen A. "The Valuation of Options for Alternative Stochastic Processes," *J. Finan. Econ.*, Jan./Mar. 1976, *3*(1/2), pp. 145–66.

Cox, John C.; Ross, Stephen A. and Rubinstein, Mark. "Option Pricing: A Simplified Approach," *J. Finan. Econ.*, Sept. 1979, *7*(3), pp. 229–63.

Cox, John C. and Rubinstein, Mark. *Options markets*. Englewood Cliffs, NJ: Prentice-Hall, 1985.

Craine, Roger. "Risky Business: The Allocation of Capital," *J. Monet. Econ.*, Mar. 1989, *23*(2), pp. 201–18.

Cukierman, Alex. "The Effects of Uncertainty on Investment under Risk Neutrality with Endogenous Information," *J. Polit. Econ.*, June 1980, *88*(3), pp. 462–75.

Dixit, Avinash. "A Heuristic Argument for the Smooth Pasting Condition." Unpub., Princeton U., Mar. 1988.

———. "Entry and Exit Decisions under Uncertainty," *J. Polit. Econ.*, June 1989a, *97*(3), pp. 620–38.

———. "Hysteresis, Import Penetration, and Exchange Rate Pass-Through," *Quart. J. Econ.*, May 1989b, *104*(2), pp. 205–28.

———. "Investment and Hysteresis." Unpub. Princeton U., June 1991.

Dornbusch, Rudiger. "Open Economy Macroeconomics: New Directions." NBER Working Paper No. 2372, Aug. 1987.

Dreyfus, Stuart E. *Dynamic programming and the calculus of variations*. NY: Academic Press, 1965.

Evans, Paul. "The Effects on Output of Money Growth and Interest Rate Volatility in the United States," *J. Polit. Econ.*, Apr. 1984, *92*, pp. 204–22.

Fisher, Anthony C. and Hanemann, W. Michael. "Quasi-Option Value: Some Misconceptions Dispelled," *J. Environ. Econ. Manage.*, June 1987, *14*(2), pp. 183–90.

Fleming, Wendell H. and Rishel, Raymond W. *Deterministic and stochastic optimal control.* NY: Springer-Verlag, 1975.

Geske, Robert. "The Valuation of Compound Options," *J. Finan. Econ.*, Mar. 1979, *7*(1), pp. 63–81.

Geske, Robert and Shastri, Kuldeep. "Valuation by Approximation: A Comparison of Alternative Option Valuation Techniques," *J. Finan. Quant. Anal.*, Mar. 1985, *20*(1), pp. 45–71.

Gilbert, Richard J. "Mobility Barriers and the Value of Incumbency," *Handbook of industrial organization.* Vol. I. Eds.: Richard Schmalensee and Robert Willig. NY: North-Holland, 1989.

Grossman, Gene M. and Shapiro, Carl. "Optimal Dynamic R&D Programs," *Rand J. Econ.*, Winter 1986, *17*, pp. 581–93.

Grossman, Sanford J. and Laroque, Guy. "Asset Pricing and Optimal Portfolio Choice in the Presence of Illiquid Durable Consumption Goods," *Econometrica*, Jan. 1990, *58*(1), pp. 25–51.

Hanemann, W. Michael. "Information and the Concept of Option Value," *J. Environ. Econ. Manage.*, Jan. 1989, *16*(1), pp. 23–37.

Hartman, Richard. "The Effects of Price and Cost Uncertainty on Investment," *J. Econ. Theory*, Oct. 1972, *5*(2), pp. 258–66.

He, Hua and Pindyck, Robert S. "Investments in Flexible Production Capacity." MIT, Sloan School of Management Working Paper No. 2102–89. Mar. 1989.

Henry, Claude. "Investment Decisions under Uncertainty: The 'Irreversibility Effect,'" *Amer. Econ. Rev.*, Dec. 1974, *64*(6), pp. 1006–12.

Hull, John. *Options, futures, and other derivative securities.* Prentice-Hall, 1989.

Ingersoll, Jonathan E., Jr. and Ross, Stephen A. "Waiting to Invest: Investment and Uncertainty." unpublished, Yale U., Oct. 1988.

Joskow, Paul L. and Pindyck, Robert S. "Synthetic Fuels: Should the Government Subsidize Nonconventional Energy Supplies?" *Regulation*, Sept. 1979, pp. 18–24.

Kester, W. Carl. "Today's Options for Tomorrow's Growth," *Harvard Bus. Rev.*, Mar./Apr. 1984, *62*(2), pp. 153–60.

Krugman, Paul R. *Exchange rate instability.* Cambridge: MIT Press, 1989.

Kushner, Harold J. *Stochastic stability and control.* NY: Academic Press, 1967.

Lam, Pok-sang. "Irreversibility and Consumer Durables Expenditures," *J. Monet. Econ.*, Jan. 1989, *23*(1), pp. 135–50.

Leahy, John. "Notes on an Industry Equilibrium Model of Entry and Exit." unpublished, Princeton U., Nov. 1989.

Lippman, Steven A. and Rumelt, Richard P. "Industry-Specific Capital and Uncertainty." Unpublished, UCLA, Sept. 1985.

MacKie-Mason, Jeffrey K. "Some Nonlinear Tax Effects on Asset Values and Investment Decisions Under Uncertainty," *J. Public Econ.*, forthcoming 1990.

Majd, Saman and Pindyck, Robert S. "Time to Build, Option Value, and Investment Decisions," *J. Finan. Econ.*, Mar. 1987, *18*(1), pp. 7–27.

————. "The Learning Curve and Optimal Production under Uncertainty," *RAND J. Econ.*, Autumn 1989, *20*(3), pp. 331–43.

Malliaris, A. G. and Brock, William A. *Stochastic methods in economics and finance.* NY: North-Holland, 1982.

Manne, Alan S. "Capacity Expansion and Probabilistic Growth," *Econometrica*, Oct. 1961, *29*, pp. 632–49.

Mason, Scott and Merton, Robert C. "The Role of Contingent Claims Analysis in Corporate Finance," in *Recent advances in corporate finance*. Eds: Edward I. Altman and Marti G. Subrahmanyam. Richard D. Irwin, 1985, pp. 7–54.

McDonald, Robert and Siegel, Daniel R. "Investment and the Valuation of Firms When There Is an Option to Shut Down," *Int. Econ. Rev.*, June 1985, *26*(2), pp. 331–49.

———. "The Value of Waiting to Invest," *Quart. J. Econ.*, Nov. 1986, *101*(4), pp. 707–27.

Merton, Robert C. "Optimum Consumption and Portfolio Rules in a Continuous-Time Model," *J. Econ. Theory*, Dec. 1971, *3*(4), pp. 373–413.

———. "On the Pricing of Contingent Claims and the Modigliani-Miller Theorem," *J. Finan. Econ.*, Nov. 1977, *5*(2), pp. 241–49.

Myers, Stewart C. "Determinants of Corporate Borrowing," *J. Finan. Econ.*, Nov. 1977, *5*(2), pp. 147–75.

Myers, Stewart C. and Majd, Saman. "Calculating Abandonment Value Using Option Pricing Theory," MIT Sloan School of Management Working Paper No. 1462–83, Jan. 1985.

Newbery, David and Stiglitz, Joseph. *The theory of commodity price stabilization*. NY: Oxford U. Press, 1981.

Nickell, Stephen J. "On the Role of Expectations in the Pure Theory of Investment," *Rev. Econ. Stud.*, Jan. 1974, *41*(1), pp. 1–19.

———. *The investment decisions of firms*. NY: Cambridge U. Press, 1978.

Paddock, James L.; Siegel, Daniel R. and Smith, James L. "Option Valuation of Claims on Real Assets: The Case of Offshore Petroleum Leases," *Quart. J. Econ.*, Aug. 1988, *103*(3), pp. 479–508.

Pindyck, Robert S. "Irreversible Investment, Capacity Choice, and the Value of the Firm," *Amer. Econ. Rev.*, Dec. 1988, *78*(5), pp. 969–85.

———. "Irreversibility and the Explanation of Investment Behavior," in *Stochastic models and option values*. Eds.: D. Lund and B. Øksendal. Amsterdam: North-Holland, 1990a.

———. "A Note on Competitive Investment Under Uncertainty," unpub., M.I.T., July 1990b.

Plummer, Mark L. and Hartman, Richard C. "Option Value: A General Approach," *Econ. Inquiry*, July 1976, *24*(3), pp. 455–71.

Roberts, Kevin and Weitzman, Martin L. "Funding Criteria for Research, Development, and Exploration Projects," *Econometrica*, Sept. 1981, *49*(5), pp. 1261–88.

Schmalensee, Richard. "Option Demand and Consumer's Surplus: Valuing Price Changes under Uncertainty," *Amer. Econ. Rev.*, Dec. 1972, *62*(5), pp. 813–24.

———. "Appropriate Government Policy Toward Commercialization of New Energy Supply Technologies," *Energy J.*, July 1980, *1*, pp. 1–40.

Tatom, John A. "Interest Rate Variability: Its Link to the Variability of Monetary Growth and Economic Performance," *Fed. Res. Bank St. Louis Rev.*, Nov. 1984, *66*(9), pp. 31–47.

Tourinho, Octavio A. "The Valuation of Reserves of Natural Resources: An Option Pricing Approach," unpublished PhD diss., U. of California, Berkeley, 1979.

Van Wijnbergen, Sweder. "Trade Reform, Aggregate Investment and Capital Flight," *Econ. Lett.*, 1985, *19*, pp. 369–72.

Weitzman, Martin with Newey, Whitney and Rabin, Michael. "Sequential R&D Strategy for Synfuels," *Bell J. Econ.*, Autumn 1981, *12*(2), pp. 574–90.

III VALUING VARIOUS REAL OPTIONS

12 The Value of Waiting to Invest

Robert McDonald and Daniel Siegel

I Introduction

Suppose that a firm is considering building a synthetic fuel plant. What is the appropriate way to decide whether or not to build? Clearly, one calculates the present values of profits and the direct costs of construction. It would be incorrect, however, simply to compare these present values and build the plant if the present value of profits exceeds that of the direct costs.

The decision to build the plant is irreversible; the plant cannot be used for any other purpose. The decision to defer building, however, is reversible. This asymmetry, when properly taken into account, leads to a rule that says build the plant only if benefits exceed costs by a certain positive amount. The correct calculation involves comparing the value of investing today with the (present) value of investing at all possible times in the future. This is a comparison of mutually exclusive alternatives.

In this chapter we explore the practical importance of the value of waiting to invest, assuming that investment timing decisions are made by risk-averse investors who hold well-diversified portfolios. We derive explicit formulas for the value of the option to invest in an irreversible project and the rule for when to invest when both the value of the project and the cost of investing are stochastic. The formulas enable us to compute exactly the optimal investment timing rule, as well as the dollar value lost by a firm that takes a project at a suboptimal time.

In Section II we present a general model of investment with the option to wait, and apply the model to real investment problems. In Section III we solve the valuation problem assuming that both the present value of benefits and the investment cost follow geometric Brownian motion, and also assuming that the present value of benefits usually follows Brownian motion but also may jump discretely to zero. In every case we assume that the option is infinitely lived.[1] Risk aversion is introduced by assuming that investment options are owned by well-diversified investors. In Section IV we compute examples of the option value and investment rule for a wide variety of parameters. The general conclusion is that timing considerations are quantitatively important. For reasonable parameter values it is optimal to defer investing until the present value of the benefits from a project is *double* the investment cost. The rule, "invest if the net present value of investing exceeds zero" is only valid if the variance of the present value of future benefits and costs is zero or if the expected rate of growth of the present value is minus infinity; the value lost by following this suboptimal investment policy can be substantial. Section V presents an example in which a firm with a Cobb-Douglas production function faces a random demand curve. We compute the option value and investment rule as a function of exogenous parameters. Section VI concludes.

A number of related papers have studied investment timing. Baldwin [1982]; Baldwin and Meyer [1979]; Brock, Rothschild, and Stiglitz [1983]; and Venezia and Brenner [1979] have all analyzed the investment timing problem under risk neutrality and have obtained many of the same comparative static results as we do. Bernanke [1983] and Venezia [1983] have added Bayesian learning, so that investors learn not only about the value of the project by waiting, but also about the underlying sto- chastic process.[2] This chapter's main contributions are providing a tractable and realistic means of incorporating risk aversion considerations into the timing problem and presenting examples that show timing considerations to be important.

II   The Investment Problem

We study the investment decision of a firm that is considering the following invest- ment opportunity: at any time t (up to a possible expiration date T), the firm can pay F_t to install an investment project, for which expected future net cash flows condi- tional on undertaking the project have a present value V_t. We emphasize that V_t is a present value; it represents the appropriately discounted *expected* cash flows, given the information available at time t. For the firm, V_t represents the market value of a claim on the stream of net cash flows that arise from installing the investment project at time t. Typically, V_t and F_t are stochastic. The installation of capacity is irrevers- ible, in that the capacity can be used only for this specific project.

We assume that V_t follows geometric Brownian motion of the form,

$$\frac{dV}{V} = \alpha_v \, dt + \sigma_v \, dz_v, \tag{1a}$$

where z_v is a standard Wiener process. Thus, the firm knows the present value of future net cash flows if it installs the project today. However, the present value may be different if the capacity is installed in the future. (We shall also consider the pos- sibility that at some [random] time in the future, the present value of net cash flows drops at once to zero.) Similarly, we assume that F_t follows:

$$\frac{dF}{F} = \alpha_f \, dt + \sigma_f \, dz_f. \tag{1b}$$

For both V and F, the geometric Brownian motion assumption is crucial for the derivation of the formulas below. This assumption is reasonable for the project value

V, but may be less so for the investment cost F. The project value V in many applications is the market value of an asset; if the project were undertaken and a company owned only this asset, V is the price for which the company's stock would sell, which is to say that V is the price of a financial asset. The rate of growth of V will equal the rate of return on the stock, less cash flow that is earned on the project and paid out. Thus, as long as the payout rate is relatively constant, the assumption of geometric Brownian motion for V is as reasonable as assuming that a stock price obeys geometric Brownian motion (a standard assumption in the finance literature), although the rate of appreciation of V will typically be less than the total rate of return on a comparable stock.[3] Nevertheless, the example in Section V will show that the assumption of geometric Brownian motion can lead to unrealistic conclusions. If V is not a present value, our analysis is still valid, but (1a) may be a less reasonable specification. The investment cost F is typically the price of a physical asset and not a present value.[4] We discuss scenarios, however, in which F is also a present value.

Examples of the Investment Problem

The essential feature of the problem is that the firm is faced with the mutually exclusive choice of taking an irreversible project today or in the future. Uncertainty about the project's value and the cost of the project is being continuously resolved. There are a number of situations embodying these assumptions. A monopolist, for example, may have an investment opportunity such that once he installs his capacity, he is protected from competition. Alternatively, one can think of a firm in a competitive industry exhibiting temporary rents. The investment opportunity consists of a project whose future net cash flows have a present value exceeding the investment cost now, but which tend on average toward the investment cost because of lagged entry. In equation (1a) this is represented by $\alpha_v < 0$. Many examples of this kind of project occur in high technology industries. When a firm is considering introducing a new product, it realizes that others may introduce similar products. As the others enter, profits disappear. These industries also provide examples of how V_t might at some point drop to zero. While the firm is waiting to introduce its product, a new, more sophisticated or cheaper version might be introduced by another firm, rendering the former's product useless.

More generally, we shall be describing a situation in which the investor can swap one risky asset (F) for another (V). This can be thought of either as a straightforward investment problem or as an asset replacement problem. The two problems are the same. For example, suppose that the government is considering building a canal through Everglades National Park. V_t represents the present value of the benefits from building the canal, while F_t represents both the direct costs and the present value of forgone benefits of the park as a recreational area.

Optimal Scrapping of a Project

By reinterpreting variables, the model can also be used to study the problem of optimal scrapping. Interpret F as the value of the project in place and V as the value of the project if it were to be sold. The model then provides the value of the option to scrap a project. In general, it will be optimal to scrap only when the selling price exceeds the project value by a positive amount.

III   Investment Timing and the Value of Waiting

This section studies the problem of the optimal timing of the installation of an irreversible investment project. We derive an optimal decision rule and the value of the investment opportunity. We begin with the case of V and F following (1a) and (1b) and then show how the correct discount rate is obtained when investors are risk averse. We then consider the possibility that V_t may suddenly fall to zero.

V and F Stochastic

To introduce the problem, suppose initially that V_t follows (1a), but that F is constant. The firm receives $V_t - F$ when it invests. The investment timing problem consists of finding a number C_t^*, for every time t, such that if $V_t/F \geq C_t^*$, the investment is undertaken, and deferred otherwise. This investment decision schedule $\{C_t^*\}$ is chosen so as to maximize the time zero expected present value of the payoff $V_t - F$.

For example, let the investment opportunity expire at T. It is obvious that if we reach T and have not already undertaken investment, then it will be optimal to do so provided that $V_T \geq F$. Thus, $C_T^* = 1$ constitutes a boundary at T, at which the investment opportunity is undertaken. In a similar way, working backwards, for any t it is possible to derive a C_t^* such that, if the investment opportunity is still unexercised at t, then undertaking it will be optimal if $V_t/F \geq C_t^*$, and not otherwise. When $V_t/F = C_t^*$, the firm invests, and the net present value of the project is then $F[C_t^* - 1]$.

For an arbitrary boundary $\{C_t'\}_0^T$, the value of the investment opportunity is the expected present value of the payoff:

$$X(T) = E_0\{e^{-\mu t'}[V_{t'} - F]\}, \tag{2}$$

where t' is the date at which V/F first reaches the boundary $\{C_t'\}$ and $X(T)$ is the time zero value of an investment opportunity that expires at T. The expectation is taken over the first passage times t', and μ is the appropriate discount rate, which we take as given for the moment.

In the special case where the investment opportunity is infinitely lived, it is possible to solve for the maximized value of (2) explicitly. When $T = \infty$, it is possible to remove calendar time from the problem. Hence C^* cannot depend on t, so $C_t^* = C^*$ for all t. Because $V_{t'} - F = F(C^* - 1)$ is constant, maximizing (2) reduces to the problem,

$$\max_{C'} F[C' - 1]E_0\{e^{-\mu t'}\}.$$

The solution to this problem is a special case of the problem we solve below.

Now consider the same problem, except that F_t is also random and follows the stochastic process (1b). The problem is formulated as a first passage problem as before, but the characterization of the boundary at which investment should occur is not as obvious. A simple argument establishes that investment should occur when the ratio V/F reaches a boundary. The problem we have been considering involves choosing a boundary B to maximize

$$E_0[(V_t - F_t)e^{-\mu t}],$$

subject to (1a) and (1b). Let $V' = kV$ and $F' = kF$, where k is an arbitrary positive number, and consider the problem of choosing a boundary B' to maximize

$$E_0[(V'_t - F'_t)e^{-\mu t}],$$

subject to

$$\frac{dV'}{V'} = \alpha_v\, dt + \sigma_v\, dz_v; \quad \frac{dF'}{F'} = \alpha_f\, dt + \sigma_f\, dz_f.$$

The two problems are formally identical, so the boundaries B and B' must be the same and hence independent of k. Since the boundary is independent of k, it is homogeneous of degree zero in V and F. Also, as before, the boundary is independent of calendar time when $T = \infty$. Thus, the correct rule is to invest when the ratio V/F reaches a fixed boundary. There is an additional question as to whether there are multiple boundaries. The Appendix proves that the solution is to invest if V/F exceeds C^*, and wait otherwise.

Because the optimal rule is to invest when V_t/F_t reaches a barrier C^*, the expected present value of the payoff is

$$E_0\{F_{t'}[C^* - 1]e^{-\mu t'}\} = [C^* - 1]E_0\{F_{t'}e^{-\mu t'}\}, \tag{3}$$

where the expectation is taken over the joint density of F_t and the first-passage times for $V_t/F_{t'}$. Fortunately, it is not necessary to derive the joint density for $F_{t'}$ and t' in order to evaluate (3). The evaluation of (3) is involved, however, so it is relegated to the Appendix. From the Appendix the value of the opportunity is

$$X = (C^* - 1)F_0 \left(\frac{V_0/F_0}{C^*} \right)^\varepsilon, \tag{4}$$

where

$$\varepsilon = \sqrt{ \left(\frac{\alpha_v - \alpha_f}{\sigma^2} - \frac{1}{2} \right)^2 + \frac{2(\mu - \alpha_f)}{\sigma^2} } + \left(\frac{1}{2} - \frac{\alpha_v - \alpha_f}{\sigma^2} \right), \tag{5}$$

$$C^* = \varepsilon/(\varepsilon - 1),$$

$\sigma^2 = \sigma_v^2 + \sigma_f^2 - 2\rho_{vf}\sigma_v\sigma_f$, and ρ_{vf} is the instantaneous correlation between the rates of increase of V and F.

The condition $\alpha_v < \mu$ ensures that $\varepsilon > 1$, so that the solution is well defined. If $\alpha_v \geq \mu$, then the growth rate of the value of the project is expected to exceed the discount rate. Consequently, the value of the investment opportunity would be infinite, and it will never pay to invest. When F is nonstochastic, (4) is Samuelson's [1970] formula for the price of an infinitely lived American call option on a dividend-paying stock. The case where T is finite has not been solved analytically [Samuelson, 1970]. The general solution procedure in such cases involves using a discrete approximation to the continuous-time problem and applying a dynamic programming argument to obtain numerical approximations to the solution (cf. Ingersoll [1977]). Numerical procedures can also be used when the parameters (α, μ, and σ) are functions of V, F, and t.

Both the value of the investment option and the level of V/F at which investment should occur are increasing functions of the variance of V/F, σ^2.[5] The reason for this is well-known: an increase in variance increases the spread of possible future values for V/F, and hence the maximum possible gain, while leaving unchanged the maximum possible loss. Note that only the variance of the proportional change in V/F, σ^2, enters the formula; this occurs since the investment rule depends only on V/F. Therefore, an increase in either σ_v^2 or σ_f^2, or a decrease in the correlation ρ_{vf}, will increase the value of the investment option.

The value of the investment option is also an increasing function of α_v and a decreasing function of α_f and μ. As we shall see in the next section, however, comparative statics for the drifts alone are uninteresting.

Optimal Scrapping[6] As noted earlier, a simple reinterpretation of the solution with V and F random (equation (4)) provides the value of the option to scrap a project. Interpret V as the random scrap value of the project. F is the random value to the firm of the project in place. The payoff from scrapping is therefore $V - F$. An argument like that above establishes that the optimal policy is to sell the asset when the ratio F/V reaches a boundary. Let c^* represent the level to which F/V must fall before it is optimal to scrap. Equation (4) then becomes

$$X = (C^* - 1)F_0\left(\frac{V_0/F_0}{C^*}\right)^\varepsilon = (1 - c^*)V_0\left(\frac{F_0/V_0}{c^*}\right)^{1-\varepsilon}, \tag{6}$$

where $c^* = (\varepsilon - 1)/\varepsilon$ and ε is given by (5).[7] Note that c^* is less than 1. Thus, in general the firm waits to scrap until the value of the project is less than its scrap value by some positive amount. The intuition here is the same as before: by waiting, the firm can benefit from increases in $V - F$, but is protected against decreases.

Computing the Correct Discount Rate

We have taken as given μ, the rate at which future payoffs are discounted. We now show that μ—which is the equilibrium expected rate of return on the investment opportunity—must be a weighted average of the equilibrium expected rates of return on assets with the same risk as V and F.

Risk aversion by investors is here introduced by supposing that options to invest are owned by well-diversified investors, who need only be compensated for the systematic component of the risk of projects and options to invest. This is in contrast to Venezia and Brenner [1979], for example, who assume that the entire project is owned by a single risk-averse investor. Assuming that investors are well diversified describes publicly owned corporations in the United States and simplifies the computation of the option value.

The actual rate of return on the investment opportunity is computed by taking an Ito derivative[8] of the option value, equation (4):

$$\frac{dX}{X} = \frac{\varepsilon\, dV}{V} + (1 - \varepsilon)\frac{dF}{F} + \varepsilon(\varepsilon - 1)(\tfrac{1}{2}\sigma_v^2 + \tfrac{1}{2}\sigma_f^2 - \rho_{vf}\sigma_v\sigma_f)\, dt$$

$$= [\varepsilon\alpha_v + (1 - \varepsilon)\alpha_f + \varepsilon(\varepsilon - 1)\tfrac{1}{2}\sigma^2]\, dt + \varepsilon\sigma_v\, dz_v + (1 - \varepsilon)\sigma_f\, dz_f. \tag{8}$$

In (8) the unanticipated component of the return on X is $\varepsilon\sigma_v\, dz_v + (1 - \varepsilon)\sigma_f\, dz_f$, which is a weighted average of the unanticipated components in the rates of change of V and F. With standard asset pricing models, the risk premium earned on an asset is proportional to the riskiness of the asset. For example, in the Capital Asset Pricing Model,

$$\hat{\alpha}_i - r = \phi \rho_{im} \sigma_i, \tag{9}$$

where $\hat{\alpha}_i$ is the required rate of return on asset i, r is the risk-free rate, ϕ is the market price of risk, and ρ_{im} is the correlation between the rate of return on the asset and that on the market portfolio. If $\hat{\alpha}_j$ is the required rate of return for an asset with unexpected rate of return $\sigma_j \, dz_j$, then from (9) an asset with unexpected rate of return $v\sigma_j \, dz_j$ will have required rate of return $r + v(\hat{\alpha}_j - r)$. Therefore, μ, which is the discount rate for future payoffs and hence the equilibrium expected rate of return on the investment opportunity, will be given by

$$\mu = r + \varepsilon(\hat{\alpha}_v - r) + (1 - \varepsilon)(\hat{\alpha}_f - r) = \varepsilon\hat{\alpha}_v + (1 - \varepsilon)\hat{\alpha}_f, \tag{10}$$

where $\hat{\alpha}_v$ and $\hat{\alpha}_f$ are determined by (9), and are the expected rates of return required by investors for assets that are perfectly correlated with, and have the same standard deviations as V and F.

Equating the required expected rate of return (10) with the actual expected rate of return on X in (8) yields a quadratic equation in ε:

$$\mu = \varepsilon\hat{\alpha}_v + (1 - \varepsilon)\hat{\alpha}_f = \varepsilon\alpha_v + (1 - \varepsilon)\alpha_f + \tfrac{1}{2}\varepsilon(\varepsilon - 1)\sigma^2. \tag{11}$$

Equation (11) has the solution,

$$\varepsilon = \sqrt{\left(\frac{\delta_f - \delta_v}{\sigma^2} - \frac{1}{2}\right)^2 + 2\frac{\delta_f}{\sigma^2}} + \left(\frac{1}{2} - \frac{\delta_f - \delta_v}{\sigma^2}\right), \tag{12}$$

where $\delta_v = \hat{\alpha}_v - \alpha_v$ and $\delta_f = \hat{\alpha}_f - \alpha_f$. $\delta_v > 0$ insures that $\varepsilon > 1$. Equation (12) is the same as (5), since (12) can be obtained from (5) by substituting $\varepsilon\hat{\alpha}_v + (1 - \varepsilon)\hat{\alpha}_f$ for μ in equation (5) and then solving the resulting quadratic equation for ε.

Equation (12) shows that the drift terms *per se* are unimportant; the value of the option and the investment rule are affected only by the difference between the actual drifts and the required rates of return on assets with the same risk as V and F. A project with α_v of -0.10 and $\hat{\alpha}_v$ of -0.05 (a project with negative systematic risk) will less likely pay off than a project with α_v of 0.10 and $\hat{\alpha}_v$ of 0.15 (a project with positive systematic risk). The two projects will be valued the same, however, since those infrequent states in which the first project pays off are states in which the market as a whole performs poorly, and thus are valued more highly than states in which the second project pays off.

The parameter δ_v represents the portion of the required return on V that is forgone by merely receiving the price increases in V. The greater is δ_v, the greater is the cost to holding the option, which amounts to holding V indirectly. Thus, if δ_v rises, investment will optimally occur at a lower V/F, and the option is worth less. Holding α_v fixed, we see that increases in the systematic risk of V will raise δ_v and lower the option value. Similarly, δ_f represents the portion of the return on F that is forgone by obtaining only the price increases in F. An increase in δ_f has the opposite effects from an increase in δ_v, since F is a cost that is deferred by waiting. The larger is δ_f, the greater is the gain from deferral. An increase in the systematic risk of F raises δ_f and the value of the option.

More insight into the roles of δ_v and δ_f can be gained by considering the formula when $\sigma_v^2 = \sigma_f^2 = 0$. In that case, it can be shown that

$$\hat{X} = (\hat{C} - 1)F_0\left(\frac{V_0/F_0}{\hat{C}}\right)^{\delta_f/(\delta_f-\delta_v)}$$

(13)

$$\hat{C} = \delta_f/\delta_v.$$

Expression (13) implies that in the deterministic case, investing is optimal only if

$$V_0\delta_v \geq F_0\delta_f.$$

(14)

This condition says that it is optimal to invest when the opportunity cost from not installing the project, $V_0\delta_v$, equals or exceeds the opportunity cost saved by deferring installation, $F_0\delta_f$. The formula is defined only for $\delta_v < \delta_f$. Otherwise it is optimal to invest immediately, or (if $V < F$) never.

When $\sigma^2 > 0$, the investment condition is

$$V_0\delta_v \geq F_0\delta_f + h(V_0, F_0); \quad h > 0.$$

(14')

When $\delta_v = 0$, there is no loss from waiting, and it is never optimal to invest; from (4) and (12) it can be verified that in this case $X = V$ and $C^* = \infty$.[9] The condition $\delta_f = 0$ is not of comparable importance, since with uncertainty the opportunity saving on F is not the only gain from waiting—there is also value from waiting (represented by h), since the option provides the ability to capture gains in V and avoid losses.

Jumps in V_t

Assume that there is a positive probability that the present value of net future cash flows, V_t, can take a discrete jump to zero. If this happens, the investment opportunity becomes worthless. Thus the stochastic process for V_t is a mixed Poisson-Wiener process of the form,

$$\frac{dV}{V} = \alpha_v \, dt + \sigma_v \, dz_v + dq,$$ (15)

where

$$dq = \begin{cases} -1 & \text{with probability } \lambda \, dt \\ 0 & \text{with probability } 1 - \lambda \, dt. \end{cases}$$

The occurrence of the Poisson event induces the process to stop, since zero is a natural absorbing barrier for a geometric Brownian motion process.

Notice that when the Poisson event occurs, it is as if the investment opportunity expires, since its value becomes zero. Thus, calculating the value of the investment opportunity when V_t can jump to zero is like calculating the value of an investment opportunity with an uncertain expiration date. The value in this case is easily calculated thanks to a result in Merton [1971].

The distribution of first occurrence times for a Poisson event with parameter λ is exponential. Suppose that the Poisson event is uncorrelated with the market portfolio and V, and that F is constant. Then the expected present value of the payoff from the investment opportunity with uncertain expiration date is

$$X^* = \int_0^\infty \lambda e^{-\lambda T} X(T) \, dT.$$ (16)

This may be integrated by parts [Merton, 1971] to give

$$X^* = \max_{\{C_t'\}} E_0(e^{-(\mu+\lambda)t'} F[C_t' - 1]).$$ (17)

This is exactly the problem we solved in subsection A above with no Poisson jump, except that the discount rate μ has been replaced by $\mu + \lambda$.[10] The formula is therefore the same as (4) with the discount rate adjusted in (5).

To compute the discount rate in this case, we can use Ito's lemma for Poisson processes [Merton, 1971] to calculate the expected rate of return on the option to invest. Assume for simplicity that F is fixed. The Ito derivative of (4) is then

$$\frac{dX^*}{X^*} = \varepsilon(\alpha_v \, dt + \sigma_v \, dz_v) + \varepsilon(\varepsilon - 1)\tfrac{1}{2}\sigma_v^2 \, dt - \lambda \, dt.$$ (18)

The only risk in (18) is due to the term $\varepsilon \sigma_v \, dz_v$, so the required rate of return on X^* is $r + \varepsilon(\hat{\alpha}_v - r)$. Equating this to the expected rate of return gives

$$[r + \varepsilon(\hat{\alpha}_v - r)] \, dt = E\left(\frac{dX^*}{X^*}\right) = [\varepsilon\alpha_v - \lambda + \varepsilon(\varepsilon - 1)\tfrac{1}{2}\sigma_v^2] \, dt.$$ (19)

Solving for ε yields

$$\varepsilon = \sqrt{\left(\frac{r-\delta_v}{\sigma_v^2}-\frac{1}{2}\right)^2 + \frac{2(r+\lambda)}{\sigma_v^2}} + \left(\frac{1}{2}-\frac{r-\delta_v}{\sigma_v^2}\right). \tag{20}$$

For the case when F is random, every occurrence of r in (20) is replaced by δ_f.

As would be expected from the analogy between an increase in the jump probability and an increase in the discount rate, an increase in λ reduces the value of the option and lowers C^*.[11] For a given C^*, if the payoff occurs, it occurs at the same time as with no jump, but has a lower present value.

IV Numerical Examples

Tables 12.1 and 12.2 display the value of the investment option and the investment rule for a wide range of parameters. For the base case we set $\sigma_v^2 = \sigma_f^2 = 0.04$ and $\delta_v = \delta_f = 0.10$. If V is interpreted as a present value, a reasonable estimate for σ_v is the average standard deviation for unlevered equity in the United States, which is about 0.20.[12] δ_v measures the extent to which expected price increases in V alone fail

Table 12.1
Value of investment opportunity when $V = F = 1$

δ_v		0.05			0.10			0.25	
ρ_{vf}	−0.5	0.0	0.5	−0.5	0.0	0.5	−0.5	0.0	0.5
σ_v^2, σ_f^2									
0.01	0.33	0.30	0.28	0.14	0.12	0.08	0.03	0.02	0.01
0.02	0.38	0.34	0.30	0.20	0.16	0.12	0.06	0.04	0.02
0.04	0.45	0.40	0.34	0.27	0.23	0.16	0.11	0.08	0.04
0.10	0.57	0.51	0.43	0.40	0.34	0.25	0.21	0.16	0.09
0.20	0.67	0.61	0.51	0.52	0.45	0.34	0.32	0.25	0.16
0.30	0.73	0.67	0.57	0.60	0.52	0.40	0.39	0.32	0.21
λ									
0.00	0.45	0.40	0.34	0.27	0.23	0.16	0.11	0.08	0.04
0.05	0.33	0.29	0.24	0.23	0.19	0.13	0.10	0.07	0.04
0.10	0.27	0.23	0.19	0.20	0.16	0.12	0.10	0.07	0.04
0.25	0.19	0.16	0.12	0.15	0.12	0.09	0.09	0.06	0.04
δ_f									
0.01	0.30	0.23	0.14	0.18	0.13	0.07	0.08	0.06	0.03
0.05	0.37	0.31	0.23	0.22	0.17	0.10	0.09	0.06	0.03
0.10	0.45	0.40	0.34	0.27	0.23	0.16	0.11	0.08	0.04
0.25	0.60	0.58	0.56	0.42	0.39	0.36	0.18	0.15	0.10

Note: Entries are calculated using (4) and (12) in the text. Base case parameters are $\sigma_v^2 = \sigma_f^2 = 0.04$; $\delta_v = \delta_f = 0.10$; $\lambda = 0.00$.

Table 12.2
Value of benefits relative to investment cost (V/F) at which investment is optimal

δ_v	0.05			0.10			0.25		
ρ_{vf}	−0.5	0.0	0.5	−0.5	0.0	0.5	−0.5	0.0	0.5
σ_v^2,σ_f^2									
0.01	2.50	2.35	2.18	1.47	1.37	1.25	1.09	1.06	1.03
0.02	2.91	2.64	2.35	1.72	1.56	1.37	1.18	1.12	1.06
0.04	3.65	3.17	2.64	2.13	1.86	1.56	1.34	1.24	1.12
0.10	5.65	4.56	3.41	3.19	2.62	2.00	1.77	1.54	1.29
0.20	8.77	6.70	4.56	4.79	3.73	2.62	2.44	2.00	1.54
0.30	11.83	8.77	5.65	6.34	4.79	3.19	3.07	2.44	1.77
λ									
0.00	3.65	3.17	2.64	2.13	1.86	1.56	1.34	1.24	1.12
0.05	2.50	2.23	1.92	1.86	1.67	1.44	1.32	1.23	1.12
0.10	2.10	1.90	1.67	1.72	1.56	1.37	1.30	1.22	1.12
0.25	1.67	1.54	1.40	1.51	1.40	1.27	1.27	1.19	1.11
δ_f									
0.01	2.31	1.89	1.46	1.64	1.43	1.22	1.25	1.17	1.08
0.05	2.85	2.38	1.86	1.83	1.58	1.32	1.28	1.19	1.10
0.10	3.65	3.17	2.64	2.13	1.86	1.56	1.34	1.24	1.12
0.25	6.42	5.96	5.49	3.35	3.09	2.81	1.62	1.49	1.33

Note: Entries are calculated using equations (4) and (12) in the text. Base case parameters are $\delta_v = \delta_f = 0.10$; $\sigma_v^2 = \sigma_f^2 = 0.04$; $\lambda = 0.00$.

to compensate investors for the risk of price changes in V. We set this value at 0.10.[13] Appropriate choices for F are less clear. If the investment cost is nonstochastic, δ_f should be the risk-free rate. If F is systematically risky (which is likely), but $\alpha_f = 0$, then it would be greater.

With no investment timing option, $\max[0, V_0 - F_0]$ would be the value of the investment opportunity because the opportunity could only be exercised now. The value of the investment timing option is the difference between the infinitely lived investment opportunity and $\max[0, V_0 - F_0]$. Table 12.1 shows that the cost of following a suboptimal investment rule can be substantial. The entries in table 12.1 represent the loss per dollar of V if the project were undertaken at $V/F = 1$, rather than waiting until the optimal time. The value of the option to invest can never exceed V, so 1.00 is an upper bound for the entries in table 12.1. For example, if $\sigma_v^2 = \sigma_f^2 = 0.02$, $\rho_{vf} = 0.00$, and $\delta_v = \delta_f = 0.10$, then the investment option is worth 16 percent of V. If the other parameters stayed the same but the drift in V were lowered by 15 percent annually, then $\delta_v = 0.25$, and the option would be worth 4 percent of V.

Table 12.2 shows that investment in the first case above would be optimal if V/F reached 1.56, and in the second case at 1.12. It is clear from table 12.2 that the level

Table 12.3
Percentage of value of investment option which is due to uncertainty

	$\sigma^2 = 0.02$	$\sigma^2 = 0.04$	$\sigma^2 = 0.10$	$\sigma^2 = 0.30$
$\delta_v = 0.02$	5.3	9.4	17.2	28.4
$\delta_v = 0.04$	12.5	20.1	32.6	47.1
$\delta_v = 0.06$	25.6	36.4	50.8	64.6
$\delta_v = 0.08$	51.4	61.9	73.0	82.1
$\delta_v = 0.10$	100.0	100.0	100.0	100.0

Note: Entries are calculated using equations (4), (12), and (13) in the text. All of these calculations assume that $V = F = 1$ and $\delta_f = 0.10$.

of V/F at which investment is optimal is typically much greater than 1.00. (From equation (5), a firm will be willing to invest at $V = F$ only when $\sigma^2 = 0.00$ or $\delta_v = \infty$.) For reasonable parameters, it is optimal to wait to invest until V is more than twice F.

Tables 12.1 and 12.2 demonstrate that both the option value and investment rule are sensitive to changes in variance. The option value and investment rule are also sensitive to a change in δ_v from 0.05 to 0.10. This sensitivity is to be expected in the vicinity of $\delta_v = 0.0$, since at that point we obtain the limiting values of $X = 1.00$ and $C^* = \infty$. X and C^* are less sensitive to changes in δ_f. For options that already have little value (for example, in the last column of table 12.1), even a dramatic increase in λ from 0.00 to 0.25 has little effect on the option value. This occurs because the option value in those cases is already primarily due to variance, because of the large δ_v.

One can compare the value of the timing option with the value the option would have under certainty. Table 12.3 presents the percentage of the option value which is due to uncertainty, computed by comparing equation (4) with equation (13). To concentrate on the "pure" uncertainty component, we assume that increases in σ^2 are not accompanied by changes in δ_v or δ_f.[14] As the table shows, increases in both δ_v and σ^2, holding δ_f constant, increase the percentage of the value attributable to uncertainty. For an investment opportunity with $\delta_v \geq \delta_f$, all of the value is due to uncertainty, since otherwise waiting would be suboptimal.

V   Example: The Investment Decision of a Monopolist

In this section we present an example in which V and the option value are derived in terms of production and demand parameters. Consider the example of a project that produces a commodity, using a Cobb-Douglas production function,

$$Q_t = \bar{K}^\alpha L_t^\beta, \tag{21}$$

where $\bar{K}$ is the fixed level of capital, and Q_t and L_t are quantity produced and labor employed at time t. The firm faces an inverse demand curve given by

$$P_t = \theta_t Q_t^{-1/\eta}, \tag{22}$$

where P_t is the price of the commodity at time t, η is the price elasticity of demand, and θ_t is a demand shift parameter following the stochastic process,

$$\frac{d\theta}{\theta} = \alpha_\theta \, dt + \sigma_\theta \, dz_\theta. \tag{23}$$

Let $\rho_{\theta m}$ be the correlation of θ with the market portfolio.

After the project is installed, instantaneous profits are given by $\pi_t = P_t Q_t - \bar{w} L_t$, where $\bar{w}$ is the wage. At each t, the firm chooses labor usage to maximize instantaneous profits. Maximized profits at t are then $B\theta_t^\gamma$, where $\gamma = [1 - \beta(1 - 1/\eta)]^{-1} > 1$ and B is a constant. When the project lives forever, the present value of expected maximized profits is

$$V(\theta_0) = B\theta_0^\gamma / (\hat{\alpha}_v - \alpha_v), \tag{24}$$

where $\alpha_v = \gamma\alpha_\theta + \frac{1}{2}\gamma(\gamma - 1)\sigma_\theta^2$ and

$$\hat{\alpha}_v = r + \phi\rho_{\theta m}\gamma\sigma_\theta, \tag{25}$$

which follows from (9) together with the fact that $\sigma_v = \gamma\sigma_\theta$ and $\rho_{\theta m} = \rho_{vm}$. Equation (24) can be rewritten as

$$\hat{\alpha}_v = \alpha_v + B\theta_0^\gamma / V_0 = \alpha_v + \delta_v, \tag{26}$$

so that δ_v represents the payout ratio of the installed project.

Table 12.4 displays the option values and investment rules corresponding to different values of the underlying exogenous parameters. It is important to realize that the comparative static experiment in this table is different from that in tables 12.1 and 12.2. In particular, a change in σ_θ not only changes the option value directly, but also changes $\hat{\alpha}_v$ and α_v. It is possible for an increase in σ_θ to lower the value of the option (see footnote 14), although this does not occur in table 12.4. For example, if $\eta = 1.0001$, $\alpha_\theta = -0.03$, and $\rho_{\theta m} = 0.95$, then an increase in σ_θ^2 from 0.0025 to 0.0050 (σ_v^2 increases by the same amount) will lower the value of the option from 0.0293 to 0.0286. The table shows sizable option values and optimal investment levels for reasonable parameters. Several of the entries are asterisked, which signifies that it is always optimal to defer investment. It is implausible, however, to expect that one

Table 12.4
Option values and investment rules

α_θ	-0.03			0.00			0.01		
$\rho_{\theta m}$	0.00	0.20	0.50	0.00	0.20	0.50	0.00	0.20	0.50
σ_θ^2									
0.01	0.0740	0.0597	0.0459	0.1890	0.1305	0.0837	0.2902	0.1890	0.1110
	(1.22)	(1.18)	(1.13)	(1.68)	(1.43)	(1.26)	(2.25)	(1.68)	(1.35)
0.04	0.2227	0.1657	0.1177	0.4127	0.2659	0.1657	0.5493	0.3257	0.1905
	(1.85)	(1.58)	(1.38)	(3.28)	(2.09)	(1.58)	(5.28)	(2.50)	(1.69)
0.10	0.4399	0.3044	0.2056	0.7545	0.4302	0.2592	*	0.4973	0.2835
	(3.58)	(2.35)	(1.76)	(13.7)	(3.47)	(2.05)	*	(4.36)	(2.20)
0.20	0.7647	0.4736	0.3053	*	0.6318	0.3631	*	0.7151	0.3874
	(14.6)	(4.02)	(2.35)	*	(7.37)	(2.80)	*	(11.0)	(3.02)

Note: Values are option values computed using (4) and (12) in the text. Values in parentheses are optimal investment levels. Technological parameters are chosen such that $V = 1$. F is nonstochastic and equal to 1. Other parameter values are $\eta = 2.0$; $r = 0.05$; $\beta = 2/3$; and $\phi = 0.50$.
* For these values $\delta_v < 0$, so the option value is undefined.

would never invest in a real asset, however large V becomes. This demonstrates a weakness of the assumption that θ follows geometric Brownian motion. The parameter θ represents a real shock; as such, it is unreasonable to expect uncertainty about future values of the shock to grow linearly with time. A mean-reverting process for θ (for which it is not possible to obtain an analytic solution) would capture the notion that in the long run, demand can be expected to be at a "normal" level.

One might expect the variance of total returns (changes in V *plus* payouts) from an investment to grow linearly with time. The variance of V, however, would not grow linearly with time if δ_v, the payout rate, increased with V.[15] This would place limits on V and induce a finite C^*.

VI Conclusion

This chapter has studied the investment timing problem and shown for quite reasonable parameters that investment timing considerations are important. In particular, the value lost by sub-optimally adopting a project with zero net present value can easily range from 10 to 20 percent or more of a project's value.

The analysis has several limitations. First, as noted, the assumption of geometric Brownian motion for V and F is most plausible when these values represent present values. Even then, however, the example in Section V demonstrated that undesirable results are possible. A more realistic specification would have payout rates and variances be functions of prices, and the result would almost certainly be lower option values. For prices which are not present values, a mean-reverting process would capture the notion that prices tend toward equilibrium levels. For these more general processes, numerical methods would likely be needed for valuation of the timing option.

The analysis also imposes implicit restrictions on the investment process. The investment is assumed to be lumpy, the importance of which can be seen by supposing that investment is not lumpy and that the marginal reward from investing is large for small investments. Some investment will then always be optimal, at least initially, and the waiting problem is less important. The analysis also ignores the possibility that the investment may be partially reversed or scrapped after the project is adopted. One could interpret V as including the value of the scrapping option, but this begs the question of how such an option affects the timing problem. Reversibility is implicitly included in the analysis to the extent that a project is deemed more reversible the more quickly it depreciates. A high depreciation rate implies a high payout rate and hence a high δ_v. The timing option is worth less for such projects.

Appendix: Derivation of $E_0\{F_{t'}e^{-\mu t'}\}$

The purpose of this Appendix is to derive the expectation on the right-hand side of (3). We discuss three results: first, we present the partial differential equation that governs the behavior of the option value; second, we derive the option value; and third, we verify that the stopping region is $[C^*, \infty)$. Let

$$L(V_3, F_3, 0) = E_0\{F_{t'}e^{-\mu t'}\}. \tag{A.1}$$

Using Theorem 7.5 from Malliaris and Brock [1982] (pp. 100–01), together with the fact that $L_3 = \mu L$, we note that L must satisfy the partial differential equation:

$$\mu L = \tfrac{1}{2}[L_{vv}V^2\sigma_v^2 + L_{ff}F^2\sigma_f^2 + 2L_{vf}VF\sigma_{vf}] + L_v\alpha_v V + L_f\alpha_f F. \tag{A.2}$$

The solution to (A.2) must satisfy certain boundary conditions: (i) $L = F$ when $C = V/F = C^*$; and (ii) $L \to 0$ as $V/F \to 0$. Assume for the moment that the stopping region is $[C^*, \infty)$. Guess that the form of L is

$$L = kF^a C^b, \tag{A.3}$$

with k a constant. This guess satisfies (A.2). Boundary condition (i) then requires that $k = C^{*-b}$ and that $a = 1$. With these constraints (A.2) can be written as

$$\mu = \tfrac{1}{2}b(b-1)\sigma^2 + b\alpha_v + (1-b)\alpha_f, \tag{A.4}$$

where $\sigma^2 = \sigma_v^2 + \sigma_f^2 - 2\sigma_{vf}$. As long as $\alpha_f < \mu$, (A.4) will have both a positive and a negative root. Boundary condition (ii) requires that $b > 0$, so the positive solution is the correct one. This is the solution given by equation (5) in the text, with $b = \varepsilon$. Therefore, (A.3), with $a = 1$, $k = C^{*-1}$, and $b = \varepsilon$ given by (10), solves the partial differential equation (A.2). This solution works for arbitrary C^*. Choosing the optimal C^*, which is done in the text, amounts to imposing an additional boundary condition, variously known as "high contact" or "smooth pasting."

The optimal scrapping problem is formally identical to the optimal investment problem, and it is again appropriate to take the positive root. This formal similarity of options to buy and options to sell is implied by Merton [1973] and Margrabe [1978].

Finally, we argue that the stopping region is $[C^*, \infty)$. Suppose, contrary to this, that it was optimal to exercise the option with $C_0 = V_0/F_0$, but that it was not optimal to exercise the option with $C_1 = V_1/F_1 > C_0$. This would imply that

$$V_1 - F_1 < X(V_1, F_1) \quad \text{and} \quad V_0 - F_0 = X(V_0, F_0). \tag{A.5}$$

It is straightforward to show by change of variable in (A.2) and the boundary conditions that X is homogeneous of degree one in V and F. (This is done by showing that (A.2) and the boundary conditions depend only upon $V/F = C$. See also Merton [1973].) Using this homogeneity property, we see that (A.5) becomes

$$X(C_1, 1) > C_1 - 1 \quad \text{and} \quad X(C_0, 1) = C_0 - 1. \tag{A.6}$$

Multiplying the left-hand side of (A.6) by C_0/C_1 and again using homogeneity yields

$$X(C_0, C_0/C_1) > C_0 - C_0/C_1 \quad \text{and} \quad X(C_0, 1) = C_0 - 1. \tag{A.7}$$

This implies that if there are two identical investment opportunities with different investment costs, it could be optimal to invest in the opportunity with the higher investment cost while leaving unexercised the opportunity with the lower investment cost. This is never optimal for call options, however, no matter how C is distributed. (See Cox and Rubinstein [1985], p. 140.) Thus, (A.6) must be false, and the stopping region must be $[C^*, \infty)$.

Acknowledgments

We thank Gregory Connor, Randy Ellis, Alan Marcus, Michael Rothschild, and especially two referees for comments, and Alex Kane and Mark Kon for helpful discussions. A previous version was presented at the 1982 NBER/KGSM Conference on Time and Uncertainty in Economics and at the 1982 NBER Summer Institute. This paper was begun while the first author was at the School of Management, Boston University, and summer research support from that institution is gratefully acknowledged.

Notes

1. Many real-life investment opportunities are not infinitely lived, but expire or become valueless at some point. We deal with this by allowing the present value of the benefit from undertaking the project to have an average downward drift and by allowing the present value of the project's cash flows to jump to zero. In the latter case the option eventually becomes valueless, but at an unknown date. The important omission in our model is the case where the option to invest expires at a known date in the future. A finitely lived patent, for example, would give the holder an option to invest with a known expiration date, and would be worth less than an infinitely lived patent. It is typically not possible to solve analytically for the option value in this case; however, numerical solutions may be obtained.

2. Bernanke also provides a useful discussion of previous papers dealing with irreversibility and their relation to financial option models and search theory models. See also Krutilla [1967]; Henry [1974]; Cukierman [1980]; Greenley, Walsh, and Young [1981]; and Myers and Majd [1983]. Roberts and Weitzman [1981] study the related problem of optimal stopping of R and D expenditures. We do not address issues of the relationship between first-mover advantages and investment timing as in Spence [1981].

3. For an installed and producing project, equilibrium requires that capital gains plus cash flow less depreciation equals the required rate of return on the project. The uninstalled project is not depreciating, so its expected price appreciation is less than the required rate of return by the cash flow net of depreciation which the project would have earned if it were installed. The earnings-to-price ratio therefore measures the extent to which α_v is less than the required rate of return.

4. Brock, Rothschild, and Stiglitz [1983] also draw this distinction, and note that the price of a financial asset should grow geometrically, unlike other prices.

5. It should be noted that this result is a consequence of the assumption that V follows geometric Brownian motion with constant parameters. Brock, Rothschild, and Stiglitz [1983] show that when the stochastic process for V has a lower absorbing barrier sufficiently close to the current value of V, then an increase in variance can lower the value of the option. With processes like (1), zero is a natural absorbing barrier, but one that is never reached in finite time.

6. Myers and Majd [1983] use numerical option-pricing techniques to value the abandonment option for a project when the option is finitely lived.

7. For the special case when V is constant, $\alpha_f = \mu$, and μ is the risk-free rate, (6) reduces to the formula obtained in Merton [1973] for the value of a perpetual put option on a nondividend paying stock.

8. If $X = g(V, F, t)$, with V and F given by (1), Ito's lemma states that

$$dX = g_t\, dt + g_v\, dV + g_f\, dF + \tfrac{1}{2}[\sigma_v^2 V^2 g_{vv} + \sigma_f^2 F^2 g_{ff} + 2\sigma_{vf} VF g_{vf}]\, dt.$$

9. Venezia [1983] also obtains a condition when waiting is optimal at any current price. This is due, however, to the value of waiting to acquire information about uncertain parameters in a Bayesian setting. Our result holds with known parameters and is driven by time-value considerations.

10. Merton [1976] first obtained this result, when he showed that the formula for a call option written on a stock for which there is a possibility of complete ruin, is obtained by replacing r with $r + \lambda$ in the Black-Scholes formula.

11. Merton [1976] shows that the possibility of complete ruin for the stock makes a call option *more* valuable. In our case the possibility of complete ruin makes the option to invest *less* valuable. Our experiment is equivalent to having both δ_v and δ_f rise with λ. Because of the assumption that the installed project earns a fair rate of return, the uncaptured cash flow from the project (as a percentage of V) is implicitly assumed to increase as λ is increased. This differs from the assumption made in Merton [1976], in which the uncaptured cash flow (a stock dividend) is held fixed. In effect, δ_f is increased, and δ_v is unchanged. Consequently, Merton obtains the opposite comparative static results.

12. From table 12.1 in Stoll and Whaley [1983] the average standard deviation of stocks on the New York Stock Exchange is approximately 0.30. Thus, the average unlevered standard deviation (assuming a debt to value ratio of $1/3$) is in the vicinity of 0.20.

13. As noted in note 3 above, the earnings-price ratio of an installed project, with earnings measured net of depreciation, would be an estimate of δ_v.

14. The tables ignore the possibility that changes in σ_v and σ_f affect the required rates of return $\hat{\alpha}_v$ and $\hat{\alpha}_f$. This assumption would be valid if the uncertainty is uncorrelated with the market portfolio or if investors are risk neutral. If the risk is systematic, then changes in σ^2 might be accompanied by changes in δ_v or δ_f; it is then possible to use an asset pricing relationship such as (9) to specify the effect on required rates of return of changes in variance (cf. McDonald and Siegel [1985]). This can lead to ambiguity in the comparative static results. Venezia and Brenner [1979] make the same point, although without distinguishing between systematic and total risk.

15. If the value of IBM's assets followed geometric Brownian motion, there would be a chance that IBM would become indefinitely large relative to the economy as a whole. It is more reasonable to suppose that there are limits to IBM's potential growth, although the total returns from investing in IBM have no such limits.

References

Baldwin, Carliss Y., "Optimal Sequential Investment When Capital is Not Readily Reversible," *Journal of Finance*, XXXVII (1982), 763–82.

——, and Richard F. Meyer, "Liquidity Preference Under Uncertainty: A Model of Dynamic Investment in Illiquid Opportunities," *Journal of Financial Economics*, VII (1979), 347–74.

Bernanke, Ben, "Irreversibility, Uncertainty, and Cyclical Investment," this *Journal*, XCVIII (1983), 85–106.

Brock, William, Michael Rothschild, and Joseph Stiglitz, "Stochastic Capital Theory," University of Wisconsin SSRI Working Paper, 1983.

Cox, John C., and Mark Rubinstein, *Options Markets* (Englewood Cliffs, NJ: Prentice Hall, Inc., 1985).

Cukierman, Alex, "The Effects of Uncertainty on Investment Under Risk Neutrality with Endogenous Information," *Journal of Political Economy*, LXXXVIII (1980), 462–75.

Greenley, Douglas A., Richard A. Walsh, and Robert A. Young, "Option Value: Empirical Evidence from a Case Study of Recreation and Water Quality," this *Journal*, XCVI (1981), 657–73.

Henry, Claude, "Investment Decisions Under Uncertainty: The Irreversibility Effect," *American Economic Review*, LXIV (1974), 1006–12.

Ingersoll, Jonathan E., Jr., "A Contingent-Claims Valuation of Convertible Securities," *Journal of Financial Economics*, IV (1977), 289–322.

Krutilla, John V., "Conservation Reconsidered," *American Economic Review*, LVII (1967), 777–86.

Malliaris, A. G., and W. A. Brock, *Stochastic Methods in Economics and Finance* (Amsterdam: North-Holland Publishing Company, 1982).

Margrabe, William, "The Value of an Option to Exchange One Asset for Another," *Journal of Finance*, XXXIII (1978), 177–86.

McDonald, Robert, and Daniel Siegel, "Investment and the Valuation of Firms When There is an Option to Shut Down," *International Economic Review*, XXVI (June 1985), 331–49.

Merton, Robert C., "Optimal Consumption and Portfolio Rules in a Continuous-Time Model," *Journal of Economic Theory*, III (1971), 373–413.

——, "Theory of Rational Option Pricing," *Bell Journal of Economics and Management Science*, IV (1973), 141–83.

——, "Option Pricing When Underlying Stock Returns are Discontinuous," *Journal of Financial Economics*, III (1976), 125–44.

Myers, Stewart C., and Saman Majd, "Calculating Abandonment Value Using Option Pricing Theory," Sloan School of Management Working Paper No. 1462–83, 1983.

Roberts, Kevin, and Martin Weitzman, "Funding Criteria for Research, Development, and Exploration Projects," *Econometrica*, XLIX (1981), 1261–88.

Samuelson, Paul A., "Rational Theory of Warrant Pricing," with Appendix by Henry P. McKean, "Appendix: A Free Boundary Problem for the Heat Equation Arising from a Problem in Mathematical Economics," in *The Collected Scientific Papers of Paul A. Samuelson*, Vol. 3, Robert C. Merton, ed. (Cambridge, MA: M.I.T. Press, 1970).

Spence, Michael, "Investment, Strategy, and Growth in a New Market," *Bell Journal of Economics*, X (1981), 1–19.

Stoll, Hans, and Robert Whaley, "Transaction Costs and the Small Firm Effect," *Journal of Financial Economics*, XII (1983), 57–79.

Venezia, Itzhak, "A Bayesian Approach to the Optimal Growth Period Problem," *Journal of Finance*, XXXVIII (1983), 237–46.

——, and Menachem Brenner, "The Optimal Duration of Growth Investments and Search," *Journal of Business*, LII (1979), 393–407.

13 Time to Build, Option Value, and Investment Decisions

Saman Majd and Robert S. Pindyck

1 Introduction

Many investment projects have the following characteristics: (i) investment decisions and associated cash outlays occur sequentially over time, (ii) there is a maximum rate at which outlays and construction can proceed—it takes "time to build"—and (iii) the project yields no cash return until it is completed. The firm's investment problem is to choose a contingent plan for making these sequential—and irreversible—expenditures over time. The arrival of new information might lead the firm to depart from the spending scenario originally planned; the firm might accelerate or decelerate the rate of investment, or simply stop the program in midstream.

Examples of industries for which these characteristics are especially important include aircraft and mining. The production of a new line of aircraft requires engineering, prototype production, testing, and final tooling stages that together can take eight to ten years to complete. The construction of a new underground mine, or the development of a large petrochemical plant are projects that usually require at least five or six years, with clear constraints on the pattern of expenditures. In other industries the lead times may be somewhat shorter, but are still important.

Traditional discounted cash flow criteria, which treat the spending pattern as fixed, are inadequate for evaluating such projects. Likewise, neoclassical investment theory,[1] which treats individual units of capital as homogeneous, interchangeable, and individually productive, fails to provide a realistic description of investment behavior under uncertainty. Adapting the neoclassical framework by introducing adjustment costs, whereby the cost of new capital rises with the rate of investment, does not deal with the fundamental problem—most real projects are composed of heterogeneous units of capital that must be installed in sequence, and are unproductive until the project is complete.[2] Indeed, the importance of sequential investment and time to build have been demonstrated by Kydland and Prescott (1982) in the context of a general equilibrium model. They have suggested that such a model yields a much better description of cyclical fluctuations than does the standard adjustment cost framework.

Our paper should be viewed in the context of several recent strands of research, all of which have helped to provide a better microeconomic foundation for investment behavior. First, Roberts and Weitzman (1981) examine projects with sequential outlays using a model that stresses the role of information gathering. In their model, each stage of investment yields information that reduces the uncertainty over the value of the completed project. This is most applicable to R&D projects in which the role of learning is critical.[3] Since the project can be stopped in mid-stream, it might pay to go ahead with the early stages of the project even though *ex ante* the net present value of the entire project is negative. Hence the use of a net present value rule for such projects, particularly one based on a single risk-adjusted discount rate, might reject investments that should be undertaken.

Second, in related papers, Bernanke (1983) and Cukierman (1980) examine investment decisions for which information about project value arrives independently of the cash outlays. They consider incentives to postpone expenditures until more information arrives. In their models the project involves a single expenditure, and there is no time to build. However, the investment expenditure is irreversible, a firm can choose only a subset of the available projects (so that investing in one set of projects excludes all others) and (unlike in Roberts and Weitzman) the firm obtains information before beginning the project. They show that uncertainty over project returns creates an incentive (an "option value") to postpone the investment and wait for more information to arrive, even if the firm is risk neutral.[4] This is just the opposite result from that in Roberts and Weitzman; here a naive net present value rule might *accept* projects that should be rejected or postponed. Both authors use their models to explain the cyclical nature of aggregate investment spending; a recession is associated with greater uncertainty over future cash flows because firms reduce their investment spending until some of that uncertainty is resolved.

The models developed in Roberts and Weitzman, Bernanke, and Cukierman are not explicitly based on valuation in financial markets. Thus, a manager following their investment criteria may not be maximizing the firm's value to stockholders. For example, although the assumption of risk neutrality allows Bernanke and Cukierman to underscore the effects of irreversibility, as distinct from risk aversion, extending their models to a more general setting is not straightforward; the correct risk premium cannot be determined independently of the optimal decision rule.

The third strand of work, and that most closely associated with this paper, is best represented by McDonald and Siegel (1986).[5] They also stress the option value of postponing an irreversible investment, but not as a means of accumulating information. Instead, the payoff from completing the project has a current value consistent with capital market equilibrium. This value fluctuates stochastically over time (independently of any investment expenditures), so that its *future* value is always unknown. Access to the investment opportunity (perhaps purchased or obtained as the result of R&D) is analogous to holding a call option on a dividend-paying common stock, where "exercising" the option is equivalent to making the investment expenditure. As with such financial options, increased risk increases the incentive to delay the investment expenditure, and for any positive amount of risk, the expenditure is made only when the project's value exceeds costs by a positive amount. These results are similar to those in Bernanke and Cukierman, but for a different reason.

This paper is also concerned with the option value of being able to delay irreversible investment expenditures, but here we focus on a series of expenditures that must be made sequentially, that *cannot exceed some maximum rate*, and that become productive only after the entire sequence is completed. For example, a project requiring a total outlay of $5 million might have a maximum rate of investment of $1 million per year, so that the minimum time to build is 5 years. Such a project can be viewed as a *compound option*: each unit of investment buys an option on the next unit. Evaluating the project requires a decision rule that determines whether an additional dollar should be spent *given any arbitrary cumulative amount that has already been spent*. That decision rule will depend on the underlying value that the project would have *today* if completed, the remaining expenditure required for completion, as well as parameters describing risk and the opportunity cost of delaying completion.

This chapter is in the spirit of recent work on capital budgeting with option-equivalent cash flows.[6] Our approach assumes that the value of a completed project is spanned by a set of traded assets and that the distribution of future values is given. Option pricing techniques are used to derive the relationship between the value of the investment program (what a firm would pay for the right to undertake the program) and the value of the project once completed.

We have several objectives. First, we show how a decision rule, applicable to each stage in the development of a project, can be derived and applied to project evaluation. Second, we show how the value of an investment program and the decision to invest depend on the maximum rate at which expenditures can productively be made (i.e., on the "time to build"). Finally, we will see how time to build interacts with uncertainty to affect investment spending, and in particular, how the depressive effect of increased uncertainty on investment spending is magnified.

The next section describes the nature of the investment program, and our assumptions regarding the distribution of future values of a completed project. It also outlines our approach to deriving the optimal investment rule. Section 3 presents numerical results for a simple example that shows how risk, opportunity cost, and time to build interact to affect the investment decision. Section 4 uses the model to examine the economic value of construction time flexibility. The concluding section discusses some implications of our results for aggregate investment behavior.

2 A Simple Model of Investment when there is Time to Build

2.1 The Model

Consider a program to build a factory. The program involves a sequence of investment outlays, corresponding to the specific steps involved in construction. The payoff to completing the program is the market value of a *completed* factory. This market value is the present value of the stream of uncertain future cash flows from operating the factory. The owner of the factory, receiving these cash flows, earns an equilibrium rate of return as determined by the market.

Note that we are *not* assuming that shares in identical factories are traded in the market and, therefore, have an observable price. We are only assuming that we could calculate the value that would prevail if such shares were traded by applying appropriate capital budgeting methods to the cash flows from the completed factory. This market value will, of course, fluctuate stochastically over time, reflecting new information about future cash flows.

We take the market value of the completed factory, denoted by V, as exogenous, and assume that, during the construction period, it evolves according to the lognormal process:

$$dV = (\mu - \delta)V\,dt + \sigma V\,dz, \tag{1}$$

where dz is the increment of a Weiner process. The last term in (1) characterizes the unexpected component of changes in V. The central feature is that future values of V are *always* uncertain, and are distributed lognormally. The degree of uncertainty depends only on how far into the future one looks. Unlike the stylized R&D projects of Roberts and Weitzman where learning takes place at each stage of investment, uncertainty about future values of V is independent of the proportion of the project already completed.[7] Nor is such uncertainty resolved by waiting, as in the models of Bernanke and Cukierman.

The parameter μ is the expected rate of return from owning a completed factory. It is the equilibrium rate established by the capital market, and includes an appropriate risk premium. Eq. (1) says that the expected rate of capital gain on the factory is less than μ; δ represents the opportunity cost of delaying completion of the project.

If the completed factory is infinitely lived, then eq. (1) also represents the evolution of V during the operating period. Specifically, δV will represent the instantaneous rate of cash flow from operating the factory. Because these payouts are not received until construction is completed, δ is the rate of opportunity cost. We assume that δ is constant. In the case of an infinitely lived project, this is consistent with future cash flows being a constant proportion of the market value of the operating factory.[8]

Eq. (1) is an abstraction from most real projects. If variable costs are positive and managers have the option to shut down temporarily when the price of the output is below variable cost, and/or the option to abandon the project completely, V will not follow a lognormal process even if the price of the output of the factory does.[9] If variable cost is positive and managers do *not* have the option to shut down (perhaps because of regulatory constraints), V can become negative, again in conflict with the assumption of lognormality. Here we ignore these possibilities (and any other options implicit in operating the completed factory) in order to focus on the options implicit in the construction phase.

There are few real projects that last forever. In principle, future investments (e.g., maintenance) can be made to maintain the productivity of the project indefinitely. To be consistent with eq. (1), we would interpret the cash payout δV, as being net of these future investments. (Another way of handling maintenance investments is discussed below.) But not all projects can be made to last forever by appropriate future maintenance investments. For example, most natural resource projects have finite lives because there is a finite quantity of reserves in the ground. For many oil and gas wells, it is common to assume an exponentially declining extraction rate, but since the price of the natural resource will not be constant, cash flows will not be a constant proportion of project value.

If the completed factory has a finite life, then eq. (1) cannot represent the evolution of V during the operating period. In particular, cash flows from operating the factory will not be a constant proportion of the market value of the factory: the last cash flow is 100 percent of the remaining value. However, under the assumptions discussed above (i.e., no operating costs or operating options during the life of the factory), eq. (1) will still represent the evolution of V during the construction period, but with a different interpretation of the constant, δ.

This can be demonstrated by the following example. Assume that the price of the output of the factory, P, evolves according to the lognormal process $dP = (\mu - \delta)P\,dt + \sigma P\,dz$, where μ is the equilibrium rate of return on a security that is perfectly correlated with P. (If the output can be stored, δP is the instantaneous convenience yield from storage, i.e., the flow of convenience benefits from holding inventory.) Let τ be the time at which construction is complete, and T be the operating life of the factory. The value of the factory at completion (i.e., the payoff to the investment program) is given by

$$V(\tau) = \int_0^T \mathrm{E}_\tau\{P(s)\}\mathrm{e}^{-\mu s}\,ds = \int_0^T P(\tau)\mathrm{e}^{(\mu-\delta)s}\mathrm{e}^{-\mu s}\,ds$$

$$= P(\tau)[(1 - \mathrm{e}^{-\delta T})/\delta] \equiv \phi P(\tau),$$

where ϕ is a constant that depends on δ and T.

Since the payoff to completing the investment program is proportional to the price of the output at completion, its present value at any earlier time (i.e., before completion) will also be proportional to the contemporaneous price of the output: $V(t) =$

$\phi P(t)$ for $t \le \tau$. Hence $dV = (\mu - \delta)V\,dt + \sigma V\,dz$, during the construction period. Here, δ is still a rate of opportunity cost, but arises from the fact that the expected growth rate of price, and hence of V, is less than the risk-adjusted return on a security that has the same risk as P. Of course the value of an *operating* factory will not evolve according to eq. (1); it will decay faster, and at a time-varying rate, because of the cash flows from operations.[10] But this is irrelevant for the investment decision, which depends only on the dynamics of V up to the time construction is complete.

The example above demonstrates the dynamics for V during the construction period [eq. (1)] do not preclude a completed project with finite life. Of course, eq. (1) will not be appropriate for all projects. More elaborate dynamics, based on different assumptions about the dynamics of output price, operating costs, etc., may be necessary. We proceed with the assumption that the dynamics of V during the construction period are given by eq. (1), in order to focus on the effects of time to build.

If, for some period of time, the payoff to completing the factory is expected to grow at the rate μ (i.e., $\delta = 0$), there will be no opportunity cost from delaying construction, but there will be a savings from delaying the investment expenditure. Hence investment will not occur during such a period. It is because the value of most real projects grows at an expected rate less μ that there is an incentive to invest.

An important assumption in our model is that the factory cannot be built overnight. There is a maximum rate at which construction and investment can proceed—it takes time to build. Because completion of the project requires some minimum amount of time, the payoff from completion is unknown during the construction period. However, we assume that the total required investment is known.

We assume that the *minimum* rate of construction and investment is zero, and that construction can be halted and later resumed without cost. In reality, we would expect some continuing costs associated with maintaining the partially completed factory (e.g., to prevent "rusting"), and with maintaining the capital and labor resources needed to resume construction. We also assume that investment is completely *irreversible*; capital in place has no alternative use, and therefore zero salvage value. For simplicity, we ignore these added features, although it is straightforward to extend our model to include them.

For expositional ease, in the example in section 3, we assume that the maximum rate of investment is constant. This is unrealistic for most real projects, where the constraints on the maximum rate of investment generally depend on the stage of construction. Our model allows the maximum rate of investment to be a (known) function of the amount of total investment remaining.

Allowing the maximum rate of investment to vary with the stage of construction also provides a way to account for any future investments required to maintain an infinite life for the completed project. If we assume that the timing and magnitude of these maintenance investments (during the infinite life of the factory) are known with certainty, we can include their present value as a required component of the investment in the final stage of construction. In other words, in the last instant before construction is completed, the investment required to complete the project includes the present value of the future maintenance investments.

To see how the constraint of time to build affects investment decisions, we must determine the *market value of the entire investment program*. This market value is what a value-maximizing firm would pay for the right to undertake the program. It will correspond to an optimal program of investment outlays, which will, of course, be contingent on the evolution of V.

We can characterize this investment decision as an optimal control problem. There are two state variables, the total amount of investment remaining for completion, K, and the current market value of a completed factory, V. The control variable is the rate of investment, I. The problem is to choose the control rule, $I^*(V, K)$, which maximizes the value of the investment program. $I^*(V, K)$ is simply a rule that determines the optimal rate of investment, given the instantaneous values of V and K. It is subject to the constraint $0 \leq I^*(V, K) \leq k$, where k is the maximum rate of investment.

Because there are no adjustment costs or costs associated with changing the level of investment, the problem has a 'bang-bang' solution: the instantaneous level of investment will be either 0 or k. In turn, the optimal decision rule reduces to a cutoff value for a completed project, $V^*(K)$, such that investment occurs at the maximum rate k for $V > V^*$, and there is no investment otherwise. As we will see, the optimal decision rule $V^*(K)$ is determined simultaneously with the current market value of the investment program.

2.2 Solution

The equilibrium market value of the investment program and the optimal current level of investment, I^*, will depend on the values of the two state variables, V and K. In our model I^* is either k or 0, depending on whether the current value of V is above or below the cutoff value, $V^*(K)$. We will find it convenient to denote the value of the investment program when $V > V^*$ (upper region) by $F(V, K)$, and when $V < V^*$ (lower region) by $f(V, K)$.

Formally, the investment program is a contingent claim. However, it is not a simple contingent claim: at every instant the manager can choose whether or not to invest and continue construction. Hence the project is a compound option, where each expenditure buys an option to make the next expenditure. Although this complicates the solution procedure, the same techniques used to value options in securities markets can be applied to value the investment program.

Using a continuous time framework, Merton (1977) derives the valuation equations for general contingent claims. His approach relies on continuous trading of specified assets to replicate the payoff to the contingent claim. Nevertheless, this approach is also valid when the assets that must be included in the replicating portfolio are not traded in financial markets. What is necessary is a capital market sufficiently complete that the new project does not change the opportunity set available to investors. If this is the case, managers need only calculate the value of the underlying asset, V, that is consistent with the equilibrium valuation model implied by the capital market. For example, if the CAPM holds and the manager can estimate the underlying asset's beta from prices of traded securities, then he can correctly calculate V. Also, given the relationship that must hold between the values of traded options and stocks, he can calculate the value of any contingent claim on V (e.g., this investment program).

Since the market value of the completed factory includes the value of any subsequent operating options, the value of these options must be included in the calculation of V. For example, the manager might have the option of shutting down (temporarily or permanently) the completed factory. Thus the calculation of V might involve more than a simple discounted cash flow analysis. As mentioned above, including the value of such operating options generally will affect the dynamics of V.

The option pricing approach yields a valuation equation relating the value of the contingent claim (the investment program) to the value of the underlying asset (the completed factory). Since the value of the investment program depends on whether the value of the completed factory, V, is above or below V^*, for notational convenience we write a separate valuation equation for each region, i.e., for $F(V, K)$ and $f(V, K)$. It is straightforward to show that F and f must satisfy the following partial differential equations:

$$\tfrac{1}{2}\sigma^2 V^2 F_{VV} + (r - \delta)VF_V - rF - kF_K - k = 0, \tag{2a}$$

$$\tfrac{1}{2}\sigma^2 V^2 f_{VV} + (r - \delta)Vf_V - rf = 0, \tag{2b}$$

subject to the boundary conditions

$$F(V, 0) = V, \tag{3a}$$

$$\lim_{V \to \infty} F_V(V, K) = e^{-\delta K/k}, \tag{3b}$$

$$f(0, K) = 0, \tag{3c}$$

$$f(V^*, K) = F(V^*, K), \tag{3d}$$

$$f_V(V^*, K) = F_V(V^*, K). \tag{3e}$$

The first boundary condition states that when the project is completed, the value of the investment program is the market value of a completed factory.

As the value of the completed project becomes very large relative to the total investment, K, the option 'premium' becomes negligible, and the value of the program approaches the value of the completed project. However, the value of the investment program will increase less rapidly than the value of a completed project. As V becomes large, construction outlays will be made at the maximum rate, k, but there is still a foregone opportunity cost. Hence for very large V, the increase in the value of the investment program for a 1 dollar increase in V is given by

$$1 - \int_0^{K/k} \delta \, e^{(\mu-\delta)t} e^{-\mu t} \, dt = e^{-\delta K/k}.$$

This condition is shown as (3b) above.

Condition (3c) states that the minimum value of the investment program is zero, and is reached when V is zero. Finally, conditions (3d) and (3e) require that the value of the investment program be continuous and differentiable at the cutoff value V^*.[11]

Eq. (2b) has the analytic solution

$$f(V) = aV^\alpha, \tag{4}$$

where

$$\alpha \equiv \{-(r - \delta - \sigma^2/2) + [(r - \delta - \sigma^2/2)^2 + 2r\sigma^2]^{1/2}\}/\sigma^2.$$

The coefficient a must be determined jointly with the solution for F in the upper region, via the shared boundary conditions (3d) and (3e). This would be straightforward if eq. (2a) also had an analytical solution; since it does not, a numerical approach is required.

First, we eliminate a using eq. (4) and the boundary conditions (3d) and (3e):

$$F(V^*, K) = (V^*/\alpha)F_V(V^*, K). \tag{5}$$

Then we numerically solve eqs. (2a), (2b), and the conditions (3a)–(3c) and (5) using a finite difference method. This procedure transforms the continuous variables V and K into discrete variables, and the partial differential equations into finite difference equations. These equations can be solved algebraically, and the solution proceeds as a backward dynamic program which incorporates the optimal investment decisions at each point. Hence the cutoff value, $V^*(K)$ (the optimal boundary between the two regions), is solved for simultaneously with the value of the investment program.[12] (Details of this procedure are in an appendix, which is available from the authors on request.)

The reader might note that the investment problem posed above is one of stochastic dynamic programming. Indeed, eqs. (2a) and (2b) are the Bellman equation under risk neutrality. As Cox and Ross (1976, pp. 153–155) have explained, given the current market value of the underlying asset, V, the contingent claims approach is equivalent to dynamic programming with risk neutrality. Any adjustment for risk is embodied in V, so that it is not necessary to know the risk-adjusted rate of return on the contingent claim.

In the next section we apply the solution procedure to a simple and stylized example. This serves to illustrate how the procedure works, and how time to build and uncertainty interact to affect investment decisions.

3   A Numerical Example

Consider an infinitely-lived project that requires a total investment (K) of $6 million, which can be spent productively at a rate no faster than $1 million per year (k). We assume the riskless rate of interest (r) is 2% per year. The value of the underlying asset, V, evolves according to eq. (1); we will vary δ and σ, but as a "base case," we take $\delta = 0.06$ and $\sigma = 0.20$ (annual rates).

Payout rates on projects can vary enormously from one project to another, so that this value of 6 percent should be viewed as reasonable, but not necessarily representative. The standard deviation of the rate of return on the stock market as a whole has been about 20 percent on average. Although this represents a diversified portfolio of assets, it also includes the effects of leverage on equity returns, and, therefore, might be a reasonable number for an average asset.

As discussed in the appendix, the solution procedure requires a discretization of the variables V and K; for this example, we assume investment outlays are made quarterly; i.e., K is measured in discrete units of $0.25 million.

The base case solution is shown in table 13.1. Each entry is the value of the investment program for different levels of V and K. Entries with an asterisk denote the cutoff value, $V^*(K)$. For example, a project with $5 million of investment outlays remaining has a cutoff value $V^*(K)$ of $9.49 million: if V is currently $9.49 million or more it pays to invest this quarter, otherwise it does not (although one would resume investing should V later rise above $9.49 million). At this critical level the value of the

Table 13.1
Value of the investment program, f, as a function of the value of the completed project, V, and the total remaining investment, K.

Value of the completed project, V	Total remaining investment, K (millions of dollars)						
	6	5	4	3	2	1	0
42.52	23.70	26.47	29.37	32.42	35.62	38.98	42.52
36.60	19.62	22.12	24.75	27.50	30.39	33.42	36.60
31.50	16.10	18.38	20.76	23.26	25.88	28.62	31.50
27.11	13.07	15.16	17.34	19.62	22.00	24.50	27.11
23.34	10.46	12.38	14.39	16.48	18.67	20.95	23.34
20.09	8.22	10.00	11.85	13.78	15.79	17.89	20.90
17.29	6.23	7.94	9.67	11.46	13.32	15.26	17.29
14.88	4.63	6.18	7.78	9.46	11.19	13.00	14.88
12.81	3.20	4.65	6.17	7.73	9.36	11.05	12.81
11.02	2.02*	3.34	4.77	6.25	7.79	9.37	11.02
9.49	1.22	2.23*	3.57	4.98	6.43	7.93	9.49
8.17	0.74	1.34	2.54	3.88	5.26	6.69	8.17
7.03	0.44	0.81	1.65*	2.93	4.26	5.62	7.03
6.05	0.27	0.49	1.00	2.12	3.39	4.70	6.05
5.21	0.18	0.29	0.60	1.42*	2.65	3.91	5.21
4.48	0.10	0.18	0.36	0.86	2.00	3.23	4.48
3.86	0.06	0.11	0.22	0.52	1.45	2.64	3.86
3.32	0.04	0.06	0.13	0.31	0.98*	2.13	3.32
2.86	0.02	0.04	0.08	0.19	0.59	1.70	2.86
2.46	0.01	0.02	0.05	0.11	0.36	1.32	2.46
2.12	0.01	0.01	0.03	0.07	0.21	1.00	2.12
1.82	0.00	0.01	0.02	0.04	0.13	0.73*	1.82
1.57	0.00	0.01	0.01	0.02	0.08	0.44	1.57
1.35	0.00	0.00	0.00	0.02	0.05	0.27	1.35
1.16	0.00	0.00	0.00	0.01	0.03	0.16	1.16
1.00	0.00	0.00	0.00	0.01	0.02	0.10	1.00
0.00	0.00	0.00	0.00	0.00	0.00	0.00	0.00*

(To conserve space, we only show values of the investment program for values of K in multiples of $1 million and for values of V up to $42.52 million.) Starred entries indicate the optimal investment rule: for each value of K, investment should be undertaken only if V is above the value corresponding to the starred entry. The value of V corresponding to each starred entry is the cutoff value, $V^*(K)$. The assumed parameters for the problem are: risk-free rate $r = 0.02$, standard deviation $\sigma = 0.20$, rate of opportunity cost $\delta = 0.06$, and maximum rate of investment $k = \$1$ million per year.

Table 13.2
Cutoff value of completed project, V^*, above which investment occurs, for different values of the rate of opportunity cost, δ, and standard deviation, σ.

Standard deviation, σ	Cutoff value	Annual rate of opportunity cost, δ (millions of dollars)		
		0.02	0.06	0.12
0.10	V^*	11.02	9.03	12.43
	V^{**}	9.77	6.30	6.05
	V^*	20.09	11.02	12.81
0.20	V^{**}	17.82	7.69	7.03
	V^*	121.51	24.53	20.09
0.40	V^{**}	107.77	17.11	9.78

Also shown is V^{**}, the cutoff value adjusted for foregone cash flows due to the opportunity cost, δV, when construction proceeds at the maximum rate (risk-free rate $r = 0.02$, total remaining investment $K = \$6$ million, maximum rate of investment $k = \$1$ million per year). *Note*: Present value of investment outflow at maximum rate of investment $K^* = \$5.65$ million.

contingent claim is $2.23 million; this is the equilibrium market value of the right to the investment program.[13]

Observe that table 13.1 can be used to make optimal investment decisions as construction of this project proceeds (i.e., as K falls from $6 million to zero). It can also be used to evaluate any project requiring a total outlay of $1, $2, ..., $6 million, but with the same values for the risk-free rate, r, the rate of opportunity cost, δ, the standard deviation, σ, and the maximum rate of investment, k.

We are interested in the sensitivity of the investment decision to the parameters σ, δ, and k. This decision is summarized by the cutoff value $V^*(K)$. Table 13.2 shows, for the initial investment decision (i.e., when $K = 6$), how the cutoff value changes in response to changes in σ and δ. (The middle entry in table 13.2 corresponds to the base case shown in table 13.1.)

Observe that V^* increases when σ is increased: i.e., with greater risk, the value of a completed project today would have to be higher to induce investment. Like most financial options, the value of the investment program, f, is a convex function of the value of the underlying asset, V, and therefore increases as the standard deviation of V increases. Recall that the only reason to invest at *any* value of V is the opportunity cost δ, which in our example of an infinitely-lived project represents the foregone cash flows. Because one is not obliged to exercise the option to invest, greater uncertainty over the future payoffs can only increase the value of the contingent claim, and increase the incentive to hold it rather than exercise it. This is an important point made by McDonald and Siegel (1986).

The dependence of V^* and δ is less obvious. One might expect that a higher opportunity cost of delaying the project, would reduce the cutoff value, V^*, and increase the incentive to invest. This would indeed be the case if the project could be built instantly, as in the model of McDonald and Siegel (1986). But the fact that it takes time to build the project creates a countervailing effect. The payoff from the project, V, is only obtained at completion and must be adjusted for the foregone cash flows during construction [the expected rate of growth of V is only $(\mu - \delta)$]. Time to build therefore reduces the value of the payoff at completion, and as δ increases, it reduces it by a larger amount. This in turn reduces the incentive to invest, i.e., increases the *current* critical cutoff value V^*. As table 13.2 shows, for high rates of opportunity cost this second effect predominates; for $\sigma = 0.10$ and 0.20, V^* rises when δ is increased from 0.06 to 0.12.

It is useful to calculate the critical cutoff value *net* of the present value of the expected flow of opportunity cost (δV), assuming that investment expenditures are made at the maximum rate. This value, V^{**}, is simply

$$V^{**} = V^* - \int_0^{K/k} \delta V^* \mathrm{e}^{(\mu-\delta)t} \mathrm{e}^{-\mu t}\, \mathrm{d}t = V^* \mathrm{e}^{-\delta K/k}, \tag{6}$$

where the second term on the right is the present value of the expected flow of opportunity cost (e.g., foregone rent) during the construction period.

Values for V^{**} are shown for each case in table 13.2. Increasing δ increases the opportunity cost of delaying the project (leading to a lower critical cutoff value), and also increases the opportunity cost *necessarily* incurred because of time to build (leading to a higher cutoff value). V^{**} corrects for the latter, and, as shown in the table, for any value of σ, it declines as δ increases.

Table 13.2 also shows the importance of the contingent nature of the investment program. A 'naive' discounted cash flow criterion would ignore flexibility during the construction period, and assume a fixed scenario for the investment outlays. Under this naive criterion, one would invest if the present value of investment outlays under the assumed scenario is less than the present value of the payoff at completion. Assuming investment occurs at the maximum rate, the present value of the payoff at completion is the current value of a completed project, V, less the foregone cash flows during construction, which is given by

$$\hat{V}(t) = V(t) - \int_0^{K/k} \delta V(t) \mathrm{e}^{-\delta\tau}\, \mathrm{d}\tau = V(t)\mathrm{e}^{-\delta K/k}, \tag{7}$$

and the present value of investment outlays is given by

$$K^* = \int_0^{K/k} k\mathrm{e}^{-r\tau}\,\mathrm{d}\tau = (1 - \mathrm{e}^{-rK/k})k/r. \tag{8}$$

For our example, the present value of investment outlays made at the maximum rate is $K^* = \$5.65$ million. Even making a rough correction for time to build by subtracting off the foregone cash flows as in eq. (6), the critical cutoff value (which would then be V^{**}) is still significantly higher than K^* for any reasonable value of σ and δ, and *much* higher if σ is large and/or δ is small. The discretionary nature of the investment program increases the threshold still further; V^* is significantly larger than V^{**}, particularly for large values of δ. For our base case of $\sigma = 0.20$ and $\delta = 0.06$, V^* is $\$11.02$ million, about *double* the present value of the investment outlays K^*.

We can obtain further insight into the ways in which uncertainty and time to build interact in affecting the investment decision by calculating V^* for different values of k, the maximum rate of investment. Figure 13.1 shows V^* as a function of k for $\delta = 0.03$ and 0.12, and $K = 6$.[14] Observe that if the rate of opportunity cost is small $(\delta = 0.03)$, changes in k have very little effect on V^*. (V then has an expected rate of

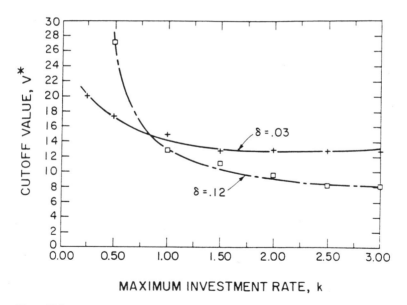

Figure 13.1
Cutoff value for investment, V^*, as a function of the maximum rate of investment, k, corresponding to two different levels of opportunity cost, δ. V^* is the value of a completed project above which it is optimal to proceed with the next stage of investment

growth close to μ, the equilibrium market rate.) Hence the ability to speed up construction has little effect on the value of the investment program, or on the investment decision. However, if the rate of opportunity cost is large ($\delta = 0.12$), V^* is fairly sensitive to k. Small values of k correspond to long minimum construction times. Hence the minimum present value of the opportunity cost during the construction period is large, reducing the value of the investment program, and increasing the *current* critical value V^*. [If V^* is adjusted for the flow of opportunity cost during the construction period, the resulting cutoff value (V^{**}) will not be very sensitive to k.] Thus time to build is more important for investment decisions where most of the return on the underlying asset is in the form of a payout stream rather than price appreciation.

Figure 13.2 shows V^* as a function of δ, for $k = 0.5$ (a 12-year minimum construction period) and 2.0 (a 3-year minimum construction period). In both cases, V^* falls as δ is increased from 0.01 to 0.04. (Remember that as the rate of opportunity cost becomes small, the critical value for investment becomes large; in the limit of zero opportunity cost one would never exercise the right to invest.) However, as δ

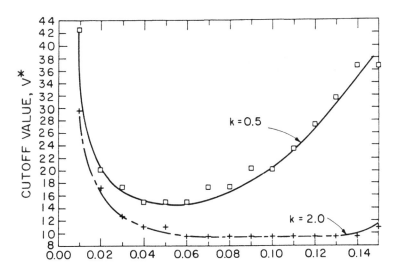

Figure 13.2
Cutoff value for investment, V^* as a function of the opportunity cost δ corresponding to two different values for the maximum rate of investment, k. V^* is the value of a completed project above which it is optimal to proceed with the next stage of investment

increases, the effect on V^* depends on the maximum rate of investment. If that maximum rate is high, V^* remains low over a wide range of δ (but is still 30–50 percent greater than the present value of the investment outlays). But if k is small, V^* can depend critically on δ. Thus for projects where the minimum time to build is long, knowledge of the rate of opportunity cost δ is a particularly critical input to the investment decision.

We have used numerical examples to illustrate how investment decisions are affected by the sequential and contingent nature of construction outlays. The difference between the results of our calculations and those based on a "naive" application of DCF rules will depend on the parameters of the problem, but as table 13.2 shows, for very reasonable parameter values, these differences can be large. Indeed, the range of values for σ in table 13.2 (0.1 to 0.4) is quite conservative. For many projects σ will exceed 0.4, so that the naive DCF rule will be grossly misleading.

4   The Value of Construction Time Flexibility

Many projects can be built with alternative construction technologies. An important way in which these technologies can differ is in terms of flexibility over the rate of construction. Generally, technologies offering greater flexibility are more costly, so that increased cost must be balanced against the value of increased construction time flexibility. Our model provides a straightforward way to determine the value of that increased flexibility.

In our model, construction time flexibility is measured by the maximum rate of construction, k. Higher k corresponds to greater flexibility, i.e., a shorter minimum construction time, K/k. The value of the investment program $f(V, K)$ increases as k increases, and the change in f corresponding to a change in k measures the value of the extra flexibility. This value of extra flexibility will depend on V and K, as well as other parameters of the problem, such as δ and σ.

We can determine the incremental value of construction time flexibility by examining the way in which the value of the investment program f changes as k changes. We calculate and compare the values of the investment program f for different values of k, holding all other variables constant. In particular, since alternative construction technologies are assumed to lead to the same completed project, its current value V must also be held constant. The incremental value of flexibility is then given by the slope of $f(k)$.[15]

Figure 13.3 shows the results of such a calculation for the base case parameters from the preceding section. We show $f(k)$ for two different values of the completed project, $V_1 = 10$ and $V_2 = 15$. As figure 13.3 shows, for each value of the completed

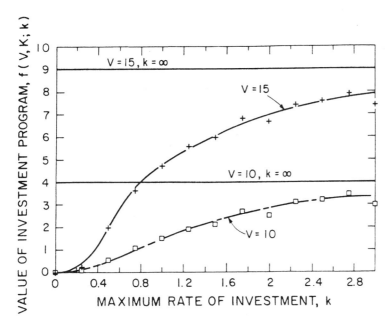

Figure 13.3
Value of the investment program, f, as a function of the maximum rate of investment, k, corresponding to two different values for a completed project, V. The horizontal lines represent the asymptotes corresponding to an infinite rate of investment (i.e. no time to build)

project, the value of the investment program increases as k increases. Note also that the incremental value of flexibility falls as k increases. For $V = 10$, the value of the investment program with *maximum* flexibility (corresponding to $k = \infty$) is 4.0, and for $V = 15$ it is 9.0, and these values are shown as horizontal lines in the figure.[16]

Consider two different construction technologies with the same total construction cost $K = 6$, but with different maximum rates of investment ($k = 0.5$ for the first, and $k = 1.0$ for the second). At $V = 10$, the incremental value of the more flexible technology ($k = 1$) is $\Delta f / \Delta k = 0.977/0.5 = 1.954$. This incremental value will be higher if the value of the completed project is higher; at $V = 15$, the incremental value is 5.520.

In general, greater flexibility might be accompanied by a different total investment K. Because the value of the investment program, $f(V, K; k)$, is not linear homogeneous in K (see footnote 15), we cannot isolate the value of the greater flexibility in such cases simply by comparing $f(V, K; k)/K$ for each technology. However, we can still rank the technologies by comparing $f(V, K; k)$.

5   Concluding Remarks

We have shown how optimal investment rules can be determined for projects with sequential investment outlays and maximum construction rates. An important feature of such projects is that the pattern of expenditures can be adjusted as new information arrives. For such projects, we have shown that traditional discounted cash flow criteria based on a fixed pattern of expenditures can lead to grossly incorrect investment decisions. As our calculations for different values of σ, δ, and k have illustrated (table 13.2, and figures 13.1, 13.2 and 13.3), the effects of time to build are greatest when uncertainty is greatest, when the opportunity cost of delay is greatest, and when the maximum rate of construction is lowest.

There are some important caveats. First, our simplifying assumption that V is lognormally distributed and that the payout rate, δ, is constant will be exact for very few projects, and for some projects may be a poor approximation. Second, our optimal investment rule critically depends on the current value of a completed project, V, as well as the parameters σ, and δ. We have assumed that these numbers are known, but in fact it may be difficult or impossible to estimate them accurately. Third, in some cases the value of the completed project, and the rate of opportunity cost δ are endogenous to the problem. This would be the case, for example, if the value of the completed project and its cash flows are affected by potential entry by competitors. Then the values of δ and V, as well as the optimal decision rule, must be determined simultaneously (e.g., as a Nash equilibrium for the resulting non-cooperative game).

Although there are many situations where the specific assumptions of our model will not be satisfied, we believe that the qualitative results will continue to hold. In particular, uncertainty is likely to have a depressive effect on the level of investment, an effect which is likely to be magnified when there is time to build.

Our primary focus in this paper has been investment decisions from the point of view of a single firm. However, our results also have implications for the behavior of aggregate investment spending, and in particular the role of risk in the economy. As in the models of Bernanke (1983), Cukierman (1980), and McDonald and Siegel (1985), we find that investment decisions can be extremely sensitive to the level of risk (which we measure by the parameter σ). Indeed, this sensitivity is greater than that suggested by traditional investment models. In our model, this greater sensitivity is due to the flexibility that the firm has in making sequential investment outlays; in the models of Bernanke and Cukierman, it is due to the reduction of uncertainty that results from learning. For different reasons, therefore, our results reinforce the view that aggregate investment spending is likely to be highly sensitive to changes in perceived risk.[17]

Acknowledgments

Financial support from the Center for Energy Policy Research of the MIT Energy Laboratory and from NSF Grant No. SES-8318990 to R. S. Pindyck is gratefully acknowledged. The authors also wish to thank James Meehan for his excellent research assistance, and Avraham Beja, John Cox, Alan Marcus, Stewart Myers, Julio Rotemberg, Richard Ruback, Daniel Siegel, an anonymous referee, and the editor, Michael C. Jensen, for their comments and suggestions.

Notes

1. See Hall and Jorgenson (1967).

2. For an overview of the adjustment cost literature, see Nickell (1978).

3. For an application to synthetic fuels, see Weitzman, Newey and Rabin (1981).

4. This notion of an "option value" is quite different from the one that we develop in this paper. In Bernanke, as in earlier papers such as Arrow and Fisher (1974) and Henry (1974), the option refers to a choice of projects (or irrevocable disposition of a natural resource in Arrow and Fisher) that is foregone once the expenditure has been made.

5. Related papers include McDonald and Siegel (1985) and Paddock, Siegel and Smith (1983). Also, Baldwin (1982) analyzes sequential and irreversible investment decisions when investment opportunities arrive randomly. She values the entire sequence of opportunities and shows that, as in McDonald and Siegel (1986), a simple discounted cash flow rule can lead to over-investment.

6. For related work, see Myers and Majd (1983) and Brennan and Schwartz (1985). For an overview, see Mason and Merton (1985).

7. We could introduce learning in our model by making σ a function of the stage of completion. Letting K denote the total amount of investment remaining for completion, we would make $\sigma = \sigma(K)$, $\sigma'(K) > 0$, and $\sigma(0) = 0$. We ignore learning in this paper in order to focus on the implications of time to build.

8. A constant payout rate, δ, and required return, μ, imply infinite project life:

$$V_0 \equiv \int_0^T \overline{CF}_t e^{-\mu t}\,dt = \int_0^T \delta V_0 e^{(\mu-\delta)t} e^{-\mu t}\,dt \quad \Rightarrow \quad T = \infty.$$

Note that this also implies that the expected rate of change of V is $\mu - \delta$.

9. For analyses of these options, see McDonald and Siegel (1985), Brennan and Schwartz (1985), and Myers and Majd (1983).

10. During the operating period $(t > \tau)$ we have

$$V(t) = \int_0^{T+\tau-t} P(s) e^{(\mu-\delta)s} e^{-\mu s}\,ds = P_t[(1 - e^{-\delta(T+\tau-t)})/\delta] \equiv \phi(t) P(t).$$

From Ito's Lemma, $dV = (\mu - \delta + \phi_t/\phi)V\,dt + \sigma V\,dz$, where the proportional rate of change, ϕ_t/ϕ, is strictly negative and varies over time.

11. See Merton's (1973) footnote 6 regarding (3e). Intuitively, if a small change in the value of the contingent claim in response to a small change in the value of the underlying asset is greater in one direction than another, moving the free boundary in that direction would result in a net increase in the value of the contingent claim.

12. See Hawkins (1982) for a similar model with analytic solutions in both regions. For an overview of numerical methods for solving option problems, see Geske and Shastri (1985). For a useful discussion of finite difference methods, see Brennan and Schwartz (1978).

13. To conserve space, the table shows only values of the investment program for values of K in multiples of \$1 million and for values of V up to \$42.52 million.

14. Our calculations are subject to numerical error because of the finite difference approximation. Absent such errors, the points plotted in figures 13.1, 13.2, and 13.3 would lie on smooth curves.

15. Another measure of the incremental value of flexibility is the change in $f(V, K; k)/K$ (the value of the investment program per dollar of total required investment) corresponding to changes in the minimum construction times K/k. Note, however, that $f(V, k; k)$ is not linear homogeneous in K, so that the resulting measure will still depend on K.

16. The case of $k = \infty$ means there is no time to build. This corresponds to a perpetual call option on a stock paying a constant proportional dividend, with exercise price K. The analytical solution is $f(V) = aV^{\alpha}$ for $V \leq V^*$ and $f(V) = V - K$ for $V > V^*$. Here α is given in eq. (4), $a = ((V^* - K)/V^*)^{\alpha}$, and $V^* = \alpha K/(\alpha - 1)$ is the cutoff value above which the option is exercised (i.e., the factory is built). In our example, $V^* = 8.6$. Since $V = 10$ and 15 exceeds this critical value, $f(V, K; \infty) = V - K$. See Merton (1973) for a derivation. Note that this is also the model used in McDonald and Siegel (1986).

17. Fischer and Merton (1984) have documented the close empirical connection between aggregate investment and the level of the stock market. Our results (like those of the authors mentioned above) suggest that aggregate investment spending might also be sensitive to the *volatility* of the stock market.

References

Arrow, Kenneth, J. and Anthony C. Fisher, 1974, Environmental preservation, uncertainty, and irreversibility, *Quarterly Journal of Economics* 88, 312–319.

Baldwin, Carliss Y., 1982, Optimal sequential investment when capital is not readily reversible, *Journal of Finance* 37, 763–782.

Bernanke, Ben S., 1983, Irreversibility, uncertainty, and cyclical investment, *Quarterly Journal of Economics* 98, 85–106.

Brennan, Michael J. and Eduardo S. Schwartz, 1978, Finite difference methods and jump processes arising in the pricing of contingent claims: A synthesis, *Journal of Financial and Quantitative Analysis* 20, 461–473.

Brennan, Michael J. and Eduardo S. Schwartz, 1985, Evaluating natural resource investments, *Journal of Business* 58, 135–157.

Cox, John C. and Stephen A. Ross, 1976, The valuation of options for alternative stochastic processes, *Journal of Financial Economics* 3, 145–166.

Cukierman, Alex, 1980, The effects of uncertainty on investment under risk neutrality with endogenous information, *Journal of Political Economy* 88, 462–475.

Fischer, Stanley and Robert C. Merton, 1984, Macroeconomics and finance: The role of the stock market, Working paper no. 1291 (NBER, Cambridge, MA).

Geske, Robert and Shastri, Kuldeep, 1985, Valuation by approximation: A comparison of alternative option valuation techniques, *Journal of Financial and Quantitative Analysis* 20, 45–71.

Hall, Robert E. and Dale W. Jorgenson, 1967, Taxation policy and investment behavior, *American Economic Review* 57, 391–414.

Hawkins, Gregory D., 1982, An analysis of revolving credit agreements, *Journal of Financial Economics* 10, 59–81.

Henry, Claude, 1974, Investment decisions under uncertainty: The irreversibility effect, *American Economic Review* 64, 1006–1012.

Kydland, Finn E. and Edward G. Prescott, 1982, Time to build and aggregate fluctuations, *Econometrica* 50, 1345–1370.

Mason, Scott and Robert C. Merton, 1985, The role of contingent claims analysis in corporate finance, in: Edward I. Altman and Marti G. Subrahmanyam, ed., *Recent advances in corporate finance* (Richard D. Irwin, Homewood, IL).

McDonald, Robert and Daniel Siegel, 1985, Investment and the valuation of firms when there is an option to shut down, *International Economic Review* 26, 331–349.

McDonald, Robert and Daniel Siegel, 1986, The value of waiting to invest, *Quarterly Journal of Economics* 101, 707–727.

Merton, Robert C., 1973, The theory of rational option pricing, *Bell Journal of Economics* 4, 141–183.

Merton, Robert C., 1977, On the pricing of contingent claims and the Modigliani–Miller theorem, *Journal of Financial Economics* 5, 241–249.

Myers, Stewart C. and Saman Majd, 1983, Calculating abandonment value using option pricing theory, Working paper no. 1462-83 (MIT Sloan School of Management, Cambridge, MA).

Nickell, Stephen J., 1978, *The investment decisions of firms* (Cambridge University Press, Cambridge).

Paddock, James L., Daniel R. Siegel and James L. Smith, 1984, Option valuation of claims and physical assets: The case of offshore petroleum leases, Unpublished working paper (MIT Energy Laboratory, Cambridge, MA).

Roberts, Kevin and Martin L. Weitzman, 1981, Funding criteria for research, development, and exploration projects, *Econometrica* 49, 1261–1288.

Weitzman, Martin, Whitney Newey and Michael Rabin, 1981, Sequential R&D strategy for synfuels, *Bell Journal of Economics* 12, 574–590.

14 Abandonment Value and Project Life

Stewart C. Myers and Saman Majd

I Introduction

Conventional capital budgeting procedure discounts project cash flows estimated for some definite project life, where the last cash flow includes an estimate of the salvage value. The only evident decision is whether or not to invest at time zero.

In real life, however, managers manage projects after time zero. As uncertainty about future cash flows is resolved, managers depart from the operating and investment plans that underlay the original cash flow forecasts. For example, the manager may switch inputs to the productions process, expand or contract the scale of operations, or shut down production altogether.[1]

In principle, all such "managerial options" should be included in project value. This chapter analyzes and values one particular option: the option to abandon a project for its salvage value.[2]

Consider the choice between two production technologies: Technology A employs standard machine tools, which have an active secondhand market. Technology B uses custom-designed, specialized equipment for which there is no secondhand market. Thus A has a higher salvage value than B at any time. The two equipment types are equally durable and produce an identical product and identical revenues. However, technology B is more efficient and has lower operating costs. If production must continue until the machines are worn out and scrapped, and if cash flows from the two technologies are discounted at the same rate, then B's net present value (NPV) is greater than A's.

These calculations presume that the duration of production is known, but it is not: if production may be halted early (before the machines are worn out) then technology A may be better than B. Technology A's higher value in the secondhand market increases its NPV relative to B's NPV.

Standard capital budgeting procedure assigns an expected salvage value to assets at the end of a definite project life. However, this misses the value of the option to extend the project's life or cut it short. In general, a project will be abandoned when the value of continuing is less than the salvage value. The total value of a project includes its abandonment value, which depends on the salvage value and the optimal time to abandon. Of course, the optimal time to abandon is not known when the project is undertaken.

Robichek and Van Horne [22] provided an early analysis of abandonment value. They recognize the value of the option to abandon a project and illustrate the option's practical importance. Their examples, however, assume that the project will be abandoned as soon as the salvage value exceeds the present value of the remaining cash flows. Dyl and Long [6] emphasized that the optimal time to abandon the project will not, in general, be the first instance where salvage value exceeds the present value of the remaining cash flows. Rather, the abandonment decision at each point must recognize that, if the project is not abandoned, the firm retains the option to abandon in the future.

Unfortunately, Robichek and Van Horne's solution procedure (as corrected by Dyl and Long) is not practical. The subsequent finance literature has not provided a practical approach either.

The option to abandon a project is formally equivalent to an American put option and can be valued by applying the techniques developed to value options on stocks. However, it is not a simple put option; the project yields uncertain cash flows and has an uncertain salvage value. These factors significantly complicate the solution procedure.[3]

The option valuation approach used in this chapter follows Merton [17], who relies on continuous trading of specified assets to replicate the payoffs to the contingent claim.[4] Hence the value of the contingent claim is the cost of forming the replicating portfolio.

At first glance, the applicability of this approach might seem questionable, since the real assets underlying these options are not traded in financial markets and their market values cannot be directly observed. Nevertheless, the option-pricing procedures can still be applied if capital markets are sufficiently complete that the new project and its associated options do not change the investment opportunity set available to investors.[5] The assumption of complete markets is also implicit in the standard discounted cash flow approach to capital budgeting.

This chapter presents a general procedure for estimating the abandonment value of a capital investment project. Section II specifies the abandonment option as a contingent claim and discusses some of the important factors that affect its value. Section III describes our simplifying assumptions and valuation procedure, and Section IV presents some numerical examples of the calculations. Section V discusses how uncertainty about the salvage value can be incorporated in the analysis. Section VI offers some concluding comments.

II Problem Specification

The option to abandon a project is formally equivalent to an American put option on a dividend-paying stock: The exercise price of the put is the salvage value of the project; the cash flows from the project are equivalent to the dividend payments on the stock. Also, the project can be abandoned at any time. This section discusses how these factors affect the abandonment value. The specific assumptions we make to implement the solution technique are described in Section III.

A   Cash Flows and Payout Ratios

The value of a project is determined by the present value of its expected cash flows. Since expectations about future cash flows are revised as new information arrives, the actual value of the project wanders randomly. The uncertainty about the future value of the project is related to uncertainty about future cash flows, although the relation is generally complex.

To apply contingent claim valuation techniques we must specify the stochastic process generating the value of the project. However, in capital budgeting we normally focus on the process generating the cash flows: project cash flows determine project value, not the other way around. Nevertheless, we can write a stochastic process for the project value provided we ensure that it is consistent with the underlying process for the cash flows.

For example, we can assume that the project value folows a lognormal diffusion process: $dP/P = \alpha\,dt - \gamma\,dt + \sigma\,dz$. Here P is the project value, α the expected total return, σ the standard deviation of the rate of change of P, and dz the standard Weiner process generating the unexpected changes. This process also includes a term $\gamma\,dt$, representing the cash flows paid out from the project. The instantaneous cash flow is expressed as a proportion of project value: $C = \gamma P$, where γ is a "payout ratio."

The following simple example shows how we restate the forecasts of cash flows in terms of payout ratios. Suppose that cash flows are forecasted to be constant over the life of the project, so that it resembles a simple annuity (figure 14.1a). Since the value of the project at any time is the present value of the remaining cash flows, we can derive the expected path of the project value over time from the forecasted cash flows. The project value will decline over time as in figure 14.1b. From these two sets of forecasts we can forecast the implied payout ratios: in this example the payout ratios will increase over time (figure 14.1c).

Forecast errors in the cash flows generally cause changes in expectations of future cash flows and project value. The way in which expectations about future cash flows are updated in response to forecast errors determines the change in project value, and together they determine the change in future payout ratios.

Different specifications of the effect of forecast errors in the cash flows on forecasted payout ratios are possible. A mean-reverting cash flow, for example, causes forecasted payout ratios to be functions of project value. More complex specifications of payout ratios as functions of time and project value are also possible.

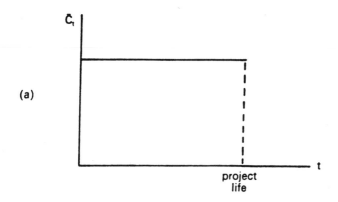

(a)

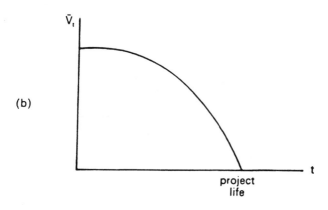

(b)

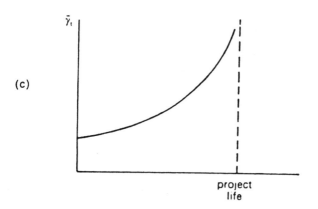

(c)

Figure 14.1
(a) Forecasted cash flows; (b) Forecasted project value implied by cash flow pattern shown in (a); and (c) Forecasted payout ratios implied by (a) and (b)

In our calculations below, we assume that the payout ratios are constant or functions of time only. The assumption that payout ratios are independent of project value may seem unduly restrictive. However, it is the usual justification for using a single risk-adjusted rate to discount future cash flows, which is standard procedure in capital budgeting.[6]

B   Asset Life and Salvage Value

What determines the "life" of a project?

The *physical* life of an asset depends on the time at which it will wear out and must be replaced. This is the maximum life of the asset. Physical life could be infinite or very long as, for example, in the cases of land or a hydroelectric facility.[7]

The *economic* life of the asset is the length of time during which the asset is being used. Thus even if the project is terminated, if the asset is put to some other use, its economic life continues.

The *project* life is not fixed, but is determined by the decision to abandon. It is solved for simultaneously with the value of the option to abandon. The determinants of the abandonment value will therefore also determine the project life.

A project might never be abandoned before the end of its asset's physical life. In that case the project life, the economic life, and the physical life will all be equal. Generally, however, the project life is less than the economic life, which is less than the physical life.

The salvage value at any time is the market value of the asset in its next most productive use. It is net of any costs of converting from one use to the other, and incorporates the value of any subsequent options to abandon. Some assets with several possible uses may be abandoned several times during their physical life. Most land, for example, has many different productive uses and infinite physical life. In such cases, the option to abandon (i.e., to switch from one use to another) is like an "option on an option": if the project is abandoned before its economic life is over, its salvage value includes the value of terminating its next tour of duty, and the next user gets another abandonment option. Therefore a completely general specification of the stochastic properties of salvage value, including its relation to project value, is not an easy thing to formulate or analyze. However, we can cope with uncertain salvage values under the assumptions described in Section V.

III   Solution Procedure

Following the methodology of Merton [17], the partial differential equation for abandonment value is:

$$1/2\sigma^2 P^2 A_{PP} + (r - \gamma)PA_P - rA + A_t = 0, \tag{1}$$

where P is the value of the underlying project, σ the standard deviation of the rate of change of P, r the riskless interest rate, γ the payout ratio, and A the abandonment value.

Two boundary conditions are: (1) if the value of the project is zero, the value of the option is the salvage value at that time: $A(P = 0, t) = S(t)$; (2) as the value of the project becomes infinitely large, the value of the option tends to zero: $\lim P \to \infty$ of $A(P, t) = 0$.

A third condition governs the decision to exercise: the value of the project is the greater of the salvage value or the value of continuing with optimal *future* abandonment. This condition is invoked at each point in time, and the optimal abandonment schedule is solved for implicitly.

Finally, a terminal boundary condition must be set to force abandonment at the physical life of the asset (the maturity of the option): $A(P, T) = \max[S(T), 0]$.

The most general specification of the abandonment option does not allow a closed-form solution because (1) future salvage values are uncertain and are related to the project value; (2) future payout ratios, as defined in the previous section, are uncertain and can depend on time and project value,[8] and (3) the abandonment option is an American option for which possible early exercise must be determined jointly with the abandonment value.

We start by assuming a deterministic salvage value, which declines at a known constant rate. We also assume that the payout ratios are functions only of time during the physical life of the asset. Project cash flows are coupled to uncertainty about project value.[9]

Since there is no closed-form solution to even this simple formulation, we must use a numerical technique. Several techniques are available: we employ an explicit form of the finite-difference method.[10]

The numerical method gives a relation between the value of the abandonment option in any period and its values in the next period. We employ this relation recursively, starting with the values at the terminal boundary, and working back to the abandonment values at the start of the project. In addition, the procedure dictates the optimal abandonment decision. Since the project value is a sufficient statistic for the value of the future cash flows, optimal abandonment is expressed as a schedule of project values over time. Should the project value fall below this schedule at any time the project will be abandoned. This schedule will not be equal to the present value of remaining cash flows (as in Robichek and Van Horne [22]) because our recursive procedure includes the value of optimal future abandonment at each point. Thus the current abandonment decision implicitly accounts for optimal future abandonment decisions.

IV Numerical Examples for the Simplified Abandonment Problem

A Base Case Assumptions

For the base case calculations we assume a constant payout ratio (constant γ), and also that:

(1) The initial project value is 100 (calculated by discounting at an assumed real risk-adjusted rate of 6%).

(2) The project payout ratio is 10%. Hence project cash flows and value are forecasted to decline by 4% per year.[11] In the absence of salvage, the project would be perpetual (i.e., economic life = physical life = infinity). However, we arbitrarily terminate the physical life of the asset in the distant future, at 70 years.[12] This is the terminal boundary where we force abandonment.

(3) The initial salvage value is 50, declining exponentially by 1% per year.

(4) The standard deviation of forecast error of project present value (PV) is 20% per year.

(5) The real risk-free rate of interest is 2% per year.

Figure 14.2 shows how the forecasted project value and salvage value change over time. Note that the initial value of 100 is based on the assumption that the project will never be abandoned prior to the end of the asset's physical life, and therefore does not include any allowance for salvage value, even at the terminal date. Therefore the abandonment value we calculate is the extra value due to the option to abandon in favor of the salvage value at any time during the project life.

B Base Case Results

Table 14.1 shows the results of the base case calculations. Each entry in the table is the abandonment value for a given project value. The first column of entries gives the abandonment value at the start of the project. Thus, since the initial forecasted value is 100, the abandonment value is about 6% of project value. If this project requires an initial investment of 100, making its NPV without abandonment value zero, the abandonment value makes the project worthwhile.

The optimal abandonment decision is also indicated in table 14.1; if at any time the project value falls below the stepped horizontal line, the project should be

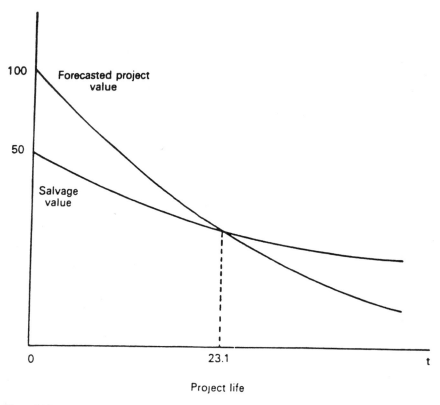

Figure 14.2
Forecasted project value and salvage value (base case example, constant payout ratio)

abandoned. For example, it should be abandoned if the project value in year 2 is less than 29.96.

The direction of the change in abandonment value can be predicted from standard option-pricing theory: other things constant, (1) an increase in the salvage value (exercise price) will increase the value of the abandonment option; (2) an increase in the volatility of the value of the project (the underlying asset) will increase the value of the option; (3) an increase in the project value (the current value of the underlying asset) will decrease the value of the option; (4) a decrease in the physical life (the maturity of the option) will decrease the value of the option. These results were verified numerically and are presented graphically in figure 14.3.

Table 14.1
Abandonment value as a function of time and project value.[a]

Project value[b]	Time[c]	70	69	68	67	66	65	64	63	62	61	60
221.41		0.00	0.00	0.00	0.00	0.00	0.00	0.00	0.00	0.00	0.00	0.00
181.27		2.31	2.09	1.88	1.69	1.53	1.37	1.24	1.12	1.00	0.90	0.81
148.41		3.49	3.15	2.84	2.56	2.30	2.08	1.87	1.68	1.52	1.37	1.23
121.51		4.50	4.06	3.66	3.30	2.97	2.68	2.41	2.17	1.96	1.76	1.59
99.48		5.63	5.07	4.57	4.12	3.72	3.35	3.02	2.72	2.45	2.21	1.99
81.45		7.00	6.31	5.68	5.12	4.62	4.16	3.75	3.38	3.05	2.74	2.47
66.69		8.68	7.82	7.06	6.36	5.73	5.17	4.66	4.19	3.78	3.41	3.07
54.60		10.78	9.71	8.75	7.89	7.11	6.41	5.78	5.21	4.69	4.23	3.81
44.70		13.35	12.05	10.86	9.78	8.82	7.95	7.16	6.46	5.82	5.24	4.73
36.60		16.57	14.93	13.48	12.14	10.93	9.87	8.89	8.01	7.22	6.51	5.86
29.96		20.59	18.53	16.69	15.07	13.57	12.22	11.03	9.94	8.95	8.08	7.28
24.53		25.47	23.03	20.71	18.65	16.86	15.17	13.66	12.34	11.11	10.01	9.03
20.09		29.91	27.48	25.16	22.95	20.85	18.85	16.96	15.27	13.80	12.42	11.19
16.44		33.56	31.12	28.80	26.59	24.49	22.50	20.60	18.79	17.07	15.44	13.88
13.46		36.54	34.10	31.78	29.57	27.47	25.48	23.58	21.77	20.05	18.42	16.86
11.02		38.98	36.54	34.22	32.01	29.91	27.92	26.02	24.21	22.49	20.86	19.30
7.39		42.61	40.17	37.85	35.65	33.55	31.55	29.65	27.85	26.13	24.49	22.94
4.95		45.05	42.61	40.29	38.08	35.98	33.99	32.09	30.28	28.56	26.93	25.37
2.72		47.28	44.84	42.52	40.32	38.22	36.22	34.32	35.52	30.80	29.16	27.61
0.00		50.00	47.56	45.24	43.04	40.94	38.94	37.04	35.23	33.52	31.88	30.33

a. Base case example, constant payout ratio. The stepped horizontal line represents the level of project value below which abandonment is optimal.
b. Project value is the present value of cash flows over the physical life of the asset. It does not include abandonment value.
c. Time measures the years of physical life remaining.

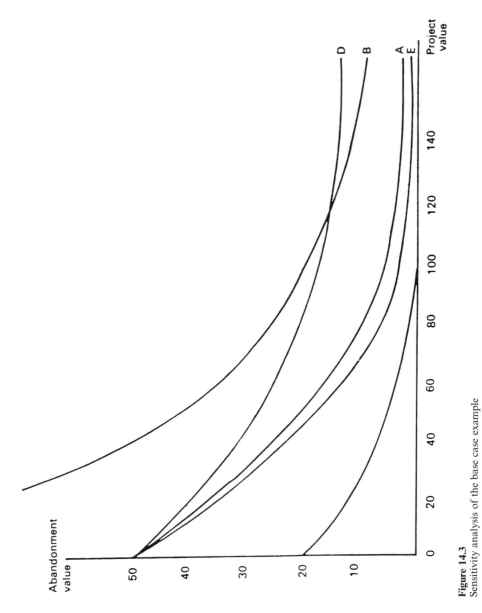

Figure 14.3
Sensitivity analysis of the base case example

C   Varying Payout Ratios

Our procedure can handle any project cash flow pattern so long as project payout ratios vary only with time. For example, consider a project with the following three-part project life cycle:

	Years	Cash flow	Payout ratio γ
1. Startup	0–5	Zero	0
2. Low profits	5–15	Low	0.02 ($= r$)
3. High profits	15 on	High	0.26

During the first five years, production has just started, a market for the product is being developed, and no cash flow is generated. In the next ten years, the project will generate a low level of cash flows. After year 15, the project will have an established market, and cash flows will be generated at a much higher rate. This implies the pattern for forecasted project value shown in figure 14.4. Assuming that the initial forecasted project value is 100, and otherwise maintaining the base case assumptions, the abandonment value is 5.54, or approximately 6% of project value.

We investigated the effect of the pattern of cash flows on abandonment value by varying the payout ratios in the three phases. There were no major surprises. Typical results are shown in table 14.2. Notice that abandonment value is highest when the initial payout ratio (γ) is highest. A higher initial payout implies a lower drift in project value, so that the abandonment put option is worth more.

V   Modeling Uncertain Salvage Values

Abandonment can occur more than once during an asset's physical life: the asset may be switched from one use to another several times. Included in the salvage value each time abandonment occurs is the option to abandon again. Hence the abandonment option is an option on a sequence of options. Unfortunately, this makes a completely general specification of the stochastic properties of the salvage value extremely difficult.

As a first step toward introducing uncertainty in the salvage value we make two simplifying assumptions. The first is that identical assets are being used elsewhere, and that these assets are held for investment and actively traded. Thus the salvage value has the usual stochastic properties of a market price. Second, we assume that the stochastic processes for the project value and the salvage value, respectively, are[13]

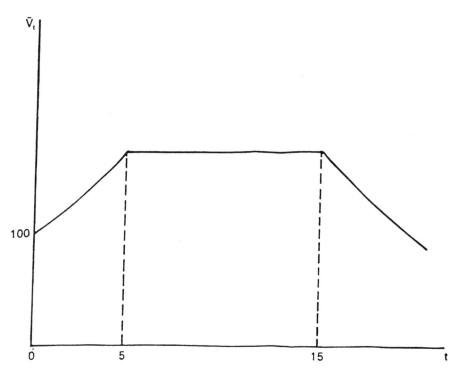

Figure 14.4
Forecasted project value (varying payout ratio)

Table 14.2
Abandonment value with varying payout ratio.[a]

Project payout ratio for years:					
0–5	0.02	0.00	−0.02	−0.04	−0.06
5–15	0.02	0.02	0.02	0.02	0.02
15–70[b]	0.25	0.26	0.27	0.28	0.30
Forecasted project life	23.10	23.10	23.10	23.10	23.10
Project value without abandonment	100.00	100.00	100.00	100.00	100.00
Abandonment value	5.56	5.54	4.78	4.51	2.61
Project value with abandonment	105.56	105.54	104.78	104.51	102.61

a. Other assumptions are as for the base case.
b. Assumed *physical* life of assets.

$$dP/P = (\alpha_P - \gamma_P)\,dt + \sigma_P\,dz_P, \tag{2}$$

$$dS/S = (\alpha_S - \gamma_S)\,dt + \sigma_S\,dz_S, \tag{3}$$

where P is the project value, α_P the expected total return, γ_P the project payout ratio, σ_P the standard deviation of the rate of change of P, and dz_P the standard Weiner process generating the unexpected changes in P. The parameters for the salvage value S are similarly defined. The project and salvage values are correlated, with the instantaneous correlation coefficient ρ.

Margrabe [12] has valued an option to exchange one risky asset for another. The assumptions above make our framework similar to his, where the stochastic salvage value can be interpreted as one of his risky assets. However, since his analysis assumes no payouts from the assets, it would not strictly apply to the abandonment option.[14]

We can use the valuation procedure developed earlier to value the abandonment option with uncertain salvage value. The appendix derives the differential equation for this option and shows that, after suitable transformation, the option's value obeys the same differential equation as applies in the case of deterministic salvage. This transformation is summarized as follows:

(1) Redefine the state variable as the ratio of project value to salvage value ($X = P/S$);

(2) The standard deviation of this new state variable is $\sigma_S^2 = \sigma_P^2 - 2\rho\sigma_P\sigma_s + \sigma_s^2$;

(3) Set the exercise price equal to unity;

(4) Substitute γ_S for the riskless interest rate.

With these four adjustments, abandonment with uncertain salvage is reduced to an equivalent option with known and constant exercise price.

Table 14.3 presents results of abandonment calculations when salvage value is uncertain. As the results indicate, the abandonment value is sensitive to changes in both the correlation between salvage and project values and the standard deviation of salvage value.

VI Conclusions

It is easy to think of the abandonment option as an American put option, and somewhat more difficult to put that insight to practical use. This paper discusses problems of application in some detail and presents numerical estimates of abandonment value for halfway realistic examples. With straightforward extensions, the

Table 14.3
Abandonment value with stochastic salvage value.[a]

Variance of salvage value (σ_S^2)	Correlation coefficient ρ.[b]				
	+0.9	+0.5	0.00	−0.5	−0.9
0.00	5.55[c]	5.55	5.55	5.55	5.55
0.04	2.18	5.55	8.83	11.45	13.13
0.08	3.75	7.80	11.45	14.63	16.18
0.12	3.88	9.85	13.50	16.53	19.63

a. For these calculations, we assume $\gamma_S = 0.07$. Otherwise the assumptions are those of the base case with deterministic salvage.
b. The variance of the rate of change of project value in units of salvage value, $X = P/S$, is $\sigma_X^2 = \sigma_P^2 - 2\rho\sigma_P\sigma_S + \sigma_S^2$.
c. When the uncertainty in salvage value is zero, the problem reduces to our base case with deterministic salvage. The difference between the abandonment value when $\sigma_S = 0$ in this table and our base case solution is due to round-off error.

procedures we have described could be applied to a large number of real-life capital projects. These procedures ought to have considerable practical importance, since project life in practice is almost never known ex ante.

Unfortunately, managers using conventional discounted cash flow rules routinely assume project life is known. In fact they have been making this assumption for so long that few seem to worry about it. It is easy to see that they should worry (or at least think) about it. Fortunately the necessary numerical procedures are not too difficult once the language and intuition of options have been learned.

Appendix

This appendix derives the partial differential equation (PDE) for the abandonment option when the salvage value is stochastic and shows that, with suitable transformation, the option value is also a solution to the PDE for deterministic salvage.

The derivation follows Merton [17], which also lists references to the supporting literature. For simplicity, the derivation that follows assumes a European abandonment option; the extension to an American option is straightforward. (The numerical results reported in the text refer, of course, to the American abandonment option.)

The stochastic processes describing the project value without salvage P and the salvage value S are given in Eqs. (2) and (3) in the text.

Let $F(P, S, t)$ be the solution to the PDE

$$1/2\sigma_P^2 P^2 F_{PP} + \rho\sigma_P\sigma_S PSF_{PS} + 1/2\sigma_S^2 S^2 F_{SS} + (r - \gamma_P)PF_P + (r - \gamma_S)SF_S - rF + F_t = 0$$

subject to the boundary conditions

$$F(P = 0, S, t) = S(t),$$

$$\lim_{P \to \infty} F(P, S, t) = 0,$$

$F(P, S, t = T) = \max[S(T) - P(T), 0]$.

From Ito's lemma,

$$dF = [F_t + (\alpha_P - \gamma_P)PF_P + (\alpha_S - \gamma_S)SF_S + 1/2\sigma_P^2 P^2 F_{PP} + \rho\sigma_P\sigma_S PSF_{PS} + 1/2\sigma_S^2 S^2 F_{SS}]\,dt$$
$$+ (\sigma_P PF_P)\,dz_P + (\sigma_S SF_S)\,dz_S.$$

Substituting from the PDE above, we have

$$dF = F_P\,dP + F_S\,dS + [rF - (r - \gamma_P)PF_P - (r - \gamma_S)SF_S]\,dt.$$

Consider the portfolio formed by investing the fractions x in P, y in S, and the remainder in riskless T-bills. The dynamics for the portfolio are

$$dY = [xY(dP + \gamma_P P\,dt)/P] + [yY(dS + \gamma_S S\,dt)/S] + (1 - x - y)Yr\,dt.$$

Choose the investment proportions according to the rules $x = F_P P/Y$ and $y = F_S S/Y$. Then,

$$dY = F_P(dP + \gamma_P P\,dt) + F_S(dS + \gamma_S S\,dt) + (Y - F_P P - F_S S)r\,dt = dF + (Y - F)r\,dt$$

If the amount initially invested in the portfolio is $Y(t = 0) = F(P, S, t = 0)$, then it is clear that $Y(t) = F(P, S, t)$ at all subsequent times. Further, the value of the portfolio Y is equal to the function $F(P, S, t)$ at the boundaries given above, which by construction are identical to the boundaries for the abandonment option. Since the portfolio has the same payoffs as the abandonment option, then to avoid dominance, the value of the abandonment option must be given by $A(P, s, t) = Y(t) = F(P, S, t)$.

The PDE for the abandonment option above can be simplified by the transformation $G(X, t) = A(P, S, t)/S$, where $X = P/S$. This leads to the PDE

$$1/2\sigma_X^2 X^2 G_{XX} + (\gamma_S - \gamma_P)XG_X - \gamma_S G + G_t = 0,$$

where $\sigma_X^2 \equiv \sigma_P^2 - 2\rho\sigma_P\sigma_S + \sigma_S^2$. The new boundary conditions are

$G(X = 0, t) = 1$,

$\lim_{X \to \infty} G(X, t) = 0$,

$G(X, t = t) = \max[1 - X(T), 0]$.

This is identical to the formulation of the abandonment option with deterministic exercise price (equal to unity), and with the riskless rate replaced by γ_S.

The intuition behind this transformation is clear: think of the salvage value as the numeraire. In these units, the project value is $P/S(= X)$, and its variance is $\sigma_X^2 = \sigma_P^2 - 2\rho\sigma_P\sigma_S + \sigma_S^2$. The exercise price is now known, constant, and equal to unity.

To see why γ_S replaces the riskless rate, consider the portfolio that is used to replicate the option. When the salvage value is uncertain and is represented by a traded asset, this asset is used to hedge against changes in the exercise price. The salvage asset earns a fair total rate of return, which includes the cash flows to the asset. However, the exercise price changes only as the price of the salvage asset. The difference between the total return to the salvage asset and the rate of change of exercise price is the opportunity cost of holding an option on the salvage asset rather than holding it directly. This difference is the payout ratio γ_S, which enters the PDE instead of the riskless rate.

Notes

1. For other examples of analysis of such "managerial options," see Paddock, Siegel, and Smith [20], McDonald and Siegel [15, 16], and Brennan and Schwartz [4].

2. Note that the project will be traded as part of the total firm once the investment is made. The market value of the project will be the sum of the present value of the underlying "unmanaged" asset and the value of the managerial options, but the asset and its options will not be observed separately. The approach outlined here is a convenient way of partitioning the total value of the project.

3. Kensinger [10] analyzes project abandonment as a put option. However, his analysis assumes that the option is of the "European" type with a nonstochastic exercise price. This is equivalent to assuming that the project can only be abandoned at one date, and that the salvage value is known with certainty. This misses important features of the option.

4. Rubinstein [23] presents an alternative approach to option valuation. He dispenses with the continuous trading and hedging assumptions and replaces them with assumptions on investor preferences and the joint distribution of asset returns. See also Brennan [2].

5. See Mason and Merton [14], especially pp. 38–39, for a more extensive discussion of this point.

6. For a discussion of the assumptions underlying use of a single risk-adjusted discount rate, see Myers and Turnbull [19]. Although we do not provide the proof here, it is straightforward to show (using the framework of Myers and Turnbull) that a multiplicative stochastic process for the cash flow and unitary elasticity of expectations, along with sequential application of the capital asset pricing model (CAPM), lead to the same multiplicative stochastic process for project value. In other words, a forecast error $\delta_t = [C_t - E_{t-1}(C_t)]/E_{t-1}(C_t)$ causes the same percentage error in project value: $P_t = E_{t-1}(P_t)(1 + \delta_t)$. Hence, the payout ratio is not changed as a result of the forecast error. These assumptions are also sufficient to justify discounting at a single risk-adjusted discount rate. However, John Cox has pointed out to us that they are not strictly necessary: it is possible to construct other examples in which a single risk-adjusted rate could be properly used.

7. Another example of an asset with very long physical life is a fleet of trucks of different vintages. A program of maintenance and replacement maintains the fleet's productive capacity and so the fleet could live indefinitely. However, it has abandonment value: its owner may decide to get out of the trucking business.

8. Options on stocks with uncertain dividend payouts can be valued given specific assumptions about the joint distribution of stock price and dividend payout ratio (see Geske [8]).

9. Note that this is not a causal relationship between the value of the project and the cash flows. The causality runs the other way, from cash flows to value.

10. For a discussion of numerical methods for solving partial differential equations and examples of their application to problems in financial economics, see Brennan and Schwartz [3], Mason [13], Parkinson [21], and Schwartz [24]. Geske and Shastri [9] provide a useful summary of the major numerical methods.

11. Since the project is expected to earn a risk-adjusted return of 6% and the payout ratio is 10%, the net drift in the project value is −4%. Similarly, the assumed decay rate of 1% in salvage value represents the difference between its expected return and payout rate. Of course, these numbers change under risk-neutral dynamics: with a riskless rate of 2%, the project value would decline at 8% and the salvage value at 5%.

12. Because our solution procedure starts at a terminal boundary and works back recursively, we need a finite horizon for our calculations. Since the base case has an infinite horizon, we approximate this by setting the boundary far in the future, at 70 years. Sensitivity analysis shows that changes in this boundary's position do not have significant effects on the initial abandonment value.

13. This implicitly assumes that there is no abandonment option for the salvage asset. If there is, then the market value of the salvage asset includes the value of this option, and the simple dynamics posited for S will no longer be appropriate. In particular, σ_s will no longer be constant and may depend on S in a complex manner.

14. Fischer [7] also values a European call option with stochastic exercise price. He describes how the CAPM can be used to infer the equilibrium expected return on a security perfectly correlated with the salvage asset if this security is not traded. Stultz [26] extends Margrabe's results to more general European options on the maximum or minimum of two risky assets.

References

1. Black, F., and M. Scholes, "The Pricing of Options and Corporate Liabilities," *Journal of Political Economy* (May/June 1973), 637–659.

2. Brennan, M., "The Pricing of Contingent Claims in Discrete Time Models," *Journal of Finance* (March 1979), 53–68.

3. Brennan, M., and E. Schwartz, "Finite Difference Methods and Jump Processes Arising in the Pricing of Contingent Claims: A Synthesis," *Journal of Financial and Quantitative Analysis* (September 1978), 461–474.

4. Brennan, M., and E. Schwartz, "Evaluating Natural Resource Investments," *Journal of Business* (April 1985), 135–157.

5. Cox, J., and S. Ross, "The Valuation of Options for Alternative Stochastic Processes," *Journal of Financial Economics* (1976), 145–166.

6. Dyl, E., and H. Long, "Abandonment Value and Capital Budgeting: Comment," *Journal of Finance* (March 1969), 88–95.

7. Fischer, S., "Call Option Pricing When the Exercise Price Is Uncertain and the Valuation of Index Bonds," *Journal of Finance* (March 1978), 169–176.

8. Geske, R., "The Pricing of Options with Stochastic Dividend Yield," *Journal of Finance* (May 1978), 617–625.

9. Geske, R., and K. Shastri, "Valuation by Approximation: A Comparison of Alternative Option Valuation Techniques," *Journal of Financial and quantitative Analysis* (March 1985), 45–71.

10. Kensinger, J., "Project Abandonment as a Put Option: Dealing with the Capital Investment Decision and Operating Risk Using Option Pricing Theory," working paper 80-121, Edwin L. Cox School of Business, Southern Methodist University, Dallas, TX, 1980.

11. Majd, S., "Applications of Option Pricing to Corporate Finance," unpublished Ph.D. dissertation, Sloan School of Management, MIT, Cambridge, MA, 1984.

12. Margrabe, W., "The Valuation of an Option to Exchange One Asset for Another," *Journal of Finance* (March 1978), 177–186.

13. Mason, S., "The Theory of the Numerical Analysis of Certain Free Boundary Problems Arising in Financial Economics," Chapter 3, unpublished Ph.D. dissertation, Sloan School of Management, MIT, Cambridge, MA, 1979.

14. Mason, S., and R. C. Merton, "The Role of Contingent Claims Analysis in Corporate Finance," in *Recent Advances in Corporate Finance*, E. I. Altman and M. G. Subrahmanyam (eds.), Homewood, IL: Irwin, 1985.

15. McDonald, R., and D. Siegel, "The Value of Waiting to Invest," *Quarterly Journal of Economics* (November 1986), 707–727.

16. McDonald, R., and D. Siegee, "Investment and Valuation of Firms When There Is the Option to Shut Down," *International Economic Review* (June 1985), 331–349.

17. Merton, R. C., "On the Pricing of Contingent Claims and the Modigliani–Miller Theorem," *Journal of Financial Economics* (November 1977), 241–249.

18. Merton, R. C., "On the Mathematics and Economics Assumptions of Continuous Time Models," *Financial Economics: Essays in Honor of Paul Cootner*, W. Sharpe and C. Cootner (eds.). Englewood Cliffs, NJ: Prentice-Hall, 1982.

19. Myers, S. C., and S. Turnbull, "Capital Budgeting and the Capital Asset Pricing Model: Good News and Bad News," *Journal of Finance* (May 1977), 321–333.

20. Paddock, J. L., D. R. Siegel, and J. L. Smith, "Option Valuation of Claims on Physical Assets: The Case of Offshore Petroleum Leases," *Quarterly Journal of Economics* (August 1988), 479–508.

21. Parkinson, M., "Option Pricing: The American Put," *The Journal of Business* (January 1977), 21–36.

22. Robichek, A., and J. Van Horne, "Abandonment Value and Capital Budgeting," *Journal of Finance* (December 1967), 577–590.

23. Rubinstein, M., "The Valuation of Uncertain Income Streams and the Pricing of Options," *Bell Journal of Economics* (Autumn 1976), 407–425.

24. Schwartz, E. S., "The Valuation of Warrants: Implementing a New Approach," *Journal of Financial Economics* (January 1977), 79–93.

25. Smith, C., "Option Pricing: A Review," *Journal of Financial Economics* (January/March 1976), 1–51.

26. Stulz, R., "Options on the Minimum or Maximum of Two Risky Assets: Analysis and Applications," *Journal of Financial Economics* (July 1982), 161–185.

15 Irreversible Investment, Capacity Choice, and the Value of the Firm

Robert S. Pindyck

Most major investment expenditures are at least partly irreversible: the firm cannot disinvest, so the expenditures are sunk costs. Irreversibility usually arises because capital is industry- or firm-specific, that is, it cannot be used in a different industry or by a different firm. A steel plant, for example, is industry-specific. It can only be used to produce steel, so if the demand for steel falls, the market value of the plant will fall. Although the plant could be sold to another steel company, there is likely to be little gain from doing so, so the investment in the plant must be viewed as a sunk cost. As another example, most investments in marketing and advertising are firm-specific, and so are likewise sunk costs.[1]

The irreversibility of investment has been neglected since the work of Kenneth Arrow (1968), despite its implications for spending decisions, capacity choice, and the value of the firm. When investment is irreversible and future demand or cost conditions are uncertain, an investment expenditure involves the exercising, or "killing," of an option—the option to productively invest at any time in the future. One gives up the possibility of waiting for new information that might affect the desirability or timing of the expenditure; one cannot disinvest should market conditions change adversely. This lost option value must be included as part of the cost of the investment. As a result, the Net Present Value (NPV) rule "Invest when the value of a unit of capital is at least as large as the purchase and installation cost of the unit" is not valid. Instead the value of the unit must *exceed* the purchase and installation cost, by an amount equal to the value of keeping the firm's option to invest these resources elsewhere alive—an opportunity cost of investing.

This aspect of investment has been explored in an emerging literature, and most notably by Robert McDonald and Daniel Siegel (1986). They show that with even moderate levels of uncertainty, the value of this opportunity cost can be large, and investment rules that ignore it will be grossly in error. Their calculations, and those in related papers by Michael Brennan and Eduardo Schwartz (1985) and Saman Majd and Robert Pindyck (1987), show that in many cases projects should be undertaken only when their present value is at least double their direct cost.[2]

The existing literature has been concerned with investment decisions involving discrete projects, for example, whether to build a factory. This chapter examines capacity choice and expansion, for example, how large a factory to build, and when to expand it. In particular, I focus on the *marginal* investment decision. This provides a simple and intuitively appealing solution to the optimal capacity problem. It also yields insight into the sources of the firm's value, and clarifies the measurement of long-run marginal cost.[3]

A firm's capacity choice is optimal when the present value of the expected cash flow from a marginal unit of capacity just equals the total cost of that unit. This total cost includes the purchase and installation cost, plus the opportunity cost of exercising the option to buy the unit. An analysis of capacity choice therefore involves two steps. First, the value of an extra unit of capacity must be determined. Second, the value of the option to invest in this unit must be determined (it will depend in part on the value of the unit itself), together with the decision rule for exercising the option. In essence, this decision rule is the solution to the optimal capacity problem.

To determine the value of a marginal unit of capacity, we must account for the fact that if demand falls, the firm can choose not to utilize the unit. In effect, a unit of capacity gives the firm an infinite number of options to produce, one for every future time t, each with exercise price equal to production cost, and can be valued accordingly. As we will show, these "operating options" are worth more the more volatile is demand, just as a call option on a stock is worth more the more volatile is the price of the stock. This suggests that the firm should hold more capacity when future demand is uncertain, but the opposite is true. The reason is that uncertainty also increases the value of the firm's investment options, and hence the opportunity cost of irreversibly investing. Although the value of a unit of capacity increases, this opportunity cost increases even more, so the net effect is to reduce the firm's optimal capacity.[4]

Note that a firm's market value has two components: the value of installed capacity (i.e., the value of the firm's options to utilize some or all of this capacity over time), and the value of the firm's options to add more capacity later. As we will see, numerical simulations suggest that for many firms, "growth options" should account for a substantial fraction of market value, and the more volatile is demand, the larger is this fraction.

Options to productively invest are important assets, which firms hold even if they are price-takers in product and input markets. How do they arise? In some cases it is the result of a patent on a production technology, or ownership of land or natural resources. More generally, a firm's managerial resources, reputation, market position, and possibly scale, all of which may have been built up over time, enable it to productively undertake investments that individuals or other firms cannot undertake.[5]

Section I clarifies the nature of the firm's options to invest and produce, and how they affect its choice of capacity and its market value. Section II then solves the capacity choice problem in the context of a specific model. As the model is developed, a numerical example is used to show how the value of a marginal unit of capital, the opportunity cost of investing, and the firm's optimal capacity depend on current demand and uncertainty over future demand. Sections III, IV, and V use the model to study the value of the firm, the behavior of capacity and capacity utilization over time, and implications for the measurement of marginal cost. Section VI concludes with caveats and limitations.

I   Optimal Incremental Investment Decisions

Consider a firm facing a demand curve that shifts over time stochastically, so that future demands are uncertain. Let θ denote the demand shift parameter, with $\partial P(Q, \theta)/\partial \theta > 0$. Suppose the firm can install units of capital one at a time, at a sunk cost k per unit, whenever it wishes. Letting K be the amount of capital currently in place, we can write the value of the firm, W, as the sum of two parts:

$$W = V(K; \theta) + F(K; \theta). \tag{1}$$

$V(K; \theta)$ is the value of the firm's capital in place, that is, the present value of the expected flow of profits that this capital will generate, given the current value of θ. $F(K; \theta)$ is the value of the firm's "growth options," that is, given that the firm has capital K in place and given the current value of θ, $F(K; \theta)$ is the present value of any additional profits that might result should the firm add more capital in the future, less the present value of the cost of that capital. Note that $F(K; \theta)$ is greater than the present value of the expected flow of net profits from *anticipated* future investments, because the firm is not committed to any investment path.

Equation (1) is just an accounting identity, but we can use it to gain insight into the firm's investment problem by noting that units of capital are installed sequentially. Assuming for now that the units are discrete, we can number them in the order they are installed. Suppose units 1 through n have been installed so far. Then, suppressing θ, we can rewrite (1) by summing the value of each installed unit and the values of the options to install further units:

$$W = \Delta V(0) + \Delta V(1) + \Delta V(2) \cdots + \Delta V(n-1) + \Delta F(n) + \Delta F(n+1) + \cdots. \tag{2}$$

Here $\Delta V(j)$ is the value of the $j + 1$st unit of capital, that is, *the present value of the expected flow of incremental profits generated by unit $j + 1$*. Of course the firm need not always utilize this (or any other) unit of capital. It has the option to utilize it at every point during its lifetime, and $\Delta V(j)$ is equal to the value of this option. Section II shows how $\Delta V(j)$ can be calculated.

The firm must decide whether to install additional capital. Given that n units are in place, $\Delta F(n)$ is the value of the option to buy one more unit, that is, unit $n + 1$, at any time in the future. If the firm exercises this option, it pays k and receives an asset worth $\Delta V(n)$. The firm also gives up $\Delta F(n)$, because once exercised, the option is dead—whether or not the firm later buys more capital, it has now paid for unit $n + 1$, and cannot disinvest. Hence $\Delta F(n)$ is also a cost of investing in this unit. The full cost of investing is thus $k + \Delta F(n)$, and this must be compared to the benefit $\Delta V(n)$.

Once the firm buys unit $n + 1$, it then faces another problem: at what point should it exercise its option, worth $\Delta F(n + 1)$, to buy unit $n + 2$, which is worth $\Delta V(n + 1)$? And so on. These options must be exercised sequentially, so the total value of the firm's options to grow is

$$F(n) = \sum_{j=n}^{\infty} \Delta F(j).$$

Letting these incremental units become infinitesimally small, we can write equation (2) for the value of a firm with capital stock K as

$$W = \int_0^K \Delta V(v; \theta) \, dv + \int_K^{\infty} \Delta F(v; \theta) \, dv. \tag{3}$$

The firm's optimal capital stock K^* is that which maximizes its net value, $W - kK^*$. Using (3), this maximization gives the following optimality condition that must hold if the firm is investing:

$$\Delta V(K^*; \theta) = k + \Delta F(K^*; \theta). \tag{4}$$

Thus the firm should invest until the value of a marginal unit of capital, $\Delta V(K; \theta)$, is equal to its total cost: the purchase and installation cost, k, plus the opportunity cost $\Delta F(K; \theta)$ of irreversibly exercising the option to invest in the unit, rather than waiting and keeping the option alive.[6]

The firm's investment problem can therefore be solved by calculating $\Delta V(K; \theta)$ and $\Delta F(K; \theta)$, and using (4) to determine the optimal capacity $K^*(\theta)$. In the next section we carry out these steps for a specific model.

II A Model of Capacity Choice

Consider a firm that faces the following demand function:

$$P = \theta(t) - \gamma Q. \tag{5}$$

(The firm might be a price-taker, in which case $\gamma = 0$.) Here $\theta(t)$ evolves according to the stochastic process

$$d\theta = \alpha\theta\,dt + \sigma\theta\,dz, \tag{6}$$

where dz is the increment of a Weiner process, that is, $dz = \varepsilon(t)(dt)^{1/2}$, with $\varepsilon(t)$ a serially uncorrelated and normally distributed random variable. Equation (6) says that the current value of θ (and thus the current demand function) is known to the firm, but future values of θ are unknown, and are lognormally distributed with a variance that grows with the time horizon. Thus even though information arrives over time (the firm observes θ changing), future demand is always uncertain.[7]

The firm's cost and production constraints are as follows: i) each unit of capital can be bought at a fixed price k per unit; ii) each unit of capital provides the capacity to produce one unit of output per time period, so that $Q \le K$; and iii) the firm has an operating cost $C(Q) = c_1 Q + (1/2)c_2 Q^2$. In general c_1 and/or c_2 can be zero, but if $\gamma = 0$ (so the firm is a price-taker), we require $c_2 > 0$ to bound the firm's size.

I assume that the firm starts with no capacity, so at $t = 0$ it must decide how much initial capacity to install. Later it might add more capacity, depending on how demand evolves. For simplicity I assume that new capacity can be installed instantly, and capital in place does not depreciate.[8] Finally, investment is completely irreversible—the firm cannot disinvest. This means there is an opportunity cost to investing. Adding a unit of capacity today precludes the possibility of waiting and instead adding the unit later or not al all.

I make one more assumption: stochastic changes in demand are spanned by existing assets, that is, there is an asset or dynamic portfolio of assets whose price is perfectly correlated with θ. (This is equivalent to saying that markets are sufficiently complete that the firm's decision to invest or produce does not affect the opportunity set available to investors.) This assumption holds for most commodities, which are usually traded on both spot and futures markets, and for manufactured goods to the extent that prices are correlated with the values of shares or portfolios. However, in some cases this assumption will not hold, for example, a new product unrelated to any existing ones.

With the spanning assumption, we can determine the investment rule that maximizes the firm's market value, and the investment problem reduces to one of contingent claim valuation.[9] This provides insight, and avoids assumptions about risk preferences or discount rates. However, as shown in the appendix, the problem can also be expressed in terms of dynamic programming.[10] If spanning does not hold, dynamic programming can still be used to maximize the present value of the firm's expected flow of profits, using an arbitrary discount rate. (Note that in such cases there is no theory for determining the discount rate; the CAPM, for example, would not hold.) $\Delta V(K)$ and $\Delta F(K)$ would satisfy differential equations nearly the same as those that will be derived below (but containing the discount rate), so the qualitative results will be the same.

Let x be the price of an asset or portfolio of assets perfectly correlated with θ, and denote by $\rho_{\theta m}$ the correlation of θ with the market portfolio. Then x evolves according to

$$dx = \mu x \, dt + \sigma x \, dz,$$

and by the CAPM, its expected return is $\mu = r + \phi \rho_{\theta m} \sigma$, where ϕ is the market price of risk. I will assume that α, the expected percentage rate of change of θ, is *less* than μ. (It will become clear later that if this were not the case, no firm in the industry would ever install any capacity. No matter what the current level of θ, firms would always be better off waiting and simply holding the option to install capacity in the future.) Denote the difference between μ and α by δ, that is, $\delta = \mu - \alpha$.

For purposes of comparison, note that if future demand were certain ($\sigma = 0$), and if $\alpha = 0$, the firm's optimal initial capacity would be $K^*(\theta) = (\theta - c_1 - rk)/(2\gamma + c_2)$, where r is the riskfree rate of interest.[11] Equivalently, the firm should add capacity only if $\theta(K) > (2\gamma + c_2)K + c_1 + rk$. We will see that uncertainty makes the optimal capacity smaller than this.

A   The Value of a Marginal Unit of Capacity

To solve the firm's investment problem we first determine $\Delta V(K)$, the present value of the expected flow of profits from an incremental unit of capacity, given a current capacity K. Because the unit need not be utilized, the profit it generates at any future time t is a nonlinear function of θ, which is stochastic:

$$\Delta \pi_t(K) = \max[0, (\theta_t - (2\gamma + c_2)K - c_1)]. \tag{7}$$

Thus $\Delta V(K)$ can be written as

$$\Delta V(K) = \int_0^\infty \int_0^\infty \Delta \pi_t(K; \theta) f(\theta, t) \, d\theta e^{-\mu t} \, dt, \tag{8}$$

where $f(\theta, t)$ is the density function for θ at time t and μ is the risk-adjusted discount rate. It is difficult, however, to evaluate (8) directly. In addition, the discount rate μ might not be known.

Instead we obtain $\Delta V(K)$ by solving the following equivalent problem: What is the value of a factory that produces 1 unit of output per period, with operating cost $(2\gamma + c_2)K + c_1$, which it sells in a perfectly competitive market at a price θ_t, and where the factory can be shut down (temporarily and costlessly) if θ_t falls below the operating cost?[12] The appendix shows that the solution to this problem, obtained using contingent claim valuation methods or equivalently via dynamic programming, is:

$$\Delta V(K) = \begin{cases} b_1\theta^{\beta_1}; & \theta \le (2\gamma + c_2)K + c_1 \\ b_2\theta^{\beta_2} + \theta/\delta - [(2\gamma + c)K + c_1]/r; & \theta \ge (2\gamma + c_2)K + c_1, \end{cases} \tag{9}$$

where

$$\beta_1 = -\frac{(r - \delta - \sigma^2/2)}{\sigma^2} + \frac{1}{\sigma^2}[(r - \delta - \sigma^2/2)^2 + 2r\sigma^2]^{1/2} > 1$$

$$\beta_2 = -\frac{(r - \delta - \sigma^2/2)}{\sigma^2} - \frac{1}{\sigma^2}[(r - \delta - \sigma^2/2)^2 + 2r\sigma^2]^{1/2} < 0$$

$$b_1 = \frac{r - \beta_2(r - \delta)}{r\delta(\beta_1 - \beta_2)} \times [(2\gamma + c_2)K + c_1]^{1-\beta_1} > 0$$

$$b_2 = \frac{r - \beta_1(r - \delta)}{r\delta(\beta_1 - \beta_2)} \times [(2\gamma + c_2)K + c_1]^{1-\beta_2} > 0$$

This solution for $\Delta V(K)$ is interpreted as follows. When $\theta < (2\gamma + c_2)K + c_1$, the unit of capacity is not utilized. Then, $b_1\theta^{\beta_1}$ is the value of the firm's option to utilize the unit in the future, should θ increase. When $\theta \ge (2\gamma + c_2)K + c_1$, the unit is utilized. If, irrespective of changes in θ, the firm had no choice but to continue utilizing the unit throughout the future, the present value of the expected flow of profits would be given by $\theta/\delta - [(2\gamma + c_2)K + c_1]/r$. (Costs are certain and so are discounted at the riskfree rate; future values of θ are discounted at the risk-adjusted rate μ, but θ is expected to grow at rate α, so the effective net discount rate is $\mu - \alpha = \delta$.) However, should θ fall, the firm can reduce output and not utilize this unit of capacity. The value of this option is $b_2\theta^{\beta_2}$.

A numerical example will help to illustrate the model. For this purpose I choose $r = \delta = .05$, $k = 10$, $c_1 = 0$, and either $\gamma = .5$ and $c_2 = 0$, or equivalently $\gamma = 0$ and $c_2 = 1$.[13] I vary θ or K, and consider values of σ in the range of 0 to .4.[14] For comparison, let $\Delta V_0(K)$ denote $\Delta V(K)$ for $\sigma = 0$, so $\Delta V_0(K) = \theta/\delta - [(2\gamma + c_2)K + c_1]/r$ for $\theta \ge (2\gamma + c_2)K + c_1$, and 0 otherwise. In this example, $\Delta V_0(K) = 20(\theta - K)$ for $\theta \ge K$, and 0 otherwise.

Figure 15.1 shows $\Delta V(K)$ as a function of θ for $K = 1$ and $\sigma = 0$, .2, and .4. Observe that $\Delta V(K)$ looks like the value of a call option—indeed it is the sum of an infinite number of European call options (see note 12). As with a call option, $\Delta V(K)$ is increasing with σ, and for $\sigma > 0$, $\Delta V(K) > \Delta V_0(K)$ because the firm need not

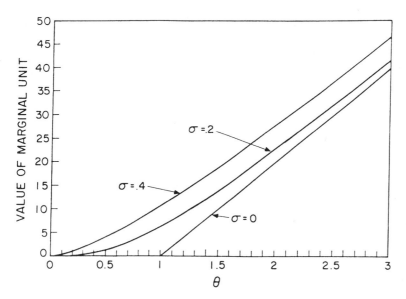

Figure 15.1
The value of a marginal unit of capacity, $\Delta V(K)$, as a function of θ ($K = 1$)

utilize its capacity. As $\theta \to \infty$, $\Delta V(K) \to \Delta V_0(K)$; for θ very large relative to K, this unit of capacity will almost surely be continuously utilized over a long period of time.

Figure 15.2 shows $\Delta V(K)$ as a function of K for $\theta = 2$, and $\sigma = 0$, .1, .2, and .4. Because demand evolves stochastically, a marginal unit of capacity has some positive value no matter how large is the existing capital stock; there is always some chance that it will be utilized over any finite period of time. The greater is σ, the more slowly $\Delta V(K)$ declines with K. Also, the smaller is K, the more likely it is that the marginal unit will be utilized, and so the smaller is $\Delta V(K) - \Delta V_0(K)$. When $K = 0$, $\Delta V(0) = \Delta V_0(K)$; with $c_1 = 0$, the *first* marginal unit will always be utilized.

The fact that $\Delta V(K)$ is larger when $\sigma > 0$ might suggest that the firm should hold more capacity, but the opposite is true. As shown below, uncertainty also makes the firm's opportunity cost of exercising its option to invest in the marginal unit larger, and by an even greater amount.

B The Decision to Invest in the Marginal Unit

Having valued the marginal unit of capacity, we can now value the firm's option to invest in this unit, and determine the optimal decision rule for investing. In the Appendix it is shown that the value of the firm's option to invest, $\Delta F(K)$, is

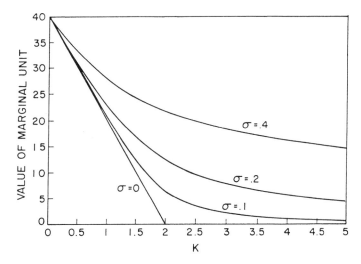

Figure 15.2
The value of a marginal unit of capacity, $\Delta V(K)$, as a function of θ ($K = 2$)

$$\Delta F(K) = \begin{cases} a\theta^{\beta_1}; & \theta \leq \theta^*(K) \\ \Delta V(K) - k; & \theta \geq \theta^*(K), \end{cases} \tag{10}$$

where

$$a = \frac{\beta_2 b_2}{\beta_1}(\theta^*)^{(\beta_2 - \beta_1)} + \frac{1}{\delta\beta_1}(\theta^*)^{(1-\beta_1)} > 0,$$

β_1, β_2, and b_2 are given under equation (9) above, and $\theta^*(K)$ is the critical value of θ at or above which it is optimal to purchase the marginal unit of capacity, that is, the firm should purchase the unit if $\theta \geq \theta^*(K)$. The critical value $\theta^*(K)$ is in turn the solution to

$$\frac{b_2(\beta_1 - \beta_2)}{\beta_1}(\theta^*)^{\beta_2} + \frac{(\beta_1 - 1)}{\delta\beta_1}\theta^* - \frac{(2\gamma + c_2)K + c_1}{r} - k = 0. \tag{11}$$

Equation (11) can be solved numerically for θ^*, and equation (10) can then be used to calculate $\Delta F(K)$.

Recall our assumption that $\delta > 0$. The reader can verify that as $\delta \to 0$, $\theta^*(K) \to \infty$. Unless $\delta > 0$, the opportunity cost of investing in a unit of capacity always exceeds the benefit, and the firm will never install capacity.[15] Thus if firms in an industry are investing optimally and some positive amount of investment is taking place, we should observe $\delta > 0$.

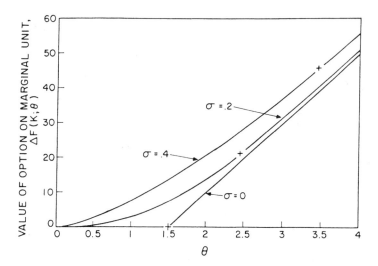

Figure 15.3
The value of the firm's option to install a marginal unit of capacity ($K = 1$)

As with a call option on a dividend-paying stock, both $\Delta F(K)$ and the critical value $\theta^*(K)$ increase as σ increases. Figure 15.3 shows $\Delta F(K)$ as a function of θ for $K = 1$ and $\sigma = 0$, .2, and .4. In each case θ^* is indicated by a "+." When $\sigma = 0$, $\theta^* = 1.5$, that is, the firm should increase capacity only if θ exceeds 1.5. For $\sigma = .2$ and .4, θ^* is 2.45 and 3.44, respectively. The opportunity cost of exercising the firm's option to invest in additional capacity is $\Delta F(K)$, which increases with σ, so a higher σ implies a higher critical value $\theta^*(K)$. Also, it is easily shown that $\theta^*(K)$ is monotonically increasing in K.

C The Firm's Optimal Capacity

The function $\theta^*(K)$ is the firm's optimal investment rule; if θ and K are such that $\theta > \theta^*(K)$, the firm should add capacity, increasing K until θ^* rises to θ. Equivalently we can substitute for $b_2(K)$ and rewrite equation (11) in terms of $K^*(\theta)$, the firm's optimal capacity:

$$\frac{r - \beta_1(r - \delta)}{r\delta\beta_1}\theta^{\beta_2}[(2\gamma + c_2)K^* + c_1]^{1-\beta_2}$$

$$- \frac{[(2\gamma + c_2)K^* + c_1]}{r} + \frac{(\beta_1 - 1)}{\delta\beta_1}\theta - k = 0. \tag{11'}$$

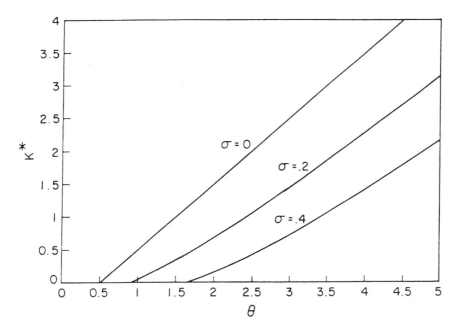

Figure 15.4
Optimal capacity, K^*, as a function of θ

Figure 15.4 shows $K^*(\theta)$ for $\sigma = 0$, .2, and .4. (For many industries .2 is a conservative value for σ—see fn. 14.) Observe that K^* is much smaller when future demand is uncertain. For $\sigma = .4$, θ must be more than three times as large as when $\sigma = 0$ before any capacity is installed.

Another way to see how uncertainty over future demand affects the firm's optimal capacity is by comparing $\Delta F(K)$, the value of the option to invest in a marginal unit, with $\Delta V(K) - k$, the net (of purchase cost) value of the unit. The optimal capacity $K^*(\theta)$ is the maximum K for which these two quantities are equal. Note from equation (10) that for $\theta \geq \theta^*$, or equivalently, $K \leq K^*$, exercising the option to invest maximizes its value, so that $\Delta F(K) = \Delta V(K) - k$, but for $K > K^*$, $\Delta F(K) > \Delta V(K) - k$, and the option to invest is worth more "alive" than "dead."

This is shown in figure 15.5, which plots $\Delta F(K)$ and $\Delta V(K) - k$ as functions of K, for $\theta = 2$ and $\sigma = .2$. Recall that $\Delta V(K)$ is larger when future demand is uncertain. As the figure shows, if the opportunity cost of exercising the option to invest were ignored, that is, if the firm adds capacity until $\Delta V(K) - k = 0$, then capacity would be about 2.3 units (as opposed to 1.5 units when $\sigma = 0$). But at these capacity levels

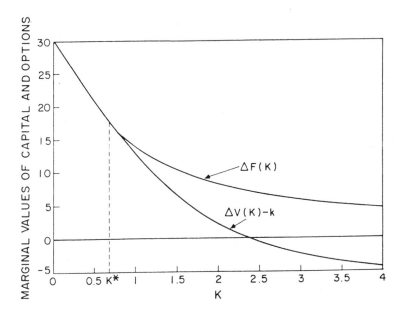

Figure 15.5
The net value of a marginal unit of capacity, and the value of the option to install the marginal unit $\Delta F(K)$

the opportunity cost of investing in a marginal unit exceeds the net value of the unit, so the value of the firm is not maximized. The optimal capacity is only $K^* = .67$, the largest K for which $\Delta F(K) = \Delta V(K) - k$, and the solution to equation (11′).

III   The Value of The Firm

As noted above, $K^*(\theta)$ maximizes the firm's market value, net of cash outlays for the purchase of capital. Recall that the firm's net value as a function of its capacity K is given by:

$$\text{Net Value} = \int_0^K \Delta V(v)\, dv + \int_K^\infty \Delta F(v)\, dv - kK. \tag{12}$$

Differentiating with respect to K shows that this is maximized when $K = K^*$ such that $\Delta V(K^*) - \Delta F(K^*) - k = 0$.

The value of the firm's installed capacity, $V(K^*)$, is the first integral in equation (12). In figure 15.5 it is the area under the curve $\Delta V(K) - k$ from $K = 0$ to K^*, *plus* the purchase cost kK^*. The value of the firm's growth options is the second integral,

Table 15.1
Value of firm ($c_1 = c_2 = 0$, $\gamma = .5$, $r = \delta = .05$, $k = 10$)

σ	θ	K^*	$V(K^*)$	$F(K^*)$	Value
0	.5	0	0	0	0
	1	0.5	7.5	0	7.5
	2	1.5	37.5	0	37.5
	3	12.5	87.5	0	87.5
	4	3.5	157.5	0	157.5
.1	.5	0	0	0.4	0.4
	1	0.23	4.3	3.4	7.7
	2	1.00	33.1	9.1	42.2
	3	1.82	80.4	20.3	100.7
	4	2.65	147.3	35.5	182.8
.2	.5	0	0	3.1	3.1
	1	0.04	0.8	13.5	14.3
	2	0.67	24.0	49.2	73.2
	3	1.37	67.1	94.6	161.7
	4	2.09	134.1	143.7	277.8
.4	.5	0	0	25.8	25.8
	1	0	0	69.7	69.7
	2	0.15	5.9	182.6	188.7
	3	0.64	36.2	307.2	343.4
	4	1.22	91.3	427.5	518.8

which in figure 15.5 is the area under the curve $\Delta F(K)$ from $K = K^*$ to ∞. As the figure shows, growth options can account for a large portion of the firm's total value.

The sensitivity of firm value and its components to uncertainty over future demand can be seen from table 15.1, which shows K^*, $V(K^*)$, $F(K^*)$, and total value for different values of σ and θ. When $\sigma = 0$, the value of the firm is only the value of its installed capacity. Whatever the value of θ, the firm is worth more the more volatile is demand. A larger σ implies a larger value for each unit of installed capacity, and a much larger value for the firm's options to expand. Also, the larger is σ, the larger is the fraction of firm value attributable to its growth options. When $\sigma = .2$ or more, more than half of the firm's value is $F(K^*)$, the value of its growth options. Even when $\sigma = .1$, $F(K^*)$ accounts for more than half of total value when θ is 1 or less. (When demand is currently small, it is the possibility of greater demand in the future that gives the firm much of its value.) And there is always a range of θ for which K^* is zero, so that *all* of the firm's value is due to its growth options.

As mentioned earlier, a σ of .2 or more would not be unusual. Thus an implication of the model is that for many firms, the fraction of market value attributable to the value of capital in place should be one-half or less. A second implication is that this fraction should be smaller the greater is the volatility of market demand. I have not tried to test either of these implications (valuing capital in place is difficult). However, calculations reported by Carl Kester (1984) are consistent with both of them. He estimated the value of capital in place for 15 firms in 5 industries by capitalizing the implied flows of anticipated earnings, and found that it is half or less of market value in the majority of cases. Furthermore, this fraction is only about 1/5 to 1/3 in industries where demand is more volatile (electronics, computers), but more than 1/2 in industries with less volatile demand (tires and rubber, food processing).

IV   The Dynamics of Capacity, Capacity Utilization, and Firm Value

If the firm begins with no capacity, it initially observes θ and installs a starting capacity $K^*(\theta)$. If θ then increases, it will expand capacity accordingly, and the value of the firm will rise. The value of its growth options will also rise, but will become a smaller fraction of total value (see table 15.1). However, if θ decreases, the firm will find itself holding more capacity than it would have chosen had the decrease been anticipated. The firm's value will fall, and depending on how much θ decreases, some of its capacity may become idle.

Because capital does not depreciate in this model, the firm's capacity is non-decreasing, but will rise only periodically. The dynamics of capacity are characterized in figure 15.6, which shows a sample path for $\theta(t)$, and the corresponding behavior of $K(t)$. (The duration of continuous upward movements in $K(t)$ is exaggerated.) The firm begins at t_0 by installing $K^*(\theta_0) \equiv K_0^*$. Then θ increases until it reaches a (temporary) maximum θ_1 at t_1, and K is increased accordingly to K_1^*. Here is remains fixed until t_2, when θ again reaches θ_1. Afterward K is increased as θ increases, until t_3 when θ begins to decline from a new maximum, and K remains fixed at K_3^*.

Thus an implication of the model is that investment occurs only in spurts, when demand is rising, and only when it is rising above historic levels.[16] Firms usually increase capacity only periodically, and this is often attributed to the "lumpiness" of investment. But lumpiness is clearly not required for this behavior.

Let us now examine the firm's capacity utilization. Clearly during periods of expansion, all capacity will be utilized. When demand falls, however, some capacity may go unutilized, but only if it falls far enough.

If the firm had unlimited capacity it would maximize current profits by setting output at $Q^* = (\theta - c_1)/(2\gamma + c_2)$. However, $K^*(\theta) < (\theta - c_1)/(2\gamma + c_2)$, and as shown in Section II, can be much less even for moderate values of σ. Thus for θ in the range $\underline{\theta}(K) \equiv (2\gamma + c_2)K + c_1 \leq \theta \leq \theta^*(K)$, capacity will remain fixed but will

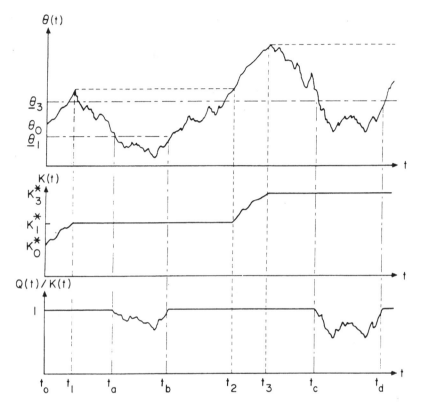

Figure 15.6
Realization of capacity and capacity utilization

be fully utilized. Capacity will go unutilized only when $\theta < \underline{\theta}(K)$. In figure 15.6 this occurs during the intervals (t_a, t_b) and (t_c, t_d).

The irreversibility of investment induces firms to hold less capacity as a buffer against unanticipated drops in demand. As a result there will be periods of low demands when capacity is fully utilized. A large drop in demand is required for capacity utilization to fall below 100 percent. Most of the time the firm's capacity K will be above $K^*(\theta)$—in figure 15.6 exceptions are during the intervals (t_0, t_1) and (t_2, t_3).

The share of the firm's value due to its growth options will also fluctuate with θ. For example, as table 15.1 shows, during periods when capacity is growing (so that $K = K^*(\theta)$), this share falls. It also falls when θ is falling and $K > K^*(\theta)$.

V   The Measurement of Long-Run Marginal Cost

The measurement of long-run marginal cost and its relationship to price are important for industry analyses in general, and antitrust applications in particular. When investment is irreversible, traditional measures understate marginal cost and overstate the amount by which it differs from price, even in a competitive market. This problem is particularly severe when product markets are volatile.

Suppose $\sigma > 0$ and $K = K^*(\theta)$. Using equation (9), the optimality condition $\Delta V(K) = k + \Delta F(K)$ can be written as:

$$\Delta V(K) = b_2\theta^{\beta_2} + \theta/\delta - [(2\gamma + c_2)K + c_1]/r$$

$$= k + \Delta F(K) \tag{13}$$

or

$$\theta/\delta - 2\gamma K/r = -b_2\theta^{\beta_2} + (c_2K + c_1)/r + k + \Delta F(K). \tag{13'}$$

If $\sigma = \alpha = 0$, equation (13') reduces to a more familiar special case:

$$\theta/\delta - 2\gamma K/r = (c_1 + c_2K)/r + k. \tag{14}$$

The left-hand side of (14) is capitalized marginal revenue. (Note that θ is capitalized at the rate $\delta = \mu - \alpha$ because it is expected to grow at the rate α but is discounted at the risk-adjusted rate μ; if $\sigma = 0$, $\mu = r$.) The right-hand side is full marginal cost: the capitalized operating cost, plus the purchase cost of a unit of capital. Equation (14) is the usual relation between marginal revenue and marginal cost when the former is increasing at a deterministic rate.

Observe that when $\sigma > 0$, two adjustments must be made to obtain full (capitalized) marginal cost, the RHS of (13'). The first term on the RHS of (13') is the value of the firm's option to let the marginal unit of capacity go unutilized, and must be subtracted from capitalized operating cost. The last term is the opportunity cost of exercising the option to invest. In our model the last term dominates the first, so that K must be smaller to satisfy (13'), and marginal cost as conventionally measured will understate true marginal cost.

If the firm is a price-taker, $\gamma = 0$ and $P = \theta$. Price will equal marginal cost, if the latter is defined correctly as in (13'). Unfortunately the first and last terms on the RHS of (13') are difficult to measure, particularly with aggregate data. But if one wishes to compare price with marginal cost, ignoring them can be misleading.[17]

VI   Conclusions

Uncertainty over future market conditions affects investment decisions through the options that firms hold—operating options, which determine the value of capital in place, and options to add more capital, which, when investment is irreversible, determine the opportunity cost of investing. By treating capital as homogeneous and focusing on incremental investment decisions, we have tried to clarify the ways in which uncertainty and irreversibility affect the values of these options, and thereby affect the firm's optimal capacity and its market value.

The assumption that firms can continuously and incrementally add capital, though common in economic models, is extreme. Most investments are lumpy, and sometimes quite so. The opposite extreme assumption is that the firm can build only a single plant, and must decide when to build it (the critical θ^*), and how large it should be (K^*). As sketched out in the Appendix, this problem can also be solved by the methods used in this paper. For our model: i) the critical θ^* at which it is optimal to invest increases with σ; ii) K^* also increases with σ (operating options are worth more, and there is only one opportunity to invest); and iii) for every θ, the value of the firm (the value of the single investment option prior to construction, and the value of the plant after construction) is less than it is when the firm can incrementally invest.

Besides ignoring the lumpiness of investment, the model presented here has other simplifying assumptions. It ignores adjustment costs and delivery lags, and includes only one source of uncertainty. It can be extended to account for these factors, but numerical methods may then be required to obtain solutions. Of course once numerical methods are used, other aspects of the model can also be generalized. For example, demand can be a nonlinear function of θ, or θ could follow some alternative stochastic process, including jumps.

It should be emphasized that the numerical results presented in this chapter are based on a specific production technology, and specific functional forms for demand and cost. Also, the assumption that the firm can incrementally invest magnifies the effects of uncertainty, as does the assumption that there is no depreciation. (If capital becomes obsolete rapidly, the opportunity cost of investing will be small.) Thus the quantitative importance of irreversibility and uncertainty may be more limited than the results here would suggest.[18]

Subject to these caveats, we find that in markets with volatile and unpredictable demand, firms should hold less capacity than they would if investment were reversible or future demands were known. Also, much of the market value of these firms is due to the possibility (as opposed to the expectation) of increased demands in the future. This value may result from patents and technical knowledge, but it also arises from the managerial expertise, infrastructure, and market position that gives these firms (as opposed to potential entrants) the option to economically expand capacity.

Do firms correctly compute and take into account the opportunity cost of investing when making capacity expansion decisions? Ignoring such costs would lead to over-investment. John McConnell and Chris Muscarella (1985), have found that for manufacturing firms, market value tends to increase (decrease) when managers announce an increase (decrease) in planned investment expenditures, which is incon-sistent with a systematic tendency to overinvest.[19] But there is anecdotal evidence that managers often base investment decisions on present values computed with dis-count rates that far exceed those that would be implied by the CAPM—diversifiable and nondiversifiable risk are sometimes confused, and an arbitrary "risk factor" is often added to the discount rate. It may be, then, that managers use the wrong method to get close to the right answer.

Appendix

Here we derive equation (9) for $\Delta V(K; \theta)$ and equations (10) and (11) for the optimal investment rule and value of the investment option $\Delta F(K; \theta)$.

The value of a marginal unit of capacity, $\Delta V(K; \theta)$, is found by valuing an equivalent "incremental project" that produces 1 unit of output per period at cost $(2\gamma + c_2)K + c_1$, that is sold at price $\theta(t)$, and where the firm can (temporarily and costlessly) shut down if price falls below cost. To value this, create a portfolio that is long the project and short ΔV_θ units of the output, or equivalently the asset or portfolio of assets perfectly correlated with θ. Because the expected rate of growth of θ is only $\alpha = \mu - \delta$, the short position requires a payment of $\delta\theta\Delta V_\theta$ per unit of time (or no rational investor would hold the corre-sponding long position). The value of this portfolio is $\Phi = \Delta V - \Delta V_\theta\theta$, and its instantaneous return is

$$d(\Delta V) - \Delta V_\theta \, d\theta - \delta\theta\Delta V_\theta \, dt + j[\theta - (2\gamma + c_2)K - c_1] \, dt. \tag{A1}$$

The last term in (A1) is the cash flow from the "incremental project"; j is a switching variable: $j = 1$ if $\theta(t) \geq (2\gamma + c_2)K + c_1$, and 0 otherwise.

By Ito's Lemma, $d(\Delta V) = \Delta V_\theta \, d\theta + (1/2)\Delta V_{\theta\theta}(d\theta)^2$. Substitute equation (6) for $d\theta$ and observe that the return (A1) is riskless. Setting that return equal to $r\Phi \, dt = (r\Delta V - r\Delta V_\theta\theta) \, dt$ yields the following equation for ΔV:

$$\tfrac{1}{2}\sigma^2\theta^2\Delta V_{\theta\theta} + (r - \delta)\theta\Delta V_\theta + j[\theta - (2\gamma + c_2)K - c_1] - r\Delta V = 0. \tag{A2}$$

The solution must satisfy the following boundary conditions:

$$\Delta V(K; 0) = 0$$

$$\lim_{\theta \to \infty} \Delta V(K; \theta) = \theta/\delta - [(2\gamma + c_2)K + c_1]/r$$

$$\lim_{\theta \to \infty} \Delta V_\theta(K; \theta) = 1/\delta,$$

and ΔV and ΔV_θ continuous at the switch point $\theta = (2\gamma + c_2)K + c_1$. The reader can verify that (9) is the solution to (A2) and its boundary conditions.

Equation (A2) can also be obtained by dynamic programming. Consider the optimal operating policy ($j = 0$ or 1) that maximizes the value Φ of the above portfolio. The Bellman equation is

$$r\Phi = \max_{j=(0,1)} \left\{ j[\theta - (2\gamma + c_2) - c_1] - \delta\theta\Delta V_\theta + \frac{1}{dt} E_t \, d\Phi \right\}, \tag{A3}$$

that is, the competitive return $r\Phi$ has two components, the cash flow given by the first two terms in the maximand, and the expected rate of capital gain. Expanding $d\Phi = d\Delta V - \Delta V_\theta \, d\theta$ and substituting into (A3) gives (A2).

Finally, note that ΔV must be the solution to (A2) and the boundary conditions even if the unit of capacity (the "incremental project") did not exist, and could not be included in a hedge portfolio. All that is required is an asset or portfolio of assets (x) that replicates the stochastic dynamics of θ. As Robert Merton (1977) has shown, one can replicate the value function with a portfolio consisting only of the asset x and riskfree bonds, and since the value of this portfolio will have the same dynamics as ΔV, the solution to (A2), ΔV must be the value function to avoid dominance.

Equation (10) for $\Delta F(K; \theta)$ can be derived in the same way. Using the same arguments as above, it is easily shown that ΔF must satisfy the equation

$$\tfrac{1}{2}\sigma^2\theta^2\Delta F_{\theta\theta} + (r - \delta)\theta\Delta F_\theta - r\Delta F = 0 \tag{A4}$$

with boundary conditions:

$$\Delta F(K; 0) = 0$$

$$\Delta F(K; \theta^*) = \Delta V(K; \theta^*) - k$$

$$\Delta F_\theta(K; \theta^*) = \Delta V_\theta(K; \theta^*),$$

where $\theta^* = \theta^*(K)$ is the exercise point, and $\Delta V(K; \theta^*) - k$ is the net gain from exercising. The reader can verify that equations (10) and (11) are the solution to (A4) and the associated boundary conditions.

The assumption that the firm can invest incrementally is extreme. At the opposite extreme, suppose that the firm can build only a single plant, and must decide when to build it and how large it should be. Now the firm has an option, worth $G(K; \theta)$, to build a plant of (arbitrary) size K. Once built, a plant of size K is worth $V(K; \theta) = \int_0^K \Delta V(v; \theta) \, dv$, where $\Delta V(v; \theta)$ is given by equation (9). It is easy to show that if K and θ are chosen optimally to maximize $G(K; \theta)$, then $G(K; \theta)$ must satisfy (A4), with ΔF replaced by G. However, the boundary conditions are now:

$$G(K; 0) = 0$$

$$V_K(K^*; \theta^*) - k = 0$$

$$G(K^*; \theta^*) = V(K^*; \theta^*) - kK^*$$

$$G_\theta(K^*; \theta^*) = V_\theta(K^*; \theta^*),$$

where θ^* is again the exercise point, K^* is the optimal plant size, that is, that K which maximizes $[V(K; \theta^*) - kK]$, and $V(K^*; \theta^*) - kK^*$ is the net gain from exercising. Using the first boundary condition, the solution is $G(K; \theta) = a\theta^{\beta_1}$, where β_1 is given under equation (9). The constant a and the critical values θ^* and K^* are determined from the remaining three boundary conditions.

Acknowledgments

I am grateful to the National Science Foundation for research support under grant no. SES-8318990, and to Giuseppe Bertola, Olivier Blanchard, Hua He, Saman

Majd, Robert McDonald, Julio Rotemberg, Lawrence Summers, and two anonymous referees for helpful discussions and comments. Any errors are mine.

Notes

1. Partial irreversibility also results from the "lemons'" problem. Office equipment, cars, trucks, and computers are not industry-specific, but have resale value well below their purchase cost, even if new.

2. Other examples are Ben Bernanke, 1983; Alex Cukierman, 1980; Carliss Baldwin, 1982; and Jeffrey Mackie-Mason, 1988. In the papers by Bernanke and Cukierman, uncertainty over future market conditions is reduced as time passes, so firms have an incentive to delay investing when markets are volatile (for example, during recessions). In the other papers cited above and in the model I present here, future market conditions are *always* uncertain. Access to the investment opportunity is then analogous to holding a call option on a dividend-paying stock; an expenditure should be made only when the value of the resulting project exceeds its cost by a positive amount, and increased uncertainty raises the incentive to delay the expenditure. Thus the results are similar to those in Bernanke and Cukierman, but for different reasons. Option value also appears in the natural resource context: if future values of wilderness areas and parking lots are uncertain, it may be better to wait before irreversibly paving a wilderness area. See, for example, Claude Henry, 1974.

3. The analysis in this chapter is closely related to that in Giuseppe Bertola, 1987, who independently developed a model of capacity choice similar to mine, using a different solution approach.

4. In Andrew Abel, 1983, and Richard Hartman, 1972, uncertainty over future prices leads to an increase in the firm's optimal capital stock when the production function is linear homogeneous. The reason is that the marginal revenue product of capital is a convex function of price, so that as in my model, a marginal unit of capital is worth more when price is stochastic. However, in Abel and Hartman investment is reversible, so the opportunity cost of investing is zero.

5. The importance of growth options and their implications for the firm's financial structure are discussed in Stewart Myers, 1977. A complete model of industry evolution would also describe the competitive processes through which firms obtain these options. Such a model is beyond the scope of this chapter.

6. Note that $\Delta V(K)$ is *not* the marginal value of capital, as the term is used in marginal q and related models of investment, such as the one in Abel and Olivier Blanchard, 1986. The marginal value of capital is the present value of the expected flow of profits throughout the future from whatever unit of capital is the marginal one, that is,

$$E \int_0^\infty [\partial \pi_t(K_t)/\partial K_t] e^{-\mu t} \, dt,$$

where μ is the discount rate. The marginal value of capital thus depends on the firm's capital stock, K_t, or its distribution, at every future t, and so its calculation can be quite difficult. Note how this differs from $\Delta V(K)$, the present value of the expected flow of incremental profits attributable to the $K + 1$st unit of capital, which is independent of how much capital the firm has in the future.

7. Analytic solutions can be obtained for any demand function linear in θ or a power function of θ; I use (5) for simplicity. Also, it is straightforward to also allow for uncertainty over future operating costs. The qualitative results would be the same.

8. Relaxing these assumptions makes no qualitative difference in the results. In fact, allowing for lead times in the construction and installation of new capacity magnifies the effects of uncertainty, as shown in Majd and Pindyck, 1987.

9. For an overview of contingent claims analysis and its applications, see John Cox and Mark Rubinstein, 1985; and Scott Mason and Robert Merton, 1985.

10. The connection between the contingent claims approach that I use and dynamic programming is examined in detail by Bertola, 1987.

11. If $\alpha > 0$, the optimal initial capacity would be smaller than this. The reason is that the cost of investing is fixed but the payoff is growing, so there is a benefit to delay, and $\Delta F(K) > 0$ for all K.

12. The valuation of a factory that can be temporarily shut down has been studied by Brennan and Schwartz, 1985; and McDonald and Siegel, 1985. Observe from equation (7) that the present value of an incremental profit at future time t is the value of a European call option, with expiration date t and exercise price $(2\gamma + c_2)K + c_1$, on a stock whose price is θ, paying a proportional dividend δ. This point was made by McDonald and Siegel, 1985. Thus $\Delta V(K)$, the value of our "equivalent factory," can be found by summing the values of these call options for every future t. However this does not readily yield a closed form solution, and I use an approach similar to that of Brennan and Schwartz, 1985.

13. With r and δ equal, $\alpha = 0$ if $\sigma = 0$ or if stochastic changes in θ are completely diversifiable (i.e., $\rho_{0m} = 0$ so $\mu = r$), but $\alpha > 0$ otherwise. Also, as can be seen from equation (9), $(\gamma = 0, c_1 = 1)$ and $(\gamma = .5, c_2 = 0)$ give the same marginal value of capital, and the same optimal behavior of the firm. In the first case the firm is a price-taker but earns inframarginal rent, and in the second case it has monopoly power.

14. As Zvi Bodie and Victor Rosansky, 1980, show, the standard deviations of annual changes in the prices of such commodities as oil, natural gas, copper, and aluminum are in the range of 20 to 50 percent. For manufactured goods these numbers are usually lower (for example, based on Producer Price Indices for 1948–97, they are 11 percent for cereal and bakery goods, 3 percent for electrical machinery, and 5 percent for photographic equipment). However, variation in the sales of a product for any one company will be much larger than variations in price for the entire industry. Thus a value of σ of 0.2 could be considered "typical" for simulation purposes.

15. $\Delta V(K)$ is a function of θ, and if $\delta = 0$, θ is expected to grow at the risk-adjusted market rate. Since the option to invest is perpetual, there would be no gain from installing capacity now rather than later.

16. If we allow for depreciation, investment will occur more often and even when demand is below historic highs, but it will still occur in spurts.

17. Robert Hall, 1986, reports that price significantly exceeds marginal cost for most two-digit industries, and finds no explanation for this disparity consistent with competition. Hall's test of marginal cost pricing is based on the relation between the marginal product of labor and the product wage. If firms set marginal operating cost equal to a (constant) proportion of price, his technique will apply, whatever the capital stock. But as shown in Section IV, there can be a wide range of prices for which the firm is capacity constrained, and the ratio of marginal operating cost to price will vary with price.

18. Also, the model examines the investment decisions of a single firm, and ignores entry and competition. If rival firms can appropriate the same investment opportunities, δ will be larger, which makes the value of the investment option smaller. Steven Lippman and R. Rumelt, 1985, examine the implications of irreversible investment for a competitive market equilibrium, and Avinash Dixit (1987a,b) studies the implications of sunk costs and stochastic prices for firms' entry and exit decisions, and for the reallocation of capital across sectors.

19. But they find the opposite true for firms in the oil industry, where there may be a tendency to overinvest in exploration and development.

References

Abel, Andrew B., "Optimal Investment under Uncertainty," *American Economic Review*, March 1983, *73*, 228–33.

———— and Blanchard, Olivier J., "The Present Value of Profits and Cyclical Movements in Investment," *Econometrica*, March 1986, *54*, 249–73.

Arrow, Kenneth J., "Optimal Capital Policy with Irreversible Investment," in James N. Wolfe, ed., *Value, Capital and Growth, Essays in Honor of Sir John Hicks*, Edinburgh: Edinburgh University Press, 1968.

Baldwin, Carliss Y., "Optimal Sequential Investment When Capital is Not Readily Reversible," *Journal of Finance*, June 1982, *37*, 763–82.

Bernanke, Ben S., "Irreversibility, Uncertainty, and Cyclical Investment," *Quarterly Journal of Economics*, February 1983, *98*, 85–106.

Bertola, Giuseppe, "Irreversible Investment," unpublished manuscript, MIT, November 1987.

Bodie, Zvi and Rosanski, Victor, "Risk and Return in Commodity Futures," *Financial Analysts Journal*, May 1980, *36*, 27–40.

Brennan, Michael J. and Schwartz, Eduardo S., "Evaluating Natural Resource Investments," *Journal of Business*, January 1985, *58*, 135–57.

Cox, John C. and Rubinstein, Mark, *Options Markets*, Englewood Cliffs: Prentice-Hall, 1985.

Gukierman, Alex, "The Effects of Uncertainty on Investment under Risk Neutrality with Endogenous Information," *Journal of Political Economy*, June 1980, *88*, 462–75.

Dixit, Avinash, (1987a) "Entry and Exit Decisions of Firms Under Fluctuating Real Exchange Rates," unpublished manuscript, September 1987.

———, (1987b) "Intersectoral Capital Reallocation Under Price Uncertainty," unpublished manuscript, November 1987.

Hall, Robert E., "The Relation Between Price and Marginal Cost in U.S. Industry," NBER Working Paper No. 1785, January 1986.

Hartman, Richard, "The Effects of Price and Cost Uncertainty on Investment," *Journal of Economic Theory*, October 1972, *5*, 258–66.

Henry, Claude, "Investment Decisions Under Uncertainty: 'The Irreversibility Effect,'" *American Economic Review*, December 1974, *64*, 1006–12.

Kester, W. Carl, "Today's Options for Tomorrow's Growth," *Harvard Business Review*, March/April 1984, 153–60.

Lippman, Steven A. and Rumelt, R. P., "Industry-Specific Capital and Uncertainty," unpublished manuscript, September 1985.

Mackie-Mason, Jeffrey K., "Nonlinear Taxation of Risky Assets and Investment, with Application to Mining," NBER Working Paper No. 2631, June 1988.

Majd, Saman and Pindyck, Robert S., "Time to Build, Option Value, and Investment Decisions," *Journal of Financial Economics*, March 1987, *18*, 7–27.

Mason, Scott and Merton, Robert C., "The Role of Contingent Claims Analysis in Corporate Finance," in E. Altman and M. Subrahmanyam, eds., *Recent Advances in Corporate Finance*, Homewood: Richard D. Irwin, 1985.

McConnell, John J. and Muscarella, Chris J., "Corporate Capital Expenditure Decisions and the Market Value of the Firm," *Journal of Financial Economics*, September 1985, *14*, 399–422.

McDonald, Robert and Siegel, Daniel R., "Investment and the Valuation of Firms When There Is an Option to Shut Down," *International Economic Review*, June 1985, *26*, 331–49.

——— and ———, "The Value of Waiting to Invest," *Quarterly Journal of Economics*, November 1986, *101*, 707–28.

Merton, Robert C., "On the Pricing of Contingent Claims and the Modigliani-Miller Theorem," *Journal of Financial Economics*, November 1977, *5*, 241–49.

Myers, Stewart C., "Determinants of Corporate Borrowing," *Journal of Financial Economics*, November 1977, *5*, 147–75.

16 Evaluating Natural Resource Investments

Michael J. Brennan and Eduardo S. Schwartz

Notwithstanding impressive advances in the theory of finance over the past 2 decades, practical procedures for capital budgeting have evolved only slowly. The standard technique, which has remained unchanged in essentials since it was originally proposed (see Dean 1951; Bierman and Smidt 1960), derives from a simple adaptation of the Fisher (1907) model of valuation under certainty: under this technique, expected cash flows from an investment project are discounted at a rate deemed appropriate to their risk, and the resulting present value is compared with the cost of the project. This standard textbook technique reflects modern theoretical developments only insofar as estimates of the discount rate may be obtained from crude application of single period asset pricing theory (but see Brennan 1973; Bogue and Roll 1974; Turnbull 1977; Constantinides 1978).

The inadequacy of this approach to capital budgeting is widely acknowledged, although not widely discussed. Its obvious deficiency is its total neglect of the stochastic nature of output prices and of possible managerial responses to price variations. While price uncertainty is unimportant in applications for which the relevant prices are reasonably predictable, it is of paramount importance in many natural resource industries, where price swings of 25%–40% per year are not uncommon.[1] Under such conditions the practice of replacing distributions of future prices by their expected values is likely to cause errors in the calculation both of expected cash flows and of appropriate discount rates and thereby to lead to suboptimal investment decisions.

The model for the evaluation of investment projects presented in this paper treats output prices as stochastic. While this makes it particularly suitable for analyzing natural resource investment projects, where uncertain prices are a particular concern, the model may be applied in other contexts also. The model also takes explicit account of managerial control over the output rate, which is assumed to be variable in response to the output price; moreover, the possibility that a project may be closed down or even abandoned if output prices fall far enough is also considered. Variation in risk and the discount rate due both to depletion of the resource and to stochastic variation in the output price are explicitly taken into account in deriving the equilibrium condition underlying the valuation model.

Two essentially distinct approaches may be taken to the general problem of valuing the uncertain cash flow stream generated by an investment project. First, the market equilibrium approach requires both complete specification of the stochastic properties of the cash flow stream and an underlying model of capital equilibrium whose parameters are known.[2] A general limitation of this approach is that it is difficult to devise adequately powerful tests of the model of market equilibrium and to obtain refined estimates of the model parameters. In the present instance, the market equilibrium approach is further hampered by the difficulty of determining the stochastic properties of the cash flow stream that depend on the stochastic process of the output price: as we have already remarked, it is often very difficult to estimate the expected rate of change in commodity prices. Therefore in this paper we resort to a second approach, which yields the value of one security relative to the value of a portfolio of other traded securities.

Our approach is to find a self-financing portfolio whose cash flows replicate those which are to be valued.[3] The present value of the cash flow stream is then equal to the current value of this replicating portfolio. When a replicating self-financing portfolio can be constructed, our approach offers several advantages over the market equilibrium approach; not only does it obviate the need for a discount rate derived from an inadequately supported model of market equilibrium but, most important in the current context, it eliminates the need for estimates of the expected rate of change of the underlying cash flow and therefore of the output price.

Construction of the requisite replicating self-financing portfolio rests on the assumption that the convenience yield on the output commodity can be written as a function of the output price alone and that the interest rate is nonstochastic. These assumptions suffice to yield a deterministic relation between the spot and futures price of the commodity, and the cash flows from the project can then be replicated by a self-financing portfolio of riskless bills and futures contracts.

Specific limitations of the valuation model include the assumptions that the resource to be exploited is homogeneous and of a known amount, that costs are known, and that interest rates are nonstochastic. Any one of these assumptions may be relaxed at the expense of adding one further dimension to the state space on which the model is defined: as a practical matter it would be difficult to obtain tractable results if more than one of these assumptions were relaxed at a time. While the model as presented here presupposes the existence of a futures market in the output commodity, it would be straightforward to derive an analogous model in a general equilibrium context similar to that employed by Brennan and Schwartz (1982a, 1982b).

To allow for dependence of the output rate on the stochastic output price the capital budgeting decision is modeled as a problem of stochastic optimal control. Stochastic optimal control theory has been applied to the investment decision in a general context by Constantinides (1978), and in the specific context of a regulated public utility by Brennan and Schwartz (1982a, 1982b). Dothan and Williams (1980) have also analyzed the capital-budgeting decision within a similar framework. Pindyck (1980), like us, applies stochastic optimal control to the problem of the optimal exploitation of an exhaustible resource under uncertainty. In some respects Pindyck's analysis is more general than ours: in particular, he allows the level of reserves of the resource to vary stochastically and to be influenced by exploration activities. On the other hand, by confining his attention to risk-neutral firms he neglects the issues of risk and valuation that are the focus of the capital-budgeting decision and of this chapter. Other writers who have recognized the importance of the option whether or not to exploit a natural resource, which is inherent in the ownership of the resource, include Tourinho (1979); Brock, Rothschild, and Stiglitz (1982); and Paddock, Siegel, and Smith (1982). These writers have not however analyzed the present value of the decision to exploit a given resource or the optimal operating policy for a given facility, as we do, and Brock et al. do not exploit the arbitrage implications of a replicating self-financing portfolio.

Miller and Upton (1985) develop and test empirically a model for the valuation of natural resources based on the Hotelling model. Although it is close in spirit to our model, in that the spot price of the commodity is a sufficient statistic for the value of the mine, unlike ours their model assumes no upper limit on the output rate and ignores the possibility of closing and reopening the mine in response to current market conditions. As they point out this may be a good approximation when output prices exceed extraction costs by a wide margin, just as the value of a stock option approaches its intrinsic value when it is deep in the money.

The general type of model presented here lends itself to use in a number of related contexts—most obviously, to corporations considering when, whether, and how, to develop a given resource; to financial analysts concerned with the valuation of such corporations; and to policymakers concerned with the social costs of layoffs in cyclical industries and with policies to avert them. The model is well suited to analysis of the effects of alternative taxation, royalty, and subsidy policies on investment, employment, and unemployment in the natural resource sector.

Section I develops a general model for valuing the cash flows from a natural resource investment. A specialized version of the general model is presented in Section II. Under the assumption of an inexhaustible resource the model allows for only a single feasible operating rate when the project is operating but includes the possibility of costs of closing and reopening the project. Section III discusses a numerical example based on the general model. Section IV considers the problem, previously raised by Tourinho (1979), of the optimal timing of natural resource investments. Section V discusses briefly the application of the model to the analysis of fixed price long term purchase contracts for natural resources.

I The General Valuation Model

The first step in analyzing an investment project is to determine the present value of the future cash flows it will generate and to compare this present value with the required investment. If the present value exceeds the investment a further decision is whether to proceed with the project immediately or to wait. We shall postpone consideration of this second, dynamic aspect of the capital-budgeting decision until Section III, and in this and the following section will restrict our attention to the problem of determining the present value of the cash flows from a project. In this section we develop a general model, a specialization of which is considered in Section II.

To focus discussion we will suppose that the project under consideration is a mine that will produce a single homogeneous commodity, whose spot price, S, is determined competitively and is assumed to follow the exogenously given continuous stochastic process

$$\frac{dS}{S} = \mu \, dt + \sigma \, dz, \tag{1}$$

where dz is the increment to a standard Gauss-Wiener process; σ, the instantaneous standard deviation of the spot price, is assumed to be known; and μ, the local trend in the price, may be stochastic.

As a preliminary to developing the valuation model it will prove useful to consider the relation between spot and futures prices and the convenience yield on the commodity. The convenience yield is the flow of services that accrues to an owner of the physical commodity but not to the owner of a contract for future delivery of the commodity (see Kaldor 1939; Working 1948; Brennan 1958; Telser 1958). Most obviously, the owner of the physical commodity is able to choose where it will be stored and when to liquidate the inventory. Recognizing the time lost and the costs incurred in transporting a commodity from one location to another, the convenience yield may be thought of as the value of being able to profit from temporary local shortages of the commodity through ownership of the physical commodity. The profit may arise either from local price variations or from the ability to maintain a production process as a result of ownership of an inventory of raw material.[4]

The convenience yield will depend on the identity of the individual holding the inventory and in equilibrium inventories will be held by individuals for whom the marginal convenience yield net of any physical storage costs is highest. We assume that a positive amount of the commodity is always held in inventory, and note that competition among potential storers will ensure that the net convenience yield of the marginal unit of inventory will be the same across all individuals who hold positive inventories. This marginal (net) convenience yield can be expected to be inversely proportional to the amount of the commodity held in inventory. Moreover, when stocks of the physical commodity are high, not only will the marginal convenience yield tend to be low, but so also will be the spot price S, and conversely when stocks of the physical commodity are low. We make the simplifying assumption that the marginal net convenience yield of the commodity can be written as a function of the current spot price and time, $C(S, t)$. Detailed modeling of the behavior of the convenience yield is beyond the scope of this paper, and in the interest of tractability we shall sometimes assume simply that the convenience yield is proportional to the current spot price.

Our assumption that the convenience yield is a function only of the current spot price, together with the further assumption which we maintain throughout the paper, that the interest rate is a constant, ρ, suffices to yield a determinate relation between the spot and futures prices of the commodity. Thus let $F(S, \tau)$ represent the futures price at time t for delivery of one unit of the commodity at time T where $\tau = T - t$. The instantaneous change in the futures prices is given from Ito's lemma by

$$dF = (-F_\tau + \tfrac{1}{2}F_{SS}\sigma^2 S^2)\, dt + F_S\, dS. \tag{2}$$

Then consider the instantaneous rate of return earned by an individual who purchases one unit of the commodity and goes short $(F_S)^{-1}$ futures contracts. Since entering the futures contract involves no receipt or outlay of funds, his instantaneous return per dollar of investment including the marginal net convenience yield, using (2), is

$$\frac{dS}{S} + \frac{C(S)\, dt}{S} - (SF_S)^{-1}\, dF = (SF_S)^{-1}[F_S C(S) - \tfrac{1}{2}F_{SS}\sigma^2 S^2 + F_\tau]\, dt. \tag{3}$$

Since this return is nonstochastic and since $C(S)$ is defined as the (net) convenience yield of the marginal unit of inventory, it follows that the return must be equal to the riskless return $\rho\, dt$. Setting the right hand side of (3) equal to $\rho\, dt$, we obtain the partial differential equation

$$\tfrac{1}{2}F_{SS}\sigma^2 S^2 + F_S(\rho S - C) - F_\tau = 0. \tag{4}$$

Thus the futures price is given by the solution to (4) subject to the boundary condition

$$F(S, 0) = S. \tag{5}$$

This establishes that the futures price is a function of the current spot price and the time to maturity. Moreover, the parameters of the convenience yield function may be estimated directly from the relation between spot and futures prices. If the convenience yield is proportional to the spot price,

$$C(S, t) = \sigma S, \tag{6}$$

then following Ross (1978) the futures price is given by

$$F(S, \tau) = S e^{(\rho - \sigma)\tau}, \tag{7}$$

independent of the stochastic process of the spot price. For more general specifications of the convenience yield it is necessary to solve (4) and (5) directly.

Finally, using (4) in expression (2), the instantaneous change in the futures price may be expressed in terms of the convenience yield and the instantaneous change in the spot price as

$$dF = F_S[S(\mu - \rho) + C]\,dt + F_S S \sigma\,dz. \tag{8}$$

We are now in a position to derive the partial differential equation that must be satisfied by the value of the mine and to characterize the optimal output policy of the mine.

The output rate of the mine, q, is assumed to be costlessly variable between the upper and lower bounds $\bar{q}$ and $\underline{q}$.[5] The output rate can be reduced below $\underline{q}$ only by closing the mine, and it is costly both to close the mine and to open it again. For this reason the value of the mine will depend on whether it is currently open or closed. The value of the mine will also depend on the current commodity price, S; the physical inventory in the mine, Q; calendar time, t; and the mine operating policy, ϕ. We write the value of the mine as

$$H \equiv H(S, Q, t; j, \phi). \tag{9}$$

The indicator variable j takes the value one if the mine is open and zero if it is closed. The operating policy is described by the function determining the output rate when the mine is open $q(S, Q, t)$, and three critical commodity output prices: $S_1(Q, t)$ is the output price at which the mine is closed down or abandoned if it was previously open; $S_2(Q, t)$ is the price at which the mine is opened up if it was previously closed; $S_0(Q, t)$ is the price at which the mine is abandoned if it is already closed. The distinction between closure and abandonment is that a closed mine incurs fixed maintenance costs but may be opened up again. An abandoned mine incurs no costs but is assumed to be permanently abandoned. It is assumed that abandonment involves no costs.

Applying Ito's lemma to (9), the instantaneous change in the value of the mine is given by

$$dH = H_S\, dS + H_Q\, dQ + H_t\, dt + \tfrac{1}{2} H_{SS}(dS)^2, \tag{10}$$

where the instantaneous change in the mine inventory is determined by the output rate

$$dQ = -q\, dt. \tag{11}$$

The after-tax cash flow, or continuous dividend rate, from the mine is

$$q(S - A) - M(1 - j) - \lambda_j H - T, \tag{12}$$

where

$A(q, Q, t)$ is the average cash cost rate of producing at the rate q at time t when the mine inventory is Q;

$M(t)$ is the after-tax fixed-cost rate of maintaining the mine at time t when it is closed;

$\lambda_j\ (j = 0, 1)$ is proportional rate of tax on the value of the mine when it is closed and open; and

$T(q, Q, S, t)$ is the total income tax and royalties levied on the mine when it is operating. While alternative forms are possible we shall assume that the tax function is

$$T(q, Q, S, t) = t_1 q S + \max\{t_2 q[S(1 - t_1) - A], 0\}, \tag{13}$$

where

t_1 is the royalty rate and t_2 is the income tax rate.[6]

The parameters λ_0 and λ_1 are interpreted most simply as property tax rates. However an alternative interpretation may be apposite in some contexts: they may represent the intensities of Poisson processes governing the event of uncompensated expropriation of the owners of the mine. Then the expected loss rate from expropriation is $\lambda_j H$ and expression (12) represents the cash flow net of the expected cost of expropriation. Under this interpretation the arbitrage strategy outlined below is not entirely risk free; however, we shall assume that there is no risk premium associated with the possibility of expropriation.

To derive the differential equation governing the value of the mine under the output policy ϕ consider the return to a portfolio consisting of a long position in the mine and a short position in (H_S/F_S) futures contracts. The return on the mine is given by (10)–(12) and the change in the futures price is given by (8). Combining these and using (1), the return on this portfolio is

$$\tfrac{1}{2}\sigma^2 S^2 H_{SS} - qH_Q + H_t + q(S - A) - M(1 - j) - T - \lambda_j H + (\rho S - C)H_s. \tag{14}$$

Ignoring the possibility of expropriation, this return is nonstochastic, and to avoid riskless arbitrage opportunities it must be equal to the riskless return on the value of the investment. Setting expression (14) equal to the riskless return ρH, the value of the mine must satisfy the partial differential equation

$$\tfrac{1}{2}\sigma^2 S^2 H_{SS} + (\rho S - C)H_S - qH_Q + H_t + q(S - A) - M(1 - j) - T - (\rho + \lambda_j)H = 0$$

$$(j = 0, 1). \tag{15}$$

The mine value satisfies (15) for any operating policy $\phi \equiv \{q, S_0, S_1, S_2\}$. Under the value maximizing operating policy $\phi^* = \{q^*, S_0^*, S_1^*, S_2^*\}$, the values of the mine when open, $V(S, Q, t)$, and when closed, $W(S, Q, t)$ are given by

$$V(S, Q, t) \equiv \max_{\phi} H(S, Q, t; 1, \phi) \tag{16}$$

$$W(S, Q, t) \equiv \max_{\phi} H(S, Q, t; 0, \phi). \tag{17}$$

The value-maximizing output and the value of the mine under the value-maximizing policy satisfy the two equations

$$\max_{q \in (\underline{q}, \bar{q})} \left[\tfrac{1}{2}\sigma^2 S^2 V_{SS} + (\rho S - C)V_S - qV_Q + V_t + q(S - A) - T - (\rho + \lambda_1)V \right] = 0, \tag{18}$$

$$\tfrac{1}{2}\sigma^2 S^2 W_{SS} + (\rho S - C)W_S + W_t - M - (\rho + \lambda_0)W = 0 \tag{19}$$

(see Merton 1971, theorem 1; Fleming and Rishel 1975, chap. 6; Cox, Ingersoll, and Ross 1978, lemma 1).

Since the policies regarding opening, closing, and abandoning the mine are known to investors, we have

$$W(S_0^*, Q, t) = 0 \tag{20}$$

$$V(S_1^*, Q, t) = \max[W(S_1^*, Q, t) - K_1(Q, t), 0] \tag{21}$$

$$W(S_2^*, Q, t) = V(S_2^*, Q, t) - K_2(Q, t) \tag{22}$$

where $K_1(\cdot)$ and $K_2(\cdot)$ are the cost of closing and opening the mine respectively. Assuming that the value of an exhausted mine is zero we also have the boundary condition

$$W(S,0,t) = V(S,0,t) = 0. \tag{23}$$

Finally, since S_0^*, S_1^*, S_2^* are chosen to maximize the value of the mine it follows from the Merton-Samuelson high-contact condition (Samuelson 1965; Merton 1973) that

$$W_S(S_0^*, Q, t) = 0; \tag{24}$$

$$V_S(S_1^*, Q, t) = \begin{cases} W_S(S_1^*, Q, t) & \text{if } W(S_1^*, Q, t) - K_1(Q, t) \geq 0, \\ 0 & \text{if } W(S_1^*, Q, t) - K_1(Q, t) < 0; \end{cases} \tag{25}$$

$$PW_S(S_2^*, Q, t) = V_S(S_2^*, Q, t). \tag{26}$$

The value of the mine depends on calendar time only because the costs A, M, K_1, and K_2 and the convenience yield C depend on time. If there is a constant rate of inflation π in all of these and if $C(S, t)$ may be written as κS, then equations (18)–(26) may be simplified as follows:

Define the deflated variables

$$a(q, Q) = A(q, Q, t)e^{-\pi t},$$
$$f = M(t)e^{-\pi t},$$
$$k_1(Q) = K_1(Q, t)e^{-\pi t},\ k_2(Q) = K_2(Q, t)e^{-\pi t},$$
$$s = Se^{-\pi t},$$
$$v(s, Q) = V(S, Q, t)e^{-\pi t},$$
$$w(s, Q) = W(S, Q, t)e^{-\pi t}.$$

Then it may be verified that the deflated value of the mine satisfies

$$\max_{q \in (\underline{q}, \bar{q})} \left[\tfrac{1}{2}\sigma^2 s^2 v_{ss} + (r - \kappa)sv_s - qv_Q + q(s - a) - \tau - (r + \lambda_1)v \right] = 0, \tag{27}$$

$$\tfrac{1}{2}\sigma^2 s^2 w_{ss} + (r - \kappa)sw_s - f - (r + \lambda_0)w = 0, \tag{28}$$

where

$r = \rho - \pi$ is the real interest rate,

$$\tau = t_1 qs + \max\{t_2 q[s(1 - t_1) - a], 0\}; \tag{29}$$

$$w(s_0^*, Q) = 0, \tag{30}$$

$$v(s_1^*, Q) = \max[w(s_1^*, Q) - k_1(Q), 0]; \tag{31}$$

$$w(s_2^*, Q) = v(s_2^*, Q) - k_2(Q); \tag{32}$$

$$w(s, 0) = v(s, 0) = 0; \tag{33}$$

$$w_s(s_0^*, Q) = 0; \tag{34}$$

$$v_s(s_1^*, Q) = \begin{cases} w_s(s_1^*, Q) & \text{if } w(s_1^*, Q, t) - k_1(Q, t) \geq 0, \\ 0 & \text{if } w(s_1^*, Q, t) - k_1(Q, t) < 0; \end{cases} \tag{35}$$

$$w_s(s_2^*, Q) - v_s(s_2^*, Q). \tag{36}$$

Equations (27)–(36) constitute the general model for the value of a mine. They suffice to determine not only the (deflated) value of the mine when open and closed, but also the optimal policies for opening, closing, and abandoning the mine and for setting the output rates. In general there exists no analytic solution to the valuation model, though it is straightforward to solve it numerically. In the next section we present a simplified version of the model.

II   The Infinite Resource Case

To obtain a model that is analytically tractable we assume that the physical inventory of the commodity in the mine, Q, is infinite. This infinite resource assumption enables us to replace the partial differential equations (27) and (28) for the value of the mine with ordinary differential equations, since the mine inventory, Q, is no longer a relevant state variable. To facilitate the analysis further we assume that the tax system allows for full loss offset so that (29) becomes

$$\tau(q, s) = t_1 q s + t_2 q[s(1 - t_1) - a]. \tag{29'}$$

Finally, we assume that the mine has only two possible operating rates, q^* when it is open, and zero when it is closed; furthermore, because it is costly to open or close the mine, costs must be incurred in moving from one output rate to the other.[7]

Under the foregoing assumptions the (deflated) value of the mine when it is open and operating at the rate q^* satisfies the ordinary differential equation

$$\tfrac{1}{2}\sigma^2 s^2 v_{ss} + (r - \kappa)s v_s + ms - n - (r + \lambda)v = 0, \tag{37}$$

where $m = q^*(1 - t_1)(1 - t_2)$, and $n = q^* a(1 - t_2)$.

If we assume that f, the periodic maintenance cost for a closed mine, is equal to zero, then the value of the mine when closed satisfies the corresponding differential equation

$$\tfrac{1}{2}\sigma^2 s^2 w_{ss} + (r - \kappa)sw_s - (r + \lambda)w = 0. \tag{38}$$

The boundary conditions are obtained by ignoring Q in (31), (32), (35), and (36) and by setting $w(0) = 0$.[8]

The complete solutions to equations (37) and (38) are

$$w(s) = \beta_1 s^{\gamma_1} + \beta_2 s^{\gamma_2}, \tag{39}$$

$$v(s) = \beta_3 s^{\gamma_1} + \beta_4 s^{\gamma_2} + \frac{ms}{\lambda + \kappa} - \frac{n}{r + \lambda}, \tag{40}$$

where the β's are constants to be determined by the boundary conditions and

$$\gamma_1 = \alpha_1 + \alpha_2, \quad \gamma_2 = \alpha_1 - \alpha_2,$$

$$\alpha_1 = \frac{1}{2} - \frac{r - \kappa}{\sigma^2}, \quad \alpha_2 = \left[\alpha_1^2 + \frac{2(r + \lambda)}{\sigma^2}\right]^{1/2}.$$

If we assume that $(r + \lambda) > 0$,[9] then $\beta_2 = 0$ since γ_2 is negative and $w(s)$ must remain finite as s approaches zero. Similarly, since $\gamma_1 > 1$, $\beta_3 = 0$ if we impose the requirement that v/s remain finite as $s \to \infty$. Thus the value of the mine when closed is given by $w(s) = \beta_1 s^{\gamma_1}$, and the value when open is

$$v(s) = \beta_4 s^{\gamma_2} + \frac{ms}{\lambda + \kappa} - \frac{n}{r + \lambda}. \tag{41}$$

If the possibility of closing the mine when output prices are low is ignored, the value of the mine is given by the last two terms in (41); thus the first term represents the value of the closure option.

The remaining constants β_1 and β_4, as well as the optimal policy for closing and opening the mine represented by the output prices s_1^* and s_2^*, are determined by conditions (31), (32), (35), and (36), which imply that

$$\beta_1 = \frac{ds_2^*(\gamma_2 - 1) + b\gamma_2}{(\gamma_2 - \gamma_1)s_2^{*\gamma_1}}, \quad \beta_4 = \frac{ds_2^*(\gamma_1 - 1) + b\gamma_1}{(\gamma_2 - \gamma_1)s_1^{*\gamma_2}},$$

$$s_2^* = \gamma_2(e - bx^{\gamma_1})/(x^{\gamma_1} - x)d(\gamma_2 - 1),$$

$$\frac{s_1^*}{s_2^*} = x,$$

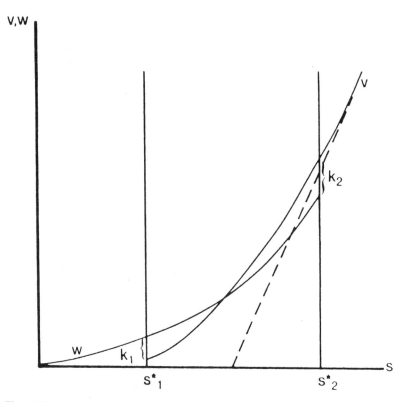

Figure 16.1
Mine value when open (v) and closed (w) as a function of the commodity price (s); k_1: cost of closing mine; k_2: cost of opening mine

where $e = k_1 - n/(r + \lambda)$, $b = -k_2 - n/(r + \lambda)$, $d = m/(\lambda + \kappa)$, and x, the ratio of the commodity prices at which the mine is closed and opened, is the solution to the nonlinear equation

$$\frac{(x^{\gamma_2} - x)(\gamma_1 - 1)}{\gamma_1(e - bx^{\gamma_2})} = \frac{(x^{\gamma_1} - x)(\gamma_2 - 1)}{\gamma_2(e - bx^{\gamma_1})}. \tag{42}$$

The solution is illustrated in figure 16.1. In this figure the dotted line represents the present value of the cash flows from the mine assuming that it can never be shut down; this is obtained by setting $\beta_4 = 0$ in equation (42). Since $\gamma_2 < 0$, the value of the closure option diminishes and approaches zero for high output prices. For very low output prices the mine is worth more when it is closed than when it is open and making losses because of the cost of closure. However, for higher output prices the

Table 16.1
Data for a hypothetical copper mine

Mine:	Copper:
Output rate (q^*): 10 million pounds/year	Convenience yield (κ): 1%/year
Inventory (Q): 150 million pounds	Price variance (σ^2): 8%/year
Initial average cost of production $a(q^*, Q)$: \$0.50/pound	Taxes:
Initial cost of opening and closing (k_1, k_2): \$200,000	Real estate (λ_1, λ_2): 2%/year
Initial maintenance costs (f): \$500,000/year	Income (t_2): 50%
Cost inflation rate (π): 8%/year	Royalty (t_1): 0%
	Interest rate (ρ): 10%/year

mine is worth more when open, and at the commodity price s_2^* it is worth just enough more to warrant the outlay k_2 to open it. It is clear from the figure and can be demonstrated analytically that as the costs of opening and closing the mine approach zero, s_1^* and s_2^* approach the same value and the mine value schedule becomes a single curve. On the other hand, as the cost of mine closure becomes very large the closure option becomes worthless, and in the limit the value schedule for the open mine approaches the dotted line. Changes in the cost of mine closure, brought about for example by government regulation, will alter the optimal policy for closing the mine, s_1^*: however, they will also affect the original decision to invest in the mine by changing the present value of the future cash flows. Such effects, or those induced by changes in the tax regime, are readily analyzed in the context of this simplified model or the general model of the previous section.

III An Example

To illustrate the nature of our solution we consider a mine example based on the stylized facts for copper. In this example there is a finite mine inventory so that the stochastic optimal control problem represented by equations (27)–(36) must be solved numerically. To simplify matters somewhat we assume that there is a single feasible operating rate when the mine is open. The mine may be closed down or opened at a cost of \$200,000 in current prices; it may also be abandoned. Other data required for this example are contained in table 16.1.[10]

Given an inventory equal to 15 years production, we find that the cost of production is 50 cents per pound, but it is not optimal to incur the cost of opening the mine until the price of copper rises to 76 cents. On the other hand, if the mine is already open and operating, it is not optimal to close it down until the copper price drops to 44 cents. Finally, the mine should be abandoned if the price drops below 20 cents. Obviously these critical prices depend on the assumed costs of opening, closing, and

Table 16.2
Value of copper mine for different copper prices

Copper price ($/pound) (1)	Mine value ($ million)		Value of fixed-output-rate mine ($ million) (4)	Value of closure option ($ million) (5)	Risk (6)	Value of mine under certainty, $\sigma^2 = 0$ ($ million) (7)
	Open (2)	Closed (3)				
.30	(1.25)*	1.45	.38	1.07		0
.40	(4.15)*	4.35	3.12	1.23		0
.50	7.95	8.11	7.22	.89	.75	1.85†
.60	12.52	12.49	12.01	.51	.66	7.84†
.70	17.56	17.38	17.19	.37	.59	13.87†
.80	22.88	(22.68)†	22.61	.27	.54	19.91†
.90	28.38	(28.18)†	28.18	.20	.50	25.94†
1.00	34.01	(33.81)†	33.85	.16	.47	31.98†

* Optimal to close mine
† Optimal to open mine

maintaining the mine: they also depend upon the remaining inventory in the mine. The greater the inventory in the mine the greater is the incentive to extract the copper immediately, since the opportunity cost of immediate extraction falls as the expected life of the mine increases. Thus the greater the inventory the lower is the price at which the mine is opened and closed and, since the mine value is a nondecreasing function of the inventory, the lower the price at which it is abandoned.

Table 16.2 summarizes the results when the mine has a 15-year inventory. Columns 1 and 3 give the present values of the future cash flows from the mine, assuming that it is open and closed, respectively, for different copper prices. These are the relevant values for the investment decision. Column 4 gives the value of the mine assuming that it cannot be closed down but must be operated at the rate of 10 million pounds per year until the inventory is exhausted in 15 years. The difference between column 4 and the greater of the values shown in columns 2 and 3 represents the value of the option to close down or abandon the mine if the price of copper falls far enough. The value of this closure option is shown in column 5: it amounts to 12% of the value of the fixed-output-rate mine when the copper price is equal to the variable cost of 50 cents per pound; of course this would represent a much higher proportion of the *net* present value of an investment in the mine.

Column 6 of the table reports the instantaneous risk of the mine at different copper prices. This is the instantaneous standard deviation of the mine value, defined as $(v_s/v)\sigma s$ when the mine is open and $(w_s/w)\sigma s$ when the mine is closed. As we would expect, the risk of the mine decreases as the copper price and hence the operating margin increases. Since the copper price is stochastic, so also is the risk of the mine and the instantaneous rate of return required by investors, pointing to the dangers of assuming a single discount rate in a present value analysis.

Ownership of a mine that is not currently operating involves three distinct types of decision possibilities or options: first, the decision to begin operations; second, the decision to close the mine when it is currently operating (and possibly to reopen it later), which we have referred to as the closure option; and third, the decision to abandon the mine early, before the inventory is exhausted.

The decision to begin operations depends in our model on the current spot price of the commodity and the mine inventory. When there is no uncertainty, so that the time path of the commodity price is deterministic, the optimal decision rule for beginning operations can be expressed in calendar time (and the mine inventory). This certainty case, which has been analyzed extensively under the rubric of the "timing option" (see, e.g., Solow 1974), corresponds to column 7, of table 2: this gives the value of the closed mine under the assumption of certainty, which may be contrasted with the uncertainty case of column 3. For our parameter values it is never optimal under certainty to close or abandon the mine, once it is open, before the inventory is exhausted,[11] so that the closure and early abandonment options are worthless. When the commodity price is in the neighborhood of the production costs the elimination of uncertainty reduces the value of the mine dramatically. Of course this depends on the particular values of the convenience yield and other parameters.

IV   The Investment Decision

Thus far, only the valuation of the cash flows from an investment project has been considered. The investment decision itself requires that a comparison be made between the present value of the project cash flows and the initial investment needed for the project. Continuing with the example of a mine, $V(S, Q^*, t)$ represents the (nominal) value at time t of a completed operating mine with inventory Q^* when the current output price is S; $V(\cdot)$ is equal to the present value of the cash flows that will be realized from the mine under the optimal operating policy. Similarly, let $I(S, Q^*, t)$ represent the investment required to construct an operating mine with inventory Q^* on a particular property: the amount of this initial investment may obviously depend on calendar time and upon the size of the mine as represented by Q^*, and S is included as an argument for the sake of generality. Then, assuming that construction lags can be neglected, the net present value (NPV) at time t of constructing the mine immediately is given by

$$\text{NPV}(S, Q^*, t) = V(S, Q^*, t) - I(S, Q^*, t). \tag{43}$$

However, once the possibility of postponing an investment decision is recognized, it is clear that it is not in general optimal to proceed with construction simply because the net present value of construction is positive: there is a "timing option" and it may pay to wait in the expectation that the net present value of construction will increase. This dynamic aspect of the investment decision is closely related to the problem of determining the optimal strategy for exercising an option on a share of common stock: the right to make the investment decision and to appropriate the resulting net present value is the ownership right in the undeveloped mine property, and the value of this ownership right corresponds to the value of the stock option.

Define $X(S, Q^*, t)$ as the value of the ownership right to an undeveloped mine with inventory Q^* at time t when the current output price is S. The stochastic process for $X(\cdot)$ is obtained from Ito's lemma, using the assumption about the stochastic process for S embodied in expression (1). Then the arbitrage argument used to derive the differential equation (15) for the value of a completed mine may be repeated to show that $X(\cdot)$ must satisfy the partial differential equation

$$\tfrac{1}{2}\sigma^2 S^2 X_{ss} + (\rho S - C)X_s + X_t - (\rho + \lambda)X = 0, \tag{44}$$

where, as before, λ represents either the rate of tax on the value of the property or the intensity of a Poisson process governing the event of expropriation.[12]

Since the origin is an absorbing state for the commodity price, S, we have the boundary condition

$$X(0, Q^*, t) = 0, \tag{45}$$

and if the ownership rights are in the form of a lease which expires at time T, then

$$X(S, Q^*, T) = 0. \tag{46}$$

Assuming that the size of the mine inventory, Q^*, is predetermined by technical and geological factors, the optimal strategy for investment can be characterized in terms of a time dependent schedule of output prices $S^I(t)$ such that

$$X(S^I, Q^*, t) = V(S^I, Q^*, t) - I(S^I, Q^*, t), \tag{47}$$

$$X_S(S^I, Q^*, t) = V_S(S^I, Q^*, t) - I_S(S^I, Q^*, t). \tag{48}$$

Equation (47) states simply that the value of the property is equal to the net present value of the investment at the time it is made. Equation (48) is the Merton-Samuelson high-contact or envelope condition for a maximizing choice of S^I.

If the amount of the accessible inventory in the mine, Q^*, depends on the amount of the initial investment instead of being determined exogenously, then we have the additional value-maximizing condition to determine the size of the initial mine inventory, Q^*:

$$V_Q(S^I, Q^*, t) = I_Q(S^I, Q^*, t). \tag{49}$$

Thus the optimal investment strategy is obtained by solving the partial differential equation (44) for the value of the ownership right, subject to boundary conditions (45)–(49). The optimal time to invest is determined by the series of critical output prices $S^I(t)$ described by (47) and (48); the optimal amount to invest is determined by the first order condition (49). Note that the boundary conditions for this problem involve $V(S, Q, t)$, the present value of the cash flows from a completed mine. Thus solving the cash flow valuation problem is a prerequisite for the investment decision analysis described in this section.

V Long-Term Supply Contracts

It is not uncommon for the outputs of natural resource investments to be sold under long-term contracts that fix the price of the commodity but leave the purchase rate at least partially to the discretion of the purchaser. Where they exist, such contracts must be taken into account in valuing ongoing projects. Therefore in this section we show briefly how these contracts may be valued and the equilibrium contract price determined.

Let $Y(S, t; p, T)$ denote the value at time t of a particular contract to purchase the commodity up to time T at the contract price p, when the current spot price of the commodity is S. The contract is assumed to permit the purchaser to vary the price rate, q, between the lower and upper bounds $\underline{q}$ and $\bar{q}$. Since the commodity is by assumption available for purchase at the prevailing spot price S, ownership of the contract yields an instantaneous benefit or cash flow $q(S - p)$.

Using Ito's lemma and the stochastic process for S, the instantaneous change in the value of the contract is given by

$$dY = (\tfrac{1}{2}\sigma^2 S^2 Y_{ss} + Y_t)\, dt + Y_s\, dS. \tag{50}$$

Then an arbitrage argument analogous to that presented in Section I implies that the value of the contract must satisfy the partial differential equation:

$$\max_{q \in (\underline{q}, \bar{q})} [\tfrac{1}{2}\sigma^2 S^2 Y_{ss} + (\rho S - C)\, Y_s + Y_t + q(S - p) - \rho Y] = 0. \tag{51}$$

The value of the contract at maturity, $t = T$, is equal to zero, so that

$$Y(S, T; p, T) = 0. \tag{52}$$

In addition, the origin is an absorbing state for the spot price S. This implies that if $S = 0$, the holder of the contract must incur certain losses at the rate $\underline{q}p$ up to the maturity of the contract, so that

$$Y(0, t; p, T) = \frac{-p\underline{q}}{\rho}[1 - e^{-\rho(T-t)}]. \tag{53}$$

Finally, for sufficiently high values of S, the value of the right to vary the purchase rate approaches zero and the value of the contract approaches that of a series of forward contracts to purchase at the rate $\bar{q}$ at the fixed price p. Noting that forward and futures prices are equivalent when the interest rate is nonstochastic (see Cox et al. 1981; Jarrow and Oldfield 1981; Richard and Sundaresan 1981), this implies that

$$\lim_{s \to \infty} \frac{\partial Y(S, t; p, T)}{\partial S} = \frac{\partial}{\partial S} \int_0^{T-t} \bar{q} F(S, \tau)\, d\tau, \tag{54}$$

where $F(S, \tau)$ is the futures price for delivery in τ periods as defined previously.

The equilibrium contract price (or price schedule) is that which makes the value of the contract at inception equal to zero, given the prevailing spot price, S, and maturity, T. Writing the equilibrium contract price as $p^*(S, T)$, we have

$$Y[S, 0; p^*(S, T), T] = 0 \tag{55}$$

In general there does not exist a closed-form solution for $Y(\cdot)$ or $p^*(\cdot)$. However, if the convenience yield can be written as $C(s) = \kappa S$, then closed-form solutions may be obtained in two special cases.

First, if the purchaser has no discretion over the purchase rate, so that $\bar{q} = \underline{q} = q^*$, then the contract is equivalent to a series of forward contracts with value given by[13]

$$Y(S, t; p, T) = q^* \left\{ \frac{S}{\kappa}[1 - e^{-\kappa(T-t)}] - \frac{p}{\rho}[1 - e^{-\rho(T-t)}] \right\}. \tag{56}$$

This implies that the equilibrium contract price is

$$p^*(S, T) = \frac{\rho S}{\kappa} \left(\frac{1 - e^{-\kappa T}}{1 - e^{-\rho T}} \right). \tag{57}$$

Second, if the contract has an infinite maturity, the value of the contract is equal to the sum of the values of two assets we have already valued: a perpetual contract to purchase the commodity at the fixed rate $\underline{q}$ and a mine with infinite inventory, an average cost of production p, feasible production rates $\bar{q} - \underline{q}$, and with no taxes, maintenance costs, or costs of opening and closing. The former may be valued using equation (56) and the latter is a special case of Section II.[14] It can then be shown that

$$
Y(S, t; p, \infty) = \begin{cases} \beta_1 S^{\gamma_1} + \underline{q}\left(\dfrac{S}{\kappa} - \dfrac{p}{\rho}\right), & S < p \\[3mm] \beta_4 S^{\gamma_2} = \bar{q}\left(\dfrac{S}{\kappa} - \dfrac{p}{\rho}\right), & S \geq p, \end{cases}
\tag{58}
$$

where

$$
\beta_1 = \frac{1}{2\alpha_2\kappa}\left[1 - \gamma_2\left(\frac{p - \kappa}{\rho}\right)\right]q^d p^{1-\gamma_1},
$$

$$
\beta_4 = \frac{1}{2\alpha_2\kappa}\left[1 - \frac{\gamma_1}{\rho}(p - \kappa)\right]q^d p^{1-\gamma_2},
$$

$$
q^d = \bar{q} - \underline{q},
$$

and γ_1, γ_2, and α_2 are as defined following equation (40). The equilibrium price $p^*(S, \tau)$ is found from the nonlinear equation obtained by setting either of the expressions (58) equal to zero.

VI Conclusion

We have shown in this chapter how assets whose cash flows depend on highly variable output prices may be valued and how the optimal policies for managing them may be determined by exploiting the properties of replicating self-financing portfolios. The explicit analysis rests on the assumption that such portfolios may be formed by trading in futures contracts in the output commodity, but the general approach can also be developed in a general equilibrium context if the relevant futures markets do not exist.

In addition to providing a rich set of empirical predictions for empirical research, this framework should be useful for the analysis of capital-budgeting decisions in a wide variety of situations in which the distribution of future cash flows is not given exogenously but must be determined by future management decisions.

Appendix

In contrast to the assumption of Section II that there are only two feasible output rates, zero and q^*, and that it is costly to shift from one to the other, we assume in this case that the output rate is continuously and costlessly variable between zero and $\bar{q}$; in keeping with this assumption, costs of opening and closing the mine are neglected and this renders the distinction between an open and a closed mine otiose.

We assume that no costs are incurred if the output rate is zero and that for positive output rates the total cost per unit time of the output rate q is $c(q) = q \cdot a(q) = a_0 + a_1 q + a_2 q^2$, where $a_1, a_2 > 0$; this represents a (linearly) increasing marginal cost schedule.

Using these assumptions in equation (27), the optimal output policy and the value of the mine satisfy

$$\tfrac{1}{2}\sigma^2 s^2 v_{ss} + (r - \kappa)vs + (1 - t_2)\max_{q \in (0, \bar{q}]}[(1 - t_1)qs - a_0 - a_1 q - a_2 q^2, 0] - (r + \lambda)v = 0. \tag{A1}$$

Carrying out the maximization we find that the optimal output policy is

$$q^*(s) = \begin{cases} \bar{q} & s > \bar{s} \\ \dfrac{(1 - t_1)s - a_1}{2a_2} & \bar{s} > s > s^* \\ 0 & s \leq s^*, \end{cases}$$

where $s^* = (a_1 + 2\sqrt{a_0 a_2})/(1 - t_1)$ and $\bar{s} = (a_1 + 2a_2\bar{q})/(1 - t_1)$. Thus the optimal output policy maximizes the instantaneous profit rate; since the profit rate is zero when the output rate is zero, the output rate is positive whenever the net-of-royalty output price exceeds the minimum average cost of production.

The after-tax cash flow from the mine under the optimal output policy, $p(s)$, is given by

$$p(s) = \begin{cases} (1 - t_2)[(1 - t_1)\bar{q}s - a_0 - a_1\bar{q} - a_2\bar{q}^2] & s > \bar{s}, \\ (1 - t_2)\dfrac{(1 - t_1)(s - a_1)^2}{4a_2 - a_0} & \bar{s} > s > s^* \\ 0 & s \leq s^*. \end{cases}$$

When $p(s)$ is substituted for the maximand in equation (A1), the complete solutions for the three regions are

$$v(s) = \beta_1 s^{\gamma_1} + \beta_2 s^{\gamma_2} \qquad\qquad\qquad s \leq s^*, \tag{A2}$$

$$v(s) = \beta_3 s^{\gamma_1} + \beta_4 s^{\gamma_2} + \delta(s) \qquad\quad \bar{s} > s > s^*, \tag{A3}$$

$$v(s) = \beta_5 s^{\gamma_1} + \beta_6 s^{\gamma_2} + \frac{ms}{\lambda + \kappa} - \frac{n}{r + \lambda} \quad s > \bar{s}. \tag{A4}$$

where

$$\delta(s) = \frac{(1 - t_2)}{r + \lambda}\left[\frac{a_1^2}{4a_2} - a_0\right] - \left[\frac{a_1(1 - t_1)(1 - t_2)}{2a_2(\lambda + c)}\right]s + \left[\frac{(1 - t_1)^2(1 - t_2)}{4a_2(\lambda + 2c - \sigma^2 - r)}\right]s^2,$$

$$m = \bar{q}(1 - t_1)(1 - t_2),$$

$$n = (1 - t_2)(a_0 + a_1\bar{q} + a_2\bar{q}^2).$$

Variables γ_1 and γ_2 are as defined following equation (40), and the coefficients β_i $(i = 1, \ldots, 6)$ are constants determined as follows. As in the case of Section II the requirements that v and v/s remain finite for very small and very large s, respectively, imply that $\beta_2 = \beta_5 = 0$. The remaining four constants are obtained by solving the four linear equations yielded by imposing the condition that the valuation schedule $v(s)$ be continuous and have a finite second derivative at s^* and $\bar{s}$:

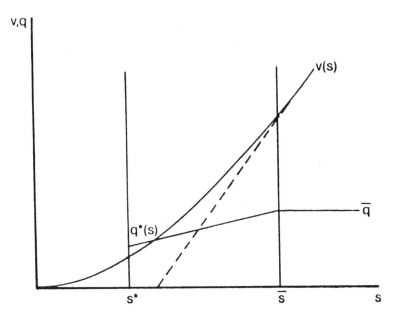

Figure 16.2
Case ii: Mine value (v) and optimal output as a function of the output price (s)

$$\beta_1 s^{*\gamma_1} = \beta_3 s^{*\gamma_1} + \beta_4 s^{*\gamma_2} + \delta(s^*), \tag{A5}$$

$$\gamma_1 \beta_1 s^{*\gamma_1-1} = \gamma_1 \beta_3 s^{*\gamma_1-1} + \gamma_2 \beta_4 s^{*\gamma_2-1} + \delta'(s^*), \tag{A6}$$

$$\beta_3 \bar{s}^{\gamma_1} + \beta_4 \bar{s}^{\gamma_2} + \delta(\bar{s}) = \beta_6 \bar{s}^{\gamma_2} + \frac{m\bar{s}}{\lambda + \kappa} - \frac{n}{r + \lambda}, \tag{A7}$$

$$\gamma_1 \beta_3 \bar{s}^{\gamma_1-1} + \gamma_2 \beta_4 \bar{s}^{\gamma_2-1} + \delta'(\bar{s}) = \gamma_2 \beta_6 \bar{s}^{\gamma_2-1} + \frac{m}{\lambda + \kappa}. \tag{A8}$$

Thus the value of the mine is given by the solution to equations (A2)–(A8) with $\beta_2 = \beta_5 = 0$. Since the equation system (A5)–(A8) is linear, it is a straightforward if tedious task to obtain an explicit valuation expression which may be used for comparative statics. The valuation schedule and the optimal output policy are illustrated in figure 16.2. In this figure the dotted line corresponds to the value of the mine if it is required to operate perpetually at its maximum rate $\bar{q}$: thus the difference between the $v(s)$ schedule and this line represents the value of the option to vary the output rate in response to changing output prices.

Acknowledgments

Research support from the Corporate Finance Division of the Department of Finance, Ottawa, is gratefully acknowledged. We especially thank the referee whose insightful comments have enabled us to eliminate several errors and to improve the presentation. We also thank Robert Pyndyck, Rene Stulz, Suresh Sundaresan, Merton Miller, and participants at seminars in London, Stockholm, Stanford, and Los Angeles.

Notes

1. Bodie and Rosansky (1980) report that the standard deviation of annual changes in futures prices over the period 1950–76 was 25.6% for silver, 47.2% for copper, and 25.2% for platinum.

2. See, e.g. the framework developed by Cox, Ingersoll, and Ross (1978); this was used by Brennan and Schwartz (1982a, 1982b) to analyze the valuation of regulated public utilities.

3. A self-financing portfolio has the property that its value at any time is exactly equal to the value of the investment and cash flow distributions required at that time. See Harrison and Kreps (1979). The notion of a replicating self-financing portfolio is closely related to the option-pricing models of Black and Scholes (1973) and Merton (1973).

4. Cootner (1967, p. 65) defines the convenience yield of inventory as "the present value of an increased income stream expected as a result of conveniently large inventories." This contrasts with our definition of the convenience yield as a flow.

5. These bounds may depend on the amount of inventory remaining in the mine and time.

6. For simplicity we have ignored depreciation tax allowances.

7. The Appendix develops the model under the neoclassical assumption of a continuously variable output rate with convex costs.

8. In the absence of maintenance costs it is never optimal to abandon a closed mine so long as there is a possibility that it will be optimal to reopen it. Hence $w(0) = 0$ and $w(s) > 0$ for $s > 0$.

9. This is necessary for the present value of the future costs to be finite.

10. The variance rate and convenience yield used in table 1 compare with a variance rate for COMEX monthly settlement prices for copper of 7.8% per year for 1971–82 and an average convenience yield of 0.7% per year computed from annual data on the May contract for the same period, using eq. (7).

11. Because the commodity price is increasing faster than the production costs.

12. An alternative assumption is that all costs inflate at the common rate π; this would convert (44) into an *ordinary* differential eq. for the deflated mine value $x = Xe^{-\pi t}$.

13. We thank the referee for this point.

14. As the referee remarks, this contract is equivalent to a perpetuity of European options on the commodity.

References

Bierman, H., and Smidt, S. 1960. *The Capital Budgeting Decision*. New York: Macmillan.

Black, F., and Scholes, M. 1973. The pricing of options and corporate liabilities. *Journal of Political Economy* 81 (May–June): 637–54.

Bodie, Z., and Rosansky, V. I. 1980. Risk and return in commodity futures. *Financial Analysis Journal* 36 (May–June): 27–40.

Bogue, M. C., and Roll, R. 1974. Capital budgeting of risky projects with imperfect markets for physical capital. *Journal of Finance* 29 (May): 601–13.

Brennan, M. J. 1958. The supply of storage. *American Economic Review* 48 (March): 50–72.

Brennan, M. J. 1973. An approach to the valuation of uncertain income streams. *Journal of Finance* 28 (July): 661–73.

Brennan, M. J., and Schwartz, E. S. 1982*a*. Consistent regulatory policy under uncertainty. *Bell Journal of Economics* 13 (Autumn): 506–21.

Brennan, M. J., and Schwartz, E. S. 1982*b*. Regulation and corporate investment policy. *Journal of Finance* 37 (May): 289–300.

Brock, W. A.; Rothschild, M.; and Stiglitz, J. E. 1982. Stochastic capital theory. Financial Research Center Memorandum no. 40. Princeton, N.J.: Princeton University, April.

Constantinides, G. M. 1978. Market risk adjustment in project valuation. *Journal of Finance* 33 (May): 603–16.

Cootner, P. 1967. Speculation and hedging. *Food Research Institute Studies* 7 (Suppl.): 65–106.

Cox, J. C.; Ingersoll, J. E.; and Ross, S. A. 1978. A theory of the term structure of interest rates. Research Paper no. 468. Stanford, Calif.: Stanford University.

Cox, J. C.; Ingersoll, J. E.; and Ross, S. A. 1981. The relation between forward prices and futures prices. *Journal of Financial Economics* 9 (December): 321–46.

Dean, Joel 1951. *Capital Budgeting; Top Management Policy on Plant Equipment and Product Development.* New York: Columbia University.

Dothan, U., and Williams, J. 1980. Term-risk structures and the valuation of projects. *Journal of Financial and Quantitative Analysis* 15 (November): 875–906.

Fama, E. F. 1977. Risk-adjusted discount rates and capital budgeting under uncertainty. *Journal of Financial Economics* 5 (August): 3–24.

Fisher, Irving. 1907. *The Rate of Interest: Its Nature, Determination and Relation to Economic Phenomena.* New York: Macmillan.

Fleming, W. H., and Rishel, R. W. 1975. *Deterministic and Stochastic Optimal Control.* New York: Springer-Verlag.

Harrison, J. M., and Kreps, D. M. 1979. Martingales and arbitrage in multiperiod securities markets. *Journal of Economic Theory* 20:381–408.

Jarrow, R. A., and Oldfield, G. S. 1981. Forward contracts and futures contracts. *Journal of Financial Economics* 9 (December): 373–82.

Kaldor, N. 1939. Speculation and economic stability. *Review of Economic Studies* 7:1–27.

Merton, R. C. 1971. Optimum consumption and portfolio rules in a continuous time model. *Journal of Economic Theory* 3 (December): 373–413.

Merton, R. 1973. The theory of rational option pricing. *Bell Journal of Economic and Management Science* 4 (Spring): 141–83.

Miller, M. H., and Upton, C. W. 1985. A test of the Hotelling valuation principle. *Journal of Political Economy* 93 (February): in press.

Myers, S. C., and Turnbull, S. M. 1977. Capital budgeting and the capital asset pricing model: Good news and bad news. *Journal of Finance* 32 (May): 321–32.

Paddock, J. L.; Siegel, D. R.; and Smith, J. L. 1982. Option valuation of claims on physical assets: The case of off-shore petroleum leases. Unpublished manuscript. Evanston, Ill.: Northwestern University.

Pindyck, R. S. 1980. Uncertainty and exhaustible resource markets. *Journal of Political Economy* 88 (December): 1203–25.

Richard, S. F., and Sundaresan, M. 1981. A continuous time equilibrium model of forward prices and futures prices in a multigood economy. *Journal of Financial Economics* 9 (December): 347–72.

Ross, S. A. 1978. A simple approach to the valuation of risky streams. *Journal of Business* 51 (July): 453–75.

Samuelson, P. A. 1965. Rational theory of warrant pricing. *Industrial Management Review* 6 (Spring): 3–31.

Solow, R. M. 1974. The economics of resources or the resources of economics. *American Economic Review* 64 (May): 1–14.

Telser, L. G. 1958. Futures trading and the storage of cotton and wheat. In A. E. Peck, ed., *Selected Writings on Future Markets*. Chicago, 1977.

Tourinho, O. A. F. 1979. The option value of reserves of natural resources. Unpublished manuscript. Berkeley: University of California.

Working, H. 1948. The theory of price of storage. *Journal of Farm Economics* 30:1–28. Reprinted in *Selected Writings of Holbrook Working*. Chicago: Chicago Board of Trade, 1977.

17 The Nature of Option Interactions and the Valuation of Investments with Multiple Real Options

Lenos Trigeorgis

I Introduction

Academics and practitioners alike now recognize that standard discounted cash flow (DCF) techniques when applied improperly often undervalue projects with real operating options and other strategic interactions. In practice, many corporate managers overrule passive net present value (NPV) analysis and use intuition and executive judgment to value future managerial flexibility.

Recently, Myers (1987), Kester (1984), Mason and Merton (1985), and Trigeorgis and Mason (1987), among others, suggest the use of option-based techniques to value the managerial flexibility implicit in investment opportunities. Managerial flexibility is a set of "real options," for example, the options to defer, abandon, contract, or expand investment, or switch investment to an alternative use.[1]

The real options literature to date has tended to focus on valuing individual options (i.e., one type of operating option at a time).[2] However, managerial flexibility embedded in investment projects typically takes the form of a *collection* of real options. This chapter demonstrates that interactions among real options present in combination generally make their individual values nonadditive. Although many readers may intuit that certain options do in fact interact, the nature of such interactions and the conditions under which they may be small or large, as well as negative or positive, may not be trivial. In particular, the chapter illustrates through a generic project the size and type of interactions among the options to defer, abandon, contract, expand, and switch use.

The combined value of operating options can have a large impact on the value of a project. However, the incremental value of an additional option often tends to be lower the greater the number of other options already present. Neglecting a particular option while including others may not necessarily cause significant valuation errors. However, valuing each option individually and summing these separate option values can substantially overstate the value of a project. Configurations of real options that can exhibit precisely the opposite behavior are also identified. Sensitivity analysis shows that, despite interactions, projects seen as collections of real options preserve a number of the familiar option properties.

The remainder of the chapter is organized as follows. Section II describes a generic investment project with multiple operating options, along with the model specification and assumptions. The nature of option interactions and option value (non)-additivity are examined in Section III. Section IV demonstrates interactions among options by first valuing various real options separately, then in combination. A summary and concluding remarks are provided in Section V.

II An Investment Opportunity with Multiple Real Options

A Project Description

Consider a generic investment opportunity with multiple real options. Construction of the project requires a series of investment outlays at specific times during a "building stage." For example, an initial outlay of I_1, followed by subsequent outlays of I_2 and I_3. The project generates its first cash flows during the "operating stage" that follows the last investment outlay, I_3.

The investment opportunity allows management the flexibility to:

a) *defer* undertaking the project;

b) permanently *abandon* construction, with no recovery, by foregoing subsequent planned investment outlays;

c) *contract* the scale of the project by reducing planned investment outlays;

d) *expand* the project's scale by making an additional investment outlay;

e) *switch* the investment from the current to its best alternative use, here modeled as a specified salvage value.

The above generic investment with its collection of real options is summarized in figure 17.1. This project could describe many practical situations. For example, a large company engaged in the exploitation of natural resources could be offered the opportunity to purchase a lease on undeveloped land with potential mineral resources. The lease, expiring in T_1 years, would give management the right to start the project within that period by making an investment outlay, I_1, for construction of roads and other infrastructure. This would be followed by a second outlay of I_2 for excavation, and a third outlay of I_3 for the construction of a processing plant. Reducing this outlay to I_3' would result in a c-percent contraction in the operation scale of this plant. If the mineral is later found to enjoy a stronger demand than initially expected, the rate of production could be enhanced by x percent by expanding the processing plant at a cost of I_4. All along, management retains the option to salvage a percentage of its investment.

As another example, a firm is considering the introduction of one of its existing patented products into a new geographic market. Management can delay introduction up to the time the patent expires, in T_1 years. Initiating the project requires an

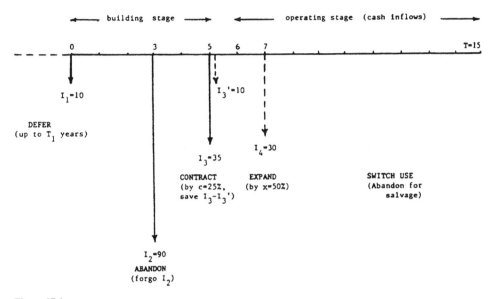

Figure 17.1

A generic project requiring a series of outlays (vertical arrows, Is), allowing management the flexibility (collection of real options) to defer, abandon, contract, or expand the investment, and switch use

outlay of I_1 to purchase land, to be followed by an outlay of I_2 to build a plant in the new area. Upon the plant's completion, management plans a large one-time advertising expenditure of I_3, which, if the product's prospects at that time seem limited, could be reduced to I_3' with a c-percent market share loss. If, a year after introduction, the product is more enthusiastically received in the new market than originally expected, management can expand the project by x percent by adding to plant capacity at a cost of I_4. If at any time market conditions deteriorate, management can salvage a portion of the investment by selling the plant and equipment. The next part illustrates traditional valuation of this project.

B Traditional NPV and Managerial Flexibility

Assume that the generic project is expected to generate annual cash flows during the operating stage, starting in year 6. Under traditional NPV analysis, these expected cash flows and the terminal project value would be discounted at an appropriate risk-adjusted rate. Assume that this calculation results in a "gross" project value of $V = 100$. This is simply the present value of expected cash flows from immediately undertaking the project, not including any required investment outlays or embedded real options. Following standard practice in the real options literature, this V (or its modified scale) will serve as the underlying asset value for the project's various real options.

Assuming the particular values shown in figure 17.1 and subtracting the present value of the planned investment outlays, $I = 114.7$,[3] the passive NPV of immediately undertaking the above project, in the absence of managerial flexibility, is

$$\text{NPV} = V - I = 100 - 114.7 = -14.7.$$

The project would be rejected because its NPV is negative. The presence of managerial flexibility, however, can make the investment opportunity economically attractive.

Management's flexibility, or collection of options, to revise its future actions, contingent on uncertain future developments, introduces an asymmetry or skewness in the probability distribution of NPV. This asymmetry expends the opportunity's true value relative to passive NPV by improving its profit potential while limiting losses. Correct valuation thus requires an expanded NPV rule encompassing both sources of a real investment opportunity's value, the passive NPV of expected cash flows, and a value component for the combined value of the flexibility represented by the project's real options,

Expanded NPV = Passive NPV + Combined Option Value.

Traditional valuation approaches that either ignore these options altogether (passive NPV) or attempt to value such investment opportunities using a constant discount rate can lead to significant valuation errors. This is so because asymmetric claims on an asset do not generally have the same discount rate as the asset itself. This asymmetry can be properly analyzed by viewing flexibility in an options framework.[4]

An options-based approach to this problem, however, must recognize that flexibility seldom takes the form of a single option but instead typically is present as a combination of options. Therefore, proper analysis must account for the possible interactions among multiple options and the extent to which option values are not strictly additive. The rest of this paper values flexibility in the form of various combinations of options written on project value, and demonstrates the degree of interaction among different option combinations. The model specification and assumptions used in the option valuation of the above project are described next.

C   Model Specification and Assumptions

The valuation of operating options in this paper is based on the log-transformed version of binomial numerical analysis described in Trigeorgis (1991b).[5] Following standard practice in the real options literature, the gross project value (V_t) is assumed to follow a standard diffusion Wiener process given by[6]

$$dV/V = (\alpha - \delta)\, dt + \sigma\, dz, \tag{1}$$

where α is the instantaneous actual expected return on the project, σ is the instantaneous standard deviation of project value, dz is a standard Wiener process, and δ is the rate of return shortfall between the equilibrium total expected rate of return of a similar-risk traded financial asset, α^*, and the actual expected return of a nontraded real asset, α (see McDonald and Siegel (1984), (1985)). (δ may also capture any proportional cash flow (dividend-like) payout on the operating project, or even the net convenience yield in the case of commodities.)

Current option values can be determined by discounting certainty-equivalent or risk-neutral expectations of future payoffs at the riskless interest rate, r. In general, any contingent claim on an asset (traded or not) can be priced in a world with systematic risk by replacing the actual growth rate, α, with a certainty-equivalent rate, $\hat{\alpha} \equiv \alpha - RP$, where RP represents an appropriate risk premium, and then behaving as if the world were risk neutral (e.g., see Constantinides (1978), Cox, Ingersoll, and Ross (1985), Lemma 4, or Hull (1989), Ch. 7). (In general, $RP = S\sigma$, where $S \equiv (\alpha - r)/\sigma$ is the asset's market price of risk or reward-to-variability ratio. Note that if the market price of risk, S, is zero, investors are neutral to the asset's risk. If the CAPM holds, then $S = S_M \rho_M$, or $RP = S_M \rho_M \sigma$, where S_M is the market price of risk of the market portfolio (M) and ρ_M is the asset's correlation with the market.) Given that $\alpha = \alpha^* - \delta$, then $\alpha - RP = (\alpha^* - RP) - \delta \equiv r - \delta$. This is equivalent to a risk-neutral valuation (e.g., see Cox and Ross (1976), Harrison and Kreps (1979)), where the actual drift (α) would be replaced by the risk-neutral equivalent drift, $\hat{\alpha} = r - \delta$. (Such a world, where expected growth rates are adjusted from α to $\hat{\alpha} \equiv \alpha - RP = r - \delta$, will be referred to as a "risk-neutral" world. In this world, instead of using actual probabilities, expectations are formulated using equivalent "risk-neutral" probabilities (Harrison and Kreps (1979), Cox and Ross (1976), Trigeorgis and Mason (1987)).) For traded assets (in equilibrium) or for those real assets with no systematic risk (e.g., R&D projects, oil exploration, etc.), $\hat{\alpha} = r$ or $\delta = 0$.

In discrete time, Log V follows an arithmetic Brownian motion, which can be approximated, over successively smaller intervals, by an equivalent binomial Markov random walk progressing in a triangular lattice as in figure 17.2, A and B. Adjustments for cash flows (dividends) and for the asymmetries introduced by real options (the discrete-time equivalent of specifying boundary conditions in continuous-time

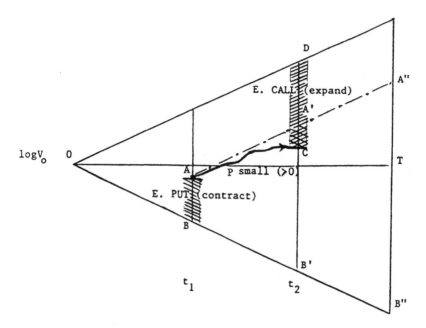

Figure 17.2A
Options of different type, approximately additive

models with partial differential equations) are made at appropriate times in a backward risk-neutral iterative process as in Trigeorgis (1991b).

The subsequent option analysis is based on the following base case input assumptions (see figure 17.1):

a. Initial gross project value, $V = 100$;[7]

b. Annual risk-free interest rate, $r = 5$ percent;

c. Variance of project value, Var $= 0.25$;

d. Expected project life, $T = 15$ years;

e. Opportunity is deferrable for $T_1 = 2$ years; the project begins with first investment
outlay of $I_1 = 10$;

f. Construction can be abandoned, with no recovery, by foregoing the second
investment outlay, I_2, of 90 in year 3;

g. The scale of the project can be contracted by $c = 25$ percent in year 5 by reducing
the third investment outlay, I_3, to $I_3' = 10$;

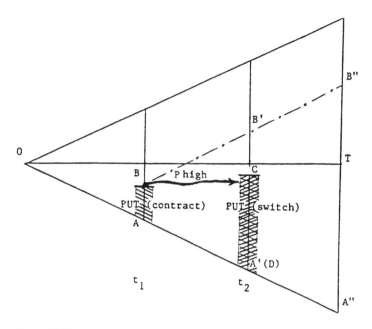

Figure 17.2B
Options of similar type, nonadditive

h. The scale of the project can be expanded by $x = 50$ percent by making an additional investment outlay, I_4, of 30 in year 7;

i. The project's salvage value is $S = 50$ percent of cumulative investment costs (i.e., it "jumps" upward by 50 percent of each new cost outlay incurred), while declining exponentially at a rate of 10 percent per year between cost outlays.

Before proceeding with the presentation and discussion of the results for valuing the above investment opportunity with its collection of embedded real options, however, it would be useful to next examine the nature of real option interactions.

III   The Nature of Option Interactions and Option Value (Non)Additivity

Additivity of individual option values is trivial when options are written on distinct assets (e.g., calls or puts on shares of IBM stock). However, option additivity is not trivial when the options are written on the same unique underlying asset. Examples of interacting financial options include putable convertible bonds, callable extendable bonds, or simply securities callable by the issuer at two distinct times. Real options also typically come as an inseparable package with a single underlying asset (the gross project value, V). In situations such as these, options can interact.

First, the mere presence of subsequent options increases the value of the effective underlying asset for earlier options. In essence, prior real options have as their underlying asset the whole portfolio of gross project value plus the then value of any future options. At an extreme, the inseparability of real options from their underlying asset allows also the possibility that exercise of a prior put option on the asset, such as the option to abandon early, may eliminate or "kill" that asset. Due to the real asset's uniqueness and unavailability of other identical assets, this may preclude exercising future options on it (e.g., later to contract the project or switch between uses).

More generally, however, exercise of a prior real option may alter the underlying asset itself and, hence, the value of subsequent options on it, causing a second-order interaction. For example, the option to contract would decrease, while the option to expand would increase the project scale, affecting the value of other options on it. Further, the (conditional) probability of exercising a latter option, in the presence of an earlier option, would be higher or lower than the (marginal) probability of its exercise as a separate option, depending on whether the prior option is of the same or of opposite type, respectively. Real options may thus interact for various reasons and to varying degrees, depending on the probability of their joint exercise during the investment's life.

To illustrate the nature of these interactions, consider having a package of two options on the same asset. The degree of interaction and (non)additivity of option values—and the extend to which the underlying asset for a prior or subsequent option is altered—will be seen to depend on a) whether the options are of the same type (e.g., two puts or two calls) or are opposites (i.e., a put and a call), b) the separation of their exercise times (influenced by whether they are European or American options), c) their relative degree of being "in or out of the money," and d) their order or sequence. All these factors affect the degree of overlap between their exercise regions and the probability of their joint exercise.

The underlying principle in this analysis is that the value of an option in the presence of other options may differ from its value in isolation. Alternatively, the combined value of two options in the presence of each other may differ from the alternative of evaluating each option separately and adding the results. Two effects may be at work here, each affecting the direction or sign of the interaction as well as its magnitude.

First, recall that the value of a prior option would be altered if followed by a subsequent option because it would effectively be written on a higher underlying asset,

V' (equal to the gross project value, V, plus the then expected value of the subsequent option). Specifically, in terms of sign, if the *first* option is a put, *its* value would be lower (giving a negative interaction), and if a call, higher (exhibiting a positive interaction), *relative to its value as a separate option.* (The magnitude of alteration in the *prior* option's value or the degree of its interaction would be larger the greater the joint probability of exercising both options, P, which depends on the similarity of the options involved.)

Second, the effective underlying asset for the *latter* option may be lower conditional on prior exercise of an earlier put option (e.g., to contract project scale), V'', than if the prior option were not exercised (i.e., maintaining project value, V). This may lead to a double negative effect if the prior option is a put.[8] If, instead, the prior option were a call (e.g., to expand project scale), the interaction can be positive, with the incremental value of both the prior and the latter option possibly being greater than their separate values.[9] In either situation, the degree of interaction between the two options would again be directly proportional to the probability of joint exercise.

If the two options are of opposite type (e.g., a pair of a put and a call) so that they are optimally exercisable under opposite (negatively correlated) circumstances, then the conditional probability of exercising the latter option given prior exercise of the former would be small—smaller than the marginal probability of exercising the latter option alone. The degree of interaction would then also be small and the options approximately additive. If the two options are of the same type (either a pair of puts or a pair of calls), then the conditional probability of exercise would be higher, and so would be the magnitude of interaction (deviation from option value additivity). Again, the sign of the interaction would depend on whether the prior option is a put (negative) or a call (positive).

One can examine further, with the aid of graphical illustrations, the possible variations in the magnitude and sign of interaction between two options, starting first from situations where option value additivity holds and extending into cases with higher degrees of interaction. First, as noted, interactions are small and the separate option values are approximately additive when the two options are of opposite type: a put (e.g., the option to contract) and a call (e.g., to expand), and are both out of the money.[10] As noted, two such European options would in fact be purely additive (i.e., their interaction would be precisely zero) only if both matured at the same time (i.e., $t_1 = t_2$). In this extreme case, although the marginal probabilities that either option may be independently exercised at (their common) maturity are positive, the joint (or conditional) probability of exercising both options is precisely zero ($P = 0$); with no interaction, each option retains its full, undistorted value as if evaluated independently, and thus their separate values are exactly additive.

The situation depicted in figure 17.2A is similar, except that there is a separation in the exercise times of the two opposite-type, out-of-the-money (European) options, with the put maturing at an earlier time. Although there is again a high positive marginal probability that the put option will be exercised at time t_1 or that the call option may later be independently exercised at time t_2, the conditional probability of exercising the latter call option, given a prior exercise of the first put ($P_{L|F}$), is nevertheless small (> 0)—smaller than the marginal probability of exercising the latter option alone, P_L. For the put option to be optimally exercised at t_1, the state variable (the log of asset value) must drop below the "exercise boundary" into the "exercise region" (shaded area) AB. Following exercise of the first option, its subsequent movement would then be constrained within the trapezoidal area $ABB'A'$ by t_2 (or $ABB''A''$ by maturity, T), which only partially overlaps with the exercise region (CD) of the subsequent option (double-shaded area $A'C$)—with only a small chance of reaching the second exercise boundary necessary for triggering exercise of the latter call option. The smaller (greater) this overlap ($A'C$), the smaller (greater) the conditional probability of joint exercise and the smaller (greater) the degree of interaction between the two option values. If it is small enough, as in this case of opposite types of options, the separate option values would still be approximately additive. If the order were reversed so that the call option preceded the put, the options would still be of opposite type with nonoverlapping exercise regions and low conditional probability of joint exercise (related to the double-shaded area $A'C$), so that their interaction would again be small—though it may be of opposite (i.e., positive) sign— and the separate options could still be approximately added.[11]

If the prior option were also a put instead of a call, as shown in figure 17.2B, the separate option values would be far from additive. As the options would then be of similar type, in this case both puts, their exercise regions would overlap significantly and the conditional probability of exercising one put, given earlier exercise of the other (as indicated by the increased double-shaded area $A'C$), would be high (< 1). Because exercise of the prior put (e.g., to contract) would reduce the project's scale and value and, hence, the other put option's (e.g., to switch between uses) with high probability, P, the expected incremental value of the latter option would be smaller. As noted, the prior put's value may also be somewhat smaller—a double negative effect—than if evaluated separately, because it is written on the project's portfolio with the future put, even though the latter may be reduced by the first-order interaction. Similarly, interactions would again be high, though *positive*, if the similar-type options were both calls (e.g., to expand the project at two distinct times) instead of puts. Of course, interactions can get more complicated if more than two options are considered. For example, if the pair of European calls (a compound European call)—or, by extension, an American call—were preceded by another put option, (potentially dominating) negative interactions could arise between the positively interacting pair and the prior put.

As a final observation, it is possible that exercising a prior real put option (e.g., to abandon the project by simply foregoing an upcoming investment outlay) may "kill" other future options. In the special but extreme case that the exercise regions of two put options overlap fully and the first option can kill the latter one with certainty (with $P_{L|F} = 1$), the expected incremental value of the latter option would be negligible. The combined value would then simply be the full separate value of the first option (essentially written only on the base-scale project, because the latter option is valueless). More generally, however, if the latter option—for example, being instead a call with nonoverlapping exercise boundaries similar to the situation in figure 17.2A—were not completely within the "shooting range" of the prior killing put so that the conditional probability is less than 1, it would not be completely "dead"; it would still retain some value as long as there were some chance it could be exercised without prior exercise of the first killing put (i.e., $P_{L|\bar{F}} > 0$).

Alternatively, if the condition for optimally exercising the one put (e.g., to abandon) also simultaneously satisfies, or is a subset of, the condition for optimally exercising the other (e.g., switching between uses), the combined value of the two options would then simply be the higher of the two separate values, an extreme case of full negative interaction. Such may also be the case when the separation between the exercise times of two similar-type options is negligible. More generally, the nature of interaction and, hence, the extent to which the values of two separate options may or may not approximately add up can be summarized as follows.

There is no (small) interaction and, hence, the separate option values would be (approximately) additive (i.e., option value additivity holds), if the conditional probability of exercising both options before maturity is zero (small).[12] Conversely, the interaction would be highest (high), making it most inappropriate to add up the separate option values, if it is certain (likely) both options will be exercised jointly (or the conditional probability of a joint exercise, $P_{L|F}$, is 1 (high)). The interaction would typically be positive if the prior option is a call and negative if a put. In the latter case (as when the separation between two similar-type options is negligible), the combined option value may be only (somewhat higher than) the higher of the separate individual values, that is, the incremental value of the lesser option may be negligible (small). Supportive numerical results based on the fairly rich generic project example described earlier in Section II are presented next.

IV   Presentation and Discussion of Results

This section presents the numerical valuation results for the generic project's multiple real options, first in isolation (i.e., one option at a time) and later in combination.

A   The Value of Separate Options

The option to *defer* alone is basically valued as an American call option on the project, with an exercise price equal to the necessary investment outlays. As shown in table 17.1, this option increases the project's Expanded NPV to 26.3, in contrast to the no-flexibility base case NPV of -14.7. Alternatively, the value of this option is 41,

Option Value = Expanded NPV − Passive NPV = $26.3 - (-14.7) = 41$.

The option to permanently *abandon during construction* is valued as a compound call option on the project. If management has only this option, then the project has an Expanded NPV of 22.1. Thus, the value of the option to abandon during construction amounts to 37 percent of V.

Table 17.1
Interactions among multiple real options (base case: $V = 100$; $r = 5\%$; Var. $= 0.25$; Life $T = 15$; Defer $T_1 = 2$ yrs.)

NPV of project without real options: -14.7				
Value with one real option:				
Defer (D)	Abandon (A)	Contract (C)	Expand (E)	Switch use (S)
26.3* (41)**	22.1 (36.8)	-7.8 (6.9)	20.3 (35)	24.6 (39.3)
Value with two real options:				
$D \& A$	$D \& C$	$D \& E$	$D \& S$	$A \& C$
36.4 (51.1)	27.7 (42.4)	54.7 (69.4)	38.2 (52.9)	22.6 (37.3)
$A \& E$	$A \& S$	$C \& E$	$C \& S$	$E \& S$
50.6 (65.3)	24.6 (39.3)	27.1 (41.8)	25.5 (40.2)	54.7 (69.4)
Value with three real options:				
$D \& A \& C$	$D \& A \& E$	$D \& A \& S$	$D \& C \& E$	$D \& C \& S$
36.8 (51.5)	68.2 (82.9)	38.2 (52.9)	57.1 (71.8)	38.7 (53.4)
$D \& E \& S$	$A \& C \& E$	$A \& C \& S$	$A \& E \& S$	$C \& E \& S$
71 (85.7)	51.9 (66.6)	25.5 (40.2)	54.7 (69.4)	55.9 (70.6)
Value with four real options:				
$D \& A \& C \& E$	$D \& A \& C \& S$	$D \& A \& E \& S$	$D \& C \& E \& S$	$A \& C \& E \& S$
69.3 (84)	38.7 (53.4)	71 (85.7)	71.9 (86.6)	55.9 (70.6)
Value with five real options:				
$D \& A \& C \& E \& S$ (All)				
71.9 (86.6)				

*Project value including option(s), i.e., expanded NPV.
**Value of option(s).

The option to *contract* the scale of operations is valued as a European put on part of the project, with exercise price equal to the potential cost savings. Including just this option increases the opportunity's value by 7 percent of V (from -14.7 to -7.8). Similarly, the option to *expand* in the base case project is worth 35 percent of the gross project value. This option is valued analogous to a European call to acquire part of the project by paying an extra outlay as the exercise price.

The option to *switch use* is valued as an American put on the project, with an exercise price equal to the value in its best alternative use, here assumed to be its salvage value. As shown in table 17.1, its value in isolation is 40 percent of V.

As explained in the previous section, the value of an option in the presence of others may differ from its value in isolation. The presence of subsequent options increases the effective underlying asset for prior options. Moreover, exercise of a prior real option (e.g., expanding or contracting a project) may alter the underlying asset and value of subsequent options on it. The valuation results for the generic project, when particular real options are valued in the presence of others, illustrate option configurations where interactions can be small or large, as well as negative or positive.

Table 17.1 shows the value of the project with different *combinations* of operating options. For example, the value of the project increases from -14.7 (without any options) to 26.3, with the option to defer only; to 36.4, with the options to defer and abandon ($D \& A$); to 36.8, with the options to defer, abandon, and contract ($D \& A \& C$); to 69.3, with the options to defer, abandon, contract, and expand ($D \& A \& C \& E$); and, finally, to 71.9, with all five options. Thus, the combined option values (shown in parentheses in table 17.1) increase from 41, with only the option to defer, to 51 ($D \& A$), to 52 ($D \& A \& C$), to 84 ($D \& A \& C \& E$), and finally to 86.6 (ALL), with all five options. These results confirm that real option values in the presence of each other are not generally additive. For example, although the value of the option to defer alone is 41 and the value of the option to abandon in isolation is 37, the value of both options present simultaneously is only 51, showing substantial negative interaction.

As noted, the degree of interaction is related to option type and the degree of overlap of exercise regions. Specifically, recall that options tend to be more additive when a) the options involved are of opposite type, that is, a call option optimally exercised when circumstances become favorable and a put option optimally exercised when circumstances become unfavorable, b) the times of possible exercise of the two options are close together, for example two European options maturing at the same time, as opposed to having distinctly different maturities or being American options, and c) the options are more "out of the money," that is, having relatively high

Table 17.2
Interaction between the options to abandon and to expand vs. separation of exercise times (as maturity of option to expand increases)

Option to abandon in yr. 3 ($A3$)	36.8						
	$E3$	$E4$	$E5$	$E7$	$E9$	$E11$	$E13$
Option to expand in yr. t (Et)	28.1	30.2	32.0	35.0	37.4	39.4	41.0
Combined option value ($A3$ & Et)	64.9	63.0	63.8	65.3	66.5	67.5	68.4
Sum of separate values ($A3 + Et$)	64.9	67.0	68.8	71.8	74.2	76.1	77.7
Interaction [($A3$ & Et) − ($A3 + Et$)]	0	−4.0	−5.0	−6.5	−7.7	−8.6	−9.3
Separation in yrs. ($= t − 3$)	0	1	2	4	6	8	10

exercise prices for calls and low exercise prices for puts (leading to lower overlap of exercise regions). As an example, because the options to contract in year 5 and to expand in year 7 are of different type (i.e., a prior put and a latter call) and have no overlap between their exercise regions, their separate values ($C = 6.9$, $E = 35$) are basically additive, i.e., C & $E = 41.8$. (As noted, interaction becomes precisely zero and the two European opposite-type options are purely additive if they are exercisable at exactly the same time as well as being out of the money.)

Table 17.2 shows the magnitude of interaction as the separation of exercise times varies between the options to abandon construction (in year 3) and to expand (by $x = 50$ percent if invest $I_E \equiv I_4 = 30$). The maturity of the option to expand, t, is allowed to vary from year 3 to year 13 (so that separation varies from 0 to 10 years). The size of interaction for a given separation is the difference between the combined option value ($A3$ & Et) and the sum of separate values ($A3 + Et$). Figure 17.3 shows that for these (opposite-type) options, (negative) interaction increases with separation at a decreasing rate.

Table 17.3 illustrates how the size of interaction between the option to abandon construction (in year 3) and the option to expand (by $x = 50$ percent if invest I_E) in year 7 varies as the exercise price (I_E) declines (or, alternatively, the scale of expansion, x, increases) and the option to expand gets relatively more deep in the money (proxied by xV/I_E). Figure 17.4 confirms that the magnitude of (negative) interaction between these (opposite-type) options increases with the relative degree of "being in the money."

Furthermore, when considering operating put options with extensively overlapping exercise regions, there is high negative interaction and the combined value is slightly higher than the separate values. Two examples are the options to contract ($C = 6.9$) and switch use ($S = 39.3$) where C & $S = 40.2$, and the options to abandon ($A = 37$) and switch use ($S = 39.3$), where A & $S = 39.3$.[13] Similarly, there is heavy negative

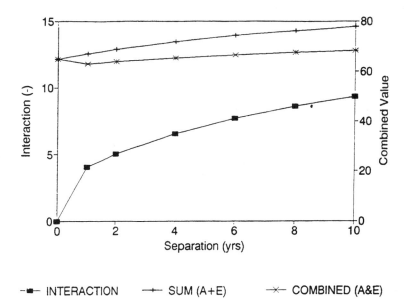

Figure 17.3
Interaction vs. separation. The degree of (negative) interaction between the opposite-type options to abandon (A) and to later expand (E), i.e., the difference between the combined option value (A & E) and the sum of separate values ($A + E$), increases with the separation of exercise times

Table 17.3
Interaction between the options to abandon and to expand vs. depth in the money (as exercise price of option to expand declines)

Option to abandon in yr. 3 ($A3$)	36.8						
Exercise price (I_E) (assuming $x = 50\%$ scale expansion in yr. 7)	∞	150	75	50	30	20	15
[or % of scale expansion (x) (assuming $I_E = 30$)	0	0.1	0.2	0.3	0.5	0.75	1.0]
Depth in the money (xV/I_E)	0	0.333	0.667	1.0	1.667	2.5	3.333
		(out of money)		(at the money)		(in the money)	
Option to expand in yr. 7 ($E7$)	0	3.2	9.7	17.6	35.0	58.3	82.2
Combined option value ($A3$ & $E7$)	36.8	39.5	45.1	51.3	65.3	84.3	104.4
Sum of separate values ($A3 + E7$)	36.8	39.9	46.5	54.3	71.8	95.1	119.0
Interaction [($A3$ & $E7$) $-$ ($A3 + E7$)]	0	-0.4	-1.4	-3.0	-6.5	-10.8	-14.6

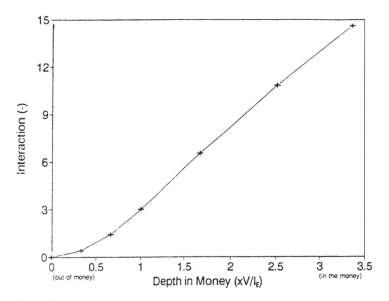

Figure 17.4
Interaction vs. depth in the money. The degree of negative interaction between the option to abandon and
to expand increases with the depth in the money (or as the exercise price of the option to expand, I_E,
declines)

interaction among the values of the options to abandon, contract, and switch use
(A & C & $S = 40.2$ vs. $A + C + S = 83$).

In addition to option type and the degree of overlap of exercise regions, affected by
separation, and depth in the money (or exercise price), the order or sequence of the
options is seen to significantly affect option additivity. As mentioned, if a put precedes a latter option, the combined option value will typically exhibit negative interaction. However, if a put follows a prior call, there can be a positive interaction.
Finally, the interaction will be positive if a call follows a prior call.

To illustrate the possibility of positive interactions, a second (European call)
option to expand the project (by 35 percent with another optional investment of 15) is
added to the basic example. Table 17.4 shows the total project value (including
options) and the option values in a number of interesting cases. Note first that if the
second option to expand has the same exercise date (i.e., year 5) as the opposite-type
option to contract, the purely additive case with precisely zero interaction is obtained,
i.e., $E5$ & $C5 = 32.1 = E5 + C5$.[14] But with two options to expand, a compound
call situation, positive interactions are large. As expected, the presence of each call
option enhances the other's value, leading to substantial positive interaction.[15]

Table 17.4
Adding a second option to expand: a case of positive interactions

NPV of project without real options: -14.7			
Value with one real option:			
Expand yr. 5 ($E5$)	Expand yr. 4 ($E4$)	Expand yr. 7 ($E7$)	Contract yr. 5 ($C5$)
10.5* (25.2)**	9.6 (24.2)	20.3 (35)	-7.8 (6.9)
Value with two real options:			
$E5$ & $C5$	$E4$ & $C5$	$C5$ & $E7$	$E4$ & $E7$
17.4 (32.1)	16.5 (31.2)	27.1 (41.8)	50.6 (65.3)
Value with three real options:			
$E4$ & $C5$ & $E7$			
62 (76.7)			
Value with six real options:			
All & $E4$			
107 (121.7)			

* Project value including option(s), i.e., expanded NPV.
** Value of option(s).

Specifically, the combined value of the options to expand in year 4 and in year 7 exceeds the sum of their individual values, that is, $E4$ & $E7 = 65.3 > E4 + E7 = 59.2$. This substantial positive interaction effect is maintained in the presence of the option to contract ($E4$ & $C5$ & $E7 = 76.7 > E4 + C5 + E7 = 66.1$) and when all other options are also jointly considered (ALL & $E4 = 121.7$ vs. ALL $+ E4 = 111$). Having illustrated the case of significant positive interactions,[16] the paper returns to the basic generic project, with just one expansion option in year 7, to examine the marginal effect on project value of having increasingly more options.

As a result of predominantly negative option interactions, the combined value of all five options (87) in the basic generic example is slightly more than half the sum of the values of each separate option (159).[17] The value of the combined flexibility is, however, of the same order of magnitude as the value of the project's expected cash inflows (87 vs. 100). Thus, ignoring the value of all real options would significantly understate the true economic value of such projects (here, by about half). But measuring the value of this flexibility by simply adding the individual option values would seriously overstate (almost double) true worth.

Ignoring certain options (typically, puts), however, would not necessarily lead to significant valuation errors because the incremental value of an additional option tends to become lower as the overlap of its exercise region with those of other included options becomes greater.[18] As can be seen from table 17.1, having only one option may be nearly half as valuable (e.g., to switch use = 39) as having all five (87); having two may be three-quarters as valuable (e.g., to abandon and expand = 65, or to defer

Total Project Value

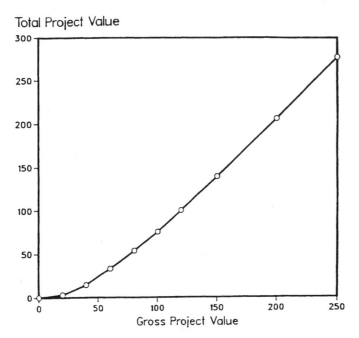

Figure 17.5A
Sensitivity of analysis of the impact of gross project value (V) on the total project value (including the value of all real options)

and expand $= 69$); and having three may be as valuable (e.g., D & E & $S = 86$ or D & A & $E = 83$) as four (e.g., D & C & E & $S = 87$ or D & A & E & $S = 86$) and as all five (ALL $= 87$). Because of this diminishing marginal option value effect, although a few particular options may have been neglected in the treatment of the generic project, the valuation results may still represent a close approximation to the true value, especially if those options that were included were appropriately selected to minimize their overlap.[19]

Finally, interacting real options do maintain a number of the usual option properties. Figure 17.5A–C examines the sensitivity of the total generic project value, including all interacting real options (determined to be 72 in the base case example above), to changes in various factors that affect option values. With other factors held constant, the total project value a) increases with V as shown in figure 17.5A; b) increases as project variance rises as seen in figure 17.5B; and c) increases with more years to defer as shown in figure 17.5C. In aggregate, this particular configuration manifests call option-like properties. Thus, the project valued as a collection

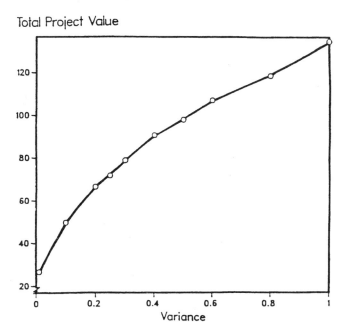

Total Project Value

Figure 17.5B
Sensitivity analysis of the impact of project variance on the total project value (including the value of real options)

of real options does preserve, despite option interactions, a number of the familiar option properties.

V   Summary and Conclusion

The chapter deviates from the current real options literature that tends to focus on valuing one type of operating option at a time. Instead, this chapter is concerned with valuing firm projects with collections of real options and quantifying the interactions among these options. Although the values of real options may not be additive, the combined flexibility that they afford management may be as economically significant as the value of the project's expected cash flows. The chapter examines the nature of option interactions, and illustrates situations where option interactions are small and, therefore, simple option additivity is a good approximation. Other situations where high interactions seriously invalidate option additivity are also identified. Interactions are seen to depend on the type, separation, degree of being in or out of the money,

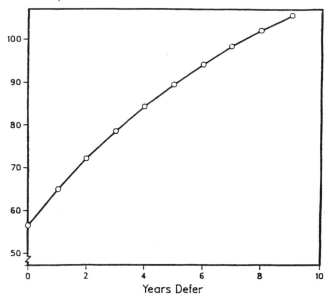

Figure 17.5C
Sensitivity analysis of the impact of years to defer (i.e., the expiration of the option to defer) on total project value (including the value of all real options)

and order of the options involved, factors that impact on the joint probability of exercise. In principle, interactions between pairs of options may be positive as well as negative. In practice, where negative interactions are more prevalent within a given project, they may so reduce the incremental value of certain options that simply ignoring them may not create any significant valuation errors. Sensitivity analysis results also confirm that projects with a variety of such interacting real options do preserve familiar option properties.

Acknowledgments

The author is indebted to Scott Mason and Stewart Myers for constant discussions and continual support during the development of this work. The author thanks George Constantinides, Richard Ruback, Lemma Senbet, *JFQA* Managing Editor Jonathan Karpoff, *JFQA* Referee Dan Siegel, and an anonymous *JFQA* referee for helpful comments. The chapter also benefited from presentation at the 1990 American Finance Association conference.

Notes

1. The option to defer investment has been examined by Tourinho (1979) in valuing reserves of natural resources, by McDonald and Siegel (1986), and by Paddock, Siegel, and Smith (1988) in valuing offshore petroleum leases. Majd and Pindyck (1987) value the option to delay sequential construction (time to build). The option to temporarily shut down operations has been analyzed by McDonald and Siegel (1985), and by Brennan and Schwartz (1985). Myers and Majd (1990) analyze the option to abandon for salvage value. Stulz (1982) values options on the maximum (and minimum) of risky assets, which may be useful in analyzing the option to switch between alternative uses. Baldwin and Ruback (1986) show that future asset price uncertainty creates a valuable switching option that benefits short-lived assets.

2. A notable exception is Brennan and Schwartz (1985) who utilize the convenience yield derived from futures and spot prices of a commodity to determine the combined value of the options to temporarily shut down (and open) a mine, and to abandon it for salvage, but do not address the interactions among individual option values.

3. The investment costs ($I_1 = 10$ in year 0, $I_2 = 90$ in year 3, and $I_3 = 35$ in year 5) are assumed known in advance and placed in an "escrow account" earning the riskless rate. Discounted continuously at the assumed risk-free rate of $r = 5$ percent, they yield a present value of $I = 114.7$.

4. For an options approach to capital budgeting, see, for example, Trigeorgis (1986), (1988), (1990), and (1991a).

5. For other numerical work on options, see, for example, Brennan (1979) and Geske and Shastri (1985); for applications to real options, see Myers and Majd (1990), and Majd and Pindyck (1987).

6. Although the precise numerical results may be somewhat different, the basic interaction effects would hold under alternative specifications of the underlying stochastic process (e.g., a mean-reverting process).

7. V is determined from discounting expected cash flows at the opportunity cost of capital. A proportional cash flow (e.g., 10 percent of current gross project value) is treated similarly to a dividend payout (see Myers and Majd (1990) for a good discussion), although here for simplicity no dividends are assumed. In general, one can incorporate any opportunity cost in delaying investment—which would be subtracted from the drift of the original project stochastic process—resulting either from a) intermediate cash flows missed by holding an option on the project (i.e., by waiting) rather than operating it immediately, or b) competitive erosion (see Trigeorgis (1986), Chapter 6).

8. This result holds unambiguously in the case of a subsequent call. If the latter option is also a put, the second effect would still be negative if exercise of the prior put reduces proportionately the scale of the latter put. However, in cases where the exercise price of the latter put is not reduced in proportion to project value, the second effect may be positive, although the net overall interaction may still be negative.

9. If exercising the prior call (e.g., in a compound call option) could expand the underlying asset or project scale (i.e., $V'' > V$), a subsequent option on that higher asset may be more valuable and interactions can be positive.

The option to defer a project—a call whose exercise does not alter the "underlying asset" for subsequent options—is more complex. First, as the cash flows and future options are pushed back allowing more time for crucial variables to change, the increased variability may make subsequent options somewhat more valuable. However, if project initiation is delayed, for example, because the project is not yet good enough, a subsequent call option to expand may be less valuable and exhibit a negative interaction, though mitigated by the above positive side effect. More important, since the option to defer is written on the portfolio of gross project value plus the value of subsequent options, it would, at first glance, appear to be more valuable, other factors being the same. At the same time, however, the presence of subsequent options may enable management to adjust better to changing circumstances, increasing the value of early investment compared with a similar situation without such flexibility. Thus, the incremental value of the option to wait would tend to decrease, relative to immediate investment. This effect typically would dominate and lead to negative overall interactions between the flexibility to defer and other subsequent real options.

10. Ironically, it is a better approximation to add up their separate values, other factors being the same, when the options are small (out of the money). To turn this around, it is least appropriate simply to add up

separate option values precisely when they are most needed, that is, when they are most valuable (in the money).

11. The options would still be approximately additive, though less so, if one of the two European options (e.g., the put) were replaced with its American counterpart, extending the possible exercise times on the same side relative to the other European option's maturity. But, the conditional probability of joint exercise, here proxied by a double-shaded trapezoidal area, and, hence, the degree of interaction would be somewhat higher.

If the American put option (e.g., to switch use) extends its potential exercise times both before and after the other (European call) option's maturity, a hybrid situation is possible. That is, negative interaction in the first part (where part of the put precedes the call) and positive in the latter part (where the call precedes part of the put). Both interactions would have small magnitude and partially cancel each other out, leading to better additive approximation.

12. In the continuous-time analogue, of course, the conditional probability is not precisely zero. Option value additivity would still approximately hold, however, if it is small enough.

13. The reader should be cautioned that, by design, the option to abandon construction with no recovery has no incremental value in the presence of the option to switch use.

14. If the additional option to expand were instead shifted to mature in year 4 so that it precedes the option to contract, then there is a slight positive interaction. $E4$ & $C5 = 31.2$ vs. $E4 + C5 = 31.1$. If the order is reversed, the options to contract in year 5 and to expand later in year 7 are still about additive, but with a slight negative interaction instead, specifically $C6$ & $E7 = 41.8$ vs. $C5 + E7 = 41.9$.

15. Assuming a proportional nature for the call options to expand, the presence of the latter call option increases the value of the first call option. This is clear since the first call option is written on the total project value, which increases in the presence of the second call option. Similarly, the possibility of exercising the first call option to expand project scale increases the value of the second proportionate call option, leading to a double positive or super-additive effect.

16. Although, in principle, there can be significant positive interactions, such as when expanding more than once, for the sequence of real options dealt with in this paper, interactions are typically negative. Positive interactions are more prevalent, however, *between* interdependent projects such as in R&D, in investments designed to gain a positioning in a new market, and in other so-called strategic investment commitments.

17. With the second option to expand in year 4 included, the joint value of all six options increases to 122, or 67 percent of their added separate values. Although the particular numbers would change when both expansion opportunities are considered, the net aggregate behavior of these options remains essentially the same.

18. The exact size of the error would, of course, depend on the type of neglected options, that is, whether they are puts or calls similar to the other options present, and the extent to which they are in the money, depending on the relative size of their exercise costs. It would also depend on the overlap of their exercise regions with those of the options included, as indicated earlier.

19. A simple selection rule is to eliminate those (usually put) options that are of similar type and are exercisable under similar circumstances as other included real options, particularly if their exercise costs are such that they are in-the-money options.

References

Abramowitz, M., and I. Stegum. *Handbook of Mathematical Functions.* (National Bureau of Standards, Washington D.C.) New York, NY: Dover Publications (1972).

Baldwin, C., and R. Ruback. "Inflation, Uncertainty, and Investment." *Journal of Finance*, 41 (July 1986), 657–669.

Black, F., and M. Scholes. "The Pricing of Options and Corporate Liabilities." *Journal of Political Economy*, 81 (May/June 1973), 637–659.

Brennan, M. "The Pricing of Contingent Claims in Discrete Time Models." *Journal of Finance*, 34 (March 1979), 53–68.

Brennan, M., and E. Schwartz. "Evaluating Natural Resource Investments." *Journal of Business*, 58 (April 1985), 135–157.

Carr, P. "The Valuation of Sequential Exchange Opportunities." *Journal of Finance*, 43 (Dec. 1988), 1235–1255.

Constantinides, G. "Market Risk Adjustment in Project Valuation." *Journal of Finance*, 33 (May 1978), 603–616.

Cox, J., and S. Ross. "The Valuation of Options for Alternative Stochastic Processes." *Journal of Financial Economics*, 3 (Jan. 1976), 145–166.

Cox, J.; J. Ingersoll; and S. Ross. "An Intertemporal General Equilibrium Model of Asset Prices." *Econometrica*, 53 (1985), 363–384.

Cox, J.; S. Ross; and M. Rubinstein. "Option Pricing: A Simplified Approach." *Journal of Financial Economics*, 7 (Sept. 1979), 229–263.

Geske, R. "The Valuation of Compound Options." *Journal of Financial Economics*, 7 (1979), 63–81.

Geske, R., and K. Shastri. "Valuation by Approximation: A Comparison of Alternative Option Valuation Techniques." *Journal of Financial and Quantitative Analysis*, 20 (March 1985), 45–71.

Harrison, J. M., and D. M. Kreps. "Martingales and Arbitrage in Multiperiod Securities Markets." *Journal of Economic Theory*, 20 (1979), 381–408.

Hull, J. *Options, Futures, and Other Derivative Securities*. Englewood Cliffs, NJ: Prentice-Hall (1989).

Jarrow, R., and A. Rudd. *Option Pricing*. Homewood, IL: R. D. Irwin (1983).

Kester, W. C. "Today's Options for Tomorrow's Growth." *Harvard Business Review* (March/April 1984), 153–160.

Majd, S., and R. Pindyck. "Time to Build, Option Value, and Investment Decisions." *Journal of Financial Economics*, 18 (March 1987), 7–27.

Margrabe, W. "The Value of an Option to Exchange One Asset for Another." *Journal of Finance*, 33 (March 1978), 177–186.

Mason, S. P., and R. C. Merton. "The Role of Contingent Claims Analysis in Corporate Finance." In *Recent Advances in Corporate Finance*. E. Altman and M. Subrahmanyam, eds. Homewood, IL: R. D. Irwin (1985).

McDonald, R., and D. Siegel. "Option Pricing when the Underlying Asset Earns a Below-Equilibrium Rate of Return: A Note." *Journal of Finance*, 39 (1984), 261–265.

———. "Investment and the Valuation of Firms when There is an Option to Shut Down." *International Economic Review*, 26 (June 1985), 331–349.

———. "The Value of Waiting to Invest." *Quarterly Journal of Economics*, 101 (Nov. 1986), 707–727.

Myers, S. C. "Finance Theory and Financial Strategy." *Midland Corporate Finance Journal*, 5 (Spring 1987), 6–13.

Myers, S. C., and S. Majd. "Abandonment Value and Project Life." *Advances in Futures and Options Research*, 4 (1990), 1–21.

Paddock, J.; D. Siegel; and J. Smith. "Option Valuation of Claims on Physical Assets: The Case of Offshore Petroleum Leases." *Quarterly Journal of Economics*, 103 (Aug. 1988), 479–508.

Stulz, R. "Options on the Minimum or Maximum of Two Risky Assets: Analysis and Applications." *Journal of Financial Economics*, 10 (July 1982), 161–185.

Tourinho, O. "The Option Value of Reserves of Natural Resources." Working Paper, Univ. of California at Berkeley (1979).

Trigeorgis, L. "Valuing Real Investment Opportunities: An Options Approach to Strategic Capital Budgeting." Unpubl. Doctoral Diss.: Harvard Univ. (1986).

————. "A Conceptual Options Framework for Capital Budgeting." *Advances in Futures and Options Research*, 3 (1988), 145–167.

————. "A Real Options Application in Natural Resource Investments." *Advances in Futures and Options Research*, 4 (1990), 153–164.

————. "Anticipated Competitive Entry and Early Preemptive Investment in Deferrable Projects." *Journal of Economics and Business*, 43 (May 1991a), 143–156.

————. "A Log-Transformed Binomial Numerical Analysis Method for Valuing Complex Multi-Option Investment." *Journal of Financial and Quantitative Analysis*, 26 (Sept. 1991b), 309–336.

Trigeorgis, L., and E. Kasanen. "An Integrated Options-Based Strategic Planning and Control Model." *Managerial Finance*, 17 (May 1991), 16–28.

Trigeorgis, L., and S. P. Mason. "Valuing Managerial Flexibility." *Midland Corporate Finance Journal*, 5 (Spring 1987), 14–21.

IV STRATEGY AND COMPETITION

18 Strategy as a Portfolio of Real Options

Timothy A. Luehrman

When executives create strategy, they project themselves and their organizations into the future, creating a path from where they are now to where they want to be some years down the road. In competitive markets, though, no one expects to formulate a detailed long-term plan and follow it mindlessly. As soon as we start down the path, we begin learning—about business conditions, competitors' actions, the quality of our preparations, and so forth—and we need to respond flexibly to what we learn. Unfortunately, the financial tool most widely relied on to estimate the value of strategy—discounted-cash-flow (DCF) valuation—assumes that we will follow a predetermined plan, regardless of how events unfold.

A better approach to valuation would incorporate both the uncertainty inherent in business and the active decision making required for a strategy to succeed. It would help executives think strategically on their feet by capturing the value of doing just that—of managing actively rather than passively. Options can deliver that extra insight. Advances in both computing power and our understanding of option pricing over the last 20 years make it feasible now to begin analyzing business strategies as chains of real options. As a result, the creative activity of strategy formulation can be informed by valuation analyses sooner rather than later. Financial insight may actually contribute to shaping strategy, rather than being relegated to an after-the-fact exercise of "checking the numbers."

In financial terms, a business strategy is much more like a series of options than a series of static cash flows. Executing a strategy almost always involves making a *sequence* of major decisions. Some actions are taken immediately, while others are deliberately deferred, so managers can optimize as circumstances evolve. The strategy sets the framework within which future decisions will be made, but at the same time it leaves room for learning from ongoing developments and for discretion to act based on what is learned.

To consider strategies as portfolios of related real options, this chapter exploits a framework presented in "Investment Opportunities as Real Options: Getting Started on the Numbers" (HBR July–August 1998). That article explains how to get from conventional DCF value to option value for a typical project—in other words, it is about how to get a number. This chapter extends that framework, exploring how option pricing can be used to improve decision making about the sequence and timing of a portfolio of strategic investments.

A Gardening Metaphor: Options as Tomatoes

Managing a portfolio of strategic options is like growing a garden of tomatoes in an unpredictable climate. Walk into the garden on a given day in August, and you will find that some tomatoes are ripe and perfect. Any gardener would know to pick and eat those immediately. Other tomatoes are rotten; no gardener would ever bother to pick them. These cases at the extremes—now and never—are easy decisions for the gardener to make.

In between are tomatoes with varying prospects. Some are edible and could be picked now but would benefit from more time on the vine. The experienced gardener picks them early only if squirrels or other competitors are likely to get them. Other tomatoes are not yet edible, and there's no point in picking them now, even if the squirrels do get them. However, they are sufficiently far along, and there is enough time left in the season, that many will ripen unharmed and eventually be picked. Still others look less promising and may not ripen before the season ends. But with more sun or water, fewer weeds, or just good luck, even some of these tomatoes may make it. Finally, there are small green tomatoes and late blossoms that have little likelihood of growing and ripening before the season ends. There is no value in picking them, and they might just as well be left on the vine.

Most experienced gardeners are able to classify the tomatoes in their gardens at any given time. Beyond that, however, good gardeners also understand how the garden changes over time. Early in the season, none of the fruit falls into the "now" or "never" categories. By the last day, all of it falls into one or the other because time has run out. The interesting question is, What can the gardener do during the season, while things are changing week to week?

A purely passive gardener visits the garden on the last day of the season, picks the ripe tomatoes, and goes home. The weekend gardener visits frequently and picks ripe fruit before it rots or the squirrels get it. Active gardeners do much more. Not only do they watch the garden but, based on what they see, they also cultivate it: watering, fertilizing, and weeding, trying to get more of those in-between tomatoes to grow and ripen before time runs out. Of course, the weather is always a question, and not all the tomatoes will make it. Still, we'd expect the active gardener to enjoy a higher yield in most years than the passive gardener.

In option terminology, active gardeners are doing more than merely making exercise decisions (pick or don't pick). They are monitoring the options and looking for ways to influence the underlying variables that determine option value and, ultimately, outcomes.

Option pricing can help us become more effective, active gardeners in several ways. It allows us to estimate the value of the entire year's crop (or even the value of a single tomato) before the season actually ends. It also helps us assess each tomato's prospects as the season progresses and tells us along the way which to pick and which to leave on the vine. Finally, it can suggest what to do to help those in-between tomatoes ripen before the season ends.

A Tour of Option Space

Instead of a garden plot, visualize a rectangle we'll call *option space*. Option space is defined by two option-value metrics, each of which captures a different part of the value associated with being able to defer an investment. Option space can help address the issues an active gardener will care about: whether to invest or not (that is, whether to pick or not to pick), when to invest, and what to do in the meantime.

Let's briefly review the two metrics, which were developed in "Investment Opportunities as Real Options." The first metric contains all the usual data captured in net present value (NPV) but adds the time value of being able to defer the investment. We called that metric NPV_q and defined it as the value of the underlying assets we intend to build or acquire divided by the present value of the expenditure required to build or buy them. Put simply, this is a ratio of value to cost. For convenience, here, we'll call it our *value-to-cost* metric instead of NPV_q, but bear in mind that *value* and *cost* refer to the project's assets, not to the option on those assets.

When the value-to-cost metric is between zero and one, we have a project worth less than it costs; when the metric is greater than one, the project is worth more than the present value of what it costs.

The second metric we'll call our *volatility* metric. It measures how much things can change before an investment decision must finally be made. That depends both on how uncertain, or risky, the future value of the assets in question is and on how long we can defer a decision. The former is captured by the *variance per period of asset returns*; the latter is the option's *time to expiration*. In the previous article, this second metric was called *cumulative volatility*.

Option space is defined by these two metrics, with value-to-cost on the horizontal axis and volatility on the vertical axis. See figure 18.1. The usual convention is to draw the space as a rectangle, with the value-to-cost metric increasing from left to right (its minimum value is zero), and the volatility metric increasing from top to bottom (its minimum value also is zero). Within the interior of the rectangle, option value increases as the value of either metric increases; that is, from any point in the

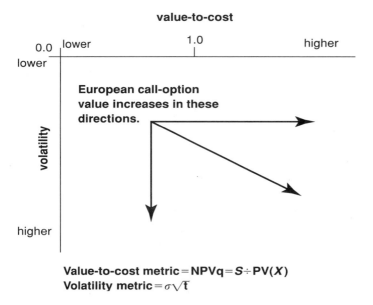

Figure 18.1
Option space is defined by two option-value metrics

space, if you move down, to the right, or in both directions simultaneously, option value rises.

How does option space help us with strategy? A business strategy is a series of related options: it is as though the condition of one tomato actually affected the size or ripeness of another one nearby. That obviously makes things more complicated. Before we analyze a strategy, let's first consider the simpler circumstance in which the tomatoes growing in the garden don't affect one another. To do that, we need to explore the option space further.

In a real garden, good, bad, and in-between tomatoes can turn up anywhere. Not so in option space, where there are six separate regions, each of which contains a distinct type of option and a corresponding managerial prescription. We carve up the space into distinct regions by using what we know about the value-to-cost and volatility metrics, along with conventional NPV.

What's the added value of dividing option space in this fashion? Traditional corporate finance gives us one metric—NPV—for evaluating projects, and only two possible actions: invest or don't invest. In option space, we have NPV, two extra metrics, and six possible actions that reflect not only where a project is now but also

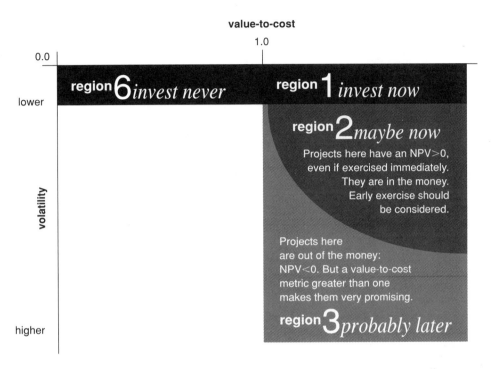

Figure 18.2
Dividing option space into regions

the likelihood of it ending up somewhere better in the future. When we return to assessing strategies, this forward looking judgment will be especially useful.

Top of the Space: *Now* and *Never*

At the very top of our option space, the volatility metric is zero. (See figure 18.2) That's so either because all uncertainty has been resolved or because time has run out. With business projects, the latter is far more likely. So projects that end up here differ from one another only according to their value-to-cost metrics, and it's easy to see what to do with them. If the value-to-cost metric is greater than one, we go ahead and invest now. If it's less than one, we invest never. Once time has run out, "now or never" completely describes our choices. It will be convenient to refer to regions by number, so let's number these extremes 1 and 6. Region 1 contains the perfectly ripe tomatoes; it is the *invest now* region. Region 6 contains the rotten ones; the prescription there is *invest never*.

Right Side of the Space: *Maybe Now* **and** *Probably Later*

What about projects whose value-to-cost metric is greater than one but whose time has not yet run out? All such projects fall somewhere in the right half of our option space but below the top. Projects here are very promising because the underlying assets are worth more than the present value of the required investment. Does that mean we should go ahead and invest right away? In some instances, the answer is clearly no, while in other cases, it's maybe. We want to be able to distinguish between those cases. The key to doing so is not option pricing but conventional NPV.

In terms of the tomato analogy, we are looking at a lot of promising tomatoes, none of which is perfectly ripe. We want to distinguish between those that, if picked right away, are edible (NPV > 0) and those that are inedible (NPV < 0). The distinction matters because there is no point in picking the inedible ones. Conventional NPV tells us the value of investing immediately despite the fact that time has not yet run out. If NPV is negative, immediate exercise is unambiguously suboptimal. In option terminology, we say that such an option is *out of the money*: it costs more to exercise it than the assets are worth. The exercise price (X) is greater than the underlying asset value (S), therefore NPV $= S - X < 0$.

The curve in our diagram separates options that are out of the money (NPV < 0) from those that are *in the money* (NPV > 0). For points above the curve in the diagram, NPV is positive; for those below the curve, NPV is negative. For points actually on the curve itself, NPV $= 0$.

Projects below the curve, which we'll call region 3, are like the inedible tomatoes that we clearly don't want to pick right away. Even so, they are very promising because their value-to-cost metric is positive and time has not yet run out. I call this region *probably later* because, even though we should not invest yet, we expect to invest eventually for a relatively high fraction of these projects. In the meantime, they should be cultivated.

Projects that fall above the NPV $= 0$ curve are even more interesting. These options are in the money. They are like tomatoes that even though not perfectly ripe are nevertheless edible. We should be considering whether to pick them early.

It may seem contradictory to consider exercising an option early when all along I've argued in "Investment Opportunities as Real Options" that it is valuable to be able to defer the investment—to wait, see what happens, and then make an optimal choice at the last possible moment. If there is value associated with deferring, why would we ever do otherwise? Sometimes, especially with real options, value may be lost as well as gained by deferring, and the proper decision depends on which effect dominates.

The financial analog to such a real option is a call option on a share of stock. If the stock pays a large dividend, the shareholder receives value that the option holder does not. The option holder may wish to become a shareholder simply to participate in the dividend, which otherwise would be forgone. Think of the dividend as value lost by deferring the exercise decision.

In the case of real options, where the underlying asset is some set of business cash flows, any *predictable* loss of value associated with deferring the investment is like the dividend in our stock example. Phenomena like pending changes in regulations, a predictable loss of market share, or preemption by a competitor are all costs associated with investing later rather than sooner and might cause us to exercise an option early. Or, to use the tomato analogy, we might pick an edible tomato early if we can predict that squirrels will get it otherwise. *Unpredictable* gains and losses, however, would not lead us to exercise our options early.

Options that are in the money (that is, those for which NPV > 0) should be evaluated to see if they ought to be exercised early. Immediate investment will not always be the optimal course of action because by investing early the company loses the advantages of deferring, which also are real. Deciding whether to invest early requires a case-by-case comparison of the value of investing immediately with the value of waiting a bit longer—that is, of continuing to hold the project as an option. I refer to that part of the option space as *maybe now* because we might decide to invest right away. Let's label it region 2.

Left Side of the Space: *Maybe Later* and *Probably Never*

All options that fall in the left half of the space are less promising because the value-to-cost metric is everywhere less than one, and conventional NPV is everywhere less than zero. But even here we can separate the more valuable from the less valuable. The upper left is unpromising territory because both the value-to-cost and volatility metrics are low. These are the late blossoms and the small green tomatoes that are unlikely to ripen before the season ends. I call this part of the option space *probably never*, and we can label it region 5.

In contrast, the lower section (of this left half of the space) has better prospects because at least one of the two metrics is reasonably high. I call it *maybe later*, and we can label it region 4. Figure 18.3 dispenses with fancy curves and simply divides the option space roughly into the six regions.

When to Harvest

As an example of what we learn from the tomato garden, consider six hypothetical projects that are entirely unrelated to one another. Table 18.1 shows the relevant data

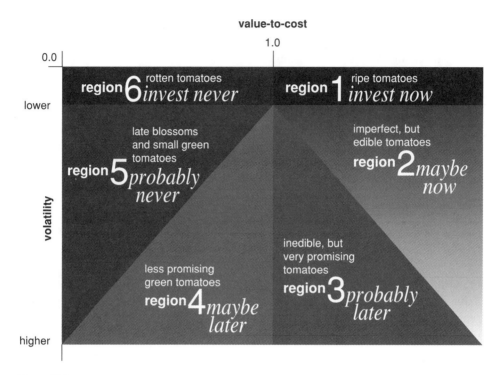

Figure 18.3
The tomato garden

for these projects, which have been labeled A through F. Note that each of them involves assets worth $100 million. Two of them (A and B) require capital expenditures of $90 million; the other four require expenditures of $110 million. So A and B each has a positive NPV of $10 million. Each of the other four has an NPV of negative $10 million. The NPV of the entire portfolio is negative $20 million or, more reasonably, positive $20 million, since the four projects with negative NPVs can be included at a value of zero. Conventional capital budgeting offers only two prescriptions—invest or don't invest. Following those rules, we'd accept projects A and B and reject all the others.

Although their NPVs are tightly clustered, the six projects have different time and volatility profiles, and hence different values for their value-to-cost and volatility metrics. Consequently, each is located in a different region of the option space. (See figure 18.4.)

Table 18.1
Vital statistics for six independent projects

Variable	A	B	C	D	E	F	Portfolio value
S Underlying asset value ($ millions)	100.00	100.00	100.00	100.00	100.00	100.00	
X Exercise price ($ millions)	90.00	90.00	110.00	110.00	110.00	110.00	
t Time to expiration (years)	0.00	2.00	0.00	0.50	1.00	2.00	
σ Standard deviation (per year)	0.30	0.30	0.30	0.20	0.30	0.40	
r_f Risk-free rate of return (% per year)	0.06	0.06	0.06	0.06	0.06	0.06	
NPVq Value-to-cost metric	1.111	1.248	0.909	0.936	0.964	1.021	
$\sigma\sqrt{t}$ Volatility metric	0.000	0.424	0.000	0.141	0.300	0.566	
Call value ($ millions)	10.00	27.23	0.00	3.06	10.42	23.24	73.95
S-X Conventional NPV ($ millions)	10.00	10.00	−10.00	−10.00	−10.00	−10.00	20.00
Region	1	2	6	5	4	3	
Exercise decision	now	maybe now	never	probably never	maybe later	probably later	

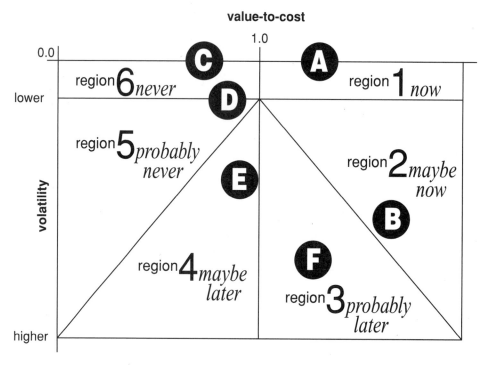

Figure 18.4
Locating the Projects in the Tomato Garden

A is a *now* project that falls in region 1; C is a *never* project in region 6. For both of them, time has run out, so the volatility metric is zero. Project B is very promising: its NPV is positive, and its value-to-cost metric is greater than one. B plots in region 2, and we should consider whether we ought to exercise our option on this project early. However, unless there is some predictable loss in future value (either a rise in cost or a fall in value), then early exercise is not only unnecessary but also suboptimal. Project F's value-to-cost metric is greater than one, but its NPV is less than zero. It falls in region 3 and is very valuable as an option, despite its negative NPV. That's because it will not expire for two years and has the highest volatility of the whole group. Hence, project F's prognosis is *probably later*.

Project E has less going for it than project F. It is in region 4 and deserves some attention because, with a year to go and the moderate standard deviation of its underlying asset return ($\sigma = 0.3$ per year), it just might make it. That's why it is classified as *maybe later*. Project D is much less promising (a *probably never*) because a decision must be made in only six months and, with a low volatility, there's not much likelihood that D will pop into the money before time runs out.

Because it can account for flexibility and uncertainty, the options-based framework produces a different assessment of this portfolio than the conventional DCF approach would. Most obviously, where DCF methods give the portfolio a value of $20 million, option pricing gives it a value of about $74 million, more than three times greater. Just as important, locating these projects in the tomato garden yields notably different exercise decisions. Instead of accepting two projects and rejecting four, our option analysis leads us to accept one, reject one, and wait and see about the other four. And as we wait, we know how each project's prospects differ. Moreover, we don't wait passively. Having only limited resources to devote to the portfolio, we realize that some wait-and-see projects are more likely to reward our active cultivation than others. In particular, we can see that projects E and F together are worth about $34 million (not negative $20 million or even $0) and should be actively cultivated rather than abandoned. At the very least, they could be sold to some other gardener.

A Dynamic Approach

Cultivation is intended to improve the crop, but it has to work within boundaries set by nature. In option space, as in nature, there are basic laws of time and motion. The most basic is that options tend to move upward and to the left in the option space as time passes. Upward, because the volatility metric decreases as time runs out. To the left, because, as a present-value calculation, the value-to-cost metric also decreases over time if its other constituent variables remain constant.

To illustrate, consider project F. Its volatility metric is 0.566, and its value-to-cost metric is 1.021. Now let a year pass, and suppose none of project F's variables changes except for t, which is now one year instead of two. Were we to recompute the metrics, we would discover that both have declined. The volatility metric falls from 0.566 to 0.400, which moves F upward in option space. And its value-to-cost metric declines from 1.021 to 0.964—that is, $100 \div [110 \div (1 + 0.06)^1]$—which moves F to the left. In fact, project F moves from region 3 (*probably later*) to the less promising region 4 (*maybe later*). Despite its initial promise, the only way project F is going to wind up in the money (that is, in region 1 or 2) and eventually get funded is if some force pushes it to the right, overcoming the natural tug to the left, before time runs out. Only two forces push in that direction: good luck and active management.

Neither force should be ignored. Sometimes we succeed by putting ourselves squarely in the way of good fortune. Other times we have to work at it. Managers actively cultivating a portfolio of opportunities are, in effect, working to push options as far as possible to the right in the space before they float all the way to the top. How is that done? By taking some action that increases either or both of our option-value metrics. Of the two, the value-to-cost metric is perhaps the more obvious one to work on first because managers are more accustomed to managing revenues, costs, and capital expenditures than volatility or time to expiration.

Anything managers can do to increase value or reduce cost will move the option to the right in our space. For example, price or volume increases, tax savings, or lower capital requirements, as well as any cost savings, will help. Such enhancements to value are obvious with or without a real-options framework. What the framework provides is a way to incorporate them visually and quantitatively into option value through the value-to-cost metric.

The real world seldom gives managers the luxury of isolating one variable and holding all others constant. Managers cannot simply declare. "Let's raise prices to increase the value of our project." More likely, they will invent and evaluate complex proposal modifications driven or constrained by technology, demographics, regulations, and so on. For example, one way to cultivate a market-entry option might be to add a new product feature. That may entail extra investment (raising X), but it will also help differentiate the product in the local market, permitting higher prices (raising S) but also adding extra manufacturing costs (lowering S), some of which are fixed. The net effect on the value-to-cost metric is what counts, and the net effect is unclear without further analysis.

Evaluating the project as an option means there is more, not less, to analyze, but the framework tells us what to analyze, gives us a way to organize the effects, and offers a visual interpretation. Observing the change in the option's location in our space tells us both whether its value has risen or fallen and whether it has migrated to a different region of the tomato garden.

There are still more considerations even in this simple example of adding a product feature. Extra fixed costs mean greater risk, which might lower the value of the project (due to the need to discount future cash flows at a higher risk-adjusted rate) and cause its value-to-cost metric to drop further. But the extra fixed costs also represent operating leverage that raises the volatility metric. That augments option value. We could hypothesize further that adding an extra feature will stimulate a competitor to match it. We, in turn, might be forced to introduce the next generation of our product (on which we hold a different option) earlier than we otherwise would have.

In general, actions taken by managers can affect not only the value-to-cost measure but also the volatility metric. In this example, both elements of the volatility metric—risk and time to expiration—are affected. And for more than one option. There is a spillover from one option to another: adding a feature reduces the length of time a subsequent decision can be deferred. For other situations, there are a myriad of possible spillover effects.

Nested Options in a Business Strategy

Once we allow options in a portfolio to directly influence other options, we are ready to consider strategies: series of options explicitly *designed* to affect one another. We can use "nests" of options upon options to represent the sequence of contingencies designed into a business, as in the following simplified and hypothetical example.

Three years ago, the WeatherIze Corporation bought an exclusive license to a technology for treating fabric to retard its breakdown in extreme weather conditions. The idea was to develop a new line of fabric especially suitable for outdoor commercial awnings, a market the company already serves with a less durable product. Now WeatherIze's engineers have developed their first treated fabric, and the company is considering making the expenditures required to roll it out commercially. If the product is well received by awning manufacturers, WeatherIze will have to expand capacity within three years of introduction just to serve awning producers.

The vice president for business development is ebullient. He anticipates that success in awnings will be followed within another two years by product extensions—similar treatment of different fabrics designed for such consumer goods as tents, umbrellas, and patio furniture. At that time, WeatherIze would expand capacity yet again. The company envisions trademarking its fabrics, expanding its sales force, and supporting the consumer products made from these fabrics with cooperative advertising.

WeatherIze's strategy for exploiting the treatment technology is pretty straightforward. It consists of a particular sequence of decision opportunities. The first step of the execution was to purchase the license. By doing so, the company acquired a sequence of nested options: to develop the product; to introduce the product; to expand capacity for manufacturing awning fabric; and to expand again to make related, branded fabrics. Just now, having developed the product, WeatherIze is part way through the strategy and is considering its next step: spending on the product introduction. That is, it's time to exercise (or not) the next real option in the chain.

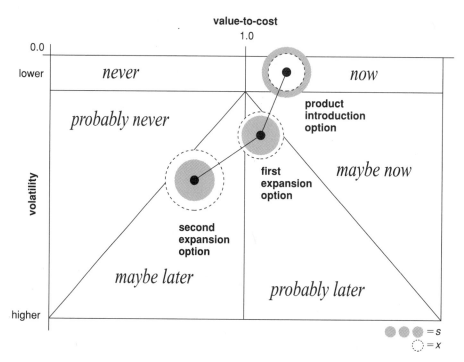

Figure 18.5
Weatherize's strategy as nested call options

WeatherIze's strategy, at this point in time, is depicted in option space in figure 18.5. Each circle represents an option whose location in space is determined by its value-to-cost and volatility metrics. The size of each solid circle is proportionate to the underlying asset value (S) for each option. The area within each dashed circle is proportionate to required expenditures (X). Thus a dashed circle inside a solid one represents an option that is in the money ($S > X$). A dashed circle outside a solid circle shows an option that is out of the money.

The line segments in the diagram indicate that the options are nested. The option to expand for awning production is acquired if and only if the option to introduce is exercised. As such, the underlying asset for the introduction option includes both the value of the operating cash flows associated with the product itself *and* the present value of the option to expand. Likewise, the option to expand a second time for commercial product production is acquired only if WeatherIze decides to exercise its first expansion option. The value of the whole strategy at this point is:

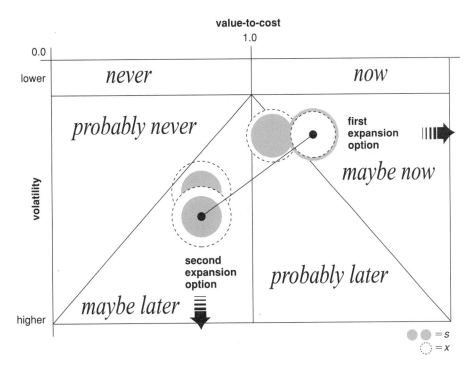

Figure 18.6
What happens if the consumer fabrics opportunities become riskier

$$PV \left\{ \begin{matrix} product \\ introduction \end{matrix} + \begin{matrix} call \\ value \end{matrix} \left[\begin{matrix} (first \\ expansion \\ option) \end{matrix} + \begin{matrix} call \\ value \end{matrix} \begin{matrix} (second \\ expansion \\ option) \end{matrix} \right] \right\}.$$

In effect, WeatherIze owns a call on a call.

The option to introduce the new awning fabric is in the money and about to expire. (WeatherIze will forfeit its license if it does not go ahead with the introduction.) As soon as this option is exercised, the picture changes. The top circle goes away; the bottom two remain linked and begin drifting upward. One of the most important factors determining whether they move right or left on their way up is how well the awning fabric does in the marketplace. But there are other factors as well. Anything that enhances the value of the second expansion option enhances the value of the first, too, because the value of the second option forms part of the value of the underlying asset value for the first option.

Suppose, for example, the risks associated with the consumer-product fabric's assets increase. Let's trace the effects in figure 18.6. The most direct effect is on the second expansion option, which moves down in the space because its volatility metric rises. The second expansion option becomes more valuable. But the increased risk also affects the first expansion option for awning fabric. Its value-to-cost metric rises because the second expansion option is part of the underlying assets (S) of the first. In fact, a change in either metric for the second option must also change the value-to-cost metric (at least) of the first.

As another example, suppose a competitor introduces a substitute fabric in the consumer goods markets that WeatherIze had planned to target. Try to visualize what will happen. Not only will the locations of the options change but so will the sizes of the circles. The solid circle, or asset value (S), of WeatherIze's second expansion option will shrink, and both the first and second expansion options will move to the left. Further, the first expansion option's underlying asset value also should shrink.

Drawing simple circles in the option space also lets us compare strategies. For example, we have been assuming that WeatherIze would not introduce branded fabrics without first expanding its awning fabric capacity. Now suppose the company could do either first, or both simultaneously, but that a larger investment would be required to make branded fabrics if the awning expansion weren't accomplished first. We could also assume that profit margins on the branded goods would be higher if the company first gained more experience with awning fabric.

These options in WeatherIze's alternative strategy are not nested, and they are no longer in the same locations. Figure 18.7 depicts the new strategy. Note that the second option, the branded-fabric option, is now farther left, its solid circle, or asset value (S), is smaller, and its dashed circle, or expenditures (X), is larger than it was originally. It is further out of the money but is now linked directly to the product introduction option. Given that the branded-fabric option is farther left under this new strategy and its solid circle is smaller, could we possibly prefer it? Yes, actually, provided it also moves down in the space—that is, if its volatility metric has increased. The pricing table in the real-options framework can tell us how far down it would have to go to compensate for any given move to the left. Finally, note that for the nonnested strategy, the value of both options directly enhances the value of the underlying asset associated with the initial product introduction. But it is no longer the case that any change in the second expansion option must affect the location of the first expansion option: each could, in fact, move around independently.

Although the options are not nested, they are very much related. Suppose, for example, that the awning expansion option pops into the money and is indeed

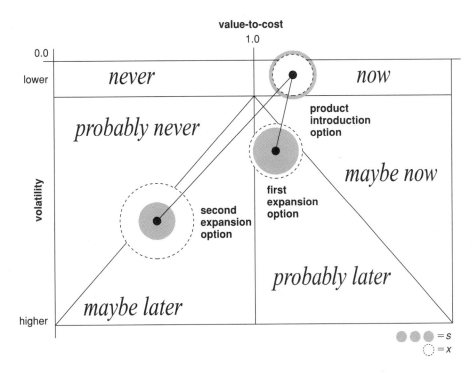

Figure 18.7
Alternative strategy

exercised first, before the consumer fabric option. The value of the latter would be enhanced because the underlying assets associated with it would be expected to produce better margins—the value-to-cost metric for the consumer fabric option rises.

To compare WeatherIze's alternative strategies, we compute the value of each strategy's introduction option. We can do that quantitatively using the real-options framework. In visual terms, we prefer the introduction option to be farther to the right and to have a larger solid circle. Whichever strategy accomplishes that is more valuable.

Learning to Garden

I argued in "Investment Opportunities as Real Options" that companies should adopt option-pricing techniques as adjuncts to their existing system, not as replacements. If WeatherIze takes that approach, there is a good chance that the "tomato garden" will help the company create and execute a superior strategy.

Strategists at WeatherIze already were thinking several moves ahead when they purchased the license. They don't need a tomato garden to tell them merely to think ahead. But option pricing quantifies the value of the all-important follow-on opportunities much better than standard DCF-valuation techniques do. And the tomato garden adds a simple but versatile picture that reveals important insights into both the value and the timing of the exercise decisions. It gives managers a way to "draw" a strategy in terms that are neither wholly strategic nor wholly financial but some of both. Managers can play with the pictures much as they might with a physical model built of Legos or Tinker Toys. Some of us are most creative while at play.

As executives at WeatherIze experiment with circles in option space, it is important that they preserve the link between the pictures they draw and the disciplined financial projections required by the real-options framework. They need to remember that the circles occupy a certain part of the space because the numbers—the value-to-cost and volatility metrics—put them there. At the same time, they need to prevent the exercise from becoming just another variation on "valuation as usual." This is the well-worn rut in which valuation analysis is used primarily to check numbers and as due diligence documentation for investments. Instead, the purpose should be to incorporate financial insights at the stage when projects and strategies are actually being created.

How does one become a good gardener? Practice, practice. I recommend starting by drawing simple combinations of projects to learn some common forms. What are the different ways you can depict a pair of nested call options? How can the pair move in the space? What are the ways to transform their configuration by changing the variables? Then move on to simple generic strategies. What does a given strategy look like when drawn in the option space? How does the picture change over time? How does it change when an option is exercised?

Next, practice translating real business phenomena into visual effects to update pictures. For example, how will the picture change if you add a direct mail campaign to your product introduction? Or how will the picture change if your competitor cuts prices when you enter a market?

Finally, try drawing your strategy and your competitors' side by side: How does the value and location of your options affect the value and location of theirs? How will they all move over time?

In most companies, strategy formulation and business development are not located in the finance bailiwick. Nevertheless, both activities raise important financial questions almost right away. Although the questions arise early, answers typically do not. For finance to play an important creative role, it must be able to contribute insightful interpretive analyses of sequences of decisions that are purely hypothetical—that is, while they are still mere possibilities. By building option pricing into a framework designed to evaluate not only hard assets but also opportunities (and multiple, related opportunities at that), we can add financial insight earlier rather than later to the creative work of strategy.

19 The Value of Options in Strategic Acquisitions

Kenneth W. Smith and Alexander J. Triantis

19.1 Introduction

In recent years, corporations have been much maligned for destroying shareholder value through acquisitions. Porter's (1987) study of acquisitions concludes that only the lawyers, investment bankers, and original sellers have benefited from these transactions, while the acquiring firms' shareholders generally have not. Recent analyses of pre- and postacquisition cash flows suggest that, on average, acquisitions have failed to increase profitability through restructuring, transfering skills, or exploiting synergies, and thus takeover premiums do not seem to be justified.[1] Not surprisingly, critics argue that many acquisitions that reduce shareholder value are driven by motives consistent with increasing managerial welfare.[2] For example, firm growth and diversification often tend to increase the value of human capital more than shareholder value.

Managers have responded to the increased concern about postacquisition value by firming up acquisition criteria so that fewer mistakes are made. For example, many companies have put in place criteria designed to limit the profit and loss (P&L) downside to acquisitions (e.g., threshold Return on Revenue or Return on Capital Employed criteria). Unfortunately, these criteria often fail to link realized returns and management's future discretionary actions to the recovery of the price paid for the acquisition. Use of conventional cash-flow valuation analyses to estimate the target enterprise's future cash flows and separately identify, schedule, and value future management actions to realize potential synergies and improve returns, place a higher standard on target selection and postacquisition management.

These approaches, however, may err on the conservative side. First, such criteria may discriminate against longer-term acquisition programs that, through a series of acquisitions over time, can significantly change an acquirer's competitive position (and even the structure of its industry) through the development of *growth options*. Cash flow analysis often fails to appropriately value alternative courses of action in such industry restructuring situations. For example, *not* pursuing an acquisition that would position the corporation in a key emerging market segment may have the effect of foreclosing important future strategic options. Moreover, allowing competitors to acquire their way into dominant positions in such segments could indeed threaten a company's current market position.

Second, firms with significant flexibility in organization, marketing, manufacturing, and financing may reap additional benefits from strategic acquisitions that involve diversification. Beyond specific actions to improve and integrate the new businesses, the resulting portfolio may open up strategic alternatives to efficiently utilize the firm's resources in the future. For example, a firm with flexible distribution channels may purchase another firm whose product demand is negatively correlated with its own and quickly adapt existing marketing and distribution, expanding its customer base to cushion the downside in periods of weak demand for its current products. An acquisition program that focuses on strategic, rather than financial, diversification will not only decrease the variance of the firm's future cash flows, but more importantly, it may significantly increase firm value by enhancing the value of the firm's *flexibility options.*

Third, conventional acquisition analysis does not always account for the option to divest parts (or all) of the acquired companies at a later date.[3] Future sale of these assets to companies that would value them at equal or close to their original purchase prices may substantially limit downside risk. For example, idle real estate may be sold off for an alternative use. While some divestitures may occur soon after an acquisition, an acquirer may instead hold on to its *divestiture options* and optimally plan the timing of their exercise.

In short, many acquisitions create valuable options. The acquirer will make decisions regarding discretionary investments, divestments, and resource allocation that depend on future conditions, analogous to financial options. Like financial options, strategic advantages associated with acquisitions introduce the ability to truncate downside risk while preserving upside potential, and thus can make a considerable contribution to shareholder value, which is not typically accounted for in a simple discounted cash flow value. Table 19.1 provides several examples of such growth, flexibility, and divestiture options as they arise in strategic acquisitions.

The rest of the chapter examines valuation considerations for strategic options associated with acquisitions. Section 19.2 discusses the purchase and development of growth options through acquisitions. Section 19.3 analyzes flexibility options and discusses the significance of acquisitions which focus on strategic diversification. Section 19.4 examines the valuation of divestiture options. Section 19.5 provides concluding remarks.

19.2   Developing Growth Options through Acquisitions

A firm's value is comprised of the value of assets in place and the value of growth options that may arise from the firm's superior technological position, significant market share, effective marketing and distribution channels, or other strategic advantages that facilitate further growth.[4] The use of the term *options* highlights the fact that the firm has some discretion over its future investments. Management can

Table 19.1
Examples of options embedded in strategic acquisitions

Growth options

A computer firm purchases another software start-up company rather than developing its own competing software.

An international airline acquires a U.S. airline to break into the U.S. market and increase traffic on existing or potential future routes.

A large publishing firm buys a smaller niche periodical firm enabling launches into related specialized periodicals in the future.

Flexibility options

A firm in the aggregates business buys undeveloped quarry sites which have future potential for municipal waste disposal.

A diversified retailer switches use of shopping mall leased space in response to varying market conditions for each business.

A newsprint maker with virgin fiber mills acquires a mill capable of using recycled fiber.

Divestiture options

An acquirer can divest real estate with a more valuable alternative use.

An acquiring airline can sell off selected routes or airport gates after purchasing another airline.

An acquirer sells companies that have not met growth targets, thereby truncating downside risk.

choose to commit capital in the future (analogous to paying the exercise price of a financial option) in order to capture the present value of subsequent cash flows associated with the project (analogous to the price of the underlying stock in the case of a stock option). Alternatively, it can decide not to pursue the investment if circumstances make the investment unattractive in the future. The growth option is valuable to the firm since it need not currently commit to undertaking the future investment, enabling the firm to truncate downside risks. Growth options are particularly valuable in high-tech or emerging industries ranging from computer hardware and software to biotechnology, new markets where there may be a very significant upside in future demand, but at the same time there is considerable technological risk and uncertainty.

Strategic acquisitions can serve as a vehicle to facilitate growth in a company. There are several ways in which growth may be enabled by acquisitions. First, a firm seeking to quickly enter into a new market niche may find it cheaper or more expedient to purchase such a growth option rather than develop it on its own. The firm may acquire a smaller "threshold company" that has developed an entrepreneurial concept and is now looking to grow but may not have the necessary manufacturing, distribution or other infrastructure or access to low-cost capital to achieve its goal. The acquirer that can best provide such a resource base will likely be able to purchase the target at a price lower than its value will be once it is integrated into the acquiring firm. Generally, a target firm may have several growth options that the acquiring firm lacks and considers especially valuable. Alternatively, an acquiring firm may have growth opportunities that it has trouble developing on its own, and thus may profit through acquisitions from the transfer of technological skills or access to distribution channels that allow marketing to new geographic locations or customer segments.

Frequently, acquisitions may involve a substantial interaction between growth options in the purchasing and acquired firms. For instance, both firms may share common opportunities for growth in a particular industry. A firm considering an acquisition may feel that joining its efforts with another firm and exploiting the resultant synergies may be valuable, especially if the move serves to strengthen its competitive position by decreasing costs or increasing the speed of developing growth opportunities.

To illustrate, consider the professional and trade periodicals industry, which is characterized by frequent new product introductions and acquisitions. Competitors such as Thomson, McGraw-Hill, and Reed International make numerous product acquisitions, most often in audience segments that they already serve. In making these acquisitions, the acquirer receives the future cash flows of acquired products and synergy values, plus three important options.

First, in combination with their own entries in the segment, these acquirers build up circulation lists and advertiser relationships overwhelmingly superior to any others in the industry, thereby enhancing the value of their options to invest in new magazine launches or other advertising products within their segment. These options may have lower exercise prices and yield larger profits, and can be exercised if and when market conditions are favorable.

Second, through such acquisitions, these firms may have enhanced the option value of acquiring other periodicals—either existing or future startups—because the operational synergies with a subsequent related periodical would be even higher than they would be with just the original slate alone. Thus, each acquisition has higher value within the broader context of the firm's long-run acquisition program.

Third, and not unrelated to the first two options, an acquirer can, through the purchase, eliminate the seller's option to grow into the market through new product launches or acquisitions. Without such acquisitions, the buyer and the seller each hold an option to reposition their products or to launch line extensions to capture a share of each other's market. Consequently, the status quo may not be a reliable base-case scenario. A firm must clearly recognize the cost of not reacting to changes in its competitive environment and may utilize acquisitions as a vehicle for the preservation of its competitive advantage.

To illustrate how one may go about valuing the growth option components involved in an acquisition, consider the following case. ABC Publishing is considering acquiring Tech Magazines for a price of $100 million. The present value (PV) of

Table 19.2
Growth option valuation (millions of $) if ABC proceeds to expand alone or if it first acquires Tech

	Proceed alone	Acquire Tech
Present value of profits (S)	10	25
PV of launching cost (Xe^{-rt})	10	15
NPV $(S - Xe^{-rt})$	0	10
Option value	1.97	11.82

Tech's cash flows based on its current publications is estimated to be $90 million. ABC also estimates that through significant consolidations in operations, there would be a cost savings of $5 million. Based on these figures alone, the Tech purchase has a negative net preset value (NPV) of −$5 million and thus does not seem attractive.

The manager of ABC's technical publications division, however, points out that both he and Tech's managers have been independently considering launching a publication on laptop computers. The market for publications in this area seems promising, but is as yet untested. ABC's manager forecasts that his firm would optimally wait for two years before deciding whether to launch such a magazine. However, he also predicts that competition with Tech would result in both firms launching the new publication after only one year if it is profitable to pursue this market at all. Based on their current market power, ABC and Tech would split the new market equally.

The cash-flow estimates required to value the growth option are given in table 19.2, both for the case where ABC expands into the new market on its own, as well as for the situation where it first acquires Tech. Note that the PV of profits from the new publication if ABC acquires Tech is more than twice than if it proceeded on its own. This is due to a reduction in operating costs through economies of scale. Similarly, by joining forces with Tech, ABC can establish economies which reduce the fixed cost of launching the magazine.

Since we assume that the growth options in each case are European, we may use the Black-Scholes pricing formula to value these options.[5] (We assume that the present value of profits has a volatility of $\sigma = 50\%$.) The last row of table 19.2 reports the estimated option values. The acquisition effectively increases ABC's growth option value by $9.85 (= 11.82 − 1.97) million, through purchasing Tech's growth option and developing both options jointly. Taking this growth option value into account, the NPV of the acquisition is in fact $4.85 million, as compared to the −$5 million valuation which ignored the growth option contribution of the acquisition.

The $9.85 million increase in growth option value comes from three sources. First, ABC purchases Tech's option to develop its half of the market. Second, there are economies of scale which are obtained from developing the larger-scale joint growth option, translating into lower costs for the launch and subsequent operation of the new publication. Note that while this synergy results in an effective increase of $10 million in the NPV shown in table 19.2, these gains are only realized if ABC does in fact exercise its growth option. Finally, by avoiding a race with Tech to reach the market first, ABC may be able to wait longer (two years, rather than one) before deciding whether it should launch the new publication or not. This incremental value of waiting contributes $1.06 million ($= 11.82 - 10.76$), where $10.76 million is the Black-Scholes value of the combined growth option with a one-year horizon.

This simple example illustrates that the value of a firm's growth option may be enhanced through acquisitions by decreasing the exercise price, increasing the present value of future profits earned upon exercise, and allowing for greater flexibility in timing the exercise of the option. Acquisitions in industries that are consolidating because of scale economies or globalization can be viewed in a similar way. Each successful acquisition can enhance the value of the option to acquire further by enlarging the size and scope of synergies with possible future targets and by reducing the risk of being left out of an industry consolidation or being structurally disadvantaged in the future.

19.3   Flexibility Options and Strategic Diversification

Synergy gains achieved through acquisitions are often a result of the consolidation of resources. Reducing duplication in administration expenses, sharing marketing distribution channels, and utilizing excess plant capacity all provide incremental value to the purchasing firm. These synergy gains, which are often estimated under a static scenario assumption regarding the markets in which the combined business units operate, can be seen to have additional value if the effects of uncertainty are more carefully analyzed.

In particular, there may be important flexibility options that derive value from the presence of uncertainty *and* diversification opportunities for an acquiring firm. If the acquiring (or integrated) firm possesses significant flexibility in organization, manufacturing, distribution, or financing, then such flexible resources may be more fully exploited by diversifying across products or lines of business whose profitabilities are not highly positively correlated. The distinction between such strategic diversification and financial diversification must be emphasized. The latter is sometimes defended by claiming that it is a means of reducing business risk. Critics of such diversification-driven acquisition programs, however, point out that shareholders can usually diversify more efficiently on their own, and that it is the acquiring firm's managers, not its

Table 19.3
Projected cash flows and present values (millions of $)

	A		B		C		A + B		A + C	
Price of oil ($/barrel)	15	25	15	25	15	25	15	25	15	25
Profit before FOC	95	75	5	25	20	20	100	100	100	95
FOC	80	80	15	15	15	15	80	80	80	80
Net profit	15	−5	−10	10	5	5	20	20	20	15
Present value	2.86		1.90		4.76		19.05		16.19	

shareholders, who stand to gain the most from such reduction in risk.[6] Besides, there may be a substantial price paid by firms who fail to "stick to their knitting."

Consider the following illustration of how an acquirer pursuing strategic diversification can enhance the value of its flexibility options. Company A, an automobile manufacturer, has followed a strategy that stresses the importance of maintaining flexible resources, including distribution channels, labor force, and manufacturing facilities. For example, it has recently modernized its production facilities and equipped them with flexible tooling such that it is now capable of producing a wide variety of different vehicles. These facilities have the capacity to produce 100,000 cars per year. Based on this capacity, the firm has an annual fixed operating cost (FOC) of $80 million. Management forecasts demand over the next year to be either 95,000 or 75,000 cars, depending on whether the price of oil (currently at $20) will be $15 or $25 a barrel, respectively.[7] The profit per car (before the FOC is covered) is $1,000.

The management of Company A is concerned about the possibility of incurring a $5 million loss should the price of oil increase to $25 next year (see first column in table 19.3). Since there is currently unused production capacity, management is considering alternatives to use this excess capacity. Since Company A does not currently have any additional new lines of its own to introduce over the next year, it is considering the purchase of one of two smaller automobile companies whose cars could be produced and sold using A's flexible resources. Company B sells only compact cars whose demand increases with the price of oil and is thus negatively correlated with that of Company A. Company C, on the other hand, specializes in vehicles whose demand is insensitive to the price of oil (and thus, uncorrelated with that of Company A). Both companies B and C have the same profit ($1,000) per car as Company A. Each has one manufacturing plant, with a capacity of 25,000 cars, and a FOC of $15,000. The cash flows for B and C are as shown in table 19.3.

The last two columns in table 19.3 show the combined cash flows of Company A should it acquire either Company B or Company C. If Company B is purchased, the combined demand for the two firms will be exactly 100,000, so A's resources are sufficient to manufacture and sell all the vehicles. Given that the fixed operating cost remains at $80 million, this would result in a $20 million profit, regardless of the price of oil.[8] If Company C is purchased instead, Company A can again choose to utilize only its own flexible resources, and can sell off C's facility. While some of C's demand can be covered by utilizing the excess capacity of A's facilities, if the price of oil decreases to $15, Company A would choose to operate at full capacity, forgoing the revenue from 15,000 of C's cars rather than keeping C's plant open at an FOC of $15,000. This would generate a combined profit (for A and C) of $20 million for next year if the price of oil declines, and $15 million if it rises.

In the last row of table 19.3, the present values for the independent companies and for the integrated companies are shown. These values are obtained using a one-period binomial option-pricing model (see Cox, Ross, and Rubinstein, 1979; or Trigeorgis and Mason, 1987). For example, given that today's oil price is $20 and assuming that $1.00 invested today in a risk-free security returns $R = \$1.05$ in one year, based on a risk-neutral probability, $p = (R - d)/(u - d) = (1.05 - .75)/(1.25 - .75) = .6$, we can calculate the value of companies A and C combined as $(.6 \times 15 + .4 \times 20)/1.05 =$ $16.19 million. The present values of A and B are similarly calculated to be 2.86 and 1.90, respectively. The present values of C and $A + B$ are easily seen to be 4.76 ($= 5/1.05$) and 19.05 ($= 20/1.05$), respectively.[9]

The values in table 19.3 indicate that Company A is better off acquiring Company B than C, assuming that it would pay a fair current market price to purchase either B or C (namely, $1.90 million for B or $4.76 million for C). The incremental value from acquiring B is $14.29 ($= 19.05 - 2.86 - 1.90$) million, while that from acquiring C is only $8.57 ($= 16.19 - 2.86 - 4.76$) million. Company B is thus a better acquisition than C, even though C appears less risky and more valuable on its own. The critical difference between these purchases is that the correlation between the demands for A and B is -1, and thus the two demands complement each other in such a way that A's capacity is always fully utilized and the demand for the cars of both A and B is completely satisfied. In addition, B's facility can be shut down resulting in considerable savings in production costs for the integrated firm.

This example illustrates that flexible production capacity can be very valuable, particularly when a firm is able to create a portfolio of products whose cash-flow streams are negatively correlated. The greater the uncertainty surrounding the demand for a firm's products, and the lower the correlation among these product demands, the more valuable will be the combined benefits of flexibility and diversification. While a typical diversification program reduces risk by narrowing the distribution of cash flows, strategic diversification can truncate the downside risk while preserving the upside potential.

The newsprint industry provides a case where firms have used acquisitions to enhance their flexibility option value. In particular, manufacturers in this industry have moved quickly to acquire recycled newsprint capacity. These manufacturers may use their sales organizations, distribution networks, and some of the same production resources to swing between recycled and virgin fiber based on market demand and pricing opportunities. A pure virgin fiber or pure recycled-based newsprint manufacturer could be equally profitable to the diversified producer if supply and demand conditions remained stable and in balance, but if market conditions change, companies with diversified production capabilities can more effectively exercise their valuable flexibility options.

In many industries, corporate real estate is considered one of the most valuable assets. This is often due, at least in part, to the fact that real estate may be one of the firm's most flexible assets. Acquisitions may introduce flexibility options by adding real estate that is flexible due to its location or zoning, or they may increase the value of the acquiring firm's existing assets by creating a diversified portfolio of businesses that is likely to exploit the flexibility of the real estate in the future.

As an illustrative example, consider the aggregates business, in which some sand and gravel operations have been converted into municipal waste disposal sites. These businesses serve different markets with entirely different products but share a valuable flexible asset, namely, real estate with certain special characteristics. A key criterion for site selection for either purpose is that the site should be sufficiently close to a major city to have favorable transportation economics, but far enough from local communities to offend as few people as possible. The operating skills are relatively simple and similar in both businesses. At some stage in the development of many aggregate resources, the property can be more valuable as a landfill site. This happens when the marginal value of further extraction falls below the value of filling in the hole with garbage. Major aggregates companies serving large urban centers are continually developing their asset bases by acquiring underdeveloped aggregates businesses and real estate. When they acquire sites that can later be used as landfill sites, they in fact acquire valuable options. In anticipation of the eventual conversion of some sites, they can invest in the protracted regulatory process and make the capital investments to convert the site, or they can exercise the option to sell the site at an appropriate time to a waste disposal company.

Another resource that is highly flexible is financial capital. Flexibility is particularly valuable in the presence of resource constraints. A firm that can easily raise additional capital on demand need not worry about integrating its various business units to ensure a balance of supply and demand for cash within the entire organization. However, most firms are, to some degree, capital rationed, if only by virtue of the costs associated with raising capital in financial markets. Of course, capital can be more or less expensive to raise depending on the prevailing circumstances in the firm's core business and in the financial markets. Thus, many acquisition programs emphasize the need to create a balanced portfolio of business units to enable cross-financing within the organization.

For example, acquisition programs can be designed to maintain a portfolio which is balanced on the basis of the stage of growth of each product or business unit. Pharmaceutical companies, for example, appear to strive for a balanced mix of marketable drugs, patents pending, and R and D activity. Uncertainties in each of these activities create currently unpredictable cash requirements at various stages of development in the future. Such future uncertainties make product diversification and the ability to cross-finance especially valuable.

19.4 Acquisition and Divestiture Options

Given the availability of appropriate financing arrangements, most firms have an option to acquire other firms or to purchase a portfolio of shares in other firms. The choice between these two alternatives centers on the relative benefits and costs of obtaining control of another business. To some firms, the option to acquire and control other firms is more valuable than it is to others because of more favorable strategic positioning. However, for all firms with valuable acquisition options, there are two important additional considerations.

The first concerns the timing of exercise of these acquisition options. Option pricing theory dictates that in certain circumstances it is worthwhile to hold on to an option even if it is "in-the-money." In the case of acquisitions in an environment characterized by an absence of competition, a firm may delay its decision to acquire while waiting for more resolution of uncertainty regarding market conditions and other economic factors such as interest rates. However, since competition for specific targets is often significant, firms in practice may not be able to wait indefinitely to acquire a target, but must instead react quickly at the right time.

The second important consideration in evaluating an acquisition has to do with the potential for partially undoing it through a divestiture option. Any acquisition investment is at least partially reversible since an investor may purchase an asset and later resell it (or parts of it). Of course, the success of such a strategy hinges on the timing of the buy and sell decisions to yield a profit, as well as on the transaction costs involved. An acquiring firm has the ability to divest an acquired business in the future—provided it does not irreversibly integrate the business with the rest of the firm—if the market price for the unit turns out to be higher than its actual value to the firm.

Often, firms acquire a business in order to realize synergy gains, but these gains may turn out to be fictitious. In such cases, divestment may effectively truncate the resulting poor returns on the acquisition investment. Clearly, the option to divest is an important consideration in risky consolidation plays. For example, during the 1980s, Maxwell Communication bought several commercial printing businesses in the United Kingdom and North America. It subsequently divested all of them (well before the death of the founder and subsequent demise of the empire). Whatever Maxwell's original strategy, and regardless of its effectiveness, the divestments clearly truncated the downside risk substantially.

An acquirer may, of course, purchase a firm with the original intent to later sell off some units but then hold the option to sell until an appropriate time to exercise the option. This may be when the business develops further or perhaps until industry consolidation progresses to the point that it becomes a seller's market. An example of the valuation and optimal timing of exercise of such a divestiture option is given below.

PJP is a large conglomerate considering the acquisition of another firm which has substantial holdings of real estate. If the acquisition goes through, PJP has plans to develop one particular piece of real estate for a distribution facility in two years' time. Based on its projected use, PJP has valued this piece at $20 million. Market conditions for the firm's business will of course cause the value of this real estate to the firm to fluctuate over the next two years. However, if the firm's business outlook turns sour and the distribution facility turns out to be unprofitable, the firm would be able to quickly sell off this centrally located land for at least $15 million. To account for this floor on downside risk in its valuation of the acquisition, PJP's management uses a simple two-year, binomial model. Management assumes that the value of the real estate to the firm will either appreciate by 50 percent or depreciate by 40 percent each year, as illustrated in the left tree of figure 19.1.

The right-hand tree in figure 19.1 illustrates the value of the land, taking into account that it can be sold at any time for $15 million. For example, in the worst-case scenario, at the end of two years the land could be sold for $15 million, mitigating the downside risk. The value in the down state at the end of the first year is calculated to be $15.71 (rather than $12) million from the discounted value of $18 and $15 million, given an annual risk-free rate of 5 percent and a risk-neutral probability of 0.5 $(p = (R - d)/(u - d) = (1.05 - .6)/(1.5 - .6) = .5)$.

Note that even though the value of the real estate to PJP as a site for its distribution facility may be only $12 million at the end of the first year, it is still not optimal

Without Divestiture Option   With Divestiture Option

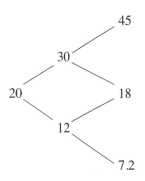
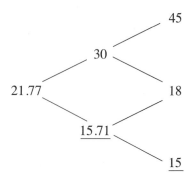

Figure 19.1
Value of real estate (millions of $)

for the firm to sell it at that time for $15 million if it can sell it for that price at the end of the second year. The firm would prefer to retain the option to develop the land at the end of the second year if business conditions improve (with a conditional value of $18 million). The incremental value of waiting to divest in this case amounts to $0.71 million at the end of the first year. The divestiture option increases time-zero value to $21.77 million. Thus, the additional value to PJP of having a divestiture option is equal to $1.77 million ($21.77 − $20 million), representing the current value of the ability to limit its downside risk in future periods. In practice, of course, a resale price for an asset is not guaranteed as assumed in this simple example, requiring the use of more sophisticated option-pricing techniques.[10] The basic intuition behind the valuation and exercise of such acquisition and divestiture options, however, is still instructive.

19.5 Implications and Conclusions

The practical necessity of introducing more stringent acceptance criteria for many acquisitions is well founded. However, it is crucially important that appropriate valuation techniques be employed to capture the various strategic considerations that could support many acquisitions. If the values of strategic options are underestimated, companies may miss valuable growth opportunities and risk losing their current competitive position.

Options valuation techniques can be very effective in capturing many strategic benefits from acquisitions. The key point is to recognize the discretionary future acquisition and divestiture decisions that must be exercised in an optimal fashion (with the benefit of waiting for additional information). Many of the strategic synergies in an acquisition are not immediately realized, but rather should be seen as growth options that are acquired (and perhaps, combined with the firm's own), developed, and potentially exercised in the future at some additional cost if they prove to be fruitful. A growth option established through an acquisition may be quite valuable even if it is not expected to be exercised within the typical time horizon used for considering capital expenditures. Furthermore, flexibility options may be valuable to firms that have or acquire flexible resources and pursue a strategic diversification policy. Although counterintuitive to many managers, such options are more valuable with increased uncertainty about product prices, demand, industry dynamics, and interest rates.

Capturing the precise benefits and costs of an acquisition program is, of course, case-specific. However, the nature of the major uncertainties faced by the firm in its market environment is certainly an important factor affecting valuation. In the long run, the options acquired, created, or developed, and the actions taken to optimally exercise these options, will determine the success of an acquisition program.

Acknowledgments

The authors are grateful to the editor, Lenos Trigeorgis, for detailed comments on an earlier draft.

Notes

1. For example, Ravenscraft and Scherer (1987) reported declines in profitability on conglomerization (pp. 75–122).

2. Morck, Schleifer, and Vishny (1990), and Amihud, Lev, and Travlos (1990) found that acquisitions are more likely to be value-decreasing when the acquiring firm's management stock ownership is low and, thus, agency problems may be prominent.

3. Porter (1987) reported the percentage of acquisitions divested for a sample of 33 large diversified U.S. companies during the period 1950–1986. He found that on average, corporations divested more than half their acquisitions in new industries and 74 percent in the case of unrelated acquisitions. Ravenscraft and Scherer (1987) also presented detailed evidence on sell-offs (see pp. 123–191).

4. The concept of modeling investment opportunities as growth options was first introduced by Myers (1977). Kester (1984) explored this framework in greater detail, discussing the critical factors that affect the value of growth options. He also provided empirical evidence showing that growth options constitute a significant portion of firm value in many industries.

5. To use the Black-Scholes formula, we must assume that the present value of profits from the new magazine is lognormally distributed (see Black and Scholes, 1973).

6. See, for example, Levy and Sarnat (1970), who argued that individual shareholders may diversify more cheaply than would a firm, which may have to pay a premium to acquire a block of the target's shares.

7. For simplicity, we are ignoring cash flows out further than one year, and we are considering only two possible oil price scenarios in each year.

8. For simplicity, we assume that Company B's production facility can be closed down, at least temporarily, without incurring significant costs. In reality, there may be substantial costs associated with closing and reopening plants. In addition, while our simple binomial structure restricts the highest value of combined demand (in this case to 100,000 cars per year), if more oil price states were allowed the total demand could potentially exceed Company A's capacity. A more complex multiperiod model would be required to address these issues.

9. Note that these values are calculated without knowing the actual probability of the price of oil increasing and without employing the firm's hurdle rate for new investments (which would likely provide a downward-biased estimate of these values).

10. See, for example, Fischer (1978) or Margrabe (1978), both of whom valued an option with an uncertain exercise price.

References

Amihud, Y., B. Lev, and N. G. Travlos (1990). "Corporate Control and the Choice of Investment Financing: The Case of Corporate Acquisitions," *Journal of Finance* 45 (June), pp. 603–616.

Black, F., and M. Scholes (1973). "The Pricing of Options and Corporate Liabilities," *Journal of Political Economy* 81 (May/June), pp. 637–659.

Fischer, S. (1978). "Call Option Pricing When the Exercise Price Is Uncertain, and the Valuation of Index Bonds," *Journal of Finance* 33 (March), pp. 169–176.

Kester, W. C. (1984). "Today's Options for Tomorrow's Growth," *Harvard Business Review* 62, 2 (March–April), pp. 153–160.

Levy, H., and M. Sarnat (1970). "Diversification, Portfolio Analysis and the Uneasy Case for Conglomerate Mergers," *Journal of Finance* 25, 4, pp. 795–802.

Margrabe, W. (1978). "The Value of an Option to Exchange One Asset for Another," *Journal of Finance* 33, 1 (March), pp. 177–186.

Morck, R., A. Schleifer, and R. W. Vishny (1990). "Do Managerial Objectives Drive Bad Acquisitions?" *Journal of Finance* 45 (March), pp. 31–48.

Myers, S. C. (1977). "Determinants of Corporate Borrowing," *Journal of Financial Economics* 5, 2 (November), pp. 147–175.

Porter, M. E. (1987). "From Competitive Advantage to Corporate Strategy," *Harvard Business Review* 65, 3 (May–June), pp. 43–59.

Ravenscraft, D. J., and F. M. Scherer (1987). *Mergers, Sell-offs and Economic Efficiency* (Washington, D.C.: Brookings Institution).

20 Capital Budgeting for Interrelated Projects: A Real Options Approach

Paul D. Childs, Steven H. Ott, and Alexander J. Triantis

I Introduction

In recent years, the classical NPV framework for making capital investment decisions has been extended to recognize the dynamic and flexible nature of investment decisions. Techniques from option pricing theory have been employed to value projects and derive optimal dynamic policies for investing in real assets. Seminal papers in this "real options" literature include Brennan and Schwartz (1985) and McDonald and Siegel (1985), (1986).[1] Further research in this area has focused on valuing specific forms of managerial or project flexibility and on determining how to optimally capture the full value of such flexibility (e.g., see Kulatilaka (1995), Pindyck (1988), Triantis and Hodder (1990), and Trigeorgis (1993)). While some of these studies have addressed interaction of flexibility options within a single project, they generally treat projects as stand-alone ventures, ignoring possible interrelationships with other projects currently in place or under consideration.

In this paper, we develop a real options model to explore the effect of project interrelationships on investment decisions and project values. Project interrelationships may arise in many forms. On one extreme, proposed projects may be mutually exclusive in the sense that they are designed to achieve the same objective; thus, at most one can be accepted. This situation often arises as firms explore competing technologies, products, or processes for production, distribution, or marketing. A particular case of mutual exclusivity that receives special attention is the replacement investment decision.[2] Of course, the option to defer investment (see, e.g., Brennan and Schwartz (1985), Dixit (1989), (1993), McDonald and Siegel (1986), and Pindyck (1991)) also presents a very special type of mutual exclusivity. In this case, the exclusivity occurs intertemporally for a single project, since a project may only be accepted once, either now or at some future point in time.

Projects may instead be partial, rather than complete, substitutes due to decreasing returns to scale or product cannibalization. Whether more than one project should be accepted in this case would depend on whether the incremental benefit of an additional project is greater than the required investment. In contrast to being substitutes, projects could be complements if implementing projects together yields synergy gains, i.e., the present value from the combined projects is greater than the sum of the present values obtained from accepting each on its own. For example, the value of a brand name is attributable to the joint implementation of several successful products. At the extreme of complementarity are projects that must be pursued in tandem, i.e., they represent different components of an integrated system.[3] Project independence represents the mid-point of a spectrum that includes mutual exclusivity on one end and complete complementarity on the other.

In addition to exploring the effect of project interrelationships on the firm's dynamic investment decisions, we also consider the impact of three common attributes of interrelated projects. First, many projects have an initial development stage before implementation of the project can begin. This initial stage actively resolves uncertainty through, for example, extensive evaluation of a project's cost and benefits, protracted contract negotiations with related business parties, a bidding process, or technological development of a process or product.[4]

Second, during the initial development stage of a particular project, information may be revealed about not only that project, but also related projects. This is the case, for example, in the development of new products. Several designs may be investigated, each of which may employ a somewhat different technology. While the technical risks for the different designs may be relatively independent, the ultimate success of the product is also subject to market risks regarding expected sales revenues, which are likely to be highly correlated across different product designs.[5]

Third, the firm may choose to conduct this initial stage investigation simultaneously for many projects or, alternatively, in some particular sequence. For instance, instead of "parallel development" of two projects and subsequent implementation of one or both, the firm may initially develop a single project and retain the option to develop the other project at some later date (i.e., "sequential development").[6]

We present an analysis of a general model of project interactions in Appendix I of the paper. For expositional purposes, however, we have chosen to focus on the mutually exclusive case in the body of the paper. The mutually exclusive projects case is a frequently encountered type of project interaction in practice, and the one that has historically received the most attention in the literature. In fact, discussions of the mutually exclusive case using a static NPV computation are commonplace in most corporate finance textbooks (see, e.g., Bierman and Smidt (1988), Brealey and Myers (1996), and Ross, Westerfield, and Jordan (1995)).

The optimal investment policy in our model involves choosing the maximum of i) the value of parallel development, ii) the maximum value of the two sequential development alternatives, and iii) zero, i.e., the value of no development. Highly correlated project values favor sequential development over parallel development since investment in one project can provide valuable information about the undeveloped project that can aid in further investment decisions. However, as the variance of project revenues increases, this effect is partially offset by the advantage offered by parallel development of the earlier receipt of the valuable option to select the better of the two projects. We find that the information advantage of developing in sequence also implies that the optimal ordering of the sequential projects does not always begin with the highest value project, contrary to what the traditional valuation technique would suggest (i.e., committing to the single project with the highest net benefit). Finally, we show that parallel development is superior for projects that have low development costs, require long periods of development, are likely to generate high cash flows when implemented, and are highly irreversible.

Our results seem consistent with development strategies observed in practice. The development of commercial aircraft at McDonnell Douglas (now part of Boeing) provides us with two examples of projects with the attributes described above. The first example involves the adaptation of the MD-11 passenger aircraft to carry freight. Among the changes necessary to convert the passenger plane for freight duty was removal of the passenger windows. Generally, two competing designs were considered. One option was to reengineer the body of the aircraft so that the window holes would not be cut.[7] This redesign process had higher initial investment costs (for design, analysis, and assembly tool modification), but the final design promised to be efficient in production and in flight and have low production costs. The alternative was to continue to cut the window holes in the body, and to develop a technique to plug the holes. On one hand, this design was easy, required few new assembly techniques or tools, and was low in initial investment cost. On the other hand, it made the plane heavier, was inefficient, and had high recurring costs. In this case, the level of correlation between project values was near zero since the risk was primarily technical, and the design solutions were quite different. These projects were developed in parallel.

As a second example, consider the development of a new airplane. This process is extremely costly (designing a new wing alone may cost a billion dollars). Further, the development process reveals information about wing design, engine choice, etc. that can be partially adapted for use in other (potentially competing) airplane designs. Thus, in this case, there is positive correlation between competing alternative types of aircraft. Whereas McDonnell Douglas developed multiple new designs for the freighter reengineering project described in the first example, it was effectively choosing to pursue a sequential strategy by first developing a single aircraft (the twin-engine MD-95) for the small jet market.[8]

The rest of the paper is organized as follows. Section II develops the model and provides distribution-free results. Section III provides closed-form solutions for the value of the investment program under parallel and sequential development assuming normally-distributed project values upon implementation. Section IV analyzes the optimal investment decision and the factors that affect the choice between sequential and parallel investment. This section also includes a discussion of empirical issues and practical implementation of the model. Section V concludes and discusses extensions of this work. Appendix I provides valuation formulas for a more general model of project interrelationships that allows for both substitutability *and* complementarity. Appendix II contains derivations and proofs.

II   The General Model and Distribution-Free Results

Consider a firm that has the opportunity to invest in two projects (a and b). Investment in each project takes place in two stages: the firm can invest $C_i \in \mathbb{R}^+$ ($i = a, b$) to "develop" a project, which resolves uncertainty regarding the project's future profitability; it can then make a further investment of $K_i \in \mathbb{R}^+$ ($i = a, b$) to "implement" a project, which enables the firm to receive revenues from the project. There are two strategies for project development that the firm may consider: parallel and sequential development.[9] These strategies are illustrated in figure 20.1 and are described below.

In the case of parallel development, the firm simultaneously invests in the development of both projects at t_0 by incurring the combined fixed costs for development, $C_a + C_b$. Once development is complete at t_1, the firm decides whether to invest K_a or K_b to implement project a or project b, respectively. The firm may, of course, decide not to implement either project.[10] Denote the present value of project i's stream of future cash flows upon implementation as X_i, and the value net of the implementation cost K_i as $x_i = X_i - K_i$. As mentioned in the Introduction, we will assume here that the projects are mutually exclusive, and will examine the more general model of project interrelationships in Appendix I. The value of the firm's investment program at t_1 under parallel development would thus be equal to $\max(x_a, x_b, 0)$, or $(x_a, x_b, 0)^+$.[11]

Under sequential development, the firm develops only one project at t_0. We arbitrarily pick this project to be project a, and later examine (in Section IV) the optimal ordering of projects under sequential development. Once development of project a is complete, the firm has two investment decisions to make at t_1: whether to spend K_a to implement project a, and whether to spend C_b to develop project b. From these two binary decisions, four feasible policies emerge.

If the firm does nothing (Policy P), the cash flow will be zero. If the firm implements project a but does not develop project b (Policy P_I), the value of its investment strategy at t_1 is simply x_a. If the firm develops project b, but does not implement a at t_1 (Policy P_D), then at the end of project b's development stage (at t_2), the firm will pick the maximum net present value of the two projects at t_2, and the program value at that time will be $(x_a, x_b)^+$. Finally, if the firm implements project a and yet also chooses to develop project b at t_1 (Policy P_{ID}), then the firm may decide to abandon project a at t_2 should project b prove to be superior, since the mutual exclusivity restriction precludes simultaneous operation of both projects. If project a is abandoned

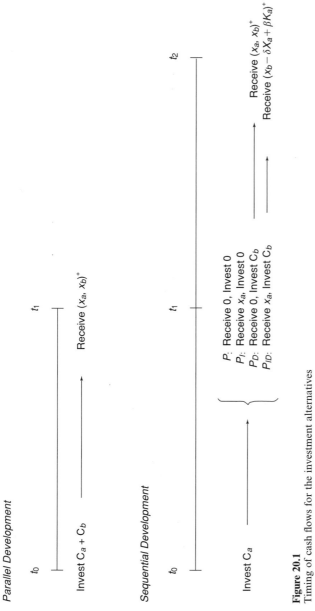

Figure 20.1
Timing of cash flows for the investment alternatives

in favor of project b, there is an opportunity cost of lost future cash flows from project a, $\delta X_a, 0 \leq \delta \leq 1.$[12] However, the firm may be able to salvage part of its implementation investment, $\beta K_a, 0 \leq \beta \leq 1.$[13] Each of the four policies will be optimal under particular parameter values and realizations of x_a at t_1. For example, if x_a is positive but not very large, the firm would likely choose to develop b at t_1 and delay possible implementation of a until t_2, when the firm can compare x_a against x_b with full information. The different investment scenarios are analyzed in much greater detail later in the paper.

Let Ω be the set of all possible outcomes for x_a and x_b. Let $\mathscr{F}$ denote the σ-field of possible events that are subsets of Ω. Define $\mathscr{F}_t^P$ and $\mathscr{F}_t^S$ as the σ-fields at time t under parallel and sequential development, respectively. The initial information about the projects is independent of the subsequent development process, so $\mathscr{F}_{t_0}^S = \mathscr{F}_{t_0}^P$. Under parallel development, uncertainty about both projects is completely resolved during the development stage $[t_0, t_1]$, i.e., $\mathscr{F}_t^P = \mathscr{F}$ $\forall t \geq t_1$. Under sequential development, all uncertainty concerning project a is resolved by t_1. In addition, knowing the outcome of x_a provides collateral learning about x_b if x_a and x_b are correlated. Thus, as long as project values are not perfectly positively correlated or perfectly negatively correlated, parallel development allows for a quicker resolution of uncertainty, i.e., $\mathscr{F}_{t_1}^S \subset \mathscr{F}_{t_1}^P$. The filtration for sequential development when $t > t_1$ depends on the investment strategy at t_1. If the firm chooses not to invest in project b, the remaining uncertainty in project b is never resolved and $\mathscr{F}_t^S = \mathscr{F}_{t_1}^S$ $\forall t \geq t_1$. Alternatively, if the firm invests in project b at time t_1, the remaining uncertainty in x_b is resolved by time t_2 and $\mathscr{F}_{t_2}^S = \mathscr{F}$. Thus, the firm's investment decisions both depend on "and affect" the pattern of uncertainty resolution.

Real options models generally assume that either i) markets are complete and claims are priced through arbitrage arguments, or ii) an equilibrium model such as the CAPM holds. The complete markets assumption would imply that the firm could learn about project values without making an irreversible investment by monitoring the value of a replicating portfolio.[14] Instead, we choose the equilibrium approach and assume that development of the projects does not alter the equilibrium pricing kernel. Given a probability measure $\mathscr{P}$, we define $\mathscr{Q}$ to be the corresponding equivalent martingale probability measure used to price assets.[15]

In order to decide whether to pursue a parallel or sequential development strategy, the firm must value the investment program under each strategy at t_0.[16] In this section, we compare these two strategies without making any specific distributional assumption for the project values x_a and x_b, thus providing some general intuition about the optimal investment strategy choice. In Section III, we assume joint normally distributed x_a and x_b in order to provide closed-form solutions for analysis and practical implementation.

The value of the program at $t_0 = 0$ under parallel development is

$$V^P = e^{-rt_1}E[(x_a, x_b)^+] - [C_a + C_b],\tag{1}$$

where E denotes the expectation with respect to the equivalent martingale measure $\mathcal{Q}$. The first term represents the discounted expected value of implementing project a, project b, or neither, while the second term is the combined development costs at t_0. This valuation can also be re-expressed as

$$V^P = (e^{-rt_1}E[x_a^+] - C_a) + (e^{-rt_1}E[(x_b - x_a^+)^+] - C_b).\tag{2}$$

Thus, one can interpret parallel development as the development of project a together with a European exchange option to replace project a with project b, maturing at t_1 and purchased at a cost of C_b at t_0.

The expression for the value of the investment program under sequential development is considerably more complex due to the firm's investment flexibility—specifically, the decisions of whether to implement project a and/or to develop project b at t_1. We define I_j as the set of x_a values for which Policy P_j is the optimal investment strategy to pursue at t_1 (e.g., I_{ID} is the set of x_a values for which Policy P_{ID}—implementation of a and development of b—would be optimal at t_1).[17] At t_1, the investment decisions are conditioned on the information in $\mathscr{F}_{t_1}^S$—specifically the value of x_a, which is fully revealed at this point.[18]

The program value under sequential development at $t_0 = 0$ is

$$V^S = -C_a + e^{-rt_1}E[x_a | x_a \in I_I] + e^{-rt_1}E[e^{-r(t_2-t_1)}(x_a, x_b)^+ - C_b | x_a \in I_D]$$

$$+ e^{-rt_1}E[x_a + e^{-r(t_2-t_1)}(x_b - (\delta X_a - \beta K_a))^+ - C_b | x_a \in I_{ID}].\tag{3}$$

The first term is simply the cost of developing project a at t_0. The second term in this expression is the present value at t_0 of implementing project a at t_1, conditional on policy P_I being optimal. The third term is the net present value of developing b (and, subsequently, choosing the better of projects a or b) when a is not implemented at t_1, conditional on Policy P_D being optimal. The fourth term is the net present value of implementing a and developing b at t_1 and then choosing between implementing b at t_2 (thus abandoning a) or continuing with project a. As in the case of parallel valuation, sequential value can be re-expressed as

$$V^S = e^{-rt_1}E[x_a^+] - C_a - (e^{-rt_1} - e^{-rt_2})E[x_a^+ | x_a \in I_D]$$

$$+ e^{-rt_1}E[e^{-r(t_2-t_1)}(x_b - (\delta X_a - \beta K_a))^+ - C_b | x_a \in I_{ID}]$$

$$+ e^{-rt_1}E[e^{-r(t_2-t_1)}(x_b - x_a^+)^+ - C_b | x_a \in I_D].\tag{4}$$

The first line of the right-hand side of equation (4) is the value of implementing project a.[19] The next two lines express the value of a European compound option to exchange project a for project b. The first stage of this compound option matures at t_1, at which time the firm pays the exercise price C_b if it chooses to exercise the option. The exercise price for the second stage of the exchange option depends on the implementation decision for project a at time t_1. If project a is implemented at t_1, the exercise price is $(\delta X_a - \beta K_a)$; if project a is not implemented, the exercise price is x_a^+.

By comparing the values of the investment program under sequential and parallel development strategies (equations (2) and (4)), it is possible to identify the relative advantages of each strategy. The program value under parallel development can be shown to be greater than that under sequential development (i.e., $V^P > V^S$) iff

$$e^{-rt_1} E[(x_b - x_a^+)^+ | x_a \in I \cup I_I] + (e^{-rt_1} - e^{-rt_2}) E[(x_a, x_b)^+ | x_a \in I_D]$$

$$+ e^{-rt_1} E[(x_b - x_a)^+ | x_a \in I_{ID}] - e^{-rt_2} E[(x_b - (\delta X_a - \beta K_a))^+ | x_a \in I_{ID}]$$

$$> C_b E[1 | X_a \in I \cup I_I] + C_b(1 - e^{-rt_1}) E[1 | X_a \in I_D \cup I_{ID}]. \qquad (5)$$

The left-hand side of this inequality quantifies the three advantages of parallel development. First, a firm that develops in parallel can always implement the higher value project. If the firm uses a sequential strategy and decides at t_1 not to develop project b, the firm may pass up the chance of implementing what might have been the superior project. This relative advantage of parallel development is captured in the first term of the first line of the left-hand side of the inequality.

Second, note that in the sequential development case where project a is not implemented at t_1 but project b is developed, the same option to select the maximum value project exists as in the case of parallel development, though it matures at t_2 rather than at t_1. At first glance, a longer maturity option may seem to be more valuable. However, the information revealed in the second period of sequential development is already known at t_1 in the parallel development case. Thus, the standard informational advantage of a longer maturity option is absent. Instead, the shorter maturity option is more valuable due to the accelerated receipt of the cash flows from implementation. This advantage of parallel development is represented by the second term on the first line of the left-hand side of inequality (5).

Third, recall that full information on both projects is available at t_1 if the firm develops in parallel. As a result, the firm can capture the entire advantage of implementing b relative to a at t_1. In contrast, under sequential development, the gain will be smaller if a is implemented at t_1 and then subsequently abandoned at t_2 in favor of project b, since the implementation investment in project a is only partially reversible, and project b's higher cash flows are delayed, starting at t_2. This relative advantage of parallel development over sequential development is captured in the second line of the left-hand side of inequality (5).

The value advantage from investing sequentially is shown on the right-hand side of the inequality. Sequential development allows the firm to make a more informed choice regarding the development of project b. First, to the extent that the project benefits are correlated, knowing the outcome of project a allows the firm to update the distribution of project b at t_1. Second, even if the project benefits are uncorrelated, knowing the outcome of project a means the firm knows the exercise price of the exchange option. For example, if development of project a shows x_a to be very high, the likelihood that x_b will exceed x_a is small and project b should not be developed. For those scenarios where x_a falls in either I or I_I, the firm does not develop project b, and thus realizes a development cost savings shown in the first term on the right-hand side of inequality (5). The second term on the right-hand side captures the present value of savings from delaying the investment outlay of C_b from t_0 to t_1 in the sequential cases where b is developed at t_1 ($x_a \in I_D$ or $x_a \in I_{ID}$).

III   The Normally Distributed Case

In order to examine the difference between parallel and sequential development strategies more carefully and to obtain explicit closed-form solutions for the value of the investment program, we now impose specific distributional assumptions on x_a and x_b. We employ the normal distribution to account for the possibility that these net present values from implementation can be negative.[20,21] We define the following parameters that completely characterize the bivariate normal density function, $g(x_a, x_b)$, under the equivalent martingale measure for the parallel case,[22]

$$E[x_i] = \mu_i, \quad i = a, b,$$

$$E[(x_i - \mu_i)^2] = \sigma_i^2, \quad i = a, b,$$

$$E[(x_a - \mu_a)(x_b - \mu_b)] = \rho \sigma_a \sigma_b,$$

where $\mu_i, \sigma_i \in \mathbb{R}$ and $\rho \in [-1, 1]$.[23] Note that the moments defined above under the equivalent martingale measure for the parallel case also apply under the sequential case since $\mathscr{F}_{t_0}^S = \mathscr{F}_{t_0}^P$.

A   Program Value under Parallel Development

Under the joint normality assumption for x_a and x_b, the expectation in equation (1) can be solved explicitly, yielding an expression for the value of the investment program under parallel development, V^P,

$$V^P \equiv e^{-rt_1} \int_{-\infty}^{\infty} \int_{-\infty}^{\infty} (x_a, x_b)^+ g(x_a, x_b)\, dx_a\, dx_b - C_a - C_b$$

$$= e^{-rt_1} \left[\int_0^{\infty} \int_{-\infty}^{x_a} x_a g(x_a, x_b)\, dx_b\, dx_a + \int_0^{\infty} \int_{-\infty}^{x_b} x_b g(x_a, x_b)\, dx_a\, dx_b \right] - C_a - C_b$$

$$= e^{-rt_1} (G(x_a, x_b) + G(x_b, x_a)) - C_a - C_b,$$

where the conditional expectation term $G(x_i, x_j)$ can be expressed as[24]

$$G(x_i, x_j) = \mu_i N_2(h_{ji}, -h_i; \alpha_j) + \sigma_i[n(h_i)N(\kappa(h_i, h_{ji}, -\alpha_j))$$

$$+ \alpha_j n(h_{ji})N(-\kappa(h_{ji}, h_i, -\alpha_j))].$$

N and N_2 are the cumulative standard normal univariate and bivariate distribution functions, respectively, and n is the univariate standard normal density function. The terms within the parentheses are defined as

$$h_i(x) = \frac{x - \mu_i}{\sigma_i}, \qquad\qquad h_{ij}(x, y) = \frac{x - \mu_i + y\mu_j}{\sqrt{(v_T(y))}},$$

$$h_i = h_i(0), \qquad\qquad h_{ij} = h_{ij}(0, 1),$$

$$\alpha_{ij}(x) = -\frac{\rho\sigma_i - x\sigma_j}{\sqrt{v_T(x)}}, \qquad \kappa(x, u, v) = \frac{u - vx}{\sqrt{1 - v^2}},$$

$$\alpha_i = \alpha_{ij}(1), \qquad\qquad v_T(x) = \sigma_b^2 - 2x\rho\sigma_a\sigma_b + x^2\sigma_a^2.$$

B Program Value under Sequential Investment

Recall that at t_1, x_b is conditionally distributed on the value of x_a, which is known since development of project a is complete. The conditional density function of x_b at t_1, $g(x_b|\mathscr{F}_{t_1}^S) = g(x_b|x_a)$, is the normal density function with mean $\mu_b' \equiv \mu_b + \rho\sigma_b((x_a - \mu_a)/\sigma_a)$ and variance $\sigma_b'^2 \equiv \sigma_b^2(1 - \rho^2)$. Let $C(x_b, \xi)$ be the value of a call option on x_b with exercise price ξ and time to maturity $(t_2 - t_1)$. The value of this call option is[25]

$$C(x_b, \xi) = e^{-r(t_2 - t_1)} \left[(\mu_b' - \xi)N\left(\frac{\mu_b' - \xi}{\sigma_b'}\right) + \sigma_b' n\left(\frac{\mu_b' - \xi}{\sigma_b'}\right) \right].$$

The values of the investment program at t_1 under the four feasible policies are as follows:[26]

P: Do not implement a and do not develop b, $V\;\; = 0$,

P_I: Implement a, but do not develop b, $V_I\;\; = x_a$,

P_D: Do not implement a, but develop b, $V_D\;\; = e^{-r(t_2-t_1)}x_a^+ + C(x_b, x_a^+) - C_b$,

P_{ID}: Implement a and develop b, $V_{ID} = x_a + C(x_b, \delta x_a - (\beta - \delta)K_a) - C_b$.

The value at t_0 of the investment program under the sequential strategy shown in equation (3) can be solved explicitly for the normally distributed case by computing the expectations as integrals, as long as we can establish that the four different investment sets, I, I_I, I_D, and I_{ID}, correspond to specific intervals of x_a values on $\mathbb{R}$: $I = (l, u)$, $I_I = (l_I, u_I)$, $I_D = (l_D, u_D)$, and $I_{ID} = (l_{ID}, u_{ID})$. There are several potential orderings of these intervals. For example, if $\rho > 0$ and $\rho(\sigma_b/\sigma_a) < \delta$, the ordering is $-\infty = l < u = l_d \leq u_d = l_{ID} \leq u_{ID} = l_I < u_I = \infty$. For low x_a values, P is the optimal policy; for higher x_a values, P_I becomes optimal; then, P_{ID} dominates; finally, for $x_a > l_I$, P_I would be the optimal policy. In contrast, if $\rho < 0$, the ordering is $-\infty = l_D < u_D = l \leq u = l_{ID} \leq u_{ID} = l_I < u_I = \infty$. These results are illustrated in figure 20.2 and proved in Appendix II.B.[27] Note in figure 20.2B that the interval $[l, u]$ is degenerate.

Solving the integrals in equation (3) explicitly yields

$$
\begin{aligned}
V^S &= e^{-rt_1}\left(\int_{I_D} V_D g(x_a)\,dx_a + \int_{I_{ID}} V_{ID}g(x_a)\,dx_a + \int_{I_I} V_I g(x_a)\,dx_a\right) - C_a \\[2mm]
&= e^{-rt_1}\left(\int_{l_D}^{u_D}(e^{-r(t_2-t_1)}x_a^+ + C(x_b, x_a^+) - C_b)g(x_a)\,dx_a\right. \\[2mm]
&\quad \left. + \int_{l_{ID}}^{u_{ID}}(x_a + C(x_b, \delta x_a - (\beta - \delta)K_a) - C_b)g(x_a)\,dx_a + \int_{l_I}^{u_I} x_a g(x_a)\,dx_a\right) - C_a \\[2mm]
&= -C_a + e^{-rt_1}\left(\int_0^\infty x_a g(x_a)\,dx_a - (1 - e^{-r(t_2-t_1)})\int_{l_D^+}^{u_D^+} x_a g(x_a)\,dx_a\right. \\[2mm]
&\quad - C_b\int_{l_D}^{u_D} g(x_a)\,dx_a - C_b\int_{l_{ID}}^{u_{ID}} g(x_a)\,dx_a \\[2mm]
&\quad + \int_{l_D^-}^{u_D^-} C(x_b, 0)g(x_a)\,dx_a + \int_{l_D^+}^{u_D^+} C(x_b, x_a)g(x_a)\,dx_a \\[2mm]
&\quad \left. + \int_{l_{ID}}^{u_{ID}} C(x_b, \delta x_a - (\beta - \delta)K_a)g(x_a)\,dx_a\right)
\end{aligned}
$$

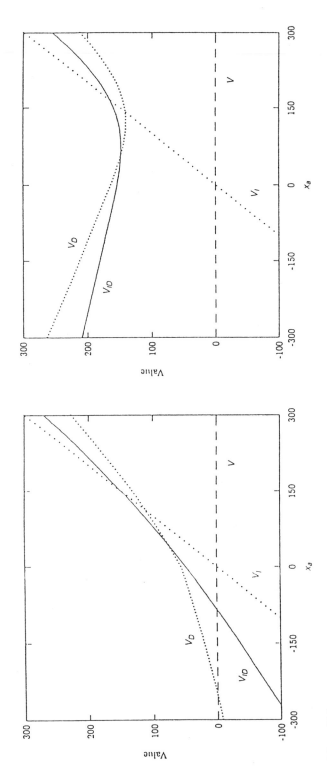

Figure 20.2
Valuation at t_1 under four feasible sequential investment strategies

$$= -C_a + e^{-rt_1}[-C_b(M_a(l_D, u_D, 0) + M_a(l_{ID}, u_{ID}, 0))$$

$$+ M_a(0, \infty, 1) - (1 - e^{-r(t_2 - t_1)})M_a(l_D^+, u_D^+, 1)$$

$$+ L(l_D^-, u_D^-, 0, 0) + L(l_D^+, u_D^+, 1, 0)$$

$$+ L(l_{ID}, u_{ID}, \delta, -(\beta - \delta)K_a)],$$

where

$$M_i(x, y, 0) = \int_x^y g(x_i)\, dx_i = N(h_i(y)) - N(h_i(x)),$$

$$M_i(x, y, 1) = \int_x^y x_i g(x_i)\, dx_i = \mu_i M_i(x, y, 0) + \sigma_i(n(h_i(x)) - n(h_i(y))),$$

and

$$L(x, y, u, v) = \int_x^y C(x_b, ux_a + v)g(x_a)\, dx_a$$

$$= \sqrt{v_T(u)}e^{-r(t_2 - t_1)}\{-h_{ba}(v, u)[N_2(-h_{ba}(v, u), h_a(y); \alpha_{ba}(u))$$

$$- N_2(-h_{ba}(v, u), h_a(x); \alpha_{ba}(u))]$$

$$- \alpha_{ba}(u)[n(h_a(x))N(\kappa(h_a(x), -h_{ba}(v, u), \alpha_{ba}(u)))$$

$$- n(h_a(y))N(\kappa(h_a(y); -h_{ba}(v, u), \alpha_{ba}(u)))]$$

$$+ n(-h_{ba}(v, u))[N(\kappa(-h_{ba}(v, u), h_a(y), \alpha_{ba}(u)))$$

$$- N(\kappa(-h_{ba}(v, u), h_a(x), \alpha_{ba}(u)))]\}.$$

The terms in the valuation expression can be interpreted as follows:

C_a	= the cost to develop project a;
$e^{-rt_1}C_b(M_a(l_D, u_D, 0) + M_a(l_{ID}, u_{ID}, 0))$	= the discounted "expected" cost of developing project b;
$e^{-rt_1}M_a(0, \infty, 1)$	= the discounted present value of project a if it were the only project;
$(e^{-rt_1} - e^{-rt_2})M_a(l_D^+, u_D^+, 1)$	= the time value of money impact of delaying the implementation decision on project a until project b has been developed;

$e^{-rt_1} L(l_D^-, u_D^-, 0, 0)$ = the discounted value of implementing project b if it is developed and if project a has negative value;

$e^{-rt_1} L(l_D^+, u_D^+, 1, 0)$ = the discounted marginal value of implementing project b vs. project a if project a has a positive value and implementation decisions are made at t_2; and

$e^{-rt_1} L(l_{ID}, u_{ID}, \delta, -(\beta - \delta)K_a)$ = The discounted marginal value of implementing project b vs. project a if project a is implemented at time t_1.

IV   The Optimal Investment Decision

The valuation formulas derived in the previous section can be used to develop greater economic intuition regarding the factors driving the choice between parallel and sequential development. We use numerical examples to illustrate our findings. The base case parameters used are listed in table 20.1. We first examine the optimal ordering of projects in the case of sequential investment, and then turn to the comparison between parallel and sequential investment strategies.

A   The Optimal Sequential Strategy

The ordering of projects for sequential development matters when projects do not have identical parameter values. The traditional capital budgeting rule would suggest simply picking the highest NPV project as the first one to develop. However, it is *not* always optimal to develop this project first. The amount of uncertainty resolved through developing a project is another important determinant of the optimal ordering decision.

Table 20.1
Base case parameters

$\mu_a = \mu_b = 147$	$t_1 = 2,\ t_2 = 4$	$\delta = 1$
$\sigma_a = \sigma_b = 150$	$C_a = C_b = 25$	$\beta = 0$
$\rho = 0$	$K_a = K_b = 25$	$r = 8\%$

This table presents the base case parameters for the numerical examples that follow. Note that μ_i is calibrated such that each project has a $100 traditional NPV at t_0.

Figure 20.3 shows it may be preferable to develop a high variance project (project b) first in order to maximize the uncertainty resolved, even if the project has a lower net present value. Since this project has high variance, it has a larger probability of achieving a very high value as revealed through development. In this case, the firm would likely implement the project immediately and avoid developing the other project. The high variance project is also more likely to have very low outcomes; however, if a low outcome occurs, the option still exists to develop the other project and then choose the highest value project for implementation. Since significant uncertainty is revealed through development of the high variance project, the firm can make a more informed decision regarding whether to expend the costs required to develop the second project. Thus, the compound exchange option mitigates the downside risk of the high variance project while preserving its upside potential. Figure 20.3A illustrates this result when the correlation between the projects is zero (all other parameter values are indicated in the figure caption).[28] Optimal sequential ordering changes once the variance of project b exceeds a threshold value. A firm that adheres to the traditional rule may be "playing it too safe" and underinvesting in high variance projects.

The literature on sequential investment has not addressed the effect of correlation between projects on optimal ordering. Figure 20.3B illustrates this effect. When the correlation is non-zero, some of the uncertainty in one project is resolved by investing in the other. If the correlation is near plus one or minus one, all or most of the uncertainty in the second project will be resolved by developing the first project. Thus, there is little difference in uncertainty resolution between the two orderings and it is better to start with the high benefit project, which is more likely to be ultimately implemented. When correlation is near zero, there can be substantially more uncertainty resolved in the first period by funding the high variance project b. It is easy to show that the uncertainty resolved between t_0 and t_1 for V_{ba}^S exceeds that of V_{ab}^S by $(\sigma_b^2 - \sigma_a^2)(1 - \rho^2)$. This quantity is maximized when $\rho = 0$ and is minimized when $\rho = \pm 1$.

B   The Parallel vs. Sequential Comparison

We now focus on how the choice to develop in parallel or in sequence depends on the various parameters in our model. Figure 20.4A shows the effect of project uncertainty on the relative values of the investment program under the two development alternatives.[29] For low variance levels, sequential development is the higher value alternative since the firm can use information from the first project's development to condition its decision of whether to develop the second project. However, as variance

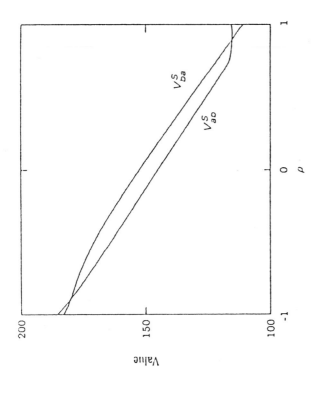

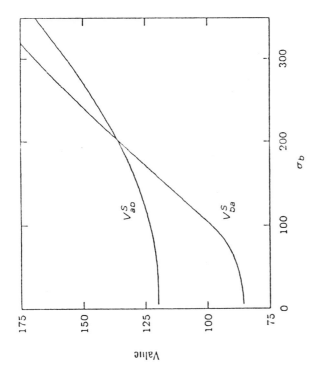

Figure 20.3
Optimal ordering for sequential development

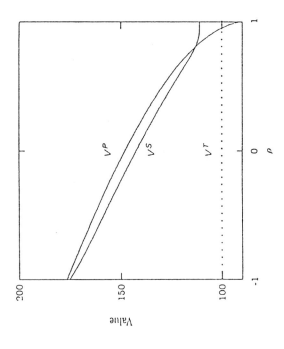

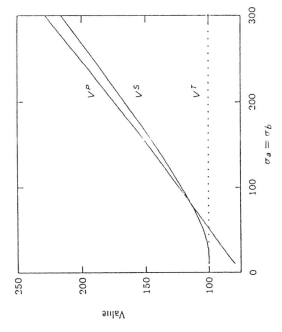

Figure 20.4
Parallel vs. sequential development: variance and covariance effects

passes a (fairly low) threshold, parallel development becomes more desirable since the exchange option to implement the higher value project has significant value and can be exercised at t_1 rather than at t_2. Note the dotted line in Figure 4A, which shows the value of the investment program under the traditional NPV rule. This value is insensitive to the variance of project value since it ignores the exchange option of the firm.

Figure 20.4B shows the effects of correlation on development choice (assuming identical projects). For very high positive correlation, sequential development is preferred as both projects will have similar values and the option to exchange is worth little. However, as correlation decreases, outcomes from the projects are more likely to be different and, thus, the exchange option becomes more valuable. The earlier this option can be exercised, the better, and, thus, parallel development becomes the optimal strategy. If correlation becomes quite negative, though, significant uncertainty is resolved about *both* project values by completing only the first project and, thus, the relative advantage of parallel development decreases.

In Figure 20.4B, we have once again included the value of the investment program under the traditional rule (100). This rule significantly underestimates the value of investment when the correlation is negative, since the exchange option is quite valuable. However, note that the value under parallel development exceeds the traditional NPV even when the correlation is equal to positive one and the exchange option has no value. The positive difference is due to the option not to implement, i.e., the firm may decide not to implement the projects if the present values, X_a and X_b, fall below the costs of implementation. In contrast, the traditional rule assumes that the firm makes a commitment at t_0 to develop *and* implement one of the projects.

Figure 20.5A displays the impact of the level of profitability of the projects on the choice of strategy. Parallel development is preferred when the two expected net present values, μ_a and μ_b, are similar, whereas sequential development is more desirable when one project clearly dominates. When project b has low value, the optimal sequential ordering is to develop project a first. The value of parallel development increases faster than the value of sequential development as the expected present value of the second project (μ_b) increases. This result occurs since the exchange option is more valuable at t_0 when expected project values are similar. If μ_b exceeds μ_a ($= 147$), project b should be developed first. For large μ_b values, sequential development may allow the firm to avoid the cost of developing a project that is unlikely to be implemented. Thus, as μ_b increases above μ_a, the marginal benefit of following the sequential development strategy is higher than that of parallel development.

Figure 20.5B shows the effect of the opportunity cost of abandoning project a on the value of sequential development. Recall that δ measures the proportion of project

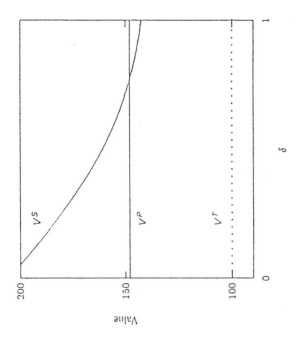

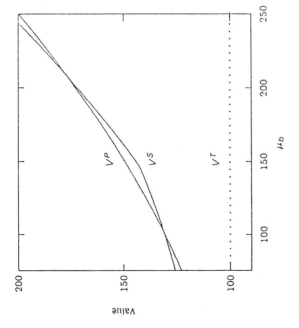

Figure 20.5
Parallel vs. sequential development: cash flow effects

a's value that is given up when project b replaces a. As this opportunity cost rises, the value of sequential development decreases. In fact, if δ becomes large enough, parallel development becomes the favorable alternative. There are two reasons why this occurs. First, the firm can avoid the sequential development situation where a is implemented at t_1, but is subsequently abandoned with minimal revenues received during $[t_1, t_2]$. Second, a large δ increases the likelihood that the firm delays any implementation until t_2 and, hence, loses time value of an implemented project.[30]

C Empirical Issues and Practical Implementation

We have shown that the decision to develop in sequence or in parallel hinges on a number of variables, including the cost of development, the correlation between project uncertainties, and the length of development. We find that sequential development is superior to parallel development when projects have low variances, high development costs, are highly reversible, and have expected present values that differ substantially, but yet whose uncertainties are highly correlated. While it may be difficult to provide a careful empirical test of the predictions of our model due to the need to collect (possibly proprietary) micro investment data about firms' development programs, anecdotal evidence suggests that our qualitative predictions are consistent with what occurs in practice.

Our results suggest that when development costs are low and implementation costs are large and not easily recovered, the parallel development strategy is favored. Such would be the case, for example, with a plant location decision, a classic example of a mutually exclusive project. Bruner (1994) provides a teaching case related to locating a chemical plant, where the decision rests not only on where to locate, but also on what technology should be used. Since it is very costly to build in one location and to later abandon in favor of another one, the development of plans for the various alternatives is typically pursued at the same time.[31]

In contrast, if project values are highly correlated, development costs are high, and implementation costs can be significantly recovered if a new design supplants the original one, then a sequential strategy would likely be optimal. In fact, we do see many firms innovating incrementally, rather than initially engaging in megaproject development. An initial low-cost design is developed, providing information about the value of a larger-scale project. Then, once the low-cost project is implemented, development of a more costly and complex design is pursued. The costs of abandoning the first design and replacing it with another are likely to be relatively low (in our model, δ is close to zero and β is close to one). The advantage of this approach is the ability to generate cash flows as quickly as possible while acquiring information gathered from development of the first project to determine optimal investment policy for later projects.[32]

In addition to providing results that seem consistent with development strategies observed in practice, our model has normative power in helping firms make more accurate investment decisions. The application of our model in practice, of course, relies on the accurate estimation of parameter values, a common challenge faced in the application of capital budgeting techniques. In fact, the parameter estimation requirements of our model are not unlike those of standard capital budgeting models, other than the estimation of one additional parameter—the correlation coefficient. The past history of development in a firm, or more generally in its industry, as well as in-house expertise regarding development risks may guide the estimation of this parameter. If this task is considered to be overly difficult, the firm could opt for the following short-cut. One can find the correlation level (or levels) at which the firm would be indifferent between developing in parallel or in sequence. The firm may then be able to quickly gauge in which region the true correlation value likely falls and, as a result, which development strategy should be pursued.

V   Conclusions and Extensions

This paper develops a real options model to examine the optimal investment policy for multiple projects that can be developed in parallel or in sequence. Several important factors drive the decision of whether to develop in parallel or in sequence: the variances of the projects, the correlation between projects' present values, the costs of development and implementation, and the time horizon for development, among others. Generally, we find that sequential development is superior to parallel development when projects are highly correlated, have low variances, have high development costs, are readily reversible, and have expected present values that differ substantially. Interestingly, when projects do have different expected present values, it is not always the one with the higher net present value that is developed first. A project with high variance may be developed first, even if it has lower value, since significant learning about *both* projects can occur through its development.

There are several extensions of our model that would be interesting to pursue. A more complex pattern of investment over time could be examined by allowing the firm more flexibility to exercise options early or to periodically review and revise its development choice. For example, consider a firm that can start development on a second project before development is completed on the first project. In this case, the real options involved in the analysis would be American in nature. Time-varying parameters and the existence of multiple decision points within the development stage of a project would introduce hybrid strategies combining parallel and sequential development at different stages of the development process. Our model provides some intuition for at least one likely scenario. If in early development stages there is rapid resolution of uncertainty or lower development costs, simultaneous development of competing projects may be optimal. As the rate of uncertainty resolution slows or the costs of further development rise, focusing on the single best alternative becomes more attractive. Adding decision points would require a numerical approximation to the solution of the problem. Once a passage to a numerical solution to the problem is made, additional assumptions can be relaxed with varying computational costs. For example, allowing uncertainty to be resolved (at a potentially slower rate) in the absence of development is possible and would introduce the option to wait, i.e., to postpone development. Such extensions would allow the model to more closely match particularly complex capital budgeting applications.

Appendix I: General Valuation Model

Consider a firm evaluating two available projects. Suppose both projects have been developed and the firm chooses to implement both of the projects. We allow each project to affect the other simultaneously implemented project's cash flows by using cash flow multipliers, $\gamma_i > 0$. Thus, $(\gamma_a x_a + \gamma_b x_b)$ represents the total value received if the projects are implemented simultaneously.[33] For example, if $\gamma_a < 1$, then project b partially substitutes for (i.e., cannibalizes) part of project a's cash flows. That is, the cash flows from simultaneous investment in both projects diminishes the size of the cash flows from project a relative to implementing project a alone. Alternatively, if $\gamma_a > 1$, project a's cash flows are enhanced by implementing a complementary project b. Finally, if $\gamma_a = \gamma_b = 1$, then the projects are independent.[34]

First, we compare joint implementation of both projects to implementation of a single project. It is better to implement both projects than just project a if

$$x_a < \gamma_a x_a + \gamma_b x_b \quad \Rightarrow \quad \frac{1 - \gamma_a}{\gamma_b} x_a < x_b. \tag{6}$$

Similarly, it is better to implement both projects than just project b if

$$x_b < \gamma_a x_a + \gamma_b x_b \quad \Rightarrow \quad \frac{1 - \gamma_b}{\gamma_b} x_b < x_a. \tag{7}$$

If both inequalities (6) and (7) are satisfied, it is optimal to implement both projects. It is easy to show that, if $\gamma_a + \gamma_b \leq 1$, then inequalities (6) and (7) describe an empty region and it is never optimal to implement both projects simultaneously. In this case, the problem is the same as the mutually exclusive scenario discussed in the body of the paper. Thus, for the valuations that follow, we assume $\gamma_a + \gamma_b > 1$.

Figure 20.6 describes the optimal implementation regions given project values (x_a, x_b). Inequalities (6) and (7) are simultaneously satisfied and both projects should be implemented in Regions II and III. In Region I, project b is implemented alone and in Region IV, project a is implemented alone.

A   Parallel Development

The value of parallel development is higher than in the mutually exclusive case if the firm finds that implementing both projects is better than implementing a single project, such as when projects are partial substitutes, independent, or complements. The value of parallel development is

$$V^P = e^{-rt_1}\left(G(x_a, x_b) + G(x_b, x_a) + H(x_a, x_b, \gamma_a - 1, \gamma_b) + H(x_b, x_a, \gamma_b - 1, \gamma_a)\right) - C_a - C_b,$$

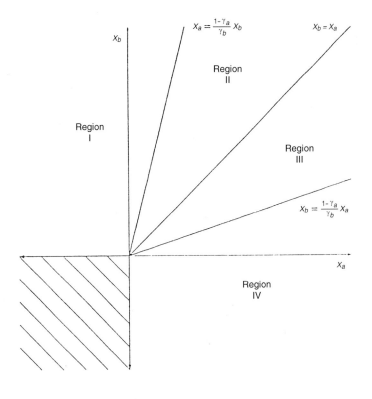

Region I	Region II	Region III	Region IV
$x_b > x_a^4$ and	$x_a^4 < x_b < \gamma_a x_a + \gamma_b x_b$	$x_b^4 < x_a < \gamma_a x_a + \gamma_b x_b$	$x_a > x_b^4$ and
$x_b > \gamma_a x_a + \gamma_b x_b$			$x_a > \gamma_a x_a + \gamma_b x_b$

Region I is the set of (x_a, x_b) pairs where it is optimal to implement project b alone. Regions II and III make up the set where it is optimal to implement both projects. Region IV is the set of points where it is optimal to implement only project a.

$$
\begin{aligned}
= (a\mu_i + b\mu_j) &\left[N_2(h_{ji}, -h_i, \alpha_j) \right. \\
&- N_2\left(h_{ji}\left(0, -\frac{a}{b}\right), -h_i; \alpha_{ji}\left(-\frac{a}{b}\right)\right) \Big] \\
+ (a\sigma_i + b\rho\sigma_b) &\left[n(h_i)\left(N(\kappa(h_i, h_{ji}, -\alpha_j)) \right.\right. \\
&\qquad - N\left(\kappa\left(h_i, h_{ji}\left(0, -\frac{a}{b}\right), -\alpha_{ji}\left(-\frac{a}{b}\right)\right)\right)\Big) \\
&+ \alpha_j n(h_{ji}) N(-\kappa(h_{ji}, h_i, -\alpha_j)) \\
&- \alpha_{ji}\left(-\frac{a}{b}\right) N\left(h_{ji}\left(0, -\frac{a}{b}\right)\right) \\
&\times N\left(-\kappa\left(h_{ji}\left(0, -\frac{a}{b}\right), h_i, -\alpha_{ji}\left(-\frac{a}{b}\right)\right)\right) \Big]
\end{aligned}
$$

Figure 20.6
Optimal implementation policies

where

$$H(x_i, x_j, a, b) \equiv \int_0^\infty \int_{-a/bx_i}^{x_i} (ax_i + bx_j)g(x_i, x_j)\, dx_j\, dx_i + (b\sigma_j \sqrt{1 - \rho^2})\left[n(h_{ji})\sqrt{1 - \alpha_j^2} \times N(-\kappa(h_{ji}, h_i, -\alpha_j)) \right.$$

$$\left. - n\left(h_{ji}\left(0, -\frac{a}{b}\right)\right)\sqrt{1 - \alpha_{ji}^2\left(-\frac{a}{b}\right)}\, N(-\kappa(h_{ji}, h_i, -\alpha_j)) \right].$$

B   Sequential Development

For simplicity, we assume that $\beta = \delta$. At time t_1, consider the value of the four policies, P, P_I, P_D, and P_{ID}. The two policies that do not lead to complete development of both projects are straightforward to value: $V = 0$, and $V_I = x_a$.

For P_D, since project a is not implemented at t_1, the opportunity cost factor (δ) does not enter the valuation. V_D is the value of implementing project a at time t_2, plus the incremental value of project b above project a in Region I, plus the incremental value of implementing both projects above implementing project a alone in Regions II and III. If $\gamma_b < 1$, then V_D can be expressed as

$$V_D = e^{-r(t_2 - t_1)}\left(x_a^+ + \int_{(\gamma_a/(1 - \gamma_b))x_a^+}^{\infty} (x_b - x_a^+)g(x_b | x_a)\, dx_b + \int_{((1 - \gamma_a)/\gamma_b)x_a^+}^{(\gamma_a/(1 - \gamma_b))x_a^+} (\gamma_a x_a + \gamma_b x_b - x_a)g(x_b | x_a)\, dx_b \right) - C_b$$

$$= e^{-r(t_2 - t_1)}\left(x_a^+ + (\mu_b' - x_a^+)N\left(d\left(\frac{\gamma_a x_a^+}{1 - \gamma_b}\right)\right) + \sigma_b' n\left(d\left(\frac{\gamma_a x_a^+}{1 - \gamma_b}\right)\right) + (\mu_b'\gamma_b + x_a^+(\gamma_a - 1)) \right.$$

$$\left. \times \left[N\left(d\left(\frac{(1 - \gamma_a)x_a^+}{\gamma_b}\right)\right) - N\left(d\left(\frac{\gamma_a x_a^+}{1 - \gamma_b}\right)\right) \right] + \sigma_b'\gamma_b\left[n\left(d\left(\frac{(1 - \gamma_a)x_a^+}{\gamma_b}\right)\right) - n\left(d\left(\frac{\gamma_a x_a^+}{1 - \gamma_b}\right)\right) \right] \right) - C_b,$$

where $d(x) = \dfrac{\mu_b' - x}{\sigma_b'}$.

If project a has been implemented and $\gamma_b < 1$, then V_{ID} can be expressed as

$$V_{ID} = x_a + e^{-r(t_2 - t_1)}\left(\int_{(\gamma_a/(1 - \gamma_b))\delta x_a}^{\infty} (x_b - \delta x_a)g(x_b | x_a)\, dx_b \right.$$

$$\left. + \int_{((1 - \gamma_a)/\gamma_b)\delta x_a^+}^{(\gamma_a/(1 - \gamma_b))\delta x_a^+} (\gamma_a x_a + \gamma_b x_b - \delta x_a)g(x_b | x_a)\, dx_b \right) - C_b$$

$$= x_a + e^{-r(t_2 - t_1)}\left((\mu_b' - \delta x_a)N\left(d\left(\frac{\gamma_a \delta x_a}{1 - \gamma_b}\right)\right) + \sigma_b' n\left(d\left(\frac{\gamma_a \delta x_a}{1 - \gamma_b}\right)\right) + (\mu_b'\gamma_b + x_a^+(\gamma_a - \delta)) \right.$$

$$\times \left[N\left(d\left(\frac{(1 - \gamma_a)\delta x_a^+}{\gamma_b}\right)\right) - N\left(d\left(\frac{\gamma_a \delta x_a^+}{1 - \gamma_b}\right)\right) \right]$$

$$\left. + \sigma_b'\gamma_b\left[n\left(d\left(\frac{(1 - \gamma_a)\delta x_a^+}{\gamma_b}\right)\right) - n\left(d\left(\frac{\gamma_a \delta x_a^+}{1 - \gamma_b}\right)\right) \right] \right) - C_b.$$

Following the approach in Section III, the value of sequential development when $\gamma_b < 1$ is

$$V^S = -C_a + e^{-rt_1}\left[-C_b(M_a(l_D, u_D, 0) + M_a(l_{ID}, u_{ID}, 0)) + M_a(0, \infty, 1) - (1 - e^{-r(t_2 - t_1)})M_a(l_D^+, u_D^+, 1) \right.$$

$$+ \mathcal{L}(l_D^-, u_D^-, 0, 0, 1) + \mathcal{L}\left(l_D^+, u_D^+, \gamma_a, \frac{\gamma_a}{1 - \gamma_b}, 1 - \gamma_b\right) + \mathcal{L}\left(l_D^+, u_D^+, 1 - \gamma_a, \frac{1 - \gamma_a}{\gamma_b}, \gamma_b\right)$$

$$\left. + \mathcal{L}\left(l_{ID}, u_{ID}, \gamma_a, \frac{\delta\gamma_a}{1 - \gamma_b}, 1 - \gamma_b\right) + \mathcal{L}\left(l_{ID}, u_{ID}, \delta - \gamma_a, \frac{\delta(1 - \gamma_a)}{\gamma_b}, \gamma_b\right) \right],$$

where

$$\mathscr{L}(x, y, u, v, w) = (\mu_b w - u\mu_a)e^{-r(t_2-t_1)}[N_2(-h_{ba}(0, v), h_a(y); \alpha_b(v)) - N_2(-h_{ba}(0, v), h_a(x); \alpha_b(v))]$$

$$+ (\rho w\sigma_b - u\sigma_a)e^{-r(t_2-t_1)}[n(h_a(x))N(\kappa(h_a(x), -h_{ba}(0, v), \alpha_{ba}(v)))$$

$$- n(h_a(y))N(\kappa(h_a(y), -h_{ba}(0, v), \alpha_{ba}(v)))$$

$$+ \alpha_{ba}(v)n(-h_{ba}(0, v))[N(\kappa(-h_{ba}(0, v), h_a(x), \alpha_{ba}(v))) - N(\kappa(-h_{ba}(0, v), h_a(y), \alpha_{ba}(v)))]]$$

$$+ \frac{w\sigma_b^2(1-\rho^2)}{\sqrt{v_T(v)}}e^{-r(t_2-t_1)}n(-h_{ba}(0, v))[N(\kappa(-h_{ba}(0, v), h_a(y), \alpha_{ba}(v)))$$

$$- N(\kappa(-h_{ba}(0, v), h_a(x), \alpha_{ba}(v)))].$$

A similar analysis holds if $\gamma_b > 1$, and the value of the sequential development program is

$$V^S = -C_a + e^{-rt_1}\left[-C_b(M_a(l_D, u_D, 0) + M_a(l_{ID}, u_{ID}, 0)) + M_a(0, \infty, 1) - (1 - e^{-r(t_2-t_1)})M_a(l_D^+, u_D^+, 1) \right.$$

$$+ \mathscr{L}(l_D^-, u_D^-, 0, 0, 1) + \mathscr{L}\left(l_D^+, u_D^+, -\gamma_a, \frac{\gamma_a}{1-\gamma_b}, \gamma_b - 1\right) + \mathscr{L}\left(l_D^+, u_D^+, 1 - \gamma_a, \frac{1-\gamma_a}{\gamma_b}, \gamma_b\right)$$

$$\left. + \mathscr{L}\left(l_{ID}, u_{ID}, \delta - \gamma_a, \frac{\delta(1-\gamma_a)}{\gamma_b}, \gamma_b\right) \right].$$

Appendix II: Derivations and Proofs

A Derivation of $G(x_i, x_j)$ for the Parallel Development Case

$$G(x_i, x_j) = \int_0^\infty \int_{-\infty}^{x_i} x_i g(x_i, x_j)\, dx_j\, dx_i$$

$$= \int_{h_i}^\infty \int_{-\infty}^{\kappa(y_i, h_{ji}, -\alpha_j)} (\mu_i + \sigma_i y_i)n(y_j)\, dy_j n(y_i)\, dy_i$$

$$= \int_{h_i}^\infty (\mu_i + \sigma_i y_i)N(\kappa(y_i, h_{ji}, -\alpha_j))n(y_i)\, dy_i$$

$$= \mu_i \int_{h_i}^\infty n(y_i)N(\kappa(y_i, h_{ji}, -\alpha_j))\, dy_i + \sigma_i \int_{h_i}^\infty y_i n(y_i)N(\kappa(y_i, h_{ji}, -\alpha_j))\, dy_i$$

$$= \mu_i[N_2(h_{ji}, \infty; -\alpha_j) - N_2(h_{ji}, h_i; -\alpha_j)] + \sigma_i[n(h_i)N(\kappa(h_i, h_{ji}, -\alpha_j)) - \alpha_j n(h_{ji})(N(\kappa_2(h_{ba}, h_i, -\alpha_j)) - 1)]$$

$$= \mu_i[N(h_{ji}) - N_2(h_{ji}, h_i; -\alpha_j)] + \sigma_i[n(h_i)N(\kappa(h_i, h_{ji}, -\alpha_j)) + \alpha_j n(h_{ji})N(-\kappa_2(h_{ji}, h_i, -\alpha_j))]$$

$$= \mu_i N_2(h_{ji}, -h_i; \alpha_j) + \sigma_i[n(h_i)N(\kappa(h_i, h_{ji}, -\alpha_j)) + \alpha_j n(h_{ji})N(-\kappa(h_{ji}, h_i, -\alpha_j))],$$

where $y_i = \dfrac{x_i - \mu_i}{\sigma_i}$, and $y_j = \dfrac{x_j - \rho\sigma_j y_i}{\sigma_j\sqrt{1-\rho^2}}$.

B   Determining the Optimal Development and Implementation Policies at t_1 under Sequential Development

The optimal development and implementation policies at t_1 depend on the revealed value of x_a. To determine the four intervals of x_a that correspond to the four investment policies, the partial derivatives of the policy values with respect to x_a are needed,

$$\frac{\partial V}{\partial x_a} = 0, \qquad \frac{\partial V_I}{\partial x_a} = 1,$$

$$\frac{\partial V_D}{\partial x_a} = e^{-r(t_2-t_1)} + e^{-r(t_2-t_1)}\left(\rho\frac{\sigma_b}{\sigma_a} - 1\right)N\left(\frac{\mu_b' - x_a^+}{\sigma_b'}\right),$$

$$\frac{\partial V_{ID}}{\partial x_a} = 1 + e^{-r(t_2-t_1)}\left(\rho\frac{\sigma_b}{\sigma_a} - \delta\right)N\left(\frac{\mu_b' - (\delta x_a - (\beta - \delta)K_a)}{\sigma_b'}\right),$$

$$\frac{\partial^2 V}{\partial x_a^2} = 0, \qquad \frac{\partial^2 V_I}{\partial x_a^2} = 0,$$

$$\frac{\partial^2 V_D}{\partial x_a^2} = e^{-r(t_2-t_1)}\left(\rho\frac{\sigma_b}{\sigma_a} - 1\right)^2 n\left(\frac{\mu_b' - x_a^+}{\sigma_b'}\right),$$

$$\frac{\partial^2 V_{ID}}{\partial x_a^2} = e^{-r(t_2-t_1)}\left(\rho\frac{\sigma_b}{\sigma_a} - \delta\right)^2 n\left(\frac{\mu_b' - (\delta x_a - (\beta - \delta)K_a)}{\sigma_b'}\right).$$

For $x_a < 0$, $V_{ID} < V_D$ and $V_I < V$, so only P_D and P can be optimal policies (i.e., it is not optimal to implement project a). If $\rho < 0$, when x_a is significantly negative, x_b is likely to be quite large and, thus, it will be optimal to develop b (i.e., follow policy P_D). If x_a is only slightly negative, the firm may or may not choose to develop b. Thus, the optimal policy ordering (as x_a increases) must be P_D, P.[35] If $\rho > 0$, this logic reverses, and the ordering will be P, P_D. If $\rho = 0$, the option to develop b is independent of the outcome of x_a, and project b will be developed iff the option to develop has positive value (i.e., one of the two intervals P and P_D will be degenerate).

If $x_a \geq 0$, then $V_I \geq V$ and, hence, P cannot be the optimal policy. For $\rho(\sigma_b/\sigma_a) < \delta$, the following comparative statics results can be easily derived,

$$\frac{\partial V_I(x_a)}{\partial x_a} > \frac{\partial V_{ID}(x_a)}{\partial x_a}, \quad \frac{\partial V_I(x_a)}{\partial x_a} > \frac{\partial V_D(x_a)}{\partial x_a}, \quad \frac{\partial^2 V_{ID}(x_a)}{\partial x_a^2} > \frac{\partial^2 V_D(x_a)}{\partial x_a^2} > 0.$$

As x_a becomes large, the value of the option to implement project b rather than project a approaches zero. Therefore, for $C_b > 0$, P_I will become the optimal policy at a significantly high x_a value, l_I. Since V_I has the largest partial derivative, if P_I is optimal at $x_a = l_I$, it is optimal for all $x_a > l_I$. Also, note that $V_D > V_{ID}$ when $x_a = 0$. Thus, if P_{ID} becomes superior to P_D after a certain point, then

$$\frac{\partial V_{ID}(x_a)}{\partial x_a} > \frac{\partial V_D(x_a)}{\partial x_a}. \quad \text{Since} \quad \frac{\partial^2 V_{ID}(x_a)}{\partial x_a^2} > \frac{\partial^2 V_D(x_a)}{\partial x_a^2}, \quad \text{once} \quad \frac{\partial V_{ID}(x_a)}{\partial x_a} > \frac{\partial V_D(x_a)}{\partial x_a},$$

it will be true for all larger x_a and P_{ID} will dominate P_D for all larger x_a. The ordering of policies (as x_a increases) would be

$$\begin{cases} P_D, P, P_{ID}, P_I & \text{for } \rho \leq 0, \\ P, P_D, P_{ID}, P_I & \text{for } \rho > 0. \end{cases}$$

C   Derivation of M and L for the Sequential Development Case

$$M_i(x, y, 0) = \int_x^y g(x_i)\, dx_i = \int_{h_i(x)}^{h_i(y)} n(y_i)\, dy_i = N(h_i(y)) - N(h_i(x)),$$

$$M_i(x, y, 1) = \int_x^y x_i g(x_i)\, dx_i = \int_{h_i(x)}^{h_i(y)} (\mu_i + \sigma_i y_i) n(y_i)\, dy_i$$

$$= \mu_i \int_{h_i(x)}^{h_i(y)} n(y_i)\, dy_i + \sigma_i \int_{h_i(x)}^{h_i(y)} y_i n(y_i)\, dy_i$$

$$= \mu_i M_i(x, y, 0) + \sigma_i (n(h_i(x)) - n(h_i(y))),$$

where $y_i = \dfrac{x_i - \mu_i}{\sigma_i}$ and $y_j = \dfrac{x_j - \rho \sigma_j y_i}{\sigma_j \sqrt{1 - \rho^2}}.$

$$L(x, y, u, v) = \int_x^y C(x_b, u x_a + v) g(x_a)\, dx_a$$

$$= e^{-r(t_2 - t_1)} \int_x^y \left((\mu_b' - u x_a - v) N\left(\frac{\mu_b' - u x_a - v}{\sigma_b'} \right) + \sigma_b' n\left(\frac{\mu_b' - u x_a - v}{\sigma_b'} \right) \right) g(x_a)\, dx_a$$

$$= e^{-r(t_2 - t_1)} \int_{h_a(x)}^{h_a(y)} \left[(\mu_b - u\mu_a - v + (\rho\sigma_b - u\sigma_a) y_a) N\left(\frac{\mu_b - u\mu_a - v + (\rho\sigma_b - u\sigma_a) y_a}{\sigma_b \sqrt{1 - \rho^2}} \right) \right.$$

$$\left. + \sigma_b \sqrt{1 - \rho^2}\, n\left(\frac{\mu_b - u\mu_a - v + (\rho\sigma_b - u\sigma_a) y_a}{\sigma_b \sqrt{1 - \rho^2}} \right) \right] n(y_a)\, dy_a. \tag{8}$$

Substituting $\kappa(y_a, -h_{ba}(v, u), \alpha_b(u)) = (\mu_b - u\mu_a - v + (\rho\sigma_b - u\sigma_a) y_a)/(\sigma_b \sqrt{1 - \rho^2})$, the integral (8) is the sum of

$$(8) = (\mu_b - u\mu_a - v) e^{-r(t_2 - t_1)} \int_{h_a(x)}^{h_a(y)} N(\kappa(y_a, -h_{ba}(v, u), \alpha_b(u))) n(y_a)\, dy_a \tag{9a}$$

$$+ (\rho\sigma_b - u\sigma_a) e^{-r(t_2 - t_1)} \int_{h_a(x)}^{h_a(y)} y_a N(\kappa(y_a, -h_{ba}(v, u), \alpha_b(u))) n(y_a)\, dy_a \tag{9b}$$

$$+ \sigma_b \sqrt{1 - \rho^2}\, e^{-r(t_2 - t_1)} \int_{h_a(x)}^{h_a(y)} n(\kappa(y_a, -h_{ba}(v, u), \alpha_b(u))) n(y_a)\, dy_a. \tag{9c}$$

We integrate using the integration rules found in Triantis and Hodder (1990),

$$(9a) = (\mu_b - u\mu_a - v) e^{-r(t_2 - t_1)} [N_2(-h_{ba}(v, u), h_a(y); \alpha_b(u)) - N_2(-h_{ba}(v, u), h_a(x); \alpha_b(u))],$$

$$(9b) = (\rho\sigma_b - u\sigma_a) e^{-r(t_2 - t_1)} [n(h_a(x)) N(\kappa(h_a(x), -h_{ba}(v, u), \alpha_{ba}(u))) - n(h_a(y)) N(\kappa(h_a(y), -h_{ba}(v, u), \alpha_{ba}(u)))$$

$$+ \alpha_{ba}(u) n(-h_{ba}(v, u)) [N(\kappa(-h_{ba}(v, u), h_a(x), \alpha_{ba}(u))) - N(\kappa(-h_{ba}(v, u), h_a(y), \alpha_{ba}(u)))]],$$

$$(9c) = \frac{\sigma_b^2 (1 - \rho^2)}{\sqrt{v_T(u)}} e^{-r(t_2 - t_1)} n(-h_{ba}(v, u)) [N(\kappa(-h_{ba}(v, u), h_a(y), \alpha_{ba}(u))) - N(\kappa(-h_{ba}(v, u), h_a(x), \alpha_{ba}(u)))].$$

When we sum these and factor out $\sqrt{v_T(u)}$, some terms cancel out, and we get the expression for L in the text.

Acknowledgments

The authors are grateful to Kerry Back, Stephen Brown (the editor), Jim Hodder, Dilip Madan, David Mauer, Lance Pekala, Howard Thompson, Tim Riddiough, and Peter Pope (the referee) for comments and suggestions related to this paper. The authors also thank their discussants at the 1996 American Finance Association meeting (Robert McDonald), the 1995 European Finance Association meeting (Cynthia Van Hulle), and the 1995 Financial Management Association meeting (Van Son Lai) for helpful comments on an earlier version of this paper entitled "Investment Decisions for Mutually Exclusive Projects: An Options Framework."

Notes

1. Sick (1995), Trigeorgis (1996), and Dixit and Pindyck (1994) provide surveys of this literature.

2. In fact, the only papers (of which we are aware) that explore the issue of project interrelationships in a real options setting both deal with this specific case. Grenadier and Weiss (1997) and Mauer and Ott (1995) examine the decision to replace an existing machine or technology with a randomly arriving new technology. They assume that the evolution of the new technology is exogenously given. In contrast, we assume that competing technologies must first be developed, and that different, possibly correlated, technologies may be simultaneously available.

3. A special intertemporal case of complementarity arises when one project is a prerequisite for a future project. Such compound options have been examined in Trigeorgis (1996).

4. See, e.g., Beidleman, Fletcher, and Veshosky (1990), who indicate that infrastructure projects often have a development phase with a duration of up to three years, Bar-Ilan and Strange (1996), who address the protracted real estate development process, and Ott (1992), who describes the ongoing process for developing fusion and solar technologies as future power sources.

5. For example, see Symonds and Matlack (1998) for a brief description of the development of the Sensor razor at Gillette in the late 1970s and early 1980s. Also, see Smith and Reinertsen (1995) for a more detailed discussion regarding technical and market risks associated with new product development, and Section IV.C of this paper where other examples are provided.

6. The economics literature contains some research related to parallel and sequential development in the context of research and development and search models. For example, see Gallini and Kotowitz (1985), Gittins (1989), Vishwanath (1992), and Weitzman (1979). These papers are based on several rather restrictive assumptions: independence of stochastic variables affecting the projects' profitabilities (or a limited form of correlation), risk neutrality, and undue constraints on project implementation in the case of sequential development.

7. Eliminating windows is not as simple as not cutting window holes. The body must be reengineered to withstand the different stresses. Further, new designs must be analyzed and/or tested depending on how much they differ from existing, certified designs.

8. Additional examples of interrelated projects are provided in Section IV.C.

9. Of course, neither project should be developed if both development strategies have negative present values.

10. For simplicity, if implementation takes place, it is assumed to occur instantaneously immediately following completion of the development stage. If implementation could be delayed after development is complete and/or if implementation takes place gradually over time, the firm would possess additional

investment options (e.g., the option to delay investment and the option to switch the implemented project). These options would, of course, only be valuable to the extent that additional uncertainty is resolved subsequent to the development stage. In order to focus on the differences between sequential and parallel development, we assume that uncertainty is resolved only when at least one of the projects is being developed. Thus, the options to delay development or implementation have no value.

11. In this paper, we use the notation x^+ in place of $\max(x, 0)$ and $(x, y)^+$ in lieu of $\max(x, y, 0)$.

12. If we were to assume that project a, once implemented, yields a perpetuity of constant cash flows, then the present value of these cash flows will be identical whether measured at t_1 or at t_2. In this case, cash flows are received by the firm during $[t_1, t_2]$, but there is no depreciation in the value of the project, i.e., $\delta = 1$.

13. Our model allows the salvage value to be any linear combination of the implementation cost, K_a, and the project value, X_a. Specifically, if the salvage value is $\beta K_a + \delta_{sv} X_a$ and the opportunity cost is δ_{oc}, then this problem maps to the formulation presented with $\delta = \delta_{oc} - \delta_{sv}$.

14. The value of the replicating portfolio would reveal project *values* but not necessarily preclude development. Development may still be required to prepare the project for implementation (even if uncertainty is otherwise resolved). For example, there may be a lengthy approval process (such as FDA approval for drugs).

15. See Rubinstein (1976) and Brennan (1979) for a utility-based application of equivalent martingale pricing in potentially incomplete markets. Recent developments in the theory of asset pricing in incomplete markets have yielded conditions under which a unique minimal martingale measure exists. For a continuous time development of this approach, see Duffie and Richardson (1991); for a discrete-time formulation, see Elliott and Madan (1998). Other decision rules have also been applied to estimate a pricing measure in an incomplete market setting. For example, see Rubinstein (1994) for an analysis involving implied probability distributions.

16. In our model, managers of the firm select an investment strategy that maximizes project value. Brennan (1990) presents an alternative rationale for developing a project. In his model, shareholders are unable to observe the value of "latent" assets, and the managers may develop a project in order to produce cash flows that serve as signals of asset value. This strategy is optimal in his asymmetric information context, despite the fact that in a symmetric information environment the costs of development (e.g., gold extraction from a mine) would, in fact, dissipate value.

17. We assume that the sets I_j are measurable with respect to the equivalent martingale measure, Q. For the normally distributed cash flow case examined in Section III, these sets are intervals on $\mathbb{R}$.

18. Note that at t_1, the distribution of x_b is conditioned on the revealed value of x_a.

19. Notice that for $x_a \in I_D$, implementation of project a, if it occurs, is deferred to t_2.

20. Brennan (1979) values a European call option on a normally distributed asset. Our analysis with normally distributed assets extends his work by providing closed-form solutions for the value of a sequential exchange option and the value of an option on the maximum of two assets.

21. See Childs (1995) for a similar analysis based on lognormal distributions for X_a and X_b. That analysis involves closed-form valuations that are similar to those found in Carr (1988), who values sequential exchange options on lognormally distributed assets.

22. We use $g(x, y)$ as the bivariate normal density function. For convenience, we also use $g(x)$ and $g(x|y)$ as univariate normal density and conditional density functions, respectively.

23. When $\rho = \pm 1$, the valuation expressions we derive must be replaced with their limiting forms.

24. The derivation of this expression can be found in Appendix II.A.

25. This call option valuation is identical to Equation (39) of Brennan (1979).

26. The identity $\delta X_a - \beta K_a = \delta x_a - (\beta - \delta) K_a$ is used to re-express V_{ID}.

27. The orderings (and proofs) for other parameter cases are available from the authors upon request. An animated graph (avi file) showing the values of the different policies as correlation changes can be accessed via the World Wide Web at http://weber.u.washington.edu/~jfqa/hold/7822.html.

28. Weitzman (1979) also shows this result in the case of statistically independent projects.

29. The value under sequential development reflects the optimal ordering of projects.

30. We have also found that, not surprisingly, increasing the interest rate or the development time (all else equal) makes waiting to obtain the exchange option more costly and favors parallel development. Also, as the firm is better able to salvage its implementation costs (i.e., β increases), sequential development becomes relatively more valuable.

31. The issue of selecting the plant size (see Dixit (1993)) also falls into this general category of decision problems.

32. See Stalk, Jr. and Hout (1990) for an illustrative example based on Mitsubishi Electric's design of its three-horsepower heat pump.

33. The specification for project interrelationships must reflect that the implementation of one project can affect the cash flows of another simultaneously implemented project. Our highly tractable specification captures these effects and allows for an asymmetric relationship for the projects (e.g., $\gamma_a < 1$ and $\gamma_b > 1$ mean that implementing project a has a complementary effect on project b, but implementing project b partially substitutes for project a).

34. The mutually exclusive cases we have examined in the body of the paper are: $\gamma_a = 0$, $\gamma_b = 1$ (implement only project b), and $\gamma_a = 1$, $\gamma_b = 0$ (implement only project a).

35. In some cases, the interval for which a policy is optimal may be degenerate. A similar note applies to the later orderings as well.

References

Bar-Ilan, A., and W. C. Strange. "Urban Development with Lags." *Journal of Urban Economics*, 39 (1996), 87–113.

Beidleman, C. R.; D. Fletcher; and D. Veshosky. "On Allocating Risk." *Sloan Management Review*, 47 (1990), 47–55.

Bierman, H., and S. Smidt. *The Capital Budgeting Decision*. London, England: MacMillan Publishing Co. (1988).

Brealey, R. A., and S. C. Myers. *Principles of Corporate Finance*, Fifth ed. New York, NY: McGraw-Hill, Inc. (1996).

Brennan, M. J. "The Pricing of Contingent Claims in Discrete Time Models." *Journal of Finance*, 34 (1979), 53–68.

――――. "Presidential Address: Latent Assets." *Journal of Finance*, 45 (1990), 709–730.

Brennan, M. J., and E. S. Schwartz. "Evaluating Natural Resource Investments." *Journal of Business*, 58 (1985), 135–157.

Bruner, R. F. "Empirical Chemicals, Ltd. (B): Merseyside and Rotterdam Projects." In *Case Studies in Finance: Managing for Corporate Value Creation*, Second ed., R. F. Bruner, ed. Chicago, IL: Irwin (1994), 258–263.

Carr, P. "The Valuation of Sequential Exchange Opportunities." *Journal of Finance*, 43 (1988), 1235–1256.

Childs, P. D. *Capital Budgeting for Interrelated Projects in a Real Options Framework*. Ph.D. Thesis, University of Wisconsin-Madison (1995).

Dixit, A. K. "Entry and Exit Decisions under Uncertainty." *Journal of Political Economy*, 97 (1989), 620–638.

――――. "Choosing among Alternative Discrete Investment Projects under Uncertainty." *Economics Letters*, 41 (1993), 265–268.

Dixit, A. K., and R. S. Pindyck. *Investment under Uncertainty*. Princeton, NJ: Princeton Univ. Press (1994).

Duffie, D., and H. R. Richardson. "Mean-Variance Hedging in Continuous Time." *Annals of Applied Probability*, 1 (1991), 1–15.

Elliott, R. J., and D. B. Madan. "A Discrete Time Equivalent Martingale Measure." *Mathematical Finance*, 8 (1998), 127–152.

Gallini, N., and Y. Kotowitz. "Optimal R&D Processes and Competition." *Economica*, 52 (1985), 321–334.

Gittins, J. C. *Multi-Armed Bandit Allocation Indices*. New York, NY: John Wiley & Sons (1989).

Grenadier, S. R., and A. M. Weiss. "Investment in Technological Innovations: An Option Pricing Approach." *Journal of Financial Economics*, 44 (1997), 397–416.

Kulatilaka, N. "Operating Flexibilities in Capital Budgeting: Substitutability and Complementarity in Real Options." In *Real Options in Capital Investment: Models, Strategies, and Applications*, L. Trigeorgis, ed. New York, NY: Praeger (1995), 121–132.

Mauer, D., and S. H. Ott. "Investment under Uncertainty: The Case of Replacement Investment Decisions." *Journal of Financial and Quantitative Analysis*, 30 (1995), 581–605.

McDonald, R., and D. R. Siegel. "Investment and the Valuation of Firms when There is an Option to Shut Down." *International Economic Review*, 26 (1985), 331–349.

———. "The Value of Waiting to Invest." *Quarterly Journal of Economics*, 101 (1986), 707–728.

Ott, S. H. *Valuing and Timing R&D Using a Real Options Pricing Framework*. Ph.D. Thesis, Univ. of Wisconsin-Madison (1992).

Pindyck, R. S. "Irreversible Investment, Capacity Choice, and the Value of the Firm." *American Economic Review*, 79 (1988), 969–985.

———. "Irreversibility, Uncertainty, and Investment." *Journal of Economic Literature*, 29 (1991), 1110–1148.

Ross, S. A., R. W. Westerfield, and B. D. Jordan. *Fundamentals of Corporate Finance*, Third ed. Chicago, IL: Irwin (1995).

Rubinstein, M. E. "The Valuation of Uncertain Income Streams and the Pricing of Options." *Bell Journal of Economics*, 7 (1976), 407–425.

———. "Presidential Address: Implied Binomial Trees." *Journal of Finance*, 49 (1994), 771–818.

Sick, G. "Real Options." In *Finance, Volume 9 of Handbooks in Operations Research and Management Science*, R. A. Jarrow, V. Maksimovic, and W. Ziemba eds. Amsterdam, The Netherlands: North Holland (1995), 631–691.

Smith, P. G., and V. G. Reinertsen. *Developing Products in Half the Time*. New York, NY: Van Nostrand Reinhold (1995).

Stalk, Jr., G., and T. M. Hout. *Competing against Time: How Time-Based Competition is Reshaping Global Markets*. New York, NY: The Free Press (1990).

Symonds, W. C., and C. Matlack. "Gillette's Edge." *Business Week* (Jan. 19, 1998). 70–77.

Triantis, A. J., and J. Hodder. "Valuing Flexibility as a Complex Option." *Journal of Finance*, 45 (1990), 549–565.

Trigeorgis, L. "The Nature of Option Interactions and the Valuation of Investments with Multiple Real Options." *Journal of Financial and Quantitative Analysis*, 28 (1993), 1–20.

———. *Real Options: Managerial Flexibility and Strategy in Resource Allocation*. Cambridge, MA: MIT Press (1996).

Vishwanath, T. "Optimal Orderings for Parallel Project Selection." *International Economic Review*, 33 (1992), 79–89.

Weitzman, M. L. "Optimal Search for the Best Alternative." *Econometrica*, 47 (1979), 641–654.

21 Flexibility and Commitment in Strategic Investment

Han T. J. Smit and Lenos Trigeorgis

Among the most common problems in corporate strategy are the timing of strategic investment and the choice of productive capacity or price setting in new or growing markets. A value creating strategy may be directed first toward building competitive advantage through an early strategic investment commitment, followed by subsequent cash-generating investments in later stages. Due to inherent uncertainty in new markets, pioneering strategies often involve a sequence of interdependent investment decisions. An early investment commitment in R&D or a pilot plant in a new market, for example, may seem unattractive based on its direct measurable cash flows when considered in isolation, but may entail substantial strategic value from improving the firm's strategic position (e.g., via reducing operating costs in a later stage or preempting competitive entry) and from generating future growth options (Myers, 1977).

Such a strategic commitment should not be seen as a one-time investment at the outset, but rather as a first necessary link in a chain of interrelated investment decisions. Growth options also provide management with valuable flexibility to alter its planned future investment decisions as uncertainty gets resolved over time. Traditional discounted cash flow (DCF) analysis has obvious shortcomings in capturing the value of flexibility in sequential investment programs. Option-based valuation has been proposed as a useful analytical tool capable of quantifying managerial operating flexibility and strategic options. The real options literature (e.g., Myers [1987], Trigeorgis and Mason [1987], McDonald and Siegel [1986], Majd and Pindyck [1987], Myers and Majd [1990], Baldwin [1982], Pindyck [1988], Ingersoll and Ross [1992], Trigeorgis [1993]) provides various examples of flexible investment strategy, but the aspect of competitive interactions merits further development. As Kester (1984), Trigeorgis (1991a), Smit and Ankum (1993), Kulatilaka and Perotti (1992), Grenadier (1996) and others point out, an options approach to strategic investing should be seen from the perspective of competitive market structure.

The goal of this chapter is to develop an integrated real options and game-theoretic industrial organization framework for strategic investments.[1] The paper departs from the standard real options optimization problem (game against *nature*) to model corporate strategy involving games against *competition*. We consider a sequence of investment decisions by a pioneer firm (involving a first-stage strategic investment commitment that can influence its relative strategic position vis-a-vis its competitor in the second stage, and subsequent cash-generating investment decisions by either competitor), and their interaction with competitive quantity or price setting in the second stage depending on the state of market demand. (The strategic investment commitment may have both a direct effect on the pioneer firm's profit value via lowering costs [or increasing demand] and an indirect or strategic effect via altering the competitor's equilibrium quantity [or price setting] or changing the market structure altogether [e.g., from Nash equilibrium to monopoly].) The paper examines how the strategic value of early commitment interacts with the option value of lost flexibility, and develops different competitive strategies depending on the nature of competitive reaction and market structure characteristics. The equilibrium outcomes of different strategic games against competition (e.g., Nash, Stackelberg leader/ follower, or monopoly) in the various states of demand become the end node or state values in a binomial option valuation tree that yields the optimal investment strategy. The optimal strategy of a pioneer firm is seen to depend not only on its own stance vis-à-vis its competitor (tough or accommodating) and the type of investment (proprietary or shared), but also on the nature of competitive reaction (reciprocating or contrarian).[2]

The rest of the paper is organized as follows. Section I discusses conceptually the real options and industrial organization framework for investment strategies under different competitive environments. Different investment strategies are modelled under contrarian quantity or reciprocating price competition in section II. Section III illustrates the various competitive strategies using numerical examples from R&D and goodwill investments, focusing on the different strategic effects. Section IV discusses critical or threshold demand values giving rise to various zones with different market structure game outcomes. By way of a summary, Section V separates out the total value of each investment strategy into its direct, strategic, and flexibility value components and concludes.

I   A Real Options and Industrial Organization Framework

A   Real Options

A strategic investment can be seen as a contingent plan of interrelated investment decisions designed to build a strategic position in a new or growing market. By investing in a strategic project, the firm essentially acquires a foothold in the market in the form of options to capitalize on valuable follow-on investment opportunities. Consider, for example, an R&D investment or a pilot project for the testing and development of an alternative, lower-cost technological process. Such a strategic investment opportunity can be viewed as a call option, having as underlying asset the present value of expected cash inflows from the completed and operating follow-on project, V_t, with exercise price being the necessary investment outlay, I. The ability to defer investment in the follow-on project under market demand uncertainty creates valuable flexibility for management. If, during the later stage, market demand develops favorably, the firm can make the follow-on investment and obtain the project's net present value at that time, $\text{NPV}_t = V_t - I$. If, however, market demand is weak, management can decide not to invest and its value would be truncated to 0.[3] (The firm may, of course, consider operating with the existing, more expensive technology if the base-case NPV is positive.) Based on the above options analogy, we can use binomial option valuation (e.g., see Cox, Ross and Rubinstein [1979], Trigeorgis and Mason [1987], or Trigeorgis [1991b]) to value the flexibility to defer the project and arrive at an optimal investment strategy.

Briefly, suppose that project value, V_t, derives from equilibrium profits, $\pi(\Theta)$, which are a function of a market demand parameter Θ that follows a multiplicative binomial process in complete markets (spanning the profit value dynamics), either moving up to $\Theta_u \equiv u\Theta$ or down to $\Theta_d \equiv d\Theta$ over the next period, where u and d are the multiplicative (up and down) binomial parameters. The value of a contingent claim on project value, C, next period will then move up (C_u) or down (C_d), in line with $V_{t+1}(\Theta_u)$ or $V_{t+1}(\Theta_d)$. Under risk-neutral valuation, the current value of this claim can be determined from its expected future up and down state values discounted at the risk-free interest rate (r), with expectations taken over risk-neutral (or "certainty equivalent") probabilities (p), as follows:[4]

$$C = \frac{pC_u + (1-p)C_d}{1+r} \tag{1}$$

The analogy between such strategic investment opportunities and financial call options is, of course, not exact. A major difference relates to the degree of exclusiveness (or sharing) of real investment opportunities, so the real option analogy must be seen in the context of market structure (e.g., see Kester [1984], Trigeorgis [1991a]). Suppose, for example, than in the first stage pioneer firm A can choose to make a strategic R&D investment in a new, cost-efficient technological process which can influence its strategic position (e.g., via lower operating costs) in the second stage, and that the market structure in the second stage will result in a duopoly, where either of two competing firms $(A$ or $B)$ may make subsequent cash-generating investments (using the new or the existing technology). In this case, instead of the standard optimization problem using the maximum of $(V_t - I, 0)$ or the deferral value in the binomial option valuation tree, the state value of the investment opportunity would now equal the equilibrium outcome of a simultaneous investment subgame. We can distinguish four basic cases: (i) when both firms invest (I) in the second stage, the game results in a Nash equilibrium; (ii) when both firms decide to defer (D), next period's market demand (Θ) is revealed and the game is repeated; and $(iii)/(iv)$ when either firm (A or B) invests first, nature moves and the other firm may then decide to invest later (as a Stackelberg follower) or not (resulting in a monopoly for the first-moving firm). The different sets of actions of the two firms result in project value payoffs at the end of each branch (node) in the binomial valuation tree, representing the equilibrium outcomes of different competitive market structure games (such as Nash equilibrium competition, a Stackelberg leader/follower game, or monopoly).

In general, the decision to invest in a strategic project should therefore be based on an *expanded* or *strategic* NPV criterion that incorporates not only the direct (or passive) NPV of expected cash flows from investing immediately, but also the option or flexibility value from adjusting future contingent decisions under active management (optimizing against nature), as well as the strategic value from competitive interactions. That is,

Expanded (strategic) net present value (NPV*)

$$= [\text{direct (passive) NPV} + \text{strategic value}] + \text{flexibility value} \qquad (2)$$

Such an expanded-NPV (or NPV*) may, in principle, be determined for any investment alternative, for example, making a strategic R&D investment in a new technological process with lower costs or not (base-case alternative of staying with the existing, more costly process). In explaining the incremental value (strategic investment vs. base case), note that a strategic investment commitment may have both a direct effect on the pioneer firm's profit value via lowering costs (or increasing demand) and an indirect or strategic reaction effect via altering the competitor's equilibrium quantity (or price setting). The total strategic value in (2) above may thus consist of this strategic reaction value (reflecting the impact of competitor's reaction on profit value via incremental changes in equilibrium quantity or price for a given market structure) and of a strategic preemption (or collusion) value from changing the market structure altogether, for example, from Nash equilibrium in the base case (staying with the existing, costlier process) to a monopoly in quantity competition (or to a collusion-type Stackelberg leader/follower game in price competition) under the strategic investment alternative.

The strategic value may be positive (e.g., if early investment in quantity competition creates a proprietary cost advantage or deters competitive entry), or negative (if early investment "proves" the market or creates shared benefits that a competitor can better exploit). We subsequently refer to the combination of the incremental direct NPV (net of the required investment outlay) and the total strategic value (reaction value + preemption value) resulting from an early capital commitment as the *net commitment* value. Thus, an early strategic investment is seen to have two main effects on value: a *net commitment effect* that influences the firm's competitive position and cash-generating ability in a later stage of the market, and a *flexibility effect* capturing the firm's ability to alter its future contingent investment decisions under demand uncertainty. Although an early strategic investment would necessarily sacrifice flexibility value, it may have either a positive or negative commitment effect (depending on the sign of the strategic value effect).[5]

B   The Strategic Value of Early Commitment

Fudenberg and Tirole (1984) have developed an interesting framework for business strategies to capture strategic interactions. We integrate these strategic interactions with real options valuation to develop a two-stage framework for thinking about competitive strategies. Following Fudenberg and Tirole, assume that firm A can make a first-stage strategic capital investment, K_A, such as in R&D or in advertising/goodwill. The value (V_i) of second-stage operating profits (π_i) for firm i in each state of nature (for $i = A$ or B) depends on the strategic investment of the pioneer firm, K_A, as well as on the firm's ability to appropriate the benefits when investing in subsequent opportunities, which is a function of competitive reaction.

Firm A $V_A(K_A, \alpha_A^*(K_A), \alpha_B^*(K_A))$ (3)

Firm B $V_B(K_A, \alpha_A^*(K_A), \alpha_B^*(K_A))$

where

K_A = first-stage strategic capital investment of pioneering firm A (potentially influencing second-stage operating costs, c, if in R&D, or market demand, Θ, if in goodwill);

$\alpha_i^*(K_A)$ = optimal (*) second-stage action of firm i (Q_i in quantity competition if R&D, or P_i in price competition if goodwill), in response to first-stage strategic investment (K_A);

$V_i()$ = the present value of operating profits (π_i) for firm i in the second stage of the market, given K_A and the optimal actions of both firms.

Given market demand, firm A must decide whether or not to make an upfront strategic investment commitment, K_A, while each firm must decide whether and when to invest in the second stage and select an optimal action (Q or P), taking the competitor's reaction into account. In some cases, pioneer firm A may invest in a strategic project in order to deter entry by making firm B's entry unprofitable (NPV$_B < 0$), thereby earning monopoly profits in the later stage of the market. The incremental impact of firm A's strategic investment (dK_A) on firm B's second-stage profit value (dV_B) is generally given by:

$$\frac{dV_B}{dK_A} = \frac{\partial V_B}{\partial K_A} + \frac{\partial V_B}{\partial \alpha_A} \frac{d\alpha_A^*}{dK_A} \qquad (4)$$

To deter entry, firm A must take a tough stance that would hurt its competitor (i.e., $dV_B/dK_A < 0$). If entry deterrence is not feasible or desirable (e.g., if it is too costly), firm A may find it preferable in some cases to follow an accommodating strategy. Firm A's incentive to make the strategic investment then depends on the impact of its incremental investment (dK_A) on its own value from second-stage operating profits, i.e.,

$$\frac{dV_A}{dK_A} = \frac{\partial V_A}{\partial K_A} + \frac{\partial V_A}{\partial \alpha_B} \frac{d\alpha_B^*}{dK_A} \qquad (5)$$

(commitment effect = direct effect + strategic effect)

It is a prerequisite for an accommodating strategy that firm A's strategic investment must result in a positive commitment value $(dV_A/dK_A > 0)$. Eq. (5) above confirms that the commitment effect consists of two components. The first term captures the direct effect of an incremental strategic investment on firm A's own second-stage profit value, with the competitor's reaction constant. The strategic effect results from the impact of firm A's strategic investment on competitor firm B's optimal second-stage action (e.g., B's output decision), $d\alpha_B^*/dK_A$, and *its* resulting indirect impact on firm A's profit value. Thus, whether firm A should make the strategic investment or not depends, in addition to the direct influence on its own profit value, on whether the indirect strategic effect via the competitor's reaction is positive or negative.

As shown in figure 21.1, the sign of this strategic effect depends on (i) whether firm A's strategic investment (K_A) would hurt or benefit its competitor's second-stage profit value, i.e., whether firm A takes a *tough* or *accommodating* position vis-à-vis its competitor (depending on whether the benefits of the strategic investment are proprietary or shared);[6] and (ii) whether competitor B's reaction to A's action, $R_B(\alpha_A)$, is *reciprocating*, as often happens in price competition, or *contrarian*, as is often the case is Cournot-type quantity competition. That is,[7]

Sign of the strategic effect (− or +)	=	whether investing results in a tough (−) or accommodating (+) position	×	whether competitive actions are reciprocating (complements) or contrarian (substitutes)

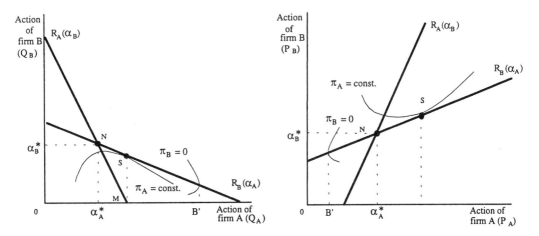

Figure 21.1
A. Contrarian competition/substitutes; down-sloping reaction curves $R_{j(\alpha_i)}$ e.g., Quantity competition, $(\alpha_i = Q_i)$

B. Reciprocating competition/complements up-sloping reaction curves, $R_{j(\alpha_i)}$ e.g., Price competition $(\alpha_i = P_i)$

Figure 21.1 illustrates the two qualitatively different cases of competitive reaction. Panel *A* shows competitive reactions that are contrarian (substitutes) involving downward-sloping reaction curves, while panel *B* illustrates reciprocating (complement) reactions, with upward-sloping reaction functions.[8] When competitive reactions are contrarian, the action of the first-moving firm substitutes for the second-stage action of its competitor, or the competitor's reaction is contrary to the leader's action. Often quantity competition, when a larger quantity produced by the leading firm (e.g., capturing a larger market share via economies of scale or a learning cost advantage) results in a lower quantity for its competitor, is regarded as contrarian and involves downward-sloping reaction functions. Competitive reactions are often reciprocating or complementary under price competition. Here, a low price setting by one firm would be matched by a low price by the competing firm (and lower marginal profits for both); both firms may thus be better off if the leading firm sets a higher price instead that the follower can also adopt.

C Competitive Strategies

As noted, with an early strategic investment the firm may enhance its relative strategic position in a later stage of the market (e.g., via a lower-cost technology) or acquire options to capitalize on follow-on investment opportunities. An offensive strategies is

Table 21.1
Sign of the strategic effect and competitive strategies following a tough or accommodating position under contrarian or reciprocating competition

	Competition	
	Contrarian (down-sloping reaction/substitutes) e.g., quantity competition	*Reciprocating* (up-sloping reaction/complements) e.g., price competition
Pioneer		
Tough position e.g., proprietary investment (hurt competition)	*Commiting and offensive* Invest (+ strategic effect) (Monopoly profits or Nash Cournot competition)	*Flexible and inoffensive* Don't invest/wait (− strategic effect) (Nash Price competition)
Accommodating e.g., shared investment (benefit competition)	*Flexible and offensive* Don't invest/wait (− strategic effect) (Nash Cournot competition)	*Commiting and inoffensive* Invest (+ strategic effect) (Leader-follower/collusion or Nash price competition)

directed at hurting competitors' profit value in the later stage so that they would not enter, creating proprietary profit opportunities for the incumbent. On the contrary, an accommodating strategy creates valuable follow-on investment opportunities that can be shared with competitors.[9] Table 21.1 also serves to illustrate various competitive strategies, depending on whether early strategic investment hurts or benefits a competitor's second-stage profit value (i.e., whether incumbent firm *A* takes a *tough* or *accommodating* position) and whether competition reacts in a *reciprocating* or in a *contrarian* fashion. The different competitive strategies are:

1. *Committing and offensive strategy (tough position with contrarian competition).* An offensive strategic investment commitment can generate a proprietary advantage and make the firm tough, hurting its competition in the second stage. Under contrarian competition where quantities are substitutes, competition will retreat and the pioneering firm can expand its share and gain (Nash Cournot) leadership as the industry grows. If demand is so low that the competitor's profit value would be negative, the pioneer may even enjoy monopoly profits. The strategic reaction effect will be positive.

2. *Flexible and offensive strategy (accommodating with contrarian competition).* Under contrarian (e.g., quantity) competition, the competitor may take advantage of the pioneer's accommodating position and capture most of the shared benefits of its strategic investment. The firm may be better off not to invest right away in the strategic project, in order to prevent the creation of valuable shared opportunities for competition. Rather, the firm should maintain an offensive posture via its option (flexibility) to wait to invest in future growth opportunities if demand uncertainty is resolved favorably over time. In case future demand grows and both firms choose to

invest simultaneously in a later period, a Nash equilibrium outcome may result. There will be a negative strategic reaction effect and a low commitment value.

3. *Flexible and inoffensive strategy (tough with reciprocating competition)*. A tough position via a strategic investment commitment may hurt competition but can invite a tough reaction by a reciprocating competitor, resulting in intensified rivalry (e.g., price competition in the airline industry). To avoid such intense (and potentially damaging) second-stage competition, the firm would not invest, staying flexible and inoffensive. If demand develops later, both firms can invest resulting in Nash price equilibrium. The strategic effect is negative.

4. *Committing and inoffensive strategy (accommodating with reciprocating competition)*. Here, early strategic investment will also benefit the competitor, who is ready to reciprocate. Thus, the pioneering firm should invest in the strategic project and be accommodating in a later stage of the market, avoiding price competition and reaping shared benefits. Through a collusion of high prices and higher profit margins, both firms can enjoy more profitable follow-on investments. The pioneer firm may act as a Stackelberg leader, with the competitor following suit. The strategic reaction effect would be positive.

II Modeling Different Competitive Strategies under Contrarian or Reciprocating Competition

In this section, we present a simple model supplementing elements of real option valuation with game-theoretic principles. We next develop the equilibrium actions (quantities or price settings), and state project values (from equilibrium profits) under the different market structures, first under contrarian quantity competition involving downward-sloping reaction functions, and later in the case of reciprocating price competition where reaction curves are upward sloping. These equilibrium outcomes of the different games against competition in the different states of demand will provide the end node values in the binomial option valuation tree to obtain the optimal investment strategy. Numerical examples based on such a binomial tree are used in the subsequent section to illustrate the qualitatively different implications of the different investment strategies in each of the two types of competitive reaction.

To help set up the problem, consider first the two-stage game in extensive form presented in figure 21.2. In the first stage, a pioneering firm must decide whether or not to make a strategic investment commitment (e.g., in R&D or goodwill) that may enhance its relative competitive position in the later stage of the market (vis-à-vis competitor B that may enter only in the second stage). This is compared with the

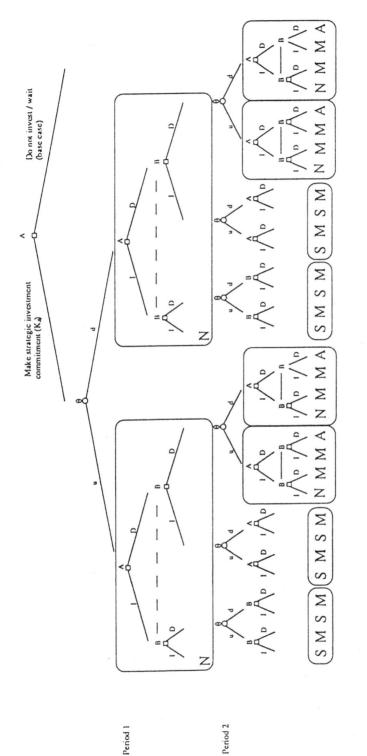

Notes: A or B (D) represents a decision to invest (I) or defer (D) by firm A or B.
θ(O) represents the state of market demand or nature's up (u) and down (d) moves.

The combination of competitive decisions (A or B) and market demand moves (θ) may
result in one of the following market structure game outcomes:

N: Nash Cournot quantity/price competition equilibrium outcome
S: Stackelberg leader (S^L)/follower (S^f) outcome
M: Monopolist outcome
A: Abandon (0 value)
D: Defer/ stay flexible (option value)

Figure 21.2
The two-stage game in extensive form under different market structures

base-case alternative of not making the strategic investment (and perhaps using the existing technology). The alternative actions of the pioneering firm to make the strategic investment or not (base case) are reflected by the tree branches in the first stage. The dynamics of market demand in the second stage, reflected by nature's (Θ) up (u) or down (d) moves, result in a range of potential investment opportunity values over time.[10] Assuming that market structure will result in a duopoly, each of the two firms A and B may invest in cash-generating projects during the second stage. To encompass various market structure possibilities, the second stage itself is assumed to consist of two periods (1 and 2). Given market demand moves, $\Theta\{u, d\}$, in each period during the second stage, each competitor's actions to invest (I) or defer (D) investment in the second-stage project are represented by the tree branches, $A \{I, D\}$ and $B \{I, D\}$. When both firms decide to invest simultaneously in the second stage (I, I), the game ends in Nash equilibrium (N); when both firms choose to defer (D, D) under low realizations of demand, nature (Θ) moves again and the game is repeated; finally, when one firm invests first, acting as a Stackelberg leader (S^L)—or in some cases a monopolist (M)—market demand is revealed again and the competitor may then decide to invest later—as a Stackelberg follower (S^F)—or to abandon (A). The competitive strategy of each firm consists of mapping the information set about its competitor's actions and the development of market demand (u or d moves in Θ) to an optimal investment action by the firm. The equilibrium set of strategies can be found by backward induction, starting with the future payoffs (state net project values) of a given competitive structure and working backward through the binomial risk-neutral valuation tree. The different market structure games (modeled in the next section) briefly are as follows:[11]

(i) *Nash (Price or Cournot Quantity) Competition (N)* If both firms decide to invest (I) in the same period (simultaneously), a Nash equilibrium is reached when each firm reacts optimally to the other firm's expected action (as expressed by its reaction function, R), i.e., $\alpha_A^* = R_A(\alpha_B^*)$ and $\alpha_B^* = R_B(\alpha_A^*)$. Thus, the Nash equilibrium actions (prices or Cournot quantities), α_A^* and α_B^*, are on the intersection of the reaction functions of both firms, shown as outcome N in figure 21.1 (and in later figures 21.3 and 21.6).[12] These Nash equilibrium actions can be obtained by substituting the expression for $R_j(\alpha_i)$ into $R_i(\alpha_j)$, or by equating the reaction functions $R_A(\alpha_B)$ and $R_B(\alpha_A)$, and solving for the optimal actions α_A^* and α_B^*.

(ii) *Stackelberg Leadership (S)* If one firm invests first in a follow-up investment and its competitor invests at a later period (e.g., if the follower faces relatively higher operating costs that require waiting until demand has risen more, or if a lag is involved for the follower to set up plant capacity), a Stackelberg leader/follower game can result. Given that the follower will observe the leader's prior action, the Stackelberg (quantity or price) leader will choose that action on the follower's reaction function, $R_B(\alpha_A)$, that will maximize its own profit value, i.e., max $V_A(\alpha_A, R_B(\alpha_A))$.[13] The Stackelberg outcome is shown in figure 21.1 (and in later figures 21.3 and 21.6) as point S where firm A's highest isoprofit curve (π_A = constant) is just tangent to firm B's reaction curve, and corresponds to a higher profit value than the Nash equilibrium.

(iii) *Monopoly (M)* In some cases (e.g., when the leader has a first-mover cost advantage and/or realized demand is low, the leader may choose an early action (e.g., a high enough quantity—above profit-breakeven ($\pi_B = 0$) point B in panel A of figure 21.1—or a low enough price—below breakeven point B' in panel B) on the follower's reaction curve such that it would become unprofitable for the follower to operate ($\pi_B(\alpha_A, \alpha_B) < 0$, or net of the required outlay, $NPV_B < 0$), preempting its entry and earning monopoly profits (π_m). The monopoly outcome is shown as point M in panel A of figure 21.1 (and in later figure 21.3), and lies on a higher iso-profit curve than the Stackelberg and Nash outcomes.[14]

(iv) *Do Not Invest/Defer (D) or Abandon (A)* Management, of course, has the option not to invest or to wait if market demand (Θ) is low and undertaking the project would thereby result in a negative value. By deferring investment, management keeps alive the opportunity that demand may improve and the project may become profitable in a future period. In case the firm does not invest up until the very last stage, or it decides to abandon, the value of follow-up investment would be truncated to 0.

A   Contrarian Quantity Competition

We now proceed to model the case of contrarian competition. Firm A (the incumbent or pioneer) can make a first-stage strategic investment, K_A, for example in R&D, which may reduce its second-stage marginal operating cost, c_A. We again assume that only firm A operates in the first stage, while in the second-stage it competes with firm B (the entrant) in quantities. Exogenous uncertainty in future market demand is characterized by fluctuations in the demand parameter, Θ_t. In the second-stage game, we assume for simplicity a linear demand function:[15]

$$P(Q, \Theta_t) = \Theta_t - (Q_A + Q_B), \tag{6}$$

where Θ_t is the demand shift parameter, assumed to follow a lognormal diffusion process (or a multiplicative binomial process in discrete-time). Q_A and Q_B are the quantities produced by firms A and B, respectively, and $P(Q)$ is the common market price as a function of total quantity ($Q = Q_A + Q_B$). The total variable production cost for each firm i ($i = A$ or B) is given by:

$$C(Q_i) = c_i Q_i + \tfrac{1}{2} q_i Q_i^2, \tag{7}$$

where c_i and q_i are the linear and quadratic cost coefficients (or the fixed and variable coefficients of the marginal cost function, $c_i + q_i Q_i$) for firm i. The second-stage annual operating profits for each firm i are given by:

$$\pi_i(Q_i, Q_j, \Theta_t) = PQ_i - C(Q_i) = [(\Theta_t - c_i) - Q_j]Q_i - (1 + \tfrac{1}{2} q_i)Q_i^2 \tag{8}$$

The gross project value (profit value), V_i, and the net present value, NPV$_i$, from the second-stage investment for firm i, assuming perpetual annual operating cash flows (profits) and a constant risk-adjusted discount rate k in the last stage, are obtained from[16]

$$V_i = \frac{\pi_i}{k}, \quad \text{and} \quad \text{NPV}_i = V_i - I = \frac{\pi_i}{k} - I. \tag{9)(9$'$}$$

Under contrarian quantity competition, the reaction function of each firm is downward sloping. Maximizing firm i's ($i = A, B$) own profit value over its quantity given that its competitor produces Q_j (setting $\partial V_i / \partial Q_i = 0$), each firm's reaction function is given by:[17,18]

$$R_i(Q_j) = \frac{\Theta_t - c_i - Q_j}{2 + q_i} \tag{10}$$

If both firms make a simultaneous investment in the second stage (I, I), a Nash Cournot equilibrium outcome will result.[19] The equilibrium quantities, Q_A^* and Q_B^*, are obtained by equating (being at the intersection of) the reaction functions of the two firms:

$$Q_i^* = \frac{(\Theta_t - c_i)(2 + q_j) - (\Theta_t - c_j)}{(2 + q_i)(2 + q_j) - 1} \tag{11}$$

In the case that firm i's early strategic investment reduces its cost (c_i) below its competitor's (c_j), then $Q_i^* > Q_j^*$. If we simplify by setting $q_i = q_j = q = 0$, this asymmetric Nash Cournot equilibrium quantity for firm i reduces to $Q_i^* = \tfrac{1}{3}(\Theta_t - 2c_i + c_j)$. (For example, if A's early strategic investment makes $c_A = 0$, $Q_A^* = \tfrac{1}{3}(\Theta_t + c_B) > \tfrac{1}{3}(\Theta_t - 2c_B) = Q_B^*$). Substituting back into profit value eqs. (8) and (9), again assuming $q_i = q_j = 0$, gives the Nash Cournot equilibrium profit value for firm i ($i = A, B$) as follows:

$$V_i^* = \frac{(\Theta_t - 2c_i + c_j)^2}{9k} \tag{12}$$

Note that $\Theta_t - 2c_i + c_j = (\Theta_t - c_i) + (c_j - c_j)$, reflecting both a profit margin for firm i and a cost advantage (relative to competitor j). In case the pioneering firm does not make an early strategic investment and both firms invest simultaneously in the second stage, a symmetric Nash Cournot equilibrium may result if the firms are otherwise identical ($Q_A^* = Q_B^* = Q^*$, with $c_A = c_B = c$ and $q_A = q_B = q$), yielding:

$$Q_i^* = \frac{(\Theta_t - c)}{(3 + q)}, \quad \text{and} \quad V_i^* = (1 + \tfrac{1}{2}q)\frac{(\theta_t - c)^2}{(3 + q)^2 k} \quad (\text{if } \Theta_t > c) \tag{13)(14}$$

(If $q = 0$, the symmetric Cournot equilibrium quantity simplifies to $Q_i^* = \tfrac{1}{3}(\Theta_t - c)$ and $V_i^* = (\Theta_t - c)^2/9k$.) Note that each firm i will eventually be profitable, net of its second-stage outlay I, if demand is such that its NPV, determined from eqs. (9') and (12) above, is positive (in this case if $\Theta_t \geq 3\sqrt{kI} + 2c_i - c_j$). If demand is too low for either firm to operate profitably they will both wait, whereas if $\Theta_t < 3\sqrt{kI} + 2c_j - c_i$ firm j will be unprofitable (NPV$_j < 0$) and firm i can earn monopoly profits.[20] It can be seen from eq. (10), with $Q_j = 0$, that the profit-value maximizing quantity for a monopolist firm i (points M in figure 21.3, where $q_i = 0$) is given by:

$$Q_i = \frac{\Theta_t - c_i}{2 + q_i} \quad (\text{with } Q_j = 0) \tag{15}$$

The monopolist firm can then set a monopolist price $[\Theta_t(1 + q_i) + c_i]/(2 + q_i)$, and enjoy monopoly profit value of:

$$V_i = \frac{(\Theta_t - c_i)^2}{(4 + 2q_i)k} \quad (\text{with } V_j = 0) \tag{16}$$

In case firm i invests first and firm j defers investment until next period (I, D), the follower will set its quantity having first observed the leader's output according to its reaction function, $R_j(Q_i)$, as in eq. (10). The Stackelberg leader i will then maximize $V_i(Q_i, R_j(Q_i))$ over Q_i, taking the follower's reaction function $R_j(Q_i)$ as given, resulting in equilibrium quantity and profit value (assuming for simplicity that $q_i = q_j = 0$) for the Stackelberg leader given by:

$$Q_i = \frac{(\Theta_t - c_i)(2 + q_j) - (\Theta_t - c_j)}{(2 + q_i)(2 + q_j) - 2}, \quad \text{and} \quad V_i = \frac{(\Theta_t - 2c_i + c_j)^2}{8k} \tag{17)(18}$$

Substituting the leader's optimal quantity from eq. (17) into the follower's reaction function in eq. (10) gives the Stackelberg follower's quantity and profit value (assuming $q_i = q_j = 0$):

$$Q_j = \frac{(\Theta_t - c_j)(2 + q_i) - (\Theta_t - c_i)}{(2 + q_i)(2 + q_j)}, \quad \text{and} \quad V_j = \frac{(\Theta_t - 2c_j + c_i)^2}{16k} \qquad (19)(20)$$

As expected, the follower's equilibrium quantity and profit value are lower than the leader's $(Q_j < Q_i, V_j < V_i)$. Further, if demand is low $(\Theta_t < 4\sqrt{kI} + 2c_j - c_i)$ the Stackelberg follower will be unable to cover its investment outlay I ($\text{NPV}_j < 0$) and will not enter; the Stackelberg leader's profit value can therefore improve (from that of eq. (18)) to the monopoly profit value shown in eq. (16) (with $q_i = 0$). The equilibrium quantities and profit values (assuming $q_i = q_j = 0$) for the various market structures above under contrarian quantity competition are summarized in table 21.2.

B   Reciprocating Price Competition

Now suppose instead that firms set their own prices and consumers determine the quantities sold. In this framework, firms may be inclined to lower prices to get a larger share of the market. But under reciprocating price competition where price settings are complements (as in ticket pricing by airlines), if one firm sets a low price so will the other; price will then be "bid down," hurting the profit margins of both firms. In many cases it may thus be preferable for both firms to avoid direct price competition and accept a higher price so that they can share collusion-type profits, competing instead on advertising, product attributes, etc. We again assume for simplicity that the demand for the good is linear in prices and Θ_t, and is given by:

$$Q_i(P_i, P_j, \Theta_{i,t}) = \Theta_{i,t} - bP_i + dP_j \qquad (21)$$

where the quantity sold by firm i is a function of its own price (P_i) as well as that of its competitor (P_j), and of a firm-specific demand shift parameter $\Theta_{i,t}$. The coefficients b and d ($b > 0, d > 0$ assuming demand substitutes) capture the sensitivities of the sold quantity to the firm's own and its competitor's price settings, respectively. The total variable cost is again of the form assumed in eq. (7). The profits of each firm i ($i = A$ or B) are then given by:

$$\pi_i(P_i, P_j, \Theta_{i,t}) = (P_i - c_i)(\Theta_{i,t} - bP_i + dP_j) - \tfrac{1}{2}q_i[\Theta_t - bP_i + dP_j]^2 \qquad (22)$$

The reaction function of each firm i is again obtained by maximizing its profit value $V_i(P_i, P_j) \equiv \pi_i/k$ over its own price P_i. Setting $\partial V_i/\partial P_i = 0$, gives:[21]

$$R_i(P_j) = \frac{(\Theta_{i,t} + dP_j)(1 + bq_i) + bc_i}{b(2 + bq_i)} \qquad (23)$$

Table 21.2
Equilibrium quantities, profits and state project values for various market structures under contrarian quantity competition in the second stage

Action[1] (A, B)	Market structure N/M/S/A/D	Equilibrium quantity Q_i^*	Equil. profit[2] π_i^*	State project value[3] NPV_i	Demand state Θ_t
Second-stage game					
(DI, DI) (II, II)	Nash Cournot (N)	$\dfrac{(\Theta_t - c_i)(2+q_j) - (\Theta_t - c_j)}{(2+q_i)(2+q_j) - 1}$	$\dfrac{(\Theta_t - 2c_i + c_j)^2}{9}$	$\dfrac{(\Theta_t - 2c_i + c_j)^2}{9k} - I$	$\geq 3\sqrt{kI} + 2c_i - c_j$
(DI, DD) (II, DD)	Monopolist (M)	$\dfrac{\Theta_t - c_i}{2 + q_i}$ $(Q_j = 0)$	$\dfrac{(\Theta_t - c_i)^2}{4}$ $(\pi_j \leq 0)$	$\dfrac{(\Theta_t - c_i)^2}{4k} - I$	$< 3\sqrt{kI} + 2c_i - c_j$
(II, DI)	Stackelberg Leader (S^L)/ Monopolist (M)	$\dfrac{(\Theta_t - c_i)(2+q_j) - (\Theta_t - c_j)}{(2+q_i)(2+q_j) - 2}$	$\dfrac{(\Theta_t - 2c_i + c_j)^2}{8}$	$\dfrac{(\Theta_t - 2c_i + c_j)^2}{8k} - I'$	$\geq 4\sqrt{kI} + 2c_i - c_j$ ($< 4\sqrt{kI} + 2c_j - c_i$)
(DI, II)	Stackelberg Follower (S^F)	$\dfrac{(\Theta_t - c_i)(2+q_j) - (\Theta_t - c_i)}{(2+q_i)(2+q_j)}$	$\dfrac{(\Theta_t - 2c_j + c_i)^2}{16}$	$\dfrac{(\Theta_t - 2c_j + c_i)^2}{16k} - I$	$\geq 4\sqrt{kI} + 2c_j - c_i$
(DD, DD)	Abandon (A)	0	0	0	
Period 1					
(I, I)	Nash Cournot (N)	$\dfrac{(\Theta_t - c_i)(2+q_j) - (\Theta_t - c_j)}{(2+q_i)(2+q_j) - 1}$	$\dfrac{(\Theta_t - 2c_i + c_j)^2}{9}$	$\dfrac{(\Theta_t - 2c_i + c_j)^2}{9k} - I$	
(I, D)	Monopolist (M)/ Stackelberg Leader (S^L)	$\dfrac{\Theta_t - c_i}{2 + q_i}$	$\pi_m = \dfrac{(\Theta_t - c_i)^2}{4}$	$\dfrac{pNPV_u^* + (1-p)NPV_d^*}{1+r} + \pi_m$	
(D, D) (D, I)	Defer (D)	0	0	$\dfrac{pNPV_u^* + (1-p)NPV_d^*}{1+r}$	

1. During period 1, (A, B) means that firm A took action A while competitor firm B took action B. During the entire second stage, (AA', BB') means that firm A took action A in period 1 and A' in period 2, while firm B took action B in period 1 and B' in period 2.

2. Calculated from $\pi_i = P_i Q_i - C(Q_i)$, assuming for simplicity $q_i = q_j = q = 0$.

3. Determined in the last stage from $NPV_i = \max(\pi_i/k - I, 0)$, where I is the required outlay and k the risk-adjusted discount rate. In the first period, it may be determined from future expanded (strategic) net present values (NPV*) in the up and down states using backward binomial risk-neutral valuation.

If both firms invest simultaneously (I, I), the Nash equilibrium prices P_i^*, P_j^* are determined from the intersection of the reaction functions of the two firms. Substituting the expression for $R_j(P_i)$ in place of P_j in eq. (23) above, gives the general asymmetric Nash equilibrium price expression:

$$P_i^* = \frac{b(2 + bq_j)[\Theta_{i,t}(1 + bq_i) + bc_i] + d(1 + bq_i)[\Theta_{j,t}(1 + bq_j) + bc_j]}{b^2(2 + bq_i)(2 + bq_j) - d^2(1 + bq_i)(1 + bq_j)} \tag{24}$$

To simplify, if we assume that $q_i = q_j = q = 0$, the Nash equilibrium prices reduce to:

$$P_i^* = \frac{2b(\Theta_{i,t} + bc_i) + d(\Theta_{j,t} + bc_j)}{4b^2 - d^2} \tag{24'}$$

If firm A does not make an early strategic investment and both firms invest simultaneously in the second stage, a symmetric Nash equilibrium price will result if the firms are otherwise identical $(P_A^* = P_B^* = P^*$, with $\Theta_{A,t} = \Theta_{B,t} = \Theta_t$, $c_A = c_B = c$ and $q_A = q_B = q$):

$$P^* = \frac{\Theta_t(1 + bq) + bc}{b(2 + bq) - d(1 + bq)} \tag{25}$$

If, for further simplicity, $q = 0$, this further reduces to:

$$P^* = \frac{\Theta_t + bc}{2b - d} \tag{25'}$$

The Nash price equilibrium quantity and profit value for firm i can be generally obtained by substituting P_i^* and P_j^* from eq. (24) or (24') back into the quantity and profit expressions in eqs. (21) and (22), respectively. For example, in the symmetric Nash equilibrium case with $q = 0$, the equilibrium quantity (Q^*) and profit value (with $\pi^* = (P^* - c)Q^*$), respectively, become:

$$Q^* = \frac{b[\Theta_t - c(b - d)]}{2b - d}, \quad \text{and} \quad V^* = \frac{b[\Theta_t - c(b - d)]^2}{(2b - d)^2 k} \tag{26)(27}$$

Both firms will have a positive Nash equilibrium quantity and earn positive profits if $\Theta_t > c(b - d)$. However, to cover their investment outlay (I) and earn a positive NPV, $V^* > I$. This would require a higher demand, namely $\Theta_t > c(b - d) + (2b - d)(kI/b)^{1/2}$. Otherwise, both firms would prefer to wait instead.

In case firm i invests first and firm j defers until next period (I, D), the leader will choose the price which maximizes its own profit value, using the reaction function of the follower. Maximizing $V_i(P_i, R_j(P_i))$ over P_i, given $R_j(P_i)$, gives a Stackelberg leader price ($q_i = q_j = 0$):

$$P_i = \frac{2b(\Theta_{i,t} + bc_i) + d(\Theta_{j,t} + bc_j - dc_i)}{4b^2 - 2d^2} \tag{28}$$

Note that the above Stackelberg leader price may exceed the Nash equilibrium price of eq. (24′). Substituting this into the follower's reaction function from eq. (23) would give the Stackelberg follower's price. In case the leader invests first (I, D) and demand is low such that it becomes uneconomical for the follower to operate profitably, the leader can improve by earning monopoly profits. A monopolist firm will maximize profit value $V_m(P_m)$ over P_m, using $Q_m = (Q_A + Q_B)$.

If $Q_m = 2(\Theta_t - (b - d)P_m) = \Theta_t - c(b - d)$,

$$P_m = \frac{\Theta_t + c(b - d)}{2(b - d)}, \quad \text{and} \quad V_m = \frac{[\Theta_t - c(b - d)]^2}{2(b - d)k} \tag{29)(30}$$

The equilibrium prices for the different market structures (for $q_i = q_j = 0$) under reciprocating price competition are summarized in table 21.3. The corresponding profits can again be obtained from $\pi_i = (P_i - c_i)Q_i$, while the second-stage project net present values from $\mathrm{NPV}_i = \max(V_i - I, 0)$, with $V_i = \pi_i/k$.

III Numerical Examples of Different Competitive Strategies and Strategic Effects

In this section we present the results of utilizing the above equilibrium state project values that result from the various competitive games in the different demand states (nodes) in the binomial option valuation tree to illustrate different competitive strategies with simple numerical examples. First, we examine an R&D example of the two-stage game under quantity competition where the production decisions of the two firms are substitutes. Later we analyze a goodwill (advertising) investment example under price competition where the price-setting decisions are complements and involve reciprocating reactions. In both competitive environments, the ability of the firm to enjoy proprietary benefits influences its strategic investment decision. The two numerical examples result in opposite strategic effects and different competitive strategies for shared and proprietary investments.

A An R&D Example (Quantity Competition)

Suppose pioneer firm A can enhance its competitive position to capitalize on future growth opportunities by an early R&D investment of $K_A = 110$ in a more cost-efficient technological process. In the second stage, either firm can invest an amount

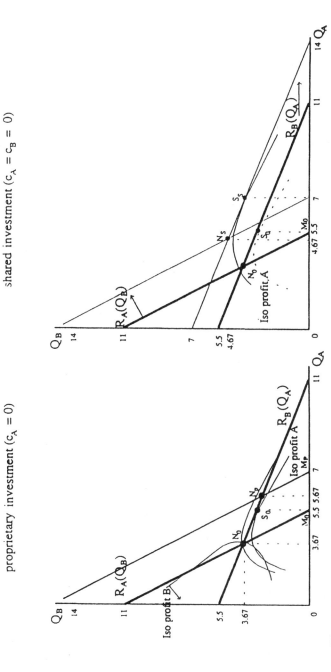

Notes:

The demand for each firm (i =A, B) is of the form $P_i(Q_A, Q_B, \Theta_t) = \Theta_t - (Q_A + Q_B)$ with $\Theta_0 = 14$ (u = 1.25, d = 0.8), and the total variable production cost for firm i is of the form $c(Q_i) = c_i Q_i$.

If no strategic investment: base-case operating costs $c_A = c_B = c = 3$ (base-case Nash equilibrium at N_0).

If proprietary investment/tough position: $c_A = 0$ ($c_B = 3$), R_A shifts to right (at N_p $Q^*_A \uparrow$, $Q^*_B \downarrow$) and $\pi_A \uparrow$.

If shared investment/accommodating position: $c_B = c_A = 0$, R_B (and R_A) shift right (at N_s $Q^*_B \uparrow$) and $\pi_B \downarrow$.

Figure 21.3A
Equilibrium Nash, Stackelberg, and Monopoly outcomes under the no strategic investment (base case), proprietary or shared investment cases assuming *contrarian* quantity competition (downward sloping reaction curves)

Pioneer firm A	Nash Cournot outcome			Stackelberg leader			Monopoly	
	N_0 base-case	N_p propriet.	N_s shared	S_0 base-case	S_p propriet.	S_s shared	M_0 base	M_p propr.
Quantity (Q^*_A)	$\frac{1}{3}(\theta_t-c)$	$\frac{1}{3}(\theta_t+c_B)$	$\frac{1}{3}\theta_t$	$\frac{1}{2}(\theta_t-c)$	$\frac{1}{2}(\theta_t+c_B)$	$\frac{1}{2}\theta_t$	$\frac{1}{2}(\theta_t-c_A)$	$\frac{1}{2}\theta_t$
base demand ($\theta_0=14$)	3.667	5.667	4.667	5.5	8.5	7	5.5	7
up ($\theta_1=u\theta_0=17.5$)	4.833	6.833	5.833	7.25	10.25	8.75	7.25	8.75
Profit (π^*_A)	$\frac{1}{9}(\theta_t-c)^2$	$\frac{1}{9}(\theta_t+c_B)^2$	$\frac{1}{9}\theta_t^2$	$\frac{1}{8}(\theta_t-c)^2$	$\frac{1}{8}(\theta_t+c_B)^2$	$\frac{1}{8}\theta_t$	$\frac{1}{4}(\theta_t-c_A)^2$	$\frac{1}{4}\theta_t^2$
base demand ($\theta_0=14$)	13.47	32.11	21.77	15.125	36.125	24.50	30.25	49
up ($\theta_1=u\theta_0=17.5$)	23.364	46.69	34.03	26.28	52.53	38.28	52.56	76.56

Notation: N_0, N_p, N_s are the Nash, and S_0, S_p, S_s the Stackelberg equilibrium outcomes for the zero, proprietary or shared investment cases; M_0 and M_p are the base-case and proprietary Monopoly outcomes. $R_j(Q_i)$ is the reaction function of firm j given the quantity of firm i (Q_i), i = A, B. Q^*_i and π^*_i fluctuate with the state of demand Θ_t.

Figure 21.3B
Equilibrium Nash, Stackelberg, and Monopoly outcomes under the no strategic investment (base case), proprietary or shared investment cases assuming *contrarian* quantity competition (downward sloping reaction curves)

$I = 100$ in subsequent cash-generating projects, depending on subsequent demand moves (where the demand parameter has initial value $\Theta_0 = 14$ and is assumed to move up or down with binomial parameters $u = 1.25$ and $d = 0.80$). The risk-free interest rate (r) is assumed to be 10% (while the risk-adjusted discount rate in the last stage is estimated at $k = 13\%$). If firm A does not make the strategic R&D investment and decides to stay with the old technology (base case) the two firms are assumed to have symmetric second-stage operating costs, using the old technology, of $c_A = c_B = 3$.

The competitive strategies can be derived by utilizing the quantity competition payoff values of table 21.2 within the two-stage game of figure 21.2. The state project values for the base case (no strategic investment) alternative in both periods during the last stage are shown for illustrative purposes in figure 21.4.[22,23] Generally, two different strategies can result as shown in figure 21.5, depending on whether the resulting investment benefits are proprietary or shared.[24]

1 Proprietary Investment: Committing and Offensive Strategy (Positive Strategic Effect)

The first (top) panel in figure 21.5 illustrates the first period of the two-stage R&D game.[25] In this case, making the strategic R&D investment commitment in the first stage results in a *proprietary* operating cost advantage for firm A when investing in follow-up capacity in the second stage. Specifically, the second-stage operating cost for firm A is reduced from 3 to 0 ($c_A = 0$) if it invests in R&D while for firm B it remains at 3 ($c_B = 3$)—as compared to the base case, $c_A = c_B = 3$, when the firm does not invest in R&D. This upfront R&D investment commitment makes the pioneer firm stronger in the second stage, preempting market share under contrarian competition. The reaction functions for this example are illustrated in figure 21.3A, where a proprietary investment causes firm A's reaction function to shift to the right changing the base-case Nash equilibrium outcome from N_0 to N_p. The equilibrium quantity (Q^*) and profits (π^*) are shown in the table of figure 21.3B for the Nash, Stackelberg leader and monopoly structures. The R&D commitment strategy in this proprietary example results in a positive strategic effect.

The first (top) panel of figure 21.5 presents the resulting valuation of the backward binomial process, given the numerical figures assumed above. Consider first the subgame (in the second box) concerning investment in follow-up capacity, following a decision to make the strategic R&D investment and a downward market demand realization ($\Theta = d$). In this state, a follow-up investment action (I) by firm A domi-

Figure 21.4 (following page)
The base-case (no strategic investment) two-stage game in extensive form under different market structures

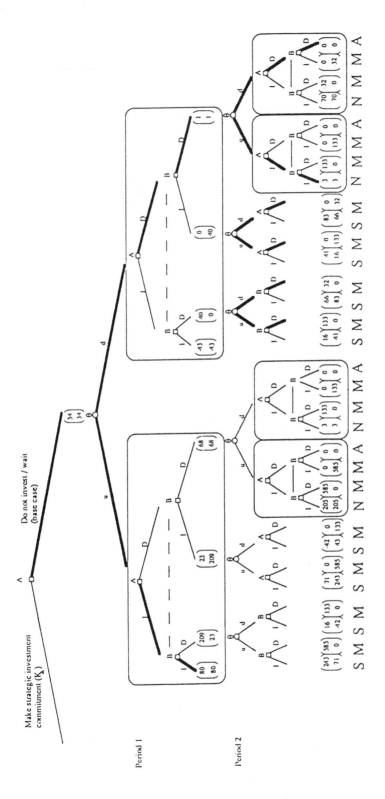

Notes: A or B (□) represents a decision to invest (I) or defer (D) by firm A or B.
θ(○) represents the state of market demand or nature's up (u) and down (d) moves.

The combination of competitive decisions (A or B) and market demand moves (θ) may
result in one of the following market structure game outcomes:

N: Nash Cournot quantity/ price competition equilibrium outcome
S: Stackelberg leader (S^l)/ follower (S^f) outcome
M: Monopolist outcome
A: Abandon (0 value)
D: Defer/ stay flexible (option value)

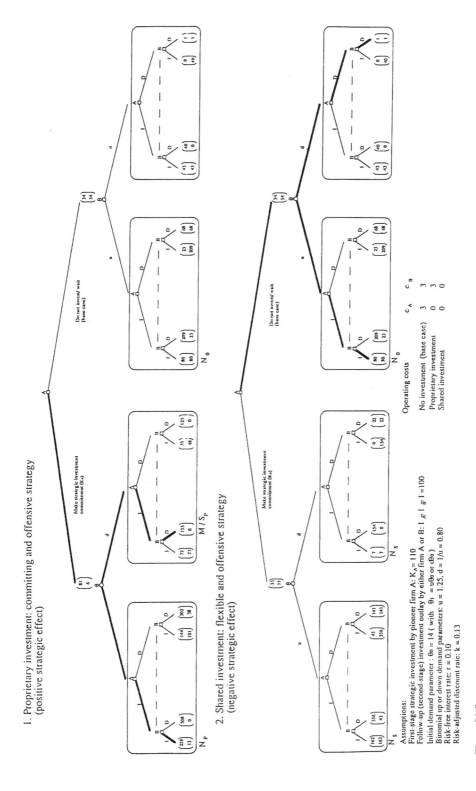

1. Proprietary investment: committing and offensive strategy (positive strategic effect)

2. Shared investment: flexible and offensive strategy (negative strategic effect)

Operating costs	c_A	c_B
No investment (base case)	3	3
Proprietary investment	0	3
Shared investment	0	0

Assumptions:
First-stage strategic investment by pioneer firm A: $K_A = 110$
Follow-up (second-stage) investment outlay by either firm A or B: $I_A = I_B = I = 100$
Initial demand parameter: $\theta_0 = 14$ (with $\theta_1 = u\theta_0$ or $d\theta_0$)
Binomial up or down demand parameters: $u = 1.25$, $d = 1/u = 0.80$
Risk-free interest rate: $r = 0.10$
Risk-adjusted discount rate: $k = 0.13$

Figure 21.5
Competitive strategies in the R&D example: proprietary vs. shared strategic investment under contrarian quantity competition

nates a deferral (D) action since it results in a higher net value for A's follow-up project regardless of whether competitor firm B decides to invest (I) or defer (D): 72 (Nash Cournot value if both invest) >35 (Stackelberg value if A defers and B invests); and 155 (monopolist or Stackelberg leader value, depending on whether B defers again or invests later) >123 (option value if both defer). Knowing that firm A has a dominating strategy to invest anyway, competing firm B would choose to defer (obtaining a value of 0 rather than -77). Thus firm A would earn monopoly profits, resulting in net present values of $(155, 0)$ for the follow-up projects of firm A and B, respectively. However, if demand moves up ($\Theta = u$) as in the first box, total market demand would be sufficient for a Nash Cournot equilibrium outcome where both firms, regardless of the other's actions, have dominant strategies to invest (I) in subsequent projects, resulting in values of $(259, 13)$ for firm (A, B), respectively.

Using backward binomial risk-neutral valuation as in eq. (1) results in expected growth option values of $(191, 6)$ when firm A makes an upfront strategic investment commitment.[26] Thus, after subtracting the required investment outlay of $K_A = 110$, the R&D investment strategy for pioneer firm A results in an expanded net present value (NPV*) of 81, as shown under the left tree branch in the first panel of figure 21.5. Since the base-case alternative of not making the strategic R&D investment or waiting (and using the existing technology) similarly results in expected equilibrium values of $(34, 34)$, firm A would find it optimal to make the strategic R&D investment ($81 > 34$).

The highlighted (bold) branches along each tree indicate the optimal actions along the equilibrium path. Pioneer firm A should commit to an offensive R&D strategy (i.e., invest K_A in the R&D project in stage 1). It should then make a follow-on commercialization investment (I) in the second stage regardless of the market demand. If market demand moves favorably ($\Theta = u$), both firms would invest resulting in a Nash Cournot quantity equilibrium value for the pioneer (259); if market demand is unfavorable ($\Theta = d$), competitor firm B would not invest and firm A's early R&D investment can result in a monopoly profit value (155).

2 Shared Investment: Flexible and Offensive Strategy (Negative Strategic Effect)
Now consider the opposite case where R&D results in a shared cost advantage, as shown in the second panels of figures 21.3 and 21.5. Here, the strategic R&D investment by firm A results in a more cost-effective technology that both competitors can exploit in the later stage of the market. Specifically, suppose the second-stage operating costs for both firms are reduced ($c_A = c_B = 0$) if firm A invests in R&D, compared to the base case of $c_A = c_B = 3$ when there is no strategic investment (and both firms use the existing technology). In this case, commitment may place the pioneer

Table 21.3
Equilibrium prices for different market structures under reciprocating price competition

Action[1] (A, B)	Market structure N/M/S/A/D	Equilibrium price,[2] P_i^* (for $q_i = q_j = 0$)
Second-stage game		
(DI, DI) (II, II)	Nash Price Comp. (N)	$\dfrac{2b(\Theta_{i,t} + bc_i) + d(\Theta_{j,t} + bc_j)}{4b^2 - d^2}$
(DI, DD) (II, DD)	Monopolist (M)	$\dfrac{\Theta_t + c(b - d)}{2(b - d)}$
(II, DI)	Stackelberg Price Leader (S^L)	$\dfrac{2b(\Theta_{i,t} + bc_i) + d(\Theta_{j,t} + bc_j - dc_i)}{4b^2 - 2d^2}$
(DD, DD)	Abandon (A)	—
Period 1		
(I, I)	Nash (N)	$\dfrac{2b(\Theta_{i,t} + bc_i) + d(\Theta_{j,t} + bc_j)}{4b^2 - d^2}$
(I, D)	Stackelberg Leader (S^L)/Monopolist (M)	$\dfrac{2b(\Theta_{i,t} + bc_i) + d(\Theta_{j,t} + bc_j - dc_i)}{4b^2 - 2d^2}$
(D, D) (D, I)	Defer (D)	—

1. During period 1, (A, B) means that firm A took action A while competitor firm B took action B. During the entire second stage, (AA′, BB′) means that firm A took action A in period 1 and A′ in period 2, while firm B took action B in period 1 and B′ in period 2.
2. Given this equilibrium price, firm i's corresponding profit can be calculated from $\pi_i = (P_i - c_i)Q_i$ (assuming $q_i = q_j = 0$), while the second-stage state net present values from $\mathrm{NPV}_i = \max(\pi_i/k - I, 0)$, where I is the required outlay and k the risk-adjusted discount rate. Period 1 values may be determined from future expanded (strategic) net present values (NPV^*) in the up and down states using backward binomial risk-neutral valuation.

firm at a strategic disadvantage by paying the cost for creating valuable investment opportunities for the competition, particularly if it enhances the competitor's ability and incentive to respond aggressively in the later stage of the market.

The incumbent firm in this case should pursue a flexible and offensive strategy, that is, do not invest in R&D but retain a flexible "wait and see" position (figure 21.5). If $\Theta = u$, each firm would find it dominating to invest (I) irrespective of the other's actions, resulting in a symmetric Nash Cournot equilibrium outcome of $(80, 80)$; if $\Theta = d$, however, both firms may choose to defer and obtain $(1, 1)$.[27] Backward binomial valuation thus gives symmetric initial expected values of $(34, 34)$. Given that R&D investment would result in initial equilibrium values of $(-33, 77)$, firm A would choose to wait.[28] The strategic reaction effect is negative.

These examples, where the knowledge from R&D can be made proprietary to the firm or it may be shared with competition, result in opposite strategic effects and different competitive strategies. This is shown in the examples of tables 21.4 and 21.5.

Table 21.4
The strategic reaction effect (when demand develops favorably) under contrarian quantity competition

Investment type	Operating costs (c_A, c_B)	Quantities Q^*_A	Q^*_B	Profit π^*_A	Direct effect	Strategic reaction	Commitment (direct + strat.)	NPV^*_A
No investment (base case)	$c_A = 3, c_B = 3$	4.83	4.83	23.4				80
Proprietary investment	$c_A = 0, c_B = 3$	6.83	3.83	46.7	128.5	+50.5	179	259
Shared investment	$c_A = 0, c_B = 0$	5.83	5.83	34.0	128.5	−47.0	81.5	161.5

Note: c_A, c_B are the second-stage operating costs (influenced by the first-stage strategic investment) for firm A, B.

Table 21.5
The strategic reaction effect (when demand develops favorably) under reciprocating price competition

Investment type	Demand parameter (Θ_A, Θ_B)	Prices P^*_A	P^*_B	Profit π^*_A	Direct effect	Strategic reaction	Commitment (direct + strat.)	NPV^*_A
No investment (base case)	$\Theta_A = 10, \Theta_B = 10$	4.83	4.83	29				126
Proprietary investment	$\Theta_A = 12, \Theta_B = 9$	5.42	4.67	39	85.5	−11.5	74	200
Shared investment	$\Theta_A = 12, \Theta_B = 12$	5.67	5.67	43	85.5	+23.5	109	235

Note: Θ_A, Θ_B is the second-stage demand (influenced by the first-stage strategic investment) for firm A, B.

To illustrate the value of the strategic effect consider, for example, the case that market demand develops favorably ($\Theta = u$), resulting in simultaneous second-stage investment by both firms and Nash Cournot quantity equilibria (highlighted leftmost branch (I, I)). Table 21.4 (and the last row of table 21.6) shows how the strategic interactions influence the investment strategy under contrarian competition when $\Theta = 17.5$. (When $\Theta = u$, the equilibrium is Nash whether making the strategic investment or not, so there is no preemption effect in this case.) The required investment outlay offsets the direct value effect (i.e., the value of incremental cash flows, basically cost savings from the new technology, assuming no competitive reaction) in eq. (5) from investing in R&D, so the strategic investment decision is determined by the strategic effect.

The Nash equilibrium values in this case are shown in the table of figure 21.3B (for $\Theta_1 = u\Theta_0 = 17.5$).[29] As noted, the incremental direct effect of the strategic R&D investment is the change in profit value compared to the base case of no R&D investment, with the competitor's reaction constant. If competing firm B would maintain its quantity at $Q_B = 4.833$ as in the base case, firm A would expand production to $Q_A = 6.333$ if the advantage is proprietary ($c_A = 0, c_B = 3$), resulting in a direct profit value of 308.5.[30] Thus, the incremental direct effect from the strategic R&D investment, determined as the strategic investment profit value when the competitor does not change its productive decision (308.5) minus the base-case profit value ($180 = 23.4/0.13$, from the table of figure 21.3 under N_0), equals 128.5.

The strategic effect of the R&D investment results from the indirect impact on firm A's profit value of the reaction in the competitor's productive decision as a result of A's R&D strategic investment ($\partial V_A/\partial \alpha_B \times d\alpha_B^*/dK_A$). The strategic (reaction) effect in the proprietary investment case has a positive value of $+50.5$ ($=$ total profit $-$ direct profit value $= 46.7/0.13 - 308.5$) as a result of A's tough position (since the strategic R&D investment reduces A's costs via the proprietary advantage that supports enlarged production) and the submissive productive reaction of competitor B. The total commitment value (direct effect + strategic effect $= 128.5 + 50.5$) is thus 179. Since this is the incremental value resulting from the strategic investment that incorporates the competitor's reaction above the base case, the proprietary investment's NPV* is base-case NPV + commitment value $= 80 + 179 = 259$. As can be seen from the last row of table 21.6 (for $\Theta = 17.5$), this case involves only a strategic reaction effect, but no strategic preemption value or flexibility value loss since both the base case and the proprietary investment case involve the same market structure (Nash) where it is optimal for both firms to invest immediately. This may not be the case for lower states of demand.

Table 21.6
Second-stage equilibrium state project values (NPV*) and strategic effects for different market structures and states of demand (Θ) for the proprietary investment case

Base case

Θ	Market structure (static)	Quantity Q_A^*	Quantity Q_B^*	Profit π_A^*	NPV$_A$	Market Structure (dynamic)	Flex. value	Base case NPV$_A^*$
7.17	Nash (invest)	1.39		1.9	−85	Defer	85	0
8.96	Nash	1.99		3.9	−70	Defer	70	0
11.20	Nash	2.73		7.5	−43	Defer (mixed)	43	0
14.00	Nash	3.67		13.4	3	Nash	0	3
17.50	Nash	4.83	4.83	23.4	80	Nash	0	80

Proprietary strategic investment

Θ	Maket structure (dynamic)	Q_A^*	Q_B^*	π_A^*	Direct value	Strategic total Reaction value	Strategic total Preemption value	Commit. value	Flex. loss	NPV$_A^*$
7.17	Defer	0		12.9	49	24	30	103	(85)	18
8.96	Monopoly/ Stackelberg	4.48		20.1	63	29	44	136	(70)	66
11.20	Monopoly/ Stackelberg	5.60		31.4	80	34	84	198	(43)	155
14.00	Monopoly/ Stackelberg	7.00		49.0	102	42	146	290	0	293
17.50	Nash	6.33	3.83	46.7	129	50	0	179	0	259

Table 21.6 shows how the equilibrium actions (Q_A^*), profits (π_A^*), state project values (NPV_A^*), and the various value components (direct value, reaction or pre-emption strategic value, and flexibility value) vary in different states of demand (Θ), involving different market structure games (for the base case and the strategic invest-ment case). The last row $(\Theta = 17.5)$ of table 21.6 corresponds to table 21.4. Under the proprietary investment, while for high demand $(\Theta = 17.5)$ a Nash Cournot equilibrium outcome results as described above, medium demand (e.g., $\Theta = 14.0$ or 11.2) may result in a monopoly or a Stackelberg leader/follower game, and low demand $(\Theta = 7.17)$ induces both firms to defer. Because of a change in market structure (from Nash Cournot equilibrium in the base case to a monopoly), when demand drops from $\Theta = 17.5$ to $\Theta = 14$ there is an additional strategic preemption effect (146) because it is no longer profitable for competitor B to operate in the future. It is interesting that a lower demand (e.g., a reduction from $\Theta = 17.5$ to 14.0) may result in a substantially higher total strategic value $(42 + 146 = 188$ vs. $50)$ when there is a switch to a different demand "zone." These "irregularities" are observed when, for the same demand parameter (e.g., $\Theta = 14.0$), the market structure is dif-

ferent (resulting in a value discontinuity) if the firm makes the strategic investment (shifting to a monopoly) than if it doesn't (base-case Nash equilibrium).[31]

The above high-demand states involved no flexibility value loss compared to a (static) Nash equilibrium base case. However, for lower states (e.g., if $\Theta = 8.96$) there is also flexibility value loss (70) since firm A would invest earlier under the proprietary investment (becoming a monopolist or Stackelberg leader) compared to a dynamic base-case alternative where the firm would defer. For $\Theta = 8.96$, the total strategic value $(29 + 44)$ added to the direct value (63) gives a total commitment value of 136; this commitment value outweighs the flexibility value loss of 70, resulting in an expanded NPV of 66 for this state.

Table 21.4 also illustrates the shared investment case that ends in Nash equilibrium for $\Theta = 17.5$. By contrast to the proprietary case above, in the game in the second panel of figure 21.5 where the cost advantage is shared by both firms $(c_B = c_A = 0)$, the shared strategic R&D commitment results in a negative strategic reaction value of -47 $(= 34.0/0.13 - 308.5)$ as a result of A's accommodating position and the competitor's aggressive (contrarian) reaction to enlarge its share from $Q_B = 4.833$ to 5.833 $(= Q_A)$. The total commitment effect in this case is thus 81.5 $(= 128.5 - 47)$, not enough to justify the required investment outlay. Given its competitor's contrarian reaction, firm A should therefore not make the strategic R&D investment but stay flexible and strong in the later stage of the market.

B   A Goodwill/Advertising Example (Price Competition)

Consider now a large one-time advertising expenditure or goodwill investment of $K_A = 85$ in an environment of reciprocating competition where price settings by competing firms are complements. A good example may be the airline or the tobacco industry where a price reduction by one firm will be met by similar price cutting by its competitor. The strategic investment in this case develops market demand and creates goodwill for subsequent investments (reflected in larger demand for the product). The basic assumptions are similar to the earlier example. Firm A can make a first-stage goodwill investment of $K_A = 85$, while either firm can invest $I = 100$ in either period during the second stage. Both firms face symmetric costs of $c_A = c_B = c = 1$. The (firm-specific) initial demand parameters are the same $(\Theta_A = \Theta_B = 10)$ in the base case of no goodwill investment (moving up or down with binomial parameters $u = 1.25$ and $d = 0.80$). The firm's own and cross price sensitivity parameters are $b = 2$ and $d = 1$.

Depending on whether the pioneering firm can achieve a proprietary or a shared advantage via the strategic goodwill investment,[32] in some cases it may be preferable to reduce prices until it is no longer profitable for the competitor to operate, while in other cases it may be better to set higher prices and share collusion-type benefits. Figure 21.6 shows the equilibrium outcomes (prices and profit values) for the different market structure games under the proprietary or shared investment cases when there is price competition (upward sloping reaction curves). The competitive strategies can again be determined using the two-stage game of figure 21.2 and the price competition project payoff values of table 21.3, as shown in figure 21.7.

3 Proprietary Investment: Flexible and Inoffensive Strategy (Negative Strategic Effect)   If the benefits of the strategic goodwill investment are proprietary to the firm and help develop a larger market share placing competition at a disadvantage, the firm should wait and maintain an inoffensive strategy if competition will reciprocate. Suppose a goodwill investment will place firm A at a competitive advantage by increasing its demand to $\Theta_A = 12$ while reducing firm B's demand to $\Theta_B = 9$ (as opposed to the symmetric base case, $\Theta_A = \Theta_B = 10$).

This example is illustrated in panel 3 (top) in figure 21.7. From a similar backward valuation process as applied earlier, the expected value of the investment opportunities for the two firms equals $(62, 62)$ for the base case of no strategic investment, while the strategic goodwill investment results in an expanded NPV of 56 for firm A (= value of growth opportunities of 141 minus goodwill investment outlay of $K_A = 85$), and 50 for firm B.[33] Thus, in this case, the base-case value (62) dominates the value of the proprietary strategic investment (56), and the strategic reaction effect is negative. The firm would pursue a flexible and inoffensive strategy by delaying investment in the strategic project. If future market demand is favorable in the second stage ($\Theta = u$), both firms will have a dominating strategy, regardless of the other's actions, to invest with Nash price equilibrium values of $(126, 126)$. If market demand is unfavorable, however, both firms may be better off to wait (or to appear unpredictable), resulting in expected values of $(13, 13)$.[34]

4 Shared Investment: Committing and Inoffensive Strategy (Positive Strategic Effect)   Now consider the case where the benefits of the strategic commitment by firm A are shared, resulting in larger demand for both competitors ($\Theta_A = 12$ and $\Theta_B = 12$). If the firm is accommodating and competition is reciprocating (i.e., the reaction functions are upward sloping), the strategic reaction effect will be positive. As illustrated in lower panel 4 in figure 21.7, the committing but inoffensive strategy results in $(156, 120)$ expected values for the growth opportunities, with a $156 - 85 = 71$ expanded NPV for the shared strategic investment of firm A.[35] This dominates the base-case alternative values $(62, 62)$.

In this case the effects are reversed, that is, the net commitment value effect overshadows the flexibility effect. The incumbent firm should thus pursue a committing

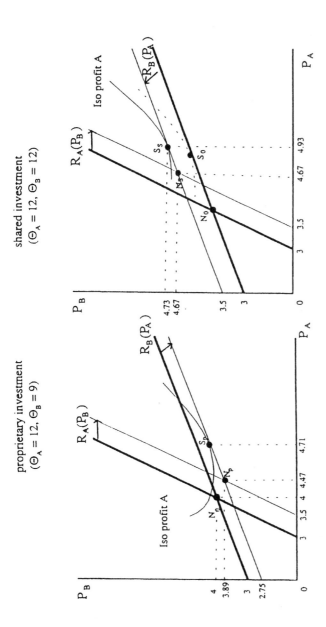

Notes:

The demand for each firm i is of the form $Q_i(P_i, P_j, \Theta_{i,t}) = \Theta_{i,t} - bP_i + dP_j$, where $\Theta_0 = 10$ ($u = 1.25$, $d = 0.80$), $b = 2$, $d = 1$, while the total variable production cost is given by $c(Q_i) = c_iQ_i$, with $c_i = 1$ ($i = A, B$).

If no strategic investment: base-case demand $\Theta_A = \Theta_B = \Theta = 10$ (base-case Nash equilibrium at N_0).

If proprietary investment/tough position: $\Theta_A = 12$ $\Theta_B = 9$, R_A and R_B shift to right (N_p P^*_A shift to right (at N_p $P^*_A \uparrow$, $P^*_B \downarrow$), $\pi_A \downarrow$.

If shared investment/accommodating position: $\Theta_B = \Theta_A = \Theta' = 12$, R_A shifts right and R_B shifts to the left (at N_s $P^*_A \uparrow$ and $P^*_B \uparrow$) and $\pi_A \uparrow$.

Figure 21.6A
Equilibrium Nash, Stackelberg, and Monopoly outcomes under the no investment (base case), proprietary or shared investment cases assuming *reciprocating* price competition (up sloping-reaction curves)

Pioneer firm A	Nash Price outcome			Stackelberg Price leader			Monopoly	
	N_0 base-case	N_p propriet.	N_s shared	S_0 base-case	S_p propriet.	S_s shared	M_0 base	M_p propr.
Price (P^*_A)	$\frac{1}{3}(\Theta+2c)$	$\frac{1}{15}(4\Theta_A+\Theta_B+10c)$	$\frac{1}{3}(\Theta+2c)$	$\frac{1}{14}(5\Theta+9c)$	$\frac{1}{14}(\Theta_A+\Theta_B+9c)$	$\frac{1}{14}(5\Theta+9c)$	$\frac{1}{2}(\Theta_A+c)$	$\frac{1}{2}(\Theta'+c)$
base demand ($\Theta_0=10$)	4	4.467	4.667	4.214	4.714	4.929	5.5	6.5
up ($u\Theta_0=12.5, u\Theta'=15$)	4.833	5.417	5.667	5.107	5.732	6	6.75	8
Profit (π^*_A)								
base demand ($\Theta_0=10$)	18	24.036	26.889	18.08	26.929	27.009	40.5	60.5
up	29.389	39.014	43.556	29.520	43.624	43.750	66.125	98

Notation: N_0, N_p, N_s are the Nash, and S_0, S_p, S_s the Stackelberg equilibrium outcomes for the zero, proprietary or shared investment cases; M_0 and M_p are the base-case and proprietary Monopoly outcomes. $R_j(P_i)$ is the reaction function of firm j given the price of firm i (P_i), i = A, B. P^*_i and π^*_i fluctuate with the state of demand Θ_t.

Figure 21.6B
Equilibrium Nash, Stackelberg, and Monopoly outcomes under the no investment (base case), proprietary or shared investment cases assuming *reciprocating* price competition (up sloping-reaction curves)

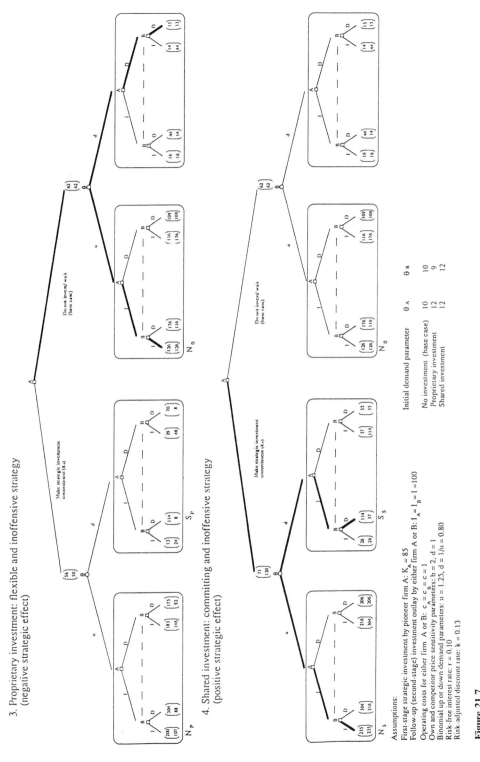

3. Proprietary investment: flexible and inoffensive strategy
   (negative strategic effect)

4. Shared investment: committing and inoffensive strategy
   (positive strategic effect)

Assumptions:

First-stage strategic investment by pioneer firm A: $K_A = 85$
Follow-up (second-stage) investment outlay by either firm A or B: $I_A = I_B = I = 100$
Operating costs for either firm A or B: $c_A = c_B = c = 1$
Own and competitor price sensitivity parameters: $b = 2$, $d = 1$
Binomial up or down demand parameters: $u = 1.25$, $d = 1/u = 0.80$
Risk-free interest rate: $r = 0.10$
Risk-adjusted discount rate: $k = 0.13$

	θ_A	θ_B
Initial demand parameter		
No investment (base case)	10	10
Proprietary investment	12	9
Shared investment	12	12

Figure 21.7
Competitive investment in the goodwill/advertising example: proprietary vs. shared investment under reciprocating price competition

but inoffensive strategy: make a strategic investment of $K_A = 85$ in the goodwill project immediately, and a follow-up investment of $I = 100$ later. If $\Theta = u$, firm B will also invest, resulting in a symmetric Nash price equilibrium; if $\Theta = d$, firm B will defer and firm A can become a Stackelberg leader.

Table 21.5 illustrates the strategic interactions for the proprietary and shared investment cases under reciprocating Nash price competition when $\Theta = u$ and both firms would invest (I, I). The direct effect in each case is 85.5 $(= (40 - 29)/0.13)$. Again, the investment outlay offsets the direct effect for firm A, so the strategic effect becomes the basis for the different competitive strategies. The proprietary or shared nature of the benefits of the strategic investment once more determine the type of investment strategy. However, these reciprocating price competition examples result in a reversal of the sign of the strategic reaction effect (-11.5 for the proprietary and $+23.5$ for the shared investment) and in opposite investment strategies, compared to the contrarian quantity competition case. To avoid intense price competition, firm A would not make an immediate strategic investment if the benefits are proprietary since a hurt competitor would retaliate, but would do so if the benefits are shared and the competitor would respond positively to an accommodating pricing strategy.

IV   Critical Demand Zones with Different Competitive Strategies

We have seen that different competitive strategies may be appropriate for different types of investment (proprietary or shared) and different types of competition (contrarian or reciprocating), and that there may be a change in market structure equilibrium in different states of demand. Figure 21.8 illustrates graphically how the state project values (expanded NPVs) for firm A (NPV_A^*) vary with the market demand parameter Θ (see also the values in table 21.6) in each of the four second-stage competitive strategies in the R&D example under contrarian competition. (The reciprocating goodwill case is illustrated later in figure 21.9). Panel A shows the base case of no strategic investment, while panels B and C show the shared and proprietary investment cases. The type of competitive strategy in a given state of demand depends on a critical or threshold market demand parameter Θ^* for each market structure. In the base case (panel A), there are three zones. If the market demand parameter Θ exceeds Θ_{NASH}^* ($= 13.8$), at the intersection of the curves whereby firm A invests or defers given that firm B invests, both firms have a dominant strategy to

Figure 21.8
Critical zones for the various competitive strategies in the second-stage project under *contrarian* competition (R&D example) for the base case, when benefits are shared, and when they are proprietary

Panel A. Base case (no strategic investment)

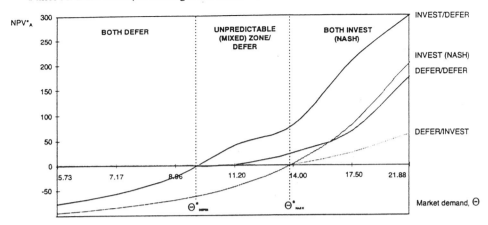

Panel B. Shared investment

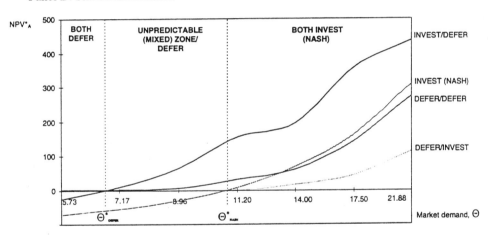

Panel C. Proprietary investment

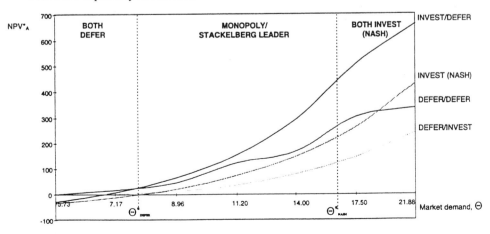

Panel A. Base case and shared investment

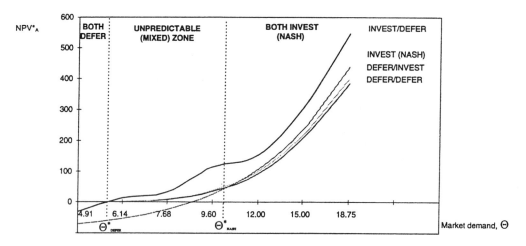

Panel B. Proprietary investment

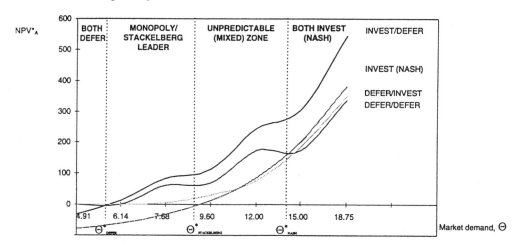

Figure 21.9
Critical zones for the various competitive strategies in the second-stage project under *reciprocating* competition (goodwill example) for the base case, when benefits are shared, and when they are proprietary

invest (regardless of whether the competitor decides to invest or not), resulting in a Nash equilibrium market structure. If Θ declines below Θ^*_{DEFER} ($= 9.8$), at the intersection of the invest/defer and defer/defer curves, both firms have a strictly dominant strategy to defer. In this symmetrical example, the critical values for both firms to defer Θ^*_{DEFER} or to invest Θ^*_{NASH} do not coincide; in fact, there arises a zone in-between where there is no pure dominant strategy for the two firms. In this "unpredictable" (or mixed) zone, investing by one firm would result in a higher value (compared to the base case where both firms defer) if the competing firm defers or the pioneer firm becomes a Stackelberg leader ($ID > DD$), but would result in a lower value if the competitor simultaneously decides also to invest, leading to Nash equilibrium ($II < DD$). The firms may equivalently choose to defer.

In panel B where the benefits of the strategic investment are shared, there are three similar zones, except that the critical Θ values are lower. Again, if Θ exceeds Θ^*_{NASH} ($= 11.1$), both firms would invest, resulting in a Nash equilibrium market structure, but if Θ declines below Θ^*_{DEFER} ($= 6.8$) both firms will defer. The lower threshold value for Θ^*_{NASH} compared to the base case (11.1 vs. 13.8) reflects the incentive of both firms to invest earlier due to the lower shared costs resulting from firm A's strategic investment.

In panel C where the benefits of the strategic investment are proprietary to the firm, the mixed (defer) zone is replaced by a larger zone where the pioneer firm dominates as a Stackelberg leader or a monopolist (A invests, B defers or invests later). The upfront strategic commitment improves the firm's strategic position via lower costs, expanding market share and preempting competitive entry. For Θ below Θ^*_{NASH} ($= 16.8$) and above Θ^*_{DEFER} ($= 7.7$), the NPV for the competitor turns negative, giving firm A the ability to preempt competitive entry and become a Stackelberg leader or a monopolist. Under contrarian competition, a proprietary investment would limit the competitor's output and incentive to invest. Thus, the critical value Θ^*_{NASH} ($= 16.8$) required for both firms to invest in the proprietary case is higher than in the base and the shared investment cases ($16.8 > 13.8 > 11.1$), reflecting the reduced incentive of the competitor to invest (being at a cost disadvantage, B invests later). Note also that the project values for the pioneer firm (NPV^*_A) in the proprietary case are higher than in the other cases (as seen by the higher curves).

Figure 21.9 illustrates the second-stage investment strategies of firm A in the goodwill investment case under reciprocating competition. Panel A shows both the base case as well as the case where the benefits of the upfront advertising investment are shared, increasing demand for both firms. Panel B illustrates the proprietary investment case. Panel A is similar to the R&D case above, except that the defer/invest value curve is now higher than the defer/defer curve (the opposite than in figure 21.8).

This is because under price competition, a high-price setting by a first-moving firm will invite a high-price setting by the competitor to their mutual benefit, regardless of who goes first. Again, if Θ exceeds Θ^*_{NASH} ($= 10.4$) both firms will invest, resulting in Nash equilibrium, while if Θ declines below Θ^*_{DEFER} ($= 5.8$), both firms will defer; in-between there is a mixed (defer) zone.

The proprietary investment case in panel B is more interesting, spanning four different zones. Here, a low-price setting by one firm will provoke intense price competition so that the Nash profit values in the proprietary investment will be lower than the Nash values in the two symmetrical cases of panel A (i.e., the Nash value curve is now relatively lower due to a negative strategic effect). Below Θ^*_{DEFER} ($= 5.8$), both firms have a strictly dominant strategy to defer. In the zone between Θ^*_{DEFER} ($= 5.8$) and $\Theta^*_{STACKELBERG}$ ($= 8.8$), firm A will become a Stackelberg leader (or a monopolist). The zone between $\Theta^*_{STACKELBERG}$ ($= 8.8$) and Θ^*_{NASH} ($= 13.5$) is unpredictable since there is no dominant strategy for both firms, resulting in a mixed equilibrium. For Θ above Θ^*_{NASH} ($= 13.5$), both firms will have a dominant strategy to invest, resulting in a Nash equilibrium. The above critical zones help illustrate graphically how the outcome may switch to a different market structure game in a different state of market demand.

V Summary and Conclusions

The standard NPV and other discounted cash flow methods have serious shortcomings in analyzing investment opportunities when future decisions are contingent on intermediate developments in an uncertain environment. Real options valuation provides a useful tool in modeling contingent decisions and evaluating managerial flexibility. Other strategic competitive interactions, however, also influence the value of a sequential strategic investment plan under uncertainty. The standard NPV decision rule should therefore be expanded by adding a strategic as well as a flexibility value component to capture these effects. In general, the expanded NPV of a strategic investment is influenced by two main effects:

(i) The flexibility effect: this arises from management's ability to wait to invest until demand develops sufficiently. An early strategic investment commitment, although it can improve the firm's strategic position and enhance the value or its future growth opportunities, would sacrifice flexibility value.

(ii) The net commitment effect: early strategic investment commitment may not only result in direct incremental future cash flows (the direct NPV), but it may indirectly also impact on value by influencing the competitor's reaction (strategic reaction effect) and the resulting competitive equilibrium, in some cases even changing the market structure entirely by deterring entry by rivals (strategic preemption effect) or by creating collusion type Stackelberg leader/follower benefits (strategic collusion effect). The nature of industry competition (reciprocal or contrarian) may thus critically influence the optimal investment strategy. In some cases, an early investment commitment may be a strategic disadvantage if it reduces the firm's ability to respond toward aggressive competitors who can exploit shared benefits from the strategic investment, or if it provokes a retaliating response and intense rivalry when competitive actions are complements.

Although an early strategic investment would necessarily reduce option or flexibility value, other things constant, it may have a high or low (even negative) net commitment value, depending on the strategic effect. The sign of the strategic effect itself may be positive or negative, depending on whether the benefits are proprietary or shared, and may be opposite for reciprocating (e.g., price) competition than for contrarian (e.g., Cournot quantity) competition.

By way of a summary, we can best see the interplay between the loss of flexibility value and the net commitment value of a strategic investment and the breakdown of the latter into its various value components, by revisiting the R&D and goodwill examples, this time using the initial (time-0), unconditional values shown in tables 21.7 and 21.8.[36] Table 21.7, Panel A shows that if the pioneer firm makes a strategic investment in a new, lower-cost technology that is proprietary (resulting in a relative cost advantage for A, with B backing down) the total expanded NPV will be 80, whereas in the base case of not making the strategic investment (staying with the old, costlier technology) firm A will obtain 34. By incurring the strategic outlay ($K_A = -110$), it will generate a net commitment value of $+69$, consisting of a direct value of $+96$ from reduction in future operating costs, a strategic reaction effect via an incremental change in the competitor's output of $+47$, and a strategic preemption effect of $+36$ from deterring competitive entry in certain states of demand. This net commitment value of $+69$ more than compensates for the loss in flexibility value of -22 from giving up the option to wait, resulting in an incremental value creation (or difference between the expanded NPVs of the strategic investment case and the base case) of $+47$ that makes the strategic investment worthwhile. Panel B shows the case of a shared investment (where the competitor also benefits from the investment technology but reacts aggressively, resulting in a negative strategic reaction value for A of -31). It is interesting that both the sign of the strategic reaction effect and of the net commitment value, as well as the difference between the net commitment value

Table 21.7
Unconditional value components of the strategic investment under *contrarian* competition when the investment is proprietary or shared

Panel A. Proprietary investment

	Base case (no investment, use old technology)	K_A	Stategic direct	Stategic reaction	Proprietary strat. investment (new technology)	Δ(Propr.-base case)
NPV	12	−110	+96	+47	45	+33
Strategic preemption	0				35	+36
						commit. +69
Flexibility value	22				0	−22
Total expanded NPV	34				80	+47

ΔNPV* = net commitment value + flexibility value
$\quad = [-K_A + (\text{direct value} + \text{strategic reaction value} + \text{strategic preemption value})] + \text{flexibility value}$
$\quad = [-110 + (96 + 47 + 36)] - 22 = +69 - 22 = +47 > 0$ (invest).

Panel B. Shared investment

	Base case (no investment)	K_A	Stategic direct	Stategic reaction	Shared strat. investment	Δ(Propr.-base case)
NPV	12	−110	+96	−31	−33	−45
Strategic preemption	0				0	0
						commit. −45
Flexibility value	22				0	−22
Total expanded NPV	34				−33	−67

ΔNPV* = net commitment value + flexibility value
$\quad = [-110 + (96 - 31)] - 22 = -45 - 22 = -67 < 0$ (don't invest).

acquired via making the strategic investment and the resulting flexibility loss, alternate between the four cases: they are positive for the proprietary investment but negative for the shared investment under contrarian quantity competition (panels *A* and *B* of table 21.5), and they reverse under reciprocating price competition (table 21.6). In the reciprocating case (table 21.6), when *A*'s investment is proprietary (panel *A*) a hurt competitor retaliates resulting in a negative strategic reaction value (−7), but if the investment is shared (panel *B*) both competitors benefit (e.g., may implicitly collude by maintaining higher prices), resulting in a positive strategic reaction value (+14). Furthermore, although higher uncertainty would increase the flexibility value loss, it may either increase or decrease strategic (preemption or collusion) value possibly by a higher amount, depending not only on which of the four cases occurs, but on the starting demand zone as well and whether variability from

Table 21.8
Unconditional value components of the strategic investment under *reciprocating* competition when the investment is proprietary or shared

Panel A. Proprietary investment

	Base case (no investment)	K_A	Strategic direct	Strategic reaction	Proprietary strat. investment	Δ(Propr.-base case)
NPV	48	−85	−53	−7	9	−39
Strategic collusion	0				47	+47
					commit.	+8
Flexibility value	14				0	−14
Total expanded NPV	62				56	−6

$\Delta NPV^* =$ net commitment value + flexibility value
$= [-K_A + (\text{direct value} + \text{strategic reaction value} + \text{strategic collusion value})] + \text{flexibility value}$
$= [-85 + (53 + -7 + 47)] - 14 = 8 - 14 = -6 < 0$ (don't invest).

Panel B. Shared investment

	Base case (no investment)	K_A	Strategic direct	Strategic reaction	Shared strat. investment	Δ(Prop.-base case)
NPV	48	−85	+53	+14	30	−18
Strategic collusion	0				41	+41
					commit.	+23
Flexibility value	14				0	−14
Total expanded NPV	62				71	+9

$\Delta NPV^* =$ net commitment value + flexibility value
$= [-85 + (53 + 14 + 41)] - 14 = 23 - 14 = +9 > 0$ (invest).

the initial demand level would shift demand past the threshold demand into a different demand zone.[37]

Based on a combination of real options valuation with basic game-theoretic principles from industrial organization we can thus distinguish various competitive investment strategies, depending on whether competitive actions are reciprocating or contrarian and whether the resulting benefits are proprietary or shared:

(1) *When competitive actions are contrarian and the benefits of strategic investment can be appropriated by the pioneering firm at the expense of its competition, the firm should commit to an offensive strategy.* Commitment makes the firm stronger in the second stage by creating a proprietary advantage when investing in follow-on projects. If competitive actions (e.g., quantities) are substitutes, competition will retreat in the later stage and the pioneering firm can become a leader as demand grows.

(2) *When the benefits of strategic investment commitment are shared and contrarian competition would respond aggressively, the firm should not invest immediately but rather follow a flexible and offensive strategy.* By delaying strategic investment, it prevents its competition from exploiting the resulting shared benefits to grow at its own expense.

(3) *When the benefits of strategic investment can be appropriated by the firm at the expense of competition and competition may reciprocate with an aggressive response, the firm should follow a flexible and inoffensive strategy.* The firm should avoid committing to the strategic project to preserve its resources and flexibility and avoid intensified price competition in the later stage of the market.

(4) *When the strategic investment benefits both firms and competition would reciprocate to an accommodating position (e.g., maintaining high industry prices), the pioneer should follow a committing and inoffensive strategy.* It may invest in goodwill to appear inoffensive in the later stage, avoiding intense price competition that would hurt the entire industry. Through (implicit) collusion of higher prices, both firms may enjoy more profitable follow-on investments.

The optimal competitive strategy may thus depend not only on the stance of the pioneer firm (tough or accommodating) and the type of investment (proprietary or shared), but also on the nature of competitive reaction (reciprocating or contrarian). The marriage of real options valuation with game-theoretic industrial organization principles enables simultaneously the determination of different market structure equilibrium games in the various states of demand (nodes) within the binomial option valuation tree, as well as proper accounting of the interdependencies among the early strategic commitment and sequential investment (along with competitive quantity or price setting) decisions in a dynamic environment.

Acknowledgments

We are indebted to Carliss Baldwin, Avinash Dixit, W. Carl Kester, Scott P. Mason, Stewart C. Myers, Michael Salinger, and William Samuelson for useful comments. The usual disclaimer applies. The paper also benefited from presentation at the European Finance Association meetings.

Notes

1. The idea that strategic considerations may provide firms with an incentive to commit capital in an earlier stage of the market to deter entry or expansion by rivals is well understood (e.g., see Spence [1977],

[1979]). However, besides sacrificing the option value of waiting, in some cases early commitment may be a strategic disadvantage if it intensifies rivalry without having an enduring competitive advantage.

2. As we explain later, a key factor in determining an appropriate competitive strategy is whether an early strategic commitment makes the pioneering firm more "tough" (i.e., whether it can appropriate the resulting benefits and hurt its competitors), or "accommodating" (i.e., whether the resulting advantage can be shared with and benefit its rivals) in a later stage of the market. A second factor is whether competitive reactions are reciprocating or contrarian, i.e., whether the competitors' reactions are similar (substitutes), or whether they are opposite (complements).

3. Besides the advantage to "wait and see," however, project deferral may involve certain disadvantages. For example, in the case of a project with an infinite or a specified expiring life, the firm would forgo the operating cash inflows when the plant is not operative, which can be treated analogous to stock dividends. As we will see, the strategic commitment value of a project must also be weighted against the option or flexibility value in determining the optimal investment timing and value.

4. Firms presumably create value by investing in projects for which the market (present) value of expected cash inflows, V, exceeds the required investment outlay, I. Therefore, the process of capital budgeting attempts to determine what a project would be worth if it were traded in the financial markets (see Mason and Merton, 1985). We here adopt the assumption of complete financial markets in which there exist portfolios of securities that replicate the dynamics of the present value of the project caused by changes in equilibrium state profits (e.g., see also Majd and Pindyck, 1987). In such complete markets, the risk-neutral probabilities can be obtained from:

$$p = \frac{(1+r)V_t(\Theta) - V_{t+1}(\Theta_d)}{V_{t+1}(\Theta_u) - V_{t+1}(\Theta_d)}$$

where $V_t(\Theta)$, $V_{t+1}(\Theta_u)$ and $V_{t+1}(\Theta_d)$ are the current, and next period's up or down equilibrium profit values. These risk-neutral probabilities are this time and state (Θ) dependent, as they endogenize competitive reaction.

5. Kulatilaka and Perotti (1992) show that under Cournot competition higher uncertainty increases the strategic value of early investment (due to increased market share) more than the flexibility value of waiting, which is contrary to the norm in the real options literature. Although this is a valid and important observation, as we point out herein it is not a universal result. Rather, it is a special case corresponding to taking a tough position involving a proprietary advantage under contrarian competition (quadrant 1 of our later table 21.1) that leads to a positive strategic effect. The strategic effect may be negative—and the above result may not hold—if (a) the strategic investment would result in shared benefits that competition can exploit under Cournot quantity competition (quadrant 2 in table 21.1); or if competition is reciprocating, as in price competition (quadrant 3 of table 21.1). In the last section we present a specific counter-example.

6. The initial strategic investment may influence the competitive position of the pioneering firm in a later stage of the market. A *tough* position depends on the firm's ability to appropriate the benefits of its strategic investment so as to hurt its competitor ($dVB/dKA < 0$). An example would be a first-mover proprietary cost advantage in the form of lower relative production costs in the later operating stage. Such a cost advantage may be the result of a learning process that is difficult to imitate and is not expected to be eliminated by subsequent technological developments. The position of the pioneering firm is *accommodating* if the resulting benefits are shared and benefit its competitor ($dVB/dKA > 0$). That may be the case if the benefits of testing, opening up the market, or developing a more cost-efficient technology are diffused to all firms in the industry. In this case, both firms can have lower costs—a *shared* cost advantage.

7. Following Fudenberg and Tirole (1984), if we assume that the (second-stage) actions of each firm are of a reciprocal nature so that $\partial V_A / \partial \alpha_B$ has the same sign as $\partial V_B / \partial \alpha_A$, and use

$$\frac{d\alpha_B^*}{dK_A} = \frac{d\alpha_B^*}{d\alpha_A} \frac{d\alpha_A^*}{dK_A} = [R_B'(\alpha_A^*)] \frac{d\alpha_A^*}{dK_A}$$

where $R_B'(\alpha_A^*)$ denotes the slope of firm B's reaction function to A's action, the sign of the strategic effect is:

$$\text{sign}\frac{\partial V_A}{\partial \alpha_B}\frac{d\alpha_B^*}{dK_A} = \text{sign}\frac{\partial V_B}{\partial \alpha_A}\left[\frac{d\alpha_A^*}{dK_A}\text{sign}(R_B'(\alpha_A^*))\right]$$

Thus, the sign of the strategic effect is crucially dependent on the sign of the slope of the reaction functions (i.e., whether they are downward sloping or upward sloping), depending on contrarian or reciprocating competition.

8. Depending on whether firms compete in prices or quantity, a reaction function assigns to every price or output level of one firm, the value-maximizing price or output for the other.

9. Under contrarian competition where the quantities produced are substitutes, the firm has an incentive to invest in a strategic project if its benefits are proprietary or it increases its ability to preempt a larger share of the market. However, in reciprocating competition where price settings are complements a strategic investment may result in lower prices via intensified rivalry. In such cases it may be appropriate to invest in strategic projects creating shared opportunities to "soften" competitive reaction in the later stage of the market.

10. Constant binomial parameters, u and d, may not be a realistic representation of the project value dynamics under endogenous competitive reaction. In the model, the binomial parameters of project value may change according to the state of market demand and equilibrium profits.

11. As noted, the state payoff values at the end of the second stage are the outcomes of different market structure games, depending on the state of demand, each firm's actions (invest, do not invest/defer) and their timing (simultaneous or lagged, at $t = 1$ or 2).

12. As noted by Tirole (1990), the reaction functions in such a simultaneous game are no more than an illustrative device since the firms have no possibility of reacting; only the final Nash equilibrium outcome at the intersection of the two reaction functions is observed. The Nash equilibrium is stable if the adjustment process converges to the equilibrium outcome from any starting position.

13. In contrarian quantity competition, an aggressive firm that invests early acting as a Stackelberg leader can acquire a larger share of the market. Under reciprocating price competition, a Stackelberg price leader would choose a price on the competitor's reaction function that maximizes its profit value. Given the prior action of the Stackelberg leader, the Stackelberg follower would then maximize its own profit value, $V_j(\alpha_i, \alpha_j)$, taking the action of the leader, α_i, as given. In the case of an accommodating price leader there need not be a first-mover advantage, as both firms can "collude" setting higher prices compared to the situation that they invest at the same time.

14. Once a leader achieves a monopoly position, it can choose the price (or quantity) which maximizes its own profit value, based on total demand for both firms, i.e., maximize $V_m(\alpha_m)$ over P_m (or Q_m), using $Q_m = (Q_A + Q_B)$.

15. A linear demand function is likely to be an unrealistic representation of true demand, particularly towards the end points. To the extent this demand equation captures realism, it is over the relevant range where uncertainty of market demand is reflected through the dynamics of Θ_t.

16. For simplicity, we assume zero taxes and depreciation so that the operating cash flows are equivalent to operating profits. The risk-adjusted discount rate k for the last stage used to determine the gross project value can be obtained from an equilibrium model such as CAPM.

17. The slope of this reaction function, given by $R_i'(Q_j) = -1/(2 + q_i)$, is determined by the quadratic cost coefficient q_i. The downward-sloping reaction function suggested by the above negative slope (for $q_i \geq 0$) results in contrarian competition where one firm can increase its quantity (or market share) at the expense of the other, as illustrated in figure 21.1, panel A, or in figure 21.3 (where $q_i = 0$). Further, the fixed marginal production cost for firm i, c_i, determines the intercept of the reaction function, $(\Theta - c_i)/(2 + q_i)$; thus, a change in this cost would cause a parallel shift in the relevant reaction function, altering the equilibrium quantities.

18. As illustrated in the example of figure 21.3 (with $q_i = 0$), if pioneering firm A's early strategic investment (K_A) would create a first-mover cost advantage (reducing c_A below c_B, say to 0) that would result in exclusive benefits and make the firm tougher, its intercept would increase and its reaction curve would shift

out to the right, increasing its equilibrium quantity (Q_A^*) while reducing that of its competitor (Q_B^*)—moving from Nash equilibrium outcome N_0 to N_p. By contrast, if firm A would take an accommodating position resulting in shared benefits with its competitor (e.g., also reducing the competitor's cost c_B, say to 0), B's reaction curve would also shift to the right, increasing its equilibrium output (Q_B^*) to that of outcome N_s.

19. Subsequently, by "Nash" we mean Cournot Nash in case of quantity competition and Bertrand Nash equilibrium in case of price competition.

20. It is assumed that the last stage is infinite (steady state) and the possibility of reentry is precluded.

21. The slope of this reaction function, given by $R_i'(P_j) = d(1 + bq_i)/b(2 + bq_i)$, is positive and is affected by the competitor's response coefficient d. These upward-sloping reaction functions, illustrated in figure 21.1 panel B (and in later figure 21.6), lead to reciprocating price competition, where a low price setting by one firm would be matched by its competitor.

22. For example, in the base case of figure 21.5 when $\Theta = d$ and both firms defer (D, D), and then Θ moves up and both firms invest (I, I), the state project value in the resulting Nash equilibrium is given by:

$$\text{NPV}_i = \frac{(\Theta_t - 2c_A + c_B)^2}{9k} - I = \frac{(14 - 2(3) + 3)^2}{9(.13)} - 100 = 3.$$

If firm A invests and B defers, A's monopoly (net) profit value is:

$$\frac{(\Theta_t - c)^2}{4k} - I = \frac{(14 - 3)^2}{4(.13)} - 100 = 133.$$

23. Subsequent figures 21.6 and 21.7 suppress the last period figures for compactness.

24. An R&D investment may create either an exclusive or a shared advantage, depending on the diffusion of knowledge. An exclusive advantage may, for example, be based on reduced costs or be the result of a learning process that is difficult to imitate and will not be eliminated by subsequent technological advances. If the benefits of opening up the market cannot be made proprietary to the pioneering firm, however, there is a free-rider problem. Competing firms entering later can take advantage of this diffusion of knowledge and replicate the pioneer's products or processes.

25. Due to space considerations, figure 21.5 does not show the last period of the game, which incorporates the equilibrium state project values for the Nash (N), Stackelberg leader/follower (S) or monopoly (M) games (summarized in table 21.2) in the various states shown in figure 21.2. These are illustrated in detail for the base case alternative in figure 21.5. All the numerical values shown in figure 21.5 are, nevertheless, the expected values derived from backward binomial option valuation based on the entire multi-stage game and the equilibrium payoff values of table 21.2. For example, in the base case (figure 21.5) with $\Theta = d$, the value $(1, 1)$ is the expected value from applying the backward binomial risk-neutral valuation of eq. (1) using the subsequent Nash equilibrium values $(3, 3)$ if Θ later moves up and both firms invest, and the $(0, 0)$ abandonment values if $\Theta = d$.

26. From eq. (1) with $p = 0.53$ (obtained from the dynamics in equilibrium state profits), the contingent claim (growth option) value for firm A is:

$$C_0 = \frac{.53(259) + .47(155)}{1.10} = 191, \text{ so that } \text{NPV}_0^* = C_0 - K_A = 191 - 110 = 81.$$

Similarly, for firm B:

$$\text{NPV}_0^* = \frac{.53(13) + .47(0)}{1.10} = 6.3.$$

27. There are two pure Nash equilibria, $(40, 0)$ and $(0, 40)$, assuming that one firm invests first and the other defers. Although once found in one of these states they wouldn't move, it is not clear how they would end up in one of these states in the first place. Both firms know that if they both end up investing they will

be worse off with $(-43, -43)$, so they might be better off to wait and receive $(1, 1)$. The same expected outcome $(1, 1)$ also obtains if a *mixed* Nash equilibrium is used instead where each competitor chooses to appear unpredictable to the other. The equilibrium probabilities that each firm will invest (such that its expected value is independent of that probability) are $P_A^* = P_B^* = 0.476$, yielding for each firm:

Expected profit value $= .476(.476)(-43) + .476(1 - .476)(40) + (1 - .476)(.476)0 + (1 - .476)^2(1) = 1$.

The expected initial values for each competitor then are $[(.46)80 + (.54)1]/1.10 = 34$.

28. If firm A had decided to make the R&D investment, whether Θ would move up or down each firm would have a dominating strategy to invest regardless of the other's action, resulting in symmetric Nash equilibrium values of $(162, 162)$ if $\Theta = u$ (first box) or of $(7, 7)$ if $\Theta = d$ (second box). In the latter case, note that both firms would have been better off to defer instead (prisoner's dilemma). From backward risk-neutral valuation, the initial (goss) value for each firm is $[.5(162) + .5(7)]/1.10 = 77$ (with $NPV_A = 77 - 110 = -33$).

29. For different values of Θ, for example $\Theta_1 = d\Theta_0 = 11.2$, similar values can be obtained for the monopoly or Stackelberg cases in the table of figure 21.5 (see later table 21.4). A simple backward valuation can then give the initial (unconditional) strategic effect values.

30. From the reaction function of equation (10), $R_A(Q_B) = \frac{1}{2}(\Theta_t - c_A - Q_B) = \frac{1}{2}(17.5 - 0 - 4.833) = 6.333$. From eq. (8) with $q_i = 0$ and $Q_B = 4.833$ (constant as in base case), the direct profit to firm A for a proprietary investment $(c_A = 0, Q_A = 6.333)$ is given by:

$$\pi_A = [(\Theta_1 - c_A) - Q_B]Q_A - Q_A^2 = [17.5 - 0 - 4.833]6.333 - 6.333^2 = 40.1,$$

giving a profit value of $V_A = \pi_A/k = 40.1/0.13 = 308.5$. A similar result obtains for a shared investment.

31. Because of these irregularities, although the direct value (from cost savings) and the strategic reaction value increase monotonically with market demand (Θ) as can be seen in table 21.6, the strategic preemption value, and hence the total commitment value, can change irregularly when there is a market structure change. Thus, even though flexibility value is higher in lower states of demand (Θ), total project value (NPV_A^*) does not increase monotonically with Θ everywhere.

32. Again, in some cases, the resulting benefits can be made proprietary to the firm. For example, a large company-focused (as opposed to product-specific) advertising investment can result in taking hold of significant market share through customer loyalty and reputation. However, in other cases the benefits may be shared with competitors as a public good of the entire industry. For example, a product-specific goodwill investment to promote a new technology or to open up the market via customer education (e.g., an advertising campaign about cellular phones when they were first introduced) or obtaining regulatory approvals benefiting the entire industry can result in a larger market demand for both firms.

33. If $\Theta = u$, both firms would invest resulting in Nash equilibrium values of $(200, 107)$. If $\Theta = d$, however, A would invest while B would defer, yielding Stackelberg values of $(114, 8)$. Backward valuation then gives:

$$NPV_A^* = \frac{.48(200) + .52(114)}{1.10} - 85 = 56, \quad \text{and} \quad NPV_B^* = \frac{.48(107) + .52(8)}{1.10} = 50.$$

34. The same expected values are obtained if both firms defer, or if a mixed Nash equilibrium results. Note that each firm would be better off to invest, given that the other would defer. However, if both firms invest they will end up worse off $(-16, -16)$. It may thus be preferable for both to defer and obtain $(13, 13)$. Alternatively, if each firm chooses to appear unpredictable, a symmetric mixed Nash equilibrium would result with investment probabilities $P_A^* = P_B^* = 0.512$ and expected equilibrium values $(13, 13)$.

35. In the case of strategic investment, if $\Theta = u$ both firms have a dominating strategy to invest, resulting in symmetric Nash equilibrium values of $(235, 235)$. If $\Theta = d$, there are multiple equilibria. To focus on the strategic effect, we use the focal point equilibrium (I, D) (the same as in the corresponding proprietary investment case). In this case firm A has a dominating strategy to invest knowing that firm B is better off to defer (37) than to also invest (26), resulting in Stackelberg values of $(114, 37)$. Backward valuation then

gives:

$$\text{NPV}_A^* = [.48(235) + .52(114)]/1.10 - 85 = 156 - 85 = 71, \quad \text{NPV}_B^* = [.48(235) + .52(37)]/1.10 = 120.$$

36. The earlier analysis of the strategic effects in section III was primarily based on a specific market structure equilibrium (Nash) conditional on a given state of demand (Θ). The values in tables 21.5 and 21.6 are obtained after applying the backward binomial valuation process using these conditional equilibrium values (e.g., for the various strategic effects) for each Θ, weighted with the appropriate risk-neutral probabilities and discounted to the beginning at the riskless rate.

37. If initial demand falls in a Nash equilibrium zone, higher uncertainty (increasing the chances of switching to a monopoly or Stackelberg equilibrium) can increase strategic preemption value. The opposite can happen if it starts in a monopoly/Stackelberg zone. For example, in the proprietary investment under contrarian competition of table 21.5, Panel A (with a base σ corresponding to $u = 1.25$), the strategic preemption value of 36 exceeds the flexibility value loss of -22; for low σ ($u = 1.12$), strategic preemption value (181) overwhelms flexibility loss (-9); however, for a high σ of $u = 1.38$ the two effects exactly offset each other (32), while for very high σ ($u = 2$) the increased flexibility value not only dominates the strategic preemption value but it also reverses the decision (making the incremental expanded NPV of the strategic investment turn negative). The above examples provide a counter example both to the standard real options implication of the impact of uncertainty on investment value as well as to Kulatilaka and Perotti's (1992) contrary assertion.

References

Baldwin, C., "Optimal Sequential Investment When Capital is Not Readily Reversible," *Journal of Finance* 37, 3 (June 1982), pp. 763–782.

Brennan, M. J. and E. S. Schwartz, "Evaluating Natural Resource Investments," *Journal of Business* 58, 2 (April 1985), pp. 135–157.

Cox, J. C., S. A. Ross, and M. Rubinstein, "Option Pricing: A Simplified Approach," *Journal of Financial Economics* 7 (September 1979), pp. 229–263.

Dixit, A., "A Model of Duopoly Suggesting a Theory of Entry Barriers," *Bell Journal of Economics* 10, 1 (Spring 1979), pp. 20–32.

Dixit, A., "The Role of Investment in Entry Deterrence," *Economic Journal* 90 (March 1980), pp. 95–106.

Dixit, A., and R. S. Pindyck, *Investment Under Uncertainty*, Princeton University Press, 1994.

Fudenberg, D., and J. Tirole, "The Fat-Cat Effect, The Puppy-Dog Ploy, and the Lean and Hungry Look," *American Economic Review* (May 1984), pp. 361–366.

Grenadier, S. R., "The Strategic Exercise of Options: Development Cascades and Overbuilding in Real Estate Markets," *Journal of Finance* 51, 5 (December 1996), pp. 1653–1679.

Ingersoll, J., and S. Ross, "Waiting to Invest: Investment and Uncertainty," *Journal of Business* 65, 1 (1992), pp. 1–29.

Kester, W. C., "Today's Options for Tomorrow's Growth," *Harvard Business Review* (March–April 1984), pp. 153–160.

Kulatilaka, N., and E. Perotti, "Strategic Investment Timing Under Uncertainty," Working Paper, Boston University, 1992.

Majd, S., and R. Pindyck, "Time to Build, Option Value, and Investment Decisions," *Journal of Financial Economics* 18 (March 1987), pp. 7–27.

Mason, S. P., and R. C. Merton, "The Role of Contingent Claims Analysis in Corporate Finance," in E. I. Altman and M. Subrahmanyan (eds.), *Recent Advances in Corporate Finance* (Homewood, IL: R.D. Irwin), 1985.

McDonald, R. L., and D. R. Siegel, "The Value of Waiting to Invest," *Quarterly Journal of Economics* 101, 4 (November 1986), pp. 707–727.

Myers, S. C., "Finance Theory and Financial Strategy," *Midland Corporate Finance Journal* 5, 1 (Spring 1987), pp. 6–13.

Myers, S. C., and S. Majd, "Abandonment Value and Project Life," *Advances in Futures and Options Research* 4 (1990), pp. 1–21.

Pindyck, R., "Irreversible Investment, Capacity Choice, and the Value of the Firm," *American Economic Review* 78, 5 (December 1988), pp. 969–985.

Reinganum, J., "Uncertain Innovation and the Persistence of Monopoly," *American Economic Review* 73 (September 1983), pp. 741–748.

Schmalensee, R., "Advertising and Entry Deterrence: An Exploratory Model," *Journal of Political Economy* 90 (August 1983), pp. 636–653.

Smit, H. T. J., and L. A. Ankum, "A Real Options and Game-Theoretic Approach to Corporate Investment Strategy Under Competition," *Financial Management* 22, 3 (Autumn 1993), pp. 241–250.

Spence, M., "Entry, Capacity, Investment, and Oligopolistic Pricing," *Bell Journal of Economics* 8, 2 (Autumn 1977), pp. 534–544.

Spence, M., "Investment Strategy and Growth in a New Market," *Bell Journal of Economics* 10 (Spring 1979), pp. 1–19.

Tirole, J., *The Theory of Industrial Organization* (Cambridge, MA: The MIT Press), 1990.

Trigeorgis, L., "Anticipated Competitive Entry and Early Preemptive Investment in Deferrable Projects." *Journal of Economics and Business* 43, 2 (May 1991a), pp. 143–156.

Trigeorgis, L., "A Log-transformed Binomial Numerical Analysis Method for Valuing Complex Multi-option Investments," *Journal of Financial and Quantitative Analysis* 26, 3 (September 1991b), pp. 309–326.

Trigeorgis, L., "The Nature of Option Interactions and the Valuation of Investments with Multiple Real Options," *Journal of Financial and Quantitative Analysis* 28, 1 (March 1993), pp. 1–20.

Trigeorgis, L., and S. P. Mason, "Valuing Managerial Flexibility," *Midland Corporate Finance Journal* 5, 1 (Spring 1987), pp. 14–21.

22 Strategic Growth Options

Nalin Kulatilaka and Enrico C. Perotti

Introduction

The goal of this chapter is to investigate the decision to make an irreversible investment under imperfect competition and uncertainty. The real options literature has led to a significant advance in understanding the valuation of investment relative to the static net-present-value (NPV) approach (see Dixit and Pindyck 1994 for an excellent survey). However, real options analysis has often been based on two very specific assumptions: (a) the firm has a monopoly over an investment opportunity, and (b) the product market is perfectly competitive. As a result, investment does not affect either prices or market structure.

On the other hand, it is often recognized that early investment is associated with a greater ability to expand in the future; usually, however, these "growth options" have been introduced as exogenous technical advantages and modeled in an ad hoc fashion. This chapter seeks to contribute to the theoretical foundations of growth options by explicitly modeling the strategic advantage gained by investment vis-à-vis competitors.

The classic real options framework is an accurate description of investment decisions such as the development of a fully owned natural resource, for which monopolistic access to the investment opportunity is secure and the impact on market structure is minimal. However, when there are other potential competitors, not investing may lead some other producer to seize the opportunity. Moreover, under imperfect competition, the commitment of an irreversible investment typically has strategic preemptive effects; immediate action may discourage entrants and enhance market share and profits (Gilbert 1989). In the early contribution by Dixit (1979), investment confers a future cost advantage vis-à-vis potential entrants, creating a strong preemptive effect.[1] Interestingly, most of the subsequent literature has not considered the impact of exogenous uncertainty on this strategic decision.[2]

We interpret the strategic value of initial investment as the acquisition of growth opportunities relative to competitors, which will be exercised if market conditions are favorable. We then contrast the value of acquiring such strategic growth options against the alternative of no investment, and offer some novel insights on the impact of uncertainty on the attractiveness of strategic investment.

In this paper, an initial investment results in the acquisition of a "capability" that allows the firm take better advantage of future growth opportunities. Specifically, in our model an initial investment in a growth option reduces future production costs, so that expansion can take place at a lower cost than for competitors without growth options. Examples of strategic investment leading to future comparative advantages may be research into building a technological advantage, an advertising campaign leading to identification and name recognition by consumers, and organizational and logistic planning leading to lower costs in building production capacity. The acquisition of this strategic advantage endogenously leads to the capture of a greater share of the market, either by dissuading entry or by inducing competitors to "make room" for the stronger competitor. This strategic advantage is particularly valuable in states of high demand when profits per unit of output are higher. Thus, strategic investment in conditions of uncertainty can be viewed as a commitment to a more aggressive future strategy.

Our main contribution is to show that, contrary to the result found in the real options literature, the effect of uncertainty on the relative value of the strategic growth options is ambiguous under imperfect competition. An important difference under imperfect competition is that profits are convex in demand, since oligopolistic firms respond to better market conditions by increasing both output and prices. Thus, expected cash flows increase with volatility, as high marginal revenues at higher levels of demand more than compensate for low revenues at low levels of demand.

When strategic investment has a significant preemptive effect, it leads to higher market share, and thus a greater (relative) convexity of ex post profits relative to the case of no investment. As a result, even though the value of not investing increases with rising uncertainty, the value of the growth option increases even more. When instead the investment confers only a modest strategic advantage, the potential profit gain is less significant relative to the cost of the investment; an increase in volatility will increase the value of not investing and thus raise the threshold for investment in the growth option. For intermediate levels of strategic advantage, increased uncertainty favors strategic investment unless the probability shift results in a much higher likelihood of entry. Finally, since maximum losses are bounded above by the initial investment, at a very high level of uncertainty a further increase favors strategic investment.

These results are confirmed in the case when more firms have access to the investment opportunity and is robust to various specifications of strategic advantages gained by the investment (Kulatilaka and Perotti 1991). However, when a systematic risk component to the volatility is introduced, we find that an increase in systematic risk discourages strategic investment, because it leads to higher risk exposure.

The rest of the chapter is organized as follows. Section 1 examines a simple benchmark model of monopoly investment under uncertainty. This section allows us to introduce several key features arising from market power. Section 2 studies the more general case of imperfect competition and the strategic effect of investment in capability. We explore the impact of uncertainty on the value of a strategic growth option and obtain a closed-form solution for the case of a log-normally distributed demand. Section 3 considers the possibility of simultaneous strategic investment and the effect of systematic risk. The last section offers some conclusive remarks.

1   A Benchmark Model: Monopoly Investment in a Growth Option

We consider as a benchmark the extreme but simple case of a firm with monopoly in both the investment opportunity and in the product market. In this context, the growth option has no strategic effect. We progressively relax these assumptions later.

At time 0, a single firm (denoted by M) has the opportunity to make an initial irreversible investment of amount I, which confers a capability for more efficient (specifically, lower cost) production.[3] This will turn out to be equivalent to the purchase of a growth option. Until time 1, when the market opens, there is uncertainty over the scale of future demand. We assume that the demand for the good is linear in prices and increasing in the random variable θ. Let $P(Q)$ be the inverse demand function expressing the market price as a function of total supply Q:

$$P(Q, \theta) = \theta - Q$$

where θ is distributed on $(0, \infty)$, with expected value $E_0[\theta] \equiv \theta_0 > 0$. Uncertainty is fully resolved at time 1 prior to production.

If no initial investment is made the firm will produce only when the market is profitable, producing at a unit cost of K. The firm will choose an output level $Q_M^N = \frac{1}{2}(\theta - K)$ with associated profits $\pi_M^N = \frac{1}{4}(\theta - K)^2$; it will not produce if $\theta < \theta_M^* \equiv K$.

In contrast, an initial investment reduces the future unit cost to κ (where $\kappa < K$), due to learning, logistic and product development improvements. If $\theta < \kappa$ the firm will not produce; else, it will choose an output level $Q_M^I = \frac{1}{2}(\theta - \kappa)$ with associated profits $\pi_M^I = \frac{1}{4}(\theta - \kappa)^2$. Thus, Q_M^N is less than Q_M^I, because investing in the growth option enhances the incentive to expand production.

Notice that these payoff functions are continuous, monotonically increasing, and convex in θ. An increase in θ has a more-than-proportional effect on payoffs because a firm with market power responds to higher demand by increasing both output and prices.

We initially assume no systematic risk (or risk neutrality) and a zero interest rate. Then the net present value of the capability investment is:

$$V_M^I \equiv E_0[\pi_M^I] - I$$

$$= E_0[\tfrac{1}{4}(\theta - \kappa)^2 \,|\, \theta \geq \kappa]\, \mathrm{prob}(\theta \geq \kappa) - I.$$

The correct investment criterion calls for a comparison between the net present values of making the investment with the NPV of not making the investment. The latter value is

$$V_M^N \equiv E_0[\pi_M^N] = E_0[\tfrac{1}{4}(\theta - K)^2 \,|\, \theta \geq K]\, \text{prob}(\theta \geq K).$$

To solve for the optimal investment decision, we define the ex post *net* gain to investment (the relative value of investment) as $\Delta^M(\theta) \equiv \pi_M^I - I - \pi_M^N$. Then the net present value of the decision to acquire the growth option (relative to not investing) is the expectation of Δ^M: $G(\theta_0) \equiv E[\Delta^M(\theta)]$. The level of expected demand $\theta_0 = \Theta^M$ such that $G(\Theta^M) = 0$ is then a point of indifference.

It is easy to show that a unique value for Θ^M exists under some simple regularity conditions, namely for the set of distributions with a strictly positive support on θ where higher mean implies first order stochastic dominance (i.e., for which given two random variables $x_1, x_2, E(x_1) > E(x_2) \Leftrightarrow x_1$ first order stochastically dominates x_2).

PROPOSITION 1. *Strategic investment is optimal when θ_0 exceeds the unique expected demand threshold Θ^M.*

PROOF. From the definition of ex post profit functions we know that $\lim_{\theta_0 \to 0} \cdot G(\theta_0) = -\tfrac{1}{4}(K^2 - \kappa^2) - I < 0$ and $\lim_{\theta_0 \to \infty} G(\theta_0) = \infty$. It is sufficient to show that $d\{G(\theta_0)\}/d\theta_0 > 0$; then uniqueness is established by the intermediate value theorem. Since Δ^M is an increasing and differentiable function of θ, the condition $d/d\theta_0 \cdot \{E\Delta[\theta(\theta_0)]\} > 0$ is satisfied for all distributions of θ under consideration. Since $G(\theta_0) > 0$ for all $\theta_0 > \Theta^M$, in this range investment in the growth option has a higher NPV than the alternative of not investing.

Figure 22.1 plots $\pi_M^I - I$, π_M^N, and Δ^M against θ for the case where $\kappa = 0$.

We now examine the impact of greater uncertainty on the relative attractiveness of investment. We define an increase in uncertainty over θ as one that does not affect its mean, thus adopting the concept of a mean-preserving spread as in Rothschild and Stiglitz (1970). Note that both π_M^I and π_M^N are convex and differentiable in θ, so by Jensen's inequality the impact of a mean-preserving spread increases their expected value. Similarly, if the net gain function Δ^M were convex or concave, the net effect of increasing uncertainty would be unambiguous. However, the net gain function has two kinks, at the points κ and K. The first kink occurs at the level of demand when a monopolist that invested in growth option starts production; the second occurs when a monopolist that did not invest starts production.

Therefore, the impact of greater uncertainty on the relative value of investment is uncertain because these entry points create discontinuities in the rate of change in

Profits

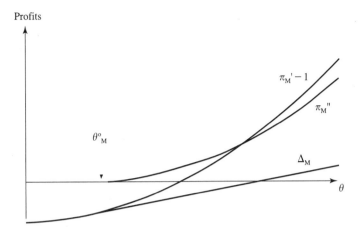

$\pi_M{}' - 1$

$\pi_M{}''$

$\theta°_M$

Δ_M

θ

Figure 22.1
Ex post net profit functions: benchmark monopoly case

marginal profits. As the next section confirms, this ambiguity is always present under imperfect competition since entry always has an impact on price and thus marginal profitability.

2 Strategic Growth Options Under Imperfect Competition

We now consider, within the framework of the model in the previous section, the possibility of a competitor entering at time 1. Now investment will have a strategic effect.

Firm 1 has a monopoly over the investment opportunity. (We relax this assumption later.) Firm 1 chooses whether to make a strategic investment at time 0, anticipating its impact on future market structure. A second firm (firm 2) may choose to enter the market at time 1, with a unit production cost of K. We assume that if both firms produce, the market outcome is Cournot competition.[4]

Consider first the case where firm 1 makes no initial investment, so that ex post it has no strategic advantage vis-à-vis the competitor. If both firms choose to produce, they face the same production cost K. As long as $\theta \geq K$, the outcome is a symmetric Cournot equilibrium in which they share the market equally; each firm produces an amount $Q_1^N = (\theta - K)/3$, which yield profits equal to $\pi_1^N = \frac{1}{9}(\theta - K)^2$. If $\theta < K$ neither will produce, as the marginal revenue falls below cost. Hence, $\theta^* \equiv K$ can be interpreted as the symmetric Cournot entry point, below which no production takes place.

If instead firm 1 invests I at time 0, market interaction is affected by its strategic advantage, which is acknowledged by firm 2 when making its output decision. It is easy to see that if both firms produce, firm 1 will choose an output level $Q_1^I = \frac{1}{3}(\theta + K - 2\kappa)$ with associated profits $\pi_1^I = \frac{1}{9}(\theta + K - 2\kappa)^2$. It is now optimal for firm 2 to choose a lower quantity, $Q_2^I = \frac{1}{3}(\theta - 2K + \kappa)$, yielding profit, $\pi_2^I = \frac{1}{9}(\theta - 2K + \kappa)^2$. Moreover, the Cournot entry point for the competitor is now higher and is defined by $\theta^{**} \equiv 2K - \kappa$.

Note the source of the market share gained by firm 1 when it invests at 0. Q_2^I is less than Q_1^I for various related reasons: first, because firm 2 faces a higher production cost; second, because it recognized firm 1's greater incentive to expand production (the post-entry dissuasion effect of strategic investment). Finally, firm 2 does not enter unless $\theta > \theta^{**}$, which is higher than θ^*. This is the entry-dissuasion effect. As a result, firm 1 acts as a monopolist for $\theta^{**} > \theta > \kappa$, charging a price $\frac{1}{2}(\theta - \kappa)$ and earning profits $\frac{1}{4}(\theta - \kappa)^2$. In general, the cost advantage derived from strategic investment increases from 1's market share and profits for all θ. We conclude that strategic investment can be seen as offering an enhanced market share.[5]

In summary, the ex post gross profits of firm 1 under not investing (π_1^N) and investment (π_1^I) are given by:

$$\pi_1^N = \begin{cases} 0 & \text{if } \theta < \theta^*, \\ \frac{1}{9}(\theta - K)^2 & \text{if } \theta \geq \theta^*, \end{cases}$$

$$\pi_1^I = \begin{cases} 0 & \text{if } \theta \leq \kappa, \\ \frac{1}{4}(\theta - \kappa)^2 & \text{if } \kappa < \theta < \theta^{**}, \\ \frac{1}{9}(\theta + K - 2\kappa)^2 & \text{if } \theta \geq \theta^{**}. \end{cases}$$

As before, these payoff functions are continuous and monotonically increasing in θ, and profit increases more than proportionately with demand. Note that profits rise faster with demand if firm 1 has invested at time 0. Because little generality is gained by a positive κ, we henceforth normalize its value to 0.

To understand the trade-off in the optimal investment problem we investigate the characteristics of the ex post *net* gain to strategic investment, defined as $\Delta \equiv \pi_1^I - I - \pi_1^N$. Figure 22.2 plots the function Δ.

We note that Δ exhibits two kinks. The first kink occurs at $\theta^* = K$ and corresponds to the beginning of production in the no-investment, symmetric Cournot case. This is the same as the kink in the monopoly case: at this point marginal profitability is continuous but not differentiable.[6] The relative gain to investment between θ^* and θ^{**} remains convex in θ, but profits rise at a lower rate.

Net Gain,Δ

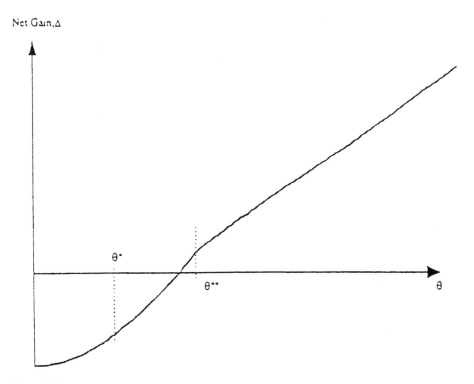

Figure 22.2
Net gain function

A more dramatic discontinuity occurs in the strategic investment case when demand is above the higher entry threshold θ^{**}. Here entry by the competitor results in a drop in the rates of increase of both price and output of the investing firm and creates a discontinuity in marginal profitability. In summary, the net gain function is piecewise convex in the region of entry dissuasion ($\theta \leq \theta^{**}$) and is linear for $\theta > \theta^{**}$.

The optimal investment decision facing firm 1 at time 0 requires comparing the relative NPV of making the strategic investment.

$$V_1^N \equiv E_0[\pi_1^N] = E_0[\tfrac{1}{9}(\theta - K)^2 \,|\, \theta \geq \theta^*]\,\mathrm{prob}(\theta \geq \theta^*),$$

$$V_1^I \equiv E_0[\pi_1^I] - I$$

$$= E_0[\tfrac{1}{9}(\theta + K)^2 \,|\, \theta \geq \theta^{**}]\,\mathrm{prob}(\theta \geq \theta^{**}) + E_0[\tfrac{1}{4}\theta^2 \,|\, \theta^{**} > \theta]\,\mathrm{prob}(\theta^{**} > \theta) - I.$$

Let $H(\theta_0) \equiv E(\Delta)$ denote the *expected net gain* from strategic investment, $V_1^I - V_1^N$. The threshold value *expected demand* such that firm 1 is indifferent whether to make the strategic investment or not is denoted by Θ and defined by $H(\Theta) \equiv 0$.

Under the regularity conditions defined in the Proposition 1, it is easy to show that strategic investment is optimal when θ_0 exceeds the unique threshold Θ.

The proof follows that of Proposition 1. Although in this case Δ nondifferentiable at θ^{**}, this does not alter the result as it occurs only at a countable number of points.

We now consider the impact of a mean-preserving spread on the relative value of investment. From the valuation expression, it is immediately apparent that the value of acquiring the growth option is strictly increasing with the uncertainty over θ. This is a result of convexity of profits created by market power and Jensen's inequality. This suggests that as uncertainty in demand increases, the incentive to invest will unambiguously increase. However, as with the real options literature, the NPV of not investing is also increasing with increasing demand uncertainty. Therefore, it is the shape of the difference in ex post marginal profits (i.e., the curvature of Δ) that will determine the overall effect of uncertainty.

As we saw also in the benchmark monopoly case, since the net gain function Δ is neither convex nor concave, the net effects of increasing uncertainty are ambiguous. The intuition is that the rate of change in marginal profits is different to the left and right of a kink. Thus, when a mean-preserving spread shifts around probability mass to more extreme values, the position of the expected level of θ relative to the kink matters a great deal.

In the benchmark case this is easy to see. Figure 22.1 (where the first kink disappears because κ is set to zero) indicates that Δ^M (the NPV of investing over non-investing) is convex for $\theta < \theta^*$ and linear for $\theta > \theta^*$. When the threshold Θ^M is in an area where Δ^M is convex in θ, more uncertainty will increase the incentive to invest; the converse is true when the threshold lies above θ^*, since the loss of profit on the downside (where Δ^M is convex in θ) is larger than the potential gain on the upside (where Δ^M is linear in θ).

In the case of imperfect competition, the effect of entry by competitors creates a second kink. Table 22.1 shows that at the entry point θ^{**}, the marginal net gain from investment drops discontinuously. When expected demand is around this point, the downside losses from a spread in probability mass will exceed the upside gain as the profits are convex for $\theta < \theta^{**}$ and linear above this range. For values of θ below θ^{**}, the payoff to strategic investment is piecewise convex; thus, in this range, a mean-preserving spread encourages investment.

Therefore, the direction of the impact of uncertainty on the relative value of investment is critically dependent on the magnitude of the strategic advantage, measured by the cost advantage K. When K is large, the entry dissuasion range of

Table 22.1
Net gain function: $\Delta = \pi_1^I - I - \pi_1^N$

Range	Δ	$\partial\Delta/\partial\theta \equiv \Delta'$	$\partial^2\Delta/\partial\theta^2 \equiv \Delta''$
$\theta < \theta^*$	$\dfrac{\theta^2}{4} - I$	$\dfrac{\theta}{2}$	$\dfrac{1}{2}$
$\theta^* < \theta < \theta^{**}$	$\dfrac{5\theta^2}{36} + \dfrac{2\theta K}{9} - \dfrac{K^2}{9} - I$	$\dfrac{5\theta}{18} + \dfrac{2K}{9}$	$\dfrac{5}{18}$
$\theta > \theta^{**}$	$\dfrac{4\theta K}{9} - I$	$\dfrac{4}{9}K$	0

demand ($\theta < \theta^{**}$) is larger, and thus the convex area of Δ is larger. As a result, the impact of higher uncertainty tends to favor investment. The opposite is true for a small K.

The conclusion is that in the case of strategic investment with strong preemptive effects, higher uncertainty will tend to decrease Θ and encourage investment; the reverse is true in the case of a weak strategic effect. In general the result is ambiguous and its exact impact depends both on the nature of the market structure *and* the nature of the distribution.

An Example: Log-Normal Distribution

We now examine the behavior of the value functions and the strategic investment threshold under the assumption that θ is log-normally distributed with expected value $E_0(\theta) = \theta_0$ and variance σ^2, i.e., $\ln(\theta/\theta_0) \sim N(-\frac{1}{2}\sigma^2, \sigma^2)$. By construction, an increase in σ will not affect the expected value of θ and would, therefore, amount to a mean-preserving spread. In all our simulations, I is normalized to 1, and κ is normalized to zero. Then the value functions have the following analytical solutions:

$$V^N(\theta_0, \sigma) = \tfrac{1}{9}[\theta_0^2 e^{\sigma^2} N(d_1) - 2K\theta_o N(d_2) + K^2 N(d_3)]$$

and

$$V^I(\theta_0, \sigma) = \frac{\theta_o^2 e^{\sigma^2}}{4}[1 - \tfrac{5}{9}N(d_4)] + \tfrac{1}{9}[2K\theta_o N(d_5) + K^2 N(d_6)] - I$$

where

$$d_1 = \frac{2\ln(\theta_o/K) + 3\sigma^2}{2\sigma}, \quad d_2 = d_1 - \sigma, \quad d_3 = d_2 - \sigma,$$

$$d_4 = \frac{2\ln(\theta_o/2K) + 3\sigma^2}{2\sigma}, \quad d_5 = d_4 - \sigma, \quad d_6 = d_5 - \sigma.$$

Table 22.2
Sensitivity of investment threshold, Θ

Cumulative volatility	Capacity cost advantage: $K - \kappa$					
	0.3	0.8	1.06	1.3	1.8	3.0
0.0	7.5000	2.8125	2.1214	2.0638	2.0047	2.0000
0.2	7.5000	2.8127	2.2046	2.0516	1.9785	1.9605
0.4	7.5000	2.8295	2.2677	2.0605	1.9139	1.8539
0.6	7.5000	2.8671	2.3117	2.0682	1.8494	1.7149
0.8	7.5002	2.9040	2.3380	2.0656	1.7887	1.5768
1.0	7.5017	2.9318	2.3495	2.0533	1.7306	1.4518
1.2	7.5058	2.9491	2.3494	2.0337	1.6749	1.3422
1.4	7.5124	2.9569	2.3408	2.0093	1.6221	1.2475
1.6	7.5201	2.9572	2.3266	1.9822	1.5729	1.1662
1.8	7.5272	2.9518	2.3090	1.9541	1.5277	1.0967
2.0	7.5328	2.9427	2.2895	1.9265	1.4868	1.0376
2.2	7.5364	2.9312	2.2697	1.9002	1.4503	0.9875
2.4	7.5381	2.9185	2.2503	1.8757	1.4181	0.9452
2.6	7.5379	2.9055	2.2319	1.8535	1.3900	0.9097
2.8	7.5363	2.8928	2.2150	1.8336	1.3657	0.8799

Table 22.2 summarizes our simulations on the effect of mean-preserving increases in volatility on the threshold point, Θ. This effect depends on the relative impact of higher uncertainty on V^I and V^N. The table clearly indicates that the net effect depends on K. A high value of K implies that strategic investment has a strong entry dissuasion effect and a marked market share advantage in a contested market.

At high levels of K, strategic investment is preferred even for low expected values of demand, and entry dissuasion is strong so that the competitor's entry threshold θ^{**} is relatively high. Figure 22.3 plots the expected values of strategic investment and no investment for such a case at two levels of uncertainty. As uncertainty increases, the value of V^N unambiguously rises; but so does V^I. The overall effect in this case is that the threshold level Θ drops with higher uncertainty. In this case, higher uncertainty leads to greater upside opportunities that outweigh the higher downside risk.

At low level of strategic advantage (low K), the entry dissuasion region is small, and the market share gain is also limited. Then strategic investment is justified only under high expected demand, when entry is almost certain. In this case growth option is less valuable. Interestingly, as volatility increases without bounds, strategic investment again is favored, as the break-even point starts falling. This is the effect of bounded losses under strategic investment.

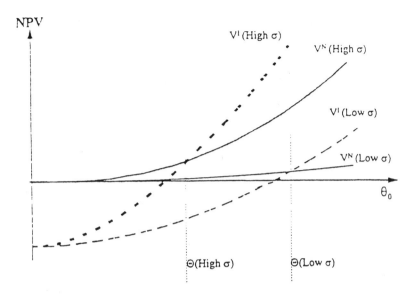

Figure 22.3
Effect of increased volatility on NPV and investment threshold

At intermediate levels of K, the impact of uncertainty depends on the position of the break-even point relative to the ex post entry threshold, θ^{**} and is in general ambiguous.

These results are consistent with our earlier general conclusions. The choice of not investing becomes more valuable under higher volatility, reflecting a lower risk exposure; however, uncertainty *may be* favorable to investment, when the extra profits from strong market share due to the deterrence or *commitment effect* out-weigh its downside risks. The ambiguity of our results arises from the very essence of imperfect competition. Strategic growth options do not exhibit the continuous features of expansion options under perfect competition: now an individual firm's investment decision has a significant impact on market structure and thus on the market price.

3   Extensions

Simultaneous Strategic Entry

We now extend the context of the basic model to the case when neither firm enjoys a monopoly on preemptive investment. In other words, both firms are able to invest at time 0 in order to reduce future capital investment costs to κ.[7]

The payoff to investment by one firm depends on the competitor's investment decision and its ex post output decision. Since the two firms decide simultaneously, neither can condition its strategy on the other's decision. The final market outcomes are monopoly, asymmetric or symmetric cost Cournot equilibrium, and no production, respectively. Each firm's belief about the other's strategy now plays a key role. In order to model ex ante identical firms, we ignore equilibria driven by asymmetric beliefs and focus only on symmetric equilibria.

There are three possible symmetric equilibria depending on the expected level of demand, θ_0. Define the following ex ante payoff functions:

$$\phi_1 \equiv E_0\left[\frac{(\theta - \kappa)^2}{9} \,\middle|\, \theta > \kappa\right] \text{prob}(\theta > \kappa) \quad \text{(simultaneous investment)},$$

$$\phi_2 \equiv E_0\left[\frac{(\theta - \kappa)^2}{4} \,\middle|\, 2K - \kappa > \theta > \kappa\right] \text{prob}(2K - \kappa > \theta > \kappa)$$

(strategic investment and no entry by competitor),

$$\phi_3 \equiv E_0\left[\frac{(\theta + K - 2\kappa)^2}{9} \,\middle|\, \theta \geq 2K - \kappa\right] \text{prob}(\theta > 2K - \kappa)$$

(strategic investment and late entry by competitor),

$$\phi_4 \equiv E_0\left[\frac{(\theta - 2K - \kappa)^2}{9} \,\middle|\, \theta > 2K - \kappa\right] \text{prob}(\theta > 2K - \kappa)$$

(no investment while competitor invests),

$$\phi_5 \equiv E_0\left[\frac{(\theta - \kappa)^2}{9} \,\middle|\, \theta \geq K\right] \text{prob}(\theta > K)$$

(no investment and ex post entry by both).

As before, in what follows we set $\kappa = 0$.

PROPOSITION 2. *The optimal investment policy is no investment by both firms when* $\theta_0 \leq \theta^R$, *randomized investment by each firm with probability* $y(\theta_0)$ *when* $\theta^R \leq \theta_0 \leq \theta^S$, *and simultaneous investment by both when* $\theta_0 \geq \theta^S$, *where:*

$$\theta^R \equiv E_0(\theta) \quad \text{s.t.} \quad I + \phi_5(\theta^R) = \phi_2(\theta^R) + \phi_3(\theta^R),$$

$$\theta^S \equiv E_0(\theta) \quad \text{s.t.} \quad \phi_1(\theta^S) = \phi_4(\theta^S) + I.$$

In addition, the equilibrium probability of entry, $y(\theta_0)$, for $\theta^R < \theta_0 \le \theta^S$ is given by

$$y(\theta_0) = -\frac{I + \phi_5 - \phi_2 - \phi_3}{\phi_1 + \phi_5 - \phi_2 - \phi_3 - \phi_4}.$$

PROOF.   See Appendix.

The optimal investment strategy is similar to the basic model. Clearly, higher expected demand favors strategic investment and reduces the value of not investing. As before, the impact of volatility depends on the degree of advantage gained by exercising the strategic investment option. Under a strong strategic advantage, higher volatility shifts downward the threshold for investment. Intuitively, when strategic gain is significant there is a stronger preemptive effect; thus the threshold level of expected demand at which investment is preferred, Θ, is low.

In contrast, a weak strategic advantage means that the competitive gain of preemptive investment is weaker on the upside, and the area of deterrence is smaller, so the reduction in profitability on the downside is greater. Since the value of not investing *increases* with volatility, the local effect of greater uncertainty in this case will be to discourage investment.

The simulation results in Table 22.3 confirm these effects of uncertainty on the probability of investment, around a parameter range when a randomized investment strategy may be optimal for both firms.

Table 22.3
Sensitivity of probability of investment, expected demand $= 3.0$

Cumulative volatility	Cost advantage: $K - \kappa$				
	0.7	0.8	0.9	1.0	1.1
0.1000	0.00	0.23	0.56	0.75	0.87
0.2000	0.00	0.23	0.56	0.75	0.87
0.3000	0.00	0.23	0.55	0.75	0.87
0.4000	0.00	0.22	0.55	0.75	0.88
0.5000	0.00	0.21	0.54	0.75	0.89
0.6000	0.00	0.19	0.54	0.76	0.91
0.7000	0.00	0.17	0.54	0.78	0.94
0.8000	0.00	0.15	0.54	0.80	0.98
0.9000	0.00	0.13	0.55	0.83	1.00
1.0000	0.00	0.12	0.57	0.87	1.00
1.1000	0.00	0.11	0.59	0.92	1.00

Systematic Risk

If an increase in uncertainty over θ induces an increase in nondiversifiable risk, our results need to be qualified. Assume that in equilibrium, the risk premium associated with uncertainty in θ is proportional to its volatility. That is, the equilibrium rate of growth of θ equals $r + \lambda\sigma$, where λ is the market price of risk associated with θ and r is the risk-free rate of interest. Since the payoffs to the firm are nonlinear functions of θ, the risk-adjusted discount rate depends on the realization of θ, which is unknown at time 0. Hence, we transform the valuation problem into its risk-neutral representation, and thereby achieve risk adjustment via adjustment to probabilities rather than the discount rate.[8]

It can easily be shown that under a risk-neutral probability measure, θ would still be log-normally distributed but its rate of return will fall short of the risk-free rate of interest by adjustment factor:

$$\ln\left(\frac{\theta}{\theta_0}\right) \sim N(-\tfrac{1}{2}\sigma^2 - 2\lambda\sigma, \sigma^2).$$

As a result of this risk adjustment, the valuation equations are modified as follows:

$$V^W(\theta_0, \sigma) = \tfrac{1}{9}[\theta_0^2 e^{\sigma^2 - 2\lambda\sigma} N(d_1) - 2Ke^{-\lambda\sigma}\theta_o N(d_2) + K^2 N(d_3)]$$

and

$$V^I(\theta_0, \sigma) = \frac{\theta_o^2 e^{\sigma^2 - 2\lambda\sigma}}{4}[1 - \tfrac{5}{9}N(d_4)] + \tfrac{1}{9}[2Ke^{-\lambda\sigma}\theta_o N(d_5) + K^2 N(d_6)] - I$$

where

$$d_1 = \frac{2\ln(\theta_o/K) + 3\sigma^2 - 2\lambda\sigma}{2\sigma},$$

$$d_4 = \frac{2\ln(\theta_o/2K) + 3\sigma^2 - 2\lambda\sigma}{2\sigma}.$$

Note that the effect of risk adjustment is equivalent to reducing θ_0, the expected value of θ. From Section 1 we know that a decrease in expected value, θ_0, will reduce $E(\pi^I)$ more than $E(\pi^W)$. Therefore, the impact of a higher risk premium will be to reduce the relative value of strategic investment. The intuition is that the strategic investment option requires the firm to bear more risk.

5 Concluding Remarks

This paper has proposed a reconciliation of the real options and the strategic approach to the optimal use of strategic investment. The real options literature assumes perfect competition and analyses the effect of exogenous uncertainty. In contrast, the strategic approach endogenizes market structure; however, it often ignores uncertainty, which is relevant for valuation even when the firm is risk neutral because of the option value of flexibility.

We show that the proper valuation of real investment must take into account both its strategic value (the preemptive effect of commitment) and the alternative value of not investing (a form of flexibility). We interpret the effect of strategic investment as lowering not just production costs but also the strike price of future expansion options. This is because choice also has a *strategic* influence on competitors' output decisions, inducing them to be less aggressive. This increases the investor's market share and, therefore, the value of its expansion option.

Our results on the effect of uncertainty on the valuation of strategic investment may be surprising in light of current practice, which tends to view volatility as a strong disincentive for new investment. In a richer intertemporal setting it would be possible to analyze how the *evolution* of strategic considerations should be contrasted with the opportunity cost of waiting to learn more about uncertain market conditions. We plan to do so in later research.

Empirically, it may be true that real investment tends to fall when uncertainty rises; however, this is probably due to a concomitant decrease in expectations over market conditions. We intend to extend further our analysis on the valuation of investment in oligopolistic markets, because we are convinced that this line of research will not only improve our theoretical understanding of optimal investment timing but may also contribute to modern capital budgeting practice and methodology.[9]

Appendix

Proof of Proposition 2

Consider the payoffs to strategic investment for firm 1. Suppose first that it invests at time 0 while firm 2 does not. If demand next period is so low that late entry by firm 2 is not profitable, i.e. $\theta < 2K$, firm 1 will be a zero marginal cost monopolist. If $\theta > 2K$, firm 2 enters, but firm 1 earns higher payoffs as a low cost, higher market share Cournot competitor. Thus firm 1's expected payoff from solitary strategic investment at 0 is:

$$E_0\left[\frac{\theta^2}{4}\,\middle|\,\theta < 2K\right] + E_0\left[\frac{(\theta+K)^2}{9}\,\middle|\,\theta \geq 2K\right] - I.$$

If instead firm 2 enters as well, they will share the market as Cournot competitors, and their expected payoff equals $E[\theta^2/9] - I$.

Consider now the payoff to not investing. If firm 1 does not invest and firm 2 does, firm 1's expected payoff equals the sum of zero when future entry is unprofitable ($\theta < 2K$) and its profits as a high cost entrant otherwise:

$$0 + E_0\left[\frac{(\theta - 2K)(\theta + K)}{9}\,\middle|\,\theta \geq 2K\right].$$

Finally, if neither firm enters at 0, their ex post payoffs are zero if $\theta < K$ and equal to the high cost, symmetric Cournot equilibrium payoffs otherwise:

$$0 + E_0\left[\frac{(\theta - K)^2}{9}\,\middle|\,\theta \geq K\right].$$

Note next that the relative payoff to investment by either firm increases monotonically with θ_0, independently of the competitor's timing of investment. To see this, assume the other firm does not invest; the net gain from entering is

$$E_0\left[\frac{\theta^2}{4}\,\middle|\,\theta < 2K\right] + E_0\left[\frac{(\theta + K)^2}{9}\,\middle|\,\theta \geq 2K\right] + E_0\left[\frac{(\theta - K)^2}{9}\,\middle|\,\theta \geq K\right] - I,$$

which can be rewritten as:

$$E_0\left[\frac{\theta^2}{4}\,\middle|\,\theta < K\right] + E_0\left[\frac{5\theta^2 - 4K^2 + 8K\theta}{36}\,\middle|\,K \leq \theta \leq 2K\right] + E_0\left[\frac{4K\theta}{9}\,\middle|\,\theta \geq 2K\right] - I.$$

In this expression, each term is positive and increasing in θ_0. If the other firm invests as well, the symmetric Cournot payoff is clearly increasing in θ_0.

The net gain equals zero at $\theta_0 = \theta^R$, the threshold value at which neither firm will invest. To verify that neither firm wishes to invest if the other firm is not expected to invest, let $y = 0$. Firm 1 will not invest if its net gain from strategic investment is negative. This occurs when $\phi_2 + \phi_3 - I < \phi_5$, which is satisfied for $\theta_0 < \theta^R$, since the net gain is monotonic in θ_0. The reasoning for firm 2 is analogous, so $y = x = 0$ is an equilibrium in this range. When θ_0 is below the threshold, neither firm invests even if certain to gain a market advantage. A similar comparison of payoffs can be made when firm 2 does invest. The net benefit (loss) of strategic investment rises (falls) with θ_0 and equals zero exactly when θ_0 equals θ^S. When θ_0 is above this threshold, both firms invest.

To verify this, let $y = 1$. Firm 1 invests today with certainty if $\phi_1 - I \geq \phi_4$, which is satisfied for all $\theta_0 > \theta^S$.

When θ_0 is in the intermediate region, both firms invest with positive probability. Let $x(\theta_0)$ be the probability of entry by firm 1 and $y(\theta_0)$ the corresponding probability for firm 2. Firm 1 will randomize between investing and not investing as long as it is indifferent to the two choices.

This occurs if:

$$yE_0\left[\frac{\theta^2}{9}\right] + (1-y)E_0\left[\frac{\theta^2}{4}\,\middle|\,\theta \leq 2K\right] + E_0\left[\frac{(\theta + K)^2}{9}\,\middle|\,\theta \geq 2K\right] - I$$

$$= yE_0\left[\frac{(\theta - 2K)^2}{9}\,\middle|\,\theta > 2K\right] + (1-y)E_0\left[\frac{(\theta - K)^2}{9}\,\middle|\,\theta \geq K\right].$$

In the game with symmetric beliefs, the equilibrium value of $y(\theta_0)$ is equal to $x(\theta_0)$ as described in Proposition 2. It is also increasing in θ_0. To verify this, notice that the numerator of $y(\theta_0)$ as defined above is always negative in the range $\theta^S > \theta_0 \geq \theta^R$, and it equals the negative of the net payoff to strategic investment when the competitor does not invest, which we have shown to be increasing in θ_0. The denominator is also negative and larger in absolute value since it equals the numerator plus $\phi_1 - I - \phi_4$ (the net gain to strategic investment when the competitors invests), which in this region is negative and decreasing in θ_0.

Notes

1. Treatments of the investment decision described costs of postponement in terms of the higher adjustment cost of rapid construction of capacity. Hartman (1972) shows that under convex adjustment costs, higher uncertainty increases the optimal amount of investment even under perfect competition. See also Abel (1983) and Pindyck (1988).

2. While considerable work has been done on the role of asymmetric information (see Tirole 1988), the only treatment of uncertain market conditions we are aware of is the partial equilibrium approach of Appelbaum and Lim (1985), who focus on production rather than investment as a form of precommitment. Their ad hoc revenue function drives entirely their results.

3. Our view of investment in growth opportunities is fairly general. Analogous results would obtain if the investment would result in greater quality or consumer appeal.

4. This is consistent with the theoretical work by Kreps and Scheinkman (1983) on capacity choice followed by price competition.

5. We find it useful to decompose the growth option gained by strategic investment in two components. First, it results in a lower "unit exercise price" for future expansion. In addition, the optimal output Q_1^I, "the number of unit production options that are optimally exercised," also increases, as other firms choose to limit their own output to make room for the stronger competitor.

6. Note that for a range of demand beyond this point the relative gain to investment is higher than for the monopoly case. This reflects the fact that not investing leads to a lower payoff because of loss of market share to competition, so in this range there is a greater incentive for investment. When demand is quite high, the monopolist benefits comparatively more from the cost advantage, while the relative market share gain declines for the investing firm.

7. It is not essential that there are only two firms; however, if we continue to increase the number of potential investors the expected value of the strategic investment option and not investing would be zero.

8. See Cox et al. 1985. For instance, in a single-factor asset pricing model, $\lambda = \rho_{\theta, M}/\sigma_M(r_M - r)$, where $\rho_{\theta, M}$ is the correlation coefficient between θ and the market portfolio, and r_M and σ_M are, respectively, the rate of return and its standard deviation.

9. We thank Marvin Freedman, Michael Manove, Alan Marcus, and Stewart Myers for helpful discussions and Avinash Dixit and two anonymous referees for their careful comments. We also wish to thank the Editor and Associate Editor for their considerable patience and inspiration. All remaining errors are our own.

References

Abel, Andrew B. 1983. Optimal investment under uncertainty. *American Economic Review* 73 228–233.

Appelbaum, Elie, and Chin Lim 1985. Contestable markets under uncertainty. *Rand J. Economics* 16 1 (Spring) 28–40.

Cox, John, Jonathan Ingersoll, and Stephen Ross. 1985. An intertemporal general equilibrium model of asset prices. *Econometrica.* 53 363–384.

Dixit, Avinash. 1989. Entry and exit decisions under uncertainty. *J. Political Economy* 97 (June) 620–638.

Dixit, Avinash. 1980. The role of investment in entry deterrence. *Economic J.* 90 95–106.

Dixit, Avinash. 1979. A model of duopoly suggesting a theory of entry barriers. *Bell J. Economics* 10: 1 20–32.

Dixit, Avinash, and Robert Pindyck, 1994. Investment under uncertainty. Princeton University Press, Princeton, New Jersey.

Gilbert, Richard J. 1989. Mobility barriers. In R. Schmalensee, and R. Willig, ed. *Handbook of Industrial Organization.* North-Holland, Amsterdam.

Hartman, Richard. 1972. The effects of price and cost uncertainty on investment. *J. Economic Theory.* 5 258–266.

Kulatilaka, Nalin, and Enrico Perotti. 1991. Strategic investment timing under uncertainty. Working Paper, London School of Economics.

McDonald, Robert, and Daniel Siegel. 1986. The value of waiting to invest. *Quarterly J. Economics* 101 707–727.

Pindyck, Robert. 1988. Irreversible investment, capacity choice, and the value of the firm. *American Economic Review* 78: 5 969–85.

Tirole, Jean. 1988. *The Theory of Industrial Organization.* MIT Press, Cambridge, Massachusetts.

Rothschild, Michael, and Joseph Stiglitz. 1970. Increasing risk I: A definition. *J. Economic Theory*, 2 (September) 225–43.

23 Investment in Technological Innovations: An Option Pricing Approach

Steven R. Grenadier and Allen M. Weiss

1 Introduction

A critical component of many firms' investment policies is a strategy for the adoption of technological innovations. Generally, firms follow different strategies: some adopt new technologies when they are first available while others postpone the adoption decision until the technology is improved. Some firms will adopt every technological improvement while others bypass the innovation altogether. The purpose of this chapter is to analyze the factors that drive the differences in such behavior.

The following example (Kaplan, 1986) illustrates two fundamental characteristics of investments in technological innovations that may account for observed behavior: the impact of past decisions on future technological options and the uncertainty over future innovation opportunities. During the 1970s some manufacturing firms invested in automatic and electronically controlled machine tools. Returns on the initial investment were reported as modest. However, microprocessor-based technologies arrived in the early 1980s, bringing about the opportunity for much more dramatic returns (greater performance at lower cost). Firms that had previously invested in electronically controlled machine tools were able to migrate quickly and cheaply to the new technology. Because operators, maintenance personnel, and process engineers were already comfortable with electronic technology, it was relatively simple to retrofit existing machines with powerful microelectronics. Companies that had deferred investment in electronically controlled machine tools quickly fell behind.

Such decisions are common for firms in modern high-technology markets. However, this is not a recent phenomenon. For example, between the world wars, marine engineering was undergoing rapid and volatile change. Shipbuilders were inclined to postpone adoption of available engines until further improvements became available. Even when the current generation of engines was an improvement over existing engines, many avoided upgrading because of expectations of impending, more dramatic improvements (Sayers, 1950). A similar phenomenon existed with improvements in incandescent lighting during the 1880s and 1890s. Passer (1953) documents how expectations of rapid technical improvement in the technology of incandescent lighting were firmly entrenched in the minds of prospective buyers. Purchasers had to decide whether to accept the current innovation in the face of expectations of potentially greater advances in the near future.

In this chapter we cast the innovation investment strategy as a sequence of embedded options. The consequences of a current innovation investment decision have ramifications on the future options available to the firm. As in Myers (1977) and

Kester (1984), a firm may view a current innovation as simply a link in a chain of future investment options. For example, when a firm must choose whether to upgrade to a new generation of technology, it must contemplate exchanging a current technology for a new generation of technology, minus the cost of upgrading. This can be interpreted as holding an "option to exchange" one innovation for the next. This form of option is derived and analyzed in Margrabe (1978). In addition, consider a firm contemplating investment in the early stage of a new technology. Not only is this firm investing in the current innovation itself, but it is also purchasing an option to upgrade in the future, as previously mentioned. That is, during the early stages of innovation, firms hold an "option on an option." These are a particular form of compound option, as analyzed in Geske (1979). Under these conditions, the challenge for a firm is determining an optimal path, or *migration* strategy, for adopting successive versions of an innovation. The application of option-pricing analysis to real investment decisions is now part of a growing literature. Excellent surveys of the real-options literature can be found in Pindyck (1991) and Dixit and Pindyck (1994).

We incorporate many of the most important characteristics of real-world technology markets. First, to highlight the dynamic features of the migration strategy, firms are confronted with a sequence of innovations. As firms choose whether or not to adopt a current version of the innovation, they consider the implications for their ability to respond to future technological innovations. Second, we assume that firms face uncertainty about both the value and the timing of future innovations. Third, we allow firms who adopt innovations to "learn by doing." Bypassing a current innovation to wait for future innovations can result in the firm losing important learning that accrues from the experience of using technology. Finally, we incorporate realistic cost concerns. For example, the cost of early adoption may be more expensive than waiting until a technology is succeeded by the following generation.

While the model includes many realistic features of technology markets, the nature of the analysis is very much a partial equilibrium framework. A richer model would allow the arrival and impact of innovations to become endogenous by including an analysis of the optimal level of research and manufacturing capabilities chosen by suppliers. In such a model, the production/research and adoption strategies would be interdependent. In addition, the model could be extended to include a game-theoretic approach to the adoption decision. A firm's choice of migration strategy would be conditioned on its expectation of its rivals' migration strategies. These extensions would entail a significant increase in the complexity of the present model.

In this chapter, we identify four potential migration strategies: (i) a *compulsive* strategy of purchasing every innovation, (ii) a *leapfrog* strategy of skipping an early innovation, but adopting the next generation of innovation, (iii) a *buy-and-hold* strategy of only purchasing an early innovation, and (iv) a *laggard* strategy of waiting until a new generation of innovation arrives before purchasing the previous innovation. A fifth potential strategy, which is for the firm to refrain from adopting any technology whatsoever (a "bystander" strategy), is easily added to the present framework, but is omitted for ease of presentation. Our model can be used to analyze the forces that determine a firm's likely innovation strategy. We compute the probability that a firm will pursue each of the four migration strategies as well as the expected time at which a firm will invest in an innovation. These computations depend on market, as well as firm-specific, factors. Our analysis shows that, depending on the nature of technological uncertainty, firms may choose to adopt an initial innovation even in the face of potentially more valuable innovations occurring in the future. We also show that firms' optimal migration strategies will differ according to their previous histories of technological adoption. That is, the future decisions of firms will be path-dependent; two firms facing the same choice will choose differently because of their previous investment decisions.

The remainder of this chapter is organized as follows. In Section 2, we present a summary of the model, including a description of the underlying assumptions. In Section 3, we derive the optimal migration strategy. Section 4 provides the main analytical result of the model, which is the likelihood that a firm will adopt any of four potential migration strategies, as well as the expected speed of adoption. Section 5 presents an analysis of the model's predictions. Section 6 concludes.

2   The Model and Its Assumptions

We consider a firm that faces a sequence of investment opportunities in technological innovations. The firm is initially confronted with an opportunity to invest in a current innovation. In addition, the firm also anticipates the possibility of a potentially more valuable technological innovation in the future. Both the arrival time and value to the firm of the future innovation are uncertain.

The existing innovation is called the *current innovation*. The firm may choose to invest in the current innovation at any time it chooses (or bypass the current innovation altogether), taking into account its expectations about the arrival of a future innovation. When the *future innovation* becomes available, the firm must then decide whether to migrate to the new technology. The firm's decision to adopt the future innovation is contingent upon its earlier decision regarding adopting the current innovation. This invokes a "path dependency" into the firm's choice of an optimal migration policy.

The model begins with the arrival of the current innovation at time 0. The value of the current innovation to the firm is denoted by P_0. At any time of its choosing, the firm can adopt the current innovation at a cost of C_e ("early adoption"). Thus, the payoff from early adoption is $P_0 - C_e$. We assume that the current innovation has a nonnegative net present value ($P_0 \geq C_e$). However, the firm can bypass the current innovation and instead await the arrival of the future innovation. For example, if a future innovation is likely to arrive in the near future, and is anticipated to render the current innovation obsolete, a firm can optimally choose to wait.

At the random time T, the next generation of technology arrives. Now, the options available to a firm will be dependent on its prior adoption policy. First, suppose the firm adopted the previous innovation. It can either adopt the new innovation, worth P_T, or hold onto its current technology. If it decides to upgrade, it receives the benefits of exchanging the current innovation for the new innovation, $P_T - P_0$, at an upgrade cost of C_u. If the firm decides not to update the previous innovation, there are no further cash flow implications. Second, suppose the firm bypassed the first innovation. Now, it has two options: leapfrog to the new innovation at a cost of C_ℓ or purchase the older innovation at the price C_d. We assume that if the firm waits until an innovation is succeeded by a new generation, it can purchase the older innovation at a lower cost than if it adopted early. Thus, $C_d \leq C_e$. We also assume that $C_\ell < C_e + C_u$, so as to prevent a form of adoption arbitrage. This condition ensures that it is always cheaper to leapfrog to the future innovation than to purchase the current innovation and instantaneously upgrade to the future innovation.

The random arrival time of the future innovation, T, will now be characterized. Let the stochastic process $X(t)$ denote the state of technological progress. As $X(t)$ rises, the arrival of the future innovation approaches. If $X(t)$ rises to the upper boundary X_h, the future innovation arrives. Thus, the arrival of the innovation is the first passage time of $X(t)$ to the boundary X_h. Mathematically, the future innovation occurs at time T where $T = \inf[t \geq 0: X(t) \geq X_h]$. This modeling approach for the arrival of innovations is analogous to much of the literature modeling bond default. As in Black and Cox (1976), Leland (1994), and Longstaff and Schwartz (1995), bond default is often triggered when a continuous-time state variable (typically asset value or firm cash flow) reaches a threshold. An alternative modeling approach would be to assume that the future innovation arrives according to a Poisson (jump) process.

Assume that $X(t)$ follows a geometric Brownian motion:

$$dX = \alpha X \, dt + \sigma X \, dz, \tag{1}$$

where α is the instantaneous conditional expected percentage change in X per unit time, σ is the instantaneous conditional standard deviation per unit time, and dz is the increment of a standard Wiener process. The parameters α and σ reflect the nature of the innovation arrival process. Markets with higher levels of the growth term, α, will be characterized by speedier innovation arrival. Markets with greater levels of the volatility term, σ, will be characterized by greater uncertainty over the arrival of future innovations.[1]

Now consider the random value of the future innovation, conditional on its arrival. We assume that the value of the future innovation P_T equals $P_0 + \varepsilon$, where ε is a random variable representing the incremental improvement (which may even be negative) over the previous generation of innovations. We assume that ε is normally distributed with mean μ and variance v^2. For simplicity, we assume that ε and $z(t)$ are independent, $\forall t \leq T$. Thus, markets characterized by greatly improving technology will have a relatively high μ, and markets with highly uncertain technological improvements will be marked by high v.

Finally, we incorporate the ability to learn through the experience of previous innovation adoption. For any given realization of the future innovation, a firm that had previously adopted the current innovation will be able to more fully reap the benefits of the future innovation. The manner in which we incorporate learning in this paper is by making the cost of upgrading from the current innovation to the future innovation, C_u, lower than the cost of leapfrogging to the future innovation without benefit of learning, C_ℓ. That is, we assume that $C_u < C_\ell$. Alternatively, we could increase the expected payoff of adopting the second innovation for firms that previously adopted the initial innovation, or permit a firm that previously adopted the current innovation to utilize the future innovation sooner through increasing α or lowering X_h.

3 The Optimal Innovation Investment Strategy

We now derive a firm's optimal technological migration strategy. The firm must decide if and when it should adopt the current innovation. In addition, it must decide whether to invest in the new innovation when it arrives. The firm's innovation adoption strategy depends on its prior decisions and its expectations of the uncertain evolution of technological opportunities in the future. This section will present only the basic outline of the solution approach. The details of the derivations appear in the appendix.

To derive the optimal migration strategy, we work backwards in a dynamic programming fashion. Thus, we begin by assuming that the firm has already adopted the current innovation, and now holds the option to upgrade to the future innovation.

Then, using this valuation, we can derive the firm's optimal decision rule for adopting the current innovation.

First, suppose the firm has already invested in the current innovation. It paid the early exercise cost of C_e, and in return received the value of the innovation, P_0. However, in addition to the direct benefit of $P_0 - C_e$, the firm has also obtained a potentially valuable option: the option to convert from the current innovation P_0 to the future innovation P_T at an upgrade cost of C_u, at the random arrival time T. It will do so if $P_T \geq P_0 + C_u$. In the parlance of the options pricing literature, this is similar to an 'option to exchange'. Margrabe (1978) values an option to exchange one asset for another, with a fixed expiration date. However, what makes this problem different is that the expiration date T is stochastic. We now proceed to value this option.

The traditional arbitrage approach to pricing cannot be used because the underlying asset, the future innovation, does not yet exist. Thus, we must instead use an equilibrium argument. For simplicity, assume risk neutrality, so that all assets are priced so as to yield an expected rate of return equal to the risk-free rate, r. This seemingly restrictive assumption can easily be relaxed by adjusting the drift rate α to account for a risk premium in the manner of Cox and Ross (1976).

Let $F(X)$ denote the value of the option to upgrade from the current to the future innovation, where X is the current state of technological progress. As shown in the appendix, $F(X)$ must satisfy the following equilibrium differential equation:

$$0 = \tfrac{1}{2}\sigma^2 X^2 F'' + \alpha X F' - rF, \tag{2}$$

subject to the boundary conditions

$$F(X_h) = \mathrm{E}[\max(P_T - P_0 - C_u, 0)], \tag{3}$$

and

$$F(0) = 0. \tag{4}$$

The first boundary condition characterizes the expected payoff of the upgrade option at the moment the new innovation arrives. Thus, when X reaches the trigger X_h, the holder of the option can choose to upgrade to the realized value of the new technology, P_T. Therefore, the expected payoff on the option to upgrade is $E[\max(P_T - P_0 - C_u, 0)]$, where expectations are taken with respect to the distribution of P_T. The second boundary condition reflects the fact that if $X(t)$ ever falls to zero, the option would never be exercised (since the new technology would never arrive), because $X(t)$ has an absorbing barrier at zero. Thus, the option would become worthless. A closed-form solution for $F(X)$ appears in Eq. (A.4) in the appendix.

We now move back a step to consider a firm's optimal investment strategy for the current innovation. When confronted with the availability of the current innovation, the firm must choose not only if but also when to adopt the current innovation. As demonstrated above, if the firm decides to purchase the current innovation, it receives not only the current payoff from adoption $(P_0 - C_e)$, but also the value of an embedded option to upgrade. Therefore, the firm holds an "option on an option" and must choose an optimal exercise policy.

The optimal exercise (investment) strategy for this option will take the following form. The optimal time at which to invest in the current innovation is when the state variable $X(t)$ falls to a lower trigger X_ℓ. This trigger will be chosen so as to maximize the value of the option $G(X)$. Intuitively, the longer the expected period before the future innovation arrives, the more beneficial the current innovation becomes, as it is less likely to be rendered obsolete in the near future. At the trigger X_ℓ, the benefits of investing in the current innovation are precisely equal to the marginal benefits of waiting. A more rigorous proof of the form of exercise policy can be derived in a manner similar to that found in Dixit and Pindyck (1994, Chapter 4, Appendix B).

Let $G(X)$ denote the value of the option to purchase the current innovation. Just as in Eq. (2), the value of this option must satisfy the following equilibrium differential equation:

$$0 = \tfrac{1}{2}\sigma^2 X^2 G'' + \alpha X G' - rG, \tag{5}$$

subject to the boundary conditions

$$G(X_\ell) = P_0 - C_e + F(X_\ell), \tag{6}$$

$$G'(X_\ell) = F'(X_\ell), \tag{7}$$

$$G(X_h) = \mathrm{E}[\max(P_T - C_\ell, P_0 - C_d)]. \tag{8}$$

The first boundary condition is the value-matching condition, which simply states that the payoff upon exercise is equal to the net benefits of investment plus the value of the option to upgrade. The second boundary condition is a smooth-pasting condition. This condition ensures the optimality of the exercise trigger, X_ℓ. The third boundary condition represents the expected payoff if the option remains unexercised at the moment the future innovation arrives. At that time, the firm will choose to either leapfrog to the new innovation $(P_T - C_\ell)$ or purchase the previous technology at a discounted price $(P_0 - C_d)$. A closed-form solution for $G(X)$ as well as the optimal exercise trigger X_ℓ is provided in Eq. (A.5) in the appendix.

Using this embedded option approach, we can now summarize the firm's optimal technological migration strategy:

Optimal technological migration strategy. *Prior to adopting the current innovation (and before the future innovation arrives), the firm holds an option to purchase the current innovation. The value of this option is $G(X)$. The firm's optimal exercise strategy is to adopt the current innovation the first moment that $X(t)$ falls below the trigger X_ℓ, prior to the arrival of the future innovation. If the firm invests in the current innovation, it will receive an option to upgrade, $F(X)$. The firm will then upgrade if and only if $P_T - P_0 - C_u \geq 0$. If the firm does not invest in the current innovation prior to the arrival of the future innovation, then it will leapfrog to the future innovation if $P_T - C_\ell \geq P_0 - C_d$. Otherwise, it will purchase the older innovation at a discounted price.*

4   The Likelihood and Speed of Migration Strategies

Having derived the optimal migration strategy, we can now use the model to help predict a firm's future innovation adoption choices. In this section we derive the probability that a firm will pursue any of the four potential migration strategies. Recall that the compulsive strategy involves purchasing every innovation, the leapfrog strategy involves bypassing the early innovation in favor of the next generation of innovation, the buy-and-hold strategy involves purchasing only the early innovation, and the laggard strategy involves purchasing the previous innovation when the new generation of innovation arrives. In addition, we derive the expected time at which a firm first invests in an innovation.

In terms of the timing of the model, we are now at the beginning of the process at time zero. Given information about the firm, the profitability of the current innovation, and the stochastic processes describing the future innovation, we consider the likelihood that a firm will adopt any of the given strategies in the future. To facilitate the derivations, it is useful to refer to the following definitions:

$$T_e = \inf[t \geq 0 : X(t) \leq X_\ell] \qquad \text{and} \qquad T = \inf[t \geq 0 : X(t) \geq X_h]. \qquad (9)$$

Thus, T_e is the first passage time of $X(t)$ to the early adoption trigger, and T is the first passage time to the value that triggers the arrival of the future innovation. A firm will adopt the current innovation early (prior to the arrival of the future innovation) if and only if $T_e < T$. Therefore, the probability of early adoption is $\Pr[T_e < T]$.

We can now characterize the probabilities that a firm will fall into any one of the four possible categories. The full analytical solutions appear in the appendix. A firm pursues a compulsive strategy if it adopts early ($T_e < T$) and exercises the upgrade option at time T ($P_T - P_0 - C_u \geq 0$). Denote the probability of a compulsive strategy, conditional upon $X(0) = X$, as $PC(X)$. Thus,

$$PC(X) \equiv \Pr[T_e < T, P_T - P_0 - C_u \geq 0]. \tag{10}$$

A firm pursues a buy-and-hold strategy if it adopts early $(T_e < T)$, but does not exercise the upgrade option at time T $(P_T - P_0 - C_u < 0)$. Denote the probability of a buy-and-hold strategy, conditional upon $X(0) = X$, as $PB(X)$. Thus,

$$PB(X) \equiv \Pr[T_e < T, P_T - P_0 - C_u < 0]. \tag{11}$$

A firm pursues a leapfrog strategy if it does not adopt early $(T_e \geq T)$, but chooses to adopt the future innovation when it arrives $(P_T - C_\ell \geq P_0 - C_d)$. Denote the probability of a leapfrog strategy, conditional upon $X(0) = X$, as $PL(X)$. Thus,

$$PL(X) \equiv \Pr[T_e \geq T, P_T - C_\ell \geq P_0 - C_d]. \tag{12}$$

Finally, a firm pursues a laggard strategy if it does not adopt early $(T_e \geq T)$, but chooses to adopt the older innovation when the future innovation arrives, rather than leapfrogging $(P_T - C_\ell < P_0 - C_d)$. Denote the probability of a laggard strategy, conditional upon $X(0) = X$, as $PG(X)$. Thus,

$$PG(X) \equiv \Pr[T_e \geq T, P_T - C_\ell < P_0 - C_d]. \tag{13}$$

We can also use the model to characterize the speed at which a firm invests in technology. Using the definitions of the stopping times T_e and T in Eq. (9), the time it takes a firm to adopt an innovation is simply $\min(T_e, T)$. The expected time of initial adoption is then $E[\min(T_e, T) \mid X(0) = X]$.

5 Innovation Adoption Behavior in Differing Technological Environments

The model provides us with the ability to fully characterize a firm's optimal migration strategy. In particular, Section 4 provides an explicit derivation of the likelihood that a firm will choose any of the four migration strategies. In this section, we explore the impact of characteristics of the technological environment on firms' migration strategies. In particular, we analyze the impact of the speed of innovation arrival, the expected benefits of pending innovations, and the uncertainty of technological progress.

First, consider the impact of the speed of innovation arrival. Many view so-called "high-technology" environments as having a rapid pace of innovation arrival. For instance, the personal computer industry is typically considered an area of rapid innovation. Industry observers report that rapid innovation in personal computers has made purchase decisions difficult. As stated in *PC Magazine* (May 28, 1996, p. 93), "in large companies, many technology managers are actually complaining about the pace of innovation: by the time they get their purchase orders approved, the products they're trying to buy have been superseded by new models." Conversely, more mature technologies are often characterized by slow progress, perhaps punctuated by minor cosmetic changes. The important question is "how does firms' optimal adoption behavior differ according to the speed of innovation arrival?"

While the firm may invest in a profitable innovation, it also anticipates the arrival of a potentially even more valuable innovation in the future. If the future innovation is expected to arrive in the near future, then there are two reasons why the firm would prefer not to adopt any innovation until the future innovation arrives. First, by purchasing the initial innovation early, the firm may very soon see the technology become obsolete when the next innovation arrives. Second, even if the firm prefers to simply hold the initial innovation and bypass the future innovation, there is little cost to waiting and taking advantage of the discounted purchase price once the future innovation arrives. Therefore, the model suggests that for markets prone to rapid innovation, firms are most likely to postpone their innovation investments until the future innovation arrives. Thus, the leapfrog and laggard strategies will be the most likely in markets with rapid innovation arrival, while the compulsive and buy-and-hold strategies will rarely be pursued in such markets.

Figure 23.1 plots the probabilities of the four migration strategies as a function of the expected arrival time, $E(T)$. For example, the curve labeled "Compulsive" is simply a plot of the solution to Eq. (10), which is presented in the appendix. Just as intuition suggests, the leapfrog and laggard strategies dominate for markets with rapid innovation (low $E(T)$), while the compulsive and buy-and-hold strategies dominate for markets with slow innovation (high $E(T)$). These results hold under a wide variety of assumed parameter values. In the base case, the future innovation is expected to arrive in two years and has an expected value of twice the value of the current innovation. These assumptions are broadly consistent with many technology-based industries.[2] In Fig. 1, $E(T)$ is varied from three months to five years by increasing the arrival trigger parameter X_h. We find that for markets prone to rapid innovation, firms are most likely to adopt the leapfrog and laggard strategies. Firms are most likely to postpone their purchase decisions until the new innovation arrives. Then, depending on the attractiveness of the new innovation, the firm will either leapfrog to the future innovation or purchase the older innovation at a discount. Conversely, for innovations that emerge only after a substantial period of time, firms are most likely to purchase the current innovation early. In this case, the firm no longer fears rapid obsolescence.

Prob.

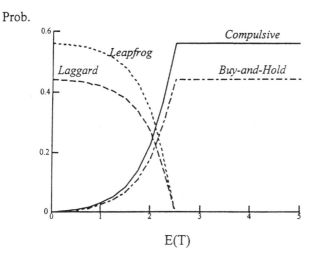

E(T)

Figure 23.1
The effect of the speed of innovation arrival on the likelihood of migration strategies. This graph shows the probability that a firm adopts a specific migration strategy as a function of $E(T)$, the expected arrival time of the future innovation. The firm may invest in a current innovation as well as a potential future technological innovation, whose value and arrival time are both uncertain. This leads to four potential migration strategies: the compulsive strategy, in which firms adopt every innovation; the leapfrog strategy, in which firms bypass the current innovation, but adopt the future innovation; the buy-and-hold strategy, in which firms adopt the current innovation, but not the future innovation; and the laggard strategy, in which firms bypass the current innovation, but adopt it later when the future innovation emerges. For technological environments with rapid innovation, the leapfrog and laggard strategies are the most likely. For technological environments with slower innovation, the compulsive and buy-and-hold strategies are the most likely. The default parameter values are $x = 0.05$, $\sigma = 0.05$, $r = 0.07$, $P_0 = 1$, $X = 1$, $\mu = 1$, $v = 1$, $C_e = 0.825$, $C_d = 0.8$, $C_l = 1.65$, $C_u = 0.85$. X_h is set in accordance with the various levels of $E(T)$.

The empirical results in Weiss (1994) for the printed-circuit assembly equipment market provide support for this prediction that firms will postpone the adoption of the first innovation under conditions of rapid technological progress. Most firms in the 1980s with automated assembly lines used the "through-hole" process for affixing electrical components to printed-circuit boards, whereby components are placed on only one side of the circuit board. However, surface-mount technology (SMT) was also available which significantly increased circuit board densities by allowing components to be placed on both sides of the boards. Although it had been developed 20 years earlier, SMT was becoming reliable enough in the 1980s for circuit manufacturers to seriously consider its adoption. It was also during this time that rapid and significant progress was being made in improving the elements of the technology (e.g., soldering and testing equipment). Weiss shows that a rapid pace of technological change (i.e., fast and significant technological improvements) led to the slow adoption of surface-mount technology (SMT) because firms bypassed early versions of the technology. Antonelli's (1989) empirical results on the adoption of open-ended spinning rotors also supports this prediction.

Technological environments differ not only according to the speed of innovation, but also according to the significance of the improvements. While a market may be prone to rapid innovation, the innovations can be evolutionary rather than revolutionary. Such markets may represent established products in which existing innovations are incrementally adapted to the needs of customers, or new technologies for which technical difficulties in early versions are eliminated. Conversely, some markets may experience rare, but significant innovations. Such market properties could be characteristic of completely new product categories in which basic technological knowledge is still being developed, or, alternatively, very mature technologies in which technological improvements occur rarely but have an enormous impact.

Consider the intuition of the model. The first, and most direct, impact of increasing the expected profitability of the future innovation is to increase the likelihood that the second innovation will be adopted. Thus, both the compulsive and leapfrog strategies become reasonable, while the laggard and buy-and-hold strategies become less compelling. The second impact deals with the effect of learning. Given that the future innovation is likely to be adopted, and given the benefits to learning by doing, firms have an incentive to purchase the current innovation. This effect increases the likelihood of both the compulsive and buy-and-hold strategies. Taking these two effects into account, the model suggests that for markets with greater expected benefits to future innovations, the compulsive and leapfrog strategies should become more likely, the buy-and-hold strategy can increase or decrease, and the laggard strategy should become increasingly rare.

In figure 23.2, the probabilities of the various strategies are graphed as the expected profitability of the future innovation, μ, increases. Just as intuition suggests, the compulsive and leapfrog strategies increase. Conversely, as the future innovation becomes more likely to be highly profitable, the laggard and buy-and-hold strategies become less likely.

These predictions have been empirically supported in several studies of innovation adoption (e.g., Griliches, 1957; Mansfield, 1968). As a specific example, Rosenthal (1984) provides extensive case study evidence of the adoption of computer-integrated manufacturing techniques (CIM). In the late 1970s and early 1980s, many firms were adopting computer-integrated manufacturing techniques. The idea behind CIM was that computer hardware, software, and databases would be joined with robots, control devices, and product design capabilities to form an integrated, highly automated

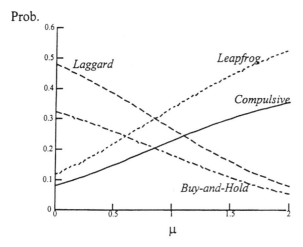

Figure 23.2
The effect of expected technological growth on the likelihood of migration strategies. This graph shows the probability that a firm adopts a specific migration strategy as a function of μ, the expected arrival incremental value of the future innovation over that of the current innovation. The firm can invest in a current innovation as well as a potential future technological innovation, whose value and arrival time are both uncertain. This leads to four potential migration strategies: the compulsive strategy, in which firms adopt every innovation; the leapfrog strategy, in which firms bypass the current innovation, but adopt the future innovation; the buy-and-hold strategy, in which firms adopt the current innovation, but not the future innovation; and the laggard strategy, in which firms bypass the current innovation, but adopt it later than the future innovation emerges. As the expected innovation growth increases, the likelihood of the leapfrog and compulsive strategies increases, the likelihood of the buy-and-hold strategy remains relatively constant, and the likelihood of the laggard strategy decreases. The default parameter values are $x = 0.05$, $\sigma = 0.05$, $r = 0.07$, $P_0 = 1$, $X = 1$, $v = 1$, $C_e = 0.825$, $C_d = 0.8$, $C_l = 1.65$, and $C_u = 0.85$. X_h is set such that $E(T) = 2$.

and flexible manufacturing system (the so-called 'factory of the future'). Future advances were expected to be highly significant. Technological progress, however, was slow because as a group, these process innovations were still being developed as basic technical knowledge was being applied to make everything work well together. Rosenthal reports that the first adopters of CIM felt they could not afford to wait until improved technologies became available. Rather, these firms were adopting CIM because they believed in learning by doing. This would allow them to take full advantage of future technological advances when they became available. Firms were pursuing a compulsive strategy of purchasing each successive innovation in a market characterized by significant, but slow, technological progress.

When we combine the previous two effects, technological environments with differing speed and significance of innovation, the model is able to provide even more specific predictions. For example, consider markets with rapid and significant progress. Recall that rapid innovation encourages delayed adoption, while significant progress encourages purchasing the future innovation. When these two results are combined, the model suggests that the leapfrog strategy should dominate in such an environment. As another example, consider markets with slow, but significant progress. Recall that slow innovation encourages early adoption of existing technologies, while significant progress encourages adopting future innovations. When these two results are combined, the model suggests that a compulsive strategy should emerge in such an environment.

By combining the effects of both the speed and significance of technology markets, the results are consistent with the previously discussed empirical results of Weiss (1994) and Rosenthal (1984). In Weiss (1994), firms respond to the rapid and significant technological improvements in surface-mount technology by adopting a leapfrog strategy; they bypass early innovations in order to jump to future innovations. In Rosenthal (1984), firms respond to the slow, but significant technological progress in computer-integrated manufacturing techniques by pursuing a compulsive strategy of purchasing innovations as they arrive.

These findings provide insight into the effects of product preannouncement behavior. In a classic antitrust case, CDC charged that IBM knowingly announced an unrealistic launch date for the IBM 360/91. According to the complaint, IBM made this announcement just prior to the delivery date of the CDC 6600 in order to forestall sales of the CDC machine. In an out-of-court settlement, CDC was awarded more than $75 million. In light of the current analysis, IBM's behavior can be viewed as an effort by a firm to induce technological expectations. According to our results, announcing a forthcoming innovation (i.e., lowering $E(T)$) would help to inspire defection to innovative products launched by competitors *only if the preannouncement also increases expectations about the extent of future improvements*. Otherwise, although firms are likely to postpone adoption, they will tend to ultimately adopt currently available technologies. Thus, our model suggests that if IBM could not credibly increase expectations about the value of their innovation, firms would not be very likely to leapfrog past the CDC machine.

A third dimension of technological markets is the level of uncertainty surrounding future innovations. Technological innovations, by their very nature, are difficult to forecast. The ability to predict the timing and impact of future innovations is likely to differ across technologies and according to the stage of the innovation cycle.[3] Similarly, sometimes the worth of one technology does not become clear until related discoveries appear. Personal computers looked like mere curiosities for hobbyists for many years; not until the first spreadsheet programs appeared did personal computers stand out as useful business tools (*Scientific American*, September 1995, p. 58).

Simulation results reveal that higher uncertainty about the future evolution of technology increases the likelihood of the leapfrog and laggard strategies, and decreases the likelihood of the compulsive and buy-and-hold strategies. Accordingly, volatility can retard the adoption of a current innovation, prompting firms to delay the investment decisions into the future.

The increased willingness of firms to postpone investment is a familiar result in real-options models (in particular, see McDonald and Siegel, 1986). At first glance, it appears that the cost of purchasing the current innovation is simply its direct cost, C_e. However, there is another, but more subtle, cost. Because the firm holds an option to postpone the decision and make its choice after more information is revealed, adopting the current innovation also involves exercising or 'killing' the option to wait. Thus, the value of this option is also a cost of adopting early. From the theory of option pricing, we know that option values increase with the underlying uncertainty. Thus, the value of the option to wait increases in more volatile technological environments, and firms become more reluctant to pursue compulsive or buy-and-hold strategies.

The ability of volatility to delay investment (even for projects with significantly positive net present values) has empirical support. For example, Hassett and Metcalf (1992) study consumers' response to investment tax credits for investments in energy conservation. While on the basis of conventional net present value calculations these subsidized investments were attractive, only a small percentage of consumers responded to the incentives. Hassett and Metcalf demonstrate that the level of ongoing uncertainty (e.g., in energy prices, or future technological advances) was sufficient to lead consumers to rationally postpone such investment.

6 Conclusion

In this chapter, we form an analogy between the adoption of innovations and the exercise strategy of a stream of embedded options. This allows us to use the tools of option pricing theory to derive and analyze a firm's optimal migration strategy under technological uncertainty. The model's results are used to predict the adoption behavior of firms in a variety of technological environments. We examine the impact of various characteristics of technological markets on a firm's decision to follow one of four distinct migration strategies.

Several extensions of the paper would prove interesting. First, while the current model analyzes optimal buyer behavior, it would be useful to endogenize the supply of innovations. This would allow an investigation of strategic efforts (e.g., increases in research and development) by suppliers of new technology. Second, it would also be useful to relate the findings of our model to empirical studies in the literature. Unfortunately, there have been virtually no systematic empirical studies of the phenomenon. Our results suggest that future empirical studies should, at the very least, distinguish between four different technological environments as characterized by high and low rates of change and timing, as distinct migration behaviors are likely to predominate in each context. If appropriate data were available, the predictions from our model could then be tested.

Appendix

A.1   Value of the Option to Upgrade

Let $F(X)$ denote the value of the option to upgrade from the current to the future innovation, where X is the current state of technological progress. Consider the instantaneous return on F over a region in which the new innovation has not yet arrived. By Itô's lemma, the instantaneous change in F is

$$dF = (\tfrac{1}{2}\sigma^2 X^2 F'' + \alpha X F')\,dt + \sigma X F'\,dz. \tag{A.1}$$

Since the option to upgrade has no interim payouts, the total return to holding this option comes in the form of capital gains, dF/F. Therefore, the total expected return on F per unit time, α_F, is

$$\alpha_F \equiv E\left(\frac{dF}{F}\right)\frac{1}{dt} = (\tfrac{1}{2}\sigma^2 X^2 F'' + \alpha X F')\frac{1}{F}. \tag{A.2}$$

Setting the expected return on the upgrade option equal to the equilibrium expected return r and simplifying yields the following equilibrium differential equation:

$$0 = \tfrac{1}{2}\sigma^2 X^2 F'' + \alpha X F' - rF. \tag{A.3}$$

Differential equation (A.3) must be solved subject to boundary conditions (3) and (4). The solution can be written as

$$F(X) = \begin{cases} \left(\dfrac{X}{X_h}\right)^{\beta_2} \cdot \left[v \cdot n\left(\dfrac{C_u - \mu}{v}\right) + (\mu - C_u) \cdot \Phi\left(\dfrac{\mu - C_u}{v}\right)\right] & \text{for } X < X_h, \\[3mm] v \cdot n\left(\dfrac{C_u - \mu}{v}\right) + (\mu - C_u) \cdot \Phi\left(\dfrac{\mu - C_u}{v}\right) & \text{for } X \geq X_h, \end{cases} \tag{A.4}$$

where $n(\cdot)$ and $\Phi(\cdot)$ are the standard normal density and cumulative distribution functions, respectively, and $\beta_2 = (-(\alpha - \sigma^2/2) + \sqrt{(\alpha - \sigma^2/2)^2 + 2r\sigma^2})/\sigma^2$. For convergence, we assume $r > \alpha$.

A.2   Solution for $G(X)$

The solution to differential equation (5), subject to boundary conditions (6)–(8), can be written as

$$G(X) = \begin{cases} P_0 - C_e + F(X_\ell) & \text{for } X \leq X_\ell, \\ A_1 X^{-\beta_1} + A_2 X^{\beta_2} & \text{for } X_\ell < X < X_h, \\ K_2 & \text{for } X \geq X_h, \end{cases} \tag{A.5}$$

where

$$X_\ell = \left[\frac{\beta_1}{\beta_1 + \beta_2}\frac{(P_0 - C_e)}{\omega}\right]^{1/\beta_2},$$

$$A_1 = C_1 \cdot \omega^{\beta_1/\beta_2},$$

$$A_2 = \omega + K_1 X_h^{-\beta_2},$$

$$K_1 = v \cdot n\left(\frac{C_u - \mu}{v}\right) + (\mu - C_u) \cdot \Phi\left(\frac{\mu - C_u}{v}\right),$$

$$K_2 = v \cdot n\left(\frac{C_\ell - C_d - \mu}{v}\right) + (C_\ell - C_d - \mu) \cdot \Phi\left(\frac{C_\ell - C_d - \mu}{v}\right) + P_0 - C_\ell + \mu,$$

$$\beta_1 = \frac{(\alpha - \sigma^2/2) + \sqrt{(\alpha - \sigma^2/2)^2 + 2r\sigma^2}}{\sigma^2} > 0,$$

$$\beta_2 = \frac{-(\alpha - \sigma^2/2) + \sqrt{(\alpha - \sigma^2/2)^2 + 2r\sigma^2}}{\sigma^2} > 1,$$

$$c_1 = \frac{\beta_2}{\beta_1}\left[\frac{\beta_1}{\beta_1 + \beta_2}(P_0 - C_e)\right]^{(\beta_1 + \beta_2)/\beta_2}$$

and where ω is the solution to the equation $c_1 X_h^{-\beta_1}\omega^{-\beta_1/\beta_2} + \omega X_h^{\beta_2} = K_2 - K_1$. Because ω is a root of the function $Q(y) = c_1 X_h^{-\beta_1} y^{-\beta_1/\beta_2} + y X_h^{\beta_2} + K_1 - K_2$, and simple manipulation of this function yields the following properties: $Q(0) = -\infty, Q(\infty) = \infty$, and $Q''(y) > 0, \forall y > 0$, then ω is positive and unique.

A.3 Probabilities of Migration Strategies

Analytical solutions to the probabilities of each of the four migration strategies in Section 4 are obtained by applying a change of variables (and some simple manipulation) to the results in Harrison (1985, Section 3.2):

$$PC(X) = H(X) \cdot \left[1 - \Phi\left(\frac{C_u - \mu}{v}\right)\right],$$

$$PB(X) = H(X) \cdot \Phi\left(\frac{C_u - \mu}{v}\right),$$

$$PL(X) = [1 - H(X)] \cdot \left[1 - \Phi\left(\frac{C_\ell - C_d - \mu}{v}\right)\right],$$ (A.6)

$$PG(X) = [1 - H(X)] \cdot \Phi\left(\frac{C_\ell - C_d - \mu}{v}\right),$$

where

$$H(X) = \begin{cases} 1 & \text{if } X \leq X_\ell, \\ (X^{-\gamma} - X_h^{-\gamma})/(X_\ell^{-\gamma} - X_h^{-\gamma}) & \text{if } X_\ell < X < X_h, \\ 0 & \text{if } X \geq X_h, \end{cases}$$

and $\gamma = -(2/\sigma^2)(\alpha - \frac{1}{2}\sigma^2)$.

A.4 The Expected Time of Adoption

Using the results of Harrison (1985, Section 3.2), the expected time of initial adoption, $E[\min(T_e, T) \mid X(0) = X]$, is

$$
\begin{cases}
\dfrac{\ln(X_h/X_\ell)}{\alpha - \frac{1}{2}\sigma^2} \left[\dfrac{X_\ell^{-\gamma} - X^{-\gamma}}{X_\ell^{-\gamma} - X_h^{-\gamma}}\right] - \dfrac{\ln(X/X_\ell)}{\alpha - \frac{1}{2}\sigma^2} & \text{if } X \in (X_\ell, X_h) \\
0 & \text{otherwise}
\end{cases}
\tag{A.7}
$$

when $\alpha \neq \frac{1}{2}\sigma^2$, and

$$
\begin{cases}
\dfrac{\ln(X_h/X) \cdot \ln(X/X_\ell)}{\sigma^2} & \text{if } X \in (X_\ell, X_h) \\
0 & \text{otherwise}
\end{cases}
$$

when $\alpha = \frac{1}{2}\sigma^2$.

Acknowledgments

We are grateful for the comments of Geert Bekaert, Michael Harrison, Jim Van Horne, and seminar participants at Ohio State University, University of Utah, INSEAD, and the 1995 American Finance Association meetings. Comments and suggestions made by Robert Pindyck (the referee) and Richard Ruback led to substantial improvements in this paper.

Notes

1. Given the default process, T, the distribution of the innovation arrival process can be obtained. Using equation (1.11) in Harrison (1985), and the application of a simple change in variables, the cumulative distribution function of the arrival time T can be written as

$$
\Pr[T \leq t] = \Phi\left[\frac{-\ln(X_h/X) + (\alpha - \frac{1}{2}\sigma^2)t}{\sigma\sqrt{t}}\right] + \left(\frac{X_h}{X}\right)^{2/\sigma^2(\alpha - (1/2)\sigma^2)} \Phi\left[\frac{-\ln(X_h/X) - (\alpha - \frac{1}{2}\sigma^2)t}{\sigma\sqrt{t}}\right],
$$

where $\Phi(\cdot)$ denotes the cumulative standard normal distribution function, and X is the current value of the arrival state variable. For $\alpha - \frac{1}{2}\sigma^2 > 0$, the expected arrival time $E(T)$ exists and is equal to $\ln(X_h/X)/(\alpha - \frac{1}{2}\sigma^2)$. The median arrival time, T_m, always exists and can be obtained by solving $\Pr[T \leq T_m] = 1/2$.

2. Microprocessors, for example, and the products on which they are based, are known to follow "Moore's Law" which predicts a doubling of performance every two years. The value of the future innovation has a standard deviation of one, or 50% of its expected value. Such uncertainty is consistent with many emerging technology markets.

3. For example, Nelson (1961) reports that RAND studies find rapid early uncertainty resolution which slows greatly as projects progress. Nelson states, "... by the time a fighter development program has proceeded to the point of a flight test or an engine program to the fifty-hour test, estimates of cost, performance, and development time are greatly improved. Many of the problems involved in radar developments were discovered quite early in the programs. Similarly with missiles."

References

Antonelli, C., 1989. The role of technological expectations in a mixed model of international diffusion of process innovations: The case of open-ended spinning rotors. *Research Policy* 18, 273–288.

Black, F., and Cox, J. C., 1976. Valuing corporate securities: Some effects of bond indenture provisions. *Journal of Finance* 31, 351–367.

Cox, J. C., and Ross, S. A., 1976. The valuation of options for alternative stochastic processes. *Econometrica* 53, 385–408.

Dixit, A. K., and Pindyck, R. S., 1994. *Investment Under Uncertainty*. Princeton University Press, Princeton, NJ.

Geske, R., 1979. The valuation of compound options. *Journal of Financial Economics* 7, 63–81.

Griliches, Z., 1957. Hybrid corn: An exploration in the economics of technological change. *Econometrica* 25, 501–522.

Harrison, J. M., 1985. *Brownian Motion and Stochastic Flow Systems*. Wiley, New York.

Hassett, K. A., and Metcalf, G. E., 1992. Energy tax credits and residential conservation investment. Working paper, National Bureau of Economic Research, Cambridge, MA.

Kaplan, R. S., 1986. Must CIM be justified by faith alone? *Harvard Business Review* 64, 87–93.

Kester, W. C., 1984. Today's options for tomorrow's growth. *Harvard Business Review* 62, 153–160.

Leland, H. E., 1994. Corporate debt value, bond covenants, and optimal capital structure. *Journal of Finance* 49, 1213–1252.

Longstaff, F. A., and Schwartz, E. S., 1995. A simple approach to valuing risky fixed and floating rate debt. *Journal of Finance* 50, 789–819.

Mansfield, E., 1968. *The Economics of Technological Change*. Norton, New York.

Margrabe, W., 1978. The value of an option to exchange one asset for another. *Journal of Finance* 33, 177–186.

McDonald, R., and Siegel, D., 1986. The value of waiting to invest. *Quarterly Journal of Economics* 101, 707–727.

Myers, S. C., 1977. Determinants of corporate borrowing. *Journal of Financial Economics* 5, 147–175.

Nelson, R. R., 1961. Uncertainty, learning, and the development of parallel research and development efforts. *The Review of Economics and Statistics* 351–364.

Passer, H., 1953. *The Electrical Manufacturers, 1875–1900*. Harvard University Press, Cambridge, MA.

Pindyck, R. S., 1991. Irreversibility, uncertainty, and investment. *Journal of Economic Literature* 29, 1110–1152.

Rosenthal, S. R., 1984. Progress toward the "factory of the future." *Journal of Operations Management* 4, 203–229.

Sayers R. S., 1950. The springs of technical progress in Britain, 1919–1939. *Economic Journal* 60, 275–291.

Weiss, A. M., 1994. The effects of expectations on technology adoption: Some empirical evidence. *Journal of Industrial Economics* 42, 341–360.

V NUMERICAL TECHNIQUES

24 A Log-transformed Binomial Numerical Analysis Method for Valuing Complex Multi-Option Investments

Lenos Trigeorgis

I Introduction

More researchers are now using numerical techniques to solve complex option-related problems. Geske and Shastri (1985) provide a comprehensive comparison of such methods. Most finance academics are familiar with the Cox, Ross, and Rubinstein (1979) multiplicative binomial model, which showed that options can be valued by discounting their terminal expected value in a world of risk neutrality. However, the Cox, Ross, and Rubinstein version of binomial approximation is not unique (e.g., see Jarrow and Rudd (1983), p. 188, and Rendleman and Bartter (1979) for alternative choices for the binomial parameters). In fact, once the return distribution of the underlying asset is known and risk-neutral valuation is accepted, other types of numerical analysis can be employed.[1] Basically, a discrete process that appropriately approximates the assumed continuous asset dynamics over successively smaller intervals must be identified.

The method proposed in this chapter can be seen as a variation of the binomial approximation with improved qualities. The variation is designed and the parameters chosen such that the valuation procedure is consistent, unconditionally stable, and computationally efficient. Consistency means that the discrete-time process used for computation has the same mean and variance for every time-step size as the underlying continuous process. Numerical stability means that the approximation errors in the computations will be dampened out rather than amplified. Efficiency refers to the number of operations or amount of computing time needed for accuracy of a given approximation.[2]

Assuming risk neutrality and diffusion asset dynamics, we show how to approximate the underlying continuous diffusion process when there is a series of exercise prices, nonproportional dividends, and interactions among a variety of options imbedded in a single underlying asset. Such features are prevalent in real investments requiring a series of capital outlays to generate expected cash flows. Real projects often afford management valuable flexibility as well. Myers (1987), Mason and Merton (1985), Trigeorgis and Mason (1987), Trigeorgis (1988), and others suggest viewing such flexibility as a collection of real options. Since our method is more useful and efficient when valuing complex real options, it is subsequently presented in that context.

The real options literature has so far focused on valuing one type of real option at a time. McDonald and Siegel (1985), (1986) value analytically the option to temporarily cease operations, and the option to wait. Majd and Pindyck (1987) value the option to delay sequential construction, and Myers and Majd (1990) analyze the option to abandon. Real-life investments are often more complex in that they may involve more than one option simultaneously. In such cases, analytic solutions may not exist and one may not even be able to write down the set of partial differential equations describing the underlying stochastic processes. Valuing each option separately and adding up the individual results is often inappropriate since multiple options may in fact interact (see Trigeorgis (1986)). The proposed method extends our valuation ability to such complex investments with multiple interacting options. Its application, together with numerical results, is illustrated here in the case of a research and development project with five imbedded real options.

The chapter is organized as follows. The theoretical design of the proposed numerical method is presented in Section II. The basic structure of the algorithm is described in Section III. Numerical comparisons with several existing numerical methods are presented in Section IV. Necessary adjustments for cash flows and real options, as well as a numerical example, are given in Section V. A summary and conclusions are contained in Section VI.

II   Theoretical Design of the Log-Transformed Binomial Method

In this section, we design a consistent, stable, and efficient numerical technique for valuing complex investment opportunities with many imbedded options. The value of the underlying asset, V, is the present value of the expected cash flows from immediately undertaking a real project. It is the gross or naked project value, not including any required investment cost outlays or any imbedded real options. To the firm, V represents the market value of a claim on the future cash flows from installing the project now.

Let the value of the underlying asset, V, follow a diffusion process of the form,

$$dV/V = \alpha\,dt + \sigma\,dz, \tag{1}$$

where α is the instantaneous expected return on the project, σ is the instantaneous standard deviation of project value changes, and dz is a standard Wiener process.

In any differential time interval, dt, $X \equiv \log V$ follows an arithmetic Brownian motion. Under risk neutrality, $\alpha = r$, and $dX = \log(V_{t+dt}/V_t) = (r - \frac{1}{2}\sigma^2)\,dt + \sigma\,dz$, with r being the risk-free rate. The increments, dX, are independent, identical, and normally distributed with mean $(r - \frac{1}{2}\sigma^2)\,dt$ and variance $\sigma^2\,dt$.

If we further let $K \equiv \sigma^2\,dt$, then dX become normally distributed with mean and variance,

$$E(dX) = \mu K; \quad \text{and} \quad \text{Var}(dX) = K,$$

where $\mu \equiv r/\sigma^2 - \frac{1}{2}$.

We approximate the continuous process above by subdividing the total period (project life), T, into N equal discrete subintervals of length τ so that $T = N\tau$. Thus, K can be approximated from $\sigma^2 T/N$. Within each discrete subinterval τ, X follows a Markov random walk moving up by an amount $\Delta X = H$ with some (risk-neutral) probability, P, or down by the same amount ($\Delta X = -H$) with probability $1 - P$. The mean and variance of this discrete-time Markov process are

$$E(\Delta X) = 2PH - H; \quad \text{and} \quad \text{Var}(\Delta X) = H^2 - [E(\Delta X)]^2.$$

For the discrete-time process to be consistent with the continuous diffusion process in (1), their corresponding means and variances should be equal,

$$2PH - H = \mu K, \quad \text{so} \quad P = \frac{1}{2}(1 + \mu K/H); \tag{2}$$

$$H^2 - (\mu K)^2 = K, \quad \text{so} \quad H = \sqrt{K + (\mu K)^2} \quad (\geq \mu K).$$

The above transformations of the state and time variables guarantee stability as well as consistency of the discrete-time approximation to the continuous process.[3] By its definition, $\text{Var}(\Delta X) \geq 0$ and, hence, $-1 \leq \mu K/H \leq 1$, which implies that $0 \leq P \leq 1$. As probabilities, P and $(1 - P)$ also and up to 1, satisfying the conditions that ensure unconditional stability in this weighted average numeric scheme with no external constraints on K and H.

III Algorithm Structure

The log-transformed binomial algorithm consists of four main steps: parameter value specification, preliminary sequential calculation, determination of terminal values, and backward iterative process. These are outlined in figure 24.1. First, parameters affecting option values (i.e., V, r, σ^2, T, and the set of exercise prices or investment cost outlays, EX's or I's), are specified, along with the desired number of sub-intervals, N. The cash flows, CF, and their timing (if discrete), as well as the type, timing, and other characteristics of the various imbedded options must be specified as well.

The second step involves preliminary calculations needed for the rest of the algorithm. Using the values of variables calculated along the way, the algorithm sequentially determines the following key variables:

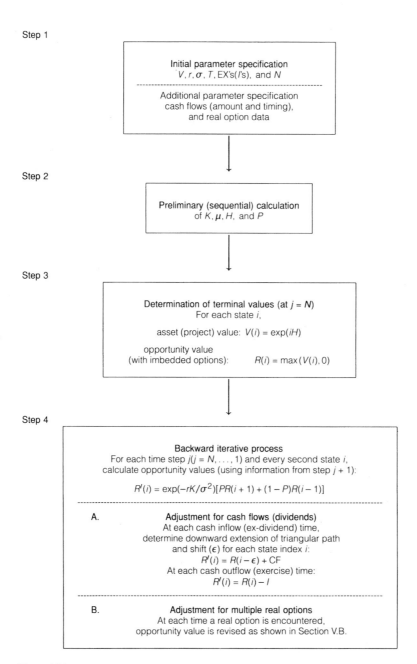

Step 1

Initial parameter specification
$V, r, \sigma, T, \text{EX's}(I\text{'s})$, and N

Additional parameter specification
cash flows (amount and timing),
and real option data

Step 2

Preliminary (sequential) calculation
of K, μ, H, and P

Step 3

Determination of terminal values (at $j = N$)
For each state i,

asset (project) value: $V(i) = \exp(iH)$

opportunity value
(with imbedded options): $R(i) = \max(V(i), 0)$

Step 4

Backward iterative process
For each time step $j(j = N, \ldots, 1)$ and every second state i,
calculate opportunity values (using information from step $j + 1$):

$$R'(i) = \exp(-rK/\sigma^2)[PR(i + 1) + (1 - P)R(i - 1)]$$

A.   Adjustment for cash flows (dividends)
At each cash inflow (ex-dividend) time,
determine downward extension of triangular path
and shift (ϵ) for each state index i:
$$R'(i) = R(i - \epsilon) + CF$$
At each cash outflow (exercise) time:
$$R'(i) = R(i) - I$$

B.   Adjustment for multiple real options
At each time a real option is encountered,
opportunity value is revised as shown in Section V.B.

Figure 24.1
Flow chart for the log-transformed binomial algorithm

(a) time-step: K from $\sigma^2 T/N$;

(b) drift: μ from $r/\sigma^2 - \frac{1}{2}$;

(c) state-step: H from $\sqrt{K + (\mu K)^2}$;

(d) probability: P from $\frac{1}{2}(1 + \mu K/H)$.

Before proceeding, it is convenient to define additional notation. Let "j" be the integer number of time-steps (each of length K), "i" be the integer index of the state variable X corresponding to the net number of ups less downs (i.e., $X(i) = X_0 + iH$), and $R(i)$ denote the total investment opportunity value (i.e., the combined value for the project and its imbedded real options) at state i.

The third step involves the determination of terminal boundary values (at $j = N$). For each state i, the algorithm fills in the underlying asset (project) values from $V(i) = e^{X_0 + iH}$ (since $X \equiv \log V = X_0 + iH$); and the total investment opportunity values from the terminal condition $R(i) = \max(V(i), 0)$.

The fourth step follows a backward iterative process, with adjustments for cash flows (dividends) and real options at appropriate times. Starting from the end ($j = N$) and working backward through a triangular path, the algorithm proceeds in a binomial dynamic programming fashion.[4] For each time-step j ($j = N - 1, \ldots, 1$) and every second state i, it calculates the total investment opportunity values (i.e., the combined values for the project with options) using information from step $j + 1$ or earlier. That is, between any two consecutive periods, the value of the opportunity in the earlier period (j) at sate i, $R'(i)$—where "$'$" indicates a new or revised value—is determined iteratively from its expected end-of-period values in the up and down states calculated in the previous time-step ($j + 1$), discounted back one period of length $\tau = K/\sigma^2$ at the rate r,[5]

$$R'(i) = e^{-r(K/\sigma^2)}[PR(i+1) + (1 - P)R(i-1)]. \tag{3}$$

Adjustments for the cash flows (dividends) and the various real options imbedded in the project need be made at appropriate times within the backward iterative process of step four. These adjustments are described in Section V. Numerical comparisons with several existing methods are presented next.

IV   Comparison with Alternative Numerical Methods[6]

Table 24.1 presents comparisons of American put values without dividends using the following methods: (1) Geske and Johnson's (1984) compound-option analytic polynomial approximation using three- or four-point extrapolation; (2) Barone-Adesi and

Table 24.1
American put values without dividends using compound analytic, quadratic, Johnson, finite difference, numerical integration, Cox, Ross, and Rubinstein (CRR) multiplicative binomial, and log-transformed binomial methods

Panel A. (EX = 100)[a]

#	r	σ	T	V	Put option value					
					Black-Scholes European	Compound analytic	Quadratic	Johnson	Finite-differences	Log-transformed binomial
1	0.08	0.2	0.25	80	18.09	20.00	20.00	20.00	20.00	20.00
2	0.08	0.2	0.25	90	9.05	10.07	10.01	10.56	10.04	10.04
3	0.08	0.2	0.25	100	3.04	3.21	3.22	3.21	3.22	3.22
4	0.08	0.2	0.25	110	0.64	0.66	0.68	0.65	0.66	0.67
5	0.08	0.2	0.25	120	0.09	0.09	0.10	0.09	0.09	0.09
6	0.12	0.2	0.25	80	17.13	20.01	20.00	20.00	20.00	20.00
7	0.12	0.2	0.25	90	8.26	9.96	10.00	10.00	10.00	10.00
8	0.12	0.2	0.25	100	2.63	2.91	2.93	2.90	2.92	2.92
9	0.12	0.2	0.25	110	0.52	0.55	0.58	0.53	0.55	0.56
10	0.12	0.2	0.25	120	0.07	0.07	0.08	0.07	0.07	0.07
11	0.08	0.4	0.25	80	19.45	20.37	20.25	20.08	20.32	20.32
12	0.08	0.4	0.25	90	12.17	12.55	12.51	12.52	12.56	12.57
13	0.08	0.4	0.25	100	6.94	7.10	7.10	7.12	7.11	7.12
14	0.08	0.4	0.25	110	3.63	3.70	3.71	3.72	3.70	3.71
15	0.08	0.4	0.25	120	1.76	1.79	1.81	1.80	1.79	1.80
16	0.08	0.2	0.50	80	16.65	19.94	20.00	20.00	20.00	20.00
→17	0.08	0.2	0.50	90	8.83	10.37	10.23	10.73	10.29	10.30
18	0.08	0.2	0.50	100	3.79	4.17	4.19	4.17	4.19	4.18
19	0.08	0.2	0.50	110	1.31	1.41	1.45	1.38	1.41	1.41
20	0.08	0.2	0.50	120	0.38	0.40	0.42	0.39	0.40	0.40

V = the underlying asset value (e.g., stock price), EX = the put option's exercise price, r = the risk-free interest rate, σ = the instantaneous standard deviation of asset returns, and T = the option maturity. Above values are on an annualized basis. # is the row reference number, and N is the number of iterations used in the discrete-time approximation.

Panel B. $(V = 100,\ EX = 100,\ T = 1)$[b]

#	r	σ	Put option value				
			Black-Scholes European	Numerical integration	Analytic polynomial	CRR binomial	Log-transformed binomial
1	0.125	0.5	13.27	14.8	14.76	14.80	14.76
2	0.080	0.4	11.70	12.6	12.58	12.60	12.61
3	0.045	0.3	9.59	10.1	10.05	10.05	10.06
4	0.020	0.2	6.94	7.1	7.12	7.11	7.12
5	0.005	0.1	3.73	3.8	3.77	3.77	3.76
6	0.090	0.3	7.61	8.6	8.59	8.61	8.62
7	0.040	0.2	6.00	6.4	6.40	6.40	6.41
8	0.010	0.1	3.49	3.6	3.57	3.57	3.57
9	0.080	0.2	4.42	5.3	5.25	5.27	5.27
10	0.020	0.1	3.04	3.3	3.22	3.22	3.22
11	0.120	0.2	3.17	4.4	4.39	4.42	4.41
12	0.030	0.1	2.63	3.0	2.92	2.93	2.92

Table 24.1 (continued)

Panel C. ($V = 40$, $r = 0.0488$)[c]

#	EX	σ	T	Put option value Black-Scholes European	Analytic polynomial	CRR binomial ($N = 500$)	Log-transformed binomial ($N = 50$)
1	35	0.2	0.0833	0.006	0.006	0.006	0.006
2	35	0.2	0.3333	0.196	0.200	0.200	0.200
3	35	0.2	0.5833	0.417	0.432	0.433	0.434
4	40	0.2	0.0833	0.840	0.853	0.852	0.851
5	40	0.2	0.3333	1.522	1.581	1.579	1.581
6	40	0.2	0.5833	1.881	1.991	1.990	1.992
7	45	0.2	0.0833	4.840	4.999	5.000	5.000
8	45	0.2	0.3333	4.781	5.095	5.089	5.092
9	45	0.2	0.5833	4.840	5.272	5.267	5.273
10	35	0.3	0.0833	0.077	0.077	0.077	0.078
11	35	0.3	0.3333	0.687	0.697	0.698	0.705
12	35	0.3	0.5833	1.189	1.219	1.221	1.221
13	40	0.3	0.0833	1.299	1.310	1.309	1.305
14	40	0.3	0.3333	2.438	2.482	2.482	2.482
15	40	0.3	0.5833	3.064	3.173	3.169	3.174
16	45	0.3	0.0833	4.980	5.060	5.060	5.059
17	45	0.3	0.3333	5.529	5.701	5.707	5.716
18	45	0.3	0.5833	5.973	6.237	6.245	6.240
19	35	0.4	0.0833	0.246	0.247	0.246	0.246
20	35	0.4	0.3333	1.330	1.345	1.348	1.343
21	35	0.4	0.5833	2.113	2.157	2.155	2.157
22	40	0.4	0.0833	1.758	1.768	1.768	1.769
23	40	0.4	0.3333	3.334	3.363	3.387	3.385
24	40	0.4	0.5833	4.247	4.356	4.352	4.354
25	45	0.4	0.0833	5.236	5.286	5.287	5.287
26	45	0.4	0.3333	6.377	6.509	6.511	6.511
27	45	0.4	0.5833	7.166	7.383	7.385	7.387

V = the underlying asset value (e.g., stock price), EX = the put option's exercise price, r = the risk-free interest rate, σ = the instantaneous standard deviation of asset returns, and T = the option maturity. Above values are on an annualized basis. # is the row reference number, and N is the number of iterations used in the discrete-time approximation.

a. From Barone-Adesi and Whaley (1987), Table IV. Implicit finite differences were computed with $N = 456$. Compound-option values computed using three-point extrapolation. In the last column, we added the log-transformed binomial values computed with only $N = 50$ iterations (except for a few typically in-the-money observations, namely row numbers 1, 6, 7, 14, 16, and 19, where we used $N = 456$).

b. From Geske and Johnson (1984), Table I. Cox, Ross, and Rubinstein (CRR) values with $N = 500$ from Hull and White (1988). We added the last column with $N = 50$ iterations.

c. Analytic values from Geske and Johnson (1984), Table I, using four-point extrapolation. Cox, Ross, and Rubinstein (CRR) values with $N = 500$ iterations from Hull and White (1988) (see also Cox and Rubinstein (1985) for $N = 150$ values). In the last column we added the log-transformed binomial values using only $N = 50$ (except for the high-variance case, $\sigma = 0.4$, where we used $N = 480$).

Whaley's (1987) quadratic approximation; (3) Johnson's (1983) heuristic technique; (4) Brennan and Schwartz's (1977), (1978) implicit finite difference scheme with $N = 456$ iterations; (5) Parkinson's (1977) numerical integration; and (6) Cox, Ross, and Rubinstein's (1979) multiplicative binomial method with $N = 500$ iterations. The proposed log-transformed binomial method is presented in the last column, using $N = 50$ iterations.[7] The set of options used in the tables has been widely employed for comparing different numerical techniques (e.g., by Cox and Rubinstein (1985), Geske and Johnson (1984), Barone-Adesi and Whaley (1987), Hull and White (1988), etc.).

To make comparisons, we need a benchmark for accuracy. Since no method can be widely accepted as being the most accurate, we resort to an ad hoc measure of accuracy. Following Barone-Adesi and Whaley ((1987), p. 312, footnote 11, and p. 316), we assume that finite differences is the most accurate method, partly because of the large number of steps used ($N = 456$). It also provides values closest to the median of all the methods compared in table 24.1, which can serve as the ad hoc benchmark for accuracy.

Panel A shows that, for a variety of parameter values (r, σ, T, and asset prices, V), the proposed log-transformed binomial method is more accurate than the analytic, quadratic, and Johnson methods, and gives identical results (within penny accuracy and less than 1-percent error) with finite differences with many fewer iterations ($N = 50$ versus 456). The greatest disagreement among the various methods occurs when the put option is slightly in the money (row reference numbers 2, 11, 12, and 17, when $V = 90$ or 80), although the log-transformed binomial and finite difference methods still give the same results. In row number 17, for example, the analytic method differs by +\$0.07 (or +0.7 percent), while the quadratic differs by −\$0.07 (or −0.7 percent), and the Johnson method by +\$0.43 (or +4 percent) from the median value (\$10.30), achieved by the log-transformed binomial and finite differences.

Panel B compares the numerical integration method with the analytic method and the two binomial methods for various at-the-money options (with varying r and σ). All methods agree within \$0.1. The log-transformed bionomial with only 50 steps seems to be as accurate as the Cox, Ross, and Rubinstein method with 500 steps, with the two methods being in agreement within \$0.01 (except for row number 1).[8] The analytic method also agrees, in most cases, with the log-transformed binomial within \$0.01. In two instances, with low standard deviation ($\sigma = 0.1$) and row r (row numbers 10 and 12), numerical integration slightly overvalues relative to the analytic and the binomial methods, which are here in agreement.

Panel C shows that, for a broader range of parameter values (EX, σ, and T), the log-transformed binomial (with $N = 50$) is again within penny accuracy of the Cox, Ross, and Rubinstein binomial (with $N = 500$) as well as of the analytic approxima-

Table 24.2
American put values with discrete cash dividends[a] using the Cox, Ross, and Rubinstein (CRR) multiplicative binomial and log-transformed binomial methods ($V = 40$, $r = 0.0488$)

				Put option value		
				Black-Scholes European	CRR binomial	Log-transformed binomial
#	EX	σ	T			
1	35	0.2	0.0833	0.01	0.01	0.01
2	35	0.2	0.3333	0.30	0.31	0.32
3	40	0.2	0.0833	1.09	1.11	1.11
4	40	0.2	0.3333	1.98	2.01	2.04
5	45	0.2	0.0833	5.33	5.41	5.41
6	45	0.2	0.3333	5.60	5.67	5.68
7	35	0.3	0.0833	0.11	0.11	0.11
8	35	0.3	0.3333	0.88	0.88	0.88
9	40	0.3	0.0833	1.55	1.56	1.56
10	40	0.3	0.3333	2.88	2.91	2.91
11	45	0.3	0.0833	5.43	5.50	5.50
12	45	0.3	0.3333	6.24	6.29	6.28
13	35	0.4	0.0833	0.30	0.31	0.31
14	35	0.4	0.3333	1.57	1.58	1.62
15	40	0.4	0.0833	2.00	2.01	2.01
16	40	0.4	0.3333	3.78	3.81	3.84
17	45	0.4	0.0833	5.65	5.70	5.70
18	45	0.4	0.3333	7.02	7.07	7.10

V = the underlying asset value (e.g., stock price), EX = the put option's exercise price, r = the risk-free interest rate, σ = the instantaneous standard deviation of asset returns, and T = the option maturity. Above values are on an annualized basis. # is the row reference number, and N is the number of iterations used in the discrete-time approximation.
a. Multiplicative (CRR) binomial values are from Cox and Rubinstein (1985). The European put values are from the Black-Scholes model adjusted by reducing the stock price by the present value of the scheduled (escrowed) dividends. A \$0.50 discrete cash dividend is scheduled in 0.5 and 3.5 months, so that one- and four-month puts ($T = 0.0833$ and 0.3333) have one and two scheduled dividends, respectively.

tion. In most cases, the analytic is even within \$0.002 of the log-transformed binomial; but in few, typically in-the-money, cases (row numbers 17, 23, 27) it slightly underestimates relative to the two binomial approaches.

Table 24.2 compares American put values with one or two discrete cash dividends using the two binomial methods for varying parameter values (for EX, σ, and T). In most instances, the two methods give results within a penny of each other—with the highest discrepancies of \$0.03 occurring under high variance ($\sigma = 0.4$). The European Black-Scholes put values are included to give a measure of the early exercise premium.[9]

Table 24.3 shows stability restrictions and consistency comparisons between implicit or explicit finite difference schemes and their log-transforms, numerical inte-

Table 24.3
Stability restrictions and consistency comparisons between implicit or explicit finite differences (and their log-transforms), numerical integration, Cox, Ross, and Rubinstein (CRR) multiplicative binomial, and log-transformed binomial methods

Method	Stability restrictions	Consistency
Implicit finite differences	$h \leq \sigma^2/|m|$[a]	Variance upward biased by square of the mean[h]
Log-transformed implicit finite differences	None[b]	
Explicit finite differences	$h \leq \sigma^2/|m|; \; k \leq h^2/\sigma^{2}$[c]	Variance downward biased[h] by square of the mean
Log-transformed explicit finite differences	$k \leq h^2/\sigma^{2}$[d]	
Numerical integration	$h^2 \geq \sigma^2 k + m^2 k^2; \; h \leq \sigma^2/|m| + mk$[e]	Yes
CRR multiplicative binomial	$k \leq \sigma^2/m^{2}$[f]	Consistent only in the limit[i] (variance downward biased by mean$^2/N$)
Log-transformed binomial	None[g]	Yes

$m = r - \frac{1}{2}\sigma^2 (\equiv \mu\sigma^2)$
$k = $ time-step $(= \tau$; note $K = \sigma^2 k)$
$h = $ state-step $(= \Delta X$; same as H earlier)
a. See Brennan and Schwartz (1978), Eq. (48), p. 470.
b. The result that logarithmic transformation can eliminate the stability restriction in the implicit finite difference scheme is well known in numerical analysis (see Forsythe and Wasow (1965)).
c. See Brennan and Schwartz (1978), Eq. (9), p. 464; and Mason (1978), Eq. (4.4), p. 21.
d. The result that logarithmic transformation in the explicit finite difference scheme can eliminate one of the two stability restrictions is shown in Mason (1978), Eq. (4.2), p. 20.
e. See Mason (1978), Eq. (4.3), p. 21.
f. See the Appendix, Part B, for derivation.
g. The condition for consistency, $h^2 = \sigma^2 k + m^2 k^2 \geq (mk)^2$, also implies $0 \leq P \equiv \frac{1}{2}(1 + mk/h) \leq 1$, which guarantees unconditional stability.
h. See Brennan and Schwartz (1978).
i. See, for example, Cox, Ross, and Rubinstein (1979), Jarrow and Rudd (1983), and Omberg (1987).

gration, the Cox, Ross, and Rubinstein binomial, and log-transformed binomial methods. All but the log-transformed binomial and the log-transformed implicit finite difference methods have specific stability constraints.[10] The log-transformation eliminates the single stability restriction in the implicit finite difference and the binomial methods, and one of the two restrictions in the explicit finite difference scheme. In terms of consistency, only the log-transformed binomial and numerical integration are consistent for every step size. Explicit finite difference methods are generally unstable and the variance of the approximating discrete process can be a downward (versus upward in the implicit scheme) biased estimate of the diffusion process.

The Cox, Ross, and Rubinstein multiplicative binomial model also may be unstable in that the error can blow up when $N < [(r - \frac{1}{2}\sigma^2)/\sigma]^2 T$. This may occur for certain parameter values because the risk-neutral probability, P, and the discrete process variance can become negative (see the appendix, part B). Moreover, the Cox, Ross, and Rubinstein approximation is consistent only in the limit (as $\tau \to 0$). In contrast, by taking the log of V as the state variable (X) that follows an arithmetic process (and expressing time in units of variance), the proposed binomial approach is stable under any conditions and is consistent for any step size, not just in the limit.

The proposed method also compares favorably in terms of computational efficiency due to the log-transformation. Geske and Shastri (1985), for example, find that when finite differences are log-transformed they become computationally more efficient, with the explicit scheme becoming the most efficient. They also find that the standard binomial approximation—which they view as being a special case of explicit finite differences with a conditional starting point allowing for improved efficiency—is still the most efficient method when evaluating one or a small number of options. Further, the log-transformed binomial method has a significant computational advantage relative to finite difference schemes since only every second node in a triangular path needs to be calculated instead of every node in a rectangular path. Moreover, as we will see next, computational efficiency is further enhanced by handling nonproportional dividends such that post-dividend nodes recombine. The adjustments for dividends and multiple real options, as well as a numerical application, are presented next.

V Adjustments and a Numerical Application

A Adjustment for Cash Flows (Dividends)

Each time the underlying asset pays a cash flow CF, $V(\equiv e^{X_0 + iH})$ is reduced by CF, i.e., $V^-(i) = V^+(i) - \text{CF}$, where the superscript signs refer to times just after $(-)$ and just before $(+)$ the payment time. Since the value of the option component is unchanged, the total opportunity (asset plus option) value after payment is given by $R'(V^-) = R(V^+ - \text{CF}) + \text{CF}$.

In terms of implementation, at each cash inflow time, the path triangle followed by $X(\equiv \log V)$ is extended downward by an amount determined by the cash flow drop; the revised value of the investment opportunity at state index i, $R'(i)$, is then obtained from the opportunity value corresponding to some lower index, $i - \varepsilon$ (with ε depending on CF), that is, $R'(i) = R(i - \varepsilon) + \text{CF}$.[11] Essentially, as we step backward

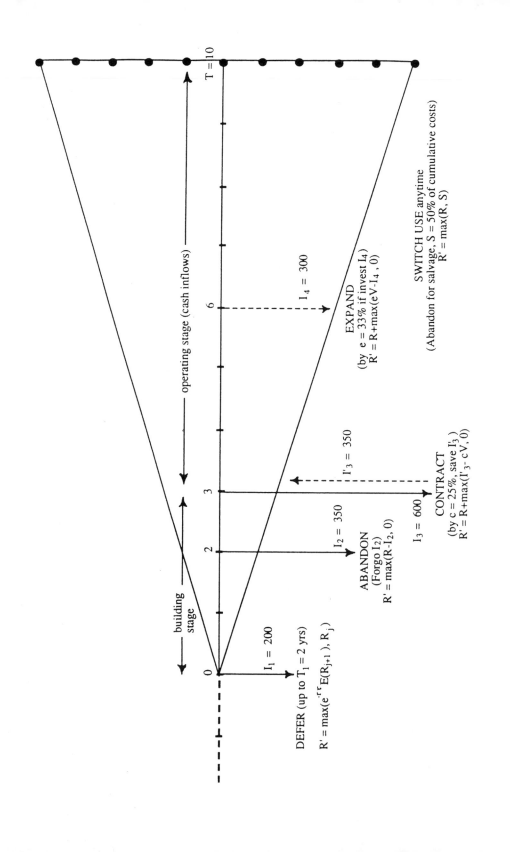

in time, this cash flow adjustment shifts the whole valuation grid upward whenever a cash inflow is encountered.

On the other hand, whenever a planned cash outflow or investment cost outlay, I, is reached, current opportunity value is revised by subtracting that outlay, i.e., $R'(i) = R(i) - I$.

B Adjustment for Multiple Real Options

If at any time, j, a real option is encountered as we move backward, the total opportunity value is revised to reflect the asymmetry introduced by that type of flexibility. To be more concrete, consider evaluating a complex multi-option project as described in figure 24.2.

Operating the project requires a series of investment outlays during a building stage (say, a first expenditure of I_1 to initiate it, to be followed by outlays of I_2 and I_3) before it is expected to generate cash inflows during a later operating stage. The project affords management the flexibility to wait for up to T_1 years. Later on, management may abandon early by forgoing a preplanned outlay (say, I_2), may contract the scale of operations by a fraction c, thereby saving part (I_3') of a planned outlay (I_3), or may expand production by a fraction e, if it makes an extra outlay (I_4). Finally, at any time, it may switch the project from the current to its best future alternative use, or abandon for its salvage value (S).

As each of the above real options is encountered, the total opportunity value (including all subsequent options) is adjusted—from R to R'—for each type of flexibility as follows:

switch use (or abandon for salvage S), $\qquad R' = \max(R, S)$,

expand by e % by investing I_4, $\qquad R' = R + \max(eV - I_4, 0)$,

contract project scale by c % saving I_3', $\qquad R' = R + \max(I_3' - cV, 0)$,

abandon by defaulting on investment I_2, $\qquad R' = \max(R - I_2, 0)$,

defer (until next period),[12] $\qquad R' = \max(e^{-r\tau} E(R_{j+1}), R_j)$.

C A Numerical Example of the Multi-Option Investment

Consider valuing an investment opportunity by a chemical company to undertake a research and development project. The project characteristics are summarized in

Figure 24.2
A complex (research and development) project with multiple options to defer, abandon, contract, expand, or switch use (abandon for salvage) with appropriate adjustments

Figure 2.[13] Further, the gross project value, V, is estimated to be 1,000 (in thousands of dollars), with a σ of 20 percent. r is 6 percent. As a benchmark for reference, the traditional NPV of the base-scale project with no options, obtained by subtracting from gross project value the present value of planned capital outlays, is[14]

NPV (no options) $= V - I = 1,000 - 1,015 = -15$.

The project would thus be rejected, unless the value of flexibility added by its real options is properly recognized. The value of each option, if determined in isolation using standard option pricing, is as follows:

option to defer investment	147
option to abandon during construction	34
option to contract project scale	62
option to expand production	133
option to switch use (abandon for salvage)	121

Adding up these separate option values, however, would substantially over-state their combined worth due to various, typically negative, interactions. Exercise of certain prior real options may kill or alter the underlying asset and value of subsequent options. Furthermore, the presence of latter options would increase the effective underlying asset for earlier ones. Taking these interactions into account, the combined value of all five options is 349 (increasing total value from -15 without options, to 334). This combined option value is just 70 percent of the sum of separate option values, although still amounting to a sizeable portion (35 percent) of total capital outlays.[15]

VI Conclusion

Unlike other methods used to value investments with only one option in isolation, this paper proposes an options-based numerical approach capable of valuing complex investments with multiple kinds of flexibility and capturing their interactions.

The proposed method offers a more intuitive framework for the analysis of complex options than alternative approaches. Its favorable technical qualities include its accuracy, consistency, unconditional stability, and computational efficiency. The latter is achieved both through log-transformation, and through a different adjustment for nonproportional dividends that allows post-dividend nodes to recombine. More importantly, it can easily handle a variety of possibly interacting options, a series of exercise prices (compound options), as well as nonproportional cash flows (dividends). Similar adjustments can be made to handle competitive jumps and other complications.[16]

A numerical example illustrating application of the proposed approach in the case of a complex multi-option capital budgeting project also was presented. The ability to value multiple interacting options also may be useful, for instance, in valuing financial instruments with interacting options such as a convertible putable bond or a callable and extendable bond; or in valuing the interacting operating lease options to purchase, cancel, or renew a lease. Its improved technical qualities and the more efficient way for handling nonproportional dividends also may be useful in the valuation of a variety of other option situations, both real and financial.

Appendix

A

This part shows that the risk-neutral probability in the log-transformed binomial model, P, converges (as $N \to \infty$) to that of the Cox, Ross, and Rubinstein (CRR) binomial model, q.

Let $m \equiv r - \frac{1}{2}\sigma^2 (= \mu\sigma^2)$. In the limit as $N \to \infty$, K^2 is negligible compared to K (as $K \equiv \sigma^2 T/N \to 0$), so that

$$H(= \sqrt{K + (\mu K)^2}) \to \sqrt{K} \text{ (in CRR, } H \equiv \log u = \sqrt{K}), \text{ and } K/H \to \sqrt{K}; \text{ so}$$

$$P = \tfrac{1}{2}(1 + \mu K/H) \to \tfrac{1}{2}(1 + (m/\sigma^2)\sigma\sqrt{\tau}) = \tfrac{1}{2} + \tfrac{1}{2}(m/\sigma)\sqrt{\tau} \ (= q).$$

B

This part derives the stability restriction for the Cox, Ross, and Rubinstein multiplicative binomial method.

As with any weighted average numeric scheme, the probabilities (weights), q and $1 - q$, must be constrained between zero and one. The condition $q(\equiv \tfrac{1}{2} + \tfrac{1}{2}(m/\sigma)\sqrt{\tau}) \geq 0$ implies that $\sqrt{\tau} \geq -\sigma/m$, while $q \leq 1$ implies $\sqrt{\tau} \leq \sigma/m$. Both conditions together require that $\tau \leq (\sigma/m)^2$ or, alternatively, (since $\tau \equiv T/N$) that $N \geq (m/\sigma)^2 T$. (Conditions on $1 - q$ lead to identical results.) If the number of iterations used is less than $[(r - \tfrac{1}{2}\sigma^2)/\sigma]^2 T$, the approximation errors may grow and the process may blow up. For example, if $r = 0.10$, $\sigma = 0.05$, and $T = 10$ years, the Cox, Ross, and Rubinstein binomial approximation may be unstable if $N \leq 40$. (The critical number of iterations below which stability problems may occur is higher for higher r and lower σ.)

Alternatively, if N does not satisfy the above condition, the variance of the approximating discrete process, which is a downward biased estimate of the continuous diffusion variance, would become *negative*, leading to stability problems. From Cox, Ross, and Rubinstein (1979), p. 249, or Cox and Rubinstein (1985), p. 200,

Var(discrete process) = Var(continuous) − mean^2/N.

Note that the downward bias, mean^2/N, disappears and the approximation becomes consistent only in the limit, as $N \to \infty$. In practice with N finite, to prevent the discrete variance from becoming negative and the process from blowing up, N must satisfy

$$N \geq \text{mean}^2/\text{var(continuous)} = (mT)^2/(\sigma^2 T) = (m/\sigma)^2 T, \text{ as above.}$$

In fact, any such method with a downward biased variance (e.g., explicit finite differences, of which the Cox, Ross, and Rubinstein binomial is a special case) may suffer from such stability problems. By contrast, methods guaranteeing a nonnegative discrete process variance such as the proposed log-transformed binomial (with variance positive by consistency design) or the log-transformed implicit finite difference scheme (with variance positive due to upward bias) may achieve weights between 0 and 1 and, hence, require no external stability restrictions.

Acknowledgments

The author is indebted to Scott Mason for initiating him to numerical analysis and for many constant discussions and support. The author also is grateful to Phelim Boyle, George Constantinides, Stewart Myers, Kuldeep Shastri, Alan White, *JFQA* Managing Editor Paul Malatesta, and especially to *JFQA* referee Ramon Rabinovitch for helpful comments. The chapter also benefited from presentations at the 1988 European Finance Association and American Finance Association conferences.

Notes

1. For example, see Boyle (1988) and Omberg (1988) for efficient trinomial processes; see also Barone-Adesi and Whaley (1987), Blomeyer (1986), Boyle (1977), Brennan and Schwartz (1977), (1978), Geske and Johnson (1984), Johnson (1983), and Parkinson (1977) for various other numerical methods in option pricing.

2. For more formal definitions of stability (using the mesh ratio) and efficiency, see Geske and Shastri (1985), pp. 53–56. See also note 3 and the appendix, part B, concerning stability restrictions.

3. For any weighted average numeric scheme—such as a binomial method or explicit finite differences used by Brennan and Schwartz (1978)—to be stable (i.e., for the error not to blow up) the weights must be constrained between 0 and 1 and add up to 1 (like probabilities), in turn restricting the admissible values of K and H to satisfy a certain condition.

4. Due to the binomial nature of this process, the possible paths followed by the state variable X are constrained within a triangular path with vertex at the current value X_0. Note also that we only need every second state for any given time, and that the highest and lowest possible values of i are each shrinking by 1 at each step as we move backward in time. These observations can result in valued computational savings.

5. To simplify the notation, subscripts "j" on the left side of Equation (3) and "$j + 1$" on its right side are dropped from R.

6. In general, there are two types of numerical techniques for option valuation: (1) those that approximate the underlying stochastic process directly and are generally more intuitive; and (2) those approximating the resulting partial differential equations. Our approach belongs in the first category, as do the Cox, Ross, and Rubinstein (1979) binomial method and Monte Carlo simulation used by Boyle (1977). Examples of the second category are numerical integration used by Parkinson (1977), and finite difference schemes used by Brennan and Schwartz (1977), (1978). Finally, Geske and Johnson (1984) proposed a compound-option analytic polynomial approximation approach, Barone-Adesi and Whaley (1987) suggested a quadratic approximation, while others such as Johnson (1983) and Blomeyer (1986) have used various problem-specific heuristic techniques.

7. Only in few typically in-the-money cases, namely row numbers 1, 6, 7, 14, 16, and 19, we used $N = 456$ (the same as for finite differences) for better accuracy.

8. This efficiency comes from log-transformation and different choice of binomial parameters. Additional efficiency would result from the different adjustment for nonproportional dividends described in Section V.

9. We also were able to confirm with close accuracy the results on the American put option to abandon for salvage obtained by Myers and Majd (1990) using explicit finite differences, both with a constant cash payout under deterministic salvage—their Table I—and with stochastic salvage—their Table III.

10. For stability restrictions in implicit finite difference schemes, see Brennan and Schwartz (1978), Equation (48), p. 470. For restrictions in explicit finite differences see their Equation (9), as well as Mason (1978), Equation (4.4), p. 21. For restrictions in numerical integration, see Mason (1978), Equation (4.3), p. 21. For derivation of the restriction in the Cox, Ross, and Rubinstein binomial see the Appendix, Part B.

11. In general, with discrete nonproportional cash flows, each node in the "tree" is shifted by a different amount (ε differs for each i). Only in the special case when cash flow is a constant proportion of project value is the whole tree shifted by a constant amount. Note also that when retrieving a revised value from a lower index $(i - \varepsilon)$, it may be necessary to interpolate between adjacent node values.

12. That is, defer one more period if the discounted expected opportunity value from initiating the project next period $(j + 1)$ exceeds the value from exercising, i.e., investing at the current period (j). This requires multiple parallel runs of the rest of the program already adjusted for other options, and pairwise comparisons conditional on project initiation in successive periods as we move backward starting from T_1 to the present.

13. Specifically, management believes it can safely wait for up to two years. To start, it must spend 200 on research (to last for two years), to be followed by planned development costs of 350, which could be forgone if research fails. A large facility is planned to be built in the third year at a cost of 600. However, management may build a 25-percent smaller facility, resulting in variable cost savings of 350 if the market outlook then seems limited. Once completed, the project is expected to generate annual cash flows equal to 10 percent of gross project value until year ten. If demand exceeds expectations, production scale and project value can expand by 33 percent upon investing an extra 300 for add-on facilities in year six. Finally, if the project fails at any time, it could be abandoned salvaging 50 percent of cumulative capital outlays net of a 10-percent annual depreciation.

14. The planned capital oulays (200 in year 0, 350 in year 2, and 600 in year 3) are assumed known in advance and placed in an escrow account earning the risk-free rate. Discounted at $r = 6$ percent, they give a present value of $I = 1,015$.

15. For a more detailed explanation of such option value calculations and option interactions, see Trigeorgis (1986), Chapter 7, and Trigeorgis (1990).

16. For example, the algorithm can be extended to handle both anticipated competitive arrivals, which can be preempted by an early investment outlay, with an adjustment similar to the discrete cash dividends above, as well as random exogenous competitive arrivals modelled as mixed jump-diffusion processes (see Trigeorgis (1986), Chapter 6).

References

Barone-Adesi, G., and R. Whaley. "Efficient Analytic Approximation of American Option Values." *Journal of Finance*, 42 (June 1987), 301–320.

Black, F., and M. Scholes. "The Pricing of Options and Corporate Liabilities." *Journal of Political Economy*, 81 (May–June 1973), 637–659.

Blomeyer, E. C. "An Analytic Approximation for the American Put Price for Options on Stocks with Dividends." *Journal of Financial and Quantitative Analysis*, 21 (June 1986), 229–233.

Boyle, P. "Options: A Monte Carlo Approach." *Journal of Financial Economics*, 4 (May 1977), 323–338.

———. "A Lattice Framework for Option Pricing with Two State Variables." *Journal of Financial and Quantitative Analysis*, 23 (March 1988), 1–12.

Brennan, M. "The Pricing of Contingent Claims in Discrete Time Models." *Journal of Finance*, 34 (March 1979), 53–68.

Brennan, M., and E. Schwartz. "The Valuation of American Put Options." *Journal of Finance*, 32 (May 1977), 449–462.

––––––. "Finite Difference Methods and Jump Processes Arising in the Pricing of Contingent Claims: A Synthesis." *Journal of Financial and Quantitative Analysis*, 13 (Sept. 1978), 461–474.

Cox, J.; S. Ross; and M. Rubinstein. "Option Pricing: A Simplified Approach." *Journal of Financial Economics*, 7 (Sept. 1979), 229–263.

Cox, J., and M. Rubinstein. *Options Markets*. Englewood Cliffs, N.J.: Prentice-Hall (1985).

Geske, R., and H. Johnson. "The American Put Option Valued Analytically." *Journal of Finance*, 39 (Dec. 1984), 1511–1524.

Geske, R., and K. Shastri. "The Early Exercise of American Puts." *Journal of Banking and Finance* (1980).

––––––. "Valuation by Approximation: A Comparison of Alternative Option Valuation Techniques." *Journal of Financial and Quantitative Analysis*, 20 (March 1985), 45–71.

Hull, J., and A. White. "The Use of the Control Variate Technique in Option Pricing." *Journal of Financial and Quantitative Analysis*, 23 (Sept. 1988), 237–251.

Jarrow, R., and A. Rudd. *Option Pricing*. Homewood, IL: R. D. Irwin (1983).

Johnson, H. E. "An Analytic Approximation for the American Put Price." *Journal of Financial and Quantitative Analysis*, 18 (March 1983), 141–148.

Majd, S., and R. Pindyck. "Time to Build, Option Value, and Investment Decisions." *Journal of Financial Economics*, 18 (March 1987), 7–27.

Mason, S. P. "The Numerical Analysis of Certain Free Boundary Problems Arising in Financial Economics." Harvard Business School Working Paper 78–52 (1978).

Mason, S. P., and R. C. Merton. "The Role of Contingent Claims Analysis in Corporate Finance." In *Recent Advances in Corporate Finance*, E. Altman and M. Subrahmanyam, eds. Homewood, IL: R. D. Irwin (1985).

McDonald, R., and D. Siegel. "Investment and the Valuation of Firms when There is an Option to Shut Down." *International Economic Review*, 26 (June 1985), 331–349.

––––––. "The Value of Waiting to Invest." *Quarterly Journal of Economics*, 101 (Nov. 1986), 707–727.

Myers, S. C. "Finance Theory and Financial Strategy." *Midland Corporate Finance Journal*, 5 (Spring 1987), 6–13.

Myers, S. C., and S. Majd. "Abandonment Value and Project Life." *Advances in Futures and Options Research*, 4 (1990), 1–21.

Omberg, E. "A Note on the Convergence of Binomial-Pricing and Compound-Option Models." *Journal of Finance*, 42 (June 1987), 463–469.

––––––. "Efficient Discrete Time Jump Process Models in Option Pricing." *Journal of Financial and Quantitative Analysis*, 23 (June 1988), 161–174.

Parkinson, M. "Option Pricing: The American Put." *Journal of Business*, 50 (Jan. 1977), 21–36.

Rendleman, R., and B. Bartter. "Two-State Option Pricing." *Journal of Finance*, 34 (Dec. 1979), 1093–1110.

Trigeorgis, L. "Valuing Real Investment Opportunities: An Options Approach to Strategic Capital Budgeting." Unpubl. Ph.D. Diss., Harvard Univ. (1986).

––––––. "A Conceptual Options Framework for Capital Budgeting." *Advances in Futures and Options Research*, 3 (1988), 145–167.

––––––. "The Nature of Option Interactions and the Valuation of Investments with Multiple Real Options." *Journal of Financial and Quantitative Analysis*, 28 (1993), 1–20.

Trigeorgis, L., and S. P. Mason. "Valuing Managerial Flexibility." *Midland Corporate Finance Journal*, 5 (Spring 1987), 14–21.

25 Finite Difference Methods and Jump Processes Arising in the Pricing of Contingent Claims: A Synthesis

Michael J. Brennan and Eduardo S. Schwartz

Since the seminal article by Black and Scholes on the pricing of corporate liabilities, the importance in finance of contingent claims has become widely recognized. The key to the valuation of such claims has been found to lie in the solution to certain partial differential equations. The best known of these was derived by Black and Scholes, in their original article, from the assumption that the value of the asset underlying the contingent claim follows a geometric Brownian motion.

Depending on the nature of the boundary conditions which must be satisfied by the value of the contingent claim, the Black-Scholes partial differential equation and its extensions may or may not have an analytic solution. Analytic solutions have been derived under certain conditions for the values of a call option (Black and Scholes [1], Merton [11]), of a risky corporate discount bond (Merton [12]), of European put options (Black and Scholes [1], Merton [11]), of the capital shares of dual funds (Ingersoll [8]), and of convertible bonds (Ingersoll [9]). In many realistic situations, however, analytic solutions do not exist, and the analyst must resort to other methods. These include the finite difference approximation to the differential equation employed extensively by Brennan and Schwartz [3, 4, 5], numerical integration used by Parkinson [13], and Monte Carlo methods advocated by Boyle [2].

Complementing the above work, Cox and Ross [6, 7] have analyzed the pricing of contingent claims when the value of the underlying asset follows a jump process rather than a diffusion process, and have shown that in the limit the jump process approaches a pure diffusion process. The major purpose of this paper is to demonstrate that approximation of the Black-Scholes partial differential equation by use of the finite difference method is equivalent to approximating the diffusion process by a jump process and that therefore the finite difference approximation is a type of numerical integration. In particular, we establish that the simpler explicit finite difference approximation is equivalent to approximating the diffusion process by one of the jump processes described by Cox and Ross, while the implicit finite difference approximation amounts to approximating the diffusion process by a more general type of jump process. As a preliminary to this, we show that certain simplifications of the numerical procedure are made possible by taking a log transform of the Black-Scholes equation. In the subsequent sections we discuss the explicit and implicit finite difference approximations, respectively.

I The Log Transform of the Black-Scholes Equation

The basic Black-Scholes equation is

$$\tfrac{1}{2}\sigma^2 S^2 H_{SS} + rSH_S + H_t - rH = 0 \tag{1}$$

where S is the value of the underlying asset, t is time, $H(S,t)$ is the value of the contingent claim, r is the riskless rate of interest, σ^2 is the instantaneous variance rate of the return on the underlying asset, and subscripts denote partial differentiation.

To obtain the log transform of (1) we define

$$y \equiv \ln S \tag{2}$$

$$W(y,t) \equiv H(S,t) \tag{3}$$

so that

$$H_S = W_y e^{-y} \tag{4}$$

$$H_{SS} = (W_{yy} - W_y)e^{-2y} \tag{5}$$

$$H_t = W_t. \tag{6}$$

Then, making the appropriate substitutions in (1), we obtain the transformed equation:

$$\tfrac{1}{2}\sigma^2 W_{yy} + (r - \tfrac{1}{2}\sigma^2)W_y + W_t - rW = 0. \tag{7}$$

Notice that (7), unlike (1), is a partial differential equation with constant coefficients. This simplifies the numerical analysis, and, as we shall see below, makes it possible to employ an explicit finite difference approximation to (7), whereas the explicit finite difference approximation to (1) is in general unstable.

II The Explicit Finite Difference Approximation

To obtain a finite difference approximation to (7), we replace the partial derivatives by finite differences, and to this end define

$$W(y,t) = W(ih, jk) = W_{i,j}$$

where h and k are the discrete increments in the value of the underlying asset and the time dimension, respectively. For the explicit approximation, the partial derivatives are approximated by

$$W_y = (W_{i+1,j+1} - W_{i-1,j+1})/2h$$

$$W_{yy} = (W_{i+1,j+1} - 2W_{i,j+1} + W_{i-1,j+1})/h^2$$

$$W_t = (W_{i,j+1} - W_{i,j})/k$$

so that the corresponding difference equation is

$$W_{i,j}(1 + rk) = aW_{i-1,j+1} + bW_{i,j+1} + cW_{i+1,j+1} \quad i = 1, \ldots, (n-1)$$

$$j = 1, \ldots, m \qquad (8)$$

where

$a = [\frac{1}{2}(\sigma/h)^2 - \frac{1}{2}(r - \frac{1}{2}\sigma^2)/h]k,$

$b = [1 - (\sigma/h)^2 k],$ and

$c = [\frac{1}{2}(\sigma/h)^2 + \frac{1}{2}(r - 1/2\sigma^2)/h]k.$

For any given value of j, (8) allows us to solve for $W_{i,j}$ ($i = 1, \ldots, n-1$) in terms of $W_{i,j+1}$. The extreme values of $W_{i,j}$, $W_{o,j}$, and $W_{n,j}$, must be given by the boundary conditions to the problem.[1] Then, given the values of $W_{i,j}$ corresponding to the maturity of the contingent claim, we may solve (8) recursively for all values of $W_{i,j}$.

Notice that the coefficients of (8) are independent of i and that $a + b + c = 1$. For the stability of the explicit solution, it is necessary that the coefficients of (8) be nonnegative (McCracken and Dorn [10]). While appropriate choice of h and k may guarantee this for (8), the corresponding coefficients of the explicit approximation to (1) depend on i, and will be negative for sufficiently large values of i, so that this explicit finite difference approximation may not be applied to the untransformed equation (1).

For the nonnegativity condition to be satisfied, it is necessary that h and k be chosen so that

$$h \le \sigma^2/|(r - \frac{1}{2}\sigma^2)|$$

and

$$k \le \sigma^2/(r - \frac{1}{2}\sigma^2)^2. \qquad (9)$$

If the conditions (9) are satisfied, the coefficients of the RHS of (8) may be interpreted as probabilities since they are nonnegative. Writing p^- for a, p for b and p^+ for c, (8) becomes

$$W_{i,j} = \frac{1}{(1 + rk)} p^- W_{i-1,j+1} + pW_{i,j+1} + p^+ W_{i+1,j+1} \qquad (10)$$

Thus the value of the contingent claim at time instant j may be regarded as given by its expected value at $(j+1)$ discounted at the riskless rate, r. The expected value of the claim at the next instant is obtained by assuming that y, the logarithm of the stock price, follows the jump process

$$
dy = \begin{cases} h & p^+ \\ 0 & p \\ -h & p^- \end{cases} \tag{11}
$$

which is formally identical to a jump process discussed by Cox and Ross [6, equation (8)], where $\mu = 0$. The local mean and variance of (11) are

$$
E[dy] = h[p^+ - p^-]
$$
$$
= (r - \tfrac{1}{2}\sigma^2)k. \tag{12}
$$
$$
V[dy] = h^2[p^+ + p^-] - (E[dy])^2
$$
$$
= \sigma^2 k - (r - \tfrac{1}{2}\sigma^2)^2 k^2. \tag{13}
$$

Thus the diffusion limit of (11) is

$$
dy = (r - \tfrac{1}{2}\sigma^2)\,dt + \sigma\,dz \tag{14}
$$

where dz is a Gauss-Wiener process with $E[dz] = 0, E[dz^2] = dt$; this implies that the diffusion limit of dS is

$$
\frac{dS}{S} = r\,dt + \sigma\,dz. \tag{15}
$$

Now, as Cox and Ross [6] have pointed out, if a riskless arbitrage portfolio can be established between the contingent claim and the underlying asset, the resulting valuation equation is preference free. Therefore we may value the contingent claim under any convenient assumption about preferences, in particular under the assumption of risk neutrality, which implies that the diffusion process for the underlying asset is (15) and that the value of the contingent claim is obtained by discounting its expected future value at the riskless rate of interest as is done in (10).

We have established therefore that the explicit finite difference approximation to the Black-Scholes differential equation is equivalent to making the permissible assumption of risk-neutrality and approximating the diffusion process (15) by the jump process (11). Notice however that the variance of the approximating jump process given by (13) is a downward biased estimate of the variance of the approximated diffusion process (14). The bias is equal to the square of the expected jump, $(r - \frac{1}{2}\sigma^2)k$. Using the stability condition (9), the upper bound on this bias is σ^4.

The recursive valuation equation (10) may be regarded as a type of numerical integration where the probabilities are taken, not from the normal density function, but from a jump process, (11), approximating the Gauss-Wiener process (14). This approach is almost identical to the numerical integration procedure employed by Parkinson [13], who also approximated the normal distribution by a related but different three-point distribution.

III The Implicit Finite Difference Approximation

The implicit finite difference approximation to (7) is obtained by approximating the partial derivatives by the finite differences

$$W_{yy} = (W_{i+1,j} - 2W_{i,j} + W_{i-1,j})/h^2 \tag{16}$$

$$W_y = (W_{i+1,j} - W_{i-1,j})/2h \tag{17}$$

$$W_t = (W_{i,j+1} - W_{i,j})/k \tag{18}$$

so that the differential equation is written in finite difference form as:

$$aW_{i-1,j} + bW_{i,j} + cW_{i+1,j} = (1 - rk)W_{i,j+1} \quad i = 1, \ldots n$$
$$j = 1, \ldots m \tag{19}$$

where

$$a = [-\tfrac{1}{2}(\sigma/h)^2 + \tfrac{1}{2}(r - \tfrac{1}{2}\sigma^2)/h]k \tag{20}$$

$$b = 1 + (\sigma/h)^2 k \tag{21}$$

$$c = [-\tfrac{1}{2}(\sigma/h)^2 - \tfrac{1}{2}(r - \tfrac{1}{2}\sigma^2)/h]k \tag{22}$$

For any value of j, (19) constitutes a system of n equations in the $(n+2)$ unknowns $W_{i,j}$ ($i = 0, 1, \ldots, n+1$). To complete the system, it is necessary to introduce two boundary conditions. Assume that these are given by knowing $W_{0,j}$ and $W_{n+1,j}$:

$$W_{0,j} = \alpha_j \tag{23}$$

$$W_{n+1,j} = \beta_j \tag{24}$$

Then we may eliminate $W_{0,j}$ and $W_{n+1,j}$ from the first and last equations of (19) to obtain:

$$bW_{1,j} + cW_{2,j} \qquad\qquad = (1 - rk)W_{1,j+1} - a\alpha_j = f_1$$

$$-\ -\ \circ\ \circ\ \circ\ -\ -$$

$$aW_{i-1,j} + bW_{i,j} + cW_{i+1,j} = (1 - rk)W_{i,j+1} \qquad\qquad = f_i \qquad\qquad (25)$$

$$-\ -\ \circ\ \circ\ \circ\ -\ -$$

$$aW_{n-1,j} + bW_{n,j} = (1 - rk)W_{n,j+1} - c\beta_j = f_n$$

This system of equations may be written in matrix form as

$$\underline{\underline{A}}\,\underline{W} = \underline{f}. \qquad\qquad (26)$$

And by recursive solution of (26), knowing the values of $W_{i,j}$ at maturity, we generate the whole set of $W_{i,j}$ values. Note that since $\underline{\underline{A}}$ is independent of j, the matrix must be inverted only once, so that each time step simply involves the multiplication of a vector by this matrix inverse. This is admittedly a more complex calculation than was required for the explicit solution: on the other hand, the implicit solution procedure is potentially more accurate.

Our objective is to demonstrate that the elements of this matrix inverse may be viewed as discounted probabilities, and that therefore the implicit solution procedure generates successively earlier value of $W_{i,j}$ by discounting the expected value at the end of the next time increment assuming risk neutral preferences.

The simple form of the matrix, $\underline{\underline{A}}$, suggests the use of Gaussian elimination to solve the equation system. We proceed by multiplying the second equation of (25) by (b/a) and subtracting from it the first equation to obtain a transformed second equation from which $W_{1,j}$ has been eliminated: we proceed in this way, multiplying each equation by (b/a) and subtracting from it its transformed predecessor, obtaining the transformed system of equations:

$$b_1^* W_{1,j} + c_1^* W_{2,j} \qquad\qquad\qquad = f_1^*$$

$$b_2^* W_{2,j} + c_2^* W_{3,j} \qquad\qquad\qquad = f_2^*$$

$$-\ -\ \circ\ \circ\ \circ\ -\ -$$

$$b_{n-1}^* W_{n-1,j} + c_{n-1}^* W_{n,j} = f_{n-1}^*$$

$$b_n^* W_{n,j} = f_n^* \qquad\qquad (27)$$

In the first equation

$$b_1^* = b, c_1^* = c, f_1^* = f_1$$

and in general

$$b_i^* = (b/a)b_{i-1}^* - c_{i-1}^* \tag{28}$$

$$c_i^* = (c/a)b_{i-1}^* \tag{29}$$

$$f_i^* = (f_i/a)b_{i-1}^* - f_{i-1}^*. \tag{30}$$

Substituting for c_{i-1}^* in (28) from (29), we obtain the difference equation for b_i^*:

$$b_i^* = (b/a)b_{i-1}^* - (c/a)b_{i-2}^*. \tag{31}$$

The solution to this difference equation, given the initial conditions $b_1^* = b, c_1^* = c$ is:

$$b_i^* = (a^2/\sqrt{b^2 - 4ac})(\lambda_1^{i+1} - \lambda_2^{i+1}) \tag{32}$$

where

$$\lambda_1 = (b + \sqrt{b^2 - 4ac})/2a \tag{33}$$

$$\lambda_2 = (b - \sqrt{b^2 - 4ac})/2a. \tag{34}$$

Then, substituting for b_{i-1}^* from (32) in (29), c_i^* may be written as:

$$c_i^* = (ac/\sqrt{b^2 - 4ac})(\lambda_1^i - \lambda_2^i). \tag{35}$$

The expression for f_i^* is obtained by substituting for b_i^* in (30) and solving recursively for $f_2^*, f_3^* \ldots$ This yields

$$f_i^* = (a/\sqrt{b^2 - 4ac}) \sum_{j=1}^{i} L_j f_j (-1)^{(i-j)} \tag{36}$$

where

$$L_j = \lambda_1^j - \lambda_2^j.$$

The matrix inversion is completed by solving the system of equations (27) starting with the last equation. Define $Z_i = \sum_{j=1}^{i} L_j f_j (-1)^{(i-j)}$.
Then

$$W_{n,j} = f_n^*/b_n^* = Z_n/aL_n$$

$$W_{n-1,j} = \frac{Z_{n-1}}{aL_n} - \frac{c}{a^2} \frac{L_{n-1}Z_n}{L_nL_{n+1}}$$

$$- - \circ \circ \circ - - .$$

$$W_{n-q,j} = \frac{L_{n-q}}{a} \left[\frac{Z_{n-q}}{L_{n-q}L_{n-q+1}} - \frac{c}{a} \frac{Z_{n-q+1}}{L_{n-q+1}L_{n-q+2}} \right.$$
$$\left. + \frac{c^2}{a^2} \frac{Z_{n-q+2}}{L_{n-q+2}L_{n-q+3}} + \cdots - + \left(\frac{-c}{a}\right)^q \frac{Z_n}{L_nL_{n+1}} \right] \tag{37}$$

$$- - \circ \circ \circ - - .$$

Set $(n-q) = i$ and collect coefficients of $W_{i,j+1}$ in (37), recalling that $f_j = (1 - rk)W_{i,j+1}$. Denoting the coefficient of $W_{i,j+1}$ by $(1-rk)p_i$, we have:

$$p_i = \frac{L_i^2}{a} \sum_{j=1}^{n} (c/a)^{j-i}(1/L_jL_{j+1}) \tag{38}$$

$$p_{i-q} = (-1)^q \frac{L_iL_{i-q}}{a} \sum_{j=i}^{n} (c/a)^{j-i}(1/L_jL_{j+1}) \tag{39}$$

$$p_{i+q} = (-1)^q \frac{L_iL_{i+q}}{a} \sum_{j=i+q}^{n} (c/a)^{j-(i+q)}(1/L_jL_{j+1}). \tag{40}$$

The values of p_{i+q} ($q = 1-i, \ldots, -1, 0, +1, \ldots n-i$) are the elements of the ith row of $\underline{\underline{A}}^{-1}$. We shall now show that as the boundaries become indefinitely remote p_{i+q} may be interpreted as the probability that the logarithm of the stock price will jump by qh. As the lower boundary becomes remote $i \to \infty$, while $(n-i) + \infty$ as the upper boundary becomes remote.

First note that

$$\frac{L_i}{L_{i+q}} = \frac{\lambda_1^i - \lambda_2^i}{\lambda_1^{i+q} - \lambda_2^{i+q}} = \frac{1}{\lambda_1^q} \frac{1 - (\lambda_2/\lambda_1)^i}{1 - (\lambda_2/\lambda_1)^{i+q}} \tag{41}$$

and that since $|\lambda_2/\lambda_1| < 1$

$$\lim_{i \to \infty} \frac{L_i}{L_{i+q}} = \frac{1}{\lambda_1^q}. \tag{42}$$

Hence as $(n-i)$, $i \to \infty$,[2]

$$\underset{\substack{i \to \infty \\ n-i \to \infty}}{\mathrm{Lim}} \; p_i = p_o^* = \frac{1}{a}\left[\frac{1}{\lambda_1} + \frac{c}{a}\frac{1}{\lambda_1^3} + \frac{c^2}{a^2}\frac{1}{\lambda_1^5}\cdots\right]$$

$$= \lambda_1/(a\lambda_1^2 - c) \tag{43}$$

and from (38) and (39)

$$\underset{\substack{i \to \infty \\ n-i \to \infty}}{\mathrm{Lim}} \; p_{i-q} = p_{-q}^* = \left(-\frac{1}{\lambda_1}\right)^q p_1^*, \quad \text{for } q = 1,\ldots,\infty \tag{44}$$

$$\underset{i \to \infty}{\mathrm{Lim}} \; p_{i+q} = p_q^* = \left(\frac{-c}{a\lambda_1}\right)^q p_i^*, \quad \text{for } q = 1,\ldots,\infty. \tag{45}$$

Consider the sum of the p_q^* $(q = -\infty,\ldots,+\infty)$, S:

$$S = p_o^*\left[\left(1 - \frac{c}{a\lambda_1} + \left(\frac{c}{a\lambda_1}\right)^2 - \left(\frac{c}{a\lambda_1}\right)^3\cdots\right) - \frac{1}{\lambda_1}\left(1 - \frac{1}{\lambda_1} + \left(\frac{1}{\lambda_1}\right)^2\cdots\right)\right]$$

$$= p_o^*\left[\frac{a\lambda_1}{a\lambda_1 + c} - \frac{1}{1 - \lambda_1}\right] = p_o^*\left[\frac{a\lambda_1^2 - c}{(1 + \lambda_1)(a\lambda_1 + c)}\right] \tag{46}$$

and, substituting for p_o^* from (43),

$$S = \frac{\lambda_1}{(1 + \lambda_1)(a\lambda_1 + c)}. \tag{47}$$

But since λ_1 is a root of the auxiliary equation of (31) and $b = 1 - (a + c)$, $(1 + \lambda_1)(a\lambda_1 + c) = \lambda_1$ so that $S = 1$. Thus the sum of the weights p_q^* $(q = -\infty,\ldots,+\infty)$ equals 1.

Moreover, each element p_q^* is nonnegative so long as[3]

$$h^2 \le \sigma^4/(r - \tfrac{1}{2}\sigma^2)^2. \tag{48}$$

Thus since the p_q^* are nonnegative and sum to unity, they may be interpreted as probabilities and we have

$$W_{i,j} = (1 - rk)\sum_{q=-\infty}^{\infty} p_q^* W_{i+q,j+1}$$

$$\simeq \frac{1}{1 + rk}\sum_{q=-\infty}^{\infty} p_q^* W_{i+q,j+1}. \tag{49}$$

Again, the value of the contingent claim at time instant j may be regarded as given by the expected value of its value at $(j+1)$ discounted at the riskless rate, r. In this case the expected value of the claim at the next instant is obtained by assuming that y, the logarithm of the stock price, follows the generalized jump process

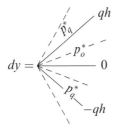

The locan mean and variance of this process are shown in the Appendix to be given by

$$E[dy] = (r - \tfrac{1}{2}\sigma^2)k \tag{50}$$

$$V[dy] = \sigma^2 k + (r - \tfrac{1}{2}\sigma^2)^2 k^2. \tag{51}$$

Taking the diffusion limit as $k \to 0$, y again follows the stochastic differential equation (14) which again implies that the stochastic process for S is (15). Notice that for finite k the variance of the jump process approximation to the diffusion process is biased upwards by the square of the expected size of the jump. This suggests that the accuracy of the implicit method could be improved by adjusting the variance used in (19) by subtracting from the true variance the square of the expected change in the logarithm of the underlying asset value obtained under the assumption of risk neutrality.

Thus the implicit finite difference approximation to the log transform of the Black-Scholes differential equation (7) is also equivalent to approximating the diffusion process by a jump process. In this case the jump process is a generalized one which allows for the possibility that the stock price will jump to an infinity of possible future values rather than just three. It would appear that this "more realistic" approximation would result in more accurate determination of the value of the contingent claim, but this conjecture must wait upon detailed numerical analysis.

IV Summary

In this chapter we have established that the coefficients of the difference equation approximation to the Black-Scholes partial differential equation correspond to the probabilities of a jump process approximation to the underlying diffusion process. The simpler explicit finite difference approximation corresponds to a three-point jump process of the type discussed by Cox and Ross [6], while the more complex implicit finite difference approximation corresponds to a generalized jump process to an infinity of possible points.

Appendix

1. Condition for nonnegativity of weights in implicit solution. (43) can also be written as

$$p_o^* = \left(b + \sqrt{b^2 - 4ac}\right) \Big/ \left(b^2 - 4ac + b\sqrt{b^2 - 4ac}\right)$$

but from (21) $b > 0$, and from (20), (21) and (22) $b^2 - 4ac > 0$. Therefore $p_o^* > 0$.

Then from (44) $p_{-q}^* > 0$, iff $\lambda_1 < 0$ which from (33) requires that $a < 0$. Then from (45), $p_q^* > 0$, also iff $c/a > 0$, so that c must also be negative. From (20) and (22), c and a are negative if and only if (48) is satisfied.

2. Mean and variance of the generalized Jump Process.

$$E(dy) = h\left[\sum_{q=1}^{\infty} q p_q^* - \sum_{q=1}^{\infty} q p_{-q}^*\right].$$

Substituting for p_q^* and p_{-q}^* from (44) and (45),

$$E(dy) = h\left[-\frac{c}{a\lambda_1}\left(1 - 2\frac{c}{a\lambda_1} + 3\left(\frac{c}{a\lambda_1}\right)^2 - \cdots\right) + \frac{1}{\lambda_1}\left(1 - \frac{2}{\lambda_1} + \frac{3}{\lambda_1^2} - \cdots\right)\right]p_i^*.$$

Summing and using (43),

$$E(dy) = h\left[-\frac{ac\lambda_1}{(a\lambda_1 + c)}2 + \frac{\lambda_1}{(1 + \lambda_1)}2\right]\frac{\lambda_1}{a\lambda_1^2 - c}$$

$$E(dy) = (a - c)h = (r - \tfrac{1}{2}\sigma^2)k.$$

$$V(dy) = \sum_{q=0}^{\infty} p_{-q}^*(-qh - (a - c)h)^2 + \sum_{q=1}^{\infty} p_q^*(qh - (a - c)h)^2$$

$$= h^2\left[\sum_{q=0}^{\infty} q^2 p_{-q}^* + \sum_{q=1}^{\infty} q^2 p_q^* - (a - c)^2\right].$$

Summing the series and substituting for p_o^* as above we obtain:

$$V(dy) = h^2\left[\left\{\frac{\lambda_1(1 - \lambda_1)}{(1 + \lambda_1)^3} - \frac{ac\lambda_1(a\lambda_1 - c)}{(a\lambda_1 + c)^3}\right\}\frac{\lambda_1}{a\lambda_1^2 - c} - (a - c)^2\right].$$

Simplifying yields:

$$V(dy) = -h^2[(a + c)b + 4ac]$$

and, substituting for a, b and c, we obtain (51).

Acknowledgments

The authors gratefully acknowledge financial support from The S. S. Huebner Foundation, The Wharton School, University of Pennsylvania. They also thank Phelim Boyle for helpful comments.

Notes

1. Note that we are implicitly assuming that the lower boundary condition is of the form $W(0, t) = Z_t$. More generally the boundary condtion may be $W(i_j h, t) = Z_t$; this will simply change the range of i in (8) without changing anything essential.

2. Since λ_1 and λ_2 are the roots of the auxiliary equation of the difference equation (31), $\lambda_1 \lambda_2 = c/a$. Therefore, $|c/a\lambda_1^2| = |\lambda_2/\lambda_1| < 1$.

3. For a proof see Appendix.

References

[1] Black, F., and M. Scholes. "The Pricing of Options and Corporate Liabilities." *Journal of Political Economy*, Vol. 81 (1973), pp. 637–659.

[2] Boyle, P. "Options: A Monte Carlo Approach." *Journal of Financial Economics* (1976).

[3] Brennan, M., and E. Schwartz. "The Pricing of Equity-Linked Life Insurance Policies with an Asset Value Guarantee." *Journal of Financial Economics*, Vol. 3 (1976), pp. 195–214.

[4] ———. "Convertible Bonds: Valuation and Optimal Strategies for Call and Conversion." *Journal of Finance* (1976).

[5] ———. "The Valuation of American Put Options." *Journal of Finance* (1976).

[6] Cox, J. C., and S. A. Ross. "The Valuation of Options for Alternative Stochastic Processes." *Journal of Financial Economics*, Vol. 3 (1976), pp. 145–166.

[7] ———. "A Survey of Some New Results in Financial Option Pricing Theory." *Journal of Finance*, Vol. 31 (1976), pp. 383–402.

[8] Ingersoll, J. "A Theoretical and Empirical Investigation of the Dual Purpose Funds: An Application of Contingent Claims Analysis." *Journal of Financial Economics*, Vol. 3 (1976), pp. 83–124.

[9] ———. "A Contingent Claims Valuation of Convertible Bonds." Unpublished Manuscript, University of Chicago (1976).

[10] McCracken, D., and W. Dorn. "Numerical Methods and Fortran Programming." New York: John Wiley and Sons, Inc. (1969).

[11] Merton, R. C. "Theory of Rational Option Pricing." *Bell Journal of Economics and Management Science*, Vol. 4 (1973), pp. 141–183.

[12] ———. "On the Pricing of Corporate Debt: The Risk Structure of Interest Rates." *Journal of Finance*, Vol. 29 (1974), pp. 449–470.

[13] Parkinson, M. "Option Pricing: The American Put." *Journal of Business* (1976).

26 Valuation by Approximation: A Comparison of Alternative Option Valuation Techniques

Robert Geske and Kuldeep Shastri

I Introduction

Recent advances in the area of asset pricing theory have generated many partial equilibrium conditions describing the "no arbitrage" paths for asset prices. Assumptions about the effects of information on asset price changes lead to valuation models based on a variety of stochastic processes. Examples are the constant-variance diffusion model of Black and Scholes [3], the pure jump model of Cox and Ross [10], the combined jump-diffusion model of Merton [28], and the changing variance diffusion model of Geske [17]. In these papers, analytic solutions exist.[1] However, if complex payout or exercise contingencies are present, analytic solutions are rare. One example is valuing an American put on a dividend-paying stock. The works of Parkinson [28], Brennan and Schwartz [5], and Cox, Ross, and Rubinstein [11] demonstrate examples of different approximation approaches to the American put problem.

Recently, Geske and Johnson [22] have presented an analytic solution to the American put problem, with or without dividends. However, many valuation problems have no known analytic solutions. Some examples are callable and convertible coupon bonds, insurance contracts, and the term structure of interest rate models for bond valuation. Because no arbitrage partial equilibrium conditions can be derived, many of these problems may be solved by numerical approximation. The purpose of this chapter is to provide a concise comparison of the approximation techniques that financial economists have used for one-dimensional valuation problems when no analytic solutions exist. Although much of the intuition presented here would carry over for higher-dimensional problems, the exact analysis and numbers would be different.

In Section II, both valuation and approximation principles are first described. Several numerical methods, including the Monte Carlo, binomial, and finite difference techniques, are discussed. The stability, rate of convergence, and accuracy conditions are described and compared.

Section III presents a comparison of the binomial and a variety of finite difference techniques based on both accuracy and efficiency criteria. *It is important for the reader to realize that results different from those presented here may arise from the use of different computer hardware and/or software.* Although comparisons and discrepancies are sensitive to the particular implementation schemes, it will be shown that fundamental differences do stand out. For example, the pure binomial approximation appears to dominate all the finite difference schemes when either there are no payouts or a small number of options are being valued. However, for fixed-cash payouts or when valuing a large number of options, the explicit finite difference approach with logarithmic transformation appears to dominate. Section IV summarizes the paper and presents conclusions.

II Valuation and Approximation Principles

The Black-Scholes partial differential equation is valid for many significant valuation problems where no analytic solutions have been found. This has led to considerable research employing numerical methods to approximate solutions. The next few pages of this paper attempt to explain some important principles and techniques for valuation by approximation.

Although the focus of this paper is on diffusion processes, different assumptions about the effects of information arrival on the changes in asset prices imply different stochastic processes; and, hence, different partial equilibrium conditions. Efficient markets imply the rapid reflection of information in asset prices. Thus, the arrival of "new" information often will be accompanied by price changes. If the underlying asset is assumed to follow a diffusion process, then price changes are continuous. Alternatively, if the underlying asset is assumed to follow a jump process, price changes are discontinuous. In the diffusion case, information is thought to arrive in a smooth, continuous fashion; price changes can have either a constant or a changing variance. The jump process signifies that the information arrival is discontinuous. A diffusion process implies that asset price changes are either Normally or lognormally distributed, while a jump process implies a Poisson distribution. Casual empiricism leads one to suspect that a combined diffusion-jump process is generating the data.

The no-arbitrage partial equilibrium conditions have been derived for the pure diffusion, pure jump, and combined processes, and some analytic solutions have been found for each case. However, in many complex but realistic problems, numerical methods must be employed to approximate the value of the asset. There is a branch of mathematics devoted to this topic and from this work financial economists have to date employed Monte Carlo simulation [4], finite differences ([5] and [6]), numerical integration [28], and binomial processes [11]. This has by no means exhausted the many methods of solution available. Collocation, finite elements, and integral transform techniques are other approaches. [2] In the next subsections, some of the techniques currently in use are described and compared in terms of truncation error, stability, and convergence. The primary focus is on the binomial and finite difference approaches applied to one-dimensional, lognormal-diffusion option valuation problems.

The constant-variance diffusion approach to asset price changes has led to the now well-known parabolic partial differential equation for option valuation. [3] This equation is

$$0 = D + V_t + \frac{\sigma^2}{2} S^2 V_{ss} + (rS - D)V_s - rV \tag{1}$$

where

V = Value of the option

S = Value of the state variable (i.e., stock price)

σ = Standard deviation of stock returns

r = Continuously compounded risk-free rate of interest

D = Dividend payout (continuous)

t = Time to expiration

and subscripts denote partial derivatives. Equation (1) is subject to a variety of boundaries regarding expiration, exercise, and payout conditions. Expiration boundary conditions differentiate put options, which give the right to sell, from call options, which give the right to buy the underlying stock S for the option's exercise price X. Holders of put options receive the maximum of the exercise price minus the stock price or zero at expiration,

$$P(S,0) = \max(X - S, 0) \tag{2}$$

and holders of call options receive the maximum of the stock price minus the exercise price or zero at expiration,

$$C(S,0) = \max(0, S - X). \tag{3}$$

If the option is American and can be exercised at any instant, the boundary conditions must be checked to see if for every possible stock price at each instant, the option is worth more held than exercised (i.e., dead or alive). Thus, if t^- is the instant before exercise and t^+ the instant after, then for put options,

$$P(S, t^-) = \max(X - S, P(S, t^+)) \tag{4}$$

and for call options,

$$C(S, t^-) = \max(C(S, t^+), S - X). \tag{5}$$

If the firm pays discrete cash dividends to stockholders at quarterly intervals, then at these ex-dividend dates occuring during the life of the option, the stock price must be reduced by the amount of the dividend to eliminate riskless arbitrage opportunities. If t^- is the instant before the ex-dividend date and t^+ is the instant after, then (in the absence of taxes)

$$S(t^-) = S(t^+) + D. \tag{6}$$

Merton [25] has shown that the exercise boundary condition for put options must be checked at every instant, but that call options may be exercised only at the ex-dividend dates. This implies that because more checks of exercise conditions are necessary, put options will be more expensive to value numerically than call options. Section III confirms this implication by showing that all approximation techniques are more efficient for call options than for put options.

The Black-Scholes partial differential equation has variable coefficients that make it more difficult to solve numerically than one with constant coefficients. Although an equation with variable coefficients can switch from a parabolic to either an elliptic or hyperbolic form, the Black-Scholes equation remains parabolic.[4] However, because the coefficients change as the state variables change with time, the approximation equations and stability conditions become more complex. Fortunately, Black and Scholes [3], Merton [25], and others have shown that by changing variables, equation (1) can be transformed into the following equation that has received considerable analytic and numerical analysis in the physical sciences

$$a\frac{\partial u}{\partial t} = \frac{\partial}{\partial x} k \frac{\partial u}{\partial x} \tag{7}$$

where a and k may be at least twice-differentiable functions of x and t. This equation may have variable coefficients and it could be nonlinear if a and k are allowed to vary with u as well as with x and t. To use established numerical schemes of high accuracy, equation (7) with variable coefficients can be converted into one with constant coefficients by making the following transformation

$$y = \int \frac{1}{k(x)} \, dx \tag{8}$$

whereupon (7) becomes

$$\frac{\partial u}{\partial t} = \frac{1}{ak} \frac{\partial^2 u}{\partial y^2}. \tag{9}$$

In terms of the original variable x, this transform scheme in y will have unequal spacing of the net points.[5] Brennan and Schwartz [6] and Mason [24] used a form of this transformation by substituting y-ln(S) into equation (1). Section III will reveal in dollars per option valued the efficiency gained by this transformation. The next sub-sections describe several alternative approximation techniques.

A   Approximation Techniques

There are a variety of techniques for approximating either the underlying stochastic process directly or the resultant partial differential equation. The classic Monte Carlo simulation or the binomial process are both approaches to approximating the stochastic process directly. It is known that a binomial distribution converges to a Normal and a Poisson distribution, depending on how the limits are taken.[6] A mixture of the two is also possible (See [12].). For the Monte Carlo method, a number of simulations can be drawn from a lognormal distribution, a Poisson distribution, or a combination of the two. Thus, both the Monte Carlo and the binomial approximations can be directly used for pure diffusion, pure jump, or jump-diffusion valuation models.

Conversely, once the underlying process is assumed, the partial equilibrium condition resulting from no-riskless-arbitrage often can be derived. If an analytic solution to the partial differential equation cannot be obtained, finite difference methods or numerical integration can be used to approximate the solution. These techniques also can be used for pure diffusion, pure jump, or combined jump-diffusion models.

All the approximation techniques are performed in a space-time hyperplane.[7] The stock price-time space is divided into a set of points in the (S, t) plane given by $S = i\Delta S$ and $t = j\Delta t$, where $i = 0, 1, 2, \ldots n$ and $j = 0, 1, 2, \ldots m$. This division results in a net (or grid or lattice) whose mesh size (or ratio) is determined by ΔS and Δt. In the transformed space, ΔS is replaced by Δx. The approximations to the put and call values given by V in equation (1) (and rewritten as P and C in equations (4) and (5)) would be $P(i\Delta S, j\Delta t)$ and $C(i\Delta S, j\Delta t)$, and are denoted by P_i^j or C_i^j. For the transformed argument in equation (9), $u(x, t) = u(i\Delta x, j\Delta t)$ is denoted u_i^j. Figure 26.1 depicts this (S, t) grid.

The increments ΔS (or Δx) and Δt are thought of as small and when considering limiting processes, they approach zero. In application, the step sizes are not zero, and they need not be equal. However, the step sizes must be chosen to ensure stable, accurate, and efficient convergence to the solution. The stock price and time solution space is bounded in both put and call option valuation problems. In the time dimension, the expiration date, t, determines the maximum time allowed. In the stock-price space, limited liability determines the lower absolute bound, $SMIN = 0$, and a derivative condition determines the necessary upper bound, $SMAX$. For puts, $SMAX$ is the stock price above which $\partial P/\partial S$ approaches zero, and for calls $SMAX$ is the stock price above which $\partial C/\partial S$ approaches one.[8] (See figure 26.1).

In the direct approximations of the underlying stochastic process, these upper and lower stock-price bounds may or may not be reached. In the Monte Carlo simula-

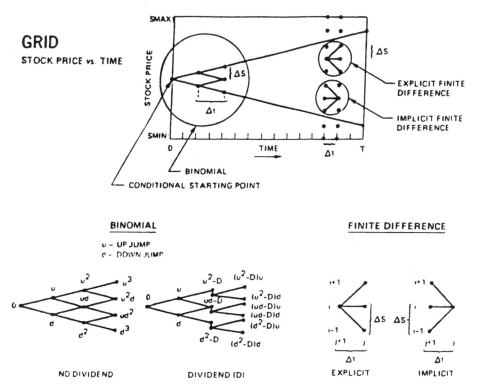

Figure 26.1
Grid of stock price vs. time

tion, achieving the bounds would depend on the number of simulations, and for the binomial process this would depend on the size of the up and down jumps and on the number of jumps or trials. The time step-size is defined as $k = \Delta t = t/m$. The range of stock prices in the binomial process is determined by the size of the up and down jumps, which depend on the estimate of the variance of the underlying stock price changes.[9] In the binomial process, the net is a cone and selecting the time step determines the number of stock price steps at any time step and thus the mesh in the stock price-time net. (See figure 26.1.)

For finite difference approximations, the time step is similarly defined by expiration. The stock price step size is defined as $h = \Delta S = (SMAX\text{-}SMIN)/n$. The finite difference net is rectangular (see figure 26.1) and selecting the mesh size is often critical for ensuring stable, accurate convergence to the solution. The critical mesh ratio is known to be sensitive to the type of differencing procedure employed. Before discussing this, a brief description is presented of the Monte Carlo technique.

The Monte Carlo valuation method [4], relies on the observation by Cox and Ross [10] that when a riskless hedge can be formed, the option can be valued by discounting the expected value at expiration by the risk-free rate. The accuracy of this method depends on the number N of simulation paths used to form the distribution of stock prices at the expiration date. Generally, the accuracy increases as $1/\sqrt{N}$, so the computation cost approximately doubles as the error diminishes by about 70 percent. The Monte Carlo method can handle complex payout and exercise contingencies. However, when valuing American options, m lognormal distributions, one for each time step, must be approximated rather than just approximating one terminal distribution. Because a full set of sample paths is generated, conditioned on the starting point, multiple options for a variety of exercise prices and expiration dates can be valued. The conditional starting point makes the Monte Carlo method less efficient for valuing options for multiple stock prices.

The finite difference techniques analyze the partial differential equations (1) or (9) by using discrete estimates of the changes in the options value for small changes in time or the underlying stock price to form difference equations as approximations to the continuous partial derivatives. There are infinitely many ways to estimate the changes in the option's value with respect to time and the stock price. Forward, central, and backward differences, along with complex averages of them, can be used.[10] Although the variety of difference choices is large, all of them lead to solutions that can be classified as either explicit or implicit. In the explicit class, each unknown option price at any node can be solved explicitly in terms of previous known option price nodes, while in the implicit class a set of simultaneous equations must be solved.

An explicit finite difference approximation to equation (9) is

$$\frac{u_i^{j+1} - u_i^j}{\Delta t} = c \frac{u_{i+1}^j - 2u_i^j + u_{i-1}^j}{(\Delta x)^2} + O(\Delta x)^2 + O(\Delta t). \tag{10}$$

An implicit approximation to equation (9) is

$$\frac{u_i^{j+1} - u_i^j}{\Delta t} = c \frac{u_{i+1}^{j+1} - 2u_i^{j+1} + u_{i-1}^{j+1}}{(\Delta x)^2} + O(\Delta x)^2 + O(\Delta t) \tag{11}$$

where i and j denote stock price and time differences, respectively. Equations (10) and (11) use forward and backward time differences, respectively, relative to the time t

(either j or $j+1$) that the stock price differences are expressed. In this notation, c is a transformation coefficient and $O(\cdot)$ represents the order of errors in the stock price and time approximations. Note that in the explicit equation (10), the unknown transformed option price at time $j+1$, u_i^{j+1}, can be solved for directly in terms of known prices at time j. However, in the implicit equation (11), the unknown transformed option price u_i^{j+1} depends on other adjacent and unknown prices at time $j+1$, and thus, a set of simultaneous equations must be solved. Figure 26.1 illustrates this distinction between explicit and implicit methods.

Figure 26.1 also shows that the binomial method is simply a form of the explicit finite difference scheme where the option price at stock price step i and time step $j+1$ is an explicit function of three previous option prices at time step j and at the stock price steps $i-1$, i, and $i+1$, respectively. In the coincident binomial technique, if a time step is skipped, then the current option price depends on three previous option prices (instead of two), exactly as in the explicit finite difference technique. Thus, the binomial technique is a special case of the explicit finite difference scheme with the major remaining distinction being its conditional starting point.

The conditional starting point for the binomial process allows for efficiency when a single option value is computed because the nodes in a cone rather than in a rectangle need to be evaluated. However, if option values for a variety of initial stock prices are desired, the binomial technique must be re-executed and becomes expensive. As an alternative to re-executing the binomial process for each initial stock price, two or more binomial processes could evolve simultaneously. Efficiency could be enhanced by eliminating near or overlapping stock price nodes. In the limit, as the number of initial stock prices became large, the binomial technique would be exactly equivalent to the explicit finite difference scheme. However, as Section III demonstrates, the pure binomial method with its conditional starting point will not be as efficient as the explicit finite difference technique when multiple options are valued for a variety of initial stock prices.

Stability of the approximation scheme in all nets of mesh $(\Delta t, \Delta x)$ often requires a specific ratio of time step to the square of stock price step, termed the mesh ratio R, defined as[11]

$$R \equiv \frac{\Delta t}{\Delta x^2}. \tag{12}$$

The explicit equation (10) can be written in terms of the mesh ratio as

$$u_i^{j+1} = q u_{i+1}^j + (1-2q) u_i^j + q u_{i-1}^j \tag{13}$$

where $q \equiv c(\Delta t/(\Delta x)^2) = cR$.

Note that if the mesh ratio R is selected to insure that $q = 1/2$, equation (13) is simplified. In matrix notation, for any stock price i, for all j,

$$u^{j+1} = Au^j \tag{14}$$

where A is a tridiagonal coefficient matrix and u^j and u^{j+1} are the successively calculated values of transformed option prices.

The implicit equation (11) can similarly be written as

$$-qu_{i+1}^{j+1} + (1 + 2q)u_i^{j+1} - qu_{i-1}^{j+1} = u_i^j. \tag{15}$$

In matrix notation, for any stock price i, for all j,

$$Bu^{j+1} = u^j. \tag{16}$$

To solve (16) for u^{j+1}, the matrix B must be inverted to yield $u^{j+1} = B^{-1}u^j$.

A general family of difference systems can be considered by taking a weighted average of the right-hand sides of the explicit and implicit methods in equations (10) and (11). If $g(x)$ is any function of x, define the differential operator ϕ so that $(\phi g)_i$ yields the central difference $g((i+1)\Delta x) - g((i-1)\Delta x)$; then the second differential, $(\phi^2 g)_i$, denotes $g((i+1)\Delta x) - 2g(i\Delta x) + g((i-1)\Delta x)$. With this notation, consider the difference system

$$\frac{u_i^{j+1} - u_i^j}{\Delta t} = \frac{\theta(\phi^2 u)_i^{j+1} + (1 - \theta)(\phi^2 u)_i^j}{(\Delta x)^2} \tag{17}$$

where θ is a constant in the interval $0 \leq \theta \leq 1$. When $\theta = 0$, the system is explicit in the form of equation (10); and when θ is not zero, the system is implicit, equivalent to the pure implicit form of equation (11) when $\theta = 1$. (The popular Crank-Nicholson scheme is $\theta = 1/2$.)[12]

Equation (17) can be written as

$$-qu_{i+1}^{j+1} + (h + 2q)u_i^{j+1} - qu_{i-1}^{j+1} = q\theta hu_{i+1}^j + (h - 2q\theta h)u_i^j + q\theta hu_{i-1}^j \tag{18}$$

where $h \equiv 1/(1 - \theta)$. In matrix notation, for any stock price i, for all j,

$$Mu^{j+1} = Nu^j \tag{19}$$

where M and N are tridiagonal coefficient matrices of dimension $(n \times n)$. Thus, to solve a general family of finite difference schemes requires the inversion of the matrix M. If M^{-1} exists, equation (19) can be written as

$$u^{j+1} = M^{-1}Nu^j \equiv Gu^j. \tag{20}$$

The next few pages demonstrate that the truncation error, stability, and convergence properties of this general family of finite difference schemes depend upon the eigenvalues of the general $(n \times n)$ matrix G often called the amplification matrix. Note that the coefficients in equation (18) are the elements of the amplification matrix G and are dependent on q, a function of the mesh ratio. Thus, the eigenvalues of the amplification matrix will be sensitive to the mesh ratio.

B Approximation Errors, Stability, and Convergence

If u_i^j in equation (9) is an exact solution and $\bar{u}(i\Delta x, j\Delta t)$ is an approximation, then the approximation error is termed $e_i^j = u_i^j - \bar{u}_i^j$, at the point $x = i\Delta x$, $t = j\Delta t$, $i = 1, \ldots, n$, $j = 1, \ldots, m$. If the errors at each stage of the approximation grow, then the technique is not stable. Alternatively, if the errors become smaller at each time step, then the approximation converges. Larger time steps would imply fewer computations when moving from a future to a current stock price, but the errors propagated may grow and make the approximation unstable. Furthermore, the approximation may converge with finite error and the solution will not be exact. One way of evaluating the approximation is to examine the behavior of the error e_i^j as $j \to \infty$ for fixed $\Delta x, \Delta t$. A second and more interesting way is to examine the error e_i^j as the mesh is refined, so that Δx and $\Delta t \to 0$ for a fixed value of $m\Delta t$, $n\Delta x$. This is more valuable because the goal of an approximation is to force the error to zero in the limit so the solution becomes exact.

The mesh ratio, $R \equiv \Delta t/\Delta x^2$, obviously is instrumental to accurate and efficient approximations. Because, in the approximation limit, the number of calculations becomes infinite and the errors may be amplified without bound, a means of establishing proper stability and convergence criteria is necessary. There are numerous methods for approaching these problems.[13] Here an examination of the eigenvalues of the solution matrices in conjunction with the errors propagated will illustrate the proper restrictions on the mesh ratio.

1 Errors and Convergence To find the order of the error, assume that the exact solution of equation (9) has continuous partial derivatives. Then do a Taylor's series expansion of u_i^{j+1}, u_{i+1}^j, and u_{i-1}^j. Because u_i^j satisfies equation (9), $\partial u/\partial t$ can be replaced by $c(\partial^2 u/\partial x^2)$, and solving for (10) in terms of these expansions yields

$$\frac{u_i^{j+1} - u_i^j}{\Delta t} - c\frac{u_{i+1}^j - 2u_i^j + u_{i-1}^j}{(\Delta x)^2} = \left[\frac{1}{2}\Delta t\left(\frac{\partial^2 u}{\partial t^2}\right)_i^j - \frac{c}{12}(\Delta x)^2\left[\left(\frac{\partial^4 u}{\partial x^4}\right)_i^j\right]\right] + \cdots \qquad (21)$$

This result demonstrates that, as stated in (10), the error for the explicit method[14] is of order Δt and $(\Delta x)^2$ as $\Delta t, \Delta x \to 0$.

2 Stability Recall equation (20) demonstrated that a family of explicit or implicit finite difference schemes could be written as $u^{j+1} = Gu^j$, where G represents a general coefficient matrix and u^{j+1} and u^j are vectors whose components are successive values of transformed option prices. Using initial values u^0 to begin the solution process, the successive row calculations are $u^1 = Gu^0$, $u^2 = Gu^1 = G^2u^0, \ldots$, so that ultimately

$$u^j = Gu^{j-1} = G^j u^0$$

where the superscripts on G are exponents.

To trace the effects of errors through the calculations suppose that the approximation has an initial error so that $e^0 = u^0 - \bar{u}^0$. Then the successive approximate calculations are again $\bar{u}^j = G\bar{u}^{j-1} = G^j\bar{u}^{-0}$ and the errors would be propagated by the same algorithm as the prices, implying $e^j = u^j - \bar{u}^j = G^j e^0$. Thus, the initial error e^0 is "amplified" by the coefficient matrix G raised to the power of j.

Whether this error expands or contracts depends on the eigenvalues of G. To see this, note that in general the eigenvalues of these tridiagonalized matrices are distinct so the eigenvectors $z_1, \ldots, z_j$ are independent. Thus, the error vectors are simply linear combinations of the eigenvectors, and

$$e^0 = \sum_i c_i z_i$$

where the c's are constants. After j steps

$$e^j = Ge^{j-1} = \cdots = G^j e^0 = \sum_i G^j c_i z_i = \sum_i c_i \lambda_i^j z_i \tag{22}$$

where λ_i is the ith eigenvalue and $Gz_i = \lambda_i z_i$. Recall that each eigenvalue λ_i will be a function of the mesh ratio R. Obviously, if the magnitudes of all G's eigenvalues are less than or equal to 1, the errors will not grow and the approximation will be stable. Imposing this condition after solving for the eigenvalues implies that for stability, when the normalized range on X is $0 \le X \le 1$, the mesh ratio must be[15]

$$0 < R \equiv \frac{\Delta t}{(\Delta x)^2} \le \frac{1}{2} \frac{1}{(1 - 2\theta)} \quad \text{if } 0 \le \theta < \frac{1}{2}$$

$$\tag{23}$$

$$\text{No restriction} \quad\quad\quad\quad \text{if } \frac{1}{2} \le \theta \le 1.$$

The most common choices for θ are 0, 1/2, 1. The implicit schemes for $\theta \geq 1/2$ are unconditionally stable. By employing such an implicit scheme, one incurs the cost of solving systems of simultaneous equations but avoids all stability worries and can choose Δt by a tradeoff based on accuracy and efficiency. In the next section, a comparison is made in terms of accuracy and efficiency between the pure explicit scheme ($\theta = 0$), equation (10), a pure implicit scheme ($\theta = 1$), equation (11), both with and without logarithmic transformations, and the binomial technique.

III Comparison of Techniques Used for Valuing Options

In this section, two explicit finite difference methods, two implicit finite difference methods, and the binomial method are compared for both their accuracy and efficiency in valuing put and call options with and without dividends. The following notation is used throughout the tables and graphs:

Black-Scholes	Analytic Solution
Binomial	Binomial Approximation
BFCD	Binomial Fixed Cash Dividend
BFDY	Binomial Fixed Dividend Yield
FDE1	Finite Difference Explicit #1
FDE2	Finite Difference Explicit #2 (Logarithmic transform of #1)
FDI1	Finite Difference Implicit #1
FDI2	Finite Difference Implicit #2 (Logarithmic transform of #1)

All comparisons are made with some or all of the following parameters:[16]

S Stock Price	$= \$40.00$
X Exercise Price	$= \$35.00, \$40.00, \$45.00$
r_F Risk: Free Rate	$= 5.00$ percent (annual)
σ Standard Deviation of Stock Return	$= 0.3$ (annual)
t Time to Option Expiration	$= 1, 4, 7$ months
D Dividend	$= \$ .50, \$1.00, \$2.00, \$3.00, \$4.00$ (quarterly)
t_D Ex-Dividend Dates	$= .5, 3.5, 6.5$ months

Sometimes this range of stock prices and exercise prices is expanded to analyze approximation efficiency of computing multiple option values.

All dividend comparisons are made solely for the quarterly $ .50 dividend except for the comparison between the binomial fixed dividend yield (BFDY) as an approximation to the binomial fixed cash dividend (BFCD), where a variety of dividend amounts are compared. The options with expirations in one, four, and seven months each have one, two, and three $0.50 quarterly dividends, respectively. In every case, the last quarterly dividend is paid one-half month prior to expiration. Assume throughout that the fixed cash dividend is not suspended except for those stock prices in the approximation grid that are less than the dividend. This suspension price could be changed easily to reflect a more realistic suspension level as was done in [19], but this change would not significantly alter the conditions.

As previously demonstrated, the stability of the approximation procedure may depend on the mesh ratio. If the method is stable as the number of steps used in each numerical method increases, convergence occurs when, to the nearest cent, the approximation value does not change for two successive increments. Options are valued using the binomial approximation by starting with 50 as the initial value for N time (and thus stock price) steps, and then by incrementing the number of steps until convergence occurred. Similarly, by using the finite difference approximations, the options were valued by starting with 50 steps in stock price (n) and 45 steps/month in time to maturity (m) and then incrementing each until convergence occurred. This approach to convergence was taken as a means of standardizing the criteria for efficiency comparisons. Thus, for some parameters, a small truncation error was tolerated but might have been eliminated by departure from the standardized mesh ratio adjustment. Finally, recall that, while all efficiency comparisons herein are naturally implementation-sensitive, such comparisons readily expose inherent fundamental advantages and disadvantages of each technique.

A   Call Options

Here the accuracy and efficiency of solution techniques for valuing American call options are compared, first without dividends and then with dividends. The no-dividend case for calls is presented as an initial calibration for comparing these numerical methods.[17] Merton [25] demonstrated the equivalence between American and European call values for stocks that do not pay dividends. Thus, all call-option values for stocks that do not pay dividends would usually be computed with the analytic Black-Scholes formula by using a polynomial approximation for the univariate normal distribution function.[18]

Approximating call values on stocks that pay fixed cash dividends is more complicated because of the positive probability of prematurely exercising just before each ex-dividend date. As will be shown, this reduces the binomial's time-skipping

Table 26.1
Call option values for $S = \$40.00$, $\sigma = 0.3$, and $r_f = 5\%$

Exercise price ($)	Solution technique	Time to maturity (months)		
		1.0	4.0	7.0
35.00	Black-Scholes	5.22	6.25	7.17
	Binomial[a]	5.22	6.25	7.17
	FDE1[b]	5.22	6.26	7.19
	FDE2[c]	5.22	6.26	7.19
	FDI1[c]	5.22	6.26	7.19
	FDI2[c]	5.23	6.26	7.19
40.00	Black-Scholes	1.46	3.07	4.19
	Binomial	1.46	3.07	4.19
	FDE1	1.46	3.08	4.20
	FDE2	1.47	3.08	4.20
	FDI1	1.46	3.08	4.20
	FDI2	1.46	3.08	4.20
45.00	Black-Scholes	0.16	1.25	2.24
	Binomial	0.16	1.25	2.24
	FDE1	0.16	1.26	2.24
	FDE2	0.17	1.26	2.25
	FDI1	0.16	1.26	2.24
	FDI2	0.17	1.26	2.25

a. The values for the binomial approximation are calculated for 300 steps.
b. The values for FDE1 are for 200 steps in stock-price and 315 steps/month in time.
c. The values for FDE2, FDI1, and FDI2 are for 200 steps in stock-price and 45 steps/month in time (for FDE2 and FDI2, $N_1 = 3$).

efficiency. In addition, because the binomial method is a path-dependent approximation to the possible stock price paths, its efficiency is diminished as the number of cash dividend payments, and thus paths, increases.

1 Calls without Dividends   Table 26.1 compares the convergence and accuracy of six solution techniques for nine call-option values when the parameters are as previously given and the underlying stock does not pay dividends. Note that all six methods first converged for the stock price and time step sizes reported. The binomial technique has no truncation error when its solution is compared to the analytic Black-Scholes solution, while all finite-difference techniques had a small truncation error of one or two cents for some parameters.

The first explicit finite difference method, FDE1, requires about seven times as many time steps per month (315 vs. 45) as the other finite difference approaches require for convergence. This disparity results because the explicit methods require a finer mesh ratio than do the implicit methods for stability. However, the log-

Table 26.2
Computing costs for results in table 26.1

Solution technique	CPU time (secs)	I/O requests	Core	Cost for 9 options[a]
Binomial $N = 300$	0.26	67	145K	$ 0.21
FDE1 $n = 200, m = 2205$	39.75	104	150K	$11.90
FDE2 $n = 200, m = 315$	3.94	108	150K	$ 1.38
FDI1 $n = 200, m = 315$	7.35	123	170K	$ 2.47
FDI2 $n = 200, m = 315$	6.60	118	160K	$ 2.21

a. Costs for computer use at the UCLA Computing Facility are calculated as: (CPU Time + (0:007) I/O Requests)(1 + 0:00135 Min (Core, 500) + 0:00015 Core)(0:24).

transformed explicit method, FDE2, converges for the same mesh ratio as do these implicit methods because the transformed equation has constant coefficients.

For the no-dividend case, this binomial approximation used a large number of time steps ($n = 300$) that produced an extra fine partition of stock prices for the final stock price vector. Then, computational efficiency was enhanced by jumping backwards over time from the final vector of stock (and thus option prices) to the initial option value. This time jumping can be done because of the binomial formula, and because with no probability of premature exercise, it is not necessary to calculate the intermediate option values. However, this is not true for the finite difference methods even with no probability of early exercise.

For the logarithmically transformed, finite difference methods ($y = \ln S$ in FDE2 and FDI2), a different stock price step size was used in the two stock price ranges from zero to one dollar, $[0, 1]$, and from one dollar to infinity, $[1, \infty]$, approximated by $[SMIN, 1]$ and $[1, SMAX]$. For computational accuracy and efficiency, it is not necessary to partition the stock price region of zero to one dollar as finely in the logarithmically transformed space of $[-\infty, 0]$ as in the symmetric region $[0, \infty]$. Thus N_1, the number of stock price steps in the zero-to-one-dollar range, was set equal to three ($N_1, = 3$) for both the explicit and implicit methods, FDE2 and FDI2.

Table 26.2 presents the computing costs for the results in table 26.1. Here the efficiency is compared for computing all nine option values for the approximation techniques.[19] The cost for nine options is primarily a function of the central processing unit (CPU) time.[20]

The least expensive solution technique is the binomial and it also uses the least CPU time (and I/O requests and core size). In fact, the ranking by least to most expensive, which is identical to the ranking by least to most CPU time, is Binomial, FDE2, FDI2, FDI1, and FDE1, respectively. Of the four finite difference techniques compared, the logarithmically transformed methods are most efficient, and the logarithmically transformed explicit (FDE2) is more efficient than the implicit (FDI2) one, because it does not require the solution of simultaneous equations.

The CPU time comprises compilation and execution times. Once either the binomial or the finite difference programs are compiled they can be executed, repetitively if necessary to compute multiple option values for a variety of time, to expiration, stock, and exercise prices without being recompiled. In general, for computing multiple option values, the binomial technique with time skipping must be executed once for each option value while the finite difference methods need be executed only once for all option values.[21]

Figure 26.2 graphically compares four of the solution techniques in table 26.2, omitting the most costly untransformed explicit method, FDE1. The graph demonstrates that as the number of options increases, the finite difference cost per option approaches zero while the binomial cost per option valued is asymptotic to the execution expense. When more than 300 (460, 610) options are being valued FDE2 (FDI2, FDI1), is less expensive per option than the binomial method. Thus, for individuals or firms computing a large number of option values, the finite difference methods may be more cost-efficient. These conclusions must be reconsidered when valuing the typical call option on a dividend-paying stock.

2   Calls with Dividends   Most financial securities have either contracted or expected payouts. While the payouts can be discrete or continuous, and either a fixed dollar amount, a fixed yield, or stochastic, the most common type of stock dividend is an expected, discrete, fixed cash dividend. The reason is that typically, corporations maintain a stable quarterly dividend policy. All payouts complicate the valuation process, but a discrete, fixed cash dividend is one of the most difficult for continuous-time option techniques because each discrete payout requires an additional boundary condition and may alter the parameters of the stochastic process.

Here, the five approximation techniques considered in the no-dividend case are re-examined when the underlying stock pays discrete quarterly dividends. The finite difference techniques can accommodate discrete cash dividends more easily than can the binomial technique because the density of the binomial grid partition increases at each ex-dividend date. To see this, recall that in the simple coincident binomial process, the number of stock price steps grows by one for each additional time increment prior to the first ex-dividend date. However, after each dividend payment, the binomial process is no longer coincident and for each additional time step the

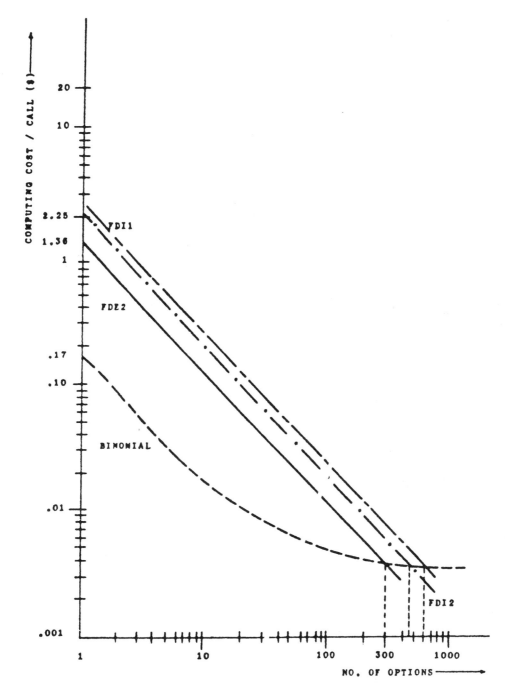

Figure 26.2
Cost comparison of binomial and finite difference methods for American calls on non-dividend paying stocks

number of stock price steps increases by $2(n + 1)$ where n is the number of the specific time step. Figure 26.1 depicts the binomial with discrete dividends. For a relatively small number of discrete fixed payouts, the binomial process "explodes," becoming computationally impractical. Currently listed stock options have a maximum expiration of nine months for a maximum of three dividends during the life of any option. One discrete cash dividend seriously compromises the efficiency of the pure binomial process, and three erode it entirely.

If a stock pays a fixed dividend yield, the binomial process will remain coincident since up/down and down/up movements after the ex-dividend date will lead to coincident points. Thus, a fixed dividend yield (BFDY) will be a more efficient binomial solution technique. However, a fixed dividend yield is an approximation to the actual fixed cash dividend that most corporations pay.

If the fixed dividend yield BFDY is a good approximation to the fixed cash dividend BFCD, this accuracy may circumvent the binomial's efficiency problems caused by the exploding grid partition. Unfortunately, the fixed dividend yield assumption will produce incorrect hedge ratios. Even with a fixed dividend yield, the efficiency of the binomial process will be reduced whenever there is a positive probability of prematurely exercising an American call option at each ex-dividend date. Here we cannot achieve the economy gained by jumping time from the final expiration date to the current date. Instead, only smaller jumps are permissible to each intermediate ex-dividend date where the boundaries for early exercise must be checked.

For all finite difference methods, the fineness of the grid partition is not affected by discrete cash dividends. Instead, the grid mesh is kept constant and interpolation is performed. Previous tables for valuing call options with no dividends showed that the implicit methods were more economical than the explicit techniques due to the former's less stringent stability requirements. Furthermore, the logarithmic transformation enhanced the efficiency of both techniques and the increased economy for the explicit method was dramatic. This increased efficiency of the logarithmic transformation is still obtainable when the stock pays discrete cash dividends. However, due to the nonlinearity of the logarithmic transformation at each ex-dividend date, the grid must be transformed from the logarithm of the stock price back to stock price space, the dividend paid, and then retransformed back to the logarithm of the stock price. Fortunately, this back and forth use of the logarithmic transformation at each ex-dividend date does not destroy its efficiency. (Figure 26.3 demonstrates this point.)[22]

Table 26.3 compares the convergence and accuracy of six solution techniques for nine call option values when the parameters are as given previously in table 26.1.

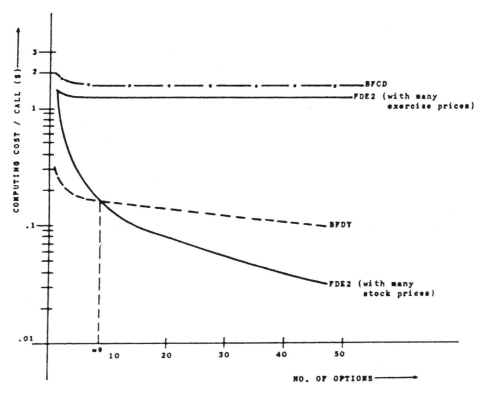

Figure 26.3
Cost comparison of binomial and finite difference approximations for American calls on dividend paying stocks (two dividend payments)

Here the stock pays a $0.50 quarterly cash dividend. The binomial fixed yield, BFDY, is 5 percent annually or 1.25 percent quarterly, which is equivalent to a $0.50 cash dividend when the stock price is $40.

First note that all six methods converged for the stock price and time step sizes reported. It was necessary to make the step sizes in table 26.3 different from those in table 26.1 because of dividends. The steps were chosen to insure convergence subject to the restriction that the dividend payments and expiration dates fall on and not between time steps. This choice avoids interpolation errors that would diminish accuracy. All the methods are accurate and are within one or two cents of each other. The binomial fixed dividend yield closely approximates the fixed cash dividend for these nine call option values. The quality of this fixed dividend yield approximation is examined in table 26.4.

Table 26.3
Call option values for $S = \$40.00$, $\sigma = 0.3$, $r = 5\%$, and $D = \$0.50$

Exercise price ($)	Solution technique	Time to maturity (months)		
		1.0	4.0	7.0
35.00	BFCD[a]	5.10	5.73	6.34
	BFDY[b]	5.10	5.74	6.34
	FDE1[c]	5.10	5.74	6.35
	FDE2[d]	5.10	5.74	6.35
	FDI1[d]	5.10	5.74	6.34
	FDI2[d]	5.10	5.74	6.35
40.00	BFCD	1.27	2.69	3.55
	BFDY	1.27	2.68	3.54
	FDE1	1.27	2.70	3.57
	FDE2	1.27	2.70	3.57
	FDI1	1.26	2.69	3.56
	FDI2	1.26	2.69	3.57
45.00	BFCD	0.12	1.04	1.82
	BFDY	0.12	1.03	1.80
	FDE1	0.12	1.04	1.83
	FDE2	0.13	1.05	1.84
	FDI1	0.12	1.04	1.82
	FDI2	0.13	1.05	1.84

a. The values for the fixed dividend approach to the binomial approximation are calculated for 140, 160, and 140 steps for 1.0, 4.0, and 7.0 month maturities, respectively.
b. The values for the fixed dividend yield approach to the binomial approximation are calculated for 140, 200, and 210 steps for 1.0, 4.0, and 7.0 month maturities, respectively.
c. The values for FDE1 are calculated using 200 steps in stock price and 320 steps/month in time.
d. The values of FDE2, FDI1, and FDI2 are calculated using 200 steps in stock price and 80 steps/month in time.

A graphical summary of the efficiency of these solution techniques is provided by figure 26.3 (other graphs are available upon request). Here the cost per call option computed versus the number of options valued is presented for two dividends. The graph shows that the logarithmically transformed finite difference (FDE2) is less expensive than the binomial fixed cash dividend (BFCD) in every case. BFDY is quickly dominated by FDE2 for valuing multiple call options with many stock prices due to the binomial's conditional starting point that necessitates re-execution for each value. However, FDE2 is dominated by BFDY when computing multiple call options with many different exercise prices.

Table 26.4 compares the binomial fixed dividend yield as an approximation to the fixed cash dividend for quarterly cash dividends ranging from $0.50 to $4 and equivalent quarterly yields ranging from 1.25 to 10 percent when the stock price is

Table 26.4
Comparison of binomial approximations: fixed cash dividend vs. fixed dividend yield $S = \$40.00$, $\sigma = 0.3$, $r = 5\%$

Exercise price ($)	Time to maturity (mos.)	Dividend amount/dividend yield									
		$0.50/1.25%		$1.0/2.5%		$2.0/5.0%		$3.0/7.5%		$4.0/10%	
		BFCD	BFDY	BFCD	BFDY	BFCD	BFDY	BFCD	BFDY	BFCD	BFDY
35.00	1.0	5.10	5.10	5.09	5.09	5.08	5.09	5.08	5.08	5.08	5.08
	4.0	5.73	5.74	5.40	5.41	5.17	5.19	5.11	5.12	5.10	5.10
	7.0	6.34	6.34	5.76	5.79	5.24	5.29	5.12	5.15	5.10	5.11
40.00	1.0	1.27	1.27	1.17	1.17	1.07	1.08	1.04	1.04	1.02	1.02
	4.0	2.69	2.68	2.39	2.38	1.92	1.91	1.58	1.60	1.38	1.39
	7.0	3.55	3.54	3.06	3.05	2.32	2.31	1.81	1.83	1.48	1.51
45.00	1.0	0.12	0.12	0.09	0.09	0.05	0.05	0.04	0.04	0.03	0.03
	4.0	1.04	1.03	0.88	0.87	0.64	0.62	0.46	0.44	0.32	0.31
	7.0	1.82	1.80	1.50	1.47	1.02	0.99	0.69	0.66	0.46	0.43

$40. It is surprising that the biases previously mentioned approximately cancel. BFDY is a very accurate approximation to BFCD for the one- and two-dividend cases (i.e., expirations of one and four months). Even in the three-dividend case, the maximum error was 5 cents for a cash dividend of $2 when the exercise price and option's expiration date were $35 and seven months, respectively.

B Put Options

At every instant, American put options have a positive probability of premature exercise regardless of whether the stock pays dividends [26]. Thus, there is always a critical stock price, independent of the current stock price, below which it is optimal to exercise the American put. Because of this possibility of early exercise, an exercise condition comparing the value of the put if held to the value if exercised must be checked at every instant.

A main advantage of the binomial method over all finite difference techniques for valuing American call options is attributable to the binomial formula that allows jumping over many time steps and computing values at only the ex-dividend dates. This computational advantage is obviously not plausible when valuing American puts, even if the stock pays no dividends. Discrete cash dividend payments will further complicate the binomial technique because of the "exploding" tree problem.

In the next few pages, the accuracy and efficiency of several solution techniques for valuing American put options are compared, first with no dividends in subsection 1, and then with dividends in subsection 2. The binomial fixed cash dividend (BFCD) approach is not presented because it is always dominated by the finite difference techniques. Only the binomial fixed dividend yield (BFDY) is presented for put valuation. To check the convergence and approximation error of the binomial fixed dividend yield, put values for a logarithmically transformed explicit finite difference method with a fixed dividend yield, (FDE2DY), are also presented in tables but not in the graphs.

1 Puts without Dividends Table 26.5 compares the convergence and accuracy of four solution techniques for nine put option values when the parameters are as previously given and the underlying stock does not pay dividends. All four methods converged to values within one cent of each other for the time and stock price step sizes reported.

Figure 26.4 presents the computational efficiency for the four solution techniques of table 26.5 for valuing multiple options. We considered a variety of exercise prices and expiration dates to value a range of put options. The binomial technique is more efficient for valuing a small number of puts; but at nine options valued, the finite

Table 26.5
Put option values for $S = \$40.00$, $\sigma = 0.3$, and $r = 5\%$

Exercise price ($)	Solution technique	Time to maturity (months)		
		1.0	4.0	7.0
35.00	Binomial[a]	0.08	0.70	1.22
	FDE2[b]	0.08	0.70	1.21
	FDI1[b]	0.08	0.69	1.21
	FDI2[b]	0.08	0.69	1.21
40.00	Binomial	1.31	2.48	3.17
	FDE2	1.31	2.48	3.16
	FDI1	1.30	2.47	3.16
	FDI2	1.30	2.47	3.16
45.00	Binomial	5.06	5.71	6.24
	FDE2	5.06	5.70	6.23
	FDI1	5.06	5.70	5.23
	FDI2	5.06	5.70	6.23

a. The values reported are for $N = 150$.
b. The values reported are for 200 steps in stock price and 45 steps/month in time (for FDE2 $N_1 = 3$)

difference methods become competitive and are dominant thereafter. As with calls, the logarithmically transformed explicit finite difference method is most efficient. The binomial computation cost per option approaches an asymptote as before because it is necessary to re-execute the program for each option valued. This re-execution is not necessary with the finite difference techniques. The binomial execution costs are much greater when valuing American puts rather than calls because time jumping is not feasible. The finite difference methods become more economical when only about ten American put options are being valued, whereas the finite differences did not dominate the binomial method until more than about 300 American call values were computed.[23] Thus, practitioners interested in efficiently valuing put options would reduce their computation costs by using finite difference techniques, even if dividend payments were not considered.[24]

2 Puts with Dividends Table 26.6 compares the binomial fixed dividend yield as an approximation to the fixed cash dividend computed by the logarithmically transformed explicit finite difference technique FDE2CD. In addition, this explicit finite difference technique modified for a fixed dividend yield FDE2DY is also computed to check the binomial put scheme BFDY. All the parameters are as given in table 26.5, and the cash dividend is $0.50, which together imply a quarterly yield of 1.25 percent. At this point of comparison, the implicit methods are dropped because they are less efficient than the explicit technique.

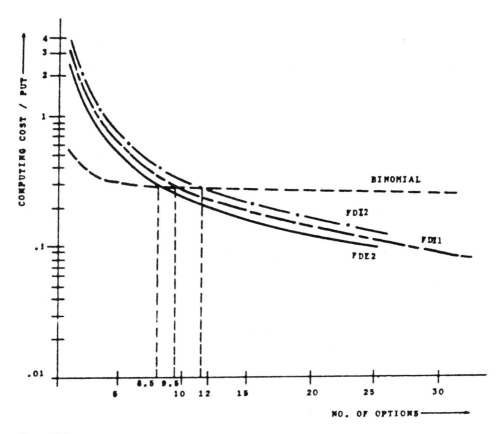

Figure 26.4
Cost comparison of binomial and finite difference approximations for American puts on non-dividend
paying stocks

First, note that all three methods converge. Again, the fixed dividend yield is
shown to be an accurate approximation to the fixed cash dividend. The maximum
discrepancy between FDE2CD and BFDY is five cents for an at-the-money put with
a seven-month expiration, and thus three scheduled dividend payments.

Figure 26.5 summarizes the cost comparisons for the three solution techniques in
table 26.6 for valuing multiple put options on stocks for two dividend payments.
Again the binomial fixed dividend yield is more efficient than the logarithmically
transformed explicit finite difference method when the multiple options are generated
by varying the exercise price for a single stock price. Conversely, when the multiple
options are valued for multiple stock prices and a single exercise price, the explicit
finite difference scheme asserts its efficiency after only a few options are valued. As

Table 26.6
Put option values for $S = \$40$, $\sigma = 0.3$, and $r = 5\%$, and $D = \$0.50$

Exercise price ($)	Solution technique	Time to maturity (months)		
		1.0	4.0	7.0
35.00	BFDY[a]	0.11	0.88	1.55
	FDE2DY[b]	0.11	0.88	1.54
	FDE2CD[c]	0.11	0.91	1.59
40.00	BFDY	1.56	2.91	3.75
	FDE2DY	1.55	2.90	3.74
	FDE2CD	1.56	2.93	3.80
45.00	BFDY	5.50	6.30	7.00
	FDE2DY	5.50	6.29	6.98
	FDE2CD	5.50	6.31	7.02

a. The values for the fixed dividend yield approach to the binomial approximation BFDY are calculated for 140, 160, and 140 steps for 1.0, 4.0, and 7.0 month maturities, respectively.
b. The values for the fixed dividend yield FDE2DY are calculated for 200 steps in stock price and 80 steps/month in time.
c. The values for the fixed cash dividend FDE2CD are calculated for 200 steps in stock price and 80 steps/month in time.

before, if the fixed dividend yield were used for the finite difference schemes, thus maintaining linear homogeneity in S and X, they would dominate the pure binomial process for both multiple exercise and multiple stock prices.

IV Summary and Conclusion

In summary, the results for puts and calls are similiar. All approximation methods analyzed converge and are accurate. The binomial technique, the implicit and the logarithmically transformed explicit, finite difference methods are "best," and each has its strong points. The binomial method works well for computing a small number of options on stocks without dividends, but is inefficient when effects of cash dividends must be analyzed. However, the assumption of a fixed dividend yield is shown to be a reasonably accurate and efficient approximation. Unfortunately, the fixed dividend yield produces an incorrect hedge ratio. The binomial technique also loses efficiency when valuing American options. Furthermore, because the binomial process has a conditional starting point it is less efficient than the two finite difference methods for valuing multiple options.

The explicit finite difference method should not be discarded for stability problems because these can be readily overcome. In addition, when transformed logarithmically, the explicit method is more efficient than the implicit method because it does not require the solution of a set of simultaneous equations. The binomial technique is

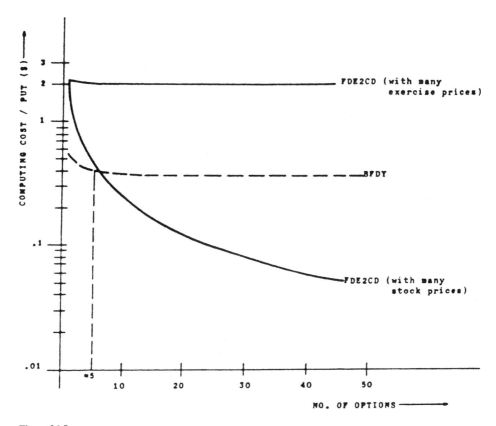

Figure 26.5
Cost comparisons of binomial and finite difference approximations for American puts on dividend paying stock (two dividends case)

more intuitive and also may be more readily implemented than the finite difference methods. Thus, it is pedagogically superior. In conclusion, researchers computing a smaller number of option values may prefer the binomial approximation, while practitioners in the business of computing a larger number of option values will generally find that the finite difference approximations are more efficient.

Acknowledgments

The authors thank the CIVITAS Foundation at the University of California, Los Angeles, and the Graduate School of Business at the University of Pittsburgh for financial support. They also thank Mark Rubinstein, the *JFQA* anonymous referees, and colleagues at UCLA and the University of Pittsburgh for helpful comments.

Notes

1. Other analytic solutions are by Cox [9], Roll [29], Rubinstein [30], and Geske and Johnson [21].

2. See [13].

3. Garman [16] has derived the fundamental partial differential equation which all assets, including derivative assets such as options, must follow under diffusion state processes. The Black-Scholes equation for options is a special case of Garman's equation. Both equations are second order because of the continuous time diffusion assumption, and specifically parabolic, rather than hyperbolic or elliptic, because their discriminant is zero. See Friedman [15] for further discussion of this.

4. In the general form of a second-order partial differential equation, if coefficients which are nonzero (or zero) can become zero (or nonzero), the form of the equation can change. Because of limited liability, this cannot happen with the Black-Scholes equation.

5. The exact form of the transformed equation depends on the change of variables. See [3], [25], [32], or [2] for examples of these transformations.

6. See [14] Chapters VI and VII.

7. The space dimension is determined by the number of stochastic variables in the problem. In the simplest valuation problems the space is one dimensional. For example, in Black-Scholes option pricing the stock price is the single underlying stochastic variable. In Merton's [25] generalization to stochastic interest rates, the state space would be two-dimensional, with both a stochastic stock price and an interest rate. The focus of this paper is on one-dimensional stochastic problems, but many of the findings would carry over to multiple dimensions.

8. Derivative boundary conditions are necessary for the finite difference approximations but not for the direct approximations to the underlying process, such as the binomial or Monte Carlo techniques. The hedge ratio derivatives, $\partial V/\partial S$, appear in equation (1). Their convergence to either zero or one for puts or calls as S increases can be determined from the Black-Scholes European solution. A useful rule of thumb is that the stock price will be about one-and-a-half times the exercise price for these derivatives to be satisfied.

9. The up jump, defined as the reciprocal of the down jump, is shown to be $u = \exp(\sigma\sqrt{t/m})$. See [11] for details.

10. Forward differences use a "forward" differencing interval while backward differences use the opposite. For example, $(t_2 - t_1)$ where t_2 is closer to the present than t_1 could be a forward difference relative to t_1; then relative to t_1, $(t_1 - t_0)$ would be a backward difference. A central difference "centers" on t_1. For example, $(t_2 - t_0)/2$ would center on t_1.

11. There is a voluminous amount of research on this subject. One excellent reference is [14], p. 388.

12. See [2].

13. Several related methods for analyzing these concepts are fourier series, energy conservation, solution boundedness, and eigenvalues. Fourier series is more versatile, and can be used with a wide degree of analytic precision; for example, which harmonics, or wave length multiples of the mesh ratio, become amplified. However, such precise information is not currently necessary in financial economics.

14. This approach also can be used to demonstrate an identical order of error in equation (11) for the implicit method. Sometimes the error order can be reduced to $O[(\Delta t)^2]$ which is the same as $O[(\Delta x)^4]$ if Δt and Δx go to zero so that $c\Delta t/(\Delta x)^2 = 1/6$. See [8] for an example of this type of accuracy improvement.

15. See [13] or [2] for reference to this stability condition.

16. These parameters were chosen to be consistent with those used in the forthcoming book by Cox and Rubinstein [12], and the published article by Cox, Ross, and Rubinstein [11]. The binomial approximation

has been discussed and used by Cox and Rubinstein [12] with and without fixed dividend yields. The finite difference approximations have been discussed by Schwartz [31]; and Brennan and Schwartz discussed and used FDE1 [7], FDE2 [6], and FDI1 [5] in those papers, respectively. Recently, Geske and Shastri [19], [20] used FDE2 and FDI2.

17. All computations were done on an IBM 3033 computer at the University of California, Los Angeles. The programming language was Fortran.

18. See [1], page 932, for examples of these polynomial approximations.

19. Although it is very inexpensive, the analytic Black-Scholes solution is not included in this comparison because it cannot be used later for the more complex option problems.

20. The formula for computing costs on this IBM 3033 is: Cost = (CPU TIME + (0 : 007)I/O REQUESTS) (1 + 0 : 00135 MIN(CORE, 500) + 0 : 00015 CORE) (0 : 24). The critical factor in this equation is CPU time. Core size and I/O requests have a small effect on cost. In fact, the standard measure is CPU time and cost alone, because the core and I/O measures have negligible impact. For example, reducing the core size by factors of 10 or 100 (i.e., from 145K to 14.5K or 1.45K) for the binomial example in table 26.2 reduces cost only form \$.21 to \$.179 and \$.175, respectively.

21. This implies the following CPU cost equations: Binomial cost = [(Compilation Cost)/(# Options Valued)] + Execution Cost; Finite Difference Costs = (Compilation + Execution Cost)/(# Options Valued). These formulas suggest that as the number of options valued increases, the finite difference techniques should become less expensive than the binomial method on a per-option basis.

22. An analytic solution to the problem of valuing an American call option on a dividend paying stock (see [29], [17], and [33]) might be more efficient than an approximation. The purpose of this paper is to compare alternative approximation techniques, so these analytic solutions are not considered.

23. The fixed dividend yield assumption maintains linear homogeneity in S and X for both the binomial and finite difference processes. Thus, if this assumption were employed for the finite difference methods, they would also dominate the binomial method for fixed dividend yield.

24. In a recent paper, Johnson [23] demonstrated that American puts without dividends can be analytically approximated. This analytic approximation is both accurate and highly efficient for reasonable parameters. Furthermore, Geske and Johnson [21] have recently presented an exact analytic solution to the partial differential equation that is computationally efficient because its evaluation requires very few critical stock price computations. It can also be sued for valuing puts on stocks with dividends.

References

[1] Abramowitz, M., and I. Stegum. *Handbook of Mathematical Functions*. National Bureau of Standards (1970).

[2] Ames, William F. *Numerical Methods for Partial Differential Equations*. Academic Press, (1977).

[3] Black, F., and M. Scholes. "The Pricing of Options and Corporate Liabilities." *Journal of Political Economy*, Vol. 81 (May–June 1973), pp. 637–659.

[4] Boyle, P. "Options: A Monte Carlo Approach." *Journal of Financial Economics*, Vol. 44 (May 1977), pp. 323–338.

[5] Brennan, M., and E. Schwartz. "The Valuation of American Put Options." *Journal of Finance*, Vol. 32 (May 1977), pp. 449–462.

[6] ———. "Finite Difference Methods and Jump Processes Arising in the Pricing of Contingent Claims: A Synthesis." *Journal of Financial and Quantitative Analysis*, Vol. 13 (September 1978), pp. 461–474.

[7] ———. "Convertible Bonds: Valuation and Optimal Strategies for Call and Conversion." *Journal of Finance*, Vol. 32 (December 1977), pp. 1699–1716.

[8] Courtadon, G. "A More Accurate Finite Difference Approximation for the Valuation of Options." *Journal of Financial and Quantitative Analysis*, Vol. 17 (December 1982), pp. 697–705.

[9] Cox, J. "Note on Option Pricing 1: Constant Elasticity of Variance Diffusions." Stanford, Unpublished (1975).

[10] Cox, J., and S. Ross. "The Valuation of Options for Alternative Stochastic Processes." *Journal of Financial Economics*, Vol. 3 (March 1976), pp. 145–166.

[11] Cox, J., S. Ross, and M. Rubinstein. "Option Pricing: A Simplified Approach." *Journal of Financial Economics*, Vol. 7 (October 1979), pp. 229–264.

[12] Cox, J., and M. Rubinstein. *Option Markets*. Englewood Cliffs, NJ: Prentice Hall (1984).

[13] Dahlquist, G., and A. Bjorck. *Numerical Methods*. Prentice Hall (1974).

[14] Feller, W. *An Introduction to Probability Theory and Its Applications*. Vol. 1. New York: John Wiley and Sons (1968).

[15] Friedman, A. *Partial Differential Equations*. Huntington, NY: Robert Krieger Publications (1976).

[16] Garman, M. "A General Theory of Asset Valuation Under Diffusion State Processes." Working Paper No. 50, University of California, Berkeley (1976).

[17] Geske, R. "The Valuation of Compound Options." *Journal of Financial Economics*, Vol. 7 (March 1979), pp. 63–81.

[18] ———. "A Note on an Analytical Method for the Valuation of American Call Options on Dividend Paying Stocks." *Journal of Financial Economics*, Vol. 7 (December 1979), pp. 275–380.

[19] Geske, R., and K. Shastri. "The Effects of Payouts on the Rational Pricing of American Options." Working Paper, University of California, Los Angeles (1982).

[20] ———. "The Early Exercise of American Puts." *The Journal of Banking and Finance*, Vol. 9 (January 1985).

[21] Geske, R., and H. Johnson. "The American Put Valued Analytically." *Journal of Finance*, Vol. 39 (December 1984), pp. 1511–1524.

[22] Ingersoll, J. "A Contingent-Claims Valuation of Convertible Securities." *Journal of Financial Economics*, Vol. 4 (May 1977), pp. 289–322.

[23] Johnson, H. "An Analytic Approximation to the American Put Price." *Journal of Financial and Quantitative Analysis*, Vol. 17 (March 1983), pp. 141–148.

[24] Mason, S. "The Numerical Analysis of Certain Free Boundary Problems Arising in Financial Economics." Working Paper 78-52, Harvard Business School (1978).

[25] Merton, R. "Theory of Rational Option Pricing." *Bell Journal of Economics and Management Science*, Vol. 4 (Spring 1973), pp. 141–183.

[26] ———. "On the Pricing of Corporate Debt: The Risk Structure of Interest Rates." *Journal of Finance*, Vol. 29 (May 1974), pp. 449–470.

[27] ———. "Options Pricing when the Underlying Stock Returns are Discontinuous." *Journal of Financial Economics*, Vol. 31 (March 1976), pp. 333–350.

[28] Parkinson, M. "Option Pricing: The American Put," *Journal of Business*, Vol. 50 (January 1977), pp. 21–36.

[29] Roll, R. "An Analytic Method for Valuing American Call Options on Dividend Paying Stocks." *Journal of Financial Economics*, Vol. 85 (November 1977), pp. 251–258.

[30] Rubinstein, M. "Displaced Diffusion Option Pricing." *Journal of Finance*, Vol. 38 (March 1983), pp. 213–218.

[31] Schwartz, E. "The Valuation of Warrants: Implementing a New Approach." *Journal of Financial Economics*, Vol. 4 (January 1977), pp. 79–94.

[32] Sommerfield, A. *Partial Differential Equations in Physics*. New York: Academic Press (1949).

[33] Whaley, R. "On the Valuation of American Call Options on Stocks with Known Dividends." *Journal of Financial Economics*, Vol. 10 (June 1981), pp. 207–211.

27 Simulation and Numerical Methods in Real Options Valuation

Gonzalo Cortazar

1 Introduction

Traditional finance literature stresses that the value of an asset is determined by future cash flows. As long as these cash flows are certain, the task of determining asset values amounts to finding adequate inter-temporal discount factors to transform these future flows into equivalent present values.

Uncertainty introduces two additional complications into asset valuation. First, we must find a way to penalize the present value of risky cash flows so that we can take into consideration not only the time value of money but also risk aversion. This may be done by determining risk premiums to be added to inter-temporal discount factors or, alternatively, by replacing expected cash flows by their certainty equivalents.

A second and somewhat more difficult issue arises when cash flows are a nonlinear function of a risky state variable. Risk premiums then become much more difficult to derive, and the contingent claims approach of finding certainty equivalents for cash flows at each state of nature becomes the only practical approach.

It has long been noted that simulation lends itself nicely to valuing assets under uncertainty. As long as cash flows may be determined using past information, a nonlinear cash flow function poses no additional burden. An example of *past-dependent* nonlinear cash flows is the *European* call option. The value of this option is nonlinear by being equivalent to the maximum value of two assets, and *past-dependent* in the sense that cash flows depend only on past information. This approach, which values a function by unfolding uncertainty as it evolves from the past, is known as *forward induction* and may be successfully applied whenever present cash flows do not depend on future events.

An additional difficulty arises when nonlinear cash flows are dependent on future information. For example, *American* options may be exercised at any of several dates. Thus, cash flows on a given date depend not only on past information but also on expectations of future events. It has long been known that whenever uncertainty can be described by a Markovian process (in the sense that all past information may be embedded in current state variable values) the value of a security may be obtained by some kind of *backward induction*. This procedure works its way into the present starting from some known future value, typically at option expiration.

A number of backward induction procedures have been proposed for valuing assets, from dynamic programming, to binomial and multinomial trees, to finite difference procedures for solving partial differential equations. All of these procedures start from some boundary conditions and solve simultaneously for the asset value and the optimal exercise policy, determining the shape of the cash flow function in such a way as to maximize asset value.

Both forward and backward induction procedures have a role in asset valuation. While forward induction handles in an easier way complex uncertain processes, including path dependent cash flows that may arise because of technical or tax reasons, backward induction is specially appropriate for handling American-type options very common in real option problems. Until recently, simulation procedures were only recommended for European-type options in forward induction implementations. In section 3 we present the basic intuition of how to use simulation for American-type options and provide an actual application to a well-known real option problem.

2   Standard Simulation and Other Numerical Approaches

2.1   European Real Option Valuation by Numerical Procedures

Some contingent claims problems may be solved through closed-form analytical expressions, but most can not. If there is no analytical solution, numerical methods must be used. To illustrate our discussion on alternative numerical approaches and compare them to a standard simulation, we define a simple real-option valuation problem and solve it using different methods.

Let's assume we want to value a project with cash flows contingent on a stochastic output price, S. The project requires no initial investment at time $T_0 = 0$ but requires an investment I_1 at time T_1, which, if undertaken, generates cash flows with a present value at T_1 of $V(S)$. Depending on the value of $V(S)$ the manager may decide not to invest at T_1, in which case the project must be abandoned at zero liquidation value. The value of this project may be modeled as a call option written on $V(S)$ with exercise price I_1 and time to maturity T_1.

We may be able to solve for the value of this project using the well-known Black and Scholes (1973) formula for a call option, provided some assumptions are made. Among them are that S is a tradable asset, that markets are sufficiently complete as to allow the hedging of output price risk and that output price returns follow a Brownian motion with constant interest rates and volatility. If these assumptions apply then there is no need to resort to numerical procedures.

Most real option problems, however, do not have closed-form analytical solutions. There are many reasons this may be the case, including a more complex uncertainty model or project-flexibility specification. In these cases, to value the contingent claim numerical solution procedures must be used.

There are many numerical methods that may be used to value a European-type contingent claim. In order to place standard Monte Carlo simulation procedures into perspective and to discuss their comparative strengths and weaknesses, we solve the above problem using three alternative numerical procedures: binomial trees, finite differences, and simulation. We assume Black and Scholes (1973) holds so we have an analytical solution that can be used as a benchmark for our approximate numerical methods.

For concreteness we assume risk-adjusted prices follow a geometric brownian motion with a discretized specification as follows:

$$\Delta S = rS\Delta t + \sigma S\sqrt{\Delta t}Z \tag{1}$$

with

$r \quad = 0.10$

$\sigma \quad = 0.2$

$\Delta t =$ time interval

$Z \quad =$ random variable with a standardized Normal distribution.

Also the investment project described earlier has the following specification:

$V(S) = aS + b$

$a \qquad = 100$

$b \qquad = 10$

$I_1 \qquad = 110$

$T_0 \qquad = 0$

$T_1 \qquad = 1$

As stated earlier, the value of this real option can be directly obtained using Black and Scholes (1973). The value of the project for an initial output price of 1 is $1.30. We now solve this same valuation problem using the three alternative numerical approaches. We implement all three numerical solutions using standard Excel spreadsheets.

2.2 Binomial Trees

Discrete tree representations of stochastic processes and their use in option valuation have been proposed by Cox et al. (1979), Rendleman and Barter (1979), and Sharpe (1978). We explain the binomial tree, which is the simplest one. Binomial trees assume that uncertainty at any time can be represented by two alternative states. These two sates are defined such that the implied price distribution matches as closely as possible the probability distribution of the underlying continuous state variable. Given our stochastic process for output price, we must restrict the values and probabilities of the two states in such a way that the expected price return over the next time interval is equal to $r\Delta t$ and that its volatility is $\sigma\sqrt{\Delta t}$. A solution is to define the two values for the state variable as Su and Sd, with probabilities p and $(1 - p)$, with:

$$u = e^{\sigma\sqrt{\Delta t}} \tag{2}$$

$$d = e^{-\sigma\sqrt{\Delta t}}$$

or

$$d = \frac{1}{u} \tag{3}$$

$$p = \frac{e^{r\Delta t} - d}{u - d} \tag{4}$$

Depending on the required accuracy we can determine the size of the time interval Δt, or equivalently, the number of subintervals in which we partition the total time to maturity. In our case the time to maturity is $T_1 = 1$, and we arbitrarily divide it into 10 subintervals, setting $\Delta t = 0.1$. Once the binomial tree that represents the underlying price distribution is obtained, it is possible to value the derivative asset (in our case the investment project) as a contingent claim on output price.

In figure 27.1 a binomial tree solution to our investment valuation problem is presented. A two-dimensional vector is specified at each binomial node: output price and option value. To obtain option values, we compute the cash flows at maturity (T_1) as:

$Max(V(S) - I_1; 0)$.

These values are presented bolded at the extreme right of the figure.

The next step is to compute the option value for each of the preceding nodes. As an example, on the top-right corner of figure 27.1 a box with three nodes is presented. The option value of **7.77** is computed as the expected option value at the two following nodes using the risk neutral probabilities:

Option Value $= [p * 8.82 + (1 - p)6.59]e^{-r\Delta t} = 7.77$

This procedure is repeated column by column from right to left. The last node represents the current option value of **1.31** for an initial output price of **1.00**. This option value is very similar to our analytical solution using Black and Scholes.

Time to Maturity

1.00	0.90	0.80	0.70	0.60	0.50	0.40	0.30	0.20	0.10	0.00
										1.88
										8.82
									1.77	
									7.77	
								1.66		1.66
								6.78		**0.59**
							1.56		1.56	
							5.86		5.67	
						1.46		1.46		1.46
						5.01		4.81		**4.62**
					1.37		1.37		1.37	
					4.21		4.01		3.82	
				1.29		1.29		1.29		1.29
				3.47		3.27		3.08		**2.88**
			1.21		1.21		1.21		1.21	
			2.80		2.59		2.38		2.19	
		1.13		1.13		1.13		1.13		1.13
		2.22		2.01		1.78		1.55		**1.35**
	1.07		1.07		1.07		1.07		1.07	
	1.72		1.51		1.29		1.04		0.75	
1.00		1.00		1.00		1.00		1.00		1.00
1.31		1.11		0.91		0.68		0.42		**0.00**
	0.94		0.94		0.94		0.94		0.94	
	0.80		0.63		0.44		0.23		0.00	
		0.88		0.88		0.88		0.88		0.88
		0.42		0.28		0.13		0.00		**0.00**
			0.83		0.83		0.83		0.83	
			0.17		0.07		0.00		0.00	
				0.78		0.78		0.78		0.78
				0.04		0.00		0.00		**0.00**
					0.73		0.73		0.73	
					0.00		0.00		0.00	
						0.68		0.68		0.68
						0.00		0.00		**0.00**
							0.64		0.64	
							0.00		0.00	
								0.60		0.60
								0.00		**0.00**
									0.57	
									0.00	
										0.53
										0.00

Information in each node:

Output Price S
Real Option Value

Figure 27.1

2.3 Finite Differences

An alternative to binomial trees is to use finite differences for solving the above valuation equation. In this case we can use standard no-arbitrage conditions to derive a partial differential equation for the value of the contingent claim. For our real option problem, the standard Black and Scholes differential equation for the value of the real option $H(S, t)$ is:

$$\frac{1}{2} H_{SS} S^2 \sigma^2 + rSH_S - rH + H_t = 0 \tag{5}$$

with the following boundary condition at maturity

$$H(S, t = T_1) = \text{Max}[V(S) - I_1; 0] \tag{6}$$

Also when the price S is worthless so is the option, thus:

$$H(0, t) = 0 \tag{7}$$

Schwartz (1977) proposed the finite difference procedure of discretizing all state variables, determining the value of the contingent claim at the boundary conditions, replacing first and second derivatives by a finite difference approximation, and solving backward using a discretized version of the partial differential equation that represents the valuation equation. There are two basic finite difference approaches: the implicit and the explicit scheme. Even though the former is more robust, we implement the latter for expositional reasons.

In our problem, the value of the project is a function of two state variables: output price, S, and time to maturity, T. Time is discretized into M intervals, and price S into N intervals as shown in Figure 27.2. The Black and Sholes differential equation is then replaced by the following difference approximations:

$$\Delta S = S \max / N \tag{8}$$

$$\Delta T = T_1 / M \tag{9}$$

$$H_S = \frac{H_{i+1,j+1} - H_{i+1,j-1}}{2\Delta S} \tag{10}$$

$$H_{SS} = \frac{H_{i+1,j+1} - 2H_{i+1,j} + H_{i+1,j-1}}{\Delta S^2} \tag{11}$$

$$H_t = \frac{H_{i+1,j} - H_{i,j}}{\Delta t} \tag{12}$$

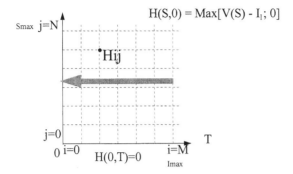

$$H(S,0) = Max[V(S) - I_1; 0]$$

Figure 27.2

Once these approximations are substituted into the differential equation, we obtain:

$$a_j H_{i+1,j-1} + b_j H_{i+1,j} + c_j H_{i+1,j+1} = H_{i,j} \tag{13}$$

with

$$a_j = \frac{1}{1+r\Delta t}\left(-\frac{1}{2}rj\Delta t + \frac{1}{2}\sigma^2 j^2 \Delta t\right) \tag{14}$$

$$b_j = \frac{1}{1+r\Delta t}(1 - \sigma^2 j^2 \Delta t) \tag{15}$$

$$c_j = \frac{1}{1+r\Delta t}\left(\frac{1}{2}rj\Delta t + \frac{1}{2}\sigma^2 j^2 \Delta t\right) \tag{16}$$

Thus, knowing the values of the contingent claim at $i+1$ we can obtain the values at i. Given that we have a boundary condition that gives initial values at $i = M$, it is possible to work backward from $i = M$ to $i = 0$.

Figure 27.3 presents an explicit finite difference solution to the investment valuation problem. The three right columns compute the constants necessary for the calculations. The next column to the left values the real option at the boundary:

Option Value at Maturity $= Max(V(S) - I_1; 0)$.

Using the above equations, the preceding columns are computed. Finally, project value for each initial price, when time to maturity is 1, is presented. It can be noted that for an initial output price of **1**, the computed option value is **1.30** (with $T_1 = 1$), again very similar to our previous results.

Real Option Value

j	Price	Time to Maturity(i)											aj	bj	cj
		1.0	0.9	0.8	0.7	0.6	0.5	0.4	0.3	0.2	0.1	0.0			
20	2.0	10	10	10	10	10	10	10	10	10	10	10	0.6931	-0.5941	0.8911
19	1.9	9.2	9.3	9.2	9.3	9.2	9.2	9.2	9.2	9.1	9.1	9	0.6208	-0.4396	0.8089
18	1.8	8.6	8.4	8.5	8.4	8.4	8.3	8.3	8.2	8.2	8.1	8	0.5525	-0.2931	0.7307
17	1.7	7.6	7.7	7.6	7.6	7.5	7.4	7.4	7.3	7.2	7.1	7	0.4881	-0.1545	0.6564
16	1.6	6.8	6.7	6.7	6.6	6.6	6.5	6.4	6.3	6.2	6.1	6	0.4277	-0.0238	0.5861
15	1.5	5.9	5.8	5.7	5.7	5.6	5.5	5.4	5.3	5.2	5.1	5	0.3713	0.0990	0.5198
14	1.4	4.9	4.8	4.8	4.7	4.6	4.5	4.4	4.3	4.2	4.1	4	0.3188	0.2139	0.4574
13	1.3	4.0	3.9	3.8	3.7	3.6	3.5	3.4	3.3	3.2	3.1	3	0.2703	0.3208	0.3990
12	1.2	3.01	2.9	2.8	2.7	2.6	2.5	2.4	2.3	2.2	2.1	2	0.2257	0.4198	0.3446
11	1.1	2.11	2.0	1.9	1.8	1.7	1.6	1.5	1.3	1.2	1.1	1	0.1851	0.5109	0.2941
10	1.0	1.30	1.2	1.1	1.0	0.9	0.8	0.7	0.6	0.4	0.2	0	0.1485	0.5941	0.2475
9	0.9	0.67	0.6	0.5	0.4	0.4	0.3	0.2	0.1	0.1	0.0	0	0.1158	0.6693	0.2050
8	0.8	0.26	0.2	0.2	0.1	0.1	0.1	0.0	0.0	0.0	0.0	0	0.0871	0.7366	0.1663
7	0.7	0.07	0.0	0.0	0.0	0.0	0.0	0.0	0.0	0.0	0.0	0	0.0624	0.7960	0.1317
6	0.6	0.01	0.0	0.0	0.0	0.0	0.0	0.0	0.0	0.0	0.0	0	0.0416	0.8475	0.1010
5	0.5	0.00	0.0	0.0	0.0	0.0	0.0	0.0	0.0	0.0	0.0	0	0.0248	0.8911	0.0743
4	0.4	0.00	0.0	0.0	0.0	0.0	0.0	0.0	0.0	0.0	0.0	0	0.0119	0.9267	0.0515
3	0.3	0.00	0.0	0.0	0.0	0.0	0.0	0.0	0.0	0.0	0.0	0	0.0030	0.9545	0.0327
2	0.2	0.00	0.0	0.0	0.0	0.0	0.0	0.0	0.0	0.0	0.0	0	-0.0020	0.9743	0.0178
1	0.1	0.00	0.0	0.0	0.0	0.0	0.0	0.0	0.0	0.0	0.0	0	-0.0030	0.9861	0.0069
0	0.0	0.00	0.0	0.0	0.0	0.0	0.0	0.0	0.0	0.0	0.0	0	0.0000	0.9901	0.0000

Figure 27.3

2.4 Standard Simulation

Boyle (1977) proposed a Monte Carlo simulation approach for European option valuation. The method is based on the idea that simulating price trajectories can approximate probability distributions of terminal asset values. Option cash flows are computed for each simulation run and then averaged. The discounted average cash flow using the risk free interest rate represents a point estimator of the option value.

There are several ways to increase estimation accuracy, the simplest one being to increase the number of simulating paths. Efficiency may also be improved by using variance reduction techniques, including the control-variate and antithetic-variate approaches (Hammersley and Handscomb [1964]). In what follows we solve our real option problem implementing the latter.

Figure 27.4 shows a spreadsheet with simulation runs to value the real option. Each run starts with an initial output price of **1**, and by using a specific set of random numbers, a price trajectory is computed. For example, our first price trajectory ends (at option maturity) with an output price of **0.88**. The next column to the right shows the option payoff for that specific price. Given that for that price the project would be abandoned, option value is zero.

To implement the antithetic variate variance reduction technique, our next row in figure 27.4 presents the price trajectory using the same random numbers as before, but with a change in sign. Given that our initial random numbers were such that output price at maturity was low (0.88), by changing random number signs this second row provides a price trajectory with high output price at maturity (1.34). For this new output price the option is now valuable, providing a cash flow of **3.44**. It is easy to see that an average of these two rows provides a lower variance estimate of actual cash flows than using any single one.

Once an adequate number of price trajectories is generated, real option value may be computed by discounting average option cash flows at the risk free rate. It can be seen that in our case with a set of only 30 independent price trajectories (60 rows including their antithetic values) we are able to obtain a very close value for our real option problem (1.30). In most cases it is necessary to make a much higher number of simulation runs to obtain accurate estimates.

2.5 Comparing Alternative Numerical Procedures

We have presented simple spreadsheet implementations of three alternative numerical approches to the same real option problem. Each of them has its own merits and is especially useful for specific types of valuation problems.

Run	Time to Maturity(i)											V(S)	NPV
	1.0	0.9	0.8	0.7	0.6	0.5	0.4	0.3	0.2	0.1	0.0		
1	1.00	0.98	0.98	0.91	1.00	0.99	0.95	0.97	0.95	0.91	0.88	0.00	0.00
	1.00	1.04	1.06	1.16	1.06	1.09	1.16	1.16	1.20	1.28	1.34	3.44	1.56
2	1.00	0.98	0.99	1.11	1.13	1.11	1.23	1.19	1.26	1.27	1.31	3.12	1.98
	1.00	1.04	1.05	0.95	0.94	0.98	0.89	0.94	0.91	0.91	0.90	0.00	1.49
3	1.00	0.98	1.07	1.09	1.06	1.01	1.06	1.00	1.06	1.08	1.25	2.50	1.30
	1.00	1.04	0.97	0.97	1.01	1.08	1.05	1.13	1.09	1.08	0.94	0.00	1.37
4	1.00	0.93	0.89	0.90	0.88	0.75	0.77	0.82	0.90	0.80	0.72	0.00	1.28
	1.00	1.09	1.16	1.17	1.22	1.43	1.41	1.34	1.24	1.40	1.58	5.81	1.68
5	1.00	0.92	0.88	0.72	0.68	0.64	0.60	0.59	0.60	0.67	0.70	0.00	1.30
	1.00	1.10	1.17	1.41	1.52	1.63	1.77	1.84	1.85	1.65	1.60	6.01	1.89
10	1.00	1.00	1.02	0.99	0.96	1.09	0.99	0.94	0.89	0.90	0.88	0.00	1.29
	1.00	1.02	1.02	1.07	1.12	1.00	1.11	1.18	1.27	1.29	1.33	3.33	1.43
15	1.00	1.07	1.08	1.15	1.09	1.14	1.24	1.43	1.45	1.54	1.61	6.10	1.33
	1.00	0.95	0.96	0.92	0.98	0.96	0.89	0.77	0.78	0.75	0.73	0.00	1.44
20	1.00	0.91	0.93	0.93	0.93	0.94	0.92	0.94	1.01	1.13	1.18	1.75	1.32
	1.00	1.11	1.11	1.13	1.16	1.16	1.22	1.21	1.15	1.03	1.01	0.10	1.37
25	1.00	1.10	1.10	1.06	1.13	1.18	1.23	1.24	1.35	1.35	1.35	3.53	1.31
	1.00	0.92	0.94	0.99	0.95	0.92	0.90	0.91	0.85	0.86	0.88	0.00	1.34
30	1.00	1.05	1.02	1.05	1.09	1.08	1.13	1.07	1.04	1.12	1.18	1.82	1.30
	1.00	0.97	1.01	1.01	0.99	1.02	0.99	1.06	1.11	1.05	1.01	0.15	**1.30**

Figure 27.4

Maybe the most important factor in choosing the appropriate numerical approach is the type of option we are trying to value. Standard simulation is a forward induction procedure, and as such presents problems for valuing American-type options. In situations when the optimal strategy is not known in advance, standard simulation procedures are not able to correctly value these options. As discussed later, many real options allow decision-makers to change production or investment levels at different points in time, and are therefore modeled as American options. Finite differences and binomial trees, on the other hand, are backward induction procedures that can determine optimal exercise policies, correctly valuing these American options.

What is a weakness for simulation in handling American-type options becomes a strength when there are path-dependent cash flows. For example, current tax payments normally depend on past profits, presenting a difficulty for all backward induction procedures. It is always possible to circumvent this problem by defining new state variables that represent path dependent information, but this may increase model complexity in a substantial way. Therefore, in the presence of path-dependent cash flows, simulation is a much better procedure than backward induction procedures.

The main characteristic that makes simulation so attractive is its ability to cope with uncertainty in a very simple way. The recent trend in modeling price uncertainty using multi-factor models is much easier to implement using standard simulation than using other numerical approaches. Something similar can be said on the use of complex stochastic processes for modeling the dynamics of these risk factors, which are simpler to implement using simulation.

Finally, the fact that the cost of computing has been going down so dramatically in the past years and that this trend shows no sign of weakening in the near future, presents a favorable prospect for increasing use of simulation. Moreover, its major drawback, the inability to successfully handle American-type options, has been tackled by new research in recent years, as described in the following section. With lower computational costs we can expect handling increasing modeling complexity, and an enhanced use of simulation techniques.

3   Simulation for American Options

3.1   Introduction

As stated earlier, there have been several recent efforts to extend Monte Carlo simulation techniques for solving American-type options. These include Barraquand and Martineau (1995), Broadie and Glasserman (1997a, 1997b), Broadie, Glasserman, and Jain (1997), Raymar and Zwecher (1997), Longstaff and Schwartz (1998), and others. These methods attempt to combine the simplicity of forward induction with the ability of determining the optimal option exercise of backward induction. In this section we give the basic intuition of this new approach and in the next the results of its application to the classical Brennan and Schwartz (1985) model for evaluating natural resource investments.

Longstaff and Schwartz (1998) propose a promising new procedure for solving American options. Their approach basically consists of estimating a conditional expected payoff function for each date for the continuation value of the American option, and comparing this value with its exercise value. Whenever the exercise value is higher than the continuation value the option should be optimally exercised, while in the opposite case it would not. To estimate the conditional expected payoff value they first run several thousand state variable paths, and at a second stage they make a backward induction analysis of when it is optimal to exercise. At any point in time (starting from the end) each path generates one observation on the optimality of exercising or not for that path. Using cross sectional regressions it is possible to estimate when it is optimal to exercise for given date and state variable values, and solve recursively backward.

Another approach (used in the next section) proposed by Barraquand and Martineau (1995) has been applied to solve some financial options. Its main insight is that in most cases it is possible to discretize and to reduce the dimensionality of the valuation problem, and still get reasonably good approximations. For example, if we assume a multi-factor process for a state variable S, the procedure calls for making

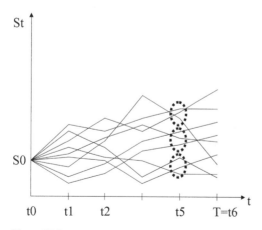

Figure 27.5

several thousand Monte Carlo simulations on S and grouping the obtained values into a fixed set of "bins," as shown in figure 27.5. Then, by making successive simulation runs, it is possible to empirically determine the transition probabilities between successive bins and finally to solve backward the valuation process using each bin as a decision unit (see figure 27.6).

One of the crucial success factors in using this methodology is the selection of the one-dimensional state variable that will represent all state variables in the problem. As Broadie and Glasserman (1997b) point out, this procedure does not ensure convergence when, for example, there are disjoint optimal exercise sectors. In this case, further increases in the number of one-dimensional bins are not able to determine the optimal exercise policy, as figure 27.7 shows.

To reduce this problem, Raymar and Zwecher (1997) recommend adding a second dimension to the bin grouping process, so the state of the economy can be represented by more than a one-dimensional vector.

Most of the literature for solving American options by simulation has concentrated on valuing financial options. In the next section we illustrate the use of the Barraquand and Martineau (1995) procedure for the more complex optimal operation of a copper mine, initially modeled in Brennan and Schwartz (1985). Other applications of simulation to real options include Cortazar and Schwartz (1998), who solve for the optimal timing of a development investment in an oil reserve using the Barraquand and Martineau (1995) procedure, and Cortazar, Acosta, and Osorio (1999) who compare different simulation alternatives for valuing real options and extend some of the results presented in the next section.

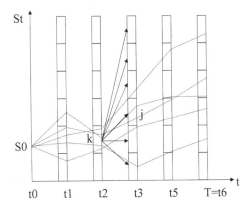

Figure 27.6

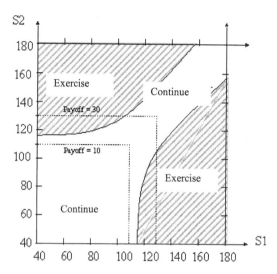

Figure 27.7

3.2   Evaluating Natural Resource Investments: Solving the Brennan and Schwartz (1985) Mine Problem Using Monte Carlo Simulation

3.2.1   The Model and Solution Procedure   Most real investments have embedded American-type options in their cash flow function. Whenever investments may be delayed, capacity expanded at different dates, and/or production suspended or resumed, the optimal timing of this decision is crucial for asset value maximization.

In this section we use the Barraquand and Martineau (1995) simulation procedure for solving the Brennan and Schwartz (1985)[1] model for valuing a copper mine which involves several American-type options. In this model, mine value depends on the discounted cash flows of future production, with copper prices following a stochastic process. The mine has finite copper reserves (Q), a constant-returns-to-scale technology with average unit cost of production $A(Q)$, a flexible tax structure, a diversifiable expropriation risk, and several American-type options including the flexibility to temporarily stop or resume production (with associated costs) or to abandon the mine. The mine has a maximum production rate and will optimally either produce at the maximum rate or close down.

Brennan and Schwartz (1985) solve their model by backward induction using finite difference numerical approximations to the partial differential equations that describe the value of the mine. They start the valuation process at known boundary conditions, including setting the value of the mine to zero when resources are exhausted or output price becomes zero.

The key elements to solve such a real option problem by simulation are: 1) the definition of a proper valuation grid, with each node representing a markovian state of the mine susceptible to be solved by backward induction, and 2) the discretization of the risk-neutral price process to simulate possible price paths.

First, to define the valuation grid, the value of the mine at any moment can be seen as depending on copper price, on remaining reserves, and on whether the mine is open or closed. It is convenient to discretize total reserves into units of production, q. Each unit of production represents total copper output that will be produced after a decision in that regard has been made and before a new review on whether or not to continue producing is made.

Depending on the current state of the mine, the feasible next stages can be determined. For example, if the mine is open and has n units of copper reserves (each one of q pounds of copper) the mine manager might decide to maintain the mine open (reducing next-stage reserves to $n - 1$ units), to close the mine (with next-stage reserves remaining the same), or to definitely abandon the mine. Each decision is associated with different cash flows. In the first case the cash flow is equal to the revenues minus the costs of production, in the second to the closing and maintenance costs, and in the third to zero.

Similarly, if the mine is currently closed and has n units of copper reserves, the manager might decide to keep it closed, to open it (reducing next-stage reserves to $n - 1$ units), or to abandon the mine. The cash flows in this case are equal to the maintenance costs for the first alternative, to the revenues minus the costs of producing a unit minus the cost of opening the closed mine for the second case, and to zero in the third alternative.

To solve for the optimal decision for each state of the mine we compute the expected value of each alternative decision, which, in turn, depends on the transition probabilities for the changes in copper prices and on the optimal continuation value once any of the three decisions is made.

The second element in solving by simulation such an evaluation problem is the definition of the stochastic process that models uncertainty. To obtain the price change probabilities we must specify the price stochastic process. Brennan and Schwartz (1985) assume a random walk process for the risk-adjusted commodity price returns. We discretize this process using the following equation:

$$\Delta S = (r - \delta)S\Delta t + \sigma S\sqrt{\Delta t}Z \tag{17}$$

where S is the commodity price, r is the (real) risk-free interest rate, δ the convenience yield, σ the volatility of price returns, Δt the time-increment, and Z a standardized Normal random variable. Even though a mean-reverting process for commodity prices might be better, we use this random walk process for comparison with the finite-difference method used in the original paper. In the next section we discuss possible model extensions that take this issue into account.

Following Barraquand and Martineau (1995), to obtain a discrete number of price states that adequately represent this stochastic process, a first set of simulation runs is performed. For each time interval, ΔT, all price paths are sorted and grouped into 200 bins, each one with the same number of observations. The average, maximum and minimum price in each bin is computed. Successive simulation runs are then performed and used to compute the transition probabilities between bins at successive time intervals.

Once transition probabilities are obtained, backward induction is used on the discrete state space that includes prices and mine states. Figure 27.8 shows a graphical representation of the grid that must be solved by backward induction. Assuming the mine is open and has 2 units of production, the arrows indicate the feasible states that could be reached with some non-zero probability. We solve the grid starting from the end and work our way backward determining the optimal operating policy for each state vector value.

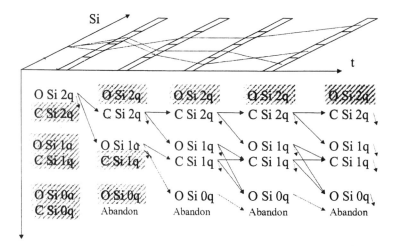

[Q, O:Open C:Closed]

Figure 27.8

3.2.2 Mine Value and Optimal Policy To check the simulation method accuracy we compare our results with those obtained by finite differences as reported in Brennan and Schwartz (1985). Table 27.1 presents a comparison of both solutions. It can be verified that the simulation method provides good approximations.

The optimal policy obtained by the simulation method is illustrated in figure 27.9. This result is reasonably close to the finite-differences optimal policy, as can be seen in figure 27.10, which compares the critical opening prices obtained by finite differences and by simulation.

3.2.3 Model Extensions The main advantage of simulation procedures for solving real option problems is its ability to handle models of increased complexity. In the following we provide some examples of model extensions that can easily be accommodated using these procedures.

The first type of possible extension deals with modeling uncertainty. There is an extensive bibliography on the appropriate number and specification of the risk factors to be used for the stochastic process that defines uncertainty (Schwartz [1997]). The simple random walk process in the last section was simply used to match the Brennan and Schwartz (1985) model, and is a very strong assumption given state-of-the-art research in commodity prices. Given that simulation is much more efficient to solve problems with multi-factor processes, simulation models can easily be extended to use more complex process specifications.

A second type of possible extension deals with the modeling of the derivative asset. The last section already considered one model extension (over Brennan and Schwartz [1985]) with the use of time as a state variable. This allows for including time-dependent information, like cost inflation or finite-time concessions for mine production. Other extensions of the derivative asset model could easily be considered.

Table 27.1

Copper price (US$/lb)	Mine value (MMUS$) Brennan-Schwartz		Mine value (MMUS$) Barraquand-Martineau		Error (%)	
	Open	Closed	Open	Closed	Open	Closed
0.4	4.15	4.35	4.19	4.39	1.0	0.9
0.5	7.95	8.11	7.97	8.17	0.3	0.7
0.6	12.52	12.49	12.53	12.53	0.1	0.3
0.7	17.56	17.38	17.57	17.37	0.1	−0.1
0.8	22.88	22.68	22.90	22.70	0.1	0.1
0.9	28.38	28.18	28.44	28.24	0.2	0.2
1.0	34.01	33.81	34.10	33.90	0.3	0.3

Critical Price (US$/lb)

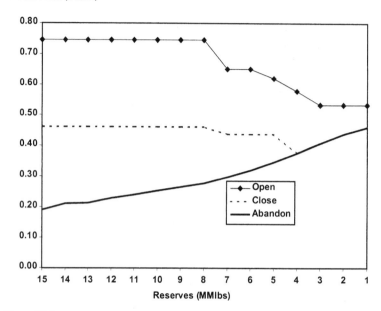

Figure 27.9

Critical Opening Price (US$/lb)

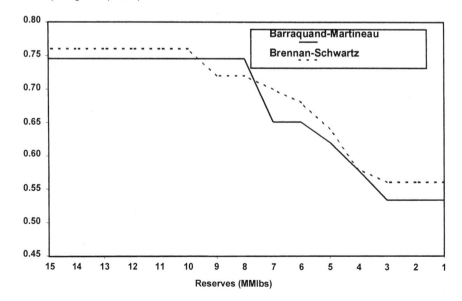

Figure 27.10

Finally, extensions of the modeling approach itself could be considered. For example, additional dimensions of the state variables could allow for a richer definition of the optimal policy, a source of considerable value in real options investments.

4 Conclusions

This chapter provided an overview of simulation and its applicability for solving real option problems. It discussed alternative numerical approaches to valuing assets and showed that (both forward and backward) induction procedures have a place in real options valuation.

To highlight the relative merits of the different numerical methods, a case-project with the option of investing in the future contingent on a stochastic output price was valued using binomial trees, finite differences, and simulation. Given that the project can be modeled as a European call option, the Black and Scholes (1973) analytical solution was used as a benchmark. The four methods provided similar results.

Standard simulation methods, even though very powerful for solving European-type options, have traditionally been considered inadequate for solving American-type options, a major drawback for their use in real option valuation. Recent research, however, has proposed extensions of simulation that combine forward and backward procedures for valuing American-type options. We presented an application of these extended simulation methods to solve Brennan and Schwartz's (1985) classic mine valuation problem. The benefits of this approach, with its better handling of complex uncertainty modeling and path-dependent cash flows, were discussed.

Acknowledgments

This research has been supported by FONDECYT-1990109. The author would like to thank Paulina Acosta and Manuel Osorio for joint research on this subject, and the editors for helpful comments.

Note

1. See chapter 16 of this book for a full presentation of this model.

References

Barraquand, J., and Martineau, D. (1995) "Numerical Valuation of High Dimensional Multivariate American Securities." *Journal of Financial and Quantitative Analysis*, 30 no. 3, 383–405.

Black, F., and Scholes, M. (1973) "The Pricing of Options and Corporate Liabilities." *Journal of Political Economy*, 81, 637–659.

Boyle, P. (1977) "Options: A Monte Carlo Approach." *Journal of Financial Economics*, 4, 323–338.

Brennan, M., and Schwartz, E. (1985) "Evaluating Natural Resource Investments." *Journal of Business*, vol. 58, no. 2, 135–157.

Broadie, M., and Glasserman, P. (1997a) "Pricing American-Style Securities Using Simulation." *Journal of Economic Dynamics and Control*, 21, 1323–1352.

Broadie, M., and Glasserman, P. (1997b) "Monte Carlo Methods for Pricing High-Dimensional American Options: An Overview." Working Paper, Columbia University.

Broadie, M., Glasserman, P., and Jain, G. (1997) "Enhanced Monte Carlo Estimates for American Option Prices." *Journal of Derivatives*, Fall 1997.

Cortazar, G., and Schwartz, E. (1998) "Monte Carlo Evaluation Model of an Undeveloped Oil Field." *Journal of Energy Finance and Development*, 3, no. 1, 73–84.

Cortazar, G., Acosta, P., and Osorio, M. (1999) "Monte Carlo Evaluation of Natural Resource Investments." Working Paper, Pontificia Universidad Catolica de Chile.

Cox, J. S., Ross, S., and Rubinstein, M. (1979) "Option Pricing: A Simplified Approach." *Journal of Financial Economics*, 7, 229–264.

Hammersley, J. M., and Handscomb, D. C. (1964) *Monte Carlo Methods*, London: *Methuen*.

Longstaff, F., and Schwartz, E. (1998) "Valuing American Options by Simulation: A Simple Least-Squares Approach." The John E. Anderson Graduate School of Management at UCLA, Finance Working Paper #25-98.

Raymar, S., and Zwecher, M. (1997) "A Monte Carlo Valuation of American Call Options On the Maximum of Several Stocks." *Journal of Derivatives*, Fall 1997, 7–23.

Rendleman, R. J., and Barter, B. J. (1979) "Two State Option Pricing." *Journal of Finance*, 34, 1092–1110.

Schwartz, E. (1977) "The Valuation of Warrants: Implementing a New Approach." *Journal of Financial Economics*, 4, 79–94.

Schwartz, E. (1997) "The Stochastic Behavior of Commodity Prices: Implications for Valuation and hedging." *Journal of Finance*, 52, no. 3, July 1997.

Sharpe, W. F. (1978) *Investments*. Englewood Cliffs, N.J.: Prentice-Hall.

VI APPLICATIONS

28 Applications of Option-Pricing Theory: Twenty-Five Years Later

Robert C. Merton

I Applications of the Option-Pricing Technology

Open the financial section of a major newspaper almost anywhere in the world and you will find pages devoted to reporting the prices of exchange-traded derivative securities, both futures and options. Along with the vast over-the-counter derivatives market, these exchange markets trade options and futures on individual stocks, stock-index and mutual-fund portfolios, on bonds and other fixed-income securities of every maturity, on currencies, and on commodities including agricultural products, metals, crude oil and refined products, natural gas, and even, electricity. The volume of transactions in these markets is often many times larger than the volume in the underlying cash-market assets. Options have traditionally been used in the purchase of real estate and the acquisition of publishing and movie rights. Employee stock options have long been granted to key employees and today represent a significantly growing proportion of total compensation, especially for the more highly paid workers in the United States. In all these markets, the same option-pricing methodology is widely used both to price and to measure the risk exposure from these derivatives (cf., Robert A. Jarrow and Andrew T. Rudd [1983] and John C. Cox and Mark Rubinstein [1985]). However, financial options represent only one of several categories of applications for the option-pricing technology.

In the late 1960's and early 1970's when the basic research leading to the Black-Scholes model was underway, options were seen as rather arcane and specialized financial instruments. However, both Black and Scholes (1972, 1973) and I (Merton [1970, 1974]) recognized early on in the research effort that the same approach used to price options could be applied to a variety of other valuation problems. Perhaps the first major development of this sort was the pricing of corporate liabilities, the "right-hand side" of the firm's balance sheet. This approach to valuation treated the wide array of instruments used to finance firms such as debentures, convertible bonds, warrants, preferred stock, and common stock (as well as a variety of hybrid securities) as derivative securities with their contractual payouts ultimately dependent on the value of the overall firm. In contrast to the standard fragmented valuation methods of the time, it provided a unified theory for pricing these liabilities. Because application of the pricing methodology does not require a history of trading in the particular instrument to be evaluated, it was well suited for pricing new types of financial securities issued by corporations in an innovating environment. Applications to corporate finance along this line developed rapidly.[1]

"Option-like" structures were soon seen to be lurking everywhere; thus there came an explosion of research in applying option-pricing which still continues. Indeed, I could not do full justice to the list of contributions accumulated over the past 25 years even if this entire paper were devoted to that endeavor. Fortunately, a major effort to do just that is underway and the results will soon be available (Jin et al., 1998). The authors have generously shared their findings with me. And so, I can convey here some sense of the breadth of applications and be necessarily incomplete without harm.

The put option is a basic option which gives its owner the right to sell the under-lying asset at a specified ("exercise") price on or before a given ("expiration") date. When purchased in conjunction with ownership of the underlying asset, it is func-tionally equivalent to an insurance policy that protects its owner against economic loss from a decline in the asset's value below the exercise price for any reason, where the term of the insurance policy corresponds to the expiration date. Hence, option-pricing theory can be applied to value insurance contracts. An early insurance application of the Black-Scholes model was to the pricing of loan guarantees and deposit insurance (cf., Merton, 1977a). A contract that insures against losses in value caused by default on promised payments on a contract in effect is equivalent to a put option on the contract with an exercise price equal to the value of the contract if it were default free. Loan and other contract guarantees, collectively called credit derivatives, are ubiquitous in the private sector. Indeed, whenever a debt instrument is purchased in which there is any chance that the promised payments will not be made, the pur-chaser is not only lending money but also in effect issuing a loan guarantee as a form of self-insurance. Another private-sector application of options analysis is in the valu-ation of catastrophic-insurance reinsurance contracts and bonds.[2] Dual funds and exotic options provide various financial-insurance and minimum-return-guarantee products.[3]

Almost surely, the largest issuer of such guarantees are governments. In the United States, the Office of the Management of the Budget is required by law to value those guarantees. The option model has been applied to assess deposit insurance, pension insurance, guarantees of student loans and home mortgages, and loans to small businesses and some large ones as well.[4] The application to government activities goes beyond just providing guarantees. The model has been used to determine the cost of other subsidies including farm-price supports and through-put guarantees for pipelines.[5] It has been applied to value licenses issued with limiting quotas such as for taxis or fisheries or the right to pollute and to value the government's right to change those quotas.[6] Government sanctions patents. The decision whether to spend the resources to acquire a patent depends on the value of the patent which can be framed as an option-pricing problem. Indeed, even on something that is not currently commercial, one may acquire the patent for its "option value," should economic conditions change in an unexpected way.[7] James L. Paddock et al. (1988) show that option value can be a significant proportion of the total valuation of government-granted offshore drilling rights, especially when current and expected future economic conditions would not support development of the fields. Option-pricing analysis quantifies the government's economic decision whether to build roads in less-populated areas depending on whether it has the policy option to abandon rural roads if they are not used enough.[8]

Various legal and tax issues involving policy and behavior have been addressed using the option model. Among them is the valuation of plaintiffs' litigation options, bankruptcy laws including limited-liability provisions, tax delinquency on real estate and other property as an option to abandon or recover the property by paying the arrears, tax evasion, and valuing the tax "timing" option for the capital-gains tax in a circumstance when only realization of losses and gains on investments triggers a taxable event.[9]

In a recent preliminary study, the options structure has been employed to help model the decision of whether the Social Security fund should invest in equities (Kenneth Smetters, 1997). As can be seen in the option formula, the value of an option depends on the volatility of the underlying asset. The Federal Reserve uses as one of its indicators of investor uncertainty about the future course of interest rates, the "implied" volatility derived from option prices on government bonds.[10] In his last paper, published after his death, Black (1995) applies options theory to model the process for the interest rates that govern the dynamics of government bond prices. In another area involving central-bank concerns, Perold (1995) shows how the introduction of various types of derivatives contracts has helped reduce potential systemic-risk problems in the payment system from settlement exposures. The Black-Scholes model can be used to value the "free credit option" implicitly offered to participants, in addition to "float," in markets with other than instantaneous settlement periods. See also Paul H. Kupiec and Patricia A. White (1996). The prospective application of derivative-security technology to enhance central-bank stabilization policies in both interest rates and currencies is discussed in Merton (1995, 1997b).

In an application involving government activities far removed from sophisticated and relatively efficient financial markets, options analysis has been used to provide new insights into optimal government planning policies in developing countries. A view held by some in development economics about the optimal educational policy for less-developed countries is that once the expected future needs for labor-force composition are determined, the optimal education policy should be to pursue targeted training of the specific skills forecast and in the quantities needed. The alternative of providing either more general education and training in multiple skills or training in skills not expected to be used is seen as a "luxury" that poorer, developing countries could not afford. It, of course, was understood, that forecasts of future labor-training needs were not precise. Nevertheless, the basic prescription formally treated them as if they were. In Samantha J. Merton (1992), the question is revisited, this time with an explicit recognition of the uncertainty about future labor requirements embedded in the model. The analysis shows that the value of having the option to change the skill mix and skill type of the labor force over a relatively short period of time can exceed the increased cost in terms of longer education periods or less-deep training in any one skill. The Black-Scholes model is used to quantify that trade-off. In a different context of the private sector in a developed country, the same technique could be used to assess the cost-benefit trade-off for a company to pay a higher wage for a labor force with additional skills not expected to be used in return for the flexibility to employ those skills if the unexpected happens.

The discussion of labor education and training decisions and litigation and taxes leads naturally into the subject of human capital and household decision-making. The individual decision as to how much vocational education to acquire can be formulated as an option-valuation problem in which the optimal exercise conditions reflect when to stop training and start working.[11] In the classic labor-leisure trade-off, one whose job provides the flexibility to increase or decrease the number of hours worked, and hence his total compensation, on relatively short notice, has a valuable option relative to those whose available work hours are fixed.[12] Wage and pension-plan "floors" that provide for a minimum compensation, and even tenure for university professors (John G. McDonald, 1974), have an option-like structure. Other options commonly a part of household finance are: the commitment by an institution to provide a mortgage to the house buyer, if he chooses to get one; the prepayment right, after he takes the mortgage, that gives the homeowner the right to renegotiate the interest rate paid to the lender if rates fall;[13] a car lease which gives the customer the right, but not the obligation, to purchase the car at a prespecified price at the end of the lease.[14] Health-care insurance contains varying degrees of flexibility, a major one being whether the consumer agrees in advance to use only a prespecified set of doctors and hospitals ("HMO plan") or he retains the right to choose an "out-of-plan" doctor or hospital ("point-of-service" plan). For the consumer making the decision on which to take and the health insurer assessing the relative cost of providing the two plans, each solves an option-pricing problem as to the value of that flexibility.[15] Much the same structure of valuation occurs in choosing between "pay-per-view" and "flat-fee" payment for cable-television services.

Many of the preceding option-pricing applications do not involve financial instruments. The family of such applications is called "real" options. The most developed area for real-option application is investment decisions by firms.[16] However, real-options analysis has also been applied to real-estate investment and development decisions.[17] The common element for using option-pricing here is the same as in the preceding examples: the future is uncertain (if it were not, there would be no need to create options because we know now what we will do later) and in an uncertain environment, having the flexibility to decide what to do after some of that uncertainty is resolved definitely has value. Option-pricing theory provides the means for assessing that value.

The major categories of options within project-investment valuations are: the option to initiate or expand; the option to abandon or contract; and the option to wait, slow down, or speed up development. There are "growth" options which involve creating excess capacity as an option to expand and research and development as creating the opportunity to produce new products and even new businesses, but not the obligation to do so if they are not economically viable.[18]

A few examples: For real-world application of the options technology in valuing product development in the pharmaceutical industry, see Nichols (1994). In the generation of electric power, the power plant can be constructed to use a single fuel such as oil or natural gas or it can be built to operate on either. The value of that option is the ability to use the least-cost, available fuel at each point in time and the cost of that optionality is manifest in both the higher cost of construction and less-efficient energy conversion than with the corresponding specialized equipment. A third example described in Timothy A. Luehrman (1992) comes from the entertainment industry and involves the decision about making a sequel to a movie; the choices are: either to produce both the original movie and its sequel at the same time, or wait and produce the sequel after the success or failure of the original is known. One does not have to be a movie-production expert to guess that the incremental cost of producing the sequel is going to be less if the first path is followed. While this is done, more typically the latter is chosen, especially with higher-budget films. The economic reason is that the second approach provides the option not to make the sequel (if, for example, the original is not a success). If the producer knew (almost certainly) that the sequel will be produced, then the option value of waiting for more information is small and the cost of doing the sequel separately is likely to exceed the benefit. Hence, once again, we see that the amount of uncertainty is critical to the decision, and the option-pricing model provides the means for quantifying the cost/benefit trade-off. As a last example, Baldwin and Clark (1999) develop a model for designing complex production systems focused around the concept of modularity. They exemplify their central theme with several industrial examples which include computer and automobile production. Modularity in production provides options. In assessing the value of modularity for production, they employ an option-pricing type of methodology, where complexity in the production system is comparable to uncertainty in the financial one.[19]

In each of these real-option examples, as with a number of the other applications discussed in this section, the underlying "asset" is rarely traded in anything approximating a continuous market and its price is therefore not continuously observable either. For that reason, this chapter, manifestly focused on applications, devotes so much space to the technical section on extending the Black-Scholes option-pricing framework to include nontradability and nonobservability [omitted here].

Acknowledgments

I am grateful to Robert K. Merton, Lisa Meulbroek, and Myron Scholes for their helpful suggestions and for so much more. Over the past 30 years, I have come to owe an incalculable debt to Paul A. Samuelson, my teacher, mentor, colleague, co-researcher, and friend. Try as I have (cf., Merton, 1983, 1992), I cannot find the words to pay sufficient tribute to him. I dedicate this to Paul and to the memory of Fischer Black.

Notes

1. See Merton (1992 pp. 423–27) for an extensive list of references. See also Gregory D. Hawkins (1982) and Michael J. Brennan and Eduardo S. Schwartz (1985a) and the early empirical testing by E. Philip Jones et al. (1984).

2. Cf., Alan Kraus and Ross (1982), Neil A. Doherty and James R. Garven (1986), J. David Cummins (1988), Cummins and Hélyette Geman (1995), and Scott E. Harrington et al. (1995).

3. Brennan and Schwartz (1976), Jonathan J. Ingersoll, Jr. (1976), M. Barry Goldman et al. (1979), Mary Ann Gatto et al. (1980), and René M. Stulz (1982). In an early real-world application, Myron Scholes and I developed the first options-strategy mutual fund in the United States, Money Market/Options Investments, Inc., in February 1976. The strategy, which invested 90 percent of its assets in money-market instruments and 10 percent in a diversified portfolio of stock call options, provided equity exposure on the upside with a guaranteed "floor" on the value of the portfolio. The return patterns from this and similar "floor" strategies were later published in Merton et al. (1978, 1982).

4. Howard B. Sosin (1980), Baldwin et al. (1983), Donald F. Cunningham and Patric H. Hendershott (1984), Alan J. Marcus (1987), Merton and Zvi Bodie (1992), Bodie (1996), Ashoka Mody (1996), and Robert S. Neal (1996).

5. Scott P. Mason and R. C. Merton (1985), Calum G. Turvey and Vincent Amanor-Boadu (1989), and Taehoon Kang and B. Wade Brorsen (1995).

6. James E. Anderson (1987) and Jonathan M. Karpoff (1989).

7. Lenos Trigeorgis (1993).

8. Cathy A. Hamlett and C. Phillip Baumel (1990).

9. George M. Constantinides and J. Ingersoll (1984), Brendan O'Flaherty (1990), William J. Blanton (1995), Paul G. Mahoney (1995), and Charles T. Terry (1995).

10. Sylvia Nasar (1992). See Bodie and Merton (1995) for an overview article on implied volatility as an example of the informational role of asset and option prices.

11. Uri Dothan and Joseph Williams (1981).

12. Bodie et al. (1992).

13. Kenneth B. Dunn and John J. McConnell (1981) and M. Brennan and E. Schwartz (1985b).

14. Stephen E. Miller (1995).

15. James A. Hayes et al. (1993) and Frank T. Magiera and Robert A. McLean (1996).

16. Mason and Merton (1985), Robert L. McDonald and Daniel R. Siegel (1985), Saman Majd and Robert S. Pindyck (1987), Alexander J. Triantis and James E. Hodder (1990), Avinash K. Dixit and R. S. Pindyck (1994), Nancy A. Nichols (1994), Lenos Trigeorgis (1996), and Keith J. Leslie and Max P. Michaels (1997).

17. V. Kerry Smith (1984), Raymond Chiang et al. (1986), David Geltner and William C. Wheaton (1989), Joseph T. Williams (1991), and F. Christian Zinkhan (1991).

18. W. Carl Kester (1984), Robyn McLaughlin and Robert A. Taggart (1992), and Terrance W. Faulkner (1996).

19. See also Hua He and Pindyck (1992). On an entirely different application, Kester's (1984) analysis of whether to develop products in parallel or sequentially could be applied to the evaluation of alternative strategies for funding basic scientific research: is it better to support N different research approaches simultaneously or just to support one or two and then use the resulting outcomes to sequence future research approaches? See also Merton (1992 p. 426).

References

Anderson, James E. "Quotas as Options: Optimality and Quota License Pricing Under Uncertainty." *Journal of International Economics*, August 1987, *23* (1/2), pp. 21–39.

Baldwin, Carliss, Lessard, Donald and Mason, Scott P. "Budgetary Time Bombs: Controlling Government Loan Guarantees." *Canadian Public Policy*, 1983, *9*, pp. 338–46.

Black, Fischer and Scholes, Myron S. "The Valuation of Option Contracts and a Test of Market Efficiency." *Journal of Finance*, May 1972, *27* (2), pp. 399–418.

―――. "The Pricing of Options and Corporate Liabilities." *Journal of Political Economy*, May–June 1973, *81* (3), pp. 637–54.

Blanton, William J. "Reducing the Value of Plaintiff's Litigation Option in Federal Court: *Daubert v. Merrell Dow Pharmaceuticals, Inc.*" *George Mason Law Review*, Spring 1995, *2*, pp. 159–222.

Bodie, Zvi. "What the Pension Benefit Guaranty Corporation Can Learn from the Federal Savings-and-Loan Insurance Corporation." *Journal of Financial Services Research*, January 1996, *10* (1), pp. 83–100.

Bodie, Zvi and Merton, Robert C. "The Informational Role of Asset Prices: The Case of Implied Volatility," in Dwight B. Crane, Kenneth A. Froot, Scott P. Mason, André F. Perold, Robert C. Merton, Zvi Bodie, Erik R. Sirri, and Peter Tufano, eds., *The Global Financial System: A Functional Perspective.* Boston, MA: Harvard Business School Press, 1995, pp. 197–224.

―――. *Finance.* Upper Saddle River, NJ: Prentice Hall, 1998.

Bodie, Zvi, Merton, Robert C. and Samuelson, William F. "Labor Supply Flexibility and Portfolio Choice in a Life-Cycle Model." *Journal of Economic Dynamics and Control*, July–October 1992, *16* (3–4), pp. 427–49.

Brennan, Michael J. and Schwartz, Eduardo S. "The Pricing of Equity-Linked Life Insurance Policies with an Asset Value Guarantee." *Journal of Financial Economics*, June 1976, *3* (3), pp. 195–213.

———. "Determinants of GNMA Mortgage Prices." *Journal of the American Real Estate & Urban Economics Association*, Fall 1985b, *13* (3), pp. 209–28.

Chiang, Raymond, Led, Tsong-Yue and Ling, David C. "Retail Leasehold Interests: A Contingent Claim Analysis." *Journal of the American Real Estate & Urban Economics Association*, Summer 1986, *14* (2), pp. 216–29.

Constantinides, George M. and Ingersoll, Jonathan E., Jr. "Optimal Bond Trading with Personal Taxes." *Journal of Financial Economics*, September, 1984, *13* (3), pp. 299–336.

Cox, John C. and Rubinstein, Mark. *Options Markets*. Englewood Cliffs, NJ: Prentice Hall, 1985.

Cummins, J. David. "Risk-Based Premiums for Insurance Guarantee Funds." *Journal of Finance*, September 1988, *43* (4), pp. 823–89.

Cummins, J. David and Geman, Hélyette. "Pricing Catastrophe Insurance Futures and Call Spreads: An Arbitrage Approach." *Journal of Fixed Income*, March 1995, *4* (4) pp. 46–57.

Cunningham, Donald F. and Hendershott, Patric H. "Pricing FHA Mortgage Default Insurance." *Housing Finance Review*, December 1984, *3* (4), pp. 373–92.

Dixit, Avinash K. and Pindyck, Robert S. *Investment under Uncertainty*. Princeton, NJ: Princeton University Press, 1994.

Doherty, Neil A. and Garven, James R. "Price Regulation in Property-Liability Insurance: A Contingent-Claims Approach." *Journal of Finance*, December 1986, *41* (5), pp. 1031–50.

Dothan, Uri and Williams, Joseph. "Education as an Option." *Journal of Business*, January 1981, *54* (1), pp. 117–39.

Dunn, Kenneth B, and McConnell, John J. "Valuation of GNMA Mortgage-Backed Securities." *Journal of Finance*, June 1981, *36* (3), pp. 599–616.

Faulkner, Terrance W. "Applying 'Options Thinking' to R&D Valuation." *Research-Technology Management*, May–June 1996, *39* (3), pp. 50–56.

Gatto, Mary Ann, Geske, Robert, Litzenberger, Robert H. and Sosin, Howard B. "Mutual Fund Insurance." *Journal of Financial Economics*, September 1980, *8* (3), pp. 283–317.

Geltner, David and Wheaton, William C. "On the Use of the Financial Option Price Model to Value and Explain Vacant Urban Land." *Journal of the American Real Estate & Urban Economics Association*, Summer 1989, *17* (2), pp. 142–58.

Goldman, M. Barry, Sosin, Howard B. and Shepp, Lawrence A. "On Contingent Claims that Ensure Ex-Post Optimal Stock Market Timing." *Journal of Finance*, May 1979, *34* (2), pp. 401–13.

Hamlett, Cathy A. and Baumel, C. Phillip. "Rural Road Abandonment: Policy Criteria and Empirical Analysis." *American Journal of Agricultural Economics*, February 1990, *72* (1) pp. 114–20.

Harrington, Scott E., Mann, Steven V. and Niehaus, Greg. "Insurer Capital Structure Decisions and the Viability of Insurance Derivatives." *Journal of Risk and Insurance*, September 1995, *62* (3), pp. 483–508.

Hayes, James A., Cole, Joseph B. and Meiselman, David I. "Health Insurance Derivatives: The Newest Application of Modern Financial Risk Management." *Business Economics*, April 1993, *28* (2), pp. 36–40.

He, Hua and Pindyck, Robert, S. "Investments in Flexible Production Capacity." *Journal of Economic Dynamics and Control*, July–October 1992, *16* (3, 4), pp. 575–99.

Ingersoll, Jonathan E., Jr. "A Theoretical Model and Empirical Investigation of the Dual Purpose Funds: An Application of Contingent-Claims Analysis." *Journal of Financial Economics*, January–March 1976, *3* (1/2), pp. 82–123.

Jarrow, Robert A. and Rudd, Andrew T. *Option Pricing*. Homewood, IL: Irwin, 1983.

Jin, Li, Kogan, Leonid, Lim, Terence, Taylor, Jonathan and Lo, Andrew W. "The Derivatives Sourcebook: A Bibliography of Applications of the Black-Scholes/Merton Option-Pricing Model." Working paper, Massachusetts Institute of Technology, 1998.

Kang, Taehoon and Brorsen, B. Wade. "Valuing Target Price Support Programs with Average Option Pricing." *American Journal of Agricultural Economics*, February 1995, *77* (1), pp. 106–18.

Karpoff, Jonathan M. "Characteristics of Limited Entry Fisheries and the Option Component of Entry Licenses." *Land Economics*, November 1989, *65* (4), pp. 386–93.

Kester, W. Carl. "Today's Options for Tomorrow's Growth." *Harvard Business Review*, March–April 1984, *62* (2), pp. 153–60.

Kraus, Alan and Ross, Stephen A. "The Determination of Fair Profits for the Property-Liability Insurance Firm." *Journal of Finance*, September 1982, *37* (4), pp. 1015–28.

Leslie, Keith J. and Michaels, Max P. "The Real Power of Real Options." *McKinsey Quarterly*, 1997, (3), pp. 4–22.

Mahoney, Paul G. "Contract Remedies and Options Pricing." *Journal of Legal Studies*, January 1995, *24* (1), pp. 139–63.

Majd, Saman and Pindyck, Robert S. "Time to Build, Option Value, and Investment Decisions." *Journal of Financial Economics*, March 1987, *18* (1), pp. 7–28.

Marcus, Alan J. "Corporate Pension Policy and the Value of PBGC Insurance," in Zvi Bodie, John B. Shoven, and David A. Wise, eds., *Issues in Pension Economics*. Chicago: University of Chicago Press, 1987, pp. 49–76.

Mason, Scott P. and Merton, Robert C. "The Role of Contingent Claims Analysis in Corporate Finance," in Edward Altman and Marti Subrahmanyan, eds., *Recent Advances in Corporate Finance*. Homewood, IL: Irwin, 1982, pp. 7–54.

McDonald, Robert L. and Siegel, Daniel R. "Investment and the Valuation of Firms When There Is an Option to Shut Down." *International Economic Review*, June 1985, *26* (2), pp. 331–49.

McLaughlin, Robyn and Taggart, Robert A. "The Opportunity Cost of Using Excess Capacity." *Financial Management*, Summer 1992, *21* (2), pp. 12–23.

Merton, Robert C. "A Dynamic General Equilibrium Model of the Asset Market and its Application to the Pricing of the Capital Structure of the Firm." Massachusetts Institute of Technology Working Paper No. 497–70, 1970.

———. "On the Pricing of Corporate Debt: The Risk Structure of Interest Rates." *Journal of Finance*, May 1974, *29* (2), pp. 449–70.

———. "An Analytic Derivation of the Cost of Deposit Insurance and Loan Guarantees: An Application of Modern Option Pricing Theory." *Journal of Banking and Finance*, June 1977a, *1* (1), pp. 3–11.

———. *Continuous-time Finance*. Cambridge, MA: Blackwell, 1992.

Merton, Robert C. and Bodie, Zvi. "On the Management of Financial Guarantees." *Financial Management*, Winter 1992, *21* (4), pp. 87–109.

Merton, Robert C., Scholes, Myron S. and Gladstein, Mathew L. "The Returns and Risk of Alternative Call Option Portfolio Investment Strategies." *Journal of Business*, April 1978, *51* (2), pp. 183–242.

———. "The Returns and Risks of Alternative Put-Option Portfolio Investment Strategies." *Journal of Business*, January 1982, *55* (1), pp. 1–55.

Miller, Stephen E. "Economics of Automobile Leasing: The Call Option Value." *Journal of Consumer Affairs*, Summer 1995, *29* (1), pp. 199–218.

Mody, Ashoka. "Valuing and Accounting for Loan Guarantees." *World Bank Research Observer*, 1996, *11* (1), pp. 119–42.

Nasar, Sylvia. "For Fed, a New Set of Tea Leaves." *New York Times*, July 5, 1992, p. D1.

Neal, Robert S. "Credit Derivatives: New Financial Instruments for Controlling Credit Risk." *Economic Review*, Second Quarter 1996, *81* (2), pp. 14–27.

Nichols, Nancy A. "Scientific Management at Merck: An Interview with CFO Judy Lewent." *Harvard Business Review*, January–February 1994, *72* (1), pp. 89–99.

O'Flaherty, Brendan. "The Option Value of Tax Delinquency: Theory." *Journal of Urban Economics*, November 1990, *28* (3), pp. 287–317.

Paddock, James L., Siegel, Daniel R. and Smith, James L. "Option Valuation of Claims on Real Assets: The Case of Offshore Petroleum Leases." *Quarterly Journal of Economics*, August 1988, *103* (3), pp. 479–508.

Smith, V. Kerry. "A Bound for Option Value." *Land Economics*, August 1984, *60* (3), pp. 292–96.

Sosin, Howard B. "On the Valuation of Federal Loan Guarantees to Corporations." *Journal of Finance*, December 1980, *35* (5), pp. 1209–21.

Stulz, René M. "Options on the Minimum or the Maximum of Two Risky Assets: Analysis and Applications." *Journal of Financial Economics*, July 1982, *10* (2), pp. 161–85.

Terry, Charles T. "Option Pricing Theory and the Economic Incentive Analysis of Nonrecourse Acquisition Liabilities." *American Journal of Tax Policy*, Fall 1995, *12* (2), pp. 273–397.

Triantis, Alexander J. and Hodder, James E. "Valuing Flexibility as a Complex Option." *Journal of Finance*, June 1990, *45* (2), pp. 549–65.

Trigeorgis, Lenos. "Real Options and Interactions with Financial Flexibility." *Financial Management*, Autumn 1993, *22* (3), pp. 202–24.

————. *Real Options*. Cambridge, MA: MIT Press, 1996.

Turvey, Calum G. and Amanor-Boadu, Vincent. "Evaluating Premiums for a Farm Income Insurance Policy." *Canadian Journal of Agricultural Economics*, July 1989, *37* (2), pp. 233–47.

Williams, Joseph T. "Real Estate Development as an Option." *Journal of Real Estate Finance and Economics*, June 1991, *4* (2), pp. 191–208.

Zinkhan, F. Christian. "Option-Pricing and Timberland's Land-Use Conversion Option." *Land Economics*, August 1991, *67* (3), pp. 317–25.

29 Scientific Management at Merck: An Interview with CFO Judy Lewent

Nancy A. Nichols

Risk, complexity, and uncertainty define the business environment of the 1990s. While there is broad agreement about the need to manage within an ever-changing context, few have suggested a framework for managing risk or a set of tools to help cope with uncertainty. Yet that is precisely what Judy Lewent, CFO of Merck & Co., Inc., and her 500-member finance team have developed to deal with the high-stakes nature of the pharmaceutical industry.

On average, it costs $359 million and takes ten years to bring a drug to market. Once there, seven out of ten products fail to return the cost of the company's capital. Raising the stakes in this already risky game is the specter of health care reform that could limit the prices of breakthrough medicines, dramatically affect a pharmaceutical product's life cycle, and permanently weaken the already poor odds of making money on a prescription drug.

Add to that uncertain scenario the standard risks borne by multinational corporations, such as interest-rate and currency-rate fluctuations, and you can see why the finance team at Merck prides itself on bringing prudent financial risk management to the routinely unpredictable pharmaceutical industry.

In this interview with HBR senior editor Nancy A. Nichols, Lewent talks about her scientific approach to finance, one that is both long-term in nature and eminently tied to Merck's overall strategy. At 44 years of age, Lewent ranks among the most powerful women in corporate America and is the only woman to hold the title of CFO at a major corporation.

A graduate of MIT's Sloan School of Management, Lewent served as division controller at Pfizer before joining Merck in 1980 in the newly created position of director of acquisitions and capital analysis. She was named CFO in 1990 after serving three years as treasurer and sits on the seven-member chairman's staff, the senior policy-making group at Merck.

HBR: *What major challenges face Merck today?*

Judy Lewent: Everywhere I look in the pharmaceutical industry today, I see increasing complexity and uncertainty. Whether I am considering health care reform, the emergence of the generic drug market, therapeutic substitution, or even currency fluctuations, I see both volatility and risk.

As finance professionals, therefore, we must not only manage the risks that lie at the core of our business, such as the inherent risks in drug research, but also hedge or otherwise manage the risks we don't want to retain, like the currency risks associated with doing business in 40 of the countries in which we operate. In addition, we must plan for and attempt to deal with the changes that health care reform will bring to the market.

To date, the risks and rewards in pharmaceutical research have mostly balanced out. In general, the returns the industry has realized on R&D have more or less equaled our cost of capital. As I look to the future, however, I see the marketplace dynamics changing, and that jeopardizes the delicate balance we have achieved.

What are the parameters of your risk/reward ratio?

Success in our industry demands a steady flow of new and innovative medicines, yet research is an increasingly costly and time-consuming proposition. That, of course, is the paradox of the pharmaceutical business: the route to success is to put more money at risk, not less.

Merck invests approximately $1 billion per year in research, which has given us extraordinary insight into the risky nature and high cost of pharmaceutical research. We know that scientists will probe an idea they feel has merit for as long as they possibly can, which is great. You get advocates, you get champions, and you never say die. The challenge from the point of view of the finance department is to put parameters around that curiosity and determine what is and what is not productive. After all, our success or failure in R&D won't result from the quality of our scientists alone; it will also come from the quality of our thinking about where to invest.

What role does finance play in those decisions?

Think about drug research for a minute. We may know at the beginning of a project that there is a market for a specific treatment that includes many thousands of people, and once we reach a certain point in the process, we may know that a certain compound may be effective. But we still aren't 100% certain that the compound will prove so safe and effective that it can be turned into a drug. So we have to ask ourselves, "Do we continue to invest?" Those are the kinds of decisions we face every day. And they aren't investments that easily lend themselves to traditional financial analysis. Remember that we need to make huge investments now and may not see a profit for 10 to 15 years. In that kind of situation, a traditional analysis that factors in the time value of money may not fully capture the strategic value of an investment in research, because the positive cash flows are severely discounted when they are analyzed over a very long time frame. As a result, the volatility or risk isn't properly valued.

If traditional financial tools aren't always helpful, how do you value your investments?

Option analysis, like the kind used to value stock options, provides a more flexible approach to valuing our research investments than traditional financial analysis because it allows us to evaluate those investments at successive stages of a project.

When you make an initial investment in a research project, you are paying an entry fee for a right, but you are not obligated to continue that research at a later stage. Merck's experience with R&D has given us a database of information that allows us to value the risk or the volatility of our research projects, a key piece of information in option analysis. Therefore, if I use option theory to analyze that investment, I have a tool to examine uncertainty and to value it.

When I look at investments from this perspective, I am able to value the project if it is successful. In other words, I know the value of a new product. But I am also able to value the project if it doesn't result in a new product, because I know we will have gained new scientific information that will help us in the future.

Now that's different from a decision to invest in a plant or buy a company. In those cases, traditional financial valuation may be warranted; although at Merck, we see opportunities to use option analysis in traditional projects as well. To me, all kinds of business decisions are options. (See box 29.1, "Option Analysis at Merck," by Gary L. Sender.)

What's Monte Carlo analysis? When do you use it?

Monte Carlo analysis is a sophisticated form of mathematical analysis that lets us come up with a range of possibilities or outcomes for a certain set of possible actions. Whereas analysts most often predict results for the total project based on isolated changes in particular variables, Monte Carlo analysis predicts results based on simultaneous changes in numerous variables. Monte Carlo analysis is ideal for us, when you consider the number of changes in our competitive environment.

For example, we know that in any array of research projects, most will do poorly and a handful will do well; roughly 1 in 10,000 explored chemicals becomes a prescription drug. But we cannot predict with any certainty how any of our research projects will fare. To try to assess our risks in this situation, I began work on a model in 1983 that today is known as the Research Planning Model. That model, which is heavily dependent on Monte Carlo analysis, marries science and finance: it takes all of our risks and shows us how they are deployed across our entire portfolio of research projects.

We begin with an estimate of the project's scientific viability and factor in the marketing and manufacturing variables. We then add in economic constraints, such as pricing, inflation, and selling costs. Extended over 20 years, the model is used by senior managers for resource allocation. It shows us not only where we have

Box 29.1
Option Analysis at Merck
Gary L. Sender

Pharmaceutical companies frequently enter into business relationships with small biotechnology companies or universities in order to gain access to early-stage research projects. Analyzing the strategic value of such projects, however, can be difficult. Because of the prolonged development phase of any pharmaceutical product (often up to a decade before the first commercial sale) and the extreme difficulty of predicting cash flows and market conditions far into the future, net-present-value techniques may not capture the real strategic value of the research.

As a result, the business agreements are often structured so that the larger pharmaceutical company will make an up-front payment followed by a series of progress payments to the smaller company or university for research. These contingent progress payments give the pharmaceutical company the right—but not the obligation—to make further investments: for instance, funding clinical trials or providing capital for manufacturing requirements. This is known as an *option contract*.

The Financial Evaluation and Analysis Group at Merck was recently presented with just such an option contract—I'll call it Project Gamma. Merck wanted to enter a new line of business that required the acquisition of appropriate technologies from a small biotech company called Gamma: product development, scale-up of the manufacturing process, coordination of regulatory requirements, and product commercialization. Under the terms of the proposed agreement, Merck would make a $2 million payment to Gamma over a period of three years. In addition, Merck would pay Gamma royalties should the product ever come to market. Merck had the option to terminate the agreement at any time if dissatisfied with the progress of the research.

When it came to analyzing the strategic value of Project Gamma, the finance group could not rely on traditional techniques. Project returns were difficult to model both because of the high degree of uncertainty regarding the size and profitability of the future market segments and because sales were not expected to commence until the latter part of the decade. But here was a project that clearly had option characteristics: an asymmetrical distribution of returns present or, in other words, an overwhelming potential upside with little current downside exposure. The group, therefore, chose to use option analysis.

Two factors determine a project's option value. The first factor is the length of time the project may be deferred. Clearly, the longer Merck had to examine future developments, the more valuable the project would be. With more time, Merck would be able to collect more information and therefore make a better investment decision. The second factor that drives option value is project volatility. The high degree of uncertainty in terms of project returns increases a project's value as an option because of the asymmetry between potential upside gains and downside losses. In this case, Merck's downside loss potential was limited to the amount of the initial investment, and substantial upside potential existed.

Merck's finance group used the Black-Scholes option-pricing model to determine the project's option value. Five factors that influence an option's price are used in the Black-Scholes model. The finance group defined those factors as follows:

• The *exercise price* is the capital investment to be made approximately two years hence.

• The *stock price*, or value of the underlying asset, is the present value of the cash flows from the project (excluding the above-mentioned capital investment to be made and the present value of the up-front fees and development costs over the next two years).

• The *time to expiration* was varied over two, three, and four years. The option could be exercised in two years at the earliest. The option was structured to expire in four years because Merck thought that competing products, making market entry unfeasible, would exist by then.

• A sample of the annual standard deviation of returns for typical biotechnology stocks was obtained from an investment bank as a proxy measure for *project volatility*. A conservative range for the volatility of the project was set at 40% to 60%.

Box 29.1 (Continued)

> • A *risk-free rate of interest* of 4.5% was assumed. This figure roughly represents the U.S. Treasury rate over the two to four year period referred to in the time to expiration of the model.
>
> The option value that the Financial Evaluation and Analysis Group arrived at from the above factors showed that this option had significantly more value than the up-front payment that needed to be invested.

competency gaps, but also where an increase in resources can help us reach our goals more quickly and where investments with only marginal returns can be cut. The Research Planning Model is a tool that is sensitive to changes in the environment and is integral to our strategic decision-making process.

So you take a scientific approach to finance?

In my mind, the two disciplines are intimately linked. Certainly no one understands risk better than a research scientist, who can spend many years on a project and ultimately see it fail. In addition, many of the tools we use for financial analysis, such as Monte Carlo simulation, are tools that scientists also use. In general, there is a healthy respect for learning, technology, and quantitative models at Merck, and there is no question that helps us in finance. Quantitative approaches, the use of models, the use of advanced math do not daunt our CEO, Roy Vagelos, or other senior managers here. They don't view our models as some black box that completely ignores the great wisdom of management and tries to mechanize the decision making of business. They understand both the potential and the limitations.

But in many companies, senior managers feel that financial professionals lack the insight to participate in strategic decision making.

I believe strongly that financial theory, properly applied, is critical to managing in an increasingly complex and risky business climate. Unfortunately, finance professionals in traditional industries have been criticized for being too shortsighted and unwilling to make strategic investments. These in-house analysts are great at doing calculations that result in one number that proclaims, "Build that plant," or "Don't build that plant." But these same analysts can't deal with the nuances of a decision that has a 30% probability of failure, even though by definition that means it has a 70% chance of success. Increasingly, the pharmaceutical industry is made up of just those kinds of decisions, and the effective finance person has to be able to deal with them and show the value of taking prudent risks.

But CFOs are not often considered able to manage for the long term. Rather, they are held responsible for the United States' inability to invest.

People who don't practice finance properly have done a great disservice to U.S. industry. Too often, when finance people are unleashed on operating people, an unhealthy tension develops between the need to invest in new projects and the need to have tight controls on spending. For that reason, finance people are often viewed as traffic cops: "You can't do this or go there." They keep the records straight, and that's that.

At Merck, we certainly work with a very sharp pencil. We are not lax. But instead of being an impediment to business, we attempt to work with the operating units and, in many cases, have been accepted as a partner in the business. I think that finance departments can take the nuances, the intuitive feelings that really fine businesspeople have and quantify them. In that way, they can capture both the hard financials of a project and the strategic intent.

For example, we had a development project in our agricultural research department for a nontraditional market segment, an antiparasitic agent called Avid that everyone was excited about. We collected the manufacturing and marketing elements and the research inputs, but the financial evaluation model showed a negative net present value for the project. If we had been traffic cops, we would have blown our whistle and gone home.

But instead, we started to take the project apart and talk more in-depth with marketing and with manufacturing. It turned out that the packaging costs were eating up the gross margins on the project. This was something that the original sponsors of the project had feared all along, but only on a conceptual level. We were able to give the project's sponsors, the marketing department, and manufacturing people a framework for talking about the product, and it suddenly became clear to all involved that the packaging size had to change. In this case, then, finance was a real resource in problem solving.

What role did your department play in Merck's $6 billion acquisition of Medco?

We were a key participant in the project from the beginning. We had to work with our marketing area to quantify the effects of different future market environments, looking at the impact of generic and therapeutic substitution on our sales and margins. We modeled factors in very specific detail, such as population in different payer groups, therapeutic class utilization, price discounts, competitive retaliation, and synergies in other areas of our business. We performed in-depth analyses of all of the companies in the pharmaceutical benefits arena and determined which factors were expected to fuel their growth. All of those factors provided a perfect frame-work for a Monte Carlo analysis to assess total risk.

With the acquisition of Medco, Merck set out to redefine the pharmaceutical paradigm, and the finance department was a key part of designing and implementing that strategy. Back in the 1950s, Merck manufactured bulk chemicals for pharmaceuticals, which we then sold to companies that actually created the prescription medicines. The company foresaw dramatic changes in medicine and wanted to draw closer to patients, the ultimate customers, so Merck merged with Sharp & Dohme, a pharmaceuticals marketer.

We had the same goal in our acquisition of Medco: to get closer to our ultimate customers by merging with Medco, a company that manages prescription drug benefits for 33 million Americans through various employer-sponsored plans. One thing that is unique about our industry is that the person who actually takes a drug does not choose which drug to take and often is not the person who ultimately pays for it. The consumer takes a drug prescribed by a doctor. The drug is usually paid for by a third party such as an insurance company. Our acquisition of Medco will help us link the various parties, providing a coordinated approach to pharmaceutical care. We will be able to link patients, doctors, pharmacists, pharmaceutical companies, and the plan sponsors who pay for benefits. We are also creating new synergies between Medco and Merck. Our job in finance, then, was to value both the strategy and the resulting synergies.

And to arrive at a price?

We knew that we would have to pay a premium to acquire Medco, so we needed to come up with a range of numbers that somehow told us what the combined synergies of Merck and Medco would be worth. Or to put it in other words, we were trying to value the access to Medco's information technology, which stores information on its 33 million patients. That volume combined with Medco's knowledge about each individual's drug needs can help us fashion competitive benefits packages.

30 Case Studies on Real Options

Angelien G. Z. Kemna

The introduction of option pricing theory (OPT) has been well received by practitioners, who have struggled with discounted cash flow (DCF) analysis for many years.[1] The ability of option pricing theory to quantify flexibility in strategic investment projects makes it a very appealing choice. This is especially so when one considers the fact that flexibility is often not explicitly taken into account by standard DCF analysis. Incorporating the value of flexibility could increase the total value of the project and may increase the probability of acceptance, an incentive for practitioners to try OPT in capital budgeting. The value of flexibility of an investment project is basically a collection of real options, which can be priced with the techniques known from financial options.

Despite this incentive, the process of adapting OPT to the practice of strategic decision-making is far from smooth. In most cases, the introduction of OPT would require practitioners to fundamentally reconsider their standard capital budgeting techniques. And when all this hard work has been done, there is still the question: how do we tell management? That question seems to lead us back to where we started. For practical purposes, we cannot afford to come up with very complicated options techniques that can only be priced with black-box computer programs.[2] The contribution of real options in practice is limited when one cannot explain what the important options are and why DCF analysis cannot be used.

In this paper, the major insights gained from practical case applications, developed in cooperation with the group planning and manufacturing functions in Shell's central offices and a number of Shell operating companies, are presented.[3] Shell's main interest was to conduct a number of exploratory studies on the use of OPT in capital budgeting decisions. The studies are part of a group planning program to adapt existing and develop new techniques for strategic decision-making. In practice, real world cases have to be simplified in order to keep the analysis tractable. This applies for the OPT as well as for a standard DCF analysis. During an initial round of discussions, a number of investment opportunities were selected which were of particular interest to Shell and appeared to be illustrative of the potential benefit of applying OPT in capital budgeting decisions. Three of these cases are described here in some detail.

Each case follows the same format. It begins with a problem and model description, followed by the presentation of the data and results. The depth of analysis differs from case to case. Sometimes more attention is paid to the model description, and sometimes more time is spent on data estimation. Since all cases are confidential, the data have been disguised and some details have been omitted, without changing the basic option-like characteristics of the decision-problem. The chapter is organized as follows: Section I analyzes the timing option in an offshore project. In Section II, a so-called growth or sequential option case is presented, where the introduction of OPT helped management to reformulate their investment proposal. Section III contains an abandonment decision of a refinery production unit. In Section IV, the important steps of the decision-making process, when options are involved, are presented. This is followed by a summary of the major insights gained by the practitioners involved. Finally, the conclusion discusses the major contributions of real options in practice.

I Timing Option

The first case deals with a decision problem that is typical for the offshore oil and gas industry. It has been simplified substantially, because, as described here, it turned out to be a nice example to illustrate the difference between OPT and DCF analysis.

In order to explore and develop an oil field, companies can buy licenses from the government. In the exploration phase, they try to estimate the amount and quantity of the oil and gas reserve within that field. Data necessary to perform the estimation are obtained from drilling holes. The license for exploration typically expires after a certain time. When the exploration time has expired, the oil company has three possible strategies, assuming that no additional information is required to obtain more accurate estimates of the volume of the reserve. It can decide:

(i) Not to develop and thus to return the field to the government;

(ii) To start and develop the reserve immediately; or

(iii) To postpone development and thus extend the exploration phase.

In order to extend the exploration phase and hold onto the license, it is necessary for the company to drill a number of extra holes at some cost. It is assumed that these holes do not provide new information for the estimation of the size of the reserve. Consequently, the only potential benefit from drilling the holes is postponing the investment for a couple of years. It is further assumed that once the alternative to extend the exploration phase has been chosen, it is only possible to start development after the expiration of the extended exploration phase.

Under standard analysis, the company should choose the alternative with the highest net present value (NPV). The first and the second alternatives do not contain any real options and can therefore be evaluated by applying standard DCF analysis. Given the estimation of reserve size, a positive NPV results in project initiation;

otherwise, the field would be returned. Initially, under the assumption that no new information on the size would occur, the third alternative was not taken seriously at all. Management wondered why anyone would be willing to incur extra costs without some concrete gain. Management did not readily recognize that deferring the investment could lead to a higher NPV in the future due to a potential increase in oil prices. Management had to be convinced that alternative three can be attractive because it provides an opportunity to postpone and therefore to wait for higher prices in the future.

Of course, the value of investing today has to be compared with the value of investing after a number of years. If the company were to accept the project now, it would forego the option to postpone. If it were to decide to postpone the investment, it would forego the net cash inflows that it could have received from the project in the meantime. If the option of waiting to invest is worth more than the additional costs, it may in fact be worthwhile to extend the exploration phase and wait for higher oil prices. Moreover, even when the NPV is negative but the option to wait net of the additional costs offsets this negative NPV, the project should also not be abandoned.

A naive application of DCF analysis assumes that the project will have to start immediately, irrespective of its future NPV. This does not recognize the opportunity for management to decide not to start the project at the end of the extended exploration phase if it is not desirable to do so. There is, of course, no obligation to start the development of the oil field, but only a right which will only be exercised if the future NPV is positive.

At this point, practitioners often come up with decision-tree analysis as an alternative. In my experience, it was necessary to point out what additional implicit assumptions are being made. Although it is well known from financial markets that the risk of an option changes over time, and with changing prices, we found it necessary to explain to management that this has consequences for the discount rates used in the decision-tree analysis. Still, when trying to determine the options embedded in the investment project, it is often convenient to use the decision-tree analysis as a basic framework.

The option to postpone the investment can be modelled more appropriately as follows. When the company buys the option to wait by incurring the costs of extra drilling, it buys the right to start development at the expiration date of the extended license, T. The benefit of exercising the option at the expiration date is the market value of the developed project, $V(T)$, and the cost is equal to the (single) investment outlay, K. In this case, the option to wait is similar to a European call option on an installed project with maturity date T. To simplify matters, it is assumed that the investment outlay is constant and irreversible in the sense that the installation can only be used for this project. It would not be difficult to extend the model for a stochastic investment outlay.[4] We subsequently define $W(V, t)$ as the value of the total investment project, which can be seen as the ownership right to an undeveloped project.

The standard OPT typically assumes that the underlying stock follows a geometric Brownian motion with a constant rate of return and a constant volatility. If OPT is applied to capital budgeting, the similarity between the underlying stock price and the present market value of a claim to the developed project is used. The total expected rate of return of the project is equal to the capital gains plus the pay-out rate on the project.[5] The pay-out rate on the project represents the opportunity cost of delaying completion of the project, or the expected net cash flow accruing from a producing project. The greater the pay-out rate on the project, the greater is the cost of holding the option.

In this offshore case, the risk of the net cash inflows of the developed project is assumed to be determined only by the natural resource prices (gas and oil); the investment outlay is assumed to be fixed. The resulting option on the cash flows of the developed field is thus analogous to a financial option on a dividend-paying stock,[6] whose value can be calculated from Merton's [13] formula:

$$W(V, \tau) = Ve^{-\delta\tau}N(h) - Ke^{-r\tau}N(h - \sigma\sqrt{\tau}), \tag{1}$$

where

V = present value of the developed reserve.

K = present value of the investment outlay.

δ = pay-out rate on the project.

τ = time to maturity ($= T - t$).

σ = volatility of the logarithmic rate of return of V.

r = riskless interest rate.

$N(\cdot)$ = univariate normal distribution function.

In this case, we do not go into detail on obtaining the necessary data. Our goal here is merely to illustrate the impact of real options on capital budgeting decisions and to show that these decisions can significantly change if the value of the option to wait is properly taken into account.

The data in this case are determined as follows. The present value of the developed reserve, $V(t)$, is assumed equal to the value of the investment outlay K, or $V(t) - K$ is equal to zero. This implies that, if there is no development lag, the NPV of developing the field immediately, $V(t) - K$, is equal to zero. The time to maturity is set equal to the expiration time of the license, which in this case was two years. Determining the time to maturity of the option to wait is not always so clear-cut. Theoretically, the time to maturity could be very long, but in practice it is often determined by the time it takes for competitors to enter the market.

The interest rate of a riskless bond with a maturity of two years was five percent (in real terms). The volatility and the pay-out rate are difficult to estimate. (In the next case, the estimation of oil price volatility is discussed in more detail.) Here, volatility is estimated at 20% (as a base case), and for sensitivity purposes it is varied between ten percent and 30% annually. The pay-out rate can be determined from the estimated cash flows of the developed field. However, if the project has a finite time to maturity the pay-out rate will not be constant, as assumed by the above model. Siegel, Smith, and Paddock [16] use a number of 4.1% as pay-out rate for a case of offshore petroleum leases. A five percent base case pay-out rate is assumed here, and for sensitivity purposes it is varied between zero and ten percent annually.[7] The cost of drilling additional holes is set equal to two percent of the investment outlay. In table 30.1, the total value of the investment opportunity, net of the cost of drilling holes, is presented as a percentage of the investment outlay.

For example, for a base case of $\sigma = 20\%$ and $\delta = 5\%$, net investment opportunity value amounts to about eight percent of the investment outlay. Of course, when volatility increases, the value of the investment opportunity also increases. When the pay-out rate of the project is large, the option to wait to invest is low. When the volatility is low and the pay-out rate is high, the drilling costs are not justified by the value of the option to wait.

Even when the market value of the project is less than the investment outlay, it may still be profitable to extend the exploration phase if the option to wait is sufficiently large. In table 30.2, the same numbers are presented assuming that the present value of the completed project's net cash inflows, $V(t)$, is only 90% of the investment

Table 30.1
Total investment opportunity value as a percentage of investment outlay (K)

Volatility (σ)	Pay-out rate (δ)		
	0	5	10
10	9.6	3.1	−0.3
20	14.3	8.2	4.0
30	19.4	13.3	8.6

Note: $V = K$; $\tau = 2$ years; $r = 5\%$ annually.

Table 30.2
Total investment opportunity value as a percentage of investment outlay (K)

	Pay-out rate (δ)		
Volatility (σ)	0	5	10
10	2.9	−0.4	−1.6
20	8.0	3.9	1.2
30	13.1	8.4	5.0

Note: $V = 0.9 \times K$; $\tau = 2$ years; $r = 5\%$ annually.

outlay K. The rest of the data remain the same. When the investment opportunity (the option to wait minus the two percent costs of drilling) is worth more than ten percent of the investment outlay, the decision to wait is justified. If the volatility is high enough and the pay-out rate is low enough, it is worthwhile to wait. Therefore, it may pay to incur additional costs in order to hold onto a temporarily unprofitable (but risky) project.

II Growth Option

The growth option considered in this section is a pioneer venture, which is typically a project with a high investment outlay and relatively low net cash inflows. It is a manufacturing project with substantial investment costs necessary to prove technology in a period when the project on its own does not appear attractive. But when economic conditions improve, it is important to have the technology proven in order to maintain and enhance market position. Therefore, from a strategic point of view, the pioneer venture may make sense.

From a traditional cash flow perspective, i.e., DCF analysis, however, the pioneer venture was not profitable on its own, where this project was considered on a stand-alone basis. The strategic value of the project derived from the fact that investing in the pioneer venture provided management with the opportunity to invest in future commercial ventures (see Brealey and Myers [2]). Production of the commercial venture could be approximately four to five times the size of the pioneer venture production.

Before reformulating the investment problem as stated below, we discussed the options embedded in the pioneer venture when considered as a stand-alone project. Management had actually tried to incorporate the value of the option to wait assuming that it takes time to build the project (see Majd and Pindyck [11]). Management understood that every time an investment outlay has to be made, it

Table 30.3
Planning situation for pioneer venture (growth option)

First stage		Second stage	
Year 0	Year 4	Year 7	Year 11
Go ahead with pioneer venture or stop	Start-up production of pioneer venture	Decision moment to start commercial venture	Start-up production of commercial venture

can decide to continue, to wait, or to stop the project. This is similar to a sequential investment problem, where the value of the total investment project consists of the values of a series of call options on the market value of the installed project.[8] In view of the fact that it would take about four years to build the project, management tried to determine the total option value using the accompanying software of Majd and Pindyck [11]. As it turned out, the calculated total option value was still insufficient to justify the investment in the pioneer venture. This further convinced management to regard the pioneer venture as an opportunity for growth instead of as a stand-alone project. In subsequent discussions, it was clarified that, due to technological reasons, there was only one time during the four years that it was possible to wait or to call off the project. In what follows, I first consider the simple base case in which no option during the building of the project is considered. Subsequently, I consider the one time at which it was possible to wait or to cancel the project.

In option pricing terms, "buying" the pioneer venture would give management the right to acquire a commercial venture by paying its investment outlay. The option will only be exercised if the commercial venture is profitable at the maturity date of the option. Investing in the pioneer venture today is thus similar to investing in a growth option. In a sense, the negative NPV of the pioneer venture is part of the cost of buying this growth option. The investment problem can therefore be restated as follows: does the value of the growth option justify the cost of buying this option? Reformulating the investment problem in this way was seen by management as a major contribution of OPT to capital budgeting.

In table 30.3, the time profile of the decision situation is presented. At present, management must decide whether to continue or not with the pioneer venture.[9] Once the decision has been made, it would take four years to build the pioneer venture. Because competition was expected to be strong, the maturity date of the option was set equal to the earliest possible time that (from a technological point of view) building of the first commercial venture could start. As mentioned earlier, the esti-mated lead on competitors is an important factor in determining the time to maturity of the option. Here, this was estimated to be in year seven, after the first three years of production of the pioneer venture. The building of a follow-up commercial venture would take another four years, ready to start production in year 11. The planning situation is illustrated in table 30.3.

Given this time schedule, the project can be formulated in option pricing terms as follows. The pioneer venture can be naively seen as a European call option on a futures contract, where the futures price, F, is equal to the value of the commercial venture in seven years. The exercise price is equal to the investment outlay in year seven. The time to maturity is equal to seven years. The nature of this standard European call option on a futures contract is given by the following equation (Black [1]):

$$W(V, \tau) = Fe^{-r\tau}N(h) - Ke^{-r\tau}N(h - \sigma\sqrt{\tau}),$$ (2)

where

$$h = \frac{\ln(F/K) + \frac{1}{2}\sigma^2\tau}{\sigma\sqrt{\tau}}.$$

$N(\cdot) =$ univariate normal distribution function.

The risk from the project's net cash inflows comes from the relative (margin) risk between the input and the output prices of both ventures. Since input prices are less sensitive to crude oil price changes than the output prices, it is assumed that most of the risk of this project comes from uncertainties involving the output price (i.e., from uncertainties in the crude oil price).

As already noted, one complication in this case is the opportunity by management to either continue or stop the investment at some specific moment during the building of the project (i.e., after one year). This implies that instead of deciding now to start and finish the whole pioneer venture, management actually only has to decide to continue with the next phase. In the first phase, starting now and ending after one year, only the investment outlay needed during that year is involved; this, in return, provides management with an option to continue with the pioneer venture (including the option on the commercial venture). At the end of this phase, management can decide to exercise the first option, which implies completion of the pioneer venture. If the option is left to expire unexercised, management basically aborts the entire investment opportunity. The decision to exercise the option depends on the remaining value of the pioneer venture, which itself is an option on the commercial venture. Thus, the decision to continue with the pioneer venture after the first year also depends on the value of the commercial venture.

The first call option, with a time to maturity of τ^*, is written on the value of the pioneer venture, which in turn depends on the value of the commercial venture. The cost of exercising this option equals the remaining (negative) NPV of the pioneer venture, defined as K^*. Exercising this first option provides a second call option with time to maturity equal to $\tau - \tau^*$. The first option is, in fact, an option on an option (a compound option), since the completion of the pioneer venture provides another option.[10] In the compound option formulation, the flexibility of multistage decision-making is explicitly taken into account, increasing the value of the option. The following formula for a compound option (see Geske [5]) can be used:

$$W(V,\tau) = Fe^{-r\tau}M(k,h;\rho) - Ke^{-r\tau}M(k - \sigma\sqrt{\tau^*}, h - \sigma\sqrt{\tau};\rho)$$
$$- K^*e^{-r\tau^*}N(k - \sigma\sqrt{\tau^*}), \tag{3}$$

where

$$h = \frac{\ln(F/K) + \frac{1}{2}\sigma^2\tau}{\sigma\sqrt{\tau}}.$$

$$k = \frac{\ln(F/F_c) + \frac{1}{2}\sigma^2\tau^*}{\sigma\sqrt{\tau^*}}.$$

$N(\cdot)$ = univariate normal distribution function.

$M(a,b;\rho)$ = bivariate normal distribution function with a and b as upper and lower integral limits, and correlation coefficient ρ.

$$\rho = \left(\frac{\tau^*}{\tau}\right)^{1/2}.$$

F_c is the critical value of the project above which the first call option will be exercised.[11] Estimates for the values of the following input variables are thus needed:

F = present value of the cash inflows of the commercial venture as of year seven.

σ = volatility of the rate of change of the commercial venture.

K = present value of the capital expenditures of the commercial venture as of year seven.

K^* = present value of first year capital expenditure of the pioneer venture.

r = riskless rate of interest.

τ = time to maturity of the simple option.

τ^* = maturity date of the first option (within the compound option).

Table 30.4
Production revenues and capital expenditure (capex) percentages

Pioneer venture										
Year	0	1	2	3	4	5	6	7	8...	25
Production						25%	50%	75%	100%...	100%
Capex	3%	18%	41%	27%	11%					
Commercial venture										
Year	7	8	9	10	11	12	13	14...	25	
Production					25%	50%	75%	100%...	100%	
Capex	20%	40%	25%	15%						

It is relatively simple to determine the last three variables. Because investors are interested in the after-tax rate of return, the appropriate riskless rate is the after-tax real return on treasury securities. This rate, based on U.S. $, was equal to two percent annually (in real terms). The time to maturity of the simple option is equal to seven years. The compound option has a time to maturity of one year and six years, respectively, which implies that τ^* is equal to one year. For all the other variables, market or project data are required. For both the pioneer and the commercial ventures, the production cash flows and the capital expenditures (capex) were estimated. Since I was not allowed to give the discount rate used by Shell, I disguised the data by presenting them as percentages in table 30.4. The percentages for the capital expenditures add up to 100%. The percentages for the production cash flows are percentages of the total production per year.

Two items should be noted. The 3% capital expenditures of the pioneer venture are treated as sunk costs and will not be taken into account. The technological uncertainty of the project is only reflected in the lower production level for the first three years for both the pioneer and the commercial venture.[12] Since management has a claim on the future net cash inflows of the commercial venture, the present value of the commercial venture as of year seven is calculated. This value should be regarded as an estimate for the market price of a futures contract for delivery of the net cash inflows of the commercial venture in year seven. It is assumed that this present value is already adjusted for the foregone pay-out rate during the time to maturity of the option. The fact that it takes time to build the project, of course, has consequences for the calculation of the present value of a producing venture, because the cash inflows arrive four years later. This is incorporated by calculating the present value of the commercial venture as of year 11, and discounting this value back to year seven. This results in a future value of U.S. $1000 million as of year seven.

Since the volatility is not observable, it must be estimated empirically. Again, the main source of uncertainty is the difference between the supply costs and the output proceeds of the project. Since the supply costs are relatively insensitive to crude oil prices compared to the output proceeds, the volatility of the rate of return in the crude oil price is used as an upper bound for the volatility of the rate of return of the PV of the commercial venture. One problem encountered when estimating this volatility measure is that only historical data are available. There are no long-term financial options on oil (yet) from which we can calculate the implied volatility. On the basis of historical data, it is clear that the volatility of oil is not stable over time. Depending on the time horizon taken (between two and ten years), oil volatility has fluctuated between 15 and 20% annually.[13] Based on forecasts by company executives, it was expected that volatility could even be as much as 25%. The results are shown for a volatility of 15%, 20%, and 25% annually.

The present value of investment outlays is derived by discounting the total capital expenditures at the after-tax real riskless rate of two percent.[14] This results in U.S. $1000 million. The total expenditures are based on the expected efficiency improvement with respect to the capital expenditures compared with the pioneer venture. For the compound option formulation, the present value of the remaining (negative) NPV of the pioneer venture is also required. This was estimated as U.S. $90 million. In short, the following values were used to determine the value of the options:[15]

F = U.S. $1000 million.

σ = 15%, 20% and 25% annually.

K = U.S. $1000 million.

K^* = U.S. $90 million.

r = 2% annually.

τ = 7 years.

τ^* = 1 year.

To calculate the simple option, Equation (2) can be used. The value of the simple option must then be compared with the (negative) NPV of the pioneer venture. When the option value exceeds this negative NPV, the pioneer venture should be continued. To calculate the NPV of the pioneer venture, its cash outflows are discounted at a riskless rate of two percent (in real terms), and all net cash inflows at the company's cost of capital (in real terms). This resulted in a negative NPV of $-300 + 100 =$ U.S. $-200 million. To calculate the compound option value, Equation (3) is used. The value of the compound option is then compared with the present value of the first-year capital expenditures of the pioneer venture. When the compound option value exceeds these costs, the pioneer venture should be continued. The present value of the first-year capital expenditures is estimated at U.S. $98 million.

Table 30.5
Total investment value in million U.S. $

	Volatility (σ)		
	15%	20%	25%
Simple option	−65	−19	25
Compound option	−41	0	43
Critical value F_c	812	730	653

In table 30.5, the option value for various volatility estimates is presented. The first row contains the value of the simple option minus its costs. The second row contains the value of the compound option net of its costs. In the third row, the critical value below which the project should be stopped after one year is also given.

The results indicate that, in case of a low volatility, the pioneer venture should not be started. However, based on the compound option value, the investment can be justified when volatility is 20% or higher. If management is able to modify its decisions more frequently, this will further increase the value of the total investment opportunity.

III Abandonment Option

In this section, the abandonment decision of a crude distiller (CD) in a refinery is discussed. At some point, management had decided to abandon this crude distiller. One reason was that during the last couple of years the supply of distillates from crude oil exceeded the demand, and despite increased rationalization in production, there was still pressure on the price of distillates produced by the refining industry. This case was analyzed because it was felt that it might yield insights useful for future abandonment decisions in this industry.

Although not considered in this section, management was also interested in applying OPT to a more general strategic problem in the refinery industry. In this competitive industry with over-capacity, management has to continuously consider whether to stay in business or to get out. The advantage of staying in business is that when other competitors get out, the company can take over their market share and ultimately extend its business. The costs of staying in business are the losses that are incurred by maintaining production at a given level. Although this strategic problem is difficult to quantify, it helps if it is structured in terms of options. It was felt by management that thinking in terms of options would force them to analyze their competitive situation more explicitly. Basically, in this situation there is an option to

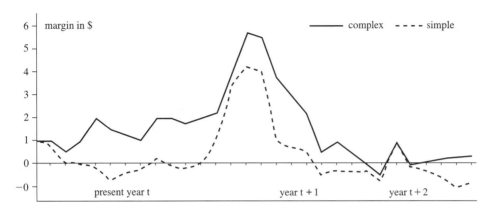

Figure 30.1
Average monthly data of the complex and simple margins on the crude distiller

abandon and an option to extend the business. Whatever management may decide, it would depend on the critical project value below which abandonment takes place and on the critical project value above which extension of production would take place.[16] However, since the abandonment decision of the CD itself was already complicated enough, the more general problem (with potential interactions) will not be presented here.

In principle, the CD produces a wide range of products, but due to the small resulting margin it was only used to bridge the shutdowns of other crude distillers. When it turned out that there existed another (cheaper) alternative to bridge the shutdowns, the justification of continued maintenance was undermined. The only reason to hold onto the CD would be a sufficient margin to justify the high upfront revision costs and the annual operating costs. Since, at the time, it was expected that the margin would be insufficient, the CD was abandoned.

The major source of uncertainty in the cash flows of the CD was the difference in value between the supply cost (i.e., crude prices) and the output proceeds determined by the yields of different products (e.g., naphtha, gasoline, fuel oil) and their respective prices on the open market. For an installation of this type, this is referred to as a "simple margin." For a crude distiller coupled with a number of other installations that further upgrade the product package, it would be called a "complex margin." For the relevant time period, average monthly data of the complex and simple margins are presented in figure 30.1.

During the two years prior to the decision, the simple margin was almost always negative. In the year of the decision, the simple margin recovered slightly and was above the acceptable level of U.S. $.40/barrel for about two or three months. A substantial increase in the simple margin above the U.S. $4.00/barrel followed in the first part of the subsequent year.

On the basis of the simple margin, it was unlikely that the operating costs would be covered. Certainly the upfront revision costs would not be justified. Even when the cash inflows would exactly offset the operating costs every year, the resulting NPV would be negative due to the upfront revision costs. In brief, the NPV of the project, based on the simple margin at the time of the decision, lead to the decision to abandon the project. However, due to the high margin in the following year, the NPV might have been positive. There are, of course, no guarantees to prevent margins from dropping again. If, in future years, simple margins could frequently be above the U.S. $.40/barrel, it might be worthwhile to hold onto the CD.

The decision to abandon the CD can be seen as owning the project and having a put option to abandon at every relevant moment (here, in every year during the technical life of the CD).[17] The project is similar to an American put option with a limited amount of exercise possibilities. The benefit of abandonment now is equal to sum of the present value of the future operating costs, $K(t)$, and the upfront revision costs, $REVC$. The loss is equal to the sum of the present value of the future cash inflows, $V(t)$, and the opportunity to abandon the CD in the future.

Unfortunately, it is relatively complicated to solve the American put problem, and therefore numerical methods are needed to calculate its value. The approach applied here is based on the method of Geske and Johnson [6]. Let us assume that the technical life of the CD is equal to $T + 1$ years. After T years, management decides whether to stop or continue the CD on the basis of the remaining NPV of the CD. If the expected cash inflows, $V(T)$, are less than or equal to the production costs, $K(T)$, production is stopped. This can be seen as exercising a put option at the maturity date. When management decides to continue the project at year T, there is no option left since the project will be stopped at $T + 1$ with certainty. At year $T - 1$, management has the opportunity to again stop or to continue. It will decide to stop production if $V(T - 1)$ is below some critical value $V_c(T - 1)$. This critical value is the value for which management is indifferent between stopping or continuing. At year $T - 1$, the value of stopping is equal to $K(T - 1) - V(T - 1)$, and the value of continuing is equal to a European put option with time to maturity of one year and an exercise price equal to $K(T)$. This implies that $V_c(T - 1)$ can be found by solving the following equation:

$$K(T - 1) - V_c(T - 1) = P[V_c(T - 1), K(T - 1), 1], \tag{4}$$

where $P(V, K, \tau)$ is equal to the value of a European put to give up V in exchange for

K with maturity τ. If $V(T-1)$ is below $V_c(T-1)$, the project should be abandoned. However, at year $T-1$, this possibility to abandon only exists when the project has not been abandoned on or before year $T-1$. Going back another year, the decision to stop can be taken at year $T-1$ and at year T, provided that the project has not been abandoned before. Management has a put option that can be exercised at year $T-1$ or year T. The put option can be divided into two separate put option values. The first put option, expiring at year $T-1$, gives the right on a second put option expiring at year T. The value of the second option is conditional on no early exercise at year $T-1$. The put option value is given by (see Geske and Johnson [6]):

$$
\begin{aligned}
P[V, K(T-1), K(T), 2] = {} & K(T-1)e^{-r}N(-k+\sigma) - VN(-k) \\
& + K(T)e^{-2r}M(k-\sigma, -h+\sigma\sqrt{2}; -1/\sqrt{2}) \\
& - VM(k, -h; -1/\sqrt{2}).
\end{aligned}
\tag{5}
$$

where

$$
h = \frac{\ln(V/K(T)) + 2(r+\frac{1}{2}\sigma^2)}{\sigma\sqrt{2}}.
$$

$$
k = \frac{\ln(V/V_c(T-1)) + (r+\frac{1}{2}\sigma^2)}{\sigma}.
$$

$N(\cdot)$ = univariate normal distribution function.

$M(a, b; \rho)$ = bivariate normal distribution function with a and b as upper and lower integral limits, and correlation coefficient ρ.

Again, this put option will only have value when the project is not abandoned at year $T-2$. This will be the case when $V(T-2)$ is above the critical value $V_c(T-2)$. This analysis can be repeated for $T-2$, $T-3$, $T-4, \ldots$ up to the present year t. At the present time, the value of a put option that can be exercised every year is computed. This put value consists of T pairs of European put options, one for each year in which abandonment is possible. All the European put options are conditional on not being exercised before that year, which results in multinomial distribution functions for the American put value at time t. These multinomial distribution functions can be approximated by a log-transformed explicit finite difference method (e.g., see Geske and Shastri [7]). The following input variables are to be estimated:

$V(t)$ = the present value of the future cash inflows.

$K(t)$ = the present value of the future operating costs.

σ = the volatility of the rate of return on $V(t)$.

r = the riskless rate.

τ = the time to maturity.

$REVC$ = the revision costs.

The last three variables do not cause any problems. The time to maturity is equal to nine years, the after-tax riskless rate, based on guilders, is set equal to 6.5% annually. The revision costs are equal to the present value of the after-tax capital expenditures necessary to upgrade the production unit, which amounted to 6 million guilders. In order to determine $V(t)$ and $K(t)$, we have to determine the cash inflows and the operating costs of the production unit. Irrespective of the number of weeks of production, the after-tax operating costs are 4 million guilders per year, that is, in case the production unit is kept ready for production. As mentioned earlier, production will only take place when the simple margin exceeds U.S. $.40/bbl. Based on the simple margin of the year in which the decision is taken (and taking into account the fact that it takes one week to start producing), it is estimated that the CD would produce for approximately eight weeks at a minimum simple margin of U.S. $.40/bbl. Using a constant exchange rate of fl 2.00/$, the yearly after-tax cash inflow would be equal to 4.8 million guilders per year.

This implies that, when the firm's after-tax cost of capital is used to discount the cash flows, the present value of the future cash inflows is equal to 30 million guilders and the present value of the future operating costs is equal to 25 million guilders. Using a standard DCF analysis, this project would be abandoned immediately since the NPV is equal to $-6 - 25 + 30 = -1$ million guilders. In order to show the sensitivity of the put option value with respect to $V(t)$, we also show the results when $V(t)$ equals 25 million (which results in an at-the-money put option) and 31 million guilders (which results in a zero NPV for the total investment opportunity).

The uncertainty of the cash inflows stems directly from the uncertainty in the simple margin. The evolution of $V(t)$ over time is determined by the development of the simple margin. In order to use the standard option pricing model, we need to adopt the assumption that the logarithmic rate of return of $V(t)$ is normally distributed with volatility σ. This volatility is equal to the volatility of the logarithmic rate of return of the simple margin assuming that the simple margin is log-normally distributed. This can be achieved by defining the simple margin as the percentage between the output proceeds and the supply costs and assuming that both are log-normally distributed. Using weekly data on the output proceeds and supply costs over the year preceding the decision moment, the volatility was estimated as low as

Table 30.6
Put option values for abandoning the crude distiller

	Volatility			
	5%	10%	15%	20%
$V = 25$	0.06	0.53	1.27	2.16
$V = 30$	0.00	0.05	0.42	1.11
$V = 31$	0.00	0.03	0.34	0.98
V_c	31.00	30.97	30.64	29.88

5.8%. However, in the subsequent year, volatility was estimated as high as 24.4%, after which it dropped to 11.3% in the following year. Therefore, the results are presented for a volatility between five and 20%. In all, the results are presented for the following input variables:

$V(t)$ = 25, 30, 31 million guilders.

$K(t)$ = 25 million guilders.

σ = 5, 10, 15 and 20%.

r = 6.5%.

τ = 9 years.

$REVC$ = 6 million guilders.

In table 30.6, the value of the put option for abandoning the crude distiller for the various $V(t)$ and volatilities is given. In the last row, the critical value of $V(t)$ below which the project should be abandoned immediately (V_c) is presented. When the value of $V(t)$ plus the value of the put option exceeds $K(t)$ plus the revision costs (= 31 million guilders), the project should not be abandoned.

From these results it follows that for $V(t) = K(t) = 25$ million guilders, the project would always be abandoned. For $V(t)$ equal to 30 million guilders, the project would not be abandoned when volatility is as high as 20%, because $V(t)$ exceeds V_c. Given the available information at the moment of the decision (a volatility of no more than ten percent), it appears that management made the right decision to abandon the project.

IV Main Insights

From the experience gained from these and other cases developed in cooperation with Shell planning group, an attempt was made to develop a more general formulation of the decision-making process when such options are involved. This resulted in conceptualizing various steps that were considered important in the decision-making process, as follows:

(i) Convince management that some proposals contain flexibility that cannot be valued by using DCF analysis and must be valued using OPT.[18]

(ii) Make a clear distinction between investment alternatives and options embedded in these alternatives, because management often considers options as alternatives, which leads to misinterpretations.

(iii) Restrict the number of options to the most important ones; more options increase complexity without necessarily adding much value.

(iv) Restate the investment problem in the following sense: Can the costs of the (additional) flexibility be justified by the benefits when the flexible alternative is compared to the alternative without flexibility?

(v) Define properly the uncertainties that management faces and, given these uncertainties, determine the most valuable option(s).

(vi) Whenever possible, incorporate the influence of competitors and other costs that may affect the value of the option(s). Sometimes management takes the option(s) for free. It may be possible that due to the specific situation of the firm, the option is cheaper to the firm than to other firms. But options are usually not free. It is also important to incorporate the effects of competition not only on the cash flow estimates, but also on the value of the option (e.g., see Trigeorgis [20]).

(vii) Focus on the value of the project including the option(s) and present sensitivity analysis, especially for volatility.

When applying OPT in practice, it is important to come to a more general approach in the decision-making process, but it seems equally relevant to find out the opinion of the practitioners involved. This provides insight into how they position the new technique and how they cope with it. Some major insights gained by practitioners involved in these cases are as follows:

(i) The same fundamental principles underlie both DCF analysis and OPT.

(ii) DCF is a simplified technique, which is appropriate for the analysis of a broad range of problems under passive management. When it is known that different elements of a cash flow are associated with different risks, this should be reflected by applying different discount rates.

(iii) DCF and OPT are complementary rather than competing techniques. OPT should be used in combination with DCF when there are future decision points which influence the riskiness of the cash flow.

(iv) OPT is rather like an appropriate combination of discounting and decision-tree analysis. It is particularly useful for analyzing the value and phasing of a series of related investments.

(v) DCF analysis has probably been sufficient for the evaluation of most traditional expansion projects. As normally applied, however, it systematically undervalues the benefits of waiting.

(vi) These techniques do not, of course, replace the need for strategic thinking and judgment in the generation and examination of business alternatives. When they are properly applied, however, they could be of invaluable support to this activity by enabling a meaningful quantification as part of the evaluation process. As one participant noted, "It's a shame to do all this hard strategic analysis and then throw it away at the arithmetic stage."

V Conclusion

The theoretical foundations of the above cases were mostly limited to the more simple option models. But even these simple option models can provide management with considerable intuition. The above cases were developed with Shell staff members, who were unfamiliar with the theory. But the basic outcomes and the sensitivities of these outcomes to changes in the underlying input variables, seemed consistent with their intuition. When applying OPT, a major problem is to decide on the most important embedded options; what are they, and which of them are potentially valuable to model? In the cases that we looked at, most problems had to be simplified, although this was also common practice when a standard DCF analysis was used.

Based on these experiences, we suggest that the main contribution of OPT in capital budgeting is twofold. First, it helps management to structure the investment opportunity by defining the different investment alternatives with their underlying uncertainties and their embedded options. A side-benefit is that it usually leads to a renewed discussion about the use of standard capital budgeting techniques. Second, OPT can handle flexibilities within the project more easily than the traditional DCF analysis. Although other models such as decision-tree analysis or Monte Carlo simulation could be used, they tend to become complicated and are frequently misapplied.[19]

The application of OPT in practical capital budgeting decisions is not without problems either. When the real options in the investment projects tend to become more complex, the OPT approach also becomes complicated and computations become increasingly difficult. It is also not always easy to find a good estimate for the uncertainty of the underlying project. It is thus not surprising that in most real world cases OPT has been applied to investment projects whose cash flows are based on quoted natural resource prices. In conclusion, I suggest that further research on real options should focus on unanswered questions arising from practical investment problems.

Acknowledgments

I would like to thank Lenos Trigeorgis (the editor) and an anonymous referee for their useful comments on this paper.

Notes

1. See, for example, Kester [9], Myers [14], and Trigeorgis and Mason [19].

2. See Triantis and Hodder [18].

3. Permission was given by Shell to present these cases. For other real option applications, see, for example, Brennan and Schwartz [3], Siegel, Smith, and Paddock [16], and Trigeorgis [21].

4. See McDonald and Siegel [12].

5. The total expected return is the equilibrium rate established by the capital market on a comparable-risk financial asset and it includes an appropriate risk premium. This is the discount rate for determining the present value of a developed project.

6. For example, see Brennan and Schwartz [3].

7. Strictly speaking, the values the volatility can take on are related to the values of the pay-out rate. This has been ignored here.

8. These options are, in fact, options on options, or compound options (see Geske [5]).

9. The project was actually already started three years before, but the major investment outlay still had to be made during the coming year.

10. See Geske [5].

11. This value can be obtained using a simple Newton-Raphson procedure.

12. There are different alternatives to deal with the technological uncertainties. One possibility is to incorporate uncertain capital expenditures (see, for example, Fisher [3]). However, management appeared relatively certain about the estimation of the capital expenditure. Another possibility is to model the first years of production as compound options, which would increase complexity substantially.

13. Pindyck [17] tests whether the oil price returns are mean-reverting or not, but could not find evidence that oil price returns are indeed mean-reverting. However, if mean reversion is assumed, this would lead to a decrease in the estimated option value.

14. This ignores the option to wait during the building period of the commercial venture. However as for the pioneer venture, this option to wait was considered irrelevant due to competition.

15. Although the numbers presented here are not the exact numbers used in the real project, the relative order is the same.

16. It must be recognized that the combined value of these two options is not equal to the sum of separate values due to interactions; see Trigeorgis [22].

17. This abandonment decision can also be seen as a sequential investment decision. Every year management has the opportunity to exercise a call option, obtaining the remaining future cash inflows by paying the cash outflow in that year. The benefit of exercising the option is equal to the net cash inflows of that year plus the opportunity to continue the project in the future. The costs are equal to the cash outflows of that year (see Myers and Majd [15]).

18. A recent paper by Kulatilaka and Marcus [10] focuses specifically on this issue.

19. An interesting method, proposed by Jacoby and Laughton [8], tries to find a balance between the standard capital budgeting techniques and the more stochastic-oriented OPT.

References

1. F. Black, "The Pricing of Commodity Contracts," *Journal of Financial Economics* (January–March 1976), pp. 167–179.

2. R. Brealey and S. Myers, *Principles of Corporate Finance*, McGraw-Hill, 4th edition, 1991.

3. M. Brennan and E. Schwartz, "Evaluating Natural Resource Investments," *Journal of Business* (April 1985), pp. 135–157.

4. S. Fisher, "Call Option Pricing when the Exercise Price is Uncertain," *Journal of Finance* (March 1978), pp. 169–176.

5. R. Geske, "The Valuation of Compound Options," *Journal of Financial Economics* (March 1979), pp. 63–81.

6. R. Geske and H. Johnson, "The American Put Option Valued Analytically," *Journal of Finance* (December 1984), pp. 1511–1524.

7. R. Geske and K. Shastri, "Valuation by Approximation: A Comparison of Alternative Option Valuation Techniques," *Journal of Financial and Quantitative Analysis* (March 1985), pp. 45–71.

8. H. Jacoby and D. Laughton, "Uncertainty, Information and Project Evaluation," MIT CEPR 90-002, January 1990.

9. C. Kester, "Growth Options and Investment: Reducing the Guesswork in Strategic Capital Budgeting," *Harvard Business Review* (March–April 1984), pp. 153–160.

10. N. Kulatilaka and A. Marcus, "Project Valuation under Uncertainty: When Does DCF Fail?," Working Paper, Boston University, October 1991.

11. S. Majd and R. Pindyck, "Time to Build, Option Value, and Investment Decisions," *Journal of Financial Economics* (March 1987), pp. 7–27.

12. R. McDonald and D. Siegel, "The Value of Waiting to Invest," *Quarterly Journal of Economics* (November 1986), pp. 707–727.

13. R. Merton, "Theory of Rational Option Pricing," *Bell Journal of Economics and Management Science* (Spring 1973), pp. 141–183.

14. S. Myers, "Finance Theory and Financial Strategy," *Interfaces* (January–February 1984), pp. 126–137.

15. S. Myers and S. Majd, "Abandonment Value and Project Life," *Advances in Futures and Options Research* (No. 4, 1990), pp. 1–21.

16. D. Siegel, J. Smith, and J. Paddock, "Valuing Offshore Oil Properties with Option Pricing Models," *Midland Corporate Finance Journal* (Spring 1987), pp. 22–30.

17. R. Pindyck, "Options, Flexibility, and Investment Decisions," MIT Working Paper presented at the CEPR Workshop on New Methods for Project and Contract Evaluation, 1988.

18. A. Triantis and J. Hodder, "Valuing Flexibility as a Complex Option," *Journal of Finance* (June 1990), pp. 549–565.

19. L. Trigeorgis and S. P. Mason, "Valuing Managerial Flexibility," *Midland Corporate Finance Journal* (Spring 1987), pp. 14–21.

20. L. Trigeorgis, "Valuing Real Investment Opportunities: An Options Approach to Strategic Capital Budgeting," Unpublished Doctoral Dissertation, Harvard University, 1986, Ch. 6.

21. L. Trigeorgis, "A Real Options Application in Natural Resource Investments," *Advances in Futures and Options Research* (No. 4, 1990), pp. 153–164.

22. L. Trigeorgis, "The Nature of Option Interactions and the Valuation of Investments with Multiple Real Options," *Journal of Financial and Quantitative Analysis* (March 1993), pp. 1–20.

31 The Value of Flexibility: The Case of a Dual-Fuel Industrial Steam Boiler

Nalin Kulatilaka

It is now widely understood that conventional economic analysis based on discounted cash flow (DCF) methods fails to capture the strategic impact of projects. In particular, DCF methods ignore the "operating flexibilities" that give project managers options to revise decisions in response to changing exogenous economic conditions. The importance of such operating options becomes critical when the environment is highly volatile and the technology is flexible, thus permitting managerial intervention at little cost. For example, when facing exogenous stochastic prices a project with operating options can protect itself against some of the adverse price movements by switching into an alternative "mode of operation" that is less affected by the adverse price realizations. In effect, the irreversibility assumption of conventional investment analysis is violated. Real options techniques, by endogenizing the optimal operating rules and explicitly capturing the flexibility and its effects on uncertainty, provide for a consistent treatment of risk in the valuation of flexible projects.

The growing literature on real options has revealed several important lessons:[1] (*i*) the *volatility* of prices becomes an important determinant of investment, both in terms of the type of investment (e.g., rigid versus flexible technologies) and in terms of the quantity of investment (in that high volatility increases the value and Tobin's *q* of flexible systems); (*ii*) the value of flexibility *per se* may be determined explicitly, given the dynamics for relative input prices; (*iii*) input price elasticities have less meaning at the microlevel than critical input *price boundaries* (i.e., the price levels at which decisions must be revised); (*iv*) switching costs may be treated realistically rather than with ad hoc costs of adjustment models; (*v*) it may be optimal for a firm to utilize a short-run inefficient technology, creating a *hysteresis* (i.e., a bias towards maintaining the status quo); and (*vi*) investment decisions take on a long-run strategic view.

While the theoretical literature on real options has provided many useful insights, specific applications have been limited and heavily stylized for mathematical tractability. In this chapter, we present a general model of flexibility that is computationally simple and is more amenable to empirical implementation than those that rely on analytical solutions.[2] We then apply the model to the case of an industrial steam boiler than can switch between using residual fuel oil and natural gas. This technology is ideally suited for such an analysis because (*i*) both flexible and rigid systems are being produced, suggesting that, at the margin, price differences between the installed cost of the two types of technologies *should* be roughly equal to the incremental value of flexibility, and (*ii*) the technology is extremely simple in that it uses a single variable input (fuel) to produce a single output (steam).

The rest of the chapter is organized as follows. In Section I, we compare investment in fixed-fuel boilers and a dual-fuel boiler to motivate the need for the special tools of option valuation. The example makes two important points: first, projects with embedded options typically call for discount rates that change *endogenously* as the value of some underlying state variable evolves (where NPV analysis takes the discount rate as fixed, or at most exogenously determined), and second, the decisions to exercise real options must be determined *jointly* with the valuation analysis, meaning that even expected cash flows (which are taken as exogenous in NPV analysis) can not be determined without a proper valuation framework. Hence, neither discount rates nor expected cash flows can be taken as strictly exogenous.

In Section II, we introduce a dynamic programming procedure that would be appropriate to project valuation in an economy with risk-neutral agents. This section shows how project valuation and option exercise interact and must be jointly determined. We then extend the analysis to show how the basic methodology can be modified to accommodate the considerations of risk-aversion. Section III presents an application of the model to the case of dual-fuel boilers. Finally, Section IV concludes.

I   Valuing Flexible-Fuel Boilers: A Simple Formulation

A simple example can illustrate both the value of real options as well as the need for a valuation methodology more sophisticated than conventional DCF techniques (such as NPV or IRR analysis).[3] Consider a firm currently planning the installation of an industrial steam boiler. The available menu fitting the engineering design specifications contains boilers that can be fired with natural gas only, residual fuel oil only, and a dual-fuel boiler that may switch between gas and oil depending on current costs. The operating cost of the flexible boiler is the *minimum* of the oil or gas costs, since in each period the cheaper input will be used to fire the flexible boiler.

For pedagogical simplicity, we choose the natural gas price as numeraire and consider it fixed at $10 per "energy unit." The current oil price is $7.50 per "efficiency adjusted energy unit." Since oil and gas burn at different thermal efficiencies, these prices are adjusted so that the unit of input of each produces an identical level of annual output. The rate of oil price increase, which for now is assumed *certain*, is five percent per year. Hence, in the first five years, oil offers a cost advantage, but in the last five years, gas is cheaper.

We assume that the boiler has a useful economic life of ten years. Suppose that both gas and oil boilers cost the same to purchase but a flexible system requires an additional investment of ΔI. The boiler output is independent of the type of fuel in use. Therefore, the choice between the boilers depends entirely on the one that can be operated with the minimum expected cost.

Using a rate of five percent to discount these cash flows, we find that the present value of operating costs for the three boilers are $61.45, $58.59, and $56.22 for the gas, oil, and flexible boilers, respectively.[4] Based on these values, the oil boiler is most preferred: it has a lower cumulative present value cost than the equally priced gas boiler, and although its costs are higher than those of a dual-fuel boiler, the cost difference is less than the additional investment needed to purchase the flexible boiler.

If future prices are uncertain, this present value analysis must be modified. The discount rate must be adjusted for a risk premium. In principle, each component of the cash flow stream—both revenues and costs—may have different risk characteristics, and therefore require its own discount rate.[5] Specifically, suppose that oil prices next year can take on values of $1.1625, $.7875, or $.4125 with equal probability, resulting in an expected value of $.7875 and providing an expected growth rate over the current price of five percent, as in the benchmark certainty NPV analysis. Thereafter, oil prices grow at five percent per year. If the appropriate discount rate for cash flows allowing for oil price risk were five percent (to keep the analysis comparable with the certainty case), the present value of expected cash flows in each period would be the same as in the certainty case. In this event, conventional DCF analysis is perfectly adequate to value the gas-only and oil-only boilers. The major complication arising from uncertainty is the determination of the discount rate.

The value of the flexible boiler, however, changes substantially. The expected fuel costs for the flexible boiler, averaging across the three scenarios, are lower in each period. The present value of costs decreases from $56.22 to $52.89. The flexible boiler can actually dominate both the oil-only and the gas-only boilers if the incremental investment required to purchase it (ΔI), is less than $\min(58.59, 61.45) - 52.89 = 5.7$.

Why does this happen? The flexible boiler creates a valuable asymmetry: when oil prices follow the low path, the cost savings are fully realized by the firm. In contrast, when oil prices follow the high path, increases in energy costs are limited by the ability to switch to a gas boiler. Thus, in contrast to the cash flows of the oil boiler, the expected cash flow of the flexible boiler is actually a function of oil price volatility, even when that volatility is symmetric around the mean price. Higher volatility increases average net cash flow since benefits accrue when oil prices fall, but losses are limited by the price of gas.

Given the *option* to choose the better energy source, one may no longer calculate cash flows using mean price paths. Instead, recognizing the option-like feature of the energy choice, one may try to exploit the analogy between this "real option" and more usual financial options to obtain pricing algorithms. The ability to obtain the best energy source ex post makes the flexible technology similar to a call option. The operator of the flexible boiler can purchase "energy" for the cheaper of the (fixed) gas price or the market price of oil. For instance, when the boiler is fired with oil, the operator has the right to buy an asset (energy) for the minimum of a strike price (the fixed gas price) or the market price of the asset (the oil price). Compared to the oil-fired boiler, the flexible boiler offers cash flows that are higher in each period by the amount $\max(P_{oil} - P_{gas}, 0)$, which is formally identical to the payoff of a call option.

Unlike the case of a call option on a stock, however, exercising this switching option gives the firm not only the underlying asset (a gas-burning boiler) but also an option to switch back to oil in the future in the event of a price reversal of sufficient magnitude. The latter is analogous to a put option on the oil price.[6] Hence, we have a nested compound option problem.

Valuation of options and option-like projects, such as the flexible boiler, is, in general, fairly complicated and, except for special assumptions, does not allow for analytic solutions. However, quite general numerical approaches to this valuation problem are now established in the literature. In the next section, we present a dynamic programming formulation (where the switching decisions become transparently obvious) that also allows for a rich variety of assumptions regarding the stochastic specifications and technology conditions.

II   General Model of Flexibility

A   A Risk-Neutral Formulation

We will first focus only on the "decision-tree" nature of the problem. We assume that all agents are risk-neutral. Later, we will show how to incorporate adjustments for risk into the analysis.

The basic concept is a "mode of operation." Modes may be "gas-fired" versus "oil-fired" or "invest now" versus "invest later." In general, there may be M modes, indexed by m, ranging from one to M. The cost of switching from mode j to mode k is denoted c_{jk}. For example, if mode j = oil and mode k = gas, c_{jk} is the cost of converting from oil to gas. Continuing in a mode entails no switching costs: i.e., $c_{mm} = 0$ for all m.

Given that the firm is operating in a particular mode, there may be a flow of income (or costs) that occurs at a rate that may depend not only on that mode, but also on some market price P (that may be either an output or input price) as well as on time, t. We denote the income flow in the time interval $(t, t + \Delta t)$ as $\Pi(P_t, m, t)$.

The present value (using the risk-free interest rate, r) of all future net profit flows *given optimal behavior henceforth* is denoted $F(P_t, m, t)$. Optimal behavior means that the firm always chooses the current mode to maximize the present value of current plus discounted expected future profits net of switching costs. This condition is the well-known Bellman equation of dynamic programming and may be written in our notation as follows (assuming that the firm arrives at time t operating in mode m):

$$F(P_t, m, t) = \max_l \{\Pi(P_t, l, t) - c_{ml} + \rho E_t[F(P_{t+1}, l, t+1)]\} \tag{1}$$

where $l, m = 1, \ldots, M$; $t = 0, \ldots, T$; and $\rho = e^{r\Delta t}$.

The above equation shows that in each period the firm must contemplate switching into a new mode (denoted by l). If it chooses mode l, it realizes profits of $\Pi(P_t, l, t)$, but pays switching costs of c_{ml} (which equals zero if $l = m$), and then arrives at the following period with value function $F(P_{t+1}, l, t+1)$. This value depends on the mode chosen this period, l, as well as on the value of the state variable next period, P_{t+1}. Because P_{t+1} is still unknown at time t, we take expectations and discount. The firm in each period chooses the mode, l, that maximizes the value of the project.

The exogenous uncertainty faced by the firm is summarized by a stochastic variable P which follows a process of the form:

$$\frac{\Delta P_t}{P_t} = \mu(P_t, t)\Delta t + \sigma(P_t, t)\Delta Z_t, \tag{2}$$

where ΔZ is standard normal distributed, and $\mu(P_t, t)$ and $\sigma(P_t, t)$ are the rate of return and volatility of P, respectively. In appendix A, we show how this process can be used in obtaining the transition probabilities that are needed to compute the expectations in Equation (1).

If it were not for switching costs, the solution to this optimization problem would be simple: choose in each period the mode that maximizes $\prod(P_t, m, t)$ in that period. However, switching costs make a forward-looking analysis necessary. For example, a firm may decline to switch from oil to gas even when gas is marginally cheaper if either the cost of switching is high or the possibility of a reversal in the relative cost advantage (which would entail further switching costs) is high. Thus, the probability distribution of *future* oil to gas price ratios affects the *current* choice of technology.

This "inertia" results in what is known as a "hysteresis band." A hysteresis band is a range of values that the state variable (i.e., the exogenous source of uncertainty that drives all other variables, such as the ratio of gas to oil prices) may take for which mode switching is passed up, even when short-term cost conditions make switching appear profitable.[7] If conversion from gas to oil is cheaper than conversion from oil to gas, there will be a bias towards remaining in the gas mode even if prices slightly favor oil. The firm will preserve its option to convert later, rather than be locked to the current mode for which later conversion is more costly.

B Risk Adjustment Techniques

We have shown how the operating decisions involved in managing real options can be made properly using tools of dynamic programming. We simplified the earlier analysis by positing risk-neutral managers. The next task, therefore, is to introduce a modification to the solution technique that accounts for asset valuation in markets with risk-averse investors.

For this, we rely on a result from Cox, Ingersoll, and Ross [4, Lemma 4] (CIR) that is akin to treating uncertainty through the use of certainty equivalent cash flows rather than through the use of risk-adjusted discount rates. Specifically, we continue to use the risk-free interest rate for purposes of discounting, but we replace the actual drift rate of the driving stochastic variable by a "certainty equivalent drift rate." This adjusted drift equals the actual drift on the variable minus the risk premium that would emerge in market equilibrium on an asset with the same risk features as the stochastic variable.

The intuition behind this result is that instead of discounting the actual expected cash flows at the risk-adjusted interest rates, we may equivalently discount at the risk-free interest rate and adjust the reduced "expected" cash flow for risk. CIR shows that the correct cash flow adjustment requires a reduction of the drift rate by the risk premium.

An alternative approach to the intuition behind this result is to imagine that we are valuing the project in an economy with risk-neutral agents. Such agents would, of course, use the risk-free rate to discount cash flows. However, all assets in this economy would be expected to earn only the risk-free rate of return—there would be no risk premia. Thus, equilibrium drift rates on securities in this risk-neutral economy would be lower than they are in our economy by the risk premium. CIR prove that asset values in this economy will be precisely equal to values in our actual economy.

1 Financial Assets For example, if the state variable was the stock price of a firm paying no dividends, the certainty-equivalent drift would be simply the risk-free rate, since the stock's expected rate of capital gains should, in equilibrium, exceed the risk-free rate by just the fair risk premium. Call μ the equilibrium drift rate on the stock (which, in this case, will equal the actual drift rate), RP the risk premium, and r the risk-free rate. Then, for the non-dividend-paying stock,

$$\mu - RP = r. \tag{3}$$

If, instead, the stock was paying dividends, say at a yield of δ, then to provide a fair total rate of return to investors, the stock would offer an expected capital gains yield of $g = \mu - \delta$, and the certainty-equivalent drift rate on the stock would be

$$g - RP = (\mu - \delta) - RP$$
$$= r - \delta. \tag{4}$$

Therefore, for traded financial securities, the certainty-equivalent drift will equal the risk-free rate minus the income yield on the security. This equals the total rate of return the risky asset offers its investors minus (*i*) the risk premium on the asset, and (*ii*) the income yield on the asset (i.e., δ). However, since $\mu - RP = r$ (by the definition of the risk premium) we need not know RP or even rely on a model of risk premia to calculate value in this case. We simply replace the drift rate, μ, with its certainty-equivalent equilibrium value, $r - \delta$, and pursue the dynamic program as previously described.[8]

2 Nonfinancial Assets   Unfortunately, in most instances, the driving variable will not be a security price. Instead, it typically will be the price of some input or output. When that price is for a commodity on which futures contracts trade, it still is relatively easy to perform the risk adjustment.

For instance, suppose P is the price of oil. To determine the equilibrium expected drift rate of oil, we compute the costs of storing oil (denoted s), the benefits of storing oil (or convenience yield, c), the expected appreciation rate, g, and the fair total rate of return (given risk) on an investment in oil, μ, and impose the equilibrium condition that $\mu = g + c - s$ or that $g = \mu + s - c$.

Next, reducing this equilibrium drift rate by the fair risk premium on oil results in a certainty equivalent drift of $g_{ce} = (\mu - RP) + (s - c) = r - \delta$, where $\delta = c - s$ is the convenience yield net of storage cost. Thus, the net convenience yield of oil plays precisely the same role as the dividend yield for stocks. Both represent the component of total returns realized from sources other than expected capital gains.

Estimating the net convenience yield still may be difficult, but at least it is open to econometric attack (e.g., see Brennan and Schwartz [1]). Moreover, when assets are traded on futures markets, δ may be computed directly with minimal effort. The reason is that oil futures prices for delivery at different dates, say τ_1 and τ_2, should obey the parity relationship that

$$\frac{F(\tau_2)}{F(\tau_1)} = e^{[(r-\delta)(\tau_2 - \tau_1)]}. \tag{5}$$

3 Goods Prices   Assets, whether financial or other, have the common property that they are stored, and therefore, the expected price appreciation relative to risk ought to be subject to equilibrium principles of risk versus return. Storage of the asset implies that agents believe that expected appreciation is sufficient to compensate for time value and risk, net of marginal convenience yield. In many cases, however, the driving state variable is an input or output price of some good that is not stored in equilibrium. The paths of these prices, therefore, are free to evolve without regard to their risk characteristics. In general, in these cases, δ will be both time- and state-dependent.

Consider, for example, the following specification for the expected change in the price:

$$E(\Delta P_t) = \lambda(P^* - P_t)\Delta t$$

$$\text{var}(\Delta P_t) = \sigma^2 P_t^2 \Delta t. \tag{6}$$

This specification states that in a small time interval, Δt, price is subject to both systematic trends and random disturbances. The random disturbances have zero mean and a standard deviation of $\sigma P_t \sqrt{\Delta t}$. But since deviations of P_t from P^* lead to disequilibrium in the asset market, prices tend toward their equilibrium values, i.e., if $P_t > P^*$, prices will tend, on average, to fall.

In this specification, drift (i.e., the expected rate of price change) has no relationship to risk. However, we can use our "δ strategy" based on the relationship that $g - RP = r - \delta$, which implies that δ is equal to the required return given risk minus the actual drift from specified price dynamics, or

$$\delta = (r + RP) - \mu. \tag{7}$$

In this case, however, there is no way to avoid the reliance on an equilibrium model of risk and return such as the CAPM. Such a model is necessary to calculate the first term on the right-hand side of Equation (7).

Still, this approach offers considerable advantages over the conventional constant-discount-rate NPV methodology. Recall that as the state variable evolves and the project becomes more or less of a "long shot," the appropriate discount rate also changes. Thus, while it might be reasonable to use an equilibrium model to estimate the discount rate appropriate to oil price risk which might be reasonably stable, it would not make sense to apply a fixed discount rate to most projects with embedded options that depend on the price of oil. For these projects, the risk level itself evolves over time. Even if the calculation of the discount rate for the asset in Equation (7) is not perfectly precise, it is likely much more precise than any attempt would be to calculate directly a rate for a project that is dependent in a nonlinear fashion on the underlying asset price.

III Valuing a Dual-Fuel Industrial Steam Boiler

Industrial steam boilers provide a perfect example to apply our model of flexibility. They embody a simple technology with a single variable input (fuel) and a single output (steam). Specifically, we analyzed a 350 hp. Package Firetube Boiler manufactured by Cleaver-Brooks, which is configured to produce steam at a pressure of 125 psig per hour (an annual output rate of approximately 1190 MBtu). This quality and rate of output can be achieved by firing it with either natural gas or No. 2 fuel oil. However, due primarily to their different combustion temperatures, the two fuel types vary in their burning efficiencies. Hence, we can focus on the efficiency differences and the resulting cost differences under the alternative input fuels to determine the value of the flexible fuel boiler.

In order to estimate the profit functions, we relied on an engineering model described by Provance [14]. The heat loss in producing steam is a function of the ambient temperature, flue gases, and the operating pressure. The principle behind Provance's model is to estimate the *stack gas losses* and *radiation/convection losses* under the alternative fuel burning configurations. Table 31.1 summarizes the efficiency estimates of the boiler under the two alternative fuel configurations.[9]

Translating the estimates in table 31.1 into the notation we used in the previous section, we can write the monthly profit functions of gas-only and oil-only boilers as:

$$\Pi(P_{gas}, gas, t) = R_t - 1469 P_{gas}$$

$$\Pi(P_{oil}, oil, t) = R_t - 1408 P_{oil}$$

where R_t is the annual revenues from the boiler, and P_{oil} and P_{gas} are the nominal prices of oil and gas expressed in $ per million Btu (MBtu), respectively. Since both

Table 31.1
A Cleaver-Brooks 350 hp. package firetube boiler

Fuel type	Efficiency (%)	Output (psig/hour)	Annual output (MBtu/year)	Input (MBtu)	Purchase cost ($)
Natural gas	81.0	125	1190	1469	63.560
No. 2 fuel oil	84.5	125	1190	1408	66.600
No. 2 oil/gas					68.760

boiler costs are for producing identical amounts of output (1190 MBtu), the problem of value maximization reduces to that of cost minimization.

We normalize costs in terms of the real price of oil relative to that of gas and express the normalized cost functions as:

$$\Psi(P_t, gas, t) = 1469$$

$$\Psi(P_t, oil, t) = 1408P_t \tag{8}$$

where $P_t = P_{oil}/P_{gas}$ is the relative price of oil. It is now evident that the single stochastic state variable affecting the relative values of the boilers is the relative price of oil to gas, P_t.

These cost functions also provide the costs of the two operating modes of a dual-fuel boiler. If the flexible boiler switches between modes costlessly, the firm would be indifferent between operating the boiler with gas or oil at a relative oil price of $P = 1469 \div 1408 = 1.04$. Using market prices of \$0.60 per gallon for No. 2 fuel oil and \$1.90/MBtu for natural gas, the relative price adjusted for Btu content equals approximately 1.2.[10] Under these prices, the above efficiency estimates suggest that a natural gas boiler would be preferred to one that is fired by oil. However, due to the volatility of the relative price of gas to fuel oil, a decision rule that takes into account the relative price dynamics may make a flexible boiler even more preferable.

Given the high degree of substitution between these two fuel sources, competitive forces would tend to drive the long-run relative price to an equilibrium where users will be indifferent between the two fuels.[11] This suggests a mean-reverting specification in estimating the stochastic dynamics of the relative price of oil to gas. We set the long-run mean to which prices revert at the level at which the two boilers would be operated at equal cost, i.e., $\bar{P} = 1.04$.[12] In other words, when the oil price (\$/MBtu) is 1.04 times greater than the natural gas price, a boiler user will be indifferent between the two fuel sources. Therefore, the law-of-one-price will tend to drive the relative prices towards this value which accounts for the efficiency difference in the combustion of the two fuels.

Specifically, we used monthly spot market prices during the sample period from January 1984 through December 1987 to estimate the following equation:[13]

$$\ln P_t = \lambda(\bar{P} - P_t) + \varepsilon \tag{9}$$

where λ is the mean-reversion adjustment factor (per month) and $E[\varepsilon^2] = \sigma^2$.[14] OLS regression results yielded the following parameter values:

$$\ln P_t = 0.0307(1.04 - P_t) + \varepsilon \quad \text{where } \sigma_\varepsilon = 0.0522. \tag{10}$$

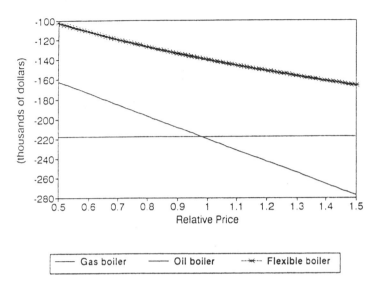

Figure 31.1
Present-value costs of industrial steam boiler

These values translate into a volatility of 18.1% ($= 5.22 * \sqrt{12}$) and a mean-reversion adjustment factor of 36.8% ($= 3.07 * 12$), on an annualized basis.

Finally, we assumed that the relative price of oil and gas has no systematic risk. Hence, the expected return on the relative price process is the risk-free rate of interest. From our results in Section II.B.3., we determined the certainty equivalent drift rate (or rate of return in a risk-neutral economy) to be $r - [r - \lambda(\bar{P} - P_t)] = \lambda(\bar{P} - P_t)$.[15]

We used the above parameter values, along with a risk-free rate of two percent per annum and an economic life of ten years, as the base case to solve the dynamic programming equations described in Equation (1).[16] Figure 31.1 plots the present value cost of operating each boiler against the current value of relative price, P_0, assuming that the boiler can be switched between the two fuels without incurring any adjustment costs. The area between the single-fuel boiler with the lower cost and the purchase cost of the flexible boiler is interpreted as the incremental value of flexibility. Figure 31.2 plots this flexibility value against the current value of the relative price.

Of course, an investment decision rule requires a comparison between the incremental value of flexibility and the additional purchase cost of the flexible boiler over the relevant single-fuel boiler. For instance, if the current relative price (P_0) is 1.2, then the gas boiler dominates the oil boiler. The value of flexibility is $26,000, which far exceeds the $5200 ($68,760 − $63,560) incremental purchase cost of the flexible

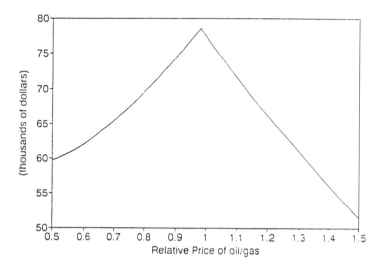

Figure 31.2
Value of flexibility (costless switching)

boiler. Note that the option to switch is most valuable around the point at which
the two fuels are indifferent. Intuitively, this is because the probability of a switch
is highest at this indifference point, making flexibility most valuable. We can also
interpret this result by appealing to an options analogy. When the flexible boiler is
operating in the oil mode (when $P_0 < \bar{P}$), the boiler contains a call option on P that
can be exercised to switch to gas. On the other hand, when it is operating using gas
(for $P_0 > \bar{P}$), the boiler contains a put option on P that can be exercised to switch to
oil. At $P_0 = \bar{P}$, both these options are at-the-money, making the nested option most
valuable.

We also performed comparative statics to study the effect of changes in σ and λ.
As expected, the option value of switching increases with increasing volatility,
but as λ increases, the option value decreases, indicating the dampening effect of
mean-reversion.

The above analysis assumed no switching costs. In practice, however, even flexible
boilers incur switching costs to switch between fuel types. These could arise from
work interruptions, recontracting costs, and the costs of physically switching fuel
types. The actual switching costs, of course, depend to a large extent on the specific
application. Based on conversations with several users, we used a value of $3000 as
the average user's cost of fuel switching, which is approximately equal to the monthly
fuel cost.[17]

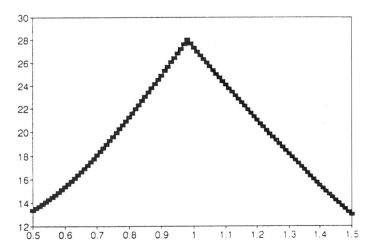

Figure 31.3
Value of flexibility (switching cost = $3000)

Figure 31.3 plots the value of flexibility in the presence of switching costs. Comparing these values with the base-case of costless switching, we see that the value of flexibility is reduced, but is still significantly greater than the additional investment cost of the single-fuel boilers. Perhaps, this explains why over 80% of the boilers sold by major manufacturers are of the dual-fuel type.

We also computed the critical boundaries of the relative price at which firms would switch between oil and gas.[18] For the above base-case parameter values and a switching cost of $3000, the firm would switch from gas to oil if the relative oil price falls below 0.92, and it will switch from oil to gas if the relative price rises above 1.15. As expected, the hysteresis band between the critical prices (see Kogut and Kulatilaka [6]) increases with increasing volatility and higher switching costs. For instance, the relative price of 1.2 (approximating current market conditions) would call for switching away from oil into gas for firms facing our base-case parameter values.

IV Concluding Remarks

We have presented a simple model of flexibility that can be used to obtain the option value to switch between different modes of operation. We then applied the model to evaluate the incremental cost saving of a dual-fuel boiler over the better of two single-fuel boilers. We found that the value of flexibility exceeds the incremental investment cost of purchasing a dual-fuel boiler.

This result not only has obvious implications for investment in flexible technologies but may also influence the equilibrium market prices of substitute fuels. In the absence of dual-fuel boilers, the large switching costs, the installed base, and the resulting hysteresis will act as a wedge between the prices of substitutable energy sources. For instance, if oil boilers were cheaper to operate under current energy prices, the threat of potential future gas price increases will tend to maintain the status quo and dissuade oil-using firms from switching into gas-operated technologies. However, the introduction of flexible technologies reduces the switching costs and enables firms to choose the lower cost alternative fuel source. Clearly, higher relative price volatility will increase the value of flexibility and create increased investment in flexible technologies. Ironically, the very presence of these flexible technologies, however, may link the markets and reduce the volatility of relative price changes, potentially reducing the future value of flexibility.[19]

Acknowledgments

The model described in this chapter is based on an earlier working paper entitled "The Value of Flexibility," MIT-EL 86-014WP. The empirical results are extensions of the results from an unpublished research project that I conducted with David Wood, with the assistance of Michael Provance and Yoshiki Ogawa at the Center for Energy Policy Research at the MIT Energy Laboratory. The project was interrupted by the untimely death of David Wood. The chapter would not be possible without his contributions, and hence is really a joint product. However, I am solely responsible for any errors.

Notes

1. See Pindyck [13] for a review of the literature on irreversible investments under uncertainty. Kulatilaka and Marcus [9] provide a more intuitive discussion of real options and their implications. Mason and Merton [10] contains a general technical discussion of issues related to the use of options techniques in capital budgeting.

2. The model is described in greater detail in Kulatilaka [7], where I also show how other previously known real options are special cases of this general model of flexibility.

3. This example is similar to that in Kulatilaka and Marcus [9].

4. Because there is no uncertainty, the five percent rate may be applied to all cash flows. Using a single rate to discount all cash flows usually is too simplistic, since different cash flows have different risk characteristics.

5. Although the issues pertaining to choice of risk-adjusted discount rates are important, initially we will limit sources of uncertainty to very simple forms to highlight the special problems surrounding the analysis of real options.

6. Furthermore, the strike price of the options (the price of gas) may be evolving stochastically. However, the switching decision depends only on the relative price of oil with respect to gas, and hence the problem reduces to a single stochastic state variable.

7. One important application of hysteresis occurs in the foreign trade literature where firms may continue buying from current suppliers even when exchange rate movements make those suppliers higher cost producers than other competitors. This behavior may make sense when either the cost of switching suppliers is high or the probability of exchange-rate reversals is significant.

8. This result was first suggested by Constantinides [3]. McDonald and Siegel [11] later derived it more formally and applied it in the context of option pricing.

9. The efficiency also depends on the utilization rate of the boiler. However, Provance [14] notes that the level of efficiency tapers off at above 30%.

10. Although we use spot market prices here, most industrial purchases take place on various contracts and discounts that are based on location and customer-specific conditions.

11. A study of fuel switching capability in the natural gas market conducted by Electric Power Research Institute [5] provides a detailed analysis of these issues. It concludes that the addition of fuel switching capabilities in the capital stock has strongly linked the prices of the substitute fuels (natural gas and residual oil).

12. Clearly, the equilibrium relative price depends on the installed base of technology that uses the two fuels and the relative efficiencies of these technologies in using the fuels. Our assumption abstracts from these more complex equilibrium issues.

13. In practice, the natural gas and residual oil markets have various contractual arrangements and local variations. Here, we assumed that the spot prices form the benchmark for transactions.

14. A more rigorous econometric analysis could use nonlinear techniques to jointly estimate λ, σ, and $\bar{P}$.

15. Note that this drift rate depends on the realization of P_t. This is analogous to having a state-dependent dividend.

16. The numerical valuation grid was formed by restricting the relative price, P, to the range 0.5 to 1.5, and using 100 discrete steps.

17. It is more likely that the marginal user's switching costs and prices will probably be reflected in the purchase prices of the flexible boilers. Our calculations abstract from these general equilibrium considerations.

18. These are the optimal exercise boundaries of the call and put options on the relative oil price.

19. These kinds of dependencies between the investment/operating decisions of a firm and the resultant prices have been the focus of an emerging literature. See, for example, Caballero [2].

References

1. M. Brennan and E. Schwartz, "Evaluating Natural Resource Investments," *Journal of Business* (April 1985), pp. 135–157.

2. R. J. Caballero, "On the Sign of the Investment-Uncertainty Relationship," *American Economic Review* (March 1991), pp. 279–288.

3. G. Constantinides, "Market Risk Adjustment in Project Valuation." *Journal of Finance* (May 1978), pp. 603–616.

4. J. Cox, J. Ingersoll, and S. Ross, "An Inter-temporal General Equilibrium Model of Asset Prices," *Econometrica* (March 1985), pp. 363–384.

5. Electric Power Research Institute, "Fuel Switching and Gas Market Risks: Volumes 1 and 2," *EPRI P-6822*, Palo Alto, CA, 1990.

6. B. Kogut and N. Kulatilaka, "Operating Flexibility, Global Manufacturing, and the Option Value of a Multinational Network," *Management Science* (1994), pp. 123–139.

7. N. Kulatilaka, "The Value of Flexibility I: A General Model of Real Options," in *Real Options in Capital Investment: New Contributions*, L. Trigeorgis (ed.), Praeger, NY, 1993.

8. N. Kulatilaka, "Operating Flexibilities in Capital Budgeting: Substitutability and Complementarity of Real Options," in *Real Options in Capital Investment: New Contributions*, L. Trigeorgis (ed.), Praeger, NY, 1993.

9. N. Kulatilaka and A. Marcus, "Project Valuation Under Uncertainty: When Does DCF Fail?," *Journal of Applied Corporate Finance* (Fall 1992), pp. 92–100.

10. S. Mason and R. Merton, "The Role of Contingent Claims Analysis in Corporate Finance," in *Recent Advances in Corporate Finance*, E. I. Altman and M. G. Subrahmanyam (eds.), Homewood, IL, Richard D. Irwin, 1985, pp. 7–54.

11. R. McDonald and D. Siegel, "Option Pricing When the Underlying Asset Earns a Below Equilibrium Rate of Return: A Note." *Journal of Finance* (March 1984), pp. 261–265.

12. R. McDonald and D. Siegel, "The Value of Waiting to Invest," *Quarterly Journal of Economics* (November 1986), pp. 707–727.

13. R. S. Pindyck, "Irreversibility, Uncertainty, and Investment," *Journal of Economic Literature* (September 1991), pp. 1110–1148.

14. M. Provance, "Industrial Boiler Fuel Cost Model," Draft-Mimeo, MIT Energy Laboratory, Cambridge, MA.

Appendix A. Discrete Transition Probabilities

This appendix shows how the discrete transition probability matrix can be approximated from the continuous-time dynamics of θ. We rely on the property that, as long as the state variable θ_t evolves continuously, we may act as though over short time intervals it has a normal distribution.

In modeling a mean-reverting process, we assume that $\Delta\theta_t$ over time period Δt is normally distributed over the interval Δt, with mean $-\lambda(\bar{P} - P_t)\Delta t$ and variance $\sigma^2 \Delta t$. (We suppress the possible dependence of $\lambda, \bar{P}$ and σ on θ_t and t for notational simplicity.)

In order to discretize the range of possible values of P_t, we assume that P_t may take one of S possible values, $P^1, \ldots, P^S$. Given a value of P_t^i (state P_i at time t), the probability of P_{t+1}^j in the next period depends on the difference $j - i$. As the absolute value of $j - i$ increases, the probability falls in accordance with the normal distribution.

It is easy to show that, consistent with the discrete version of the cumulative normal distribution, a transition from state i to state j occurs with probability

$$P_{ij} = \Phi\left[\frac{-\lambda(\bar{P} - P^i)\Delta t + (j - i + \frac{1}{2})\Delta P}{\sigma P^i \sqrt{\Delta t}}\right] - \Phi\left[\frac{-\lambda(\bar{P} - P^i)\Delta t + (j - i - \frac{1}{2})\Delta P}{\sigma P^i \sqrt{\Delta t}}\right] \tag{A1}$$

where $\Phi[\cdot]$ is the cumulative standard normal distribution, and the step size $\Delta P = P^{i+1} - P^i$, for all $i = 1, \ldots, S$.

Special care must be taken with respect to the end points P^1 and P^S. Lumping all exterior values to the boundary, we obtain the transition probabilities

$$P_{iS} = 1 - \Phi\left[\frac{-\lambda(\bar{P} - P^i)\Delta t + (S - i + \frac{1}{2})\Delta P}{\sigma P^i \sqrt{\Delta t}}\right].$$

$$P_{Si} = \Phi\left[\frac{-\lambda(\bar{P} - P^i)\Delta t + (1 - i + \frac{1}{2})\Delta P}{\sigma P^i \sqrt{\Delta t}}\right].$$

Using the above equations, it is easy to take the necessary expectations in Equation (1). Given the current value of P_t, we may now calculate the probability associated with any value of P_{t+1}. We can, therefore, use these probabilities to calculate the expected value of $F(P_{t+1}, m, t + 1)$ as we proceed along the backward iterative process.

32 A Real Options Application in Natural-Resource Investments

Lenos Trigeorgis

I Introduction

This chapter demonstrates the application of an options-based numerical analysis methodology in the case of a natural-resource investment opportunity that was recently being considered by a major multinational company.[1] The company executives felt that their traditional valuation techniques did not fully capture all the opportunity's value. Despite a negative NPV of forecasted cash flows, they felt that the project's inherent flexibility and "strategic" potential might justify its undertaking. The "hard numbers" could not justify such a decision, however, and so the company executives turned outside, looking for alternative valuation frameworks that would help them understand better the value trade-offs, and eventually decide whether the flexibility or strategic worth was sufficiently large to make up for the negative value of cash flows.

The following options-based analysis was the author's response to help company executives facing such dilemmas gain a better understanding of the relative importance to project value of various elements of operating flexibility. In the case of this minerals project, flexibility consists of the options to cancel during construction, expand production, abandon early for salvage value, or even defer project initiation. As such real options may interact when present in combination, however, their separate values (as may be determined by standard option-pricing models) may not be additive, necessitating the use of options-based numerical analysis. Sensitivity results also provide an indication of the degree to which various factors influence flexibility value, reinforcing the degree of management's confidence in making judgments about its relative importance in project valuation.

The rest of the paper is organized as follows. Section II describes the mineral project's characteristics. Section III presents the base-case options analysis. Sensitivity tests to a variety of factors are presented in Section IV. The last section contains implications and conclusions.

II Project Description

The project to be analyzed is a natural-resource investment, producing a certain mineral. The base-scale project consists of two main phases, as shown in figure 32.1. The construction phase starts with the commitment of the first outlay (in year 0) and ends when capacity comes on line with the last planned capital outlay (in year 4). Overall, a series of five annual capital outlays must be incurred until construction is

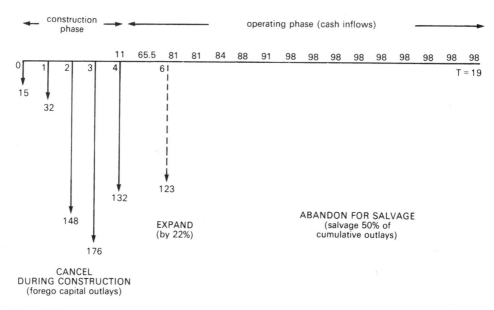

Figure 32.1
The minerals project with indicated capital outlays during the construction phase and expected cash inflows
during the operating phase (in millions of dollars)

completed (years 0–4). This capital investment will result in a production capacity of
400,000 tons of mineral annually for the base-scale project, starting after year 4.
However, several years are required to penetrate the domestic market, resulting in a
gradual buildup of sales, and so production is not expected to reach full capacity
until after year 10.[2] The mineral can be sold in the domestic market at a price of $330
per ton. Given this selling price, sales projections, and known maintenance and
operating costs (M&O),[3] the expected cash inflows during the project's operating
phase from year 4 onward are determined to be as shown in figure 32.1. The real risk-
adjusted discount rate is estimated to be 10%.

Although currently uncertain and remote, corporate executives feel that an export
potential could be developed by year 6. At that time they could consider adding stage
II to expand the base-scale project. An additional $123 million investment in plant
and equipment in year 6 (spread over two years) would increase the mine capacity by
50%, producing an additional 200,000 tons per year that could be fully absorbed by
the export market from year 8 onward. At the lower export price of $168 per ton, this
capacity expansion translates into a 22% increase in the "gross" value of the base-
scale project (i.e., the present value of its expected cash inflows).[4,5]

Company executives can furthermore identify four types of operating flexibility embedded in this mineral project:

(1) *Cancellation during construction.* In case mineral prices turn particularly unfavorable, construction can be cancelled and the developer can walk away from any subsequent planned capital outlays with no cancellation penalty. This option might be exercised at any time during the five-year construction phase.

(2) *Expansion.* At a given time (year 6), management can decide to add stage II, expanding production capacity by 50%, as discussed above. If this additional production is sold at export prices, there will be an expansion in project value by about 22% (50% if it can be sold at the higher domestic prices).

(3) *Abandonment for salvage.* At any time the entire project may be abandoned for its salvage value (or may be repositioned into an alternative use). In case of abandonment, salvage value would amount to 50% of accumulated capital outlays net of a 10% annual depreciation.[6]

(4) *Deferral.* Project initiation may be delayed for up to two years without any adverse (e.g., competitive) consequences.

The value of these real options and the operating rules that should guide managerial decisions as to when to exercise each of these elements of flexibility are implicit in the options analysis, as discussed below.

III   Base-Case Options Analysis

In addition to the project characteristics described above, subsequent analysis is also based on the following base-case assumptions (although sensitivity tests of some of these factors are presented in the next section):

(1) All figures are in real terms.

(2) Capital outlays and M&O costs are known with relative certainty.

(3) The (real) riskless interest rate is 2%.

(4) Expected project life is 20 years (assuming no early abandonment).

(5) The annual standard deviation of gross project value (or of the present value of expected cash inflows) is 20% (i.e., variance = 0.04).[7]

Before presenting the valuation results that capture the value of flexibility, it would seem appropriate first to determine the base-scale project's traditional discounted cash flow (DCF) value, with no flexibility, as a benchmark that would enable a better appreciation of the relative importance of operating flexibility.

Under traditional DCF, one would first discount the expected cash inflows generated by the base-scale project during the operating phase at the risk-adjusted rate of 10% to determine the gross project value (V), here found to be $V = \$465.6$ million. The present value of known capital outlays planned to be incurred during the construction phase (discounted at the riskless rate) is then determined to be $I = \$476.2$ million. The difference, of course, gives the NPV (in millions of dollars) of the base-scale project with no flexibility: $V - I = 465.6 - 476.2 = -10.6$.

Traditional valuation therefore does not justify acceptance of this project. To this value, however, must be added the values imparted by operating flexibility. The value (in millions of dollars) of each component of flexibility determined separately (using standard option pricing) is as follows:

Cancellation during construction   41.4
(valued as a compound call option on project value with exercise prices the series of capital outlays)

Expansion   17.4
(valued as a European call on part of the project, here 22% of V, with exercise price the additional investment outlay of $123 million in year 6)

Abandonment for salvage[8]   85.1
(valued as an American dividend-paying put on current project value V, with exercise price the salvage value).

Unfortunately, these individual real-option values are not necessarily additive due to various interactions. For example, if the project is cancelled during construction, it cannot later be expanded. If the base-scale project is, in fact, expanded, that would alter the underlying asset (project scale) and value of the last option (to abandon for salvage). Moreover, the mere presence of the last two options (i.e., to abandon for salvage or to expand) would increase the effective underlying asset for earlier options. In essence, prior options (i.e., to defer, or cancel during construction) have as their underlying asset the whole portfolio of gross project value plus the then value of any subsequent options.

Because of such interactions, the combined value of a collection of such real options can only be captured correctly through properly designed options-based numerical analysis valuation techniques (see Trigeorgis [11] for an examination of the nature of such interactions, and Trigeorgis [12] for a numerical-analysis approach that can properly account for them). In the above minerals project, the combined value of all three options taking their interactions into account is determined to be $98.5 million (about 21% of the $476.2 million total capital outlays needed), increasing total project value (from the no-flexibility NPV of −10.6) to $87.9 million.[9]

In addition to the value of flexibility, the options-based analysis simultaneously imputes a set of operating schedules or rules that can serve as the basis for an optimal operating policy. For example, "expand capacity if mineral price goes above $X at the time of decision (year 6)," or "abandon if the price falls below $Y in year t, Y' in year $t + 1$, etc."[10] These operating rules underscore the need to manage investment projects actively over time in response to future market developments, as opposed to the naive treatment depicted by a passive, mechanistic accept/reject decision at the beginning.

IV   Sensitivity Analysis

To get a better feel for how sensitive the value of flexibility is to various factors, table 32.1 tabulates the results of sensitivity analysis with respect to project value volatility, salvage value estimates, and riskless interest rate variation.

As expected, a somewhat higher project value uncertainty (mainly driven by the volatility in mineral prices) makes the various components of project flexibility sig-

Table 32.1
Sensitivity tests of combined flexibility value to variation in project standard deviation, salvage value, and riskless interest rate

Variable	Combined flexibility value (millions of dollars)
Project standard deviation	
0.1	64.6
0.15	80.7
0.2[a]	98.5
0.3	137.3
Salvage value (%)	
10	62.2
30	78.4
50[a]	98.5
70	123.0
Real riskless interest rate (%)	
0	89.5
1	93.7
2[a]	98.5
3	103.9
4	109.7

a. Base-case assumption.

nificantly more valuable. For example, a 50% increase in the standard deviation (from 0.2 to 0.3) brings about a 40% increase in the combined flexibility value (from 98.5 to 137.3). Similarly, a 50% reduction (from 0.2 to 0.1) results in a 35% flexibility value decline (from 98.5 down to 64.6).

The value of flexibility is also quite sensitive to the percentage of capital investment that can be salvaged in case of abandonment. For example, a 40% decline in this percentage (from 50 to 30%) would result in a 20% reduction in the combined flexibility value (from 98.5 down to 78.4).

By contrast, the results do not appear strongly sensitive to variation in the riskless interest rate. A 100% increase in the riskless rate (from 2% to 4%) would result in an increase in flexibility value of about 11% (from 98.5 to 109.7).

Finally, if the output from potential expansion (stage II) could be fully absorbed at the higher domestic price rather than be sold at the export price, the expansion option would surpass in significance the ability to abandon, becoming the most valuable component of flexibility (alone rising in value from $17.4 to $125.7 million). The value of all three elements of flexibility taken together would then rise from $98.5 to $170.4 million (about 36% of capital outlays). If the option to defer the project for up to two years is also included, the combined value of all four options would increase further to $210.4 million (or 44% of capital outlays).

Figures 32.2–32.5 show graphically the sensitivity of total project value, including the value of flexibility, to changes in several factors. With other factors being constant, total project value

(1) increases with project variance (figure 32.2),

(2) rises with salvage value (figure 32.3),

(3) increases with more years to defer (figure 32.4),

(4) rises with gross project value V (figure 32.5), behaving in aggregate as a "super–call option."

These sensitivity tests suggest that the project with its collection of real options, despite their interactions, maintains the basic option properties.

V Implications and Conclusion

This chapter describes the application of options-based analysis to a real natural-resource project in order to sharpen managerial judgment concerning operating flexibility and its potential value. It has been demonstrated that the value of flexibility imparted by the options to cancel during construction, expand capacity, abandon for

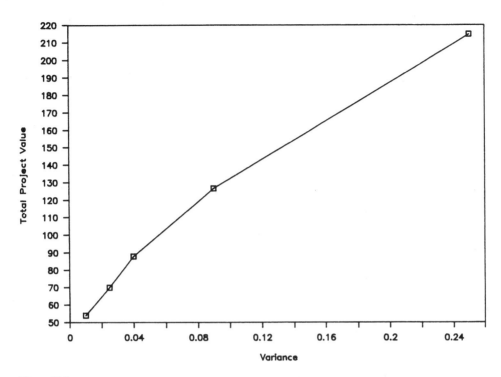

Figure 32.2
Total project value vs. variance

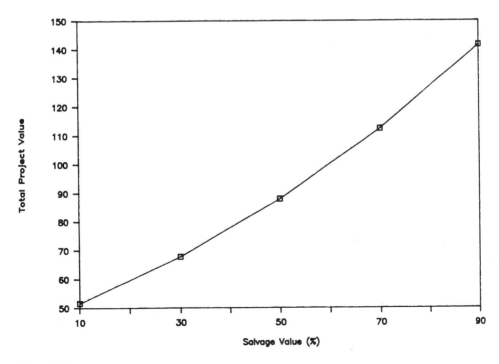

Figure 32.3
Total project value vs. salvage value

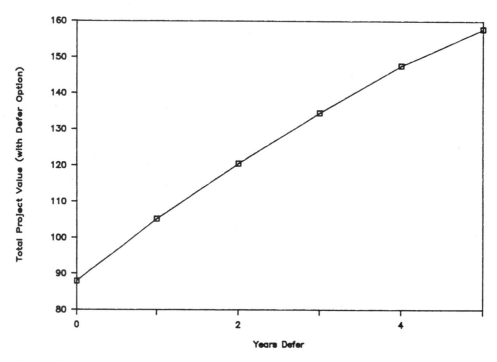

Figure 32.4
Total project value vs. years deferred

salvage, or even defer project initiation amounts to a substantial percentage of the total value of capital outlays. Special care is taken to account for possible inter- actions among these options that may violate option value additivity.

The combined value of flexibility justifies going ahead with the minerals project, despite its negative NPV of expected cash flows. Options-based analysis not only may thus reverse the traditional DCF-based decision, but also underscores the importance of active management of the project over time while providing guidelines for its optimal operation. Sensitivity tests of the project with flexibility are also presented suggesting that, despite option interactions, it maintains basic option properties.

Acknowledgments

I thank Henry D. Jacoby and Scott P. Mason for their help and ideas, as well as company executives for providing data and help in formulating the application.

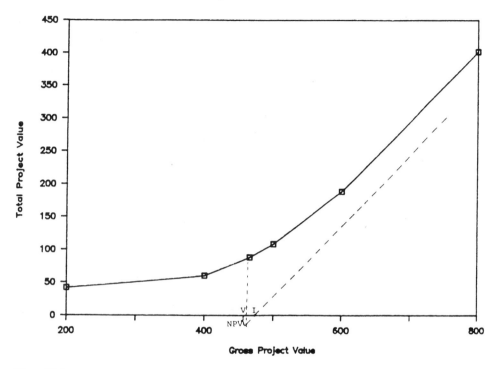

Figure 32.5
Total project value vs. gross value

Notes

1. There is a growing "real-options" literature that uses option pricing to value capital-budgeting projects. For example, see Majd and Pindyck [3], Mason and Merton [4], McDonald and Siegel [5, 6], Myers and Majd [this volume], Trigeorgis [10], and Trigeorgis and Mason [13]. Other applications to natural-resource investments include the work of Brennan and Schwartz [2], Siegel, Smith, and Paddock [8], and Tourinho [9].

2. Projected sales during the operating phase are (in thousands of tons per year): 67 in year 4, 284 in 5, 340 in 6 and 7, 350 in 8, 363 in 9, 372 in 10, and 400 (fully capacity) from years 11 to 19.

3. For the base-scale project, fixed M&O costs are $8 million in year 4, and $16 million from year 5 onward. Variable M&O costs are $44/ton.

4. For simplicity, it is assumed that all the output of stage II, if in fact built, would be exported, while that of the base-scale project is sold in the domestic market. In reality, if export demand is still not satisfied, it might be possible to export any unused capacity (i.e., the difference between production capacity and domestic sales) from the base-scale project. Similarly, if future domestic sales were to exceed base-scale capacity, part of stage II production could be sold to satisfy the excess demand at home at the higher domestic prices. Ignoring these possibilities would lead to a small underestimate of the option to expand and of project value.

5. The additional annual fixed M&O cost for stage II is $3 million from year 8 onward, while the variable M&O cost is unchanged ($44/ton).

6. The salvage value would include a portion of any additional outlays on the stage II expansion.

7. The volatility in project value is, of course, a key determinant of the value of flexibility, and should be estimated with utmost care. As well known, operating flexibility is more valuable in a more uncertain environment. The project standard deviation value of 0.2 used here is about the same as that of the average stock traded in financial markets—which also represents a claim to future cash flows and is therefore analogous to the variable of interest here. For many real assets such as commodities, oil, mineral, and other natural resources, the standard deviation of price is between 0.2 and 0.4. Thus, it is not unreasonable to assume a standard deviation of 0.2 for the base-case calculations for this mineral project. In any event, sensitivity results are presented over the range from 0.1 to 0.3.

8. In this case, the ability to get out of the project seems to exceed the value of the opportunity to expand it (so long as the stage II output is sold at the lower export prices).

9. If the option to defer initiating the project for up to two years is also included, the combined value of all four options rises to $131.1 million (about 28% of the $476.2 capital outlay), increasing total project value to $120.5 million.

10. The value of flexibility determined above should be viewed as an upper bound since it will only be fully realized if the optimal operating rules are in fact followed, i.e., the project is actually cancelled, expanded, or abandoned precisely when indicated. To the degree that actual operation departs from the optimal rules, the flexibility value actually realized will be below its theoretical value as calculated above.

References

1. Black, F. and Scholes, M. "The Pricing of Options and Corporate Liabilities," *Journal of Political Economy* 3 (1973), 637–659.

2. Brennan, M. and Schwartz, E. "Evaluating Natural Resource Investments," *Journal of Business* 58 (1985), 135–157.

3. Majd, S. and Pindyck, R. "Time to Build, Option Value, and Investment Decisions," *Journal of Financial Economics* (March 1987), 7–27.

4. Mason, S. P. and Merton, R. C. "The Role of Contingent Claims Analysis in Corporate Finance," in *Recent Advances in Corporate Finance*, E. Altman and M. Subrahmanyam (eds.). Chicago, IL: Irwin, 1985.

5. McDonald, R. and Siegel, D. "Investment and the Valuation of Firms When There Is an Option to Shut Down," *International Economic Review* (1985), 331–349.

6. McDonald, R. and Siegel, D. "The Value of Waiting to Invest," *Quarterly Journal of Economics* 101 (November 1986), 707–727.

7. Myers, S. C. "Finance Theory and Financial Strategy," *Midland Corporate Finance Journal* (Spring 1987), 6–13.

8. Siegel, D., Smith, J. and Paddock, J. "Valuing Offshore Oil Properties with Option Pricing Models," *Midland Corporate Finance Journal* (Spring 1987), 22–30.

9. Tourinho, O. "The Option Value of Reserves of Natural Resources," working paper, University of California—Berkeley, 1979.

10. Trigeorgis, L. "A Conceptual Options Framework for Capital Budgeting," in *Advances in Futures and Options Research*, Vol. 3, F. J. Fabozzi, (ed.), pp. 145–168. Greenwich, CT: JAI Press, 1988.

11. Trigeorgis, L. "The Nature of Option Interactions and the Valuation of Investments with Multiple Real Options," *Journal of Financial and Quantitative Analysis* (1993), 1–20.

12. Trigeorgis, L. "A Log-transformed Binomial Numerical Analysis Method for Valuing Complex Multi-option Investments," (1991), 309–326.

13. Trigeorgis, L. and Mason, S. P. "Valuing Managerial Flexibility," *Midland Corporate Finance Journal* (Spring 1987), 14–21.

33 Managing Investment Opportunities under Price Uncertainty: From "Last Chance" to "Wait and See" Strategies

Petter Bjerksund and Steinar Ekern

Problems easily arise when using traditional discounted cash flow analysis to evaluate projects involving both uncertainty and decision flexibility. Difficulties are caused by simultaneous interrelations between the expected cash flow, the risk-adjusted discount rate, the optimal strategy, and the values obtained. Option pricing theory and contingent claims analysis offer both a suitable conceptual framework and improved analytical tools for simultaneously determining project values and optimal strategies. A number of recent studies have used the contingent claims framework to explore various applications to the capital budgeting area [2, 3, 4, 6, 8, 9, 11, 12, 14, 15, 16, 18, 19, 24, 25, 26, 27, 28, 31, 34, 35, 36].

A productive investment opportunity which is irrevocable once undertaken is considered here. The fundamental source of uncertainty is the output price being generated by a stochastic process. Various degrees of flexibility are primarily expressed in terms of possibilities for delaying the final investment decision itself. The essence is how to obtain both explicit values for the investment project and optimal managerial decision rules consistent with the uncertainty and flexibility assumed.

The objectives are:

(i) Modeling the risky output price as the basic source of uncertainty and as a sufficient statistic in decision rules and valuation;

(ii) Providing a comprehensive, unified, and mostly self-contained treatment of various degrees of flexibility assumed for the investment decision;

(iii) Taking a managerial perspective in modifying decision rules which are not appropriate in a flexibility context, preserving the general format of the traditional rules;

(iv) Keeping the basic structure simple to allow for analytical solutions when possible, and otherwise not requiring more computing power than available on a pocket calculator; and

(v) Showing that for hypothetical but reasonable parameter values the effects of investment flexibility are considerable, whereas the results from adding operating or abandonment options may be negligible in comparision (Trigeorgis [35] deals with option interactions and shows that the valuation errors from ignoring particular options, in the presence of other options, may be small).

Several related studies [15, 19, 25, 26] of the value of waiting to invest introduce uncertainty by means of the stochastic value of a completed project which is either producing or ready for production. In contrast, this study goes one step further in tracing the elementary source of uncertainty down to the risky spot output price, which is assumed to follow a geometric Brownian motion.[1] In the option interpretation of the investment opportunity, the underlying asset becomes the output itself and not the project if undertaken. This distinction is neither a simple matter of reinterpreting state variables nor a question of convenience, but an issue with substantial theoretical, empirical, and practical ramifications.[2] The spot price of the output turns out to be a sufficient statistic for valuation and the relevant state variable for decision rules.[3]

Aspects of most issues discussed are scattered around in the literature referred to above, but not within any single contribution. A sequence of models with an increasing degree of investment flexibility will be examined. A basic building block is the current value of a commitment to a project without any flexibility whatsoever. In two traditional models, the accept/reject case and the old optimal timing models, the analysis is performed as if it were the "last chance" to invest in the project or the opportunity would be lost forever. In contrast, three different "wait and see" models explicitly bring in possibilities for making the investment decision later. These latter models differ with respect to the assumptions as to when the decision may be made, resulting in European, perpetual American, and finite-maturity American option interpretations, respectively. Two additional models allow for additional managerial flexibility. For each alternative a relevant decision scenario is described, the decision rule is formulated, and the project value is derived.

Casual observations suggest that managers are more comfortable in relating to observable market prices than to nonobservable net present values. The net present value rule in traditional project evaluation is therefore often operationalized in terms of a critical break-even price, whose value is no longer valid under investment timing flexibility. It may be quite a challenge to achieve managerial acceptance of the insight from option-based formulations as relevant decision support. However, a modified break-even rule of the form, "Invest the first time the output price exceeds an adjusted break-even price," is both intuitively appealing and familiar from cases in which decision flexibility is not an important feature.

The methods used here for investigating the effects of decision flexibility are standard for contingent claims analyses. Still, many academic economists, and probably almost all managers, will find the mathematical apparatus of stochastic calculus prohibitively difficult (for a brief introduction to stochastic calculus, see Ingersoll [10, Ch. 16] and Smith [33, Appendix]). Furthermore, actually solving realistic and complex models may involve complicated numerical methods and extensive computer runs, outside the range of anyone but a few specialists. The following analysis has therefore been restricted to simple structures for which either closed-form analytic solutions exist or the required computations are not more difficult than finding the internal rate of return in traditional analyses. In that way, a user may easily experiment with different parameter values and thus gain both more experience with the models and confidence in the results.

At first sight it may appear excessively restrictive to allow decision flexibility only with respect to when to make a final investment decision. The analysis is therefore extended to allow for additional managerial flexibility—in particular, possibilities for switching production on and off as well as irreversibly abandoning the project forever. For the base case parameters, investment flexibility alone doubles the break-even output price compared to the traditional one computed by ignoring any flexibility. In turn, introducing operating or abandonment flexibility affects adjusted break-even prices and project values only on the order of one percentage point. This indicates that the additional managerial flexibility influences optimal investment strategies and values only marginally and may be rather unimportant, considering the estimation risk present for the required input parameters.

The discussion is phrased in terms of a deferrable opportunity to develop an oil field. The approach, however, is quite general. The economic relevance of the results is not limited to oil-related projects or to valuing other natural resources.

I Assumptions and Commitment Value

A The Economy

The first basic premise is that the dynamics of the spot price of oil is described by a geometric Brownian motion

$$\frac{dS}{S} = \alpha\, dt + \sigma\, dz. \tag{1}$$

In this equation, the drift term α is the instantaneous expected relative price change per unit time and represents a trend, if any. The parameter σ is the assumed constant instantaneous standard deviation of the relative price change, per unit time. The term dz is the increment of a standard Wiener process, uncorrelated across time, and at any one instant satisfying $E(dz) = 0$, $E(dz^2) = dt$, and where E denotes the expectations operator. In other words, Equation (1) says that random successive relative price changes are independent and identically distributed normal variables. The spot price of oil follows a continuous sample path, with no jumps.[4]

Next, let $\hat{\alpha}$ be the equilibrium expected rate of return per unit time for a tradable asset perfectly correlated with the spot price of oil, if such an asset exists. This hypothetical "twin asset" has the same volatility σ as oil. Its mean rate of return α may contain both capital gains and a payout component. Such an asset might be a producing oilfield with zero extraction costs.

The second basic premise is that the equilibrium required rate $\hat{\alpha}$ exceeds the growth rate α of the expected spot price of oil:

$$\delta \equiv \hat{\alpha} - \alpha > 0. \tag{2}$$

Note that this positive difference δ is independent of whether both $\hat{\alpha}$ and α are measured in nominal or real terms.

This "rate of return shortfall," δ, is the instantaneous opportunity cost of holding oil rather than the equally risky "twin asset."[5] It represents the portion of the risk-adjusted required return, $\hat{\alpha}$, which is forgone by merely receiving the expected price increase α in spot oil. An analogy would be that δ corresponds to a proportional dividend yield on a stock.

Alternatively, δ may be interpreted as instantaneous marginal convenience yield net of storage costs to an owner of the physical asset (i.e., oil) for whom positive storage is optimal. Then δ is similar to a liquidity premium for holding cash.

Assume that the risk-free rate of interest, r, is known and constant through time. Borrowing and lending, at the same rate r, are unrestricted. In addition, invoke the usual perfect market assumptions of continuous trading, no restrictions on short selling, no transactions costs or differential taxes, and that traded assets are fully divisible.

B The Project

The project is described by a production plan and by a cost schedule for construction and operation. Define the conditional function $q(\tau|t)$ as the rate of production at project time τ, counting time since the project decision at t. Similarly, the function $k(\tau|t)$ gives the rate of combined investment and production costs at calendar time $(t + \tau)$ for development initiated at t. Assume full and perfect information about these costs and output quantities. Once undertaken, the project is irreversible. Uncertainty enters the model only through the stochastic oil price.

The third basic premise is that deferring the development decision has no effect on the output profile by project time, whereas the future cost rate at a fixed project time will grow exponentially. Formally,

$$q(\tau|t) = q(\tau), \tag{3}$$

and

$$k(\tau|t') = e^{\pi(t'-t)}k(\tau|t), \tag{4}$$

where t and t' are alternative development times and τ is the project time since start of development. Equation (3) is a stationarity assumption and implies that the total quantity of oil, $Q(0) \equiv \int q(\tau)\,d\tau$, is a known constant. The parameter π in Equation (4) is a cost escalation factor. The cost profile $k(\tau|t)$, the cost escalation factor π, and the risk-free rate of interest r, are stated either all in nominal terms or all in real terms.

C Investment Flexibility

A petroleum reserve represents an opportunity—but not an obligation—to develop the field. The fourth basic premise is that an immediate decision on when to undertake the project, if ever, is not required. The development decision may be made either now, later at a fixed date T, sometime between now and the expiration date T of the investment opportunity, or possibly at any arbitrary time whatsoever. Different assumptions on decision deferral opportunities will cause different decision rules and different project values.

Observe that this kind of decision flexibility refers to possibly postponing the investment decision itself, allowing for optimal "wait and see" strategies. This assumption is quite different from the "last chance" perspective of the traditional optimal timing literature on immediately determining the preferred time for phasing in a project.

D Valuing Future Output

As a prelude, consider the value at time t of one output unit (e.g., one barrel of oil) available at $t' > t$. The expected output price is $E_t[S(t')] = e^{\alpha(t'-t)}S(t)$. The appropriate discount rate for cash flows of the risk class of spot oil is $\hat{\alpha}$, by assumption. Therefore, the value at t of the expected spot price at t' is

$$V_t\{E_t[S(t')]\} = e^{\alpha(t'-t)}S(t)e^{-\hat{\alpha}(t'-t)}$$
$$= e^{-\delta(t'-t)S(t)}, \tag{5}$$

where V is a general valuation operator. The valuation rule is to discount the current price $S(t)$ at the rate of return shortfall $\delta \equiv \hat{\alpha} - \alpha$, for the time interval $(t' - t)$.

If δ is interpreted as proportional convenience yield accruing to some holders of the physical asset (oil), then an arbitrage argument based on self-financing replicating cash flows shows that

$$V_t[\tilde{S}(t')] = e^{-\delta(t'-t)}S(t), \tag{6}$$

where the left side of Equation (6) evaluates the uncertain cash flow $S(t')$ and not its expected value $E_t[S(t')]$.[6]

Alternatively, consider a hypothetical future contract at time t for delivery of one barrel of oil at time t'. The futures price at t is

$$F_t(S(t')] = e^{(r-\delta)(t'-t)}S(t), \tag{7}$$

by costless arbitrage (see Brennan and Schwartz [3] and Ross [29]). Discounting both sides of Equation (7) at the constant riskless rate r yields Equation (6).

E   Commitment Value

It is a useful preliminary to have the value of a project where there is no flexibility whatsoever. For some unspecified reason the firm is contractually or legally obliged to implement the project according to the previously fixed investment, production, and cost schedules. Suppose the project is initiated at time t. The cash flow at project time τ is

$$X(t + \tau|t) = S(t + \tau)q(\tau) - k(\tau|t). \tag{8}$$

Here the only stochastic term is the future oil price $S(t + \tau)$, which may be evaluated by Equation (6) or (7). The assumed certain costs are discounted at the riskless rate r. Hence, the value of $X(t + \tau|t)$ at decision time is

$$V_t[X(t + \tau|t)] = e^{-\delta\tau}S(t)q(\tau) - e^{-r\tau}k(\tau|t). \tag{9}$$

By integrating Equation (9) over all project times τ, the present value of the project commitment, C, is given by

$$C = C(S, \delta, r|t) = A(\delta)S(t) - K(r|t), \tag{10}$$

where

$$A(\delta) \equiv \int e^{-\delta\tau}q(\tau)\,d\tau, \tag{11}$$

and

$$K(r|t) \equiv \int e^{-r\tau}k(r|t)\,d\tau. \tag{12}$$

A is a time-adjusted quantity of oil found by discounting the output $q(\tau)$ at the rate of return shortfall δ. It is independent of development time t. The ratio $A/Q(0)$ indicates the amount of oil immediately available which would be equivalent to having one barrel available according to the fixed production profile. K is the present value at development time of future costs.[7]

II Immediate Development Decision

A The Traditional Accept/Reject Case

The analysis is performed as if it were the last chance to invest in that particular project. One illustrative example is a newly discovered but marginal reservoir that can only be profitably exploited if linked to the facilities of a neighboring field which is otherwise about to be abandoned.

The value of such an investment opportunity is given by

$$U = \max\{C, 0\}, \tag{13}$$

as the voluntary commitment of course will be rejected if it has a negative value. Recall from Equation (10) that the commitment value C is linear in the current spot price $S(t)$. Hence, the value U of the oil field is a nonnegative kinked linear function of the current output price.

Alternatively, rewrite Equation (10) as

$$C = A(\delta)S_{BE}(t)\left[\frac{S(t)}{S_{BE}(t)} - 1\right], \tag{14}$$

where the break-even price $S_{BE}(t)$ is given by

$$S_{BE}(t) = S_{BE}(\delta, r|t)$$

$$= \frac{K(r|t)}{A(\delta)}, \tag{15}$$

The net present value rule may thus be transformed into the break-even price rule

Develop now if and only if $S(t) > S_{BE}(t)$, $\tag{16}$

for the accept/reject case.

A naive NPV model, which appears to be popular among some practitioners, discounts all cash flow elements at a common and constant risk-adjusted discount rate (RADR) of ρ.[8] In the present formulation, this corresponds to

$$C = A(\rho - \alpha)S(t) - K(\rho|t). \tag{17}$$

Suppose that by chance ρ equals $\hat{a}$. From Equations (10) and (17) it is clear that the revenues are then correctly discounted, whereas the costs are discounted at a too high rate. The consequence of including a risk premium for assumed certain costs is a too high NPV and a too low break-even price. Otherwise, the qualitative results remain.

B   Traditional Optimal Timing

Consider a commitment made at time t to develop at time $T \geq t$. Compared with immediate development, the revenue stream in effect has to be discounted for additional $(T - t)$ periods at the rate δ. The costs increase at the escalation rate π during the delay, but are then discounted back at the risk-free rate r. Thus, the present value at time t of a precommitted development at T is

$$C_t(T) = e^{-\delta(T-t)}A(\delta)S(t) - e^{-(r-\pi)(T-t)}K(r|t). \tag{18}$$

Suppose there are no restrictions on the choice of project initiation time, T, except that it must be fixed immediately. This may occur because of regulatory constraints imposed by the government when granting the license.[9] Also, assume that the parameters satisfy[10]

$$r - \pi > \delta. \tag{19}$$

Then, maximizing Equation (18) with respect to T, the optimal lag is given by

$$\hat{T} - t = \max\left\{0, \frac{\ln\{[(r-\pi)K]/[\delta AS(t)]\}}{r - \pi - \delta}\right\}. \tag{20}$$

The project should be undertaken immediately whenever

$$S(t) > \hat{S}(t) \equiv \left[\frac{(r-\pi)}{\delta}\right]S_{BE}(t) > S_{BE}(t). \tag{21}$$

Inserting the optimal $\hat{T}$ from Equation (20) into Equation (18), note that the commitment value $C_t(\hat{T})$ is an increasing concave function of current price $S(t)$, strictly concave for $S(t) < \hat{S}(t)$ and linear thereafter. Also, from Equation (21) it is seen that the current price exceeding the traditional break-even price is not a sufficient reason for launching the project at once. Both the strict concavity for parts of the value function and the adjustment to the traditional break-even price are typical features to be found in the "wait and see" models, where deferral of the investment decision is allowed. In the formulation above, however, these properties only arise for particular parameter values satisfying the restriction in (19). They are caused by a perceived "last chance" of immediately choosing the start-up time optimally.

Rather than literally committing to an immediate choice of investment timing, some managers might be tempted to follow an ad hoc procedure for apparently taking decision flexibility into account. It builds on considering a future investment date as only tentative, as long as the project has not been irrevocably launched. Instead of computing the optimal investment time once and for all, the output price $S(t)$ is continuously monitored and compared to an updated adjusted break-even price $\hat{S}(t)$ given by Equation (21). Such a myopic approach would be an improvement compared to a usual accept/reject decision formulation. Unfortunately, even though the decisions are in fact sequentially reexamined, the procedure itself fails to take the effect of future revisions explicitly into account. Because each timing date or adjusted critical price is computed as if it were the last one in the sequence, it underestimates the value of waiting to make the ultimate decision. The misconception causes a systematic tendency to initiate projects too early. That problem is ameliorated by option based approaches.

III Development Decision at a Fixed Future Date

Regard the oil field as an investment opportunity where the decision has to be made at a preset future date T. One case is that T is the time when a license expires if development has not been initiated. Another possibility is that the government may have imposed a freeze on field development. Water or gas injection projects aimed at prolonging the production period of an existing field also exemplify the issue to be discussed below.

Recall that by Equation (10) the net present value of committing to a project is a linear function of the spot price at the time of development. Thus the value at the future time T of implementing the project at that time is stochastic and may be negative. As the project will only be accepted if profitable, the stochastic value of the oilfield at the future point in time T is

$$X(T) = \max\{C[S(T), \delta, r|T], 0\}. \tag{22}$$

Using the break-even version, Equation (14), of the present value, this equation translates into

$$X(T) = A(\delta) \max[S(T) - S_{BE}(T), 0], \tag{23}$$

where $S_{BE}(T) = [K(r|T)]/[A(\delta)]$ by Equation (15). Combining the latter expression with Equation (4) on the cost escalation resulting from postponing development yields

$$S_{BE}(T) = e^{\pi(T-t)}S_{BE}(t). \tag{24}$$

Thus, future break-even prices also grow exponentially at the rate π.

The term to be maximized in Equation (23) is, in fact, the future pay-off at maturity of a European call option, with one unit of oil as the underlying asset. Hence, the investment opportunity represents $A(\delta)$ European call options maturing at time T, written on one barrel of oil and with the break-even price $S_{BE}(T)$ at maturity as exercise price.

The stated assumptions are sufficient to call upon the constant proportional dividend yield version of the famous Black-Scholes formula, with suitable reinterpretations of parameters.[11] The following value of the investment opportunity is obtained:

$$W_E = A(\delta)[e^{-\delta(T-t)}S(t)N(d_1) - e^{-(r-\pi)(T-t)}S_{BE}(t)N(d_2)], \tag{25}$$

where

$$d_1 \equiv \frac{\ln\{[S(t)]/[S_{BE}(t)]\} + (r - \pi - \delta + 0.5\sigma^2)(T - t)}{\sigma\sqrt{T - t}}, \tag{26}$$

and

$$d_2 \equiv d_1 - \sigma\sqrt{T - t}, \tag{27}$$

and $N(\cdot)$ is the univariate standard normal distribution function and the subscript E indicates a European option.

The positive value W_E of the investment opportunity increases with higher spot price $S(t)$, lower rate of return shortfall δ, higher risk-free rate of return r, lower cost escalation factor π, and higher volatility σ. Contrary to the case with financial stock options, the effect of extending the time to maturity is ambiguous. The direct effect of higher T is positive, whereas the indirect effects of higher exercise price through escalating break-even price, as well as increased opportunity cost of a prolonged rate of return shortfall, are both negative. A positive shift in the production profile $q(\tau)$ increases the value, whereas a positive shift in the conditional cost function $k(\tau|t)$ decreases W_E.

Assume the choice to be between immediate development and having the opportunity to make an accept/reject decision at the fixed future time T. One illustrative case is that a producing field currently has available capacity, which may either be used for a satellite field or committed to another producer for the time up to T.

If immediate development is to be the optimal choice, the present value U of accepting the project now has to exceed the option value W_E of the future investment opportunity. Hence, a positive present value is not a sufficient condition for launching the project rather than waiting to invest. Similarly, the current spot price of oil exceeding the break-even price is not an obvious "go" signal.

As the values of both immediate development and future investment opportunity are increasing functions of $S(t)$, let $S_E^*(t)$ be the unique spot price at t for which the two values are equal:

$$U[S(t)] = W_E[S(t)] \Rightarrow S_E^*(t) = S(t). \tag{28}$$

The modified decision rule is then

Develop now if and only if $S(t) > S_E^*(t)$. $\tag{29}$

The difference between the adjusted break-even price and the traditional one, $S_E^*(t) - S_{BE}(t)$, becomes an additional profitability hurdle for immediate development to overcome.

IV Development Decision at Any Time

Relax the constraint that development may only commence now, at a fixed date T, or never. Rather, the irrevocable development decision may be made at any time before or on T. Thus, at any point in time up to T, the oil field is an opportunity to acquire the future production by committing to pay the future investment and production costs. Drawing upon the discussion of the previous section, the field is equivalent to $A(\delta)$ American options, where each option is written on one barrel of oil, the exercise price is the current break-even price $S_{BE}(t)$ growing exponentially over time at the rate π, and the rate of return shortfall δ plays the role of constant proportional dividend yield.

The focus is mainly on the limiting case where T goes to infinity, such that the development decision may be arbitrarily postponed if so desired. This turns the field into perpetual American option, for which closed-form solutions are available (e.g., see Barone-Adesi and Whaley [1], Majd and Pindyck [15], McDonald and Siegel [19], Samuelson [30], or Smith [32]).

McDonald and Siegel [19] consider an infinitely lived investment opportunity in which both the underlying asset value and the exercise price follow correlated geometric Brownian motions. The current formulation is somewhat different. Here the underlying asset is one unit of the commodity (oil), not the project's present value excluding investment costs (a developed field ready for production). Thus, in this case production costs are incorporated in the exercise price and not handled by the underlying asset value as in McDonald and Siegel.[12] Also, to focus on output price uncertainty, the exercise price is nonstochastic. Still, the McDonald and Siegel results serve as a convenient departure point.

A   Valuing the Investment Opportunity

As long as it is optimal to keep the option alive by leaving the oil field undeveloped, its value is given by[13]

$$W_{AP} = A\left(\frac{1}{\varepsilon - 1}\right) S_{BE} \left[\left(\frac{\varepsilon - 1}{\varepsilon}\right)\left(\frac{S}{S_{BE}}\right)\right]^{\varepsilon}, \tag{30}$$

where the subscript AP indicates a perpetual American option. In this equation, the time-adjusted quantity of oil A is given by Equation (11), S is the current spot price, S_{BE} is the current traditional break-even price according to Equation (15), and the exponent ε is given by

$$\varepsilon \equiv \left[\frac{1}{2} - \frac{(r - \pi) - \delta}{\sigma^2}\right] + \sqrt{\left[\frac{(r - \pi) - \delta}{\sigma^2} - \frac{1}{2}\right]^2 + 2\frac{r - \pi}{\sigma^2}}. \tag{31}$$

Observe that the exponent ε is a function of the "rate of return shortfall" δ of oil, the difference $(r - \pi)$ between the riskless rate of interest and the cost escalation factor, and the volatility σ of oil price changes.[14] The assumption[15] in Equation (2) of $\delta \equiv \hat{\alpha} - \alpha > 0$ ensures that $\varepsilon > 1$ and thus a positive value of the investment opportunity.

Rewrite Equation (30) as

$$W_{AP} = Q\frac{A}{Q}\left(\frac{1}{\varepsilon - 1}\right) S_{BE} \left[\left(\frac{\varepsilon - 1}{\varepsilon}\right)\left(\frac{S}{S_{BE}}\right)\right]^{\varepsilon}. \tag{32}$$

The value of the nondeveloped oil field may then be explained as follows. Q represents total quantity of oil in the ground, received according to the production plan. The ratio A/Q takes the time-distribution of the production into account. It represents the quantity of delivered oil spot that is equivalent to owning a one-barrel share of the future production. The last factors represent the value of one barrel in the ground which (if optimal) immediately can be transformed into one barrel of oil spot.

B   The Adjusted Break-Even Price

By equating the value U of immediate development in Equation (14) and the option value W_{AP} in Equation (30), it is easy to verify that the two values coincide at a critical oil price S_{AP}^*, given by

$$S^*_{AP}[\varepsilon, S_{BE}(t)] = \frac{\varepsilon}{\varepsilon - 1} S_{BE}(t). \tag{33}$$

Thus, for a perpetual investment opportunity, there is an explicit relationship between the adjusted break-even price S^*_{AP} and the accept/reject break-even price S_{BE}. For corresponding expressions, see [1, 15, 19, 30, or 32].

The optimal strategy is expressed as

Develop now if and only if $S(t) > S^*_{AP}(t)$. \tag{34}

The values U, W_E, and W_{AP} are all increasing functions of the spot price $S(t)$. Also, as optimal development may occur at any point in time rather than at the fixed date T, the American option value W_{AP} is higher than the European option value W_E. Hence, the relation between corresponding break-even prices is

$$S^*_{AP}(t) > S^*_E(t) > S_{BE}(t). \tag{35}$$

Next, relate the value of the oil field to the critical price. Three alternative closed-form expressions for the option value W_{AP} are of interest. From solving Equation (33) for the traditional break-even price S_{BE} and substituting in Equation (30) the following values are obtained:

$$W_{AP} = A(\delta)(S^*_{AP} - S_{BE})\left(\frac{S}{S^*_{AP}}\right)^{\varepsilon}, \tag{36}$$

$$W_{AP} = A(\delta)S^*_{AP}\left(\frac{1}{\varepsilon}\right)\left(\frac{S}{S^*_{AP}}\right)^{\varepsilon}, \tag{37}$$

and

$$W_{AP} = K\left(\frac{1}{\varepsilon - 1}\right)\left(\frac{S}{S^*_{AP}}\right)^{\varepsilon}. \tag{38}$$

In all cases the term to be raised to the εth power is the ratio of current price to adjusted break-even price. Multiplied by the intermediate term of the two former equations, it gives the value of one output unit available for immediate extraction. The $A(\delta)$ term reflects both the size of the reservoir and the time distribution of production. The latter equation brings in directly the present value of costs K. All valuation expressions are homogenous of degree one, such that changing the currency unit of prices and costs yields a consistent value expressed in the new currency.

C   The Flexibility Factor

The critical ratio of adjusted critical price to the traditional break-even price,

$$\varphi(\varepsilon) \equiv \frac{S^*_{AP}}{S_{BE}} = \frac{\varepsilon}{\varepsilon - 1},\tag{39}$$

may be termed a flexibility factor. It expresses by how much the traditional break-even price has to be adjusted upwards because of flexibility to make the development decision at any time. It depends only on economy-wide parameters: δ, r, π, and σ. Project specific assumptions on output profile $q(\tau)$ and costs $k(\tau|t)$ are not used for computing ε or φ.[16] It can be verified that the flexibility factor φ increases with lower "rate of return shortfall" δ, higher risk-free interest rate r, lower cost escalation rate π, and higher volatility σ.

Further, it is easily seen that when the rate of return shortfall approaches zero, the flexibility factor $\varphi = S^*_{AP}/S_{BE}$ will grow to infinity. Assume for the moment that δ is very close to zero. Then, there will be no significant opportunity cost from keeping oil in the ground. Hence, there will be almost no incentive to develop the oil field today—that is, the adjusted break-even price will be very high. The analogy to the perpetual investment opportunity in question is a perpetual American option written on a nondividend-paying stock. With no dividend, there is certainly no reason to "kill" the option before it matures.

D   An Expiring Investment Opportunity

In many practical applications it may be possible to defer the development decision for some limited time, but not forever. That is, the investment option expires if not being used by a fixed date; e.g., leases of natural resources most often have a finite time horizon. The investment opportunity then corresponds to an American option of finite maturity. Therefore, closed-form solutions for the field value or for the break-even price for immediate development are no longer available.

However, the formulas above may still serve as analytical bounds on the investment opportunity value W_{AF} and the corresponding critical price S^*_{AF}, where the subscript AF indicates a finite American option. The perpetual formulation allows for a nonfeasible possibility of optimal development to occur after the fixed horizon T. It therefore exaggerates the project value and the appropriate break-even price. Because of the rate of return shortfall δ on oil, it might on the other hand be optimal to develop before any preset date T', not beyond the maturity considered T. Even when optimizing the particular fixed date T' for which the accept/reject decision is to be made, the resulting values will be too low. In short,

$$W_{AP} > W_{AF}(T - t) > \max_{T' \leq T} W_E(T' - t), \tag{40}$$

and

$$S_{AP}^* > S_{AF}^*(T - t) > \max_{T' \leq T} S_E^*(T' - t) > S_{BE}, \tag{41}$$

where the argument in the two latter equations is the time to maturity.

If such bounds are considered insufficient, explicit values and adjusted break-even prices may be found by numerical methods surveyed by Geske and Shastri [7]. Barone-Adesi and Whaley [1] have developed an analytical approximation for nonperpetual American options. The binomial approach of Cox, Ross, and Rubinstein [5] may yield reasonably accurate results.

V Additional Managerial Flexibility

So far it has been assumed that once investment has been initiated, the oil field represents an obligation to produce according to the fixed schedule. If the output price were to drop low enough, however, closing down the oil field temporarily or even abandoning the entire project might be desirable actions. The scope of the analysis may be extended by introducing additional managerial flexibility, beyond the one associated with timing the investment decision. Formulas for adjusted critical prices as well as project values can be found in the appendix.

A Special Case Assumptions

Suppose that the firm may at any time irreversibly decide on costlessly abandoning a developed field. Alternatively, specify as the second special case assumption that production may be costlessly switched off or on at a developed field. In either case these decisions are supposed to be made based on future emerging information rather than being fixed at the outset. These extended flexibility properties are referred to as abandonment and operating options, respectively. (Previous related studies of such flexibility aspects include Brennan and Schwartz [3], McDonald and Siegel [18], Myers and Majd [25], and Trigeorgis and Mason [36].)

When the investment flexibility is combined with either abandonment or operating flexibility, the analysis is simplified by postulating a particular form of the production profile, viz. that the output rate is proportional to the exponentially declining remaining quantity in the reserve:[17]

$$q(\tau) = \gamma Q(\tau). \tag{42}$$

For further expositional simplification, also assume that investment is instantaneous and immediately yields a field ready for production.[18] Furthermore, assume that there is an initial unit variable cost c, no cost escalation (i.e., $\pi = 0$), and no fixed production costs. Investment costs are stationary, with a present value of I regardless of the development time. Finally, allow the various decisions to be made at any arbitrary time, corresponding to perpetual American options.

B Asset in Place

Suppose the reserve has been developed and consider the question of maintaining the fixed production schedule $q(\tau)$. Let $B(t)$ denote the present value of operating costs associated with a production commitment when shutting down production either temporarily or permanently is infeasible. With proportional output parameter γ and constant unit operating cost c, the present value of future production costs is

$$B(t) = \frac{\gamma}{\gamma + r} cQ(t). \tag{43}$$

The time-adjusted quantity of oil is

$$A = \frac{\gamma}{\gamma + \delta} Q(t). \tag{44}$$

The ratio

$$\left(\frac{B}{A}\right) = \left(\frac{\gamma + \delta}{\gamma + r}\right) c, \tag{45}$$

would be the critical price for executing a "last chance" possibility to scrap the project.

With abandonment flexibility, the critical price P_{AB} for scrapping the project is less than the ratio (B/A). The reason is that lasting abandonment opportunities may make it worthwhile to maintain production at a current operating loss in order to preserve the potential for later profitable operations. Operating flexibility subsumes abandonment flexibility, as it allows for temporary shutdowns of arbitrary length and not only permanent closure. Thus, with operating flexibility, the critical price P_{OP} at which production will be switched either off or on, as the case might be, is greater than P_{AB}.

C Asset Not Yet in Place

Return to an investment opportunity such as an undeveloped oil reserve. By paying the investment costs, I, the owner acquires a developed reserve equipped with either a production switch or the possibility of early abandonment. The investment opportunity is then an (investment) option on an (operating or abandonment) option, that is, a compound contingent claim.

Because of option interaction effects, there are no longer analytical expressions for the critical prices at which investment will be undertaken. With joint investment and operating flexibility, the break-even output price S_{IO} for investment equals the corresponding break-even price with the asset in place, multiplied by a correction factor to be determined from an implicit equation. A similar relation holds for the trigger price S_{IA}, with compound investment and abandonment flexibility.

For a current output price $S(t)$ below S_{IO} with operating options, or below S_{IA} with abandonment options, the field remains undeveloped and the project value is entirely the value of the compound option. For output prices exceeding the investment break-even prices, investment should take place. The project value then consists of the investment commitment value plus an option premium associated with the corresponding asset in place option.

VI   A Numerical Example

A   Investment Flexibility Only

The numerical example has been adapted from an applied research report (in Norwegian), prepared in 1988 and available from the authors on request. The numerical market-wide parameter values below equal those of the report. The numerical project specific parameter values below are hypothetical, whereas the report uses investment and production profiles submitted by the Norwegian Ministry of Oil and Energy. The qualitative results are quite similar, but the report also provides a series of graphs illustrating the sensitivity of the results to the chosen parameter values.

Assume:[19]

δ	$= 0.04,$	rate of return shortfall on oil spot;
$r - \pi$	$= 0.02,$	risk-free rate of interest less cost escalation rate;
σ	$= 0.245,$	volatility of oil price changes;
A	$= 100,$	time adjusted equivalent oil quantity;
K	$= 1,000,$	present value of investment and production costs; and
T	$= (t + 4),$	
or $T \to \infty,$		expiration time of investment opportunity.

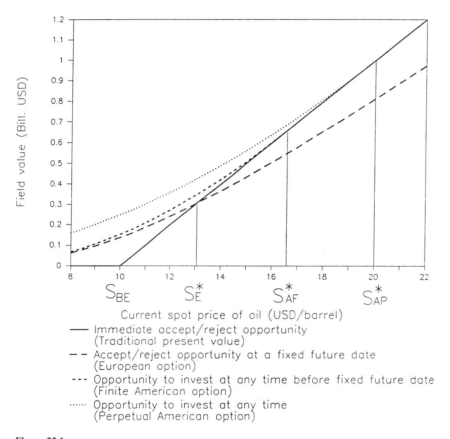

Figure 33.1
The value of the oil field

Using these parameter values, figure 33.1 shows the value of the oil field as a function of the spot price, under different assumptions as to feasible alternatives for postponing the development decision.[20] The traditional present value is a kinked, linear function, whereas the option interpretations yield increasing nonlinear functions.

When considered as an immediate accept/reject opportunity only, the field has a traditional break-even price of $S_{BE} = 10$ USD/barrel of oil. At a current price of $S(t) = 10$, however, the opportunity to make an accept/reject decision in exactly $T - t = 4$ years is worth $W_E = 139$ million USD. The corresponding field value is $W_{AF} = 154$ million USD, provided a possible decision to go ahead with the project may be made at any time within the next $T - t = 4$ years. If the development decision may be made at any time whatsoever, the field is worth $W_{AP} = 250$ million USD, when the current price equals the traditional break-even price.

Suppose there is a choice between making the accept/reject decision either immediately or only in exactly 4 years. Then, for current prices below the adjusted break-even price $S_E^* = 13.05$ USD/barrel, postponing the decision is the preferred alternative. At a price of $S(t) = 13.05$, both opportunities are worth $U = W_E = 305$ (million USD). With $S(t)$ increasing further, immediate acceptance is the superior decision.

There will be more decision flexibility if the investment decision may be exercised any time within the next 4 years. Immediate development is then a preferred choice only for a current price being above an adjusted break-even price of $S_{AF}^* = 16.62$.

Let the investment opportunity be perpetual. With the stated parameter values, immediate development is then only preferable if the current price equals or exceeds twice the traditional break-even price. That is, the adjusted break-even price $S_{AP}^* = 20.00$ (USD/barrel). At that price the field value $U = W_{AP}^* = 1,000$ (million USD).[21]

Note that with either American option interpretation, the option value and the traditional present value coincide for spot prices at or above the respective critical price at which the option is exercised. In contrast, for the European option case, the option value curve intersects the traditional present value line for acceptance. The reason is that for high spot prices, it is better to make a commitment immediately rather than putting off the decision for a fixed time.

With $\delta > (r - \pi)$, the parameter values of this example violate the condition in (19). The traditional optimal timing problem of an immediate choice of a preferred development time degenerates to the standard accept/reject case.

B Abandonment or Operating Flexibility in Addition

Retain the parameter values $\delta = 0.04$ for rate of return shortfall, $\sigma = 0.245$ as the output volatility, and $T = \infty$ for a perpetual investment opportunity. For the special case also assume:

γ	$= 0.10$,	proportional output rate factor;
r	$= 0.02$,	risk-free rate of interest;
$Q(0)$	$= 140$,	initial volume of recoverable reserves;
π	$= 0.00$,	cost escalation rate;
c	$= 3$,	constant unit production cost; and
I	$= 650$,	net present value of investment costs.

By the special case assumptions, the commitment net present value of production cost is $B = cQ(0)[\gamma/(\gamma + r)] = 350$. The time equivalent oil quantity is $A = Q(0)[\gamma/(\gamma + \delta)] = 100$. Net present value of total costs is $K = B + I = 1,000$. Thus, the special case parameters are consistent with those in the previous section, where only investment flexibility was assumed.

Suppose the investment has been undertaken, such that investment costs I are sunk cost. With the asset in place, the critical price for abandoning the project permanently is neither the unit cost $c = 3.00$ nor the "last chance" dismissal price $(B/A) = 3.50$. Rather, from Equation (B2), the project should be scrapped at a break-even price[22] of $P_{AB} = 2.00$. The borderprice for indifference between operating or temporarily closing down is $P_{OP} = 4.00$ by Equation (C1) (with the asset in place the operating break-even price P_{OP} is simply the abandonment break-even price $P_{AB} = 2.00$, multiplied by the flexibility factor $\varphi = 2.00$ from the simple investment case).

To find the effect of such additional flexibility on the investment opportunity itself, the implicit Equations (B4) and (C3) first have to be solved. Then substitute back into Equation (B3) to get the adjusted break-even price $S_{IA} = 19.76$ for flexibility with respect to both investment and abandonment. Similarly, Equation (C2) yields $S_{IO} = 19.64$ as the triggering price for executing the investment, when there are subsequent possibilities for temporarily switching off production several times.

Thus, either operating or abandonment flexibility lowers the adjusted critical price for going ahead with the investment project. The effect is largest for the option to switch on or off production, as such decisions may be made repeatedly, whereas the abandonment decision is irreversible. The important thing to note is that such additional flexibility has only a minor influence on the relevant break-even price: compare $S_{IA} = 19.76$ and $S_{IO} = 19.64$ to $S_{AP}^* = 20.00$ when there is only investment flexibility.

Table 33.1 compares the value of a perpetual investment opportunity under different flexibility assumptions: none, investment only, investment and abandonment, or investment and operating. Observe that the major difference in value is found in going from the traditional accept/reject model to a model incorporating the flexibility to postpone the investment decision. The additional effect on project value from adding on either abandonment or operating flexibility is quite small, on the order of one percentage point. Thus, the bias from ignoring managerial flexibility for an asset in place appears to be almost negligible. Estimation risk for parameters such as volatility σ and rate of return shortfall δ may be more important than complicating models by supplementary flexibility features.

Even considering the inherent dangers of generalizing from one particular case, this example seems to justify the focus on just the deferrable investment opportunity while disregarding further flexibility for the asset once in place.

Table 33.1
Asset value—asset not yet in place (in million USD)

Spot price (USD)	Traditional immediate accept/reject	Investment flexibility only	Option models investment and abandonment flexibility	Investment and operating flexibility
1.00	0	3	3	3
2.00	0	10	10	10
3.00	0	23	23	23
4.00	0	40	40	40
5.00	0	63	63	63
6.00	0	90	91	91
7.00	0	123	123	124
8.00	0	160	161	162
9.00	0	203	204	205
10.00	0	250	252	253
11.00	100	303	305	306
12.00	200	360	363	364
13.00	300	423	426	427
14.00	400	490	493	495
15.00	500	563	566	569
16.00	600	640	645	647
17.00	700	723	728	730
18.00	800	810	816	819
19.00	900	902	909	912
20.00	1,000	1,000	1,007	1,011
21.00	1,100	1,100	1,107	1,110
22.00	1,200	1,200	1,206	1,209

C Flexibility Factors

Once again assume that the only flexibility of interest concerns the timing of the initial investment decision. For the perpetual investment opportunity, table 33.2 shows how sensitive the ratio of the adjusted break-even price to the traditional one is to changes in the parameters δ, $(r - \pi)$, and σ^2 from their base case values.[23] This flexibility factor $\varphi = S_{AP}^*/S_{BE}$ increases with lower rate of return shortfall δ, higher margin $(r - \pi)$, and higher volatility σ.

Returning to the case in which the investment opportunity is only available at a fixed future date, there is no closed-form solution for the adjusted break-even price S_E^*. The flexibility factor $\varphi = S_E^*/S_{BE}$ for adjusting the traditional break-even price upwards is project specific, as it depends on both the production profile $q(\tau)$ and the cost schedule $k(\tau|t)$. Assume that the development decision may be taken neither before nor after a fixed maturity of 4 years.

Table 33.2
Flexibility factor for perpetual investment opportunity

$r - \pi$	δ	σ^2 0.01	σ^2 0.04	σ^2 0.06	σ^2 0.09
0.00	0.02	1.25	2.00	2.50	3.25
	0.04	1.13	1.50	1.75	2.13
	0.06	1.08	1.33	1.50	1.75
	0.08	1.06	1.25	1.38	1.56
0.02	0.02	1.64	2.62	3.19	4.00
	0.04	1.21	1.71	2.00	2.42
	0.06	1.12	1.43	1.63	1.91
	0.08	1.08	1.31	1.45	1.66
0.04	0.02	2.43	3.41	4.00	4.84
	0.04	1.42	2.00	2.32	2.76
	0.06	1.19	1.58	1.80	2.10
	0.08	1.11	1.39	1.55	1.78

δ = rate of return shortfall on oil spot;
$r - \pi$ = risk-free interest rate less cost escalation rate;
σ^2 = instantaneous variance of oil spot;
S_{BE} = traditional break-even price;
S_{AP}^* = adjusted break-even price for perpetual investment opportunity (perpetual American option);
ε = exponent, given by Equation (31); and
$\varphi(\varepsilon) = S_{AP}^*/S_{BE} = \varepsilon/(\varepsilon - 1)$, flexibility factor for perpetual investment opportunity.

Table 33.3 presents a sensitivity analysis of the ratio of the two alternative break-even prices, S_E^* and S_{BE}, for this European option formulation. As expected, lower rate of return shortfall δ, higher risk-free rate of interest rate r, and higher variance σ^2 increase the flexibility factor. The numerical values are project specific and also depend on the investment opportunity occurring only at $T = t + 4$.

VII Concluding Remarks

An important class of capital budgeting problems is the evaluation of investment projects characterized by both output price uncertainty and flexibility to make an irrevocable accept/reject decision at a later time rather than immediately. The traditional net present value based approaches of immediate accept/reject and optimal timing problems ignore the option properties of the investment opportunity. Hence, both the project value and the associated break-even price for triggering acceptance of the project now have to be adjusted upwards. How much upward adjustment is required depends both on the actual parameters of the problem at hand and on the degree of flexibility present for postponing the decision. Explicit guidelines for eval-

Table 33.3
Flexibility factor for fixed date investment opportunity

$r - \pi$	δ	σ^2			
		0.01	0.04	0.06	0.09
0.00	0.02	1.08	1.27	1.39	1.55
	0.04	1.03	1.14	1.22	1.31
	0.06	1.01	1.08	1.13	1.20
	0.08	1.00	1.05	1.09	1.14
0.02	0.02	1.22	1.49	1.62	1.81
	0.04	1.07	1.22	1.31	1.42
	0.06	1.03	1.13	1.18	1.26
	0.08	1.01	1.08	1.12	1.18
0.04	0.02	1.92	1.99	2.08	2.23
	0.04	1.16	1.35	1.44	1.56
	0.06	1.06	1.18	1.25	1.34
	0.08	1.02	1.11	1.16	1.22

δ = rate of return shortfall on oil spot;
r = risk-free interest rate;
σ^2 = instantaneous variance of oil spot;
S_{BE} = traditional break-even price;
S_E^* = adjusted break-even price for investment opportunity at a fixed date only (European option); and
$\varphi = S_E^*/S_{BE}$, flexibility factor for perpetual investment opportunity only available in exactly 4 years.

uating option-like investment projects and computing critical prices when there is decision flexibility are provided here.

The models examined are based on having the trade-off between realism and simplicity tilted in favor of simplifying assumptions, in most cases allowing analytical solutions while preserving the major insight. The highlight has been concentrated on the importance of explicit modeling of option features at the investment stage, as further managerial flexibility endogenizing production seemed to have less effect. Other analysts might prefer to model the oil price as, say, a mean-reverting process rather than a geometric Brownian motion. (Pindyck [27] states that both a geometric Brownian motion and a mean-reverting process are consistent with observed data for oil prices, such that an analyst might pick either price process.) Introducing additional sources of uncertainty or allowing parameters to change over time may be extensions for later research (Gibson and Schwartz [8, 9] are important contributions along these lines). For some practical applications, tax considerations and incentive structures may induce distortions.

Even with more realistic assumptions leading to more complex models, the qualitative essence of the results presented will remain. However, the project values and adjusted break-even prices, as computed by the methods suggested above, are then no longer quite as appropriate. Nevertheless, the lesson remains: do not take values and break-even prices from traditional discounted cash flow analysis at face value when price uncertainty and decision flexibility are present. The need for such adjustment to traditional procedures is rather recently being recognized by academic economists. Although some companies are beginning to use contingent claims analysis of real investment projects, the potential for actual corporate applications remains largely untapped.[24] Corporate managers should be encouraged to include the contingent claims approach as a powerful decision support in their capital budgeting activities.

Acknowledgments

We thank John J. Dran, Jr., Rajna Gibson, Bruce Grundy, Peter Jennergren, Diderik Lund, Eduardo Schwartz, and anonymous referees for helpful comments and discussions.

Notes

1. Brennan and Schwartz [3], Lund [12], MacKie-Mason [14], and Pindyck [27] also model the output price as a stochastic process. The three former studies are far more complicated than ours and the scope is partly different. Lund and MacKie-Mason are concerned with tax effects and reflect more the perspective of a social planner than that of a corporate manager.

2. Compare the difference between postulating an exogenous share price process for a leveraged firm and making assumptions about the dynamic behavior of the value of the firm's assets. In the latter case, the share price may be derived from interpreting it as an option on the firm value (Smith [33]), and a stock option becomes a compound option on the underlying assets. In the present context, with positive extraction costs and output prices generated by geometric Brownian motion, the value of an asset in place (i.e., after investment) does not follow a corresponding stochastic process. Whether the Brownian motion assumption is most reasonable for the output or for the asset in place is an empirical issue which we do not address. For many practical applications the output will be widely traded in competitive markets, simplifying assessment of crucial input parameters such as volatility. On the other hand, using market data to deduce appropriate parameters for an investment opportunity with more or less unique properties may be more than difficult; e.g., Paddock, Siegel, and Smith [26] have to resort to a dubious "one-third" rule of thumb outside their model.

3. The output spot price is also a sufficient statistic in the Miller and Upton [23] model, which does not use the contingent claims approach. Gibson and Schwartz [9] postulate the existence of a term structure of convenience yields and then use seven months ahead futures prices to compute steady-state spot prices rather than simply using observed spot prices.

4. The assumed price dynamics may equivalently be stated in terms of the ratio of the uncertain future spot price $S(t')$ at time t' to current spot price $S(t)$. Equation (1) implies that the price relative is

$$\frac{S(t')}{S(t)} = e^{(\alpha - 0.5\sigma^2)(t'-t) + \sigma z(t'-t)},$$

where the Wiener process term $z(t'-t)$ is normally distributed with mean zero and variance $(t'-t)$. The price ratio is then log-normally distributed, with mean $e^{\alpha(t'-t)}$. The logarithmic rate $\ln[s(t')/s(t)]$ is thus normally distributed, with mean $\mu(t'-t) = (\alpha - 0.5\sigma^2)(t'-t)$ and variance $\sigma^2(t'-t)$.

5. McDonald and Siegel [17] coined the term "rate of return shortfall" for assets earning a below-equilibrium expected rate of return. Lund [13] provides an illuminating discussion of various interpretations of δ. Further examples can be found in, e.g., Brennan and Schwartz [3], Majd and Pindyck [15], McDonald and Siegel [18, 19], Myers and Majd [25], and Paddock, Siegel, and Smith [26].

6. When using arbitrage arguments, it should be noted that with a rate of return shortfall δ, the borrower of the asset will need to compensate the lender for this shortfall, unlike standard short-selling cases. Also, similar valuation results may be obtained without explicit arbitrage, by calling upon equilibrium models such as the Intertemporal Capital Asset Pricing Model originated by Merton [21].

7. Note that by Equation (10) the commitment value C is a linear function of the spot price S. Its slope coefficient A is determined by the project specific production profile q as well as the market-wide rate of return shortfall δ. The project specific intercept term K is the present value of costs.

In contrast, the "one-third" rule of Paddock, Siegel, and Smith [26] would give the net present value of a producing reserve as

$$C = \left(\frac{1}{3}\right) S(t) Q(t).$$

The assumed constant proportionality factor $(\frac{1}{3})$ does not explicitly depend on either project specific properties or on market parameters. Furthermore, the rule corresponds to zero (or price proportional) unit extraction costs.

8. Even elementary corporate finance textbooks tell students to use different discount rates if the cash flow components have different risks. This prescription may be easily overlooked in practice. In publicly available analyses of huge real-life projects, we have been surprised to observe one common discount rate being used for the entire cash flow stream.

9. In some countries the government retains the right to approve any field development plans, including the timing. For macroeconomic planning purposes, it may be important for the government to have the corporate development activities fit into a socially desired activity pattern. Letting the firm itself determine the phasing in, conditional on giving immediate notification, is a rather mild form for exercising the governmental prerogatives vis a vis the license holders.

10. Equation (19) follows from the second-order condition. It may be interpreted as the benefit rate of delayed cost $(r - \pi)$ initially outweighing the opportunity cost rate δ of delayed revenue.

11. The conversion from our real option to the more usual financial option is as follows. First, by Equation (1), the spot price of the underlying asset (oil) follows a geometric Brownian motion, as otherwise assumed for the stock price. Second, when valuing an option written on oil, the assumed "rate of return shortfall" on oil defined in Equation (2) is to be treated as if oil yields a constant, proportional dividend payout. Third, the exercise price equals the future break-even price, which by Equation (24) is the current break-even price growing exponentially. Some minor algebraic manipulations then yield Equations (25)–(27). For a review of the constant proportional dividend version of the Black-Scholes formula, see e.g., Kemna [11], McDonald and Siegel [17], Merton [20], or Smith [32].

12. The difference between two log-normal variables, or the difference between a log-normal variable and a constant, is not itself log-normally distributed. Therefore, if output prices are generated by a geometric Brownian motion, then the stochastic process for the discounted cash flows net of production costs cannot belong to the same family.

13. The value W_{AP} of the nondeveloped oil field is obtained from Equation (4) of McDonald and Siegel by inserting S as the value of the underlying asset and S_{BE} as the exercise price. Equation (30) then occurs from multiplying by the quantity $A(\delta)$ of options being held.

14. In the similar Equation (12) of McDonald and Siegel, the exponent ε depends on the "rate of return shortfalls" on both the underlying asset and the exercise price, which in our formulation are δ and $(r - \pi)$, respectively. Also, with a deterministic exercise price the relevant variance measure is that of the underlying asset and not the variance of the ratio of two log-normally distributed variables.

15. In practical applications it is not trivial to estimate the required rate of return $\hat{\alpha}$ and the mean price change α, and one may have to resort to "guesstimates." Equations (10), (25), and (30) demonstrate that the guessing game may be reduced to the difference $\delta = \hat{\alpha} - \alpha$. When observations from futures markets are available, Equation (7) will provide estimates of the rate of return shortfall δ. Unfortunately, the empirical evidence of Kemna [11] suggests that δ is not constant over time. In Gibson and Schwartz [8] both S and δ are stochastic, following correlated Brownian motions.

16. These project-specific assumptions, combined with market-wide rates δ and r, determine the traditional break-even price S_{BE}. Thus, whereas the flexibility factor φ itself is independent of project-specific characteristics, the adjusted critical price S_{AP}^* is project dependent through S_{BE}. This fact explains why a spot price increase may cause a particular reserve to be developed whereas other higher-cost reserves remain undeveloped.

17. Equation (42) implies that $Q(\tau) = e^{-\gamma\tau} Q(0)$. Paddock, Siegel, and Smith [26] note that this is a standard assumption in the literature on petroleum extraction and reflects geological constraints on extraction. In their specific example, Brennan and Schwartz [3] assume that the quantity of resources in the ground is infinite. Majd and Pindyck [15] use a level output flow in their example.

18. McDonald and Siegel [19] also disregard construction time, whereas the principal focus of Majd and Pindyck [15] is just on the effects of time to build. Bjerksund [2] allows a fixed time lag between the irrevocable investment decision and the first possible production date, yielding far more complex expressions.

19. Let the required rate of return of an asset perfectly correlated with the oil spot price be $\hat{\alpha} = 0.07$ (in real terms). Suppose the increase in expected spot price of oil is $\alpha = 0.03$ (in real terms). Then the rate of return shortfall $\delta = 0.04$, whether in real or nominal terms. The risk-free rate of interest has been set at $r = 0.02$. Costs are supposed to remain constant in real terms, i.e., $\pi = 0.00$. The oil volatility $\sigma = 0.245$, corresponding to a variance of $\sigma^2 = 0.06$. The expected logarithmic growth rate is then $\mu = 0.03 - (0.06/2) = 0.00$. The equivalent oil quantity $A(\delta) = 100$ million barrels is found by discounting the production profile $q(\tau)$ at the rate $\delta = 0.04$. Risk-free discounting of the cost profile $k(\tau|t)$ yields the current present value of costs $K = \$1,000$ million. The investment opportunity either disappears in 4 years $(T - t = 4)$, or the option is perpetual $(T \to \infty)$.

20. The traditional present value, the European option value, and the perpetual American option value are computed by Equations (10), (25), and (30), respectively. The finite American option value is computed by the approximation method of Barone-Adesi and Whaley [1].

21. Note that by Equation (31) the exponent $\varepsilon = 2.00$. Thus, by Equation (39), the flexibility factor $\varphi(\varepsilon) = S_{AP/S_{BE}}^* = \varepsilon/(\varepsilon - 1) = 2.00$. As long as it is optimal not to develop, the field value is by Equations (36), (37), or (38) proportional to the square of the ratio of current price to adjusted break-even price; in fact, $W_{AP} = 1,000(S/S_{AP}^*)^2$.

22. From Equation (A3), the factor $\beta = -(\frac{4}{3})$. The ratio $\beta/(\beta - 1) = (\frac{4}{7})$ is the flexibility factor for an abandonment option, with asset in place.

23. To give the parameter values at least some empirical flavor, we report some scattered obervations. As for oil price uncertainty, Paddock, Siegel, and Smith [26] used a volatility $\sigma = 0.142$ based on the 1974–1980 period, but they also allowed for increasing uncertainty by reporting results for $\sigma = 0.25$. Pindyck [27] reported a standard deviation of 0.17 for the years 1965–1986. Kemna [11] found a crude oil volatility of about 0.15 for the years 1980–1984 and about 0.20 for 1985–1986. Based on a particular quality of North Sea oil we have computed a standard deviation of about $\sigma = 0.23$ for the period 1975–1986. As for the rate of return shortfall δ, Paddock, Siegel, and Smith suggested a value of 4.1% based on the payout rate of a producing oil reserve. From futures market data—compare our Equation (7)—Kemna found excessively high rates of return shortfall, but settled for a 0–10% range for δ. Keeping a fixed risk-free rate of interest of $r = 2\%$ in real terms, the reported values for $(r - \pi)$ cover both increasing, constant, and decreasing costs over time.

24. In the spring of 1988 there was a lively public, political, and corporate debate in Norway, regarding starting up development of a huge offshore oil field ("Snorre"). "Real options" aspects were among the important issues in that debate. There was considerable support among both professional and academic economists for postponing the development decision, showing option values exceeding one billion USD.

However, the ultimate decision makers seemed to think that only "rubber stamping" previous decisions remained when the option considerations were introduced.

References

1. G. Barone-Adesi and R. E. Whaley, "Efficient Analytic Approximation of American Option Values," *Journal of Finance* (June 1987), pp. 301–320.

2. P. Bjerksund, "A Contingent Claims Analysis of an Oil Reserve," Doctoral Dissertation, The Norwegian School of Economics and Business Administration, Bergen, 1989.

3. M. J. Brennan and E. S. Schwartz, "Evaluating Natural Resource Investments," *Journal of Business* (April 1985), pp. 135–157.

4. ———, "A New Approach to Evaluating Natural Resource Investments," in *The Revolution in Corporate Finance*, J. M. Stern and D. H. Chew, Jr. (eds.), Oxford, Basil Blackwell, 1986.

5. J. C. Cox, S. A. Ross, and M. Rubinstein, "Option Pricing: A Simplified Approach," *Journal of Financial Economics* (September 1979), pp. 229–263.

6. S. Ekern, "An Option Pricing Approach to Evaluating Petroleum Projects," *Energy Economics* (April 1988), pp. 91–99.

7. R. Geske and K. Shastri, "Valuation by Approximation: A Comparision of Alternative Option Valuation Techniques," *Journal of Financial and Quantitative Analysis* (March 1985), pp. 45–71.

8. R. Gibson and E. S. Schwartz, "Stochastic Convenience Yield and the Pricing of Oil Contingent Claims," Working Paper No. 15-1989, Anderson Graduate School of Management, UCLA, July 1989.

9. ———, "Valuation of Long Term Oil-Linked Assets," in *Stochastic Models and Option Values: with Applications to Resources, Environment, and Investment Problems*, D. Lund and B. Øksendal (eds.), Amsterdam, North-Holland, 1990.

10. J. E. Ingersoll, Jr., *Theory of Financial Decision Making*, Totowa, NJ, Rowman & Littlefield, 1987.

11. A. G. Z. Kemna, "Options in Real and Financial Markets," Doctoral Dissertation, Erasmus Universiteit, Rotterdam, November 1987.

12. D. Lund, "Investment, Taxes, and Uncertainty, with Applications to the Norwegian Petroleum Sector," Memorandum No. 1/87, Department of Economics, University of Oslo, February 1987.

13. ———, "Stochastic Models and Option Values: An Introduction," in *Stochastic Models and Option Values: with Applications to Resources, Environment, and Investment Problems*, D. Lund and B. Øksendal (eds.), Amsterdam, North-Holland, 1990.

14. J. K. MacKie-Mason, "Nonlinear Taxation of Risky Assets and Investment, with Application to Mining," NBER Working Paper No. 2631, June 1988.

15. S. Majd and R. S. Pindyck, "Time to Build, Option Value, and Investment Decisions," *Journal of Financial Economics* (March 1987), pp. 7–27.

16. S. P. Mason and R. C. Merton, "The Role of Contingent Claims Analysis in Corporate Finance," in *Recent Advances in Corporate Finance*, E. I. Altman and M. G. Subrahmanyam (eds.), Homewood, IL, Richard D. Irwin, 1985.

17. R. McDonald and D. Siegel, "Option Pricing When the Underlying Asset Earns a Below-Equilibrium Rate of Return: A Note," *Journal of Finance* (March 1984), pp. 261–265.

18. ———, "Investment and the Valuation of Firms when there is an Option to Shut Down," *International Economic Review* (June 1985), pp. 331–349.

19. ———, "The Value of Waiting to Invest," *Quarterly Journal of Economics* (November 1986), pp. 707–727.

20. R. C. Merton, "Theory of Rational Option Pricing," *Bell Journal of Economics and Management Science* (Spring 1973), pp. 141–183.

21. ———, "An Intertemporal Capital Asset Pricing Model," *Econometrica* (September 1973), pp. 867–887.

22. ———, "On the Pricing of Contingent Claims and the Modigliani-Miller Theorem," *Journal of Financial Economics* (November 1977), pp. 241–249.

23. M. H. Miller and C. W. Upton, "A Test of the Hotelling Valuation Principle," *Journal of Political Economy* (February 1985), pp. 1–25.

24. S. C. Myers, "Finance Theory and Financial Strategy," *Interfaces* (January/February 1984), pp. 126–137.

25. S. C. Myers and S. Majd, "Abandonment Value and Project Life," *Advances in Futures and Options Research* (1989).

26. J. L. Paddock, D. R. Siegel, and J. L. Smith, "Option Valuation of Claims on Real Assets: The Case of Offshore Petroleum Leases," *Quarterly Journal of Economics* (August 1988), pp. 479–508.

27. R. S. Pindyck, "Options, Flexibility, and Investment Decisions," Presented at the Workshop on New Methods for Project Evaluation, Center for Energy Policy Research, M.I.T., March 1988.

28. ———, "Irreversible Investment, Capacity Choice, and the Value of the Firm," *American Economic Review* (December 1988), pp. 969–985.

29. S. A. Ross, "A Simple Approach to the Valuation of Risky Streams," *Journal of Business* (July 1978), pp. 453–475.

30. P. A. Samuelson, "Rational Theory of Warrant Pricing," *Industrial Management Review* (Spring 1965), pp. 13–39.

31. D. R. Siegel, J. L. Smith, and J. L. Paddock, "Valuing Offshore Oil Properties with Option Pricing Models," *Midland Corporate Finance Journal* (Spring 1987), pp. 22–30.

32. C. W. Smith, Jr., "Option Pricing: A Review," *Journal of Financial Economics* (January/March 1976), pp. 3–51.

33. ———, "Applications of Option Pricing Analysis," in *Handbook of Financial Economics*, J. L. Bicksler (ed.), Amsterdam, North-Holland, 1979, pp. 289–330.

34. O. A. F. Tourinho, "The Valuation of Reserves of Natural Resources: An Option Pricing Approach," Ph.D. Dissertation, University of California, Berkeley, 1979.

35. L. Trigeorgis, "The Nature of Option Interactions and the Valuation of Investments with Multiple Real Options," *Journal of Financial and Quantitative Analysis* (1993), pp. 1–20.

36. L. Trigeorgis and S. P. Mason, "Valuing Managerial Flexibility," *Midland Corporate Finance Journal* (Spring 1987), pp. 14–21.

Appendix A: Break-Even Prices and Project Values

Finding the adjusted break-even prices and project values, under the special case assumptions of Section V, is an exercise in standard methods of contingent claims analysis, which the manager will probably leave to the specialists. Basically, it involves solving a sequence of stochastic differential equations, with appropriate boundary conditions. The procedure is briefly indicated below, in conjunction with a presentation of some useful results. The results for the operating flexibility case are developed in detail in Bjerksund [2]. The corresponding abandonment flexibility results below follow from similar computations. A concise, general formulation can be found in Merton [22]. Mason and Merton [16] contains numerous illustrations. McDonald and Siegel [19] sketch the derivation of results similar to those found in Section IV.

The starting point is to observe that the project may be interpreted as a contingent claim whose market value must satisfy a fundamental stochastic partial differential equation. Consider the asset in place situation and assume initially that at the current output price the optimal strategy is to continue producing. The value U of the optimally producing field then satisfies the partial differential equation

$$0.5\sigma^2 S^2 U_{SS} + (r - \delta)SU_S - rU - \gamma QU_Q + \gamma Q(S - c) = 0. \tag{A1}$$

This equation is a special case of Equation (1) of Merton [22]. His D_1 instantaneous "dividend" to holders of the underlying asset is here represented by δS. His D_2 "dividend" rate to holders of the contingent claim here corresponds to $\gamma Q(t)[S(t) - c]$. The partial derivative wrt. calendar time t is $U_t = -\gamma Q(t)U_Q$, where U_Q is the partial derivative of the field value U wrt. the total remaining quantity of oil Q.

From solving Equation (A1) with the appended boundary conditions, the value U of the developed and optimally producing oil field is given by

$$U[S(t)] = aS(t)^\beta + AS(t) - B. \tag{A2}$$

The exponent β is defined by

$$\beta \equiv \left(\frac{1}{2} - \frac{r - \delta}{\sigma^2}\right) - \sqrt{\left(\frac{r - \delta}{\sigma^2} - \frac{1}{2}\right)^2 + 2\frac{r + \gamma}{\sigma^2}}, \tag{A3}$$

which is negative and somewhat related to ε defined in Equation (31) above. The constant a depends on the kind of flexibility assumed. The product aS^β then yields the value of the assumed flexibility by itself. The additional terms $AS - B$ are recognized as the commitment value with the asset in place.

Appendix B: Abandonment Flexibility

The decision rule for optimal abandonment is to abandon the project permanently the first time t' when

$$S(t') < P_{AB}. \tag{B1}$$

In turn, the critical price for scrapping the project is

$$P_{AB} = \left(\frac{\beta}{\beta - 1}\right)\left(\frac{B}{A}\right). \tag{B2}$$

The ratio $\beta/(\beta - 1)$ is another flexibility factor, positive but less that unity. Note the similarity of Expressions (33) and (B2).

An undeveloped field is then an option on acquiring a developed field with abandonment possibilities, by paying the investment costs I. Let S_{IA} be the critical price at which investment should occur, given that the project may be abandoned later. Define

$$S_{IA} \equiv \lambda_{IA} P_{AB}. \tag{B3}$$

That is, the break-even price for investment is the break-even price for abandonment, multiplied by a factor λ_{IA}. This factor is given implicitly by the equation

$$(\beta - \varepsilon)(\lambda_{IA})^\beta + \beta(\varepsilon - 1)\lambda_{IA} - (\beta - 1)\varepsilon\left(\frac{B + I}{B}\right) = 0. \tag{B4}$$

Like computations of internal rates of return, Equation (B4) may be solved by trial and error or by an iterative procedure.

The field value, with both investment and abandonment flexibility, is given as

$$W_{IA} = \left(\frac{\beta}{\beta - \varepsilon}\right)(\lambda_{IA}B - B - I)\left[\frac{S(t)}{S_{IA}}\right]^\varepsilon, \tag{B5}$$

as long as investment has not been triggered, i.e., $S(t) < S_{IA}$. Thus, it is proportional to an "excess cost" measure and to the ratio of current to critical price, raised to the εth power.

If immediate investment is called for, the field value is the sum of the commitment value plus a premium for the abandonment possibility:

$$W_{IA} = -\left(\frac{1}{\beta-1}\right)B\left[\frac{S(t)}{P_{AB}}\right]^{\beta} + AS(t) - (B+I). \tag{B6}$$

Appendix C: Operating Flexibility

The critical price at which production will be switched either off or on is given by

$$P_{OP} = \left(\frac{\beta}{\beta-1}\right)\left(\frac{\varepsilon}{\varepsilon-1}\right)\left(\frac{B}{A}\right). \tag{C1}$$

The operating flexibility factor is thus the product of the flexibility factors for the abandonment asset in place and the standard investment case, respectively.

With operating flexibility, investment will only be profitable for output prices exceeding S_{IO}, given by

$$S_{IO} \equiv \lambda_{IO}P_{OP}. \tag{C2}$$

As for the combined investment-abandonment case, the correction factor is defined implicitly by an equation to be solved by trial and error or by an iterative search procedure:

$$(\lambda_{IO})^{\beta} - \beta\lambda_{IO} + (\beta-1)\left(\frac{B+I}{B}\right) = 0. \tag{C3}$$

For a current output price $S(t)$ below S_{IO}, the field will remain undeveloped, with value

$$W_{IO} = \left(\frac{\beta}{\beta-\varepsilon}\right)\left[\left(\frac{\varepsilon}{\varepsilon-1}\right)\lambda_{IO}B - B - I\right]\left[\frac{S(t)}{S_{IO}}\right]^{\varepsilon}. \tag{C4}$$

If $S(t) > S_{IO}$, investment should take place. Because of the operating flexibility, the project's value once again consists of the commitment value plus an option premium:

$$W_{IO} = \frac{\varepsilon\beta}{(\beta-1)(\beta-\varepsilon)}\left[\frac{S(t)}{P_{OP}}\right]^{\beta} + AS(t) - (B+I). \tag{C5}$$

34 Urban Land Prices under Uncertainty

Sheridan Titman

Land prices in west Los Angeles are among the highest in the United States. Yet, we can observe a number of vacant lots and grossly underutilized land in this area. A good example of this is a parking lot, owned by the University of California-Los Angeles, in an area of Westwood where land has been known to sell for more than $100 per square foot. The university could probably raise a considerable amount of money by selling two-thirds of the parking lot and constructing a parking structure on the remaining land to satisfy the demand for parking. Although this may be one of the best examples of underutilized land in west Los Angeles, it is by no means the only example. There are many underutilized and vacant urban lots throughout Los Angeles and the rest of the world, held by private investors who presumably wish to maximize their wealth.

The fact that investors choose to keep valuable land vacant or underutilized for prolonged periods of time suggests that the land is more valuable as a potential site for development in the future than it is as an actual site for constructing any particular building at the present time. Hence, in order to understand why certain urban lots remain vacant, we must determine how the land is valued under the two alternatives. Valuing the land as a site for constructing a particular building at the current time is fairly straightforward. It is simply the market value of the building (including the land) minus the lot preparation and construction costs (this is referred to in the real estate literature as residual value). However, valuing the vacant land as a potential building site is not as straightforward since the type of building that will eventually be built on the land, as well as the future real estate prices, are uncertain.

The model developed in this chapter provides a valuation equation for pricing vacant lots of this type. Although the model is very simple, it provides strong intuition about the conditions under which it is rational to postpone building until a future date. Furthermore, the pricing model can be adapted to provide realistic estimates of urban land values in much more complex settings.

The notion that it is often optimal to delay irreversible investment decisions has previously been considered in the environmental economics and capital investments literature.[1] The basic intuition in these papers is that it may be advantageous to wait for additional information before deciding upon the exact specifications of the investment project. While the authors demonstrate that it is often valuable to delay investment, and maintain the option to choose a better investment project in the future, they do not explicitly show how this option affects the value of other related assets in their models.

This chapter adapts the methods first used by Fisher Black and Myron Scholes (1973) and Robert Merton (1973), to value options and other derivative securities, to determine explicit values for vacant urban land. The valuation model is particularly close in its approach to the binomial option pricing models of John Cox, Stephen Ross, and Mark Rubinstein (1979), and Richard Rendleman and Brit Bartter (1979). The intuition being that a vacant lot can be viewed as an option to purchase one of a number of different possible buildings at exercise prices that are equal to their respective construction costs. This approach provides a valuation formula that is a function of observable variables and is independent of the investor's preferences.

This valuation technique should be contrasted to the standard textbook approach to valuing vacant land under uncertainty.[2] Richard Ratcliff (1972), for instance, suggests that appraisers determine the most probable future use of the land, appraise the property as of that future time and that use, and then discount this future value to the present. This method ignores the fact that the type of building that will be constructed in the future is generally unknown, and will be determined by real estate prices at that time. The analysis in this paper demonstrates that the amount of uncertainty about the type of building that will be optimal in the future is an important determinant of the value of vacant land. If there is a lot of uncertainty about future real estate prices, then the option to select the type of building in the future is very valuable. This makes the vacant land relatively more valuable and makes the decision to develop the land at the current time relatively less attractive. However, if there is very little uncertainty about future real estate prices, the option to select the appropriate type of building in the future is relatively less valuable. In this case, the decision to develop the land at the current time is relatively more attractive.

My analysis provides more than just a novel method for valuing land under uncertainty. It enables us to address issues, previously unexplored, that pertain to the effect of uncertainty on real estate markets. My results relating to how uncertainty about future real estate prices affect current real estate activities has important policy implications. For example, the analysis suggests that government action intended to stimulate construction activities may actually lead to a decrease in such activities if the extent and duration of the activity is uncertain. The analysis also has policy implications regarding the imposition of height restrictions on buildings. It is shown that the initiation of height restrictions, perhaps for the purpose of limiting growth in an area, may lead to an increase in building activity in the area because of the consequent decrease in uncertainty regarding the optimal height of the buildings, and thus has the immediate affect of increasing the number of building units in an area.

The paper is organized as follows: Section I examines the type of building, characterized by its size, that will be built at a given date if the land is to be developed at that time. Section II presents a simple two-date, two states of nature, model for determining the value of the vacant land for the case where the future price of building units, and hence the size of the building that is to be constructed, is uncertain. A simple numerical example that illustrates this valuation technique is presented in Section III. Section IV presents a comparative static analysis of this valuation model which includes, among other things, an analysis of the effect of uncertainty on vacant land value. Section V examines a model where the current price and rental rate on building units as well as land values are endogenous and Section VI provides a numerical example which illustrates how the valuation technique can be applied to value land with many possible building dates and many possible states of nature corresponding to each date.

I   The Optimal Building Size

Buildings, is this model, are characterized by their size, or number of units, q. The cost of constructing a building on a given piece of land, C, is an increasing and convex function of the number of units, that is, $dC/dq > 0$ and $d^2C/dq^2 > 0$. The rationale for the second assumption is that as the number of floors in a building increases, labor costs per floor increase and the foundation of the building must be stronger. It is also assumed that subsequent to completing a building of a certain size, it is prohibitively expensive to add additional building units.

Given these assumptions, the building size that maximizes the wealth of a landowner who wishes to construct a building at the present time will satisfy the following maximization problem:

$$\operatorname*{Max}_{(q)} \Pi(p_0) = p_0 q - C(q), \tag{1}$$

where p_0 is the current market price per building unit.

Differentiating (1) with respect to q, it follows that the solution to this maximization problem is to choose a building size which satisfies the condition,

$$dC/dq = p_0. \tag{2}$$

The building size that satisfies this equality will be denoted q^*. Given this optimal decision, it follows directly that the value of the land for building at the present time, $\pi(p_0)$, is an increasing and convex function of p_0. It should be noted that the convexity results because the landowner can change q^* in response to changes in p_0.

I will later demonstrate, within a more specialized model, that because of this convexity property, greater uncertainty about the future unit price of buildings increases the current value of vacant land. The basic intuition behind this result can be seen by comparing the expected value of the land for building at date 1, over uncertain realizations of $\tilde{p}_1$, with the value of the land given a known date 1 price of $\hat{p}_1 = E(\tilde{p}_1)$. It follows from Jensen's inequality that

$$E(\Pi(\tilde{p}_1)) > \Pi(E(\tilde{p}_1)). \tag{3}$$

Hence, uncertainty increases the expected future value of the vacant land. This implies that uncertainty causes current vacant land values to increase at least for the case where investors are risk neutral.[3]

II Valuing Urban Land under Uncertainty

Here I present a simple model for valuing land under uncertainty. Although the model makes no assumptions about investor preferences, other simplifying assumptions are made. The model consists of only two dates, so if the landowner chooses not to build at the present date (date 0), he or she will develop the land at date 1 if $\pi(p_1) > 0$. Holding vacant land is assumed to generate no revenues or costs. Uncertainty, in this model, enters in a very simplistic manner. First, the only source of uncertainty pertains to the market price of building units. Per unit construction costs are known and constant. Furthermore, $\tilde{p}_1$, the date 1 price of building units takes on one of only two possible values, p_h and p_l, where $p_h > p_l$. Given that building units can take on only two possible prices on the second date and building costs are constant, it follows that the land at date 1 can take on only two possible values, $\pi(p_h)$ and $\pi(p_l)$. It should be noted that these simplifying assumptions are relaxed considerably in Section VI. It is also assumed that a risk-free asset exists with a return of R_f. The per unit rental rate, R_t, is initially assumed to be exogenous; however, this variable is determined endogenously in the model presented in Section V. Finally, it is assumed that markets are perfect in that there are no taxes, no transaction costs, and no short-selling restrictions.[4]

The vacant land can be considered what the finance literature refers to as a contingent or derivative security. Its date 1 value is completely determined by (or derived from) an exogenously priced asset, the date 1 price of building units. In the finance literature, options and other contingent securities are valued by forming a hedge portfolio, consisting of the risk-free asset and the exogenously priced primitive asset, that is perfectly correlated with the contingent security. In the absence of riskless arbitrage, the contingent security must have the same value as this hedge portfolio.

The vacant land can be similarly valued in this model. Since there exist three investments (land, building units, and the risk-free asset) that take on at most two possible values, the returns of the vacant land can be exactly duplicated by a linear combination of the returns of the building units and the risk-free asset. Hence, in the absence of risk-less arbitrage, the price of the vacant land can be determined as a function of these investments.

An easy way to solve this pricing problem is to first determine the state prices (i.e., the cost at date 0 of receiving one dollar in one of the two date 1 states of nature and zero dollars in the other), and then sum the products of these state prices and the land values in the two states of nature. These state prices, s_h and s_l, must satisfy the following two equations that express the date 0 price of building units and the price of a discount bond as functions of their date 1 cash flows:

$$p_0 = s_h p_h + s_l p_l + R_t(s_h + s_l) \tag{4}$$

$$1/(1 + R_f) = s_l + s_h. \tag{5}$$

Solving these equations yields the following state prices for high and low price states of nature, respectively:

$$s_h = \frac{p_0 - (p_l + R_t/1 + R_f)}{p_h - p_l} \tag{6}$$

and

$$s_l = \frac{(p_h + R_t/1 + R_f) - p_0}{p_h - p_l}. \tag{7}$$

Given these state prices, it follows that if no opportunities for riskless arbitrage exist, the price of vacant land at date 0 must be

$$V = \Pi(p_h)s_h + \Pi(p_l)s_l. \tag{8}$$

If the value of the vacant land, as specified in equation (8), exceeds the profit from building at the present date, $\Pi(p_0)$, the wealth-maximizing landowner will choose to have the land remain vacant. Otherwise, he or she will build at date 0 the size building that satisfies equation (2).

III   A Simple Numerical Example

Consider the example where an investor owns a lot that is suitable for either six or nine condominium units. The per unit construction costs of the building with six and nine units is $80,000 and $90,000, respectively. The current market price of the units is $100,000. The per year rental rate is $8,000 per unit (net of expenses) and the risk-free rate of interest for the year is 12 percent. If market conditions are favorable next year, the condominiums will sell for $120,000; if conditions are unfavorable, they will sell for only $90,000.

Since the marginal cost, per unit, of building nine rather than six units is $110,000, the investor will build a six-unit building and realize a profit of $120,000 if he builds at the current time. However, if he chooses to wait one year to build, he will construct a six-unit building if market conditions are unfavorable and realize a total profit of $60,000, and will build a nine-unit building and realize a total profit of $270,000 if favorable market conditions prevail. Substituting these numbers into equation (8) yields a current value for this land, if it is to remain vacant until next year, of $141,071. Since this is greater than the profit that would be realized by building immediately, it is better to keep the land vacant.

If the land sells for less than this amount, investors can earn arbitrage profits by purchasing the land, and hedging the risk by short-selling the condominium units. For example, if the land sold for $120,000, investors could realize a risk-free gain with no initial investment by purchasing the land, short-selling seven condomium units, and investing the net proceeds from the transactions in the risk-free asset. The seven condominium units completely hedges the risk from owning the vacant land since the difference between the value of the units in the good and bad states of nature, $210,000, exactly offsets the difference in land values in the two states. Hence, the above investment yields a risk-free gain of $23,600. Since such gains cannot exist in equilibrium, investors will bid up the price of the land to its equilibrium value of $141,071.

IV Comparative Statics

The above numerical example illustrates the effects of the current price of the building units, the interest rate, and the rental rate on the current value of vacant land. Recall that in order to hedge the risk from owning the vacant land, individual building units were sold, with the proceeds invested in the risk-free asset. If the price of the building units increases, the proceeds from the short sale increase, so the vacant land becomes more valuable. Similarly, if the interest rate increases, the income from the risk-free asset increases so the vacant land becomes less valuable. Conversely, if the rental rate increases, the cost of maintaining the short position increases, so the value of the vacant land decreases.

These comparative static results can be shown formally by differentiating equation (8) under the assumption that p_h and p_l are fixed:

$$\partial V/\partial p_0 = \frac{\Pi(p_h) - \Pi(p_l)}{p_h - p_l} > 0, \tag{9a}$$

$$\partial V/\partial R_f = \frac{\Pi(p_h)(p_l + R_t) - \Pi(p_l)(p_h + R_t)}{(p_h - p_l)(1 + R_f)^2} \lesseqgtr 0, \tag{9b}$$

$$\partial V/\partial R_t = \frac{\Pi(p_l) - \Pi(p_h)}{(p_h - p_l)(1 + R_f)} < 0. \tag{9c}$$

The preceding analysis implicitly assumes that the current price and rental rate on building units are unaffected by changes in the risk-free rate. Alternatively, we can examine the case where R_t is constrained to equal $R_f p_0$. A change in the risk-free rate accompanied by a proportional change in the rental rate can then be analyzed by substituting $R_f p_0$ for R_t in equation (8) to yield

$$V = \Pi(p_h)\left(\frac{p_0 - p_l}{(p_h - p_l)(1 + R_f)}\right) + \Pi(p_l)\left(\frac{p_h - p_0}{(p_h - p_l)(1 + R_f)}\right). \tag{8'}$$

It is clear from the above equation that the value of the vacant land decreases if an increase in interest rates is accompanied by a corresponding increase in rental rates.

The valuation technique presented in Section IV above also enables us to analyze the effect of increased uncertainty on land values. This is done by considering the effect of increasing the spread between p_h and p_l in such a way that state prices remain constant, and are consistent with both current rental rates and the prices of building units remaining constant. Hence, the effect of uncertainty on land values established here is applicable to cross-sectional comparisons holding current building prices constant.

One can easily verify that if p_h increases by x dollars and p_l decreases by xs_h/s_l dollars, the state prices remain unchanged. Also, the value $p_h s_h + p_l s_l = p_0 - R_t/1 + R_f$ remains unchanged. This is consistent with, but does not require, p_0 and R_t to remain unchanged. However, the value of vacant land,

$$V = \Pi(p_h + x)s_h + \Pi(p_l - (xs_h/s_l))s_l, \tag{10}$$

is an increasing function of x. This can be seen by differentiating V, in equation (10), with respect to x:

$$dV/dx = \Pi'(p_h + x)s_h + \Pi'(p_l - (xs_h/s_l))s_h.$$

It follows from the convexity of $\Pi(p)$ that

$$dV/dx > 0 \quad \text{since } \Pi'(p_h + x) > \Pi'(p_l - (xs_h/s_l)).$$

This result indicates that if the amount of uncertainty increases, the value of the vacant land increases, decreasing the relative attractiveness of constructing a building at the current time. Developing the land at the current time becomes less attractive because the increased uncertainty about future prices makes the size of the building that will be optimal at the future date more uncertain, which in turn makes it more likely that the optimal building size at the current time will be suboptimal in the future. If the building size (q^*) that will be constructed in the future is known, perhaps because of height restrictions, then the amount of uncertainty about future prices will not enter the decision as to whether to build now or to build in the future. The decision will instead be determined by a comparison between the rental rate and the return from investing the construction expenses in the risk-free asset. This can be seen by comparing the value of the land for constructing a building with q^* units at the current time period:

$$\Pi = p_0 q^* - C(q^*), \tag{11}$$

with its value as a building site for next period:

$$V = s_h[p_h q^* - C(q^*)] + s_l[p_l q^* - C(q^*)]. \tag{12}$$

Substituting equation (7) into (12) yields

$$V = p_0 q^* - R_t q^*(s_h + s_l) - C(q^*)(s_h + s_l), \tag{13}$$

which suggests that the building should be constructed at the present date if and only if

$$(C(q^*) + R_t q^*)/(1 + R_f) > C(q^*),$$

which simplifies to

$$R_t q^* > R_f C(q^*). \tag{14}$$

Since condition (14) is less restrictive than the condition $\Pi(p_0) > V$ (for the case where there are no building restrictions), a particular piece of land may be developed at the present date (if height restrictions are imposed), in circumstances under which it would not be developed otherwise. Hence, the imposition of height restrictions can conceivably have the immediate effect of increasing the number of building units in a particular area.

The effects of changes in future building prices, which do lead to changes in current building prices, can also be examined within this model. An increase in p_h, holding p_l, s_l, s_h, and R_t constant, will increase p_0 by the amount s_h (see equation (4)), which in turn will increase the profit from developing the land at the current date by the amount

$$d\Pi/dp_h = \Pi'(p_0)s_h. \tag{15}$$

From equation (8), this increase in p_h leads to an increase in the value of the vacant land of

$$dV/dp_h = \Pi'(p_h)s_h. \tag{16}$$

If p_h exceeds p_0, $\Pi'(p_h)$ will exceed $\Pi'(p_0)$ since $\Pi(\cdot)$ is convex. In this case, an increase in building prices in the good state of nature increases the current value of the vacant land relative to its value if developed. Hence, it becomes less attractive to build at the current date. In the less likely case where the price of building units in the favorable state of nature is lower than the current price, an increase in p_h makes it more attractive to build at the current date.

Similarly, a decrease in p_l, holding the other variables constant, decreases current building unit prices by s_l, which in turn leads to a decrease in the profit from developing the land at the current date by the amount

$$d\Pi/dp_l = \Pi'(p_0)s_l. \tag{17}$$

This decrease in p_l leads to a corresponding decrease in the vacant land value of

$$dV/dp_l = \Pi'(p_l)s_l. \tag{18}$$

It follows, from the above equations, that a decrease in p_l will lead to a decrease in the profit from developing the land at the current date that is greater (less) than the corresponding decrease in the value of the vacant land if p_0 exceeds (is less than) p_l. The above analysis suggests that any increase in the $p_h - p_l$ spread makes it relatively more valuable to delay developing the land as long as $p_h > p_0 > p_l$. This conforms to the basic intuition that increased uncertainty increases the value of having open alternatives. However, this intuition does not necessarily hold when either $p_0 > p_h$, or $p_0 < p_l$.

V A Simple Examination

Here I present a simple examination of the effect of increased uncertainty on equilibrium prices and building activity. Up to this point, I have not addressed issues relating to the effect of uncertainty on the current prices and rental rates of building units. In order to do this, I must add structure to the model. The following analysis examines a simple economy that consists of N identical lots that are initially vacant. If, in equilibrium, all the lots are developed at date 0, then there will exist no vacant lots to value. Conversely, if none of the lots are developed, no building units will exist. Hence, it makes sense to restrict the analysis to equilibria in which some, but not all, of the lots are developed at date 0. This suggests that, in equilibrium, the date 0 value of a vacant lot must equal the profit from developing it at that time:

$$V_0 = \Pi(p_0). \tag{19}$$

The demand for building units at date 0 is expressed as a decreasing function of their rental rate:

$$Q = nq^* = f(R_t), \tag{20}$$

where Q, the number of building units demanded, is equal to the product of n, the number of lots that are developed in the current period, and q^*, the number of building units constructed per lot. The function $f(R_t)$ is assumed to be continuous and differentiable with df/dR_t less than zero.

Equations (1), (2), (4), (8), (19), and (20), along with the exogenous p_l, p_h, and R_f, define a well-specified equilibrium.[5] The effect of uncertainty on this equilibrium can be explored in the manner developed in the previous section; by increasing p_h by x and decreasing p_l by xs_h/s_l so that $p_0 - (R_t/(1 + R_f))$, s_h and s_l remain unchanged.

As was shown previously, an increase in uncertainty of this type leads to an increase in V. This implies that $\Pi(p_0)$ must increase, which in turn implies that both p_0 and q^* must increase. Since $p_0 - (R_t/(1 + R_f))$ remains constant with changes in x, R_t must also increase. From equation (20) we see that Q decreases with increases in R_t. Since q^* increases and Q decreases, it must be the case that n decreases. In other words, if uncertainty is increased in a manner that keeps the state prices constant, prices of both land and building units as well as rental rates will increase, a larger portion of the land will remain vacant, but taller buildings will be constructed.

VI Extensions and Practical Applications

Because of tractability considerations, the valuation model developed in Section II was kept simple. The model consisted of only two dates, with only two possible states of nature at the second date, and construction costs were assumed to be fixed. While these assumptions allow us to easily analyze the effects of uncertainty on land prices, they can be relaxed if our only interest is in developing a practical technique for valuing urban land.

The assumption that construction costs are certain can easily be relaxed. The profit from constructing the optimal size building in each date and state of nature can be calculated as long as the construction costs and the per unit price of buildings is specified for each date and state. Substituting these profit levels into equation (8) yields the value of the vacant land.

The pricing model can also be generalized to allow for more than two dates. This can be done by specifying that for each date t state of nature, two possible date $t + 1$ states of nature can occur. The date 0 land value can then be solved by backwards induction. For each state of nature at the second to last date, the vacant land value is given by equation (8). The larger of this value and the profit from developing the land in each state of nature at this date can then be substituted for Π into equation (8) to calculate the values of vacant land at the third to last date for the different states of nature. By continuing this process, we not only obtain the current value of the vacant land, but also determine at which future dates and states of nature the land is developed. Note also that by making the time periods between dates arbitrarily small and the number of dates arbitrarily large, we can have an arbitrarily large number of states of nature for each future time period. Hence, the assumption of only two date $t + 1$ future states of nature for each date t state is not really restrictive.

The following numerical example illustrates this valuation method. It assumes three dates. The profit from developing the land, the per unit building price, and the rental rate is given for each date and state of nature in figure 34.1. The value of the vacant land in the two date 1 states of nature are calculated in the manner specified in Section II. Since the value of the vacant land in the favorable state of nature ($408,635) exceeds the profits from developing the land in this state of nature, the land will remain vacant. However, the value of the land is only $254,545 in the unfavorable date 1 state of nature. Since this value is less than the profit from developing the land at that date, the land will be developed if the unfavorable state of nature occurs. Substituting the larger of the value of the vacant land and the profit from developing the land in each state of nature for $\Pi(p)$ in equation (8) yields the date 0 value of the vacant land. Since this value ($317,168) exceeds the profit from developing the land at date 0, the land will remain vacant at this date.

VII Conclusion

The model developed in this paper provides a valuation equation for pricing vacant lots in urban areas. The analysis demonstrates that the range of possible building

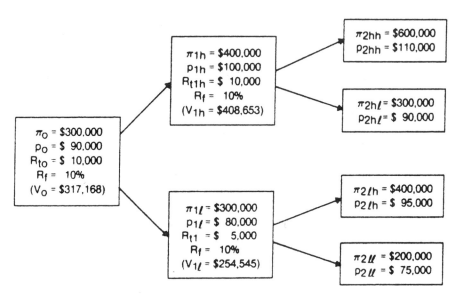

Figure 34.1

sizes provides a valuable option to the owner of vacant land that becomes more valuable as uncertainty about future prices increases. An implication of this relationship between uncertainty and vacant land values is that increased uncertainty leads to a decrease in building activity in the current period.

The relationship between building activity and uncertainty may have important macro implications. An article by Lawrence Summers (1981) and my 1982 article suggest that an increase in anticipated inflation leads to an increase in housing prices, which in turn leads to an increase in construction activity. The analysis presented here suggests that if the government initiates a monetary policy (or any other policy) to stimulate building activity, the policy may actually lead to a decrease in building activity if there is uncertainty about its duration or its effect.

The model also provides insights into the role of real estate speculators who purchase vacant lots, and rather than develop them immediately, choose to keep them vacant for a period of time. By waiting until some future date to build, the speculator is able to construct a building that is most appropriate given economic conditions at that time. Since the exact nature of these economic conditions are unknown at earlier dates, a building constructed earlier will not in general be the optimal size for the future. The decision to build or not build can thus be thought of as weighting the opportunity costs associated with keeping the land vacant against the expected gain from constructing a more appropriate building in the future.

It should also be noted that the framework developed here can easily be extended to analyze other issues relating to real estate pricing under uncertainty. For example, the analysis can easily be augmented to determine the value of houses that may or may not be torn down in the future so that the land can be used to develop large condominium complexes. The framework can also be used to determine when it is optimal to demolish a small building for the purpose of constructing a larger building, and under what conditions it is optimal to renovate an apartment house or convert it to condominiums. One could also use similar techniques to analyze the effect of uncertainty on the optimal durability of buildings.

Acknowledgments

I thank Fred Case, Nai-Fu Chen, Margaret Fry, Mark Grinblatt, Frank Mittelbach, and Brett Trueman for helpful comments.

Notes

1. See, for example, John Krutilla (1967), Alex Cukierman (1980), Douglas Greenley, Richard Walsh, and Robert Young, (1981), and Ben Bernanke (1983).

2. I am unaware of any extant land pricing models that consider uncertainty. However, Donald Shoup (1970), Chapman Findlay and Hugh Howson (1975), and James Markusen and David Scheffman (1978) have examined some of the issues analyzed here within certainty models. Also, René Stulz (1982) suggested that the model he developed for pricing options to purchase one of two risky assets could be applied to price land in some specific cases.

3. For the special cases where $\tilde{p}_1$ is normally distributed, or where $C(q)$ is quadratic, the expected future value of land is monotonically increasing in the variance of $\tilde{p}_1$.

4. The assumption of frictionless markets, generally assumed in models of security prices, is considered by some to be less realistic when applied to real estate markets. However, it should be noted that securities represent indirect claims on factories and equipment that are probably much less liquid than real estate. Yet we can price these assets as if they were perfectly liquid because the securities are traded on (almost) frictionless markets. Similarly, a large fraction of real estate is held by publicly traded firms. If the real estate investments of these firms are chosen in a manner consistent with value maximization, then real estate prices will be determined in equilibrium as if markets were really frictionless.

5. Note that the above equations are all continuous and that the variables are all finite and nonnegative. Hence, the existence of this equilibrium follows directly from Brouwer's fixed-point theorem.

References

Bernanke, Ben S., "Irreversibility, Uncertainty, and Cyclical Investment," *Quarterly Journal of Economics*, February 1983, *97*, 85–106.

Black, Fisher and Scholes, Myron, "The Pricing of Options and Corporate Liabilities," *Journal of Political Economy*, May/June 1973, *81*, 637–59.

Cox, John C., Ross, Stephen A. and Rubinstein, Mark, "Option Pricing: A Simplified Approach," *Journal of Financial Economics*, September 1979, *7*, 229–63.

Cukierman, Alex, "The Effects of Uncertainty on Investment under Risk Neutrality with Endogenous Information," *Journal of Political Economy*, June 1980, *88*, 462–75.

Findlay, M. Chapman and Howson, Hugh R., "Optimal Intertemporal Real Estate Ownership, Valuation, and Use," *American Real Estate and Urban Economics Association Journal*, Summer 1975, *3*, 51–66.

Greenley, Douglas A., Walsh, Richard G. and Young, Robert A., "Option Value: Empirical Evidence from a Case Study of Recreation and Water Quality," *Quarterly Journal of Economics*, November 1981, *95*, 657–73.

Krutilla, John V., "Conservation Reconsidered," *American Economic Review*, September 1967, *57*, 777–86.

Markusen, James and Scheffman, David T., "The Timing of Residential Land Development: A General Equilibrium Approach," *Journal of Urban Economics*, October 1978, *5*, 411–24.

Merton, Robert C., "Theory of Rational Option Pricing," *Bell Journal of Economics*, Spring 1973, *4*, 141–83.

Ratcliff, Richard U., *Valuation for Real Estate Decisions*, Santa Cruz: Democrat Press, 1972.

Rendleman, Richard J. and Bartter, Brit J., "Two-State Option Pricing," *Journal of Finance*, December 1979, *34*, 117–34.

Shoup, Donald C., "The Optimal Timing of Urban Land Development," *Regional Science Association Papers*, 1970, *25*, 33–44.

Stulz, René M., "Options on the Minimum or the Maximum of Two Risky Assets: Analysis and Applications," *Journal of Financial Economics*, July 1982, *10*, 161–85.

Summers, Lawrence H., "Inflation, The Stock Market, and Owner-Occupied Housing," *American Economic Review Proceedings*, May 1981, *71*, 429–34.

Titman, Sheridan, "The Effects of Anticipated Inflation on Housing Market Equilibrium," *Journal of Finance*, June 1982, *37*, 827–42.

35 Investments of Uncertain Cost: An Application to the Construction of Nuclear Power Plants

Robert S. Pindyck

Introduction

In most studies of investment under uncertainty, it is the future payoffs from the investment that are uncertain. The emphasis on uncertainty over future payoffs also applies to the growing literature on irreversible investment. Much of that literature [see Dixit (1992), Pindyck (1991), and Dixit and Pindyck (1993) for an overview] studies optimal stopping rules for the timing of sunk costs of known magnitude in exchange for capital whose value fluctuates stochastically.

Sometimes the cost of an investment is more uncertain than the future payoff, particularly for large projects that take considerable time to build. An example is a nuclear power plant, for which total construction costs are hard to predict due to both engineering and regulatory uncertainties. Although the future value of a completed nuclear plant is also uncertain (because electricity demand and costs of alternative fuels are uncertain), construction cost uncertainty is much greater than revenue uncertainty, and has deterred utilities from building new plants. There are many other examples, including large petrochemical complexes, the development of a new line of aircraft, and urban construction projects. Moreover, large size is not a requisite. Many R&D projects involve considerable cost uncertainty; the development of a new drug by a pharmaceutical company is an example.

In addition to their uncertain costs, all of the investments mentioned above are irreversible. Expenditures on nuclear power plants, petrochemical complexes, and the development of new drugs are firm- or industry-specific, and hence are sunk costs that cannot be recovered should the investment turn out, *ex post*, to have been a bad one. In each case, the investment could turn out to be bad either because demand for the product is less than anticipated or because the cost of the investment turns out to be greater than anticipated. Whatever the reason, the firm cannot 'disinvest' and recover the money it spent.

This chapter studies the implications of cost uncertainty for irreversible investment decisions. With projects that take time to complete, two different kinds of uncertainty arise. The first, which I call *technical* uncertainty, relates to the physical difficulty of completing a project: Assuming prices of construction inputs are known, how much time, effort, and materials will ultimately be required? Technical uncertainty can only be resolved by undertaking the project; actual costs and construction time unfold as the project proceeds.[1] These costs may be greater or less than anticipated if impediments arise or if the work progresses faster than planned, but the total cost of the investment is only known for certain when the project is complete. Also, technical uncertainty is largely diversifiable. It results only from the inability to predict how difficult a project will be, which is likely to be independent of the overall economy.

The second kind of uncertainty relates to *input costs*, and is external to what the firm does. It arises when the prices of labor, land, and materials needed to build a project fluctuate unpredictably, or when unpredictable changes in government regulations change the cost of construction. Prices and regulations change regardless of whether or not the firm is investing, and are more uncertain the farther into the future one looks. Hence input cost uncertainty is particularly important for projects that take time to complete or are subject to voluntary or involuntary delays. Also, this uncertainty may be partly nondiversifiable; changes in construction costs are likely to be correlated with overall economic activity.

This chapter derives decision rules for irreversible investments subject to both types of cost uncertainty. For simplicity, I first assume that the value of the completed project is known with certainty, and then show how the model can be extended so that this value is also stochastic. The decision rules I derive allow for the possibility of abandoning the project midstream, and maximize the value of the firm in a competitive capital market. These rules have a simple form: *Invest as long the expected cost to complete the project is below a critical number*. Also, the derivation of the decision rule yields the value of the investment opportunity, i.e., the value of the right to undertake the project. I explore how this value, and the critical expected cost to completion, depend on the type and level of uncertainty.

Both technical and input cost uncertainty increase the value of an investment opportunity. The reason is that the payoff function is $\max[0, V - K]$, where K is the cost and V the value of the completed project. The investment opportunity is like a put option; the holder can sell an asset worth an uncertain amount K for a fixed 'exercise price' V. Like any option, its value is increased by an increase in the variance of the price of the underlying asset. (In my model, the firm actually has a more complicated compound option; it can spend an uncertain amount of money in return for an option to continue the partially completed project.)

However, the two types of uncertainty affect the investment decision differently. Technical uncertainty makes investing more attractive; a project can have an expected cost that makes its conventional NPV negative, but it can still be economical to begin investing. The reason is that investing reveals information about cost, and therefore has a shadow value beyond its direct contribution to the completion of the project; this shadow value lowers the full expected cost of the investment.[2] Also, since information about cost arrives only when investment is taking place, there is no value to waiting.

As an example, a project requires a first phase investment of $1. Then, with probability 0.5 the project will be finished, and with probability 0.5 a second phase costing $4 will be required. Completion of the project yields a certain payoff of $2.8. Since the expected cost of the project is $3, the conventionally measured NPV is negative. But the conventional NPV ignores the value of the option to abandon the project should the second phase be required. The correct NPV is $-1 + (0.5)(2.8) = \$0.4$, so the firm should proceed with at least the first phase.

Input cost uncertainty makes it less attractive to invest now. A project with a conventional NPV that is positive might still be uneconomical, because costs of construction inputs change whether or not investment is taking place, so there is a value of waiting for new information before committing resources. Also, this effect is magnified when fluctuations in construction costs are correlated with the economy, or, in the context of the Capital Asset Pricing Model, when the 'beta' of cost is high. The reason is that a higher beta implies that high-cost outcomes are more likely to be associated with high stock market returns, so that the investment opportunity is a hedge against nondiversifiable risk. Put another way, a higher beta raises the discount rate applied to expected future costs, which raises the value of the investment opportunity as well as the benefit from waiting rather than investing now.

For example, suppose an investment can be made now or later. The cost now is $3, but next period it will either fall to $2 or rise to $4, each with probability 0.5, and then remain at that level. Investing yields a certain payoff of $3.2. Assume the risk-free rate of interest is zero. If we invest now, the project has a conventional NPV of $0.2. But this NPV ignores the opportunity cost of closing our option to wait for a better outcome (a drop in cost). If we wait, we will only invest if the cost falls to $2. The NPV if we wait is $(0.5)(3.2 - 2) = \$0.6$, so it is better to wait. Now suppose the beta of cost is high, so that the risk-adjusted discount rate is 25% per period. Because the payoff from completing the project is certain, this discount rate is only applied to cost. Hence the NPV if we wait is now $(0.5)(3.2 - 2/1.25) = \$0.8$. The higher beta raises the present values of net payoffs, and thereby increases both the value of the investment opportunity and the value of waiting.

Since technical and input cost uncertainty have different effects on investment, it is important to incorporate both in the analysis. In doing so, the model developed herein offers guidance as to the types of projects (e.g., nuclear power plants versus R&D) for which one source of uncertainty or the other will exert the primary influence on investment decisions.

This work is related to several earlier studies. The value of information gathering has been explored by Roberts and Weitzman (1981), who develop a model of sequential investment similar to mine in that the project can be stopped in midstream, and the process of investing reduces both the expected cost of completing the project as well the variance of that cost. They derive an optimal stopping rule, and show that it may pay to go ahead with the early stages of an investment even though the NPV of the entire project is negative.[3] Grossman and Shapiro (1986) also study investments for which the total effort required to reach a payoff is unknown. They model the payoff as a Poisson arrival, with a hazard rate specified as a function of the cumulative effort expended. They allow the rate of progress to be a concave function of effort, and focus on the rate of investment, rather than on whether one should proceed or not. The result in this chapter complements the work of these authors, but my model is more general in its treatment of cost uncertainty, and yields relatively simple decision rules.

This chapter is also related to the basic model of irreversible investment by McDonald and Siegel (1986). They consider the payment of a sunk cost I in return for a project worth V, where V and I evolve as geometric Brownian motions. The optimal investment rule is to wait until V/I reaches a critical value that exceeds one, because of the opportunity cost of committing resources. Also, Majd and Pindyck (1987) study sequential investment when a firm can invest at some maximum rate (so that it takes time to complete a project), the project can be abandoned before completion, and the value of the project, received upon completion, evolves as a geometric Brownian motion. In this chapter the firm can also invest at a maximum rate, but it is the cost rather than the value of the completed project that is uncertain.

Other related work includes that of Baldwin (1982), who analyzes sequential investment decisions when investment opportunities arrive randomly and the firm has limited resources. She values the sequence of opportunities and shows that a simple NPV rule leads to overinvestment, i.e., there is a value to waiting for better opportunities. Likewise, if cost evolves stochastically, it may pay to wait for the cost to fall. Also, Myers and Majd (1984) determine the value of a firm's option to abandon a project in return for a scrap value, S, when the value of the project, V, evolves as a geometric Brownian motion (the firm has a put option to sell a project worth V for a price S), and show how this abandonment value affects the decision to invest.

An Application to the Construction of Nuclear Power Plants

This section examines the decision to start or continue building a nuclear power plant in the context of market conditions in late 1982 or 1983. This was about three years after Three Mile Island and a time of considerable uncertainty over nuclear plant construction costs, which had begun rising sharply. Many utilities faced difficult decisions about whether to go ahead with planned or ongoing construction, and some utilities canceled plants that were well on their way towards completion.[4] Examining this investment problem will show how the model can be used and provide insight into the evolution of nuclear power in the U.S.

Consider an investment opportunity F in such a nuclear power plant (or any project) whose actual cost of completion, K, is uncertain, with expected (mean) cost $E(K)$. The plant takes time to complete, proceeding at a maximum rate of investment K. Upon completion, the firm receives the value of the completed plant, V, which is assumed known with certainty. The value of the investment opportunity in the nuclear power plant, $F(K)$, and the critical expected cost to completion, K^*, are related to the degree of technical uncertainty, β, input cost uncertainty, γ, the maximum rate of investment, k, the correlation with the market, ϕ, and the (real) risk-free return through the following relationship (for derivation see the original article, section 2, and its Appendix):

$$\tfrac{1}{2}\beta^2 IKF_{KK} + \tfrac{1}{2}\gamma^2 K^2 F_{KK} - IF_K - \phi\gamma KF_K - I = rF, \tag{1}$$

To apply the model, we need estimates of the expectation and variance of the cost of building a kilowatt of nuclear generating capacity, a decomposition of that variance into technical (β) and input cost (γ) components, the maximum rate of investment (k), and the value of the unit of capacity. The last two numbers are relatively straightforward. Perl (1987, 1988) has shown that given the prices of alternative fuels during the early- and mid-1980s, the value of a unit of capacity was about \$2,000, with fluctuations in real terms within only a $\pm 10\%$ range. (Unless otherwise noted, all numbers are in 1985 constant dollars.) The *actual* construction time for nuclear plants varied through time and across plants during the late 1970s and 1980s, from six to as long as sixteen years, but tended to move proportionally with realized costs, and increased over the years as (real) costs increased. During the early 1980s, however, estimates of *expected* construction time were clustered around ten years, so a good estimate of the maximum rate of investment (k) is 10% of expected cost or \$144 per year.

To estimate the expectation, variance, and variance decomposition of cost, I use survey data on individual nuclear plant costs published by the Tennessee Valley Authority (TVA) and a cross-section regression analysis by Perl (1987, 1988) that explains differences in these costs across plants. The TVA obtained quarterly estimates of expected cost for nuclear plants planned or under construction in the U.S. These numbers, published in the TVA's "Costs per Kilowatt Report for U.S. Nuclear Plants," provide data on the expected cost of a kilowatt of generating capacity on a plant-by-plant basis. The variance of cost and its decomposition can be estimated from the time-series and cross-sectional variation of these numbers, using the fact that the variance of cost due to technical uncertainty is independent of time, but the variance due to input cost fluctuations grows with the time horizon.

In any year, expected costs per kilowatt will vary across the 50 to 60 plants in the TVA survey, but part of this variation can be explained by differences in the type of plant, the experience of the contractor, region of the country, etc. Consider the cross-section regression:

$$COST_{it} = a_0 + a_1 X_{1it} + a_2 X_{2it} + \cdots + \varepsilon_i, \tag{2}$$

where $COST_{it}$ is expected cost for plant i in year t, and the X_{it}'s are a set of explanatory variables. This regression filters out the predictable part of the cross-sectional variation. Then, for plant i in year t, an estimator of the variance of cost due to technical uncertainty is the variance of the cross-sectional forecast error for $COST_{it}$ from the regression equation (2), given the values of X_{1it}, X_{2it}, etc. that apply to plant i.

A lower bound on this variance is the (squared) standard error of the regression, which would be the variance of the forecast error if, for plant i, X_{kit} for each k were equal to its cross-sectional mean. In general, the X_{kit}'s for any plant will differ from the means, so the variance of the forecast error will exceed the squared standard error of the regression. (The reason is that the true coefficients a_1, a_2, etc. are unknown, and only estimated.) An upper bound on the variance of the forecast error is the cross-sectional sample variance of $COST_{it}$. Hence, I consider values of the degree of technical uncertainty that correspond to forecast error variances ranging from the squared standard error of the regression to the sample variance.

Perl ran such regressions in logarithmic form for 1977–1985, using the TVA data on $COST$ for the last quarter of each year, with a set of up to ten explanatory variables that included: the log of the real wage, the log of the net design electric rating (reflecting the scale of the plant), the log of the experience of the architect/engineer (measured in number of plants designed), and dummy variables for the region of the country, the type of rock foundation, whether the plant was the first or subsequent built by the utility, whether it was a boiling water reactor, whether the utility served as its own construction manager, and whether the plant had a complex cooling tower. (Only variables that were statistically significant were retained, so regressions for some years included only a subset of the above.) I infer values of technical uncertainty β from his results, using the 1982 data and regression. Converting to levels, the mean expected cost for that year was \$1,435 per kilowatt, with a standard error of regression of 17%. This is a lower bound on the standard deviation of the cross-sectional forecast error, and implies $\beta = 0.24$.[5] The upper bound is the sample stan-

Table 35.1
Critical cost of kilowatt of capacity at end of 1982[a]

Degree of technical uncertainty, β	Degree of input cost uncertainty, γ		
	0	0.07	0.20
0	$K^* = 1550$	$K^* = 1251$	$K^* = 867$
	$F(\bar{K}) = 121$	$F(\bar{K}) = 194$	$F(\bar{K}) = 465$
0.24	$K^* = 1609$	$K^* = 1260$	$K^* = 871$
	$F(\bar{K}) = 131$	$F(\bar{K}) = 201$	$F(\bar{K}) = 469$
0.59	$K^* = 1881$	$K^* = 1293$	$K^* = 887$
	$F(\bar{K}) = 215$	$F(\bar{K}) = 228$	$F(\bar{K}) = 487$

a. Based on $V = \$2,000$ per kilowatt, $r = 0.045$, $k = \$144$ per year, and $\phi = 0$. Mean expected cost was $\bar{K} = \$1,435$ per kilowatt.

dard deviation, which for 1982 was 46% of expected cost and corresponds to $\beta = 0.59$.

Next, I estimate the variance due to input cost uncertainty γ by fitting the annual time series for mean expected cost to a geometric random walk. The drift and standard deviation of percentage changes in mean expected cost are 0.12 and 0.06, respectively, for 1977–1985, and 0.11 and 0.07 for 1977–1982. Since I consider decisions at the end of 1982, I use the latter numbers. However, an estimate of the drift based on six years of data (1977–1982) is very imprecise, and an expected real rate of increase of mean cost of 5% per year would have been reasonable at the time. This rate of increase would yield an estimated standard deviation of 0.20, so 0.07 to 0.20 is used as a reasonable range for input cost uncertainty γ. Also, most input cost uncertainty was due to continual and unpredictable regulatory change, rather than factor price fluctuations. Since regulatory change is largely uncorrelated with the economy, I set $\phi = 0$.

Table 35.1 shows solutions for $\beta = 0$, 0.24, and 0.59 and $\gamma = 0$, 0.07, and 0.20. In each case, $V = \$2,000$ per kilowatt, $k = \$144$ per year (10% of the $1,435 mean expected cost in 1982), $\phi = 0$, and $r = 0.045$. (The average yield on three-year and ten-year Treasury bonds in 1982 was 13%. Using the 1979–1982 average rate of inflation of 7% in the PPI and 10% in the CPI as estimates of expected inflation puts the real risk-free rate, r, at about 3–6%.) The table shows the critical expected cost to completion, K^*, and the value of the utility's investment option (per kilowatt) for an actual expected cost equal to the mean of $1,435.

Observe that absent input cost uncertainty $(\gamma = 0)$, K^* ranges from $1,609 to $1,881, so that these investments would have been largely economical. (Technical uncertainty increases K^* by 4–21% compared to its value of $1,550 when $\beta = \gamma = 0$.)

But input cost uncertainty lowers K^* considerably, making the average plant uneconomical. Even for $\gamma = 0.07$, in most cases it would have been preferable to wait to see how regulations (and the expected costs they implied) evolved. And for $\gamma = 0.20$, it would have been economical to stop construction on plants that were 40% complete. This would seem to justify the decisions that some utilities made at the time to cancel planned or ongoing construction. Also, the TVA surveys were available to all U.S. utilities, so presumably they could have performed the same analysis.

The results are not very sensitive to the maximum rate of investment, k. Taking $\beta = 0.24$ and $\gamma = 0.07$, if $k = 288$ (so expected construction time is five years instead of ten), K^* rises to \$1,397. If $k = 96$ (so construction is expected to take fifteen years), K^* falls to \$1,154. Thus for a reasonable range of expected construction times, K^* varies by $\pm 10\%$.

These results show that for nuclear plants, the investment decision is most affected by input cost uncertainty, even though there is substantial technical uncertainty. The results also show the importance of incorporating both types of uncertainty in the analysis, rather than treating them separately. Note from the table that the dependence of K^* on β is much less when γ is 0.07 or 0.20 than it is when γ is 0. If one first calculated the change in K^* due to, say, a β of 0.59 (holding $\gamma = 0$) and then the percentage change due to a γ of 0.07, the result would be a K^* of about \$1,518 rather than the correct value of \$1,293.

Appendix: Mean and Variance of $\tilde{K}$

Here I show that if $K(t)$ follows a controlled diffusion of the form

$$dK = -k\,dt + \beta K(k/K)^{\alpha}\,dz,\tag{A.1}$$

then $K(t)$ is indeed the expected cost to completion. Let

$$M(K) = E_t\left[\int_t^{\tilde{T}} k\,d\tau \mid K(t)\right],\tag{A.2}$$

where $\tilde{T}$ is the first passage time for $K = 0$. We will show that $M(K) = K$.

We make use of the fact that the functional $M(K)$ must satisfy the Kolmogorov backward equation corresponding to (A.1):

$$\tfrac{1}{2}\beta^2 k^{2\alpha}K^{2-2\alpha}M_{KK} - kM_K + k = 0,\tag{A.3}$$

subject to the boundary conditions (i) $M(0) = 0$ and (ii) $M(\infty) = \infty$. [See Karlin and Taylor (1981), ch. 15).] Clearly $M(K) = K$ is a solution of (A.3) and the associated boundary conditions. Now consider a more general solution of the form $M(K) = K + h(K)$, where $h(K)$ is an arbitrary function of K. By direct integration,

$$h_K(K) = C\exp\left[\frac{2K^{2\alpha-1}}{(2\alpha-1)\beta^2 k^{2\alpha}}\right].\tag{A.4}$$

But since $\lim_{K\to\infty} h_K(K) = C$, the constant C must equal zero to satisfy boundary condition (ii). Hence $M(K) = K$.

For the case of $\alpha = \frac{1}{2}$ (technical uncertainty), we can also find the variance of the cost of completion, i.e.,

$$\text{var}(K) = E_t \left[\int_t^{\bar{T}} k \, d\tau \,|\, K \right]^2 - K^2(t). \tag{A.5}$$

Let $G(K) = E_t[\int_t^{\bar{T}} k \, d\tau | K]^2$. Then $G(K)$ must satisfy the following Kolmogorov equation:

$$\tfrac{1}{2}\beta^2 kK G_{KK} - kG_K + 2kK = 0, \tag{A.6}$$

subject to the boundary conditions $G(0) = 0$ and $G(\infty) = \infty$. [See Karlin and Taylor (1981, p. 203).] The solution to (A.6) is $G(K) = 2K^2/(2 - \beta^2)$, so the variance is

$$\text{var}(K) = \left(\frac{\beta^2}{2 - \beta^2} \right) K^2. \tag{A.7}$$

Acknowledgments

This research was supported by the M.I.T. Center for Energy Policy Research and by the National Science Foundation under Grant No. SES90-22823. My thanks to Alexandar Angelus and David Chariton for their excellent research assistance, to Barbara MacMullan and Lewis Perl of National Economics Research Associates for making available their nuclear power plant cost data and regressions, and to John Cox, Gene Grossman, Paul Joskow, Richard Lester, Mark McCabe, Lewis Perl, William Pounds, Richard Ruback, Robert Taggart, and Martin Weitzman for helpful comments and suggestions.

Notes

This chapter is only a part of the original article, focusing on an application to the construction of nuclear power plants. Sections 2, 3, and 5 of the original paper, which developed the theoretical model resulting in eq (1) herein, were omitted. Please refer to the original paper for the theory part.

1. This is a simplification, in that for some projects cost uncertainty can be reduced by first undertaking additional engineering studies. The investment problem is then more complicated because one has three choices instead of two: start construction now, undertake an engineering study now, and then begin construction only if the study indicates costs are likely to be low, or abandon the project completely.

2. It is analogous to the shadow value of production arising from a learning curve, which lowers the full cost of production; see Majd and Pindyck (1989).

3. Weitzman, Newey, and Rabin (1981) use this model to evaluate demonstration plants for synthetic fuels, and show that learning about costs could justify these investments. MacKie-Mason (1991) extends

the Roberts and Weitzman analysis by allowing for investors (who pay the cost of a project) and managers (who decide whether to continue or abandon the project) to have conflicting interests and asymmetric information. He shows that asymmetric learning about cost leads to inefficient overabandonment of projects. Finally, Zeira (1987) develops a model in which a firm learns about its payoff function as it accumulates capital.

4. For example, Virginia Electric Power canceled its Northanna III and IV units, which were 10% completed, Public Service of Indiana canceled Marble Hill (35% completed), Washington Public Power Supply Systems canceled four of its five plants (5% to 50% completed), and Cleveland Electric Illuminating canceled its Zimmer plant, which was more than 90% completed.

5. Note that this accounts for construction experience and movement down the learning curve. For a discussion of the impact of experience on nuclear plant *operating* costs, see McCabe (1991). McCabe also examines technology adoption with uncertain operating cost, and argues that utilities buy a mix of technologies in order to reduce the variance of operating cost.

References

Baldwin, Carliss Y., 1982, Optimal sequential investment when capital is not readily reversible, *Journal of Finance* 37, 763–782.

Dixit, Avinash, 1992, Investment and hysteresis, *Journal of Economic Perspectives* 6, 107–132.

Dixit, Avinash and Robert S. Pindyck, 1993, *Investment under uncertainty* (Princeton University Press, Princeton, NJ).

Grossman, Gene M. and Carl Shapiro, 1986, Optimal dynamic R&D programs, *RAND Journal of Economics* 17, 581–593.

Karlin, Samuel and Howard M. Taylor, 1981, *A second course in stochastic processes* (Academic Press, New York, NY).

MacKie-Mason, Jeffrey K., 1991, Sequential investment decisions with asymmetric learning, Unpublished working paper (NBER, Cambridge, MA).

Majd, Saman and Robert S. Pindyck, 1987, Time to build, option value, and investment decisions, *Journal of Financial Economics* 18, 7–27.

Majd, Saman and Robert S. Pindyck, 1989, The learning curve and optimal production under uncertainty, RAND *Journal of Economics* 20, 331–343.

McCabe, Mark J., 1991, Industrial structure and technological change in the nuclear power industry, Ph.D. thesis (Massachusetts Institute of Technology Cambridge, MA).

McDonald, Robert and Daniel R. Siegel, 1986, The value of waiting to invest, *Quarterly Journal of Economics* 101, 707–728.

Myers, Stewart C. and Samon Majd, 1984, Calculating abandonment value using option pricing theory, Working paper no. 1462-83 (Sloan School of Management, Massachusetts Institute of Technology, Cambridge, MA).

Perl, Lewis J., 1987, Testimony before public utility commission of Texas on behalf of Gulf States Utilities Co., Docket nos. 7195 and 6755, April 13th.

Perl, Lewis J., 1988, Testimony before City Council of City of New Orleans on behalf of Louisiana Power & Light Co., Application no. CD-86-11, Jan. 15th.

Pindyck, Robert S., 1991, Irreversibility, uncertainty, and investment, Journal of Economic *Literature* 29, 1110–1152.

Roberts, Kevin and Martin L. Weitzman, 1981, Funding criteria for research, development, and exploration projects, *Econometrica* 49, 1261–1288.

Tennessee Valley Authority, Cost per kilowatt report for U.S. nuclear plants, Quarterly surveys, 1977 to 1985.

Weitzman, Martin, 1979, Optimal search for the best alternative, *Econometrica* 47, 641–654.

Weitzman, Martin, Whitney Newey, and Michael Rabin, 1981, Sequential R&D strategy for synfuels, *Bell Journal of Economics* 12, 574–590.

Zeira, Joseph, 1987, Investment as a process of search, *Journal of Political Economy* 95, 204–210.

36 Operating Flexibility, Global Manufacturing, and the Option Value of a Multinational Network

Bruce Kogut and Nalin Kulatilaka

Introduction

The theory of the multinational corporation has traditionally sought to explain why a firm can successfully invest in overseas operations. As Hymer (1960) noted, a foreign company operates at a disadvantage relative to local firms; it must control the operations over longer distances and it is at a handicap in a foreign culture. Thus, he concluded, direct investment must be motivated by a competitive asset that provides the foreign firm with an advantage.

Around this central perspective, the work in both economics and management has developed a substantial and complementary body of research. In the field of the economics of the multinational corporation, considerable attention has been paid to the theoretical and empirical investigation of firm-level advantages and foreign direct investment. In the area of management, a principal line of inquiry regards the costs of managing foreign operations due to differences in culture, labor relations, and human resource practices. The management literature, in effect, has investigated in detail Hymer's supposition of the higher costs of managing in foreign countries.

This central perspective, however, loses considerable relevance for the investigation of the economic and competitive behavior of multinational corporations. There is a distinction between the economic and management aspects of a firm's first and subsequent investments in a foreign country. Nor is this distinction minor when it is considered that around 40% of U.S. trade stems from the transfer of goods among affiliates within a corporation and that the predominant proportion of U.S. direct investment is in the form of reinvested earnings in already existing subsidiaries.[1]

An indication of the use of foreign subsidiaries as part of an internationally coordinated strategy is given in table 36.1. This table shows the sales of affiliates within the corporation and to the outside. The degree of internal transfers is quite high, especially for the Asian region which provides a platform for global sourcing.

The coordination of a network of subsidiaries dispersed throughout the world provides an "operating flexibility" that adds value to the firm. This operating flexibility is an advantage gained by being a multinational corporation. As developed below, it can be conceived as owning the option to respond to uncertain events, such as government policies, competitors' decisions, or the arrival of new technologies in some parts of the world.

The following chapter develops a formal model of the option value of multinationality. For purposes of illustration, we use the example of global manufacturing, where building plants in two countries is shown to generate additional value for

Table 36.1
Destination of shipments of U.S. manufacturing affiliates abroad

	As fraction of total sales		
Area	Local sales	Third country sales	U.S. sales
Canada	61.9%	3.4%	34.8%
Europe	60.2%	34.2%	5.6%
Japan	83.3%	7.8%	8.9%
Other Asia and Pacific	60.9%	18.0%	21.1%
Latin America	78.6%	23.0%	13.6%

Notes: Aggregation due to presentation of Original Data.
Source: 1989 Benchmark Survey of U.S. Direct Foreign Investment Abroad.

the firm by shifting production depending on the real exchange rate. Using stochastic dynamic programming, simulations are generated by varying the volatility and speed by which the exchange rate returns to parity. We expand the across-country option of production shifting to include the creation of the within-country growth option.

In the last part of the chapter, we show that this model is more than normative but captures changes in the organization and information systems of multinational corporations. By examples from the recent management literature, the observed changes in internal accounting and pricing heuristics of the multinational corporation are argued to reflect the efforts to provide the correct information and incentives required for exercising operating flexibility. We show how the control system must be altered to support the transformation of a "dyadic" relationship between headquarters and subsidiaries to a network structure.

In this sense, our treatment of the option value of a multinational corporation has a more general implication. The network structure of the multinational corporation provides the organizational capability to coordinate subsidiaries flexibly across borders. The economic merits of the international firm as a network are derived from the option value of multinational operating flexibility under the critical condition of uncertainty. The network structure of the multinational firm is an evolutionary response to the uncertainty of international markets.

1   Operating Flexibility and Multinational Options

Options are valuable due to three conditions: uncertainty, time dependence, and discretion. That flexibility is valuable only when there is uncertainty is obvious. Yet, often, the problem of understanding the source and properties of the uncertainty is substantial. A simple example is the difficulty of describing the probabilities attached to the arrival of new technologies.

A more subtle feature is time dependence. The application of option analysis to investments is important, because it captures the value in the dependence of decisions over time. To provide a counterexample, some investments, such as those characterized by easy entry and exit into perfectly competitive markets, can largely be analyzed independent of how today's decision influences future decisions.

These two conditions imply that the value of an option stems from the investment in the capability to respond profitably to future uncertain events. A critical issue is, then, the third condition, that is, that this capability is accompanied by the discretion to exercise the option. For example, the option to withdraw from a country is of little value, if the firm is encumbered by restrictions on laying-off workers or by the requirement to make burdensome severance payments.[2]

It is important to note that an investment in a foreign country generates two kinds of options. One kind is a "within-country" growth option which, by establishing a brand label or simply knowledge of the market, provides a platform for the introduction of new products. This kind of option applies also to an investment by a domestic firm. The second kind is an "across-country" option provided by operating flexibility.

Within-country options are significant in the international case because of the Hymer condition mentioned above, that is, the first international investments are made by firms which lack the organizational knowledge and supporting assets in the foreign market. The first investment carries, consequently, a large option value, as it opens the market for subsequent expansion. But the creation of these options is not itself an advantage of being international, but rather an aspect of the process by which the firm expands in a foreign country. In fact, as the firm grows in the foreign market, the value of these options to launch new products or to diversify within the country becomes the same as for a purely domestic corporation.[3]

The advantage of operating across borders relative to a purely domestic firm lies, then, not in being international, but in the ownership of options to coordinate flexibly *multinational* activities within a network. The option value of multinationality is different from that of the benefits of geographic diversification. The benefits of diversification are created by the reduction in variance of the overall portfolio of subsidiary results.[4] An option, on the other hand, is valuable because it gives *managerial discretion* to respond profitably to the realization of uncertain events.

In this sense, a real, as opposed to a financial, option differs in an important sense. (By real, it is meant an investment in operating activities rather than the purchase of financial instruments.) The exercising of a financial option is rarely impaired by institutional impediments; prices are easily available from markets and trading is relatively easy to carry out. But the exercise of a real option faces important impediments that cannot be ignored. A firm must be able to gather the appropriate information to know when the option should optimally be exercised; even when the information is known, exercise may be hindered by organizational features that obstruct flexibility.

We investigate these issues more formally be analyzing the problem of evaluating the value of manufacturing in two different countries. The source of uncertainty is the fluctuation in the real exchange rate; time dependence arises because the flexibility to shift production can only be realized by investing in two plants; managerial discretion is achieved by creating the proper accounting and organizational practices.

As our intention is not to model the extant manufacturing location problem, we focus only on the aspects of interest to our argument, that is, the increase in value gained through operating flexibility. We lay out first the formal model of the value of shifting production in response to exchange rates. We extend the results to consider a generalized global sourcing from more than two countries, hysteresis and growth options. Then, we turn to examining the accounting and pricing rules required to support the exercise of operating flexibility in a multinational network.

2   Global Manufacturing and Production Shifting

The literature on global manufacturing planning models has largely focused on the problem of plant location and scheduling in the absence of multiperiod flexibility. Recent advances have tried to embed the location and scheduling problem within the context of a network of production and distribution facilities (Cohen et al. 1989, Cohen and Lee 1989). Whereas these approaches have progressed considerably in analyzing cost minimization of multinational operations within a network, they do not incorporate the value of flexibility under uncertainty. The effect of uncertainty in a single-period model has been addressed in a mean-variance approach (Hodder and Jucker 1985a, Hodder and Jucker 1985b). This approach addresses uncertainty as a penalty to be minimized; multinationality, via diversification effects, is valuable only insofar as the variance of the portfolio of manufacturing sites decreases with geographical dispersion.

An attempt to capture the value of flexibility under uncertainty is provided in the one-period stochastic model of production shifting of de Meza and van der Ploeg (1987). A multiperiod stochastic model explicitly incorporating the option valuation of production shifting in a network is qualitatively described in Kogut (1983, 1985) and formally analyzed in Kogut and Kulatilaka (1988). It is this multiperiod stochastic formulation that is explored below.[5]

To analyze the value of multinational coordination of manufacturing, consider a firm with assets dispersed to various parts of the world. The decision facing the firm is

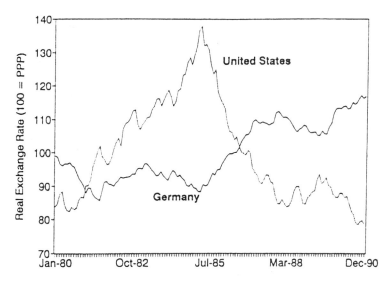

Figure 36.1
Trade weighted real exchange rates

to minimize total cost producing in a single location or switch flexibly between two sites located in different countries. Factor prices and final demand are given and known. Uncertainty arises through fluctuations in exchange rates. By treating prices and output as given, we are able to focus on the effect of location switching on value.[6]

Though a number of factors generate economic shocks which are likely to influence the value of investing in flexibility, fluctuations in exchange rates are certainly one of the more potent sources of disturbance. The variance in real exchange rates is illustrated in figure 36.1 which shows the (trade weighted movement) of the Deutsche mark and dollar over the period 1976 to August 1992. The monthly variance of these rates about the mean of 1.00 (i.e. if PPP holds true) is in the order of magnitude of 8% and the total band is given by the range (0.6, 1.4). These violations of PPP point to substantial disparities in prices in the real-goods markets. Clearly, in the absence of arbitrage between goods markets—an assumption which is eminently reasonable for labor and for sticky energy pricing—there is a value in investing in the option of where to produce.

2.1 A Simple Formulation: Costless Switching

The principal elements of our argument can be most clearly examined by modeling a simple example. Consider a firm which is evaluating a project to invest in two manufacturing plants—one in the U.S. and the other in Germany. The plants are identical in their technological characteristics and differ only in the prices (evaluated in dollars) of the local inputs. The firm carries redundant production capacity, so that total demand, which is known and nonstochastic, can be met with either plant. (This formulation also accommodates the case where only part of the production is shifted in response to changing exchange rates.) The product of the firm is priced in a world market, say in U.S. dollars, and fluctuations of the DM/$ exchange rate do not affect the dollar market price.[7]

Suppose some input factors of production are also priced in the world market. Other inputs (e.g, labor) are priced in the local currency and their prices do not comply with the law of one price, due to institutional and government regulatory factors. Since short-term wage movements tend to be independent of short-term movements in exchange rates, the law of one price frequently is violated for the case of labor. Consequently, the wage rates in the two countries are equated not by the nominal exchange rate but by the *real* exchange rate:

$$w_\$ = \theta w_G \tag{1}$$

where $w_\$$ is the wage rate in the U.S. expressed in \$, $w_G = w_M S(\$/M)$ is the dollar value of the wage rate in Germany, w_M is the German wage rate in Deutsche marks, $S(\$/M)$ is the nominal exchange rate, and θ is the effective *real* exchange rate (i.e., deviation from the law of one price). In such a world, if the firm could shift its production between the two plants, the production location will be determined by the relative price of the locally sourced input. In addition, taxes (subsidies), tariffs, trade and financial barriers, and transportation costs can affect the dollar value of the locally-sourced input.

2.2 Modelling Uncertainty

The option value to switch production can be affected by a number of sources of uncertainty, including labor unrest, government policies or threats, or local suppliers' demands. Clearly, however, one of the most important sources of uncertainty, as suggested by figure 36.1, is the volatility of the exchange rate. For simplicity, we let uncertainty in the model only arise from the real exchange rate. It is important to note that this assumption eliminates other relevant uncertainties facing the firm, and, thus, underestimates the total value of the option to switch.

In order to elucidate the insights of our model, we choose a discrete time specification for the real exchange rate which is affected by factors beyond the control of the firm.[8] Hence, the firm faces an exogenous stochastic process that affects its production decision. It is reasonable to assume that the stochastic process is one where θ tends to revert towards its equilibrium value, $\bar{\bar{\theta}}$. In this context, we can think of the mean reverting property of the real exchange rate as arising from the goods market equilibrium conditions that motivate purchasing power parity. In fact, models of overshooting exchange rates implicitly assume that the real exchange rate tends to revert back towards its long-term purchasing power parity, i.e., $\bar{\bar{\theta}} = 1$.[9]

With increasing volatility in the foreign exchange markets, the probability of deviating from equilibrium becomes greater. When the real exchange rate (θ) is greater than one, it is cheaper to produce in Germany. However, as discussed below, when switching is costly, the decision rule is not simply to switch when the threshold of $\bar{\bar{\theta}}$ is crossed.

The discrete-time mean reverting stochastic process for the real exchange rate can be written as

$$\Delta\theta_t = \lambda(\bar{\bar{\theta}} - \theta_t)\Delta t + \sigma\theta_t\Delta Z_\theta \tag{2}$$

where ΔZ_θ are the increments of a discrete-time Wiener process and are normally distributed with mean 0 and variance Δt, $\sigma\theta_t$ is the standard deviation of θ per unit of time, and λ is the mean reverting parameter. Randomness is introduced via the ΔZ term. The parameter λ acts as an elastic force which serves to bring the price indices in the two countries towards parity. For example, when $\lambda = 1$, any random shock which affects the real exchange rate would be corrected (i.e., purchasing power parity is restored) within one period. For $\lambda < 1$, only partial adjustment will take place during that period.

It should be clear that the parameter values depend on the particular currency and must be scaled to adjust for the chosen length of the unit time period. For example, if the PPP disparities are corrected by 50% in one month, it will be corrected by 0.875 in three months. Since the variance of ΔZ_θ is linear in Δt, the estimated σ varies with the square root of the time interval.

2.3 The Relative Cost Function

Under our assumption that the output price is set in the world market in dollars, the production decision will be based entirely on the lower cost alternative. Suppose the plant in the U.S. is facing input prices $P_\$$ (a vector of input prices), the minimum cost of producing one unit of output within a time interval Δt is given by the unit *dollar* cost function $\psi^\$ = \psi(P_\$)$. Furthermore, since the technologies are identical, the unit *dollar* cost function of the plant in Germany must be $\psi^G = \psi(P_G\theta(\$/M))$, where P_G is input price vector faced by the German plant and is expressed in U.S. dollars. Since by definition $\psi(\cdot)$ is homogeneous of degree 1 in prices, $\psi(P_G) = \psi(\theta P_\$) = \theta\psi(P_\$)$.

The advantage of focusing on cost functions is to isolate the relationship between the two relevant parameters (i.e., λ and σ) in our model, since, by assumption, other outputs are not affected by the real exchange rate and revenues are held constant. Notice that when $\theta < 1$, $\psi^{\$} > \psi^{G}$, making the firm choose to produce in Germany; when $\theta > 1$, $\psi^{\$} < \psi^{G}$ and the firm will produce in the U.S. Hence it is the relative cost of production that determines the production location choice.

Without loss of generality, we normalize the costs of the U.S. plant as one: $\psi(P_{\$}) = 1$. If *all* input prices are locally determined then the dollar value of the German costs equals

$$\psi^{G}(\theta) = \psi(\theta P_{\$})/\psi(P_{\$}) = \theta.$$

In general, when only some of the input factors are locally priced the normalized cost function of German production can be expressed as $\psi^{G}(\theta)$.

3   Value of Flexibility

Given the above macro and microeconomic description, the option value of flexibility can be solved as a dynamic program. To be evaluated are the stream of costs from the plants each with an economic life of T periods of length Δt. At the beginning of a period, the firm knows with certainty the realized values of all relevant variables, including the real exchange rate θ, for that period.

If switching between locations is costless, then the time T present value of the costs under the flexible production arrangement obtained by choosing the location with the minimum costs over the last time period is

$$\mathscr{F}(\theta_T) = \min[1, \psi^{G}(\theta_{T-1})]. \tag{3}$$

At any previous time t, the value of the project will be the sum of costs from the optimal operation in the period beginning at time t and the (minimized) value function at time $t+1$. By this logic, we arrive at the following recursive equation for $\mathscr{F}(\theta_t)$:

$$\mathscr{F}(\theta_t) = \min[1, \psi^{G}(\theta_t)] + \rho E_t \mathscr{F}(\theta_{t+1}), \quad t = 0, \dots, T, \tag{4}$$

where E_t is the expectations operator conditional on information at time t and ρ is the one-period risk-free discount factor.[10] This recursive system of equations states the fundamental proposition in our model. It expresses the value of the project as the discounted flow of a temporal series of options.[11]

3.1 When Switching Is Costly

In practice, it is costly to switch between plants due to costs associated with shutdowns and startups, labor contracting, and managerial time commitments. If the decision to switch production takes into account the costs of switching multiple times over the life of the plants, the switching decision becomes also a function of the current mode of operation. Compared to the costless case, cost differences must move sufficiently to justify switching production. We denote the cost to switch from location i to j, as κ_{ij}. When the U.S. is defined as location 1 and Germany as location 2, κ_{12} is the cost of switching manufacturing from the U.S. to Germany.

This problem is more complex than the previous one, as it involves solving a compound option where the value function depends on the operating location chosen during the previous period. For example, if the firm operated at location 1 during the period $t-1$, then the value function at t is given by

$$\mathscr{F}(\theta_t, 1) = \min\left\{ \underbrace{[1 + \rho E_t \mathscr{F}(\theta_{t+1}, 1)]}_{\text{cost of using location 1}}, \quad \underbrace{[-\kappa_{12} + \psi^G(\theta_t) + \rho E_t F(\theta_{t+1}, 2)]}_{\text{cost if switch to location 2}} \right\} \tag{5}$$

where $\mathscr{F}(\theta_t, l)$ is the value of the flexible project at time t (when θ_t is realized) when the location l was in operation during the period $t-1$. The first argument of the minimum operator is the cost if the firm chooses to use location 1 for the period beginning at time t, and is computed in a manner similar to Equation (6). The second argument of the minimum operator gives the cost when the firm switches to employ location 2 and incurs a cost κ_{12}.

Similarly, the value of the project when operating in location 2 during the previous period is

$$\mathscr{F}(\theta_t, 2) = \min\left\{ \underbrace{[1 - \kappa_{21} + \rho E_t \mathscr{F}(\theta_{t+1}, 1)]}_{\text{cost if switch to location 1}}, \quad \underbrace{[\psi^G(\theta_t) + \rho E_t \mathscr{F}(\theta_{t+1}, 2)]}_{\text{cost of using location 2}} \right\}. \tag{6}$$

Another way to think about the problem of coordinating two plants located in different countries is to consider what are the optimal exchange rates at which production is shifted. If switching costs are zero (i.e., $\kappa_{12} = \kappa_{21} = 0$), then the optimal exchange rate would be independent of the current operating mode. No matter, then, if Equation (5) or (6) were to govern the value of the project, the timing of switching between the two plants would occur at the same optimal exchange rate. At this threshold exchange rate, the value of the two cost functions are identical.[12]

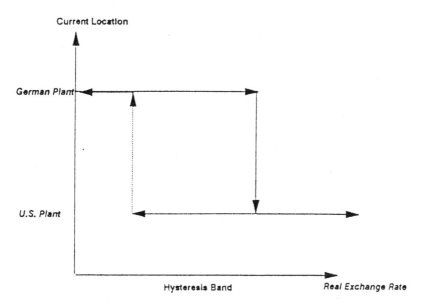

Figure 36.2
Hysteresis and real exchange rates

However, when costs are incurred, the boundary conditions are not the same. These costs cause the threshold exchange rates for shifting production to deviate from the break-even rate for costless switching.

If it were not for switching costs, the solution to the optimization problem would be simple: choose in each period the location l that maximizes $\psi^l(\theta_t)$ in that period. However, switching costs make a forward-looking analysis necessary. A firm may decline to switch locations if the possibility of a reversal in the relative cost advantage due to subsequent exchange rate movements is high. The probability distribution of *future* real exchange rates affects the *current* choice of technology. This band of inaction is commonly called a *condition of hysteresis*. In figure 36.2, we provide a stylized representation of hysteresis in production switching between two locations. Except for a few degenerate processes, this band widens with the degree of uncertainty and switching costs.[13]

3.2   Global Sourcing: The General Formulation

In general, when there is a set $\mathscr{L} = \{1, \ldots, L\}$ possible production locations with associated cost functions ψ^l, the valuation equations can be written as

$$\mathscr{F}(\theta_t, l) = \min_{m \in \mathscr{L}}[-\kappa_{l,m} + \psi^m(\theta_t) + \rho E_t \mathscr{F}(\theta_{t+1}, m)], \quad l \in \mathscr{L}. \tag{7}$$

Parenthetically, the model becomes intractable for multiple-exchange rate processes, but it should be recalled that since most currencies are pegged to the dollar, ECU, or yen, the model can be reduced to considering two exchange rates.[14]

Neglecting transportation and factor cost differentials, the intuitive solution to this more generalized problem is to choose to locate a plant in a country whose exchange rate is the most volatile. Given plants in $n-1$ countries, the selection of a new site will be influenced by its correlation with the portfolio of current and potential operating locations as well as volatilities. The lower the correlation, the greater the contribution to overall volatility and to increasing the value of the underlying options. In this sense, correlations matter: pure volatility contributes directly to increase the project values.

Differences among firms in the covariance structure of the cost movements of their international plant locations will influence competitive interactions among multinational corporations in a nontrivial way. Much of the anecdotal discussion of the effects of exchange rates on Japanese and American competitors is a reflection of this influence. A more complete rendering of the influence of exchange rates on the competition among international firms requires a specification of pricing and production decisions as dependent on exchange rates and competitors' responses.[15] Other variations of this model include differences in the technology, uncertainty arising from more than one source, restrictions imposed by host governments on some factor use, transportation costs, and multiple-product manufacturing strategies. Each of these modifications complicates the implementation of the above model, but the fundamental results are conceptually similar to the simple version above.

4   A Numerical Example

Insight into the significance of the option value to switch can be gained by a numerical analysis. Through the numerical solutions, the magnitude of the value in across-border coordination is analyzed by varying the parameter values of the exchange rate variance and adjustment coefficient. The major issues in specifying the simulations is to characterize the technologies (cost functions), the nature of uncertainty, and the associated parameter values.

For the purpose of identifying the contribution of changes in exchange rate variance to the option value, we specify a linear cost function of the form $\psi(\theta) = -\alpha + \beta\theta$, where α and β are constant coefficients (i.e., Leontief functional form).

More complex functional specifications, such as scale economies and carrying-costs of excess capacity, would give essentially the same results, though dampened in magnitude. (Some of the dampening effect is captured in our switching costs parametrization.) Since total demand is treated as constant, revenues are not affected by switching. Thus, the cost side is driving the location choice.

When we use a characterization of uncertainty such as the mean reverting process given by Equation (2) the expectations must be computed numerically. We do so by discreting the state space.[16] Suppose at any time t, θ_t can only take one of M discrete values, $\theta^1, \theta^2, \ldots, \theta^M$ (say between 0.5 and 1.5). If we observe θ_t to be θ^i (e.g., $\theta_t = 0.95$), then the probability $\theta_{t+1} = \theta^j$ (e.g., $\theta_{t+1} = 1.05$) is the transition probability from state i to j which we denote by p_{ij}.[17]

In this discrete state-space we can rewrite Equation (7) as

$$\mathcal{F}(\theta_t = \theta^j, l) = \min_{m \in \mathcal{L}} \left[-\kappa_{l,m} + \psi^m(\theta^j) + \rho \sum_{i=1}^{M} \mathcal{F}(\theta_{t+1} = \theta^i, m) p_{j,i} \right]. \tag{8}$$

The parameter values consist of five factors: time horizon, duration of the intervals during which switching is not possible, switching costs, variance of the real exchange rate (σ), and the adjustment coefficient (λ). The first three factors are fixed at 20 years, quarterly intervals, and 2.5% of mean (i.e., when $\theta = 1$) quarterly costs per switch for all the simulations.[18] Switching costs capture expenses associated with adjusting labor schedules, inventory, and start-up.

Because our central focus is on the effect of the real exchange rate variance and, though less so, the PPP adjustment coefficient, we vary σ and λ over simulations. In the initial runs, we set $\lambda = 0.05$, and let σ vary from 5% to 10% (base case) and 20%. These exchange rate variances are not substantially different from the estimated variances given by figure 36.1. In the second set of simulations, we let the adjustment coefficient vary from 5% to 20%, with σ set to 10%.[19]

4.1   Discussion of Principal Results

The simulations provide an opportunity to investigate the incremental profitability of production shifting to changes in the parameters, especially that of the real exchange rate variance. Figure 36.2 provides a graphical illustration of the values of flexibility for three values of volatility: $\sigma = 5\%$, 10% and 20%. (λ is held at 5%.) As is apparent, the incremental profitability is far from insignificant. Of particular interest is the relationship of the expected value of flexibility given the initial real exchange rate, with the greatest percent increase in profitability expected when θ is close to one.

Table 36.2
Sensitivity of value of flexibility to parameter changes

	$\sigma = 0.05$	$\sigma = 0.10$	$\sigma = 0.20$
$\lambda = 0.05$	5.58%	11.09%	17.45%
$\lambda = 0.10$		8.34%	
$\lambda = 0.20$		5.99%	

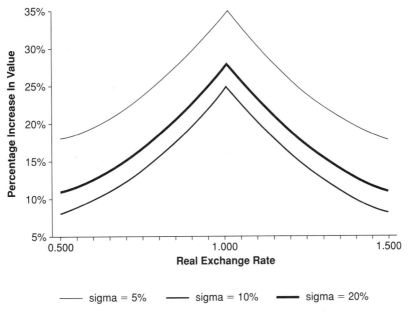

Figure 36.3
Value of flexibility

The explanation of these peaks is transparent on reflection. Since the likelihood of a change in the real exchange rate crossing the boundary (of one) is greatest when the current rate is close to one, the value of the option must also reach a minimum at this boundary. To borrow from the terminology of financial option markets, the option to switch is deepest in the money when $\theta = 1$. Conversely, as the deviation from PPP increases (i.e., the real exchange rate moves away from 1), the likelihood of a boundary crossing is reduced.

A more precise illustration of the sensitivity of the value of the option to switch production is given in table 36.2. The center column gives the numerical values of the percentage increase in profitability shown by figure 36.3. At the mean exchange rate

($\theta = 1$), the value of flexibility increases from about 5.5% when $\sigma = 5\%$ to 17.5% when $\sigma = 20\%$. Having the flexibility to move production to locations with lower input prices has the effect of insuring against detrimental movements of the real exchange rate. Increased exchange rate volatility will increase the upside benefits while the insurance feature of value derived from location flexibility is greater in periods of volatile exchange rates. The value of multinationality increases with greater volatility.

These numerical results give a simple static decision rule. The project, building the second plant, should be undertaken if the increased value due to flexibility is greater than the required initial investment.

4.2   Extension: Hysteresis and Within-country Options

So far, we have analyzed the value of multinationality as arising from the across-country coordination of production. This development has been couched in the context of a *vertical* direct investment decision, that is, whether to build one or two plants. Clearly, there are also implications for the economics of the "horizontal" direct investment whereby a plant is built in a country to support local sales in that market. The horizontal investment decision can be seen as part of a well-documented sequence by which a firm expands from exporting to investing in local production.[20] The sequence by which a firm expands from exports to local investment is, conceptually, a product of the exercise of a *within-country* option established by the investments made in country-specific goodwill and experience to support exports.

In this wider context, the band of inaction is generated by two components of hysteresis. We call the component associated with switching costs between plants in two locations "production hysteresis." (See the discussion in §3.1.) There is also a hysteresis effect resulting from the more fundamental decision whether or not to invest in goodwill (e.g., brand labels and sales force recruitment) to serve a market through exports; these effects have been discussed in Dixit (1989a), Baldwin and Krugman (1989), and Dumas (1988). We call this component "export hysteresis."

While the investment in goodwill leads to a condition of hysteresis, it leads to increase the likelihood that the initial export activity will eventually be followed by investments in manufacturing. These observations imply that any subsequent investment can benefit from the initial establishment of goodwill. The accumulation of goodwill generates what Myers (1977) first called a growth option, that is, it serves as a platform by which a firm expands in the future.

Growth options are not acquired per se by the establishment of multinational investments; they represent opportunities gained by investing in a current activity, no matter if this investment is made by a domestic or international firm. However, they

Table 36.3
Threshold values of real exchange rate

	Threshold θ
Naive investment	1.0
First entry (when entry can be delayed)	1.5
Subsequent switch to German plant	0.975
Exit from German market	0.575

are important in underscoring the likelihood that foreign investors will persist in a market once they have initially entered. As general experience and goodwill are gained, the cost of launching new products in the foreign market is reduced. The combination of hysteresis, along with the acquisition of growth options, underscore the argument that the initial entry into a country increases the likelihood of subsequent investments.

Some insight into this pattern can be gained from table 36.3, which provides the threshold exchange rates for entry for the first time and subsequent entries. Assuming that later products can enjoy the initial investment in goodwill, then subsequent products can be introduced at a significantly lower critical exchange rate than the case when exporting began. (These values are estimated by assuming the same production function for the initial and subsequent products.) In this sense, the initial investment establishes a growth option for future product entries.

5   Heuristic Rules and Operating Procedures

An important objection to the above model is the question of whether labor can be treated as variable. However, the benefits of production shifting rely less on the feasibility of layoffs than on rules for labor flexibility. It is important to recall that direct labor costs are an increasingly insignificant proportion of total production costs (Johnson and Kaplan 1987). The main cost drivers are materials and energy, the prices of which are determined by domestic market forces and government regulations. A more general characterization is to treat W as a vector of those inputs that are priced locally in the country where the plant is located.

Along these lines, an alternative, and more appropriate, way to understand the above model is to treat the investment in two countries as the creation of excess capacity in the overall system. Plants are never closed. Rather, what is shifted is overtime production. Even if the value of production shifting is realized by savings from material and energy usage, labor policy still remains important in terms of creating flexible overtime.

These considerations raise the general question whether this operating flexibility is discretionary. One way to address this question is to consider whether the effect of costs of operating flexibility, e.g., establishing contracts for flexible overtime, on the hysteresis band eliminates the plausibility of switching.[21] But another way to understand this issue is by focusing on the often overlooked question of whether managers have the information and institutional flexibility to identify and exercise these options. It is this avenue we explore by analyzing internal accounting practices, and pricing.

5.1   Internal Accounting Practices

What should be the control system appropriate to the coordination of cross-border activities in response to fluctuating exchange rates? Because floating exchange rates only were introduced in the mid-1970s, it is possible by reviewing a few empirical and prescriptive studies to trace how evaluation systems have developed to provide information, and incentives, for across-border coordination. What is striking is how the heuristic rules of international accountability have changed to meet the environmental pressures of multinational competition and coordination.

The canonical problem in international performance evaluation of foreign subsidiaries is how to treat the effects of exchange rate movements on accounting variances. This problem can be most simply stated as the choice of exchange rate values by which to budget and to monitor performance. Between the time of budgeting and monitoring, exchange rates move. The control problem is what exchange rate should be applied and who should be held accountable for exchange rate effects. Clearly, if the control system removes the effect of exchange rates on operating decisions and results, there is no mechanism by which to trigger the shifting of production.

The seminal prescriptive analysis of this problem was given by Lessard and Lorange (1977). Table 36.4, taken from their article, depicts the combinations of three exchange rates that can be used for control purposes: the spot exchange at the

Table 36.4
Possible combinations of exchange rates in the control process

Rate used for determining budget	Rate used to track performance relative to budget		
	Actual at time of budget	Projected at time of budget	Actual at end of period
Actual at time of budget	A-1	A-2	A-3
Projected at time of budget	P-1	P-2	P-3
Actual at end of period (through updating)	E-1	E-2	E-3

Source: Lessard and Lorange (1977)

time of budgeting, the spot exchange rate at the time of tracking performance, or some kind of forward rate determined at the time of budgeting. Four cells are crossed out as they represent illogical combinations.

Each combination carries particular behavioral consequences. For example, for any combination where the same rate is used, the foreign subsidiary bears no risk for the effect of exchange rate movements. When the rates for budgeting and tracking differ, the local subsidiary bears the full risk of exchange rate movements. In this latter case, there is an incentive for the local subsidiary to hedge. Even if not permitted to do so by engaging in financial positions, it may do so by building up inventory or by insisting on local manufacture to support local sales.

The combination that Lessard and Lorange prescribed was the use of forward rates for budgeting and tracking. In this case, the subsidiary and the central controller's office have the incentive to establish accurate forward rates for purposes of budgeting, with the spot rate at the time of tracking or the forward used for evaluation. Empirical studies showed that one of these two combinations tended to prevail during the 1970s. (See, for example, Business International 1976).

It is interesting to note the unstated assumptions of this approach. In the Lessard and Lorange formulation which represented best practice at the time, the control problem was headquarters assessing the performance of a subsidiary. In other words, the control problem was perceived as "dyadic," that is, involving only two players. The effect of the ability to coordinate production across borders is not built into the performance evaluation.

In addition, the competitive effects of exchange rates were largely neglected. This neglect is permissible as long as the international competition is American, and hence all competitors are exposed to the same exchange rate. However, as competition becomes more multinational in character, exchange rates carry implications for prices and quantities.[22]

But this innovation to use forward rates to budget and to track performance entails a number of assumptions that were not suited to the competitive environment of the 1980s. As documented initially by Doz (1978), the internationalization of markets began to lead to the rationalization of production into global plants. Similarly, Flaherty (1986) has described global sourcing policies as the standardization of manufacturing across geographically-dispersed plants. In short, the coordination of global manufacturing has increasingly become part of the competitive strategy of the firm (Cohen et al. 1989).

The internal sourcing of production as part of a coordinated international strategy conflicts with the assumptions of the original Lessard/Lorange proposals. The evaluation problem is no longer the dyadic control by headquarters of each subsidiary.

Rather, the transfers across subsidiaries require that the evaluation of performance be conceived in the context of a network with the flexibility to shift production in response to exchange rates. The decision to transfer production from one country will depress the operating results of that subsidiary, but to the gain of operations elsewhere. Sterilizing operating results from exchange rates removes the incentive to coordinate production multinationally.

Control within a network requires minimally two related changes, as recognized in the subsequent writings of Lessard. First, since the advantage of multinational shifting is to schedule production where real costs are minimized, the selection of the appropriate exchange rate is much more complicated. One possibility is to budget and track at the PPP rate (Stewart 1983). But while this rate will give a more accurate appraisal over longer periods of time, it fails to provide the incentives for operating flexibility.

The recommendation, made by Lessard and Sharp (1984) and Jacque and Lorange (1984), is to establish the PPP rate as the benchmark, but to work out the implications of deviations from these rates on operating results. Thus, the second change proposed by Lessard and Sharp is to develop, at least implicitly, a set of contingent budgets to be used for tracking depending on the actually-realized exchange rate. These contingent budgets incorporate, for example, the expectation that production will be shifted contingent on the real exchange rate that prevailed during the period under evaluation. If operating flexibility is to be built on the exercise of discretionary options, then the control system must itself build in the flexibility in the choice of benchmarks by which to evaluate operating results.[23]

5.2 Market and Transfer Pricing

Despite the substantial impact of exchange rates on operating performance, the diffusion of new evaluation techniques has been slow. Moreover, the internal performance evaluation methods clearly influence other decisions, such as pricing. If effects of exchange rates on comparing operating costs across subsidiaries are ignored, then the tendency will be to use accounting procedures and estimates based on the home market.

The relationship between control systems and pricing has been documented in a number of studies. In his field research, Sharp (1987) found that a number of American multinational operations continued to price by adding a mark-up to the American unit costs. While these practices made sense when the competition was American and all competitors were following similar pricing policies, the persistence of these pricing heuristics led, Sharp found, to poorer performance for the firms facing multinational competition.

These practices show up in a few popular MBA teaching cases. Caterpillar Tractor is described as using cost-plus pricing rules, with the cost estimates derived from U.S. plant experiences. "Because the company used a uniform dollar pricing policy, dealers all over the world were billed in dollars, irrespective of the origin of the machines. The prices were often based on U.S. manufacturing cost, and when the dollar was strong, the company had to engage in price-cutting" (Caterpillar Tractor Co., Harvard Business School 1985). In the mid-1980s, it switched to competitive pricing, as Komatsu began to make severe in-roads in the United States and elsewhere.

Matsushita, interestingly, seems to be following a similar pricing rule. "In general," it is noted in the case, "the (Japanese) plant was expected to absorb the effect of any changes in its costs during the year, while the subsidiary was expected to deal with changes in market conditions *without modifying the transfer price*" (Matsushita Electric Industrial Company, Ltd., Insead-Harvard 1987). Where Japanese companies face foreign competition, prices tend to be set to-the-market; where they face only Japanese competitors, pricing tends to be set on the basis of Japanese costs, much like the earlier experience of American multinationals (Marston 1990). The pricing and control policies of Matsushita reflect their dominant position in their major market, VCRs, which is only challenged by other Japanese competitors. In this respect, these policies mirror American practices of the 1970s when world competition was more U.S. based.

In summary, the pricing rules and evaluation systems tend to reflect the degree of multinationality in the competitive environment and of the firm. As corporations establish foreign subsidiaries and as they face competition from competitors from many countries, the potential to gain an advantage through international coordination can be achieved only through the development of the appropriate systems of evaluation and operating heuristics. The ownership of the option to shift production is of little value if the managerial information is poor, if the incentives are tied to the wrong benchmarks, and if pricing rules do not capture the value of the flexibility to manufacture at the lowest cost site. It is not surprising, consequently, that a number of firms in a recent survey reported a break with traditional practice by denominating transfer prices in the source country currency (Business International 1990).

6 Conclusions

The above model has analyzed the benefits of multinationality as the ownership of dispersed international operations that provide valuable operating flexibility through multinational coordination. As an illustration, we have used the example of production shifting and global manufacturing. For this particular example of multinationality, there remains a number of areas requiring further work. One area is the important question of whether contracts can be designed to provide these benefits. It may well be possible, as appears in the case in the international apparel industry, to write short-term contracts that allow the buying firms to switch suppliers based upon changes in costs and exchange rates. Another area requiring development is a fuller comparison against other alternatives, such as flexible manufacturing systems, that might be used to change inputs or market segments in response to cost shocks.[24]

Despite the simplicity of the above model of production shifting, it captures the importance of the element of flexibility within a network of subsidiaries. It is this element of flexibility that underlies the recent management treatment of the multinational firm as consisting of the ability to exercise the option to coordinate and transfer resources internationally.[25] This ability is not one simply of insurance through the buffering of the firm against uncertainty. Rather, it is the expression of why multinationality, as a result of these options, can be a source of value due to uncertainty.

The formal model presented above allows an abstract and general format by which to frame the management discussion on the organization and practice of the multinational corporation. This framework of the option value of multinationality, we are aware, can be generalized to cover other applications, such as acquisitions, investments in new skills and knowledge, and platforms into new technologies. But the option application to multinationality is especially apt, because the high variance of international markets increases the value of operating flexibility and global coordination. Despite the popular notion of the riskiness of international markets, it is this uncertainty that drives the opportunities available to the firm that it is multinational, as opposed to only domestic, in its investments and operations.

Appendix A: Calculating Expectations

In order to calculate the expectations in Equation (7) we must obtain the transition probability distributions associated with each realization of θ_t. Merton (1982) shows that as long as the state variable θ_t evolves continuously, we may act as though over short time intervals it has a normal distribution. (The mean and variance of that distribution, however, may change over time. Therefore, over longer time periods, the ratio θ_t/θ_0 may be quite unlike a normal distribution. For example, if we let the mean change in θ_t be proportional to the level of θ_t in each period, then θ_t/θ_0 will be log-normally distributed, even if the distribution of changes in each small time period is approximately normal.) Therefore, for the process described in Equation (2) we assume that $\Delta\theta_t$ over time period Δt is distributed normally, with mean $\lambda(\bar{\bar{\theta}} - \theta_t)\Delta t$ and variance $\sigma^2\theta_t^2\Delta t$.

Next we discretize the range of possible values of θ_t. We assume that θ_t may take one of S possible values, θ^i for $i \in \mathscr{S}$, $\mathscr{S} = \{1, \ldots, S\}$.[26] Given a value of θ_t^i, the probability of θ_{t+1}^j in the next period depends on the difference $j - i$. Hence, as the absolute value of $j - i$ increases, the probability falls in accordance with the normal distribution.

Consistent with the discrete version of the normal distribution with parameters $N(\lambda(\bar{\bar{\theta}} - \theta_t)\Delta t, \sigma^2 \theta_t^2 \Delta t)$, a transition from state i to j occurs with probability

$$p_{ij} = \Phi\left[\frac{-\lambda(\bar{\bar{\theta}} - \theta^i)\Delta t + (j - i + (1/2))\Delta\theta}{\sigma\theta^i\sqrt{\Delta t}}\right] - \Phi\left[\frac{-\lambda(\bar{\bar{\theta}} - \theta^i)\Delta t + (j - i - (1/2))\Delta\theta}{\sigma\theta^i\sqrt{\Delta t}}\right] \quad (9)$$

where $\Phi[\cdot]$ is the cumulative standard normal distribution and the step size $\Delta\theta = \theta^{i+1} - \theta^i$, $\forall i \in \mathscr{S}$.

Special care must be taken with the end points θ^1 and θ^S. Lumping all exterior values to the boundary we obtain the transition probabilities

$$p_{is} = 1 - \Phi\left[\frac{-\lambda(\bar{\bar{\theta}} - \theta^i)\Delta t + (S - i + (1/2))\Delta\theta}{\sigma\theta^i\sqrt{\Delta t}}\right], \quad (10)$$

$$p_{si} = \Phi\left[\frac{-\lambda(\bar{\bar{\theta}} - \theta^i)\Delta t + (1 - i + (1/2))\Delta\theta}{\sigma\theta^i\sqrt{\Delta t}}\right]. \quad (11)$$

Using Equations (9)–(11), it is easy to take the necessary expectations in Equation (8). Given the current value of θ_t, we may now calculate the probability associated with any value of θ_{t+1}. We therefore use these probabilities to calculate the expected value of $\mathscr{F}(\theta_{t+1}, m, t + 1)$ as we proceed along the backward solution.

Appendix B: A Continuous-time Formulation

In the main body of the paper, for the purpose of exposition, we modeled the decision to switch as a discrete-time dynamic program. This treatment is in accordance with the discrete-time nature of production scheduling. It also allows greater transparency of the economics of the switching decision.

In this appendix we analyze the general model of flexibility when the stochastic variable follows a lognormal process.[27] We then apply it to study the problems of multinational coordination of production. For a special case we derive closed-form solutions.

Consider a single underlying stochastic state variable θ which summarizes the uncertainty faced by the firm, and that θ follows geometric Brownian motion:

$$d\theta_t/\theta_t = \alpha_\theta \, dt + \sigma_\theta \, dZ_\theta \quad (12)$$

where dZ_θ is a standard Wiener process. This assumption is strong, but necessary for the derivation of the analytical solution.

The general problem we consider is the following: a firm has an investment opportunity which can be undertaken at a cost F. If undertaken, it has a continuous payoff rate of $\psi(\theta_t, t)$. In the interim, there is a cash flow $\pi(\theta_t)$ which is no longer received once payoff $\psi(\theta)$ is obtained. Again for the sake of an analytical solution we assume that the investment opportunity is infinitely lived. We ask two questions: (a) When should the firm pay the fixed cost F? (b) What is the value of the option to invest $\psi(\theta)$?

We assume that the investment option is valued and exercised by a firm that is owned by risk-averse, well-diversified investors. The equilibrium argument in Cox et al. (1985) implies that the option to acquire ψ has a value V which obeys the partial differential equation

$$\pi(\theta_t, t) = rV(\theta_t, t) + V_t(\theta_t, t) + (r - \delta)\theta_t V_\theta(\theta, t) + \tfrac{1}{2}\sigma^2\theta_t^2 V_{\theta\theta}(\theta, t) = 0 \quad (13)$$

where subscripts on $V_t = \partial V/\partial t$, $V_\theta = \partial V/\partial\theta$, $V_{\theta\theta} = \partial^2 V/\partial\theta^2$, and r is the risk-free rate of interest. Assume that $\pi(\theta)$ and $\psi(\theta)$ both have the form

$$a_i + b_i\theta^{c_i}, \quad i = \pi, \psi. \quad (14)$$

The parameter δ measures the extent to which α_θ, the expected return on an asset with price θ, is below the required rate of return on an asset with the same risk as θ. Thus, for example, suppose that a stock with price P follows the process

$$dP_t/P_t = \bar{\alpha}\,dt + \sigma_p\,dZ_\theta. \tag{15}$$

Notice that the stochastic term in (15) is the same as that in (12). If the stock has an expected rate of return of $\bar{\alpha}$, this is the *required* rate of return for an asset with the same risk as θ. We define

$$\delta = \bar{\alpha} - \alpha_\theta, \tag{16}$$

i.e., δ measures the extent to which the actual expected rate of return on θ falls below the required rate of return on an asset with the same risk. δ can be defined in this way whatever the form of the equilibrium asset pricing equation, as long as it is based on mean-variance efficiency.

The solution to (13) then has the form

$$V(\theta_t, t) = \gamma_1 \theta^{\varepsilon_1} + \gamma_2 \theta^{\varepsilon_2} + \frac{\alpha_\pi}{r} + \frac{\beta_\pi}{r - \delta_\pi} \theta^{c_\pi} \tag{17}$$

where

$$\delta_\pi = c_\pi(r - \delta) + \tfrac{1}{2}c_\pi(c_\pi - 1)\sigma_\theta^2,$$

$$\varepsilon_1 = \left[\frac{1}{2} - \frac{r - \delta}{\sigma_\theta^2}\right] + \left[\left(\frac{1}{2} - \frac{r - \delta}{\sigma_\theta^2}\right)^2 + \frac{2r}{\sigma_\theta^2}\right]^{1/2} > 0,$$

$$\varepsilon_2 = \left[\frac{1}{2} - \frac{r - \delta}{\sigma_\theta^2}\right] - \left[\left(\frac{1}{2} - \frac{r - \delta}{\sigma_\theta^2}\right)^2 + \frac{2r}{\sigma_\theta^2}\right]^{1/2} < 0.$$

If we let θ^* denote the value at which it is optimal to act, then the following free boundary condition must be satisfied:

$$V(\theta^*) = \mathrm{PV}[\psi(\theta^*)] - F, \tag{18}$$

where $\mathrm{PV}[\psi(\theta)]$ is the present value of an infinitely-lived stream of cash flow arriving at rate ψ. Furthermore, in order to ensure continuity and differentiability of V the derivatives of V and ψ with respect to θ must also be equal.

This is the Merton-Samuelson *high-contact* condition:[28]

$$V'(\theta^*) = \mathrm{PV}'[\psi(\theta^*)]. \tag{19}$$

B.1   An Example: Production Location Choice Problem

Here we will show how the above general model can be used to evaluate a flexible project consisting of plants in the U.S. and Germany. The relevant stochastic variable θ, is the real exchange rate which we assume follows the process in Equation (12).

Let $\psi(\theta_t)$ be the dollar value of the profit flow when producing in Germany and value of U.S. and $\pi(\theta_t)$ be the dollar profit flow when producing in the U.S. The cost of switching from U.S. to German production is k_1 and from German to U.S. production is k_2. Since the only relevant stochastic variable is θ the value of both production locations will be governed by the partial differential equation (PDE) in Equation (13).

Suppose $V(\theta_t, t)$ and $W(\theta_t, t)$ are the values of the U.S. and German production, respectively. Let $\bar{\theta}$ and $\underline{\theta}$ be the critical real exchange rates at which the firm switches from U.S. to German plant and vice versa. At these free boundaries the firm will be indifferent between continuing at the current operating mode and incurring the switching cost to change the production location, i.e.,

$$V(\bar{\theta}) = -k_1 + W(\bar{\theta}),$$

$$V'(\bar{\theta}) = W'(\bar{\theta}),$$

$$W(\underline{\theta}) = -k_2 + V(\underline{\theta}),$$

$$W'(\underline{\theta}) = V'(\underline{\theta}).$$

Examining the limiting cases of $\theta \to 0$ and $\theta \to \infty$, we note that $V_\theta > 0$ and $W_\theta < 0$. Furthermore, since both V and W follows the PDE in (13), the solutions must be of the form

$$V(\theta_t, t) = \underbrace{\gamma_2 \theta^{\varepsilon_2}}_{\text{option to switch to U.S.}} + \underbrace{\frac{\alpha_\pi}{r} + \frac{\beta_\pi}{r - \delta_\pi} \theta^{c_\pi}}_{\text{value of fixed U.S. production}},$$

$$W(\theta_t, t) = \underbrace{\gamma_1 \theta^{\varepsilon_1}}_{\text{option to switch to Germany}} + \underbrace{\frac{\alpha_\psi}{r} + \frac{\beta_\psi}{r - \delta_\psi} \theta^{c_\psi}}_{\text{value of fixed German production}},$$

where γ_1, γ_2, $\bar{\theta}$, and $\underline{\theta}$ satisfy

$$\gamma_2 \bar{\theta}^{\varepsilon_2} + \frac{\alpha_\pi}{r} + \frac{\beta_\pi}{r - \delta_\pi} \bar{\theta}^{c_\pi} = -k_2 + \gamma_1 \bar{\theta}^{\varepsilon_1} + \frac{\alpha_\psi}{r} + \frac{\gamma_\psi}{r - \delta_\psi} \bar{\theta}^{c_\psi},$$

$$\gamma_2 \varepsilon_2 \bar{\theta}^{\varepsilon_2 - 1} + \frac{\beta_\pi c_\pi}{r - \delta_\pi} \bar{\theta}^{c_\pi - 1} = \gamma_1 \varepsilon_1 \bar{\theta}^{\varepsilon_1 - 1} + \frac{\beta_\psi c_\psi}{r - \delta_\psi} \bar{\theta}^{c_\psi - 1},$$

$$\gamma_1 \underline{\theta}^{\varepsilon_1} + \frac{\alpha_\psi}{r} + \frac{\beta_\psi}{r - \delta_\psi} \underline{\theta}^{c_\psi} = -k_1 + \gamma_2 \underline{\theta}^{\varepsilon_2} + \frac{\alpha_\pi}{r} + \frac{\beta_\pi}{r - \delta_\pi} \underline{\theta}^{c_\pi},$$

$$\gamma_1 \varepsilon_1 \underline{\theta}^{\varepsilon_1 - 1} + \frac{\beta_\psi c_\psi}{r - \delta_\psi} \underline{\theta}^{c_\psi - 1} = \gamma_2 \varepsilon_2 \underline{\theta}^{\varepsilon_2 - 1} + \frac{\beta_\pi c_\pi}{r - \delta_\pi} \underline{\theta}^{c_\pi - 1}. \tag{20}$$

These equations are linear in ε_i but nonlinear in $\underline{\theta}$ and $\bar{\theta}$.[29] The range $[\underline{\theta}, \bar{\theta}]$ forms the hysteresis band.

In search of analytical solutions we consider two special cases. First, consider the case when U.S. profits are normalized to 1 and the German plant has linear profits, i.e., $\pi(\theta, t) = 1$ and $\psi(\theta, t) = \theta_t$. The above nonlinear equations are now simply as follows:

$$\gamma_2 \bar{\theta}^{\varepsilon_2} + \frac{1}{r} = -k_2 + \gamma_1 \bar{\theta}^{\varepsilon_1} + \frac{\bar{\theta}}{r - \delta},$$

$$\gamma_2 \varepsilon_2 \bar{\theta}^{\varepsilon_2 - 1} = \gamma_1 \varepsilon_1 \bar{\theta}^{\varepsilon_1 - 1} + \frac{1}{r - \delta},$$

$$\gamma_1 \underline{\theta}^{\varepsilon_1} + \frac{\underline{\theta}}{r - \delta} = -k_1 + \gamma_2 \underline{\theta}^{\varepsilon_2} + \frac{1}{r},$$

$$\gamma_1 \varepsilon_1 \underline{\theta}^{\varepsilon_1 - 1} + \frac{1}{r - \delta} = \gamma_2 \varepsilon_2 \underline{\theta}^{\varepsilon_2 - 1}.$$

Now we have a simpler set of nonlinear equations to solve for the γ_i's and the threshold exchange rates. However, even these equations can not, in general, be solved in closed form. In the very special case, when $k_1 = k_2 = 0$ and $\delta = 0$, we get the obvious solution $\underline{\theta} = \bar{\theta} = 1$ and $\gamma_1 = \gamma_2 = 1/r(\varepsilon_1 - \varepsilon_2)$.

When $\alpha_\psi = 0$ and $c_\psi = b_\psi = 1$, and $a_\pi = b_\pi = c_\pi = 0$, i.e., θ is the cash flow from the export operation, then we can solve the equations in closed form. This is similar to the problems handled by Dixit (1989a) and McDonald and Siegel (1986).

B.2   When Real Exchange Rate Follows an Ornstein-Uhlembeck Process

The general continuous-time analog to the discrete-time stochastic process in Equation (2) is given by the Ornstein-Uhlembeck Process:

$$d\theta_t = (\alpha - \beta \ln \theta_t)\theta_t \, dt + \sigma \theta_t \, dZ \tag{21}$$

where dZ is a standard Wiener process. The PDE in (13) now becomes

$$\pi(\theta_t, t) - rV(\theta_t, t) + V_t(\theta_t, t) + (\alpha - \beta \ln \theta_t)\theta_t V_\theta(\theta, t) + \tfrac{1}{2}\sigma^2 \theta_t^2 V_{\theta\theta}(\theta_t, t) = 0. \tag{22}$$

This is equivalent to having a state-dependent δ in Equation (13). In general, analytic solutions are not available to this *PDE* and numerical solution techniques must be employed.

Acknowledgments

This research has been supported by a grant from the Reginald H. Jones Center and the Huntsman Center for Global Competitiveness at the Wharton School. We thank Bernard Dumas, Donald Lessard, and anonymous referees for helpful comments.

Notes

1. See Kogut (1983) for a discussion.

2. For an interesting case illustrating these kind of restrictions, see Badger (Belgium) N. V., Harvard Business School, 1981.

3. Of course, they carry substantial implications. For example, the predominant means of entering a foreign country is by acquisition, which represents an immediate way to gain brand label and distribution platforms for other products.

4. This diversification, because shareholders can achieve it more efficiently through capital markets, has empirically been shown to be of minor value to the multinational corporation. See Jacquillat and Solnik (1978).

5. This model has been expanded to explore critical exchange rates at which optimal exercise occurs (Kulatilaka and Kogut 1990). Huchzermeier (1990) and Cohen and Huchzermeier (1991) have embedded this model in the context of a richer formalization of the logistical and distribution network.

6. In this formulation marginal costs do not equal price at each point in time; rather profits fluctuate with the exchange rate. This condition need not be a violation of perfect competition in a dynamic setting; see Dixit (1989b).

7. To use the terminology of Flood and Lessard (1986), the currency habitat of the output product price in U.S. dollars.

8. In an Appendix we analyze the possibility of modeling uncertainty within a continuous-time framework. Analytic solutions can only be obtained for a very restrictive class of problems.

9. See, for example, Dornbusch (1976).

10. Cox et al. (1985) have shown that when θ is the price of a traded security or if does not contain systematic risk the appropriate discount rate is the risk-free rate. Furthermore, even when θ is not the price of a traded asset and when it contains systematic risk, a simple adjustment to the transition probabilities allows the use of risk-neutral discounting. See Hull (1989) for a good intuitive discussion of this point.

11. In order to solve this recursive system we must specify a stochastic process for θ, such as in Equation (2). Under certain very restrictive assumptions about the process we can obtain closed-form solutions for F. See Kulatilaka and Marcus (1988) where the option values are derived in closed form when θ follows geometric Brownian motion.

12. The equivalence of the two cost functions satisfies one of two boundary conditions; the other condition is smooth-pasting. See the Appendix for a discussion.

13. See Baldwin (1989), Dixit (1989) and Baldwin and Krugman (1989). It is important to note that the magnitude of the hysteresis band is time invariant only when the horizon is infinite. In a finite-time horizon problem, as the firm approaches the terminal time the band widens since the firm has a shorter time period to recoup the switching costs.

14. See Baillie and Bollerslev (1989) for an analysis of the common root in multiple-exchange rate movements.

15. For an exploration, see Dornbusch (1987).

16. See the appendix for details.

17. For stationary processes p_{ij} is time independent.

18. Quarterly intervals were suggested by discussions with plant managers and are longer, in fact, than those attributed to Japanese production planning. See Abegglen and Stalk (1985). We can very easily reduce the intervals and permit continuous switching. This situation can also be thought of as a way of endogenizing the switching intervals.

19. In the numerical simulations we restricted the possible range of θ values between 0.25 and 1.75. In order to avoid distortion from end-point approximations we only report the value of flexibility for the θ ranging from 0.5 to 1.5. Note that these bounds are close to those empirically estimated from figure 36.1, as reported earlier.

20. See Davidson (1980).

21. See Kulatilaka and Kogut (1990) for an analysis.

22. See Dornbusch (1987) and Flood and Lessard (1986) for a discussion.

23. A recent Business International (1989) publication showed that the most common current policy is to sterilize operating results of exchange rate effects, though a number of firms were reported to calculate exchange rate variances to evaluate the responses of subsidiaries.

24. For work on production flexibility as an option, see Fine and Freund (1990) and Kulatilaka (1987).

25. See Bartlett and Ghoshal (1989), Prahalad and Doz (1987), and Hedlund (1986).

26. The end values θ^1 and θ^S, and the number of discrete values (S) are chosen so that the desired accuracy to the continuous-time process is achieved.

27. This appendix draws from working notes of Nalin Kulatilaka and Robert McDonald.

28. It is also known as the *smooth-pasting* condition.

29. Note that in general we must solve this set of $2M$ nonlinear equations using numerical techniques.

References

Abegglen, James C. and George Stalk, *Kaisha, The Japanese Corporation*, Free Press, New York, 1985.

Badger, (Belgium) N. V., Harvard Business School, Boston (9-481-127), 1981.

Baillie, Richard T. and Tim Bollerslev, "Common Stochastic Trends in a System of Exchange Rates," *J. Finance*, 44 (1989), 167–180.

Baldwin, Richard E., "Sunk Cost Hysteresis," NBER Working Paper, No. 2911, March 1989.

—— and Krugman, Paul, "Persistent Trade Effects of Large Exchange Rate Shocks," *Quart. J. Economics*, 104 (1989), 636–654.

Bartlett, Chris and Sumantra Ghoshal, *Managing Across Borders. The Transnational Solution*, Harvard Business School Press, Boston, 1989.

Brennan, Michael and Eduardo Schwartz, "Finite Difference Methods and Jump Processes Arising in the Pricing of Contingent Claims: A Synthesis," *J. Financial and Quantitative Analysis* (September 1978), 461–474.

Business International, *Operating in a Floating Rate World*, Business International Corporation, New York, 1976.

——, *Evaluating the Performance of International Operations*, New York: International Corporation, 1989.

——, *Protecting Profits from Market Turmoil: Strategic Financial Risk Managing for the 1990s*, New York: International Corporation, 1990.

Caterpillar Tractor Co., Harvard Business School, Boston (385-276), 1985.

Cohen, Morris, Marshall Fisher, and Ramchandran Jaikumar, "International Manufacturing and Distribution Networks: A Normative Model Framework," in Kasra Ferdows (Ed.), *Managing International Manufacturing*, North-Holland, Netherlands, 1989, 67–93.

—— and Arnd Huchzermeier, "Valuing Manufacturing Flexibility Under Foreign Exchange Uncertainty," Working Paper, Wharton School, Department of Decision Sciences, University of Pennsylvania, 1991.

—— and Hau Lee, "Strategic Analysis of Integrated Production-Distribution Systems: Models and Methods," *Oper. Res.*, 36 (1989), 216–228.

Cox, John, Jonathan Ingersoll, and Stephen Ross, "An Intertemporal General Equilibrium Model of Asset Prices," *Econometrica*, 53 (1985), 363–384.

De Meza, David and Frederick van der Ploeg, "Production Flexibility as a Motive for Multinationality," *J. Industrial Econ.* 35 (1987), 343–352.

Dixit, Avinash, "Entry and Exit Decisions Under Uncertainty," *J. Political Econ.*, 97 (1989a), 620–638.

——, "Hysteresis, Import Penetration, and Exchange Rate Pass-through," *Quart. J. Econ.*, 104 (1989b), 205–228.

Dornbusch, Rudiger, "Expectations and Exchange Rate Dynamics," *J. Political Econ.*, 84 (1976), 1161–76.

——, "Exchange Rates and Prices," *American Econ. Review*, 77 (1987), 93–106.

Doz, Yves, "Managing Manufacturing Rationalization with Multinational Corporations," *Columbia J. World Business*, (1978).

Dumas, Bernard, "Perishable Capital and Hysteresis in Capital Formation," Rodney White Center Working Paper, 1988.

Fine, Charles and Robert Freund, "Optimal Investment in Product-Flexible Manufacturing Capacity," *Management Sci.*, 36 (1990), 449–466.

Flaherty, Therese, "Coordinating International Manufacturing and Technology," M. E. Porter (Ed.), *Competition in Global Industries*, Harvard Business School Press, Boston, MA, 1986.

Flood, Eugene and Donald Lessard, "On the Measurement of Operating Exposure to Exchange Rates: A Conceptual Approach," *Financial Management*, 32 (1986), 25–35.

Hodder, James and James Jucker, "International Plant Location under Price and Exchange Rate Uncertainty," *Engineering and Production Econ.*, 9 (1985a), 225–229.

—— and ——, "A Simple Plant-Location Model for Quantity-Setting Firms Subject to Price Uncertainty," *European J. Oper. Res.*, 21 (1985b), 39–46.

Hedlund, Gunnar, "The Hypermodern MNC: A Heterarchy," *Human Resource Management*, (1986), 9–35.

Huchzermeier, Arnd, "Global Manufacturing Strategy Planning under Exchange Rate Uncertainty," Ph.D. Thesis, University of Pennsylvania, 1990.

Hull, John, *Options, Futures, and Other Derivative Securities*, Prentice-Hall, Englewood Cliffs, NJ, 2000.

Hymer, Stephen, "The International Operations of National Firms," Ph.D. Thesis, Massachusetts Institute of Technology, Cambridge, MA, 1960.

Jacque, Laurent and Peter Lorange, "The International Control Conundrum: The Case of 'Hyperinflationary' Subsidiaries," *J. International Business Studies*, 15 (1984), 185–201.

Jacquillat, Bertrand and Bruno H. Solnik, "Multinationals are Poor Tools for Diversification," *J. Portfolio Management*, Winter (1978), 8–12.

Johnson, H. Thomas and Robert Kaplan, *Relevance Lost: The Rise and Fall of Management Accounting*, Harvard Business School Press, Boston, MA, 1987.

Kogut, Bruce, "Foreign Direct Investment as a Sequential Process," Charles P. Kindelberger and David Audretsch (Eds.), *The Multinational Corporations in the 1980s*, MIT Press, Cambridge, MA, 1983.

——— "Designing Global Strategies: Profiting from Operating Flexibility," *Sloan Management Review*, 26 (1985), 27–38.

——— and Nalin Kulatilaka, "Multinational Flexibility and the Theory of Foreign Direct Investment," Working Paper No. 88-10, Reginald H. Jones Center for Management Policy, Strategy and Organization, University of Pennsylvania, July 1988.

——— and ———, "Multinational Flexibility, Growth Options, and the Theory of Foreign Direct Investment," mimeo, Wharton School, University of Pennsylvania, 1991.

Kulatilaka, Nalin, "The Value of Flexibility," Working Paper, MIT Energy Laboratory, MIT-EL 86-014, revised May 1987.

——— and Bruce Kogut, "Direct Investment, Hysteresis, and Real Exchange Rate Volatility," mimeo, Wharton School, University of Pennsylvania, 1990.

——— and Alan Marcus, "A General Formulation of Corporate Operating Options," *Research in Finance*, (1988), 183–200.

Lessard, Donald and Peter Lorange, "Currency Changes and Management Control: Resolving the Centralization-Decentralization Dilemma," *Accounting Review*, July 7 (1977), 628–637.

——— and David Sharp, "Measuring the Performance of Operations Subject to Fluctuating Exchange Rates," *Midland Corporate Finance J.*, 2 (1984).

Marston, Richard, "Pricing to Market in Japanese Manufacturing," *J. International Econ.*, 29 (1989), 217–236.

Matsushita Electric Industrial (MEI) in 1987, European Institute of Business Administration (INSEAD), Harvard Business School, Boston (388-144).

McDonald, Robert and Daniel Siegel, "The Value of Waiting to Invest," *Quarterly J. Economics*, 101 (1986), 707–727.

Merton, Robert, "Theory of Rational Option Pricing," *Bell J. Econ. and Management Sci.*, (1973), 41–83.

——— "On the Mathematics and Economics Assumptions of Continuous-time Models," in W. F. Sharpe and C. M. Cootner (Eds.), *Financial Economics: Essays in Honor of Paul Cootner*, 1982; reprinted in *Continuous Time Finance*, Robert Merton, Basil Blackwell Inc., Cambridge, MA, 57–96, 1990.

Prahalad, C. K. and Yves Doz, *The Multinational Mission*, Free Press, New York, 1987.

Sharp, David, *Control Systems and Decision-making in Multinational Firms: Price Management Under Floating Exchange Rates*, Ph.D. Thesis, Massachusetts Institute of Technology, Cambridge, MA, 1987.

Stewart, George, "A Proposal for Measuring International Performance," *Midland Corporate Finance J.*, 1 (1983), 56–71.

VII EMPIRICAL EVIDENCE

37 Option Valuation of Claims on Real Assets: The Case of Offshore Petroleum Leases

James L. Paddock, Daniel R. Siegel, and James L. Smith

I Introduction

One of the most fruitful areas of research in financial economics has been the development of the theory of valuing stock options. Since the seminal work of Black and Scholes [1973] and Merton [1973] appeared, many papers have used this method of analysis to value other financial assets with "option-like" characteristics. See Smith [1976] for a survey of this literature.

More recently, it has been observed that there are contractual claims to real assets that also display option-like characteristics, which suggests that the Black-Scholes-Merton analysis might be useful in valuing such claims. (See Brealey and Myers [1984] and Mason and Merton [1985].) Examples include the following: McDonald and Siegel [1985], who study project valuation where the firm has the option to shut down production; McDonald and Siegel [1986] and Myers and Majd [1983], who study the valuation of investment and scrapping opportunities; and Brennan and Schwartz [1985], who study natural resource investments.

This chapter uses option valuation theory to develop a new approach to valuing leases for offshore petroleum. Our treatment makes several contributions to the literature on valuing "real options." First, we demonstrate how to integrate an explicit model of equilibrium in the market for the underlying real asset (developed petroleum reserves) with option-pricing theory to derive the value of a real option. The necessity of this type of integration follows from McDonald and Siegel's [1984] point that valuing real options may require a deeper understanding of equilibrium in the market for the underlying asset than valuing options on financial assets. Second, by using oil leases as an example, we specify a valuation problem in sufficient detail to allow close examination of the many theoretical and practical issues involved in extending financial option valuation theory to real options. Finally, the detail of the valuation problem allows us to consider informational and computational economies of the option valuation methodology relative to conventionally applied discounted cash flow techniques. In particular, we show the efficient use made by option valuation of market data, which mitigates the need to use (among other things) expected future commodity prices or risk-adjusted discount rates.

The valuation of offshore leases is an important issue in itself. Firms perform valuations as inputs to their bidding decisions. The government uses valuations to establish presale reservation prices and to study the effect of policy changes on revenues it expects to receive from lease sales. Because the bidding process involves billions of dollars, it is important to obtain accurate valuations. Government valuations have tended to underestimate industry bids. Using the same geological and cost data as the government, our option valuations are closer to industry bids.

Embedded in any approach to valuing petroleum leases is a rule specifying when and if a firm should explore and develop a particular leased property (i.e., exercise its options). Deriving the optimal rule is often difficult, especially using conventional discounted cash flow techniques. The option valuation approach we develop, however, leads to a straightforward form for this rule, which depends only upon observable variables. Using this analysis, we are able to study the effects of exploration and development costs and lags, and relinquishment requirements[1] on exploration and development investment-timing decisions. We also demonstrate empirically the form of the decision rule.

The chapter is organized as follows. Section II discusses relevant economic and technological characteristics of offshore petroleum leases. Section III discusses discounted cash flow valuation techniques as currently used by firms and the government, and points out their weaknesses. Section IV develops the option valuation approach, along with the investment-timing rule. Section V presents empirical results drawn from a sample of offshore petroleum leases. We compare valuations based upon the discounted cash flow approach (from government calculations) and the option valuation approach (using government cost and geological data) with actual industry bids. Finally, we explore the empirical effect of lessor policy and economic variables on tract value, and characteristics of the investment-timing rule. Section VI summarizes and discusses extensions of this research.

II   Economic and Technological Characteristics of Offshore Petroleum Leases

The holder of an offshore petroleum lease must pass through three stages before he can obtain hydrocarbons above the ground: exploration, development, and extraction. The exploration stage involves seismic and drilling activity to obtain information on the quantities of hydrocarbon reserves present in the tract, as well as the costs of bringing them out. If the exploration results are favorable, the firm may then proceed to the development stage, which involves putting the equipment in place to extract the oil: for example, constructing platforms and drilling production wells. The development expenditures convert *undeveloped* reserves into *developed* reserves; the latter are defined as reserves with productive capacity. The government subjects the leaseholder to relinquishment requirements that dictate how long a company can wait before beginning exploration and development. Often, holders of leases will relinquish the lease by deciding not to explore or develop a tract before the lease runs out. Thus both the exploration and development stages represent options of the leaseholder. If he does explore and develop the tract, the extraction stage involves using the installed capacity to take the hydrocarbons out of the ground. The proper valuation of a petroleum lease involves valuing the cash flows from this multistage process.

III Tract Valuation by the Discounted Cash Flow Approach

In the discounted cash flow (DCF) approach, expected future cash flows to lease-holders are determined, discounted to the present, and summed to yield the lease value. To determine expected cash flows and proper discount rates, it is first necessary to specify statistical distributions (not necessarily independent) for exploration costs, quantities of hydrocarbon reserves, development costs, hydrocarbon prices, and operating costs. For each set of realizations from these distributions, an analyst must determine whether it is optimal for the firm to explore, develop, and extract. To complicate matters further, the analyst must also make assumptions about the *timing* of exploration and development, as well as the rate of extraction. Then, using the prices, costs, quantities, and timing decisions from a particular set of realizations, the time path of cash flows is determined. The path of expected cash flows is found by integrating over all possible sets of realizations from the statistical distributions. As typically applied, this DCF analysis involves multivariate Monte Carlo simulations. A set of risk-adjusted discount rates is derived in principle by determining the co-variance of these respective cash flows with other assets in the economy and using a pricing model such as the Capital Asset Pricing Model.

The popularity of the DCF approach derives from its sound theoretical foundations. If the set of discounted cash flows is correctly determined, then the sum of these flows (net of the acquisition cost) yields the market value addition to the firm acquiring the lease. Performing these calculations correctly, however, is very difficult, and the DCF approach as applied has five major weaknesses that inhibit correct lease value determination.

1. The proper timing of exploration and development is not transparent. The choice of timing for the DCF calculations is therefore typically arbitrary and subject to error. This problem leads to valuations that are divergent between companies, the government, and the capital markets.

2. Different companies, as well as the government, may have different assessments of future statistical distributions, and thus expected paths, of hydrocarbon prices, none

of which need conform to the aggregate expectations held by capital markets. This also leads to divergent valuations.

3. The process of choosing the correct set of risk-adjusted discount rates in the presence of the complex statistical structure of the cash flows is a difficult task, which is also subject to a great deal of subjectivity and error. For example, the investment-timing rules used by the firm will affect the risk of the cash flows in complicated ways. Thus, the optimal investment-timing rule will need to take account of this relationship. Companies, as well as the government, often resort to simple rules of thumb such as "use 20 percent for the exploration phase and 10 percent thereafter." The choice of discount rates is crucial, however, because the DCF valuations are very sensitive to the rates chosen.

4. The DCF calculations, particularly Monte Carlo applications, are very complex and costly.

5. Because tract information is often relatively sparse at the bidding stage, the assessments of geological and cost distributions can vary, perhaps widely, across companies and the government. This also causes large discrepancies among respective valuations.

The next section develops the option valuation methodology and shows how it is not subject to the first four of these problems. Because it is purely a financial valuation tool, however, the problems associated with number 5 above remain.

IV Tract Valuation by the Option Valuation Approach

As was discussed in Section II, valuing a lease involves valuing the cash flows from a three-stage process. These stages form a nested set of options and each of these stages has distinct characteristics relevant to the option valuation (OV) approach. By making plausible assumptions about the underlying price processes, we shall be able to use option-pricing techniques to value this nested set of options.

A Characteristics of the Stages

Exploration The exploration stage consists of the option to make the exploration expenditures and to receive undeveloped reserves. This is analogous to a stock option, which confers the right to pay the exercise price and receive the stock. Just as a stock option has an expiration date, the leaseholder is subject to relinquishment requirements which stipulate that it must give up the lease if it does not explore and develop by a certain date. There are important differences, however, related to uncertainties in the exploration process.

The primary uncertainty surrounding the exploration stage is the quantity of hydrocarbons. This uncertainty is resolved by exploring. Because offshore development costs are primarily driven by factors related to economies of scale, exploration also resolves uncertainty about development costs. We can represent the exploration stage as the option to spend the expected exploration costs $\bar{E}$, and receive the expected value of undeveloped reserves,

$$X^*(V) = \int QX(V, T - t; D(Q)) \, dF(Q), \tag{1}$$

where

Q	$=$ random quantity (possibly zero) of recoverable hydrocarbons in the tract
$D(Q)$	$=$ per unit development cost (in real dollars), a function of quantity[2]
V	$=$ *current* value of a unit of developed hydrocarbon reserves
$F(Q)$	$=$ probability distribution over the quantity of hydrocarbons
$X(V, T - t; D(Q))$	$=$ *current* per unit value of undeveloped reserves given the *current* per unit value of a developed reserve and per unit development cost
t	$=$ current date
T	$=$ expiration date.

We can represent the current value of the reserves obtained after exploration as the expectation over the value of the undeveloped reserves, because the quantity risk is almost entirely technological and geological. The risk is therefore nonsystematic and requires no risk premium. Thus, this "risk-neutral" technique is appropriate.[3] We assume here that exploration is instantaneous; later, we show how to relax this assumption.

Development   Once exploration has provided an indication of the quantity of hydrocarbons and the magnitude of development costs, the leaseholder has the option to pay the development costs and install productive capacity. Therefore, ownership of an undeveloped reserve is an option to obtain developed reserves by paying the development cost. This option has value $X(V, T - t; D(Q))$. As with exploration, we shall for now treat development expenditures as occurring in one instantaneous lump sum. We again relax this assumption below.[4]

Extraction   Once the leaseholder has exercised its development option, he owns developed reserves. He then has the option to extract the hydrocarbons if he chooses. Valuation of the developed reserves requires assumption about oil quality, future extraction rates and costs, tax and royalty regimes, and hydrocarbon prices. Fortunately, a firm can observe the value that competitive asset markets place on similar developed reserves. There are active secondary markets in properties containing developed reserves, so that a firm knows or can determine within a reasonable tolerance, the market value of a given quantity and type of developed reserves. This market value reflects the value of reserves with similar extraction rates and operating costs, quality of hydrocarbons and tax regime as for the tract being valued. Of these, extraction rates and operating costs for a particular tract are the most difficult to predict, ex ante. Fortunately, extraction rates and operating costs do not vary as much as exploration and development costs across tracts. For a given hydrocarbon quality and tax regime, this leads to a relative homogeneity in the market value of developed reserves. The option valuation technique we develop uses this market information about the value of developed reserves in an explicit and straightforward manner.[5] Our use of market values for developed reserves mitigates possible errors in explicitly modeling extraction, as in Brennan and Schwartz [1985].

B   Valuation

The above discussion indicates that a hydrocarbon lease can be modeled as a compound option, where the unexplored tract is an option on the development option. The extraction option is already incorporated in the current market value of a developed reserve. Valuing compound options has been explored by Geske [1979] in the context of financial options. As we now show, extending this theory to valuing real options requires some important modifications. One important feature of valuing stock options is that, other than specifying a stochastic process for the underlying stock price, it is not necessary to understand equilibrium in the market for the stock itself. As we now show, this is not true for valuing unexplored tracts or undeveloped reserves. To see this, we first characterize the behavior of developed reserve prices, using a model of equilibrium in the market for petroleum reserves. We then demonstrate how to integrate this model with option pricing techniques, valuing first the development option and then the option to explore. (The equilibrium model that follows is based upon the model in McDonald and Siegel [1983].)

Petroleum Reserve Market Equilibrium   In equilibrium the expected net payoff from holding a developed reserve (payouts plus capital gains) must compensate the owner for the opportunity cost of investing in that reserve. Let B_t be the number of units of petroleum in a developed reserve, V_t be the value of a unit of developed reserves, and R_t be the instantaneous per unit time net payoff from holding the reserve, all at time t. Assume that the rate of return to the owner follows the diffusion process:

$$R_t\, dt/B_t V_t = \alpha_v^*\, dt + \sigma_v\, dz_v, \tag{2}$$

where α_v^* is the required (expected) rate of return to the owner, σ_v is the instantaneous per unit time standard deviation of the rate of return, and dz_v is an increment to a Wiener (diffusion) process. If the owner is to be compensated for the opportunity cost of investing in the reserve, α_v^* must equal the expected rate of return on a stock with risk $\sigma_v\, dz_v$.

The assumption that the total rate of return to holding a developed reserve follows a diffusion process is as plausible as the assumption that stock rates of return follow such a process.[6] Like a stock price, $B_t V_t$ represents the market value of an asset whose owners expect to be compensated for their investment. In fact, there are several companies listed on the New York Stock Exchange (Permian Basin Royalty Trust, for example) and the London Stock Exchange (LASMO, for example) whose assets consist largely of producing developed reserves.

The net payoff R_t comes from two sources: (1) the profits from production: and (2) the capital gain on holding the remaining petroleum. Suppose that production from a developed reserve follows an exponential decline:[7]

$$dB_t = -\gamma B_t\, dt. \tag{3}$$

Then the net payoff can be written as

$$R_t\, dt = \{\gamma B_t P_t\, dt\} + \{(1 - \gamma\, dt) B_t (V_t + dV_t) - B_t V_t\}, \tag{4}$$

where the net payoff is over a short interval dt. P_t is the after-tax operating profit from selling a unit of petroleum. Substituting (4) into (2) yields the process for the value of a producing developed reserve:[8]

$$\frac{dV}{V} = (\alpha_v^* - \delta_t)\, dt + \sigma_v\, dz_v$$

$$\equiv \alpha_v\, dt + \sigma_v\, dz_v, \tag{5}$$

where

$$\alpha_v = \alpha_v^* - \delta_t,$$

$$\delta_t = \gamma[P_t - V_t]/V_t.$$

δ_t is the payout rate of the producing developed reserve,[9] and α_v is the expected rate of capital gain. Therefore, V follows a diffusion process.

It is clear from (5) that in equilibrium no agent will hold a nonproducing developed reserve.[10] The expected rate of return from a strategy of holding nonproducing developed reserves, α_v, is less than the required rate of return, α_v^*, on an asset with risk $\sigma_v dz_v$. The rate of return shortfall to the strategy would be the payout rate δ_t. Note that δ_t can be estimated using observable variables. (See Section V for a detailed discussion of how to estimate δ_t.) The behavior of V has important implications for the proper valuation equation for both undeveloped reserves and unexplored tracts, which we now discuss.

Valuing Undeveloped Reserves   We now turn to the problem of determining the value of an undeveloped reserve on a tract that has already been explored, $X(V, T - t; D)$. This is of interest in its own right, as firms often wish to value these reserves. It is also the first stage in the valuation of unexplored tracts.

Table 37.1 summarizes the analogy between an undeveloped reserve and a stock call option. Because the firm can begin development at any time before expiration of the lease, the analogy is with an American option.

For simplicity, assume that α_v^*, σ_v, and δ_t in (5) are constant over the life of the lease.[11] Then V follows geometric Brownian motion. One way to find the value of the undeveloped reserve, $X(V, T - t; D)$, would be to invoke standard arbitrage arguments that rely on replicating the undeveloped reserve's payoff by holding a portfolio of developed reserves and riskless bonds [Merton, 1973]. There are, however, two

Table 37.1
Comparison of variables for pricing models of stock call options and undeveloped petroleum reserves

Stock option	Undeveloped reserve
Current stock price	Value of developed reserve discounted for development lag
Variance of rate of return on the stock	Variance of rate of change of the value of a developed reserve
Exercise price	Per unit development cost
Time to expiration	Relinquishment requirement
Riskless rate of interest	Riskless rate of interest
Dividend	Net production revenue less depletion

Note: This table is modified for unexplored tracts by replacing the development lag by the combined exploration and development lag, and the per unit development cost by the combined per unit expected exploration and development cost.

ways to accomplish this replication: (1) by holding nonproducing developed reserves; and (2) by holding producing developed reserves. The equilibrium model above demonstrated that $\alpha_v < \alpha_v^*$. McDonald and Siegel [1984] have shown that in this case the first replication strategy is inefficient because it entails holding an asset which carries a rate of return shortfall δ. The resulting undeveloped reserve value will be too high. The second replication strategy is efficient, because the holder of a developed reserve who produces from it earns a fair rate of return. In this case, the payout (at rate δ) is identical to a proportional dividend on a stock, and the partial differential equation characterizing the value of an option on such a stock is appropriate for valuing an undeveloped reserve.

Alternatively, because effecting the actual arbitrage would be difficult, one can value the undeveloped reserve using the equilibrium analysis in Constantinides [1978]. This approach yields the same partial differential equation as the arbitrage analysis:

$$\frac{\partial X}{\partial t} = rX - (r - \delta)\frac{\partial X}{\partial V} - \frac{1}{2}\sigma_v^2 V^2 \frac{\partial^2 X}{\partial V^2}, \tag{6}$$

where r is the riskless rate of interest, assumed constant over the life of the lease (on the undeveloped reserve). The link between the equilibrium model of petroleum reserves and option pricing comes in a straightforward way through the parameter δ. Note that there is no measure of the systematic risk of V in equation (6).

Following Merton [1973] and McDonald and Siegel [1986], the main boundary condition of equation (6) arises from a stopping rule that says the reserve should be developed when the ratio $C_t = V_t/D$ strikes a hitting boundary $\{C_t^*\}$ ($t \in [0, T]$) from below for the first time, or

$$X(V_t, T - t; D) = V_t - D \quad \text{if} \quad C_t = C_t^* \quad \text{and} \quad C_s < C_s^* \quad \text{for all } s < t. \tag{7}$$

$\{C_t^*\}$ is determined as the boundary that maximizes the solution to (6) and is independent of V and D. Therefore, this boundary will apply to *all* leases with an expiration date of T. To illustrate, figure 37.1 shows the values of $\{C_t^*\}$ for a sample of offshore petroleum leases that will be discussed below. The hitting boundary declines toward unity as we move through calendar time because the option value implicit in the undeveloped reserve declines with time. With no time left, there is no option value, and it is optimal to develop if and only if the value of the developed reserve exceeds the development cost.

Two other boundary conditions are

$$X(0, T - t; D) = 0 \quad \text{for all } t, \tag{8}$$

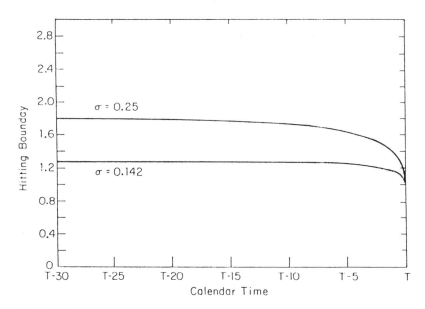

Figure 37.1
Hitting boundaries

and

$$X(V_T, 0; D) = \max[0, V_T - D] \quad \text{if } C_s < C_s^* \quad \text{for every } s < T. \tag{9}$$

For $T < \infty$, there are no closed forms for the solution to (6) or for $\{C_t^*\}$, but numerical solutions are easy to obtain. We provide examples in Section V.

Valuing Unexplored Tracts We now determine the value of an unexplored tract, which is the same as valuing the option to make the expected exploration expenditures $\bar{E}$ and receive the expected value of undeveloped reserves $X^*(V)$, defined in (1). In general, valuing the unexplored tract involves complications arising out of the properties of the development option and optimal development timing. To avoid these problems, we make the simplifying assumption that it is optimal to begin development immediately after successful exploration has occurred. We discuss the appropriateness of this assumption below. Using our simplifying assumption, we can "collapse" the development option into the exploration option. Formally, if the development option will always be exercised immediately, then it will have value,

$$X(V, T - t; D(Q)) = V - D(Q). \tag{10}$$

Combining (1) and (10), it is clear that exercising the exploration option requires paying $\bar{E}$ and receiving

$$X^*(V) = \int Q[V - D(Q)]\,dF(Q)$$

$$= V\int Q\,dF(Q) - \int QD(Q)\,dF(Q). \tag{11}$$

Alternatively, we can view exercising the exploration option as paying

$$\int QD(Q)\,dF(Q) + \bar{E} = \bar{D} + \bar{E} \tag{12}$$

and receiving

$$V\int Q\,dF(Q) = V\bar{Q},$$

where $\bar{D}$ and $\bar{Q}$ are the expected total development cost and expected reserve quantity, respectively. Using the homogeneity of the valuation discussed above (see footnote 2), we can represent the value of an unexplored tract as

$$\bar{Q}W(V, T - t; S); \qquad S = (\bar{D} + \bar{E})/\bar{Q}, \tag{13}$$

where $W(V, T - t; S)$ is the current value of an option to receive a unit of developed reserves by paying the per unit combined expected exploration and development cost S.

The option value $W(V, T - t; S)$ can be solved in the same way as the value of an undeveloped reserve $X(V, T - t; D)$ can be solved. $W(V, T - t; S)$ must satisfy the partial differential equation (6) and meet the boundary conditions (7), (8), and (9), with the development cost D replaced by the expected combined exploration and development cost, S. The hitting boundary will be the same because the underlying asset, developed reserves, is the same and because the boundary only depends upon the ratio of the developed reserve to the (expected) expenditure required to obtain the developed reserve (D for undeveloped reserves and S for unexplored leases).

With no geological uncertainty, collapsing together the development and exploration options is always appropriate. If V/S exceeds the hitting boundary, then so will V/D because $S > D$. However, with geological uncertainty and economies of scale to development of reserves, it is quite possible that V/S can exceed the hitting boundary, but that $V/D(Q)$ will be below the hitting boundary for Q sufficiently below $\bar{Q}$. Thus, one may explore and find that the quantity of reserves found is small enough that it is optimal to wait to develop because the size of the per unit development costs is large. Thus, the collapsing technique gives a lower bound to the true option value. We believe that this does not represent a significant problem for our analysis. First, we show below that the economies of scale for development are moderate. Second, exploration costs are an important component of total investment costs in our sample. Finally, this problem is present only for small values of Q, and this will have a small impact on the valuation.

Exploration and Development Lags   In the above analysis we have assumed that the holder of the undeveloped reserve receives the developed reserve immediately upon beginning development and that the holder of the unexplored tract receives the developed reserve immediately upon beginning exploration (and therefore development). In fact, he receives it only after a lag equal to the development time for the undeveloped reserve and the combined exploration and development time for the unexplored lease. Let $\hat{t}$ be the length of this lag. The value of a claim at time t to receive a developed reserve at $t + \hat{t}$ is simply the present value,[12]

$$\hat{V}_t = e^{-\alpha_v^* \hat{t}} E_t[V_{t+\hat{t}}] = e^{-\alpha_v^* \hat{t}} V_t e^{(\alpha_v^* - \delta)} = e^{-\delta \hat{t}} V_t. \tag{14}$$

Since by beginning development (or exploration and development) at t, the firm receives such a claim (rather than the developed reserve itself), the actual asset underlying either the development or the exploration option is the present value with price $\hat{V}_t$. Notice, however, that $\hat{V}_t$ also follows (5), so that we can simply replace V_t everywhere by $\hat{V}_t$, for both the exploration and development option.

Optimal Investment Timing   As discussed above, the optimal hitting boundary will be the same for both the exploration and the development options. This boundary provides an investment rule for the firm: begin development or exploration the first time C_t ($= \hat{V}/D$ for development and $\hat{V}/S$ for exploration) hits $\{C_t^*\}$ from below. Notice that C_t depends only upon the observable variables $V_t, \delta, \hat{t}$, and D or S.

Two interesting insights about investment timing arise from this analysis. First, for a given $\hat{t}$, C_t is a decreasing function of per unit investment costs. Thus, reserves with low investment costs will hit the boundary before those with high costs and will be explored or developed first. This is consistent with Herfindahl's [1967] equilibrium. Second, for a given S or D, C_t is a decreasing function of $\hat{t}$. Thus, properties with shorter investment lags will be explored or developed before those with longer lags (see (14)).

Comparative Statics   The comparative statics of the solution to (6) are the same as those for a stock call option. The value of the unexplored tract or undeveloped reserve is increasing, ceteris paribus, in the time to relinquishment, riskless rate of interest, and the standard deviation of the rate of change in the value of a developed reserve.

C   Comparison of Option Valuation and Discounted Cash Flow Approaches

One of the most important features of models used to price stock options is the small number of input parameters needed. These same advantages are present in pricing an unexplored tract or an undeveloped reserve using our option valuation approach, particularly when compared with DCF analysis. Table 37.1 provides a list of parameters needed to solve equation (6). Because exploration and development costs are in real dollars, all other parameters will also be in real terms. Of these parameters, only the standard deviation of the rate of change in developed reserve value and the real riskless rate are not directly observable. We shall discuss how to estimate them below. As with stock option pricing, the most important parameters not on the list are risk-adjusted discount rates or expected future prices (e.g., of petroleum or developed reserves). Therefore, as with stock option pricing, one does not need to know the systematic risk of the underlying asset. Comparing these information requirements with the substantial requirements for standard discounted cash flow analysis discussed in Section III demonstrates the power of the option valuation approach to reduce information requirements.

There are several ways in which the option valuation approach reduces information requirements relative to standard discounted cash flow analysis. The discounted cash flow approach typically explicitly models the extraction stage. This requires the analyst to make assumptions about expected future oil prices and optimal extraction-timing. As discussed above, the option valuation approach lets the market place a value on developed reserves, by finding market prices of developed reserves similar to those that the firm would acquire after exploration and development. In fact, the DCF approach could also use the market value of developed reserves to avoid modeling the extraction stage.

There are, however, two important advantages of the OV approach over DCF that are present, even if the DCF analyst uses the market value of developed reserves. First, the OV approach reduces information requirements by eliminating the need to estimate future developed reserve values. Even using the market value of developed reserves, the DCF analyst would still need to make assumptions about the expected rate of appreciation of the value of a developed reserve, α_v. Second, the OV approach eliminates the need to determine risk-adjusted discount rates. As discussed in Section

III, this is an important consideration, because the optimal investment-timing decision must take account of the feedbacks between the investment-timing rule and the risk of the resulting cash flows. In practical applications this is nearly an impossible task. This problem is not present with the OV approach.

V Empirical Results

In this section we use the option valuation approach to arrive at estimates of the market value of selected offshore petroleum tracts awarded to the industry in federal lease sale No. 62. The option valuation estimates we generate are then compared with value estimates prepared by the U.S. Geological Survey (USGS) using the DCF method. Both sets of estimates are compared with industry bids on the same tracts. Finally, we demonstrate empirically the comparative statics results discussed in the preceding section.

A Tract Sample and Data Sources

Federal lease sale No. 62 was held on November 18, 1980, and covered western and central portions of the Gulf of Mexico. In total, 67 tracts were awarded in the sale; however, we have been able to gather consistent data on only 21 of these tracts. All of these are one-sixth royalty tracts.[13] The tract-specific data we do have were provided by the USGS. Data elements provided by the USGS include the following items for each tract:

(1) mean and variance for quantities of recoverable oil reserves

(2) mean and variance for quantities of recoverable condensate reserves

(3) mean and variance for quantities of recoverable gas reserves

(4) probability that the tract is dry

(5) expected exploration cost

(6) expected development cost

(7) USGS estimate of tract value.

Items (1) through (6) are a subset of the input parameters used by the USGS in their DCF analysis of tract values (results of which are given by item (7)).

The means and variances of reserve quantities reported by the USGS (items (1)–(3)) are conditional on the tract not being dry (i.e., not devoid of recoverable hydrocarbons). The USGS provides separately its (subjective) probability that each tract is in fact dry (item (4) above). We assume that, conditional on a tract being wet, the statistical distribution of oil[14] and gas reserves for a given tract is joint lognormal.[15] Therefore, the joint distribution of oil and gas reserves for each tract has a spike at the origin equal to the probability that the tract is dry, and a continuous distribution in the positive quadrant equal to the wet tract probability times the appropriate joint lognormal density.[16]

B   Inputs into the Valuation Equation

Using the data provided by the USGS, along with the market data described below, we construct each of the inputs to the valuation equation (6), which are summarized in table 37.1 and are discussed below.

Developed Reserve Value   It is necessary for our purposes to establish the market value of developed reserves of oil and gas as of November 1980. Gruy et al. [1982] analyzed a number of private sales of developed oil reserves that occurred around this time and their results indicate that a value of approximately $12 per barrel of oil reserves is appropriate. This value is also supported by an analysis (see Paddock [1982]) of the Oil Production Stocks of the London and Scottish Marine Oil Co., Ltd., which are traded on the London Stock Exchange, as well as of similar securities traded on exchanges in the United States, such as the Permian Basin Royalty Trust (which is traded on the New York Stock Exchange). These securities are financial claims to the net revenues of developed oil reserves, and are valued and marketable in developed capital markets.

Gas is a bit more problematic. Strictly on a BTU-equilibrating basis, the value of an mcf of gas (at burner tip) would be approximately one sixth the value of a barrel of oil, i.e., $2. However, there are many reasons to doubt that such a direct relationship links the in-situ values of the two fuels: e.g., natural gas is a preferred fuel in many applications, and is also subject to different extraction, transportation and storage costs, and taxes. Consequently, $2 per mcf provides a benchmark, but not the best estimate of the value of developed gas reserves. Private correspondence with investment bankers who were actively involved in the market for developed gas reserves indicates that a figure closer to $3 per mcf would be a better reflection of market values for the latter part of 1980.[17] Due to the guesswork in our estimate of this parameter, and to illustrate the sensitivity of our results to it, we report two sets of results based alternatively on gas reserve values of $2 and $3 per mcf.[18]

The values for developed oil and gas reserves that we use here are for illustrative purposes. In applying the OV method to a particular property, the analyst must be careful to choose the market value of a reserve that has the same hydrocarbon quality, cost structure, and tax regime, as discussed above. We do not have this kind of detailed information for the tracts we study. However, given the active markets in developed reserves, firms that are in the market for reserves would have access to these values.

Variance   The variance of the rate of change in the value of developed reserves is an input parameter that must be estimated. One technique would be to estimate this variance from past data on market values of developed reserves. Unfortunately, while developed reserves are traded in competitive markets, market value data are not publicly available at regular enough intervals to estimate this variance directly. We can, however, get a reasonable estimate using a result in Gruy et al. [1982] (which is also commonly used by industry participants) that developed reserve prices tend to be about one third of crude oil prices. This approximate relationship has held for a number of years, so (at least for illustrative purposes) we can use the variance of the rate of change of crude oil prices as a proxy for the variance of the rate of change of developed reserve prices. Using monthly data for the period 1974–1980, the annualized variance of the real (CPI deflated) refiner cost of imported crude oil is about $\sigma^2 = 0.02019$, implying that $\sigma = 0.142$.[19]

The period 1974–1980 is probably representative of the type of period that market participants might have expected to occur from 1980 on. It includes periods of crisis, as well as periods of relative tranquility. To further validate this variance estimate, we have constructed 95 percent confidence intervals for future crude oil prices implicit in the variance estimate. To capture a possible increase in perceived uncertainty, we also examine a variance of $\sigma^2 = 0.0625$ ($\sigma = 0.250$). The ranges of future prices shown in table 37.2 are 95 percent confidence intervals for years 1 through 10. We assume that the expected rate of increase in value is 3 percent for $\sigma = 0.142$ and 5 percent for $\sigma = 0.250$.[20] While recent experience has demonstrated that crude prices can fall well outside of the confidence interval for $\sigma = 0.142$, we are interested in market expectations in late 1980. We believe that this confidence interval better captures those expectations than that for the higher standard deviation. Therefore, we have adopted the value $\sigma = 0.142$ as our base case, but we also report results based on the assumption that $\sigma = 0.250$.

Expected Exploration and Development Costs   Expected exploration costs reported by the USGS are before tax. About 90 percent of these expenditures are "intangible" and can be expensed for tax purposes.[21] The remaining 10 percent are depreciated. Because such a high proportion of these costs can be expensed, we simply multiply these costs by $(1 - \tau)$, where τ is the corporate income tax rate, taken to be 46 percent.[22]

Table 37.2
Per barrel crude oil wellhead price ranges implicit in standard deviations; year 0 is 1980 with a price of $36 per barrel

Year	$\sigma = 0.142$		$\sigma = 0.250$	
	Lower	Upper	Lower	Upper
1	27.37	48.30	21.56	58.62
2	24.57	54.86	17.31	71.21
3	22.67	60.63	14.58	82.44
5	20.04	71.36	11.05	103.45
10	16.18	97.51	6.54	154.42

Note: The ranges of future prices are 95 percent confidence intervals for years 1 through 10, assuming that oil prices are distributed log-normally:

$$\ln\left(\frac{S_t}{S_0}\right) \sim N\left(\left(\alpha_e - \frac{1}{2}\sigma_e^2\right)t, \sigma^2 t\right),$$

where S_t = crude oil price at t.

Whereas the USGS reports only the expected development cost for each tract, it is necessary for our purposes to derive a development cost function that relates development cost to reserve size. Assume that (real) total development costs are of the deterministic form:

$$D_j = A_j[6Q_{oj} + Q_{gj}]^{\beta}, \tag{15}$$

where Q_{oj} and Q_{gj} are quantities of recoverable oil and gas reserves on the jth tract, and A_j is a tract-specific scaling parameter that might vary with parameters such as water depth and drilling depth.[23] The term in square brackets in equation (15) represents total reserve volume measured in terms of cubic feet of gas equivalent.[24] We have set the economy of scale parameter, β, equal to $\frac{2}{3}$, which is consistent with at least one recent study of development costs in the Gulf of Mexico.[25] To arrive at the tract-specific parameters A_j, we use the following fitting procedure. First, we take the expectation of a second-order Taylor Expansion of (15) to yield

$$\bar{D}_j = A_j(6\bar{Q}_{oj} + \bar{Q}_{gj})^{\beta} + (18\sigma_{oj}^2 + \sigma_{gf}^2/2 + 6\sigma_{ogj})A_j\beta(\beta - 1)(6\bar{Q}_{oj} + \bar{Q}_{gj})^{\beta 2}, \tag{16}$$

where σ_{oj}^2 and σ_{gj}^2 are variances of oil and gas quantities, σ_{ogj} is the covariance between them, and bars represent expected values. We then make the arbitrary assumption that $\sigma_{ogj} = 0.5\sigma_{oj}\sigma_{gj}$, and solve (16) for the equilibrating value of A_j for each tract using the tract-specific means of the distributions for D_j, Q_{oj}, and Q_{gj} provided by the USGS.[26] The resulting set of tract-specific development cost functions is an approximation to the true development cost functions used by the USGS, which are not available to us.

Approximately 50 percent of development expenditures in the Gulf of Mexico are intangible and can be expensed for tax purposes.[27] The remainder are tangible expenses that are depreciated.[28] Therefore, after-tax development costs will be about 77 percent $(1 - (0.46)(0.50))$ of actual development costs.

Relinquishment Requirement Contract provisions for all leases issued in sale 62 set the term to relinquishment (time to expiration) at five years.

Riskless Rate Constantinides [1978] shows that the riskless rate appears in (6) because it is the certainty-equivalent of the required rate of return on the underlying asset. Because investors are interested in after-tax rates of return, the appropriate certainty-equivalent is the return on riskless tax-free bonds or the after-tax return on treasury securities for an investor who is indifferent between taxable and tax-free riskless debt. Skelton [1983] estimates that this marginal tax rate varies from the low 20s for long-term bonds to about 50 percent for short-term bonds. Until recently, a common estimate of the average (pretax) real riskless rate was about 2 percent. We therefore use a real riskless rate of 1.25 percent. Note that using a real model as we do gives more plausibility to the assumption of a constant riskless rate than using a nominal model.

Delta We derive an estimate for δ from equation (5), for a producing reserve, defined at time t.

M_t = market price of crude oil, per barrel

OC_t = operating cost, per barrel (including royalty)

DA_t = depreciation allowance, per barrel

x $= OC_t/M_t$, assumed constant over time

y $= DA_t/M_t$, assumed constant over time.

After-tax barrel profit from production is

$$P_t = M_t - OC_t - \tau(M_t - OC_t - DA_t)$$
$$= M_t(1 - x) - 0.46M_t(1 - x - y). \tag{17}$$

With the "one-third" rule discussed above, $M_t/V_t = 3$, and (17) becomes

$$P_t = 3V_t(1 - x) - (0.46)(3)V_t(1 - x - y)$$
$$= 1.62V_t(1 - x + 0.85y). \tag{17'}$$

Substituting (17′) into (5) yields

$$\delta_t = \gamma[1.62V_t(1 - x + 0.85y) - V_t]/V_t$$

$$= \gamma[0.62 - 1.62x + 1.377y]. \qquad (18)$$

We assume that $x = 0.30$, $y = 0.20$, and $\gamma = 0.10$, which are consistent with data from late 1980. Using these parameter values to solve (18) yields $\delta = 0.041$. Given our assumptions, δ will be constant over time. Alternative assumptions can easily be incorporated into the analysis. For example, x and y can be made functions of M_t, and therefore of V_t. δ will then be a function of V_t. Similarly, δ can be made to vary deterministically with time. In either case (6) can be solved in a straightforward manner numerically.

Combined exploration and development activities in the Gulf of Mexico take place in about one year. Therefore, given this value of delta, $\hat{V}/V = e^{-\delta \hat{t}} = e^{-0.041} = 0.959829$. The present values of the developed reserves are therefore \$11.52 for oil, and \$1.92 and \$2.88 for gas. These values will be used in the option valuation below.

C   Option Valuation Comparisons

Based on the input data described above, we have computed option valuation estimates using equation (6). We provide summary statistics for comparisons between our option valuation estimates, USGS estimates and industry bids. There are several considerations in evaluating these comparisons.

Comparison with USGS Estimates

a. Because our underlying geological and cost data are provided by the USGS, differences between the option valuation estimates and USGS estimates should be due primarily to differences in the financial valuation techniques.

b. By statute, the USGS must assign a small positive value to tracts that they estimate to have a zero or negative value. To increase the fairness of the comparisons, we have assigned a zero value to these tracts.

c. The USGS's values are examples of values derived using discounted cash flow techniques. As was discussed above, other analysts might derive significantly different discounted cash flow values using the same geological and cost data.

Comparison with Industry Bids   The comparison of option valuation estimates to industry bids is less straightforward.

Table 37.3
Simple correlation coefficients between valuations ($N = 21$)

	$2 per mcf gas				$3 per mcf gas			
	OV	USGS	GB	HB	OV	USGS	GB	HB
OV	1.00				1.00			
USGS	0.99	1.00			0.98	1.00		
GB	0.39	0.39	1.00		0.38	0.39	1.00	
HB	0.21	0.18	0.55	1.00	0.24	0.18	0.55	1.00

a. The cost and geological data used by the USGS (and therefore by the option valuation) may deviate from industry expectations on these particular tracts, for both quantities of hydrocarbons and development costs.

b. Even if the underlying USGS data match industry expectations, we still do not observe industry valuations directly. The bids that we observe are not simple relevations of bidders' internal valuations or reservation prices. Instead, they are the outcome of a strategic bidding process. Theoretically, the high bid tendered for an item of uncertain value should be strictly lower than the item's expected value, but should converge to it as the number of bidders grows large (see Wilson [1977] and Milgrom and Weber [1982]). Some practitioners argue, however, that winning bids in OCS lease sales appear to systematically exceed true expected underlying tract values—the "winner's curse" (see Capen, Clapp, and Campbell [1971] and Lohrenz and Dougherty [1983]). Recent experimental evidence (see Kagel and Levin [1986]) gathered in controlled bidding environments, where experienced subjects put real money at stake, also shows that high bids tend to exceed true expected underlying values. Because of these contrary views on what high bids do represent, we present both high bids and geometric mean bids as indicators of industry valuations for the OCS tracts in our sample.[29]

Results   To preserve confidentiality of USGS data, we are not able to provide tract-specific results. Tables 37.3 and 37.4 provide summary measures for the comparisons between option valuation, USGS and industry bid values. We use the following notation:

OV   = option valuation

USGS = USGS discounted cash flow valuation

GB   = geometric mean of industry bids

HG   = high (winning) industry bid.

Table 37.4
Mean and standard deviations for valuations ($N = 21$) (millions $)

| Valuation methodology | $2 per mcf of gas | | |
	Sample mean	Sample standard deviation	Standard error of the mean
OV	4.13	5.56	1.21
USGS	4.93	6.32	1.38
GB	6.03	3.58	0.78
HB	18.95	16.07	3.51
OV-USGS	−0.79	1.26	0.27
GB-OV	1.90	5.33	1.16
HB-OV	14.81	15.88	3.47
GB-USGS	1.11	5.94	1.30
HB-USGS	14.02	16.19	3.53

| Valuation methodology | $3 per mcf of gas | | |
	Sample mean	Sample standard deviation	Standard error of the mean
OV	8.20	9.42	2.06
USGS	4.93	6.32	1.38
GB	6.03	3.58	0.78
HB	18.95	16.07	3.51
OV-USGS	3.27	3.50	0.76
GB-OV	−2.17	8.69	1.90
HB-OV	13.22	16.52	3.60
GB-USGS	1.11	5.94	1.30
HB-USGS	14.02	16.19	3.53

Note: OV-USGS represents the tract-by-tract difference in OV and USGS valuations, etc.

Table 37.3 presents simple correlation coefficients that measure the degree of linear association between the alternative measures of tract value. It is immediately apparent that the OV and USGS estimates are very highly correlated. In view of the common data inputs (cost and geological) they share, this is not surprising. In spite of the high correlation, there are significant disparities between the OV and USGS estimates that will be pointed out shortly.

It is also apparent from table 37.3 that the USGS estimates are not highly correlated with the level of industry bids. This has been a recurrent problem for the USGS, and undoubtedly reflects the well-known fact that USGS appraisals of geological potential differ markedly in many cases from the individual assessments of private firms. The OV estimates also correlate poorly with industry bids, since the OV estimates rely on the same underlying geological data used by the USGS.

We turn next to a comparison of average tract values, which are recorded in Table 37.4. The results are sensitive to the value chosen for gas. For a $2 per mcf value for gas (implied by strict BTU pricing parity), the OV estimates are, on average, below the values from the USGS and both industry measures. For the $3 per mcf value (drawn from market sources), the OV estimates are, on average, above both the USGS values and the average of mean industry bids. They are, however, well below the mean high bid. As this experiment is meant to be a broad test of the plausibility of the OV approach, these results are quite promising. Uman et al. [1979] find that there is no apparent bias in USGS ex ante geological estimates, even though they are subject to large errors. That the OV approach with the preferred $3 per mcf value for gas falls between the two industry measures provides room for optimism.

We can only speculate about how the OV technique might perform in conjunction with geological assessments more in line with industry expectations. However, on the basis of the present results, we are greatly encouraged to try such an experiment. The most valid comparison would be an OV estimate compared with industry valuations based on the same geological and cost assumptions. This is not possible at present due to data restrictions.

D   Comparative Statics

In Section III we discussed how increases in reserve price variability and relinquishment time limits unambiguously increase the OV value of undeveloped reserves and unexplored tracts. However, neither extending relinquishment time limits nor increasing the variance has significant effects for the tracts in sale 62. The variance effect arises because of the possibility of not exploring and developing. In our data set, nearly all of the tracts are very much in the money (conditional on the presence of hydrocarbons), meaning that the developed reserve value greatly exceeds combined exploration and development costs. Therefore, given that oil and gas have been found, there is little likelihood that exploration and development will *not* occur immediately. Hence the variance effect is not important. Relaxing the relinquishment requirement does not have much effect for reasons we discuss below.

To demonstrate how variance and time limits would affect tract value in areas subject to *higher* unit investment costs, we value a set of hypothetical undeveloped reserves that have cost structures representative of those found in Alaska and the North Atlantic region. These tracts have the following: (a) 100 million barrels of oil are proven; and (b) $\hat{V}/D$ ratios varying from 0.7 to 1.0. We increase the standard deviation of the rate of change in the value of a developed reserve from 0.142 to 0.250 and increase the relinquishment time limit from five to both ten and fifteen years. (The USGS has granted ten-year limits on certain high cost tracts.) Table 37.5

Table 37.5
Valuations for OV for different variances and expiration times: hypothetical high-development cost of undeveloped reserves (millions $)

Variance and expiration times	Value to development cost ratio (V/D)			
	0.70	0.80	0.90	1.00
$\sigma = 0.142, \bar{T} = 5$	10.78	26.06	51.51	88.25
$\sigma = 0.142, \bar{T} = 10$	21.76	40.49	67.14	102.41
$\sigma = 0.142, \bar{T} = 15$	28.04	47.65	74.28	108.65
$\sigma = 0.250, \bar{T} = 5$	73.74	106.47	142.96	182.06
$\sigma = 0.250, \bar{T} = 10$	116.50	149.64	184.19	219.70
$\sigma = 0.250, \bar{T} = 15$	139.67	171.84	204.76	238.19

Hypothetical High Cost Parameters
Reserve value $= \$11.52$
Hydrocarbon reserves $= 100$ million barrels
$\bar{T} = T - t$.

presents valuations for these tracts. Clearly, increasing volatility from $\sigma = 0.142$ to $\sigma = 0.250$ has a large impact on high-cost undeveloped reserve values. The effect dampens as $\hat{V}/D$ increases, because the tract becomes more likely to be developed. For example, for $\bar{T} = T - t = 10$, increasing the volatility increases the reserve value by 435 percent for $\hat{V}/D = 0.70$ and by 115 percent for $\hat{V}/D = 1.0$. Relaxing relinquishment requirements can also have a significant effect on tract values. For example, for $\sigma = 0.142$, increasing the time to relinquishment from five to fifteen years increases the reserve value by 160 percent for $\hat{V}/D = 0.70$ and by 23 percent of $\hat{V}/D = 1.0$. Again, the effect diminishes as $\hat{V}/D$ increases. Thus, the option of waiting to explore and develop is quite valuable to companies leasing tracts in high-cost areas, especially during periods of great uncertainty about future hydrocarbon prices. Since the government appears to capture at least all residual economic rents on OCS lease sales (see Mead et al. [1983]), the private option to wait is then also valuable to the government, which could expect to receive commensurately larger bonus bids.[30] The only exception arises if some distortive element of the tax or royalty system would somehow be aggravated by lengthening the term to relinquishment, resulting in less efficient extraction.[31]

E   Exploration and Development Timing

As discussed above, embedded in the option valuation is the solution of the optimal investment timing problem. Figure 37.1 gives hitting boundaries based on the same parameters that were used in the valuations above; i.e., $\sigma = 0.142$, and $\sigma = 0.250$. As discussed above, this boundary is appropriate for either valuing an unexplored tract (assuming that immediate development is always optimal) or an undeveloped reserve.

Each curve represents the boundary that $C = \hat{V}/S$ or $\hat{V}/D$ must hit for immediate investment to be optimal. As would be expected, the boundary for the higher volatility is above that for the lower volatility. With greater volatility the firm wants to allow for the possibility that prices may become very high.

The most interesting feature of both hitting boundaries is that they are relatively flat before diving to 1.0 at expiration. This indicates that tracts with certain cost and geological characteristics should be explored or developed immediately, while others should be held either until close to the expiration of the relinquishment time limit or until developed reserve prices increase sufficiently to induce explorations or development. In particular, low-cost tracts will be explored or developed immediately and higher cost tracts will be held from exploration or development. This is a particularly simple form of an investment rule, given that the hitting boundary will be the same for all tracts. The firm need only calculate $C = \hat{V}/S$ or $\hat{V}/D$ to decide whether a tract should be explored or developed immediately.

VI Summary and Extensions

This chapter has extended financial option theory by developing an approach to valuing a claim on a real asset: an offshore petroleum lease. We have addressed several theoretical and practical problems, not present in applying option pricing theory to financial assets. Most importantly, we show the necessity of combining option pricing techniques with a model of equilibrium in the market for the underlying asset. Our new approach has several advantages over currently used discounted cash flow techniques. First, it requires significantly less data because it efficiently uses market information. Second, it has less computational cost and is less subject to error. Third, it provides a guide for the optimal timing of development. Finally, it provides important insights for both government policy and company behavior. Empirical application of the approach suggests that the approach has significant promise.

There are three important extensions of this work. The first involves obtaining good measures of the market value of developed reserves. While companies have access to these values from their dealings in active secondary markets, it would be useful to be able to obtain these values from more public sources. One possibility is to try to extract these values from the (traded) stock prices of companies whose assets consist solely of developed reserves (producing properties). These companies exist both in the United States and in the United Kingdom. Controlling for variables such as differing tax regimes, price controls, cost structures, and oil quality will be an important consideration.

The second extension involves a more complex specification of the development decision. We have modeled development as a lump instantaneous expenditure. Actually, companies have latitude in varying the rate of development. It may, for example, be optimal to develop slowly to take advantage of new information. This gives the company the *option* to discontinue further development if it becomes unprofitable. This option effect must be weighed against possible economies of proceeding more rapidly. The resulting analysis would be similar to that in Majd and Pindyck [1987].

Finally, there are many other real assets with option-like characteristics. The kinds of informational economies, insights, and problems discussed here in relation to valuing petroleum leases should be present in valuing claims on other real assets as well.

Acknowledgments

The work has been supported by the United States Geological Survey and the U. S. Department of Energy—Energy Information Administration under contract No. EX-76-A-01-2295, and by the U. S. National Science Foundation under Grant No. DAR 78-19044. The work also has been supported by the M.I.T. Center for Energy Policy Research. However, any opinions, findings, conclusions, or recommendations expressed herein are those of the authors and do not necessarily reflect the views of any of the sponsors. We thank Yuk-Shee Chan, Greg Connor, Steinar Ekern, Robert Hodrick, Ravi Jagannathan, Scott Mason, Stewart Myers, Anjan Thakor, and an anonymous referee for useful comments. We are particularly indebted to Robert McDonald for his many contributions to our thinking. The usual disclaimer applies.

Notes

1. Relinquishment requirements put a limit on the time a firm can hold a petroleum tract before exploring and developing it.

2. As McDonald and Siegel [1986] discuss, $X(\cdot)$ is first degree homogeneous in V and D.

3. There are certainly systematic components to development cost uncertainty. Costs of steel, concrete, platform crews, ships, and other factors of production will all move somewhat systematically. However, these systematic sources of variability are quantitatively unimportant when compared with geological uncertainty and tract-specific cost factors. The only reason for a systematic component to geological risk is the unlikely event that a field could be large enough such that the realization of Q could affect all other assets in the economy in a perceptible way. Certainly, movement in other assets will not affect geological risk.

4. See Adelman and Paddock [1980] for a discussion and justification of this "collapsing" technique. This sum is essentially the present value of development expenditures. There are two possible objections to this

approach. First, the developed reserves are not obtained until after a lag equal to the development time. We shall explicitly account for this lag. Second, the firm has latitude over the speed and quantity of development, which it can vary as new information arrives. We discuss this problem in Section VI.

5. In current practice the DCF method does not typically use this market information. While this information could be incorporated into a DCF valuation, it would be much more difficult than in the OV approach. See below for a detailed discussion of this point.

Tourinho [1979] suggests looking at petroleum reserves as options. However, he lumps development and extraction costs together as the exercise price and considers the option to extract the petroleum. This formulation does not lead to a usable valuation scheme because it does not separately address the critical development option, and does not make efficient use of market information. Brennan and Schwartz [1985] also discuss natural resource extraction in an option framework. They do not, however, address the important issues arising out of our discussion of equilibrium in the market for developed reserves.

6. The finance literature has modeled stock rates of return by a continuous-time random walk because if information flows into the market continuously, then in an efficient market participants must update their expectations and valuations continuously.

7. This is a standard assumption in the literature on petroleum extraction (see Adelman and Jacoby [1979]) and reflects geological constraints on the extraction rate.

8. Note that $dt\,dV_t = 0$. α_v^* and α_v can vary with time.

9. This is similar to the payout rate in Myers and Majd [1983].

10. Note that P will exceed V because one would prefer a barrel of oil above the ground to one in the ground due to extraction costs and the time it takes to extract the oil. This will be true as long as storage costs above the ground are small relative to extraction costs and the time value costs associated with waiting until a barrel of oil can be extracted.

11. As is true with standard option pricing, α_v^* can vary with the state variables of the problem without changing the valuations. In Section V below, we justify the assumption that δ_t is constant. If σ_v or δ_t is a function of state variables, more complex numerical techniques than those we use can be employed.

12. If α_v^* varies with the state variables of the problem, then $\hat{V}_t$ can be priced using (6). The resulting value of the claim will again be (14).

13. A more complete specification of contract terms appears in the *Federal Register*, Vol. 45, no. 202, pp. 68866–883. We have chosen to look only at one-sixth royalty tracts because our developed reserve values are most appropriate for this type of tract.

14. We combine oil and condensate by adding means and variances. While oil and condensate may not be independently distributed, we have no estimate of the covariance to work with. Because the quantities of condensate are very small, this procedure should not affect our results in a significant way.

15. This is the usual distributional assumption (empirically supported) for hydrocarbon quantities. See Reece [1978, p. 371] for a discussion.

16. See Press [1982] for a discussion of the joint log-normal distribution.

17. Government forecasts made in 1981 indicated that delivered prices for new gas would jump to nearly $7 per mcf (1980 dollars) when scheduled decontrol measures took effect in 1985 [U. S. DOE, 1981]. This was the expected price level supporting in-situ values of $2 to $3 per mcf in 1980. The dramatic fall that has since occurred was not foreseen in 1980.

18. Notice that the oil and gas reserve market values include deductions for expected taxes and royalties, as well as allowances for depreciation of tangible development costs associated with the producing reserve. When a company purchases a developed reserve, it receives any unused depreciation allowances associated with the reserve. The depreciation allowance it receives will depend upon the magnitude of the exploration and development costs. It is not likely, however, that this will cause great variability in the market value of developed reserves across tracts with different exploration and development costs.

19. Imported crude is more appropriate than domestic crude, because domestic crude was controlled during this period and decontrolled soon after.

20. See Jacoby and Paddock [1983] for a discussion of these price forecasts. Note, however, that the confidence intervals are not very sensitive to these forecasts.

21. This proportion is taken from the National Petroleum Council [1981].

22. We use undiscounted expected exploration costs because most drilling lags are short.

23. In Section IV we did not distinguish between oil and gas. It is necessary to view the option to develop as the option to obtain $V_o Q_o + V_g Q_g$, where V_o and V_g are the values of developed reserves of oil and gas, respectively. The exercise price is now the *total* development cost. As mentioned above, homogeneity of the value of an undeveloped reserve allows this transformation.

24. We have converted oil to equivalent gas quantities on a BTU basis, using the conversion factor: 1 barrel = 6 mcf.

25. Mansvelt Beck and Wiig [1977] tabulate total development expenditures in the Gulf of Mexico as a function of field size, for both gas and oil fields (see their tables C3 and C4). Their data imply a gas-field scale parameter (β) precisely equal to 0.66, and an oil-field scale parameter equal to 0.80. Because federal sale No. 62 consisted predominantly of gas prospects, we have used the lower value. Experimentation with higher values, however, shows that our results are not affected appreciably by the presumed magnitude of scale economies.

26. Because of Jensen's Inequality, it is not proper to simply insert expectations in (15) to arrive at A_j.

27. See the National Petroleum Council [1981].

28. Depreciation allowances can only be taken once production has begun. As we discussed above, depreciation allowances associated with the producing developed reserve will be reflected in the market value of the reserve.

29. Because the distribution of industry bids is so markedly skewed, it is customary in the literature to use the geometric mean as a measure of central tendency.

30. By extending the term to relinquishment, the government does reduce the present value of its option to resell the tract if the tract is unexplored when relinquishment occurs. However, to the extent that a relinquishment requirement forces a company to explore and develop earlier than is optimal, extending the term to relinquishment should have an overall positive effect on total rents. However, we have not estimated this effect explicitly. See footnote 31 for a discussion of when this may not be true.

31. Royalties and excise taxes generally cause the developer to postpone production. If longer terms to relinquishment accommodate this, they also would reduce the total net social value of the lease. We do not propose, however, that the government attempt to neutralize the tax distortion by manipulating the relinquishment terms. In any event, the effect of extending relinquishment on bonus bids would be as described in the text. The developer postpones production only if doing so increases the net private value of the tract, and this increment in value is captured by the government via the competitive bidding process.

For a given number of years to expiration at date T, if $C = V/D(V/S)$ is less than C^*, the firm defers development (exploration and development). If C exceeds C^*, investment should proceed immediately. σ represents the standard deviation of the rate of change of V. To account for investment lags, replace V by $\hat{V}$.

References

Adelman, M. A., and H. D. Jacoby, "Alternative Methods of Oil Supply Forecasting," *Advances in the Economics of Energy and Resources*, Vol. 2, Robert Pindyck, ed. (Greenwich, CT: J.A.I. Press, 1979).

Adelman, M. A., and J. Paddock, "An Aggregate Model of Petroleum Production Capacity and Supply Forecasting," MIT Working Paper No. MIT-EL 79-005WP, July 1980.

Black, F., and M. Scholes, "The Pricing of Options and Corporate Liabilities," *Journal of Political Economy*, 81 (1973), 637–54.

Brealey, R., and S. Myers, *Principles of Corporate Finance*, 2nd ed. (New York, NY: McGraw Hill Book Company, 1984).

Brennan, M. J., and E. S. Schwartz, "Evaluating Natural Resource Investments," *Journal of Business*, 58 (1985), 135–57.

Capen, E. C., R. V. Clapp, and W. M. Campbell, "Competitive Bidding in High-Risk Situations," *Journal of Petroleum Technology*, 23 (1971), 641–53.

Constantinides, G. M., "Market Risk Adjustment in Project Valuation," *Journal of Finance*, 33 (1978), 603–16.

Federal Energy Administration, *Monthly Energy Review*, issues from 1974–1981.

Federal Register, XLV, 1980.

Geske, R., "The Valuation of Compound Options," *Journal of Financial Economics*, 52 (1979), 63–81.

Gruy, H. J., F. A. Garb, and J. W. Wood, "Determining the Value of Oil and Gas in the Ground," *World Oil*, 194 (1982), 105–08.

Herfindahl, O., "Depletion and Economic Theory," *Extractive Resources and Taxation*, M. Gaffney, ed. (Madison, WI: University of Wisconsin Press, 1967).

Jacoby, H. D., and J. L. Paddock, "World Oil Prices and Economic Growth in the 1980's, *Energy Journal*, 4 (1983), 31–47.

Kagel, J. H., and D. Levin, "The Winner's Curse and Public Information in Common Value Auctions," *American Economic Review*, 76 (1986), 894–920.

Lohrenz, J., and E. L. Dougherty, "Bonus Bidding and Bottom Lines: Federal Offshore Oil and Gas," Society of Petroleum Engineers Paper No. 12024, 1983.

Majd, S., and R. S. Pindyck, "Time to Build, Option Value, and Investment Decisions," *Journal of Financial Economics*, 18 (1987), 7–27.

Mansvelt Beck, F. W., and K. M. Wiig, *The Economics of Offshore Oil and Gas Supplies* (Lexington MA: D. C. Heath and Co., 1977).

Mason, S. P., and R. C. Merton, "The Role of Contingent Claims Analysis in Corporate Finance," *Recent Advances in Corporate Finance*, E. I. Altman and M. G. Subrahmanyam, eds. (Homewood, IL: Richard D. Irwin, 1985).

McDonald, R., and D. Siegel, "Asset Market Equilibrium, Investment and the Price Behavior of an Exhaustible Resource," Northwestern University Working Paper, May 1983.

———, and ———, "Option Valuation when the Underlying Asset Earns a Below-Equilibrium Return: A Note," *Journal of Finance*, 39 (1984) 261–66.

———, and ———, "Investment and the Valuation of Firms When There is an Option to Shut Down," *International Economic Review*, 26 (1985), 331–49.

———, and ———, "The Value of Waiting to Invest," *Quarterly Journal of Economics*, 101 (1986), 707–27.

Mead, W. J., A. Moseidjord, and P. E. Sorenson, "The Rate of Return Earned by Lessees under Cash Bonus Bidding for OCS Oil and Gas Leases," *Energy Journal*, 4 (1983), 37–52.

Merton, R. C., "The Theory of Rational Option Pricing," *Bell Journal of Economics and Management Science*, 4 (1973), 141–83.

Milgrom, P. R., and R. J. Weber, "A Theory of Auctions and Competitive Bidding," *Econometrica*, 50 (1982), 1089–122.

Myers, S., and S. Majd, "Abandonment Value and Project Life," *Advances in Futures and Optional Research* 4, 1–21.

National Petroleum Council, "Working Paper #39 of the National Petroleum Council's Committee on Arctic Oil and Gas Resources, Appendix 11," December 1981.

Paddock, J. L., "Financial Market Valuation of Developed Oil Reserves," mimeo. M.I.T. Energy Laboratory, 1982.

Press, S. J., *Applied Multivariate Analysis*, 2nd ed. (Malabar, FL: Robert K. Kreiger Publishing Co., 1982).

Reece, D. K., "Competitive Bidding for Offshore Petroleum Leases," *Bell Journal of Economics*, 9 (1978), 369–84.

Skelton, J., "Banks, Firms and the Relative Pricing of Tax-Exempt and Taxable Bonds," *Journal of Financial Economics*, 12 (1983), 343–56.

Smith, C. W., "Option Pricing: A Review," *Journal of Financial Economics*, 3 (1976), 3–52.

Tourinho, O. A. F., "The Option Value of Reserves of Natural Resources," unpublished, University of California, Berkeley, 1979.

Uman, M. F., W. R. James, and H. R. Tomlinson, "Oil and Gas in Offshore Tracts: Estimates Before and After Drilling," *Science*, 205 (1979), 489–91.

U. S. Department of Energy, Office of Policy, Planning and Analysis, "A Study of Alternatives to the Natural Gas Act of 1978," DOE/PE-0031, 1981.

Wilson, R. B., "A Bidding Model of Perfect Competition," *Review of Economic Studies*, 44 (1977), 511–18.

38 Empirical Testing of Real Option-Pricing Models

Laura Quigg

Despite extensive testing of option-pricing models for financial assets, virtually no research has addressed the empirical implications of option-based valuation models for real assets.[1] This research is the first effort that examines the empirical predictions of a real option-pricing model using a large sample of market prices. Real options that have been valued in the academic literature include capital investments and natural resources, as well as urban land. The model we consider incorporates the option to wait to invest in the valuation of urban land. This paper provides empirical information about the option-based value of land, relative to its intrinsic value and its market price.

Using data on 2700 land transactions in Seattle, we find a mean option (time) premium of 6% of the theoretical land value. This premium ranges from 1% to 30% in various subsamples. We define the "option premium" as the difference between the intrinsic value and the option model value, divided by the option model value.[2] We also find that the option model has explanatory power over and above the intrinsic value for predicting transaction prices. Therefore, to the extent that it is possible to coordinate and time an investment, valuation models should account for the option to wait. We believe that the premia for more speculative properties might be much larger than the values given here.[3]

In addition, we estimate implied standard deviations of individual commercial real estate asset prices in the range of 18 to 28% per year. This result is a contribution in itself, as a lack of repeat sales data for this class of assets makes it difficult to estimate the price variance directly. The implied variances we estimate are equivalent to Black-Scholes implied volatilities from stock options.

Previous research that evaluates the prices obtained from a real option model is limited to Paddock, Siegel, and Smith (1988). Paddock *et al.* develop an option-based model that values offshore petroleum leases as a function of the market price of oil. For 21 tracts, they compare the prices computed from this model both to the government's discounted cash flow model (which uses the same underlying data inputs) and to industry bids (both highest and geometric mean). The Paddock *et al.* and government models give very highly correlated values, and neither comes close to predicting industry bids. The highest industry bid would generally correspond to the market price, providing a comparison between real option values and transaction prices. While these high bids are more than twice either the option-based or government valuations, the mean industry bid is within the range (either above or below depending on the assigned value for gas) of the alternative valuations. As the authors point out, due to a "winner's curse," the high bid may exceed the true expected tract value.

In Section I we discuss our model that prices land, incorporating the option to wait to develop. The option value is a function of the building developed on the site and development costs. In Section II, the marginal prices of each building's characteristics are estimated using hedonic estimation on a separate sample of 3200 developed properties. Using these results, we calculate the value of an optimally scaled building for each of 2700 undeveloped properties. In Section III we evaluate the theoretical land values given by the option-based model relative to the intrinsic values and to market prices. We present conclusions in Section IV.

I The Model

The model we consider is a fairly general, infinite-horizon, continuous-time model that in form most closely resembles Williams (1991a), but also tests the implications of Titman (1985). The principal features of previous optimal timing models are incorporated.

Through ownership of an undeveloped or underdeveloped property, the landholder holds a perpetual option to construct an optimal size building at an optimal time, subject to zoning restrictions. The cost of development is,

$$X = f + q^{\gamma} x_1, \tag{1}$$

where f represents fixed costs, q is the square footage of the building, γ is the cost elasticity of scale, and x_1 is the development cost per square foot. Development costs are assumed to follow a geometric Brownian motion with a constant drift, α_x, and a constant variance, σ_x^2,

$$dX/X = \alpha_x \, dt + \sigma_x \, dz_x. \tag{2}$$

We assume that the price P of the underlying asset, the building, is observable. The implications of this assumption are discussed in Section III.B. P is given by $P = q^{\phi}\varepsilon$, where ε is a function of other attributes of the property and ϕ is the price elasticity of scale.[4] The complete formulation and estimation of P are discussed in Section III.A. P follows a geometric Brownian motion with constant drift, α_p, and constant variance, σ_p^2,

$$dP/P = (\alpha_p - x_2) \, dt + \sigma_p \, dz_p, \tag{3}$$

where x_2 are payouts to the developed property and $\rho \, dt$ is the constant correlation between dz_x and dz_p. We require that the cost elasticity of scale, γ, exceed the price elasticity of scale, ϕ.[5]

We also make the following assumptions. There is a known riskless instantaneous interest rate, r, which is constant through time and equal for borrowers and lenders. Land owners are price takers, giving a partial equilibrium model.[6] The investment is irreversible, i.e., once the investor has built on the property, it no longer has any optimal timing value. βP is the income to the undeveloped or underdeveloped property.[7]

Finally, we assume that there is an equilibrium in the economy in which contingent claims on the pair of processes for the development costs and building price (X, P) are uniquely priced.[8] We will represent the corresponding pricing operator by taking the expectation of future cash flows under the risk-adjusted probability measure and discounting at the risk-free rate. This is carried out by changing the drifts of X and P, α_x and α_p, respectively, to $v_x \equiv \alpha_x - \lambda_x \sigma_x$ and $v_p \equiv (\alpha_p - x_2) - \lambda_p \sigma_p$, where λ_x and λ_p are constant parameters representing the excess mean return per unit of standard deviation. We can then express the value of the undeveloped property, $V(X, P)$, as the solution to the fundamental valuation equation:

$$0 = 0.5\sigma_x^2 X^2 V_{xx} + \sigma_{xp} XP V_{xp} + .5\sigma_p^2 P^2 V_{pp} + v_x X V_x + v_p P V_p - rV + \beta P, \tag{4}$$

subject to appropriate boundary conditions.

Making a change of variables, $z \equiv P/X$ and $W(z) \equiv V(X, P)/X$, we obtain:

$$0 = 0.5\omega^2 z^2 W'' + (v_p - v_x)z W' + (v_x - r)W + \beta z, \tag{5}$$

where

$$\omega^2 = \sigma_x^2 - 2\rho \sigma_x \sigma_p + \sigma_p^2.$$

To solve this differential equation, we assume that there is a ratio of the building price to development costs, z, at which it is optimal to build. The investor exercises optimally at this "hurdle ratio," z^*, giving the "smooth-pasting" condition. The appendix provides a more detailed solution and description of these conditions.

The solution is given as follows:

$$V(P, X) = X(Az^j + k), \tag{6}$$

where,

$$A = (z^* - 1 - k)(z^*)^{-j},$$

$$z^* = j(1 + k)/(j - 1),$$

$$k = \beta z/(r - v_x),$$

$$j = \omega^{-2}(.5\omega^2 + v_x - v_p + [\omega^2(.25\omega^2 - v_p - v_x + 2r) + (v_x - v_p)^2]^{.5})$$

$$z = P/X$$

The intrinsic value of the option can be found by taking the limit of (6) as the variance ω goes to zero. This result is given by,

$$V^I(X, P) = P - X, \quad z \geq 1 + k$$

$$V^I(X, P) = \beta P/(r - v_x), \quad z < 1 + k \tag{7}$$

If the ratio $z \equiv P/X$ exceeds $1 + k$, the landowner will build immediately. Otherwise he will hold the land for the income it generates.[9]

For tractability, the optimal scale or building square footage, q^*, is determined by the initial values of P and X, and is therefore the same for both the option-based value, $V(P, X)$, and the intrinsic value $V^I(P, X)$. This assumption understates the value of the option, as we discuss further in Section III.B. q^* is found by maximizing the value of the undeveloped property, $V(q) = P(q) - X(q) = q^\phi \varepsilon - (f + q^\gamma x_1)$, over q. The solution is,

$$q^* = (\gamma x_1/\varepsilon\phi)^{(\gamma/(\phi-\gamma))} \quad q^* < \delta$$

$$q^* = \delta \quad q^* \geq \delta, \tag{8}$$

where δ is the maximum size permitted by the zoning regulations.

Our empirical work examines the option-based value given by (6), compared to the intrinsic value (7) and compared to market prices. The building is assumed to be built to the optimal scale in (8), and the optimal time to build is when the ratio of building price to development costs exceeds z^* in (6).

II The Data

The primary data set consists of a large number of real estate transactions within the city of Seattle.[10] All properties are within the city limits and are zoned for investment purposes: business, commercial, industrial, or low- and high-density residential.[11] The data cover the second half of 1976 through the end of 1979 and include the characteristics of 3200 transactions of developed properties (developed to a reasonable approximation of the permitted zoning) and 2700 transactions of unimproved land parcels. The data on the developed properties are used in the hedonic estimation of the potential building values. The unimproved parcels represent the real options, the land which the owner has the option to develop.

The cost function is given by (1). These costs are estimated using the Marshall Valuation Service. This service provides indexes of per-square-foot construction costs for various types and qualities of buildings and assigns multipliers for adjusting these unit costs to particular years and localities.[12] Estimation of the cost scale parameter γ is described in Section III.C.

III   Empirical Results

A   Estimates of Building Values

Land is valued as an option, for which the underlying asset is the building that potentially would be built on that site. The price of this building is not observable, and thus must be estimated. The method we employ is hedonic estimation. Hedonic theory focuses on markets in which a generic commodity can embody varying amounts of each of a vector of characteristics or attributes Z. A hedonic price function $p(Z)$ specifies how the market price of a commodity varies as these characteristics vary. Rosen (1974) provides a theoretical framework in which $p(Z)$ emerges as the equilibrium price arising from bids and offers of the suppliers and demanders of the good. The distribution of the quantity, as a function of Z, that is supplied and consumed is also endogenously determined.

We separate the sample into years (1976–1977, 1978, and 1979) and into five zoning categories (commercial, business, industrial, low-density residential, and high-density residential), to improve the predictive power of the coefficients.[13] For each subsample, we regress the log price for an improved property on its characteristics,

$$\log P_i = c + \phi \log q_1 + \psi \log LSF_i + a_1 HT_i + a_2 HT_i^2 + a_3 AGE_i + b' L_i + d' Q_i + e_i$$
$$(9)$$

The independent variables included are the log of square footage of the building (q), the log of the lot (LSF), and the height and age of the building. L is a vector of six dummy variables, obtained by combining groups of census tracts in the city. These are abbreviated n (north), w (west), ce (central east), cw (central west), se (southeast), and sw (southwest). Q is a vector of dummy variables representing the quarter in which the property was sold, with the last quarter of each subsample omitted. This functional form is used because its Box-Cox transformation gives the highest log likelihood, lowest standard error, and highest R^2.

From these equations we estimate the coefficients to be used to determine the potential building value on an undeveloped plot of land. The results from each of these regressions are presented in tables 38.1 to 38.5. The fit of the regressions is good

Table 38.1

Hedonic estimation for business properties in Seattle $(\log P_i = c + \phi \log q_i + \psi \log LSF_i + a_1 HT_i + a_2 HT_i^2 + a_3 AGE_i + b'L_i + d'Q_i + e_i)$. For each property, i, P is the price; q and LSF are the building and lot sizes, respectively, as measured in square feet. Height (HT) is measured in stories and age in years. L and Q are dummy variables representing the location and quarter in which the sale took place. The last quarter of each time period and Central West are omitted variables. N is the sample size. The regression is estimated separately for each of the three time periods.

	1976–1977			1978			1979	
R-squared	0.922			0.843			0.878	
Std. Error	0.312			0.457			0.426	
F-statistic	156.11			67.31			82.86	
N	215			177			164	
Variable	Coeff.	Std. error		Coeff.	Std. error		Coeff.	Std. error
Constant	−0.741	0.463		3.210	0.575		1.152	0.527
$\log(q)$	0.565	0.039		0.495	0.058		0.314	0.057
$\log(LSF)$	0.875	0.063		0.507	0.067		0.935	0.061
HT	0.126	0.053		0.163	0.066		0.255	0.094
HT^2	−0.011	0.006		−0.006	0.004		−0.019	0.011
AGE	−0.003	0.001		−0.005	0.002		−0.003	0.002
Locations								
North	−0.158	0.089		−0.074	0.147		−0.185	0.134
West	−0.101	0.094		0.070	0.158		−0.262	0.148
Central east	−0.355	0.100		−0.434	0.172		−0.276	0.146
Central west	0			0			0	
Southeast	−0.340	0.094		−0.117	0.172		−0.198	0.159
Southwest	−0.415	0.105		−0.511	0.166		−0.332	0.155
Quarters								
76-3	−0.202	0.078	78-1	−0.258	0.097	79-1	−0.190	0.143
76-4	−0.075	0.065	78-2	−0.167	0.098	79-2	−0.136	0.147
77-1	−0.067	0.081	78-3	−0.007	0.112	79-3	−0.120	0.148
77-2	−0.045	0.070						
77-3	−0.039	0.084						

for all zoning categories and all years, with R^2 ranging from 80.2 to 95.6. Each of the price elasticities of size is less than one and significantly greater than zero at conventional levels. The elasticity of lot size is fairly large, in most cases greater than 0.5. The elasticity of building size ranges approximately between 0.3 and 0.5. This situation is reversed for low-density residential properties, for which the elasticity of the building size is much higher than that of the lot. The estimates vary across years; the variation might reflect that each data set consists of the differing properties that have sold each year. However, because of the unknown time series properties of this data, it is possible that the standard errors are understated. Therefore, we cannot reject the hypothesis that the true elasticities are constant across time.

Table 38.2
Hedonic estimation for commercial properties in Seattle ($\log P_i = c + \phi \log q_i + \psi \log LSF_i + a_1 HT_i + a_2 HT_i^2 + a_3 AGE_i + b'L_i + d'Q_i + e_i$). For each property, i, P is the price; q and LSF are the building and lot sizes, respectively, as measured in square feet. Height (HT) is measured in stories and age in years. L and Q are dummy variables representing the location and quarter in which the sale took place. The last quarter of each time period and Central West are omitted variables. N is the sample size. The regression is estimated separately for each of the three time periods.

	1976–1977			1978			1979	
R-squared	0.885			0.856			0.893	
Std. Error	0.336			0.397			0.326	
F-statistic	108.9			54.26			75.05	
N	229			133			131	
Variable	Coeff.	Std. error		Coeff.	Std. error		Coeff.	Std. error
Constant	1.887	0.366		2.854	0.476		0.853	0.469
log(q)	0.419	0.036		0.501	0.064		0.415	0.050
log(LSF)	0.702	0.038		0.513	0.067		0.804	0.061
HT	0.051	0.068		0.151	0.076		0.209	0.059
HT^2	0.002	0.011		−0.004	0.005		−0.014	0.004
AGE	−0.006	0.001		−0.004	0.002		−0.000	0.002
Locations								
North	−0.119	0.090		0.080	0.146		−0.055	0.103
West	0.144	0.085		0.151	0.154		−0.064	0.102
Central east	−0.208	0.100		−0.267	0.160		0.075	0.127
Central west	0			0	0		0	0
Southeast	−0.283	0.134		0.090	0.261		−0.065	0.185
Southwest	−0.325	0.104		−0.199	0.178		−0.285	0.116
Quarters								
76-3	−0.148	0.079	78-1	−0.228	0.092	79-1	−0.092	0.098
76-4	−0.086	0.078	78-2	−0.122	0.105	79-2	−0.026	0.092
77-1	−0.079	0.073	78-3	−0.008	0.104	79-3	0.059	0.094
77-2	−0.084	0.087						
77-3	0.017	0.067						

For business and commercial properties, the downtown area (central west, *cw*) is the eliminated locational dummy variable. For all other subsamples the north is eliminated due to the lack of data points in the downtown area. From these estimates it is clear that Seattle is not a monocentric city, and that a simple variable measuring the distance from the city center would not capture important locational features. In particular, the area east of downtown (central east, *ce*) is a location that has negative price effects. North and west generally add to value, while central west is not always the most attractive location.[14]

When the coefficient for age is statistically significant, age has a negative impact. For the height levels that make up most of the sample, the effect of height on value is

Table 38.3

Hedonic estimation for industrial properties in Seattle $(\log P_i = c + \phi \log q_i + \psi \log LSF_i + a_1 HT_i + a_2 HT_i^2 + a_3 AGE_i + b'L_i + d'Q_i + e_i)$. For each property, i, P is the price; q and LSF are the building and lot sizes, respectively, as measured in square feet. Height (HT) is measured in stories and age in years. L and Q are dummy variables representing the location and quarter in which the sale took place. The last quarter of each time period and North are omitted variables. N is the sample size. The regression is estimated separately for each of the three time periods.

	1976–1977			1978			1979	
R-squared	0.824			0.948			0.956	
Std. Error	0.464			0.318			0.252	
F-statistic	22.0			26.8			45.5	
N	75			33			41	

Variable	Coeff.	Std. error		Coeff.	Std. error		Coeff.	Std. error
Constant	2.740	0.907		2.866	0.923		1.989	0.512
$\log(q)$	0.332	0.085		0.373	0.105		0.289	0.058
$\log(LSF)$	0.728	0.082		0.681	0.110		0.789	0.054
HT_2	−0.329	0.422		−0.177	0.283		0.171	0.202
HT^2	0.085	0.108		0.037	0.042		0.013	0.030
AGE	0.000	0.003		−0.004	0.004		0.001	0.003
Locations								
North	0			0			0	
West	−0.224	0.222		−0.079	0.372		−0.230	0.234
Central east	*			−0.144	0.372		−0.651	0.293
Central west	*			0.225	0.422		1.011	0.316
Southeast	−0.491	0.225		−0.102	0.186		−0.330	0.159
Southwest	−0.288	0.149		−0.108	0.176		−0.277	0.147
Quarters								
76-3	−0.590	0.278	78-1	−0.548	0.302	79-1	−0.353	0.189
76-4	−0.460	0.259	78-2	−0.431	0.241	79-2	−0.262	0.178
77-1	−0.412	0.253	78-3	−0.308	0.233	79-3	−0.169	0.195
77-2	−0.283	0.263						
77-3	−0.107	0.258						

* No transactions in this region.

increasing at a decreasing rate, although the coefficients on these variables often are only marginally significant.

In order to predict the building value that corresponds to a particular plot of land, we need to estimate the size and height of the building. From Section I, the building price is given by $P(q) = q^\phi \varepsilon$ where the building size, q, and the price elasticity of scale, ϕ, are the same as in the hedonic equation (9), and ε is a function of other attributes of the property. We assume that the investor develops the optimally sized building, $q = q^*$, as given by equation (8).

We base the height estimates on existing property heights, so that the estimated height, $\widehat{HT}$, of a given property is equal to the average height for the relevant zoning

Table 38.4

Hedonic estimation for low-density residential properties in Seattle ($\log P_i = c + \phi \log q_i + \psi \log LSF_i + a_1 HT_i + a_2 HT_i^2 + a_3 AGE_i + b'L_i + d'Q_i + e_i$). For each property, i, P is the price; q and LSF are the building and lot sizes, respectively, as measured in square feet. Height (HT) is measured in stories and age in years. L and Q are dummy variables representing the location and quarter in which the sale took place. The last quarter of each time period and North are omitted variables. N is the sample size. The regression is estimated separately for each of the three time periods.

Variable	1977 Coeff.	1977 Std. error		1978 Coeff.	1978 Std. error		1979 Coeff.	1979 Std. error
R-squared	0.820			0.815			0.856	
Std. Error	0.288			0.282			0.254	
F-Statistic	112.2			112.7			121.6	
N	361			319			259	
Constant	2.560	0.400		3.611	0.350		0.948	0.306
$\log(q)$	0.800	0.036		0.622	0.374		0.637	0.034
$\log(LSF)$	0.279	0.044		0.378	0.044		0.631	0.042
HT	0.195	0.114		−0.152	0.159		0.022	0.041
HT^2	−0.054	0.031		0.051	0.046		−0.001	0.002
AGE	−0.006	0.001		−0.005	0.001		−0.001	0.001
Locations								
North	0			0			0	
West	0.127	0.047		0.040	0.052		0.046	0.048
Central east	−0.292	0.047		−0.467	0.049		−0.064	0.053
Central west	*			*			*	
Southeast	−0.073	0.044		−0.072	0.051		−0.097	0.056
Southwest	−0.399	0.057		−0.358	0.052		−0.072	0.050
Quarters								
76-3	−0.359	0.060	78-1	−0.333	0.045	79-1	−0.287	0.061
76-4	−0.309	0.061	78-2	−0.213	0.046	79-2	−0.243	0.045
77-1	−0.241	0.048	78-3	−0.117	0.047	79-3	−0.010	0.044
77-2	−0.235	0.048						
77-3	−0.191	0.047						

* No transactions in this region.

and location. We then conclude that the estimated value of a building developed on each of the 2700 land transactions is given by,

$$P_i = q_i^{*\phi} LSF_i^{\phi} \exp\{c + a_i \widehat{HT}_i + a_2 \widehat{HT}_i^2 + b'L_i + d'Q_i + e_i\} \tag{10}$$

where the L, LSF, and Q represent the actual location, size, and date sold of each parcel.

B   Observation Errors

There are a number of sources of error in our estimation. Consistent with the assumption of an exogenously given building price process, the estimated building

Table 38.5

Hedonic estimation for high-density residential properties in Seattle ($\log P_i = c + \phi \log q_i + \psi \log LSF_i + a_1 HT_i + a_2 HT_i^2 + a_3 AGE_i + b'L_i + d'Q_i + e_i$). For each property, i, P is the price; q and LSF are the building and lot sizes, respectively, as measured in square feet. Height (HT) is measured in stories and age in years. L and Q are dummy variables representing the location and quarter in which the sale took place. The last quarter of each time period and North are omitted variables. N is the sample size. The regression is estimated separately for each of the three time periods.

	1977			1978			1979	
R-squared		0.859			0.848			0.802
Std. Error		0.379			0.353			0.350
F-statistic		161.3			119.4			54.8
N		413			269			175
Variable	Coeff.	Std. error		Coeff.	Std. error		Coeff.	Std. error
Constant	3.181	0.274		2.637	0.401		2.472	0.492
$\log(q)$	0.595	0.045		0.772	0.050		0.548	0.063
$\log(LSF)$	0.407	0.051		0.315	0.062		0.593	0.071
HT	0.090	0.069		0.149	0.110		0.015	0.122
HT^2	−0.004	0.010		−0.031	0.020		−0.002	0.023
AGE	−0.007	0.001		−0.003	0.001		−0.003	0.001
Locations								
North	0			0			0	
West	0.118	0.058		*			*	
Central east	−0.159	0.053		0.018	0.070		0.021	0.094
Central west	0.156	0.391		−0.178	0.055		−0.080	0.693
Southeast	−0.056	0.073		0.152	0.089		0.007	0.126
Southwest	−0.282	0.073		−0.203	0.094		0.068	0.136
Quarters								
76-1	−0.296	0.069	78-1	−0.249	0.064	79-1	−0.221	0.123
76-2	−0.252	0.069	78-2	−0.189	0.064	79-2	−0.273	0.126
77-1	−0.254	0.068	78-3	−0.001	0.064	79-3	−0.174	0.124
77-2	−0.212	0.058						
77-3	−0.140	0.059						

* No transactions in this region.

values do not account for a possible depression in prices due to additions to supply. This would tend to overstate the value of the building if the true price process reflects a downward sloping demand curve. The intrinsic value of the land would tend to be overstated and the option premium correspondingly understated. However, the sample consists of many scattered, mostly small, heterogeneous lots in a market which at the time was neither saturated nor underdeveloped. The supply of land available for development was fairly limited. The building on each of these lots probably does not have much impact on the price. Therefore, the potential for substantially overstating the building value due to the assumption of exogeneity is much smaller than for a large tract of similar properties.

In addition, we may tend to overstate the true price because we observe prices only for those undeveloped or developed properties that sell. However, we also assume that the observable characteristics of existing buildings have the same marginal prices as the new buildings, and we only control for the depreciation of the existing stock in a simple way. This assumption would tend to understate the true price. Note that we do not assume that the new building is developed to the maximum density. We assume only that its value is estimated based on values of other buildings in the same zoning classification, which generally are not developed to the maximum density.[15] In sum, the building value estimation introduces several potential biases, the net impact of which is difficult to gauge.

The state variable to the option model is the ratio z of the building price to development costs. Both these values are likely to be observed with error. Since z enters into the model in a nonlinear way, the expected value of the land is affected by the estimation error. To be specific, if we assume that the estimation error is normal and multiplicative, i.e., if $\ln \hat{z} = \ln z + \varepsilon$ and ε is distributed $N(0, \sigma_\varepsilon^2)$, then,

$$E[W(\hat{z})] = Az^j \exp(j^2 \sigma_\varepsilon^2 / 2) + k > W(z). \tag{11}$$

The presence of this bias means that we are more likely to reject the null hypothesis, and therefore that our tests tend to be more conservative than stated. In addition, in our regressions of theoretical prices on actual prices, the presence of errors-in-variables problems biases the slope coefficient downward and the intercept upward.[16]

We assumed that the building price is observable. For many reasons, including building delay, the value is usually not observable. As was shown in Flesaker (1991), this uncertainty can lead to errors of omission, in which the option is not exercised when it should be, or errors of commission, in which the option is exercised when it should not be, and uniformly lowers the value of the option itself. However, if the developer retains the option to alter the building plans during the building process, the option value may possibly increase.

C Results from Tests of the Land Valuation Model

In this section we discuss the results of the estimation and specification tests. As with the hedonic estimation, we break the sample into the five data classes organized by zoning category, for which the parameters are assumed constant across each class. We evaluate real option values, (6), relative to market prices and to the intrinsic values, (7).

In order to calculate the model prices, we must make assumptions about several parameters. We assume that the risk-adjusted drift parameters $v_p = v_x = 0.03$ and the interest rate $r = 0.08$. The model does not appear to be very sensitive to these assumptions. We find, however, that the theoretical values are extremely sensitive to assumptions regarding the values of the development cost scale parameter, γ, and the payout to the underdeveloped property, β. Since we lack information about the true values of these variables, we estimate values that minimize the pricing errors in our sample. We estimate a value for β ranging from 0.3% to 3% of the developed building value. Our priors were that γ should be less than but close to one, giving some economies of scale. The values we estimate range from 0.9 to 1. The prices we calculate are extremely sensitive to γ, primarily through its function in determining the optimal building size. Only a small fraction of the sample was developed to the maximum density.

Because both the intrinsic value and option-based value models depend in the same way on the building value, development costs, and land payout, the estimates of γ and β, the optimal building size q^*, and the height assumptions should affect the option model and intrinsic value equivalently.[17] That is, for positive variance, reasonable changes in these values do not alter the theoretically positive difference between the option model price and intrinsic value.

Table 38.6 shows variance estimates that are "implied" from the real option model. The parameter we estimate is ω^2, given by (5), which is the variance of the developed property value and development costs. The standard errors of the estimates are very low. We then present values for the variance and standard deviations of the developed property value only, assuming $\rho = 0$ and $\sigma_x = 0.05$. We find annual standard deviations ranging from 18.55% to 28.07%, with no significant differences among the different property types.[18] We can reject that the variance is constant, but we do not find any uniform movement up or down in the variance estimates across the years.

Because these figures represent the annual standard deviation of individual properties, based on actual prices rather than on appraisals, it is difficult to find comparable numbers in the literature. The closest we find comes from a recent study by Case and Shiller (1989) of repeat sales; the study reports a 15% annual standard deviation of individual housing prices, from 1970 to 1986, in Atlanta, Chicago, Dallas, and San Francisco-Oakland. Titman and Torous (1989) estimate an implied property value standard deviation of 15.5% using their commercial mortgage-pricing model.[19] There is a fundamental inconsistency in utilizing a model that assumes constant variance to estimate implied variances that are allowed to change. This issue has been addressed in several papers. Preliminary findings of Sheik and Vora (1990) show that, under certain circumstances that allow for changing variance (such as a constant elasticity of variance diffusion process), implied volatilities measure the average volatility of the underlying stocks' returns fairly accurately.

Table 38.6

Variance estimates implied from the option model. We estimate $\text{Var}(P, X)$, the variance of developed property value, P, and development costs, X, from the option model (equation (6)), which incorporates the option to wait to develop land. The standard error is of this estimate. The variance and standard deviation of developed property value, P, are calculated assuming a 5% annual standard deviation of development costs and zero covariance.

	n	$\text{Var}(P, X)$	Standard error	$\text{Var}(P)$	Standard deviation (P)
Business					
1977	76	0.0369	0.0030	0.0344	0.1855
1978	64	0.0616	0.0053	0.0591	0.2431
1979	48	0.0571	0.0046	0.0546	0.2337
Commercial					
1977	102	0.0503	0.0024	0.0478	0.2186
1978	90	0.0533	0.0032	0.0508	0.2254
1979	73	0.0526	0.0024	0.0501	0.2238
Industrial					
1977	62	0.0525	0.0037	0.0500	0.2236
1978	43	0.0813	0.0038	0.0788	0.2807
1979	25	0.0658	0.0073	0.0633	0.2516
Low-density residential					
1977	490	0.0720	0.0011	0.0695	0.2636
1978	401	0.0577	0.0017	0.0552	0.2348
1979	340	0.0488	0.0016	0.0463	0.2152
High-density residential					
1977	224	0.0475	0.0014	0.0450	0.2121
1978	336	0.0647	0.0031	0.0622	0.2494
1979	360	0.0699	0.0022	0.0674	0.2595

Based on our assumptions and estimates, most properties would not be developed if the investor correctly accounts for the option to wait. For most properties the current ratio of building price to development costs, z, is still less than the optimal development ratio, z^*. However, most properties would be developed in the intrinsic value case, where a null variance is assumed. We lack information about the actual development of these properties,[20] and therefore cannot test whether the developer follows an optimal strategy.

In table 38.7, we present summary statistics for the option-based model price and the intrinsic value. As expected, the former exceeds the latter in every subsample, and in some cases by a substantial margin. Based on these values, we calculate the option (time) premium as the mean percentage difference between the option model price and the intrinsic value. These premia range from 1% to 30%, with a mean of 6%.[21] In support of the theory, they are consistently positive. There is no reason for the estimated option premium to be constant across the sample, since properties bought for

Table 38.7
Summary statistics and option premia. Average land values given by the option model (equation (6)), which incorporates the option to wait to invest, and the intrinsic value (equation (7)) which does not value this option. The option premium for each parcel is defined as: (option model price—intrinsic value)/option model price. We present the mean option premium for each subsample (not the option premium of the average values). Sample sizes are as given in table 38.6.

	Option model ($)	Intrinsic value ($)	Option premium
Business			
1977	30,550	29,090	0.0377
1978	115,092	112,578	0.0222
1979	84,773	74,998	0.0449
Commercial			
1977	144,237	136,844	0.0518
1978	180,221	177,735	0.0095
1979	184,477	171,792	0.0256
Industrial			
1977	146,670	122,124	0.2980
1978	337,196	291,904	0.1757
1979	147,812	140,696	0.0219
Low-density residential			
1977	90,106	84,603	0.0489
1978	47,207	43,968	0.1120
1979	51,148	49,192	0.0117
High-density residential			
1977	58,147	54,148	0.1040
1978	40,981	37,512	0.0586
1979	51,227	48,404	0.0189

current development should have a premium of zero, while more "speculative" transactions could have premia approaching 100% of the value. We consider that these numbers represent a lower bound on the option premium for land, since our sample consists of urban land during a period of expansion in a city with tight growth controls.[22] Some larger figures appear, especially for industrial properties.[23] When the industrial properties are excluded, the average premium is 5%. As previously discussed, our assumptions and imputations should not affect the existence of a premium for the option to wait. However, the standard errors may be large despite the narrow confidence intervals given by the variance estimates.

Finally, we perform several regressions to ascertain the comparative fit and explanatory power of the option-pricing model. In these regressions, errors-in-variables bias the slope coefficient downward and the intercept upward. In table 38.8 we regress theoretical prices for both the option and intrinsic value models given in equations (6) and (7), respectively, on actual prices, where all prices are per square foot. Both

Table 38.8
Regressions of per square foot market prices on model prices.

	Option model					Intrinsic value				
	Constant a	Std. error	Coeff. b	Std. error	R-square	Constant a	Std. error	Coeff. b	Std. error	R-square
Business										
1977	0.7355	0.0957	0.7814	0.0179	0.963	0.6609	0.0798	0.9110	0.0171	0.975
1978	−0.5551	0.2962	1.0913	0.0373	0.932	−0.6102	0.2662	1.1606	0.0354	0.945
1979	0.0919	0.1780	0.9781	0.0296	0.960	1.2966	0.1193	0.9666	0.0234	0.974
Commercial										
1977	0.6387	0.0900	0.8234	0.0166	0.961	1.3372	0.0791	0.7985	0.0163	0.960
1978	−0.8580	0.3470	1.1364	0.0293	0.945	0.1117	0.3533	1.0826	0.0304	0.935
1979	1.8306	0.2857	0.7705	0.0304	0.900	2.1786	0.3027	0.8182	0.0360	0.878
Industrial										
1977	−0.1859	0.1584	1.0786	0.0365	0.936	0.1157	0.1163	1.1502	0.0301	0.960
1978	−0.4262	0.1212	1.0973	0.0196	0.987	0.6801	0.1481	0.9998	0.0255	0.974
1979	2.0889	0.1367	0.6173	0.0264	0.960	2.3146	0.1737	0.5993	0.0349	0.928
Low-density residential										
1977	−1.4781	0.1864	1.1566	0.0211	0.860	1.9440	0.1092	0.9131	0.0080	0.964
1978	−0.3560	0.1079	1.0662	0.0128	0.945	0.1129	0.1103	1.0307	0.0133	0.938
1979	0.6242	0.0727	0.8807	0.0068	0.981	1.3223	0.0656	0.9142	0.0067	0.982
High-density residential										
1977	−0.5059	0.1200	1.1068	0.0146	0.963	−0.3230	0.1494	1.1261	0.0189	0.941
1978	0.8254	0.3344	0.9001	0.0545	0.449	2.3718	0.2671	0.7261	0.0475	0.412
1979	1.1399	0.0818	0.7987	0.0103	0.944	2.6650	0.0762	0.6772	0.0105	0.921

The models are well specified if the coefficients are not significantly different from zero, and the constants are not significantly different from one. Option model: Market Price/SF = $a + b$*Option Model Price/SF + e. Option model price (equation (6)) incorporates the option to wait to invest. Intrinsic value: Market Price/SF = $a + b$*Intrinsic Value/SF + e. Intrinsic value (equation (7)) does not value this option. It equals the option model price for which the variance is zero in the limit. Sample sizes are as given in table 38.6.

Table 38.9
Regressions per square foot.

	Constant a	Std. error	Coeff. b	Std. error	Coeff. c	Std. error	R-square
Business							
1977	0.3412	0.0753	0.9372	0.01361	0.6993	0.09605	0.985
1978	−0.7711	0.2431	1.1721	0.03203	0.3739	0.18748	0.956
1979	1.2424	0.4509	0.9700	0.03601	0.0424	0.34273	0.979
Commercial							
1977	0.4839	0.1730	0.8924	0.02261	0.7835	0.14528	0.969
1978	−1.0618	0.5015	1.1508	0.03611	1.3296	0.42118	0.942
1979	1.4745	0.3358	0.8390	0.03356	0.6439	0.18164	0.898
Industrial							
1977	0.1332	0.0670	1.0705	0.01881	0.5285	0.04791	0.987
1978	0.3627	0.0746	0.9821	0.01211	0.6352	0.05281	0.994
1979	1.5415	0.1651	0.7318	0.03203	0.5581	0.06866	0.960
Low-density residential							
1977	0.5663	0.2016	0.9679	0.01021	0.6537	0.08228	0.968
1978	−0.0838	0.0742	0.9719	0.00929	1.2678	0.057	0.972
1979	−0.2634	0.1327	1.0217	0.0099	1.2962	0.09926	0.988
High-density residential							
1977	0.0782	0.1086	1.0093	0.01544	0.9332	0.06207	0.971
1978	−0.0537	0.5213	0.9939	0.06778	1.5105	0.28259	0.458
1979	0.3955	0.1520	0.8963	0.01573	1.0843	0.06712	0.954

Market price of land parcel/SF = $a + b$ intrinsic value/SF + c(option model value/SF—intrinsic value/ SF). Option model price (equation (6)) incorporates the option to wait to invest. Intrinsic value, given by intrinsic value (equation (7)) does not value this option. Sample sizes are as given in table 38.6.

models perform fairly well as measured by their R^2, although overall we reject the joint hypothesis that the coefficient is one and the constant is zero.

In order to assess the incremental effect of the option to wait, we also run the regressions using the observed land values as the dependent variables, with the intrinsic values and the difference between the option model values and the intrinsic values as independent variables (values per square foot). The latter is a measure of the option premium, in dollar terms. Results are presented in table 38.9. The difference between R^2 in table 38.9 and those in the right side of table 38.8 represent the additional explanatory power of the option premium, over and above the intrinsic value. We find evidence of some contribution based on this criteria, but not generally a significant one.

If the option valuation model were a perfect description of land values the constant would equal zero and the other coefficients would equal one. We find that the constant is not far from zero. The intrinsic value has a coefficient that is close to one. We also find that the coefficients for the option premium are uniformly positive and statistically significant in all but one subsample. While in most cases we would reject the hypothesis that the coefficient equals one, in most subsamples it lies between 0.5 and 1.3, supporting the hypothesis that the option valuation model has some explanatory power for prices, over and above the intrinsic value.

IV   Conclusion

This chapter provides evidence, based on a large sample of actual real estate transactions, that the real option-pricing model has descriptive value. Market prices reflect a premium for optimal development, which based on our estimates has a mean of 6% of the land value. The basis behind the theory, that the option to wait has value, appears to ring true. To the extent that it is possible to take advantage of the optimal timing option, its value should not be neglected. We also estimate that the annual standard deviation of individual commercial real estate asset values ranges from 18 to 28%, without relying on time series of property prices or appraised values.

These results encourage further research in this field: using the techniques employed here to test other real option applications, including more speculative properties where we would expect the variance and option premium to be higher. An alternative test might also examine the exercise policy of the developer to gauge whether development did actually occur at the optimal point predicted by the option-based model.

Appendix

We wish to solve equation (4). The solution has the form, $W(z) = Az^j + k$. Inserting the values of W, W', and W'' into equation (4), we obtain values for k and j, given in equation (5).

At the hurdle ratio, z^*, the value of the option is its intrinsic value, giving the first boundary condition, $W(z^*) = Az^{*j} + k = z^* - 1$.

The second boundary condition is the smooth pasting condition, which is based on an assumption of rational exercise, $W'(z^*) = jAz^{*j^1} = 1$.

The solutions for z^* and A follow.

Acknowledgments

The author thanks Peter Berck, Peter Colwell, Robert Edelstein, Bjorn Flesaker, Steven Grenadier, Hayne Leland, Jay Ritter, Anthony Sanders, René Stulz, Sheridan Titman, Nancy Wallace, Joseph Williams, and seminar participants at the University of Illinois, the 1992 Western Finance Association Meetings, and the Norwegian School of Management, and two anonymous referees for useful comments.

Notes

1. The exception is the Paddock, Siegel, and Smith (1988) empirical study discussed below. Theoretical real option-pricing models include Titman (1985), Brennan and Schwartz (1985), McDonald and Siegel (1985, 1986), Majd and Pindyck (1987), Morck, Schwartz, and Stangeland (1989), Brennan (1990), Gibson and Schwartz (1990), Triantis and Hodder (1990), and Williams (1991a).

2. The mean of 6% is an unweighted average across all sample observations.

3. The finding of small but consistently positive premia seems reasonable given that Seattle experienced moderate growth during the sample period (1976 to 1979). However, the exact figures obtained for Seattle may not be representative of the overall economy, given the city's dependence on a single industry (aerospace).

4. We allow for $\phi < 1$, giving a concave relationship between price and building size in the option model, which is consistent with the relationship estimated in the hedonic function described in Section III.*A*. This concave relationship may exist for several reasons. Colwell (1992) argues that the cost functions are concave because the exterior walls increase less than proportionally to the floorspace. Concavity in the industry offer curves requires, in turn, that the lower envelope of the offer curves, and hence the hedonic function, must be concave. For the building as a whole, the marginal cost curve must intersect the marginal price curve from below in order to obtain an interior solution for the optimal building size. In the market for commercial space, there might be a downward sloping demand curve for a given location, and it is likely that as the building size grows, the prime rentable space decreases as a proportion of the total space (e.g., more interior offices). In the market for residential space doubling an apartment's size does not normally double the rent, since it would still suit one family and have one kitchen.

5. Williams' (1991a) model assumes that unit development costs (x_1) and unit cash inflows to the developed property (x_2) are the underlying stochastic variables, both following lognormal processes. The data that we have provides information about building prices, but not about the rents generated by the building. Therefore, we alter the Williams' model with the assumption that the building price and total construction costs, both dependent on scale, are the state variables. Williams solves for price as a linear function of unit cash inflows $(P = \pi q x_2, \pi$ constant$)$, and he assumes that total development cost is a linear function of unit development cost $(X = x_1 q^\gamma)$. Therefore the two derivations are formally equivalent. However, we are not required to make the assumption, as Williams does, that price is a linear function of scale and therefore that development costs must exhibit decreasing returns to scale (in order to obtain an interior solution to the optimal scale problem). Instead, with our formulation we require only that the scale cost parameter exceed the price elasticity of scale, thus allowing for either increasing or decreasing returns to scale.

6. The model assumes that an individual's decision to develop has no impact on the market price of buildings. The empirical implications of this assumption are discussed in Section III.*B*. Williams (1991b) models a Nash equilibrium among developers.

7. The payouts to the undeveloped property are thereby assumed to be proportional to the developed property value.

8. This assumption is sometimes derived as a consequence of no arbitrage opportunities in an economy in which there exist tradeable securities whose prices are perfectly correlated with P and X. See, e.g., Titman (1985) and Brennan and Schwartz (1985). Given the nature of the underlying processes, we find it more palatable not to explicitly rely on a hedging argument. An equilibrium similar to the one we assume was explicitly derived by Rubinstein (1976) and applied by Milne and Turnbull (1991). An intermediate solution assumes that the component of the risk in (P, X) that is priced in equilibrium can be dynamically spanned by tradeable securities.

9. This "hurdle ratio," $1 + k$, corresponds to the ratio z^* in the option-based model. It is found by taking the limit of z^* as $\omega \to 0$ $(j \to 1)$.

10. The source of the data is the Real Estate Monitor Corporation.

11. The Seattle Zoning Code classifies these zoning categories cumulatively. The lowest (i.e. most inclusive) zoning category is industrial. Commercial includes nonretail business and light manufacturing. The

purpose of business zoning is to provide for retail and office uses. The lowest residential use (high rise and mixed use) is not included in our sample because there were few data points and a large amount of heterogeneity. Therefore, what we term high-density residential is actually medium density (midrise). Low-density residential includes duplexes and triplexes.

12. We calculate the 1977 to 1979 square foot costs for building types according to the purpose of each zoning category (apartment, store, office, warehouse, and industrial building) for an average quality C and a good quality B building, and chose values at the middle of each range. These costs range from \$23 per square foot to \$34 per square foot. We assume fixed costs of \$10,000.

13. A Wald test of the restrictions that the parameters are the same across zoning categories is statistically significant in nearly all cases. Therefore, we separated these groups in this first estimation, and also in the tests of the land valuation model.

14. Our goal was to estimate coefficients that serve as predictors of marginal prices. We separated the city into as many regions as possible, given the number of data points in each region.

15. Because the zoning is cumulative, we attempted a search over all possible building types for a given zoning category, e.g., allowing an industrial parcel to be developed commercially. The prices obtained were unreasonably high, indicating that the industrial parcel could not command the same marginal prices as a commercially zoned parcel. The fact that the land was zoned as industrial conveys information about its location and potential. Moreover, the marginal prices we estimate for the industrial parcel are based only on other industrially zoned lots, which are not necessarily developed to the maximum density.

16. See Theil (1971), for example.

17. In the intrinsic value case, the building is either developed immediately, a function of the factors which affect P and X, or held as income-producing land, a function of P and β.

18. Clearly, different cities and different sample periods would generate different results. The results obtained in this study provide an indication of how the model fares empirically, but do not purport to be representative.

19. By comparison, Cox and Rubinstein (1985) report individual stock standard deviations ranging from 17% (for utilities) to 68% (for Winnebago) during the 1980 to 1984 sample period.

20. From 1977 to 1979 Seattle experienced a steady increase in building permits for all property types, but building activity subsequently dropped off. No trend can be seen in our data which reflects the statistics.

21. This mean is calculated across all observations, i.e., $\sum_{t=1}^{15}(N_i op_i)/N$, where for each subsample i, N_i is the number of observations and op_i is the option premium, and N is the total number of observations (2734).

22. We would expect higher premia in locations where very little building is currently taking place, indicating that the value in the land is mostly as an option to build far out in the future. The overall expansion in Seattle during this period indicates that many options are "in the money."

23. The premia for the industrial properties are not driven by just a few outliers. The industrial properties have by far the widest range of sizes and prices compared to the other zoning categories. The land prices and lot sizes are also the largest. Given the small sample size and heterogeneous data, it is quite possible that the building values fitted from the hedonic regressions are less representative of the sample of vacant lots than for the other categories. It is also possible that the industrial properties in 1977 and 1978 do have a larger option premium.

References

Brennan, Michael, 1990, Latent assets, *Journal of Finance* 45, 709–730.

――― and Eduardo Schwartz, 1985, Evaluating natural resource investments, *Journal of Business* 58, 1135–1157.

Case, Karl E., and Robert J. Shiller, 1989, The efficiency of the market for single-family homes, *American Economic Review* 79, 125–137.

Colwell, Peter F., 1992, Semiparametric estimates of the marginal price of floorspace (comment), *Journal of Real Estate Finance and Economics*, Forthcoming.

Cox, John C., and Mark Rubinstein, 1985, *Options Markets* (Prentice-Hall, Englewood Cliffs, N.J.).

Flesaker, Bjorn, 1991, Valuing European options when the terminal value of the underlying asset is unobservable, BEBR Working Paper No. 91-0175, University of Illinois.

Gibson, Rajna, and Eduardo S. Schwartz, 1990, Stochastic convenience yield and the pricing of oil contingent claims, *Journal of Finance* 45, 959–976.

McDonald, Robert L., and Daniel R. Siegel, 1985, Investment and the valuation of firms when there is an option to shut down, *International Economic Review* 26, 331–349.

———, 1986, The value of waiting to invest, *Quarterly Journal of Economics* 100, 707–727.

Majd, Saman, and Robert S. Pindyck, 1987, Time to build, option value, and investment decisions, *Journal of Financial Economics* 18, 7–27.

Marshall Valuation Service, 1986, Marshall and Swift, Los Angeles.

Milne, Frank, and Stuart Turnbull, 1991, A simple approach to interest rate option pricing, *Review of Financial Studies* 4, 87–120.

Morck, Randall, Eduardo Schwartz, and David Stangeland, 1989, The valuation of forestry resources under stochastic prices and inventories, *Journal of Financial and Quantitative Analysis* 24, 473–488.

Paddock, James L., Daniel R. Siegel, and James L. Smith, 1988, Option valuation of claims on real assets: The case of offshore petroleum leases, *Quarterly Journal of Economics* 102, 479–508.

Rosen, Sherwin, 1974, Hedonic prices and implicit markets: Product differentiation in pure competition, *Journal of Political Economy* 82, 34–55.

Rubinstein, Mark, 1976, The valuation of uncertain streams and the pricing of options, *Bell Journal of Economics* 7, 407–425.

Sheik, Aamir, and Gautam Vora, 1990, The robustness of volatilities implied by the Black-Scholes formula and using implied volatilities to infer the parameters of stock-price processes, Working paper, Indiana University.

Theil, Henri, 1971, *Principles of Econometrics* (John Wiley and Sons, New York).

Titman, Sheridan, 1985, Urban land prices under uncertainty, *American Economic Review* 75, 505–514.

——— and Walter Torous, 1989, Valuing commercial mortgages: An empirical investigation of the contingent-claims approach to pricing risky debt, *Journal of Finance* 44, 345–375.

Triantis, Alexander J., and James E. Hodder, 1990, Valuing flexibility as a complex option, *Journal of Finance* 45, 549–566.

Williams, Joseph T., 1991a, Real estate development as an option, *Journal of Real Estate Finance and Economics* 4, 191–208.

———, 1991b, Equilibrium and options on real assets, Working paper, University of British Columbia.

39 Investor Valuation of the Abandonment Option

Philip G. Berger, Eli Ofek, and Itzhak Swary

1 Introduction

We investigate whether investors use balance sheet information about a firm's assets to value their option to abandon the continuing business in exchange for the assets' exit value. As uncertainty about future cash flows is resolved, investors might choose to exercise their option to abandon the firm for its exit value. This abandonment option is like owning an insurance policy that pays off if the firm performs below expectations. The option thus has value, and information about the exit value of the firm's assets should affect its market value.

One area to which our study contributes is the real options literature. This body of research recognizes that investment decisions often involve choices about a variety of control opportunities, such as when to invest (McDonald and Siegel, 1985; Majd and Pindyck, 1987; Lee, 1988; Pindyck, 1988), how to modify operating plans during a project's life (Stulz, 1982; Johnson, 1987; Kensinger, 1988; Triantis and Hodder, 1990), and whether to abandon an investment in midstream (Robichek and Van Horne, 1967; Bonini, 1977; Kensinger, 1980; Myers and Majd, 1990). Despite the theoretical development of real option-pricing models for these and other embedded options, almost no research has examined the models' empirical implications. Two exceptions are Paddock, Siegel, and Smith (1988) and Quigg (1993), both of which examine the effect of the option of waiting on the price of specific capital investment (offshore oil leases or land). In contrast, our paper tests the empirical implications of abandonment option-pricing models on the price of the entire firm.

Our paper also contributes to the large body of accounting research that attempts to identify value-relevant accounting attributes. Much of this research has explored the relation between income statement disclosures and stock prices. Less evidence exists, however, on the role played by the balance sheet in assessing firm value. Foster (1986, p. 446) states that "one area of equity valuation where important unresolved questions exist is the link between the level of equity security prices and the values of the individual assets and liabilities owned or controlled by the firm." Recently, a number of theoretical and empirical papers have addressed the valuation effects of balance sheet items. Most of these papers examine the potential for balance sheet disclosures to provide incremental information about the expected level of future going-concern cash flows (see, for example, Ohlson, 1996; Penman, 1992). In contrast, our examination of the abandonment option's effect on firm value assesses the extent to which balance sheet information affects firm value *given* the level of expected going-concern cash flows. Thus, rather than exploring an area of valuation in which the balance sheet's role is incremental to that of the income statement, we study one for which balance sheet information is vital.

The abandonment option is equivalent to an "American" put option on a dividend-paying stock. Our analysis of this option leads to predictions about how exit value affects firm value. All else equal, the abandonment option results in firms with a greater exit value being worth more to investors. We therefore predict that *after* we control for the relation between market value and the present value of expected cash flows (*PVCF*), market value will be positively related to exit value.

Exit values for going concerns are generally unobservable. Moreover, we are interested in the association between balance sheet information and the abandonment option's value. Therefore, we estimate the relation between book value and exit value for major asset classes by using the "discontinued operations" footnotes of 157 firms with sufficiently detailed information. We find that a dollar's book value produces, on average, $0.72 in exit value for receivables, $0.55 for inventory, and $0.54 for fixed assets. To provide estimated exit values, we apply these estimates of exit value per dollar of book value for cash asset category to the book values of each asset category disclosed by firms in the full sample.

We use discounted analysts' forecasts of future earnings as proxies for *PVCF*. Kaplan and Ruback (1995) find that for a sample of 52 highly levered transactions, firm-value estimates based on discounted cash-flow forecasts consistently outperform those based on industry-median cash-flow multipliers.

After controlling for *PVCF*, we find a positive, highly significant relation between market value and estimated exit value. This relation holds both across each year in the 1984–1990 sample period, and after we control for factors that affect market value and which might not be completely captured by the *PVCF* proxy. We provide further assurance that correlated omitted variables do not drive the results through the fact that the positive relation between exit and market values holds in changes as well as levels.

Option-pricing theory suggests that the abandonment option's value is increased more by less-specialized assets because their value is less correlated with *PVCF*. Thus, if *PVCF* becomes disappointing, the value of the firm's generalizable assets will not decline as much as the value of its specialized assets. We find support for the prediction that less-specialized assets produce more abandonment option value. We find that a dollar's book value of current assets adds more market value than a dollar's book value of fixed assets. Noninventory current assets create more value than inventory, and land enhances the option's value more than other fixed assets.

Finally, we hypothesize that the probability of the abandonment option being exercised is a function of other variables, such as the probability of financial distress and the likelihood of managers (who control the option's exercise) delaying abandonment past the optimal time for the firm's investors. Variation around a given level of exit value has more effect on market value when the probability of the option being exercised is higher. Consistent with this prediction, we find that firms with higher probabilities of either financial distress—as measured by the inverse of Altman's (1968) Z-score—or timely abandonment have market values that are more sensitive to variation in estimated exit values.

Section 2 describes the abandonment put option theory and develops our predictions. Section 3 describes the estimation of exit values, details the construction of $PVCF$ from discounted analysts' forecasts, and presents the sample selection and description. Section 4 describes the empirical tests and results, and Section 5 provides our summary and conclusions. The appendix presents additional details on variables construction.

2   Theory and Predictions

In the capital budgeting literature, the abandonment option has been discussed for over 25 years. [The option to redeploy or liquidate assets has also received attention in the accounting literature. Burgstahler and Dichev (1994) and Hayn (1995) address how the likelihood of redeployments and liquidations, respectively, might affect the relation between accounting numbers and firm value.] Robichek and VanHorne (1967) include the abandonment option as a contingency in the forecast of cash flows used for calculating the net present value or internal rate of return of an investment project. Their contingency approach (as corrected by Dyl and Long, 1969) does not, however, provide a practical procedure for calculating the abandonment option's value. This has motivated attempts to model the option's value directly. Kensinger (1980) does this, but his analysis assumes that the option is "European" and that it has a nonstochastic exercise price. Myers and Majd (1990) improve on Kensinger's approach by recognizing that the abandonment option is equivalent to a complex "American" put with both an uncertain underlying stock value (the cash flows) and an uncertain exercise price (the exit value).

Beginning with the intuition provided by Myers and Majd, we develop our hypotheses on the relation between firm value and the firm characteristics that determine the abandonment option's value. The hypotheses are explained through the following equations:

$$VALUE = PVCF + P(PVCF, EXIT, SDEV),\tag{1}$$

$$\left(\frac{VALUE}{PVCF} - 1\right) = P\left(1, \frac{EXIT}{PVCF}, SDEV\right). \tag{2}$$

where

$VALUE =$ the firm's market value,

$PVCF \quad =$ present value of the firm's expected operating cash flows,

$P \qquad =$ operator representing an American put option,

$EXIT \quad =$ exit value of the firm's assets,

$SDEV \quad =$ standard deviation of the ratio of $PVCF$ over $EXIT$.

Eq. (1) shows that the firm's market value equals the sum of the value of its expected operating cash flows plus the value of the abandonment option. Note that the abandonment option need not represent disposal of the entire firm. The option to sell subsets of the firm's assets, such as lines of business, is also valuable to investors. The additive form of Eq. (1) is strictly appropriate only when the abandonment option involves the choice of selling the entire firm. When a firm exits only some lines of business, proceeds can be reinvested in the firm to produce operating cash flow, thus creating an interaction between $PVCF$ and the put's value.

When we divide each term of Eq. (1) by $PVCF$ and rearrange terms in Eq. (2), the result is an expression of the *abandonment option value* (the percentage by which firm value exceeds $PVCF$) as a function of the option's parameters. We present the relation in this form because it facilitates hypothesis development. As Myers and Majd point out, a general specification of the abandonment option does not allow a closed-form solution. The empirical tests therefore address only the relations suggested by Eq. (2), rather than an exact functional form.

The value of the option is a function of the ratio of $EXIT$ to $PVCF$, which we call *excess exit value*. Eq. (2) shows that excess exit value can be viewed as the stochastic strike price of a put option with a normalized value of one on its underlying stock. When excess exit value equals one (i.e., exit value equals the value of expected cash flows), the abandonment option is at the money. As the exit value increases, the option moves farther into the money. When the value of expected cash flow increases, the option moves father out of the money. Thus, excess exit value is positively related to abandonment option value.

Abandonment option theory gives rise to the prediction that for a given current value of assets, more abandonment option value is created when the assets are less specialized. Ronen and Sorter (1973) and Williamson (1988) argue that when the firm's cash flows become disappointing, redeployable assets can be liquidated for relatively high values. Shleifer and Vishny (1992) contend that the reason specialized assets are more likely to drop in value is because, when the seller's cash flows are disappointing, potential buyers are themselves likely to be experiencing problems.

Myers and Majd (1990) use an example to clarify this point. Consider two firms that differ only in the nature of their assets: Firm A's assets are standard and have an active secondary market, whereas firm B's assets are custom-built and have no secondary market. If both firms have the same *PVCF* and both are certain to continue operating until their assets are completely worn out, investors are indifferent between them. When investors might sell the firm's assets if cash flows are disappointing, firm A is preferred to firm B, because the higher exit value of firm A's assets provides greater risk protection.

The preceding example implies that given current asset value and *PVCF*, market value decreases with asset specialization. The current value of the firm's assets is unobservable, thus we are interested in how investors use book values to price their abandonment option. We therefore test whether, after holding constant *PVCF* and book value of assets, market value decreases with asset specialization. We discuss with the empirical results the potential effects on our inferences of using book values to measure current values. To categorize assets by degree of specialization, we follow Ronen and Sorter (1973) in classifying current assets as less specialized than fixed assets, noninventory current assets as less specialized than inventory, and land as less specialized than other fixed assets. These classifications enjoy wide acceptance in both the literature on liquidation values and in financial accounting.[1]

Abandonment option theory shows that for given levels of *PVCF* and exit value, market value is more sensitive to variation in exit value when there is a higher probability of the option being exercised. We propose two factors that could affect investors' assessment of the probability of exercise: the likelihood of financial distress and the level of agency problems between investors and managers. Financial distress can force liquidation of the firm. We therefore predict that firms with higher financial distress probabilities have market values that are more sensitive to variation in estimated exit values.

Although investors hold the abandonment option, they might be unable to effect exercise when they wish due to agency problems with the managers who control the abandonment decision. For example, Ofek (1993) finds results indicating that entrenched managers are more likely to avoid taking actions, such as discontinuing operations, when a firm becomes distressed. If variations in agency problems result in some managers being more likely to delay exit past the optimal time for investors, then investors will value the abandonment option more highly when the probability of delayed exercise is lower. We therefore predict that, when investors attach a higher probability to timely exercise of the option, firm value is more sensitive to variation around a given excess exit value.

Our final predictions are for the bounds of the relation between excess exit value and abandonment option value. If there is no probability that the abandonment option will be exercised, information about exit value has no effect on firm value, and the slope of the relation is at its lower bound of zero. At the other extreme, when the abandonment option is certain to be exercised, an extra dollar of exit value increases firm value by one dollar.

3 Empirical Approach

3.1 Estimating Exit Values

The exit value of a firm's assets is not observable, whereas the book value is. We therefore use firms with discontinued operations to estimate how many cents per dollar of book value each of three major asset classifications produces when sold. We then apply these estimates to all sample firms to construct the excess exit value variable.

We obtain the information about discontinued operations from the National Automated Accounting Research Service (NAARS) library of Lexis/Nexis, using the search "discop w/seg (write-down or write-off)" for the years 1984–93. This produces 1,043 observations. "Write-down" and "write-off" are used in an attempt to restrict the cases identified to those in which the motive for discontinuance is to abandon operations whose cash flows have become disappointing. The observations we obtain represent both the sales of the discontinued line of business to a single buyer and "fire sale" liquidations of separate assets of the business line to multiple buyers. Observations are retained if information is available on the discontinued segment's book value, its exit value, and the proportion of its book value in non-inventory current assets, inventory, and fixed assets. In addition, the assets of the discontinued line of business must be sold to unrelated parties. These requirements result in a sample of 157 observations.

The regression we perform on this sample and the estimation results are as follows (t-values in parentheses):

$$EXITBOOK_i = 0.715 \ NONINV_i + .5470 \ INV_i + 0.535 \ FIXED_i, \qquad (3)$$
$$ (12.25) \qquad\qquad (8.07) \qquad\quad (15.52)$$

Adjusted $R^2 = 0.85$.

where

$EXITBOOK_i$ = ratio of exit value to book value for firm i's discontinued operations,

$NONINV_i$ = proportion of book value in noninventory current assets for firm i's discontinued operations,

INV_i = proportion of book value in inventory for firm i's discontinued operations,

$FIXED_i$ = proportion of book value in fixed assets for firm i's discontinued operations.

The regression is performed with no intercept because, by construction, the independent variables sum to one. The estimates show how many cents per dollar of book value each asset category produces when exit occurs and the asset's line of business is discontinued. Noninventory current assets are disposed of for $0.72 on the dollar, inventory for $0.55, and fixed assets for $0.54.

We use the estimates from the preceding regression to construct the exit value of equity for our full sample. For each sample firm, we multiply each of the three components of book value (noninventory current assets, inventory, and fixed assets) by the estimated exit value per dollar of book value, and subtract the book values of payables and debt. Note that the cash and short-term marketable securities components within the noninventory current assets category are multiplied by one rather than by 0.72.

3.2 Proxies for the Present Value of Cash Flows

We use analysts' earnings forecasts to calculate the $PVCF$ proxy. The fact that analysts are forecasting earnings, rather than distributable cash flows, offers both an advantage and a disadvantage. The advantage is that because accountants measure going-concern earnings, a $PVCF$ proxy based on forecasts of these earnings does not incorporate the abandonment option's value. If analysts' were instead forecasting distributable cash flows, their forecasts would presumably incorporate cash flows expected from non-going-concern events (i.e., exit). The disadvantage is that earnings differ from cash flows. Thus, the present value of going-concern earnings must be adjusted to obtain the present value of going-concern cash flows. Adjustments must be made because capital expenditures might not equal depreciation, and growth in working capital is not subtracted from earnings. An adjustment for capital structure changes is not required, because we assume that such changes are not foreseeable.

Eq. (4) illustrates the construction of the *PVCF* proxy from analysts' discounted earnings forecasts:

$$PVCF = \sum_{t=1}^{n} \frac{EARN_t}{(1+r)^t} + \sum_{t=n+1}^{10} \frac{EARN_2 * (1+gr)^{t-2}}{(1+r)^t} + \frac{EARN_2 * (1+gr)^9}{(r-tg)}$$

$$* \frac{1}{(1+r)^{10}} - CAPEX\ ADJUST - WC\ ADJUST, \tag{4}$$

where

PVCF	= present value of analysts' predicted going-concern cash flows,
$EARN_t$	= analyst's forecast of year t after-interest earnings,
r	= expected CAPM return, described below,
gr	= consensus forecast of five-year earnings growth,
tg	= terminal growth rate of earnings,
n	= number of years for which earnings are forecast,
t	= year index,
CAPEX ADJUST	= reduction to the present value of analysts' earnings forecasts to adjust for the difference between capital expenditures and depreciation,
WC ADJUST	= reduction to the present value of analysts' earnings forecasts to adjust for growth in working capital.

The expected CAPM return is defined as

$$r = r_f + \beta_e * [r_m - r_f], \tag{5}$$

where

r_f	= risk-free rate,
β_e	= the firm's beta or systematic risk (from the CRSP beta file),
$r_m - r_f$	= risk premium of the stock market over the risk-free rate.

In implementing Eq. (5), we assume that the relevant investment horizon is short-term. Therefore, we use the one-month Treasury-bill rate as a proxy for the risk-free rate and a risk premium of 8.67% (the arithmetic average spread from 1926 to 1991 between the return on the S&P 500 and the return on Treasury bills).

As Eq. (4) shows, the analyst-forecast approach uses five components to proxy for the present value of after-interest cash flows. First, expected earnings from analysts' forecasts are discounted and summed. These forecasts are available for at least two years for all sample firms. The second term projects earnings for the period from the last forecast earnings through year 10 by using analysts' consensus long-term (five-year) earnings growth forecasts, then discounts and sums these expected inflows.[2] The third term calculates the present value of the perpetuity for the earnings from year 11 forward by assuming a constant 4% nominal terminal growth rate applies for all observations. The fourth term subtracts the present value of the excess of future capital expenditures minus future depreciation. This adjustment for future excess capital expenditures is needed because analysts are forecasting earnings, not distributable cash flows, and earnings growth typically requires capital investment in excess of depreciation charges. The fifth term makes a similar subtraction for the present value of working capital growth.

Three factors lead us to project firm-specific growth for ten years. First, although our earnings growth forecasts are for five-year growth, it seems unrealistic to assume that earnings growth moves immediately from its firm-specific rate to a terminal rate in year 6. Second, ten is the most common number of years for the management cash flow forecasts of the 52 firms studied by Kaplan and Ruback (1995). Third, we compare the *PVCF* figures that result from projecting firm-specific growth for 5, 10, 15, and 20 years, and find that ten years performs best in terms of minimizing the variance of the log of the ratio of equity value to *PVCF*. Minimizing this variance is a desirable feature for the *PVCF* proxy, because true *PVCF* is presumably quite close to equity value for most firms. Regarding the 4% terminal growth rate, Kaplan and Ruback (1995) present results using nominal growth rates of 4%, 2%, and 0%, but state that they feel "the 4% rate is economically the most appropriate."

Because we start from forecast earnings to calculate discounted cash flows, we adjust for future excess capital expenditures, which are a major source of the difference between future earnings and future cash flows. Forecasts of excess capital expenditures are, however, unavailable. We could attempt to develop our own forecasts from historical figures, but for extreme values historical variation in excess of capital expenditures tends to overstate future variation.

The rank order of historical excess capital expenditures is, however, a good predictor of the rank order for future excess capital expenditures. Using 20 years of Compustat data, we find that firms with relatively high (low) excess capital expenditures in a given year have an increased likelihood of having relatively high (low) excess capital expenditures the following year, and an increased likelihood of having a more negative (positive) percentage change in excess capital expenditures in the following year. Therefore, we adjust each future years' earnings by a fixed percentage that depends on the decile ranking of the historical level of excess capital expenditures. The decile rankings are based on the ratio of the sum of capital expenditures to the sum of depreciation expense, with the sums calculated using those observations within the most recent three years that have available information.

After grouping observations into deciles, we calculate the median amount to subtract from discounted earnings as the median ratio of the present value of future excess capital expenditures to equity value. Eq. (6) shows how this ratio is calculated:

$$CAPEX\ ADJUST = \frac{(CAPEX_0 - DEPN_0)/(r-g)}{EQUITY_0}. \tag{6}$$

where year 0 is the year for which $PVCF$ is calculated and the variables not previously defined are:

$CAPEX_0$ = year 0 capital expenditures,

$DEPN_0$ = year 0 depreciation expense,

$EQUITY_0$ = year 0 market value of equity,

g = growth rate of excess capital expenditures, set to -4%.

We set the growth rate of excess capital expenditures to a negative value because we expect the gap between capital expenditures and depreciation to shrink as earnings growth declines to its terminal rate. The median value of $CAPEX\ ADJUST$ is 12%. We use increments of 2% of discounted earnings to increase the amount deducted from firms in each historical excess capital expenditures decile. Therefore, we subtract 3% of discounted earnings from all observations in the smallest decile and 21% for observations in the largest decile, resulting in a median deduction of 12%.

Earnings do not capture expenditures made to increase working capital. The amount spent on future working capital growth depends on both the historical level of working capital and the future growth of the firm. Therefore, we adjust each future year's earnings by a fixed percentage. The percentage depends on the decile ranking of the product of expected earnings growth times the ratio of average net working capital[3] to average assets. We calculate the averages over all of the most recent three years that have this information.

We calculate the median amount to subtract from discounted earnings as the median ratio of the present value of future working capital growth to equity value. Eq. (7) shows how this ratio is calculated:

$$WC\ ADJUST = \frac{([0.5(gr) + 0.5(tg)] * 0.5[NETWC_0])/r}{EQUITY_0},\tag{7}$$

where the variable not previously defined is $NETWC_0$, the average net working capital for the three years ending in year 0.

The median value of $WC\ ADJUST$ is 5.5%. The numerator of $WC\ ADJUST$ is a weighted earnings growth rate times half of average net working capital, all discounted at the expected CAPM return. The weighted earnings growth rate is the equal-weighted average of the five-year analysts' growth rate and the 4% terminal growth rate. This rate is multiplied by only half of net working capital to recognize that working capital growth may be less than earnings growth and that some of the growth in working capital is in the form of interest-bearing assets.

We use increments of 1% of discounted earnings to increase the amount deducted from firms in each working capital growth decile. Therefore, 1% of discounted earnings is subtracted from all observations in the smallest decile, and 10% is subtracted for observations in the largest decile, resulting in a median deduction of 5.5%.

Several factors introduce potential measurement error in the $PVCF$ measure. Discounting future earnings using the expected return implied by the CAPM reflects each firm's systematic risk, but does not incorporate risk factors that may be omitted from the CAPM. Analysts' optimistic forecasts during the sample period are another potential source of measurement error in the $PVCF$ proxy.[4] Measurement error is also introduced by the lack of forecast information for excess capital expenditures and working capital growth. Finally, the $PVCF$ proxy is sensitive to the assumed terminal growth rate and to the year in which terminal growth is assumed to begin.

We address the measurement error potential in the $PVCF$ proxy in three ways. First, we include variables in the regressions that could be correlated with the portion of true $PVCF$ omitted from our proxy. Second, we assess the sensitivity of our results to the assumed terminal growth rate, and to the year in which growth is assumed to reach its terminal rate. None of our inferences are sensitive to changing these assumptions within reasonable ranges. Third, we perform all of the reported tests using an alternative $PVCF$ proxy that is constructed by multiplying an industry-median capital-to-cash-flow multiplier by the firm's cash flow. The resulting proxy is analogous to the Berger and Ofek (1995) earnings-based measure for imputing the values of segments of diversified firms. None of the main results is sensitive to the use of the alternative $PVCF$ proxy.

3.3   Sample Selection and Description

We obtain data for those firms covered by the Institutional Brokers Estimate System (IBES) that have forecasts of earnings for at least two years ahead and for five-year

Table 39.1
Descriptive statistics for a 1984–1990 sample from the IBES summary tape with at least two years' earnings forecasts, a five-year growth rate forecast, at least $20 million in sales, and available data on Compustat and CRSP, for a total of 7,102 observations

Variable	Median	Mean	STD	High	Low
Market value of equity ($ millions)[a]	525	1.518	2.662	21.381	5
Unadjusted *PVCF* from forecast EPS[b]	0.128	0.144	0.080	0.622	−0.645
Unadjusted *PVCF* from 10 years' forecast growth[b]	0.420	0.413	0.086	1.161	0.037
Unadjusted *PVCF* from 4% terminal growth[b]	0.437	0.443	0.120	1.521	0.084
PVCF/unadjusted *PVCF*[c]	0.801	0.810	0.073	0.960	0.711
Abandonment option value[d]	0.115	0.275	0.704	2.989	−0.750
Excess exit value[e]	−0.761	−0.666	0.414	3.000	−1.000
Excess book value[f]	−0.308	−0.156	0.627	3.000	−1.000
Fixed assets/total assets[g]	0.336	0.383	0.256	0.971	0.001
Noninventory current assets/current assets[h]	0.598	0.599	0.201	1.051	0.001
Land/fixed assets[i]	0.052	0.075	0.082	1.000	0.000
Replacement value/total assets[j]	1.281	1.370	0.370	6.107	0.499

a. Market value of the firm's equity at the time of the earnings forecast.
b. The fraction of the net present value of future earnings generated from each of the following three components: (1) the present value (PV) of the consensus earnings forecast by analysts (for at least years 1 and 2), (2) the PV of the earnings projected from the time of the last analyst forecast through to year 10 by multiplying the last specifically forecast positive earnings (say, year 2) by the analyst forecast of five-year earnings growth, and (3) the terminal value calculated at a 4% terminal growth rate.
c. The ratio of the present value of future cash flows to the present value of future earnings.
d. The ratio of market value of equity to $PVCF$, minus 1.
e. The ratio of exit value of equity to $PVCF$, minus 1. Exit value is defined as: cash + 0.72 ∗ receivables + 0.55 ∗ inventory + 0.54 ∗ fixed assets − payables − total debt.
f. The ratio of book value of equity to $PVCF$, minus 1.
g. The ratio of property, plant, and equipment to total assets in the year before the forecast.
h. The ratio of cash, marketable securities, and receivables to current assets in the year before the forecast.
i. The ratio of book value of land to property, plant, and equipment in the year before the forecast.
j. The ratio of replacement value of assets to total assets in the year before the forecast.

earnings growth. Each observation's first earnings forecast must be made at least six months before the firm's fiscal year-end, thus ensuring that we correctly align the year in which exit value is estimated from the balance sheet with the year for which *PVCF* is calculated. All available IBES observations with sales above $20 million, and Compustat and CRSP data, are included in the sample. The minimum sales requirement is imposed because the *PVCF* proxy is likely to be less accurate for extremely small firms.

Table 39.1 provides descriptive information on the IBES sample. Because of skewness in the distributions, we emphasize medians. Rows 2–4 provide information on the first three components of *PVCF*, whose sum we refer to as unadjusted *PVCF*. For the median firm, 13% of unadjusted *PVCF* is due to the earnings forecast by analysts (usually for years 1 and 2), 42% is due to the earnings projected from the time of the last analyst forecast through year 10, and 44% is due to the perpetuity calculated from year 11 forward. The median ratio of *PVCF* to unadjusted *PVCF* is 80%, showing that the adjustments for excess capital expenditures and working capital growth reduce unadjusted *PVCF* by 20%.

The abandonment option's value (see the appendix for calculation details) is 12%, consistent with the median firm having a positive-value abandonment option. Note that the figure of 12% is very sensitive to assumptions about the rate of terminal growth and the year in which growth reaches its terminal rate (see table 39.8). Therefore, this figure is not an accurate estimate of the abandonment option's relative value. Excess exit value (see Appendix) is −76%, showing that the median firm's exit value is 24% of its *PVCF*. *Excess book value* (see Appendix), which captures the percentage difference between the book value of the firm's net assets and the value of its after-interest cash flows, is −31%, showing that book value represents 69% of *PVCF*.[5]

The median sample firm has fixed assets equal to 34% of total assets. Less-specialized assets—cash, marketable securities, and receivables among current assets, and land among fixed assets—represent 60% of current assets and 5% of fixed assets. Finally, we use a control variable in the asset structure tests, the ratio of replacement value (see Appendix) to book value, with a median value of 1.28.

4 Empirical Results

4.1 Exit Value and Firm Value

Table 39.2 reports the results of regressions on the pooled 1984–1990 analyst forecast sample. These regressions test whether, after contolling for *PVCF*, equity value is positively related to the exit value of net assets. Column 1 reports the regression of equity value of *PVCF* and exit value. The variables in this specification are undeflated, thus providing assurance that the common deflators used in later specifications do not affect the inferences. We therefore take logs of all variables to reduce the influence of outliers. In addition, all of the table 39.2 regressions include fixed factors for each year (coefficient estimates are not reported).[6] The column 1 results show that the coefficient estimates on both the log of *PVCF* and the log of exit value are positive and significant at the 0.001 level.[7]

Theory shows that the ratio of exit value of *PVCF*, rather than exit value itself, is the stochastic strike price of the abandonment option. Therefore, in column 2, we report the results when the log of exit value is replaced by excess exit value. The coefficient of 1.024 on the *PVCF* variable shows that after controlling for the option's

Table 39.2

Regression estimates of the relation between market value of equity and exit value of assets. The sample includes all 1984–1990 observations in the IBES summary tape with at least two years' earnings forecasts, a five-year growth rate forecast, at least \$20 million in sales, and available data on Compustat and CRSP. *P*-values (in parentheses) are based on the White-adjusted standard errors. All regressions include fixed factors for each year, whose coefficient estimates are not reported

Dependent variable	Regression					
	1	2	3	4	5	6
	ln(equity)[a]		Market equity/ sales		Abandonment option value[b]	
Observations	4718	5745	5753	5076	5076	5115
Adjusted R^2	0.910	0.900	0.681	0.696	0.236	0.309
Constant	0.297[h] (0.000)	0.283[h] (0.000)	0.200[h] (0.000)	0.159[h] (0.000)	0.420[h] (0.000)	0.275[h] (0.000)
ln($PVCF$)[c]	0.786[h] (0.000)	1.024[h] (0.000)				
ln(exit value)[d]	0.241[h] (0.000)					
$PVCF$/sales			0.679[h] (0.000)	0.659[h] (0.000)		
Exit value/sales			0.939[h] (0.000)	0.920[h] (0.000)		
Excess exit value[e]		0.489[h] (0.000)			0.491[h] (0.000)	
Excess book value[f]						0.577[h] (0.000)
(Capital expenditures—depreciation)/ total assets				1.530[h] (0.000)	1.053[h] (0.000)	1.164[h] (0.000)
Sales/$PVCF$					0.084[h] (0.000)	0.009 (0.133)
R&D/sales				1.439[h] (0.000)	1.683[h] (0.000)	1.904[h] (0.000)
Change in cash flow year 0 to year 1[g]				0.099[h] (0.000)	0.125[h] (0.000)	0.134[h] (0.000)

a. The natural log of the market value of equity at the time of the earnings forecast.

b. The ratio of market value of equity to $PVCF$, minus 1. $PVCF$ has the following five components: (1) the present value (PV) of the consensus earnings forecast by analysts (for at least years 1 and 2), (2) the PV of the earnings projected from the time of the last analyst forecast through to year 10 by multiplying the last specifically forecast positive earnings (say, year 2) by the analyst forecast of five-year earnings growth, (3) the terminal value calculated at a 4% terminal growth rate, with terminal growth beginning in year 11, (4) a reduction to the present value of analysts' earnings forecasts to adjust for the difference between capital expenditures and depreciation, and (5) a reduction to the present value of analysts' earnings forecasts to adjust for growth in working capital. The annual discount rate is calculated by using the CAPM. The risk-free rate is the one-month Treasury bill rate in the month of the forecast, the beta is calculated over the calendar year prior to the forecast, and the market premium over the risk-free rate is 8.67%.

c. See footnote b in this table.

d. Exit value is defined as: cash + 0.72 * receivables + 0.55 * inventory + 0.54 * fixed assets − payables − total debt.

e. The ratio of exit value of equity to $PVCF$, minus 1.

f. The ratio of book value of equity to $PVCF$, minus 1.

g. Cash flow in year 1/cash flow in year 0, minus 1. Cash flow is defined as earnings before interest, taxes, and depreciation.

h. Denotes significance at the 1% level for a two-tailed test.

strike price, the market value of the firm's equity increases approximately one for one with increases in the present value of after-interest cash flows. The significantly positive estimate on the excess exit value variable continues to support the inference that the abandonment option makes a significant contribution to firm value beyond that made by *PVCF*.

In columns 3 and 4, to adjust for size differences across observations, we normalize equity value, *PVCF*, and exit value by sales. We use no controls in column 3, whereas controls are added in column 4. The controls address the concern that rather than capturing the intended economic constructs, *PVCF* and estimated exit value could be nothing more than labels for measures that capture a single economic construct. Specifically, if estimated exit value contains information about going-concern cash flows that is not captured by estimated *PVCF*, then a positive coefficient estimate on excess exit value could reflect the association between equity value and future cash flows, rather than equity value and abandonment value. The control variables, the tests of the additional implications of abandonment option theory, the analysis performed in changes, and the sensitivity tests are all consistent with our measures capturing the intended economic constructs. We cannot completely dismiss, however, the possibility that the exit value and *PVCF* measures capture the same underlying construct.

Because it is a growth proxy, a source of difference between earnings and cash flows, and is related to the vintage of the firm's tangible assets, the first control variable, capital expenditures minus depreciation (scaled by assets), could affect both future cash flows and estimated exit value. Similarly, R&D/sales could affect both future cash flows and estimated exit value.[8] The change in cash flow for the first year following the observation year is used as an *ex post* control for future cash flows potentially omitted from *PVCF*.

The coefficient estimates on the *PVCF* and exit value variables are similar without (column 3) and with (column 4) the inclusion of the controls. The estimates on both variables are positive and significant at the 0.001 level. To gauge the relative economic effects of variation in *PVCF* and exit value, we multiply the estimates reported in column 4 for each variable by the variable's standard deviation. The results are that a one-standard-deviation change in *PVCF*/sales leads to a 0.641 change in equity value/sales. For exit value/sales, the associated change is 0.265. These results show that exit value has an economically significant effect on equity value. The significantly positive estimates on all the controls show that these variables are significant in controlling for growth opportunities not captured by *PVCF*.

In columns 5 and 6 we present regressions whose functional form corresponds to that used in the hypothesis development. This functional form directly relates the value of the abandonment option to the option's strike price. The 0.491 coefficient estimate on excess exit value in column 5 shows that the option's strike price is significant and positively related to abandonment option value. The estimate falls between the theoretical lower and upper bounds of zero and one. The adjusted R-squared of 24% indicates that the independent variables explain a substantial portion of the variation in abandonment option value. We add to the control variables the ratio of sales/$PVCF$ because sales, due to its more direct link to future cash flows, is likely to capture any information about future cash flows that exit value captures. As in column 4, all of the controls have significant, positive coefficient estimates.

We also perform an unreported regression like that in column 5, but with lagged excess exit value used in place of the contemporaneous value. Using the lagged value checks against the possibility that analysts are unable to distinguish transitory from permanent earnings shocks, which could affect the results. If analyst forecasts of future earnings are too high (low) when earnings are temporarily high, our proxy assigns too high (low) a $PVCF$, resulting in abandonment option value being too low (high). If estimated exit values are more stable than earnings, excess exit value will also be too low (high) in the same year. Thus, transitory earnings shocks could result in a positive relation between contemporaneous excess exit value and abandonment option value. Using lagged excess exit value avoids this possibility, since current year earnings do not affect this variable.

The inferences using the lagged variable are consistent with those for the reported results. The coefficient estimate of 0.164 on lagged excess exit value is significant at better than the 0.001 level, and the adjusted R-squared of the regression is 0.170.

Measurement error is introduced into the estimated exit values because we apply the same estimate of exit value per dollar of book value to all sample observations for each of the three asset categories. As a sensitivity test for this concern, we use untransformed book values in column 6 as our measure of abandonment value. The column 6 results show that the inferences are not sensitive to whether total book value is used to measure abandonment value. The coefficient estimate of 0.577 on excess book value is positive and highly significant.

We wish to investigate the variation over time in the relation between excess exit value and abandonment option value, and to address the concern that the pooled observations may not be independent because of the inclusion of the same firm for multiple years. Thus, table 39.3 reports the results from performing the table 39.2, column 5 regression by year. The results continue to show a strong, positive relation between the estimated exit value of the firm's net assets and the market value of its equity. The magnitude of the relation does not exhibit an obvious pattern over the 1984–1990 period. Each of the yearly estimates on excess exit value is between zero

Table 39.3
Regression estimates of the relation between market value of equity and exit value of assets, by year. The sample includes all 1984–1990 observations in the IBES summary tape with at least two years' earnings forecasts, a five-year growth rate forecast, at least $20 million in sales, and available data on Compustat and CRSP. P-values (in parentheses) are based on the White-adjusted standard errors

	Regression						
	1	2	3	4	5	6	7
	Abandonment option value in year[a]						
Dependent variable	1984	1985	1986	1987	1988	1989	1990
Observations	133	878	826	815	882	951	585
Adjusted R^2	0.417	0.254	0.230	0.187	0.184	0.200	0.167
Constant	0.430d (0.008)	0.592d (0.000)	0.547d (0.000)	0.574d (0.000)	0.277d (0.000)	0.532d (0.000)	0.485d (0.000)
Excess exit value[b]	0.772d (0.000)	0.560d (0.000)	0.482d (0.000)	0.496d (0.000)	0.327d (0.000)	0.530d (0.000)	0.449d (0.000)
(Capital expenditures—depreciation)/total assets	1.145f (0.089)	1.480d (0.000)	1.564d (0.000)	1.112d (0.001)	0.310 (0.389)	0.878d (0.003)	1.045e (0.032)
Sales/$PVCF$	0.116d (0.000)	0.076d (0.000)	0.108d (0.000)	0.093d (0.000)	0.088d (0.000)	0.084d (0.000)	0.044d (0.000)
R&D/sales	1.781 (0.174)	2.656d (0.000)	4.302d (0.000)	1.891d (0.001)	0.901e (0.032)	0.997e (0.007)	−0.985f (0.065)
Change in cash flow year 0 to year 1[c]	0.224d (0.000)	0.193d (0.000)	0.154d (0.000)	0.120d (0.000)	0.086d (0.001)	0.048f (0.075)	0.154d (0.000)

a. See footnote b, table 39.2.
b. See footnote e, table 39.2.
c. See footnote g, table 39.2.
d. Denotes significance at the 1% level for a two-tailed test.
e. Denotes significance at the 5% level for a two-tailed test.
f. Denotes significance at the 10% level for a two-tailed test.

and one, consistent with an extra dollar of exit value providing an increment to firm value of between zero and one dollar. Finally, the coefficient estimates on all of the controls are consistently positive, and are generally significant at the 0.10 level.

We perform an analysis in changes to further mitigate any concern that inferences may be affected by the exit value measure capturing a portion of the true *PVCF* omitted from our proxy. The dependent variable is the percentage change in equity value. The independent variables are percentage changes in *PVCF*, exit value, and *EBITD*, as well as the level of *EBITD*/sales. The two *EBITD* variables are included as controls for changes in the true *PVCF* omitted from the proxy measure.

The sample consists of all first differences of the observations from the levels analysis that meet sample selection restrictions. We require that the first earnings forecast occur no later than the fourth month after the date exit value is measured. This ensures that the changes in exit value and *PVCF* are aligned correctly in time for each firm. The percentage change in equity value is meant to capture the effect of operational decisions, not the effects of issuances and redemptions. Therefore, we eliminate observations with issuances or retirements. (See the Appendix for additional details about the construction of the percentage change variables.)

The results for the changes specification are presented in table 39.4. As expected, the coefficient estimate of 0.114 on the percentage change in *PVCF* is larger than the estimate of 0.042 on the percentage change in exit value. However, the fact that the latter estimate is significantly positive provides strong evidence that the relation we documented earlier between exit and equity values was not driven by exit value and the *PVCF* proxy both measuring different portions of true *PVCF*. The constant component of any relation between exit value and the omitted portion of true *PVCF* is eliminated by examining changes rather than levels. Therefore, continuing to find the strong, positive relation between exit and equity values in the changes analysis reinforces our confidence in the inferences from the levels analysis.

4.2 Asset Structure and Firm Value

Theory suggests that exit values are closer to going-concern values for redeployable versus specialized assets. Moreover, using asset sell-offs from 157 firms, we found that the number of cents per dollar of book value produced from exit is higher for noninventory current assets than for either inventory or fixed assets. We therefore examine the effect of asset structure on the abandonment option's value. Table 39.5 reports the results of regressing the abandonment option value on excess book value, several asset-structure variables, the control variables, and a replacement-to-book variable. The significantly negative estimate in column 1 of −0.134 on the portion of assets that are fixed shows that for a given level of excess book value, firms have less

Table 39.4
Regression estimates of the relation between changes in market value of equity and changes in exit value

Dependent variable	Regression 1—Percentage change in equity value[a]
Observations	1577
Adjusted R^2	0.226
Constant	0.003
	(0.885)
Percentage change in $PVCF$[b]	0.114[d]
	(0.000)
Percentage change in exit value[c]	0.042[d]
	(0.002)
Percentage change in $EBITD$	0.054[d]
	(0.000)
$EBITD$/Sales	0.547[d]
	(0.000)

The sample includes first differences of all 1984–1990 observations in the IBES summary tape with at least two years of earnings forecasts, a five-year growth rate forecast, at least $20 million in sales, available data on Compustat and CRSP, a first earnings forecast that occurs no later than the fourth month after the date exit value is measured, and no issuances or retirements exceeding 2% of either equity value or of the number of shares outstanding. P-values (in parentheses) are based on the White-adjusted standard errors.
a. The ratio of market value of equity to lagged market value of equity, minus 1.
b. The ratio of the present value of cash flows to the lagged value of same, minus 1.
c. The ratio of exit value to lagged exit value, minus 1.
d. Denotes significance at the 1% level for a two-tailed test.

abandonment option value when more of their assets are long-term. The significantly positive estimate of 0.175 on the portion of current assets that are noninventory shows that firms with more of their liquid assets in noninventory items have higher market values of equity. Both results are consistent with more specialized assets creating less abandonment option value per dollar of book value. Column 2 adds the portion of fixed assets in land as an additional explanatory variable. The significantly positive estimate of 0.284 on this variable indicates that firms with more of their fixed assets in land have higher equity values. This result is consistent with land creating more abandonment value per dollar of book value, because of its less specialized nature.

Because we observe only book values (not current values) for each asset category, the extent to which book values reflect current values could affect the asset-structure results. Explaining these results on the basis of accounting rules is, however, very difficult. The first result is that increasing the ratio of inventory/current assets decreases equity value. Noninventory current assets generally have book values that approximate current values. Thus, for accounting rules to explain the result, book

Table 39.5
Regression estimates of the relation between market value of equity and asset structure. The sample includes all 1984–1990 observations in the IBES summary tape with at least two years' earnings forecasts, a five-year growth rate forecast, at least $20 million in sales, and available data on Compustat and CRSP. *P*-values (in parentheses) are based on the White-adjusted standard errors. All regressions include fixed factors for each year, whose coefficient estimates are not reported

| | Regression | |
| | 1 | 2 |
Dependent variable[a]	Abandonment option value	
Observations	4787	2852
Adjusted R^2	0.311	0.298
Constant	0.257[b] (0.000)	0.326[b] (0.000)
Excess book value	0.600[b] (0.000)	0.574[b] (0.000)
Fixed assets/total assets	−0.134[b] (0.006)	−0.201[c] (0.019)
Noninventory current assets/current assets	0.175[b] (0.000)	0.182[b] (0.009)
Land/fixed assets		0.284[d] (0.070)
Replacement value/total assets		−0.057[c] (0.040)
(Capital expenditures—depreciation)/total assets	1.199[b] (0.000)	1.100[b] (0.000)
Sales/*PVCF*	0.008 (0.241)	0.015 (0.130)
R&D/sales	1.473[b] (0.000)	1.379[b] (0.000)
Change in cash flow year 0 to year 1	0.128[b] (0.000)	0.134[b] (0.000)

a. See footnotes b–e and g in table 39.2 for variable definitions.
b. Denotes significance at the 1% level for a two-tailed test.
c. Denotes significance at the 5% level for a two-tailed test.
d. Denotes significance at the 10% level for a two-tailed test.

value must overstate the current value of inventory (so that having a larger portion of book value in inventory provides less current value). However, generally accepted accounting principles require the use of the lower-of-cost-or-market basis for most inventory reporting purposes.[9] Using this method, book values never overstate current values for inventory. Similarly, for accounting rules to explain the negative estimate on the portion of assets that are fixed, book value must overstate the current value of fixed assets more than current assets. Book value's reflection of current value is probably similar, however, between fixed and current assets.[10] Thus, the only asset-structure variable whose results could plausibly be affected by accounting rules is land/fixed assets. It is possible, though not necessarily likely, that the ratio of book value to current value is higher for nonland fixed assets than for land.

To address potential concerns about book values being used to proxy current values, we control for the variation in the ratio of replacement-to-book value. This variation can arise from differences in asset structure and vintage. For example, a firm with mainly old, fixed assets could have a higher book value, but a lower current asset value, than a firm with mainly liquid assets. The replacement-to-book variable controls for this concern, because replacement value is calculated with an algorithm that adjusts assets for inflation based on asset age (see Appendix). Controlling for inflation's effect with the replacement-to-book variable in column 2 does not affect the inferences from the asset-structure variables. This result increases our confidence that the asset-structure results reflect, at least in part, investors' expectation that more-specialized assets will produce less abandonment value per dollar of current value.

4.3   The Abandonment Option's Sensitivity to Financial Distress Likelihood and Agency Conflicts

Abandonment option theory shows that market value is more sensitive to variation in exit value when there is a greater probability of the option being exercised. For given levels of *PVCF* and exit value, one factor that could increase the probability of abandonment is the likelihood of financial distress. We therefore examine whether, all else equal, abandonment option value is more sensitive to variation in excess exit value for firms that have a higher probability of experiencing financial distress. Table 39.6 presents the results of regressing abandonment option value on excess exit value, the controls, and a variable that interacts excess exit value with the probability of financial distress. In column 1, the interactive variable is multiplicative, and the probability of financial distress is measured as the inverse of the Altman (1968) Z-score.[11] In column 2, the interactive variable is an indicator set equal to excess exit value for firms with a Z-score in the bottom quartile of the sample, and to zero

Table 39.6
Regression estimates of the relation between abandonment option value and financial distress likelihood

	Regression	
	1	2
Dependent variable[a]	Abandonment option value	
Observations	3013	3013
Adjusted R^2	0.260	0.260
Constant	0.168[d] (0.003)	0.183[d] (0.000)
Excess exit value	0.160[d] (0.002)	0.251[d] (0.000)
Excess exit value × probability of financial distress[b]	0.598[d] (0.003)	
Excess exit value for firms with high financial distress probability[c]		0.107[e] (0.036)
(Capital expenditures—depreciation)/total assets	0.881[d] (0.002)	0.911[d] (0.001)
Sales/$PVCF$	0.133[d] (0.000)	0.129[d] (0.000)
R&D/sales	2.208[d] (0.000)	2.234[d] (0.000)
Change in cash flow year 0 to year 1	0.129[d] (0.000)	0.131[d] (0.000)

The sample includes all 1984–1990 observations of industrial firms (SIC codes between 2000–3999) in the IBES summary tape with available data. P-values (in parentheses) are based on the White-adjusted standard errors. Both regressions include fixed factors for each year, whose coefficient estimates are not reported.
a. See footnotes b–e and g in table 39.2 for variable definitions.
b. The product of excess exit value and 1/Z-score.
c. Excess exit value if the firm's Z-score is in the bottom quartile of all firms in the sample, 0 otherwise.
d. Denotes significance at the 1% level for a two-tailed test.
e. Denotes significance at the 5% level for a two-tailed test.

otherwise. The sample for both regressions includes all observations of industrial firms (SIC codes between 2000 and 3999) on the IBES summary tape with available data for the 1984–1990 period. Nonindustrials are excluded, because Altman estimated the parameters used to calculate Z-scores only for industrial firms.

The results show that a given excess exit value is valued more highly when the likelihood of experiencing financial distress is high. The coefficient estimates on the interactive indicators are significantly positive in column 1 (0.01 level) and column 2 (0.05 level). One concern we have with the Table 39.6 tests is that firms with higher financial distress probabilities are likely to have higher financial distress costs, and that these costs tend to be omitted from the $PVCF$ estimate because analysts are forecasting going-concern earnings. Therefore, the reported results could be sensitive to the assumptions used to calculate *PVCF*.

We have performed sensitivity tests to assess this concern, and we find that the magnitude and significance of the coefficient estimates on the interactive indicators are sensitive to the assumptions used to calculate *PVCF*. The reported results are therefore fragile, and should be interpreted with caution.

The probability of abandonment can also increase when agency conflicts between owners and managers are reduced. To investigate the importance of agency problems to holders of the abandonment option, we test whether a given excess exit value is associated with more option value when there is a higher probability that managers will exit when investors wish them to do so. We assume rational expectations, and therefore use the *ex post* exercise of the abandonment option through partial exit as an indicator of a higher *ex ante* probability of timely exercise.

Table 39.7 presents three regressions of the abandonment option value on excess exit value; the controls; and an interactive indicator set equal to excess exit value for firms that subsequently had a partial exit, and to zero otherwise. The three regressions in table 39.7 differ in their definition of partial exit. The first regression defines partial exit as having an asset sale of at least $100 million, the second as having a one-time dividend equal to at least 10% of equity value, and the third as either of these two events. The sample used for these regressions includes only 1986 observations. We use 1986 as the base year, thus facilitating searching forward for partial exits. The subsample used for the first and third regressions includes only those 1986 observations with a market value of equity of at least $1 billion. We impose the market value of equity requirement because our sample of large asset sales is drawn from the John and Ofek (1995) sample, and includes only sales of at least $100 million. Therefore, we restrict the sample to firms large enough to realistically contemplate a partial exit of at least $100 million.

The coefficient estimates on the interactive indicators are significantly positive (0.01 level) in all three regressions, indicating that an extra dollar of exit value is more highly valued when partial exit is about to occur. The results are thus consistent with some managers delaying abandonment beyond the time that investors consider optimal.

4.4 Sensitivity Tests

We assess the sensitivity of the reported results to the calculation of *PVCF* by performing regressions in which *PVCF* is calculated under alternative assumptions. We vary *PVCF* along three dimensions. The first dimension is whether or not *PVCF* is adjusted for excess capital expenditures and working-capital growth. The second

Table 39.7
Regression estimates of the relation between abandonment option value and future partial exit through large asset sales or liquidating dividends

Dependent variable[a]	Regression		
	1	2	3
	Abandonment option value		
Observations	272	826	272
Adjusted R^2	0.207	0.236	0.219
Constant	0.744[e]	0.549[e]	0.739[e]
	(0.000)	(0.000)	(0.000)
Excess exit value	0.241	0.479[e]	0.228
	(0.137)	(0.000)	(0.160)
Excess exit value if had a major asset sale, 0 otherwise[b]	0.490[e]		
	(0.002)		
Excess exit value if paid at least 10% of equity as dividend, 0 otherwise[c]		0.419[e]	
		(0.006)	
Excess exit value if either asset sale or dividend payment, 0 otherwise[d]			0.509[e]
			(0.005)
(Capital expenditures—depreciation)/total assets	0.979	1.553[e]	1.017
	(0.341)	(0.000)	(0.414)
Sales/$PVCF$	0.099[e]	0.108[e]	0.102[e]
	(0.001)	(0.000)	(0.001)
R&D/sales	4.920[e]	4.280[e]	4.878[e]
	(0.001)	(0.000)	(0.001)
Change in cash flow year 0 to year 1	0.343[e]	0.151[e]	0.329[e]
	(0.000)	(0.000)	(0.000)

The sample includes only 1986 IBES forecasts. In columns 1 and 3 the sample is restricted to firms with at least $1 billion in equity value. P-values (in parentheses) are based on the White-adjusted standard errors.
a. See footnotes b–e and g in table 39.2 for variable definitions.
b. A variable that equals excess exit value if the firm sold assets of $100 million or more in the period 1986–1988, 0 otherwise.
c. A variable that equals excess exit value if the firm paid a one-time dividend of at least 10% of its equity in the period 1986–1988, 0 otherwise.
d. A variable that equals excess exit value if the firm either sold assets of $100 million or more or paid a one-time dividend of at least 10% of its equity in the period 1986–1988, 0 otherwise.
e. Denotes significance at the 1% level for a two-tailed test.

Table 39.8
Descriptive statistics for the abandonment option's value[a] with various *PVCF* calculations

Method of calculating *PVCF*[b]	Median	Mean	STD	Q3	Q1
Terminal growth = 4%, 10 years with specific growth	0.115	0.275	0.704	0.594	−0.226
Unadjusted for capex-depreciation and WC changes	−0.104	0.023	0.548	0.266	−0.369
Terminal growth = 0%	0.223	0.380	0.705	0.702	−0.118
Terminal growth = 2%	0.157	0.315	0.694	0.628	−0.177
Terminal growth = 6%	−0.011	0.140	0.645	0.433	−0.324
Terminal growth starts at year 6	0.333	0.494	0.754	0.881	−0.068
Terminal growth starts at year 16	−0.061	0.067	0.586	0.337	−0.357
Terminal growth starts at year 21	−0.142	−0.023	0.542	0.223	−0.418

The sample includes all 1984–1990 observations in the IBES summary tape with at least two years' earnings forecasts, a five-year growth rate forecast, at least $20 million in sales, and available data on Compustat and CRSP.
a. The ratio of market value of equity to *PVCF*, minus 1.
b. The *PVCF* calculation has five steps, as listed below. Row 2, table 39.8, calculates *PVCF* without making the adjustments described in steps 4 and 5, whereas the remaining rows of table 39.8 calculate *PVCF* with differing terminal value calculations from those described in step 3. The five components of *PVCF* are: (1) the present value (*PV*) of the consensus earnings forecast by analysts (for at least years 1 and 2), (2) the *PV* of the earnings projected from the time of the last analyst forecast through to year 10 by multiplying the last specifically forecast positive earnings (say, year 2) by the analyst forecast of five-year earnings growth, (3) the terminal value calculated at a 4% terminal growth rate, with terminal growth beginning in year 11 (see Eq. (4) in the text), (4) a reduction to the present value of analysts' earnings forecasts to adjust for the difference between capital expenditures and depreciation (see Eq. (4) in the text), and (5) a reduction to the present value of analysts' earnings forecasts to adjust for growth in working capital (see Eq. (4) in the text). The annual discount rate is calculated by using the CAPM. The risk-free rate is the one-month Treasury bill rate in the month of the forecast, the beta is calculated over the calendar year prior to the forecast, and the market premium over the risk-free rate is 8.67%.

dimension is the terminal growth rate. The third is the year in which growth is assumed to reach its terminal rate.

Table 39.8 provides descriptive information on how excess equity value, the dependent variable in the sensitivity regressions, is affected by varying the *PVCF* calculation along each of the three dimensions. The table's first row reports information for the version of *PVCF* used in the reported results (i.e., with adjustment for excess capital expenditures and working-capital growth, using a 4% terminal growth rate, and assuming the terminal growth rate begins in year 11). The median abandonment option value is 0.115. The remaining rows describe what happens to abandonment option value when one dimension of the *PVCF* calculation is changed from that used in the reported results. When no adjustment is made to *PVCF* for excess capital expenditures and working capital growth, *PVCF* is increased and the median abandonment option value is lowered to −0.104. The same effect occurs if the assumed rate of terminal growth is increased, or if the year in which terminal growth starts is postponed. Thus, the median abandonment option value falls from 0.223 with 0%

terminal growth to -0.011 with 6% terminal growth, and from 0.333 when terminal growth starts in year 6 to -0.142 when it starts in year 21.

Table 39.9 presents the sensitivity regressions. It is readily apparent that varying the assumptions used in calculating *PVCF* has little effect on the inference from the excess exit value variable. The column with terminal growth starting in year 11 is the original result, which we presented in column 5 of table 39.2. The estimate on excess exit value is between 0.4 and 0.5, and is significant at the 0.001 level. The same is also true in each of the seven sensitivity regressions. Moreover, as either the rate of terminal growth or its starting year is increased, no trend is evident in the magnitude of the coefficient estimate on excess exit value. The estimate decreases from 0.494 to 0.479 as the terminal growth rate is increased from 0% to 2%, but then it increases when terminal growth is raised to 4% (the original results), and decreases again when the growth rate is changed to 6%. Similarly, the estimate on excess exit value is greater when terminal growth begins in year 11 instead of year 6, but thereafter it becomes smaller as the starting year for terminal growth is increased. With the control variables, the striking pattern is that the estimates on the controls generally become smaller as the year of starting terminal growth is increased. Thus, extending firm-specific growth further in time appears to reduce the extent to which growth opportunities are omitted from the *PVCF* proxy. Overall, the sensitivity regressions provide strong evidence that, within reasonable ranges, our inferences are not affected by changing the assumptions used to calculate *PVCF*.

5 Conclusions

As uncertainty about future cash flows is resolved, investors have the option to abandon the firm for its exit value. Theory suggests that this option is priced as an American put, whose value increases with exit value. We estimate exit value based on the relation between book value and exit value for major asset classes, as disclosed by firms with sufficiently detailed discontinued operations footnotes. We measure the abandonment option value as the percentage by which equity value exceeds going-concern, after-interest cash flows. The present value of these cash flows is calculated using analysts' earnings forecasts. Specific earnings forecasts are discounted and summed, earnings for the period from the last forecast through year 10 are projected based on analysts' consensus earnings growth forecast, and a perpetuity for the earnings from year 11 forward is added by assuming that a constant 4% nominal terminal growth rate applies for all observations. The present value of future earnings is then adjusted to arrive at the present value of future cash flows distributable to equity holders. Adjustments are made for the present value of future capital expen-

Table 39.9
Regression estimates of the relation between abandonment option value and exit value for various *PVCF* calculations

	Regression							
	1	2	3	4	5	6	7	8
		Abandonment option value						
	Not adjusted	Terminal value growth rate =			Terminal value start at			
Dependent variable[a]		0%	2%	6%	year 6	year 11	year 16	year 21
Observations	5013	5049	5061	4998	4906	5076	4817	4749
Adjusted R^2	0.208	0.226	0.225	0.231	0.212	0.232	0.244	0.249
Constant	0.213[b]	0.508[b]	0.443[b]	0.304[b]	0.612[b]	0.420[b]	0.272[b]	0.203[b]
	(0.000)	(0.000)	(0.000)	(0.000)	(0.000)	(0.000)	(0.000)	(0.000)
Excess exit value	0.403[b]	0.494[b]	0.479[b]	0.451[b]	0.476[b]	0.491[b]	0.452[b]	0.427[b]
	(0.000)	(0.000)	(0.000)	(0.000)	(0.000)	(0.000)	(0.000)	(0.000)
(Capital expenditures—depreciation)/total assets	0.330[b]	1.018[b]	0.988[b]	0.860[b]	1.543[b]	1.053[b]	0.524[b]	0.416[b]
	(0.003)	(0.000)	(0.000)	(0.000)	(0.000)	(0.000)	(0.000)	(0.001)
Sales/*PVCF*	0.074[b]	0.069[b]	0.074[b]	0.085[b]	0.063[b]	0.084[b]	0.083[b]	0.088[b]
	(0.000)	(0.000)	(0.000)	(0.000)	(0.000)	(0.000)	(0.000)	(0.000)
R&D/sales	1.217[b]	1.602[b]	1.689[b]	1.869[b]	2.546[b]	1.683[b]	0.845[b]	0.614[b]
	(0.000)	(0.000)	(0.000)	(0.000)	(0.000)	(0.000)	(0.000)	(0.001)
Change in cash flow year 0 to year 1	0.095[b]	0.130[b]	0.124[b]	0.112[b]	0.133[b]	0.125[b]	0.089[b]	0.075[b]
	(0.000)	(0.000)	(0.000)	(0.000)	(0.000)	(0.000)	(0.000)	(0.000)

The sample includes all 1984–1990 observations in the IBES summary tape with at least two years' earnings forecasts, a five-year growth rate forecast, at least $20 million in sales, and available data on Compustat and CRSP. *P*-values (in parentheses) are based on the White-adjusted standard errors. All regressions include fixed factors for each year, whose coefficient estimates are not reported.
a. See footnotes b–e and g in table 39.2 for variable definitions.
b. Denotes significance at the 1% level for a two-tailed test.

ditures minus future depreciation, and for the present value of working capital growth. After controlling for the value of future cash flows, we find a positive and highly significant relation between market value and estimated exit value. This relation holds in levels, in changes, and for various methods of estimating the value of future cash flows.

Option-pricing theory suggests that if future cash flows become disappointing, the value of the firm's generalizable assets will not decline as much as the value of its specialized assets. We therefore investigate whether more generalizable assets produce more abandonment option value. We find that a given amount of book value has a more positive effect on market value when more of the book value derives from certain categories of assets. These results are consistent with assets producing more abandonment value when they are more generalizable.

In addition to depending on the ratio of exit value to *PVCF*, the probability of the abandonment option's exercise is posited to depend on the firm's likelihood of experiencing financial distress, and on the level of agency problems between the firm's investors and its managers. Abandonment put option theory predicts that market value is more sensitive to variation in exit value when the probability of the option being exercised is higher. We find support for the prediction that an extra dollar of exit value is valued more highly when the likelihood of experiencing financial distress is higher, although this result is sensitive to the assumptions made in controlling for future cash flows. In addition, tests that use a subsample of firms that made large divestitures or paid large special dividends support the hypothesis that investors attach more value to the abandonment option when the probability of timely exit by the manager is higher.

Appendix

Abandonment Option Value

$$Abandonment\ option\ value = \left(\frac{Market\ value\ of\ equity}{PVCF}\right) - 1. \tag{8}$$

Extreme abandonment option value measures are excluded from the analysis, with extreme defined as values above 3 or below −0.75.

Excess Exit Value

$$Excess\ exit\ value = \left(\frac{Estimated\ exit\ value\ of\ equity}{PVCF}\right) - 1. \tag{9}$$

Estimated exit value of equity is defined as: *cash + 0.72 * receivables + 0.55 * inventory + 0.54 * fixed assets − payables − total debt*. Excess exit value is winsorized at −1 and at 3.

Excess Book Value

$$Excess\ book\ value = \left(\frac{Book\ value\ of\ equity}{PVCF_{analyst}}\right) - 1. \tag{10}$$

Excess book value is winsorized at -1 and at 3.

Percentage Change in Equity Value

$$Percentage\ change\ in\ equity\ value = \left(\frac{Market\ value\ of\ equity_t}{Market\ value\ of\ equity_{t-1}}\right) - 1. \tag{11}$$

Observations are excluded with issuances or retirements that create a change in value, or in the number of shares outstanding, exceeding 2%. One additional observation is eliminated because it is an extreme outlier.

Percentage Change in PVCF

$$Percentage\ change\ in\ PVCF = \left(\frac{PVCF_t}{PVCF_{t-1}}\right) - 1. \tag{12}$$

Percentage change in $PVCF$ is winsorized at its 99th percentile (4.3).

Percentage Change in Exit Value

$$Percentage\ change\ in\ exit\ value = \left(\frac{Exit\ value_t}{Exit\ value_{t-1}}\right) - 1. \tag{13}$$

Percentage change in exit value is adjusted in cases where either or both the year $t-1$ and the year t exit values are negative. If both are negative, the percentage change is set to zero. If the year $t-1$ value is negative (positive) and the year t value is positive (negative), the percentage change is set to 1 (-1). Finally, the percentage change in exit value is winsorized at its 99th percentile (3.24).

Replacement Value of Assets

The replacement value is estimated using a modification of the Lindenberg and Ross (1981) algorithm. Plant and equipment are valued by setting up an acquisition schedule and adjusting for price-level changes and depreciation as suggested by Lindenberg and Ross, while the technological change parameter of Lindenberg and Ross is (following Smirlock, Gilligan, and Marshall, 1984) assumed to be zero. Specifically, we assume that the value of the physical plant in 1970 (or the first year with available Compustat data) is equal to book value. Following Smirlock, Gilligan, and Marshall, we reduce the value of plant and equipment by 5% each year to compensate for depreciation, and then adjust it for inflation using the GNP deflator. We then apply the Lindenberg and Ross formula. For inventories, we apply the Lindenberg and Ross algorithm directly.

Acknowledgments

We appreciate helpful comments from Ron Adiel, Andrew Alford, Jacob Boudoukh. Paul Fischer, Bob Holthausen, Kose John, Anthony Lynch, Krishna Palepu (the referee), Josh Ronen, Rick Ruback (the editor), Richard Sloan, Robert Whitelaw, and workshop participants at the American Accounting Association annual meeting, the Third Harvard Summer Financial Decisions and Control Workshop, the Sixth Annual Conference on Financial Economics and Accounting, and the University of Pennsylvania. We gratefully acknowledge the contribution of I/B/E/S Inc. for providing earnings per share forecast data, available through the Institutional Brokers Estimate System. Berger acknowledges the financial support of Coopers & Lybrand and the Wharton Junior Faculty Research Fund.

Notes

1. For example, Shleifer and Vishny (1992) note that whereas "commercial land can be used for many different purposes," fixed assets often "have no reasonable uses other than the one they are destined for." Moreover, financial accounting classifies cash, current marketable securities, and current accounts receivable as liquid assets, but excludes inventory, which is viewed as more illiquid (Stickney and Weil, 1994).

2. In calculating the second term, we assume earnings from year 2 will grow at the consensus growth rate through year 10. If the year 2 forecast earnings are negative, year 1's (or else year 3's) are used if positive, or, if positive earnings are not forecast, the observation is eliminated.

3. We define net working capital as current assets minus current liabilities plus short-term debt.

4. See, for example, Philbrick and Ricks (1991), Freeman and Tse (1992), and, for a summary of the evidence, Schipper (1991).

5. The abandonment option value, excess exit value, and excess book value variables do not exhibit a time trend during the 1984–1990 period.

6. Throughout the paper, all regressions that pool observations across years include unreported fixed factors for each year.

7. In most of the reported regressions, the White test rejects the null of homoskedasticity at the 0.01 level. Therefore, we calculate reported significance levels using White (1980) heteroskedasticity-consistent standard errors.

8. Firms with R&D less than 1% of sales are not required to disclose their R&D expenditures. We therefore treat unreported R&D as being equal to zero.

9. During our sample period, approximately 90% of surveyed companies used lower-of-cost-or-market to price all or a portion of their inventories (AICPA, 1987, 1992).

10. Noninventory items represent 60% of the book value of current assets (see table 39.1), so book value likely represents a large portion of current value for current assets, on average. This suggests that market-to-book ratios for current assets are slightly greater than one. Since the mean of the median market-to-book ratios for total assets for the years 1986–1985 is 1.2 (Penman, 1992), the relation of market-to-book is likely similar, on average, between fixed and current assets.

11. We add 1.4 to all Z-scores in order to make the minimum Z-score greater than one. This ensures that the probability of financial distress measure has values between zero and one.

References

AICPA, 1987, *Accounting trends and techniques*, edited by J. Shohet (AICPA, New York, NY).

AICPA, 1992, *Accounting trends and techniques*, edited by J. Shohet (AICPA, New York, NY).

Altman, E. I., 1968, Financial ratios, discriminant analysis and the prediction of corporate bankruptcy, *Journal of Finance* 23, 589–609.

Berger, P. and E. Ofek, 1995, Diversification's effect on firm value, *Journal of Financial Economics* 37, 39–65.

Bonini, C., 1977, Capital investment under uncertainty with abandonment options, *Journal of Financial and Quantitative Analysis* 12, 39–54.

Burgstahler, D. and I. Dichev, 1994, Earnings, adaptation, and equity value, Working paper (University of Washington, Seattle, WA).

Dyl, E. and H. Long, 1969, Abandonment value and capital budgeting: Comment, *Journal of Finance* 24, 88–95.

Foster, G., 1986, *Financial statement analysis* (Prentice-Hall, Englewood Cliffs, NJ).

Freeman, R. N. and S. Y. Tse, 1992, Security price responses to unexpected earnings, *Journal of Accounting Research* 30, 185–209.

Hayn, C., 1995, The information content of losses, *Journal of Accounting and Economics* 20, 125–153.

John, K. and F. Ofek, 1995, Asset sales and increase in focus, *Journal of Financial Economics* 37, 105–126.

Johnson, H., 1987, Options on the maximum or the minimum of several assets, *Journal of Financial and Quantitative Analysis* 22, 277–283.

Kaplan, S. N. and R. S. Ruback, 1995, The valuation of cash flow forecasts: An empirical analysis, *Journal of Finance* 50, 1059–1093.

Kensinger, J. W., 1980, Project abandonment as a put option: Dealing with the capital investment decision and operating risk using option pricing theory, Working paper 80-121 (Edwin L. Cox School of Business, Southern Methodist University, Dallas, TX).

Kensinger, J. W., 1988, The capital investment project as a set of exchange options, *Managerial Finance* 14, 16–27.

Lee, C. J., 1988, Capital budgeting under uncertainty: The case of optimal timing, *Journal of Business Finance and Accounting* 15, 155–168.

Lindenberg, E. B. and S. A. Ross, 1981, Tobin's q ratio and industrial organization, *Journal of Business* 54, 1–32.

McDonald, R. and D. Siegel, 1985, Investment and the valuation of firms when there is an option to shut down, *International Economic Review* 26, 331–349.

Majd, S. and R. Pindyck, 1987, Time to build, option value, and investment decisions. *Journal of Financial Economics* 18, 7–27.

Myers, S. C. and S. Majd, 1990, Abandonment value and project life, *Advances in Futures and Options Research* 4, 1–21.

Ofek, E., 1993, Capital structure and firm response to poor performance: An empirical analysis, *Journal of Financial Economics* 34, 3–30.

Ohlson, J. A., 1996, Earnings, book values and dividends in security valuation, *Contemporary Accounting Research*, forthcoming.

Paddock, J., D. Siegel, and J. Smith, 1988, Option valuation of claims on real assets: The case of offshore petroleum leases, *Quarterly Journal of Economics* 103, 479–508.

Penman, S., 1992, The articulation of price-earnings ratios and market-to-book ratios and the evaluation of growth, Working paper (University of California, Berkeley, CA).

Philbrick, D. and W. Ricks, 1991, Using value line and IBES analyst forecasts in accounting research, *Journal of Accounting Research* 29, 397–417.

Pindyck, R., 1988, Irreversible investment, capacity choice, and the value of the firm, *American Economic Review* 78, 969–985.

Quigg, L., 1993, Empirical testing of real option-pricing models, Journal of Finance 48, 621–640.

Robichek, A. and J. Van Horne, 1967, Abandonment value and capital budgeting, *Journal of Finance* 22, 577–590.

Ronen, J. and G. H. Sorter, 1973, Relevant accounting, *Journal of Business* 46, 258–282.

Schipper, K., 1991, Analysts' forecasts, *Accounting Horizons* 5, 105–121.

Shleifer, A. and R. W. Vishny, 1992, Liquidation value and debt capacity: A market equilibrium approach, *Journal of Finance* 47, 1343–1366.

Smirlock, M., T. Gilligan, and W. Marshall, 1984, Tobin's q and the structure performance relationship, *American Economic Review* 74, 1051–1060.

Stickney, C. P. and R. L. Weil, 1994, *Financial accounting: An introduction to concepts, methods, and uses* (Dryden Press, New York, NY).

Stulz, R., 1982, Options on the minimum or the maximum of two risky assets: Analysis and applications, *Journal of Financial Economics* 10, 161–185.

Triantis, A. and J. Hodder, 1990, Valuing flexibility as a complex option, *Journal of Finance* 45, 549–565.

White, H., 1980, A heteroskedasticity-consistent covariance matrix estimator and a direct test for heteroskedasticity, *Econometrica* 48, 817–838.

Williamson, O. E., 1988, Corporate finance and corporate governance, *Journal of Finance* 43, 567–592.

Sources

2. S. C. Myers. "Finance Theory and Financial Strategy." *Interfaces* 14, 1 (January–February 1984): 126–137; reprinted in *Midland Corporate Finance Journal* 5 (Spring 1987): 6–13.

3. W. C. Kester. "Today's Options for Tomorrow's Growth." *Harvard Business Review* 62, 2 (March–April 1984): 153–160.

4. L. Trigeorgis and S. P. Mason. "Valuing Managerial Flexibility." *Midland Corporate Finance Journal* 5 (Spring 1987): 14–21.

5. A. Dixit and R. S. Pindyck. "The Options Approach to Capital Investment." *Harvard Business Review* (May–June 1995): 105–118.

6. L. Trigeorgis. "A Conceptual Options Framework for Capital Budgeting." *Advances in Futures and Options Research* 3 (1988): 145–167.

7. L. Trigeorgis. "Real Options and Interactions with Financial Flexibility." *Financial Management* 22, 3 (1993): 202–224 (first part only, up to 216, plus conclusion & references).

8. M. Brennan and E. Schwartz. "A New Approach to Evaluating Natural Resource Investments." *Midland Corporate Finance Journal* (Spring 1985): 37–47.

9. A. Dixit. "Investment and Hysteresis." *Journal of Economic Perspectives* 6 (Winter 1992): 107–132.

10. N. Kulatilaka and L. Trigeorgis. "The General Flexibility to Switch: Real Options Revisited." *International Journal of Finance* 6, 2 (1994): 778–798.

11. R. S. Pindyck. "Irreversibility, Uncertainty, and Investment." *Journal of Economic Literature* 29, 3 (1991): 1110–1148.

12. R. McDonald and D. Siegel. "The Value of Waiting to Invest." *Quarterly Journal of Economics* 101 (November 1986): 707–727.

13. S. Majd and R. Pindyck. "Time to Build, Option Value, and Investment Decisions." *Journal of Financial Economics* 18 (March 1987): 7–27.

14. S. C. Myers and S. Majd. "Abandonment Value and Project Life." *Advances in Futures and Options Research* 4 (1990): 1–21.

15. R. Pindyck. "Irreversible Investment, Capacity Choice, and the Value of the Firm." *American Economic Review* 78 (December 1988): 969–985.

16. M. Brennan and E. Schwartz. "Evaluating Natural Resource Investments." *Journal of Business* 58 (April 1985): 135–157.

17. L. Trigeorgis. "The Nature of Option Interactions and the Valuation of Investments with Multiple Real Options." *Journal of Financial and Quantitative Analysis* 28, 1 (1993): 1–20.

18. T. Luehrman. "Strategy as a Portfolio of Real Options." *Harvard Business Review* (September–October 1998): 89–99.

19. K. W. Smith and A. Triantis. "The Value of Options in Strategic Acquisitions." In *Real Options in Capital Investment*, ed. L. Trigeorgis. Praeger (1995).

20. P. Childs, S. Ott, and A. Triantis. "Capital Budgeting for Interrelated Projects: A Real Options Approach." *Journal of Financial and Quantitative Analysis* 33, 3 (September 1998): 305–334.

21. H. T. J. Smit and L. Trigeorgis. "Flexibility and Commitment in Strategic Investment." Working paper, Tinbergen Institute, Erasmus University (1993).

22. N. Kulatilaka and E. Perotti. "Strategic Growth Options." *Management Science* 44, 8 (August 1998): 1021–1031.

23. S. Grenadier and A. M. Weiss. "Investment in Technological Innovations: An Option Pricing Approach." *Journal of Financial Economics* 44 (1997): 397–416.

24. L. Trigeorgis. "A Log-transformed Binomial Numerical Analysis Method for Valuing Complex Multi-Option Investments." *Journal of Financial and Quantitative Analysis* 26 (September 1991): 309–326.

25. M. Brennan and E. Schwartz. "Finite Difference Methods and Jump Processes Arising in the Pricing of Contingent Claims: A Synthesis." *Journal of Financial and Quantitative Analysis* 13 (September 1978): 461–474.

26. R. Geske and K. Shastri. "Valuation by Approximation: A Comparison of Alternative Option Valuation Techniques." *Journal of Financial and Quantitative Analysis* 20 (March 1985): 45–71.

28. R. C. Merton. "Applications of Option-Pricing Theory: Twenty-Five Years Later." *American Economic Review* 88, 3 (June 1998) [pp. 336–340 and references only].

29. N. Nichols. "Scientific Management at Merck: An Interview with CFO Judy Lewent." *Harvard Business Review* 72, 1 (1994) [pp. 89–94 only].

30. A. Kemna. "Case Studies on Real Options." *Financial Management* 22, 3 (1993): 259–270.

31. N. Kulatilaka. "The Value of Flexibility: The Case of a Dual-fuel Industrial Steam Boiler." *Financial Management* 22, 3 (1993): 271–279.

32. L. Trigeorgis. "A Real Options Application in Natural Resource Investments." *Advances in Futures and Options Research* 4 (1990): 153–164.

33. P. Bjerksund and S. Ekern. "Managing Investment Opportunities Under Price Uncertainty: From "Last Chance" to "Wait and See" Strategies." *Financial Management* 19, 3 (Autumn 1990): 65–83.

34. S. Titman. "Urban Land Prices Under Uncertainty." *American Economic Review* (June 1985): 505–514.

35. R. Pindyck. "Investments of Uncertain Cost." *Journal of Financial Economics* (August 1993) [sections 1, 4, 6 only].

36. B. Kogut and N. Kulatilaka. "Operating Flexibility, Global Manufacturing, and the Option Value of a Multi-national Network." *Management Science* 40, 1 (1994): 123–139.

37. J. Paddock, D. Siegel, and J. Smith. "Option Valuation of Claims on Real Assets: The Case of Offshore Petroleum Leases." *Quarterly Journal of Economics* (August 1988): 479–508.

38. L. Quigg. "Empirical Testing of Real Option-pricing Models." *Journal of Finance* 48, 2 (1993): 621–640.

39. P. Berger, E. Ofek, and I. Swary. "Investor Valuation of the Abandonment Option." *Journal of Financial Economics* 42 (1996): 257–287.

Index